STOLEN LIGHTNING

Daniel Lawrence O'Keefe

STOLEN LIGHTNING

The Social Theory of Magic

CONTINUUM · NEW YORK

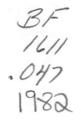

1982

The Continuum Publishing Company
575 Lexington Avenue, New York, N.Y. 10022

Printed in the United States of America

Library of Congress Cataloging in Publication Data

O'Keefe, Daniel Lawrence, 1928–
Stolen lightning.

1. Magic.   I. Title.
BF1611.047   133.4′3   81–9688
ISBN 0–8264–0059–0   AACR2

FOR AND WITH
DEBORAH

"Painful are these things to relate, painful
is silence, and all is wretchedness."

Aeschylus, *Prometheus Bound*

CONTENTS

Preface: HOW TO DO IT

IN most modern cities the traveler is seldom far from a storefront fortune teller. She is not there to amuse tourists. She is a diviner with a busy local practice. If a neighbor comes to her with a problem or secret affliction, she will give him a magical diagnosis through an oracle (tarot cards, crystal ball, tea leaves). She may tell him his difficulty was caused by a ghost, or a distant star. For an extra fee, she will give him magic medicine: an amulet, a spell against an enemy; or she will burn candles for him. She may refer him to other specialists—faith healers, astrologers or mentalists, people most of us did not realize lived nearby. When someone walks in her door he enters an ancient province of meaning whose tail reaches back at least to the Neolithic. For this is the perennial magical medical complex. The whole zoo of magic medical occupations is still here— diviners, oracles, medicine men—thousands of them. And so are the centuries' accumulation of newer variants, from strokers, magnetists and spiritualists to neuropaths and wild psychotherapists—so many "caretakers" (Erikson[1]) that we have become a "therapeutic society" (Rieff[2]) and may develop a "therapeutic state" (Szasz[3]). But magic medicine is only one of the provinces of magic. Another, "the paranormal," is more active with us than in primitive society: To-day some scientists, think tanks and intelligence agencies join the ESP band-wagon. Still another magic, the magic of millenarian sects, sweeps across the underdeveloped world, two thirds of humanity. Newer magics of pseudo-science, mental technology and mass manipulation are invented almost daily. Occasionally, an "occult revival" like the present one becomes so blatant that we notice this persistence of magic; but usually we dismiss it as an exception and go on believing magic belongs to the past. As a result, the difference between modern and primitive societies is not that they had magic and we do not. The difference is that they accepted the magic around them, whereas we deny it.

A General Theory

This is an attempt to write a general theory of magic: that means a complete explanatory account of the whole thing, past and present, all the provinces, rather than a single hypothesis. This has not been done. Malinowski's *Magic, Science and Religion* was really just one hypothesis: He said magic builds confidence in situations of uncertainty.[4] Frazer's explanation was one proposition: Sympathetic magic is based on association of ideas.[5] Actually, both men studied magic in several books and a reader could dig propositions out of these to put together a rudimentary general theory. I have done this in a footnote,[5a] but neither Malinowski nor Frazer did it. Most theories of magic play just one tune. The exception is Hubert and Mauss, who at least wrote a "sketch" (*esquisse*) of a general theory.[6] But it was so condensed it was misunderstood even by its English editor.[7] An American reviewer, Schleiter,[8] writing in 1919, attacked it because, he said, it was not one but "six different theories" which he outlined in six sentences—demonstrating that he thought a general theory had only one idea in it.

A complete explanation of magic must be general and theoretical. It cannot break down into separate chapters on witchcraft, shamanism, exorcism and so on, as popular treatments do, for that is too slack to explain anything.[9] Nor can it merely lay out magic historically, though magic has a history. On the other hand, a taxonomy would be too static.[10] So I will use general propositions about the dynamics of magic, each one applying to all magic. I will organize these generalizations into a system of postulates, a neo-scholastic approach effective again in our day: used, for example, by Bloomfield[11] in linguistics, and Shor[12] in hypnotism studies. But I will not do it so formally. For this is *not* a "hypothetico-deductive system," like that of Hull[13] in psychology, Keynes[14] in economics, Russell and Whitehead in philosophy.[15] It cannot be, for magic is so far insufficiently analyzed. Instead I will use a dozen broad propositions and then discuss them more informally.

What follows is a nondeductive system of empirical propositions. The texture is descriptive-analytical. The approach is positivist, but not, I think, insensitive. The postulates organize what we know about magic at an abstract level so we can see how these pieces fit together. The data consist of most of the best studies of magic made in several fields: psychiatry, anthropology, sociology, philosophy, history—but the organizing viewpoint will be sociological theory, for magic is social. The data are from primary sources, field reports, but also from theories attempting partial organizations of these data. But this is *not* a critical reduction of theories: It is not what Gouldner[16] called "the rhetoric of convergence," nor a history of ideas, nor the old Aristotelian approach of arriving at a theoretical position through a process of elimination. Instead, I use theories as data, along with primary data. For there are really no raw data in this field. As Tillich said, the interpretation begins in the dream. As the text will show, magic itself is already an interpretation. Using studies from different fields this way will put the pieces together. It will show we know more about magic than we think we do. Maybe, with effort, we can recover primitive man's insight into this ineluctable human labyrinth.

Magic Is Real

Writing a general theory of magic presupposes that its numerous provinces form a unity, enough to generalize about. They do. Even the vaudeville magician uses remnants of sorcery rites; yogic meditation recapitulates magicians' initiation; sect magic is a kind of medical magic. It all hangs together and travels together. There is a remarkable pattern consistency all over the world—witches usually fly, ESP is usually confirmed by small groups agreeing to agree, sects usually begin with miracles, and so on.

Nowadays we are not supposed to write about global subjects like magic. The British language-censors and the American nominalists (e.g., Goldenweisser[17]) tell us that things like totemism or magic do not exist. They are just "constructs," words we make up. We cannot talk about caste systems, totemism, magic, anxiety and so forth, and so we are helpless when we bump into these harsh realities. The truth is that the social world is largely made up of overdetermined symbolic complexes like these. Just because they are hard to describe does not mean they are less real. We understand sub-atomic particles, DNA and stellar evolution better than things like religion, personality, mental illness or magic. And yet the latter are formed, have histories and predictable patterns. Marcel Mauss called them "total social facts."[18] Their complexity can only be grasped by a theoretical approach. That is really true in everyday life, too. We all live by theories about what to expect from the social world around us. When our ability to make theories is hurt we are mentally ill.

But how are we to understand such immensities scientifically? One way is to make up an abstract model; a better way is to describe real examples.[19] Instead of "ideal types," Mauss uses "extreme cases."[20] I would call them "natural ideal types." These are real institutions, strikingly *formed* so inherent tendencies are clearest. A good example is Evans-Pritchard's[21] work on the magical medical complex in Zandeland. It is put to the same use as ideal types ("comparison," "model," etc.). For forty years anthropologists have either found the same complex or showed how variations are related to differences in social structure. I share the social realism of Durkheim and Mauss. I will use real rather than nominalist definitions,[22] and actual cases rather than ideal types, because they focus better the social reality of magic.

A Difficult Subject

Magic is not an attractive subject. I came to it for theoretical reasons. I wondered, if the classics of sociological theory are so much about religion (Durkheim, Weber), where does magic fit in? Why does magic persist? What *is* it? I found that it is not a pretty subject, and not an easy one if one cannot tolerate ambiguity. Many social facts are dialectical and ambiguous; magic is more so than many. Typically, magic is an attempt to help that makes a botch. But magic helped make man human, and man remains in many ways a magic animal. Freud said, in *The Future of an Illusion*,[23] that he hoped mankind could get along without certain beliefs, but he would not bet on it. In the modern age, the extension of scientism to society and self has produced a backlash. The magic self bounces back armed with the tools of science to renew agreement on the paranormal.

Today the occult is debated with an intensity not seen since the wars of religion. A new intellectualism attacks any skepticism about it as closed-minded, while older rationalists organize to put pressure on publishers not to print occultism. Both sides may be offended by my argument. I tend to feel, with

Adorno,[24] that the occult is "the metaphysics of the dopes." But I also think that dismissing magic as merely "superstitious" is a circular position and pointless. Is it not better to find out what magic is all about and why it persists?

But I confess that I sometimes feel little more comfortable with some of my guides in this study. Durkheim, for example, admired social integration a bit too much for my tastes. His earnest, normal-school pedagogy, not to mention his advocacy of corporativism, is enough to make one want to cry out, "Anomie is good for you." "Teach us to sit still," T.S. Eliot prayed in "Ash Wednesday." Religion often does that, and so perhaps does sociology. In scores of journal articles it uses chi square to prove that if anything changes people get sick. Perhaps it is not surprising therefore that sociological theory overvalues religion. After all, does not Durkheim teach that religion is the projection of society? So is not the study of society apt to turn the water back into wine again? And maybe the classics of sociological theory are sociology's own theology, the "sacred canopy"[25] to which it retreats when it loses confidence. But these ruminations do not dissuade me, for Durkheim, Mauss and the others at least appreciated complexity, overdetermination, total social facts—and that is the right attitude for penetrating something as complicated as magic.

How This Began

This study began with a problem in sociological theory, especially with Durkheim and Weber. Why did Max Weber use the word magic on almost every page and never define it? What is magic? I got my first lead from two short sections in Durkheim's impressive study of religion as the worship of society.[26] In thirteen sharp pages it stated that magic is something anti-religious that develops *out of* religion. Why? In certain writers in the Freudian tradition[27] I saw a hint of an answer: Magic is symbolism expropriated to protect the self against the social.

Later I discovered that Marcel Mauss had a part of such a theory, though he did not complete it, in my view. The Durkheim-Mauss tradition in France has produced something not too far from my account. I wish it were better known here. My paper shows that a theory of magic is possible; but in their work a sustained theory already exists, at least in part. I have used many other sources, but wherever possible in this paper I will develop ideas from the French school, especially those of Mauss.

Marcel Mauss

Now that the hundred-odd, widely scattered journal articles Mauss published during his lifetime have been republished, assembled in a few large collections,[28] it is hard to resist the recognition that magic was his main preoccupation. The "Sketch" or "Outline (*Esquisse*) of a General Theory of Magic,"[29] which he wrote with Hubert in 1902, began a debate he frequently reentered. He wrote other papers on magic: for instance, on initiation of Australian magicians.[30] *Primitive Classification*[31] provides a deeper key to sympathetic magic than Frazer does; and *The Gift* tells us how magic fostered trade and law. From the time he joined his uncle Durkheim in Bordeaux in the 1890's until his death in 1950, the sacred was Mauss' specialty and he found it full of magic. Today Lévi-Strauss tries to claim him as the forerunner of structuralism;[32] Gurvitch portrays him as a loyal Durkheimian.[33] But his lasting contribution was to show that magic is society's first tool for engineering spontaneity in its individuals.

Marcel Mauss was an eccentric but gregarious figure. He held an academic post of prominence but did not finish his doctorate. Honigsheim[34] depicts him as a maverick even in his own small group. Listening to a colleague he was apt to say, "Ah, but there again you merely show how stupid you are." Bouglé called him *"un homme bizarre."*[35] He kept the Durkheim group together after his uncle's death, convening them regularly at their *"dinées Proudhon"* in Parisian restaurants picked for good food, scenes reminiscent of Roger Shattuck's *The Banquet Years.* He never saw publication of a book that was entirely his own in his lifetime, but he helped to publish the works of fallen colleagues after World War I, and started *L'Année Sociologique* again after Durkheim's death. He was independent and eccentric yet loyal and intensely devoted to several small publics; he was an active member of several learned societies and two socialist parties and contributed to their journals in half a dozen fields including Sanskrit and Hebrew studies; he was a sociologist but also headed an anthropological institute. He taught almost everyone of consequence in French social science for two generations; his students were loyal; his reputation was the product of close contact, small groups and tiny publics. He is the giant of French social science, little known here, and his real subject was magic. I will frequently refer to his works. But this paper is my theory, not a gloss on Mauss.

About Sources

My first sources were *the Durkheimians.* Several dozen anthropologists, sociologists, philosophers and psychiatrists in France extended Mauss's ideas about magic. I have used many of them: Davy, Gurvitch, Caillois, Douttéo, Eliade, Barthes, Ellul, Fauconnet, Pradines, Gusdorf, Rony, Loisy, Allier, Cazeneuve, Huvelin, Bastide, Hocart, others. I also made use of Durkheim himself and the original Durkheimians—Halbwachs, Hubert, Hertz, Bouglé etc.—and of related figures: Lévy-Bruhl, LeBon, Van Gennup, de Coulanges, Granet, Bloch, Massonneau, Lot. Works by Lévi-Strauss, Piaget and the structuralists are also used.

But much has been accomplished since Mauss's day, above all in anthropological fieldwork and in psychiatry. So I have used many other sources, though not miscellaneously. Instead I looked attentively into a number of traditions which have developed important theoretical statements about magic: 1. *The Freudians.* I consulted most of Freud's works, but also the spectacular ideas about magic developed by Róheim, Stekel, Nunberg, Ferenczi, Fenichel, Arieti, Kris, others. I have examined some non-Freudians too: Werner, Storch, Becker, Sullivan, etc. 2. *Max Weber.* His works are useful in showing how the theory can be generalized to advanced civilizations and help explain social change. 3. Other traditions in sociological theory are also consulted: Simmel, Mannheim, Parsons, Marx,

Feuerbach, etc. The Frankfurt School is important, for it shows how the modern world comes to seem demonic through the alienation of reason. 4. Classic theories of magic by Lang, Michelet, Frazer, Malinowski, Hegel, are also examined, along with the mana theorists in Britain, France and America. 5. The study makes prominent use of *the anthropologists*, especially the British group stimulated by Evans-Pritchard and influenced by Durkheim, who studied magic in Africa. 6. Some of the Oxford-Cambridge classicists were influenced by Durkheim and think like anthropologists: Gilbert Murray, Jane Harrison, Francis Cornford, Guthrie, etc. 7. *Psychologists*. Some have interesting theories of magic, including B.F. Skinner, Schachtel. Also relevant are some special topics in psychology like hypnosis, modeling theory, etc. 8. *Some philosophers* with theories of symbolism demonstrate its magical effects: Cassirer, Langer, Duncan. Ludwig Wittgenstein was especially helpful; he reached a social realism position close to Durkheim's. 9. Some accounts of the current occult revival and works spawned by it were also consulted. 10. *Historians of magic* in Western civilization were useful, including Thorndike, Lea, Kittredge, Notestein and the new Oxford group who cross-fertilize with the anthropologists: MacFarlane, Keith Thomas.

A thousand sources are not enough to cover the universe of magic. But, guided by some initial hypotheses, I tried to pick them well. My aim is to write a general theory of magic, putting the pieces together.

Notes

1. Erik H. Erikson, *Identity and the Life Cycle, Psychological Issues* Monograph, vol. 1, no. 1, 1959, cf. David Rapaport Introduction, p. 15.
2. Philip Rieff, *The Triumph of the Therapeutic* (N.Y., 1968), pp. 35–36.
3. Thomas S. Szasz, *Law, Liberty and Psychiatry* (N.Y., 1963), pp. 212–222.
4. Bronislaw Malinowski, *Magic, Science and Religion* (N.Y., 1954), p. 79 ff.
5. James George Frazer, *The Golden Bough* (N.Y., 1960).
5a. Using several books by Frazer and Malinowski instead of one, we could construct a rudimentary *general* theory for each as follows:
Frazer:
a. Magic depends on the association of ideas. (From *The Golden Bough*)
b. Magic enables clever men to dominate others, become kings, set up the first states, become immortalized as gods after death. (From *The Divine King*)
c. Magic provided the first sanctions backing up private property and the integrity of the individual. (From *Psyche's Task*)

Malinowski:
a. Magic builds confidence in situations of uncertainty. (From *Magic, Science and Religion*)
b. Magic provides a ceremonial framework for trade. (From *Argonauts of the Western Pacific*)
c. Magic often organizes collective work. (From *Coral Gardens and Their Magic,* vol. I)
d. Magic works by exerting social pressures. (From *Sexual Life of Savages*)
e. Myths are charters for magic; just reciting the myth has magic effects. (From *The Foundations of Faith and Morals*)
f. Magic is largely verbal and uses a special stilted language different from both work language and sociability language. (From Supplement to Ogden and Richards, *The Meaning of Meaning*)
g. Magic is an extreme case illuminating the action function of language, and all language is magical at first. (From *Coral Gardens,* vol. II)

h. Magic loopholes evade reciprocity laws but most magic conservatively supports inequalities in primitive society. (From *Crime and Custom in Savage Society*)

i. Magic is confirmed by miracles which are generated by faith. (From *Sex and Repression in Savage Society*)

6. Henri Hubert and Marcel Mauss, "Esquisse d'Une Théorie Générale de la Magie," *L'Année Sociologique* (Paris, 1902–1903). Republished in Claude Lévi-Strauss, ed., *Marcel Mauss Sociologie et Anthropologie* (Paris, 1950, 1966), pp. 6 – 137.

7. Marcel Mauss, *A General Theory of Magic*, trans. by Robert Brain, foreword by D.F. Pocock. (Routledge & Kegan Paul, London & Boston, 1972); paperback ed. (Norton Library, N.Y., 1975). Care should be taken with the English edition: e.g. the name of the co-author, Henri Hubert, is left off the book. A foreword added by David Pocock, of the School of African and Asian Studies, University of Sussex, makes the claim that Mauss in this essay "dissolves" the concept of magic (I suppose he means the way Lévi-Strauss claimed Goldenweisser "dissolved" the concept of totemism). Mauss does not in fact do this.

8. Frederick Schleiter, *Religion and Culture* (N.Y., 1919), pp. 109–110.

9. Dozens of books are written which examine magic that way, with chapters on various magical arts. The most respectable authors, such as Kurt Seligmann, Julio Caro Baroja and Idries Shah, at least try to demonstrate historical diffusion paths. But the data remain too raw to be explanatory, and the authors are often true believers. These books are tedious and I have consulted only a few dozen—by Bergier and Pauwels, Arthur Lyons, Nat Freedland, Colin Wilson, Richard Cavendish, Arthur Koestler, W.B. Crow, R.E.I. Bonewitz, Theodore Roszak, Jacob Needleman and others. Some of these writers are *part* of the occult revival.

10. I cannot just break down magic into its "elements" as Hubert and Mauss do in part ("rites, representations, actors"). Anyway, I want to cover far more than they do (they neglect sects, psychological magic, etc.), and the elements vary in some provinces.

11. Leonard Bloomfield, "A Set of Postulates for the Science of Language," *Language*, 2.153–64 (1926), reprinted in Sol Saporta and Jarvis R. Bastian, *Psycholinguistics* (N.Y., 1966), pp. 26–33.

12. Ronald E. Shor, "Hypnosis and the Concept of the Generalized Reality-Orientation," *American Journal of Psychotherapy*, vol. 13 (1959), pp. 582–602; and "Three Dimensions of Hypnotic Depth," *International Journal of Clinical and Experimental Hypnosis*, vol. 10 (1962), pp. 23–38. Both reprinted in Charles T. Tart, ed., *Altered States of Consciousness* (N.Y., 1972), pp. 239–267.

13. Clark L. Hull, *A Behavior System* (New Haven, 1952, N.Y., 1964).

14. John Maynard Keynes, *The General Theory of Employment, Interest and Money* (N.Y., 1936).

15. Bertrand Russell and Alfred North Whitehead, *Principia Mathematica* (Cambridge, 1910, short edition to *56, 1967).

16. Alvin W. Gouldner, *The Coming Crisis of Western Sociology* (N.Y., 1970), p. 17.

17. Alexander Goldenweisser, "Totemism, An Analytical Study," *Journal of American Folklore* XXIII (1910). See Lévi-Strauss comments in *Totemism* (Boston, 1963), pp. 4, 5, 75. Goldenweisser's anti-Durkheim position is made clear in his *Ancient Civilization: An Introduction to Anthropology* (N.Y., 1922), ch. 16.

18. Mauss, *Essais Sur le Don*, Lévi-Strauss, ed., *Marcel Mauss Sociologie et Anthropologie* (Paris, 1950, 1966), pp. 273–284. Engl. ed., *The Gift* (N.Y., 1967), pp. 76–81.

19. Max Weber's "ideal types" examine our constructs more than the phenomena they refer to. An ideal type is a whole theory written in the style of a long definition. (Weber's ideal type of bureaucracy runs 11 pages.) Weber's excuse is that we use words like capitalism and totemism with complicated meanings anyway, so we might as well make the content explicit. Making it up before our eyes is like the waiter who cooks the crêpes at the table—you can see everything that goes into it. (Weber, *The Methodology of the Social Sciences*, Glencoe, Ill, 1949, "Objectivity in Social Science and Social Policy," pp. 49–112.) But there is a nominalist skepticism in this operation which, paradoxically, produces dogmas. For ideal types are too complicated to be tested or "falsified." (Karl R. Popper, *The Logic of Scientific Discovery*, N.Y., 1965, Ch. 4, pp. 78–92.) They are usually based on surreptitious inductions but foreclose induction. We know that Weber's ideal type of bureaucracy is generalized from the Chinese and Prussian civil services, but we are not supposed to say this or check its accuracy. So ideal types float in the air like transcendent archetypes; they some-

how actualize their inherent forms, like Aristotle's entelechies. They belong in catechisms. Durkheim rightly calls this "the method of idealism." (*Les Règles de la Methode Sociologique*, Paris, 1950, ch. 1.) If you put your whole theory in your initial definitions, you do not have to do any investigation.

20. He develops this idea explicitly in "Essai Sur les Variations Saisonnières Des Sociétés Eskimos: Etude de Morphologie Sociale" in Lévi-Strauss, ed., *Marcel Mauss Sociologie et Anthropologie*, pp. 389–475.

21. E.E. Evans-Pritchard, *Witchcraft, Oracles and Magic Among the Azande* (Oxford, 1937).

22. See Melford E. Spiro, "Religion: Problems of Definition and Explanation" in M. Banton, ed., *Anthropological Approaches to the Study of Religion* (London, 1966), pp. 85–126.

23. Sigmund Freud, *The Future of an Illusion* (Garden City, N.Y., 1964), p. 83 ff.

24. Theodore Adorno, "The Stars Down to Earth: The Los Angeles Times Astrology Column," *Telos*, no. 19, Spring, 1974, pp. 13–90, and "Theses Against Occultism," same issue, pp. 7–12, cf. p. 9.

25. Peter L. Berger, *The Sacred Canopy* (N.Y., 1967), cf. ch. 2.

26. Emile Durkheim, *The Elementary Forms of Religious Life* (London, 1915), pp. 42–47, 355–362.

27. Especially, Géza Róheim, *Magic and Schizophrenia* (Bloomington, Ind., 1955). To be discussed (in ch. 9).

28. Marcel Mauss, *Oeuvres* (Les Editions de Minuit, Paris, 1968), ed. Victor Karady, 3 vols. By agreement, this contains everything except the important papers collected in *Marcel Mauss Sociologie et Anthropologie* (P.U.F., Paris, 1950, 1966), ed. Claude Lévi-Strauss, and the unimpressive *Manuel d'Ethnographie* compiled from stenographic notes of his lecture course and published as he lay ill, 1947, republished Paris, 1967. Karady also omitted some letters, and Mauss's Introduction to Durkheim's book on socialism (Emile Durkheim, *Socialism*, N.Y., 1958), on the peculiar grounds that these mild five pages were "ideology" rather than sociology. So the three volumes edited by Karady and the one by Lévi-Strauss contain almost all of Mauss. A few of his longer monographs have been translated into English and published as books. Besides the *General Theory of Magic*, already mentioned, we have: Mauss, *The Gift* (N.Y., 1967); Emile Durkheim and Mauss, *Primitive Classification* (Chicago, 1963); Henri Hubert and Mauss, *Sacrifice, Its Nature and Function* (Chicago and London, 1964). One of his shorter pieces was translated in *Psychoanalytic Review*, vol. 55, no. 3 (1968): Mauss, "A Category of the Human Spirit," pp. 457–481.

29. i.e., "*Esquisse d'une Théorie Générale de la Magie.*" *Esquisse* means sketch, outline, plan.

30. Mauss, "L'Origine des Pouvoirs Magiques dans les Sociétés Australiennes," 1904, republished in *Oeuvres*, vol. I, pp. 319–369.

31. Durkheim and Mauss (Chicago, 1963).

32. In Introduction to *Marcel Mauss Sociologie et Anthropologie*; in *Structural Anthropology*, etc.

33. Georges Gurvitch, *La Vocation Actuelle de la Sociologie*, vol. II (Paris, 1963) pp. 59–174. And see Jean Cazeneuve on the controversy: *Sociologie de Marcel Mauss* (Paris, 1968). Also the Karady Introduction to Mauss, *Oeuvres*, vol. I. Other useful essays include Maurice Merleau-Ponty, "De Mauss à Claude Lévi-Strauss," *Eloge de la Philosophie* (Paris, 1953, 1960), pp. 145–169; Lawrence Krader in issue of *Psychoanalytic Quarterly* cited above; Evans-Pritchard's Introduction to *The Gift*; Rodney Needham's to *Primitive Classification*; references in Lucien Goldman, *The Human Sciences and Philosophy* (London, 1969); E.E. Evans-Pritchard, *Theories of Primitive Religion*, (Oxford, 1965), ch. 3.

34. Paul Honigsheim, "Reminiscences of the Durkheim School," in Kurt H. Wolff, ed., *Essays on Sociology and Philosophy by Emile Durkheim et al.* (N.Y., 1964), pp. 309–314.

35. *Ibid.*, p. 311.

Introduction: WHAT IS IT?

WITTGENSTEIN considered language a great mirror.[1] It really does reflect what is there—especially what is there in society, in culture. When you begin studying something complicated, you can look at the phenomenon itself, or you can first look for its reflection in the great mirror. And we can see magic very clearly in the mirror of language. For magic is first of all a universal human idea, a concept so widespread and distinct that it is almost a "category of the human spirit," like time, space and mass. A word for magic is found in many languages—often it is a derivative of the local "mana" word (which frequently means some kind of social power). And in many languages the word for magic refers to the same thing—a group of well-known, clearly identified and unmistakable institutions. The most important are medical, ceremonial, religious, occult, paranormal, sectarian and black magic.

Now turn away from the mirror and look at these institutions themselves. They are real. They are almost everywhere—in every era, in almost every society. For these are "real social facts" in Durkheim's sense. They possess all three of his criteria for objective reality: "externality," "coerciveness" and "generality" (and did he not say that two out of three were enough?).[2] They also have what I consider to be Mauss's fourth criterion—they are "formed."[3] These institutions are too consistently patterned to be explained away by a nominalist analysis. They are found in almost every society above the Paleolithic band stage, and many, many cultures recognize them and call them magic. What are they for? They appear to be related to religion and to help the individual. They were active at earlier stages when they left marks on other institutions. But some are still quite active now, above all medical magic, paranormal magic and the protest magic of sects.

Now look back at the great mirror again, for there is more to be seen. There are haloes, auras, metaphors. Besides referring to clear-cut magic institutions, the word magic appears to be a seemingly indispensable metaphor for making statements about certain striking qualities of human action, speech and thought. This is as true of our own culture as that of primitive man. In our time, these metaphors of magic are elevated into theory language and are used in several disciplines as explanations of human behavior. Psychiatrists characterize neurotic symptoms as "magical" operations. Philosophers like Langer and Cassirer see "magical" qualities in all human symbolization. Any thorough explanation of magic must also explore these metaphors, for they are shadows cast by something real.

1

The Seven Provinces

But the main task of a general theory must be to explain the real magical institutions, magic in the strict sense.

1. Medical Magic

Consider, for example, one of the larger provinces of magic: the magical-medical scenario with its dramatic cast of characters, both real (diviners, oracles, witchdoctors) and imaginary (ghosts, evil spirits, witches, etc.). It is still so vivid among our primitive contemporaries that it is the object of earnest investigations today by Western psychiatrists like E. Fuller Torrey[4] and Ari Kiev[5] who seek to discover what modern medicine should learn from it. It is so pattern-consistent that it is the subject of a widely agreed-upon "natural ideal type" (my term)— the one developed by Evans-Pritchard in *Witchcraft, Oracles and Magic Among the Azande*.[6] In Zandeland anyone who gets sick first consults a mechanical oracle (and may later see a diviner) to get a diagnosis. He may be told his illness was caused by a sorcerer, a ghost, an evil spirit, a broken taboo or a natural cause —but in Zandeland, he is usually told that a witch did it. He may go to higher oracles for confirmation. He may then seek out a witchdoctor to get magic medicine to fight his spiritual tormentor, or he may go to the dumbfounded accused "witch" himself and demand that he climb down. He may later join a thaumaturgical sect to get protection from witches. Meanwhile, he may suspect that the local witchdoctor is also a sorcerer. (Witches kill spiritually without magic—magic is used as a *defense* against them. Sorcerers kill by means of magic: spells, medicines, etc.)

Evans-Pritchard did not intend to produce a natural ideal type, and elsewhere he insisted on variability in primitive religions (based on their differing worldviews). But many anthropologists in Africa (and other continents) have confirmed his patterns. Almost everywhere they find oracles and diviners as diagnosticians, and witchdoctors or shamans or medical cults as healers, providing magic as a defense. And almost everywhere they find the same major diagnoses of illness: witchcraft, sorcery, ghosts, broken taboos, evil spirits. They usually find a witch pattern distinct from a sorcery pattern, with witches using imaginary weapons (such as sending their souls flying through the air to suck out a man's liver while he sleeps) and sorcerers using "real" (potentially do-able) magic (like the jealous neighbor who burns someone in effigy—or poisons him). Moreover, where the patterns vary, the variations reflect features in the social structure. While Zandeland attributes most illnesses to witchcraft, Dobu[7] and the Paiute[8] emphasize sorcery more; there is a greater emphasis on taboo-breaking in Maori[9] diagnosis, while spirits are the main pathogens among the Dinka[10] and Nuer.[11] Max Marwick[12] and others show *there is always a social reason* for these variations. (All this is discussed in Chapter 11.)

The medical complex as a whole also varies in the prominence it has in each society; again, this reflects worldview and social structure. In Zandeland magic medicine swamps religion and all other magics; it takes the place of theodicy, cosmology; people are so busy thinking about witches that they do not think about gods. Witches explain almost everything that happens. By contrast, among the Plains Indians[13] another aspect of religion, the vision quest associated with tribal initiation, swamps other magic and religious institutions. Still other people, like the Nuer, are so theistic that their magic is rudimentary and they have to use religious rites (like sacrifice) for magical purposes[14] for want of adequate magic. So the magic medicine complex varies both in importance and in internal emphasis—but it is almost always present, Evans-Pritchard admits, in rudimentary or prominent form, and all the familiar elements are there to some degree.[15]

The magical medical complex is present in our own society, where diviners and oracles are called by other names (fortune tellers, clairvoyants, astrologers, etc.) and the occupations of medicine men or curers are so spectacularly varied it would take a Rabelaisian gusto to enumerate them all. In addition to Jungians, Sullivanites and transactionalists, we have Scientologists, Reichians, gestaltists and T-group leaders; technicians for every hatha, karma, bhakti, Vajrayana and mechanical yoga; snake handlers, faith healers, holy rollers, logolaliacs, primal screamers and other commotions; personifications of all past curers including strokers, magnetists, spiritualists and hypnotists; and every spice in the melting pot including brujos, gurus, santeros, voodoos, Macumbas and Catholic exorcists; acupuncturers, kundalinis and mantra-tantras; all the Subuds, Babas, Zens and Sufis; guides for every trance and drug; plus macrobioticians, biorhythmers, guided imagers, behavior controllers and wild psychologists.

Their numbers are enormous. In 1968 Truzzi[16] estimated 10,000 full-time and 175,000 part-time astrologers alone in the U.S.—these are just diviners, and only one kind. Ellul in 1973 estimated 6,000 fakirs, soothsayers and fortune tellers in France.[17] And even if we do not consult them, they flood our communications media with their obsessive magical advice on how to live our lives carefully and safely.

Yet social science until recently often ignored or denied their presence. (This is now changing.[18]) For example, sociologist Ann Parsons did a study of an Italian-American woman in Boston who was killed by the magical medical complex, yet she interpreted it differently.[19] Parsons diagnosed Mrs. Perella as psychotic, because she suffered delusions after her ninth pregnancy, claimed one of her friends was hexing her with the evil eye, and then committed suicide. Ms. Parsons contrasted the "dysfunctional" delusions about black magic that psychotics like Mrs. Perella have with the "socially-integrating functions" she claimed black magic institutions had in primitive society. But in Ms. Parsons' own account, Mrs. Perella committed suicide only after she had consulted a fortune teller. The fortune teller confirmed her own self-diagnosis of evil eye and gave her some magical medicine to fight the spell. Did Mrs. Perella commit suicide because her delusions were dysfunctional, or because the magic medicine complex was still around and *it* was dysfunctional? Does anyone really imagine that people go to fortune tellers because they are idly curious about the future, or to astrologers just as an amusement? When one considers all the subcultural magics in our melting pot, and how world civilization preserves magics from all past ages, and how jaded cosmopolitans take up even the primitive magics anthropologists uncover, the total number of full and part-time magical specialists may run in the millions. And that means that the people who seek magical help because they experience magical illnesses or interpret illness that way may run in the hundreds of millions.

Medical magic exists. It is a cluster of actual rites, representations and actors; it is a group of institutions with large professional staffs of real people. But it is only one of the provinces of magic. In a rough and ready way, I discern seven. Besides medical magic, there are:

2. Black Magic

Black magic overlaps medical magic, for some of its actors cause the diseases medical magic fights: e.g., witches and sorcerers. But it is logically distinct from medical magic, and separate in several real ways. For one thing, it is probably older. As for imaginary witches and how they fit into magic, the thing to grasp is that the *accusation* of witchcraft is the magical act. I suspect that it may have been man's first magical counterattack on the superego; it neutralized moral entrepreneurs who used to cause voodoo death. Witchdoctors who fight witches are often suspected of being sorcerers, because that is what they were originally. (The antiquity of black magic is demonstrated in Chapter 11.) But black magic is separate from medical magic for another reason—it includes a lot more than the agents of disease. Black magic, one might say, runs a continuum from the mild aggressions of love magic (not always so mild, according to Malinowski[20]), to trivial spite magic, to defensive magic that counterattacks the enemy, all the way to the darker counties of witchcraft, sorcery and demonology.

Evans-Pritchard distinguished witchcraft from sorcery on the grounds that witchcraft is an "impossible" crime while sorcery is an "improbable" crime.[21] This needs to be discussed. He meant that witches kill by imaginary, "spiritual" means which even primitives find mysterious, such as sending their doubles to eat the inner organs of their enemies. This is clearly impossible. By contrast, sorcerers kill by conceivable but unlikely magical means (such as spells and effigies.) Evans-Pritchard thought this could happen but that it was more likely to be yet another delusion, like witchcraft. That may be true in Zandeland, but it is debatable elsewhere. In some societies sorcerers are out in the open, organized into collegia, flaunting their wiles and self-identified as mean individuals out to do us harm. There are leopard cults, for example. There are black magics owned by particular families: in Dobu,[22] elsewhere. And only in fairy tales do sorcerers stick to non-physical magic alone. Among the Barotse,[23] they bushwhack people with "bush guns," handmade blunderbusses that can blow a person's head off. In many societies, they are poisoners. There is, in fact, an immemorial folk association between poisoning and sorcery. It is only in modern civilization that we clearly distinguish physical from psychological agencies: Primitive sorcerers would just as soon poison an enemy, shoot him, burn down his house or kill his chickens. And even the "impossible" crime of witchcraft tends to come into being, probably through "modeling" and "acting out" of a familiar archetype, though as a rule it is imaginary. Most accounts of witches, such as those the Navajo gave Kluckholn,[24] are based on tradition and imagination, rather than encounters. But in some few societies visible, black magicians turn up whose actions, symbols or propaganda about themselves include details from the witch complex. Occasionally there are witch-like complexes with reports of actual encounters. Technically, these are sorcerers who imitate as best they can the witch archetype's frightfulness. In today's occult revival, some people in California will tell you they are witches. It is beside the point to tell them they are using the wrong word. They read all the books and do the best they can.

In modern terms, perhaps, a witch is someone whose sullen, unconscious or hidden hatred somehow gets one down. By contrast, a sorcerer is a rival or real enemy who actively uses "dirty tricks." We have our own sorcery patterns: for instance, Southerners who burn down a neighbor's barn, people who write poison pen letters, and so on. The C.I.A. engaged in a kind of sorcery when, according to a Senate investigation, it tried to put chemicals onto the soles of Castro's shoes to cause his beard to fall out (thus destroying his charisma, his mana?).[25] And if, in our world, that is only sorcery in a metaphorical sense, it is no fault of the C.I.A.'s. They and other intelligence agencies back so much research in magic and ESP that they are among its modern "carriers."[26]

3. Ceremonial Magic

Individual health is not the only end to which magic is put. There is also the magic of collective purpose: such as rain-making magic; agricultural magic; the ritual magic of great occasions; and hunting magic, fishing magic, work magic in general, a topic so often studied by Malinowski.[27] I will call all this ceremonial magic, because typically it is performed as a public ceremony. Whereas most magic, like medical magic, falls into the client-professional pattern, one person ministering to another, ceremonial magic is performed for the community. Often it is led by an official of the community, either a headman or chief, or a member of a magician caste that has been coopted for official ends (as in Australia) It is distinct from more surreptitious and individual magics this way, but it is also distinct from religious magic. For typically it works for profane or quasi-profane if collective ends. Ceremonial magic also adds to the pomp of chiefs and kings, as Budge,[28] Childe,[29] etc., have shown.

4. Religious Magic

In a strict sense, this term applies only to some clearly magical institutions that have gotten embedded within religions, often in response to other magic. The clearest case is exorcism, which is religion's own medicine man magic to fight black magic. There are recognized exorcists within the Catholic Church, for example: not many, and they do not accept many cases, but their presence helps certify that belief in magic which is part of official church credo. Another clear-cut case is theurgy, the use of magical means, within a religion or church, to worship or get close to god. Theurgy was prominent in Egyptian religion and in Hinduism. But in addition to these hard-core institutions of religious magic in the strict sense, other religious rites are magical in a metaphorical sense and this will be explored. These include magical uses of prayer, myth and above all sacrifice and the many sacraments derived from it. I will show that these institutions are magical "in the weak sense," and that their historical function was to "model" the inherent sympathetic properties of religious rites in a way that stimulated the development of real magic.

5. The Occult Sciences (and the Theosophies)

The occult sciences developed partly out of magic medicine, for many of them were originally some particular society's *divination system.* I Ching, astrology, dream analysis, etc., then became rationalized as systems of learning within civilizations, beginning with the castes of priests and magicians that states set up to centralize magic. Douttée,[30] Thorndike[31] and others have suggested that divination procedures go a separate path from the rest of magic because they predict while magic seeks immediate effects—so they become pseudo-sciences of forecasting and may lead to real science through feedback of observations. But Evans-Pritchard has shown[32] that divination systems are embedded in medical and black magic systems so complex that all statements are circular and self-confirming and there is no falsification. Moreover, diagnosis by divination is itself a magical act with magical results.[33] Not empirical results but inherent logics are what make divination systems rationalize themselves. Many tend to be binary oracles to begin with ("she loves me, she loves me not"). First the priestly collegia of Near East empires systematized the most popular divinations from diverse peoples; then Hellenic rationalism further rationalized them into a permanent part of the planetary magical heritage. A similar process occurred in China, where divination was unusually important in magic, and where it spawned many games we play as well as occult sciences: chess, dominoes and so on. The binary operators and other systematics inherent in divination systems caused them to be further rationalized, beyond occult sciences to theosophies—which are magical philosophies generalizing from a large number of occult sciences[34] (the way Hellenistic gnosticism, for example, made use of astrology, kabbalah, alchemy, etc.). Theosophies like Hermeticism, gnosticism, Vedanta, etc., compete with religious theologies. They significantly increase a society's belief in all forms of magic. Astrology itself became a theosophy, and provided the sacred canopy for at least three occult upsurges. Thus Angus has shown[35] that magical beliefs waxed with astrology in the Hellenistic period; Keith Thomas[36] showed that acceptance of astrology by the intelligentsia provided the basis for official support of witch beliefs in the early modern period; and Truzzi has demonstrated the centrality of astrology in the current occult revival.

6. The Paranormal

Extrasensory perception, altered states of consciousness and paranormal experiences in general cannot be left out of any complete account of magic.

They seem like natural phenomena but they are often produced by small groups using traditional magical means and their expectations are patterned by magical archetypes. As for the possibility that there may exist some core ESP phenomena that are real, I will simply "bracket" it, leave it open. It is a subject beyond the scope of this study. Here is my justification: In so many paranormal studies (flying saucers, ESP, etc.), the typical approach is to discard 99 percent of the cases as fraudulent or badly reported, and concentrate on the one percent that seem best documented. I think it is just as important to study the 99 percent which are discarded. To throw the 99 percent away as mere superstition is to throw away valuable data. What we need to understand is why mankind constantly forms itself into small groups to produce and confirm paranormal experiences. Whether some small core of phenomena mixed in these experiences contains some objective reality is perhaps less significant than how this province works, as magic. The apostles of the occult would like to fixate our attention on whether there is "something in" ESP; those who challenge this accept battle on terms laid down by the enemy. But if there are a few objective phenomena mixed up in ESP, we will eventually discover them and add them to science, as we added electricity and many other things. Meanwhile, let us not assume that this is an acid test that admits everything. The occultists are monists who think that way, and would like us to do so; they hope with any demonstration to bring back not just ESP but shamanism, exorcism, all seven provinces.

So we must study all the various ESP phenomena, and we must also study the studiers of these phenomena and note how their institutes and collegia and sects are socially organized. We must study, as data, certain institutions that call themselves sciences. Under the same heading, we must explore hypnosis, borderline psychological states of all kinds, and all socially patterned intoxications and the latest research on psychoactive drugs together with the social structures that collect around them. We must also study yoga and meditation—yes, and "mysticism" too. All these are perennial, patterned, widespread social experiences; and all are related to small groups embedded in magical institutions. The mystic's ascent to god, for example, recapitulates the universal practice whereby a magician, with the aid of drugs or suggestion, ascends to heaven to get powers from god during his initiation.

7. Magic Cults and Sects

Finally, there is the quasi-rebellious magic of cultic groups. These include the thaumaturgical societies that offer primitive man protection against witches. They also include sects and cults born of initiation and medicine lodges. As society becomes more complex, they develop into sects protesting, challenging, changing or augmenting established religions in an endless and spectacular symbolic struggle. "Charisma" is magic as Max Weber demonstrated; that is the key for including all charismatic sects and movements in a study of magic. This implies that new religions *begin* as magic, and that must be explored, too, for it seems to challenge a more basic finding that magic comes after religion and derives from it. The answer will be dialectical.

This is not an exhaustive list and there are overlaps. The seven provinces might be charted as an interlinked chain of Venn circles moving out of religion (which is suggestive), with religious magic overlapping ceremonial magic which overlaps medical, occult, paranormal, sectarian and black magics.

Lesser Provinces

There are also lesser provinces of magic worth mentioning, though most are derivative or decay products and will get less attention:

1. *"Magic tricks."* Stage and hobby magic is an enormous subculture which preserves symbols of more serious magic in play form. The Indian rope trick, for example, is a remnant of a hallucinatory experience of dismemberment that took place in magicians' initiations.[37] Tricks of palming and sleight of hand derive from shamanic skills at planting objects on a patient's body and then removing them as symbols and persuasions that the disease is being removed. Hypnosis is a modern, socially patterned variant of magical trance. Stage magic intersects numerous other folk institutions that preserve magic symbolism: carnivals, circuses, pantomimes and so on. Truzzi has done valuable studies of this. Real magic can often be found in these worlds, and getting interested in stage magic sometimes leads to more hard-core magical pursuits.

2. *Folk magic.* Folk remedies and magics are the masses' first line of defense against magical illnesses. Keith Thomas showed that in the Renaissance this province possessed enormous resources. Bypassed and outdated sciences, as well as magics driven underground, often sink down into folk magics. This is magic *alla casa lingua*, magic done at home, without calling in a specialist. It shades imperceptibly into practices that are magical only in a metaphorical way but no less necessary: from "magic" kisses for baby's injuries to all sorts of psychic home remedies.

3. *Occupational magics.* Other magics persist in the various professions and arts: law and theater, and the good luck magics of longshoremen, loggers, sailors and so on. Several investigators, seeking to confirm Malinowski's theory of magic as a device to increase confidence in uncertainty, have done studies of these.[38]

A General Theory Deduced From the Classics

What a General Theory Might Accomplish

I want to explain all these provinces in a unified way, what they have in common. Although some of my propositions concern one province more than another, all apply somewhat to all of them.[39] For I want to keep them at a level of generalization where they can connect with classical sociological theory, from which my initial definition and hypothesis were derived. I hope thereby to test, renew and challenge classic theory. A general theory of magic will also make special contributions to the sociology of knowledge, the sociology of religion, the theory of social action and sociological psychology. And since understanding any strategic "total social fact" will help us understand the others it intersects, the theory will throw light on mental illness, human personality, suicide, millenarian movements and other interesting matters.

What Do the Classics Say About Magic?

Concern is frequently expressed (by Geertz,[40] Roland Robertson,[41] Block and Hammond,[42] Gouldner[43]) that sociology has been living too long off a limited heritage of classical theory (this means mostly Weber and Durkheim), and that this intellectual capital will soon be exhausted unless it is somehow "renewed." But if the classics are still the nearest thing to an overarching body of theory in sociology, then it is surely striking that *religion* is such a central topic in them. This preoccupation–in an allegedly secular age–appears to be more than just a conservative reaction to modern society (as Nisbet[44] would have it). The classics score some of their best hits when they do a sociology of religion. Marx stated that sociology *begins* with the study of religion. Durkheim devoted two of his greatest studies to religion,[45] and used it to explain the development of human thought. Many of Weber's books are about religion. But with one exception the classics themselves do not contain a developed theory of magic. That is odd.

Consider the Marxist tradition, which seems to have neglected magic despite its considerable anthropological interest, and despite Hegel. Hegel wrote one of the earliest theories of magic, in which he handed on to modern social science the ethnocentric view that reason triumphs in a magic-to-religion-to-science sequence.[46] Hegel's account anticipated many later ideas. He remarked that magic operates through a *tradition*; that it concerns a *"power"* obtained by knowing and operating on the *quality* of things; that religion and magic engage in a *dialectic*; that magic has to do with mastery of social forces through *mastery of self*, and so on. But his student Marx did not develop these ideas.

Marx felt that sociology, while it must begin with the analysis of religion, must move beyond it. Henri LeFebvre[47] has shown that Marx's dialectic is based, not so much on synthesis as on "overcoming," going beyond. The "truth of religion," what it really is, is discovered by going beyond it, to philosophy. But we do not linger there, for the "truth of philosophy," what *it* really is, is discovered in politics. Nathan Rotenstreich asserts[48] that the turning point was Marx's "Theses on Feuerbach," in which he explicitly repudiated the technique of studying religious projections of society in which Feuerbach had anticipated Durkheim. Somewhere Marx called Feuerbach "our own venerable Saint Max," suggesting that a social-theory reconstruction of religious phenomena could itself turn into a religion. Marx had a point. Since religion is really about society, sociology can sound like religion. Even Durkheim's sociology, enshrined as the official educational philosophy of the Third Republic,[49] bore at least a metaphorical resemblance to the state religion Robespierre and Comte had called for. In *The German Ideology*[50] Marx denounced the sociology of religion as unrevolutionary.[51]

Marx's decision entailed that he never got around to producing a theory of magic. I find no study of magic in the works of Marx and Engels. Even Engels' account of the transition from matriarchy to patriarchy ignores magic.[52] So does his discussion of the chiliasms of the peasant wars.[53] Not even the very Hegelian early writings of Marx,[54] which work with suggestive categories like "alienation," fraud and "false consciousness," develop a theory of magic, though they might have. (The potential for a theory of magic is perhaps present, as later Marxists of a Feuerbachian persuasion, like Ernst Bloch,[55] have shown.)

The Durkheim school does have a sustained theory of magic in its second figure, Marcel Mauss, but his work is little known here. If we stick to Durkheim himself, we find only one excellent but short statement on magic, set out in 13 pages and not mentioned again.[56] This statement is seldom commented on in the United States, where magic is treated as a footnote to the sociology of religion, if at all. My investigation began with Durkheim's hint and I want to make Mauss better known, even though his theory does not cover all of magic.[57] (Several dozen French writers in the Durkheim-Mauss tradition *do* cumulatively say a lot about magic.[58])

Max Weber gave no definition of magic, but his books about religion are saturated with the subject. His *Sociology of Religion* seems to be about magic as much as religion; it is mentioned constantly and basic religious phenomena are frequently referred to as magical.[59] The preoccupation continues through his books on the religions of India, China and Israel, and essays such as "The Social Psychology of The World Religions."[60] We are told how Upanishadic and Confucian rationalism left the masses behind, abandoned to magic; how the Brahmins were really a caste of magicians, not priests; how Christ was a magician, and so on—all these tantalizing statements without definitions. References to magic are so frequent that Parsons[61] considers it a main concern of Weber's. (Parsons' own attempt to develop a one-proposition theory out of all this oversimplifies.) Weber himself does not develop his numerous insights into an explicit theory of magic.[62] Yet some of Weber's hypotheses about religion—such as "routinization of charisma"—are partly hypotheses about magic. A challenging partial theory of magic could be developed out of Weber alone by making these statements explicit. In particular, Weber emphasizes what Mauss and Durkheim leave out—the magic of mass charisma and sects, of new religions and of the endless dialectic between magic and religion that is part of social change in advanced societies and civilizations.

At very least a theory of magic might synthesize what is already implicit in the classics. This might help renew them, extend their meaning and vitality. But sociology by itself does not contain an adequate understanding of magic. We need the painstaking field investigations of anthropology to go further, and also the clinical discoveries of psychiatry. The perspective of history is essential. And other subjects have important investigations to contribute: psychology, philosophy, theology, studies of symbolism, etc.

So my study *starts* with the classics, with Durkheim and Weber especially. But my approach is an analytical-empirical survey of evidence, not a critical reduction of classic theories. The latter method has inherent defects, and it is too loose. Besides, there would be little justification for leaving out thoughtful theories in related subjects like anthropology (Marett, Malinowski, Frazer, etc.), psychology (B.F. Skinner), not to mention theology (Otto, Van der Leeuw, Bloch, etc.) Theory reduction on that large a scale would be a meat grinder. So

I begin with Durkheim-Weber style definitions, but then investigate the *phenomena* of magic rather than theories about it.[63]

Definitions of Magic

With a subject as vast as magic, the old Durkheim double-bind about initial definitions is particularly painful. On the one hand Durkheim said, do not even begin with minimal hypotheses in studying a raw, little understood subject: this will cause too much premature theory ("the method of idealism"). On the other hand, he insisted one must have a clear simple *definition* in advance and study everything that falls under it so as to avoid "picking one's cases."[64]

The best students were quite reluctant to pre-define the vast subject of magic. Weber gave *no* definition of magic. And Hubert and Mauss were reluctant to give one because "our aim is not...to define words, but to set up natural classes of fact...we cannot know *a priori* its limits.... We must first make a kind of inventory of these facts."[65] They did give a minimal definition anyway, but I share their reluctance. I would almost prefer an "ostensive" definition—"By magic I mean that and that and that, all those provinces."

And what about all the metaphors of magic applied to so many aspects of human action and speech? What definition could include them? Yet it is precisely my desire to explain this metaphorical penumbra as well as real magic that makes a clear initial definition necessary. For without a definite standard of comparison, how can I evaluate the metaphors? To call something "magical" this way would be meaningless. So I will use a formal definition for the real magical institutions, and an open, cumulating definition for magic in the weak sense. One way of avoiding equivocations on a subject that is real on several levels is to use several definitions. "Category errors"[66] can be avoided by making sure that any sentence which designates phenomena in more than one of these definitions asserts a functional relation between the two.

In the Weak Sense

While my definition of magic "in the strict sense" will refer to real magical institutions, mainly to the seven provinces, magic in "the weak sense" will refer to the metaphors of magic. I will not even define the latter initially, but wait and see what the study picks up. However, it might be well to give a preview here. This study will discover that metaphors of magic, "magic in the weak sense," refer to several things that are very real on symbolic and psychological levels: 1. The inherent "sympathetic" effects of language, which trace back to primitive classification systems. 2. The inherent "sympathetic" effects of all religious rites, in which religion strikingly "models" the magical potentials of symbolism. 3. Certain ego actions of the human self which was nourished historically by magical institutions and retains a magical character. 4. Certain magical aspects of social action, in which actors use the "sympathetic" effects of symbolism to affect each other. 5. In addition, there are of course *defective* metaphors of magic, as when we label certain forceful or successful actions "magical" which are not magical at all.

In the Strict Sense

How is magic in the strict sense to be defined? How can we give a simple definition to something so seemingly diverse? I began with the conviction that these data possess Durkheim's three criteria of "social facts," of objectivity: they have "externality, constraint and generality." I was struck by the fact that they also have what I consider to be Mauss's fourth criterion: "formedness." I also noted that they possess still another attribute which might be a criterion for the objectivity of a cultural fact: common usage, common report of mankind. That is to say many languages have words for magic, indeed whole clusters of words which refer to many of the magical institutions. This degree of formedness and this frequency of common usage inspired in me the intuition that magic is a "total social fact" in Mauss' sense, an important ganglionic human institution. I might therefore hope that even a simple definition, which perhaps covered only a few attributes, might nonetheless be a safe way to begin for it would enable me to hit this phenomenon in my researches, and its inherent wholeness would then lead me to other parts of it.

The alternative was to use elaborate ideal types, but that requires too much premature specification of theory. For example, Weber's ideal type of bureaucracy is a kind of definition that runs about a dozen pages. Ideal types are perhaps useful in studying middle-sized entities, but I think they can become arbitrary when applied to enormous "total social facts." They are perhaps most useful in defining entities which have more "construct" than actual case in them to begin with, such as "the market." But ideal types have limitations: 1. They tend to be transcendent typifications, with the presumption that the form is forever coming into being like an entelechy; hence propositions about ideal types can be hard to falsify (because maybe the thing has not fully developed yet.) 2. They are surreptitious inductions that foreclose the operation of induction. We know that Weber's ideal type of bureaucracy was generalized partly from the Prussian and Chinese civil services, but we are not allowed to test the accuracy of this induction. 3. Finally, too much premature specification of theory prevents that differential sedimentation of knowledge which makes *new* propositions more testable. Pierre Duhem has observed that all the theories of a science are implicitly retested in every experiment; but older theorems have been tested for a long time so we can safely assume that the new hypothesis we are testing now is the one that is most proven or disproven. In an elaborate ideal type, however, scores of propositions may be advanced *all at once*, all complexly interrelated, and it is hard to devise a test for all this.

If we are to avoid elaborate ideal types, however, and begin instead with a simple definition pointing to a few real elements in a complex, then with what elements should we start? Here we encounter another problem, which Wittgenstein illuminated in his *Philosophical Investigations*. It is usually impossible, when defining a broad entity like, for example, "games," Wittgenstein observed, to find a criterion that will fit every kind of game. These phenomena are actually clusters related by "family resemblances," rather than sets with sharply demarcated borders or domains. A realist definition of magic, therefore, might include a few elements that *tend* to be true of the cluster, but they need not be true in every case.

Which elements should be included in a minimal definition? Here I felt that it would be an advantage to build on definitions used in the classics of sociological theory. Examining Durkheim and Weber (and Mauss) I found that they all used a variant of Robertson Smith's "peripheral hypothesis" (i.e. religion is central rite; magic is peripheral rite.) Two of them also emphasized more precisely the tendency of religion to be congregational while magic is administered in a one-to-one professional-to-client relationship. Here again, we are only dealing with family resemblances, for this criterion obviously does not fit what I call "ceremonial magic," which is typically performed officially, by a headman, for the social group as a whole. Since the problem of family resemblances is inescapable, and since I want to build on the sociological classics so as to help test and renew them, I decided nonetheless to make the occupational criterion a central feature of my definition.

There are other elements in my definition, and, more than that, conjectures behind it. I have decided to admit these as I build the definition. I am not setting up an elaborate ideal type by including all these hunches, just revealing what was on my mind when I began this study.

Building a Definition

Here is how I constructed my definition of "magic in the strict sense," i.e. real magical institutions:

1. The occupational distinction. Neither Weber nor Durkheim gave a formal definition of magic. But Durkheim's thirteen-page description makes sharp distinctions of magic from religion and almost constitutes a definition by contrast.[67] Weber said much more *about* magic, but did not come closer to an explicit definition. Both, however, really reported the same thing about what magic is. Both Weber and Durkheim used *occupational relation* to distinguish magic from religion. In contrast to the priest, who works for the collectivity to which all his flock also belong, the magician is more often on a private professional basis with the person who seeks his help.

Durkheim insists: magicians may form collegia among themselves but clients are not admitted, there is no church of magic.[68]

Weber makes a similar contrast of magician and priest.[69] Priests work as officials of a collectivity, whereas the magicians are often in private practice.

Hubert and Mauss did give an explicit definition of magic. Despite considerable evidence they amassed about the official role of magicians in ceremonial magic, their definition employs the Robertson Smith "peripheral hypothesis" and thus perhaps implies the same occupational distinction.[70]

Magicians do more often tend to work on an *ad hoc* basis, for individuals or groups that are fractions of a collectivity. I found notable exceptions to this, but it is largely true.

2. *Other definitional elements.* There are other ideas in the classics that lead toward a definition:

a. From Durkheim: the idea that magic derives from religion rather than vice-versa.

b. From Weber: the seemingly opposite idea that *new* religions begin in magic ("charisma").[71] Putting Weber and Durkheim together we discover dialectical sequences in which magical protests against existing religion produce new cults that renew religion.

c. From both Durkheim and Weber: the idea that magic is frequently hostile to religion. "Magic takes a sort of professional pleasure in profaning holy things," Durkheim writes.[72] Weber stresses the corresponding hostility of (ethical) religion toward magic.

d. From Durkheim: the idea that religion is the "projection of society."

e. From Freud: the suggestion that magic defends the ego.

f. My deduction: Magic defends the self against society.

What, then, is magic? If religion is the projection of the overwhelming power of the group, and if magic derives from religion, but sets itself up on a somewhat independent basis to help individuals, and is, at the same time, frequently reported to be hostile toward religion...then is not the answer apparent? Magic is the expropriation of religious collective representations for individual or subgroup purposes—to enable the individual ego to resist psychic extinction or the subgroup to resist cognitive collapse.[73] Therefore, magic must have something to do with the parturition of individual monads out of the collective whole, and with the separation of subgroups from it. That was my initial deduction from Weber, Durkheim and Freud.

And that is the working hypothesis that told me where to look, what to investigate. Durkheim's advice about "no initial hypothesis" will not work on a subject this vast—one needs something to thread the labyrinth. This idea was my golden string and it led me to many corridors most theories of magic ignore: such as psychiatry, the study of sects, the development of law and other institutions supporting the individual. I am admitting this initial hypothesis and admitting that it colors my simple definition of magic in the strict sense.

Definition

Magic "in the strict sense," then, will refer to certain well-known sacred institutions (especially what I call the main provinces of medical, ceremonial, paranormal, occult, sectarian, religious and black magic), institutions which are widely designated as magical in many societies, which are derived from religion, associated with religion or respond to religion, which are often of a secret or illicit or peripheral nature, or tend at least to organize themselves separately from (or within) religion, more often on a professional-client rather than community relationship, and which tend to serve fractional rather than fully collective ends, especially those of individuals and of subgroups in any collectivity.

Synopsis

Magic is multi-dimensional but overdetermined and a unity. All facets must be pictured to project the "total social fact." My paper is organized into three Books of four postulates each, which penetrate magic in different dimensions synthesizing findings of several sciences.

Book One, on Symbols, is phenomenological; it looks closely at the symbolic texture of magic to show that it consummates real social action, action that makes something or changes something (Postulate 1); and that it wields a mainly verbal symbolism, highly traditional, which gives man some purchase on the transcendent in his life (Postulate 2). The magic of names, of single words, of sentences as speech acts is probed—and also those latent affinities between words which spawn "sympathetic magic" (they are afterglows of primitive classification systems elaborated by mythic propositions working like a logic of classes). Magic expropriates many of its symbols from religion, then rigidifies the scripts lest they lose their efficacy, thereby creating a miraculous language different from ordinary speech which gives man courage to think, speak and act (Postulate 3). Magic achieves its striking effects through simple agreement: the perennial experimental magic seance group uses some traditional device to relax the objective frame of cognitive orientation, and then overvalues and interprets the paranormal phenomena which ensue according to traditional agreements (Postulate 4).

Book Two, on Religions, is institutional and dialectic: it illuminates the endless argument of magic and religion out of which the individual will emerge. Magic uses stolen scripts to challenge religion, but thereby renews it, keeps it in touch with the changing pluralist social order that projects it; even the so-called ethical world religions begin this way as partly magical protest sects (Postulate 5). But religion comes first and magic emerges out of religion, not vice versa (Postulate 6). This first happens at the tribal stage of social organization, through what Durkheim called "the generalization of mana," when religious symbols of society, reflecting its increasing complexity, become more abstract, hence easier to detach, expropriate from particular rites and extrapolate to instrumental or individual purposes (Postulate 7). In general, religion creates or "models" magic; certain core ceremonies that arise when membership becomes problematical in more complex societies (initiation and sacrifice) are especially transparent in modeling the sympathetic magical potential of language and rite. They are magical "in the weak sense," but their striking, explicit, instrumental modeling of magical potential invites magical institutions "in the strict sense" to spin off from religion just when society needs their agency to help engineer the greater autonomy it now requires from individuals (Postulate 8).

Book Three is functionalist and historical; it demonstrates that the manifest function of magic in man's development has been to serve as the midwife of the self and as a co-founder of the individual. Postulate 9 reconstructs the psychoanalytic theory of magic to show that ego operations are magical in the weak sense and that magic defends the self against the social. But magic also helped create the legal-rational institutions of the individual which encase the self—by contributing to the early development of individual law and property, law of contracts, the person category, etc. (Postulate 10). Postulate 11 tests propositions about magic's intimate relation to the individual and the self, by showing black magic to be a strain gauge registering pressure on either entity. Magic continues to advance with civilization and Postulate 12 examines its curious persistence in our times and the possibility that magic is the appropriate religious projection of post-modern society. When either the self or the individual is forced to contract—but also when either adventurously seeks to conquer new powers—magic often appears in various guises.

Notes

1. Cf. James K. Feibleman, *Inside the Great Mirror* (The Hague, 1958).
2. Emile Durkheim, *The Rules of Sociological Method* (N.Y., 1964), pp. 1–13.
3. There are traces of this idea in the Eskimo essay, the last chapter of *The Gift*, and the Prologue to the *Esquisse*.
4. E. Fuller Torrey, *The Mind Game* (N.Y., 1973).
5. Ari Kiev, ed., *Magic, Faith and Healing* (N.Y., 1964).
6. E.E. Evans-Pritchard (London, 1937). Discussed in ch. 11.
7. R.F. Fortune, *The Sorcerers of Dobu* (N.Y., 1963), pp. 133–153.
8. Beatrice Blyth Whiting, *Paiute Sorcery* (N.Y., 1950), section, "The Theory of Disease."
9. Marcel Mauss, "Effet Physique Chez l'Individu de l'Idée de Mort Suggérée par la Collectivité," ch. 4, "Types de Faits Néo-Zélandais et Polynésiens," pp. 323–330, in Lévi-Strauss, ed., *Marcel Mauss Sociologie et Anthropologie*, (Paris, 1950, 1966).
10. Godfrey Lienhardt, *Divinity and Experience, The Religion of the Dinka* (Oxford, 1961), ch. 5, 6, 7, pp. 219–321.
11. E.E. Evans-Pritchard, *Nuer Religion* (Oxford, 1956, 1970), ch. 3 & *passim*.
12. Max G. Marwick, *Sorcery in its Social Setting* (Manchester, 1965). Also "Witchcraft As a Social Strain-Gauge," ch. 24 in Max Marwick, ed., *Witchcraft and Sorcery* (Harmondsworth, Middlesex, England, 1970), pp. 280–295.
13. Robert A. Lowie, *Primitive Religion* (N.Y., 1924, 1970), "Crow Religion," ch. 1, pp. 3–32.
14. Also certain clans among the Murngin, according to W. Lloyd Warner, *A Black Civilization* (N.Y., rev. ed., 1958), ch. 7, p. 193ff.
15. E.E. Evans-Pritchard, *Nuer Religion* (Oxford, 1970), p. 315.
16. Marcello Truzzi, "The Occult Revival as Popular Culture," *The Sociological Quarterly*, vol. 13, Winter 1972, pp. 16–36.
17. Jacques Ellul, *The New Demons* (N.Y., 1975), p. 133. French ed, *Les Nouveaux Possédés*, was 1973.
18. This is indeed changing. An empirical sociology of the occult has been emerging. Marcello Truzzi kept track of it for years with his witty newsletter, *The Zetetic*. Studies now appear in anthologies like Irving I. Zaretsky and Mark P. Leone, eds., *Religious Movements in Contemporary America* (Princeton, 1974), and Edward A. Tiryakian, ed., *On the Margin of the Occult* (N.Y., 1974). Studies of contemporary cults inevitably use categories like shamanism: e.g. Robert S. Ellwood, Jr., *Religious and Spiritual Groups in Modern America* (Englewood Cliffs, N.J., 1973). So far these studies offer, at best, what Merton called "middle-level theory"; more often they confirm a low-level generalization. At worst, some are written by true believers or by "participant observers" who are cult members. Many are too quick to offer functionalist rationalizations: e.g., Edward J. Moody shows how satanism "integrates" marginal personalities without considering cultural consequences (Zaretsky and Leone, pp. 355–382). Meanwhile, some sociologists seem to join the occult revolution: e.g. Philip Slater, *The Wayward Gate* (Boston, 1977). Mircea Eliade notes how

historians of ideas and religious scholarship have stimulated the occult: e.g. Dead Sea Scrolls, Nag Hammadi library, the great oriental scholars (*Occultism, Witchcraft and Cultural Fashions*, Chicago, 1976; *The Quest*, Chicago, 1969). Recent spectacular news stories about aberrations of Scientology, Synanon and the Jim Jones church will surely stimulate this empirical sociology. But so far this new field has produced no general theory; one has to turn back to Durkheim, Mauss, Weber, Malinowski and the grand theorists of an earlier day to find one.

19. Anne Parsons, *Belief, Magic and Anomie* (N.Y., 1969), ch. 7, "Expressive Symbolism in Witchcraft and Delusion, A Comparative Study."

20. B. Malinowski, *The Sexual Life of Savages* (N.Y., 1929), ch. 11, "The Magic of Love and Beauty," pp. 344–383.

21. *Witchcraft, Oracles and Magic Among the Azande*, p. 64, p. 404, etc.

22. R.F. Fortune, *The Sorcerers of Dobu* (New York, 1963), p. 144, etc.

23. Barrie Reynolds, *Divination and Witchcraft Among the Barotse of Northern Rhodesia* (Berkeley & Los Angeles, 1963), chs. 1–2.

24. Clyde Kluckhohn, *Navajo Witchcraft* (Boston, 1967), cf. pp. 13–21.

25. *Alleged Assassination Plots Involving Foreign Leaders*, Interim Report of the Select Committee to Study Government Operations with Respect to Intelligence Activities, U.S. Senate (N.Y., 1976),.p. 72, ff.

26. John Wilhelm, *In Search of Superman* (N.Y., 1976), conversations.

27. Bronislaw Malinowski, *Coral Gardens and Their Magic*, Volume One: The Description of the Gardening (London, 1935), pp. 62–80, 435 –51; *Magic, Science and Religion* (N.Y., 1954) pp. 69–92.

28. E.A. Wallis Budge, *Egyptian Magic* (N.Y., 1971), p. xi, *passim*. Budge stresses Egyptian use of magic to *command* gods.

29. V. Gordon Childe, *What Happened In History* (London, 1942, 1965), p. 124ff.

30. Edmond Douttée, *Magie et Religion dans l'Afrique du Nord* (Algiers, 1908), cf. ch. 1.

31. Lynn Thorndike, *A History of Magic and Experimental Science During the First 13 Centuries of Our Era*, vol. I (N.Y., 1923).

32. *Witchcraft, Oracles and Magic Among the Azande*, cf. p. 475ff.

33. Divination systems mobilize all the permutations and combinations in a society's classification system to focus on and back up one feeble individual. This horoscope, or tarot reading, or I Ching calculation seems magically to mobilize the whole cosmos behind him, so that he can *act*. Diagnosis by itself is a powerful procedure affecting the outcome. But of course divination *can* provide a nucleus for observation. I once heard a master Fuller Brush district sales manager lecture a hall full of people on how to size up prospects by their head sizes. Phrenology may be a pseudo-science, but as divination magic it worked, helping anxious salesmen decide what to say and how to act, and perhaps focusing their attention on customers' personalities so that, around this nucleus of pseudo-science, they could begin to size them up accurately.

34. Hermeneutic plays an important role in the rationalization of occult sciences and other magics into theosophies. Eliade describes one such sequence in the ancient world. Mircea Eliade, *Rites and Symbols of Initiation* (N.Y., 1958, 1965), pp. 109–115.

35. S. Angus, *The Mystery-Religions* (N.Y., 1975), pp. 33, 36, 48, 164–170.

36. Keith Thomas, *Religion and the Decline of Magic* (N.Y., 1971), pp. 283–385.

37. Mircea Eliade, *Yoga* (Princeton, 1969), pp. 321–323.

38. E.g., Paul Blumberg, "Magic in the Modern World," *Sociology and Social Research*, Jan. 1963, vol. 47, no. 2, pp. 147–160. Shows magic is found in uncertain professions like mining, boxing, among sailors, etc. Cf. also David F. Aberle, "Religion, Magical Phenomena and Power, Prediction and Control," *Southwest Journal of Anthropology*, vol. 22, no. 3, Fall 1966, p. 221ff.

39. Postulates 1, 2 and 3 apply especially to ceremonial magic. Postulate 4 has special relevance to paranormal magic. Number 5 applies especially to magical sects; 8 especially to religious magic; 9 especially to medical magic; 10 in part to magics of professions. Postulate 11 is about black magic.

40. Clifford Geertz, "Religion as a Cultural System," in *Anthropological Approaches to the Study of Religion*, ed. Michael Banton (London, 1968) pp. 1–3.

41. Roland Robertson, *The Sociological Interpretation of Religion* (N.Y., 1972), ch. 2 & *passim*.

42. Charles Y. Glock & Phillip E. Hammond, eds., *Beyond the Classics?* (N.Y., 1973). This is the import of the volume as a whole.

43. Alvin W. Gouldner, *The Coming Crisis of Western Sociology* (N.Y., 1971), chs. 1, 4 & *passim*.

44. Robert A. Nisbet, *The Sociological Tradition* (N.Y., 1966), pp. 21–46, 221–263.

45. I refer to *The Elementary Forms of Religious Life* and *The Social Division of Labor*.

46. Georg Wilhelm Friedrich Hegel, *Lectures on the Philosophy of Religion* 1840, London 1895, vol. 1, pp. 290–298, reprinted in Norman Birnbaum and Gertrud Lenzer, eds., *Sociology and Religion* (Englewood Cliffs, N.J., 1969).

47. Lefebvre, *The Sociology of Marx* (N.Y., 1969), pp. 4–5.

48. Nathan Rotenstreich, *Basic Problems of Marx's Philosophy* (Indianapolis, 1965), pp. 3–22.

49. A former Durkheim colleague, Gaston Richards, complained bitterly of this in "L'Athéisme Dogmatique en Sociologie Religieuse," *Revue d'Histoire et de Philosophie Religieuses*, 1923, vol, 3, pp. 125–137.

50. Marx & Engels, *The German Ideology* (N.Y., 1965) p. 6ff.

51. The criticism was in part unfair; Feuerbach's Hegelian dialectic made it possible for him to demonstrate, as in his essay on the future, that through religious representations man could also act back on society. Cf. his Principles of the Philosophy of the Future, reprinted in Zawar Hanfi, ed., *The Fiery Brook, Selected Writings of Ludwig Feuerbach* (N.Y., 1972), pp. 175–245.

52. Frederick Engels, *The Origin of the Family, Private Property and The State* (N.Y., 1942, 1971).

53. Engels, *The Peasant War in Germany,* in *The German Revolutions*, ed. Leonard Krieger (Chicago, 1967), cf. index & *passim*.

54. T.B. Bottomore, *Karl Marx Early Writings* (N.Y., 1964).

55. Ernst Bloch, "Man's Increasing Entry into Religious Mystery," in *Man On His Own* (N.Y., 1970), pp. 147–240.

56. Emile Durkheim, *The Elementary Forms of Religious Life* (London, 1915), pp. 42–47, 355–362.

57. Hubert and Mauss largely focused on professional magic done by trained magicians and committed sorcerers—mainly, that is, on ceremonial magic, religious magic, medical magic and black magic. They threw out excellent but excessively short hints about paranormal and occult magic. Statements on sect magic were minimal. They gave no attention to magic in the weak sense.

58. More convincingly than the occultists, the sensitive positivists of the Durkheim-Mauss tradition make us startlingly aware of some invisible dimensions of our social world—of shadows and forces projected by real corporate powers. Like Wittgenstein, they discover empirical foundations for ideal entities in agreements people make—and so establish their social reality (Wittgenstein, *Remarks on the Foundations of Mathematics*, Cambridge, Mass., 1967, esp. pp. 94–98). Like the Freudians, they demonstrate that these entities are overdetermined and massive—and hence show that they are powerful and deeply constitutive of our lives. And so, like "imaginary gardens with real toads in them" (Marianne Moore, "Poetry"), the Durkheimians create a socially reductionist landscape which is nonetheless peopled with sacred forces, active Platonic ideas, communicating through hidden logical codes, and even spirits and ghosts, all reconstituted on a social basis. Thus Robert Hertz shows us that prolonged rites must take place before a second and final burial among primitives because the person who has died really is, as a social idea, a persistent and troublesome entity (a ghost) that must be laid to rest (*Death and the Right Hand*, Aberdeen, 1960), pp. 27–86, cf. esp. p. 82.

59. The lapse is not unusual; he resisted stating even a definition of religion at the beginning of his general work on the subject because the phenomenon is too vast, he said.

60. In Gerth & Mills, eds., *From Max Weber* (N.Y. 1946, 1958), pp. 267–301.

61. Talcott Parsons, Introd. to Weber's *The Sociology of Religion*, (Boston, 1964), pp. xxx, xxxii, xlvii, xlix, L.

62. Parsons contrasts the immediate gratifications of magic with the more long-circuited projects of religion to suggest that Weber's whole point is that religion leads to higher, more disciplined culture. This idea is present in Weber, but his understanding of the magic-religion dialectic is much richer than this.

63. Alan Blum has shown (*Theorizing*, London, 1974, pp. 1–34) how the old Aristotelian approach of critical reduction of theories "suppresses dialectic" by consigning alternative viewpoints to the prehistory of the allegedly correct theory. I think he casts doubt on the logical soundness of all critical reductions and "rhetorics of convergence" (Gouldner) as a means of getting at the truth. (Alvin W. Gouldner, *The Coming Crisis of Western Society*, N.Y., 1970, p. 17). Look how Parsons distorted Durkheim in *The Structure of Social Action*, for example, to make him "converge" with Weber, Marshall and Pareto in Parsons' superposing version of The Truth.

64. Rodney Needham has shown how, in practice, the Durkheimians explained away data which did not fit their definitions as "survivals" or "degenerate cases." (Introd. to Durkheim & Mauss, *Primitive Classification*, Chicago, 1967, pp. xvi–xvii.)

65. *A General Theory of Magic*, p. 7.

66. See the *Encyclopedia of Philosophy* under "Categories," for Aristotle's ideas about "category errors."

67. *The Elementary Forms* (London, 1915), esp. the section pp. 42–47.

68. Durkheim writes: "*There is no Church of magic. Between the individuals themselves...there are no lasting bonds.... The magician has a clientele and not a Church, and it is very possible that his clients have no other relations between each other.... It is true that in certain cases, magicians form societies ... but when these societies of magic are formed, they do not include all the adherents of magic, but only the magicians; the laymen...are excluded ... A church is not a fraternity of priests; it is a moral community formed by all the believers in a single faith, laymen as well as priests.*" Emile Durkheim, *The Elementary Forms of Religious Life* (London, 1915), pp. 44–45.

69. Weber insists on the interpenetration of magic and religion; they are hard to distinguish: "Applied to reality, this contrast is fluid...it may be thought that what is decisive for the concept of priesthood is that the functionaries...be actively associated with some type of social organization...in contrast with the magicians, who are self-employed. Yet even this distinction...is fluid in actuality. The sorcerers not infrequently are members of an organized guild..." Max Weber, *The Sociology of Religion* (Boston, 1964), pp. 28–29. But finally, Weber does settle on the key distinction, which is occupational: "It is more correct for our purpose...to set up as the crucial feature of priesthood the specialization of a particular group of persons in the continuous operation of a cultic enterprise...related to specific social groups." (*Ibid.*, p. 30)

70. Hubert and Mauss: "*A magical rite is any rite which does not play a part in organized cults—it is private, secret, mysterious and approaches the limit of a prohibited rite.*" (*General Theory of Magic*, p. 24.) So Durkheim, Weber and Mauss all use W. Robertson Smith's "*peripheral hypothesis*" (from *Religion of the Semites*, London, 1889, N.Y. 1962, p. 90, etc.) that religion is central rite, magic is peripheral rite. But Weber and Durkheim translate it into *role relationships*; membership vs. clientship, church vs. colleagues. Magician and client do not have the same *membership* status.

71. Weber uses "charisma" and "magic" interchangeably and virtually defines charisma *as* magic. For example, he frankly identifies charisma *as* a mana word, *his* mana word: "It is primarily, though not exclusively, these extraordinary powers that have been designated by such special terms as 'mana,' 'orenda,' and the Iranian 'maga' (the term from which our word 'magic' is derived). *We shall henceforth employ the term 'charisma' for such extraordinary powers.*" (p. 2; italics added). He actually distinguished two types of charisma: one based on natural endowment and one based on stage management. By charisma he usually means the kind of magic that is exerted before groups of people. Of course, magic always has an audience, even at medical seances in small societies, as Lévi-Strauss has shown (*Structural Anthropology*, ch. 9). But Weber is particularly interested in the crowd effects exerted by the messianic leaders of new sects. His idea helps us see how mass magic works in large, complex civilizations.

72. *Elementary Forms*, p. 43.

73. See Rollo May's idea of ego implosion, in *The Meaning of Anxiety* (N.Y., 1950), pp. 68–70 & *passim*.

A GENERAL SOCIOLOGICAL THEORY OF MAGIC

BOOK ONE: SYMBOLS

Postulate 1:   Magic Is A Form of Social Action.
Postulate 2:   Magic Social Action Consists of Symbolic Performances — and Linguistic Symbolism Is Central to Magic.
Postulate 3:   Magical Symbolic Action Is Rigidly Scripted.
Postulate 4:   Magical Scripts Achieve Their Social Effects Largely by Pre-Existing Or Pre-Figured Agreements.

BOOK TWO: RELIGIONS

Postulate 5:   Magic Borrows Symbolism from Religion and Uses It to Argue with Religion in a Dialectic that Renews Religion.
Postulate 6:   Logically, and in Some Observable Historical Sequences, Magic Derives from Religion Rather Than Vice Versa.
Postulate 7:   Magic Is a Byproduct of the Projection of Society in Religion.
Postulate 8:   Religion Is the Institution that Creates or Models Magic for Society.

BOOK THREE: INDIVIDUALS AND SELVES

Postulate 9:   Magic Tries to Protect the Self.
Postulate 10:   Magic Helped Develop the Institution of the Individual.
Postulate 11:   Magic – Especially Black Magic – Is An Index of Social Pressures on Selves and Individuals.
Postualte 12:   Magic Persists as an Expression of Certain Aspects of Civilization.

POSTSCRIPT: HISTORY

Postulate 13:   Magical Symbolism Travels Easily and Accumulates a History.

BOOK ONE

SYMBOLS

Postulate 1: MAGIC IS A FORM
OF SOCIAL ACTION.

MAGIC is real action. Something really happens, often something violent, usually something of consequence. People are shaken, influenced, healed, destroyed, transformed. The social situation is altered. Magic is not mere illusion just because its efficacy depends on beliefs in illusory entities. Many observers have insisted that the essence of magic *is* action, though some claim that it is a kind of pseudo-action, or defective action, or proto-action. It is important to demonstrate that it is effective social action in order to show that the phenomenon is real. The derivation of the word for magic in several languages from roots meaning "action" is well known and suggestive: *factum* in Latin and *Zauber* in German are words meaning magic that come from verbs "to do"; and "in India the word which best corresponds to our word ritual is *karman*, action."[1] Loisy[2] considers sacrifice and magic both to be "efficacious mystical action." Jane Harrison characterizes magic as sacred action;[3] and Suzanne Langer portrays it as symbolic action.[4] To Róheim[5] it is counter-phobic action; to Malinowski[6] it is counter-phobic action that organizes collective efforts. But many Freudians regard it as sick, defensive action; and to Sartre[7] it is defective or pseudo-action, or at least some magic is so.

Ideas of defective, sick or pseudo-action seem to suggest that magical action is still in some sense not real. It will be necessary to criticize such theories. But first, it can be shown that magic is real action to the extent that it fits very easily into the various schemas of sociological action theory. Thus the three principal "elements" of magic which Hubert and Mauss[8] use to organize their theory—the *magician*, his *actions* (the rites) and the *representations*—can be fitted, for example, into the "general theory of action" of Parsons and Shils.[9] Magic is only done, in fact, when these elements come together in unified social action, such as is described in Talcott Parsons' model which brings together the representations ("culture patterns"), the actors ("personalities") and the actions (as patterned by "situations," "orientations," etc.).

In Max Weber's model, in turn, "action" is human behavior which has "subjective meaning," and "social action" is action which also "takes account of the behavior of others": By this definition all magic is at least "action" and all magic in the strict sense is "social action."[10] Freund[11] objects that behavior directed at inanimate objects cannot be termed social. But magic is often performed on ob-

25

jects, with the action really oriented to the behavior of others. The "objects" have social meaning, the rites and representations are traditional,[12] and other people are involved, at least implicitly. In fact, magic is more often than not *collective* social action. Solitary-seeming magics such as yoga and mysticism and the study of occult arts also have social objectives: in practice they translate into "withdrawal and return" (Toynbee), the pursuit of power, prestige and authority over others. Magic in the strict sense, then, is "social action."[13]

Can we say that magic is any particular kind of social action? Parsons' pattern variables do not suggest anything that is not either uninteresting or misleading about magic.[14] Nor do the four "functional aspects" discussed in his *Working Papers*[15] help us to say anything interesting: magic can be either "adaptive," "instrumental," "expressive" or "integrative." As for Weber's classification of action according to four modes of orientation, magical phenomena could fit under all four: "means-end," "absolute values," "affectual orientations" and "traditional orientations."

The sweeping simplification of Weber's schema of action effected by Habermas—symbolic interaction versus rational-purposive action—offers us one tempting possibility.[16] One is tempted to say that magic is the form of social action in which the language appropriate to ordinary talk, to "symbolic interaction," is inappropriately applied to work, to the praxis of "rational-purposive action." But that is just a more exact way of saying something which is often said, and which is inaccurate—i.e., the familiar idea that magic dim-wittedly addresses objects like people and physical work as if it were a matter of persuasion. Frazer intended something like this with his notion of magic as a "defective theory of causality," and Kenneth Burke (inaccurately) hinged his slender distinction of magic from rhetoric on this basis.[17] Anyway, the idea is incorrect, first, because magic is also applied to the proper domain of symbolic interaction where it is notably effective, as in psychological healing, for example. Second, Malinowski[18] and many others have shown that magic can be a useful overlay in rational-purposive action as well. It is not inappropriate: it helps. It not only "inspires confidence" in practical action but helps to organize action. Third, assertions about the ability of primitives to distinguish effective techniques from magic overlays have been often criticized, e.g., by the Waxes,[19] Hsu[20] and S.F. Nadel[21] who remind us that no age has full knowledge of its own techniques, just as we did not know until recently how aspirin works. So some techniques are "magical" in that they use forces we do not yet understand, others because they contribute nothing to the result and we just have not found that out yet. In still other cases we fool ourselves about the result. Sometimes the woman you saw throwing away her crutches at a faith healing session can later be seen hobbling home on them[22] — and neither she nor the audience can see any contradiction. A final reason why there is no pure praxis is that confidence magic and leadership magic and the magic that organizes collective social action are often necessary for the outcome. "Magic" in all these senses seems to refer to residual elements within praxis which we might formally summarize as: a. practices that do not really work but we do not know it yet; b. undiscovered physical forces that magic operations really do manipulate in ways we do not yet understand (as alchemy once did); c. a useful psychological overlay that encourages and organizes rational-purposive action; and, d. finally, results that are self-fulfillingly obtained or obtained only because we agree they are.

In addition, insofar as certain sciences are constructivist, insofar as they consist in a continuous agreement to agree that we have agreed in the Wittgenstein sense[23] and insofar as they constitute a "technique" in the Ellul sense[24] which has a "self-fulfilling" effect, the gulf between magic and science and hence between magical and praxis action is not always that great. As Dunlap has observed,[25] magic, science and religion are all forms of praxis, aimed at doing something. And Bryan Wilson[26] has edited a collection of anthropologists' essays which often show that magic is usually rightfully considered to be "rational" action within the social frames in which it is performed.

It is therefore not accurate to claim magic exclusively for either the realm of symbolic interaction and communication or of rational-purposive action and communication; it works in both quite properly. Is magic a special kind of action in any other sense? Is it, for example, deceptive action? Not in every case. But in later sections on magic as rhetoric or logic, we will see how magic often takes the form of a first person singular speaking or acting as a first person plural and getting away with it. Magic is often sacred action which gets free of collective religious action. We will later on study ways in which magic is counterphobic action, rebellious action, logical or abstract symbolic action.

Magic Makes Something or Changes Something

There is, however, something definite and important that can be said about what kind of social action magic is. And once again hints can be found in various languages. The Latin verb *facere*, for example, has the dual meaning of *to do*—and *to make*: a *factum* is something made. When a magician says "I'll do, and I'll do, and I'll do," what he usually does is to make something. Jane Harrison[27] observes that *sacra*, the Greek word for magic, etc., means "things done." In Harrison's view, all rites are makings which construct new entities—for example, a god can arise out of any of them. Thus Zeus ("the greatest Kouros") is born of the *kouretes*, the young armed males dancing in the initiation rite; and the Titans perhaps derive etymologically from the "*titanes*" or "white-faced" ones (elders who have painted their faces for the rite). Gods can crystallize out of any of man's artifacts, too, because these also are human makings, just like magic rites, and hence revered in the same way. A shield, for example, is a sacred making that may give rise to a god—e.g., the Palladion and Athena.[28] (See also Mendenhall on a god coming out of the ancient kingly "aegis."[29]) Childe has similarly shown that ideas of magic attached to the first manufactures, such as metallurgy and smithies, in which man made remarkable new things.[30] Some observers have shown that "elf bolts" (i.e., prehistoric stone spearheads) were considered sacred by primitive men precisely because they had been made by the mysterious human races that went before. Malinowski has observed (as part of his formulation that "myths are charters for magic") that important myths in turn are usually about the original makings of magic by culture heroes (or gods) and that all myths are therefore creation myths.[31] In several of his books[32] he stresses that magic is felt to be intrinsically human, belonging to man or given him at the start, and connected with man's ability to make things.

Magic actions are rituals that make or change something. They operate mysteriously and what they create is mostly mystical—but these mysterious actions have social effects. Hubert and Mauss do a sensitive content analysis of what the mystical actions appear to be: They often create an object or a change of state, usually by a transfer of a quality or infusion of a power. A characteristic is imposed or suppressed; very prominent are images of someone being tied or untied; of something added or subtracted; often something goes or comes back; objects are connected, united or confounded.[33] But this mystical doing and making (only dimly understood by the participants) has the effect, by virtue of their beliefs, of bringing about a real social doing or making, as surely as the minister ties when he "pronounces" you man and wife or the judge changes your status with his "sentence." That is why magic is "efficacious mystical action" in Loisy's sense[34] and not just any "social action" in the Parsons-Weber sense.[35] Although, as we will see, the magic worldview is typically monist, there is usually a dualism in magic action which is simultaneously mystical and physical-social—thus the Zande witch eats the "spiritual" analogues of the victim's inner organs, and the real organs sicken until he dies.[36]

Which Is Magical: Social Action or Social Action Theory?

Magic makes something and so does human action in general; no wonder magic easily fits schemas of social action theory. Maybe this is because human action is "magical" in some weak sense—but maybe it is because the social action schema is itself too mentalist. At least one critic has voiced this suspicion. Goran Therborn has asserted, in an article titled "Social Action, Social Magic,"[37] that the theory of social action does not describe real action at all (so even if magic fits that schema it still would not be social action). For example, Parsons' theory of action is only a theory of "mentalist choice," in Therborn's view (whereas Marx wrote a theory of true action that changes the world). Like the noblesse de la robe whom Lucien Goldmann[38] saw as the carriers of Jansenist intellectualism because they were alienated by but dependent on the system, Therborn portrays action theory as the product of old-fashioned bourgeois academic intellectuals who are unhappy during the trend to monopoly but tied to the system, hence impotent, and who therefore lapse into "magical thinking" in the form of abstract, formal, social theories that leave the world alone. This criticism is persuasive. Parsons, Weber, MacIver, Schutz, etc., do indeed stress mental operations as the springs of action—"subjective meaning," "plan," "dynamic assessment" and so on.[39] Nothing seems to happen in these schema; maybe alienated conservatives really are using such theories as magic, in the sense of mental magic as a substitute for real action.

The mentalist focus of the action schema is notorious, but Therborn's effective critique of it does not entail that magic itself is therefore pseudo-action. Magic will fit other schemas of action as well as the theory of social action; and there is indeed something about human action, as we shall see, that is "magical" —in the weak sense. Yet the pejorative sense in which Therborn uses the phrase magic action is a very common usage. Magic is frequently identified with action that is mere wishful thinking, or defective action or not quite action, a usage possibly based in part on a popular understanding of psychoanalysis, which has exposed certain ritualistic actions symptomatic of illness and often labeled them "magical." But far from saying that these rituals are therefore all non-action, the psychoanalysts found they had remarkable effects that could be arranged on a continuum from almost-action through various degrees of defective action to almost effective social action.

The paradigmatic extreme case of magic as non-action is perhaps found in some schizophrenic syndromes, but even these are seen as action that failed.[40] In Freud's essays, the psychoses are conceptualized as bundles of magical symptoms that are really attempts to get well.[41] The original illness was the capitulation of the ego to the id and its withdrawal from a world that frustrated the id; the withdrawn cathexis may then have been put on the ego, as in the heightened narcissism of paranoia, or on the loved object taken back into the ego via identification, in melancholia, etc. But the psychosis the doctor sees (i.e., the symptoms), is, like fever, an attempt to get well, to get back to the world. But it is a kind of magical action that often fails. In schizophrenia it often works by constructing an imaginary world within the ego, so the ego can act again—hence the magical actions of the schizophrenic syndrome are indeed the nearest paradigm of magic as pseudo-action, for they are directed not at the real world, but at the disorganized, badly reconstructed, imaginary world of the patient, and cannot even be understood as action by other people. This world is not only imaginary; it is also too fragmented and disorganized to serve even as a hypothetical "model" for action in the real world because, as Freud puts it, the ego has been swamped or disorganized by the id; or, as Róheim puts it,[42] in the destruction of the real world the ego has been destroyed as well and so cannot organize even its own fantasies; or because the intense affect produced by ego self-cathection overwhelms cognition, as Jung formulates it, producing Janet's "*abaissement du niveau mentale.*"[43]

But some of these same investigators show that mental magic of this kind, if it is organized, can work to some degree. Consider the other psychoses and neuroses in Freud's works. They could be arranged on a continuum from unreal to real action. Schizophrenic magic does not often work, but paranoia sometimes works. Freud writes that this partial recovery is carried out by projection.[44] Perhaps because the delusional world of the paranoid is relatively coherent, it can serve as a crude, inaccurate but focused model of the real world; i.e., action can be projected out into the real world by acting on the imaginary world as if it were the real world. This action may be mad, but it will have some consistency. And since, as we will see, all action must be based on abstract "models" (Goldstein) or "plans" (Schutz) or "projects" (Heidegger), which are themselves in part theories of limited accuracy about the world, paranoid action has a chance of being accepted as real action.

When we come to the neuroses, the magic action of symptoms approaches even nearer to effective action. Neurosis is a conflict between ego and id[45] in which the ego remains in contact with the world and even represses some of the id in allegiance to reality. Now repression is not yet the neurosis or the magic action. The neurosis emerges in the "return of the repressed"—those remarkable double-faced symbolic symptoms which are partly unreal and self-defeating actions, but also partly real and gratifying. For example, as Freud showed in *The Problem of Anxiety*,[46] obsessional-compulsive symptoms are partly symbols for the self-punishing act of repression itself (and Diamond has characterized obsessional magic as the failed magic of our time, i.e., magic turned against the self[47]). But the symptoms also simultaneously symbolize (and partly *gratify*) the repressed impulse: and that is closer to real action. And of course neurotic symptoms sometimes punish other people or express aggression. In this way they do have effects on others; they are social action.

Finally, in *Group Psychology and the Analysis of the Ego*,[48] we see magic at work in effective *collective* action. A close reading of this book (and of Becker's *Denial of Death* which interprets it[49]) shows that the interaction between leader and followers can be understood as magical action. Here, however pathologically, magical action is shown to *organize* group action (just like the work magic in Malinowski's *Coral Gardens*).

This continuum in turn can be fitted on to the wider continuum of all human action which might be said to run from pure, psychotic non-action to an opposite ideal type of pure praxis which contains no surplus affect, no overlay of confidence or leadership magic and no techniques that will later be found to contribute nothing to the outcome. Most human action, in fact, lies between these extremes, and there is little pure praxis just as there is little pure non-action.

Magic Is Not Pseudo-Action: Refuting the Theory of Sartre

The doubt persists, however, in conceptualizations of magic action as somehow unreal—e.g., the preoccupation with "magic thinking" as a psychiatric topic. It appears prominently, for example, in some French psychiatrists influenced by Mauss' theory of magic: such as in Odier's *Anxiety and Magic Thinking*,[50] Bastide's *Sociologie et Psychanalyse*,[51] etc.; and a special issue of the *Revue Française de Psychanalyse* devoted to the subject with contributions by Marie Bonaparte, H. Codet, R. LaForgue, J. Leuba, etc., in 1934.[52] (There is also a related continental tendency to homologize infantile, primitive, psychotic and magical in such theorists as Heinz Werner.[53]) Sartre drew on this tradition, and also on Janet, in formulating an impressive theory of some magic as pseudo-action, and it provoked an equally impressive refutation by Schachtel.

Sartre's real aim in *The Emotions, Outline of a Theory*[54] is to show that the emotions are magical and therefore pseudo-action; magic is thus derogated incidentally. In a book whose French title is reminiscent of that of Hubert and Mauss' treatise,[55] Sartre characterizes the emotions as "magical" because they change things subjectively without really changing them objectively. Turning on an emotion is a form of escape, a substitute pseudo-action undertaken when real action is blocked and the organism has a strong motivation to do something. This is chosen behavior, not unconscious but simply "unreflected," so that the emotion seems to seize from outside. Emotion then is a change or "degradation" of consciousness which alters the world by altering our perception of it, as tinted glasses do. Our perception of our world is already "furrowed" and twisted by our own acts and needs.[56] Magic is wishful thinking that dodges blocks in this furrowed world that we have ourselves partly constituted. Magic joy, for example, moves time ahead so that we can experience anticipated good outcomes vicariously in the present and so cash in prematurely without doing any work. Anger similarly changes our perception of the whole field. Thus consciousness, through willed but unreflected behavior, creates a "magic" world which holds itself captive, as in a trap.[57]

Interesting here is Sartre's idea that the body is used as an "instrument" to change consciousness: action is performed on the body instead of on the world. Emotion is a disturbance of the body which produces this new perceptual experience and belief in it; to believe in magical behavior it is necessary to be highly disturbed physically. The whole idea of acting on the body in order to act on the world is an old one in the world tradition of magic; it is crystallized in many theosophies—in, for example, the basic "as below, so above" formula of the Hermetic books. Eliade[58] has demonstrated that these ideas often take practical form in "mystic physiologies" that show up in yoga, astrology, alchemy, in which parts of the body are identified with parts of the universe, so action on one produces like action upon the other. Sartre's speculations, in other words, resonate to something fundamental in magic, but he is wrong in saying that the emotions are not action, because at the very least they communciate to others. Before developing this critique, however, we should consider first the criticism which Ernest Schachtel leveled against Sartre's position in his book *Metamorphosis.*[59]

Schachtel takes issue with the view that all "affect" is mere subjective disturbance and the opposite of action. Freud, he writes, thinks that in normal action all the affect goes entirely and efficiently into the action and none is left over, save the experience of tension-reduction itself. Wrong, he says: even a nursing child shows eagerness and zest and this helps him find the breast. Schachtel then makes a distinction, calling the disorganized emotion that can be a mere alternative to action "embeddedness affect," by which he means mere diffuse discharges of tension, perhaps reminiscent of the fetal state. But "activity affect," on the other hand, helps to concentrate the action; its function is precisely to establish an effective emotional link between the organism and the environment. Schachtel claims that Sartre's theory of emotion applies only to "embeddedness affects." Thus "magic joy" is an expectation of future embeddedness. And so is "magic hope" that is vague about its anticipated object. But there is such a thing as realistic hope, an "activity affect" that is tied to praxis and motivates it. Anxiety is typically *the* magical emotion; it reacts to the threat of separation from embeddedness. But even anxiety, when it is faced with the attitude of "resoluteness" (Heidegger's *"Entschlossenheit"*), can be an activity affect that helps organize action to explore new freedom.

More interesting is a point Schachtel mentions without development: emotion (even magical, diffuse emotion) is communicative. The science of ethology has developed abundant evidence that emotions communicate and this helps organize social behavior among animals. *Stimmung* or mood is a basic category to Portmann in *Animals As Social Beings,*[60] for example; he finds it even among dragonflies. Derek Wragg Morley finds among social ants individuals he calls "excitement centers," ants that excitedly start to do something; their behavior alters the behavior of others who then imitate their action.[61]

Lower organisms do perhaps communicate their emotions. At a higher level this is stylized and emotion is *symbolized*: e.g., in postures that signal attack and capitulation (cf. Konrad Lorenz[62]). Maclay and Knipe in *The Dominant Man*[63] have synthesized numerous studies showing how, perhaps by natural selection working to conserve the species, destructive fights-to-the-finish are replaced by symbolic interchanges in which the competitors signal their moods until one gives way, with binding social effect. The underlying idea is that pecking orders have survival value, for they dispose toward sexual selection of the best specimens, whose health is tested by their emotional mettle in these ritual face-downs.

But very early, it appears, these formal "ritual" gestures begin to get detached from any one-to-one correspondence with the emotion they symbolize or any underlying mettle or strength it expresses. In the famous rat slum experiments on the effect of overcrowding, for example,[64] those famous rats who managed to preserve their families from pathology by defending an adequate corner of space for them were not always the strongest rats. Wolfgang Wickler in *The Sexual Code*[65] shows how dominance competitions make increasing use of the natural symbols of sex, with female sex behavior mimicked widely as a symbol of capitulation. Maclay and Knipe observe that in street fights among boys it is not usually the largest one who wins, but that often the larger man is made the leader because he symbolizes the idea of winning in a face-down. This is what strategy theorist Thomas C. Schelling calls a "rallying point."[66]

Thus emotion is so intrinsically communicative that it apparently evolves into a symbolization of itself; with human beings, perhaps, it is entirely symbolic communication. There is a temptation to identify substitution of protosymbols for action among animals with prototypical magic; but even in the "weak sense," we must reserve all definitions of magic for the human species alone (for reasons to be discussed in the section on symbolism). Perhaps the signaling of emotions in dominance competitions among animals is an important element in the phylogenetic background out of which the human capacity for magical action developed. It has often been noted that the most primitive form of magic grows out of direct expression of emotion: the evil eye phenomenon, for example, is interpreted as a direct communication of emotions.[67] But as we will see later, there are better, more sociological explanations for the weak sense of magic, to be found in the nature of human symbolization and its history.

Anyway, it is well documented that a "magic" change in mood is *not* a pseudo-action, for it communicates to others, often quite persuasively.[68] Magic or emotion that has no effect is possible, at a limit in certain extreme social situations. A person may sometimes do something to himself that has little influence on the world; he may perform Hermetic magic on his body via the James-Lang effect and have no impact whatsoever because no one is paying attention to him. Sartre's idea of magic emotion as utterly without effect perhaps applies as a limit in a modern, secularized, bureaucratic world, a world in which our emotions do not impress others the way they would in primitive society, a world in which our little piques and threats and sullen depressions will be steadfastly ignored by the management. Perhaps in a cool, bureaucratic setting personal human magic is crippled, as Diamond suggests, and interaction becomes a non-zero-sum game with randomization as the only saddle point and even blandness a tactic. But pure bureaucracies of the Weberian ideal type are rare and in most human settings the communication of emotion is significant social action that has some effects. So Sartre's extreme case of a purely passive emotional magic that is non-action is rare or non-existent.

Sartre anyway was writing only about one kind of "magic," not magic in general. At the end of the book, Sartre sketched the outlines of an exciting general theory of magic according to which the social world only *seems* solid. Occasionally it breaks open to reveal a startling glimpse of its underlying "magical" nature (he means its construction out of social interaction); this revelation is accompanied by either "wonder" or "horror" depending on whether the insight was sought or is forced upon us.[69]

So attempts to characterize magic as non-action are unsuccessful. Even in the two extreme test cases of "magic" emotions and "magic symptoms of mental illness" (both magical in the weak sense), we find social effects, communication, action. Some of this action is more effective, some less so, and we can imagine a continuum. Somewhere on such a continuum would be found all the alleged varieties of "crippled magic," magic that has little effect on others because the individual uses it on himself, to turn himself off and accomodate to society. Certain neuroses typical of our society (e.g., obsessional-compulsive neurosis) are perhaps of this order. But how magical any action is said to be will depend somewhat on the viewpoint, and a great deal on the outcome. We can conclude, then, not only that most magic is indeed social action, but that a magical element may be present in much social action. Is there perhaps, as well, something basically magical about the nature of human action?

Some writers have thought so. Róheim was the most explicit. He identified the whole sequence of thought...speech...action *as* magical, with thought the magical proto-action that shapes a plan that makes action possible:

> We suggest, therefore, that *thinking*, which at its apex is very much an ego activity, is deeply rooted in the libido, and that between the two

we must place the mental image as magic. (p. 203).... People practice
love magic or war magic or canoe magic...first they perform the incantation and then they proceed to realistic behavior.... That is, they could
not do these things successfully without believing in their ability to do
them. (p. 11).... *everyone* practices magic... or the counterphobic attitude, that is everyone who believes that he does his work well. If people
have the opposite attitude ("inferiority complex") the superego is
triumphant and their magic is defeated (p. 84).... Magic is the counterphobic attitude, the transition from passivity to activity. (p. 18)[70]

And thus, Róheim writes, "I would go further than Malinowski" (p. 9) who
identifies magic with action that is surrounded by uncertainty. In between the
pleasure principle and the reality principle is "the magical principle," which is
the transition to action. The notion of thought as a plan of action necessary to
action is found also in Heidegger's concept of "a project," in Goldstein's idea of
an "abstract model" of behavior (which is impaired in brain injuries)[71] and in
Schutz's notion of the prior projection of action, by thought, into the "future
perfect tense."[72] Schutz even adds this, in his later works, as a third essential
criterion of social action to Weber's two criteria (subjective meaning and orientation to the behavior of others): i.e., social action is also conscious behavior
according to a plan (a mental symbolization of action before action).

We cannot learn more about the sense in which action is "magical" without
first undertaking the discussion of symbolism. But it is clear already that magic
is action. It is action of a certain kind, namely social action that makes something or changes something. It is usually effective in some way. Far from being
illusory, magic is among man's first actions, certainly his first individual actions.
In magic the individual first learns to use collective ideas in order to think—and
collective rituals in order to act—spontaneously.[73] Even bodily gestures may be,
in part, remnants of collective rituals.[74] With social symbols and rituals bent to
private uses by magic, individual players first begin to emerge from the social
chorus. As the discussion will later demonstrate, magic is the beginning of the
individual—and when man totally loses these symbolic powers, he loses his ability
to act.[75]

Notes

1. Henri Hubert and Marcel Mauss, *A General Theory of Magic* (London & Boston, 1972),
p. 19.
2. Alfred Loisy, *Essai Historique Sur le Sacrifice* (Paris, 1920), ch. 1.
3. Jane Ellen Harrison, *Themis* (Cambridge, England, 1927), p. xv, ch. 3, etc.
4. Suzanne Langer, *Philosophy in a New Key* (New York, 1948), p. 129ff, etc.
5. Géza Róheim, *Magic and Schizophrenia* (Bloomington, Ind., 1955), pp. 18–19.
6. Bronislaw Malinowski, *Magic, Science and Religion* (Garden City, N.Y., 1954), p. 98ff.
7. Jean-Paul Sartre, *The Emotions: Outline of a Theory* (New York, 1948), e.g. p. 58.
8. *A General Theory of Magic*, ch. 3.
9. Talcott Parsons & Edward A. Shils, eds., *Toward a General Theory of Action* (New
York, 1954).
10. "In 'action' is included all human behavior when and in so far as the acting individual
attaches a subjective meaning to it. Action in this sense may be either overt or purely inward

or subjective.... Action is social in so far as...it takes account of the behavior of others..."
Weber, *The Theory of Social and Economic Organization* (London, 1947), p. 80.

11. Julien Freund, *The Sociology of Max Weber* (New York, 1968), p. 102ff.

12. Cf. Hubert and Mauss on traditional symbols, *A General Theory of Magic*, e.g. p. 78.

13. Because it has both criteria: "subjective meaning" and "orientation to the behavior of others." Magic in the weak sense—whatever is denoted by those inevitable metaphors about the "magical" qualities of human speech, thought and action—would at least qualify under Weber's definition of *action*, because it has subjective meaning, whether or not it also comes over the threshold of *social* action oriented to others' behavior.

14. For example, it is misleading to say that magic is always "instrumental" rather than "moral" (Eliade has demonstrated the theurgic and devotional element in magic in a dozen books). Magic does often have a "private" rather than a "collective orientation," but this is less true of ceremonial and religious magic, and not completely true even of medical magic. And in fact, polar ideal types of magic, like those of Frazer and Goode which we criticize later, are unhelpful or misleading precisely because they are based on vague antinomies like the pattern variables. Cf. Talcott Parsons, *The Social System* (Glencoe, Ill., 1951), pp. 46–67.

15. Talcott Parsons, Robert F. Bales and Edward A. Shils, *Working Papers in the Theory of Action* (Glencoe, Ill., 1953), pp. 63–109.

16. Habermas formulates two systems of communication derived from two different kinds of action: the reflexive language of the humanities derived from symbolic interaction (for which the hermaneutics of Dilthey is the appropriate interpretation); and the empirically grounded but transcendent constructions of scientific language derived from the praxis of rational-purposive action (for which the philosophy of Peirce is the best kind of interpretation, in Habermas' neat demonstration). Jürgen Habermas, *Knowledge and Human Interests* (Boston, 1971), chs. 5–8.

17. Kenneth Burke, *A Rhetoric of Motives* (Cleveland, 1950, 1962), pp. 564–568.

18. See Malinowski, *Coral Gardens; Magic, Science and Religion*, etc. For critique, cf. S.F. Nadel, "Malinowski on Magic and Religion" in Raymond Firth, ed., *Man and Culture, An Evaluation of the Work of B. Malinowski* (London, 1957), pp. 189–209.

19. Rosalie and Murray Wax, "Magic and Monotheism," in *Proceedings of the 1964 Annual Spring Meeting of the American Ethnological Society*: Symposium on New Approaches to the Sociology of Religion; "The Notion of Magic," *Current Anthropology*, vol. 4, no. 5 (Dec. 1963), pp. 50–61; "The Magical World View," *Journal for the Scientific Study of Religion*, vol. 1, no. 2 (1962), pp. 179–188.

20. Francis L.K. Hsu, *Religion, Science and Human Crises* (London, 1952), cf. chs. 7–8. During this account of an epidemic in a small Yunnan Province city in the 1940's, the author reported that many sensible Chinese protected themselves both by Western medicine and the more magical Chinese kind. Many of the health measures undertaken for magical reasons, moreover, had side effects that were healthy, while others were dysfunctional.

21. S.F. Nadel, *op. cit.* Nadel claims Malinowski ignores the problem of distinguishing magic from mistaken empiricism.

22. Louis Rose, *Faith Healing* (London, 1968, 1971), ch. 6.

23. L. Wittgenstein, *Remarks on the Foundations of Mathematics* (Cambridge, Mass., 1967), pp. 94–97, etc.

24. Jacques Ellul, *The Technological Society* (New York, 1964), pp. 3–22.

25. Knight Dunlap, *Religion, Its Functions In Human Life* (N.Y., 1946), p. 35ff.

26. Bryan R. Wilson, ed., *Rationality* (New York, 1970).

27. Jane Ellen Harrison, *Themis* (London, 1927). Harrison writes that magic is "a thing re-done and pre-done, a thing enacted or represented. It is sometimes re-done, commemorative, sometimes pre-done, anticipatory. (p. 43).... Language here speaks clearly enough. The Latin *factura* is a magical "making," witchcraft; the Sanskrit *krtya* is doing and magic... The German *zauber* connected with O.H.G. *zouwan*, Gothic *tanyan*, to do... (p. 82)."

28. "The shield...is sacred because it is a shield, a tool, a defensive weapon, part of man's personality.... But it is not the goddess Pallas Athena who lends sanctity to the Palladion; it is the sanctity of the Palladion that begets the godhead of Pallas Athena." (*Ibid.*, pp. 86–87.)

29. George E. Mendenhall, *The Tenth Generation: The Origins of the Biblical Tradition* (Baltimore, 1973), p. 43ff.

30. V. Gordon Childe, *What Happened in History; Man Makes Himself,* etc. There are even suggestions in some theories (such as those of Malinowski and Hammond) that magic is in part a *celebration* of man's own powers.

31. Malinowski, *The Foundations of Faith and Morals* (London, 1936, 1969), pp. 11, 20, 30, 45.

32. Malinowski: see especially *Argonauts,* and *Coral Gardens,* part I.

33. *General Theory of Magic,* p. 61.

34. Alfred Loisy, *Essai Historique Sur le Sacrifice* (Paris, 1920), ch. 1.

35. Alfred Schutz's action theory stresses making something, as Weber's does not. We first discover the idea that social action *makes* something at the core of the phenomenological schema Schutz uses (in *The Phenomenology of the Social World,* Chicago, 1967, pp. 54, 56ff.) to build a sound logical foundation for the whole tradition of "interpretive sociology" that runs from Dilthey and Rickert through Weber to today's social action theory. Later, Schutz developed an action schema of his own which magic would also fit, in *Collected Papers,* vol. I, (The Hague, 1962), pp. 67–96, 207–259. In that later schema magic would be action, i.e., "conduct with a plan;" and magic in the strict sense would be "overt action" and hence a "working" that "gears into the outside world" and accomplishes something.

36. E.E. Evans-Pritchard, *Witchcraft, Oracles and Magic Among the Azande* (London, 1937), ch. 3.

37. Goran Therborn, "Social Action, Social Magic," *Acta Sociologica,* 1973, pp. 157–174.

38. Lucien Goldmann, *Le Dieu Caché* (Paris, 1959).

39. But it is probably extreme to say Parsons and Weber are both really writing about the structure of *religious* action, as Therborn says, and that *this* is why they overdramatize that precious moment of "value choice."

40. Róheim, in *Magic and Schizophrenia* (Bloomington, Ind., 1955, 1962), uses the idea of schizophrenia this way. Perhaps some ideal type of pure autism could also represent the pole of non-action. In works like Bruno Bettelheim's *The Empty Fortress* (New York, 1967) we occasionally encounter case histories in which there is perhaps no action of any kind —neither real action nor magical pseudo-action—because there is no one home, no actor. But in actuality, autist cases are quite varied. Even the polar case of schizophrenic "magic" can be a "positive disintegration," as postulated by Kazimierz Dabrowski in *Positive Disintegration* (Boston, 1964), and developed almost into an ideology by R.D. Laing, especially in *The Politics of Experience* (New York, 1967) and *Self and Others* (New York, 1969). This is some sort of action. The sub-types of schizophrenia could themselves be arranged on a continuum showing the degree to which they approach effective action. Harry Stack Sullivan, especially in *Clinical Studies in Psychiatry* (New York, 1956; chs. 7, 9, 14), attempted something like this, characterizing paranoid schizophrenia as a reorganization that sometimes works, catatonia as a rigid defense against further disorganization, and only hebephrenia as total disorganization devoid of meaningful action.

41. Freud, *General Psychological Theory: Papers on Meta-Psychology* (New York, 1963), chs. 2, 10.

42. Géza Róheim, *Magic and Schizophrenia* (Bloomington, Ind., 1955), p. 83.

43. C.G. Jung, *The Psychology of Dementia Praecox* (Princeton, 1974), p. 185.

44. Freud, *General Psychological Theory* (N.Y., 1963), ch. 2, "On The Mechanism of Paranoia," pp. 29–48.

45. *Ibid.,* chs. 10 & 12.

46. Freud, *The Problem of Anxiety* (London, 1936), *passim.*

47. Stanley Diamond, Lectures, New School For Social Research (N.Y., 1967).

48. Freud, *Group Psychology and the Analysis of the Ego* (N.Y., 1965).

49. Ernest Becker, *The Denial of Death* (New York, 1973), cf. ch. 7, pp. 127–158.

50. Charles Odier, *Anxiety and Magic Thinking* (N.Y., 1956).

51. Roger Bastide, *Sociologie et Psychanalyse* (Paris, 1950, 1972).

52. *Revue Française de Psychanalyse,* 7th Year, 1934.

53. Heinz Werner, *Comparative Psychology of Mental Development* (N.Y., 1948), *passim* & cf. ch. 11, pp. 337–376.

54. Jean-Paul Sartre (New York, 1948). The French title was *Esquisse d'Une Théorie des Emotions.*

55. Hubert and Mauss' title was *Esquisse d'Une Théorie Générale de la Magie. Esquisse* means sketch, outline, rough draft or plan. This treatise has been influential with 20th century French philosophers, sociologists, anthropologists, psychiatrists. Sartre does not cite Mauss, however.

56. In the "hodological" sense of Lewin's field theory.

57. As the James-Lang hypothesis asserts, the more it flees, the more frightened it is; anxiety is always larger than its object.

58. Mircea Eliade, *Yoga* (Princeton, 1970), pp. 112–113, 129–138, 227–252.

59. Ernest G. Schachtel, *Metamorphosis* (New York, 1959), pp. 19–77.

60. Adolf Portmann, *Animals as Social Beings* (N.Y., 1964), pp. 120–135.

61. Derek Wragg Morley, *The Ant World* (London, 1953), pp. 73, 76ff.

62. Konrad Lorenz, *On Aggression* (N.Y., 1966), cf. ch. 5, "Habit, Ritual, Magic," pp. 57–84.

63. George Maclay and Humphry Knipe, *The Dominant Man* (N.Y., 1972), pp. 35–42 & *passim.*

64. Calhoun's experiments are described in Edward T. Hall, *The Hidden Dimension* (Garden City, N.Y., 1966), pp. 21–29.

65. Wolfgang Wickler, *The Sexual Code* (Garden City, N.Y., 1973), pp. 46–58 & *passim.*

66. Thomas C. Schelling, *The Strategy of Conflict* (N.Y., 1963), pp. 83 118. Strategy games are non-zero-sum games, i.e., variable sum games, for which game theory approaches like those of Anatol Rapoport in *Two-Person Game Theory* (Ann Arbor, 1966), or John Von Neumann and Oskar Morgenstern in *Theory of Games and Economic Behavior* (N.Y., 1964) have been unable to work out determinate (mathematical) solutions, because of imperfect information. Mere randomization of response to make action unpredictable as in poker is impossible (see John McDonald, *Strategy in Poker, Business and War* [N.Y., 1950]) because there are more than two parties, or there are mixed goals. Some convergence is required, and that is where rallying points enter in. A man is picked to lead because he looks like what most people think most people think a leader looks like—i.e., because he symbolizes a leader. Armies will often fight by a stream because each general will think that the other will think he will make his stand there. Etc.

67. A non-sociological but reasonable and informative account of this phenomenon is given by Frederick Elworthy, *The Evil Eye* (N.Y., 1970).

68. Emotions communicate perhaps in hundreds of ways, many of which we do not even know about yet. Even the dilation of pupils communicates emotion. Margaret Mead used photography to discover "subliminal" communications. Prof. Ray Birdwhistle and his school in "kinesics" have found that much direct communication of emotions goes on through gestures.

69. An excerpt will demonstrate the theory's remarkable power (Sartre wrote that he planned to enlarge this theory elsewhere, but I'm not aware that he ever did): "...in emotion, consciousness is degraded and abruptly transforms the determined world in which we live into a magical world. But...this world itself sometimes reveals itself to consciousness as magical instead of determined, as was expected of it...the category 'magical' governs the interpsychic relations of men.... The magical, as Alain says, is 'the mind dragging among things'.... It is an inert activity, a consciousness rendered passive. But it is precisely in this form that others appear to us.... Thus, the meaning of a face is a matter of consciousness to begin with...but an altered, degraded consciousness, which is, precisely, passivity.... Thus, man is always a wizard to man, and the social world is at first magical. It is not impossible to ...build rational superstructures upon this magical world. But this time it is they which are ephemeral and without equilibrium; it is they which cave in when the magical aspect of faces, of gestures, and of human situations, is too strong.... The abrupt passage from a rational apprehension of the world to a perception of the same world as magical, if it is motivated by the object itself and if it is accompanied by a disagreeable element, is horror, if it is accompanied by an agreeable element it will be wonder.... In horror ...we suddenly perceive the upsetting of the deterministic barriers." (Sartre, *Ibid.*, pp. 83–85.)

70. Géza Róheim, *Magic and Schizophrenia* (Bloomington, Ind., 1955), pp. 201, 203, 11, 84, 18.

71. Kurt Goldstein, *Human Nature in the Light of Psychopathology* (N.Y., 1963), cf. ch. 3; and *The Organism* (Boston, 1963), cf. ch. 7. For a more up to date summary of such

research with a slightly different slant, see Howard Gardner, *The Shattered Mind* (N.Y., 1975).

72. Alfred Schutz, *Collected Papers*, vol. I (The Hague, 1962), pp. 68–73.

73. Cf. Hubert and Mauss, *A General Theory of Magic*, pp. 139–142.

74. Cf. Marcel Mauss, "Les Techniques du Corps" in Claude Lévi-Strauss, ed., *Marcel Mauss Sociologie et Anthropologie* (Paris, 1950, 1966), pp. 365–386.

75. Grand theories of society-and-the-individual are constructed by using Weber's social action theory to conceptualize the subjective side, and Durkheimian accounts of collective representations to generate the objective side. But in a sense systems like Parsons and Shils' *Toward a General Theory of Action* (Cambridge, Mass., 1954) and Berger and Luckmann's *The Social Creation of Reality* (Garden City, N.Y., 1966) are conceptual mismarriages, for they unite empirical and objective traits of cultural systems with ideal-typical and mentalist constructions of individual action. Weber uses these logical ideal types to generate the whole social system out of imaginary individual atoms. It is less well known that Durkheim's objective-empirical construction shows how individuals can be generated historically and empirically out of social systems. So it is not necessary to mismarry a mentalist Weberian theory of action with an empirical study of culture, for the Durkheim tradition has its own excellent empirical account of individuals as social emergents.

Postulate 2: MAGICAL SOCIAL ACTION CONSISTS OF SYMBOLIC PERFORMANCES— AND LINGUISTIC SYMBOLISM IS CENTRAL TO MAGIC.

MAGIC works with symbols, as does almost all human action, but magic puts a special accent on them. It appears sometimes to be a celebration of them, a half-exuberant, half-terrified flexing of their dangerous powers, or a dawning discovery and exploration of their remarkable uses. Above all, magic frequently appears to be the use of these symbolic powers to counter the terrors of the symbolic world that man has created and to get some control over it. Suzanne Langer emphasizes the effervescence, the overflowing sense of power that magic discovers in language.[1] Lévi-Strauss speculates about the billowing "surplus meaning" that boiled up fast when language was first invented, and theorizes that magic puts this surplus meaning to positive use repairing breaks in the social-symbolic networks in which egos subsist.[2] Some investigators, such as Peter Berger[3] and Loren Eiseley,[4] put greater emphasis on the terrors of the symbolic world that language creates; and Eiseley even suggests that the sudden explosion of man's brain size was required by the evolutionary necessity of somehow surviving in this new spiritual dimension that man himself had made—a dimension in which he constantly risked "falling into the deep well of himself." Presumably, only those large-brained people capable of defensive magical manipulation of the symbols could survive in this fourth dimension:

> O the mind, mind has mountains, cliffs of fall
> Frightful, sheer, no-man-fathomed...[5]

Magic combats the uncertainties and dangers of this symbolic universe by giving man control over some of the most potent of the symbols. Man uses this power in his first efforts to get control of his own attentionalities and emotions and hence organize and direct his behavior and the behavior of others. This use of magic probably gave man the concentration he needed to win against the other animals.

The Power of Symbols: Control of the Transcendent

What is this power that symbols have and why do symbols seem to generate magic? The numerous theories of symbolism disagree because it is seemingly impossible to pick one defining characteristic that will fit all the different kinds of signs and symbols: thus terms like "stands for," "indicates," "denotes," "names," etc. in definitions of symbols fit some cases but not others.[6] Perhaps we should call the whole cluster a "motley" united only by "family resemblances" in the manner of Wittgenstein.[7] But in the various triadic or four-term theories of Langer,[8] Peirce,[9] Morris, Schutz[10] and others (e.g., Langer's "subject, symbol, conception and object") there is some minimal and useful consensus: Many theorists could now be said to agree that a symbol is a conventional collective representation that refers to something that is *transcendent* in one of a number of senses—either the object is not present, or it is an abstract entity or a class. Schutz tries to simplify the whole problem with Husserl's idea[11] of "appresentation"—i.e., one object almost always evokes another when it is presented and the appresented object is in a transcendent realm. William James observed this even of everyday perception of ordinary objects. Few things are ever merely presented: presentation of an object also "appresents" its "inner and outer" horizon (Schutz), its "fringe" (James),[12] the way the front of a house sometimes makes you think of the back that you cannot see. The other person's body and especially his face appresent his mind as we imagine it (which is one reason why Sartre[13] thinks the face has always seemed to possess occult properties). This other mind, unknown to us and conjectured in the face, seems mystical to us for it appresents a non-shared biography, unknown intentions and also the transcendent we-relation between the two of us.

To many writers, therefore (Langer, Husserl, James, Schutz, Cassirer, etc.), symbols, by their very nature, have the property of referring to something transcending immediate experience. And manipulating symbols (as magic does) helps us get these transcendent dimensions of our experience under control.

In magic, individuals are able to take over especially powerful collective symbols (i.e., the sacred symbols of religion) and use them to think and to act effectively in the dangerous symbolic world in which man lives. As society evolves, these symbols become more powerful because they become more abstract, reflecting a social evolution from simple forms of organization to more complex social systems, a process Durkheim calls "the generalization of mana."[14] More elaborate social organization projects a more elaborate sacred cosmology containing more abstract and powerful symbols—and these become available to individuals to help them organize their "projects" or "plans" or "models" of action just at the time when society "needs" individuals. Then magic helps train them for autonomy by providing them with powerful symbols to use in modeling their action.

The recognition that magic consists of manipulating symbols of transcendent entities helps explain some other questions. It helps us understand, for example, why magic is "mystical action," why it often "doubles" things, so that it works on abstract or mystical doubles of the entities it seeks to affect—like the witch who eats the "soul" of her victim and causes his body to die. These doubles are none other than the symbolic ideas or classes or abstract entities which are manipulated by this symbolization. It also helps us understand the "weak sense" of magic suggested by the observation of Róheim, Goldstein and others that all human action involves prior thought that makes a "model" of the projected action. In abstract symbols lies the very possibility of abstract model-making as a guide to action. (Lienhardt observes that the magic twist of grass thrown behind by the fugitive is not really thought to impede the pursuer, but it helps the fugitive focus his own efforts by making a "model of his actions."[15])

Linguistic Symbols Are Central

Although magic uses material symbols too, the ultimate reference is usually to the verbal symbols of language. Evans-Pritchard disputed Malinowski on this in an early essay,[16] claiming Malinowski's theories applied to certain types of societies and not others—not to Africa, for example, where "medicines" are the core of magic. But even medicines are usually "sung," and even particularistic material symbols that seem to be merely heaped up together in nonverbal rites (such as we see in the Ndembu rituals described by Turner[17]) refer *through* linguistic symbols and derive their efficacy from them, as we will see. For in the background of the symbols lie the primitive classification systems, worked over by myths, which are the projection of the society, and the "sympathetic" effects of the material symbols derive from this background, which is a linguistic configuration.

Rites as well as representations are clearly a matter of symbolism. (In Cazeneuve's *Sociologie du Rite*,[18] rites are symbolic performances that create religious order or fight, via magic and taboo, the contrasting disorder this precipitates. There is a similar idea in Caillois[19] and in Mary Douglas' *Purity and Danger*;[20] in *Natural Symbols*[21] Douglas prefers to call this whole process and rites of any kind "magical.") Though rites also use material and gestural symbols, linguistic symbols are often central. Malinowski produced evidence of this. In *Argonauts of the Western Pacific*,[22] he demonstrated that the verbal magic of a spoken "spell" (incantation) is the core of any magical rite among the Trobrianders. This is the effective part; the materials and the actions are public knowledge, but it is the words of the incantation that are owned, kept secret, handed on or sold. And the Trobrianders say that this is the powerful part. In the simplest types of Trobriand magic, the action of the rite consists of little more than facing the object or putting it within range of the voice or aiming at it, so that the magic words will penetrate it.[23] The complications of more elaborate rites are just extra means of transference to make sure that the quality in the words passes into their objective. And the core of the incantation is usually a simple statement of the end that is desired. Malinowski observes that the native believes in the power of mere statements if they are made right.

In the serious work magic described in *Coral Gardens and Their Magic*,[24] Malinowski again emphasizes the centrality of the solemn spoken "spell." This is official magic, led by the professional magician appropriate to each activity (who may be the chief); it makes use of important sacred myths, which are of course verbal symbolism. In the less central love and beauty magic described in *The Sexual Life of Savages*, Malinowski shows material elements, such as cosmetics and lustrations, to be important.[25] But even here, the accompanying incantation is crucial, for its simple statement of the desired end is the engine of the magical effect.[26]

We can understand the power of a love spell as a social statement. The girl who is the object of love magic soon learns of it; the boy focuses public opinion on her by his daring, open display of magic. All the forces of tradition and belief in magic add to the pressure. Field reports from other societies confirm this aspect of magic as public statement (or rumor) applying social pressure. Sorcerers, for example, apparently sometimes start rumors about their intentions (though this can be dangerous for them) as part of the social-symbolic pressure they apply to make their victims sicken. In Trobriand love magic, the pressure of stated intention becomes quite overtly aggressive; it passes ultimately to physical pressure such as touching and even inculcating magical substances into the food of the beloved. In some societies, rejected love magic is believed to turn automatically into death magic.[27]

There is evidence from other investigators on the centrality of verbal magic. Hutton Webster,[28] synthesizing a vast number of field reports, sees a movement in magic from wish *through word* into action; pure wish magic is proto-magic and it is found in pure form in the evil eye phenomenon. Raymond Firth,[29] analyzing a society which he says lacks any real magic, looks for characteristic actions which might assimilate to magic and finds them in attempts by individuals to obtain specific objects by mere statement in words of what they wish. And it is hard to find any examples of medical magic in which incantations are not basic.

The numerous field studies of medical magic surveyed by Torrey[30] confirm this impression by the strategic importance they place on assigning meaning and a name to illnesses. Systems like that of Ruesch[31] can be comfortably assimilated to field reports of medical magic to explain magical illnesses as "disturbed communication" and treatment as "therapeutic communication," orally performed in both cases. Even where drugs are part of magic, linguistic symbols may dominate. Harner[32] and his school, in studying the role of drugs in magical and religious experiences, emphasize the verbal reconstruction of the experience afterwards as the determining element, as does Castenada.[33] There are some societies, such as the Azande studied by Evans-Pritchard,[34] in which the incantation is rudimentary and diagnosis is often made by mechanical non-verbal "oracles." More often, however, the diagnosis is made by a person who takes and interprets an oral case history, and the witchdoctor who cures does so with verbal incantations and references to myth that work against a linguistic background of meaning to help the patient withstand suffering, as Lévi-Strauss has shown.[35]

Magical rites frequently make use of myth. Some magic is virtually all action but what it acts out non-verbally is a (verbal) narrative from a myth. Primordial myths are often present in rites as unspoken scripts for the performance, as Lévy-Bruhl emphasized in his four main later works,[36] or as "charters" for magic, in Malinowski's formulation.[37] Malinowski proposes that the myths which serve as charters for magic are themselves stories of primordial magical acts performed by culture heroes, and that all rite-certifying myths are therefore creation myths. The magical rite reenacts and so reproduces the original magical creation which is revealed in the myth that charters the rite. It is well known what capital Eliade[38] has made of similar ideas.

Of what elements, then, does magic's verbal symbolization consist? It will be convenient to break this down under the heading of 1. magical words, 2. magical relations between words, and 3. magical sentences. Under magical words we will discuss their powers over concepts and other non-physical entities. Under magical links between words we will discuss "sympathetic magic" and the primitive classification systems that lie behind it. Under magical sentences we will discuss the myths that elaborate those classification systems in the sacred cosmos of each society.

I. Magical Words

There is abundant evidence that single words can be magical all by themselves, independent of sentences or of sympathy links with other words. There is, for example, the familiar magic of exotic, archaic, foreign or mumbo-jumbo words. "Abracadabra," for example, has maintained its potency across national and even civilizational lines, and the British Old Testament scholar John M. Allegro[39] claims to have traced it back through Aramaic to its original meaning in drug-centered religious cults of ancient Sumeria, with the alleged Sumerian mushroom phrase AB-BA-TAB-BA-RI still resonating in the "Our Father" (Abba, father) of a Christian prayer. Whatever the merits of this philology (not to mention Allegro's curious thesis about esoteric early Christianity as a drug cult), the mystery of "abracadabra" and other words like it remains. The grimoires are full of them. Some, like "presto," seem to be mere intensifiers, or one-word expressive sentences. They seem to simply stand for (and urge on) the magic effect itself—they say, in effect, be it so, *soit*—and Hubert and Mauss have suggested that even "mana" is used this way.[40] Other single magic words or syllables, like the mantras of Tantrism, come laden with theories about how they operate directly and physically on the universe. But their real power seems to derive from some old rite in which they were used as a hypnotic. No doubt many magic words can be explained as particles detached from more complete religious texts. But there exists at least one group of words possessing magical potency by themselves and outside of texts—and these are names.

A. Magic Names

Everyone is familiar with practices whereby the name of the god is kept secret because it is so magically powerful (e.g., Yahweh). The names of persons are also kept secret (as in the fairy tale of Rumpelstiltskin). Mauss tells us in his essay on prayer[41] that in India only the Brahmins could pray, presumably for this reason, and Frankfort[42] and Budge[43] report on the important magical uses of divine names. Words are so powerful that the name of the deity is more potent than the deity, which is not surprising since that is often how he began. *Nomen* is *numen*, name is linked to soul or self.[44]

I think also that the evidence of Codrington[45] and Hertz[46] strongly implies what Cassirer boldly states, which is that the problem of ghosts is the problem of the persistence of names, especially strong names (of strong people).[47] What is the power inherent in a name all by itself? Obviously, a name is thought to give some control over the object referred to. A name, moreover, is a creative idea; in the sense of a naming, it can also participate in the making of a *nomos*. "In the beginning was the word" is a phrase that turns up in many primitive cosmologies.[48] It is an old idea that naming things creates order. Harvey Cox suggests that the Hebrews, with their experience of creating a society through a social contract, were more aware of this than were the Greeks.[49] So the Hebrews said that, whereas god created the things of the world, he let man name them. By contrast, the naming of things was a problem for the Greeks that resulted in such conceptualization as Plato's theory of ideas.

B. Borrowed Words

Another group of words which seem to possess potency by themselves are words that are borrowed from some other context, so they come to plain speech with mysterious halos of surplus meaning wrenched from their previous contexts but now incompletely understood. Kenneth Burke, in his book *The Rhetoric of Religion,*[50] has developed a theory of this. The gist of it is that the supernatural is a cosmos constructed by words that are "borrowed" from the natural sphere. These words are made numinous by this use—and then we can "borrow them back" to achieve numinous effects. These effects he characterizes as "religious language." There is a real possibility for a theory of magic here, but Burke dodges it (as he dodges magic in his general statement on rhetoric, to be discussed later),[51] perhaps because he does not seem to like that category. The borrowed-back words he is talking about are mostly words about religion—for example, theological words.[52] But I would like to suggest that "borrowing back" can also be useful in explaining some magical words. Sacred words that are borrowed back and put to instrumental use in the secular sphere would be magical words.

Borrowing back is a very important way of generating new meaning in language. Take economic theory, for example, which, perhaps because so much of it was initiated by the British, deliberately used simple everyday words as symbols for its key concepts. The result was that plain words like "supply" and "demand" were given special meanings, and now have new effects in everyday speech when they are borrowed back. In "A Category of the Human Spirit,"[53] Mauss notes that the original word for "person" came from the word for mask in the quasi-specialized usage of the theater. Krader[54] remarks on the possibility that new categories are frequently formed like this, when words are taken from specialized use into general use.

Borrowing back is a very important source of mystification and reification.[55] In their original public language games, these words had clear meanings; and even in the initial act of borrowing, their special meanings were often precisely defined. While they remained within their specialized contexts, the newly defined words remained in touch with their specialized referents. But when the words are reintroduced into public language games their new special senses can become half understood ghost concepts or mystifications. There is a dimension of alienated meaning as well as power-through-meaning in the "borrowed-back" words that magic employs.

The most important borrowed-back words used by magic, of course, are religious words. Magic borrows them from dying religions, dead religions and foreign religions as well as from official contemporary religion. Dupre observes that religion can be conceived of as an intensification of man's natural process of symbolization.[56] Eliade[57] cites the frequently noted fact that shamans possess vastly larger vocabularies than ordinary people. Truly, religion has been a fountain of language, constantly coining new meanings from which not just magic but all the emerging professions have borrowed.

C. Words as Concepts

But there is a deeper explanation for some of the power of individual words used in magic, and this is the fact that many words are concepts —they refer to abstract entities or classes, and they are ideas that light up experience and generate thought.[58] The probable reason why words are believed to give power over the objects they denote is precisely because they are so convincingly felt to give power over the concepts that they connote. The connoted concepts can be more easily manipulated than the denoted objects. Even proper nouns that denote a single object (e.g., names) may also in a sense connote a conception (e.g., a concept or image of the person bearing that name)[59]—and, to primitive man, concepts of persons are experienced as the invisible "souls" or "spirits" of persons that magic attacks or defends in order to attack or defend the person himself.

Suzanne Langer writes that because words are concepts man can easily build with them.[60] It is as natural for man to use symbols as for bees to build hives; our talk is mainly about ideas and we are excited by them. She therefore views magic and religion as effervescence caused not by social interaction but by the sheer chance and urge to talk, the overflow of language's richness. Religions are the social creation of this talk, but man talking is magic. However, like Durkheim, she recognizes that magic uses religious material and evolves out of it, not vice-versa: "We are often told that savage religion begins in magic; but the chances are, I think, that magic begins in religion. Its typical form—the confident, practical *use* of a formula...is the empty shell of a religious act."[61] But our symbols are not originally utilitarian; they are lush, rank, prodigal and they make us exuberant. Man exults in their use because, as he soon discovers, he can transform something by them. He can transform concepts. Concepts can be rearranged, combined, even created by thought, and manipulating one concept causes effects on others:

> Magic has not its origin in fraud.... Its roots lie much deeper than any conscious purpose...|in| the human need for expressing such ideas. Whatever purpose magical practice may serve, its direct motivation is the desire to symbolize great conceptions. (p. 39).... The power of conception—of "having ideas"—is man's peculiar asset, and awareness of this power is an exciting sense of human strength. Nothing is more thrilling than the dawn of a new conception. The symbols that embody ideas of life and death, of man and the word, are naturally sacred. (p. 122)[62]

It is on this realm of concepts that magic works, not on nature, though magic cooperates with the movement of nature. ("No savage tries to induce a snowstorm in midsummer.... He dances *with* the rain."[63]) Goldstein observes that common nouns refer to classes of objects and involve an abstract attitude, which man needs to orient experience in his symbolic world. When brain injury impairs the abstract attitude, the result is terror and the "hunger for meaning"[64] found in anxiety states (which the magician may repair with his "surplus meaning" as Lévi-Strauss shows[65]). Abstraction is the heart of that "plan" or "project" that precedes action as the "counterphobic attitude" in Róheim's sense,[66] that organizes it in Schutz's definition.[67] Durkheim[68] has suggested that magic itself arose when mana as a real social force was conceptualized as a category, in "mana words."[69] In its essence, magic presupposes a certain ability to abstract and extrapolate, to apply symbols as concepts that impose themselves on reality.

Although Langer admits that some magic is tired and works with worn symbols, she mainly analyzes the triumphant sense of power that younger, healthier magic celebrates. By contrast, Cassirer puts greater stress on our grave human vulnerability to magic.[70] He demonstrates how man's whole environment and self are so woven out of concepts that his very being trembles when they are manipulated by magic. For just as Johannes Von Uexkull has shown that each species lives in its own "world" or "species-specific environment"—the fly in a "fly world" filled mostly by "fly things," for example—man lives entirely in the world of concepts which he has created.

It is this transcendent realm of concepts that is ultimate reality for man; here he registers many of his experiences; here his ego is born and grows. Individual words that ripple the texture of this symbolic ether have remarkable effects when the self is still primitive—words can evoke, create, change and summon entities. There is little doubt that gods, for example, condensing out of rites or artifacts or just mana, are finally crystallized by words. Usener in 1896 propounded the theory of "momentary divinities" —with the first personifications of mana appearing literally as visions when the name of the god was uttered.[71] Hubert and Mauss cite similar evocations—tongues of flame and flashes of light actually experienced during magical ceremonies.[72]

Something seems to steal a primitive man's attention, as if by magic; he is caught and held by the image. When the ego, as a category of the human spirit, was not much developed, intentionality was not sufficiently organized to control attentionality, and men were singularly vulnerable to "fascinations." Consider, for example, such phenomena as "olanism," which persisted into this century among Tatar peoples—it is the compulsive imitation of some forceful gesture that could seize a whole Cossak regiment.[73] Rasmussen[74] demonstrated that one of the functions of the shaman was to defend small vulnerable societies from deadly chain reactions caused by such fascinations. Ellul[75] and Marcuse[76] have shown how the compulsive fascination of the word can be used in propaganda to compel action even among civilized peoples. Studies of the evil eye phenomenon make it plain that it was not just the (hostile or envious) emotion communicated that made this proto-magic deadly—but also the "fascination" it exerted. The usual defense was the amulet, intended to fascinate the fascinator and so provide a distraction.[77]

Man's attentionality is especially vulnerable to words since they constitute his species-specific environment. Thus it is extremely hard for primitive man to believe that striking ideas in his stream of consciousness do not come to him from the outside. E.R. Dodds[78] has shown that in Homeric civilization the conventional explanation for inventive ideas was a "monition" from outside, from gods, perhaps, and that emotions came that way too—like the *ate* or divine madness that blinded Agamemnon. Nilsson[79] has noticed that the heroes in the *Iliad* were quite worried about their unstable moods. For until the personality as a "category of the human spirit" (Mauss), or the "discovery of the mind" (Bruno Snell[80]), or the "development of the soul" (A.E. Taylor[81]), or the "magical construction of the self" (De Martino[82]), has proceeded to some degree, intentionality can provide attentionality with little protection against the evocative power of words. And so, German scholars, such as Wilamowitz and Walter Otto,[83] report that "the gods were *there*," powerfully evoked by their names.

The magic of words is of the same stuff as the world that made us, and so it can go *straight into us*. Harry Stack Sullivan,[84] for example, has demonstrated how simple verbal formulae can work just below the surface of consciousness (e.g., in hysterics). The hysteric has been frustrated by his employer; he reflects on it and precipitates some mental phrase like, "This thing will drive me crazy!" just before going to bed. A few hours later, he wakes up in a terrible state which confuses and punishes everyone. The mechanism is shallow, but his doctor is unlikely to turn up the magical phrase by which he programmed himself unconsciously.

But magic is not so much these vulnerabilities and effects as it is the use to which they are put. In magic, man concentrates his efforts, gets some control over these phenomena and ultimately over his own attentionality. "Faith in magic is one of the earliest and most striking expressions of man's awakening self-confidence. Here he no longer feels himself at the mercy of natural or supernatural forces. He begins to play his own part..."[85]

D. Natural Symbols as Class Concepts

"Natural symbols" are perhaps among the first general operators that help to get the floating world of symbols under control for emerging selves. The scholarly study of natural symbols, their distribution and alleged universality as archetypes can be an antiquarian or Platonic sidetrack, however. Jung, for example, could not penetrate with certainty the exact meaning of the prehistoric classification systems that lay behind myths he studied, so the "archetypes" he found in them tended to be derived myths. Lévi-Strauss, more witty, admits that when he tries to decipher the natural symbols of myths he is really just writing a new version of the myth. Or we might put it this way: theorists like Lévi-Strauss and Jung are really writing magic theory, or theosophy, which is a very important process of rationalization generated within magic itself. Even with a Durkheimian like Mary Douglas, a preoccupation with natural symbols can lead toward theosophy.[86]

However, Victor Turner has shown us the important thing about natural symbols, which is the strategic use to which they are put. They are obvious rallying points for "condensation symbols"[87] that bring the beginnings of conscious rationalizing order to symbolic universes and hence control to men. Condensation symbols are symbols for classes of symbols, hence concepts for classes of concepts. Here, surely, the magical power of the single word reaches its primitive apogee. In powerful meta-symbols like "blood" and "milk" or "red" and "black" man begins to get control of the social symbols that distract him. When this happens, we move from the magical power *of* words to power *over* words, which is the birth of real magic. For the development of magic goes hand in hand with an incipient process of rationalization worked on the faded remains of older classification systems.

II. Magical Relations Between Words

We turn now from the seemingly independent potency that some words have to the much more common case of a magical effect being achieved through mysterious relations between words. At this point we are talking about traditional relationships that exist between words even in advance of their use in sentences. These connections offer man even more sweeping symbolic powers, for they make it possible to use one word to act upon another, and hence upon its concept and the class of objects in that concept's domain. As an example, consider the social impact of metaphors. In metaphors, connections are referred to between several words and therefore between the concepts or classes of objects they connote and so the appresentational power of symbols is magnified. James Fernandez writes that metaphors "get control" of strange situations by relating them to "familiar circumstances";[88] thereby they allay anxiety, provide tools for a plan of action and so make action possible (like Róheim's mental "plans" of action). Moreover, metaphors in action influence other people, because, as Fernandez colorfully puts it, "society is a movement of pronouns in quality space."[89] He means that every metaphorical connection stated in speech influences the social position of entities, things and persons, and by so much "magically" affects their standing, status and power. But metaphors are not often individual adventitious relations; they are usually conventional and based on relations that already subsist between the words.

This brings us, of course, to the phenomenon of so-called "sympathetic magic." Frazer's familiar theory of the types of sympathetic magic, developed in Chapter Three of *The Golden Bough*,[90] is actually a mere non-explanatory classification, and an incomplete one at that. "Homeopathic" (or imitative) and "contagious" magical effects, based respectively on association by similarity and association by contact or contiguity, do indeed appear in many sympathetic connections of words, but not in all; and anyway the classification does not explain these links. It is intended to, however, because a theory derived from English associationalist psychology comes along with it. It can be demonstrated by consulting a good history of psychology, such as that of Boring,[91] that both "similarity" and "contiguity" appear as principles in the fundamental theories of the "association of ideas" in the works of John Locke,[92] Hume, Hartley and other classical associationalist writers. "Contiguity" is also one of the principles used in their metaphysical accounts of causality. Thus Frazer is really saying that sympathetic links are sedimented by the association of ideas.

Sympathy Links Are Based on Tradition. But as Hubert and Mauss demonstrate, the associations between words used in sympathetic magic are conventional.[93] The possible associations of ideas are infinite in number but only a limited number are used—those which tradition ordains. These are cultural links, not psychological associations of ideas. They also point out some obvious additional principles of sympathy that Frazer left out—and others including Freud have added to this list.[94] And so, besides "similarity" and "contiguity" there is "the part standing for the whole," "it happened before," "condensation," "displacement," "transformation into opposites," etc. And there are large provinces of magic in which the major connections are not mainly based on sympathy at all: sacrifice, for example. Thus Frazer's principles of sympathy cannot explain magic; they cannot even explain all of sympathetic magic, which in turn does not cover all magical word-links. And anyway, it is not mere association of words for its own sake that goes on here; what is significant in most rites is the transfer of qualities across links between words which are established by tradition.

Primitive Classification Systems Are the Origin of Sympathetic Magic. The word links of sympathetic magic are conventional; they make use of an existing tradition. What are Hubert and Mauss talking about? What comes to mind are those primitive, often totemic classification systems that early man projects as an image of his society, with, for example, the kangaroo group including kangaroos and also grubs because kangaroos eat them, but also the sun (perhaps because it sets in the West and the kangaroo group sits on the west side of the campsite) and other objects for other reasons that have been forgotten and could never now be fathomed. I strongly suggest that this is what the authors had in mind, for Durkheim and Mauss were even then embarked on their study, *Primitive Classification*, which would be published barely a year later in *L'Année Sociologique*.[95] They did not explicitly put it together in the *Esquisse*, but we can do it for them because it clearly provides the answer. Mysterious links often exist between words because, originally, they were linked together in primitive classification systems. These links remain (and perhaps seem even more mysterious) when the reasons for classifying them together (and even the whole classification system) have been forgotten. At the very least, there is evidence that sympathetic word links derive from *myths*, and we will later show that myths work rationalizing operations on primitive classification systems. Thus a certain medicine is used because myth says it was sacred to Apollo, on whose day the rite is performed—etc. But even after ages of myth, primitive classification systems retain their own mystical prestige. In *Primitive Classification* Durkheim and Mauss[96] argue that both the *I Ching* and the system of astrology brought into the Greek world from Mesopotamia derive from and perpetuate primitive classification systems. Much of their occult power stems from mysterious connections between objects and qualities; their very uncanniness, I suggest, comes from the half-forgotten nature of these links—content is remembered but meaning is lost. Our own classification systems have become so rationalized by science and logic that we forget that they too are social creations. We assume that they reflect the order of the universe, and primitives have the same attitude toward their classifications. Sympathetic word links are born here—between the names of objects which are associated in the same classes, for forgotten reasons.

Sympathy links between words are only part of the way in which even sympathetic magic works. In one of his later books, for example, Lévy-Bruhl[97] demonstrated that three links are involved, not one, and the word-to-word association is perhaps the least important of the three. To recast his thought into the language of Langer and Cassirer, Lévy-Bruhl might be said to be specifying these three links:

1. *First, there is the link between the word as a symbol and the concept which it appresents.* We have seen that words designate concepts and that this is one source of the primitive's experience of a mystic reality. Lévy-Bruhl emphasizes this. Everything has a double aspect—there is an invisible entity, he writes, associated like shadow or soul with almost every visible entity. Lévy-Bruhl is especially interesting on psychic entities that duplicate persons, such as the soul.[98] There is abundant evidence from all over the world that it is these entities rather than their physical doubles that are most vulnerable to magic. Among the Azande,[99] for example, it is *mbisimo mangu* or the spirit of witchcraft (itself a physical part of the witch) which does the work; the witch's spirit in turn leaves her own sleeping body when she travels to do her mischief; and she harms her victim by eating the spiritual doubles of his internal organs, not the organs themselves. That is the first sympathetic link: between the word and the spiritual double of a thing.

2. *The second link is between the spiritual entity and the physical entity.* When the spirit of one's liver is eaten by a witch, the liver itself sickens; when the soul becomes afflicted, the body wastes. We understand some of this, but only some, with our modern idea of psychosomatic medicine. The power of magic is deeper, for in some cases the spiritual double actually constitutes the real entity out of raw experience: e.g., the self. Attacks on one's self or one's soul can be devastating; consider, for example, the effect even now of an attack on one's name or status or identity. Walter Cannon's "The Voodoo Death"[100] and Mauss' "*Effet Physique Chez l'Individu de l'Idée de Mort Suggérée par la Collectivité*"[101] have shown how lethal and rapid is the physical effect. Primitives will physically sicken and die when the witch doctor or a broken taboo condemns them. And just as Hegel says that "magic works by getting things on their weak side,"[102] it is frequently reported that sorcerers attack people who are already sick and vulnerable; their psychological attack is fatal in these circumstances if it cannot be repelled by magical counteraction. And of course magical illnesses are still found abundantly among civilized peoples, and sometimes can only be arrested by "magical" therapies which operate on the psychic entities that are so potent in affecting physical organisms.

3. *The third link,* Lévy-Bruhl writes, *is the mere associative link between ideas* —and it is the least important of all! So much for Frazer's theory of sympathy, which is a partial and inadequate explanation of this verbal link.

I propose, then, that sympathetic magic comes down to links between words provided by primitive classification systems, which are used for the transfer of qualities between concepts in suggestive statements aimed at affecting these entities, which in turn affect their physical referents. Spells can "go right into" a person's psychic organization, because it is itself constituted out of words. Peter Berger, with his concept of "plausibility structures,"[103] has shown how such entities as identity are built up in conversation and must be sustained by talk. Howard Gardner,[104] in surveying recent studies of stroke damage to help decide the old question about localization vs. holism in brain functions,[105] finds a mixed picture and makes an interesting suggestion. The self may be little more than "a metaphor" which the individual constructs in the course of his biography to use as a comparison with which continuously to scan his own mental content; if so, that metaphor may be located somewhere in the frontal lobes. Whether it is so located or not, that metaphor or cluster of metaphors consists of verbal material in large measure, and thus it can certainly be pierced by verbal spells. Modern man's relative immunity to spells is based on several special factors. First of all, the older classification systems on which sympathetic magic is based have faded much more for us; their prestige has been almost totally undermined by the classifications of modern science; their curious connections have lost all compulsion. But second, even against an incantation aimed at us in our own language we have a much more complex verbal apparatus of self and much more formidable "nihilating processes" than primitive man. (See Freud, for example, on the mental operation of "negation" as a powerful defense, enabling ego to de-fuse dangerous messages without the risk of losing conscious access to them that the alternative process of repression poses.[106]) Of course, external "magic" is getting pretty complicated, too, and some of the assaults on our integrity are made with magical engines more intricate than those devised by primitive man (such as chi square!). So the struggle goes on.

Real magic does not long remain at a level of mere inert associations between words. The power of single words and of sympathy connections between them is more like the possibility than the actuality of magic; it is more like "magic in the weak sense." Actual magical rites more often involve putting the effects together in sentences, just as magic as a category of action requires some degree of abstraction and generalization to have developed in the religious ideas it expropriates. High magic really begins when the possibilities of sympathetic word connections are eventually used to assert magical sentences of various kinds, beginning with myth and going on to further rationalizations and finally theories of magic (the theosophies). In fact, there is a theoretical element implicit in every magical act and new magic is generated by theories of magic. The rise of magic is associated, as we will later see, with an incipient ability to generalize stimulated by the evolution of society toward more complex forms.[107]

Transition to Magical Sentences. In Victor Turner's Ndembu we perhaps can see a transitional society, on the verge of "the generalization of mana" but not yet putting the magic words together into sentences. Looking again at several of Turner's works[108] from this standpoint, we find that the curious massing of symbols that occurs in Ndembu ritual seems to suggest words still connected almost entirely by their original classificatory affinities and not yet formulated into any kind of generalizations. In *The Ritual Process* and *The Forest of Symbols* Turner observes that the Ndembu have no theories, do not build cosmologies or systems —they do not even have many *myths.* Instead, they express meaning by over-determined massing of symbols in their rituals, material objects in such use being saturated with dozens of intersecting associations so that the whole constitutes a "forest" of reiterated symbols. The Ndembu do not themselves even understand all the ramifications and connections of these symbol networks, much less have a theory of it.[109] Now it is interesting that this society with its low level of generalization has very little magic. Communal rites of a religious nature are prominent here. Except to notice the derivation of some magical medicine from religion, there is little expressly about magic in Turner's several accounts of this society. One major exception is the material on witchcraft and sorcery.[110] Since witchcraft is the oldest magical idea, this finding would not conflict with the impression of a society lacking prominent magic because religious symbols are not yet generalized.

But perhaps we can see the generalization of sympathy effects beginning here in the centrality of what Turner calls "condensation symbols," particularly intense symbols which are the nexi of a larger than average number of interconnections.[111] These condensation symbols are already "dominant symbols," which could be interpreted as an incipient rationalization of a classification system into more general *genera*. Another process of rationalization may perhaps be seen in the polarization of symbols. Turner does not say all this (and presents his material more in structuralist terms), but I am persuaded that the Ndembu could be used as an example of a people nearing the point of transition toward more general mana categories, and straining toward them through massive reiteration of connections. Whether Ndembu social morphology would fit such an interpretation is less certain.[112]

The symbols heaped up in Ndembu rites are objects—things—but the sympathy links are between the words they imply. Hubert and Mauss have shown how non-verbal sympathy links can be expressed via substances—"cuisine, pharmacy, chemistry"—or materials which the magician "sculpts, models, paints, draws, embroiders, knits, weaves, engraves," to make objects such as "gree-grees, scapulars, talismans, amulets," etc.[113] But it is the names of the objects as linguistic symbols that carry the sympathy connections because these depend on primitive classification systems. At low levels of generalization, characteristic of polysegmental societies, these classificatory affinities may be expressed almost entirely without words, just by piling up the objects as symbols in a rite; and in advanced magics as well some use will be made of objects, which carry their meaning only implicitly, thereby adding to the mystification. Tribes at low levels of generalization like the Ndembu will, conversely, also use some purely verbal spells, but in these, too, we may expect the words to be more "heaped up" to establish their sympathetic connections, than logically ordered. This heaping together of symbols, with strategic connections implied by strong "condensation symbols," is perhaps a transition to magical sentences.

III. Magical Sentences

The full magical potential of traditional affinities between words can be most realized when the words are associated in the verbal magic of spells and incantations. These speech acts can be analyzed as sentences, and a systematic account of them would be useful. Help in building one can be found in the philosophical study of religious language, a branch of analytical philosphy which has developed a fair-sized literature in the last 25 years, with contributions by Flew, Braithwaite, Bultmann,[114] Wittgenstein, Kenneth Burke,[115] etc. We can use the useful synthesis of Anders Jeffner[116] as a platform from which to suggest what a theory of magic sentences might cover. We can begin, as he does, with a "neutral definition": magical sentences are sentences "connected with" magic. And just as Jeffner notes that there are in general four kinds of sentences and examines what religious sentences might be under each heading—1. "expressions," 2. "statements" (i.e., propositions), 3. "prescriptions" and 4. "performatives"—we can do the same for magical sentences:

1. The simplest magical speech acts would be *expressions*, sentences which just put together a few words of emotion or intention in a way that has a social (and is thought to have a mystical) effect: "Boil and bubble!" 2. Magical *pro-*

positions assert something to be the case; they may simply repeat something from myth or tradition as the groundwork for a magical implication, or may already involve a magical interpretation or bending of tradition: *"Great is the power of Satan!"* or *"It is written, but I say unto you..."* 3. Magical *prescriptions* state something that should be done; they are common in wish magic and are often used in expropriating and detouring religious values toward magical ends: *"Those who do not gather will scatter!" "He that denies me shall die!"* 4. But perhaps most typical of magic are *performative* sentences, statements that by themselves create a new state of affairs—*"I vow..."* or *"I name thee..."* 5. And most potent of all are an intermediary form that Jeffner calls *"power prescriptions"* (they really function as performatives)—these are sentences that create what is prescribed because their very utterance changes a social situation. Even in secular life power prescriptives have dramatic, magic-like consequences: *"We herewith declare war...," "We pronounce outlawry upon...," "I sentence you to be hanged by the neck until you are dead."* Magical power prescriptives employ the same social-consensual forces but work more surreptitiously and more mysteriously: *"Arise and walk!"* One very deadly type of magical power prescription is the curse, which by its mere assertion tends to produce the state of affairs which it asserts. Its social effect is to move the victim's self, as a concept, into dangerous regions of "quality space" as defined by tradition, where it may wither, thereby causing the biological individual to sicken and perhaps to die. In general, the main types of sentences seem so adaptable to magic ends that the thought occurs that sentence forms perhaps began in magico-religious practice, as surely as poetry did.

The "anchorage" of all these sentences, to use another Jeffner term, is the relation between the speech act and our supposition concerning the existence of a certain state of affairs. The "localization" of sentences refers to the world of reference, which could be the real world, a fictional world, etc. "Indirect sentences" are those located in a fictitious world but thought to have an important relation to or meaning or effect in the real world. I think that magical sentences are usually believed to be "direct" sentences by their believers, anchored in the existence of real entities.[117]

One can imagine a logical progression toward generality in the kinds of sentences used in magic. In a society like the Ndembu, the few magical sentences used are of a low level of generality—usually just expressive sentences. As societies evolve more complex organization, they start to rationalize their classification systems (which are projections of society) and they make increasing use of propositional sentences in their religious scripts, which assert general relationships between words and classes of objects. Thus the religious cosmos is elaborated. Much of this is done by the propositions contained in myths. As Durkheim and Mauss have shown,[118] a myth about, for example, the direct birth of Athena from Zeus has the effect of a general proposition asserting a connection between the class of all Zeus objects (sky, thunder, etc.) and the class of all Athena objects (owl, war, wisdom, shield, Athens, etc.).

But powerful magic in action tends to use "power prescriptive sentences" and "performative sentences." These are often directly copied from prescriptives and performatives used in religious rites. But they are also derivable, at least in principle, by deduction from propositional sentences in the worldview projected by religion. In general it is from the overarching system of beliefs projected by religious propositions that, according to Durkheim, magic derives its credibility and hence its potency.[119] And it is only when religion begins to speak more in general propositions, when, moreover, general rites such as sacrifice appear, that the generalization on which magical expropriation and extrapolation depend becomes possible.

Sentences of a power prescriptive or performative sort also appear in the core of religious practice, and magic in many cases just borrows these. And no doubt performative and prescriptive verbal rites also spring up within magic out of their own efficacy, without implication from religious propositions. Moreover, the relation between religious and magical sentences is reciprocal. Marett has demonstrated that continued belief in the religious worldview is sustained by the "real" (i.e., intersocial) effects of magical practices. An important part of these are magical speech acts; because they really do "psych out" the other person, induce altered states of consciousness and other striking phenomena, they renew faith in the propositions of the religious worldview. Thus some performative sentences work as "miracles" (e.g., "Arise and walk!") to renew religious faith.

Magic and religion sustain each other reciprocally, in other words, and this could be analyzed in terms of the types of sentence used. As Durkheim said, the worldview projected by religion provides the possibility for magical action; this could be thought of as propositions of religious myths from which other propositions could be deduced as a setting for performative and power prescriptive sentences. But religion uses performatives too, and magic borrows them directly. And new performatives spring up in magic which, by their dramatic effects, renew faith in religious propositions. When a religion becomes too cognitive and its own magic dries up, either faith in the propositions of its worldview will weaken, or else magical challenges will appear at the periphery in the form of new sects using striking performatives to overthrow or renew the religion.

Performatives and power prescriptives can continue to have "magical" power even after belief in religion wanes: e.g., in the legal system. ("I now pronounce you man and wife.") Power prescriptives and performatives may also continue to have lasting "magical" effects in the weak sense—even after the religions from which they are derived have waned—by being perceived as "indirect sentences." Religious propositions are often so conceived today. Take, for example, what Jeffner calls "the problematical set of religious statements"; this is what Bultmann calls the "kerygma"; Jeffner writes that it refers to a fictional world of myth but somehow has meaning in our own real world. This "indirect localization" is even more substantial in magical practice. We know that beliefs about black cats and Friday the thirteenth are myths but we also have a sense of minimizing psychic risks.

We can observe the different types of sentences at work in magical incantations recorded by anthropologists. In many published by Malinowski (cf. *Argonauts*, ch. 18), the sentences in the key middle part of incantations are mainly power prescriptives. Expressive sentences are also important according to other field reports. Henry Munn[120] reproduces one brilliant incantation that expresses dramatically the shaman's sheer joy at the power of speech; it recalls what Suzanne Langer alleged about magic as an exuberant display of man's symbolic powers:

> "I am he who speaks, he who searches, says. I am he who looks for the spirit of the day, says.... Where there is the fear, says. Where there is the terror, says." (pp. 113—114)

Performative and power prescriptive sentences are the powerful means which magic uses for major symbolic transformation: the laying of a curse, the key sentences in purification and forgiveness rites. New states of social existence are created by magical oaths, curses, declarations of outlawry, etc.

But propositions are also important in magical ceremonies. This is immediately apparent in all the numerous reports (e.g., Lévy-Bruhl, Malinowski, Eliade, etc.) about the recitation of religious myths during magical performances. The myths contain propositions, though it might be argued that their performance is intended as a global performative to recreate the time and event they narrate. Sometimes, as in the song magic of the Papago Indians,[121] for example, simple statements apparently in narrative form in the first person are so difficult to interpret that they appear to be simultaneously propositions, performatives, expressions and prescriptions. There is a sense in which all magical speech acts are partly performative, tending to change the nature of something or create something.

Notes

1. Suzanne Langer, *Philosophy in a New Key* (N.Y., 1942, 1948), chs. 6, 7, pp. 116—164.
2. Lévi-Strauss' theory of magic can be put together basically from four sources: A. A section in *The Savage Mind* (Chicago, 1962), on the magician as "bricoleur" or handyman patching things up with bits of old traditions (pp. 16—36). B. Chs. 9 & 10 of *Structural Anthropology* (N.Y., 1963), pp. 167—205, on how the sorcerer cures through surplus meaning. C. pp. 66—68 of *Totemism* (Boston, 1963) criticizing affect theories of magic and showing that the emotions are part of the script. D. The Introduction to *Sociologie et Anthropologie* (Paris, 1950, 1966) relating "surplus meaning" to the beginnings of language and showing how it is used to reintegrate individuals who threaten to become "private symbol systems" (e.g., psychotics), pp. IX—LII.
3. Peter L. Berger, *The Sacred Canopy* (Garden City, N.Y., 1967), p. 55, etc.
4. Loren Eiseley, esp. *The Immense Journey* (N.Y., 1956), chapter on the brain; *The Mind as Nature* (N.Y., 1962); and *Man, Time and Prophecy* (N.Y., 1966). Also, *The Invisible Pyramid* (N.Y., 1970); *The Unexpected Universe* (N.Y., 1964); *The Night Country* (N.Y., 1971); *All the Strange Hours* (N.Y., 1975); plus speeches, articles, conversations.
5. Gerard Manley Hopkins, "No Worst, There Is None."
6. William P. Alston, "Sign and Symbol," *Encyclopedia of Philosophy* (N.Y., 1967), vol. VI & VII, pp. 437—441.

7. Ludwig Wittgenstein, *Philosophical Investigations* (N.Y., 1968), p. 32ff, etc.

8. Suzanne Langer, *Ibid.*, ch. 3.

9. Charles S. Peirce, *Values In a Universe of Chance*, ed. Philip S. Wiener (Garden City, N.Y., 1958); Justus Buchler, ed., *Philosophical Writings of Peirce* (N.Y., 1955); also James K. Feibleman, *An Introduction to the Philosophy of Charles S. Peirce* (Cambridge, Mass, 1970).

10. Alfred Schutz, "Symbol, Reality and Society," *Collected Papers* (The Hague, 1962), vol. 1, pp. 287–356.

11. Edmund Husserl, *Cartesian Meditations* (The Hague, 1960), p. 108ff.

12. William James, *The Principles of Psychology* (N.Y., 1890, 1950), vol. 2, ch. 20. And cf. Schutz, *op. cit.*, p. 108.

13. Jean-Paul Sartre, *The Emotions: Outline of a Theory* (N.Y., 1948), p. 84.

14. Emile Durkheim, *The Elementary Forms of Religious Life* (London, 1915, 1954), Book II, ch. 7.

15. Godfrey Lienhardt, *Divinity and Experience: The Religion of the Dinka* (Oxford, 1961), ch. 7, "The Control of Experience: Symbolic Action," cf. p. 283.

16. E.E. Evans-Pritchard, "The Morphology and Function of Magic," *American Anthropologist*, n.s. 31, 1929, pp. 619–640.

17. Victor Turner, *The Forest of Symbols* (Ithaca and London, 1967); *The Ritual Process* (London, 1969); *Dramas, Fields and Metaphors* (Ithaca & London, 1974).

18. Jean Cazeneuve, *Sociologie du Rite (Taboo, Magie, Sacré* (Paris, 1950).

19. Roger Caillois, *L'Homme et le Sacré* (Paris, 1950).

20. Mary Douglas, *Purity and Danger* (London, 1970).

21. Mary Douglas, *Natural Symbols* (N.Y., 1950).

22. B. Malinowski, *Argonauts of the Western Pacific* (N.Y., 1961), chs. 17–18, pp. 376 463.

23. Malinowski, *Ibid.*, p. 403.

24. Malinowski, *Coral Gardens and Their Magic* (London, 1935), vol. I, pp. 62–80, 435 451.

25. Malinowski, *The Sexual Life of Savages* (N.Y., 1929), ch. 11, "The Magic of Love and Beauty," pp. 344–383.

26. Modern advertising uses a similar frank statement of wishes.

27. Ken Brower, conversation, July, 1978.

28. Hutton Webster, *La Magie Dans Les Sociétés Primitives* (Paris, 1952), cf. ch. 4, p. 96ff.

29. Raymond Firth, *Tikopia Ritual and Belief* (Boston, 1967), ch. 9, pp. 195–212.

30. E. Fuller Torrey, *The Mind Game: Witchdoctors and Psychiatrists* (N.Y., 1973) p. 15 ff.

31. Jurgen Ruesch, *Disturbed Communication* (N.Y., 1957); and *Therapeutic Communication* (N.Y., 1973).

32. Michael J. Harner, ed., *Hallucinogens and Shamanism* (London, 1973), *passim*.

33. Carlos Castenada, *The Teaching of Don Juan: A Yaqui Way of Knowledge* (N.Y., 1968), cf. Part 2.

34. E.E. Evans-Pritchard, *Witchcraft, Oracles and Magic Among the Azande* (London, 1937, 1969).

35. Claude Lévi-Strauss, "The Sorcerer and His Magic," *Structural Anthropology* (N.Y., 1963), ch. 9.

36. Lucien Lévy-Bruhl: see especially *La Mythologie Primitive* (Paris, 1935). In addition, see *Primitives and the Supernatural; L'Expérience Mystique et Les Symboles Chez les Primitives;* and *Les Carnets de Lucien Lévy-Bruhl.*

37. Bronislaw Malinowski, *The Foundation of Faith and Morals* (London, 1936), cf. p. 11ff, etc.

38. Mircea Eliade: see especially *Cosmos and History* (N.Y., 1959) and *The Sacred and the Profane* (N.Y., 1959).

39. John M. Allegro, *The Sacred Mushroom and the Cross* (N.Y., 1970), p. 160.

40. *A General Theory of Magic*, pp. 108–121.

41. Marcel Mauss, "La Prière et les Rites Oraux," *Oeuvres*, vol. 1, ch. 4, pp. 357–477.

42. Henri Frankfort, et al., *Before Philosophy* (London, 1949), cf. index under "names."

43. E.A. Wallace Budge, *Egyptian Magic* (N.Y., 1971), ch. 5, p. 147ff.

44. Ernst Cassirer, *Language and Myth* (N.Y., 1946), ch. 4, "Word Magic," pp. 44–61.

45. R.H. Codrington, *The Melanesians* (N.Y., 1972), p. 125.

46. Robert Hertz, "A Contribution to the Study of the Collective Representation of Death," *Death and the Right Hand* (Oxford, 1960), pp. 27–88.

47. *Ibid.*, p. 52.

48. *Ibid.*, p. 45.

49. Harvey Cox, *The Secular City* (N.Y., 1965), pp. 73–75.

50. Kenneth Burke, *The Rhetoric of Religion* (Berkeley and L.A., 1961, 1970), ch. 1.

51. Kenneth Burke, *A Rhetoric of Motives* (Cleveland & N.Y., 1950, 1962), p. 564ff.

52. Sometimes numinous concepts are borrowed by sociology: e.g., Max Weber's importation of the term "charisma" from biblical studies.

53. Mauss, "A Category of the Human Spirit," *Psychoanalytic Review,* vol. 55, no. 3, 1968, pp. 457–481.

54. Lawrence Krader, "Person, Ego, Human Spirit in Marcel Mauss, Comments," *Psychoanalytic Review*, vol. 55, no. 3, 1968, pp. 482–490.

55. I am leaning on Kenneth Burke's idea here but he did not say this.

56. Wilhelm Dupre, *Religion in Primitive Cultures* (The Hague, Paris, 1975), pp. 141–149.

57. Mircea Eliade, *Shamanism* (Princeton, 1964), p. 96ff & *passim.*

58. Suzanne Langer, *Philosophy In a New Key* (N.Y., 1948), ch. 1, pp. 1–19.

59. *Ibid.*, pp. 48–52.

60. *Ibid.*, cf. chs. 6, 7, pp. 116–165.

61. *Ibid.*, pp. 125–126.

62. *Ibid.*, pp. 39, 122.

63. *Ibid.*, p. 129.

64. Kurt Goldstein, *Human Nature in the Light of Psychopathology* (Cambridge, Mass., 1940), pp. 54, 74, 77, 79, 81, 83.

65. Claude Lévi-Strauss, "The Sorcerer and His Magic," *Structural Anthropology* (N.Y., 1963), ch. 9, pp. 167–185.

66. Géza Róheim, *Magic and Schizophrenia* (Bloomington, Ind., 1955), p. 18.

67. Alfred Schutz, *Collected Papers,* vol. 1 (The Hague, 1962), pp. 67–74, 83–85, etc.

68. Emile Durkheim, *The Elementary Forms of Religious Life* (London, 1915, 1954), Bk. 2, ch. 7, pp. 205–239.

69. Cf. Georges Gurvitch, "La Magie, La Religion et le Droit," *La Vocation Actuelle de la Sociologie,* vol. 2 (Paris, 1963), p. 80ff.

70. Ernst Cassirer, *Language and Myth* (N.Y., 1946), ch. 4, pp. 44–61.

71. Cited by Cassirer, pp. 17–18.

72. Hubert and Mauss, *A General Theory of Magic,* p. 95.

73. Ernesto de Martino, *The World of Magic* (Hong Kong, 1972), p. 81ff.

74. Knud Rasmussen, *Intellectual Culture of the Iglulik Esquimos* (Copenhagen, 1930), ch. 5.

75. Jacques Ellul, *Propaganda* (N.Y., 1968), p. 25–32; and *The Political Illusion* (N.Y., 1967), p. 55, etc.

76. Herbert Marcuse, *One Dimensional Man* (Boston, 1966), p. 84, ff.

77. Frederick Elworthy, *The Evil Eye* (London, 1958), chs. 4, 5, 6, pp. 115–232.

78. E.R. Dodds, *The Greeks and the Irrational* (Berkeley, 1951, 1973), pp. 2–8.

79. Discussed pp. 13–15 in E.R. Dodds, *op. cit.* And cf. Martin P. Nilsson, *A History of Greek Religion* (N.Y., 1964); *Greek Piety* (N.Y., 1969), *passim.*

80. Bruno Snell, *The Discovery of the Mind* (N.Y., 1960).

81. A.E. Taylor, *Socrates* (N.Y., 1954); and *Plato, the Man and His Works,* (London, rev., 1929).

82. Ernesto de Martino, *The World of Magic* (Hong Kong, 1972), pp. 84–110.

83. Walter F. Otto, *Dionysus, Myth and Cult* (Bloomington, Ind., 1965), p. xvii & *passim.*

84. Harry Stack Sullivan, *Clinical Studies in Psychiatry* (N.Y., 1969), *passim.*

85. Ernst Cassirer, *An Essay on Man* (N.Y., 1970), p. 101.

86. Mary Douglas, *Natural Symbols* (N.Y., 1973). Once she has unleashed her copula, there is no stopping her. We finally get the formula of "tight" societies (i.e., extreme mechanical solidarity) identified with much use of bodily symbols, much use of magical

rites, and a speech pattern analogous to the "restricted speech code" Basil Bernstein associates with the lower classes. Whereas societies which are "loose" (e.g., nomad societies like the Nuer) use fewer bodily symbols, fewer magical rites, and "elaborated" speech like upper-middle-class Londoners. Thus even the positivistic categories of the Durkheim school can be turned into theosophy if the quest for natural symbols becomes obsessive. The big defect of these theosophies is that they do not detach their categories from their primitive data, so that the unanalyzed links derived from faded classification systems determine their own formulations as more accretions to myth. One feels that the idea of "tightness" as an unanalyzed primitive concept (and perhaps a bodily symbol) playing upon unstated classifications is what operates this whole formulation. (Cf. ch. 5, pp. 92–112.)

87. Victor Turner, *The Forest of Symbols* (Ithaca and London, 1967), pp. 28–30. In "Color Classification in Ndembu Ritual" (in Michael Banton, ed., *Anthropological Approaches to the Study of Religion*, London, 1968, pp. 47–84), Turner asserts that the three-color system he finds among the Ndembu (white for life, semen and milk; black for void; and red an intermediate, standing for blood, for killing but also for life) is virtually universal. He demonstrates it in India, and in the "four elements" of Empedocles, etc. If investigators of Turner's caliber took his pains to study natural symbols at work in individual societies and then compared notes, some propositions about the distribution of bodily symbols might well supplement the emphasis on social-morphological symbols, that Douglas claimed Mauss called for (in *Techniques du Corps* perhaps?). But it is *not* certain that such demonstrations would tell us much that is important.

88. James W. Fernandez, "Persuasions and Performances: Of the Beast in Every Body.... And the Metaphors of Everyman," in Clifford Geertz, ed., *Myth, Symbol, and Culture* (N.Y., 1974).

89. He is referring to the "semantic differential scales" of Osgood, which, being tripartite, could be arranged like our concept of space in an X-Y-Z coordinate system of the three qualities ("activity," "goodness" and "potency") which Osgood thinks are fundamental to all the languages of the world. In all this there are perhaps echoes of Wittgenstein's "logical space" or perhaps the vector space of matrix algebra. Charles E. Osgood, George J. Suci, Percy Tannenbaum, *The Measurement of Meaning* (Urbana, 1957).

90. Frazer, *The Golden Bough* (N.Y., Macmillan abridged ed., 1960), ch. 3, "Sympathetic Magic," pp. 12–55.

91. Edwin G. Boring, *A History of Experimental Psychology* (N.Y., 1950), chs. 9–10, pp. 157–202.

92. John Locke, *An Essay Concerning Human Understanding* in E.A. Burtt, *The English Philosophers from Bacon to Mill* (N.Y., 1939), pp. 283–316.

93. Hubert and Mauss, *General Theory of Magic*, pp. 60–68, 97–108.

94. Sympathy is not the whole of magic, and Frazer's principles do not even explain all of sympathy, Hubert and Mauss show. First, they demonstrate some sympathetic magic not covered by contiguity or similarity, e.g., the part standing for the whole, or the presence in a rite of objects previously medicated or prepared (as by entry or exit rites). Following their examples, other writers keep pointing out new principles of sympathetic magic not covered by contiguity or similarity: Leuba mentions "*it happened before*" (so it will again); *repetition* of a symbol; *abreaction*; and simple *will projection* at a distance. (Leuba, *A Psychological Study of Religion*, N.Y., 1912, ch. 8, p. 151ff.) See also Chapter 9 of this paper for Freud's numerous additions. In addition, Hubert and Mauss dig more deeply into Frazer's own principles and show they are superficial in formulation: Behind "contiguity" actually lie nascent ideas of logical transitivity; and behind ideas of "similarity" perhaps lies a nascent consciousness of the nature of symbolization itself. The two principles can also be shown to blur into each other. Finally, sympathy, which Frazer's principles do not fully cover, is only one part of magic—along with the trained magician, the audience constituting the magical milieu, and so on. *A General Theory of Magic*, pp. 63–79.

95. Emile Durkheim and Marcel Mauss, *Primitive Classification*, trans. and intro. by Rodney Needham (Chicago, 1963, 1967). The monograph was originally published as *De Quelques Formes Primitives de Classification, Contribution à l'Etude des Représentations Collectives*, republ. in vol. 2 of Marcel Mauss *Oeuvres*, pp. 13–89. It appeared originally in *L'Année Sociologique*, vol. 6, 1903. The *Esquisse* was published in the *Année* number for 1902-3. It is likely that some of these matters therefore occupied Mauss's thoughts simultaneously.

96. Durkheim and Mauss, *Primitive Classification*, pp. 67–76.

97. Lucien Lévy-Bruhl, *L'Expérience Mystique et les Symboles Chez Les Primitives* (Paris, 1938), cf. ch. 6.

98. In an earlier work he also showed interest in invisible entities that anticipate the concept of class. Thus folkloric figures like "Br'er Rabbit" or just "Rabbit" or "Bear" are simultaneously *any* substantial bear or rabbit and also the *genus* of rabbit or bear. Lévy-Bruhl, *The Soul of the Primitive* (Chicago, 1966), p. 64, etc. & *passim*.

99. E.E. Evans-Pritchard, *Witchcraft, Oracles, and Magic Among the Azande* (London, 1937), chs. 1–3.

100. Walter B. Cannon, "Voodoo Death," *American Anthropologist*, vol. 44, no. 2 (April–June, 1942), pp. 169–181.

101. Mauss, in Lévi-Strauss, ed., *Sociologie et Anthropologie*, pp. 313–332.

102. G.W.F. Hegel, *Lectures on the Philosophy of Religion*, 1840 (N.Y., 1962), vol. I, part 2, pp. 290–317.

103. Peter L. Berger, *The Sacred Canopy* (N.Y., 1967), pp. 17, 79, etc.

104. Howard Gardner, *The Shattered Mind* (N.Y., 1975).

105. —so endlessly debated by "holists" like Goldstein (*op. cit.*) and Maurice Merleau-Ponty, *The Structure of Behavior* (Boston, 1963).

106. Freud, "Negation" (1925), in *General Psychological Theory* (N.Y., 1963), pp. 213–217.

107. The passages in Durkheim's *Elementary Forms...*on "the generalization of mana" (London, 1915, pp. 196–198) were considered very important by Lukes (*Emile Durkheim*, N.Y., 1972); Gurvitch ("La Magie, La Religion et le Droit," *La Vocation Actuelle de la Sociologie*, vol. 2, Paris, 1963); and D'Halbwachs (*Sources of Religious Sentiment*, Glencoe, Ill., 1962, pp. 71–74). The idea is that as society evolves from polysegmental forms to hierarchical, tribal organization, religion as projection of society changes from the fragmentation of sacred objects in totemism to more powerful general symbols (such as "mana"). This generalization makes it possible for people to get hold of the sacred and apply it to other purposes; magical expropriation of religion's power becomes possible.

108. *The Forest of Symbols* (Ithaca, 1967); *The Ritual Process* (Baltimore, 1969); *Schism and Continuity...* (Manchester, 1957); *Dramas, Fields and Metaphors* (Ithaca & London, 1974).

109. Turner, *The Forest of Symbols* (Ithaca, 1967), cf. p. 26, etc.

110. Here (*The Forest of Symbols*, ch. 5, pp. 112–130), as in his book on lineage fission (Turner, *Schism and Continuity in an African Society,* Manchester, 1957), his emphasis, after the manner of the Oxford school, is on the *accusation* as an act reflecting social pressures.

111. Turner's "condensation symbols," Mary Douglas' "natural symbols," Fernandez's "metaphors," Lévi-Strauss' "operators" are perhaps words for the same thing. And Malinowski suggests that homonyms may also serve to condense symbols. (*Coral Gardens...*, N.Y., 1935, vol. 11, pp. 71–73).

112. In *Schism and Continuity...* Turner characterizes the Ndembu as an unstable society lacking strong political forms. Ostensibly it has attained a tribal organization and even the rudiments of a state, but the central king is weak, still just a ritual chief. Fragmentation extends down to the village level, where the struggle for the job of headman frequently splits these small hamlets. The result is that in actuality, the matrilineal, virilocal lineage unit, supplemented by some "followers" of headmen or candidates for headmen, is virtually the unit of the society. Perhaps this is because the Ndembu drifted into the country in small groups. It is hazardous to speculate until Turner's reports are complete, but this morphology is extremely suggestive. Whether by political regression or some other factor, the Ndembu seem thrust back virtually to the clan-centered stage of organization, though they possess a shadowy tribal structure. Durkheim associated "the generalization of mana" with the transition from clan *to* tribal organization. When clans are more hierarchically knit into tribes, the primitive intuits the *general idea* of social power as something inhering in a *class* of phenomena, and develops more general concepts of it, such as "mana." The Ndembu, with a fragmentary social structure that bears a crude similarity to clan organization, perhaps for that reason do not have general categories. Cf. Turner, *op. cit.*, ch. 5 & *passim*.

113. Hubert and Mauss, *A General Theory of Magic*, pp. 53–54.

114. Rudolf Bultmann, *Kerygma and Myth* (N.Y., 1961).

115. Kenneth Burke, *The Rhetoric of Religion, A Rhetoric of Motives.*

116. Anders Jeffner, *The Study of Religious Language* (London, 1972).

117. It is true that what Lévy-Bruhl calls "the affective category of the supernatural" (that creepy feeling primitives get around strange or sacred events) does distinguish the supernatural world from the natural world to some degree even for primitives; but the two are interpenetrated. At later levels of sophistication (cf., Bultmann), when some separation is imagined, religious sentences may be "indirect sentences," referring to the ideal world of Kerygma but believed to achieve effects in the natural (social) world—in such sophistication the magical effects of religious statements come close to consciousness.

118. Durkheim and Mauss, *Primitive Classification*, p. 78.

119. Durkheim, *The Elementary Forms of Religious Life*, pp. 42–47.

120. Henry Munn, "The Mushrooms of Language," *Hallucinogens and Shamanism*, ed. by Michael J. Harner (London, 1973), ch. 7, pp. 86–122.

121. Ruth Murray Underhill, *Singing for Power* (N.Y., 1973), cf. the poems excerpted in text.

Postulate 3: MAGICAL SYMBOLIC
ACTION IS RIGIDLY SCRIPTED.

MAGIC speech is not like ordinary speech. It is often extremely odd speech, full of mumbo-jumbo words, archaisms, neologisms and nonsense syllables; it is repetitious, alliterative and full of figures. It may be said in a peculiar tone of voice: chanted or sung or mumbled or sing-songed. Above all, it is usually scripted speech, said in a certain way and that way only, often using fixed expressions handed down. Magic speech is neither the practical speech of workaday action, nor is it the relaxed conversation of human sociability.[1] The overall impression is of an archaic script that has been borrowed from some other context, committed to memory and repeated just so, even when the meaning of the words is forgotten. In sections that lie ahead, we will see that this is indeed the case: magic speech is neither shop talk nor palaver; instead, it consists of sacred scripts, many of them borrowed or stolen from religion and put to special use.

A Third Type of Speech?

Would it be possible, then, to speak of a third kind of speech pattern, magical speech, deriving from magical praxis, and distinguish it from both symbolic-interaction speech and rational-purposive action speech (in the sense of Weber and Habermas)? At least one anthropologist has really done this, if one puts together some little known chapters he wrote. This was Malinowski, and the first place to look is a special article which he contributed to Ogden and Richards' volume, *The Meaning of Meaning*.[2] There Malinowski described the other two types of talk in a manner anticipating Habermas; he began with a very ideal account of purely social talk, what he called "phatic communication." His account resembles Habermas' symbolic interaction talk, or Simmel's description of "pure sociability."[3] This speech seems to "stroke," placate, amuse, hearten, warm, identify, etc., more than it communicates facts. In some primitive languages, in which words may be even more fluid and vary even more with context than in modern languages, where the distinction between grammatical and lexical forms is not as clear, the sheer lack of cognitive content in such amiable interactive speech is even more striking than in our own, and this reveals its essential function. Meaning is less important in such speech than the establishment of community. Fernandez[4] presents still another picture of it in his account of men of the neo-Bantu Fang people talking in their palaver house. The art with which they "slice the talk" (they are woodsmen and use woodsmen's metaphors) is judged for its balance and appropriateness rather than for any information it might convey. Many field reports of palaver house talk confirm the widespread existence and importance of "phatic communication," of talk that is "pure sociability."

Malinowski distinguishes phatic talk from talk connected with practical work. He uses as his example of practical talk the talk the Trobriander men use in net fishing. This is talk wherein, "Each utterance is essentially bound up with the context of the situation and the aim of the pursuit....The vocabulary....is not less surbordinate to action."[5] This is the talk Weber and Habermas associate with rational-purposive action. But it, too, is flexible in its way, to its purposes and needs:

> ...a word of command is passed here and there, a technical expression or explanation which serves to harmonize their behavior... Short, telling exclamations fly about, which might be rendered by such words as: "Pull in," "Let go," "Shift further," "Lift the net"; or again technical expressions completely untranslatable except by minute description of the instruments used, and of the mode of action.[6]

Thus even in a praxis setting the meaning of words is tied to specific actions and varies with this context. And phatic speech is even more flexible. (He later abandoned the distinction between them in *Coral Gardens and Their Magic*.)[7]

Now Malinowski would distinguish both types of normal, flexible speech from magical language. For later he wrote descriptions of magical language which make it clear that it fits neither type. In *Coral Gardens* he insisted that magic uses fixed scripts.[8] In a late chapter of *Argonauts*,[9] he observed that magic language has striking eccentricities, including: A. rigid verbalisms with many strange words, neologisms, archaisms, chopped up words; B. fixed figures of speech such as alliteration, onomatopoeia, pedantic enumerations; C. strange arrangements and repetitions; D. rigid sequences including a traditional introduction and conclusion (which remind me of the "entry and exit rites" Hubert and Mauss noted in *Sacrifice*). Moreover, magic speech is not spoken like ordinary language, but is "whined," or said in a sing-song or monotone manner. It is full of words not understood by the laity and there can be no reciprocal dialogue on an even footing with this language. Hugh Dalziel Duncan comments on Malinowski's account:[10]

> ...there is another kind of language, which is not like the pragmatic language of work or purely social talk. This is magic. The language of magic is sacred; it is fixed, like the language of religious ritual (p. 36) .... magical words are...pronounced according to a special phonology, in a sing-song, with their own rhythm...there is a specific use of...rhetorical devices, such as...repetition...and question-with-answer. All such devices create a clear breach of continuity between...magical and ordinary speech. (pp. 38–39)

It Derives From Sacred Action

This suggests the possibility that magical speech derives from a third kind of action, which is neither the action of work nor the interaction of sociability. What is it? Would it tell us anything simply to say that it derives from "magical action," which has an enormous extent in primitive societies? Malinowski, who seems to suggest this neutral definition, actually *explains* magic itself in terms of an alleged phenomenal base in the wish-speech of infancy. Malinowski's explicit theory (as seen in *Magic, Science and Religion*)—i.e., magic as a confidence builder using expressions that erupt out of human wishes—is really a psychological theory. At best it is an "eruption" theory, i.e., an only half-sociological explanation, which has magic erupting from a psychological base (wishes, emotions) and then getting coöpted and formed into social institutions by sociological needs (the need for group confidence, for the organization of collective action, etc.). But it is far from clear how emotional "eruptions" would get patterned into the stiff, scripted speeches of magic.[11] And it is hard to think of any real examples of the "eruption" and institutionalization of spontaneous wish magic that have ever been observed. Even when a brand new magical practice develops which is so simple that one could imagine it as a spontaneous new creation, it is often stereotyped and scripted from the beginning and may derive from a long tradition. An example is the extremely simple mantra magic that lies at the heart of several popular new religions in post-War Japan[12] and India,[13] and such mechanical yogas as the so-called Transcendental Meditation. Mystified, rigid, authoritarian and unexplicit about their basic practices, these movements actually revive fixed traditional techniques that go back thousands of years in Hindu, Buddhist, Tantric and even Vedic practice, and the familiar fetishism about form is always present in them.

Anyhow, there is an alternative that is less tautological: We can derive magical speech from a third form of action—from *sacred praxis* in general, or in other words, largely from religion. Durkheim made the point that magic derives its efficacy from the religious worldview; this is the cognitive aspect. But, more concretely, Hubert and Mauss have demonstrated[14] that magic expropriates many of its scripts wholesale and ready-made from religion—incantations, ceremonies, the whole apparatus of sacrifice, for example.

Now Kenneth Burke has characterized sacred ritual action as a kind of dramaturgy;[15] to Burke, sacred action is dramatic action of great significance, apt to be about grand themes such as "guilt, redemption, hierarchy, victimage,"[16] etc. And of course, it is well known that drama quite literally originated in sacred action, and that drama requires scripts, in the literal sense. The word "literal" is important, for it is fashionable to speak of "dramas" and "scripts" loosely in symbolic interaction theory when referring to action that is relatively more open. There the word "script" is a figure of speech and refers to the fact that people are often in some sense playing "roles" and trying to speak somewhat as they are expected to. But sacred dramas are scripted in a literal sense—the words used in magic and religion are memorized and must be said just right; sometimes they can kill you if they are said wrong. We should confess some hesitation about letting the matter rest there, for there seems to be something even more rigid in magical scripts than in religion, and this needs to be explained. Is not the communal reciprocity and group excitement and fellow-feeling of a religious ceremony at least partly reminiscent of "phatic speech" or "pure sociability"? There is more of a participative side to religion than to magic, is there not? Diamond[17] and others stress the continual process of collective creation that goes on through religious rites in a healthy primitive community, with the rite never said the same way each time, with individual ad-libs coloring it. And although there is much in primitive religion that is as reminiscent of mumbo-jumbo as magic is, there are these other, more interactive, more participative aspects. Religion, in other words, tends to be partly symbolic interaction speech and partly sacred scripted speech. But magic tends to be entirely sacred scripted speech.

If therefore magical talk has been derived from sacred religious praxis, then something has happened to it. It has become more rigid, more fixed. The most likely explanation is that something that has been expropriated from its legitimate context because of the effects it has is preserved with rigid detail *lest those effects be lost.* Religious rites can be more spontaneous, in other words, but derived formulae, scripts taken from sacred dramas and used magically, would have to remain letter perfect so as not to lose their borrowed efficacy. Thus Duncan writes:

> Magic spells must be handed down, without change. The slightest alteration from the original pattern would be fatal. (p. 318)

Scripting for Certainty

What is the purpose of scripted action in the first place, as distinguished from work action and sociable interaction? Why should people ever want to memorize and speak scripts? The creation of *nomos* in religion is an enormous topic and belongs to the sociology of religion—but a few suggestions here might be useful. We have seen how hard it is to understand either sociable speech or workaday speech independent of the situations to which they are tied. One result of this is that, in retrospect, people often do not have too clear an idea of what they said or of what happened. It is notorious that eye witnesses never agree. Surely men must hunger at times for some definite agreement about what is happening, for some definite reports they can hold onto as basing points for their experience.

Indeed, it is surprising that people can even agree about what is happening well enough to be able to get along together. Laing, Phillipson and Lee, in *Interpersonal Perception* (London, 1966), have outlined the whole problem of the faulty fit of "meta-perspectives"—e.g., what "he thinks she thinks he means" is never what "she thinks he means," etc. Wittgenstein has emphasized that communication is basically problematical.

Sacred action, therefore, might be characterized as dramatic action in which a group of people act out things together following a script, so that the action is predetermined and is interpreted identically by all the participants, the interpretation being part of the script. Thus, in at least part of their actions, human beings can be sure of what is happening and what they are doing. Rational-purposive praxis has its regularities, too, but it is adaptive to the situation, as Malinowski showed. And sociable speech continually reinterprets what is happening. Somewhere in their lives men have to know exactly what they are doing and saying. Sacred action is dramatic action that is rigidly scripted to provide that certainty.

The certainty about action which scripted rites provide would help explain the often reported utility magic has in organizing collective action, even economic action. See, for example, Malinowski on how work magic organizes the work gang, in *Argonauts*. Duncan writes:

> If the magician were to stop mumbling his incantations a complete disorganization of the work of the whole community would follow. (p.40)

Praxis is often doubtful as to how its results are produced. The manipulation of only partly understood forces and chemicals is a common event in the history of science (e.g., aspirin). B.F. Skinner's "reinforcement theory" of magic suggests that many irrelevant ingredients of actions persist in early science simply because they were reinforced by a favorable outcome appearing shortly thereafter. By contrast with praxis, which gets results but does not always know how, scripted sacred action is definite as to what is happening during its execution— but the outcome itself is more vague. Very often, it takes the form of a mild, over-valued, subjective state of consciousness. But the rite itself covers this by trying to pattern as well the definition of the outcome.[18]

It is this factor of providing a bench mark for experience that enables sacred dramas as religion to sustain social reality, and as magic to concentrate individual action as well. Durkheim noted that individual streams of consciousness are in flux, and that it is only fixed social experience that brings any order to them. And he observed that even when the religious effects are not experienced by the individual, he supposes that *some* people experience them and he continues his allegiance because of the *order* which these suppositions give to his experience.[19] Lienhardt, speaking of the Dinka, asserts that magic gives them a sense of control over their own actions. Magic is not thought of as mechanical causality, but as certainty as to what is happening. Take rain magic, for example: They know when it is going to rain. Their magic "moves with the rhythm of the world...not merely attempting to coerce it."[20] A man who has done magic "has produced a model of his desires." This will focus his efforts.[21] And so these symbolic actions have real effects on how the Dinka experience these events.[22]

Magic provides a definite model of action to help the individual concentrate his attention and the group to coordinate its effort. This is not just a matter of supplying meaning when there is anxiety and doubt, in the manner of Lévi-Strauss' sorcerer,[23] or confidence in the face of uncertainty, as Malinowski puts it. Both individual and group are assailed not only by doubt and anxiety but also by confusion; and the rite provides the certainty of an authoritative definition of what is happening and what has happened. In medical magic, that is sometimes enough to effect a cure. It is not so much that magic provides confidence (a psychological category more applicable to individual "magic" in the weak sense). Sociologically, magic provides what strategy theorists like Schelling call "a rallying point,"[24] a piece of action we all experience the same way. It is like synchronizing watches before a battle.

Besides providing collective certainty, sacred scripts can be borrowed by magic to provide some certainty for the individual. In fact, they make it possible in the first place for him to be able to *think* or *speak* or *act* in his uncertain symbolic world. Animals have no trouble acting spontaneously as individuals; but once man creates his terrifying symbolic environment with its "cliffs of fall," he is tongue-tied and needs memorized scripts to help him speak. Once reality is transmuted into a kaleidoscope of symbols, the individual is confused and he needs powerful magical operators just to be able to think. And once action becomes symbolic and radiates infinite meaning, individual man, paralyzed, can act only by following a script "in closed ranks." Let us consider individual speech, motor action and thought in that light:[25]

Magic and the Courage to Speak

It is a curious fact that in many ages memory has been associated with magic, and various mnemonic arts have been occult sciences. Giordano Bruno's secret magic was a memory magic, according to Frances Yates.[26] Campanella, Fludd and other Renaissance maguses also had memory magics. Memorizing the Vedas, the Brahmanas or their equivalent and saying them letter perfect was the power base of the herald or Brahmin. All this is not surprising, for consider the predicament of the terrified primitive with a weak ego—to speak, he has to seize some of the collective representations and dare to use them as his own. It is small wonder that ordinary speech tends to be conventionalized, right down to standard exchanges. And when we consider someone who dares to speak before the multitude, it is easy to grasp the necessity and the magical power of memorized scripts.

Magic and the Courage to Act

In his fascinating essay on the "techniques of the body," Marcel Mauss[27] anticipated the science of gestures or "kinesics"[28] but gave a much deeper explanation of patterned action than the familiar kinesic explanation in terms of social modeling. Gestures are not merely imitated; they are actively taught, usually orally, for they are really *rituals*. For example, Mauss noted that the way French boys dive had been changed during his lifetime because their gym instructors had begun to teach them to dive with their eyes open; they used to keep them closed. Many human gestures, he hints, are in effect remnants of ancient sacred rituals—or else they are new rituals in the sense of being taught, like diving. We underestimate the degree to which gestures are taught—consciously and usually orally. Thus Maori women orally teach their daughters to wag their hips when they walk. And I am informed that into the sixties anyway, Smith College undergraduates had to pass a course in "Basic Motor Skills" which culminated in such final tests as walking in high heels while carrying suitcases.

Mauss defines "techniques of the body" as "traditional effective techniques" (note the similarity to magic), and states that they give confidence to one's actions and a kind of "forward momentum" to them.[29] I think this could be generalized. There is a sense in which *any* gesture, however trivial, has a magical effect, and must be done right, because it may be the "entry rite" or the "exit rite," as it were, to some purposive action or at very least it is needed to give continuing confidence and "forward momentum" to any ongoing action sequence. Action is the "counterphobic attitude," Róheim wrote; but it must be "appropriate action" to avoid anxiety, Goldstein demonstrated.[30] Just perform one public gesture in an eccentric fashion and watch the instant effect—on yourself as well as on others. Scripted gestures help forfend the sense of "uncanniness" which Sullivan[31] for one identified with anxiety. So it is quite likely that many human actions are patterned gestures because they were originally rituals in the strict sense (just as those which are orally taught in our posture, swimming and drill classes today are rituals metaphorically). Not that hominids could not walk, sit, climb, jump, but that man, once "fallen into the deep well of himself" through creation of his symbolic world, had to pattern gestures ritually to control meaning. Thus V.S. Naipaul,[32] examining Gandhi's autobiography, speculates on the relation between the weak egos of Hindu India and the magical prescriptions surrounding every gesture that young Gandhi grew up with—right down to when and how to use the bathroom. Similarly, Mauss was interested in "*la position de la main dans la miction.*" At first man can indeed only act by scripted actions. "Magic gives form and shape to those poorly coordinated or impotent gestures by which the needs of the individual are expressed, and, because it does this through ritual, it renders them effective."[33]

Magic and the Courage to Think

Hubert and Mauss suggest that magic produces all forward reasoning operations such as transitivity. Beyond that, it is a main conclusion of their essay that in "mana" concepts are born the original "categories of human thought" (such as force, matter, power, space, time) and that these are self-starting operators enabling human individuals to think with collective representations.

> We are confident that...we shall find magical origins in those early forms of collective representations which have since become the basis for individual understanding...we believe that we have shown with regard to magic, how a collective phenomenon can assume individual forms.[34]

The idea is obscure but challenging. Thus mana gives the will to deduce, to connect; and from it are born logical operators enabling individuals to put the social symbols together in quite individual ways—or, in other words, to think. In this, they write, magic resembles science, which also consists of collective representations, but which grows only when individual scientists pick them up and do something with them.

The Durkheim school has done impressive work in tracing the major categories of thought to sacred action, and in showing that they depend on its definite, scripted certainty. They traced all such ideas back to primitive religion. Hubert and Mauss then showed that these categories, as super-concepts, are taken over by magic and used as logical operators enabling individuals to assemble, rearrange and manipulate collective representations for private ends. Thus "mana" itself, as a prototype of the category of force, is used expressively—"*mana!*"—to try to urge along that transitive transfer of qualities along sympathetic connections at which the spell aims.[35]

The Categories

What do the Durkheim school sociologists mean by "the categories"? The term is used a bit pretentiously and with echoes of some musty neo-Kantian philosophy that was popular at Ecole Normale Supérieur when they were students. An ancient essentialism is implicit in it, for the reference is to Kant and Aristotle. To Aristotle, the categories were the highest *genera* and he held that every expression in a sentence signifies, denotes, refers to things falling in at least one of these *genera*: "substance, quantity, quality, relation, place, time, posture, state, action and passion." These are distinguished from logical expressions, such as "not," "or," "some," etc. The basic use to which the list was put was in explaining certain logical fallacies and how to avoid them: e.g., certain equivocations could be understood as "category errors," for example. Whereas Aristotle applied the term "category" to non-logical expressions, to *genera*, Kant also used them as basic ways of classifying the forms of sentences, and so included logical expressions. Thus every statement has quantity (number), quality (it is negative or affirmative), etc., and all these are thought to reflect the structure of the human mind. Neo-Kantians tend to view that structure as being constituted culturally, in society as it evolves historically. The often Neo-Kantian "philosophy of science" is especially interested in those categories which have become central to science, and so refined definitionally that they appear in physical formulae, such as time, space, mass, distance, etc. See, for example, Max Jammer's *Concepts of Mass*,[36] which shows how this seemingly clear and simple variable in physical equations has a long history and evolved out of more complicated, even magical, ideas. (Some phenomenological research—e.g., Bergson,[37] Husserl[38]—also attempts to probe for roots in human experience for such ideas.) But there is no broad consensus in philosophy today that accords to any list of "categories" a special status, with the possible exception of time and space. The others seem to be of intermediate status, much more general than most concepts, but not as basic as the logical constants, for example.

The Durkheim school uses the term "category" loosely—for example, Mauss calls the idea of "the person" a category.[39] "Person" did not appear on either

Aristotle's or Kant's list. "Categories," in this new Durkheimian usage, just tends to mean extremely influential *ideas*. Now it is significant that Durkheim solved the philosophical problem of the status of ideas. He did so in a manner very similar to that of Wittgenstein. Both rejected both the idealist and empirical explanations. Radical empiricism or nominalism is wrong; ideas do exist; they are real— but this does not entail a belief in idealism. For they are social, Durkheim would say.[40] (They are conventions created by agreement, Wittgenstein would say.[41]) They exist, but not in hyperspace: they are collective representations imposed on data. The categories, as very important and formative conventional ideas, are susceptible to the same sociological explanation; and in discussing them Durkheim even approaches Wittgenstein's language. If men did not agree on these essential, orienting ideas of time, space, cause, etc., then all communication between them would be impossible, he writes.[42]

For several decades the Durkheim school had an ambitious program of systematically studying the key "categories" one by one, as important organizing ideas in human life. Their approach was a kind of historical and social epistemology, with the categories evolving through the ages, but in most cases tracing back ultimately to religious or magical projections, which were considered to be man's first and formative projections. In this light, Mauss studied "mass" as a kind of category in the twenties, "the person" in 1938,[43] "matter" in 1939[44] and "money" several times.[45] Hubert did a similar study of "time."[46] These ideas were shown to become self-actualizing archetypes moulding human perceptions and even human individuality in the case of the idea of "the person." They are always present as something added to and organizing empirical data. Modern science, in fact, emerges when empirical observation is combined with a mathematical-logical abstract organization derived from these category ideas. The main point of the Durkheim school (as distinguished from the structuralists) is that these ideas are all purely social and historical in their formation and may change tomorrow.[47]

Thus science does not derive entirely from the praxis of rational-purposive action as Habermas suggests; its organizing concepts came from the categories forged in dramatic sacred action. Lévi-Strauss even thinks this is what enabled modern science to overcome the "Neolithic paradox"—i.e., the apparent inability of merely empirical scientific effort to get very far (as exemplified in the stagnation of science after the Neolithic advances).[48] We will see later how the productive, mathematical worldview of modern science emerged in the Renaissance not merely via use of categories derived long ago from sacred dramas—it also required a fresh infusion of magical thought in the form of Kabbala and the Hermetic worldview to create mathematically organized, technologically oriented modern science.[49]

In modern society the "categories" serve to anchor man's everyday frame of reference to the deepest laws of contemporary science. Words like "time" and "space" are used in everyday discourse in a way that could be translated into the meaning they have when they appear as variables in scientific equations—as "x" or "y" or "z," in Descartes' analytical geometry, or "time" or "distance" in the

Lorentz transformation equations.[50] The "vagueness" of the primitive supernatural world has been considerably reduced by a social consensus anchoring key ideas so precisely to a physicalist and scientific consensus. When "supernatural" phenomena attempt to storm this universe of discourse, it is not difficult to repel them through careful reference to the consensual frame. "Cognitive minorities" that attempt to project a different cosmology suffer cognitive dissonance with this frame, and until recently could maintain their "plausibility structures" only through the extreme isolation of "intellectual ghettoes."[51] Thus it is a fascinating paradox that many of the important ideas, or "categories," which sustain the frame that repels the supernatural were developed originally out of religious and magical projections. The original religious cosmos as a projection of society, when first generalized, created the possibility for belief in magic. Before the emergence of the objective frame that repelled the supernatural, magic itself was the first defense of the ego. The modern frame now affords the protection magic used to give and thereby makes it less necessary. But at one time magic helped organize primitive categories into a worldview, and magic itself was a very important category at that time. (Closely accompanying mana words in many primitive societies is a word for "magic" itself, e.g., *magia*, and it too is a "category.") Lévy-Bruhl has suggested that these were "affective" categories, more felt than thought.[52] These magical categories at one time organized a universal frame of reference the way time-space does today. That frame gave man a measure of orientation and control just as ours does. Within its provenance, the newer categories took shape, growing out of the ritual of sacred drama.

Hubert's essay on "time"[53] is an example of these category studies—although it is burdened with a special philosophical argument and it untypically concentrates entirely on showing how civic time *began* in primitive mentality, instead of examining its entire later evolution, as Mauss does with "the person." Hubert's basic theory is that the idea of time does not grow up around natural events like the seasons (because there are too many of them that could be chosen), but rather, around religious events. Civic time, as distinguished from phenomenal time or subjective *durée* in the sense of Husserl[54] and Bergson,[55] is originally just a calendar of religious feasts. And this religious time is "non-isotropic"; it is pulled out of shape by the sacred feasts in it. Thus Hubert postulates that: A. Critical religious dates interrupt the continuity of time, creating absolute breaks that are periods of danger. B. The time between two sacred dates is indivisible (like "The Twelve Days of Christmas") and this sacred stretch of time has its rites of entry and exit just like sacrifice. C. The critical dates (the sacred holidays) are therefore equivalent to the intervals that they limit. ("The Twelve Days of Christmas" *are* Christmas.) D. Similar parts are equivalent (there are cyclical repetitions, etc.). E. Quantitatively unequal durations are equalized and equal durations are unequalized. The presence of sacred events in one expanse of time "stretches" it, makes it "longer" than an equal secular segment. Hubert's essay also contains ideas similar to some later developed by Eliade in a dozen books,[56] such as: A. The idea that "sacred time" is outside of time altogether, relates to "myth time" and is simultaneously the holy past, the mysterious destination of the future, and "eternal now" of the mystic present. B. The idea that historical events are assimilated to myths and real time is collapsed into eternal time (but in addition, historical time *renews* sacred time).

There is also a heavy philosophical argument in this essay, centered in Hubert's insistence that "sacred time" and "religious time" are not the same thing: religious time (the original civic time) is a third kind of time created by the intersection of "sacred time" (which is eternal and really "timeless") into profane time (at first just subjective *durée*). Hubert may have had several philosophical problems on his mind when he wrote this. First, the problem of the instantaneous and transcendent present, an old issue going back to Augustine and renewed in philosophy in modern times by George Herbert Mead,[57] William James,[58] Jean-Paul Sartre,[59] etc. Augustine developed the paradox while considering such problems as why god who is infinite would create man in time.[60] Second, in Hubert's solution (religious time created by intersection of sacred and profane time) we hear echoes of the theory of relativity, which are in fact found throughout the essay. Hubert's essay was published in the book *Mélanges d'Histoire des Religions* in 1909, but Mauss tells us that it first appeared as a journal article in 1905.[61] Einstein's "Special Theory of Relativity"[62] was published in 1905. Essays by Poincaré[63] and Whitehead[64] that anticipated it on philosophical grounds came out at the same time or a bit earlier. Lorentz and others did essays struggling with the same physical problems that brought Einstein to relativity, before 1905. The idea was in the air. The problem that was solved by relativity was similar to the problem of the "absolute" nature of sacred time in Hubert's phrasings: How does one fit the "absolute" (unchanging) speed of light into a Galilean coordinate system? Transformation equations which do this seem to suggest deductively the possibility of the time relativity.[65] Similarly, in Hubert, the intersection of "absolute" sacred time with profane time produces "religious time" which is relative; it increases or changes shape according to the religious festivals contained in it. The echoes of relativity are quite pronounced. In one example Hubert cites a Macedonian tale of a hero who takes 30 years to descend to the antipodes and 12 years to come back—but he has spent altogether only 30 years away from home. This hero could have been an astronaut traveling at close to the speed of light in a popular exposition on relativity.

But I think relativity ideas are being used in the background simply to demonstrate the *magical* plasticity of the category of time: the title of the essay after all derives time from magic as well as religion,[66] and it is published in a book along with Mauss' essay on the initiation of Australian magicians and an introduction that continues the argument of their joint monograph on magic.[67] Religious feasts that bend time out of shape, that produce special effects on our perception of the world, all this recalls Durkheim's idea that the religious worldview makes belief in magic and hence magical efficacy possible. The categories, as our deepest social contracts, are so deeply sedimented that they seem almost biological as they did to Kant. But their formation was social, in magic and in religion, and religion always reserves the right to reopen discussion of them at any time—this is part of its "profundity." Since magic is, in its essence, audacious individual use of existing powerful symbols, just as religion is the constituting action that forms those symbols, neither enterprise is intimidated by its creations, and both are willing to amend the constitution. Magic as man's exploitation of symbols achieves some of its most profound effects in fact by challenging and bending these ultimate symbols, the categories that sustain the objective frame of reference. "Bending the categories" relates to magic's exploitation of "altered states of consciousness."

The derivation of the categories from magical-religious projections means that the conceptual frameworks of science, what Thomas Kuhn calls "paradigms," use concepts derived ultimately not from praxis but from the highly scripted performances of sacred drama and superimposed on empirical data.[68] Just as Cornford[69] showed that the key categories of the ancient Ionian physicists were primitive religious concepts (*moira*, or "order" being the Greek "*dharma* word," for example), so that he characterized philosophy as "the analysis of religious material," so philosophy in turn has imported much of that magical-religious material deep into the paradigms of science. Sometimes it is this framework, rather than the data, which emits many of the metaphysical messages that come from science. Such as, for example, the suggestion of Nagel and Newman[70] that Gödel thought his proof demonstrates that numbers "subsist," like Platonic ideas. Thus Bronowski[71] has demonstrated that the relativity of time can be deduced from the Pythagorean theorem alone; this is supposed to indicate that the theorem tells us something fundamental about time and space. Thus the constant discovery of "god's footprints" by paradigm-oriented scientists who overvalue the logical and mathematical framework. Surprises are perhaps built into this framework from the beginning by the magic-derived categories out of which it is constructed. For example, the existence of black holes was deduced (by Chandrasheka) from Einstein's gravity theory[72] and began to threaten our entire world picture before any black holes were actually discovered or verified. Some say the idea might have been deduced from Newton's inverse square law alone.[73]

There is a tendency to think of paradigm as absolute, or approaching the absolute, since the science it organizes demonstrably squares with reality. But that fit improves with history and has always been faulty; moreover, paradigm does adapt to changes in the underlying empirical findings, however slowly, though it predates them. Meanwhile, the reification of paradigm provides the opportunity for the magical potential inherent in categories derived from sacred drama to be realized. Gödel's proof, the distribution of primes, Planck's constant and other constants that show up in both microcosm and macrocosm and other such Hermetic messages are artifacts of scientific paradigms that derive from social categories forged originally in sacred dramas and imposed on experience. Such messages constantly threaten to reopen discussion of our deepest social agreements. Thereby they raise the possibility of an alteration in the frame that would admit the possibility of magic. And it might be added that religion itself constantly reserves the right to reopen this discussion. Magic, in turn, continuously demands constitutional amendments. In at least one of its seven major provinces (the "paranormal") magic works largely by attempting to challenge and change the social consensus about the categories. This is just one of the ways in which magic challenges religion and social consensus. In commenting on the category studies, Mauss says somewhere that by such investigations sociology will replace philosophy. With its understanding of the categories as *social contracts,* sociology may be more immune to irrationalist attack than philosophy or psychology have been.

Theology of Hope: Magic Hope

In the present-day "theology of hope," we see a typical example of religion insisting on its right to keep open the discussion of the categories. Writers like Bloch[74] and Pannenberg[75] are actually attacking the evolved category of time that helps form the contemporary frame, time as it has continued to develop after its origin in religion—isotropic, unilinear, secular time—and the effect of their theologies is really magical. The domination of the future in their world picture abolishes the past and hence secular time. The past does not realize its meaning until the future, Bloch writes; in other words, it is continuously redefined (as in a totalitarian state, one might add). But is not the true historicity of secular unilinear time (in everyday language) defined by the once-and-for-all pastness[76] of the past, rather than by the "plunge into the future" which these philosophers romanticize? Popper has shown how certain philosophers preoccupied with change are actually terrified of it, so that "historicism" aims at abolishing history.[77] The theology of hope similarly appears to idolize but actually abolishes time and attempts to re-enter the absolute realm of "sacred time," of myth time, which is at once the mythic past, the all-defining future, and the eternal now of the mystic present. In the theology of hope god *becomes* the future, and "he is that that he will be," like Jehovah. But the true experience of time (in ordinary language) is the experience of irrevocable pastness, from which we infer the future in the future perfect tense of our plans for action in the present. To sanctify the future is to refuse to let the past go; the past will be saved with the resurrection of the dead. In the theology of hope we see a combination of religious and magical thinking used once more to transform the categories and hence alter the socially objective frame of reference whereby we perceive reality. Once again, this alteration aims at making magical action possible—in this case the collective, Sabellian, millenarian magic of building the future as a timeless Utopia here on earth. In reopening the Feuerbach approach, Bloch and his followers have served to underscore what Marx was attempting to turn away from in dropping the sociological study of religious ideas. Changing a category and hence the frame is like turning on an emotion in Sartre's sense; the theology of hope is surely a vivid example of what Sartre called "magic hope."[78] Bloch writes that he values even magic, for it shakes the world[79]; in the New Testament it is propaganda in favor of the future; the first prophets are shamans; the miraculous brings above all the possibility of new definitions; all miracles are indications of the coming of the end. Miracles explode current states of affairs: "We shall all be changed, in a moment, in the twinkling of an eye." We live now in a "*Zeitwende*," transition time, when man is "*unterwegs*," on the way to something.[80] Pannenberg says that god dominated the past by the possibility of his coming in the future. He is the "power" of the future, writes Pannenberg; he is the "wave of the future," one suspects, for Bloch. In order to be open to the future, Altizer and Ritschl[81] call for liberation from the past. All these philosophers praise the ancient Hebrews for their courageous acceptance of unilinear history, but one suspects that the mystical overvaluation of the future is actually one more magical attack on the secular category of time that provides an objective framework for that history. As such, it is full of obvious voluntarist, decisionist, irrational and magical undertones. By altering the category of time under the guise of worshipping time, this magical attack on the social framework of understanding helps prepare the way for miracles.

To summarize this section: The symbolic action of magic differs from other action and speech in the use of rigid scripts. These are borrowed from the sacred dramas of religion, where they give a core of certainty to collective experience, and then are used by magic to help the individual speak, act and think. The most powerful symbols of all are those that are most fixed—the "categories" of human thought, which were forged in the sacred dramas. They provide logical operators enabling individual minds to work with spontaneity on collective representations. And both religion and magic remember better than science does that these categories were sacred creations which can be altered tomorrow to disintegrate the conventional frame of reference and produce miraculous effects.

Notes

1. That is, in Jürgen Habermas' terms, it is neither the practical-technical-scientific language that develops out of "rational-purposive action," nor is it the humanistic language that develops out of "symbolic interaction." It is too rigid, traditional, inflexible to fit either of these. *Knowledge and Human Interests* (Boston, 1971), chs. 5–8, pp. 91–186.

2. Malinowski, "Supplement I: The Problem of Meaning in Primitive Languages," in C.K. Ogden and I.A. Richards, *The Meaning of Meaning* (N.Y., 1923), pp. 296–336.

3. *The Sociology of Georg Simmel*, Kurt H. Wolff, ed. (Glencoe, Ill., 1950), part I, ch. 3, "Sociability," pp. 40–57.

4. James Fernandez, in *Myth, Symbol and Culture*, ed. by Clifford Geertz (N.Y., 1974).

5. Malinowski, in *The Meaning of Meaning*, p. 311.

6. *Ibid.*, p. 311.

7. Malinowski later changed this formulation. The article distinguishing "phatic" from "practical" speech (with magic speech comfortable in *neither* formulation) appeared in the Ogden and Richards volume in 1923. But in 1934 (London pub.), Volume Two of *Coral Gardens and Their Magic* offered a new distinction—"pragmatic" vs. "mystical" (i.e. magical-religious) speech, and "phatic" speech seems to have dropped out. (pp. 52–53, etc.) This is perhaps because the book presents Malinowski's new behaviorist theory of speech in which the "meaning" of words is simply the effects these speech acts have: both phatic and practical talk collapse into the same kind of *action*. (The volume also contains a theory of

magic speech as an "extreme case" which demonstrates the pragmatic nature of all speech. Speech begins in the magic speech-acts of infancy; all speech is magical at first; this development permanently colors language.)

8. "...the language of magic is sacred, set and used for an entirely different purpose to that of ordinary life...too great liberties must not be taken with it." Vol. II, *Coral Gardens and Their Magic* (N.Y., 1935, 1978), p. 213. Zaretsky shows how in spiritualist churches the "argot" must be used just right; and it may only be used in full by the medium-ministers. Irving I. Zaretsky, "In The Beginning Was The Word..." Zaretsky and Leone, *Religious Movements In Contemporary America* (Princeton, 1974), pp. 166–219.

9. Malinowski, *Argonauts of the Western Pacific* (N.Y., 1961), ch. 18, "The Power of Words in Magic–Some Linguistic Data," pp. 428–463.

10. Hugh Dalziel Duncan, *Communication and Social Order* (London, 1962, 1970), pp. 36, 38–39.

11. Moreover, such a theory commits equivocations unless it simultaneously employs two definitions of magic: magic in the strict sense and magic in the weak sense. Thus Malinowski at best is saying that magic (in the weak sense) erupts in human wishes, emotions and speech, and is somehow formed into magical institutions (in the strict sense of magic). Durkheim has shown (*Les Règles...*, ch. 2) that only social facts can account for other social facts: A weak definition of magic has some uses as we shall see, but should not be used as a ruse for bringing in a psychological theory by the back door–that would be a "category error." (Aristotle)

12. See H. Neill McFarland, *The Rush Hour of the Gods* (N.Y., 1967, 1970).

13. It is remarkable how many of the new Hindu cults come down to mantra or a simple trance-inducing chant. There is a long tradition in India of such movements.

14. Hubert and Mauss, *A General Theory of Magic*, esp. pp. 40–60.

15. Cf. Hugh Dalziel Duncan, *op. cit.*, chs. 8–12.

16. *Ibid.*, ch. 10.

17. Stanley Diamond, *In Search of the Primitive* (New Brunswick, N.J., 1974); *Primitive View of the World* (N.Y., 1964).

18. The same way that Wittgenstein shows that pain language comes to substitute for the incommunicable experience of pain. *Philosophical Investigations* (N.Y., 1968), pp. 89, 448–449, etc.

19. Durkheim, *The Elementary Forms...*, pp. 360, 368.

20. Godfrey Lienhardt, *Divinity and Experience* (Oxford, 1961), p. 280.

21. *Ibid.*, p. 288.

22. *Ibid.*, p. 291.

23. Lévi-Strauss, *Structural Anthropology* (N.Y., 1963), ch. 9, pp. 167–185.

24. Thomas C. Schelling, *The Strategy of Conflict* (Oxford, 1963), p. 74.

25. Note the idea that individual thought, speech and action may be facilitated by magic (in the strict sense) is logically distinct from the possibility that there may be something inherently "magical" (in the weak sense) ABOUT human thought, speech and action. These are two different matters, though one might be the explanation for the other.

26. Frances A. Yates, *Giordano Bruno and the Hermetic Tradition* (N.Y., 1964, 1969). Yates relates Renaissance memory magic to the Hermetic idea of the mind reflecting the universe (p. 191, seq.).

27. Mauss, "Les Techniques du Corps," Claude Lévi-Strauss, ed., *Sociologie et Anthropologie* (Paris, 1950, 1966), pp. 365–386.

28. e.g., Dr. Ray Birdwhistle on "Kinesics," or Edward Hall, *The Hidden Dimension* (N.Y., 1966).

29. Mauss, "Les Techniques du Corps," *op. cit.*, ch. 4, pp. 384, 386.

30. Géza Róheim, *Magic and Schizophrenia* (Bloomington, 1953); Kurt Goldstein, *Human Nature in the Light of Psychopathology* (N.Y., 1963), p. 159, etc.

31. Harry Stack Sullivan, *The Fusion of Psychiatry and Social Science* (N.Y., 1964), p. 231, etc.; *The Interpersonal Theory of Psychiatry* (N.Y., 1953), pp. 313, 315ff.

32. V.S. Naipaul, "India, A Defect of Vision," *The New York Review of Books*, August 5, 1976, pp. 9–14. Reprinted in Naipaul, *India, A Wounded Civilization* (N.Y., 1977), ch. 5, pp. 101–123.

33. Hubert and Mauss, *A General Theory of Magic*, p. 142.

34. *Ibid.*, p. 144.

35. *Ibid.*, p. 122ff.

36. Max Jammer, *Concepts of Mass in Classical and Modern Physics* (N.Y., 1964), *passim.*

37. Henri Bergson, *Time and Free Will*: cf. discussion in Schutz, *op. cit.*, p. 85ff.

38. Edmond Husserl, *The Phenomenology of Internal Time Consciousness* (Bloomington, Ind., 1969).

39. Mauss, "A Category of the Human Spirit," *Psychoanalytic Review*, vol. 55, no. 3, 1968, pp. 457–481.

40. *The Elementary Forms of Religious Life*, esp. Conclusion, pp. 415–447.

41. Wittgenstein, *Remarks on the Foundations of Mathematics* (Cambridge, 1967), p. 97, etc.

42. *The Elementary Forms of Religious Life*, p. 17.

43. Mauss, "A Category of the Human Spirit." Also, "L'Ame, Le Nom et la Personne" (1923), Marcel Mauss *Oeuvres*, vol. 2 (Paris, 1968), pp. 131–135.

44. Mauss, "Conceptions Qui Ont Precédé la Notion de Matière" (1939), *Oeuvres*, vol. 2, p. 161–166.

45. Mauss, "Les Origins de la Notion de la Monnaie" (1914), *Oeuvres*, vol. 2, pp. 106–112, "Debat Sur Les Fonctions Sociales de la Monnaie," *Oeuvres*, vol. 2 (1934), pp. 116–120.

46. Henri Hubert, "Etude Sommaire de la Représentation du Temps dans la Religion et la Magic," in Hubert & Mauss, *Mélanges d'Histoire des Religions* (Paris, 1909).

47. This point is often missed by the structuralists—and even by friendly critics of Durkheim such as Lukes—who do not grasp that Durkheim and Mauss are extreme conventionalists, and will not be intimidated by the fact that categories evolving in society increasingly seem to "fit" objective reality. (Cf. Lukes' objections in *Durkheim, His Life and Works*, London, 1972, p. 447 ff). Mauss and Hertz developed a sociobiology showing how even biological structures, such as left-handedness, may be socially derived. So the Kantian argument about faculties is not saved by a retreat to a biological base. More serious is Lukes' repetition of the familiar problem of logic. (Cf. Keynes' attempt to homologize the inductive verifiability of probability with its deductive basis in logic. J.M. Keynes, *A Treatise on Probability*, N.Y., 1962). But the correspondence of logic with the laws of nature exists *because we say it does*, though perhaps not for that reason alone. Logic itself is still evolving; it has carried notorious flaws for centuries. Much of it is either transparently simple, or so complicated that it may be flawed. Consider what Wittgenstein says (*Remarks on the Foundations of Mathematics*, Cambridge, Mass, 1967, pp. 73, 80–81, etc.), about the *Principia Mathematica*—no one could possibly follow those long chains of deductive reasoning. They cannot be "taken in." Errors could creep in, and who would know? Of course, ultimately logic turns into something that programs very fast computers, but then, have we discovered something about reality or have we created a machine?

48. This expresses a typical neo-Kantian idea which had currency in France. We see it, for example, in Pradines' idea that science necessarily contains a "mystical" element, namely, "reason" (its philosophical or paradigm component), which is superimposed on data to escape the "tyranny" of raw empiricism, of the senses. (*Esprit de la Religion*, Paris, 1941, cf. Introduction).

49. Cf. Frances A. Yates, *The Rosicrucian Enlightenment* (London and Boston, 1972), ch. 8 & *passim*.

50. Einstein, *Relativity, The Special and General Theory* (N.Y., 1961), ch. 11, pp. 30–34.

51. The terms are from Peter L. Berger, *The Sacred Canopy, The Precarious Vision*, lectures.

52. Lucien Lévy-Bruhl, *L'Expérience Mystique et les Symboles Chez les Primitives* (Paris, 1938), ch. 2.

53. Henri Hubert, *op. cit.*, 1909.

54. *The Phenomenology of Internal Time Consciousness* (Bloomington, Ind., 1969).

55. *Time and Free Will*. Cf. Schutz, *op. cit.*, p. 85.

56. Mircea Eliade, *Cosmos and History* (N.Y., 1959), etc. Eliade knew the Durkheim School well and may have found some elements for his *idée maîtresse* here.

57. George Herbert Mead, *Mind, Self, and Society* (Chicago, 1934).

58. William James, *Principles of Psychology* (N.Y., 1950), vol. 1, ch. 10, "The Consciousness of Self," pp. 291–401.

59. J.P. Sartre, *The Transcendence of the Ego* (N.Y., 1957), *passim.*

60. Augustine, *Concerning the City of God Against the Pagans* (London, 1972), Book II, ch. 4.

61. Mauss made an outline and critique of the paper for *L'Année Sociologique*, and in a footnote he tells us it was published in *Annuaire de l'Ecole Pratique des Hautes-Etudes Section des Sciences Religieuses*, 1905 (Mauss, *Oeuvres*, vol. 1, p. 50–52).

62. Einstein, *Relativity, The Special and the General Theory*, 1905. Banesh Hoffmann, *Albert Einstein, Creator and Rebel* (N.Y., 1972), records that in the special theory, first published as an article, in 1905, Einstein's reasoning was physical, empirical, rather than philosophical like Whitehead's.

63. Henri Poincaré, "The Relativity of Space," now ch. 7, pp. 93–116, in *Science and Method*, the undated (N.Y., 195–) Dover paperback. This paper came out in 1905, according to Banesh Hoffmann (*op. cit.* p. 78) and Poincaré had the sense of the idea of relativity earlier.

64. Whitehead's paper "On Mathematical Concepts of the Material World" was submitted to the Royal Society in 1905, according to Victor Lowe, in Paul Arthur Schlipp, ed., *The Philosophy of Alfred North Whitehead* (Evanston & Chicago, 1941), p. 34.

65. On this point Hoffmann insists Einstein thought physically, not deductively. (*Ibid.*, and conversation with Hoffmann.)

66. The full title was *Etude Sommaire de la Représentation du Temps dans la Religion et la Magie.*

67. Hubert's essay on time was collected in *Mélanges D'Histoire des Religions*, Hubert and Mauss (Paris, 1909), which contained also their joint paper on *Sacrifice,* and Mauss' essay on Australian magicians' initiation (*L'Origine des Pouvoirs Magiques dans les Sociétés Australiennes*, originally pub. in *Rapports Annuels de l'Ecole des Hautes Etudes*, Paris, 1904). It also contained, as an introduction, an essay that continued the argument of their *General Theory of Magic—Introducton à L'Analyse de Quelques Phénomènes Religieux* (which had first appeared in 1906 in *La Revue de l'Histoire des Religions*, 58, pp. 163–203). In short, this was a *book about magic*, or the magical component of religion.

68. Thomas S. Kuhn, *The Structure of Scientific Revolutions* (Chicago, 1970), pp. 43–51.

69. F.M. Cornford, *From Religion to Philosophy* (N.Y., 1957), p. 17, etc.

70. Ernest Nagel and James R. Newman, *Gödel's Proof* (N.Y., 1964), p. 99.

71. J. Bronowski, "The Clock Paradox," *Scientific American*, Feb., 1963, pp. 134–144. It may indeed tell us something about how our category of space developed as a social product; it was greatly influenced by the arithmetical geometry of the magical Pythagorean brotherhood.

72. On gravitational collapse: Harrison, Thorne, Wakano & Wheeler, *Gravitation Theory and Gravitational Collapse* (Chicago, 1965).

73. J. Taylor, *Black Holes* (London, 1975).

74. Ernst Bloch, *Man on His Own* (N.Y., 1970); & *On Karl Marx* (N.Y., 1971).

75. Wolfhart Pannenberg, ed., *Revelation As History* (N.Y., 1968); and *Theology and the Kingdom of God* (Philadelphia, 1968). See also John B. Cobb, Jr., *God and the World* (Philadelphia, 1969), pp. 51–71.

76. One German word for the past is *Die Vergangenheit*, the "gone-ness."

77. Karl R. Popper, *The Open Society and Its Enemies* (Princeton, 1950), pp. 11–36.

78. Jean-Paul Sartre, *The Emotions: Outline of a Theory* (N.Y., 1948), pp. 62, 70–71, etc.

79. Ernst Bloch, "Man's Increasing Entry Into Religious Experience," in *Man On His Own* (N.Y., 1970), pp. 147–240.

80. Turner suggests that man's human qualities are most apparent in transitions. See "Betwixt and Between: The Liminal Period in *Rîtes de Passage*," ch. 4, *The Forest of Symbols* (Ithaca, 1967), pp. 93–111; and "Liminality and Communitas," ch. 3 in *The Ritual Process* (London, 1974), pp. 80–118.

81. According to John B. Cobb, Jr., *op. cit.* pp. 31–32, 34.

Postulate 4: MAGICAL SCRIPTS
ACHIEVE THEIR SOCIAL EFFECTS
LARGELY BY PRE-EXISTING
OR PREFIGURED AGREEMENTS.

FRAZER was in the minority when he supposed that primitive man gradually perceived that magic fails. Most investigators testify that, socially speaking, magic works. (Marett even declared that its efficacy was the source of the whole supernatural realm—men were so surprised by the effects we call magic that all their supernatural beliefs were engendered because of this.[1]) How does magic achieve its remarkable effects? We have seen that it is real social action, that it manipulates some of society's most powerful symbols, embodying them in potent scripts (which are often borrowed from powerful religious rites). But this is not enough to explain its striking social efficacies. How, after all, is it able to induce altered states of consciousness, cure illness, actually kill people and do other remarkable things? The many explanations that are heard could be classified under major subheads including: 1. human *interaction* as the source of magical fireworks; 2. suggestion, fascination or some other form of individual *persuasion;* 3. theories deriving magic from some *experiential base* such as trance, drugs, hypnosis, ESP, etc. We cannot consider all variants of these possibilities, and since our interest is theoretical, we will instead analyze whether magic fits certain theoretical frameworks appropriate to some of these major types of explanation. For most of these explanations, rather than wrong, are incomplete, partial, low-level generalizations or just aspects of the truth—and not the strategic sociological aspects. A theoretical approach is necessary to give a comprehensive explanation of these phenomena.[2]

Therefore, to assess various explanations of magical effects as the result of suggestion or persuasion, we will consider whether magic fits the classical paradigm of rhetoric. To consider all notions that magic arises from interpersonal effects, we will see how well it fits the paradigms of "symbolic interaction" theory. After that, we will examine the possibility that magical efficacy derives from some experiential base—before finally turning to a sociological explanation.

Theories of Magical Effects

1. Does Symbolic Interaction Theory Help Us Understand How Magic Achieves Its Effects?

Not very much, and this is itself interesting. Symbolic interactionism is perhaps more useful as an account of constituting action than of constituted action like magic. It tends to be about action that is to an important degree reciprocal, whereas magical action is to a great extent rigidly scripted, predetermined and relatively uninflected by reciprocal reactions. Magic is also apt to be authoritarian, with one actor the speaker and the others listeners or mere chorus. Even the reactions of the client and the attendant chorus of onlookers are stereotyped, produced on cue by the rite itself and patterned by tradition. Typical symbolic interaction processes of "mirroring," "taking on the role of the other," reciprocal response and mutual interaction found in the formulations of Mead,[3] Cooley,[4] Blumer,[5] etc. seem more appropriate in describing formative, constitutive or relatively free interactive situations than in describing the constituted, stereotyped monologues of magic. Therefore, symbolic interactionism will probably not be as useful in describing ceremonies that are traditional and set, as it is in accounting for the formation of a new custom out of free interaction. Of course, Blumer and others accept constituted institutions as frameworks; interaction goes on *against* a cultural frame. But as Peter McHugh[6] has pointed out, this background tends to be taken for granted (as "the definition of the situation"), with the spotlight thrown on current, moving, reciprocal interaction. McHugh and, to a lesser degree, Blumer do emphasize that continuous tacit mutual agreement is required to sustain these taken-for-granted frameworks, but do not give the matter deep attention. Certain new interactive theories which do emphasize continuous creation of the frame, by the ethnomethodologists[7] and Goffman, have gone further in showing how the assumptive frame is manipulated by individuals. But classical interactionist theory like that of Mead and Cooley is more appropriate to free or constitutive interaction than to the authoritarian, formularized scripts of magic.[8]

Magic will not easily fit symbolic interaction schemas, for it is too fixed and scripted. This theoretical excursus suggests that we must therefore reject all attempts to derive magic from some kind of social interaction—from groups of people somehow stimulating each other or psyching each other out—such as we find in such diverse descriptions as those of Gurvitch[9] or Marett.[10] It is true that the constituted social world once in a while opens up a gap so that men have glimpses of the precariousness of what is taken for granted; then they may be reminded that stable structures were originally constituted in social interaction, and they may indeed experience this revelation with Sartre's sense of "horror" or the "terror" that Berger writes about. But magic is not that horror or terror but rather one of the oldest defenses against it. Gurvitch is wrong to derive religion from society and magic from interaction, as if the two institutions existed on separate planes. And when Marett attempts to derive magic from interaction we know what he means but he is using the words incorrectly. He means that magical practices impress people; but that is no proof that they began in such impressions. More often, what impresses was borrowed ready-made from another context, and being impressed on cue is contained in the script.

2. Is Magic a Kind of Rhetoric?

The effects of magic are sometimes attributed to "suggestion," "persuasion" or other personal influence. Instead of considering these possibilities diversely, we can focus on one theoretical framework, the theory of rhetoric as a paradigm of persuasion. Magic will not fit this framework either. Kenneth Burke claims that it almost does. In *The Rhetoric of Religion*[11] he states that religious language is rhetoric because both rhetoric and religious language are forms of persuasion; but in *A Rhetoric of Motives*[12] he writes that magic is not exactly rhetoric. His basic idea, though, is that magic *aims* at rhetoric; it is not a proto-science but a proto-rhetoric of symbolic persuasion attempting to organize social action. He denies it the full status of rhetoric because it is a language that goes wrong—i.e., it jumps the track and "is used to address things instead of people."[13] This hurdle aside, Burke is willing to identify magic as a forerunner of rhetoric: magic persuades people to act; it organizes social action. But his analogy is weak.

For attempts to assimilate magic to rhetoric (or any other paradigm of persuasion) will founder again on the scripted rigidity of magic. Rhetoric has its formal rules, of course, but it presupposes an open mind that can be persuaded, and there is much more give-and-take to it than we find in the memorized scripts of magic. Rhetoric has therefore little in common with magic in the strict sense, with the obdurate, fixed institutions of ceremonial magic, shamanism, divination, the occult sciences and so on.

What writers like Burke (and others who stress theories of persuasion, like Frank[14]) are really picking up is an analogy to magic "in the weak sense." Rhetoric in the ancient world was a training in symbolic powers that enabled an individual man to have an effect on his small society in the agora, the way primitives experience their own symbolic powers when they participate in a collective rite; both cases are "magical" in the weak sense only.[15]

Most ancient philosophers had good things to say about rhetoric, and like Burke they defended the use of figures and other devices. For rhetoric was considered to be a rational process: "lively" inventions should be chosen over dull ones, but truth would win out in free discourse. Plato's scorn was directed, not against rhetoric, but against sophistry, the mystification of argument by experts who could then make the worse appear the better cause. Aristotle[16] elevated rhetoric to be the counterpart of dialectic, both having to do with such things as fall within the realm of common knowledge, with rhetoric as public discussion of these things. The use of devices, even emotional devices, to persuade is legitimate, because one is talking about, and to, the consensus, and its logos will be elicited by public persuasive discourse.

The classical theories should make it obvious that rhetoric and magic are different. Rhetoric presupposes that the assent of the audience can be freely won;

it assumes more flexibility and freer argument than magic with its stereotyped rites and automated assents. Rhetoric, after all, is discourse with and about the "general will"; as such it is more appropriate in the center of society and homologizes better to religion, with its more flexible and community-wide rites. It is a poor analogy for magic. Magic may indeed help to focus and even organize some kinds of collective action, but magic is not pow-wow or palaver or the logos of the general will. Magical speeches are not extemporaneous or composed, but entirely traditonal; and audience response is preordained.

Recent studies of domination in communication, by writers like Habermas,[17] Schroyer,[18] Mueller,[19] Wellmer,[20] Marcuse[21] and Ellul,[22] homologize better to analogies of magic than do conceptualizations of rhetoric. Marcuse's notion that the non-critical language reflecting the techno-structure, "purified" by linguistic philosophy, is a compulsive language aimed at producing action rather than thought, is suggestive.[23] Ellul expresses similar ideas in his argument that propaganda aims not at instilling orthodoxy, but "orthopraxy,"[24] i.e., an action. Comments on this trend of language have been with us since Orwell.[25] Claus Mueller has demonstrated empirically how the new magic command language works, with his brilliant coup in obtaining actual grammatical and stylistic rules laid down by two modern totalitarian regimes.[26] Trent Schroyer builds a similar account of the new compulsive public language on Habermas' theories of "repressive communication":[27] The main idea is that public communications today increasingly consist of "imperatives" derived unambiguously from the alleged rationality of the underlying technological system—just as, we might observe, magic derives its imperatives from religious assumptions. The notion that ideology gets "embedded" in something physical, in the underlying structures of society, is a characteristic viewpoint of the whole Frankfurt school[28] (and of Wilhelm Reich[29]). Putting the core of the value system down into the "ground" of technology (or biological character) where it cannot be discussed is a curious modern variation on the traditional process of putting these values "up in the sky"[30] of the sacred cosmos. Magic more closely resembles the restrictive language codes of totalitarian societies than it does rhetoric or any other paradigm of "persuasion." Magical language is more authoritarian than persuasive; it does not try to "persuade" but to compel.

But there is one interesting idea from classical rhetoric that is suggestive and worth a moment's reflection. This is Aristotle's enthymene, or "artistic proof." Basically, this is a syllogism which did not exist before the argument (as logical truths do), but is made up as a means of persuasion. This may work by the speaker getting the audience to identify with his premise. In a syllogism in *Barbara*, for example, the speaker might phrase some generalization about the public interest in a way that is close enough to the unorganized consensus as to gain unreflected assent from his audience, yet slanted in such a way as to lead to the conclusion he seeks. His argument then syllogistically persuades the audience of the intended conclusion; they are led toward it because they have let him phrase the major premise and have consented to it. Enthymenes are much more effective than arguments by example, Aristotle says.

The enthymene suggests something about the frequent report that magical action works with traditional ideas yet is always to some degree surreptitious. The enthymene operates by identification, and so does magic. The rhaetor states a premise in a persuasive manner so as to get the people to identify their own inarticulated consensus with his intention. "We all agree," the speaker says, and then gives his own definition of some principle that sounds close enough to the general will so that the crowd will go along with him. Once agreement on the major premise is secured, the conclusion is clinched. I would like to characterize this operation as "a first person singular speaking in the first person plural" and getting away with it. I think this operation is significant for magic in both the strong and the weak senses. For even in real institutional magic, there is often an underlying reasoning in which the major premise is from the religious consensus universe of discourse and slanted; this makes possible the deduction of a magical effect. In magic in the weak sense, persuasion often takes the form of speaking in the management voice before you belong to the management.[31]

There is a sense in which even science proceeds this way. Each science begins by redefining some of the major premises in the social consensus, and then, with its experiments and proofs and other dramas of agreement, drills the society as a whole into going along. As these premises are accepted, science unfolds its worldview until ultimately the universe seems to work "like a syllogism in *Barbara*," as Peirce has put it.[32] Alan Blum[33] has shown how Aristotle laid the foundations of his own sciences, the first formal sciences—with enthymenes in effect. Many of us can recall enough Aristotle to remember how he starts each science—i.e., by reflecting on his own stream of consciousness to discover the consensual knowledge his own society sedimented in it. As Blum puts it, Aristotle often begins by saying, in effect, "We all agree that..." Since he is defining the first person plural agreement for his own purposes, this smacks more of enthymene than syllogism. He also consigns opposing viewpoints to the prehistory of scientific discussion via his "genetic" account of their shortcomings. This uses a kind of rhetoric of convergence; it also suppresses the dialectic in Aristotle's own mind. Alternative interpretations are no longer present as challenging arguments. Blum's point is that in saying "we all agree," Aristotle is wrenching the consensus and foreclosing it. Plato, too, appeals to "we agree," but tries to keep it transparent through continuing dialogue; his thought remains more consensual and therefore is "religious," according to Blum. Whereas Aristotle interrupts the endless reflexive meditation on what we agree about that is culture, and persuades the people to accept scripted formulae as premises from which effects can be deduced.[34] There is some resemblance to magic in this operation—in the attempt to suspend communal dialogue, in the first person singular speaking as first person plural, in the partialism of the viewpoint.

Blum fails to see that in this weak sense of magic, everyone speaks magically whenever he speaks in any way. An implicit unstated part of every communication is "I am he who says this by right of who I am." Another part consists of implicit or half-stated references to consensual premises which are colored by him who speaks. Whenever someone speaks influentially, or on his own behalf, he must assume the abstract attitude of him who speaks within the consensus, knowing its premises, knowing exactly who he is, and knowing how far he can bend those premises to make the enthymenes of everyday individual speech possible. And so in the weak sense of "magic," most social speech is magical,[35] affecting the position of pronouns in quality space, as Fernandez neatly put it. Brain-damaged people (Goldstein[36]) and schizophrenics (Sullivan[37]) experience anxiety when they lose this contact with the nomos so they cannot speak with appropriate enthymenes; and in strange situations it can be difficult for anyone. Then shaman figures who know the nomos better than the crowd may be pressed into service to speak with their enormous vocabularies, for the "We." And charismatic individuals may emerge when the people demand their services, to challenge the nomos on their behalf by saying, "It is written, but I say unto you." And if they get away with it, then we say, "it's magic," or words to that effect.

But not all metaphors of magic are apt metaphors, and not everything referred to as "magical" is magic, not even in the weak sense. Often common speech simply deceives itself, confounding the effects of magic with magic itself. Sometimes other people move us deeply with gesture or speech that is spontaneous or free, and we call this "magical," but it is not— it is simply that the effect on us reminds us of magic. Some metaphors of magic are just inaccurate.

The language game of rhetoric did perhaps approach this fitness of metaphor to some degree, because it was patterned by tradition. The crowd anticipated the figures, the wind-up, the peroration, and having gone to the same school, subjectively patterned its own psychological effects. If people expect to be impressed, they are impressed. If they believe they believe, their belief is strengthened.[38] As it was played in the ancient world, the public language game of rhetoric did entail the likelihood that listeners would be persuaded; and to that degree of patterning rhetoric perhaps approached the status, metaphorically, of magic "in the weak sense." But in the strict sense, magic institutional practice is far too rigid to be explained by the framework of rhetoric or by any theory of persuasion, which is much freer and more plastic.

3. Does Magic Symbolism Achieve Its Compelling Effects by Logic – Or Illogic?

If an enthymene, why not a syllogism? The notorious rigidity of logic, with its preexisting outcomes determined by the rules of a tradition, is certainly more suggestive of magic's scripted formulae than is the free discourse of rhetoric. Does magical symbolism perhaps compel by a kind of logic? The idea frequently occurs, at least metaphorically, to Hubert and Mauss. In one passage they suggest that mana seems to be used like the logical copula, joining together arguments,[39] or perhaps it works like a universal middle term in magical syllogisms.[40] In another, they suggest that spells often read like "syllogistic reasoning," with a "major premise" clearly stated, and the desired result elicited by implication.[41] They even suggest that it works like Kant's "synthetic a priori," another logical idea.[42] There do sometimes seem to be implicative links between sentences used in magic, and magic is somewhat logical to this extent. ("The central topic of logic is implication," writes David Mitchell.[43]) For the links between ideas in sympathetic magic are not just "traditional" links as Hubert and Mauss insist in their critique of Frazer—there is also a kind of logic to them based on the fact that they refer ultimately to primitive classification systems.[44] Operations performed by sympathetic magic on these primitive classifications seem to entail a kind of logic of classes.[45] Hubert and Mauss also hint that the idea of logical transitivity is latent in contagious magic; and perhaps it is in homeopathic magic, too.[46]

In magic there is always a curious tension between the traditional and the surreptitious, and hence between syllogism, implication from accepted truth, and an enthymene that bends consensus to private ends. Magic gets its effects through expropriated sacred solemn scripts which it hesitates to change lest it weaken their power. Yet magic must often bend the sacred to its private or subgroup ends. Depending on how official or how illicit the magic is, we might say that in it implication runs in a continuum from consensual syllogism to rhetorical enthymene (and quite beyond, to outright reversals).

But magic uses implication only in part, and logical necessity can account for only a part of magic's effects. Moreover, any attempt to derive the compelling power of magical symbolism in general from the implicative force of the syllogism would founder on the problem that the nature of logical necessity itself is not entirely clear:

> We have not succeeded in discovering concepts which are more basic than that of logical necessity and in terms of which logical necessity can be defined...the notion of necessity is left unexplained.[47]

All his life Wittgenstein kept asking himself in his various notebooks, how does logical necessity work? It has something to do with negation, "and that is not nothing." But how could so much turn on a mere "twiddle"?[48] (as he called the curled symbol for negation). "That necessity is not exclusively a logical notion seems likely," writes Mitchell.[49] In other words, the logical sequitur itself is too uncertain to explain the compelling force of magical symbolism. There are some who would derive *both* compulsions from convention.[50]

Prelogical vagueness and magic. What about the alternative view, that primitive thought is illogical and that magic derives its force from the logical vagueness of the primitive worldview? Logical vagueness might at least help explain why magic is not "falsified" in Popper's sense,[51] why its failures do not condemn it—though it is less certain that vagueness can offer anything more than a tautological explanation of the real effects magic does sometimes produce. Thus Evans-Pritchard (who was influenced by Lévy-Bruhl) showed how Azande witch beliefs were unfalsifiable because their very complexity and logical vagueness left loopholes to explain any failures of techniques.[52]

The outcome of the famous debate on whether primitive thought is "illogical" is uncertain, but it raised some sensitive issues worth exploring. Lévy-Bruhl opened it with his charge in 1910 that primitive thought was "pre-logical." In the first of seven books devoted to the subject[53] he made several charges that come down to one charge. He said primitive thought used representations containing emotional elements derived from magic and ritual, non-cognitive elements, so that representations could not be reduced to homogeneous concepts in a sustained ratiocination. For these reasons—and also because primitive thought lacked "the principle of contradiction"—it could not build deductively. But his whole argument could be reduced to the absence of the principle of contradiction, i.e., the basic rule of Western logic which says "It is not true both P true and P false"— $\sim (P \cdot \sim P)$.[54] Primitives do not have any such orienting conception; they believe it is possible to be two persons or in two places at once, both dead and alive, right and wrong, here and there; and if they believe that they will believe anything. The whole idea is that primitives' superstitions (and presumably also magic) stem from their not having any rule of contradiction. There is an additional, subordinate argument in the first book about "participation," the blurring of entities and concepts, which might also help explain magic.

Now Durkheim and Mauss, even though they were busy showing how the categories of modern thought slowly evolved originally out of primitive religious thinking, criticized this idea for portraying too sharp a gulf between primitives and moderns.[55] Under criticism from his colleagues, Lévy-Bruhl switched his emphasis in his next two books to give greater attention to what had been his secondary explanation: mystic participation. In *The Soul of the Primitive*,[56] he stressed participation and the confounding of the individual with the species. But this is still a kind of logical deficiency; the primitive yet has no pure notion of a set and the species is just a more generalized image of an individual: eg., "Bear" or "Coyote." This book is Lévy-Bruhl's equivalent of Durkheim's "Homo Duplex" essay.[57] In *Primitive Mentality* Lévy-Bruhl stressed not so much prelogical thought as "mystical" beliefs (we would say "magical"), especially mystical beliefs about causality. Major attention is given here to the fact that primitives ask their causality theory to tell them, not merely "how" but "why" something happened—there are no pure accidents.[58] Evans-Pritchard, who developed this idea so clearly in his book about the Azande,[59] has in several places hinted at a debt to him and usually writes of him with respect.[60]

But it was in his last three books that Lévy-Bruhl completed the switch from "prelogical" thinking to what we would call "magical" thinking as his explanation of the cultural gulf between primitive and modern thought. The key idea, first set forth in *Primitives and the Supernatural*,[61] is that the first logical sets are organized not on the basis of properties that can be expressed in cognitive terms but on the basis of feelings. "I saw you last night and got that old feeling!" —So run the lyrics of a popular song from the 1930's. It was as if we organized a logical set such that the "property"[62] that mapped the "elements" within the "domain" of the set were an affect, namely that "old feeling." Lévy-Bruhl gives almost all his attention to one such set, "the affective category of the supernatural," which is the set of all objects, symbols or events that provoke a particular creepy feeling which we associate with the supernatural. (It is obviously similar to the feeling provoked by the sacred—the *mysterium, tremendum* and *fascinans* of Otto.[63]) Primitive sets are also organized around "dispositions," which are also more affectual than cognitive—e.g., "friendly" spirits, ghosts, sorcerers, circumstances, etc., would be one set; "unfriendly" might be another. "Lucky" is an additional set, whose domain is mapped by an affectual property. This new argument has the effect of making magic thinking the explanation for illogicality, rather than the reverse, which was his initial position.

This particular book[64] contains Lévy-Bruhl's major statements on magic; it is here that he discusses witchcraft, evil eye, supernatural powers. And he states here that belief in these phenomena is maintained by the very vagueness of what is asserted about them; vagueness makes falsification difficult—another idea that Evans-Pritchard perhaps developed from Lévy-Bruhl. If Lévy-Bruhl had constructed an explicit theory of magic it might have been built on this base; and it might have stated that the possibility of magic derives from a worldview making use of affectual categories and sets, in which the objects participate with one another and the set as a whole, and in which anything postulated as happening in this framework is difficult to falsify. But this is really not too helpful, for it amounts to saying that magical thinking makes magic possible. If not tautological, this position is not exactly explanatory.

Later, Lévy-Bruhl seemed to move toward an explanation of magic in terms of myth (which is closer to the ideas of Hubert and Mauss with their emphasis on magic's use of traditional materials). In *La Mythologie Primitive*[65] he shows how myths can be used as magical instruments; because of their evocations, myths have power and he assimilates myths to spells. But in *L'Expérience Mystique et Les Symboles Chez les Primitives*,[66] his last book published before his death, the idea of sets mapped by affective properties is further developed. Lévy-Bruhl is now increasingly under Mauss' influence and he now stresses that affectual categories are prototypes of the cognitive categories and are a start toward the logical organization of experience.

By this time, Lévy-Bruhl had dropped altogether his notion that lack of contradiction creates primitive mentality with its superstition and magic. But in his posthumously published notebooks, he returned to the problem of "illogicality" and finally solved it, in my opinion. In *Les Carnets*,[67] which he scribbled on buses and in parks during his last year, he finally made a clinching connection between his later ideas about affectual concepts and his original thought about logic. It is 1939; he is in his 80's and he has gone back to brood on his first works on primitive mentality. (According to the Leenhardt preface, Lévy-Bruhl asked that the *Carnets* be arranged in six sections bearing on his six main books on primitive mentality.) Now he specifically denies that primitives do not recognize contradiction; the human mind is the same everywhere—but its categories evolve culturally. He is now in total agreement with Mauss. We have deduction because we have categories that invite it, that define their own definiteness. He is also close, at the end, to the later Wittgenstein. It is not that primitives do not recognize contradictions when they see them. The problem is not logical but "physical," he writes. Primitive physical concepts are not sharply defined in a way that would sharply delineate all the contradictions that we see. Primitives do recognize such contradictions as their rather affectual, cloudy representations reveal to them; but where they miss others that we recognize it is not because they deny contradiction, but because their categories for space and time and mass and extension themselves do not have the sharp cutting edges that ours have. But of course this is really a conceptual, logical matter after all, and not a "physical" one. In this final statement, Lévy-Bruhl is very close to the extreme conventionalist position of Wittgenstein.[68] Wittgenstein's idea is that the principle of contradiction became a Western institution which progressively hardened our concepts of all the physical entities so as to build contradiction right into them. The sharp edges that objects have for us are all conceptual: "...it is not the property of an object that is ever 'essential,' but rather the mark of a concept....if you talk about *essence*, you are merely noting a convention...to the *depth* that we see in the essence there corresponds the *deep* need for the convention."[69] Clearly, objects that are defined in isotropic, three-dimensional space, objects whose properties are described according to other categories of modern thought, will obey the principle of contradiction because such exclusion is built right into our concepts of them.

One could say, then, that Lévy-Bruhl's original argument is saved. It has not been abandoned but has been reformulated: primitive thought lacks the principle of contradiction not in the sense that it does not obey simple contradiction but because its basic concepts lack the sharp edges that the principle of contradiction as a social institution builds into them over the long course of civilization. But ordinary recognition of contradiction *is* there in the primitive mind. It is there in the fundamental antithesis of sacred and profane which does generate a few sharp edges indeed: those dangerous borders that must be crossed through the careful rituals of entry and exit rites as in sacrifice. It is there in practical pursuits, when it needs to be. But primitive religion and magic know nothing of the deductive and sometimes ideological modes of thinking Western society built on exclusionary logic.

Logic As a Group of Social Categories. The suspicion begins to arise that what is peculiar is not primitive thought—but Western thought, which has made contradiction a dominant institution that built such edges into all our concepts so that we see the world in black-and-white. Mauss has accustomed us to view the Aristotelian categories as social and historical, capable of changing tomorrow—why not the Kantian categories, why not the "principles" and "constants" of *logic*? It is possible that contradiction and the related ideas of identity and excluded middle originally grew out of *polemos.*[70] After all, formal logic emerges out of a tradition of sophistry that was very much related to public debate as a vehicle of class war in Greek city states. The operation of negation—"You're wrong!"—is central in such debate. Identity, excluded middle and contradiction all turn on negation. Most attempts to reduce logic from laws down to just the operation of the logical constants, and these down to just a few, come down to "not." Thus the *not-and* system of the *Principia Mathematica*[71] and Quine's M.L.[72] Or the *not-or* system that Quine, in his book *Elementary Logic,*[73] says is just as possible. *Not-and* or *not-or*: either way, *not.*[74] Wittgenstein even tried to reduce the whole thing *just to not* in the *Tractatus* through repeated operations of negation, by means of Sheffer's double-negation sign.[75]

It would have been interesting if Wittgenstein had tried to analyze negation as a "language game," or if Mauss had studied it as a "category." Negation, contradiction, identity and excluded middle are interdefinable. Primitives knew contradiction but it seldom applied, for their concepts lacked sharp edges; but negation—it is *not!*—is the strategic new element that makes the binary thinking of logic possible and with its prestige reforms all our concepts. But this is a cultural historical event, not a theophany. The idea of contradiction wavers even in Aristotle; in his earlier work, *The Topics*, according to Bochenski,[76] he postulated four types of contradiction—including the contrary (e.g., just-unjust), the opposition between privation and possession (e.g., blindness vs. sight), as well as contradictory opposition (e.g., just vs. not just). Bochenski goes on to observe that he quickly did develop the correct account of contradiction, provided the words used were not ambiguous. But this turned on applying negation across the boards, he wrote. And Aristotle continued to doubt,[77] as Wittgenstein would,[78] the universal applicability of the law of the excluded middle. Lévi-Strauss has shown that primitives were well aware of contradiction and had several forms approximating to it;[79] we are suggesting that what they lacked was a true operation of negation, which makes contradiction clear-cut, and that attaining it was a historical development. The phatic speech of a palaver house in a consensus-ridden society at the stage of "mechanical solidarity" is *not* fertile ground for *polemos* or the idea of negation that emerges from it.

Lévi-Strauss vividly demonstrates that primitives are able to recognize contradiction; they are in fact fascinated by it, but they cannot resolve it. They weave funny patterns with contradiction in myths, and Lévi-Strauss almost gets away with calling this a kind of "proto-logic" (even though he undercuts himself by having to admit that the logic is a. unconscious; b. polyvalent; c. uses operations that are not understood by the users; d. does not settle anything or make any deductive "progress"). Whether it is equivocation to call this "proto-logic" or not, what comes through Lévi-Strauss' several books is that primitives are tormented by contradiction, and that they weave complex patterns in myths to attempt "to attenuate the logical scandal," to use the phrase Lévi-Strauss quotes from Durkheim. He even affects to see prototypes of the principle of contradiction or of the copula, or of other logical constants, in certain repeated "operations" or "connectives" he observes in primitive myths. One of these we might call "the ratio connective," which takes the form "A is to B as C is to D." Thus, a primitive, confronted with a contradiction, does not say that A is *not* B; instead, in a myth, he will say something like this: Life is to death as peace is to war. That "attenuates" the tension of the contradiction. Or he will use what might be called the "triadic connection" to give my own name again to the other main connective described in Lévi-Strauss' *Structural Anthropology*. Confronted with a stark contradiction—e.g., male vs. female—mythic thinking handles it, "attenuates" it, by inventing a middle term: e.g., a bisexual god (or, later, a "scientific" theory of bisexuality!). So strong is the tension of contradiction that Lévi-Strauss seems to think that the triadic connective, as an operator solving logical-cognitive problems, precipitates changes in social morphology, such as tripartite organization. (This is Lévi-Strauss' typical idealist tendency to "reverse" Mauss and Durkheim and show social morphology as a projection of an emerging logic instead of vice versa.) The reason why primitive myths proliferate in their repetition of forms is because contradiction without negation settles nothing, so the logical scandal must be continually worked over. And whatever the medium—bits of action endlessly shuffled in myth; "gustemes" of sweet and sour in cuisine; colors reversing themselves in an endless visual symphony in artifacts and dress—the whole force behind the movement is unresolved contradiction, according to Lévi-Strauss.

An analogy to the role played by "negation" in Freud's metapsychology is suggestive, though it is a different concept on a different level, of course. To Freud "repression" is often a primitive and unsuccessful way of handling a "contradiction,"[80] e.g., the contradiction of some id impulse with the reality principle. In neurotic repressions (i.e., repressions that "miscarry") nothing is settled, any more than primitive mythic operations with contradiction settle anything. In fact, the same kind of endless elaboration of the contradiction is observed in the unconscious that Lévi-Strauss demonstrates in primitive myth. The proliferating neurotic symptoms try to attenuate the contradiction.[81] The symptom represents both "the return of the repressed," partially gratified in disguised form, and the renewed operation of repression. And the contradiction spreads (just like Lévi-Strauss' myths), first in the unconscious, where it rapidly multiplies symbolic variations, and then in the proliferating double-faced symptoms which both repress and gratify the contradicted impulse. Freud compares the results of unsuccessful repression with the much more efficient operation of *negation*.[82] Negation consciously refutes a cognitive implication of a threatening impulse; the ego remains in touch with it and so is enriched by the diversity of content; meanwhile, energy is not locked up in unconscious contradiction, so it does not proliferate symbolic expressions. The matter is settled.[83]

Both primitive myth and Western logic are binary systems based on contradiction. But primitive contradiction is mere sustained apposition of contradictories, such as sacred and profane, whereas Western logic profanely settles the contradiction—with negation. Hence deduction (and not mere elaboration) is possible. Deduction based on negation, itself the outcome of the social experience of *polemos*, becomes a convention which increasingly builds negation into all our concepts: the not-I, not-here, not-now, not-this, sharp edges of our world. This logicalization of concepts considerably reduces the "participations," the "mystic identifications," the "vagueness" and the "affectual content" of the conventional frame of the wide-awake state and this lessens to some degree our susceptibility to magic. But outside the specialized languages of mathematics, logic or Rudolf Carnap, words are never entirely stripped of their haloes, transcendental horizons, echoes, ambiguities, contextual adaptations, pragmatic flexibilities, associations, shadows, ghosts or mysteries. They continue to refer to transcendent concepts and to have striking effects on them. So the possibility of verbal magic is still present. But its ability to sweep all before it, to turn on altered states of consciousness, to dissolve egos, to vaporize structures and to change entities is greatly reduced by the isomorphisms of our interlocking rationalized frames of reference. The logical objective frame of reference of the paramount reality, then, is a protection of the ego against the supernatural, just as personal magic once was; the necessity for ego-defense magic is in fact reduced thanks to this institutionalized protection.

In certain limited ways, then, magic's stereotyped compulsions do seem closer to the mechanical outcomes of logic than to the much freer language games of rhetoric or symbolic interaction. But logic will explain only certain aspects of magical scripts and their efficacy. And *illogicality* does not so much explain the efficacy of magic as the social process of logic explains the modern cognitive framework which tries to deny magic. It is almost as if logic were a competing class of mechanical mental formulae, rather than the genus that contains the species. As a social process, logic has been an engine machine-tooling categories for a physicalist worldview that nullifies magical formulae. So while there is a resemblance (a primitive might almost consider logic to be our deepest magic), magic will not fit into the framework of logic, for logic itself seems to be part of a competing cluster of conventions that substitute for magic.

We leave theoretical frames now to discuss raw empirical data which strongly suggest that magic arises from an *experiential* base, whether psychological, biological or paranormal. Since magic is conventional, in my view, I must refute these claims before proceeding.

4. Is Magic Perennially Refreshed From Some Experiential Base?

The problem remains: How does magic *work*? Evidence that it does "work" is abundant, even in modern society. Just consider the psychic curing of psychoanalysis, for example. Some decades ago Eysenck[84] attempted to cast doubt on whether it had any effects at all, using statistics to show that it only obtains a "cure" rate roughly equal to the rate of spontaneous remission of neurotic symptoms (approximately two-thirds in both cases). But more recent analyses by Allen Bergin[85] and Dorothy Tennov[86] suggest that these results are produced because all subjects are powerfully affected — adversely as well as favorably — by psychotherapy, with the percentage of those harmed subtracted from those markedly improved so the net improvement rate is about equal to the rate of spontaneous remission. Either way, something *happens*. But we do not have to confine ourselves to the metaphor of psychological curing. Millions of people have experiences of a much franker magical nature; their clamorous reports constantly assault the scientific frame and until recently were kept down only by a sustained effort of social denial.

We have to consider, therefore, the possibility that magical efficacy has some psychodynamic, biological or other experiential basis. There are, of course, innumerable theories deriving magic from some such base. Freud, for example, derived both magic and religion from psychopathology, characterizing religion as "the universal obsessional neurosis of humanity,"[87] and in another paper, hinted that neurotic symptoms are "magical ceremonies"[88] (that postpone the breakthrough of repressed desires by projecting them into the future). The word "magic" constantly appears in his texts and those of other analysts in discussing symptoms.[89] A detailed explanation of sympathetic magic, more sensitive than Frazer's, could perhaps be pieced together from Freud's many concepts, with "pathological" operations like displacement, projection, etc., taking the place of Frazer's principles of association. Paul Radin[90] also derives magic and religion from psychopathology. He is one of many (LaBarre, Róheim, etc.) who emphasize the role of "sick" individuals (the shamans) who exploit their symptoms. We need not dwell on which pathological processes various theorists of this stripe emphasize — whether obsessionalism (Freud), dreams (Róheim),[91] schizophrenia (La Barre),[92] "neurotic-epileptoid character" (Radin),[93] etc.

The possibility that magic derives from a psychological source seems weighty when we consider the large numbers of people who report personal experiences with borderline psychological states easily interpreted as "supernatural." Millions undergo frank, psychotic hallucinations at some time in their lives. Hundreds of thousands report experiences of extra-sensory perception. Thousands have "seen" ghosts; or think they have had experiences of precognition. Underlying these reports there seems to be a striking human capacity for altered states of consciousness in response to collective suggestion. In the "Latihan" ceremony of the currently imported Subod sect,[94] for example, people simply go into an auditorium once a week and immediately go into trance just because they expect to. A dozen schools of psychology show us in different ways our dizzying susceptibility to one another. The Festinger group show in cognitive dissonance studies[95] that individual perception cannot withstand group influence; Hadley Cantril's group used to do something similar.[96] The Bandura group who study "modeling" show that it is impossible *not* to learn behavior that we see emitted by others.[97] Hilgard[98] links the capacity for hypnosis with a "normal" tendency people have to go in and out of momentary light trances all day long in response to one another. Phenomena like *latah* and *olonism* in more primitive societies suggest how deep these propensities may be biologically.

Drugs seem to produce similar experiences, and Castenada,[99] Harner and others have suggested that magical efficacy and religious belief are both refreshed at this source. Suggestions that the familiar witch delusions (e.g., magic flight) may owe their worldwide similarities to a common drug experience are not new. At first the Spanish Inquisition tended to regard witchcraft as a delusion caused by the "inunction of drugs," according to Henry Charles Lea.[100] This may have been echoing an old belief, for medieval churchmen had speculated that the delusion was caused by the use of a "witch ointment," according to Harner.[101] Baroja finds passages in Petronius, Lucan, Horace and other classical authors that contain similar suggestions about a chemical basis for the experience.[102] Research into the drug origins of magic and religious experience is a small industry nowadays, with attempts to find the secrets of all mystery religions throughout history in a few common drugs. Thus Furst[103] thinks the "soma" of the Vedas was fly argeric, and maybe it was also used in the Eleusinian Mysteries. Allegro[104] suspects a drug cult at the heart of original esoteric Christianity. It is suggested that an origin in something as homogeneous as a few common drugs might help explain the universal sameness of so much magical phenomena the world over.[105]

Is there a special province of human experience from which magic naturally arises? Certainly it has often been noticed that magic makes reference to marginal states and marginal worlds. First, magic uses the symbolism of sacred drama, which is already a different frame of reference from work or social interaction. Second, even within the sacred, magic makes reference to especially marginal realms insofar as it is illicit, or anti-religion. Third, magic, even more than religion, has historically cultivated altered states of consciousness. Fourth, it is claimed that magic is related to real paranormal experiences, such as ESP and other phenomena not yet fully understood. Fifth, beyond that, is the possibility that magic depends on some real spiritual experience. We cannot in this investigation undertake to tell whether ESP or "spiritual" experiences are real; questions of this sort will be bracketed. But surely it will be helpful to show how many of these phenomena can be explained sociologically, and at least partly demystified by some strategic subtractions. First of all, magic may indeed manipulate some forces not yet fully understood—but presumably these will be one day claimed for science. Thus, magic may be partly constituted by undiscovered sixth senses or by remnants of old faculties no longer socially useful and screened out by our present social frame of reference. After all, we communicate in many more ways than we have yet discovered. Kinesics as a science of non-verbal gestures is relatively new. New signals are still being discovered. Changes in skin color, eye flicker pattern and voice level communicate reliably though unconsciously. ESP itself may consist of remnants of old social senses from a time when our ancestors were more tightly bound chemically as social groups. In other words, many of the "paranormal" realms of experience may be social or remnants of an older biosocial dimension.

It is also quite likely that religion itself helps *create* all this just by being extraordinarily sensitive to otherwise ineffable experiences. Even when latter-day science discovers some physical basis, such as the correlation of alpha waves with yoga states of meditation, these pointer readings are not immediately translatable into determinate "experience," nor are they even very definite biologically. Theta waves induced by biofeedback, for example, reduce tension in some people but seem to elicit anxiety in others; alpha emissions are not "healthy" or "good" or anything determinate by themselves (they seem, in fact, to correlate with underachievement in some studies of students).[106]

It is the very vagueness of all these "senses," states of mind and other experiences that undercuts any notion that magic *derives* from them—they have to be socially patterned even to be *noticed*. The vagueness of all sacred experience in general is notorious. Phenomenologies of the sacred such as that of Van der Leeuw[107] are extremely impressionistic; and categories to describe religious experience such as "the *mysterium*, the *tremendum* and the *fascinans*" of Otto[108] are extremely vague. So, too, is the "enthusiasm" of Ronald Knox[109] and other churchmen. Some American psychologists (William James,[110] Gordon Allport,[111] Knight Dunlap[112]), while themselves proposing superficial psychological theories of religion (as the servant of individual needs) have done a service in persuasively demonstrating that there is *no particular religious emotion*. Allport reminds us how many different attitudes or emotions have been named as "the" religious feeling by philosophers: e.g., Schleiermacher's[113] "dependence" or "taste for the infinite." James observes that there is "religious fear, religious awe, religious hope" and so on. The same stricture surely applies to magic which, by all reports, is less emotional than religion. In *Totemism* Lévi-Strauss insists that an explanation of a vague entity like magic in terms of a still vaguer phenomenon, such as anxiety for example, adds little to understanding.[114] Rather, he observes, magical rites are mechanical and prosaic and cannot be explained by an emotion; instead, they elicit emotions on cue. (In this statement, Lévi-Strauss is echoing Durkheim[115] and Mauss,[116] especially their writings about obligatory keening in funeral rites.)

The Oxford analysts have shown that numerous subjective states of feeling (e.g., "twinge of pain," "a pang of anxiety") are so vague as to be almost impossible to communicate; as a result, "painspeech" behavior, for example, does not so much communicate the experience of pain as substitute for "subjective pain behavior."[117] Many sacred or supernatural experiences are of this order, so vague themselves that they require language even to be structured subjectively, as the sorcerer's "surplus meaning" (Lévi-Strauss[118]) and "large vocabulary" (Eliade[119]) help clients control anxiety by giving it meaning. Some experiences that are not talked about much may remain relatively unstructured, but religion is on the opposite pole because it is talked about endlessly, or at least it used to be. While some experiences, such as orgasm, may remain relatively undelineated since people do not often discuss its qualities (at least not until recently), so that a highly developed "orgasm language" has not yet emerged, this is far from being the case with anything religious. Religious and magical experiences are among the vaguest and mildest experiences that human beings ever manage to notice in their streams of consciousness, but for millennia they have been patterned by a torrent of discussion. By agreement, experiences as mild as the glow felt after a good meal are described as "mountaintop experiences," and their varying qualities sensitively evaluated. The much sought mystical experience, for example, or currently fashionable mild states of meditation, are virtually talked into existence.[120] They can hardly be said to burst upon the scene and sweep all before them. The same considerations apply to the reporting, the discussion, the magnification and the collective overvaluing of all so-called paranormal experiences. They are more often the result of patient attention sharpened by traditional belief and ritual practice than the spontaneous cause of those institutions.

Even those theories which stress more normal psychological experiences as the source of magic—such as desire (Malinowski) or rewarded action (B.F. Skinner)—still have to face the problem of how raw experiences become organized and patterned into the rigid institutionalized scripts of magic. Malinowski can describe the eruption but not the patterning. His basic idea is that magic performances erupt out of wish or desire, like "follow-through" motions, and then are taken over and institutionalized as rituals that give confidence before uncertain actions.[121] But almost all the spells Malinowski actually reports are traditional and fixed; moreover, he observes, most magic is dull, mundane, practical,[122] leaving little trace of its original spontaneity and effervescent overflow. How, then, is the psychological eruption socially patterned?[123] Malinowski's explanation of the "institutionalization" of useful eruptive magic is also psychological rather than sociological. Institutionalization proceeds, he suggests, by a kind of natural selection, and what is selected is spells that fill individual needs. But this is still psychological and it does not tell how those social scripts rigidify. The explanation is at best quasi-sociological, like social psychology. There is little explanation of how these mere outbursts are culturally patterned. How do we get to those archaisms, strange language and rigid scripts that Malinowski noted elsewhere?[124]

It is common for basically psychological theories, which derive magic from some psychological "eruption" (normal, pathological or paranormal), to explain also the social patterning of this eruptive material through some equally psychological process. A great many of these explanations go in terms of what is loosely called "suggestion." Even when large numbers of people are involved the effects are still conceived psychologically—as common denominators in individual reactions in Le Bon's study of atomized crowds[125] or as summed individual reactions in Tarde's imitation studies.[126] Explanations in terms of imitation, modeling, suggestion, mass suggestion or crowd excitement are all psychological or social-psychological explanations. In such theories magic erupts on to the social scene as some kind of raw psychological experience; it is then patterned by some kind of psychological "mass drill" suggestion, modeling or what have you as if raw unpatterned data could be a model for behavior that is as precisely scripted as magic. "Magic fixes upon these...rudimentary rites and standardizes them into permanent traditional forms," Malinowski writes vaguely.[127] Imitation, modeling or suggestion could perhaps explain the perpetuation of the rite, not its original, rigid patterning.[128]

Suggestion is often invoked to explain the efficacy of medical magic; but once again this psychological category can give only a partial explanation. Jerome Frank[129] shows that the social assumptive frame, as an objective social fact, is more important than the suggestive actions of the curer, and E. Fuller Torrey[130] postulates assumptive frame and patient expectations as key elements in a cure (though both Frank and Torrey nonetheless manage to take it for granted and study suggestion as the strategic variable). A more penetrating study by Louis Rose[131] points to a more sociological explanation. Rose spent several decades studying faith cures. He reports seeing numerous faith cures shortly after the miracle; the patient is still sick or else the symptoms have come back, yet he still defines his experience as a cure and so do the other participants in his seance. This strongly suggests what we can now propose as a solution to the problem of explaining how magic works: i.e., it works because people agree it works.

How Magic Works: A Sociological Explanation

Theories which derive the origin and efficacy of magic from a normal, abnormal or paranormal *experiential* source, then, are psychologistic in a double-barrelled sense. First, they reduce a highly traditional, highly patterned institution to an alleged eruptive source which is private, psychological, raw and unstructured. Secondly, they imagine that this raw experience is then patterned and institutionalized by some process that is *also* a matter of individual psychology—such as "suggestion." What we need, to replace both processes, are two sociological processes. We need first a sociological explanation of the odd experiences that are often seen to "erupt" in new magical movements. And then we need a sociological explanation of how they are patterned. Our two sociological categories, to replace the psychological categories of "eruption" and "patterning by suggestion" will be: 1. Deviation via temporary *relaxation of the normal social frame* of orientation; and 2. overvaluation and patterning of the resulting experiences by *social agreement.* We will find that magic continually recycles itself back into religion and social consensus by this highly patterned and traditional process of systematically relaxing the frame to produce exceptional experiences and then interpreting and patterning them according to the traditional agreements of the culture.

A. Relaxation of the Social-Cognitive Framework

All these insistent phenomena—normal outbursts of wish or intention, pathological eruptions and paranormal demonstrations—can be raised to the level of sociological phenomena by considering them as departures from a social frame of reference. We can, as Berger demonstrates,[132] suppose that what is problematical is not deviation but normality, not chaos but order, and by this reversal remain within the realm of social facts instead of chasing reductive psychologisms. If we use what William James calls the frame of reference of "the paramount reality," or what Schutz[133] calls the "wide-awake state," or what Ronald Shor[134] calls "the generalized reality orientation" or even what Berger calls the "social nomos"[135] as our point of departure, "eruptions" that depart from it can be understood in terms of it, often as patterned in it or by it.

The normal cognitive frame is not merely a social construction; it is an abstract construction and extremely fragile. When the framework is even slightly disturbed, an "altered state of consciousness" supervenes, according to one current conceptualization.[136] It is extremely easy to alter the framework. I. First of all, the state of attention that sustains it can be altered, to use the summary of Arnold M. Ludwig,[137] 1. by reduction of exteroceptive or motor stimulation (e.g., sensory deprivation, highly patterned data as in a *ganzfeld*, boredom, highway hypnosis, hypnopompic or hypnogogic states, sleep, immobilization, etc.); 2. by increase of stimulation (excitement from overload, crowd contagion, ecstatic trance, inner turmoils, berserk, latah, whitico psychoses, acute schizophrenic states, etc.); 3. increased alertness or mental involvement (e.g., long watches, mental absorption, listening to charismatic speaker, etc.); 4. decreased alertness or relaxation of critical faculties (passive states like satori, samadhi, nirvana, cosmic consciousness, brown study, reverie, autohypnotic trances, music trance, etc.); 5. presence of somatological factors (drugs, hypoglycemia, dehydration, hyperventilation, temporal frontal lobe seizures, dreamy states, etc.). But all this can be reversed to emphasize the fragility of the social frame and the inputs constantly necessary to sustain it: adequate stimulation, adequate attention, adequate somatological basis, etc.

II. The frame can also be altered by social cognitive means, too, such as resocialization, brain-washing, inputs of occult "information," philosophy that challenges *Weltanschauung*, etc. Nor do the deeply sedimented "categories" underlying the frame prevent cognitive assault; experimental agreement-to-agree in small act-as-if groups, if sufficiently ghetto-ized as to avoid cognitive dissonance with the public frame, can quickly alter the frame of orientation. Deviant plausibility structures can easily be substituted in cognitive minorities, if they manage to isolate their members intellectually, as so many cults succeed in doing today. Thus psychology emphasizes the events that seem to alter the frame; but sociology emphasizes how hard it is to sustain this abstract social framework all the time.

The paramount reality is so fragile that any mere lapse of attention seems sufficient to produce a "*siddhi.*" Patanjali reported that the careful practice of Yoga would induce a veritable swarm of paranormal experiences and fantastic "magical powers" (the "*siddhis*") which the true yogin must decline as a dangerous distraction from his divine goal.[138] The introduction of hypnosis in the nineteenth century immediately led to paranormal experiences culminating in the spiritualist phenomenon.[139] Every yoga has its siddhis, it seems. Even free-association on a psychoanalyst's couch relaxes the frame enough to elicit such reports. About twenty-five years ago, before Albert Ellis showed how certain analysts were eliciting them by their own expectations, these were taken very seriously and produced numerous papers like those gathered in the volume edited by George Devereux.[140] Such experiences immediately came to Freud's attention and he kept an open mind about them.

The eruptions of unusual material are not only rationalized by the frame. They also have to be taken over and patterned, for the protection of the paramount reality. Religion has always done this. As the social frame becomes increasingly scientific and the religious frame seems increasingly to detach itself from it and become marginal, the religious frame seems by comparison, in a secular age, to be relatively more preoccupied with these phenomena. But this is in part because religion as the original frame of overarching reality had to protect itself against this chaos by inventing patterns to contain it. Part of the tension between magic and religion is due to the comparatively greater use that magic deliberately makes of frame-relaxing phenomena which religion attempts to control. Churches try to monopolize magic in part because they are always suspicious of these phenomena, even of mysticism. The framework of orientation of the religious worldview always remains closer to the frame of the paramount reality, which used to nest within it; whereas magic purposely cultivates paranormal phenomena in experimental act-as-if groups as draft legislation for the creation of frame alterations.

Since the paramount frame becomes increasingly abstract in a positivist age, "exceptional" experiences proliferate and it takes a considerable social effort to ignore them. Failing to recognize that they are in fact artifacts of frame myopias, society periodically undergoes a wave of pseudo-discoveries of these spurious remainders—especially when religion, chasing after the secular worldview to try to reencapsulate it within its overarching cosmos, so minimizes the paranormal as to divest itself of rationalizing formulae for containing these phenomena. When rationalizations for them are forgotten, they seem new and urgent, just as witches seemed to proliferate in African societies when the Europeans outlawed witch-finding ordeals. This may help explain those "sudden swings" from "rational" to "irrational" postures which Baroja[141] claims to see in the history of Christianity.

Apologists for the latest occult revival propound an explanation that is similar to this, but on different grounds. They too say that our frame of orientation is fragile—because it is "artificial." It does indeed require a constant effort of denial to screen out paranormal experiences—because these experiences are "real." Bonewitz[142] suggests that we have to fight so hard to resist such messages that we even do so physically, and he coins terms for our most typical resistances to ESP—e.g., "catapsi" (the static of muscle tightness); "splodging" (emotional bursts of anxiety); and "negapsi" (sending conflicting messages). (The use of involuntary muscle tightness to ward off messages from the unconscious has of course been thoroughly explored by psychoanalysts like Wilhelm Reich.[143]) Without such efforts, the spirits, the angels, the archetypes or whatever will get through to us. The occultists are certainly right about the narrowness of this amblyopic frame, and about how much it screens out—but the forces they imagine to be struggling to get through were actually invented as encapsulating archetypes to protect the frame in past cultures.

For the objective frame does not merely screen out the paranormal; it defines and takes over some of it. The patterns it creates to contain these attacks produce the cultural archetypes about the paranormal that later help elicit them. For what is real is the abstract, socially-constructed frame, not the chaos outside it—it is in the frame itself (or previous historical versions of it) that the archetypes were formed. By themselves, subjective experiences of frame reduction are experiences of confusion, terror, disorientation or mere vagueness.[144] They become draft legislation for a debate on the constitution only as they are socially patterned. Without social patterning, many paranormal experiences would remain as inarticulate as attacks of indigestion. Most of those we do hear about, however, are stamped with ages-old archetypes, originally invented by sacred institutions that sought to control these experiences. They are revived from century to century by publishing booms. Pathological experiences are adopted into religion as a way of neutralizing them, and in some cases they become positive cults within religion. Some cults make use of carefully patterned, strictly controlled paranormal experiences to help confirm collective belief in the existence of a supernatural realm. This is especially likely to occur in "crisis cults" (in the La Barre sense[145]) or "possession and protest cults" (in the sense of I.M. Lewis[146]). In these cases the sacred cosmos projected by a religion will indeed differ from the paramount reality, for it is the projection of a subjugated or disadvantaged subculture. Magic is always an important element in protest cults. Ecstatic or ritualized drug experiences may serve to confirm the existence of a realm important to the protest theodicy, as Gerald Weiss shows.[147] Thus memory of the ancient explanations religion used to rationalize the common experience of logolalia, kept alive in books, presents assimilation cults like the Pentacostalists with a social pattern that is releasing for groups undergoing acculturation and having difficulty with a new language. Erika Bourguignon,[148] looking at the Murdock 1967 Ethnographic Atlas, shows that 90 per cent of the societies in it institutionalize the cultivation of such states of consciousness. And it is well known how many seemingly cooler and steady religious institutions are simply outgrowths of the earlier patterning by religions of such challenges.[149] And of course these experiences are not just patterned after they occur—scripted procedures come to pattern *expectations* of their occurrence and hence to *elicit* them.

No account of how paranormal or "magical" experiences are generated through relaxation of the frame is complete without a further explanation of how this experience is patterned. This brings us to the next point:

B. The Agreement to Agree

The notion of "agreeing to agree" comes from the extreme Wittgenstein of the *Remarks on the Foundation of Mathematics.*[150] It is inadequate to characterize Wittgenstein as a "conventionalist" on logic and mathematics, as Dummett[151] does. Wittgenstein's position is sometimes even more extreme. For he not only asserts that we agree on conventional definitions when we do math or logic and on how they work; we must also agree continuously as we go along that we *are* following a rule (when this cannot be proven) and, when we finish, that we *have* followed a rule. And more than that, we agree that we *have* agreed, and so on.[152] Later he said that mathematicians are people who agree much more than other scientists, and that if they did not agree that much they would not be called mathematicians.[153] We not only agree about rules, we agree about how we weight them. Rules about the categories are like the incest taboo: we weight them very heavily. Our agreement to agree on such matters is one of our deepest social contracts. Joseph Cowan[154] observes that Wittgenstein thus does to deduction what Hume did to induction. He means that deduction works because we say it does, and we have to say so for it entails the minimal essential agreements we need to make about the very possibility of agreeing in order to communicate with one another at all. But communication is always problematical. We literally do not hear what other people say half the time, and simply agree tacitly to suppose that we did hear. Communication does not break down completely only because it is continuously papered over by such agreements.

We can borrow this powerful concept and use it to explain how strange experiences that erupt when the cognitive frame weakens are patterned. They are patterned, defined, institutionalized and overvalued—*by agreement*. The experiences are so varied and subjective that we have to agree that we are agreeing. We even have to agree that anything at all has happened. That is basically how magic works; it systematically weakens the frame to produce some vague experience, and then the small experimental act-as-if magical group *agrees* to define this experience as significant and momentous.

We can demonstrate agreement to agree at work behind seeming psychological processes like modeling and suggestion. Even something as biological-seeming as hypnosis is revealed, by recent research, to be the outcome of latent social contracts, of role-playing according to patterns of behavior stamped in by tradition. We can consider this research as a critical test of the paradigm: Hypnosis is certainly an example of group-altered states of consciousness that are produced deliberately, systematically and socially; the particular milieu in this case is the scientific laboratory or the doctor's consulting room (or the theater), and the experience is meticulously patterned by the language, lore and expectations accumulating there. Trance phenomena, in fact, were largely lost in the West by virtue of not possessing any systematic patterning whereby they could come to official attention, *until* they were repackaged in this new "medical" pattern. Now a line of inquiry begun by White's paper in 1941[155] has led to the hypothesis that hypnosis is a social drama involving agreed-upon roles. White viewed hypnosis as the result of two intertwined processes: 1. "goal-directed striving" which, 2. takes place in an altered psychological state. But he emphasized the first. He defined hypnosis as meaningful, goal-directed striving, its most general goal being *to behave like a hypnotized person*, as this is continuously defined by the operator and understood by the subject. Followers of White tended to emphasize the "goal striving" at the expense of his second factor, the altered state of consciousness. Sarbin,[156] for example (1950), put White's theory into social psychology language, with White's "striving" now called "role-taking." Sarbin viewed even the deepest hypnotic phenomena as a kind of "act-as-if" behavior, which is not a sham but involves the submergence of the self so deeply into the role playing that the subject can no longer perceive the situation in any other way. Some investigators have considered this to be the core of the hypnotic experience. This has been much criticized. But the important point is that many if not most psychologists and social psychologists who study hypnotism nowadays represent this phenomenon of mutual agreement on roles as at least an important element in the experience. Even Ernest Hilgard, the skeptical, extremely empiricist doyen of hypnosis studies, criticizes only the essentialism of those who say that hypnosis "is *only* role playing."[157] There really is an altered state of consciousness as well, he insists; subjects report feelings of spinning, dizziness, floating, etc. The evidence seems to support Hilgard. The "induction" phase of hypnotism does seem to be important; it cannot be explained away as mere initial cues for role playing; it does seem to center on the induction of an altered state of consciousness. During it consciousness blurs; then it is reestablished with a different kind of clarity and "the hypnotist inside." Hilgard's conclusion is that hypnotic induction furnishes conditions for transition to a "hypnotic state" which is characterized only in part by "heightened suggestibility" (i.e., role playing); there is also "trance" as an altered state of consciousness.

Now in recent years an attempt has been made by Ronald E. Shor[158] and others to build on the role-playing findings of White and Sarbin while also incorporating an adequate social explanation of trance itself, instead of denying it. The initial formulation of Shor was that hypnotism consisted of two elements: role-playing and trance, and he formulated trance as a sociological phenomenon by conceptualizing in terms of the weakening of the objective frame of reference, just as we have done. In Shor's theory, which because of its history we might call the "White-Sarbin-Shor hypothesis," hypnotic phenomena can be seen as the outcome of the two processes we are discussing—1. weakening of the frame, and 2. patterning of resulting phenomena through mutual agreement (or "role playing" as Shor puts it). Shor stresses that the frame, which he calls "the generalized reality orientation," is extremely fragile. Mere drowsiness, inattention or distraction causes sections of it to blur or erase themselves. The hypnotist avails himself of this vulnerability to erase parts of the frame during hypnotic induction. Having done so, he can then develop his own modified frame, in which he is central. With all attention focused on the hypnotist, the new role-playing game becomes the only orientation possible in the distorted frame; the subject then experiences whatever phenomena are suggested to him because it is now extremely important for him to play the role of a hypnotized subject.

Shor insists that the generalized reality orientation fades easily and does not retain its regnancy without constant effort. Hilgard supposes that there are so many ordinary experiences in everyday life that can weaken the frame and so many gestures and statements that make other people more susceptible to suggestion that we are constantly inducing mild hypnotic states in one another by coaxing, role-defining speech ("You, as a successful executive, would probably agree...") and frame-weakening stimuli (drinks, music, the boredom of our company, etc.). Shor emphasizes that the generalized reality orientation develops slowly through life; that it is made up of numerous processes such as "the self" (we would say "categories") that have long social histories (the Durkheim school showed this), and also long personal histories as these categories are structured in socialization (as Piaget showed).

The White-Sarbin-Shor hypothesis offers a schema for handling the relationship of all strongly affectual, abnormal or paranormal experience to scripted magical symbolism—i.e., "weakening the frame" followed by "role-playing" about the results (I prefer to say "agreement to agree").[159] If even a strikingly "psychological" phenomenon like hypnosis can be thus conceptualized sociologically, then perhaps all the alleged individual experiential bases for magic can be uprooted and grafted on to the sociological institution itself: When the fragile social frame is relaxed, the strange experiences that result are patterned by traditional agreements just as hypnosis is patterned by playing the traditional role of a hypnotized subject.

And there does indeed exist abundant field evidence showing that, whenever a magical rite makes use of paranormal experiences in its clients, it usually elicits them in the first place, and then systematically patterns the form they take, by agreement. The shaman or therapist interprets the experience or, better still, gets his clients to do so within a paradigm: the important thing is to get mutual agreement about what has happened. In psychotherapy and brain washing, this takes the form of having the subject himself produce his own interpretation but do so in the light of an archetype.[160] In Yoga, the content of the meditation is rigidly patterned by the traditional instruction in the techniques. Mystic experiences, both sought for and spontaneous, are patterned by a long tradition. In the ecstatic sects that break out on the peripheries of some religions, similar templates are always priorly available. The people may be said to be perennially awaiting a messiah and to have a precise tradition for evaluating any charismatic bids that are made for the job. Ecstatics always develop *traditional* symptoms; they would be misunderstood and rejected otherwise. Tradition also ordains how the person who cures his own seizures will cure others, and what relationship will then ensue between the curer and his patients. Usually this takes the form of "analysis interminable,"[161] a pattern found in almost every society. The core phenomenon is a group of people who continuously agree to agree about what is happening, how the symptoms are defined, what they mean and how they are "cured."

Finally, we have some very vivid examples of agreement as the basis of patterning even of drug magic and drug cults. Harner[162] and his associates demonstrate how the shaman talks to and leads the patient all during the drug seance, telling him what he is experiencing; he and the client also discuss it afterwards and pattern it. Siskind[163] similarly demonstrates that when the Sharanahua Indians of Eastern Peru use the hallucinogenic ayajuasca the shaman talks to the users about myth and belief, structuring their visions with songs all during the drug seance itself. There is a different song for each disease and for each thing they are supposed to see. Without the songs they just see snakes. If they saw something that was not in the system, Siskind observes, they could not communicate it and so the experience would fade. In the same collection, Kenneth Kensinger[164] tells how the Peruvian Cashinahua, using banisteriopsis, talk all during the experience and validate it collectively afterwards; as a result they see the same things. Both Kensinger and Castenada[165] speak of how the Indians regard these hallucinations as a form of "knowledge"; the hallucinations are "learned" through a process of group agreement; experiencing them means that one "knows" in a very noetic way the fundamental images of the group's *Weltan-*

schauung. Castenada's analysis of how the teachings of Don Juan work is entirely consistent with the theory that magic obtains its effects through agreement. In his "structural analysis" of this Indian system of "knowledge," his main point is that with the aid of an "ally," i.e., a drug, a "man of knowledge," i.e., a shaman, inducts an initiate into this experience by means of a "rule." The rule consists of agreeing on interpretation, and so a realm of "non-ordinary reality" is built up and corroborated by what he calls "a special consensus." The special consensus is the agreement to agree of a small group undergoing the experience, in this case two people. Don Juan accomplished the patterning 1. by having the student tell his experiences; 2. by providing a system to interpret them; 3. by using the different properties of different drugs to guide special consensus about non-ordinary reality.

Magical seances sometimes need to agree not merely about what is happening, but also *that* something is happening. This is strikingly the case where the effect is nothing more than the institution of a new state of being. In ordinary life we go in and out of many such states, initiated by performative sentences and validated by agreement. The state of being "in love," for example, is more than just the "overvaluation of the sex object" that Freud imagined; it is also a social state which, like war, exists upon being declared. We usually agree to sustain one another's performatives, and the proper negative response to a declaration of love is to say "But I don't love you," rather than to refuse to agree to the existence or possibility of such a magical state.[166] The participants at a magical or religious rite may feel nothing whatsoever; but they all agree to the possibility that the rite may provoke some feelings in some of them, or that it has moved someone, somehow, somewhere. This is one of the many reasons for the importance of ecstatics in magic and religion. They "witness." They serve to demonstrate that something can happen.

Our agreements about what is happening in magic are turned back on normal, abnormal and paranormal experience to pattern it from the second it is elicited, and indeed to elicit it. In this sense agreement rather than weakening the frame is the more important process. Agreement can work even when the frame is not successfully weakened, even when nothing whatsoever happens. We can all agree that nonetheless the spirit has been raised. Even when an experiential base is involved, patterning begins before the experience. We agree beforehand on what is going to happen; then we agree that it is happening; and our agreement that it is happening helps make it happen.

Whenever "new" magics erupt, they often consist of very old scripts of agreement borrowed from antiquarian sources (e.g., Vedic mantras) that are edited into a new form to elicit the phenomena in small act-as-if groups offering draft legislation for a change in the categories to the great society. The members agree to agree that something is happening, and hope that this will cause something to happen. It is not important whether or not the individual participants believe in it. It is well known that magicians themselves are skeptical about magic: this is part of the antinomian atmosphere of magic, part of the irreverence, the *détour-*

nement (Huvelin), the "compulsion and doubt" (Stekel). They will nonetheless be impressed by the supraindividual phenomenon of everyone testifying that it is indeed happening, even though they know that this is part of the script.

It is well known that people "play at" many of these practices, but playing leads to involvement. Ellul[167] has shown that a particular occult fad may begin as a *blague*, with a film that satirizes vampirism, diabolism or magic, for example; but then the films become more serious as a lucrative magic public is recreated to which the industry panders. Or take the current interest in astrology: Truzzi has shown that the vast majority of those who follow the astrology columns are not merely skeptical; they actually say that they do not believe in astrology.[168] And yet it influences them, and they influence one another, if only by creating a public and an occult publishing boom. Adorno[169] has vividly demonstrated that even playing at such an interest changes one's attitudes toward reality. When the astrologer Madame Soleil appeared on French private radio in 1970, this was considered a novelty; but suddenly she started getting 25,000 letters and phone calls a day, and a new vogue of astrology swept France, according to a French public opinion study.[170]

Every new magic, every tedious revival of some fragment of mantra-tantra or old rite torn from a dead religion is an attempt to achieve mild subjective states of consciousness which are then overvalued by mutual agreement within an act-as-if group bidding for substitute status and offering "draft legislation" for the repeal of some categories. The descriptions of what is supposed to be happening are built right into the scripted action itself. Nowadays these new magics often have a "scientific" cast. A scientific establishment which is itself based on an agreement-to-agree (and whose agreements are constantly renewed by "proof" and by "experiment," two new ways of voting that agreement) is lately showing itself to be a pushover before this revival and is actually offering it new language for patterning agreement. Thus, for example, it is "discovered" that the yogins had something after all, because Yoga turns on the alpha wave. As if *that* "pointer reading" meant anything more definite than what yogins who read Patanjali used to agree was happening in their stupors. What, after all, is the significance of an alpha wave? Nothing very definite; but the experiments which demonstrate its presence become part of the magical process in which people agree to agree on overvaluing the significance of these mild experiences.

What do the members of these act-as-if groups hope to accomplish with their radical "legislative" proposals? Several things: 1. The scripts themselves define anticipated personal benefits. These include all kinds of magical states of well-being, but many have as their common denominator some increment in personal social power. Crow[171] and other occultists have admitted that the aim of magic is power. 2. The act-as-if group itself provides prestige and substitute status. 3. The "draft legislation" carries the message of "Say it isn't so" to the cruel world; it aims at repealing large sections of reality. At the same time it is in part antinomian, antisocial and vengeful against the indifferent great society. But in the end it does not matter whether anyone actually feels the experiences or obtains any benefit; if the scripts are read together and more people come to play the act-as-if game, then they are all going to wind up on the cover of *Time* magazine. If wild science cooperates these groups may be able to negotiate a society-wide agreement about changes in the categories. At first, the new agreement may be minimal, a mere matter of style. We might say that a new agreement already exists that takes this form: it is now considered ignorant, "Jesuitical," closed-minded and old-fashioned to be *too* skeptical about the occult. Black holes have punctured our four-dimensional coordinate systems and a new worldview threatens to emerge that might legitimize the magical sciences. Magic, moreover, is increasingly vested and funded. A new consensus is emerging that positivism somehow leads to My Lai and therefore must be wrong. While we have not yet altered the categories of time and space, legislation has at least reached committee stage that would require us to agree to listen more attentively to all attempts to do so. The new agreement legitimizes the sale of occult books; old scruples are neutralized and reputable publishers put their imprint on books that would have been crimes in ancient Rome.[172] The new legislation, in effect, makes us all part of an experimental society-wide group which is going to "keep an open mind about" all occult phenomena. This means that we are all going to allow the frame to weaken more often, and we are going to consider patterning any resulting phenomena with the self-inflating language of the occult.

Some observers, like Truzzi, are so impressed with the play-acting quality of this mass involvement that they minimize its significance. To Truzzi it represents something like the final abreaction of the spooks; playing with the occult will lay it to rest at last. But this is not what is happening at all: instead we are all agreeing to agree that these things may be possible and useful and should be elicited and studied. Truzzi forgets that previous occult revivals (e.g., in Greece and Rome) had many of the same qualities of fad and game-playing initially. There is, however, one sense in which he could be partly right. The categories undergirding the rational frame of the paramount reality are today rooted deeply in society as never before. They are rooted not merely in a science that gets results, but a technology on which the whole society depends. Marcuse and Habermas speak of the "embedding" of this rationality as undiscussible ideology in the technological infrastructure of the society, and this might protect us from the goblins. One can almost detect, in the current game-playing with the occult, a feeling of freedom from danger, a sense that one can play with strange phenomena without inviting the Valkyries to return, because this time the technostructure makes this impossible.

But the vulnerability of modern science itself to the occult suggests that this confidence may be ill founded. That the two are not absolutely antithetical is revealed by Wittgenstein's analysis of how agreeing-to-agree works in science too. Wittgenstein develops a remarkable analysis of deductive proof and inductive experiment as devices of agreement. Modern science is based less and less on direct observation (the phenomenological revolt had little influence outside of psychology and philosophy) and increasingly on formal "proofs" and "experiments." Wittgenstein's main point is that a "proof" is a "picture" of an experiment, and that an experiment is a pedagogical ritual to engineer agreement. Experiments are indeed pedagogical devices in part. John Herman Randall, Jr.[173] tells how, among the Averroest Aristotelians on the eve of the Renaissance, experiments and proofs were thought of as teaching devices as much as methods of investigation. We forget that experiments are used this way much of the time. Most science courses in the curriculum have laboratory hours in which the science is taught by means of its experiments. But even new experiments are pedagogical; they are offered as draft referenda and are voted in only as they are reproduced again and again in different laboratories around the world. It is well known that Mannheim was criticized on this ground by Popper after he attempted to extend his sociology of knowledge to the realm of science. Science transcends the sociological influences that determine other ideas, Popper said, because science is a body of men engaged in checking one another's experiments. But isn't that precisely a social organization producing an idea? Popper proved himself a better sociologist of knowledge; he had revealed the particular social articulation of that organized intersubjectivity which we call scientific "objectivity." It is a social process of agreement.

> This is a demonstration for whoever acknowledges it as a demonstration. If anyone *doesn't* acknowledge it...then he has parted company with us even before it comes to talk... This is use and custom among us, or a fact of our natural history.[174]

New legislation is produced by a new experiment; it is endlessly repeated and if it not only works but fits existing scientific paradigms it is gradually agreed upon, the various stages of "hypothesis," "theory," "law," etc., being like the stages of a bill going through Congress. Once the "bill" finally passes, the rule is a law and the experiment that legislated it is packaged to become part of the curriculum for all science students, who endlessly repeat it. The teacher-guided student group performing the experiment reproduces the social structure of the magical seance. Outside of the laboratory, deductive proofs are used which cite the experiment as a picture. And common speech arguments, carried on within the frame of the paramount reality, cite these proofs and these experiments as ultimate authorities, more ultimate today than scripture. Why then are we surprised as the thing unfolds? Because as part of the game we agree to psych ourselves.

> Because I alternatively look at what is shown as essential and as non-essential... because I think of these properties alternatively as external and internal. Because I alternatively take something as a matter of course and find it noteworthy. (p. 26, *Ibid.*)

Our scientific agreements create the basic "grammatical rules" by which we structure reality. The proof itself is said to be following certain laws and it may, but it does not really have to if people will only agree that it does; any more than Soviet dialecticians are necessarily obeying the laws of dialectical materialism when they change their minds and then claim that it was inevitable. A new proof or a new experiment is a draft for a new social contract which is put up for approval. If there is agreement, then it becomes a training device for eliciting continuous agreement that there is agreement. This agreement will go so far as to include a willingness to say we are following the new law even when we are not. And that will not be hard, for as Paul Feyerabend has demonstrated, each new law will train us to see data a certain way. Today, there is even a new form of demonstration, mid-way between a proof and an experiment—namely, a statistical test—where everything is done on paper so that science as a step-by-step process of sheer agreement is quite transparent. In certain fields, like psychology, "mental experiments" or experiments done on paper sometimes replace acted-out experiments.

It is true that science in our time makes solid discoveries which appear to validate its agreements. But the possibility of creating instead edifices of ideology through magical dramas that engineer agreement remains in those sciences which are less in touch with definite evidence and tend to produce self-fulfilling results. This is not so much the case, interestingly, with sociology, despite the usual claims about "too many variables" and so on, for sociology relies more on free observation and free reasoning than on mechanical proofs and scripted experimental seances. As Yogi Berra once said, "You can observe an awful lot just by looking." But there is one social science, a science which denies that it is social, which does sometimes practice magic in the sense of using experiment and proof in mechanical, circular, self-confirming ways to create social agreements about alleged subjective phenomena in bids for social power. This is academic experimental psychology, and it is worth a minute to examine it to show how close a formal modern science can still come to magic:

In psychology, experiment replaced direct observation very early; today great reliance is placed on mental experiments and on statistical tests: Step by step we agree to agree: on confidence limits, null hypothesis, etc. The thing can be done after the experiment, after the fact, or even without experiment, with mere oral instructions or other short cuts. And the results are seldom published if the real hypothesis is not proven. As experiments are increasingly designed by philosophy-of-science logic and formulated with statistical tools, they increasingly resemble mathematical proofs. But in the end there is not as much agreement as in math, because findings, being so often artifacts of concrete experiments, are different with different experimental apparatuses and even with different experimental animals.[175] Bertrand Russell has noticed that experimenters seem to pick organisms which confirm their theories: To demonstrate insight, the gestalt psychologists used apes; to demonstrate trial-and-error, Skinner used rats and pigeons. Hull used duller, blinder rats than did the cognitive theorist Tollman. There is also a fit between apparatus and theory: mazes to prove proprioceptive-muscular guidance of action; T-maze choice-points to show cognitive choice; Skinner boxes to demonstrate operants. More frank than many, Skinner has revealed that his discovery of operants emerged from his apparatus and his contingencies of reinforcement from experimenter convenience (he was low on pellets when he tried "periodic reinforcement"). This suggests artifact as well as serendipity. Skinner has said that previous experiments must be done again in Skinner boxes to be accurate and comparable with his own results; mazes are too complex. So the schools maintain their adherents by having students repeat the packaged experiments using their apparatus and animals. The designs of many of these experiments are too "systematic" rather than "representative" (Brunswick). Thus some have shown that Pavlov's dogs were practically tortured to get the desired results (Merleau-Ponty[176]), that the tortured random behavior which confirms trial-and-error theories is just an artifact of restricting an animal; it is sick behavior performed in an unnatural environment (Lorenz). The fetish of experiments leads to an excessively narrow empirical base for the science: there is no use of sampling in choice of subjects or design; there is constant extrapolation from one species to others. Experiments usually cannot be confirmed outside the school that sticks to these narrow methods, so in psychology, experiments become *mainly* pedagogical devices. The restrictions of systematic design produce results that do not explain normal behavior but perhaps the procedures create abnormal behavior, for laboratory behavior tends to replace normal behavior as a self-fulfilling prophecy through the transformation of the world into a psychology laboratory in which the ambit of stimulus and response is restricted.

Interestingly, moreover, parts of psychology have in recent years become "wild sciences" (Roszak) producing unusual effects (such as biofeedback) which resemble the traditional products of magic. In these social dramas experiment as a pedagogical device takes the place of magical scripted seances in engineering an act-as-if group to agree to agree; the product may be some mild subjective state which is then defined and overvalued as part of the script. From pedagogical experiment to experiment, from proof to proof and from small group session to session, psychology as a cognitive minority recruits new members and offers new magics: abreaction sessions, sexual rituals, techniques of propaganda, interrogation devices. And even when the artificial S-R's of the laboratory do not really work in practice, it does not really matter: much of applied psychology consists of an agreement to agree that applied psychology works. In the end, insofar as any of it works, it works because people are made increasingly to behave like laboratory animals—or like primitives at a magical seance. Since the elaborate models that guide the experiments cannot be empirically falsified at their core by means of the apparatus and design from which they spring, models themselves can be modified only by logical criticism, which further deflects science from observation. Such a science becomes a kind of philosophy of science. Operationalism itself is ultimately solipsistic and subjective, and operationalism as philosophy of science comes to replace real psychological theory which was itself premature. Such metatheory-theory-experiment systems are social systems that provide almost invulnerable higher-order ideological defences for professions, institutions and practices in the real world fostering unreason and unfreedom through magical devices for manipulating, derogating and screening people in more and more strategic areas of life. (For example, some New York gynecologists once required the dubious MMPI "personality test" to test parenthood suitability before they would treat infertility.)

Contrary to the conventional Hegel-Frazer-Weber formula which portrays man historically evolving away from magic toward science, Arthur Clarke,[177] Louis Pauwels[178] and others offer suggestive evidence that scientific advance can create new magics and stimulate a revival of old magic. After all, rapid scientific advance breaks old paradigms in the Thomas Kuhn sense[179]—and the transitional period of paradigm fluidity is a social analogue of the relaxation of the frame of the paramount reality in an individual! Everything seems up for grabs, and until timespace is restructured there is always a chance for the goblins to break through. Beyond that, in every age, some sciences *are* doing magic. Psychology today is the source of much of what Roszak[180] calls the "wild sciences" that feed the current occult boom: para-psychology, dream research, "altered states of consciousness," hypnotic age regression, biofeedback and the like.

We can conclude discussion of "agreement" with an analogy to the "synthetic a priori" of Kant. Modern logical philosophy declares that no such thing can exist: all propositions must be either "analytical" (true by definition) or "synthetic" (empirical and hence provable or "falsifiable").[181] Anything else is "meaningless" or metaphysical nonsense.[182] So there can be no "synthetic a priori," no empirically derivable statement which is somehow also true logically, metaphysically or a priori. But whether or not such statements can exist in logic, the fact is that they *do* exist socially, because human beings make them up all the time and live by them. I would like to call them "synthe*sized* a prioris."[183] Wittgenstein broached something similar in the *Tractatus,*[184] when he observed that certain of physics' most basic laws were really strategies. Later, the *Philosophical Investigations*[185] pursued this in logic. Specifically, Wittgenstein observed that we synthesize universals not out of particulars or essences but out of arbitrary taxonomic arrangements of "family resemblances." C. I. Lewis[186] called something similar "pragmatic a prioris." They work by agreement to agree on them. We might say that something analogous happens in magic through the process of agreement in defining exceptional experiences systematically produced by the weakening of the objective reality frame. In general, the sacred as a whole is renewed this way, both in religious and in magical rites.

The idea of calling these operations "synthetic a prioris" occurs to Hubert and Mauss, who continued their preoccupation with finding a possible logic in magic all through their essay. These speculations culminate in their none-too-clear ruminations about how magic works like a synthetic a priori.[187] But it seems to me that what they really mean is that it works by agreement.[188] In short, the idea of a synthetic a priori (or, as I prefer to call it, a synthe*sized* a priori) shows how the two processes of "weakening the frame" and "agreement to agree" work together to provide the social experiential base that renews the belief on which magical efficacy depends. Magic laws are a priori inductions from exceptional situations which are regularly and mechanically produced with the help of expectations and definitions engendered by those very a priori laws. Magic works by authorized individuals performing syllogism-like operations on traditional collective ideas which, because collective, come to individual minds as synthetic a prioris. And all of this in turn is embedded in the traditions of virtually every known society. The a prioris are not only to all practical intents unfalsifiable (as Evans-Pritchard showed); they actually get abundant confirmation, for the essence of the whole procedure is to agree to it.

In conclusion: Magical symbolic action achieves its effects through the traditionally patterned agreement of the participants.[189] But where do the agreements magic uses come from? They may be renewed by the results magic produces, but most are not born there. Magic does not resemble small group discussion or putting ideas up for a vote. Most typically, the magician runs the whole show and the spectators just watch. We have seen that the agreements magic uses are "conventional" or "traditional"; they precede the rite and seem to derive from the community as a whole, whereas magic in practice is two or three people pursuing private ends. The suspicion arises that magic borrows or expropriates something, that it makes use of, manipulates and channels the social power implicit in agreements, conventions and traditions that have already been forged elsewhere. In the next postulate we will show that magic borrows its agreements, along with the scripts that embody them—from religion.

Notes

1. Frazer supposed that religion arose because men came to recognize that magic did not work, a non sequitur he never clarified. Marett supposed the reverse, that religion arose *because magic worked* and so engendered the supernatural beliefs that underpin religion. Either way, both were saying that religion arose for credential reasons from magic, which is the opposite of the Durkheim position: that magic arises from religion because the supernatural worldview of religion makes belief in magical efficacy possible. Contrast Durkheim's *Elementary Forms...* (London, 1954), pp. 42–47; 361–362, with J.G. Frazer, *The Golden Bough* (abridged ed., N.Y., 1960) ch. 4, pp. 56–68; and R.R. Marett, *The Threshold of Religion* (London, rev. ed., 1914), ch. 1, (title essay).

2. And it must be a sociological approach, for magic is a sociological matter par excellence. It is an individual but highly traditional manipulation of social-consensual assumptions, and its whole power comes from society.

3. George Herbert Mead, *Mind, Self and Society* (Chicago, 1934), cf. pp. 154–156.

4. Charles Horton Cooley, *Human Nature and the Social Order* (N.Y., 1964), cf. pp. 168–210.

5. Herbert Blumer, *Symbolic Interactionism, Perspective and Method* (Englewood Cliffs, N.J., 1969), cf. ch. 3, pp. 78–89.

6. Peter McHugh, *Defining the Situation* (Indianapolis, 1968).

7. Cf. Harold Garfinkel, *Studies in Ethnomethodology* (Englewood Cliffs, N.J., 1967); Roy Turner, ed., *Ethnomethodology* (Baltimore, 1974); Aaron V. Cicourel, *The Social Organization of Juvenile Justice* (N.Y., 1968). Such studies portray the frame itself as so subject to immediate ongoing interactive effects as to seem "magical"—in the weak sense. Such discoveries converge with those of Edelman, Boorstin, Barthes, Ellul, on what might be called the "magical" texture of the modern world.

8. Goffman might be said to show us how, in ordinary interaction, people *try* to achieve spell-like, *fixating*, magical effects. Thus they mystify their objectives; they struggle to control definitions. In *The Presentation of the Self in Everyday Life* (N.Y., 1957) most of the

struggles are still fair fights in free interaction. In *Behavior in Public Places* (N.Y., 1963) attempts of actors to achieve positions of advantage are constantly challenged. In *Strategic Interaction* (Philadelphia, 1969), more conflictful struggles for definition are described; and in *Interaction Ritual* (N.Y., 1967) the beginnings of deference and differential distribution of power to define a situation are studied. In *Stigma* (Englewood Cliff, N.J., 1963) and *Asylums* (N.Y., 1957), we do see the effect of definitions that stick and sediment as constituted action.

9. Georges Gurvitch, "La Magie, La Religion et le Droit," in *La Vocation Actuelle de la Sociologie* (Paris, 1963), vol. 2.

10. R.R. Marett, *The Threshold of Religion* (London, 1914), ch. 1.

11. Kenneth Burke, *The Rhetoric of Religion* (Berkeley & Los Angeles, 1970), pp. v-vi, 12, etc.

12. Burke, *A Rhetoric of Motives* (Cleveland and N.Y., 1962), pp. 564–566.

13. This is a familiar misconception about magic, as we have seen. In truth, it is a very common magical form to address things in order to communicate with people.

14. Jerome D. Frank, *Persuasion and Healing* (Baltimore, 1961), e.g. ch. 6.

15. In an ideal, "healthy" primitive society, members may experience religious rites in a participative, creative way, never doing the ritual the same way twice, thereby renewing and creating the social *nomos* through their flexible performances. This is a kind of unalienated personal "magic," at least in the weak sense. In Rousseau's ideal of direct democracy (*The Social Contract*) this primitive continuous creation is recovered mechanically, by constitutional arrangements. Rousseau used a "natural ideal type," Periclean Athens, for his model. Rhetoric was the educational preparation of citizens for this participation. Cf. Mark Van Doren, *The Liberal Arts* (N.Y., 1943), W.W. Capes, *University Life in Ancient Athens* (N.Y., 1922), ch. 3, pp. 53–95.

16. Selections from Aristotle's *Rhetoric*, in Dudley Bailey, ed., *Essays on Rhetoric* (N.Y., 1965), pp. 55–83.

17. Jürgen Habermas, *Knowledge and Interest; Theory and Practice; Toward A Rational Society; Legitimation Crisis*, etc.

18. Trent Schroyer, *The Critique of Domination* (N.Y., 1973).

19. Claus Mueller, *The Politics of Communication* (N.Y., 1973).

20. Albrecht Wellmer, *Critical Theory of Society* (N.Y., 1974).

21. Herbert Marcuse, *One-Dimensional Man* (Boston, 1964).

22. Jacques Ellul, *Propaganda; The Political Illusion; The New Demons; The Technological Society.*

23. In his chapter on "The Closing of the Universe of Discourse," pp. 84–122, in *The One-Dimensional Man* (Boston, 1964), Marcuse writes:

"Magical, authoritarian and ritual elements permeate speech and language. Discourse is deprived of the mediations which are the stages of...cognitive evaluation. (p. 85) .... It is the word that orders and organizes, that induces people to do, to buy and to accept....the sentence is abridged and condensed and condemned in such a way that no tension, no space is left between the parts of the sentence. This linguistic form militates against a development of meaning. (p. 86) .... The noun governs the sentence in an authoritarian...fashion and the sentence becomes a declaration to be accepted—it repels demonstration, qualification..." (p. 87)

24. Ellul, *Propaganda* (N.Y., 1968), pp. 25–32.

25. George Orwell, "Politics and the English Language," *Essays* (Garden City, N.Y., 1954), pp. 162–176.

26. Claus Mueller, *The Politics of Communication* (N.Y., 1973), pp. 25–42.

27. Trent Schroyer, *The Critique of Domination* (N.Y., 1973). Schroyer contrasts this command language, which hides its assumptions elsewhere, beyond discussion, with normal speech: "...normal communication involves a self-reflexivity which makes human symbolic communication its own meta-language....the manifest message...is accompanied by a meta-communication that expresses the individuatedness of that communication." (p. 161)

28. For a summary of Adorno, Horkheimer, Neumann, Marcuse, etc., see Martin Jay, *The Dialectical Imagination* (Boston, 1973).

29. Reich, *The Mass Psychology of Fascism* (N.Y., 1970). Reich converged with the Frankfurt idea of the "embedding" of ideology in technostructure with his "left Freudian" theory that ideology gets "embedded" in the sexual-biological character structure of individuals (e.g., ch. 6).

30. See the formulation of John Robinson, *Honest to God* (Philadelphia, 1963).

31. If you succeed, they will call you a "take-charge guy" in some firms.

32. Jürgen Habermas, *Knowledge and Human Interests* (Boston, 1971), p. 122–123, quotes Peirce, *Elements of Logic*, II, p. 710.

33. Alan Blum, *Theorizing* (London, 1974), pp. 1–38.

34. Of course, a kind of dialogue then continues within the new scientific community. Popper has shown how this new "intersubjectivity" works, with each scientist theoretically able to check, by repeating the experiment, any new result that is alleged. Karl R. Popper, *The Open Society* (Princeton, 1950), ch. 23. But the public is no longer competent to speak on those matters that the scientific brotherhoods, like magicians' collegia, carve out of consensus and claim as their own provinces.

35. Hubert and Mauss noticed this resemblance of science and magic: in both cases there is a preexisting body of collective representations, and then the individual scientist or magician goes to them and does some action upon them which may augment them. (*A General Theory of Magic*, pp. 139–140).

36. *The Organism* (Boston, 1963), ch. 7, pp. 298–368.

37. *Clinical Studies in Psychiatry*, chs. 9, 14, 15, pp. 182–190, 304–378.

38. In an unpublished paper, psychologists Clyde Hendrick and Martin Giesen of Kent State University reported using false feedback reports of belief or unbelief from a "belief meter"; subjects thus told that their responses indicated that they "believed" something, tended subsequently to show greater objective evidence of belief, in an honest measure of their statements on a given subject. "Self-attribution of Attitude: The Psychology of the Belief Meter," 1974.

39. *A General Theory of Magic*, p. 122.

40. *Ibid.*, p. 114.

41. *Ibid.*, p. 61.

42. *Ibid.*, p. 97.

43. David Mitchell, *An Introduction to Logic* (N.Y., 1970), p. 4.

44. Durkheim and Mauss wrote about primitive classification systems about a year later, but Hubert and Mauss did not explicitly connect them with sympathetic magic in the *Esquisse*.

45. Since Aristotle's logic of terms can be rewritten in the modern logic of classes and since his syllogistic is built on the logic of terms, it is not surprising that sympathetic magic, which is built on primitive classification systems, should suggest syllogism to Mauss' classics-trained mind.

46. *A General Theory of Magic*, pp. 67, 69. The latent idea in both cases is that when things are similar or touching each other then the quality that is being imparted by the spell or rite to change something or create something can *pass through* the media so linked to attain its ultimate target.

47. David Mitchell, *op. cit.*, p. 194.

48. Cf. Wittgenstein, *Notebooks, 1914-16* (Oxford, 1961), pp. 33–34, etc.

49. Mitchell, *op. cit.*, p. 195.

50. See Michael Dummett, "Wittgenstein's Philosophy of Mathematics," in G. Pitcher, ed., *Wittgenstein, The Philosophical Investigations* (Garden City, N.Y., 1966), pp. 420–477. The rigid scripts and preordained outcomes of magic do resemble logic in part, but this may be because there is something "magical" about logic, and the former frame may be a better explanation of the latter than vice versa.

51. Karl R. Popper, *The Logic of Scientific Discovery* (N.Y., 1965), pp. 40–43.

52. Evans-Pritchard, *Witchcraft...Among the Azande* (London, 1937). Starting on p. 475 he offers a remarkable list of 22 reasons why they do not see the futility of their magic. Fragmentation of knowledge, the mutual support elements of the system give each other, weight of tradition are important, but the decisive element is the sheer complexity of a system made up of vague and mystical elements: it offers too many outs. Cf. pp. 475–478.

53. *Les Fonctions Mentales dans les Sociétés Inférieures* (Paris, 1910), trans. as *How Natives Think* (N.Y., 1966), pp. 61–63.

54. "By prelogical we do not mean to assert that such a mentality constitutes a kind of antecedent stage, in point of time, to the birth of logical thought.... It is not anti-logical; it is not alogical either. By designating it prelogical I merely wish to state that it does not bind itself down, as our thought does, to avoiding contradiction.... Thus oriented it does not ex-

press delight in what is contradictory...but neither does it take pains to avoid it." *How Natives Think*, p. 63.

55. Jean Cazeneuve, *Lucien Lévy-Bruhl* (N.Y., 1973), p. 11.

56. Lucien Lévy-Bruhl, *The Soul of the Primitive* (Chicago, 1966), e.g., pp. 59–86.

57. Durkheim, "The Dualism of Human Nature and Its Social Conditions," *Essays on Sociology and Philosophy by Durkheim et al.*, ed. by Kurt H. Wolff (N.Y., 1964), pp. 325–340.

58. Lévy-Bruhl, *Primitive Mentality* (Boston, 1966), pp. 43–44.

59. E.E. Evans-Pritchard, *Witchcraft, Oracles and Magic Among the Azande*, p. 64ff.

60. E.g., Evans-Pritchard, *Social Anthropology and Other Essays* (N.Y., 1962) *passim*; and *Theories of Primitive Religion* (Oxford, 1965), p. 78ff.

61. Lévy-Bruhl, *Primitives and the Supernatural* (N.Y., 1935), pp. 30–32, etc.

62. B. Baumslag and B. Chandler, *Theory and Problems of Group Theory* (N.Y., 1968), p. 1.

63. Rudolf Otto, *The Idea of the Holy* (N.Y., 1958), pp. 12–40.

64. I.e., *Primitives and the Supernatural*.

65. Lévy-Bruhl, *La Mythologie Primitive* (Paris, 1935), ch. 1.

66. Lévy-Bruhl, *L'Expérience Mystique et les Symboles Chez Les Primitives* (Paris, 1938). The "why me" problem of causality is more explicitly developed in this book, and Evans-Pritchard, who may have gotten his clue from Lévy-Bruhl's earlier hint, is now cited for his empirical confirmation among the Azande. Cf. ch. 1 on "Chance and Magic."

67. *Les Carnets de Lucien Lévy-Bruhl* (Paris, 1949).

68. Wittgenstein, *Remarks on the Foundations of Mathematics* (N.Y., 1967).

69. *Ibid.*, p. 23.

70. Cf. Martin Heidegger, *An Introduction to Metaphysics* (N.Y., 1961) pp. 51, 121.

71. Alfred North Whitehead and Bertrand Russell, *Principia Mathematica* to *56 (Abridged ed., Cambridge, 1967).

72. Willard Van Orman Quine, *Methods of Logic* (N.Y., 1950).

73. Quine, *Elementary Logic* (N.Y., 1965).

74. Samuel Beckett parodies Wittgenstein, and also modern logical man, in his novel *Watt*, whose principal character has endless problems with contradictions, seeks definitions, and finally goes to live in the house of "Mr. Knott," where, at the end, he is speaking like this: "od su did ned taw? *On.* Taw ot klat tonk? *On.* Skin, skin, skin. Tonk ot klat taw? *On.* Tank ta kool taw? *On.*" *On* is "no" spelled backwards and perhaps resembles "*om.*"

75. Wittgenstein, *Tractatus Logico-Philosophicus* (London, 1963), pp. 97–99. But I do not think this notation really is "atomic"; it is used *several* ways and so breaks open, containing "and" inside of it.

76. I.M. Bochenski, *Ancient Formal Logic* (Amsterdam, 1968).

77. *Ibid.*, pp. 40–41.

78. Wittgenstein, *Remarks on the Foundations of Mathematics* (N.Y., 1964).

79. Lévi-Strauss, Works. See especially *The Savage Mind*, chs. 2 and 3 (Chicago, 1966); *Structural Anthropology* (N.Y., 1963), chs. 11 and 12.

80. Freud, *General Psychological Theory* (N.Y., 1963), ch. 5, "Repression," pp. 104–116. See also *The Problem of Anxiety* (N.Y., 1936); *The Ego and the Id* (London, 1957); *The Psychopathology of Everyday Life* (N.Y., 1938); *A General Introduction to Psychoanalysis* (N.Y., 1935).

81. See esp. *The Problem of Anxiety*.

82. Freud, *General Psychological Theory* (N.Y., 1963), ch. 14, "Negation."

83. Just because the Freudian idea of psychodynamic negation homologizes to the social function of negation in logic, myth or other text, we must not imagine a psychological source for it. On the contrary, the source for the psychological dynamism is social. Freud speculates that the mental operation of negation no doubt works by the mind presenting to itself "the symbol of negation." (*General Psychological Theory*, p. 214). Thus negation, as a category of the human spirit, becomes one more social pattern available to the individual ego to protect and pattern itself.

84. H.J. Eysenck, *Uses and Abuses of Psychology* (London, 1953).

85. Allen E. Bergin, "Psychotherapy Can Be Dangerous," in *Psychology Today*, Nov., 1975, p. 96ff.

86. Dorothy Tennov, *Psychotherapy: The Dangerous Cure* (N.Y., 1975).

87. Sigmund Freud, *The Future of an Illusion* (Garden City, N.Y., 1964), pp. 70–71.

88. "Obsessive Actions and Religious Practices," *Character and Culture*, in *Collected Papers* (N.Y., 1963), ch. 1, pp. 17–26.

89. It is plain, for example, that he thinks of all the "dynamisms" as magical. The operations he sees at the roots of all of them are "undoing" and "isolation." And both are magical. To undo, to "blow away" as he puts it, is found in magic and religion as well as in neurosis. It is a kind of "negative magic" (p. 53). "In compulsion neurosis...'undoing' is...encountered in...symptoms in which the individual's second act...nullifies the first...(p. 54) The effect of ...isolation is the same...but intensified by motor means and with a magic intent." (p. 55) Sigmund Freud, *The Problem of Anxiety* (N.Y., 1936).

90. Radin, *Primitive Religion* (N.Y., 1957), eg. pp. 107–111, 132–133. Cf. also *The Trickster* (N.Y., 1972); *Primitive Man as Philosopher* (N.Y., 1957).

91. Cf. Géza Róheim, *The Gates of the Dream* (N.Y., 1969), pp. 154–258.

92. Weston La Barre, *The Ghost Dance* (N.Y., 1972), pp. 94–96, etc.

93. Radin, *Primitive Religion*, ch. 6.

94. Jacob Needleman, *The New Religions* (N.Y., 1972), ch. 4, "Subod," p. 102–27.

95. Leon Festinger, *A Theory of Cognitive Dissonance* (Stanford, 1957).

96. E.g., in Hadley Cantril *et al.*, *The Invasion from Mars* (Princeton, 1940).

97. Albert Bandura, *Principles of Behavior Modification* (N.Y., 1969); *Psychological Modeling: Conflicting Theories* (Chicago, 1971).

98. Ernest Hilgard, taped interview, May 1974.

99. Castenada, *The Teachings of Don Juan* (N.Y., 1969), *passim*.

100. Henry Charles Lea, "Witchcraft," in *A History of the Inquisition in Spain* (N.Y., 1906–7, 1966), vol. 4, ch. 9.

101. Michael J. Harner, "The Role of Hallucinogenic Plants in European Witchcraft," in Michael J. Harner, ed., *Hallucinogens and Shamanism* (N.Y., 1973), pp. 125–150.

102. Julio Caro Baroja, *The World of the Witches* (Chicago, 1965), pp. 17–40.

103. Furst, *Flesh of the Gods: The Ritual Use of Hallucinogens* (N.Y., 1973).

104. Allegro, *The Sacred Mushroom and the Cross* (N.Y., 1971).

105. Lévi-Strauss comments on this in ch. 1 of *The Savage Mind* (Chicago, 1966), pp. 1–34.

106. Marvin Karlins and Lewis M. Andrews, *Biofeedback* (N.Y., 1973), *passim*.

107. G. Van der Leeuw, *Religion in Essence and Manifestation* (N.Y., 1963).

108. Rudolf Otto, *The Idea of the Holy* (N.Y., 1958), pp. 12–40.

109. Ronald Knox, *Enthusiasm* (Oxford, 1950), ch. 1.

110. William James, *The Varieties of Religious Experience* (N.Y., Modern Library ed.), ch. 2, pp. 28–29.

111. Gordon W. Allport, *The Individual and His Religion* (N.Y., 1960), p. 6ff..

112. Knight Dunlap, *Religion: Its Function in Human Life* (N.Y., 1946), ch. 5 & *passim*.

113. Friedrich Schleiermacher, *On Religion: Speeches to Its Cultural Despisers* (N.Y., 1958), p. 103, etc.

114. Claude Lévi-Strauss, *Totemism* (Boston, 1963), pp. 66–71.

115. Emile Durkheim, *Elementary Forms of Religious Life* (London, 1915), Book 3, ch. 5, "Piacular Rites...," pp. 389–414.

116. Mauss, "L'Expression Obligatoire des Sentiments (Rituals Oraux Funéraires Australiens)," 1921, in *Oeuvres* (Paris, 1968), vol. 3, pp. 269–279.

117. Ludwig Wittgenstein, *Philosophical Investigations* (N.Y., 1968). See also such studies in "philosophical psychology" as Donald F. Gustafson, ed., *Essays in Philosophical Psychology* (N.Y., 1964); and V.C. Chappell, ed., *The Philosophy of Mind* (Englewood Cliffs, N.J., 1962).

118. Claude Lévi-Strauss, *Structural Anthropology* (N.Y., 1963), chs. 9 & 10, pp. 167–205.

119. Mircea Eliade, *Shamanism* (Princeton, 1972), pp. 510–511, etc. & *passim*.

120. See Becker on how even the drug experience of marijuana is defined collectively: Howard S. Becker, *Outsiders* (N.Y., 1963), ch. 3, "Becoming a Marijuana User," section 2, "Learning to Perceive the Effects," p. 48ff.

121. In B. Malinowski, *Magic, Science and Religion* (Garden City, N.Y., 1954), pp. 79–81.

122. Malinowski, *op. cit.*, pp. 69–70.

123. Malinowski's theory of language, in vol. II of *Coral Gardens*.... (N.Y., 1979,) perhaps specifies some intermediary stages, with its notion that wishful magic impulses shape language. (cf. vol. II, p. 247, etc.)

124. Bronislaw Malinowski, *Argonauts of the Western Pacific* (N.Y., 1961), ch. 18, pp. 428–463; and "The Problem of Meaning in Primitive Languages," in C.K. Ogden & I.A. Richards, *The Meaning of Meaning* (N.Y., 1923), pp. 296–336.

125. Gustav Le Bon, *The Crowd* (London, 1947), chs. 1–4, pp. 23–78.

126. Gabriel Tarde, *On Communication and Social Influence* (Chicago, 1969), ch. 3, pp. 177–194.

127. Malinowski, *Magic, Science and Religion*, p. 90.

128. The social paradigm of suggestion, of course, is trance, but there is little evidence that magic is originally patterned by trance and more evidence that trance is patterned by the magical effects that are sought. There are a few societies, like the Bali described in Margaret Mead and Martha Wolfenstein, eds. pp. 37–98, *Childhood in Contemporary Cultures*, Chicago, 1955, where large parts of the audience may go into trance; and intermediary institutions, like the "shaking tent" among the Arapaho described by Ake Hultkrantz ("Spirit Lodge, A North American Shamanistic Seance," in Carl-Martin Edsman, *Studies in Shamanism*, Stockholm, 1967), in which some borderline trance may be experienced by onlookers. But in general, the shaman alone goes into trance and the audience merely watches, impressed. The magician does not usually hypnotize his client. In fact, some writers, like Weston LaBarre (*The Ghost Dance, Origins of Religion*, N.Y., 1972, pp. 156–160 & *passim*) and Gerald Weiss (in Michael Harner, ed., *Hallucinogens and Shamanism*, N.Y., 1973), suggest that drugs have to be introduced to enable the audience to share the shaman's experience; they speculate that this may be part of his transition from shaman to priest.

129. Jerome D. Frank, *Persuasion and Healing* (N.Y., 1963), p. 20ff.

130. E. Fuller Torrey, *The Mind Game, Witchdoctors and Psychiatrists* (N.Y., 1973), pp. 52–63.

131. Louis Rose, *Faith Healing* (London, 1970), p. 175ff.

132. Peter L. Berger, *Invitation to Sociology* (N.Y., 1963), etc.

133. Alfred Schutz, in *Collected Papers*, vol. I (The Hague, 1962), p. 226ff.

134. Ronald E. Shor, "Hypnosis and the Concept of the Generalized Reality-Orientation"; and "Three Dimensions of Hypnotic Depth," chs. 15 & 16, in Charles T. Tart, ed., *Altered States of Consciousness* (Garden City, 1972), pp. 235–267.

135. Peter L. Berger, in *The Sacred Canopy* (Garden City, N.Y., 1967), reminds us that religion is that projection of society which creates a *nomos* (or *rta, ma'at, tao*, etc); that it is about reality, not about unreality; and that it endeavors to *rationalize* all marginal states which threaten *nomos*, including dreams, insanity, death. The religious framework was the frame of order within which the natural framework originally nested; it was the meta-space, meta-time and meta-organization of normal reality rather than being opposed to it. For our own society, the normal frame is the one that William James calls the "paramount reality." Alfred Schutz ("On Multiple Realities," *Collected Papers*, vol. I, The Hague, 1962, pp. 207–259) has synthesized James, Bergson and Brentano to produce a phenomenological description of the frame. It is characterized by 1. wide-awakeness; 2. suspension of doubt as to the reality of reality (the so-called "epoché of the natural attitude," of Husserl); 3. use of "civic" or conventional time reference. This frame is the orientation for both rational-purposive action *and* symbolic interaction, i.e. intersubjectivity which presumes a *lebenswelt* of other minds similar to our own. In modern times, according to Husserl, this is conceived of as millions of Galilean coordinate systems, with ego at the O origin of one, and other egos each with their own coordinate systems, and many of these precisely located on ours, so that for many the necessary transformation equations are known; for others they are knowable.

136. Shor, *op. cit.*, p. 242ff.

137. Arnold M. Ludwig, ch. 1, in Tart, *Altered States of Consciousness*, pp. 11–24.

138. Patanjali, *Yoga Sutras*, ed. by Archie J. Bahm (N.Y., 1961); Mircea Eliade, *Yoga* (Princeton, 1970), pp. 85–94.

139. Slater Brown, *The Heyday of Spiritualism* (N.Y., 1972), pp. 1–14, & *passim*.

140. George Devereux, ed., *Psychoanalysis and the Occult* (N.Y., 1970), cf. Jule Eisenbud's "review," pp. 3–15.

141. Julio Caro Baroja, *The World of the Witches* (Chicago, 1964), pp. 70–71 & *passim*.

142. P.E.I. Bonewitz, *Real Magic* (Berkeley, 1971), pp. 75–79.

143. Wilhelm Reich, *The Sexual Revolution* (N.Y., 1945); *The Function of the Orgasm* (N.Y., 1961); *Character Analysis* (1963), etc.

144. For example, the ultimate incommunicability of extreme schizophrenia. It has even been considered the result of affectual or organic toxins. For summary of current hypotheses about incommunicable altered states of consciousness in schizophrenia, see Solomon H. Snyder, *Madness and the Brain* (N.Y., 1975); and Malcolm B. Bowers, *Retreat From Sanity* (Baltimore, 1974).

145. Weston La Barre, *The Ghost Dance* (N.Y., 1972), pp. 32, 41–44, etc.

146. I.M. Lewis, *Ecstatic Religion* (London, 1971), ch. 2.

147. Gerald Weiss, "Shamanism and Priesthood in the Light of the Campa Ayahuasca Ceremony," ch. 4, in Harner, ed., *Hallucinogens and Shamanism* (N.Y., 1973), pp. 40–47.

148. Erika Bourguignon, *Altered States of Consciousness and Social Change* (Columbus, 1973), cf. Introd., ch. 8, and "Epilogue."

149. Some students, such as Arvid S. Kapelrud, see traces of shamanic ecstasy even in the Old Testament prophets, for example: cf. "Shamanic Features in the Old Testament," in Carl-Martin Edsman, *Studies in Shamanism* (Stockholm, 1967).

150.(Cambridge, Mass., 1967), pp. 20–21, 23, 34, 90, 96–97.

151. Michael Dummett, "Wittgenstein's Philosophy of Mathematics," in George Pitcher, ed., *Wittgenstein, The Philosophical Investigations* (Garden City, N.Y., 1966), pp. 420–447.

152. "The prophecy does *not* run, that a man will get *this* result when he follows this rule in making a transformation–but that he will get this result when we *say* that he is following this rule. (p. 94).... Now the result of these experiments is that human beings agree in their calculations, or that they agree in what they call agreeing and so on and so on. It could be said that science would not function if we did not agree regarding the idea of agreement." (p. 96–97). Wittgenstein, *Remarks on the Foundation of Mathematics*.

153. The question of why the ideal entities thus produced fit reality is easily disposed of. For one thing, there are latent empirical assumptions in some of them. But mainly, math corresponds to reality because we say it does (and we are not bothered by the fact that Newton's gravitational equations are approximations, for example).

154. Joseph L. Cowan, "Wittgenstein's Philosophy of Logic," in K.T. Fann, ed., *Ludwig Wittgenstein, The Man and His Philosophy* (N.Y., 1967), pp. 284–296.

155. R. White, "A Preface to a Theory of Hypnotism," *Journal Abnormal Soc. Psychology*, vol. 36 (1941), pp. 477–506.

156. T. Sarbin, "Contributions to Role-Taking Theory: I. Hypnotic Behavior," *Psychological Review*, vol. 57 (1950), pp. 255–270.

157. Ernest Hilgard, *The Experience of Hypnosis* (N.Y., 1968); also, taped interview, May, 1974.

158. Ronald E. Shor, "Hypnosis and the Concept of the Generalized Reality-Orientation," Charles T. Tart, ed., *Altered States of Consciousness* (Garden City, N.Y., 1972), pp. 239–256.

159. Shor also considered in a later article the possibility of a third independent variable in hypnosis, something similar to "transference" in psychoanalysis, which he refers to as the "dimension of archaic involvement." This regulates the "depth" of the hypnotic trance. Ronald E. Shor, "Three Dimensions of Hypnotic Depth," in *Altered States of Consciousness*, ed. by Charles Tart, ch. 16, pp. 257–267.

160. Cf. Robert J. Lifton, *Thought Reform and the Psychology of Totalism* (N.Y., 1968); W. Sargant, *The Struggle For the Mind*, etc.

161. Cf. Sigmund Freud, "Analysis Terminable and Interminable," 1937, in *Collected Papers*, vol. 5, ed. by James Strachey (London, 1957), pp. 316–357.

162. Michael J. Harner, ed., *Hallucinogens and Shamanism* (N.Y., 1973), Intro. & ch. 2, pp. 15–27.

163. Janet Siskind, "Visions and Cures Among the Sharanahua," ch. 3 in Harner, ed., *Hallucinogens and Shamanism*, pp. 28–39.

164. Kenneth M. Kensinger, "Banisteriopsis Usage Among the Peruvian Cashinahua," ch. 1 in Harner, ed., *Hallucinogens and Shamanism*, pp. 9–14.

165. Carlos Castenada, *The Teachings of Don Juan* (N.Y., 1968), Part II, "A Structural Analysis," pp. 201–255.

166. Weber's whole theory of the legitimation of authority, all his different kinds of legi-

timation, could be viewed as simple agreements to accept such authority. And these agreements must be continuously renewed, though often by unreflected behavior. The possibility that all Weberian legitimacy of authority is magic based on agreement is further glimpsed in the priority he gives to charismatic legitimacy, out of which legal-rational legitimation develops by later routinization.

167. Jacques Ellul, *The New Demons* (N.Y., 1975), p. 135. (Thus 1950's films like "La Sorcière" and "Et Mourir de Plaisir" are quite different from today's "Exorcist." My example.)

168. Marcello Truzzi, "The Occult Revival as Popular Culture: Some Random Observations on the Old and the Nouveau Witch," *Sociological Quarterly*, vol. 13 (Winter, 1972), pp. 16–36.

169. Theodore W. Adorno, "The Stars Down to Earth: The Los Angeles Times Astrology Column," *Telos*, Spring, 1974, no. 19, pp. 13–90.

170. Claude Fischler, "Astrology and French Society: The Dialectic of Archaism and Modernity," from *Le Retour Des Astrologues,* Issue 3, *L'Obs*, Club du Nouvel Observateur, Paris, 1971, reprinted in Edward A. Tiryakian, ed., *On the Margin of the Visible* (N.Y., 1974), pp. 281–293.

171. W.B. Crow, *A History of Witchcraft, Magic and Occultism* (Hollywood, 1972).

172. Cf. Eliane Massonneau, *Le Crime de Magie et le Droit Romain* (Paris, 1933), p. 19ff & Part II.

173. John Herman Randall, Jr., *The Career of Philosophy*, vol. I (N.Y., 1970), pp. 284–300.

174. Wittgenstein, *Remarks on the Foundations of Mathematics* (Cambridge, Mass., 1967), p. 20.

175. B.F. Skinner, *Contingencies of Reinforcement* (N.Y., 1969). Other sources for this section: Melvin H. Marx, *Theories in Contemporary Psychology* (N.Y., 1963); Sigmund Koch, ed., *Psychology, A Study of a Science*, vols. 1, 2 (N.Y., 1959); Edwin G. Boring, *Sensation and Perception in the History of Experimental Psychology* (N.Y., 1942); Ernest R. Hilgard and Gordon H. Bower, *Theories of Learning* (N.Y., 1948); Floyd H. Allport, *Theories of Perception and the Concept of Structure* (N.Y., 1955); Estes, Koch, et al., *Modern Learning Theory* (N.Y., 1954); Edna Heidbreder, *Seven Psychologies* (N.Y., 1933); K. Koffka, *Principles of Gestalt Psychology* (N Y , 1963); William James, *Principles of Psychology* 2 vols. (N.Y., 1950); T. Adorno, "Sociology and Psychology," *New Left Review*, vol. 46 (1967), pp. 67–80, & vol. 47 (1968), pp. 79–97; W. Reich, "Dialectical Materialism and Psychoanalysis" in *Studies on the Left*, vol. 6 (1966), pp. 5–45; Robert S. Woodworth, *Contemporary Schools of Psychology* (N.Y., 1948); John B. Watson, *Behaviorism* (Chicago, 1963); Edward Chace Tolman, *Behavior and Psychological Man* (Berkeley, 1961); Clark L. Hull, *A Behavior System* (N.Y., 1964); John Dewey, *Human Nature and Conduct* (N.Y., 1930); Wolfgang Köhler, *Gestalt Psychology* (N.Y., 1947); Max Wertheimer, *Productive Thinking* (N.Y., 1945, 1959).

176. Maurice Merleau Ponty, in *The Structure of Behavior* (Boston, 1963), passim.

177. Arthur C. Clarke, in addresses and conversations, suggests that some modern scientific advances seem to us "virtually indistinguishable from magic."

178. Louis Pauwels and Jacques Bergier, *The Morning of the Magicians* (N.Y., 1968), p. 46ff & *passim*.

179. Thomas S. Kuhn, *The Structure of Scientific Revolutions* (Chicago, 1970), ch. 10.

180. Theodore Roszak, *Unfinished Animal* (N.Y., 1975). See also *Where the Wasteland Ends* (Garden City, N.Y., 1973), and the chapter on magic in *The Making of a Counter-Culture* (Garden City, N.Y., 1969), pp. 239–268.

181. Karl R. Popper, "Falsifiability," ch. 4 in *The Logic of Scientific Discovery* (N.Y., 1965), pp. 78–92.

182. A.J. Ayer, *Language, Truth and Logic* (London, 1946).

183. The term is meant to emphasize that *we* do it, we "synthesize" the a priori, in the sense that our social group agrees to it. In other words, "this proposition is universally true *because we say so*." But it is also synthetic (empirical) as well as a priori, because we live by it and confirm it through our collective experiences. It is easy to confirm it empirically *because we say that it is confirmed*. In this sense, synthetic a prioris do exist, abundantly, as collective representations, as social facts.

184. Ludwig Wittgenstein, *Tractatus Logico-Philosophicus* (London, 1961), p. 143 & *passim*.

185. Wittgenstein, *Philosophical Investigations* (N.Y., 1968), p. 46, etc.

186. C.I. Lewis, *Mind and the World-Order* (N.Y., 1956), chs. 7–8.

187. *A General Theory of Magic*, pp. 96–97, 123–126, 130–132.

188. "...Magic should be considered as a system of a priori inductions operating under the pressure of the needs of groups of individuals." p. 126, *Ibid*.

189. Many of the institutions derived from magic still retain, long after they have lost magic's superstitious quality, its synthetic quality—i.e., the agreement to agree on what is happening. Theater, for example, is a game played by players, audience and critics who agree that someone is usually entertained and that this event has been significant. All this leads to the overvaluation of the experience of sitting in a darkened room watching players. Similarly, the law comes to us trailing clouds of glory and we agree that something deliberate and learned and determinate happens when lawyers and judges do their work. And the result of our agreement is that it works.

BOOK TWO

RELIGIONS

Postulate 5: MAGIC BORROWS SYMBOLISM FROM RELIGION AND USES IT TO ARGUE WITH RELIGION IN A DIALECTIC THAT RENEWS RELIGION.

MAGIC is real social action using highly scripted symbolism that works by traditional agreements. But the scripts are so rigid in use that it is hard to discern any process of *forming* agreement going on in this action. So the suspicion arises that something ready-made has been borrowed from some other place. Where did the scripts and the agreements they activate come from? The evidence is strong that both symbolism and agreements that make it work were largely borrowed from religion, which is the traditional symbolic projection of the community. It is well documented that magical rites and representations contain many elements traceable to old religions, foreign religions, dead religions; they may even contain archaisms from forgotten religions. But such correspondences could be cited to support the opposite thesis—that religion borrows its material from magic—by those who, in the Hegel-Frazer tradition, seek to prove that magic is prior to religion. They could explain correspondences by saying magic scripts resemble religious scripts only because they are earlier drafts of them. And this might be hard to disprove where conjectured evolutions are lost in the mists of prehistory. But suppose we could demonstrate magic borrowing rites from a new religion—new rites, fresh forms of worship. This would be a test case. And in fact we can demonstrate this with all the historical world religions. The case is clearest with Christianity. Consider how Christianity transformed magic in Western Europe.

Christian symbolism had grown so prestigious among magicians in Renaissance England that it virtually swamped pagan elements, according to Keith Thomas.[1] The Church itself modeled this magic for the masses by making increasingly explicit magical use of its own symbolism—the church sold miracles, gave Holy Eucharist as a defense against illness, used holy water on crops, used the mass as a mechanical magical rite to attain special ends (even maleficent ends according to Arthur Lyons[2] who notes that the "mass of death" was a sufficient problem that it had to be condemned). Masses for good weather, for safe journeys, for women in labor, for prosperity, against plague, etc., were common. Magical precautions still surrounded the Eucharist: rules about fasting, avoidance of chewing, etc., were more serious then, and retention in the mouth for magic powers was common. Multiplication of masses or prayers (e.g., rosaries) was as common as Buddhist prayer wheels in Ceylon, the familiar magical obsession with quantification of power. The magical nature of sacraments was very explicit in these days; being "bishoped" (confirmation) was thought to have physical effects; extreme unction was feared as a rite that hastened death; there was a special rite of "churching" women, readmitting them to the congregation after the magical pollution of childbirth; and priests were widely regarded as sorcerers. The medieval church was, in fact, a vast reservoir of magic power that could be tapped for any human purpose, as Rydberg[3] put it. Churchly modeling of magic (the selling of amulets, adoration of relics, excommunication of insect pests, blessing of the fields) practically invited the people to use Christian symbolism as magic.

This busy church magic was so prestigious that it was taken over wholesale by private magicians (the "wizards," "cunning men," "white witches" and the other members of the Elizabethan magical zoo). And it virtually swamped earlier magics derived from pagan religions or archaic folk traditions. Religious prayers were widely used by magicians—sometimes they were said backwards. Some "white witches" (folk curers) simply said a Hail Mary to cure people. The Bible was used as an instrument of divination. Kabbalists sought to find prophecies hidden in it, or names of angels numerologically coded in the text. Pagan magic remained, in part due to early syncretistic compromises that had turned pagan festivals into Christian feast days, and underground cults also existed. But co-optation of Christian symbolism by magic had begun very early, with the cult of saints in the Dark Ages, as Dill[4] has demonstrated. Illiteracy provided an initial check on the full assimilation of Christian forms by the folk. But Christian magic later expanded, especially magical defenses against demons modeled by the church, as education recovered and the Christian ethos more fully saturated the culture of the masses. Elworthy[5] has shown that crosses appeared on amulets designed to distract the evil eye; and making the sign of the cross became universal popular defensive magic.

The Christian case is simply the best documented; similar demonstrations could be given for almost any era and culture, of magic continuously taking over rites from new historical religions. When Mohammedanism swept across North Africa, a new magic based on use of inscriptions from the Koran arose here.[6] The so-called world religions always influence magic wherever they spread: meditation becomes an important instrument of magic wherever there is Buddhism or Hinduism, for example. As to further proof of continual or fresh borrowing, Hubert and Mauss note that magic in each society resembles that society's religions to a great degree; and if, for example, there is no sacrifice in the local religions it is usually lacking in the local magic.[7] Thus, the Muslim religion is relatively free of ritual and consists largely of the direct expression of wish—and Muslim magic similarly tends to be a simple, direct, wish magic.[8]

But besides these striking expropriations from new historical religions, we can also cite magical borrowings from ancient religions to support the thesis. For after all it would be forced and far-fetched always to suppose that a magic which uses the symbolism of a vanished religion does so because it is itself the origin of that religion—why should the prototype always survive the type itself? We have plenty of evidence of magic borrowing from older, bypassed, wounded or more primitive religions. In the ancient world, for example, the magical rites of the mystery cults were in many cases borrowed from primitive rural religions.[9] Magic is, in fact, quite industriously antiquarian. Because magic travels easily, accumulates in cosmopolitan civilizations once committed to writing, is preserved and easily revived in occult renewals, remnants of quite remote religions can persist within magical amalgams. Religious ideas from other societies often first penetrate a culture as magic (just as the stranger's religion always seems magical). And they persist in a magical afterglow when they are vanquished (just as outlawed religions are condemned as magical). Dead or dying religions are a major source of magic, especially when the stricken cults are denigrated as magical by their successors, the way Christianity declared the gods of Rome to be demons. Henry Charles Lea[10] proposed that demons in general arise in this way from dead religions.

What does magic borrow from religion? Everything, or a bit of everything, in fact every kind of religious ritual and representation, according to Hubert and Mauss.[11] For example, magic reproduces the rite of sacrifice. It takes over the whole intricate apparatus—a "primitive technology" Becker has called it[12]—with all its elaborate elements, including a consecrated place, pre-medicated materials, entry and exit rites, sacrifier and sacrificer, etc.[13] The black mass is only one example of a magical sacrifice.

Magic also makes use of prayers, even prayers to the gods of religion. Use of religious hymns is also common and so is recitation of religious myths. Another religious element frequently borrowed is scripture. The Bible, the Vedas, the Koran have provided texts for spells throughout the world.[14] A. Dieterich even found Mithraic scriptural passages within the magical Great Papyrus of Paris.[15] Douttée presents dozens of remarkable plates and sketches of North African amulets, charms and other magical objects literally encrusted with inscriptions from the Koran.[16]

Another elaborate religious rite borrowed by magic is initiation. The magician's powers are conveyed by a special initiation rite that is itself an elaboration of the more common religious rite of initiation open to all young men.[17] Like sacrifice, initiation has a tendency to be used as an all-purpose rite or at least parts of it have. Symbols of death and rebirth, descent beneath the earth, ascent into heaven, mystical death with replacement of bodily organs are virtually universal in magical initiations,[18] where they dramatically represent the role transitions that initiations effect. And then parts of this rite are used in an all-purpose way: above all in the shamanic drama of soul loss and recovery (deriving from initiation symbolism in which the individual dies to one role and is reborn to another). Shamanic trance, ascent to heaven, etc., get used in almost every kind of magical seance.

Magic may even take over religious ends as well as means—considerable bodies of magic are "theurgic," devotional, spiritual. Much Jewish medieval magic was of this sort, using religious symbols to manipulate angels and occult powers as a means of reaching god, according to Trachtenberg.[19] Budge has shown[20] that Egyptian magic was similarly theurgic, though so ambitious as to try to manipulate gods as well as communicate with them. All these religious rites and representations—initiation, sacrifice, prayer, hymns, myth, scripture—are frequently burlesqued, done backwards or otherwise travestied, because magic has its own aims which are always somewhat illicit and often hostile to religion.[21] But the material thus used or abused by magic is no less religious in origin on that account. Hubert and Mauss generalize that what magic mainly uses is "the obligatory beliefs of a society," which are mainly its conventional religious symbols. *Magic is, in general, a case of "expropriating social forces."*[22]

A Curious Dialectic

But a curious dialectic is set off by this expropriation, which generates many paradoxical processes. For one thing, when magic borrows from religion, it frequently borrows those elements which are already themselves most "magical," at least in the weak sense. And then it is apt to use these borrowed weapons to argue with religion, or even to attack it. But in so doing, it may turn these borrowed elements into the nucleus of new counter-culture cults and ultimately into new religious sects. But this process may in fact *renew* religious experience, by restoring magic the people need which had been leached out. Magic protests may arise against excessively rationalized religions, restoring ritual and charisma to them. All these processes need careful analysis:

1. Magic Challenges Religion

Magic borrows religious scripts and then uses them to argue with religion, to make exceptions to its rules, to bend and challenge them. Malinowski shows how magic struggles for loopholes, offsets that cancel religious sanctions: e.g., counter-magics to prevent broken taboos from killing someone.[23] The limit of magic is black magic which reverses every value of religion and appears utterly hostile to it. But this tendency is present in all magic; all the provinces of magic have an antinomian thrust. Even quasi-official ceremonial magic and the magic that is part of religion have an anti-religious potential that must be carefully curbed. This is one reason that the Catholic Church insists on certifying its own saints and mystics.

"Magic takes a sort of professional pleasure in profaning holy things," Durkheim writes.[24] Magic tends to be anti-social as well as anti-religious, which is not surprising since religion is the projection of society. "A fascination with the 'occult'...with astrology, spiritualism, magic, and the like, is generally, I suspect, a symptom of social alienation," writes W.H. Auden.[25] One reason why foreign religions are so often regarded as magical is precisely because they are presumptively hostile to the established cult: thus in some societies all strangers are considered magicians. Huvelin[26] and others of the Durkheim school trace this hostility of magic toward religion to the revolt of the individual.

Even when new magics begin for medical reasons, they easily turn into cults and their challenge to religion is not long in appearing. A large percentage of new religions begin as medical magic. One reason they become cults is that magical curing puts a great emphasis on worldview to do its work and this can have revolutionary consequences (for a modern example, R.D. Laing's shaman-like identification with the schizophrenic experience as a cognitive indictment of postindustrial society[27]). Medical magic necessarily creates cognitive projections as an assumptive frame for doctor and patient; in fact, as E. Fuller Torrey,[28] Jerome Frank,[29] Louis Rose,[30] William Sargant,[31] Una Maclean[32] and other students of primitive medicine have observed, this frame of expectations is essential to the cure. Many evolve into cults that develop their own metaphysics and ultimately even gods (e.g., the "thetons" of Scientology). Kardecism, for example, is a healing cult with a metaphysics and with spirits.

Another reason why they become cults is that they turn diseases into statuses and they tend to model and perpetuate the diseases they cure. Magical medicine creates many of the diseases that it cures. Only Malaysians do amok or latah, in part because their magical medicine teaches them how to do it. Today the psychiatric professions teach us how to "do" other illnesses which they in part make up. In primitive society, these socially created diseases sometimes becomes sects, and in modern society some diseases are trying to turn into sects once more.

Magical curing, moreover, has in many cultures a propensity to become what Freud called "analysis interminable."[33] Like a permanent member of A.A. or Synanon, the client is never really cured but remains relatively symptom-free only by staying inside the cognitive minority established around his disease and its curer. And so, in many cases, magical sects are actually *illnesses* spread by symbolism which catch people and force them to belong; membership in them is a lifelong chronic illness in a manner which suggests some respect for Freud's proposition that religion is the universal obsessional neurosis of mankind. The shaman defends the people against possession, his presence also *guarantees that this affliction will be a problem*, for he models the behavior. (Certain social facts really are very "catching," as Durkheim thought of suicide.) The cure takes the form of permanent attachment to the shaman's cult. This process never really ends, even in modern society. Louis Rose estimates that there are thousands of pure faith healers in the United Kingdom;[34] Ellul reports[35] at least 3,000 soothsayers, visionaries, fortunetellers in practice in Paris. Many of these gather little groups of permanent patients and faithful around them.

Psychoanalysis developed a new type of curing seance that, perhaps inevitably, generated magical phenomena (e.g., ESP during free association due to weakening the frame). Karen Horney[36] charged that Freud's categories imported surplus meaning into therapy from the very start, a charge disputed by the Jacques LeCan group, the structuralists and the Frankfurt school, who claim these categories get at precisely what is sociological in mental illness. In any event, orthodox psychoanalytical institutes, whether out of "the triumph of the therapeutic" or "routinization of charisma," do keep down magical outbursts. However, the movement unintentionally modeled the revival of the primordial magical medical seance for modern society. And many deviant psychotherapies that derived from the model turned into sects, just as primitive shamans sometimes accumulate a permanent gang of analysands as followers. Jungian psychoanalysis, for example, widened into an antinomian theosophy complete with its own ambivalent gods and spirits (Abraxos, "the shadow," etc.). Jungian analysands tend to remain within the movement by developing a continuing preoccupation with its interests, by common report. Scientology began as a kind of lay analysis ("Dianetics"); today it is a kind of cult preaching magical ideas (UFO's, ESP, prophecy, divination, etc.). Gestalt psychotherapy turned into T-groups which turned into the Encounter Movement. As Frank[37] has observed, the very unclarity of the situation in non-directive therapies increases their influencing power by gradually deepening involvement, subtly fostering dependency. The individual who, as in Chinese cadre training and brain washing (Lifton[38]), gradually builds up for himself a new assumptive frame which he dimly knows corresponds to what is sought, is more deeply influenced than is a patient to whom the blueprint is delivered didactically by a directive therapist. Thus the non-directive psychiatric seance can become a powerful instrument for destructuring the objective frame, producing magical phenomena and developing allegiance.[39] Sargant[40] has shown how manipulation of transference phenomena plays a key part in conversion experiences.

But of course magical revolts against religion and social consensus occur in all the magical provinces, not just in magical medicine.

2. Religion Fights Back, But Its Resistance Precipitates More Magic

Religion often feels itself threatened by magic, and may take action against it. Halbwachs cited "the marked repugnance of religion for magic, and, on the other hand, the hostility of the latter to the former."[41] Massonneau reveals that even a religion itself as saturated with magic as the Roman religion could work with the state to legislate against magic.[42] But the counterattack tends to create more magic, in several ways: 1. As religion purifies itself, it may expel some ceremonies which may then become illicit magic. 2. Religion typically fears alien religions because of their possibly potent magic and typically it therefore proscribes the entire rival cult as magical—if it succeeds the obloquy sticks and the suppressed rite becomes magical indeed in its underground afterlife. 3. But in addition, religion actively invents new counter magics to defend itself against dangerous magic: A. Some of these inventions are projections of imagination which may then pattern or even elicit the acting out of nightmares. B. Other inventions are real institutions of defensive magic established to fight the projections. A striking instance of both types is provided by the witch persecutions in Western Europe. Here a long struggle with Platonic, Manichean and gnostic dualisms colored existing black magic stereotypes to precipitate a new vision of demonology. This forever enriched black magic in the West, providing new forms such as sabbats and black masses that were occasionally acted out. At the same time new defensive magics were created to fight the demons. Official church exorcism grew rich in lore. Other rituals were colored by the obsession, so that the Catholic funeral service almost to this day reads like the last act in the struggle with "the enemy," as Satan was called in the ceremony. Religious defense against magic bred so much new magic that Hubert and Mauss could observe that the Catholic Church is one case they could be sure of in which belief in magic is asserted as dogma.[43] And so the remedies feed on each other, but this is nothing new. Most primitive magic consists of defenses against black magic, to begin with. Similarly much church magic consists of exorcism, purifications and other devices to protect the faithful from "the enemy." And "the enemy" in turn is none other than the personification of (real or imagined) magical anti-religious rites. Hubert and Mauss[44] in fact show that demons are the rationalizations of magical rites the way Jane Harrison[45] shows gods to be personifications of religious rites.

3. But Magical Attacks May Renew Religion

Even more curious, the symbolism that is borrowed from religion by magic and then turned against it is frequently used to *renew* religion—by creating new cults within it or more vigorous religions to replace those that are dying. Even the magic within religion may effervesce and renew religious experience, as when, for example, an older church magic is recovered (such as glossolalia) and the magical demonstrations of protest movements become new institutionalized religious magic when these movements turn into sects.

All magic has this potential to renew religion, though some of it may remain quiescent for long periods. Even the medical-magic complex may be in equilibrium, without generating witch-finding cults that threaten to become new sects, if there exist adequate, officially tolerated magical means to keep real sorcery and the delusions of witchcraft under control. But equilibrium is the exception; normally all seven major provinces of magic are in ferment.

The continual magical renewal of religion is an engine for dynamic adjustments in the sacred that express and to some degree may facilitate social change. All the provinces are involved. Occult sciences and theosophies may color syncretistic world religions; black magic begets religious demonology; churches split over the issue of religious magic (e.g. iconoclastism). And the province of medical magic is the breeding ground par excellence of movements that renew religous experience.

4. Most New Religious Sects Are Initially Magical in Coloration

Bryan Wilson's researches on sects demonstrate that new religious movements often begin as magic, even though he did not stress this point himself. In a first book on sects[46] Wilson took the dialectic out of Troelstch's classical formulation[47] on the grounds that denominations are more settled now than in the heyday of Christian millenarianism from which Troeltsch generalized. But in fact that period of ferment is more typical of religion than was the relative quiescence of the fifties and sixties from which Wilson generalized his own static ideal types.

Defining "sects" in the traditional manner as voluntary bodies with conscious allegiance, exclusivity and membership taking precedence over other allegiances, Wilson then reclassified them in a typology which diffused and de-emphasized their magical similarities. In his more recent book, *Magic and the Millennium*,[48] he undertook an extremely useful study by gathering together many dozens of field reports from primitive societies about the familiar witch-finding movements, medicine cults and other protest cults that spring up and attempt to become sects. But instead of developing an explanatory theory, he simply classified them under his earlier typology, thereby confirming ideal-typical distinctions in the Parsonian manner.

Virtually all Wilson's types ("conversionist, revolutionist, introversionist, manipulationist, thaumaturgical, reformist and utopian") are just different flavors of magic.[49] For consider what he finds: First, he states that most primitive protest cults are either "thaumaturgical"[50] or "revolutionist," and "thaumaturgical" cults in turn are by far the more prevalent of the two. (This, he explains, is because primitive religion is magical, so protest takes that form.) Next, he admits that the "revolutionist" movements are also magical at base, but he makes little of this. In addition, his two categories of "reformist" and "utopian" sects are fine-haired distinctions that could easily be collapsed with "revolutionist" sects, so the same would apply to them. Later, he defines "manipulationist" sects (prominent in poor countries undergoing economic advances) as the "magical sects of *modern* life"; they use scientific vocabularies but are magical. That leaves only "withdrawal" sects and "conversionist" sects. (And A.D. Nock[51] has shown that conversionist sects were magical in the ancient world, while a close examination of many practices of withdrawal cults will reveal magical elements.[52])

Wilson has done what no one else has found time to do—he has read all the chapters in anthropological field studies on witch-finding movements, cargo cults, ecstatic new sects, not merely from primitive societies but also developing countries, and put them together. And though he did not emphasize it, the overwhelmingly magical nature of new cults arising among two-thirds of humanity undergoing traumatic change is clear in his descriptions. Extremely important are the witch-finding cults, which we encounter in all the primary sources such as Evans-Pritchard, Lucy Mair, Max Marwick, Kerhari and Bouquet, and so many others who report on the magical medical complex in Africa. This is the most common "thaumaturgical cult," and Wilson gives useful accounts of several—of the Tigari cult of West Africa, for example, which tried to reinstitutionalize belief in magic; of the many "Zionist" sects in South Africa inspired by missions from Alexander Dowie's Christian Catholic Apostolic church in Zion of Chicago: their leaders resemble diviners and witch finders and they use baptism as a magical defense against witchcraft. Since he advances no theory of magic here, Wilson gives scant attention to the main reason for these thaumaturgical movements— which those whose field work he summarizes did *not* miss: they fill a vacuum created when colonial authorities outlaw witch ordeals and other native defenses against black magic. Since sorcerers really do exist in Africa (and use poison and bush-guns as well as mystical weapons[53]) and since witch fears will be a problem with any primitive society undergoing rapid social change,[54] this exposed the people to great dangers. The new cults offered new magic to substitute for forbidden magic in fighting black magic. Typically the witch-cleansing cults use mass ecstatic rites of detection and purification in which victims are given magical protections and witches are neutralized and forgiven. Wilson notices that these movements are usually volatile and ephemeral; they sweep from one society to another, but most do not last. The Lele Tribe in the Belgian Congo alone had seven anti-sorcery movements between 1910 and 1952. Thaumaturgical cults are the most common type in developing societies where the newly urbanized masses flock, for example, to the possession cults of Brazil such as Umbanda and Macumba and the local version of spiritualism, Kardecism.[54]

In chapter after chapter Wilson must return to the thaumaturgical movements; they virtually swamp his whole book; the other categories are skimpy by comparison, but he draws few conclusions from this. And those cults that he does describe under the other categories sound magical, too. This is especially true of "revolutionist" cults—e.g., the "Ethiopian" sects derived from evangelical missions that preach war against the whites and promise magical immunity to their warriors. But Wilson draws no conclusions about perennial magical revolts that renew religion as new sects. Instead he spends his last chapter dusting off his ideal types and berating rival classification systems.

Surely the cultic ferment of two-thirds of humanity—happening right now in the developing countries where it can be observed—is useful data. More penetrating studies do point toward the hypothesis that protest movements which renew religions start in magic. For what Wilson failed to do with the broadest survey, other investigators have done using narrower surveys. La Barre,[55] for example, summarized findings on *crisis cults* and Lewis summarized field reports of *ecstatic cults.*[56] The narrower base in both cases helped introduce theoretical prejudices and both men postulated that the type of cult they study reveals what is most essential about religion. Despite these defects both attempts are more explanatory than Wilson's static classifications.

Consider ecstatic cults first: According to Lewis,[57] ecstatic religiosity arises among weak or peripheral groups (such as women in patriarchal societies); it expresses protest against oppression through impressive demonstrations of spirit possession in virtuosi (mediumistic trance) which then become the center of a cult. Typically, this is a medical cult and the leader is shamanistic; his initial spirit possession is interpreted as an illness which he overcomes. His conquest gives him some power over spirits and enables him to cure others, who are actually made more susceptible to similar seizures by his modeling of the behavior. Those whom the shaman-leader cures attach themselves to him as a permanent following. In primitive societies under stress, these followings are soon on their way to becoming a sect that challenges the existing religion. The new sect may overthrow it, but more often it nests inside it as a subcult, whereupon the religion may attempt to tame its charisma. If charisma is too rationalized, however, new spirit possession will erupt and challenge. Lewis views trance behavior as sociological rather than biological or psychological, a form of role playing. Especially valuable are two of his findings: 1. The cult itself provides archetypes for the psychological illness which it cures. 2. The whole process is a religious complex with a culturally determined probability that magical protest cults will erupt on the periphery and then embed themselves in the central cult in response to pressure on marginal groups.

Crisis cults reveal similar features when numerous studies of them are examined. La Barre[58] takes cargo cults as most typical of crisis cults (just as Lewis focused on ecstatic cults with possession cults as the most typical). All religions, La Barre claims, begin as crisis cults (of which cargo cults and nativistic movements like the Ghost Dance are most typical). They combine the best of the old and the new in a new synthesis. They are led by a "shaman"; he means any charismatic cult leader. In La Barre's theory, shamans are transitional figures; they are magicians who become priests as the new magic protest becomes a sect. And it is clear that the whole process is magical. The shamans' messages come in altered states of consciousness prepared by mental instability and cultivated by drugs, fasting or other means. Building on Róheim's work on dreams,[59] La Barre says that, in effect, shamans cultivate "dream behavior" and then try to induct followers into their dreams. La Barre's theoretical apparatus[60] need not concern us. What is valuable is that once again a mass of new religions have been examined and shown to originate in magical phenomena: exploitation of dreams, magic powers of charismatic leaders, etc.

The three summaries of new religions provided by Wilson, La Barre and Lewis help put this widespread pattern into focus; but of course the proposition could also be massively documented from dozens of primary sources. New cults emerging as magic and moving toward secthood are found in the background of anthropological field reports from virtually every society on earth.

5. The Religious Cultural System "Patterns" the Magical Protest Sects

The perennial nature of magical protest cults in most societies, the highly consistent manner in which they repeat endlessly a few simple patterns, suggest that they are part of the religious complex as a whole and are patterned by the central cult. Thus Jesus was declared to be the messiah because it was part of the Hebrew religion to *expect* messiahs, and Amos may have been a functionary who spoke his challenges as part of his office. Even cargo cults derive their symbolism and ideas from the pre-existing religion.[61] La Barre's findings about the typical nativism of these movements is further evidence that they are part of the system. Magical protest sects are often fundamentalist or primitivist; they often reach back for content in the original religious tradition which has been leached out. Usually, what has been leached out and what is restored is some of the magical content of religion. Standing back and viewing any society over a period of generations, it sometimes appears that a determinate probability for religious mutation via magical protest and renewal is built into the religion itself as a total cultural system radiating out into the society.

In secularized, cosmopolitan cultures, exotic or foreign religions often take the place of nativist revivals, but even here they may fit into preexisting patterns of acceptance—Renaissance Kabbala fitting old gnostic patterns, for example. The "new religions"[62] of this decade in America are not merely exotic imports from the Orient, they work as magic protests. Their coming fills a vacuum created by the rationalization of native American religious traditions: men in need of magical help turn to religion and find that religion has turned to science, so they look to other traditions for aid. The new imports derive especially from the extremely magical Hindu and Buddhist traditions,[63] and within those traditions are themselves far along toward the mechanical and magical poles: e.g., Transcendental Meditation. Besides the imports, there *are* nativistic religious renewals in America based on digging up old magic leached out of the Christian tradition: Thus, the alleged biblical origins of the snake-handling cults;[64] glossolalia as an old Christian tradition; and the various Jesus sects that are perhaps closer to primordial Christianity than orthodox parishioners would care to admit. And even in America, nativistic magical sects arise within the magical medical complex. Thus spiritualism had some magico-religious movements as offshoots, such as Christian Science.

Altogether it is as if there were a certain expectation of such revolts built into the system, like certain genetic mutations that occur with a regular probability.[65]

6. Some Religions Systematically Institutionalize Magical Protest Sects

The religious organization itself may deliberately certify magical protests, putting them to various uses. Church organizations frequently try to turn originally deviant groups away from protest sects and into subcults and set them to work in specialized jobs—the Dominicans to fight the witches, the "secular institutes" and "pious unions" to perform good works. Most religions are as a result so amorphous that their total ramifications are unknown to the majority of members: this amorphism is the precipitate of the constant proliferation and certification of cults which nest in the structure in accordance with varying patterns of acceptance. This is one of the means whereby national Christian Churches in some countries (e.g., Protestant and Catholic churches in pre-war Holland) came to resemble the multi-organization structure of totalitarian movements as described by Neumann[66] and Arendt[67]: partly out of the ferment of new associational movements are fashioned those endless sodalities and unions, men's groups, women's groups, Knights of Columbus, children's groups, that attempt to organize all of social life. In addition to being a community or a congregation, such a church in action is a congeries of voluntary associations that have in many cases their own histories, interests and even deviant aims but are harmonized by a massive organizational *gleichschaltung*.

The Catholic Church even has a large body of law and practice concerning the gradual acceptance and certification of these new movements as they arise— which serves to routinize their magics and bend them to useful tasks. The "secular institutes" of the Catholic Church, for example, since the Apostolic constitution known as *Provida Mater Ecclesia* by Pius XII in 1947, have been quasi-legitimized and are patterned in ascending stages of acceptance. Thus these spontaneous eruptions are now partly elicited by a known pattern of legitimation. As of 1963, according to *Les Instituts Seculiers*, a handbook published privately in Paris, there were worldwide several thousand associations loosely known as "pious unions" moving in this direction; 250 had already asked permission to become "secular institutes" proper. Staged recognition gives the Church ample time to investigate and screen these spontaneous movements, which sprang up (like the friars before them) long before they were recognized. Any new form of social congregation is a possible source of magical, latihan-like behavior (tongues, ESP, prophecy, etc.) and one defense for established religion is to provide procedures for certification. Secular institutes tend toward the extreme of taking all three vows of poverty, chastity and obedience while members remain at worldly occupations ("monks in business suits"). They clearly express alienation from the modern world and a hunger for primal religious experience; unsupervised they could become chiliastic. For magical sects have frequently grown up in and split off from even the Catholic Church by a similar process, even in modern times.[68] The medieval friars themselves were suspected of sorcery and heresy (and executed for it under John XXII).

Just as the Catholic Church has patterns for assimilating such spontaneous movements as subcults—all the friars,[69] all the orders, all the institutes and pious unions are of course subcults—most religions adopt this mode of defense. And the result is not merely to pattern but also to *elicit* more such magical revolts.

7. What Magic Protests

But what, exactly, does magic protest when it erupts on the periphery of religion? What magic usually protests is religion—or its absence. This is not as paradoxical as it sounds, because in both cases what is really protested is the absence of certain kinds of magic inside religion. When there is too little religion, then the magic that travels with religion may also be missing. Then magical movements may arise to protest the *absence* of "religion," in the sense of sacral-magical religion. Or the dominant religion may be very pervasive but excessively intellectualist, or it may be ethical and anti-magical, like the missionary churches that stripped African peoples of their traditional defenses against witchcraft and so provoked new ones. Or the religion may monopolize magic; magic itself easily becomes alienated and oppressive; a religion may pullulate magic but it may be official magic or the magic of an elite, and not the people's magic. Then a magical protest sect may arise to protest oppressive church magic or to restore magic to the people for the defense of their egos. Such a movement may seem antimagical, for it may attempt to sweep away official priestly magic and its success may indeed result in a net reduction of magic even though the movement may be powered by the masses' hunger for personal magic. While Christianity in one sense rid the world of a great deal of oppressive magic such as astrology (cf. Angus[70]) it also democratized magic with its promise of personal salvation and immortality. Becker interprets it as a restoration to individuals of human symbolic powers that had been monopolized by official religions.[71]

Religion itself is protested when it is projected by an oppressive social structure (e.g., then ecstatic possession cults may erupt among disadvantaged classes in the manner Lewis has described), or when it is oppressive in the sense of making difficult or impossible ethical demands. (Thus John the Baptist's Hellenic mystery-religion rite of baptismal forgiveness was an antidote to a Hebrew religion that projected moral guilt as a byproduct of a serious emphasis on social justice and provided no easy sacramental "out" to lift the resulting sense of sin.) Magic especially protests the enormous ego pressure exerted by the social consensus which is projected in religion. Then magic may steal some of the sacred, like Prometheus, to protect man's ego. In the formulation of Huvelin,[72] magic is seen as a literal "turning" or detouring (*"détournement"*) of religious power for individual ends.

But magic and magical sects also arise when there is "too little religion" as in the case of excessive rationalization. Magic erupts then because the rationalization of religion has removed the defenses that magic provides against 1. black magic, and 2. the magical illnesses. This happened in modern times when the shock of the Protestant revolutions stripped whole nations of their defensive magics at a time when the revived theosophies of the ancient world engendered belief in black magic even among the elites.

Even when the magical worldview has declined so that black magic is no longer a threat, there is still the problem of the magical illnesses: the neuroses, the character disorders and the functional psychoses. When culture becomes too secularized, defenses against magical illnesses fall into disrepair. Mental illness probably did not increase in incidence during the nineteenth century, if studies like that of Goldhammer and Marshall[73] can be believed, though this is by no means certain. But people in recent times had become more aware of magical illnesses and were more frightened of them precisely because they had had no context of meaning within which they could be contained. Fourcault[74] has shown how modern Europe became increasingly uneasy about madness; Fourcault and Huizinga[75] relate this to the breakup of the medieval synthesis and the uncertainties of the modern world. (It was also related to the futility of knowledge by Erasmus[76] at a time when whole universes of books were being junked by social change: e.g., the scholastic philosophies, and what Pauwels and Bergier[77] call "the hundred thousand unread books of alchemy.") There was a similar transitional time during the late nineteenth century when religion was simultaneously so rationalized that it abandoned virtually all magical defenses against magical illnesses, yet at the same time it was still powerful and laden with guilt, capable of causing considerable magical illness itself. This religious pressure generated constant magical revolt despite an extremely resistant positivist social frame.

8. Magical Protest and Assimilation As the Hidden Pluralism of Primitive Society

In primitive societies the men's houses are often magic lodges that dispute with the central cult. The societies that put on ceremonies in accounts given by Malinowski, Turner, etc., are often embryonic subcults. This dialectic of revolt and reassimilation enables religion to transform itself and adjust to underlying changes in social morphology. It prevents religion from becoming totally alienated from the society that projects it. Through the process of magical protest and cultic evolution men create diversity in primitive society and recreate small communities within cosmopolitan cultures. Again and again, alienated man, through magical protest, recreates or renews a small viable community in which he can breathe. Weber is our most valuable theorist in showing how this dialectic of magic and religion is related to social change.

Although Weber's dialectic is to some degree an event that is worked out largely in the realm of ideas, and although religion is in that sense transcendental for him as for Wach, there is a kind of social mechanics in his theories. For insofar as the ideas of a religion are exceptionally transcendent, so much greater, according to Weber, is their potential for changing society, via a not-too-easily compromised ideal. De Unamuno,[78] Richard Niebuhr[79] and others grasp this; this is almost a kind of mechanical principle. (Weber uses the familiar Archimedes metaphor of a lever that could move the world if it had a "place to stand.") We might formulate the difference between Durkheim and Weber this way: Both are, to some degree, dialectical in their accounts of the interaction between religion and society. But Weber tends to stress the influence that religion has on society, more than he emphasizes the influence that society has on religion. Durkheim, by contrast, emphasizes how society literally determines religion as a reflection of its own morphology. As to the reverse reaction, Durkheim has several passages about religious idealization, showing how religion as a realm of fantasy and vagary changes easily and how these collective representations may in turn work back on society to influence it. But he clearly intends that this reverse action is of minimal importance, and I have even found a passage where he explicitly says this. The quote is in his discussion of altruistic suicide in the book *Suicide* (pp. 226–227, English edition):

> Among peoples as well as individuals, mental representations function above all as an expression of a reality not of their own making; they rather spring from it and, if they subsequently modify it, do so only to a limited extent. Religious conceptions are the products of the social environment, rather than its producers, and if they react, once formed, upon their own original causes, the reaction cannot be very profound.

Religions surviving in cosmopolitan civilizations are sometimes nothing more than the projections of dead political groupings, or of political groups that have lost their states. The DNA analogy has occurred to many modern writers (e.g., Parsons[80] and Geertz); but to extend the analogy it is well known that genes that break loose from chromosomes may become viruses. Foreign religions loose in a culture are like genes on the loose, or viruses that would settle down in a host chromosome the way a new magical cult often nests inside an existing religion when it finally comes to rest.[81]

The Problem of the "Ethical" World Religions

Contrary to conventional wisdom, all these processes apply to the "world religions" or "ethical reform religions" as well as to primitive cults and sects: In their origins, many of the world religions are also magical protest sects that 1. borrow material from older religions; 2. use it to challenge existing religions; 3. thereby renew religious experience. As a rule, they, too, are 4. following a pattern for protest sects given in their religious cultures; 5. protesting the inadequacy of existing magic; and 6. thereby effecting or reflecting social change.

In accepting this formulation, conventional wisdom has two hurdles to overcome. First, there is the popular conception, theologized by Hegel, Frazer and the evolutionists, that mankind evolves away from magic, through religion, to science—so it is expected that these new religions must be somehow less magical than what they replace. Second, lying across our path is the theoretical corpus of Max Weber, which, despite its spectacular dialectics and great sensitivity to these issues, is oversimplified by interpreters to rigidify a similar position: i.e., the idea that ethical reformist religions purge the world of magic and so make science possible. The notion that the "ethical world religions" are steps away from magic is treated empirically in a later postulate which demonstrates just the opposite to be the case. But a few words anticipating these arguments can be given here:

Do the great world religions evolve away from magic? The opposite is often the case. Many of the aims and uses of religion become more magical with the advance of civilization, more magical than in primitive society. Religion comes increasingly to serve the magical individual, rather than the religious community. Individuals increasingly seek extremely magical ends from it—such as immortality, salvation, psychological equilibrium, power, peace, release, escape from social karma, etc.

As for Max Weber, the curious fact is that he is both the source of general formulations suggesting that ethical religions cast out magic—and also of empirical demonstrations that the world religions begin as new magics and attract their followings by their magics. This is what "charisma" is all about. Weber's *Sociology of Religion* is partly a sociology of magic. Outside of Durkheim and Mauss, Weber is the best theoretician we have of magic; above all, of the mass magic of charismatic movements in large societies undergoing change. Durkheim-Mauss on the magic of primitive societies must be supplemented by Weber on the mass magic of complex and changing civilized societies. This is not to deny that Weber had a theory suggesting a propensity of ethical religions, by driving out older magics or simplifying magic, to make an opening for science. But there were many slips and reversals along the way; all Weber's processes are paradoxical and nothing is guaranteed.

There is not space in this chapter to demonstrate exhaustively how the world religions began as magical protest sects. I will therefore focus my discussion here in large part on Weber's own demonstrations (he wrote four books on this) to show how he qualified his theory of "ethical reformist" sects "driving out magic" when he confronted actual historical processes with all their slips and reversals. The following section therefore will give special attention to Weber's *Religion of India, Religion of China, Ancient Judaism* and *Protestant Ethic*, though some other sources are also used:

Buddhism

Until recently, the romantic legend of the Buddha and the purity of some teachings associated with it have obscured for the West the extremely magical nature of this whole movement. As Buddhist religions leak into the West, however, observers like Bharati,[82] Pauwels,[83] Johannson,[84] Stcherbatsky,[85] Needleman[86] make us increasingly aware of their magic. It might almost be said, in Durkheimian terms, that Buddhism is the "generalization of the mana" in Hinduism, itself a religion crackling with particularistic magics. In pristine Buddhism we have a simplification, a focusing, a generalization of the most powerful magic of Hinduism, above all mechanical techniques of meditation aimed at producing altered states of consciousness which are then defined by agreement as escapes from social misery. Weber comments that Buddhism simplified Indian religion to its essential aim: cultivation of an anxiety-free state of mind.[87] It is well known now that the end product of the Buddhist movement was a swarm of some of the most magical religions in the world: Mahayana, Zen, Tantrism, etc. Even the "pure" Minayana was a magical revolt—against the Brahmin religion, against the caste system it supported, against the Brahmin monopoly of magic. It sought to put psychological magic into the hands of all men. Its basic thrust was a simplification of magic. That is still the thrust of Buddhism today—of Zen, Tantrism, TM, Soka Gakkai, etc.[88]—it is always trying to make magical escape simpler, more mechanical, more accessible to all, via prayer wheels instead of prayers, mantras instead of metaphysics, "direct entry" into altered states of consciousness instead of prolonged mystical preparation. The mystical *aims* of Buddhism, even of the pure Minayana, are as magical as its means. Nirvana and later concepts like Satori run a continuum from mere altered states of consciousness up to the familiar magical goal of sitting up in the sky (Bodhavistas). The nihilism of pure Minayana is no obstacle to this interpretation, but just one more instance of magic's antinomianism. Even extinction of the ego (which Stcherbatsky and Bharati demonstrate to work gnostically via a Wittgenstein-like logical reduction) is just one more device serving the familiar magical aim of altering the objective frame of reference of the paramount reality. Even escape from the wheel of rebirth is just a particularly violent reversal of the usual magical aim of godhood — escape from life as the ultimate magical chutzpah defeating all the forces of the world. (It is merely the reverse of the more typical magical goal of immortality, or of becoming an angel or a god, like the god of each "Yuga," who, in the more optimistic Vaishnavite sect, is just an extremely powerful yogin who *thought* himself up there.[89]) Buddhist simplicity, its avoidance of metaphysics and spirits in order to concentrate on practical meditation, can be understood as the typical practical attitude of magic.

The heart of classic Buddhism is its preoccupation, from the beginning, with techniques of meditation to induce altered states of consciousness. Nirvana (or "nibbana" in the original Pali) is to be understood as a psychological state, according to Johannsen.[90] Techniques of meditation were present in Indic culture very early; figurines in the lotus posture have been recovered from Mohenjo Dari.[91] Buddhism carried these techniques further; and the Hindu religion became more magical partly to keep up with Buddhist magic—the classical Hindu Yoga was formulated later, as a reaction to Buddhism: To this day Tantric Buddhism is associated with so-called "higher" (more magical) yogas. Yogic techniques resemble shamanic trance on the one hand and initiation rites for magicians on the other. (Magic is always a problem in Yoga. Even in the pure theist Hindu Yoga of Patanjali, magical powers constantly erupt along the yogin's path as he attains higher and higher states; because the goal is theist, the adept is taught to disregard them. But Hindu literature is full of examples of yogins who exploit their powers, and such exploitation is present in Buddhism.[92]) It is also well known that whereas Hindu variants of Yoga retain its cognitive, gnostic side as a "path of knowledge," this tends to drop out in Buddhism's more practical, magical orientation toward results. Some Hindu yogas still try to attain knowledge of the illusory nature of the world, as well as provide escape into magical states, but Buddhism, typically, is interested only in immediate entry.

But what *is* this constant allegation of unreality, this accusation of magic against the world itself that is so basic to both Hinduism and Buddhism? Partly it is a glimmering of the sociological imagination turned against itself, turned to despair and passivity. But it is also none other than the typical device of initiating magical experiences by an assault on the objective frame of reference of the paramount reality. Buddhism and Hinduism assert that the world is made-up, magical, mâya—these ideas can actually help induce trance. But as a philosophy this insight rigidifies the very social reality shown to be illusory. In Hinduism it reinforces the social power of the dominant magicians who made the system. In Buddhism the passive "escapes" offered the faithful have that effect indirectly. The very propensity of Buddhism and Hinduism to rid the world of gods or to make them illusions (mere avatars of monistic mana forces) is part of the propensity of magic to restore the priority of mana over spirits.

Buddhism sociologically was a Kshatriya revolt against the caste system (Weber associates it with urban palaces)[93]; but in practice it took the form of a competition in magic. As a revolt against caste it failed, and Bouglé[94] blames this on Buddhist acceptance of Hindu ideas of monism and reincarnation. Perhaps it would be more exact to say that magical purposes distracted from social aims and magical satisfactions provided substitutes. The noble literati who revolted attempted to undermine the philosophical prestige of the Brahmins by abolishing metaphysics altogether; emphasis was shifted from metaphysics to salvation, from gnosis to techniques of meditation. Later Buddhism became more magical still, especially the Mahayana and above all Tantrism, which as Bharati[95] has shown, arose in both Buddhist and Hindu traditions and converged.[96] Bharati characterizes Tantrism as psycho-experimental speculation, with a kind of analytical-linguistic philosophical foundation, which attempts to storm *samadhi* without prolonged ascetic devotions but directly, through mechanical methods like mantra, sexual ecstasy, psychological experiments on the self. But as scholars like Rune Johanssen have shown,[97] the original Buddhist "nibbana" was a psychological state which Buddhism approached in a mechanical, optimistic, you-can-do-it mode. The Buddhist idea that "we are not awake," made popular in the West by Gurdjieff,[98] is prefigured by the universal primitive complex of the magician's "death" and "rebirth" during his initiation into a higher level of spiritual awareness.

Christianity

We have already noted how magical Christianity had grown in practice by the Renaissance. Consider now its magical *origins*. Christianity begins as a typical mystery religion based on a mystic rite: baptism. The Christian era opens with John the Baptist, who offered a cheap magical sacrament on a mass basis.[99] The Hebrews had practiced ritual immersion for ritual impurity only, not for sin; as they matured toward acceptance of the idea of guilt as social responsibility they resisted offering easy magical answers at first. Guilt was overcome by the forgiveness of god in whom we must, Job-like, trust; maybe also by good works. Belatedly, reluctantly, they also added sacrifice; but that was always expensive and Roman limitation of sacrifice to Jerusalem made it impossible for most. Moreover, some sects (e.g., the Sadducees) never approved of sacrifice. Meanwhile, the Hellenized urbanized masses added sick Oedipal guilt (Dodds[100]) at the weakening of patriarchy to the Hebrews' mature sense of sin based on social justice compacts. Then came John, who baptized for sin, not just impurity, in a mass baptism without cultic membership or too much unseemly magic. He won immediate mass acceptance.

There is disagreement about why or how Jesus changed this sacrament, agreement only that he did change it and make it more magical still. Morton Smith cites many texts to suggest that Jesus went into a trance during his own baptism, an experience easily accessible to him from the proliferating shamanistic practices of the heterodox masses, if he was not already a shaman himself.[101] The evidence that he then developed an esoteric sect of ecstatic experience based on trance or drugs comes to us not merely from modern commentators like Allegro[102] or Morton Smith: the oral tradition of its existence had to be literally shouted down at a hundred church councils in which the bishops gradually agreed to agree that it had never happened. Lynn Thorndike[103] provides a good summary of all the Apocryphal gospels that represented Christ as a sorcerer (e.g., Thomas) and he traces persuasively remnants remaining in the canonical gospels.

However true these claims, by the time we come to Paul, baptism has changed; it is strikingly more magical than John's rite. And some commentators believe that Paul's position was actually a compromise, between that of the Libertines and the Conservatives led by James. Morton Smith speculates that after John's original rite but before Paul's compromise came the extreme magical baptism of

Jesus, which involved a trance experience during which the initiate "ascended to heaven" (the typical magical initiation experience according to Jane Harrison, Mauss, etc.). Whether this is true or not, differences between the sacrament of John and that of Paul are wide. John's rite was public; required or effected repentance; was accompanied by confession of sins; demanded performance of good works in the future; was performed as a preparation for the coming kingdom of God; was not connected with any teaching about the holy spirit; and did not establish membership in anything. We might say that it compromised with the magical demands of the populace but still showed Judaic restraint. In contrast, by the time we get to Paul, baptism: 1. is essentially a means of uniting an initiate with the Messiah; 2. causes his spirit to take magical "possession" of the man; 3. which leads to the magical-ecstatic experience of speaking in tongues; 4. involves stripping off of clothes (which symbolizes the magic trip to the underworld); 5. is an initiation rite admitting a person to membership in a community; 6. which is part of a mystical "kingdom" (or magical state) already partly realized. Moreover, by the time we get to Paul, there are other sacraments as well, branching off from the same idea: e.g., eucharist with mystic communion and possession through eating the god.

The Bruno Bauer proposal (popularized by Homer Smith[104]) that Christ did not exist but was made up by church propaganda is better known than the magician hypothesis. Both are responses to the extreme paucity of information about Jesus contained in the Gospels. Contemporary evaluations of this "synoptic problem" approach consensus. Bultmann,[105] classifying incidents in the narratives like Lévi-Strauss working on "mythemes," peels off virtually everything and attributes it to the church, leaving only eschatology to Christ. Sandmel[106] surveys rabbinical, Hellenic and Alexandrine literature to remind us how little collateral evidence for the Gospel stories exists. And yet they have the compelling idiosyncratic reality of archetypically real events, which makes the Bauer hypothesis unlikely. The less well known magician hypothesis may reconcile these contradictions, explaining a story that is all-too-true, fits a pattern, but has dropped details in order to "clean it up." But not many have pursued this troubling idea. Max Weber toyed with it in his *Sociology of Religion.*[107] He was sufficiently troubled by the matter of miracles as to try to distinguish miracles from magic.[108] Some German scholars were similarly interested, but had little impact (references to them may be found in Morton Smith's latest book and its bibliography).[109] Certainly his story resembles the popular "aretologies" of wonder-workers of the day (Hadas).[110] This section relies partly on Morton Smith's three books, and in view of the shrill statements contained in the last of these, I used them with some trepidation. But Smith at least has the virtue of getting the obvious discussed, after centuries of neglect.

In the libertines and the gnostics, in figures like Simon Magus[111] and Apollonius,[112] who continued to dog the church as rival magicians, we see many hints that the extreme magic that is forever suppressed in Christianity like a guilty secret stems from its very core, from Jesus, whom Max Weber several times called "a magician."[113] In fact, the evidence that Jesus adopted the magician's style of communication lies right under our noses, in the familiar Gospel stories, if we can only overcome their familiarity and look at them with pristine eyes.[114] Morton Smith has done this work for us, and his content analysis is so perspicuous that recognition leaps from every sentence. In *Clement of Alexandria and a Secret Gospel of Mark*,[115] he offers an account of Jesus Christ as a magician in the strict sense, and of the New Testament as the story of a magician doing magic that attracts a following which turns into a sect:

1. Jesus possesses (and uses) a power to make anyone he wishes follow him. 2. He practices exorcism, including exorcism at a distance. (Weber, in fact, portrays him mainly as a shaman who cures illnesses by casting out demons.[116]) 3. He thus performs miraculous cures. 4. He also gives his disciples powers over demons. 5. He stills storms. 6. He raises Lazarus from the dead. 7. He walks on water, makes himself invisible, performs magical escapes, miraculously provides food. 8. He changes shape (in the transfiguration we learn that his familiar form is a disguise). 9. He has foreknowledge. 10. He introduces new rites which mystically unite his followers to him by a kind of spirit possession (baptism and the eucharist). 11. These are not merely "miracles" in the Max Weber sense[117]—i.e., single, theophanous breaks in regular law which are seen as exceptional and hence are less magical. They are systematic, regular events. This is above all evident in the training which Jesus gives to his apprentices. In addition to command over demons, they are given the power systematically and regularly to perform magic. Above all, there is a magician's initiation involved—this is the esoteric form of baptism for which Smith assembles evidence. It confers "the keys to the kingdom"; the initiate is thereafter *in* the "kingdom," which is *now*. The nakedness or quasi-nakedness of the rite symbolizes the descent into the underworld, and the rest of the imagery strongly suggests the ascent to storm heaven and obtain magic power from god which Mauss has shown to be part of magicians' initiations the world over.[118] This ascent is induced apparently by fasting for six days, perhaps also by trance, drugs or other orgiastic experiences at which Morton Smith darkly hints.[119] When Christian apologists say Christ performed miracles but not magic, they leave out not merely this initiation and training in systematic magic, but also many of his quotidian magical performances which were systematic and regular. The most obvious is his curing, which was prolific. Christ's title, "the son of god," was a common appellation for powerful magicians in Palestine of this time.[120]

In his more recent book,[121] Morton Smith employs synoptic criticism to bend every detail of the Gospels to support his thesis; and he weakens his case by extreme statements and polemics. Willing to accept the most scandalous gossip from Christ's enemies, he all but justifies the Roman execution. Even if his magician hypothesis be true, he betrays a remarkable lack of sympathy for a tormented people's magus who expressed their suffering. Yet once Smith has opened the issue we find that he is far from being our only source. There may be more to the thesis than Morton Smith has turned up. The apocryphal gospels, for example, hint at *black* magic.[122] Christian apologists make much of the fact that Christ's miracles were done so often without magical apparatus, e.g., without charms, amulets, medicines, etc. Morton Smith explains that this was typical of demonic possession magic, and that with Jesus techniques of magic took the place of apparatus, above all bodily techniques—the laying on of hands, touching, rubbing, manipulating, etc. But another answer is possible: absence of magical apparatus is characteristic of the witchcraft complex, according to Evans-Pritchard's natural ideal type. Although witchcraft is imaginary, in actual practice witch patterns blend with sorcery patterns; we find sorcerers' guilds which at least *try* to create dire effects through mystical means (i.e., without apparatus[123]). Christ's antinomian message, his break with the law, with the Jewish tradition of social justice, his libertinism, his wrath, the examples of his terrible vengeance in the apocryphal books (e.g., Thomas[124]) would be consistent with an interpretation of a magician near the sorcerer type.

He was such a powerful magician, according to Smith, that his apprentices turned his collegium into a sect after his death by divinizing him, as so many magicians are divinized posthumously in a pattern widely documented since Frazer's researches.[125] We must remember, of course, that it is quite typical for the founder of a new religion to be branded a sorcerer by his enemies, and that Smith is using early enemies of Christianity as his sources. Nonetheless, this hypothesis might help to solve some historical mysteries, such as the emergence of Simon Magus almost as a double for Christ, the mystery of gnosticism, which is saturated with magic and seems intimately related to the endemic outbreaks of libertinism that Christianity seems to foster (e.g., the Carpocratian orgies, the libertine outbursts in Corinth where incest was valued). It would explain the peculiar Manicheist, libertine twist that so many Christian heretical outbreaks take across the centuries. It would help explain why a religion born in magic and saturated with it seems constantly to be struggling against it (in a way Brahminism does not) as if it feared the return of the repressed. It would also help explain the persecution by the Romans, who tolerated Oriental cults including Judaism even after repeated Judaic uprisings based on religion. Following a policy opposite to that of the Confucian mandarins, Rome tolerated foreign religions but legislated against magic, above all because it feared attacks on the state by black magic.[126] Both Jews and Romans in the ancient world accused the Christians of being sorcerers, and as late as Constantine they were on the defensive against such charges. Even in later centuries, there is an inner esoteric toleration of occultism in the higher reaches of the church, even while the church persecutes it among the laity—e.g., the Renaissance popes, perhaps the Templars, occultism among the French clergy in the nineteenth century, etc.

The very alacrity with which the papal literati adopted the new magics revived in the Renaissance was one provocation of the Protestant counter-revolution against magic; Kramer and Sprenger[127] were allowed to become adepts in the Hermetic philosophy (in whose esoteric power they ardently believed) in order to fight fire with fire. The rumor of secret libraries echoes across the ages, and in France especially, demonological and satanic cults developed among the clergy themselves.[128] Gilles de Rais continues to fascinate this kind of Catholic mind[129]: it rationalizes the fascination in terms of the miracle of god's forgiveness of de Rais after his penance. Perhaps it is because Christianity almost failed by virtue of its magical reputation that it constantly fights its own original esoteric nature, and that may be why it is both a highly magical and a highly rationalizing religion. It often rationalizes against magic; then, quickly, it must revive exorcism and other magical defenses against the demons which its own imagination stimulates.[130]

Just as the magical nature of Hinduism is most vividly evident in some of its key myths and images,[131] Christian myths have a magical texture too, which we perceive only unconsciously because they are so familiar. The familiar nativity scenes of Christmas haunt us all with magic hope. The magicians who come from the East; the magical foreknowledge of the event; the magical song of the "herald" angels; the child himself, that central image of magic's first borrowing from religion (the initiation rite); the scene in the manger so reminiscent of the Indo-European king of the beasts—what warms us at Christmas is not the social burden of religion but the hope of human magic. Pagan magics cling to Christmas by natural affinity rather than by accident. So it is not surprising that the Santa Claus figure, which is perhaps derived from Robin Goodfellow or even a devil, gets associated with Christmas, not to mention Saturnalia. The human personality is born out of magic and sustained by its miracles; the birth of Christ symbolizes our own emergence; Christmas calls forth libertinism rather than fasting just as Christ and his disciples "came eating and drinking." It is magic and ourselves that we love in Christmas, not religion or god.[132]

Christianity emerged out of a religious milieu (including popular magic and secret societies[133]) which patterned its own magical protest cults; Christianity began as one such cult. Once established, Christianity in turn patterns its own magical protest cults. Because of its tormenting inner conflict about magic, Christianity is forever expelling magic, thereby making a vacuum, and then creating new magic to fill it. This is how it patterns its own magical protest sects; it is merely a more violent case of the universal tendency of religions to evoke and pattern magical protest.

Even Protestantism evokes new magic systematically by its antimagical attacks. At least three such processes were at work in the early modern era: 1. First, extreme Protestant anti-magic, by cancelling various sacraments, stripped the people of defenses against witchcraft and new magics had to be created or adopted (e.g., witch ordeals and trials) to fill the vacuum. 2. Second, some Protestant movements, like most new sects, brought in *new* magics when they started – drawing on gnostic, Manichean or occult ideas—to signal their ascendancy with marvels. (See Ronald Knox, for example, on the links between the Quakers and the Anabaptists and the tendency of Quakerism to become ecstatic and occult until it saved itself by the swerve into deism.[134]) 3. Finally, the tension of Calvinism's *decretum horribile* was so strong that the people were forced later to invent some fresh magics to provide themselves with relief. Weber[135] and Richard Niebuhr[136] have shown that an anti-magical index of the various sects can be given by how many sacraments they abolished. But this extreme Protestant rationalism created a new vacuum, which was filled first by popular magic and later by magical offsets which Protestantism itself ultimately had to provide. First, the extreme Job-like submission to god, which eschewed magical manipulation, became in time a kind of magical *bhahkti*. Even in the "purer," ascetic Calvinist church, which stayed closer to Calvin's doctrine that there is no way of knowing who is elect, the compromise dogma was that knowledge of election comes only by "faith." This soon translated into magical self-confidence.[137] (In time, the power of Protestant confidence magic tries to conquer the universe—Tillich defines Protestant confidence as "the courage to accept acceptance" even if you are not acceptable and there is no "Acceptor"; i.e. it "transcends theism."[138]) And if Protestants removed the frankly magical aspects of traditional prayer—the spell-like manipulations, the mechanical quantifications—they introduced new elements of magic. Avoidance of manipulation sometimes turned toward mere openness to God; but this quickly took on aspects of what Keith Thomas calls "divinatory prayer";[139] it was often close to a trance-like experience. Prayer was also frequently accompanied by fasting and personal austerity. The Protestant practice of translating the Bible into the vernacular made its many magics, both Old Testament and New, more widely available to the masses. Finally, in the Protestant breakout many of the perennial gnostic heresies of Christianity's alter ego found expression. Voegelin[140] and Ronald Knox[141] have traced this development. Frances Yates has shown how, at a still later stage, liberal Protestantism in England and Germany cultivated the occult arts of the Renaissance, and figures like John Dee hoped to find with their aid an overarching theosophy that would reunite Christianity on the basis of a higher wisdom.[142]

Weber's classic interpretation showing that few Protestant sects retained their Job-like submission to god after the first generation or so, can be interpreted to read that they relaxed their anti-magic one way or another and found some route back to magic. Lutheranism, with its magical pieties and good works; Pietism with its cultivation of a pious state of mind (seen first as a sign of salvation but later as magically causing it); Methodism with its cultivation of magical conversion; Baptism with its magical seizure of the spirit; and even later Calvinism with its cultivation of self-confidence as a sign (and no doubt instrument) of election ...so even "worldly asceticisms" lapsed back into magic.[143] And of course Protestantism spawned frankly magical, immanentist and occult minor sects by the dozen.[144] Extreme Calvinism downgraded all sacraments (as magical) and even lessened social ties (e.g., the weakening of old friendship patterns described by Nelson,[145] or of communalistic patterns described by A. D. J. MacFarlane[146])—but this relative "desocialization" freed men to serve impersonal goals of social usefulness that were potentially transformative. In true Calvinism the only sign of election is "expectant faith," which itself is not even causative but results from grace. The only possible stance in such a terrifying predicament is to "act as if." This was too harsh for almost anyone, so pastoral advice watered it down to two ideas: 1. It is one's duty to consider oneself as chosen. 2. One must absolutely fight all doubts that one is not chosen. Surely even the pure Calvinist creed is one of the most dynamic magics the world has ever seen. Calvinist thought *requires* confidence (or at least the willingness to act as if confident) and this produced an explosion of world-transformative action. And that, in the weak sense at least, is powerful magic.

Hinduism

Hinduism is so magical that it is almost difficult to conceptualize it as a religion, but here is a way of doing so: You might say that in Hinduism the typical process whereby religions pattern magical protest sects has become the whole performance. Hinduism is like a stage on which one magical protest after another is performed; Hinduism is a set of plans for constructing new magical sects preaching the same old story generation after generation; Hinduism is a loose baggy assembly of cults that constantly provoke new magical protest sects, all of them working over endlessly the same few threadbare ideas. This is only one aspect of Hindu fragmentation, of course; there is also the social structuralism dimension tending toward virtually a separate cult for every caste, subcaste and biradiri, almost suggestive of a regression to something like totemism or the clan religions de Coulanges describes in early Rome,[147] and all this reflecting and supporting caste fragmentation. How Hinduism supports the caste structure is a fascinating subject that cannot be treated in this chapter.[148]

But what attracts notice in Hinduism, and what gets exported, are the effervescent sects, and it is almost as if there were no core that they protest against, so miscellaneous has the menagerie become. One way world religions become more magical is through constant assimilation, as subcults, of magical protests that spring up around them. This also tends to produce a very amorphous structure, so that critics like Joachim Kahl[149] can claim, for example, that "there is no such thing as Christianity," just a collection of cults. Amorphism reaches a kind of limit in Hinduism, where even the main "denominations" like Saivism and Vaishnavism are themselves collections of sects with little organizational structure, no churches, etc. And the whole thing is organized around a caste of magicians, rather than priests, and rationalized by magical theosophies rather than religious theologies. Hinduism thus resembles totemic systems of individual caste and family cults (it is called "Arya Dharma" or "Aryan Duty" by its members[150]) supplemented by magical sects, with no formal organization, no theology, magicians rather than priests at the center, and the only overarching cognitive unity provided by a succession of magical theosophies (Vedanta, the Upanishads, etc.) rather than religious theology. These magical theosophies, working like archetypes, in turn program the magical protest movements that spring up endlessly around them, so Hinduism looks less like a solid house than an arena in which this is staged. All this is the result of some extraordinary historical circumstances which cannot be detailed here. To shorten the present discussion I will concentrate on Max Weber's study.

In *The Religion of India* we see that magic for Weber is not the opposite of rationality nor is it necessarily related to ecstatic experience. For the Brahmins are an intellectual elite who *rationalize* magic, making it more ritualistic, detached, non-ecstatic.[151] We see how paradoxical Weber's processes are when we read that intellectuals working on religious material to "rationalize" it often make it more irrational or more magical—their "rationalization" might be said to resemble the mental operations in obsessional neurosis. Weber repeats this idea in *Ancient Judaism*[152] when he observes that the Levites' rationalization of the Hebrew social compact was saved from irrationality only because they were on the side of the masses. In India, however, Brahminical rationalization consists of an endless elaboration rather than synthesis, a constant increment of taboos, prohibitions and ceremonial additions, much incoherent cataloguing and obsessional detail. Weber does not explain why rationalization sometimes goes in this retrograde direction, while in other cases it moves toward logic, secularization, etc., but we might surmise that magical operations on old classification systems are more involved in the former case. Hocart's suggestion[153] that Brahmins are a particular kind of magician is also helpful: if they indeed derive from the heralds who spoke the spells at sacrifices which they memorized and had to repeat precisely, rather than from shamans, for example, we can understand their intellectual, non-ecstatic magic better.

To Weber the Hindu religion is a historical anomaly and it needs to be explained: it is a case where a caste of magicians conquered power without becoming priests. Falling back on the old occupational distinction which is the root agreement between Weber and Durkheim (i.e., church = congregation = priest as servant of the community) Weber documents the very striking fact that Brahmins as a rule will not serve as priests of any of the congregationalist cults or denominations that grow up within syncretistic Hinduism. For to be a "servant of the community" is to be a Sudra; even to accept the job of temple priest could degrade a Brahmin socially; the work is beneath the dignity of this caste.[154] Some Brahmins may indeed work in temples of Vishnu but their social relationship to Hindu sect members is quite different from that of an occidental sect with its employed ministry: they are always paid fees for each magical service, rather than a stipend (and Mauss has shown that these fees still have the status of magical gifts[155]). Why the Brahmins dominate and why there is a caste system are two matters Weber links together. To explain caste he begins sensibly with a focused-eclectic position similar to that of Bouglé[156] and Hutton[157]: i.e., caste is caused by all those historical divisive factors such as invasions, weak states, racial heterogeneity, etc.—but magical-religious ideas were decisive.[158] Weber speaks of the rising prestige of magic in this society (fostered by the Brahmins), and ultimately he gives a very precise hypothesis as to what happened. This explanation in turn is the most striking instance to be found in his works showing the degree to which his whole approach to religion is transcendental, idealist, with ideas moving social structure rather than vice versa.

Weber notes that the caste system is a beautifully "logical construction"— so logical that it must have existed as a finished idea long before it conquered even the greater part of North India, much less the rest. The combination of caste legitimacy with the karma doctrine and this with the specific Brahmin theodicy was a stroke of genius, the product of thought rather than economic conditions, he claims. Weber's basic idea is that Hinduism was a rationalization of magical ideas in the form of a blueprint for a social system which then sold itself on the basis of its intellectual prestige. Dumézil[159] has shown how it crystallized the traditional three- or four-caste social structure of the Aryan peoples, as Plato attempted to do in the West. As a logical perfection of tradition, Hinduism was irresistible; it shaped social structure instead of being its projection—and it did so in a very definite way.[160] Weber imagined that Hinduism spreads because the ruling classes of various tribes and states, attracted by its prestige and seeking to pacify their masses, call the Brahmin genealogists in as consultants (the way Dion of Syracuse called in Plato!). The Brahmins come with their social blueprints and impose the caste system.[161] Once imposed, it is virtually unbreakable because of the promises it gives to the oppressed (status improvement through 1. reincarnation, 2. nirvana; all this *and* 3. heaven, too)— not to mention the incomparable legitimation it provides for the ruling strata. Hence there was never any Jacquerie in India, never any peasant revolt as in China; only the ruling classes revolted, the cultivated Kshatriyas who resembled the nobles of Provence; they were destroyed (for their sins, the Brahmins said) and replaced by the illiterate Rajput mercenary lords.[162] In India, magic protest cults are so patterned by the religious system that they reinforce it instead of overthrowing or changing it.

Chinese Religions

In *The Religion of China*[163] Weber describes another literati with a non-theistic rationalist "religion" which also drove the masses into the irrational. The Confucians were not exactly anti-magical but anti-sacred; they saw religions as potential centers of revolt (e.g., the Puritan anti-magical T'ai P'ing revolt) and suppressed them; they were more tolerant of popular magic (in the way V. Gordon Childe suggests[164] that Middle Eastern empires often were in hopes of keeping the people quiet). Specifically, they tolerated the mysticism of the Lao-Tzu tradition as a kind of official opposition, and popular magicians flocked to its banner and made it more magical still. The gods of the popular pantheon were believed to be magicians who rose into the sky, in the familiar pattern reported by Frazer; magic had the usual practical ends with a special emphasis here on attaining health and old age by avoidance of stress.

The rise of protest sects was inhibited by Confucian policy, while Confucian toleration of magic provided an alternative outlet. At some periods so-called philosophical movements probably functioned as disputing protest sects.

Needham and Waley have shown that many of them were deeply colored by the characteristic magic of Taoism. Taoist magicians sometimes created congregations, but in general religiosity did not strongly develop in this manner; and Taoism remained more an organization of magicians (and of environmentalist mystics and ecology-minded recluses).

This rather practical, sensible and even healthy magical tradition became, curiously, the religion of the urban middle class businessman—it would be hard to think of a Western parallel. (In Weber's "decisionist" interpretation, an urban bourgeoisie might have a greater presumptive "elective affinity" for a more rationalistic religion, but it does not automatically project one in a Durkheimian, much less a Marxist, manner.)

It is interesting that popular magic in imperial China was associated with a culture that, despite conspicuous social horrors, seems in general quite humanistic to Westerners, while Indian society, led by a magician's caste, has always seemed life-negating. To explain this purely as an emphasis of worldview, as Evans-Pritchard might, is perhaps merely to reassert the problem. Is the difference to be found entirely in vast underlying social differences (huge clans instead of castes, a rationalizing civil service and state instead of social fragmentation) or does it perhaps, in part, also have something to do with the *kind* of magic that was central in each case? In India, the kerux-Brahmin who expropriated the social ceremony has seemed to many observers to approach sorcery,[165] whereas Chinese Taoist magic seems more like shamanistic, health-giving white magic. There is a considerable body of evidence from Granet,[166] Needham,[168] Waley[168] and others on the centrality of Taoism and its derivation from shamanism.

Israel and Islam

But the world religions are not all equally magical—far from it. Some really do fit Weber's ideal of ethical religions that fight magic. And some do not quite fit my schema of new religions arising as magical protests. This is above all the case where religions arose as political movements and political protests. Mendenhall[169] has summarized the evidence that the Hebrews under Moses were a confederation of Apirus, a typical slave revolt; in his view religion arose out of their social contract by a process of "ceremonialization." Judaism later assimilated so much magic as to be a creative source of it in the Renaissance (e.g., Kabbala). But in its origins Judaism does not fit the schema.

It *can* be shown that early Judaism patterned magical protest sects around it (e.g., the Prophets, the secret societies, etc.) but not that core Judaism itself arose out of such a magical revolt. The difference was the political nature of pristine Judaism. True, it was a revolt patterned by previous *political* revolts, if Mendenhall's account of the Apirus' tradition is accepted; and it is also well known that political contracts were ceremonialized and projected deities in this culture area.[170] But it would be too forced to try to push this limiting case entirely into a schema which I am satisfied to assert merely as a tendency found in most religions.

According to Weber's *Ancient Judaism*,[171] Yahweh was not originally a god of Israel, but a god from afar, adopted as the symbol of the social contract—this remoteness saved the religion from immanence, curbed magic and abetted rationalization. Moses did work miracles to certify his leadership, but miracles are unusual exceptions in the normal world, discrete theophanies, not expressions of immanence or a magical worldview. One gets the impression that consciousness of society as a social contract inhibits magical expropriation of social rites. The ancient Hebrews were aware that magic is often a distraction from social justice.

At a later date, after the Iranian influences of the Babylonian exile, Israel would become a fertile source of magic for the world. And Weber does recognize that, once established as a religion, Judaism anticipated and patterned its own magical revolts just like any other religion. In *The Sociology of Religion*[172] he characterizes prophecy as a magical process—with the prophet a shaman, ecstatic or visionary who collects a group of supporters, and with the central religion patterning such movements via traditional expectations, certification and cooptation.

Mohammedanism also developed some magic in its later stages, though less than Judaism, and it too had a political origin—as the nucleus of a military state. On the other hand, its beginnings do resemble the magical pre-patterned sect phenomenon, unlike Judaism. Bouquet[173] and Gibb[174] have shown that a pattern already existed for wandering visionaries ("hanifs"); that Mohammed lapsed into this state after personal traumas and experienced ecstatic revelations as hallucinations. A. J. Arberry[175] has shown how the later Sufis always try to link their own monotheistic magic to the prophet's early mystical experiences. Although one could conceptualize Judaism as purely political in origin, with a social contract, Mohammedanism begins within the periphery of the Judaic prophet complex. This is Judaism's own assimilation pattern for its own magical protests. Christianity began as a protest sect within this culture system. This Judaic complex had diffused to Arabia and was colored by local visionary traditions. The Muslim religion began as a protest sect in this milieu. But after the visions, Mohammedanism swiftly established a political-military organization; Mohammed claimed no miracles besides revelation and the movement became anti-magical, anti-mythic, legalist and rational.

Yet magic persists in this culture, and the marabout system and the sects delineate the familiar pattern of assimilating protests. Douttée[176] demonstrates that many magical elements of the "religion of the Semites" described by Robertson Smith[177] are still present in Moslem cults of saints. Equally striking is Douttée's demonstration that even the pure monotheistic faith in Allah works as wish magic.[178]

Even in the "world religions," it seems, magic keeps borrowing symbolism from religion and using it to argue with religion; and magical protests keep turning into new cults within religion. This formulation even fits the great ethical religions—most of them, anyway, for not only do they begin with magic promises to attract followers but much of their magical symbolism is derived from the old religious culture which they protest. Thus Buddhism and Hinduism arise within Brahminism; Christianity and Islam within and against the Hebrew religious heritage.

What is the source of this endless "dialectic" of magic and religion? Some trace it to logical oppositions found in sacred symbolism, above all the opposition of sacred to profane. Roger Caillois[179] and Claude Lévi-Strauss have shown the tendencies toward endless fission and triadic synthesis that lie in these logical operators. The sacred always risks falling into the profane, thereby harming it and itself. But the sacred splits into the holy vs. the polluted; and in part the polluted is a precipitate of the interaction of the sacred with the profane. The sacred fissions, then the parts fission: thus priest vs. magician; white magician vs. black magician; sorcerer vs. witch—endless fission. But thus also the impure, a third category. Cazeneuve,[180] Douglas,[181] etc. explain this in logical cognitive terms: the sacred is order, which creates disorder as a remainder, and taboo and impurity at the border between them. Class structure sometimes reflects these antinomies, in part projects them—e.g., the sacred upper classes, the profane lower classes (and what about the "impure" middle classes based on the magic of money?).[182] There is a dialectic of fission and opposites built into sacred symbolism itself—e.g., sacred words in some languages have double and opposite meanings, such as *sacer* (holy, accursed) in Latin, *Gift* (gift, poison) in German. But it is best not to pursue this logic because that way lies the arid Platonism of the structuralist school.

Let us turn to the more obvious and sociological source—social structure itself. The distinction of central vs. peripheral rites goes back to Robertson Smith[183] and is effectively revived by Gurvitch.[184] Religion is the central cult of the society; magic tends to concern peripheral ceremonies of subcultures or marginal groups.[185] Smith's distinction of central vs. peripheral rites was a system on which to hang all his rationalist prejudices—ascribing to central rites more rationality and to magic more irrationality than was accurate. But his insight that magic is peripheral stands up in research.[186] His idea is alive today in the French school—in, for example, Gurvitch's account of the magic lodges that grow out of initiation rites and challenge the central clan religion. The peripheral theory is also alive in Weber's account of new sects representing sub-groups that challenge the larger society.

There is a third source of this dialectic. This is the struggle of the individual with society, which goes on even inside the individual, as Durkheim showed in his remarkable "Homo Duplex" essay.[187] A chapter will be devoted to this later on. There is considerable evidence that magic develops to assist at the birth of the self.

In general, it can be said that both the ego hypothesis and the peripheral hypothesis are fruitful explanations of the dialectic of religion and magic.

Magical protest speaks both for the individual ego *and* for the marginal groups. Magic springs up, as Van Gennup showed, as the magical god Hermes symbolized, at borders—borders between peoples but also the border between the individual and the society. Nor can we totally exclude consideration of the more structuralist investigations concerning the paradoxes of sacred symbolism itself. The endless dialectic of magic and religion results from all three oppositions.

Always, magic and religion lead back to each other. Religious revivals revive magic; new religions bring new magics. And magic revivals and new magics strengthen or create religious institutions. (The relation of magic to science is much less intimate and far less certain.) Magic revivals lead back to the same old thing—a few mild subjective experiences validated and patterned by the agreement to agree of a small act-as-if group or a large public reading secondary reports, all patterned by a cultural tradition that accumulates historically. The evidence is very strong, moreover, that magic and religion are projections of society; the converse evidence that they influence the course of history (like "switchmen" as Weber put it[188] or "gear wheels" in Mauss' words) is more conjectural. Finally, there is evidence that the importance of both phenomena declines, as Durkheim showed, during the growth of economic society ("organic solidarity"). Religion is important in helping us to understand the development of early society; but as both Durkheim and Marx understood, we must go beyond the sacred to understand contemporary society. Attempts of some sociologists like Parsons to turn the sociology of religion into an ideological functionalism are mistaken, for they project onto contemporary society a centrality of religion that is appropriate only in earlier societies. Religion is distinctly *not* the "command code" of modern society as Parsons would have it.[189] The DNA analogy may be appropriate for primitive societies or small societies that have lost their states. But modern society is far too complex and religion is far too confused for it to serve as the "genetic code."

By dialectic, then, I mean that religion and magic affect each other in strange and dynamic ways. These processes are paradoxical. Thus religion and magic overlap. Magic borrows symbolism from religion; but it often fights religion. On the other hand, it sometimes enters into a permanent relation with religion; religion takes it over. These paradoxes make it hard to say which precedes the other. Contemporary sociology tends therefore to abandon the question or to say that it does not matter. Despite these ambiguities, however, religion and magic can be distinguished and it is possible to say which process is basic. Moreover, both questions are important. They are the subject of the next two sections.

Notes

1. Keith Thomas, *Religion and the Decline of Magic* (N.Y., 1971), chs. 2–9, pp. 25–282.
2. Arthur Lyons, *The Second Coming: Satanism in America* (N.Y., 1970), ch. 4, pp. 63–86.
3. Viktor Rydberg, *The Magic of the Middle Ages* (N.Y., 1879). Translated from the Swedish, ch. 2.
4. Sir Samuel Dill, *Roman Society in Gaul in the Merovingian Age* (N.Y., 1966), ch. 2, "Saints and Miracles," pp. 395–438.

5. Frederick Elworthy, *The Evil Eye* (N.Y., 1970), ch. 4, p. 118, etc.
6. Edmond Douttée, *Magie et Religion Dans L'Afrique du Nord* (Algiers, 1908), pp. 593–595.
7. Hubert and Mauss, English ed., *A General Theory of Magic*, p. 52.
8. Douttée, *op. cit.*, especially Conclusion, p. 598ff.
9. If we accept the proposition that the Hellenic mystery religions were largely magical cults or carried much magic with them, then the demonstrations of Angus, Jane Harrison, Gilbert Murray, Nilsson and Dodds that these cults derived from cruder, rural versions of the same religions that had been rationalized into anthropomorphic pantheons in the cities is relevant. Zeus of the Kouretes, the "greatest Kouros," Zeus born of the ecstatic religious initiation rite, is rationalized into an Olympian with no ecstatic or animal features. Whereupon the urban masses immediately import Dionysus and his satyrs, who is simply a bumpkin form of the pristine Zeus of the Kouretes. But now the borrowed religious material is put into a much more magical cast in mystery cults serving the psychological needs of deracinated urban masses.
10. H. C. Lea, *Materials Toward a History of Witchcraft* (N.Y., London, 1957), p. xxvi and chs. 1–3.
11. *A General Theory of Magic*, ch. 3, "The Elements of Magic," p. 25ff.
12. Ernest Becker, *Escape From Evil* (N.Y., 1975), cf. chs. 1 & 4, and p. 21.
13. *A General Theory of Magic*, p. 52.
14. *Ibid.*, ch. 3, p. 25ff.
15. *Ibid.*, p. 55.
16. Douttée, *Ibid.*, p. 598ff.
17. Jane Harrison, *Themis*, ch. 3, "The Kouretes, The Thunder Rites & Mana."
18. Cf. Marcel Mauss, *L'Origine des Pouvoirs Magiques Dans Les Sociétés Australiennes*, vol. 2, *Oeuvres*, pp. 319–369.
19. Joshua Trachtenberg, *Jewish Magic and Superstition* (Cleveland, 1961), p. 15.
20. E. A. Wallis Budge, *Egyptian Magic* (N.Y., 1971), pp. xi, 4, 6.
21. Hubert and Mauss, French ed.: *Esquisse d'Une Théorie Générale de la Magie* (in Lévi-Strauss, ed., *Sociologie et Anthropologie*), p. 80, etc.
22. ". . . et nous serons amenés a l'idée que ces individus n'ont fait que *s'approprier des forces collectives*" (italics added.) Hubert and Mauss, *Esquisse. . .*, p. 83.
23. B. Malinowski, *Crime and Custom in Savage Society* (Totowa, N.J., 1976), pp. 80–83.
24. Durkheim, *The Elementary Forms of Religious Life*, p. 43.
25. Auden, *The New York Review of Books*, Feb. 17, 1966, p. 5.
26. P. Huvelin, "Magie et Droit Individuel," *L'Année Sociologique*, 1905–1906, pp. 1–47.
27. R. D. Laing, *The Divided Self* (Baltimore, 1965); *The Politics of Experience* (N.Y., 1967); *Self and Others* (N.Y., 1969); with A. Esterson, *Sanity, Madness and the Family* (London, 1964).
28. E. Fuller Torrey, *The Mind Game* (N.Y., 1973), pp. 53–56, 67–68.
29. Jerome D. Frank, *Persuasion and Healing* (N.Y., 1963), pp. 30–35.
30. Louis Rose, *Faith Healing* (London, 1970).
31. William Sargant, *Battle For the Mind* (N.Y., 1971).
32. Una Maclean, *Magical Medicine, A Nigerian Case Study* (London, 1971).
33. Freud, "Analysis Terminable and Interminable," 1937, in *Collected Papers*, James Strachey, ed. (London, 1957), vol. 5.
34. Louis Rose, *Faith Healing* (London, 1971), p. 72ff., etc.
35. Jacques Ellul, *The New Demons* (N.Y., 1975), p. 133.
36. Karen Horney, *New Ways in Psychoanalysis*, etc. (N.Y., 1939), ch. 2.
37. Jerome D. Frank, *Persuasion and Healing* (N.Y., 1963), pp. 109, 113, 152ff.
38. Robert Jay Lifton, *Thought Reform and the Psychology of Totalism* (N.Y., 1961).
39. See essays in G. Devereux, ed., *Psychoanalysis and the Occult* (N.Y., 1970), e.g., Albert Ellis, pp. 297–313.
40. William Sargant, *Battle for the Mind* (N.Y., 1971).
41. Maurice Halbwachs, *Sources of Religious Sentiment* (Glencoe, Ill., 1962), p. 22.
42. Eliane Massonneau, *Le Crime de Magie et le Droit Romain* (Paris, 1933), cf. ch. 2 on saturation of Roman religion with magic, Part II on repression of magic.
43. Hubert & Mauss, *A General Theory of Magic*, p. 92.
44. *Ibid.*, pp. 79–86.

45. Jane Ellen Harrison, *Themis* (Cambridge, 1927), chs. 1, etc.

46. Bryan Wilson, *Religious Sects* (N.Y., 1970), chs. 6–9.

47. Ernst Troeltsch, *The Social Teaching of the Christian Churches* (N.Y., 1974). Wilson charged that Troeltsch was culture-bound in classifying sects by dogma, an element more important in Western religions than elsewhere. But classification by dogma at least emphasized challenge and conflict, whereas Wilson's own classification by "response" (without a direct object) is abstract and leads to further abstract refinements (such as the sterile exercise of regrouping the seven types under further classifications as "objectivists," "subjectivists" and "relationists").

48. Bryan Wilson, *Magic and the Millennium* (N.Y., 1973).

49 It is surprising that Wilson even *used* his own earlier typology, derived from Western sects in quiescence, on the violently churning millenarian movements of the developing countries. Nonetheless, it is possible to reduce his classifications logically, factor out his definitions, and show how easily many of his types can be collapsed into magic.

50. The definition for this type is closest to being explicitly a matter of magic, though he fudges it with the awkward word "thaumaturgical" (which the OED refers first to miracles and marvels and which is not exactly the *mot juste*). *Shorter Oxford English Dictionary.*

51. A. D. Nock, *Conversion* (London, 1961), p. 74, etc.

52. See Eliade's study of Yoga, for example: *Yoga* (Princeton, 1969).

53. Barrie Reynolds, *Magic, Divination and Witchcraft Among the Barotse of Northern Rhodesia* (Berkeley and Los Angeles, 1963), chs. 1–2.

54. Later, Wilson must admit that most "messianic" religions are more thaumaturgical than revolutionist (though he claims that where a *future* messiah is expected rather than an immanentist leader, the effect is more revolutionary).

55. Weston La Barre, *The Ghost Dance* (N.Y., 1972). See also his *They Shall Take Up Serpents* (N.Y., 1969).

56. I. M. Lewis, *Ecstatic Religion* (London, 1971).

57. We can bracket Lewis' neo-animism and some of the restrictive essentialisms that go with it (his assertion that spirits are what religion is basically about and that spirit possession is the core religious phenomenon).

58. Weston La Barre, *The Ghost Dance* (N.Y., 1972), cf. pp. 41–48.

59. Géza Róheim, *The Gates of the Dream* (N.Y., 1952, 1969), ch. 3, "Dreamers and Shamans," pp. 154–251.

60. La Barre makes some sweeping generalizations. *All* religions begin as crisis cults, he claims; all religions are maladaptive: they are to be explained in Freudian Oedipal terms. There is also an evolutionary schema of the familiar Frazerian M . . . R . . . S pattern superimposed on a Róheimian-Freudian analysis. While claiming to avoid an evolutionary approach, La Barre recasts it in Freudian developmental terms: Magic is the pre-Oedipal oral phase of dual-unity, omnipotence of thought and word magic; religion is an Oedipal struggle with, worship of, ambivalence about the father and hence latently homosexual; in science man grows up. In spite of his schema La Barre gives us a valuable descriptive account of how religion is renewed or new religion created by magical protest.

61. The prophetic revolution is usually in some sense a restoration.

62. Cf. Jacob Needleman, *The New Religions* (N.Y., 1972) for accounts of Baba, Subud, etc.

63. Needleman thinks that Buddhism and Hinduism translate into the same magical core-metapsychology: Buddhism's no-Atman (no-ego) principle is really not far from Hinduism's notion that the divine being is the diverse, impersonal world and that the self IS this being. In fighting "mâya," both are piercing the illusion of the (social) world that leads us to believe in the reality of such constructs as the self. But this is just magic's typical assault on the objective frame of the paramount reality. If Buddhism and Hinduism really are a kind of sociological insight into the made-up nature of social reality it is interesting that, historically, this gnosis seems to have fostered passivity rather than action.

64. Weston La Barre, *They Shall Take Up Serpents* (N.Y., 1969), cf. chs. 2, 7.

65. Diabetes, for example, is not merely inherited but may be renewed by continued mutations, according to one theory. Before insulin, many diabetics would die without reproducing themselves, yet the frequency of the disease continued high. This could be visualized as a DNA tape with a loose molecule on it that had a certain high probability of being knocked off by mere heat motion.

66. Franz Neumann, *Behemoth* (N.Y., 1942, 1966), Part I, ch. 2, etc.

67. Hannah Arendt, *The Origins of Totalitarianism* (Cleveland, 1958), pp. 364–388.

68. For example, the Garrison investigation into the assassination of President Kennedy in New Orleans brought to light the "Orthodox Old Catholic Church of North America," a deviant sect dating back to an obscure schism in Utrecht, Holland, in the 18th century, which, after numerous permutations, had become occult and homosexual in orientation, according to testimony concerning David Ferrie and others of its members. Paris Flammonde, *The Kennedy Conspiracy* (N.Y., 1969), pp. 37–8.

69. The new movements arise, of course, in response to changes in social structure, and taking them over enables religions to adapt to these changes. Henri Pirenne, for example, shows that the Franciscans and the Dominicans were originally mystic urban mendicants spreading from city to city; established in orders, they lived on the alms of the new bourgeoisie, were recruited from it and exercised their apostolate for their sake. Coopting them helped the Church keep its foothold in the new bourgs. Henri Pirenne, *A History of Europe* (Garden City, N.Y., 1956), vol. I, p. 223.

70. S. Angus, *The Mystery-Religions* (N.Y., 1975). See reference to the burden of astral pessimism, p. 249ff.

71. Ernest Becker, *Escape From Evil* (N.Y., 1975). Becker writes that the new "era of the son" promised to democratize magic and restore it to the individual as in primitive society. (The tendency of churches to monopolize magic and thus produce magical revolts in the laity seeking some new magic of their own which the church in turn ultimately takes over, may be one source of the process we will later describe by which the world religions historically became MORE magical rather than less so.) Cf. p. 69ff.

72. P. Huvelin, "Magie et Droit Individuel," *L'Année Sociologique*, 1905-6, pp. 1–47. Hubert and Mauss use the term "expropriation."

73. Herbert Goldhammer and Andrew Marshall, *Psychosis and Civilization* (Glencoe, Ill., 1949). Cf. also (on the Hutterites) Joseph W. Eaton and Robert J. Weil, *Culture and Mental Disorders* (Glencoe, Ill. 1955).

74. Michel Foucault, *Madness and Civilization* (N.Y., 1967).

75. J. Huizinga, *The Waning of the Middle Ages* (Garden City, N.Y. 1956), pp. 9–30.

76. D. Erasmus, *In Praise of Folly*.

77. Louis Pauwels and Jacques Bergier, *The Morning of the Magicians* (N.Y., 1968), p. 109ff.

78. Miguel de Unamuno y Jugo, *The Agony of Christianity and Essays on Faith* (London, 1972).

79. Richard H. Niebuhr, *The Social Sources of Denominationalism* (N.Y., 1929).

80. Talcott Parsons, "Durkheim on Religion Revisited," in Charles Y. Glock and Phillip E. Hammond, *Beyond the Classics?* (N.Y., 1973), pp. 156-180.

81. But the "command code" analogy suffers from serious weaknesses which immediately become evident if it is taken too literally: 1. Religion is far too inchoate and vague to be the DNA codescript for anything. 2. This analogy would be more appropriate in primitive society when religious symbolism was central.

82. Agehananda Bharati, *The Tantric Tradition* (Garden City, N.Y., 1970).

83. Louis Pauwels and Jacques Bergier, *The Morning of the Magicians* (N.Y., 1968), *passim.*

84. Rune E. A. Johannsen, *The Psychology of Nirvana* (Garden City, N.Y., 1970).

85. Th. Stcherbatsky, *Buddhist Logic* (N.Y., 1962), vol. 1.

86. Jacob Needleman, *The New Religions* (N.Y., 1972).

87. "This *certitudo salutis,* however—the present enjoyment of the tranquillity of the saved—is indeed, psychologically, the psychic state sought, in the last analysis, by the religions of India . . . (Buddhism's) specific accomplishment consisted in having pursued this and only this goal, abolishing without consideration all holy means which had nothing to do with it." Max Weber, *The Religion of India* (New York, 1958), pp. 205-206.

88. Cf. H. Neill McFarland, *The Rush Hour of the Gods* (N.Y., 1967), on sects in post-war Japan.

89. Heinrich Zimmer, *Myths and Symbols in Indian Art and Civilization* (Princeton, 1972), pp. 51–52.

90. R. Johanssen, *The Psychology of Nirvana* (Garden City, N.Y., 1970), pp. 2-3.

91. Eliade, *Yoga,* p. 355.

92. The pure monism associated with these practices can be viewed as the typical magical

worldview. (The classic Hindu Yoga of Patanjali, though itself theist, is closely related to the monist Samkya philosophical system, which is in the mainline tradition of Brahmin metaphysics running from the Upanishads through Samkhya to the Vedanta.) This pure monism is nothing other than an intellectual rationalization of the typical magical ("Machian") view: of a universe unified by magical force. In Hinduism the impersonal self is part of the impersonal divine being. In Buddhism the self is nonexistent, there is only the stream of consciousness, but it in turn reproduces the chaotic reality of the world.

93. Max Weber, *The Religion of India* (N.Y., 1958), pp. 205.

94. Celestin Bouglé, *Essais Sur Le Regime des Castes* (Paris, 1935).

95. Agehananda Bharati, *The Tantric Tradition* (N.Y., 1965).

96. One feels that in merging with more popular and ancient magics in Tantrism and the Mahayana, Buddhism was merely finding its way home. Some years ago, Gilbert Highet, in *Man's Unconquerable Mind,* noted that Buddhist art was non-representational at first. After Alexander's invasion, Greek art took root in India, and Highet claims that the face of Buddha was copied from statues of Apollo. He thought it ironical that this meditative figure could thus be based on art representing the god of Greek rationalism. But of course, as Dodds has shown, the cult of Apollo, derived immediately from Asia Minor perhaps, is thought to have come originally from afar, from central Asia. What Apollo really stands for, Dodds writes, is individual trance, as distinguished from the mass ecstasy of Dionysus, despite Nietzsche's attempt to schematize a broad gulf between the two (in *The Birth of Tragedy*). So when the head of Apollo modeled the image of the entranced Buddha, perhaps something else had come home, too.

97. R. Johanssen, *The Psychology of Nirvana* (Garden City, 1970), chs. 1, 5, 6, 8.

98. Louis Pauwels, *Gurdjieff* (N.Y., 1972).

99. Morton Smith, *Clement of Alexandria and A Secret Gospel of Mark* (Cambridge, Mass., 1973), cf. ch. 4. A summary of this book is found in Morton Smith, *The Secret Gospel* (N.Y., 1973).

100. E.R. Dodds, *The Greeks and the Irrational* (Berkeley & Los Angeles, 1951, 1973), ch. 2, pp. 28-63.

101. Morton Smith, *Clement of Alexandria . . .,* pp. 219 seq.

102. John M. Allegro, *The Sacred Mushroom and the Cross* (N.Y., 1971).

103. Lynn Thorndike, *A History of Magic and Experimental Science* (N.Y., 1923), vol. I, ch. 16.

104. Homer W. Smith, *Man and His Gods* (N.Y., 1956), p. 190.

105. Rudolf Bultmann, *Primitive Christianity* (N.Y., 1974), *Kerygma and Myth* (N.Y., 1962).

106. Samuel Sandmel, *We Jews And Jesus* (N.Y., 1965, 1973), p. 19, etc.

107. Max Weber, *The Sociology of Religion* (Boston, 1964), p. 47, etc.

108. I.e., miracles are once-over exceptions which do not flout reason as regularly as magic.

109. Morton Smith, *Jesus The Magician* (N.Y., 1978), pp. 211-220.

110. Moses Hadas, *Hellenistic Culture* (N.Y., 1959), Ch. 13, "Aretologies and Martyrdoms," pp. 170-181.

111. Cf. Lynn Thorndike, *op. cit.,* ch. 17.

112. Cf. Philostratus, *Life of Apollonius,* ed. G. W. Bowersock (London, 1970).

113. Max Weber, *The Sociology of Religion* (Boston, 1964). See, for example, p. 47; pp. 148-9; p. 184; p. 191. Almost every reference to Jesus states or implies that he was a magician.

114. There is a folk knowledge of this: Peasants in Greece today call Jesus a magician. Richard and Eva Blum, *The Dangerous Hour* (London, 1970), p. 81.

115. Morton Smith, *Clement of Alexandria and a Secret Gospel of Mark* (Cambridge, Mass., 1973), pp. 224-225.

116. Weber, *The Sociology of Religion,* pp. 184, etc.

117. Max Weber, *Ancient Judaism* (Glencoe, Ill., 1952), p. 394ff and see "miracles" in the index.

118. Mauss, "L'Origine des Pouvoirs Magiques Dans les Sociétés Australiennes" in *Oeuvres,* vol. 2, pp. 319-70. Morton Smith writes: "And we have also seen some reason to believe that there was in Palestine in Jesus' time a magical technique for ascending and causing others to ascend into the heavens." (*Clement of Alexandria . . .,* p. 236).

119. *Ibid.*, p. 236; also in *The Secret Gospel* (N.Y., 1973), p. 114.

120. Morton Smith, *Clement of Alexandria . . .*, p. 222.

121. *Jesus the Magician* (N.Y., 1978).

122. Lynn Thorndike, *A History of Magic . . .*, ch. 16.

123. For example, the Barotse; cf. Barrie Reynolds, *op. cit.* See also Victor Turner's discussion of witch patterns in sorcery complexes in "Witchcraft and Sorcery," ch. 5, *The Forest of Symbols* (Ithaca, 1967), pp. 112–130.

124. R. M. Grant, *The Secret Sayings of Jesus* (Garden City, N.Y., 1959); also J. Doresse, *The Secret Book of the Egyptian Gnostics* (London, 1960).

125. J. G. Frazer, *The Magic Art and the Evolution of Kings,* condensed as first 17 chs. of *The Golden Bough,* abridged ed. (N.Y., 1960), pp. 1–205.

126. Cf. Eliane Massonneau, *Le Crime de Magie et le Droit Romain* (Paris, 1933).

127. Heinrich Kramer and James Sprenger, *The Malleus Maleficorum* (N.Y., 1971).

128. Cf. Ronald Knox, Huysmans, James Webb, *ops. cit.,* on this.

129. For an account of his career see Jules Michelet, *Jeanne D'Arc* (Paris, 1948), p. 253ff.

130. Bellah has shown that a wave of "protestant," anti-magical, ethical reformist sects hit most of the world religions, not just Christianity. Robert N. Bellah, *Beyond Belief* (N.Y., 1970), ch. 2, pp. 20–52.

131. H. Zimmer, *Myths and Symbols in Indian Art and Civilization* (Princeton, 1974).

132. The perennial banal protestations against the "commercialization of Christmas," or its alleged degradation into a mere celebration and jollity, perhaps express the discomfort some people have at the return of this repressed knowledge.

133. Even more important than the Dead Sea Scrolls, perhaps, in understanding this milieu and these secret societies is the current deciphering of the Nag Hammadi Gnostic library. Cf. John Dart's popularization, *The Laughing Savior* (N.Y., 1976).

134. Ronald Knox, *Enthusiasm* (Oxford, 1950), ch. 8.

135. Max Weber, *The Protestant Ethic and the Spirit of Capitalism* (London, 1948), ch. 4.

136. H. Richard Niebuhr, *The Social Sources of Denominationalism* (N.Y., 1957).

137. Weber, *Ibid.*, pp. 98–128.

138. Paul Tillich, *The Courage To Be* (New Haven, 1959), pp. 163ff.

139. Keith Thomas, *Religion and the Decline of Magic* (N.Y., 1971), pp. 117-8.

140. Eric Voegelin, *The New Science of Politics* (Chicago, 1952), ch. 5, "Gnostic Revolution—The Puritan Case," pp. 133–161.

141. Ronald Knox, *Enthusiasm* (Oxford, 1950), chs. 1, 7, etc.

142. F. Yates, *The Rosicrucian Enlightenment* (London & Boston, 1972), chs. 3, etc.

143. Weber, *The Protestant Ethic . . .*, ch. 4

144. Even when the apparatus is almost entirely rationalized the old promise of magic is always there. Some people read a Tillich or a Bultmann because of the "angle thrown out for the half-believer," as one critic put it (Austin Farrer, "An English Appreciation," in Rudolf Bultmann and 5 Critics, *Kerygma and Myth*, ed. H. W. Bartsch, N.Y., 1961, pp. 212–223, cf. p. 212). They hope these snares will be magic carpets that will enable them to fly after all. Just as a new mathematics begins with the fewest, sparest concepts possible, and then soars, Protestant theology today (which has become a popular commodity, "theology as theater" with new plays every season) catches the unbeliever where he is, in his unbelief, and yet offers him the hope of flying. Even from atheism we may still deduce something remarkable, is the popular, magically-appealing promise. Adorno comments on the hopeful mentality of the purveyors who "have gradually come to intone their Te Deum wherever God is denied, because at least his name is mentioned." Theodore Adorno, *Negative Dialectics* (N.Y., 1979), p. 372.

145. Benjamin Nelson, *The Idea of Usury* (Chicago & London, 1969), pp. 141–164.

146. A. D. J. MacFarlane, *Witchcraft in Tudor and Stuart England* (N.Y., 1970), ch. 18.

147. Fustel de Coulanges, *The Ancient City* (N.Y., 1955), pp. 11–41.

148. Hinduism as projection and defense of the caste system is illuminated in numerous studies including: E. A. H. Blunt, *The Caste System of Northern India* (Oxford 1931); J. J. Hutton, *Caste in India* (London, 1946); C. Bouglé, *Essais Sur le Régime des Castes* (Paris, 1935); G. S. Ghurye, *Caste and Race in India* (London, 1932); Louis Dumont, *Homo Hierarchicus* (Chicago, 1970); Bouquet, *Hinduism* (London, 1948); A. M. Hocart, *Kings and*

Councillors (Chicago, 1970); A. M. Hocart, *Caste* (London, 1950); Claude Lévi-Strauss, *The Elementary Structures of Kinship* (Boston, 1969), ch. 25, "Clans and Castes," pp. 406–421; S. V. Viswanatha, *Racial Synthesis in Hindu Culture* (London, 1932); Radharkrishnan, *Eastern Religions and Western Thought* (Oxford, 1939), ch. 9. How the Hindu family transmits these operators and shapes personality to fit the social structure is described in Margaret Cormack, *The Hindu Woman* (N.Y., 1953); Gardner Murphy, *In the Minds of Men* (N.Y., 1953); David G. Mandelbaum, "The Family in India," *Southwestern Journal of Anthropology,* vol. 4, no. 2, summer, 1948. A bitter critique of the modern outcome is found in V. S. Naipaul, *India, A Wounded Civilization,* (N.Y., 1977).

149. Joachim Kahl, *The Misery of Christianity* (London, 1971), pp. 25–6.

150. A. C. Bouquet, *Comparative Religion* (London, 1954), ch. 7.

151. Max Weber, *The Religion of India* (N.Y., 1958), pp. 137–162

152. Max Weber, *Ancient Judaism* (N.Y., 1960), ch. 7.

153. A. M. Hocart, *Kings and Councillors* (Chicago & London, 1970), ch. 14, esp. pp. 194–5. See also *Caste* (London, 1950).

154. Max Weber, *The Religion of India,* ch. 4.

155. Mauss, *The Gift* (N.Y., 1967), pp. 53–59.

156. Celestin Bouglé, *Essais Sur le Régime Des Castes* (Paris, 1935.)

157. J. J. Hutton, *Caste In India* (London, 1946).

158. In this amalgam, Lévi-Strauss surmises that hypergamy was decisive, while Dumont points to hierarchy and Bouglé and Hutton to purity ideas.

159. Georges Dumézil, *Les Dieux Des Indo-Européens* (Paris, 1952).

160. Weber's theory of the origin of caste is only one of many. A more complete explanation is possible, but there is no space to treat it here. See ch. 13.

161. Weber, *The Religion of India* (N.Y., 1958), pp. 9-11.

162. Celestin Bouglé, *op. cit.*

163. Weber, *The Religion of China* (N.Y., 1964), ch. 5.

164. V. Gordon Childe, *Man Makes Himself* (N.Y., 1951); *What Happened in History* (London, 1954).

165. In a recent book Aubrey Menon refered to the Brahmins as a caste of "witches."

166. Marcel Granet, *Chinese Civilization* (N.Y., 1958); *La Pensée Chinoise,* (Paris, 1974); *Etudes Sociologiques Sur La Chine* (Paris, 1953).

167. Joseph Needham, *Science and Civilization in China,* especially Vol. 11, Section 10. (Cf. pp. 83–86, "Taoism and Magic.") Also Vol. I (Cambridge, 1954); Vol. III (Cambridge, 1959); and Introduction to Vol. IV (Cambridge, 1962).

168. Arthur Waley, *The Way and Its Power* (N.Y., 1958).

169. George E. Mendenhall, *The Tenth Generation, The Origins of the Biblical Tradition* (Baltimore, 1973); also chs. 1, 2, 5 in Edward F. Campbell, Jr., and Noel Freedman, eds., *Biblical Archeologist Reader* No. 3 (Garden City, N.Y., 1970).

170. George E. Mendenhall, "Covenant Forms in Israelite Tradition," ch. 2 in Edward F. Campbell, Jr. and David Noel Freedman, eds., *Biblical Archeologist Reader No. 3* (Garden City, N.Y., 1970), pp. 25–53.

171. Weber, *Ancient Judaism* (Glencoe, Ill., 1952), p. 156ff., etc.

172. Max Weber, *The Sociology of Religion* (Boston, 1964): see index under "Prophets."

173. A. C. Bouquet, *Comparative Religion* (London, 1955), ch. 10, "Islam," pp. 264–283.

174. H. A. R. Gibb, *Mohammedanism* (N.Y., 1955), pp. 27-30.

175. A. J. Arberry, *Sufism* (N.Y., 1970), pp. 11-30.

176. E. Douttée, *Magie et Religion Dans L'Afrique du Nord* (Algiers, 1908), chs. 11, 12.

177. W. Robertson Smith, *The Religion of the Semites, The Fundamental Institutions* (N.Y., 1972).

178. Douttée, *Ibid.,* "Conclusion," p. 598ff.

179. Roger Caillois, *L'Homme et le Sacré* (Paris, 1950), pp. 38-70.

180. Jean Cazeneuve, *Sociologie du Rite. Taboo, Magie, Sacré* (Paris, 1971), ch. 11.

181. Mary Douglas, *Purity and Danger* (London, 1966), pp. 11-16.

182. Cf. Ossowski on fluctuations between dyadic and triadic concepts of class structure in classic Marxist theory. These could have been related to the sacred, the profane–and the

impure; but he makes no such connection. Stanislaw Ossowski, *Class Structure in the Social Consciousness* (N.Y., 1963), ch. 8, etc.

183. W. Robertson Smith, *The Religion of the Semites;* and cf. T. O. Beidelman, *W. Robertson Smith and the Sociological Study of Religion* (Chicago, 1974), p. 61ff.

184. Georges Gurvitch, "La Magie, La Religion et Le Droit," in *Vocation Actuelle de la Sociologie* (Paris, 1965), vol. 2.

185. Robertson Smith is a possible link between the young Hegelians (e.g., Feuerbach) and Durkheim. According to T. O. Beidelman he derived his inspiration from the "higher criticism" initiated by Hegelians Bauer and Strauss and was deeply read in this school. His idea that sacrifice was joyful social integration comes from Wellhausen; he passed it on to Durkheim. (Beidelman, *op. cit.,* p. 31ff.)

186. For Robertson Smith magic is peripheral in another manner: the outer edges, the unknown. The demons are *djinn,* personifications of the wild beyond the campfire. As society grows, religion expands and absorbs magic; magic explores the unknown like a vanguard of religion.

187. Durkheim, "The Dualism of Human Nature and Its Social Conditions," in Kurt H. Wolff, ed., *Essays on Sociology and Philosophy by Emile Durkheim et al.* (N.Y., 1964), pp. 325-340.

188. Max Weber, "The Social Psychology of the World Religions," in H. H. Gerth & C. Wright Mills, *From Max Weber: Essays in Sociology* (N.Y., 1958), pp. 267 301.

189. Talcott Parsons, "Durkheim on Religion Revisited," in C. Y. Glock and P. E. Hammond, *Beyond the Classics?* (N.Y., 1973), pp. 156-180.

Postulate 6: LOGICALLY, AND IN SOME OBSERVABLE HISTORICAL SEQUENCES, MAGIC DERIVES FROM RELIGION RATHER THAN VICE VERSA.

IT is because the interactions of magic and religion are so complicated and paradoxical (overlap, hostility, expropriation, rejection, synthesis, etc.) that there has been such confusion as to which preceded which, magic or religion—and even as to which is which: 1. First, there has been outright disagreement as to whether particular phenomena can be classified as magic or religion. For example, Durkheim considered totemism to be the world's most primitive *religion*, while Frazer thought it was a mere "confederation of *magic.*" And a third group including both critics of Durkheim (e.g., Van Gennup[1]) and some who try to save his position (Jane Harrison[2]) asserted that totemism is really neither: it is the underlying social structure itself. 2. And even when investigators agree on which is which, magic and religion overlap so conspicuously and beg, borrow and steal from each other so outrageously that there is disagreement about priority. Either sequence could be asserted from the same data. Here, for example, is a religion that contains conspicuous magical elements. Has that religion *grown from* magic, or is it growing magic? Or did both grow from some primordial "magico-religious" mix? Some writers throw up their hands and say there is no determinate sequence, neither can magic and religion be distinguished. Yet both sequence and distinction can be established and are important.

Which Is Older?

Which came first, magic or religion? Two main sequences are asserted by anthropological theories: the R...M sequence of the French and the M...R sequence of the English school. But there are additional elements in most of these unprovable evolutionary theories. The most important additional element is "science." In fact, a good deal of evolutionary social theory in the West has consisted of an endless musing about the alleged sequence of magic-to-religion-to-science that goes back at least to Hegel.[3] Frazer, Tyler and Spencer all assert the Hegelian sequence M...R...S. There are variations, of course. Frazer considers religion to be an obscurantist *detour,* and magic to have a thrust directly toward science, so his view might be diagrammed like this:

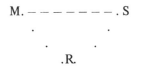

Whereas Weber sees the advance to true religion as a steep grade which, once ascended, coasts on easily to science. His view might be diagrammed like this:

.R . . . . S
                    .
M . . . .   .

The possible variations on these arrangements are three-factorial, and most are asserted by someone. An interesting new theory put forward by such writers as Pauwels[4] is: ΔS...M...R. Spectacular advances in science wake up a dreary, ossified, positivistic worldview; scientific breakthroughs smash the objective frame and make magic thinkable again, and the ensuing revival of magical phenomena stimulates in turn a revival of faith.[5] The French school, in reversing the English M...R sequence, does not handle science directly, but introduces a fourth term, which might be called philosophy (or logic), which could be abbreviated Phil. Comte's sequence is really: MR...Phil...Science.[6] And Durkheim really asserts two separate sequences: R...M, and R...Phil...Science.[7] Thus while religion throws off magic as an epiphenomenon (R...M) it also forges the logical categories of thought which lead to science. This might be diagrammed as follows, if we want to put some emphasis on the sequence leading to science and try to find grounds for an underlying agreement with Weber's position:

Durkheim: R . . . . Phil . . . . S
                        .
                   .M

Other theorists attempt to make "worldview," which is merely part of religion for the Durkheimians, a third province of the sacred, and some of them (the Waxes,[8] Hammond,[9] Mowinckle, etc.) then assert sequences that involve all three: magic, religion *and* worldview (WV). The original mana theorists did this too. Marett, for example, was implicitly asserting this sequence: M...WV...R. That is, magic, because it works (achieves intersocial effects through "suggestion"), precipitates "the magical worldview" which makes belief in religion possible. A very close reading of Durkheim shows that he was really asserting something like the *reverse* of this when he wrote that magic grows out of religion. Durkheim wrote that magic is stimulated by religion because religion precipitates a supernatural worldview, the world of the sacred, which is different from the natural world, and makes belief in magic possible. So Durkheim is really saying:

R...WV...M. Or rather, since worldview is an intrinsic part of religion to Durkheim and so must be a grace note in this sequence, he is saying: R...wv...M. Lévy-Bruhl seems to be asserting that worldview is the *primum mobile immobile* of the whole sequence. Thus, his position is: WV...M, R.

Other theorists dispute many of these sequences. Malinowski[10] and Hubert and Mauss,[11] for example, strongly assert: ~ (M...S): i.e., it *is not true that* magic develops into science. The French school emphasizes the strong relation of magic and religion and finds the connection to science more remote and less determinate, and so do I. Hubert and Mauss do admit, however, that perhaps: M...Tech (magic develops into technology). And some writers (Lévi-Strauss, etc.) who deny M...S, hint that M...SS (magic is perhaps a prototype of social science).

The Decadence Theory

Some who agree with the Durkheimians on the R...M sequence do so for different reasons. Durkheim asserts R...M because R...wv...M, and Hubert and Mauss, Huvelin, etc., show how it works: by expropriation. But Andrew Lang,[12] various medieval theologians, certain German anthropologists and some historians like Steiner[13] assert: R...M (*by decadence of religion*).

The main parallel along these lines to the French school is the so-called *Ur-monotheismus* school of Austria and Germany, which sees magic developing out of the decadence of a primal monotheism. Father Wilhelm Schmidt, founder of the school, and some others clearly mean by this that men in early times practiced a purer religion because they were present at the creation and remembered god; Ivar Lissner's popularization of these views was titled *Aber Gott War Da*[14] in the German edition. As man moved successive generations away from it, god's original theophany was slowly forgotten and religion was perverted into use for practical ends: this was the origin of magic. More scientific members of this school, such as Froebenius who founded the Frankfurt Institute of Social Anthropology and his disciple Jensen[15] play down this theology and empirically study how magic arises out of the fertility preoccupations of agriculture, for example. But the trend is always downward in *Urmonotheismus* thinking, and these theorists propose more or less the same sequence: 1. An original high god who in historical times has become a mere shadow to whom one does not pray— he comes first either because man was present at the creation, or because he reflects the noble simplicity of savages, etc. 2. The higher, "natural" magics, which make use of the sacred by devolving lower gods as avatars of the high god and then manipulating them for practical but legitimate purposes, above all agriculture. 3. Ranker, blacker magic that results from a further falling off. Has it been noticed that these systems resemble gnosticism? The theory that magic is produced by the decay of old religions is also an old idea of Christian theology. Despite its relations to Catholic apologetics, however, this school is useful in facing a logical problem about modern religion which never interested the Durkheimians but is of interest here: if magic arises from religion, then possibly modern religion and the modern world are growing more magical, not less. Thus this school might assert: R...M...S—and science is not much of an improvement! Andrew Lang, in fact, claims in *Magic and Religion*[16] that science is merely magic with legitimate hypotheses.

The school was inspired by Andrew Lang's polemic against Frazer. Frazer's *Golden Bough* was an implicit attack on Christianity; the evolutionary school was simultaneously showing that religion began in magic and retained the mark of its magical origins. John Vickery, in *The Literary Impact of the Golden Bough* (Princeton, 1973), has shown how the book grew out of the climate of "dissolvent literature"; what was most devastating were the clear similarities between Christianity, allegedly a unique historical theophany, and innumerable corn gods, gods of the year, gods who were put to death, etc. Besides stimulating Freud, Durkheim and the anthropologists, Frazer's influence helped to reduce Christianity to one myth among many in the several literary traditions it affected: the symbolists, Joyce, Yeats, etc. Lang counterattacked in a series of tendentious books aimed at salvaging Christianity.[17] In them he developed his theory of an original high god, still present in the background of most primitive pantheons. According to Eliade,[18] Lang first got the idea from reading A. W. Howitt's account[19] of the "All Fathers" or "Sky Beings" of the southeastern tribes of Australia. Lang "Christianized" his interpretation of these beings,[20] and looked for similar figures elsewhere. Spencer and Gillen[21] had found the high being Atnatus among the Kaitish in the interior. Some other anthropologists had also noticed high gods. Usually they were "otiose," idle, without function. They were not the object of any cult; no one prayed to them. This suggested to Lang a universal primal monotheism that had decayed.

Lang's idea had great influence in the German countries. Father Wilhelm Schmidt of Vienna made exhaustive searches for traces of high gods in anthropological literature. One of his works on this subject, *Der Ursprung der Gottesidee,* is thousands of pages long.[22] To Father Schmidt, the original high god of primitive man is none other than god himself in person. For the "origin of the god idea," to Schmidt, is simply god's creation of man and man's remembering it. Men turned to magic because they eventually forgot god as the generations passed, and magic works all too well. It is also typical of these theories to imagine, like Ficino or Pico, that there is a hierarchy of magics—some "natural" magics being relatively high and pure, and after them a gradual falling off until the abyss of black magic. In various Catholic countries this is still an influential theory. Eliade tells us[23] that Raffaele Pettrazzoni, Graebner, Froebenius, etc., developed the idea. Popularizers like Ivar Lissner make Schmidt's theory available here.[24] Part of its gnosticism is a Rousseau-like romance about natural man. Just as William Golding pictures Neanderthals (in *The Inheritors*[25]) as spiritually superior to Cro-Magnon man, Lissner asserts that the human brain has not grown since Neanderthal man. He attempts, in *Man, God and Magic,* to trace the gradual decline of the *Urmonon* idea through its various symbolizations: the bear god of the Aurignacian culture still found among the Gilyaks of

Siberia which for 20-30,000 years, he alleges, was the demiurge for circumpolar man; before it, the idea of the lord of the mountains, forests and seas. Before that, Lissner asserts, early man could speak directly to god, like Job.

Through several Catholic institutes, Schmidt's ideas even influenced French anthropological fieldwork in Africa, where R...M by decadence reinforced the R...M by expropriation viewpoint of the dominant Durkheim school. Thus Trilles,[26] a missionary of the Holy Spirit order and teacher at the Catholic Institute of Paris, who was also a contributor to Schmidt's journal *Anthropos*,[27] tried to demonstrate that the Pygmies, singled out as being even more primitive than Durkheim's Australian aborigines, had a pure monotheism and less magic than the more advanced Bantu tribes around them. These people, moreover, still worship their high god, though he is otiose and does not answer them. "God has deserted us because of our sins," is their faithful, Job-like theodicy. The anthropologists working with the Griaule family and its institute also frequently showed that primitive peoples have extremely lofty religions complete with quite thoughtful theologies. Marcel Griaule's works on the Dogon[28] describe this transitional society as possessing a metaphysics "as impressive as those of the Graeco-Roman religions and Christianity." This system of knowledge, which old men acquire in stages like merit badges, with its demiurges and great chain of being, immediately struck me as gnostic in content, and I wondered about possible diffusion from those philosophers the Middle Ages believed had fled to Africa after Justinian closed the schools in Athens. Later I found that the thought had occurred to others, including Victor Turner.[29] It takes a certain attitude of mind to find gnostic theosophies "impressive." Others influenced by Griaule have found high theologies in other African societies.[30] Thus Rouch found[31] that the Songhay have numerous religions and magics adhering to different occupational and territorial groups and partly a matter of choice, but all are viewed as "pathways" of knowledge and at the top is a high god, Ndebi, toward whom several of the religions ascend. Ndebi is actually the demiurge who rules the world.[32] The logical link to *Urmonotheismus* in the Griaule group studies is to be found in this preoccupation with typically gnostic systems whose "great chain of being" idea serves to rationalize (at least for the anthropologists) polytheistic systems to an overarching monotheistic unity—just as Windleband has suggested that this was the logical impetus behind Hellenic gnosticism itself.[33]

The *Urmonotheismus* school has led to some interesting results, including the useful studies of myth by Jensen and a productive revival of diffusionism. For, however mystical its origins, this theory was on the right track about the R...M sequence, and it inspired Jensen[34] and his colleagues to do several useful things: 1. First, they had a greater ideological commitment to the R...M sequence than the Durkheimians and this led them to marshal masses of useful evidence, tending to provide further support for the hypothesis that magic takes over religious symbolism for its own purposes. 2. They reintroduced a historical dimension into anthropology; neo-diffusionism was born out of this school in the works of Froebenius and Heine-Geleme. Radin was influenced by them (though he rejected their excesses as pseudo-history); it shows in his insistence that Western civilization is a conquest culture which has debilitated the "primitive" societies it now studies as inferior.[35] Jensen, similarly, claims that we misperceive primitives. In the matter of magic, for example, while vastly underestimating the magical nature of our own religions and cultures, we overemphasize the magic that we see in primitive societies. Primitives are not terribly obsessed by magic; moreover, the magic we see in their cultures is not a primal stuff away from which religion will gradually advance; it is, rather, something relatively new that is intruding as they decay toward civilization.

Even moderate, scientific investigators in this tradition like Jensen still cling to the school's theory of decadence. In his introduction to *Myth and Cult,* Jensen objects to a German reviewer who has accused him of pursuing the Schmidt degeneration theory; he claims that he is not, but his only real modification is to describe degeneration and call it something else. The basic process, he writes, is "application"—primal religious ideas get "applied" by man for purposes of his own. Increasingly these are private or personal purposes; Jensen calls them "pseudo-purposes." But what the whole process of "application" comes down to is the development of magic out of religion by the application of religious myths and rites to instrumental or private purposes.

Myth is the axial category in Jensen's system and degradation in myth parallels Schmidt's account of man's gradual forgetting of god. He assumes a primal stage of myth that still retains in story form some memory of man's original understanding of god. By the time we get to myths applied in religious rituals (what Lévy-Bruhl[36] calls myth as a "script" for a rite or what Malinowski[37] calls myth as a "charter" for a rite) we have already advanced one long stage toward "application," Jensen's term for degeneration into magic. Myths employed in rites are associated with the "dema-deities," the earth or subterranean gods associated with agriculture that are part of the fragmenting of the original religious vision. Like Dumézil, he imagines that gods proliferate by fission of original images, as avatars; this reflects in part the growing complexity of society (i.e., it is the projection of classes), but it is also part of the tragedy of forgetting. The dema-deities are approached, supplicated, manipulated by religious rites, as the otiose high god, who remains a shadowy and remote figure, is not. But myth deteriorates still further; the partial recollection of god that illuminated religious rites is in turn forgotten; now we have etiological myths that try to explain rituals which are no longer understood. (This is the phase Jessie L. Weston wrote about in *From Ritual to Romance,*[38] reinterpreted as evidence of the fall of man.) Still later we have a stage of frank magic, in which mere fragments of uncomprehended myths are used as blind instruments in magical spells. "Application" instead of "degeneration" sounds more scientific than Father Schmidt's formulation, but this version is actually more pessimistic, for it brands all human applications of intelligence (e.g., scientific technology) as decadent magic by implication (a viewpoint we also find in Ellul).[39] This is truly a Brahmin-like view, reminiscent of Hindu ideas like the "Kali Yuga."[40] Jensen recognizes that his theory entails that the "great" world religions are far down this path. He handles this suavely by admitting that there is something "fine" in Buddhism and the others, namely the useful application they make of primal religious material to "aid man's spirit." What he is saying is what Max Weber hints repeatedly beneath the surface of his dialectic: most of the world religions are magical salvation cults. These religions "have their own grandeur," Jensen says patronizingly.

Related to Jensen's idea of the decline of myth is Eliade's interesting notion of a fall of image and metaphor into the literal. In "Mephistopheles and the Androgyne,"[41] he claims that androgynous myths were originally logical counters in creation myths of deep insight; as these myths decay the image passes to the literal: e.g., the hermaphrodite. In *Yoga* he shows how literalness about sacred imagery is associated with the Kali Yuga, or fallen world, and gives one horrendous example in which a degenerate sect of ascetics fiendishly act out imagery of cemeteries, cadavers and death that were originally metaphors in a yogic tradition.[42] Magicians are "literalists of the imagination."

Empirical Evidence Supports the Priority of Religion

The trouble with the evolutionary M...R...S sequence is, first, that it is prehistory and cannot be proven. By the time we get to any primitive tribe still existing, we have religion. (The primitiveness of shamanism presents no problem: Eliade, Jensen, others have shown it is a diffusing magical-medical cult which nests within existing religions; there are always gods and religious cults associated with it.) Some investigators like Frazer attempt to hold their position by name-calling; they say primitive religions are "magical"; but in fact they are sometimes less so than our own. A second problem with the M...R...S theory is that it is rigidly asymmetrical; it cannot explain the "reversals" in history, when men "relapse" into magic. Whereas the R...M sequence can, for we have shown how the rites magic borrows from religion are endlessly used to renew and change religion: R...M...R... etc. Furthermore, the M...R...S sequence is premature grand theory, meant to be universal: whereas the R...M sequence is empirical and fits hundreds of local situations that can be observed.

In addition to evidence of the Durkheimians, and researches of the Urmonotheismus school, anthropological field reports of magical movements show us magic endlessly arising out of rites borrowed from religion. The data prove the thesis in several ways. First, content analysis of magical rites and representations reveals elements which can be traced to immediate or distant religions. Second, throughout the third world we have a vast laboratory in which we can see new magics arising by expropriating religious material. Whatever the unobservable prehistorical sequences, we are confronted every day with these *new* sequences, which *can* be observed. And even if the dialectic action gets complicated, as when the magic movements try to turn back into religions, the Durkheim R...M thesis can be understood as true in a logical sense. Since magic shows itself to be the use of expropriated religious symbolism, religion is logically prior to magic.[43] Finally, more evidence for R...M can be found by observing the high correlation between magic and level of culture. As primitive tribes advance to hierarchical tribal organization and division of labor, as they come into contact with civilizations and become civilized themselves, they develop *more* magic. Extremely primitive tribes (like the Pygmies) or regressed tribes may have very little magic.[44] A notable exception is the witchcraft complex; it is found among the most primitive peoples: Australian aborigines, Pygmies, etc. This is because it is the oldest magic.[45]

There is a sense in which both the Durkheim and *Urmonotheismus* traditions are neo-diffusionist. It might be said that while the sequence M...R...S is the typical matrix of evolutionary theories, the sequence R...M seems to be a characteristic approach of neo-diffusionism. M...R...S is an ideology of human progress through the evolution of reason, derived from Hegel. R...M, though influenced by the holistic prejudices of French "sociologism" and the Christian prejudices of German *Urmonotheismus,* is a simpler, empirical paradigm that seems to fit better the actual ups and downs of history. Hocart, who is not of the French school but deeply indebted to it, is a transitional figure who makes the neo-diffusionism of the Mauss approach explicit. Hocart is not a frank diffusionist; he does not try to trace actual pathways for ideas, an often impossible enterprise. But his account of cultural archetypes that have actual historical distribution implies this diffusion.[46]

Opponents of the R...M sequence cannot refute it by opposing to it the evolutionary sequence M...R...S, because this is imaginary prehistory. A stronger argument is advanced by many who think primitive religions are hard to distinguish from magic, so perhaps both magic and religion derive from an original "magico-religious" mixture. Thus some American anthropologists today seem to think that any determinate sequence is unprovable and not worth discussion; and many lean by default to the formula MR, M, R.[47] An immediate criticism of this is that we do find some societies with little or no magic (e.g., the Pygmies), though none in which there is no religion. Cases like the Pygmies are rare, however; most known societies have both magic and religion, and most do seem to mix magic and religion together.

The real trouble with the theory of "magico-religious" origins (RM) is that RM...R, M says nothing; it abdicates from the inquiry. We could say "RM" of almost any religion in existence anywhere. Precisely because religion and magic interpenetrate at all times, any sequence logical or historical that derives them both from some vague "magico-religious" phenomenon does not explain anything. For if the two are still so interpenetrated at present, how could they once have been so much more so as to have been something else, and in that case, what would that be?

Solution : RM = R

But the intimate mixture of magical and religious elements does pose a danger for the R...M sequence. For how can we say that "magic comes out of religion" if religion is very magical to begin with? There is even some seeming disagreement on this within the Durkheim school. For while Durkheim categorically states that R...M,[48] Hubert and Mauss lean toward RM...R, M.[49] The full solution will not emerge until the next postulate, where it is shown that religion *models* magic for the community. But meanwhile we can defend the R...M sequence against evidence for RM...R, M by showing that RM is really R. In other words we can show that those "primal magico-religious phenomena" are basically religious.

There are two ways of doing this. First, working with that seeming disagreement between Durkheim and Mauss, we can show how "mana" translates RM into R. Secondly, working with investigators like Jane Harrison,[50] Van Gennup[51] and Mendenhall,[52] who show that primal religious rites are the core of the early social structure itself, we can show that RM is really R because both are non-sacred customs in origin.

1. RM = R Because Both Derive from Mana.

Let us consider the position of Hubert and Mauss first. They did say that magic and religion separated out of a primal magico-religious amalgam. But they also derived both magic and religion from "mana," and even imagined that this was a causal explanation of both. What does this mean? Because their language was vague, especially on the relation of "mana" and the sacred,[53] they were misunderstood and this stimulated a lot of dualist elaboration among their followers, such as Cazeneuve,[54] Gurvitch[55] and Caillois.[56] This whole development, with its endless distinctions of sacred mana vs. non-sacred mana (Gurvitch), "taboo, sacred and magic" (Cazeneuve) and "sacred, profane and polluted" (Caillois) is intellectually somewhat thin, so we deal with it in a footnote.[57] But what Mauss and Hubert apparently intended is quite simple and can be understood when it is recalled that for the Durkheim school "mana" is just man's first recognition (half-cognitive, half-emotional) of society, and that religion in turn is the projection of society (by means of object-symbols representing mana). With this in mind, Mauss and Hubert can be shown to be in full agreement with Durkheim's religion-to-magic sequence. The argument might be set out thus:

RM...R, M (Hubert and Mauss)
But also: Mana...R, M. (Hubert and Mauss)
But Mana = recognition of Society (All Durkheimians)
And Religion = projection of Society (All Durkheimians)
So RM = Mana = f(Society) = Religion
Therefore RM = R
And so (RM...R, M) = (R...M)

In other words, Hubert and Mauss derive both magic and religion from mana. And mana, in Durkheim's[58] later, clearer formulation which built on them, is simply man's first recognition of society. (It takes the form of a feeling of circumambient power which is then symbolized by sacred objects.) Religion, in turn, is the projection of society that crystallizes like a map around the sacred objects symbolizing the mana of its constituent groups. Therefore mana is logically related much more closely to religion than it is to magic—it arises from communal activities, it is the basis of religion. So to say that manistic experiences give rise to both religion and magic is to say that socio-religious experiences are the source of religion and magic and of primal magico-religious experiences.

2. RM = R Because Both Are Social

We can come at this from another angle. At least one of the critics of Durkheim's *Formes Elémentaires* said that he had erroneously designated "totemism" as a religion whereas it was no religion at all: it was the social system itself.[59] Precisely. In using the genetic method to go back to what he believed to be the world's most primitive religion, Durkheim also thought he was going back to the beginning of religious projection. Jane Harrison[60] developed Durkheim's leads into an explicit theory of the form: Soc...R...M. In other words, back behind primordial religion lies no confused amalgam of religion and magic, but society itself, and mere social customs not yet sacralized. Mendenhall said something similar[61] when he characterized religion as the "ceremonialization" of certain key social and political institutions.[62]

Jane Harrison came by this formulation, I think, as a way of synthesizing Frazer and Durkheim. In her earlier book, *Prolegomena to the Study of Greek Religion*,[63] she was under the influence of Frazer in his preanimist phase. She concentrated then on showing how, behind anthropomorphic Greek gods, lay vaguer ideas of spiritual "hosts" and behind them mana-like ideas of force. (The preanimists tend to associate mana exclusively with magic, and to overlook its roots in community, in religion. So when they say *Mana...Gods*, they mean M...R.) But in the years between the *Prolegomena* (1903) and her greatest work, *Themis* (1911), she came, by her own report,[64] under the influence of the Durkheim school, and now her position changed. It is my interpretation that the new position saves Frazer and Durkheim both by showing how the sequence of the former can fit into that of the latter as an important moment in it. To be succinct, her way of synthesizing Frazer's preanimist M...R with Durkheim's R...M was to write in effect: *Soc...M...R*, while identifying Soc (society) with R (religion). In other words, R(Soc)...M...R. That is to say, religion begins as social customs become self-consciously ceremonialized; magic immediately expropriates this symbolism and applies it to practical ends; and magic's elaboration of rites in turn enriches and elaborates later religion.

Themis is constructed somewhat like *The Golden Bough*, endlessly circling around a rite implied in a hymn to Diktaean Zeus, the way Frazer circles around the legend of the priesthood at Nemi. The Hymn of Diktaean Zeus was sung by a chorus of armed warriors, called Kouretes, to invoke a daimon, "the greatest Kouros," who was not only a Frazerian *Eniautos* or Year-Daimon but, at a deeper, earlier level, a projection of this *thiasos* or band of his worshipers. Harrison's key idea is that all this grew from an initiation ceremony which inducted a young man into the tribe, evidently during a period of transition from matriarchy to patriarchy, and that the greatest Kouros is a projection or personification of the mana of the rite on its way to crystallizing into a god.[65] The daimon invoked is not present; he is commanded to come and dance with the armed young men. Now the hymn from which she infers the rite relates a myth that has presumably grown out of the rite: It tells how shielded "nurturers" took away an immortal child and hid him to protect him. In the course of the hymn, "Titans" lure the child away and tear him limb from limb, but later he is put back together. All this is quite obviously the imagery of an initiation rite. The child first lives with the mother; later he is taken into the men's house where the old men teach him the lore of the tribe, "take him apart and put him back together." According to Harrison titans means *titanes,* the "white clay men," men with faces daubed white with gypsum in the initiation rite. The child is taught a wholly new path in life; he may be renamed; his soul is "congregationalized;" he is received into his church, his *thiasos.* Because Zeus originated in Crete, had a *thiasos* according to some myths, etc., Harrison associates the Kouros youth of the hymn with Zeus and claims that this god of patriarchy crystallized out of such initiation rites. According to the later legend, his mother Rhea concealed Zeus as a child to protect him from his son-devouring father, Kronos, whom Harrison imagines to have been a magician-god of matriarchy. Whatever the version, all this is really about an initiation rite, and the various myths built on it take as their point of departure the primal symbols by which the participants represented the significance of the rite to themselves.[66]

The typical symbols of an initiation rite are the symbols of death and rebirth —for the initiate dies to one role and is reborn in another. The symbolism is so basic that it probably helped shape man's earliest ideas about actual death and life. Harrison does not say this, but Hertz[67] and others of the French school have observed, for example, that death is thought of as one more social transition or initiation. Harrison does assert that the central feature of the rite was a *dromenon* or enaction of a New Birth into the tribe—and that this initiation idea of rebirth is prior to the idea of the rebirth of nature in the spring to which this social symbolism, expropriated by magic, is later applied. In other words "corn god" fertility rites, which Frazer[68] portrayed as one of the magical roots of religion, are already an expropriation by magic of something that is communal (hence incipiently religious), namely, initiation rites that create membership.

Harrison[69] finds this pattern of symbolism endlessly repeated and put to varied uses in the Greek world. Dionysus and his satyrs are the same phenomenon as the greatest Kouros, or Zeus, and his *thiasos*—when Zeus becomes too rationalized as an Olympian, the urban masses will import Dionysus from the bumpkins. His dithyrambs are another *thiasos,* and therefore so is the chorus of the Greek drama that grows out of them and is gradually transformed into an audience that forgets that it was originally part of the play and that all the characters are projections of itself. Greek "heroes" are often projections of such initiation rites, too, as Gilbert Murray and Francis Cornford have shown.[70]

And almost immediately, while the mythic representations are still primitive, magic expropriates them and uses this ready symbolism for its own ends, beginning with fertility rites as a kind of communal magic. (In this, Harrison is close to Jensen and the *Urmonotheismus* school.) I think that this formulation saves the preanimist position (M...R) and Frazer's derivation of mystery religions from corn god magic, by showing his sequence to be a moment within the broader Durkheimian process whereby religion generates magic. It shows how magic is generated so early from socio-religious rites that it in turn has the chance to help shape the further development of religion. And so, some of Frazer's other valuable formulations are allowed to nest within the basic theory that magic derives from religion. The valuable researches Frazer did on the divine king, the emergence of some kings and hence states from magic, and the further development of religion made possible by state organization can thus be saved and assimilated to a Durkheimian position without contradiction. When magicians make themselves kings and establish states, more formal religions (with priestly functionaries) crystallize as the representations of this new order, etc. For Harrison clearly intends to say that magical use of the symbolic apparatus of initiation happens right away, before the god is even crystallized out of the rite. The daimon is still just the greatest Kouros, projection of the Kouretes, and not yet Zeus, when magicians take over the whole drama and use it for their own purposes.

The magicians turn initiation rituals into something specialized. As an example she infers a primitive magical rite from a fragment of Euripides' "The Cretans," preserved by Porphyry, which tells of a rite on Mt. Ida involving Idaean Zeus, "a Bacchos of mailed priests, etc."[71] She thinks this was also an initiation rite, but a specialized one, inducting medicine men, and she notes that Epimenides of Crete, a typical ancient medicine man, was called "the new Kouros." Certainly the themes of mystic death, symbolic bodily reconstruction, ascent into heaven, rebirth, etc., are similar to themes that show up in the initiation of medicine men the world over (which Mauss has summarized in his useful account of Australian magicians' initiation[72]).

As for religion, it both grows out of the same social ritual of initiation, and is further stimulated by the growth of magic from which it "borrows back" (Burke) symbolism. In other words, while the god is slowly crystallizing out of the initiation ceremony, magic simultaneously expropriates and elaborates that social ritual into a rite—which the sacred community promptly borrows back as an important nucleus of its incipient religion. This is easy because original magic is public, official, for the community though done by specialists. To Harrison, the basic sacraments of religion, above all sacrifice, are magical rites originally, but they spring from the same matrix as religious ceremonialization itself: namely, purely social practices. So religion comes out of social practices both directly (through crystallization of deities from manistic experience) and indirectly (by "borrowing back" early magical elaborations of these same practices). Thereby, Jane Harrison retains the Frazerian sequence by showing that magical expropriation begins at once, before religion is really formed, so key instruments of religion like sacrifice are developed first by magic and then borrowed by emerging religion: thus the Frazerian sequence (M...R) fits into the Durkheimian sequence (R...M) as a moment in it. For magic's earliest borrowings are from the same social matrix that is simultaneously projecting religion. All this could be outlined as follows:

$$M...R \text{ (from Frazer)}$$
$$R...M \text{ (from Durkheim)}$$
$$\left. \begin{array}{l} \text{But Soc...M} \\ \text{And Soc...R} \end{array} \right\} \text{ (from Harrison)}$$

And R = projection of society (Durkheim)
So M...R fits into R...M, thus:
    Soc...R (direct emergence of R from society)
       ...M...R (R *borrows back* rites from M)
Or simply, Soc (R)...M...R.

In other words, the sequence M...R is a "borrow back" sequence within the more general sequences whereby religion generates magic. So the solution to the paradox of "magico-religious" mixtures is that the primal sacred *looks* like "MR" because *both* M and R are arising simultaneously and interacting. But what is prior to both and generative of them is merely social customs or practices that become self-conscious and get ceremonialized.

Magic goes on using the sacred-social, and it tends to use and reuse a few simple doings over and over again. Initiation imagery is most of it, in fact. Communion feasts in turn grow out of initiation, and Harrison thinks that even the basic rite of sacrifice originates this way. Initiation symbolism or fragments of it become the all-purpose technology of primitive magic. Mauss has shown[73] that the magician gets his social power from a special initiation rite that is merely an intensification of the ordinary rite. But then the magician keeps using fragments of this ritual experience as an all-purpose technique. For example, Jensen has observed[74] that the shaman's trance is not a formless experience—he goes into trance in order to reexperience and then report a drama that reconstructs some familiar religious drama; and very often, it is the drama of his own initiation. Thus in the course of driving out a patient's demons the entranced shaman may pursue his patient's lost soul to hell the way he followed his own in his initiation. He may storm heaven again to seek help, and be born and illuminated once more. In short, he reexperiences, or tries to make the crowd think he reexperiences what he underwent during the initiation that gave him social power.

But these reproduced experiences in turn seem to have this special quality — the *transmutation* of mythic-symbolic representations *into literal experience*. Eliade and the *Urmonotheismus* writers have noticed the tendency of magic to make symbolism more literal. Symbolic death and rebirth originally meant the initiate's transition from one status to another, but now it is experienced more literally by the magician. With the help of drugs, vision quest, gnostic insight or training, the magician in his initiation tries to experience literally what the normal initiate experiences as symbolism. And in his regular practice thereafter, the shaman uses this ability to turn symbolism into literal experience as his principal technology. What is trance but the ability to transmute symbolism into literal experience? And surely this profound drama of acting out meaning gives the shaman power over symbolism and hence over the social reality it structures.

It may seem curious that this single drama of initiation gets reenacted as an all-purpose magic, for everything from divination to curing boils. But all-purpose rites are the rule rather than the exception in magic. Thus Evans-Pritchard shows us that among the Nuer[75] sacrifice is used as an instrument for every purpose: to celebrate office, to cure ills. Catholic sacraments are used the same way: in masses for the dead, for crops, for peace. And perhaps psychoanalysis does something similar by seeming to prescribe the same treatment for every illness and even (at one extreme) the same diagnostic interpretation: variations on the Oedipus complex. In fact, does not psychoanalysis really ask the patient to do the same thing as the shaman in its all-purpose drama? And is not the reliving of the Oedipal struggle in the transference like a belated coming of age in an initiation?

Whether we use mana or presacral social customs as our factoring device, then, primordial "magico-religious phenomena" can be shown to be community projections and hence basically religious. The fact that magical and religious representations get all mixed up together is therefore no problem. Magic emerges immediately and enters into a dialectic with religion, but it always originates in religion. The whole sequence could be summed up as follows: 1. Soc...M...R where Soc = R (lim); so R...M. 2. And R...dM but dM...dR. That is, new magic (d for increment) comes out of a religious tradition but may lead to the establishment of new or modified religion.

Science does not emerge out of magic, which has to do with the sacred. It is, however, stimulated by philosophy which grows out of religion, and by technology which is accompanied by magic, is stimulated and often organized by magic but is different from magic. Thus:

$$R \ldots \text{Phil.}$$
$$S$$
$$M \ldots \text{Tech.}$$

The full constellation might be diagrammed as follows:

Soc. (R) . . . . R

. . . . Phil . . . . S

. . . . . . (M) . . . . R

. M. . . . Tech . . . .

In short, evidence that early religion has magical elements does not contradict the basic thrust whereby magic originates in religion.

Notes

1. A. Van Gennup, *L'Etat Actuel du Problème Totemique* (Paris, 1920), ch. 2.

2. Jane Ellen Harrison, *Themis* (Cambridge, 1927), ch. 1, etc.

3. G. W. F. Hegel, *The Philosophy of History* (N.Y., 1900); *The Phenomenology of Mind* (N.Y., 1967), Preface, pp. 67–130; *Lectures on the Philosophy of Religion* (N.Y., 1962), vol. I, part 2, pp. 290–317.

4. Pauwels and Bergier, *The Morning of the Magicians* (N.Y., 1968), p. 119, 128ff, etc.

5. There are far more empirical historical studies attempting to prove the older M . . . R . . . S sequence about science than there are confirming studies for the newer theories, however. But it is the sequence of M and R alone that mainly interests me in this paper, for I have shown that magic is intimately related to religion—whereas its effects on science are less determinate.

6. August Comte, *Cours de Philosophie Positive* (Paris, 1943).

7. Durkheim, *The Elementary Forms . . .*, on magic, 42–7, 361–2; on the sequence to logic and science, 9–23, 431–445 (London, 1915, 1954).

8. Murray and Rosalie Wax, "The Notion of Magic," *Current Anthropology*, Dec., 1963, vol. 4, no. 5; "The Magical Worldview," *Journal for the Scientific Study of Religion*, 1962, vol. 1, no. 2, 179–88; "Magic and Monotheism," *Proceedings of American Ethnological Society:* Symposium on New Approaches to the Study of Religion, Spring, 1964, pp. 50–60.

9. Dorothy Hammond, "Magic, a Problem in Semantics," *American Anthropologist*, vol. 72, 1970, 1349–1356.

10. Bronislaw Malinowski, *Magic, Science and Religion* (Garden City, N.Y., 1954), *passim.*

11. Though magic sometimes enriched science. *A General Theory of Magic*, pp. 131–144.

12. Andrew Lang, *Magic and Religion* (N.Y., 1901), ch. 3.

13. George Steiner, *In Bluebeard's Castle* (New Haven, 1971), pp. 53–56.

14. Ivar Lissner, *Man, God and Magic* (N.Y., 1961); in German, *Aber Gott War Da* (1958, Walter-Verlag, Olten).

15. Adolf E. Jensen, *Myth and Cult Among Primitive Peoples* (Chicago, 1963), pp. 209–264.

16. Andrew Lang, *op. cit.*, ch. 3.

17. Consider how tendentious is the chapter (ch. 4) in *Magic and Religion* (1901) that tries desperately to disprove Frazer's idea that Christianity is an exemplar of a corn god who is killed and reborn. For a hundred pages Lang tries to show that a sacrifice like the Sacaea at Babylon involved killing a criminal who served as a mock-king, not a real king. Laborious obscurantism sometimes suggests ideological resistance.

18. Mircea Eliade, *Australian Religions, An Introduction* (Ithaca and London, 1973), ch. 1.

19. A. W. Howitt, *Native Tribes of Southeast Australia* (London, 1904).

20. Mircea Eliade, *op. cit.*, ch. 1.

21. Spencer & Gillen, *The Northern Tribes of Central Australia* (London, 1904).

22. Eliade, *op. cit.*, ch. 1.

23. *Ibid.*, ch. 1.

24. Ivar Lissner, *Man, God and Magic* (N.Y., 1961).

25. William Golding, *The Inheritors* (N.Y., 1962).

26. R. P. Trilles, *Les Pygmées de la Forêt Equatoriale* (Paris, 1931), pp. 61-197; 501-505.

27. According to Du R. P. Pinard de la Boullaye, Introduction to Trilles, *Les Pygmées.* . . .

28. Marcel Griaule, *Les Masques Dogon* (Paris, 1938); *Dieu d'Eau, Entretiens Avec Ogotemmeli* (Paris, 1948, 1966), preface, chs. 1-2.

29. Victor Turner, chapter on Griaule group in *Dramas, Fields and Metaphors* (Ithaca, 1974).

30. For example, R. P. Tempels, *La Philosophie Bantoue* (Paris, 1945); S. de Ganay, *Les Devises* (Paris, 1941).

31. Jean Rouch, *La Religion et la Magie Songhay* (Paris, 1960), ch. 1.

32. Interestingly, the strongest, frankest magic in this system belongs to the Sohantye magicians, who are literally family descendents of Sonni Ali who founded a once powerful but long-vanquished Songhay empire via a movement based on a nativist cult of this high god. It is surely interesting that here a defeated religion turns into magic, though Rouch does not underline the point.

33. More precisely, Windleband characterizes gnosticism as solving the logical problem of monotheism vs. dualism inherent in Christianity's mixing together of Judaic and Hellenic elements. The theory of "emanations" from the "one" can also rationalize polytheism to monotheism, and we have numerous examples, from Dinka "divinity" ideas to Hindu "avatars." W. Windleband, *History of Ancient Philosophy* (N.Y., 1900, 1956), pp. 355-361.

34. Adolf E. Jensen, *Myth and Cult Among Primitive Peoples* (Chicago & London, 1973).

35. Arthur Vidich, Introd. to Paul Radin, *The Method and Theory of Ethnology* (N.Y., 1966), pp. vii-cxx. Also see Radin, *The Trickster* (N.Y., 1972); *Primitive Man as Philosopher* (N.Y., 1957); *Primitive Religion, Its Nature and Origin* (N.Y., 1957); *The World of Primitive Man* (N.Y., 1960).

36. Lucien Lévy-Bruhl, especially in *La Mythologie Primitive* (Paris, 1935).

37. Bronislaw Malinowski, especially *The Foundations of Faith and Morals* (London, 1936, 1969).

38. Jessie L. Weston, *From Ritual to Romance* (Garden City, N.Y., 1957).

39. Jacques Ellul, *The New Demons; Propaganda; The Technological Society; The City; The Great Illusion.*

40. In the typically cyclic time dimension of Hinduism, four world ages or "yugas" of unimaginable length are endlessly repeated in a cycle of decadence and regeneration. The last and worst is the Kali yuga, a time of decadence and disorder. (See Zimmer, *Myths and Symbols* in *Indian Art and Civilization,* Princeton, 1972, ch. 1.) What seems to be disturbing Hindu mythologists about this period is that it is a time when caste barriers break down and lower castes rise economically, through trade. Then "each thing meets in mere repugnance," as Coriolanus said. Horror at caste disorder and the rise of money magic lies behind many conservative fears of "decadence": "We know what fate falls/ On families broken;/ The rites are forgotten,/ Vice rots the remnant/ Defiling the women,/ And from their corruption/ Comes mixing of castes;/ The curse of confusion . . ." (*Bhagavad-Gita,* Mentor edition, New York, p. 33).

41. Mircea Eliade, "Mephistopheles and the Androgyne or the Mystery of the Whole," Ch. 2 in *The Two and the One* (N.Y., 1965), pp. 78-124.

42. ". . . there is a class of Sivaist ascetics, the Aghoris or Aghorapanthis, who have at times interpreted this symbolism of the 'cemetery' and 'corpses' materially. . . . The connections with Tantrism are patent. These Aghoris eat from human skulls, haunt cemeteries, and still practiced cannibalism at the end of the 19th century. . . ." (p. 296, Eliade, *Yoga.*)

43. But what about sequences in which religions do grow more rational, more secular, gradually disenchanting the world, expelling magic? These could be understood as sequences of the form R1 . . . R2, where society moves from "very magical religions" (R1) to "religions that are antimagical" (R2). Nothing of the form M . . . R need be asserted.

44. There are problems with any generalization this sweeping. For example, Australian magic cannot be entirely explained away by assuming it is all religious magic, with the magician a functionary of the group, though that is true in part. For Mauss' account of the

initiation of Australian magicians suggests the presence here of the classical magical pattern. And Eliade has noted the relationship between this magic cult and the otiose high gods rather than totemism. But Eliade in the same book (*Australian Religions*) has exploded the notion that Australia was hermetically sealed from the rest of the world; the magician cult has perhaps diffused here.

45. This is discussed in chapter 11.

46. In this sense he is less in the tradition of Bastian's *Elementargedanken,* which prefigure structuralism, and more of Friedrich Ratzel who insisted "the earth is small" so that Fiji and India might indeed share culture patterns for historical reasons. (See Rodney Needham, Introd. to A. M. Hocart, *Kings and Councillors,* Chicago, 1970, pp. xiii–xcix.) The same tacit assumptions lie in the background of many studies by Mauss and his colleagues. There is a similar implied neo-diffusionism also behind the researches of Dumézil. (Cf. C. Scott Littleton, *The New Comparative Mythology,* Berkeley, 1973.) Since magic symbolism travels easily, develops a history, is preserved with writing and accumulates a tradition, the historical dimension cannot be overlooked.

47. Some preoccupied with shamanism are inclined to this formulation, who, lacking the insight of an Eliade, think it hard to say whether a shaman is a magician or a priest. So, for example, La Barre states that first we have an undifferentiated "magico-religious" complex characterized by the shaman, and out of it grow both the magic of magicians and the religion of priests.

48. Durkheim, *Elementary Forms of Religious Life* (London, 1915, 1954), pp. 42–47, 361–2.

49. See discussion of mana in *A General Theory of Magic.*

50. Jane Harrison, *Themis* (Cambridge, 1927), ch. 1, etc.

51. Arnold Van Gennup, *L'Etat Actuel du Problème Totemique* (Paris, 1920).

52. George E. Mendenhall, *The Tenth Generation: The Origins of the Biblical Tradition* (Baltimore, 1973).

53. See esp. *A General Theory of Magic,* p. 119.

54. Jean Cazeneuve, *Sociologie du Rite: (Taboo, Magie, Sacré),* (Paris, 1971).

55. Georges Gurvitch, "La Magie, la Religion et le Droit," *La Vocation Actuelle de la Sociologie,* vol. 2 (Paris, 1963).

56. Roger Caillois, *L'Homme et le Sacré* (Paris, 1950).

57. In Hubert and Mauss mana force and mana concept are not clearly distinguished. More serious, the relation of mana to the sacred is blurred. They say that mana and the sacred are practically the same, but they also say that they get "confounded" and they define neither. Then they say that mana is larger than the sacred and comprises also taboo. This seems to suggest that mana is a set of which the sacred is a subset. It also suggests that taboo is somehow separate from the sacred. (*General Theory of Magic,* p. 119).

Some later followers of Mauss saw in these elliptical statements the possibility of new distinctions. Thus we have Roger Caillois struggling with the idea of taboo as pollution, a third province caused by the interaction of sacred and profane. Jean Cazeneuve divided "rite" into "the sacred, magic and taboo." Gurvitch set mana up as fundamentally distinct from the sacred. He derived religion from the sacred and magic from mana. Also, religion from anxiety and magic from fear. (The reverse would make equal sense.) Religion is associated with the clan and matriarchy, magic with patriarchy and the men's lodges. Finally, religion is related to society, but magic is linked to intersocial interaction, as with Marett. The whole towering edifice of dichotomies is reared on a distinction that Hubert and Mauss are alleged to have made (they never did) between *"mana sacré"* and *"mana nonsacré."* A careful search of both the French and English editions reveals that Hubert and Mauss nowhere use the expressions *"mana sacré"* vs. *"mana non-sacré."* Gurvitch has perhaps inferred the distinction (along with the terminology) from the passage (p. 119) in which the authors suggest that mana is a genus that includes the species sacred: by deduction there must also exist some mana that is *not* sacred: thus *"mana non-sacré."* (Gurvitch cites two other sources in Mauss but once again he is reading in.)

Hubert and Mauss use mana as a "final-cause" *explanation* of magic; this is the weakest part of their essay and has been much criticized. In any event, though their statements are confusing enough, they did explicitly say that 1. mana is at the origin of BOTH magic and religion; and 2. mana represents society, and is social.

58. *The Elementary Forms of Religious Life,* p. 194ff, 62ff, 199ff, etc.

59. Arnold Van Gennup, *L'Etat Actuel du Problème Totemique* (Paris, 1920), ch. 1.

60. Harrison, *Themis*, ch. 1.

61. George E. Mendenhall, *The Tenth Generation* (Baltimore, 1913). He writes that a "liturgical movement" does this (p. 9).

62. It is almost possible to establish this by logical reduction alone. For if you go back far enough there are no collective representations because man, or his ancestors, do not yet possess culture or even speech. At some stage, there is just a social group, and later there is society projecting consciousness of itself in religion.

63. Jane Ellen Harrison, *Prolegomena to the Study of Greek Religion* (Cleveland, 1959).

64. Harrison, *Themis*, Introduction.

65. Harrison, *Themis*, ch. 1.

66. Jane Harrison goes on to imagine Kronos as a magician god of matriarchy, who takes counsel with Earth his mother against Ouranos. Later, Olympian Zeus becomes the leader of the pantheon of patriarchy, which in Harrison's view reaches such a stage of abstract representation that it is hardly a religion any more: those fixed "anthropomorphic" figures almost embody abstract ideas (like Zoroaster's pantheon).

67. Robert Hertz, *Death and the Right Hand* (Aberdeen, 1960), pp. 27–86.

68. Frazer, *The Golden Bough*, abridged ed. (N.Y., 1960), pp. 463–518, etc.

69. Jane Ellen Harrison, *Themis*, ch. 5.

70. In a contributing chapter, Gilbert Murray continues Harrison's derivation of Greek drama from these rites. (Murray, "Excursus on the Ritual Forms Preserved in Greek Tragedy," in Harrison, *Themis*, pp. 341–363 in 1974 Gloucester, Mass. ed. See also his *The Rise of the Greek Epic*, N.Y., 1967.) He shows that the traditional forms in Greek drama— the prologue, the Agon, the Pathos, the Messenger's speech, the Threnos, the Anagnorisis, the final Theophany—derive from ritual forms in the dromena of the *Eniautos-Daimon*. These ritual forms are combined with plots and characters from Homer. When the Ionians left their old lands their traditional *Eniautos-Daimons* broke loose from their rites and their myths changed in an abstract direction. The genius of Attic drama (pp. 341–363) was to put the rationalized heroes, gods and myths that broke loose from ritual forms back into their original ritual sequences of prologue, Agon, Pathos, etc. So Greek dramas are stories of de-daimonized daimons placed back within the daimonic form—tragedy being about the daimon's death, and comedy about his wedding feast, in the formulation of Cornford (*The Origin of Attic Comedy*, Garden City, 1961), and Gaster (*Thespis*, Garden City, N.Y., 1961). Cornford contributes another chapter ("The Origin of the Olympic Games," *Themis*, ch. 7) which similarly derives the Olympic games and the heroes who figured in them from initiation rites turned into fertility magic. Death followed by rebirth is like a contest followed by victory and he supposes that the winner of the footrace became the *Eniautos-Daimon* of the year.

71. Harrison, *Themis*, ch. 3.

72. Mauss, "L'Origine des Pouvoirs Magiques dans les Sociétés Australiennes," *Oeuvres*, vol. 2, pp. 319–369.

73. Mauss, *Ibid.*

74. Jensen, *Myth and Cult* . . . (Chicago, 1973), pp. 226–233.

75. E. E. Evans-Pritchard, *Nuer Religion* (Oxford, 1956), pp. 197–230.

Postulate 7: MAGIC IS A
BYPRODUCT OF THE PROJECTION
OF SOCIETY IN RELIGION.

RELIGION is obviously connected with the community: magic, less clearly so. A magical rite may involve only a specialist and his client; a religious rite is more apt to be congregational. Many investigators have recognized that magic is somehow more closely connected with the individual than is religion (though they often substitute for each other). And if all this is so, then we may be sure that religion precedes magic, for we know that society precedes the individual.

The relation of religions to society has been expressed in many ways, from Royce's idea of god as "the spirit of the beloved community,"[1] to Hegel's notion of the world spirit[2] as a cultural ideal. Theories of religion as the projection of society are especially persuasive in covering all the empirical facts. It is possible that a theory of magic could be comfortable with quite different theories of religion; it is possible that we could even make some sense in reporting on the endless arguments of magic with religion without saying *what* religion is. But a theory of religion as the projection of society is especially compatible with the theory of magic developed here. First, it helps pin down logically the priority of religion. Second, it raises the possibility of detecting just what is projected. It suggests that magical representations can be "read," like myths, for what they reveal about social formations and conflicts.[3] Above all, it suggests that in arguing endlessly with religion, magic is engaged in some kind of argument with society itself. And this is indeed the case; later on we will see that magic is related to the emergence of subgroups and individual egos out of the social whole.

Religion As the Projection of Society

For some years now the researches of the Hegel-Feuerbach tradition, the Durkheimian sociologists, the British anthropologists in Africa, the Oxford and Cambridge classicists influenced by Durkheim have all been accumulating evidence of correspondence between social morphologies and religious representations. Students of myth like Dumézil,[4] archeologists like V. Gordon Childe,[5] and investigators in many other disciplines add to the evidence, which is persuasive.[6]

Almost any social group or relationship will project a superstructure of collective representations. Even as small an institution as a marriage will have its own *nomos* (traditions, family customs, shared beliefs, etc.), as Berger and Kellner[7] have shown. And if a microcosmic institution like a marriage has a sort of "religion," it may also be said to have some sort of "magic"—such as the manipulation of the family values by one party for his own ends. Classes will have either religions (e.g., "chapel" in England) or ideological parties.[8] In our society, business corporations spent millions to project the ideology of "free enterprise" after production restrictions during World War II led them into the serendipity of "institutional advertising."

In fact a great many social phenomena largely *are* projections (cf. MacIver on government[9]), but not all of these projections are religious. We might say that social projections tend to be especially religious in primitive societies organized by "mechanical solidarity" (Durkheim's term for integration by belief, with everyone necessarily believing the same thing to hold the group together). Such an intense consensus tends to "heat up," and generate "mana" feeling, which gives the projections a sacred coloring. But in more advanced societies of "organic solidarity" (Durkheim's term for economic integration through division of labor), fewer projections will be religious—though many institutions will still be projections.

Projections of Dominant Parts

Swanson proposes that the projections most likely to form a society's main religion are not those that mirror the society as a whole, but rather those that reflect the "dominant corporate groups" in it.[10] In various cultures, this may be the tribe or the state or Pharaoh or a Sumerian temple. Such entities "transcend" human beings. As outcomes of diverse intentionalities, they go beyond us and outlast us and ultimately we cannot fathom them. So we "represent" them to ourselves—we symbolize or personify them in our attempt to grasp them, and *that* is religion. These "collective representations," these cultural reflections are religion, but what is really "super-natural" is what they reflect, the dominant corporate groups that project them. And what is particularly supra-individual about these "dominations and powers, principalities and thrones" is what Swanson calls their "constitutions," i.e. the social contracts underlying these institutions, particularly their latent parts in which unexpected powers lie. Religion is an attempt to fathom these social mysteries and get some control over them. (To Durkheim religious projection is always an attempt at understanding; to Lévi-Strauss it is man beginning to think; to Lienhardt both religion and magic are attempts to understand the order of the world.[11]) And so, in language similar to Luckmann's[12] on the transcendence of the ego in the socialization process, Swanson is saying that society really is miraculous in a way, and therefore not surprisingly represented as god.

Swanson proves his thesis by using statistical techniques on well-summarized anthropological data. Working with a random sample of societies picked from Murdock's list, he finds the following correlations: 1. *Monotheism* correlates with societies in which there are (counting out from the individual) three or more tiers of hierarchical sovereignty—e.g., clan, city, empire. 2. *Polytheism* correlates with the dominance of classes. 3. *Ancestor worship* correlates with societies in which the extended family is paramount. 4. *Reincarnation* is found in societies of small village communities in which individuals make a deep impress on one another.

Projections of the Whole

Religions do project dominant groups as Swanson suggests, but Durkheim has shown that they project all the other groups as well, so that the "sacred cosmos" can be deciphered as a kind of "map" of the social geomorphology.[13] And society as a whole is also projected; there are gods who stand for the whole, even where there is no monotheism. The ultimate explanation for the otiose "high gods" studied by the *Urmonotheismus* school is probably found in such global social projections. One example of particular lucidity is provided by certain mysterious Greek goddesses who stood above and before the Olympians: namely, Themis and Dike. Jane Harrison tells us that they stood explicitly for the social order itself.[14] Themis seems to us almost an abstraction, like law, justice, right. She is associated with political order, but before she was goddess of the polis she was goddess of the tribe. In Homer she convened and dissolved the assembly. Themis bears a remarkable resemblance to the "otiose high gods" whom Lang, Schmidt and Jensen discovered standing above so many primitive pantheons.[15] Jane Harrison does not make this connection herself, at least not in *Themis,* but it would be easy to demonstrate from what she does tell us about Themis[16] that she is this kind of divinity. And this suggests a way in which the *Urmonotheismus* school could be sociologized via a Feuerbachian strategy. Perhaps these omnipresent primitive high gods are all Themis figures, and hence projections of the whole. In that case perhaps the high god really does have something to do with man's being "present at the creation." But it was the creation of society as a moral "world" rather than the creation of the physical world, and what the high gods project is social man's dim memory of how he created himself.

Themis and the other high gods are the immediate, minimal projection of any consciously contrived social arrangement.[17] Harrison says that Themis is the spirit of the assembly incarnate. She is somewhat unformed. She trembles on the verge of deity as the Greeks who project her trembled on the verge of Durkheimian insight.[18] Religion begins when this social order represents itself to itself.[19] To Harrison representation is something that naturally accompanies ritual the way affect accompanies action; it is a parallel expression of human society. But it is also associated with the growing self-consciousness of power that is generated in a group by the re-enacted group custom—the Durkheimians would identify this as mana.

Themis is *social* order. Related to her are ideas of the *natural* order of the world. In some cultures these are already metaphysical principles—like the RTA of the Hindus, and the MA'AT of the Egyptians. In these concepts, ideas of social order are projected on to physical nature. In the Greek case, this is expressed by Themis having a daughter, Dike, who stands for the physical order of nature. And the primordial magic of all religions consists in the attempt to transmit qualities from Themis to Dike: "Deep rooted in man's heart is the pathetic conviction that moral goodness and material prosperity go together, that, if man keeps the RTA he can magically affect for good nature's ordered going."[20] The group, becoming conscious of the symbolic efficacy of its repeated customs, now uses them as metaphors of mastery for magical purposes. This is the origin of the magic within religion.

How Self-Conscious Is Religious Projection?

In Durkheim religious projection is a natural process of social man coming to consciousness; in Marx it is the opposite of self-consciousness, and a matter of alienation.[21] Since Durkheim studied primitive society and Marx studied modern society, this difference suggests that projection may be more conscious, even transparent, in simpler societies. Mendenhall and Jane Harrison suggest this in showing how projection grows naturally out of any repeated social custom. It is like a family which goes four years in a row to the Macy's Thanksgiving Day Parade and, noticing this at last, declares "we always go to the parade—it's our family custom." As such, we might well expect the process to be somewhat more self-conscious when we are still near the beginning of its formation, or when the society projected is still reasonably simple and easy to understand. It is therefore not surprising that, as many anthropologists report, many primitive peoples seem to know that the gods are "nourished" or "rejuvenated" by the rite, that they in some sense require the rite, and that the people make the gods.[22] For they literally see themselves doing this, when they assemble in their small groups. This understanding tends to be a flickering, unconsolidated insight, however, because until sacred symbols are generalized, primitives lack strong concepts for putting these insights together. Turner shows that it may take an outside observer to grasp the complicated system behind their symbols. But the insights are there nonetheless and they are very much on primitive man's mind. In many primitive societies religion is central to community life, and since religious symbols are projections of society, this means that however unconsciously or fragmentarily, primitive man is a sociologist who is constantly preoccupied with the meaning of human society.

When religions become less important and the societies they project simultaneously grow more complicated, consciousness of projection may dim and alienation may grow. In Durkheimian terms, this happens after evolution from "mechanical" to "organic" solidarity: Society is no longer held together by common religious beliefs but is instead integrated economically, by the division of labor which makes everyone dependent on everyone else. This is characteristic of more complicated societies which are already harder to understand; and since in them religion with its sociological insights is also less central and more apt to be a specialized pursuit of a priestly caste, its symbols tend to become alienated from the people. A further complication, which we will consider later, is that modern religions are more saturated with magic than are primitive religions, and although magical operations are performed in the service of the ego or of oppressed groups, each victorious magical creation is a Pyrrhic victory that expropriates and mystifies communal symbols and further helps to alienate them.

But even in complex modern religions consciousness of projection is more frequently present than our tradition admits. What keeps breaking through in philosophical form (e.g., in Hegel's "absolute") is frankly present in the idea of the Holy Spirit in early Christian communities. Wilson cites one modern sect whose members openly know that their doctrine symbolizes their community.[23] Consciousness of religion as the projection of the group is so close to the surface in some Protestant ceremonies that it takes prodigious acts of bad faith to keep it under.[24] There they are in their white bare churches, speaking of "spirit" in only the vaguest of terms while dressed in all display of rectitude and worth—surely they must know that what they are worshipping is their own fine idea of themselves.

Self-consciousness about the social meaning of religious representations is especially apt to exist when the society is new or its constitution is recent: then even complicated groups may remember that *they* designed the social system and that their religion is a celebration of it. Nowadays, when the social contract theorists have been long dismissed as the mere political ideologists of a bygone age, we lack theoretical categories for adequately appreciating the very large degree to which men create, by conscious agreements, not only their states but even their societies. But the evidence[25] keeps forcing itself upon us—in Childe's account[26] of the settlement of Sumeria by mixed ethnic groups who formed compacts to clear the marshes; in Eliade[27] on compacts groups made for the creation of new cities; in an increasing appreciation by historians (e.g., Pirenne[28]) of the conscious creation of new communities. Lévi-Strauss[29] has demonstrated that even kinship organization is created by millions of social contracts as men attempt to remain brothers after lineage fission by reconnecting the severed segments in marriage alliances with which they.endlessly tinker. If society is constantly being created, or at least reconstituted, by social contracts, then men must at times remember that they made up some of the system and its ceremonial projections, at least for a few generations.

Mendenhall demonstrates what happens as they gradually forget.[30] Within about ten generations, he claims, men in the ancient Middle East would so forget that they had made the system that they would grow alienated from it. Societies would then break down and have to be reconstituted by new social contracts with new religious projections to ceremonialize them. In dramatic formulations like this we catch some of the pathos of the *Urmonotheismus* vision of man's gradual forgetfulness of god—but what man really forgets is that he is his own creator.

This memory lapse breeds not only alienation, but also magic, for its stolen scripts, rigid formulae and mystifications thrive on the unconscious force of half-forgotten meanings.

Mendenhall is best known for his romantic reconstruction of the theory formulated originally when the Amarna tablets were first discovered at the turn of this century, the theory which identified the mysterious marauding "Apirus" of those 14th century B.C. consular reports with the Hebrews of the biblical tradition.[31] As against theories which derived the word Hebrew from words meaning "people who came from afar," and which emphasized the allegedly primitive nature of their "tribes," the Mendenhall group reconstituted the Amarna theory via an etymological approximation of Hebrew = Apiru. Several tablets at Amarna are written by an Egyptian official or vassal from Byblos complaining to Egypt of attacks by the Apirus. Mendenhall identifies them as an internal proletariat who have become stateless because they have revolted against slavery and the near-slavery of rent-racked peasantry under the bureaucratic empires. If the Hebrews were Apirus, part of a tradition of revolt for freedom, this would explain much about the biblical tradition.

In one article Mendenhall also demonstrated that what are called "tribes" in this period were really political compacts organizing diverse people according to a traditional social form.[32] Every urban settlement for which we have good records from the Bronze Age Semitic world, he claims, shows a mixed ethnic population. The "tribe" pattern that organized them may have derived from traditional kinship patterns, but it was used as a flexible political form of organization (like "tribes" at Rome or *demes* at Athens). Just as regiments may be reconstituted with remnants of diverse battalions after battles, "tribal" organization was used here to restructure societies disintegrated by war, revolution or migration. Such groups were usually formed by an oath, with a god included in the compact as a symbol of it. One common form was the device used by the Hebrews: constituting the political "tribe" as the vassal of a god, with the social contract written as a compact with him.[33]

It was against this background and tradition of Apirus' revolt and "tribal" federations created by social contracts that a group of helots broke out of Egyptian control under Moses and allied themselves with other stateless peoples. According to Mendenhall, they were not primitive; they were the social debris of oppressive civilizations now in disorder and decay. Working with Apiru patterns of revolt and covenant to restructure themselves into "tribes," they added an uncompromising ethical ideal that created an enduring tradition: They would not *be* slaves or *keep* slaves. That was the basic idea of their covenant (and hence the abomination of slavery under bureaucratic empires was the real source of what Nietzsche called their *"ressentiment."*) They preserved this ideal because, as Max Weber has shown,[34] their priestly tribe, the Levites, always identified with "the mountain," with the people; in addition, there were the Prophets whose job it was always to remind the people of history. The importance of history for the Hebrews was not the mystical entity that German higher criticism has made it, the sense of unilinear progress into the infinite future (which so easily merges with magical ideas). The purpose of a preoccupation with history was just the opposite of future-mysticism for the Hebrews: it was remembrance of the past, which meant social realism. Israel had to remember that it was founded on a social contract guaranteeing freedom and justice; it would not permit forgetfulness because it could not allow reifications and still be Israel: "What stake have we in David? To your tents, O Israel." (I Kings 12:16)

Much of what we know about the ancient Hebrews could be made to fit this romantic reconstruction: Yahweh, as a kind of god of the Spartacists, is purposely picked because he is alien and afar; he is not a culture god and cannot be manipulated by magic. He demands only justice, which means social justice. Slavery is outlawed, indentured servants are employed instead and are decently treated; the *gerim* also have their rights, as Max Weber showed. Religion is perceived by the people as a compact for a certain way of life; only gradually does it become "ceremonialized" into a way of worship; but even then there is always someone like Amos to remind the people that neither feasts nor solemn assemblies but justice is their bond.

Mendenhall gives more detail about the Apiru movements in his later book, *The Tenth Generation.* These are basically political movements, rebelling against oppression but also trying to create order out of disorder; they are stateless people creating states by struggle and covenant. The Apiru tradition is so demonstrably connected with the Hebrew, Mendenhall writes, that when David fled the enmity of his king, the Philistines labeled him and his gang "Apiru."[35] But the Hebrews were not the only Apirus; far from it: Jericho apparently fell to Apiru hordes several centuries before Moses led the tribes out of Sinai, and there is an Akkadian equivalent word, *etequ.*[36]

I reconstruct Mendenhall's account to provide background for the remarkable statements he makes about the *consciousness* these people had of religion as a projection of their social compacts. He claims that at the beginning of new states people did not merely suspect that the gods represented themselves or their state; they literally *knew* this, because many of them had been in on the creating of these arrangements and had witnessed gods being used pragmatically as traditional symbolic operators in their compacts. Mendenhall's study of the widespread symbol of the "aegis" (or winged disk),[37] for example, leads him to pronounce that such religious representations were not merely felt to be projections of the state; they *were* the state (itself a "projection" as MacIver has shown). Mendenhall connects religious projection more with the state than "society" in general (that "vaguely inert abstraction"); in Swanson's terms he would agree that religion is projected by the dominant corporate group, and in his period of bureaucratic empires that was the state.[38] And like Jane Harrison he claims that at the beginning religion is virtually indistinguishable from these social institutions, that "projection" begins in identity: They are intertwined for they are just different aspects of the same collective actions that establish order. Athena, Assur, Roma *are* both gods and states.[39]

Only later do religions separate themselves from order, as mere "ceremonialization" of it in Mendenhall's formulation.[40] At their births (or rebirths), religious representations are active instruments in the creative movement that establishes a new social order. (This is one reason why religion is obsessed with creation: its symbols are operators in *actual* creations.) In the Hebrew covenant, the escaped slaves and revolting Apirus constituted themselves a political confederacy under the kingship of Yahweh, who, as an alien god, was not a tradition-encrusted culture god but one who could say, "I am that that I shall be." Yahweh representations were not mere shadows of rigid social structures already present. Rather, these new representations were part of the conscious thought and action that went into making the new constitution. Harrison stresses the same idea that representations are simultaneous with constitutive action.

Conversely, there is a correlation between how conscious a religious projection is and how constituting it *can* be, how much it can transform infrastructure. We are trained by the sociology of religion to place main emphasis on religions of alienation and their capacity to block social change and support the existing order. We think of "the ancient, monumental, cruel and elaborate religions of Hindustan,"[41] or the massive, unfathomable Christian religions of our own tradition, whose projection literally into the skies of shadows of social structure has been so complete that it was an astounding insight when Feuerbach and Durkheim rediscovered it. And we usually assume, with Weber, that it is precisely such religions that are most apt to influence society, usually in a negative way—by blocking capitalism, as the Hindu religion is alleged to do by Weber, or simply by letting capitalism happen, as some less magical religions, like Protestantism, do. So we are surprised, for example, when the Black Muslims[42] transform black communities.

The degree to which religious projection is conscious is underestimated by the sociology of religion. This is part of the general underestimation of the degree to which communities are founded by social contracts. The works of Eliade[43] on the foundations of ancient cities and of V. Gordon Childe on Sumerian states[44] have been cited. Historians of the Hellenistic age such as Bury,[45] Tarn,[46] Cary,[47] Cloche,[48] provide ample later instances of the simultaneous foundation of cities and cults for political purposes—e.g., the deliberate, thoughtful reconstruction of the god Sarapis by a group of Greek sophists who understood national character, working for the Ptolemies of Alexandria. Tarn and Cary are also instructive on the popular understanding by Greeks and Romans of the political nature of the deification of deodachs and emperors.

But where does religious projection begin, where do we draw the line? Durkheim once said that a reunion of citizens celebrating a new law is similar to a religious gathering. But Louis Schneider[49] worries that too wide a use makes the definition of religion too loose. He wonders whether Shils and Young on the 1952 British coronation as a "religious" ceremony, or Bellah on the so-called American "civic religion,"[50] are abusing the terms in a way that damages clarity. A solution could be found in Mendenhall's concept of ceremonialization. As social-contract symbols gradually lose their quality of creation operators, and become mere ceremonializations of the new constituted social order which they continue to accompany, we get pure religion. (Mendenhall himself regards this as the "end" process of religion, not its beginning.[51]) But modern political symbolism has lost its religious vocabulary with the advance of secularization. Our political symbols are projections, but the language is not religious. The community-political process is still reasonably effective in American society, still self-creative, so we have probably not yet come to pure ceremonialization. A respect for the constitution and the other institutions of democracy is not yet a religion, in other words, but a practical attitude favoring effective participation. So what would a "civic religion" be here? The cult of the flag is a possible example; if it were to grow while the constitution waned as a rally point, then we might have a civic religion in a stricter sense. Of course, Edelman, Ellul, Boorstin and others claim to see a process already well established whereby seemingly effective political action translates into merely symbolic action—in which case we have reached the stage of ceremonialization. If anti-trust legislation, for example, is totally ineffective, as Edelman claims,[52] and serves merely to celebrate our ideal of anti-trust (while lulling the people about the actual relentless advance of monopoly), then at least some political institutions have turned into religion.

Mendenhall's emphasis on the political nature of religion raises another problem. When we speak of religious projection as self-conscious and part of social constitution, this makes it hard to maintain a distinction between religion and what we call ideology. Modern totalitarian ideologies are often labelled "religions," but the intention is usually not literal. Mendenhall faces this issue more squarely: to him not only are modern ideologies truly religions, but most ancient religions were also ideologies of power.[53] Or in other words, we might reverse the Engels of The Peasant War[54] who said that early political revolts took religious form because that was the "language of the day," and say that in our contemporary world religious revolts (which are revolts over how community shall be constituted) take the form of political ideologies because that is our language.

A strong case can be made for the proposition that symbolic superstructure influences and shapes sociopolitical infrastructure only insofar as superstructure is formulated in terms of conscious social prescriptions, of ideologies and imperatives telling exactly "what is to be done," in Lenin's phrase.[55] The Weberian system often seems to suggest transcendent ideas working out their own inner logic and affecting social structure theophanously. But much of the written content of religious traditions actually consists precisely of prescriptions for social structure and an ideology to support them as imperatives to action. To a large extent, for example, the Code Manu, with its horrendous caste regulations, *is* Hinduism.[56] There is a lot of mere traffic regulations, of sheer Deuteronomy, in the core content of most religions. As for the abstract content, a good deal of this is social ideology giving reasons why the rules should be put into effect.

Dumézil has given a great deal of attention to religious projections as ideology in this sense.[57] He recognizes that these projections do not merely *reflect* a certain social structure, but also *call for* it. Dumézil devotes his attention to the polytheistic pantheons of the various Indo-European peoples which project, as Swanson's investigations would indicate,[58] a class-structured society. In India, in ancient Rome, in Iran and among the Teutons and Celts he finds the gods arranged in three tiers corresponding to the three Indo-European classes (which become the magic-frozen "twice-born" castes in India): the priest-magicians, the warriors, and the cultivators (Brahmins, Kshatriyas, Vaisyas). To these in every Indo-European society correspond three orders of deities: Varuna-Mitra; Indra and the Maruts; the Asvins and Sarasvati in India. Or Jupiter, Mars and Quirinus at Rome (the latter representing the class that became the curiales). Or Othinn, Thorr and Njordr. But the system shows up even in literary rationalizations and hence works as ideology, as for example in Plato's *Republic.* Or Zoroaster's abstractions, with Asa and Vohu Manah as Varuna and Mitra respectively, and Xsathra as Indra, etc.[59] Plato's *Republic,* of course, is the charter myth for a lasting tradition of literary Utopias in the Western world, and many Utopias since then have projected the three-class sytem[60] and, more than that, called for the elevation of the Brahmins, or the intellectuals, as the governing elite.[61]

The Hindu tradition is never far from being explicit on this score of prescribing a certain social order. Just as World War II broke out, Radhakrishnan[62] wrote a book about the influence of Hindu philosophy on the West in which, in the climactic chapter, he categorically asserted the social organization by varnas to be man's most natural and harmonious state. The wise must rule, the warriors must defend, and so on. Most occultist religions and philosophies coming from the Hindu culture area bring this ideology with them. It is no accident that occultist thinkers in our tradition also often call for rule by religious or magical elites: the tradition goes back to Plato. There is even a risk of such prescriptions in Durkheimian sociologism; and in Dumont's *Homo Hierarchicus*[63] we witness only the latest in a long tradition of attempts to assert that this arrangement is man's natural order. Finally, the peculiar role which the party plays in modern totalitarian movements, and which the army must also play to defend these experiments, also tends to recreate the three-tier social system under fascist and communist systems.[64]

Part of the anti-capitalist animus of the second, third and fourth worlds is tinged with old magico-religious ideas of the Kali Yuga, the fallen world in which castes are disarrayed, and mere businessmen and materialists (*Vaisyas* or worse) rule over them. It is not just the "necessity" of a ruling party but an intellectual tradition going back to Platonic Utopianism that puts the modern world in touch with the West's perennial prescriptive religious projections. In Nazism there were perhaps more direct links—through the Hindu and occultist dabblings of so many key Nazi figures from Von Eckhardt through Himmler.[65]

Many religious representations are rules, or social imperatives. But even the inert projections of religion can move society—even the representations that are passive shadows of society itself. For one thing, they do not stand still; religious symbols interact, like symbols in the unconscious. Religious myth is fertile and self-generative and its propositions weave new connections in the classification systems that are projected by social morphology and underlie sympathetic magic. Durkheim himself did not think these representations could have much effect on social structure, but he did emphasize that religious representations constitute a volatile realm of fantasy and association, like poetry or imagination. But even the part that is a one-to-one projective-geometry reflection of social morphology can be creative, because what is projected is often an idealization of the society: for example, what Unamuno calls "the agony of Christianity."[66] Taking the religious tradition literally can sometimes be revolutionary. We tend to think of religion as inducing cultural lag because in our society technology changes so much more rapidly by comparison. But for millennia technology was the inert factor and religion was volatile.

Projection and Community vs. Magic and Protest

If a religion is a prescription for a certain type of community,[67] the prescription may be revolutionary, as it was with the Hebrews, or conservative, as it is with Hinduism, Platonism and other projections of Aryan social structure. But what about magic? Magic's argument with religion is in part an argument with society. We have seen how sectarian ferment can reflect the social protest of disadvantaged groups. But despite all this, there is a conservative trend in magic. Religion as operative symbols of community can bolster an old community— or overturn it and create a new one. But magic, with its texts often wrenched away from consensus, has to stick to the script to retain the consensual power that is in it. In religion, society is conscious, self-constituting, agreeing. In magic, constituted agreements are borrowed by a smaller group and applied. They *may* be used like minority reports to try to amend consensus.

But most often the expropriated scripts are used mechanically. Religions, by contrast, are more plastic (until they are alienated). Magic, because it borrows its scripts, must say them letter-perfect to retain their effects. But religions, in touch with their communities, can express *new* consensus. Many primitive religious rituals are flexible, done differently each time. Sometimes they are partly made up on the spot; e.g., some Dinka and Nuer prayers are ad-libbed, according to Lienhardt[68] and Evans-Pritchard.[69] New agreements are always possible; more spirit can be raised, more mana.

Religions are probably most revolutionary and least magical when they are actively constitutive, part of the movement that creates a social order. There is no alienation and little magical expropriation then, because a self-actualizing community is present. Lévi-Strauss has demonstrated how frequently primitive creation myths preserve the memory of recent changes in the social order, often accomplished by conscious compacts. These primitive histories were dismissed by some anthropologists as "shallow," because in them the "world" was created just a few generations back. But often these people really did indeed amend their societies a few generations back, and with the myth's help they remember "creation." Here we find, cast in the language of myth, the same self-consciousness of social and historical creation that seems a marvel in the ancient Hebrews. It reflects some health in a society that is still making itself.[70]

We might therefore expect to find less reliance on magic where there is still a self-determining community, and more magic when there is alienation, but it would be hard to test for this factor since it is only one among several with which magic correlates. Absence of magic may also be associated with ethical ideals, but perhaps that is simply because in healthy, self-constituting communities (which tend to have less magic) these ideals are actualized. The alleged relation of anti-magic to rationality is even less certain.[71]

The Mechanics of Projection: Durkheim's Mana Model

How does religious projection work, exactly? Mendenhall speaks of the "ceremonialization" of group practices; Jane Harrison imagines that representation is a parallel expression of group action. These formulations are somewhat vague. But Durkheim has a very precise model of the process of projection, scattered through *The Elementary Forms.*[72] It has never been made entirely explicit before and it should be, for it is good. So just as Rappaport[73] tried to reconstruct the basic mechanistic images at work in Freud's theory (the so-called "hydraulic model"), I want to show how the machinery of projection works in Durkheim, exactly how the gears and flywheels fit together in a close reading of his text. And the whole thing, we will find, is somewhat "hydraulic," too, for it is powered by "mana" just as Freud's model is powered by libido. What is most brilliant in Durkheim in fact is that he takes mana away from the preanimists, who identified it with magic, and shows it to be the origin of religion, while linking magic, not with the raw electrical energy of mana itself, but with concepts about mana, which come later.

Reading between his lines, we might say that the projection of society in religion works for Durkheim like this: People first become conscious of the mana *feeling* during dramatic group activities; they symbolize these feelings with *objects* which gradually establish and populate the *sacred* sphere; beliefs and rites grow up *around these objects;* when these beliefs and rites are *organized* we have religion—and lo and behold the organization of these objects falls into place as a classification system that is a cosmological map projecting social morphology onto nature like a magic lantern.[74] Let us examine those steps more carefully.

The key element for Durkheim is the division of the world into sacred vs. profane. What the sacred consists of, elementarily, is *objects,* things. These objects do not possess their sacredness intrinsically; it is projected on to them. This happens because the objects are used as symbols; they are among man's earliest symbolizations. And the first and immediate designata which are symbolized by these pristine object-symbols are *feelings,* affects. These feelings, which exist long before they are ever coherently conceptualized into mana *words,* are collective affects or excitements aroused during group activities. More than that, they are feelings that are partly perceptions and also tremble at the edge of cognition—of society. Society makes itself felt for the first time in this excitement, which is mana.

The sacred objects are symbols of mana. It is clear that Durkheim intends that they are ultimately symbols of society; but what they immediately symbolize is the mana feeling that trembles on the edge of the cognition of society. This feeling arises in group acting. We avoid circularity by supposing, like Jane Harrison, that these primordial group practices were not at first religious.[75] We may suppose that mere repetition of certain group actions, everyone doing it together, would be the occasion for arousing an affectual sense of the group's presence and power. It is this feeling which is then symbolized by sacred objects.

As these objects collect, the world is gradually divided into the two realms of sacred and profane. All this means is that after a while there are a lot of these anointed things around—trees, stones, birds, emblems—all the objects that have been used at one time or another, by one family or another, to symbolize that old feeling, that immanent excitement of power, that "affectual category of the supernatural" which we now call mana. One does not touch these things casually, or even things connected with them. There are a lot of these things because the mana feeling spreads: from one object to the whole class of that object, etc. Soon the whole world seems divided up between objects that symbolize something uncanny and objects that do not. The division of the world into sacred and profane, then, is simply a distinction of objects that are merely what they seem to be from objects that have become symbols of society.

The sacred objects themselves are the first "collective representations." But now there also grow up secondary cognitive representations *about* these objects (i.e., beliefs) and more self-conscious group practices oriented toward these objects (i.e., rites). Durkheim designates each ganglion of rite and belief a "cult," noting (as against those who charge him with misconceiving primitive religion as monolithic) that every religion has quite a number of such "cults." In totemism, for example, there is at least one cult for every lineage. Note that in this formulation there is not as yet a cult, much less a religion, until secondary representations develop—i.e., rites and beliefs directed to sacred objects which symbolize mana.

A religion is the system that emerges when a number of sacred things and their cults are seen to sustain relations of coordination with one another. This formulation[76] entails that some degree of rationalization and organization occurs before we confront religion in the strict sense. That is a useful idea; it helps us to delineate logically the proto-religious stage suggested in Mendenhall and Harrison, when group practices are becoming ceremonialized but are not yet fully religious. In proto-religions, there will be some sacred objects and maybe a few cults, but as yet no organization of the cults, hence no real religion in a strict sense.[77] Once a cult is established, the mana experience can be evoked deliberately, with increasing self-consciousness, through the rituals enacted toward the mana object, in the "crowd effervescence" of scheduled group rites. Religion grows out of mana feelings, but masters them and learns how to elicit them, on cue, as part of script.

The mana affect, then, is not the ultimate "origin" of religion; it is a half-cognitive experience that mediates man's recognition of society. Society is the object and origin of religion. Like Lévy-Bruhl's "affective category of the supernatural," the mana affect is simply the first crystallization of collective attentionality, the first group experience of "there it goes again" or "that same old feeling" in which begins the cognitive experience of the group becoming aware of its constituted and self-constituting power.

Therefore a number of separate steps are implied in Durkheim's account of religious projection. Having discussed them in detail, I can now summarize them schematically:

1. *Repetition.* Primordial human or quasi-human groups find themselves repeating collective behaviors, whether out of convenience or mere habit.

2. *Affect.* Sheer coordination of action produces a resonation and amplification of stimuli among organisms exquisitely sensitive to one another.[78] Out of collective action arises an experience, half affectual, half perceptual, of power. This collective affect which trembles at the edge of cognition we now call mana.

3. *Symbolization.* Mana feelings of group power cry out for expression and they get symbolized, in a very raw way, by objects—objects that may serve as flags or emblems or even more dramatic approximations of the group affect, such as bullroarers that make rousing sounds.

4. *Accumulation of the sacred.* These things then become objects of awe themselves, and can evoke the mana affect by themselves. These objects accumulate—soon there are many flags, many emblems, many anointed objects, whole genuses, classes, even places. This proliferation of mana-symbolizing, mana-stimulating objects *is* the sacred sphere.

5. *Secondary representations.* These objects invite thought; they provide focus for action, and now the true collective representations begin. On the cognitive side, there are beliefs—myths, explanations for the sacred objects, and even before that there is the process of giving them names. On the active side, rites develop that are directed toward the sacred objects. Note that rites are to be distinguished from the raw group practices which first generated mana affects—rites are always performed with respect to sacred objects; they are already meta-practices. Rites are group practices oriented toward objects that symbolize that funny old feeling which *raw* group practices engendered.

6. *Coalescence into cults.* Collections of rites and their associated beliefs cluster around each group of sacred objects to become cults.

7. *Organization of cults into religion.* When the various cults and their objects are interrelated and rationalized, we have a religion.

8. *Cult objects map a cosmology.* All during this process, the people have been unwittingly precipitating a cosmology which reflects the layout of their society. Worldview as a classification system mapping social morphology is the ultimate destination of the process for Durkheim and the significant core of the finished religious system.

Cosmologies are originally primitive classification systems. Their classes map social cells in one-to-one correspondences. Each clan will project its mana feeling onto chance objects, and all objects used as symbols by one particular clan will later be felt to relate to one another: dingo dogs, grubs, the moon, whatever. All the objects symbolizing *another* clan will also be felt to hang together. If there are six clans, there will be six grand classes of sacred objects. If there are two allied tribes with phratries and clans and separate marriage groups, the classification system will reflect all this. Later, myths will assert general propositions making connections between one class of cult objects and another: this process will reflect changes in social morphology (perhaps toward more hierarchical, tribal structure).

During this process religion also projects society onto the natural world and then proceeds to assimilate that natural world into social classifications. Robertson Smith[79] imagines that this happens as religion expands to absorb the outer edges beyond the campfire where mysteries and terrors lie. Jane Harrison and the *Urmonotheismus* writers propose that it is magic which later on applies social symbols to the natural world to obtain sympathetic effects. But Durkheim and Mauss in *Primitive Classification* show how the natural is incorporated into the social very early, as part of the initial symbolization. After all, natural objects—stars, stones, trees, animals—have been used from the beginning as sacred symbols of each group, so it will be easy to imagine that the moon, all emus and everything else used to symbolize the falcon clan belong together.[80] Eventually, cosmology may become thoughtful; it may struggle with the problem of evil, offer a theodicy; in more advanced civilizations it will provide a "sacred canopy," an "overarching structure of meaning," a "worldview" that helps to rationalize and buttress the socio-religious system. But at heart cosmology is just a classification system derived from the arrangement of cult objects that symbolize society's individual cells and thereby project a map of their social layout.

Durkheim does not specifically say all this, or tell *how* social structure is mapped, via some process of sacred projective geometry, as a cosmology. In *Primitive Classification*[81] he and Mauss simply describe the one-to-one correspondences of social morphology and cosmologies. But we may infer all this from what he does tell us.

Society is originally very simple, agglomerative or "polysegmental" as Durkheim calls it. It may consist of just a collection of clans, each like the other, as repetitive as wallpaper. Or, as a result of the process described by Mauss,[82] Davy,[83] Fauconnet[84] and Lévi-Strauss,[85] lineage fission under population pressure may lead to contracts restoring reciprocity between severed halves in the form of gift exchanges[86] and marriage exchanges[87] that make societies more federative and complex. Any one of these social cells can raise a mana affect as its members go through some routine. Hence every one will get symbolized by various sacred objects. A particular clan may have gotten symbolized several dozen ways over a period of time—by a stone, by a mountain, by a totem animal, etc. As its cult becomes more coherent, these objects will be recognized as belonging together in the same class. Eventually, people will forget why certain stones, all pheasants, a lofty mountain and half a dozen other things fall under the "pheasant totem." Later, when the affinities seem even more mysterious because the reasons for them have been half forgotten, they will become the vehicle of sympathetic magic.

Through this religious process of cosmological projection, society creates its first map of its own structure, and starts to become conscious of itself. And magic requires this dawning self-consciousness before *it* can come into being.

On Third Provinces of the Sacred

Sacred symbolism tends to fission and proliferate dialectically—and this is no less true of theories about it. We have already considered some French and British writers who imagine, in addition to the categories of the sacred and the profane, a third category, which they identify with pollution or taboo. We need not discuss Roger Caillois' interesting idea[88] that the sacred and profane interact to precipitate the polluted, or Mary Douglas' idea[89] that the sacred, as "order," precipitates the possibility of "disorder" or pollution. (The Greek word *miasma* can mean either.) Nor need we take space for Cazeneuve's equally stimulating formulation,[90] in which order (the sacred, or religion) precipitates disorder which is fought by two means—injunctions (taboo) and magic "raids." (Magic raids across the border that taboo guards, into disorder, in derring-do razzias aimed at strengthening order and ego against fear of disorder by showing it can be beaten.) The dialectics of Cazeneuve, Douglas, Caillois and also Gurvitch[91] are always stimulating, and there is no doubt that pollution ideas can be causative in social reality (e.g., mésalliance in Hindu castes) or that taboo rules much of primitive life. But these processes are secondary to the dialectic of religion and magic, for pollution and taboo are concepts about borders rather than provinces. Religion's ego pressure and magic's counterpressure are the main engine of dialectic; turning the borders between them into a separate province would be cumbersome.

Such complexity results, I think, from taking Durkheimian distinctions as absolutes—magic vs. religion, sacred vs. profane—whereas they were part of a unitary process for Durkheim himself. Durkheim's theory is a unity, with mana as a perception of society facilitating its projection in a religious worldview.

In this process the sacred is just the collection of symbols resulting from the projection, and magic is an epiphenomenon of all this. It is wrong to make the distinction of religion and magic absolute as Gurvitch has done, deriving them even from different phenomenal bases (anxiety vs. fear, passivity vs. action, sacred mana vs. non-sacred mana—and ultimately religion from society and magic from social interaction). But Cazeneuve, Caillois, Gurvitch, etc., are always intelligent as they explore the logic of the sacred vs. profane dialectic— even if such preciousness was part of the intellectualism that helped divert the Durkheim-Mauss tradition into structuralism and ultimately "inverted" it, as Stanley Diamond put it, so that now social structure seems to be the projection of myths rather than vice versa.[92] Despite these hazards, such analysis is acute and it helps make us sensitive to the logic of the magic-religion dialectic.

Less impressive are the attempts of some American writers to wrench some of the main gears out of the machinery of religious projection and set them up as separate entities. They do this notably with mana (which is simply man's recognition of society, in Durkheim), and with "worldview" (which is simply the end product of religious projection to him). They make either mana or worldview (or both, in a confused identification of one with the other) into a third province of the sacred on an equal footing with magic or religion. These less well known theorists (Rosalie and Murray Wax,[93] Dorothy Hammond,[94] Norbeck,[95] Mowinkel[96]) one way or another designate mana and/or worldview as a third province, separate from magic or religion, related more to metaphysics and to nature. Since these arguments are quite confused there is no space for them here, except in a footnote.[97]

Worldview is an interesting subject, however: it is the "sacred canopy" of Berger,[98] the "overarching values" of so many sociology-of-knowledge theorists.[99] But Durkheim has shown that it is an intrinsic part of religion, not a separate entity but the end product of projection, the crystallization of religious representations into a system that maps society. Just as societies differ, so will their projections and their worldviews and also the cultural ideals that emerge from them. Since Nietzsche's *Birth of Tragedy*[100] writers have tried to characterize the style of different civilizations by their worldviews. Thus Toynbee and Spencer, thus also Geertz's concept of cultural "style"[101] and the Benedict-Mead-Gorer idea[102] of "national character," etc. Evans-Pritchard's[103] works have demonstrated how the worldview each social system projects will also influence which branch of the sacred dominates—theism in Nuer, witchcraft in Zandeland, etc. Durkheim was genuinely interested in worldview as the core of religion because he believed that philosophy, logic and science grow out of the categories of the human spirit that are forged in it. (Following his lead, Cornford[104] showed concretely how the first philosophy and the beginnings of science grew out of primitive worldview concepts among the Ionian Greeks, and he defined early philosophy as "the analysis of religious concepts.") But to Durkheim this is all part of a unitary process in which mana perception of society, crystallized by sacred symbols, gradually produces a map of society. He even links magic to religion through worldview, which makes belief in magic possible.[105] In other words, religion creates not just the rites, symbols and mechanisms that magic borrows, but also the cloud-cuckoo-land in which magic is possible (not to mention the classification systems on which sympathetic magic effects are based). In short, the sacred is one process, from mana through worldview projection with magic an offshoot; the one distinction worth making is magic vs. religion, because although they both derive from the same process their arguments help create individuals and social change.

There is an ultimate divergence between the magical and religious worldviews, however, which is worth mentioning. But it has to be grasped that the magical worldview is a late development, not the primordial vision of man as Frazer supposed.[106] Magic develops through a process of abstraction and generalization; in the next section we will see how its beginnings are stimulated by "the generalization of mana" in religion. Generalization continues as magic advances. An important stage is the development of the occult sciences, which are, basically, rationalized divination systems. (Astrology, I Ching, and the like were originally some society's divination procedure.) The occult sciences in turn are further generalized by the syncretistic theosophies—by gnosticism, for example, which synthesized occult sciences and magics of different peoples, including Babylonian astrology, Hellenic mystery cult magic, Iranian angel magic, Jewish mysticism, etc. Magic tends to become international in cosmopolitan cultures, to accumulate historically, to be revived in occult renewals and further synthesized. In the end it converges toward a homogeneous outlook that transcends particular societies. Magic, moreover, strikes similar attitudes everywhere (whatever the religion, magic is often against it, whatever the black magic threat, magic defends against it); similar postures of defense and contention gradually give it a sameness everywhere. That is why Lévy-Bruhl was able to write of *the* primitive worldview, "prelogical" or "mystical" as he variously called it, and still make some sense despite Mauss' charge that he lumped too many societies together. For there does tend to grow up, internationally and historically, a more or less standard magic worldview, which is what Lévy-Bruhl was really writing about. This general magic worldview comes, in time, to color religious worldviews (which is one reason that religions grow more magical, not less, as civilization advances). By the time we get to our own era, the magical worldview is everywhere virtually the same historical, syncretistic outlook, whereas religions reflect individual societies, reflect their differences and generalize only as they incorporate more magical content (the growing theosophical and magical content of the so-called world religions). So the magical worldview does come to differ with the worldview of particular religions in particular societies; and later ethical religions arise which specifically single out the magical worldview for attack. But the magical worldview is a *late* development, and *not* the origin of magic, which depends for its start on the particular religious worldviews of particular societies.

The Discovery of Mana

Mana is an almost visceral perception of the presence of society. That is the key to Durkheim's theory, the best theory of religious projection we have. Mana is an emotional reaction to the power of the social; symbols of mana really symbolize society and initiate the religious process. But when mana was first discovered by Codrington, it was thought to be the origin of *magic*, rather than of religion. Many theories, even within the Durkheim school, linked mana with magic; this was the so-called "preanimist" position. These theories are not without some insights. There is no space to discuss here all the variously stimulating ideas of the preanimists—including the English preanimists (Marett, Frazer, Hartland[107]) who mainly used the discovery of mana to support the Hegelian M...R...S sequence; the German preanimists (Vierkandt, Preuss); some sociologically perceptive American mana theorists who came close to seeing mana as the origin of religion and not merely of magic (such as Irving King[108]) and their critics Leuba and Frederick Schleiter.[109] It was mainly in England that mana became identified with the preanimist dogma according to which there existed, prior to spirits and religion, an Age of Magic in which mankind was preoccupied with an impersonal force (mana) which men manipulated by magical means. Even in England this view was not unanimous. Hartland wrote in 1914 that mana is the origin of religion. Frazer took over preanimist theory and used it, in later editions, to bolster the M...R...S sequence, according to Vickery,[110] though in practice he shunted mana aside and characterized the magic stage as a kind of prescientific reasoning based on association of ideas.[111]

It will be useful to examine Codrington's work itself and recall what exactly his discovery was.[112] Between 1863 and 1887, from his base at the Melanesian Mission on Norfolk Island, R. H. Codrington studied Melanesian Islanders and found that their entire culture was saturated by one mysterious idea. The gist of his argument is this: Melanesian religion, magic, witchcraft, etc. are all very vague; one thing that gives them unity and clarity is the mana idea which dominates and seems to be behind them all. The purpose of cannibalism, of sacrifice, of ritual is to get mana. Mana in turn makes magical efficacy possible. Mana itself is a kind of force, like electricity, that appears to inhere in any kind of efficacy; it is impersonal, but it attaches to persons. It is efficacy of any kind, but social efficacy seems uppermost and may be the basic model. It is manifested in results. When someone has it, he can use it, but it can also break out at any time or place. All conspicuous success is a proof that a man has mana; his influence depends on the impression made on others that he has mana; he becomes chief by virtue of the mana he is thought to have. Moreover, a man's political or social power is mana, or is thought to be. Any efficacy is mana: if a man is successful in battle, it is not his right arm but mana that brings success.

Mana is impersonal but hopelessly tangled up with persons: not only does it attach to people, it is also carried by spirits and ghosts.[113] When a human person has mana usually there is a spirit present in him that brings him the mana. All spirits have mana. But spirits here appear to be little more than carriers of the mana, suggesting the mere beginnings of personification. In at least one place, on Florida Island[114] the Tindalo or mana-bearing spirit—who confers the power to do magic—was originally a person; usually he is the ghost of a powerful dead man. This, too suggests a derivation of spirit from mana, for in this case mana is the social power of important people which becomes a logical problem after their death and is likely to precipitate ideas of ghosts and spirits in the manner that Hertz[115] and Ernst Cassirer[116] have suggested. The whole process is also reminiscent of Frazer's account of powerful magicians who are deified after death because memory of their power is a logical problem. Interestingly enough, men who become powerful ghosts were not only socially powerful in life; their posthumous power is also proven by miracles done in their name after death. (This is similar to tests for canonization in the Catholic Church, which require proof of miracles performed, not by the alleged saint, but in his name after his death.)

It seems likely, in a close reading of Codrington (though he seldom speculates), that he himself intends some notion of *mana as social power.* At the same time he clearly intends to show that all branches of the sacred are based on mana and all use it at every turn—religion, magic, also witchcraft and sorcery. Codrington does not explicitly put these two findings together. But very close to the surface in his book is an implicit theory that 1. mana is social power; and that 2. since mana underlies religion and magic, these in turn are in some sense representations of social power.

Though perhaps the emphasis is on magic, Codrington seems to derive both religion and magic from mana, as Durkheim and Mauss later would do. There is no iron-clad connection between mana and magic to the exclusion of religion. But Codrington's pages clearly do suggest that spirits are emerging out of mana. This suggested to the preanimists that mana comes first, then spirits; and since they associated mana narrowly with magic this meant to them that magic precedes religion. (But as we will see later, spirits in heaven could be projections of individualism emerging on earth, and when individuals begin to have mana, then magic is emerging out of religion.[117] As for the curious fact that mana is impersonal but always associated with persons, nothing is more characteristic of social forces, and above all magic, than this. They are impersonal because they draw on the collective representations; but they act only in and through persons speaking officially or expropriating authority.)

Anyway, Codrington does explicitly say that the mana idea is the foundation of both magic and religion.[118] In associating mana with both religion and magic, and in indicating that what mana represents is social power, he is really closer to Durkheim and Mauss than to his preanimist interpreters.[119]

The discovery of mana influenced many theorists of the time. Even the nominalist Goldenweisser[120] applauded it as a useful idea. But two early interpretations were decisive and influenced the others: the preanimist theory of Marett and the "mana theory" of Hubert and Mauss. For it should be recognized that Hubert and Mauss wrote their monograph on magic very soon after Codrington's discoveries, very much under its influence, and that they too offered a "mana theory of magic," though not a preanimist version.[121] They imagined that magic could actually be explained by mana, and this is the greatest weakness of their monograph.[122] But they did make some suggestions that led to Durkheim's final clarification: above all their insistence that mana is social power and the origin of both magic and religion. The charter theorist of preanimism, Marett, also recognized these same two principles, though he gave his interpretation a different direction.

It is quite apparent that Marett thought that mana was a social phenomenon deriving from social interaction.[123] This side of his work is usually overlooked while attention is given to sheer sequence (mana...spirits = M...R). The social basis of mana, however, is not precisely the same in Marett as it is in Durkheim: Durkheim emphasizes the projection of the corporate group, whereas Marett emphasizes inter-social interaction. It is almost a social-psychological theory.

Marett begins, as Malinowski does,[124] with psychological eruption: we feel an emotion, a wish and we project it. This projection of our subjective state onto others has dramatic effects on them—it moves them. Verbal magic is especially effective in penetrating the other person.[125] All this startles us. Our impact on one another produces a feeling of awe—and this feeling (mana) is the root of both magical and religious experience. It gets designated by mana concepts as men become conscious of it.

The intersocial theory of magic is probably the first one that occurs to common sense. It is the main positivist rival to the true sociological theory of magic. There is plenty of evidence that the latter theory is the more correct, however: magic is not directly developed out of face-downs, assertiveness training or one-to-one suggestion. Magic is borrowed, fully formed, from religious projections of the corporate group.

Although mana was often used to support the "preanimist" M...R sequence, Marett himself insisted that the whole sequence is religious. Much of what has hitherto been classed as magic is really religion of an elementary kind, he wrote.[126] In other words, the early magical stage is really the stage of "magical religion," hence: $R_1...R_2$. And mana does not leave off when the magical stage is passed; it is the root-religious experience, the *das Heilige* of Otto,[127] at any stage of religion.[128] He specifically denies that we have a preanimist stage followed by an animist stage.[129] Instead, we have a single primitive magico-religious stage in which there are spirits already, but in which power is what counts—and he prefers to call this the "mana stage of religion" rather than preanimism.

Marett's protestations had no more effect than Marx's claim, *"Moi, je ne suis pas Marxist."* His interpretation of Codrington was interpreted as the basis for the preanimist position; and other theorists drew conclusions about a primordial age of magic from it. This was reinforced by the discovery of mana-like words in other societies. Webster has given a good summary of these.[130] (Lévy-Bruhl,[131] Harrison[132] and others even noticed groups of words meaning "hosts" of spirits. This suggested a refinement of the preanimist sequence: mana–hosts–gods.) Among the earliest confirmations were the discovery of orenda, manitou[133] and wakan among American Indians, but their meanings are not identical. Webster noticed subtle differences. Orenda, for example, designates personal or social power, whereas wakan seems to mean pure power or life force, and manitou stresses the personal power of individuals more.[134] It is also worth noting that a number of non-mana theorists have discerned root religious feelings that sound suspiciously like mana and have given them other, made-up names. For example, we have phenomenologies like that of Otto,[135] whose *"mysterium, fascinans* and *tremendum"* are really just aspects of mana; or Van der Leeuw, who hypothesizes that "religion is about power."[136] Van der Leeuw relates certain classical Greek words (*pneuma, charis, dynamis, doxis*) to mana, and says they are all theory words for power. He is also acute in making a direct relation of mana and taboo. "Taboo is thus a sort of warning: 'Danger! High voltage!' "[137] In addition, an interesting study could be made of mana concepts hidden in the course of Western philosophy, from Anaxagoras' *nous* to Hegel's "spirit." Mauss had something similar in mind when he traced the categories of force, cause and substance to mana.[138]

But dissatisfaction with loose usage of mana terms in theory was not long in appearing. Early critics such as Frederick Schleiter[139] accused the mana theorists of being extremely vague as to how mana is supposed to work. Later critics like Firth[140] criticized anthropologists for using the term themselves in many different senses. Mana is a primitive attempt at explanation. Properly defined, there is a use for mana terms, because there is a universal human social experience present to which these terms refer. It is something similar to Simmel's idea of "pure sociation,"[141] overlaid with affects of power, fear, dependence. It has something to do with dawning self-consciousness about society. At the same time it is significant that there are mana words in many primitive societies.[142] Primitive mana words are to be understood as primitive social science, as first steps toward understanding social reality. So we need theories about both—the phenomenon that mana words try to designate, and the generation of mana words as an important early stage of social insight. Confusion occurs when the mana experience and the mana concept are confounded. To sort all of this out it will be necessary to keep distinct several different usages of mana: 1. mana as a primitive term which may or may not refer to something definite; 2. mana as a term used by anthropologists, which may or may not be carefully defined; 3. finally, the likely existence of some real social experience which mana words, both primitive or modern, may or may not be successfully expressing.

Confusions between the mana experience and mana concepts are striking in Hubert and Mauss' *General Theory of Magic*. They are its main defect, one cause of the essay's poor reception in Anglo-Saxon countries and the main reason why this monograph fails to present a fully adequate theory of magic. First of all,

Hubert and Mauss do not distinguish explicitly between the mana *affect* and the mana *concept;* it remained for Durkheim to show how momentous the distinction is. Secondly, Hubert and Mauss do not define mana as a scientific construct; they simply take over and use the primitive concept. They use "mana" as if it were a simple word with an obvious definition, so they confound the entity, the primitive name and the scientific concept. Merleau-Ponty[143] objects to this use of "enigmatic notions," derived from primitive language and undefined, as scientific explanations, and notes that Mauss does the same thing (in *The Gift*)[144] with the Polynesian concept of "hua" (the force in a gift that makes it return to its owner). In both cases, moreover, Mauss not only uses a primitive concept in lieu of a scientific construct, but also employs it as a final cause explanation—he imagines that he has explained magic when he has related it to mana (or gift-giving when he refers to *hua*). But mana is no explanation of magic or of religion by itself;[145] Durkheim's formulation shows that mana is simply part of the apparatus whereby society projects itself in religion.[146]

Confounding mana affect with primitive concepts for it, using primitive concepts instead of precisely defined scientific constructs, and even employing them as final cause explanations of magic—these are serious faults indeed. But the solutions to some of these problems are implicit in the text. After all, the great attention Hubert and Mauss gave to mana as the first "category" of human understanding, out of which the categories of force, substance and cause evolved, demonstrates that they knew after all that mana is both an affect and a conception about that affect. But it remained for Durkheim to emphasize the distinction and build on it, just as he took over their recognition that mana is at the root of religion as well as magic, and that mana is basically a perception of the social.

The Generalization of Mana

For Durkheim, mana, as it were, happens twice. Mana first of all is an affect that men become conscious of in social ceremonies and symbolize with objects that become sacred as a result—that is the start of religion. But later still, self-consciousness about the mana feeling attains the stage where it is given a name and is conceptualized—and that is the start of magic. First there was just the feeling and objects to symbolize it; now there is a *word*—mana, orenda, manitou or whatever. This is a definite event and it corresponds to a particular stage of social organization.[147] This "generalization of mana" makes magical extrapolations and magical efficacy possible. Magic is a possibility that reveals itself once mana is generalized and religious projections are somewhat rationalized. If a cosmos, then action at a distance; if a classification system, then sympathetic magic; if a generalized concentrated mana, then the possibility of the expropriation of mana.

Finally, we might add, mana "happens" a third time, when the social science of an advanced civilization discovers mana words in primitive societies and either borrows them (Mauss) or redefines them as scientific constructs (Durkheim) to help explain human society and religion.

Mana words are associated with the "generalization of mana," which means a recognition that the various experiences of mana which different clans symbolize with assorted sacred objects are all the same thing. When you find words for mana in primitive vocabulary, you can suspect that mana is now generalized, which means that the people now recognize that this sacred object, that cult and these rituals all have the same effects; they evoke mana.[148] Before mana concepts emerged, these affects and the objects and rituals that evoked them were entirely fragmented, particularized, parceled out among the various totemic subcults and the people perhaps could not grasp their general principle.

Societies that primitive have mostly vanished, but Durkheim claims that certain Australian tribes are still in the later part of this stage of non-generalized mana;[149] they are on the threshold of generalizing but have not taken the final step yet. But even here, mana concepts are already starting. Some words exist here which express various *aspects* of mana. There is a word among the Arunta, for example, *Arungouiltha,* which means "evil mana"—a partial abstraction, not the whole idea.[150] (It is very interesting, by the way, that the first idea of mana to emerge here refers to evil mana; this suggests that black magic may have been the first magic to arise. There is considerable evidence for this, which is discussed in a later section.[151])

These Australian tribes have no completely general idea of a single and universal mana for a very good reason. According to Durkheim, that can only come at a later stage in society when tribal hierarchy has become dominant and a tribal religion grows up which accentuates the tribe over its constituent clans. Whereas these people are still at the stage of totemism, in which, for each different position in the system, there is a different cult. Durkheim is more extreme than Marx regarding the social determination of thought, and he intends to say that it is *just not possible for these men to think in general terms*—until their social structure is generalized. In primitive, "polysegmental" societies such as these—loosely associated clans—men literally cannot *see* that their separate cults duplicate each other. But when tribal organization dominates the clan mosaic and projects its own general tribal religion, *then* men can see that the cults and sacred objects are similar and refer to the same "mana" experience. Cognition evolves with social structure and is determined by it; only as structure is "generalized" can a general concept of mana emerge.

For decades these passages (pp. 196 seq.) in Durkheim's *Elementary Forms of Religious Life* were mostly overlooked by his commentators and critics. An early exception was Halbwachs, who wrote a short book to summarize and popularize Durkheim's volume in 1925[152] and gave major attention to the idea. In the forties, Gurvitch[153] made it the axis of his own theory of the emergence of magic. Among later commentators, Lukes noticed it.[154]

The point is that when there is no true mana word yet, there is very little magic. Mana as a concept, as a generalization, corresponds with the emergence of magic. The reasoning is this: magic involves the expropriation of religion to use in some *other* context. But if religion is purely particularistic, each rite massively concrete, referring directly to one group, it is hard to expropriate, extrapolate or otherwise put to another use. As Róheim[155] and the psychiatrists have shown, an element of abstraction is involved in magic. Similarities between situation A and situation B have to be recognized, implicative reasoning, if-then, must be carried out. This is only possible after the generalization of mana.

When the idea of generalized mana does emerge, it is associated with magic, though which causes which is murky in Durkheim. At one point he writes that mana emerges *out of magic,* for magic is more loose in this system than is religion, which is bound to particular clans.[156] Such magic as exists is already somewhat out of structure, or is associated with evil, hence it is already somewhat generalized. Therefore magic will be the embryo out of which the more tribe-oriented tribal religion will emerge to replace the clan religion. Thus, Durkheim is saying simultaneously that general ideas of the sacred make magic possible, and that magic itself is a loose and general use of the sacred that helps general ideas of it emerge. This is not contradictory; it simply means that generalization and magic *advance together,* for magic is a general use of sacred symbolism that detaches it from its particularistic, communal basis and puts it to miscellaneous uses. The two emerge together, in other words, with magic's generalized practice stimulating the general conceptualization of mana ideas, and these generalizations in turn facilitating magical extrapolation.

Simultaneously with this joint emergence of magic practice and mana ideas, a new stage of religion arises—the tribal stage—and there is more magic in religion than before. Thus the first major evolution of religion takes place due to the addition of magic to primal religion rather than through some Frazerian process of "outgrowing" magic. And thus both magic and religion emerge out of mana: but religion emerges out of its "first coming" (the mana *feeling*), and magic emerges out of its "second coming" (the mana *concept*).

The generalization of mana is, of course, an evolutionary hypothesis about a largely prehistoric process and therefore hard to prove. But there is evidence in historical times that magic advances with the generalization and rationalization of religious material. Greek rationalization of Babylonian astronomy-divination, for example, created a magical occult science that has haunted mankind ever since. And there is also some presumptive evidence in social anthropology for the hypothesis. Gurvitch has summarized it, showing how several things seem to appear together—the tribal stage of religion, initiation lodges for young men that develop magic, and so on. We will come back to this in a later chapter.

Magic seems, in its inception, associated with generalization, even with rationalization, and may even abet these processes. But then magic particularizes obsessively. The possibility of magic is created in self-conscious religious projections; but in wrenching these representations from the consensual community, magic cuts them off from collective consciousness. Expropriation by magic abets mystification.

Magic abounds in paradoxes. It is ignited by the generalization of mana, but it particularizes it again in the magical cults that replace the clan cults. Magic is made possible by consensus, but fragments it. Magic is born in the generalization of mana and requires a minimal degree of self-consciousness about the social nature of religious representations—but its expropriation of symbolism dulls that self-consciousness. Magic is a kind of cunning insight into the social construction of reality, but it darkens that insight. If religion is primitive sociology, with all the holistic grasp of the sociological imagination that implies, magic tends to be primitive psychology, whose narrow truths are derived from the general view but which quickly loses its bearings in self-confirming pseudo-knowledge of its own mechanical efficacies. Magical efficacy, like the primitive classifications that lie behind sympathetic magic, depends above all on what is half known and half forgotten, half understood and half mystified, half believed and half denied. Magic may begin in the individual's attempt to participate in consensus, to affect it and move it—but it may have the effect of precipitating alienation. Magic is sometimes a protest against the burden of culture, but successful magical operations precipitate more culture. Magic protests the terrifying superego pressure of communal religion, but its protests cumulatively precipitate those subcults that are the ugliest warts on religion's thick and scaly hide. Magic protests against the superego, but if the protest is effective, it sets up on Park Avenue, starts defining all neuroses as character neuroses and works increasingly as a superego figure. Magic is an ego-defense mechanism and the heart of all curing, but it is probably the most iatrogenesis-infected branch of medicine, primitive or modern. Revolutionary and nativist, original and banal, magic is forever renewing sacred experience yet is forever the same old thing. Magic is energy struggling against a mold, but all magic hardens with time into new molds. Magic is man's intimate resource, his personal symbolic power, but ultimately all magic is objectified, belongs to someone else, and confronts us as Other.

The end result is an alienation of symbolic powers, which now belong neither to the individual nor the community, but to the magicians, the Brahmins, the specialists. One almost has to fall back on gnostic imagery—on cosmic eggs that condense and diffuse—to characterize magic: Communal symbolism condenses in self-determining, religious self-consciousness, but this makes magic possible and the egg cracks, diffusing its energy again. Hegelian imagery also comes to mind, for magic is the very paradigm of the rule that action is self-alienating for it objectifies mind. Burdened by the heaped-up mind of the centuries, individual man cannot fathom it; his action is paralyzed until he can perform those magical operations of generalizing, abstracting, forming a model and using it to manipulate social reality—and the result is always more consequences, more history, more culture. Magic turns into religion as the "I" precipitates the "me," as action produces alienation. Magic is made possible by taking the broad view, and then it proceeds to apply it in ways that narrow the view.

Something is born and something is lost in this agonistic struggle—for out of it the self and the individual emerge, freed from Eden but imprisoned from the beginning in magical structures of alienation and evil which have made this birth possible. But before we contemplate this tragic drama, we must make a final effort to distinguish magic from religion. We have already considered which came first. Now we must determine which is which. And why does one give birth to the other?

Notes

1. J. Royce, *The Problem of Christianity* (N.Y., 1913, 1967), pp. xv–xvi, 70, 92; ch. 2.

2. G. W. F. Hegel, *The Philosophy of History* (N.Y., 1900), Intro., pp. 19–28ff.

3. Ludwig Feuerbach, *The Essence of Christianity* (N.Y., 1957), ch. 1, pp. 1–32.

4. Georges Dumézil, *Les Dieux des Indo-Européens* (Paris, 1952), *passim*.

5. V. Gordon Childe, *Man Makes Himself* (N.Y., 1951); *What Happened in History* (London, 1959); *Social Evolution* (Cleveland, 1951); *The Pre-History of European Society* (London, 1958), etc.

6. Religions have histories. Even in cosmopolitan cultures they may be the projections of fragmented or dispersed groups—guest peoples, ethnic minorities or even subcultures and classes. Roland Robertson notes that in pluralistic societies religions may come to represent alternate lifestyles and compete for allegiance (Robertson, *The Sociological Interpretation of Religion*, N.Y., 1970, p. 157ff.). It is *here* that the DNA analogy *is* useful, though only as a metaphor. Religions as projections of fragmented, scattered or amalgamated societies, might be likened, via the DNA analogy, to viruses, which genetic science tells us are "genes on the loose." Religions as competing blueprints might indeed tend, insofar as they are accepted, to bring a particular moral community into existence—the way Hutterites create isolated farming communities; or Sōka Gakkai (see H. Neill McFarland, *The Rush Hour of the Gods*, N.Y., 1967, pp. 194–220) creates a political party; or Pentecostal Protestantism assimilates certain immigrants to the economic ethic of America. Religion is the projection of a community; but today's new cultic movements tend to bring into being the community they envision. If the cultic representations succeed in separating a cognitive minority from the broad society, the possibility for deviant or anti-social development is very great, since these religious representations are *nothing more than* the reflection and blueprint of the special community.

7. Peter Berger and Hansfried Kellner, "Marriage and the Construction of Reality," *Diogenes*, No. 46, Summer 1964, pp. 1–24.

8. Philip Slater, in *Microcosm* (N.Y., 1966), claimed to see Durkheimian projection and the formation of something like religious symbolism of the group in an experimental small group. However, he assigned group members to read William Golding's *The Lord of the Flies* beforehand. Golding's novel about boys abandoned on an island setting up a sacrifice cult fits Durkheim's theory so perfectly as to suggest that Golding modelled it on *The Elementary Forms* . . . In actually *assigning* the book, Slater perhaps seeded the mine. (cf. p. 37.)

9. Robert MacIver (*The Web of Government*, N.Y., 1947, chs. 1, 3) has shown how the state, for example, is a projection from society, one that becomes autonomous. Functionalism depends, for any truth it possesses, on the fact that most of the institutions it "integrates" are themselves projections, i.e., representations of social relationships, and hence ideas. Religion can help integrate the state, marriage and all those other institutions *because* they are ideas, too, just like religion, which perhaps works like a general idea influencing the orientation of the others (cf. Geertz's notion of "style," in *Myth, Symbol and Culture* [N.Y., 1975]; or Geoffrey Lienhardt's idea of integration and control of experience [*Divinity and Experience: The Religion of the Dinka*, Oxford, 1961, pp. 250, 288–291] or Parsons on "value orientations" [*Toward a General Theory of Action*, Cambridge, Mass., 1954, pp. 159–189], and so on).

10. Guy E. Swanson, *The Birth of the Gods* (Ann Arbor, 1960), pp. 20–21ff.

11. Godfrey Lienhardt, *Social Anthropology* (London, 1966) ch. 6, pp. 115–149.

12. Thomas Luckmann, *The Invisible Religion* (London, 1967), pp. 48–49.

13. *The Elementary Forms of Religious Life, passim.*

14. Harrison, *Themis*, ch. 11.

15. See discussion under Postulate Six, "The Decadence Theory."

16. Harrison, *Themis,* ch. 11.

17. Harrison claims that the Greek word Themis and our (archaic) word "Doom" have the same meaning. Doom is the thing set, fixed, settled, that begins in convention, in public opinion, and ends in a statute: ". . . Doom is your private opinion but that is weak and ineffective. It is the collective doom, public opinion, that, for man's common convenience, crystallizes into law. Themis like Doom begins on earth and ends in heaven. On earth we have our Doomsday which, projected into high heaven, becomes the Crack of Doom, the Last Judgment. Out of many dooms, many public opinions, arose the one goddess; Themis out of many *themistes,* many conventions. They stood for what the Greeks held civilized; the ordinances which society compels." (*Themis,* p. 483).

18. "Here the social fact is trembling on the very verge of godhead. . . . Themis was before the particular shapes of gods; she is not religion but she is the stuff of which religion is made." (*Themis,* p. 485).

19. "It is the emphasis and representation of the collective conscience . . . (*Themis,* p. 485).

20. *Ibid.,* p. 531.

21. For a compendium of various statements by Marx about religion see Reinhold Niebuhr, ed., *Marx and Engels on Religion* (N.Y., 1964). Cf. also *Theses on Feuerbach* (reprinted and discussed in Nathan Rotenstreich, *Basic Problems of Marx's Philosophy,* Indianapolis, 1965, pp. 23–26); Marx and Engels, *The German Ideology* (N.Y., 1963) and *Karl Marx Early Writings* (T. B. Bottomore, ed., N.Y., 1964).

22. Louis Schneider, drawing on Merton's paradigm, makes the interesting suggestion that when religion becomes more conscious of itself *as* effective symbolism (distinguish this from society becoming conscious of itself through religion), then latent functions become manifest functions. (Louis Schneider, "The Scope of 'the Religious Factor' and the Sociology of Religion, Notes on Definition, Idolatry and Magic," *Social Research* vol. 41, no. 2, Summer 1974, pp. 340-361.) I want to suggest that latent functions made manifest increase the magical coloration of such practices.

23. "(They) do not know it from Durkheim . . . but they know it in a way in which sociologists do not always care for latent functions to be evident to those who benefit from them." (B. Wilson, "The Exclusive Brethren," in Weilson, ed., *Patterns of Sectarianism,* p. 337; quoted in R. Robertson, *The Sociological Interpretation of Religion,* N.Y., 1970, p. 156.)

24. See Josiah Royce, *The Problem of Christianity* (N.Y., 1913), chs 1–2.

25. Berger and Luckmann do use a kind of implicit contract model in a Weber-style ideal-typical analysis that seems to generate society out of the interaction of individual terms in *The Social Creation of Reality* (N.Y., 1966). What I am suggesting is that greater attention should be paid to major social contracts as actual events constituting large social structures.

26. V. Gordon Childe, *What Happened in History* (London, 1964), pp. 97–120.

27. Mircea Eliade, *Cosmos and History* (N.Y., 1959), pp. 6–17.

28. Henri Pirenne, *Medieval Cities* (Princeton, 1969), pp. 56–76; also, "A History of Europe," Vol. 1 (Garden City, N.Y., 1958), pp. 197–209, etc.; and *Economic and Social History of Medieval Europe* (N.Y., 1937), pp. 70–71ff.

29. Claude Lévi-Strauss, *The Elementary Structures of Kinship* (Boston, 1969), pp. 99ff, *passim.*

30. Mendenhall, *The Tenth Generation: The Origins of the Biblical Tradition* (Baltimore, 1974); also Edward F. Campbell Jr., and D. N. Freedman, eds., *The Biblical Archeologist Reader 3* (Garden City, N.Y., 1970), chs. 1, 2 and 5.

31. Cf. chs. 3, 5, 6, divers authors, *Biblical Archeologist Reader 3;* and ch. 5, Mendenhall, *The Tenth Generation,* pp. 122–141.

32. George E. Mendenhall, "Covenant Forms in Israelite Tradition," *Biblical Archeology Reader 3,* ch. 2, pp. 25–53. See also "Tribe and State in the Ancient World: The Nature of the Biblical Community," *The Tenth Generation,* ch. 7, pp. 174–197.

33. "Covenant Forms in the Israelite Tradition," *Ibid.*

34. Max Weber, *Ancient Judaism* (Glencoe, Ill., 1952), pp. 217–18.

35. Mendenhall, *The Tenth Generation,* p. 136.

36. *Ibid.*, p. 140.

37. *Ibid.*, ch. 2, "The Mask of Yahweh," pp. 32–66.

38. Mendenhall himself displays contempt for these power religions ("paganisms ancient and modern,") and he also heaps scorn on all theology that equates god with our "ground of being." Immanent gods not only become "culture gods" as Harvey Cox has put it (*The Secular City*, N.Y., 1966, pp. 257–258ff); to Mendenhall they become power gods. The biblical tradition is an advance over this, a third stage that goes beyond primitive religions that project mere economic and kinship order, and civilized religions that project political power. The biblical religion instead projects an ideal of justice.

39. "At the grass roots level of religion, behavior is often not overtly religious in a formal way, except after a long . . . accumulation of traditions. . . . Then, characteristically, a 'liturgical movement' attempts to sanctify every important facet. . . . This . . . is the end point of religion, not its beginning. (*The Tenth Generation*, p. 9) . . . Assur-the-god *is* Assur the state. (p. 47). . . . The identification of names of god and state is well illustrated from *Assur* to *Athena* to *Roma* . . ." (p. 191).

40. Mendenhall, *The Tenth Generation*, p. 9.

41. Thomas De Quincy, *Memoirs of an English Opium Eater* (N.Y., 1966).

42. Cf. C. Eric Lincoln, *Black Muslims in America* (Boston, rev. Beacon ed.), *passim*.

43. Mircea Eliade–See especially *Cosmos and History* (N.Y., 1959), ch. 1.

44. V. Gordon Childe, *What Happened in History*, ch. 5.

45. J. B. Bury, *A History of Greece* (N.Y., Modern Library ed.), pp. 759, 814.

46. W. W. Tarn, *Hellenistic Civilization* (N.Y., 1961).

47. M. Cary, *A History of the Greek World, 323 to 146 B.C.* (London, 1972). Cf. p. 371ff on recreation of Sarapis cult.

48. Paul Cloche, *La Dislocation d'un Empire: Les Premiers Successeurs d'Alexandre le Grand* (Paris, 1959).

49. Louis Schneider, "The Scope of the Religious Factor and the Sociology of Religion . . ." *Social Research*, Vol. 41, No. 2, Summer, 1964, pp. 340–361.

50. Robert Bellah, *Beyond Belief* (N.Y., 1970), pp. 168–192.

51. Mendenhall, *The Tenth Generation*, p. 9.

52. Murray Edelman, *The Symbolic Uses of Politics* (Urbana, Ill., 1967), pp. 28, 40, 43.

53. Mendenhall, *The Tenth Generation*, p. 199.

54. Friedrich Engels, *The Peasant War in Germany*, in *The German Revolutions* (Chicago, 1967).

55. This is a book title: V. I. Lenin, *What Is To Be Done?* (N.Y., 1929).

56. See for example, C. Bouglé, *Essais Sur le Régime des Castes* (Paris, 1935).

57. G. Dumézil, *op. cit.* See also C. Scott Littleton, *The New Comparative Mythology* (Berkeley & Los Angeles, 1973), pp. 144–145, etc.

58. Guy E. Swanson, *The Birth of the Gods* (Ann Arbor, 1968), pp. 82–96.

59. Very important also is the tendency of the tiers to split, which I think reflects the dialectic of magic and religion. In many pantheons the first tier includes both a magician god, one who creates order by "tying and binding" (e.g., Varuna and Uranos), and a god *of the order that is precipitated* by this magical creation of reality (e.g., Mitra). Dumézil sees here the progression from mere magical oath guarantees of order to stable contract, but in a larger sense it represents the routinization of charisma.

60. Utopias often elevate intellectual elites.

61. But too much of Dumézil's effort is devoted to problems of forcing recalcitrant data to fit an overschematic theory—e.g., the trouble he has with Mithra who derives from Mitra but seems to be a second-tier or Indra figure in Mithraism; or his attempts to re-mythify what he considers to be myth turned into pseudo-history by finding his primordial three tiers of Roman gods among the alleged early "kings" of Rome.

62. S. Radhakrishnan, *Eastern Religions and Western Thought* (Oxford, 1939, 1959), p. 355ff.

63. Louis Dumont, *Homo Hierarchicus: The Caste System and Its Implications* (Chicago, 1970, 1974).

64. Even those who seem only to be *reporting* the facts cynically (like the elitist theorists Pareto, Mosca, etc.) often seem to betray a nostalgia for the alleged order that existed before the Kali Yuga.

65. Cf. Pauwels and Bergier, *The Morning of the Magicians.* See also Dusty Sklar, *Gods and Beasts, The Nazis and the Occult* (N.Y., 1977). Sklar also delineates a marriage of evolutionist and Hindu ideas in influential racist thinkers like Gobineau. (Cf. ch. 2, p. 7ff.)

66. Miguel de Unamuno y Jugo, *The Agony of Christianity and Essays on Faith* (London, 1972).

67. The DNA analogy occurs to some: e.g., Talcott Parsons, "Durkheim on Religion Revisited . . .", in Charles Y. Glock & Philip E. Hammond, eds., *Beyond the Classics?* (N.Y., 1973), p. 160.

68. G. Lienhardt, *Divinity and Experience* (Oxford, 1961), ch. 6, p. 204ff.

69. E. E. Evans-Pritchard, *Nuer Religion* (Oxford, 1956, 1970), pp. 24–27.

70. The Utopian archeologists of today's occult revival carry Lévi-Strauss' insight to extremes. As against Eliade's finding that myth translates real history into cyclical myths, the new seers think that myths preserve accurate memories even of pre-history.

71. Weber has shown how magic too undergoes its own processes of rationalization, and he and Mannheim, with their distinction of functional vs. substantive rationality, show how reason itself can be alienated and mystified.

72. This is a free-handed reconstruction of Durkheim's theory of religious projection, drawing on interpretations by commentators as well as the original. Strategic in this is Durkheim's actual usage of the term mana, which becomes clearer later in this chapter.

73. David Rapaport, *The Structure of Psychoanalytic Theory: A Systematizing Attempt,* Monograph 6 in Psychological Issues series (vol. 2, no. 2, N.Y., 1960).

74. ". . . as if a magic lantern threw the nerves in patterns on a screen." (T. S. Eliot, "The Love Song of J. Alfred Prufrock.") According to Durkheim this projection enables society to become conscious of its own social-historical forms. It builds the first categories of human understanding out of these social reflections. Later, structuralists like Lévi-Strauss would instead assert that the magic lantern mirrors *innate* logical structures of the human mind.

75. Like Harrison, we suppose that Soc . . . R, M, where Soc − R (Lim).

76. Durkheim, *Elementary Forms . . .*, pp. 37–41.

77. "When a certain number of sacred things sustain relations of coordination or subordination with each other in such a way as to form a system . . . the totality of these beliefs and their corresponding rites constitutes a religion . . . a religion is not necessarily contained within one sole and single idea. . . . Each homogeneous group of sacred things . . . constitutes a center of organization about which gravitate a group of beliefs and rites, or a particular cult." *Ibid.*, p. 41.

78. Otto would say, some experience of *"mysterium, tremendum, fascinans."*

79. W. Robertson Smith, *The Religion of the Semites.*

80. Emile Durkheim and Marcel Mauss, *Primitive Classification* (Chicago, 1963), pp. 10–26.

81. *Ibid.*, chs. 1–2.

82. Marcel Mauss, *The Gift* (N.Y., 1967).

83. Georges Davy, *La Foi Jurée: L'Etude Sociologique du Problème de Contrat* (Paris, 1922), cf. Introduction.

84. Paul Fauconnet, *La Responsabilité* (Paris, 1920).

85. Claude Lévi-Strauss, *The Elementary Structures of Kinship* (Boston, 1969), *passim.*

86. The Davy-Mauss-Lévi-Strauss link is explored in Postulate 10.

87. Lévi-Strauss, *op. cit.*, clearly sets marriage in this context of exchanges.

88. Roger Caillois, *L'Homme et le Sacré* (Paris, 1950), pp. 39–47.

89. Mary Douglas, *Purity and Danger* (Baltimore, 1970), pp. 11–16.

90. Jean Cazeneuve, *Sociologie du Rite: Taboo, Magie, Sacré* (Paris, 1971), ch. 11.

91. Georges Gurvitch, "La Magie, La Religion et le Droit," in *La Vocation Actuelle de la Sociologie*, vol. 2 (Paris, 1963).

92. Stanley Diamond, "The Inauthenticity of Anthropology: The Myth of Structuralism," ch. 10 in *In Search of the Primitive* (New Brunswick, N.J., 1974), pp. 292–331.

93. Rosalie & Murray Wax, "Magic and Monotheism" in *Proceedings of the 1964 American Ethnological Society Spring Meeting: A symposium on New Approaches to the Sociology of Religion*, pp. 50–60; "The Notion of Magic," *Current Anthropology*, vol. 4,

no. 5, Dec. 1963; "The Magical Worldview," *Journal for the Scientific Study of Religion,* vol. 1, no. 2, 1962, pp. 179–188.

94. Dorothy Hammond, "Magic, A Problem in Semantics," *American Anthropologist,* vol. 72, 1970, pp. 1349–1356.

95. Edward Norbeck, *Religion in Primitive Society* (N.Y., 1961), pp. 50–51, etc.

96. Mowinkel is discussed in the articles by the Waxes.

97. Dorothy Hammond (*op. cit.*) proposes that "Religion" as a whole consists of three provinces: religious rites in the strict sense, magic and "worldview," which she identifies with mana. Now mana as a concept does become an important category *in* worldview, but saying the two are the same is like saying that mass is physics.

Murray and Rosalie Wax (*op. cit.*) draw on Redfield's distinction of "lesser vs. greater tradition," Weber's idea that ethical religions "disenchant" the world and Sigmund Mowinkel's theory that magic is a mentality and a "world." They state that magic *is* this "lesser tradition," this "enchanted world," this "magic world," in short, this worldview. This revives the ethnocentrism of the M . . . R . . . S sequence, and Lévy-Bruhl's ideas of "primitive mentality." But the worldview of magic is really a secondary and later development. Magic depends, for its initial efficacy, on religious worldviews. And to identify magic with its own worldview, without telling where that comes from, is no explanation at all. It repeats Lévy-Bruhl's phlogiston-like circularity in saying that superstition is caused by superstitious thinking.

In Norbeck (*op. cit.*) these sophistries are carried to Parsonian lengths of logical elaboration. He, too, imagines three provinces: magic, religion and what he calls "mana," ideas of impersonal power which he thinks are independent of magic. And all three types of action—mana, magic and religious—can be done in either a "personal" or "impersonal" way (according to the Ruth Benedict polar ideal type often used to distinguish magic from religion). Crossing "mana, religion and magic" against "personal vs. impersonal," 3 times 2, he generates six Parsonian cells. But he also classifies by "means vs. ends," potentially generating 12 cells. Thus, for example, a magical act might be used in a religious fashion (e.g., ceremonial magic) but for a magical end, and so on. The result is confusion and sterility.

98. Peter L. Berger, *The Sacred Canopy* (Garden City, N.Y., 1967), chs. 1–2.

99. E.g., Karl Mannheim, *Ideology and Utopia,* etc.; Talcott Parsons, *The Structure of Social Action,* etc.

100. F. Nietzsche, *The Birth of Tragedy from the Spirit of Music,* in *The Philosophy of Nietzsche* (N.Y., 1927), pp. 951–1088.

101. Clifford Geertz, "Religion as a Cultural System," in Michael Banton, ed., *Anthropological Approaches to the Study of Religion,* A.S.A. Monograph 3 (London, 1968), pp. 1–46.

102. Ruth, Benedict, *The Chrysanthemum and the Sword* (Boston, 1946); Margaret Mead & Rhoda Métraux, eds., *The Study of Culture at a Distance* (Chicago, 1953); Margaret Mead & Martha Wolfenstein, eds., *Childhood in Contemporary Cultures* (Chicago, 1955); Margaret Mead, *And Keep Your Powder Dry* (N.Y., 1942). Geoffrey Gorer, *Exploring English Character* (N.Y., 1955); *The American People* (N.Y., 1948).

103. Lowie also demonstrates different institutions within religions getting special emphasis depending on the worldview of different societies: Robert A. Lowie, *Primitive Religion* (N.Y., 1948, 1970), Part 1, pp. 3–98.

104. F. M. Cornford, *From Religion to Philosophy* (N.Y., 1957), p. 125ff.

105. ". . . the faith inspired by magic is only a particular case of faith in general. . . . Behind the mechanisms, laical in appearance, which are used by the magician, . . . (is) a background of religious conceptions and a whole world of forces, the idea of which has been taken by magic from religion." (Durkheim, *Elementary Forms . . .,* pp. 361–362).

106. Frazer's reasoning that the unity of magic vs. the diversity of religion proves the priority of the former is a simple non-sequitur. Selections on magic excerpted from Part 1 of *The Golden Bough* in Sir James George Frazer, *Man, God and Immortality* (N.Y., 1927), esp. pp. 217–223.

107. Cf. R. R. Marett, *The Threshold of Religion* (London, 1914), title essay, ch. 1; E.S. Hartland, *Ritual and Belief* (London, 1914), ch. 1, p. 26ff.

108. Irving King, *The Development of Religion* (N.Y., 1910), ch. 6.

109. Frederick Schleiter, *Religion and Culture* (N.Y., 1919), ch. 7. Leuba, *A Psychological Study of Religion* (New York, London, 1912), chs. 3, 4, 8. Leuba denied direct link of mana to either magic or religion. Both have other, rich psychological bases. Cf. p. 164ff.

110. Cf. John B. Vickery, *The Literary Impact of the Golden Bough* (Princeton, 1973), chs. 1-2.

111. He did admit, on p. 43 of the abridged edition (Frazer, *The Golden Bough,* N.Y., 1960), that logically this mistaken association of ideas presupposed some kind of psychical or material medium, as physics requires its ether. But elsewhere he said that most of primitive magic is practical, not theoretical.

112. R. H. Codrington, *The Melanesians* (Oxford, 1891; N.Y., 1972), *passim.*

113. Later writers have stressed that spirits are associated with mana in Codrington's account. But the spirit associated with this or that physical entity is usually not the spirit *of* that beach or sea but a mana spirit *in* the beach or sea. This suggests a transition in progress from mana ideas to animism; obviously this is what Marett had in mind, so it is unfair to him to say that he overlooked the role of spirits in Codrington's account of mana.

114. Codrington, *op. cit.,* pp. 124-5.

115. Robert Hertz, *Death and the Right Hand* (Aberdeen, 1960), pp. 29-88.

116. Ernst Cassirer, *Language and Myth* (N.Y., 1946), p. 52.

117. This is discussed in Postulate 10.

118. "By whatever name it is called, it is the belief in this supernatural power that is the foundation of the rites and practices which can be called religious; and it is from the same belief that everything which may be called Magic and Witchcraft draws its origin. Wizards, doctors, weather-mongers, prophets, diviners, dreamers all alike, everywhere in the islands, work by this power." Codrington, *op. cit.,* p. 192.

119. In at least one island Codrington noticed the existence of a pre-Christian, otiose but fully formed "high god" standing distant and above all these half-formed spirits (Qat, in the Banks Islands), which is of course grist for the *Urmonotheismus* mill. (Codrington, p. 154).

120. A. A. Goldenweisser, *Early Civilization, An Introduction to Anthropology* (N.Y., 1922), chs. 10-11, pp. 184-235.

121. Hubert and Mauss' *Esquisse d'Une Théorie Générale de la Magie* appeared in *L'Année Sociologique* for 1902-1903.

122. *General Theory of Magic,* English ed., pp. 108-121.

123. R. R. Marett, *The Threshold of Religion* (Rev. ed., London, 1914), pp. 48-54.

124. I.e., in *Magic, Science and Religion* (Garden City, N.Y., 1954), pp. 79-82.

125. "Nothing initiates an imperative more cleanly . . . than the spoken word. Nothing, again, finds its way home to another's mind more sharply. It is the very type of a spiritual projectile." Marett, *op. cit.,* p. 54.

126. Marett, *op. cit.,* Introduction.

127. Rudolf Otto, *The Idea of the Holy* (N.Y., 1958), p. 5ff.

128. ". . . if there be reason to hold that man's religious sense is a constant and universal feature of his mental life, its essence and true nature must then be sought, not so much in the shifting variety of its ideal constructions, as in that steadfast groundwork of specific emotion whereby man is able to feel the supernatural precisely at the point at which his thought breaks down. Thus from the vague utterance of the Omaha, 'the blood pertains to wakanda,' onwards, through animism to the dictum of the greatest idealist philosopher, 'the universe is a spiritual whole,' a single impulse may be discerned as active—the impulse . . . to bring together and grasp as one the That and the What of God." (Marett, p. 28).

129. Marett, *op. cit.,* ch. 4 "The Conception of Magic."

130. H. Webster, *La Magie Dans Les Sociétés Primitives* (Paris, 1952), ch. 1, "Puissance Occulte," pp. 9-44.

131. Lucien Lévy-Bruhl, *La Mythologie Primitive* (Paris, 1935). These words (bugari, ungud, etc.) usually refer to dema, ancestors, "first ones." Cf. ch. 1.

132. Jane Ellen Harrison, *Prolegomena to the Study of Greek Religion* (Cleveland & N.Y., 1959), esp. ch. 5, pp. 163-256.

133. E.g., "The Algonkin Manitou," *Journal of American Folklore,* vol. XVIII, July-Sept., 1905, pp. 183-190.

134. Webster, ch. 1 plus footnotes, pp. 9–44. Some tribes have a connotation of "hot" associated with their mana word. For others, significantly, the word mana is also used to designate their rites and magic formulae. Hubert and Mauss observe that the Hindu mana word Brahmâ, neuter, which also became the impersonal stuff of the pantheist universe in Upanishadic formulations, originally meant ritual prayer or spell.

135. Rudolf Otto, *The Idea of the Holy* (N.Y., 1958), pp. 12–40.

136. G. Van der Leeuw, *Religion in Essence and Manifestation* (N.Y., 1963), vol. 1, pp. 23ff.

137. Van der Leeuw, *op. cit.,* p. 44.

138. Hubert and Mauss, *A General Theory of Magic,* p. 114, etc.

139. Frederick Schleiter, *Religion and Culture* (N.Y., 1919), ch. 7.

140. Raymond Firth, "An Analysis of Mana: An Empirical Approach" (1940), in Firth, *Tikopia Ritual and Belief* (Boston, 1968), pp. 174–194.

141. George Simmel, "Sociability" in Kurt H. Wolff, ed., *The Sociology of George Simmel* (Glencoe, Ill., 1950), pp. 40–57.

142. Lévi-Strauss offers the only serious attempt at dismissing all this with his (somewhat unclear) notion that mana words are blank words, deuces-are-wild words that every language needs. Introduction to C. Lévi-Strauss, ed., *Marcel Mauss Sociologie et Anthropologie* (Paris, 1950, 1966), P. XLIV. He cites the American slang word "oomph" as an example. But mana words have much more content than that; they also generate secondary words which have rich meanings and rich applications, many of them consistent over many culture areas. (E.g., mana as money, mana as social power of chiefs, mana as ritual power, etc.) "Oomph" was applied to Betty Grable, but not to Franklin D. Roosevelt, Jesus Christ or the Yankee dollar.

143. Maurice Merleau-Ponty, "De Mauss à Claude Lévi-Strauss," in *Eloge de la Philosophie et Autres Essais* (Paris, 1953, 1960), pp. 145–169.

144. Marcel Mauss, *The Gift* (N.Y., 1967), pp. 8–10.

145. The excessive reliance on mana as an explanation is not even necessary for Mauss' theory (or for Durkheim's). One reason why the *Esquisse* is still valuable is that even if the passages using mana to explain magic are cut, the basic theory still stands. For Mauss (and for Durkheim as well) mana, as just a perception of society, is a *non-essential middle term* in their equations. If philologists were to explode the mana edifice tomorrow the Durkheimians could fall back on a simpler, more general statement of religion as the projection of society, without using the intermediate mana term.

146. There are differences among the Durkheimians. While Durkheim sees mana as an affectual perception of society that gets symbolized in sacred objects, Hubert and Mauss, in a more rough-and-ready way, simply identify mana with the sacred (almost). Gurvitch splits mana into the mana affect of "anxiety" aroused by society as a corporate personality (that is religion), and the mana affect of "fear" aroused in intersocial interaction (that is supposed to be the basis of magic). Douttée identifies mana instead with desire, like Malinowski's theory of magic. Bastide tries to relate mana to libido to effect a synthesis of Durkheim and Freud.

147. Durkheim, *The Elementary Forms of Religious Life,* pp. 196–197, etc.

148. This is *not* circular, for although sacred objects are initially used as symbols to catch and designate *spontaneous* mana experiences, rituals get organized around these objects which now can provoke mana automatically, as part of the script.

149. Durkheim explains that while each totemic clan is a sort of "chapel" in the group religion, it is quite independent; the particular totem, for example, is sacred only to it. The feeling of a *universal* force like mana can only arise as tribal structure becomes stronger, and tribal gods sit above totems; this stirs up the sense of a broad unity, and awakens the idea of power. *op. cit.,* p. 196.

150. *Ibid.,* p. 197.

151. Cf. Postulate 11.

152. Maurice Halbwachs, *Les Origines du Sentiment Religieux* (Paris, 1925), translated as *Sources of Religious Sentiment* (Glencoe, Ill., 1962), pp. 71–74.

153. The Gurvitch theory is discussed in Postulate 10.

154. Lukes writes: "(Durkheim) presented religious forces among the Australians as 'localized in definite and distinct social contexts' and thus 'diversified and particularized in the image of the environments in which they are situated.' In this way he explained the

fact that the Australians did not generalize the totemic principle . . . and see it more abstractly and generally as an 'anonymous and diffused force,' such as the mana of the Melanesians, the wakan of the Sioux and the orenda of the Iroquois." Steven Lukes, *Emile Durkheim, His Life and Work* (London, 1972), p. 464.

155. Géza Róheim, *Magic and Schizophrenia* (Bloomington, Ind., 1955), pp. 82–83 and *passim.*

156. "Thus among these different peoples, while the properly religious forces do not succeed in avoiding a certain heterogeneity, magic forces are thought of as being all of the same nature . . . This is because they rise above the social organization and its divisions and subdivisions . . ." *Elementary Forms . . .*, pp. 197–8.

Postulate 8: RELIGION IS
THE INSTITUTION THAT CREATES
OR MODELS MAGIC FOR SOCIETY.

IF religions are projections of society as society is becoming conscious of itself, why do they persist? Consciousness is attained and religion persists; from this it is inferred that religion serves some function. Its integrative function gets most attention; and its magical functions are not deeply probed. Religions originally are systems of symbols that project society, but these symbols are used in important ways. Frazer and Harrison show their magical application in regenerating agricultural fertility. Lloyd Warner[1] demonstrates that where magic is lacking, purely religious ceremonies can be substituted in magic healing. Evans-Pritchard[2] similarly reports that the extremely theistic Nuer people, who have very little magic proper, use religious sacrifice as an all-purpose rite for many ends. Hocart[3] has shown that the effects of core religious ceremonies are themselves magical, in the sense of being "life-giving," and Eliade[4] has made a similar point. Conversely, Lienhardt,[5] expanding Durkheim's[6] insight that individual funeral rites really aim at healing the wound to the whole group, speculates that any magical-medical treatment of any individual has secondarily this collective, "religious" healing effect on the group as a whole.

All this is extremely suggestive. It is as if magic not only borrowed from religion, but religion itself were ready to assist such borrowing; at times it almost seems that religion emits magic.

Which Is Which?

Undertaking this discussion will necessitate reviving another old debate. In Chapter 6 it was useful to revive the old debate about which came first, magic or religion. Now it is important to raise the old question of which is which, and whether indeed magic and religion can be distinguished. A number of theorists conclude that they are hopelessly intertwined, but they have taken different attitudes on this. Some postulate that they are indistinguishable, that there is only one "MR" or "magico-religious" phenomenon. But if taken literally, this is a case of identity—M = R or "all magic is religion and all religion is magic." Most of those who say this do not really mean it, and they wind up qualifying it. Mary Douglas, for example, postulates the identity of magic and religion in one book, only to distinguish magic as rite and religion as belief in another.[7]

210

Those who say that religion and magic are the same thing usually have some such reservations: some things are more magical and some are more religious than vice versa. So M = R is no solution; it is not even serious, and it permits logical slovenliness. "Polar ideal types" or "magico-religious continua" are the worst solutions of all; they reify logical confusion into formulae.

Magic and religion are hard to distinguish yet impossible to identify with each other. This difficulty is not surprising because their interrelationships are complicated. In practice, field workers find: 1. Most significant magic is found outside religion, in institutions distinguishable from it. 2. But there is also considerable magic inside religion. 3. Magic borrows from religion (and of course religion borrows from magic); moreover, the borrowed religious rite, turned into magic, sometimes turns back into religion and becomes embedded as a new subcult in it. 4. Some magic may be intrinsic to religion. Many of its basic rites, such as sacrifice, seem "magical" in at least the weak sense. Because of all this, some theorists identify particular parts of religion with magic. Thus Van Gennup[8] asserts that the rites used in religion are magical. Some theorists face the overlap problem with class inclusion statements, saying, for example, that all magic is religion (but not all religion is magic). In the end all possible *A* and *I* propositions and their obverses are asserted. Some say all magic is religion; others say all religion is magic; others say *some* R is M; etc. These statements come closer to reality than M = R, but they are still too static; they do not take account of the fact that magic is constantly moving out of religion or moving into religion—being spread by it, or ejected by it, or attacked by it.

The Province of Religious Magic

Before attempting to solve this problem, consider the magic that is deeply embedded within religion. We have already spoken of "religious magic" as one of the seven main magical "provinces," referring to such institutions as exorcism.[9] These are fully magical complexes—and magical in the strong sense since they are institutionalized—which are part of many religious organizations or churches. In many cases there are officials, a staff, a small church bureaucracy with its own rationalized procedures. Consider, for example, the several institutions of magic within the Roman Catholic church. The cult of saints is an official church procedure whereby constituted authorities declare some popular exemplars of piety posthumously to be saints, mainly on the basis of miracles performed in their name after their deaths. This is plainly an institution of magic. So was the early medieval cult of relics, which Dill has described.[10] Exorcism is another official procedure inside the Catholic Church which has a wholly magical purpose: driving out demons. It has obvious roots in New Testament accounts of the practice of Christ himself. The procedure was standardized by the publication in 1614, on the request of Paul V, of the *Rituale Romanorum,* according to Oesterreich.[11] Numerous quasi-official manuals on the subject prescribed how exorcism was to be carried out—in the name of god, after prayer and fasting, if possible in a church or consecrated place.[12] Another partly magical institution within the Church was the Holy Office, because it was once very active in the detection and suppression of black magic. As late as the 19th century, according to Lea,[13] the Holy Office acted on cases of sorcery (though witchcraft actions ended long before) and potentially it could still act, since, as Hubert and Mauss point out, belief in black magic is an article of Catholic dogma. Also worth mentioning are the numerous religious shrines and spas, such as Lourdes, which most religions maintain or certify and which practice magical curing.

But the province of religious magic is easy enough to conceptualize: "Religion has some magical institutions." It is not the problem. More puzzling is the fact that some of the core rituals of religion itself seem to have "magical" qualities—such as sacrifice, all sacraments, prayer, mysticism.[14]

Religious Practices Seem Magical

To say that religions are essentially magical, or magical in certain key aspects, is trivial if no distinction between magic and religion is maintained. If one assumes an undifferentiated "magico-religious phenomenon," then discovering the magical aspect of particular religious practices merely affirms an uninteresting identity. But some writers are more specific and say exactly what elements in religion are magical. A common solution is to say that all of the *means* which religion uses may be thought of as magical. This is the second position of Mary Douglas,[15] taken up when she identified magic with sacred rites of all kinds, and also that of Van Gennup, who similarly defined magic as "the technique of religion."[16] Cazeneuve comments that this would entail that religion had no technique of its own.[17] But Van Gennup clearly accepts this possibility, and suggests that what is purely religious in the mixture is just the *belief* content of the practice.[18] (This is the same position Pradines takes[19] when he suggests that insofar as religion is not magical it tends to be philosophy.) But Cazeneuve, Pradines and Van Gennup overlook other aspects of religion that might be considered religion per se or the religious "shell" that houses magical rites—above all organization, membership, what Durkheim ethnocentrically calls a "church."

Nonetheless, the idea that the rites and practices of religion are what is magical about it says something that holds us. Loisy[20] in effect makes the same claim when he postulates that 1. sacrifice is the main religious instrumentality, and 2. sacrifice is magical in nature.[21] And we might also consider how many other basic instruments of religion a penetrating student like Max Weber characterizes as "magical." In various passages in *The Sociology of Religion,*[22] Weber hangs the adjective "magical" on prophecy, charisma, sacrifice, all sacraments, prayer, ritual in general, religious protest sects, most priestcraft and mysticism.

Furthermore, Weber is right; and not just the means but many of the aims of religion are magical, especially the more individualistic aims that are added later in more "civilized" or "ethical" religions. Weber mentions "salvation" as a magical aim.[23] A good case could be made that immortality is the same. At first immortality was promised only to the gods in the myth of Marduck; later, in Egypt, magicians ascended to heaven and became immortal gods; still later Pharaohs attempted to achieve immortality by means of the pyramid magic complex; finally, with the victory of Osiris, the magic of immortality was promised to the people in answer to their demands. But a persuasive case might be made that the hope of immortality is not instinctive but is rather a cultivated human desire. It is originally a projection of something else. Notions of the immortality of the gods are projections of the relative immortality of the social group (as compared with the individual). The religious idea of divine immortality is later expropriated by magic and used to foster individual immortality. But the desire to do this has to be cultivated, for the hunger after personal immortality is a projection in another sense. The main purpose of magic for the individual, as we shall later see, is to save him not from physical death but from *psychic* death, from implosion of the ego by the social superego, from failure of the courage to be. Immortality as escape from physical death is probably, in the beginning, a mere "projection" (i.e., symbolization as an attempt to understand) of that protection from psychic death which magic affords the individual. Men do not originally want to live after death; they do not want to be ghosts, a horrid idea. But men do want to "live" and prosper; Hocart[24] and Becker[25] show how religious ritual gives "life" in the sense of health and prosperity and avoidance of premature death.

There is even a magical dimension to morality, especially to Puritan ideas of freedom from sin. I am not just talking about "good works," or morality for the sake of salvation, which anti-magical religions like Calvinism condemn. Even morality for its own sake sometimes has a magical coloring—if it is the morality of *"integer vitae,"* the "good life" as the source of health, happiness, power or "grace." Primitive man well understood that immoral behavior could produce magical illnesses, such as the psychosomatic effects of guilt or shame. C. S. Lewis[26] avers that Christian morality is a path of perfection, which, once begun, takes hold of us like a yoke, so that Christ's will can be worked in us, which is nothing less than to transform us into "gods and goddesses, radiant immortal creatures"—i.e., the old magical aim of becoming a divinity so carefully documented by Frazer. Finally, some writers such as Hammond[27] have suggested that what seems most modern in religion, its celebration of man, is magical. There may even exist a "theology of magic," in the sense that some modern theology (e.g., Tillich, Bonhoeffer) celebrates "grown-up" man and his "courageous" use of his symbolic powers. It is also possible that Luckmann's "invisible religion,"[28] and the whole trend toward the privatization of religion is magical. This is the subject of a later discussion.

Religious Rites Are Magical "In the Weak Sense"

But having said all this, we should now emphasize that it is mainly "in the weak sense" that all these things are "magical." True, sacrifice, mysticism, prayer and the rest are institutions, which is one criterion for magic "in the strict sense," but they are institutions of religion, intrinsically bound up with its central aims. They are not peripheral institutions, like sorcery lodges, magical medicine complexes, occult sciences, magical protest movements. (The exception is "religious magic," such as exorcism, curing shrines and witch prosecution, but these institutions refer outwards to the provinces of black magic and medical magic.) It is in the undefined weak sense of magic that we detect something magic-like in the awesome machinery of sacrifice, the power-seeking discipline of Yoga or the elaborate rituals of the sacraments. In leaving the definition of magic in the weak sense open, so as to pick up all its spectral lines, we stipulated that any discussion of it would be meaningful only if it could be functionally linked to magic in the strict sense. What is the link here? The answer will be that the weak-sense magic in religion "models" the possibility of the magical effects of symbolism for the community and thus leads to the creation of institutions of magic in the strict sense.

It is precisely because religious practices have this aspect of being magical in the weak sense that they are readily borrowed and turned into magical cults and practices in the strict sense. Society, first perceived in mana feelings and symbolized by sacred objects, increasingly elaborates rites and beliefs oriented toward these sacred objects. It is but a small step from sacrifice as the celebration of the social order to sacrifice as ritual apparatus that gives life to this order. And it is but a short additional step to the agricultural magic of Neolithic religions, which use social rituals to regenerate the natural world.

It might therefore be said that religion not only makes magic seem possible; it models it for society in its ritual. We will return to that point.

This core of magical practices inside religion is important: just as myths die when cut off from their ritual base, and observance wanes with conviction, perhaps all religions are doomed to sicken when they separate themselves from their magical means.

Let us examine the evidence for the "magical" nature of certain core religious phenomena, including: 1. sacrifice; 2. mysticism; 3. myth; 4. prayer.

1. Sacrifice—and the Miracle of Selfhood

Consider first sacrifice, by all agreement one of the most basic of religious rites. Obviously it is the archetype for many other sacraments and rites of religion. Yet there is fundamental disagreement, even within the French school, as to whether it is magical or religious in nature. Hubert and Mauss lay it down that it is the religious rite par excellence,[29] that it stands on the farthest end of the religious pole on any magic-religious continuum. Yet their own account of it crackles with a sense of magic[30] and they later report that studying it was what led them to their study of magic.[31] For Durkheim[32] and Robertson Smith,[33] it is the main religious rite. But Gusdorf,[34] in a sensitive phenomenological investigation, discovers it to be thoroughly magical. And to Loisy[35] it is the paradigm of "mystical action" or magic. Which is it? To get the answer we must try to determine what sacrifice is all about.

Many books have been written arguing one or another of the half-dozen most prominent theories of sacrifice – sacrifice as a *communal* totemic *meal* (Robertson Smith); sacrifice as a *free gift* to the gods (Tylor[36]); sacrifice as a *manipulative gift* trying magically to compel the gods (Lang[37]); sacrifice as a *bridge* between the sacred and the profane (Hubert and Mauss); sacrifice as a gift at first that later becomes a bridge when sacred and profane separate (Gusdorf). All these theories catch part of the truth but all are inadequate because they miss the central meaning of sacrifice. That meaning is apparent in any close reading of Hubert and Mauss' study, even though they themselves did not state it formally. In *Sacrifice* they use what Mauss elsewhere called "the method of the extreme case,"[38] what I call a "natural ideal type" (the opposite of an abstract "ideal type" in the Weber manner), what Evans-Pritchard[39] called a highly focused "analytical description." This description seems to convey noetically the meaning of sacrifice in a far more convincing manner than the didactic passages in which Hubert and Mauss set forth their formal theory. Their explicit theory is that sacrifice "builds a bridge" between the profane world and the dangerous sacred world, so the sacred can "renew" the profane, and vice versa, without damaging each other. But what really comes through in the description is that the victim is a symbol of the sacrifier, the person for whom the rite is performed.[40] That means, an individual sacrifices his self to the god symbol of the group—and gets this self back, strengthened.[41]

In sacrifice or in any sacrament which derives from it, an individual (or a congregation) offers up a symbol of its own living selfhood to the god that represents the social group. An individual thereby acknowledges the utter dependence of his ego on the social group, but at the same time draws nourishment from the ceremony and has his courage-to-be strengthened. Any sacrificial act symbolizes the dependence of the self on the group—in circumcision a vital piece of the self is literally given up, but in many rites this act symbolizes coming-of-age and legitimizes private use of the diminished organ. And in bloody sacrifice the self is symbolically destroyed to act out the deep mystery of its utter dependence on the group from which it nonetheless mysteriously separates. The individual who makes the sacrifice both gives and gets; he pays his dues (that is the religious side). Yet at the time the ceremony seems to suck some of the mana out of the godhead to strengthen individual power and spontaneity (that is the magic side).

The "magic" of sacrifice consists in acknowledging this debt, this origin, this utter dependence symbolically, by sacrificing this personal self which is a social product—but then *getting it back* unscathed with its charter and right-to-be strengthened by this renewal at the communal fount. Some of the sacrifices in the Old Testament almost shout this interpretation at us. Abraham's tested willingness to sacrifice his son is precisely what excuses him from the act, and wins him favor and power. Job's "though he slay me yet will I love him" is a sacrificial oath of fealty. Job's afflictions are mythic versions of sacrifices from which he emerges richer than ever, almost like the winner of a divine potlatch. Ernst Becker has in fact suggested a symbolic similarity between sacrifice and potlatches.[42] For the individual, sacrifice is also similar to the shaman's dramatic trick of conquering his superego through ecstatic possession and its abreaction, which consists of overcoming some of the predominantly social part of his own self by first giving himself up to it and then controlling it, thereby achieving social power.

Yet the rite is basically religious, for its main effect is to strengthen the *community*. For the community its meaning is an act of allegiance. Often the sacrifier is the congregation as a whole, symbolizing its mutual interdependence and unity.

A few writers have built theories of sacrifice on the idea that the victim represents the sacrifier.[43] Several empirical investigators have recognized this, without casting it into formal theory. Gusdorf[44] does a kind of content analysis of the symbols and a phenomenology of the act which seems to suggest persuasively that it has this meaning. Lienhardt[45] picks it up in describing sacrifice among the Dinka, a very theistic people. Evans-Pritchard openly states it in describing sacrifice among a neighboring people, also very theistic, the Nuer.[46] Evans-Pritchard speaks of the "substitution" of the victim for the sacrifier, so does Lienhardt. (Both the Nuer and Dinka have very little magic, and use cattle sacrifice as a kind of all-purpose rite, for everything from religious ceremonies to healing.) Evans-Pritchard incidentally makes an interesting point in criticizing the Hubert and Mauss theory of a sacred bridge: half the time natives do not want to build any such bridge, they want to "get the sacred off their backs" and sacrifice is one way of paying their dues and doing this.[47]

Precisely because sacrifice (like initiation symbolism) is such an all-purpose rite, it is hard to tell whether it is magical or religious. It is sometimes used for individual ends, sometimes for the community. But things get more complicated. Even sacrificial ceremonies conducted for individuals seem to help the group, as Durkheim has observed of funeral rites[48] and Lienhardt[49] of curing rites, and of course the reverse is also true as Hocart demonstrates.

We can solve the problem by saying that sacrifice is basically religious, but that it is one of the key rites in which religion "models" the possibility of magical effects for the community. It is religious because it tends to be congregational. Thus, the spearmasters' clan that leads the Nuer rite of cattle sacrifice[50] begins with oral rites mixing both prayer and incantation but containing ad-libbed sections basically, which the fluent spearmasters make up on the spot: this is alien to rigidly scripted magic. By contrast, in late Vedic ceremonies we see the heralds expropriating the community rite and turning it into something purely for specialists: the Brahmins must speak the incantations just so, errors can cause death, and indeed, only the Brahmins can pray.[51] Here sacrifice is becoming more magical. But in either case, a core religious rite is demonstrating the sympathetic effects of symbolism to the community. It is natural that such a rite can then be applied as an all-purpose instrument. Lloyd Warner[52] shows us a branch of the Australian Murngin who lack magic: so they simply substitute religious ceremonies when they want to achieve a magical effect such as curing. Religion has shown how sacrifice seems "magically" to renew the gods, renew society and renew the confidence of individuals; it almost invites the people to apply it magically to renew nature and cure individual disease. The solution as to whether sacrifice is magical or religious is that it is fundamentally religious, but that it is also magical "in the weak sense," in the sense of modeling the magical possibilities of this symbolism for the community. Religion does this by applying its own ceremonies for instrumental ends, and ultimately purely magical institutions spring up that expropriate this modeled symbolism and use it for practical purposes.

Sacrifice is an interface between the individual and the group just as it is a link between magic and religion. It is religion modeling magic and magic expropriating religion; it is also the individual symbolizing his dependence on the social community and at the same time sucking mana out of it to increase his autonomy. Other theories catch aspects of this drama, for none of the classic theories is actually wrong, just incomplete. Sacrifice is indeed a gift– but the important point is that it is a gift of *self.* Certainly, it is *"do ut des,"* give and take (and maybe mostly take as Andrew Lang thought) but what one takes back is oneself, strengthened by official approval of one's right to be. Certainly, it is a bridge built to the sacred as Mauss said, but the purpose is to raid the sacred of some of its mana. True, it is a ceremonial feast as Robertson Smith and Durkheim claimed, that strengthens collective representations of the god and of the group. Since, moreover, the making of individuals is one of the most august functions of religion itself, mere association with strengthening the individual does not thereby make it magical. Yet sacrifice is above all a primal model for magic in its basic idea that the individual can be strengthened through the expropriated collective act. Sacrifice is already close to expropriation; the self that is no longer killed, but has a substitute killed to strengthen itself–already this smacks of magic's "detouring" of the sacred (Huvelin[53]). Hubert and Mauss write that there is a terrifying aura of the surreptitious, even of crime, about sacrifice. In sacrifice is modeled the idea that the individual can magically take something away from the sacred community.

2. Mysticism – and the Symbols of Initiation

It is perhaps because the Christian religion, out of its mixed fear of magic and desire to monopolize magic, has so constricted mysticism, that we in the West are familiar mostly with its clean versions and think of it as a particularly pure kind of religious phenomenon. Where mysticism is not contained and rigidly patterned by an official church, however, its *siddhis* and outrages, its *grandeurs* and degradations are more apparent.[54] Basic techniques of mysticism are strongly related to patterns of magical training that are spread all over the world. In both cases, the drama of sacrifice is repeated with a self strengthened by its own surrender; and in both cases it is the dramatic social symbolism of initiation which is used. These similarities in turn suggest a relationship between sacrifice and initiation, and hence between the two enormous provinces of symbolism for which these two basic rites are the archetypes.

Rudolf Otto has written, in his study *Mysticism East and West,*[55] that mysticism is not a metaphysics but is usually considered a way of knowledge, or a "path" to a certain mental state. It is easy to homologize any such "path" or "way" or "formation" to the more explicitly mechanical formation of "Yoga," and thence to an initiation. It is also easy to assimilate any "knowledge," "wisdom" or "understanding" alleged for mystic experience with an altered state of consciousness that is culturally patterned. Mysticism is more magical than sacrifice or initiation, for it is a secondary application. In brief, mysticism is the frank cultivation of an *individual* manistic experience, expropriated from the collective manistic experiences that are renewed in religious rites. Obviously, too, mysticism is associated with trance phenomena, such as are found in shamanism. In shamanism and mysticism is reenacted the drama of soul loss and recovery that figures in the magical use of sacrifice and of initiation rites for individual ends. All four have to do with the strengthening of a vulnerable, weak ego, which experiences pain in its own individuation from the collectivity, by plunging it back into that collectivity by sacrificing it to religious representations. In shamanism, mysticism and sacrifice, what happens is symbolically similar to the action of the magician who, in his initiation as Mauss has shown, dies, goes underground, is reborn, ascends to heaven and steals power from the gods. Mystics storm heaven just like magicians, and most of them return. Most mystics have always been like the "worldly ascetics" that Weber discerns in Calvinism[56]; mysticism has always been a game of "withdrawal and return," as Toynbee calls it.[57] It is only in the extreme or limiting case that the *unio mystico* is a true surrender; some of this is mirrored in the extinction of self into the godhead or the neutral being of the universe found in Hinduism and Buddhism. (Here again, we are confronted with Hinduism's magical literalness about symbols. Whenever symbolism moves toward magical applications, the symbols are taken more literally.[58]) As a rule, the mystic comes back with power, and maybe even a message, which is why he is distrusted by the priest. Mystic or trance or shamanic experiences are culturally patterned the world over as the source of those magical or "ecstatic" (Lewis[59]) initial experiences of a prophet who will begin a magical protest cult. Morton Smith[60] has suggested that esoteric early Christian baptism may have involved some sort of ascent to heaven which gave initiates magical power (including power over demons).

There is not room to develop the point exhaustively. But if we compare Mauss on the training of Australian magicians[61] with Eliade on Yoga,[62] that Charles Atlas course in spiritual power, we find some striking similarities. Mauss begins his monograph by observing that he is continuing the study begun in the *Esquisse;* now he is concentrating on how magic power is generated. Magic is social and it is usually practiced by qualified magicians; therefore, in their formation and initiation may be found the source of their social power. Mauss is writing about an early stage in which magicians as specialists are still part of the community cult, that early stage just before the full "generalization of mana."[63] And once again, just as in Jane Harrison,[64] the group initiation rite is the primal social ceremony which the magicians take over and use for the specialized purpose of developing their magical powers. Thus the magician's initiation rite is just an intensification of the group's ordinary initiation rite, and symbolism borrowed from it becomes the main tool of the magician.

Magical power is developed by 1. birth, 2. revelation or 3. initiation by other magicians.[65] But Mauss' whole theory is that magic's power is social power, and that it is socially conferred. The group determines who will have an experience of revelation. It patterns expectations and elicits the response from the type of person it seeks. Initiation is therefore the decisive means of election. Even in societies stressing election by birth or by revelation, training and initiation by other magicians are required supplements. Election by birth is not common in Australia; it is associated with more advanced societies with greater division of labor in which certain clans specialize in sacred rites. Among the aboriginal Australians, magic power is usually first indicated by revelation, which is patterned by cultural expectations and eliciting rituals, as in American Indian vision quest.[66] But revelation must always be followed by training under other magicians, culminating in magical initiation. Mauss uses the typical Australian magicians' initiation as an "extreme case," what I call a "natural ideal type," and then compares it with similar ceremonies from other cultures throughout the world, to show that it is indeed the typical pattern.

From Mauss' description it would be plain to Jane Harrison that Australian magicians' initiation is modeled on ordinary initiation, with the familiar enactment of death and rebirth, symbolizing the passage from one role to another. Very common in many such rites, Mauss finds, are these elements: 1. *Symbolic death,* usually associated with going underground, as to Hades. (This of course persists as a widespread pattern in myth, *e.g.,* Orpheus. And Diogenes Laertius tells us, with contempt, that Pythagoras once dug a hole, had himself "buried alive" for several days, while his mother sent down notes on what was going on, then came up white and emaciated and strode down to the agora of Crotona telling everyone he had been to Hades.[67] Thus do magicians use their meager stolen symbolism to seize social power.) 2. *Symbolic reconstitution* during death. This symbolizes the initiate's training, which has "taken him apart and put him back together again." During a long sleep, or during "death" in the underworld, the spirits replace the inner organs of the initiate. A magical substance may be injected or palmed onto the body at this point. Often this is a piece of quartz crystal, suggesting "a piece of the sky" and perhaps the "mystic light" so often reported in shamanism (cf. Eliade[68]). 3. *Ascent to the heavens,* including communion with the gods who give the initiate divine power. In ordinary initiations, this symbolizes rebirth. In a magician's initiation, there is more of a sense that heaven is stormed and that the magical powers are expropriated from the gods. This brings to mind the whole cycle Frazer so eminently documented of magicians who become gods. Breasted and others have hinted that some Egyptian gods were actually magicians who ascended to the stars: e.g., Thoth.[69] Note also the ascent of Osiris to the solar cult. The idea that any form of contemplation leads up to heaven is an old metaphor, found even in Parmenides and Plato.[70]

In what way exactly does the magicians' initiation differ from the ordinary social rite from which it is copied; in what sense is it an intensification of this rite? Comparing the descriptions of Jane Harrison and Mauss, and recalling Eliade's suggestion that magic assumes a certain literal-mindedness toward symbols,[71] we find the answer: The magician's initiation rite attempts to experience the social symbolization of initiation *as literal experience.* We have seen that selection by revelation must be confirmed by initiation; but conversely, even in societies where selection is solely by initiation, this initiation ceremony is expected to produce some experience of revelation. That is, magicians' initiation is a ritual that produces revelation as a *mystical experience.* Morton Smith has suggested that in esoteric early Christian baptisms, the candidate went into trance and hallucinated an actual ascent to heaven.[72] It does not matter what means are used—whether drugs, trance, or the long vigils of a vision quest. What it comes down to is an altered state of consciousness during which ordinary initiation symbolism of death and rebirth is experienced as *literal* death and rebirth.

And it is this literal experience of social symbols that is reproduced in the trained mysticisms of various cultures. Mysticism, like the initiation of a magician, is culturally patterned and trained behavior which provokes an altered state of consciousness during which social symbols are experienced as literal events.

As Shirokoroff, Mauss and so many others report, the shaman or magician, after his initiation, will in some social sense be considered literally "dead" to the others, a ghost, not quite human, a spiritual rather than a human person. The event may produce permanent psychological change in the individual, as Bogoras, Rasmussen and so many have shown. The magician is someone who has experienced literally the symbolism of ritual death, lived in it as in reality; he has been to hell and to heaven and he will never be the same again. Mauss speculates that marginal individuals (epileptics, strange-looking people, etc.) are purposely selected for this election, to help complete their distancing from normal humanity. We therefore reach the formulation that mysticism is highly trained behavior, derived from magical initiation, that attempts to produce religious-social symbolism as *literal experience.*

Even after initiation, magical power must be conserved; certain ascetic practices are required, and occasional mystic experiences as confirmation of the presence of power are expected. The whole literal-minded idea is to put the magician outside of common life, merged with spirits, endowed with new bodily organs and maybe an extra soul, surrounded by taboos to preserve his sacred power. Above all he is possessed by a spirit or group of spirits, and this is precisely his power. But it exists only by virtue of social consensus, which is engineered by the tests and trials of his public initiation. Thus the magician is a being whom society determines and pushes to "fulfill his social personage" (Mauss[73]).

Having shown that magical initiation is mystic, we can now show that mystical experiences conversely are patterned adaptations and survivals of magical initiation symbolism. Until recently, induced mystical experiences have been so marginalized in the West that our typical image for mysticism has been James' romantic evocation of the unbidden, unexpected "moment of illumination" that transforms lives.[74] Until recently we have ignored how even these seemingly spontaneous experiences are patterned, by prayer, asceticism or just reading, in a tradition. But in most societies mystical experience is the foreordained outcome of a "technique," in the Mauss or Ellul sense.[75] Yoga is the very paradigm of mystical experience, and far from being spontaneous it is the result of a long effort: Yoga means "yoke." (The derivation of the word of yoga or yoke in turn from roots meaning to bind or tie is interesting, in view of the Indian tradition of associating binding with magic: e.g., Varuna as the god of magic "who binds and ties."[76]) Yogas consist of submission to a long and arduous program of spiritual labor and ascetic sacrifice. In the Mauss sense, we could conceive of Hindu Yoga as the "extreme case" of mysticism, the naturally appearing ideal type which is so formed and homogeneous that it reveals what all mysticism aims at.[77] And what is most remarkable about this most typical of mysticisms is that the symbolism of classical Yoga (e.g., Patanjali's system[78]) can be shown to reproduce the same symbolism Mauss focused for us in his natural-ideal-type study of magicians' initiations.

Eliade's remarkable book on Yoga[79] shimmers on every page with a recognition that Yoga is a magical quest for power, freedom, being and immortality. It is an escape from karma or determinism, from mâya, the illusions of society, the partialism of roles, into the Absolute, brahman, which in turn derives from the power of ritual. And from the very start Eliade points out Yoga's resemblance to initiation rites:

> The analogy between Yoga and initiation becomes even more marked if we think of the initiatory rites—primitive or other—that pursue the creation of a "new body," a "mystical body" (symbolically assimilated, among the primitives, to the body of the newborn infant) ... Yoga takes over and, on another plane, *continues the archaic and universal symbolism of initiation*.[80]

The basic symbolism of the Yoga quest recalls the magicians' initiation at every stage. The yogin *"dies"*—to fleshly pleasures. He *ascends to heaven*. He is *reborn* with a new spiritual body. In a sense he is *dismembered and re-membered*, as he sunders one earthly appetite after another. Ascending to heaven, he acquires divine powers. The ultimate goal is to enter *Samadhi*, a mystical experience which is an altered state of consciousness similar to the entranced state in which the magician-initiate was able to live the sacred symbolism of his society literally. This literal experience of symbolism in turn confers upon him magical powers (though the orthodox yogin renounces them).

Eliade portrays the entire enterprise as an attempt to obtain for the individual what is truly real, which is the sacred. (Is this not "expropriation"?) But notice that in Yoga-Samkhya it is not just the profane world that is unreal (or real only due to our ignorance) but the cosmos itself. Like gnosticism, the Yoga-gnosis is magic so antinomian that it appears to reject even the religious tradition—which actually patterns it. The emphasis on emancipation, so basic in Hindu religion, reflects the burden of Hindu caste society, while deflection of rebellion into socially patterned autistic magic has the effect of reinforcing that system. As Mauss has shown, there is a great development of the idea of the self as part of this magic, but it is then literally extinguished.[81] One almost might say that the Hindu religious system is a fraud of cosmic proportions in which antinomian magic is deliberately cultivated but short-circuited through a literal *overplaying* of the archetypical sacrificial drama of soul-loss and recovery with the balance tipped toward soul-loss through extinction in *nirvana* or other patterns of dissolution.[82] Destruction of the self is carried to such extremes that in orthodox Yoga one is expected to destroy even the magic that naturally develops out of this magical formation. Magical powers (the *siddhis*) erupt like St. Elmo's fire all along the path to divine annihilation, but the orthodox yogin is supposed to suppress them just as he "burns" his own soul. That most yogins in practice prefer the more profitable and typical pattern of "withdrawal and return," stopping short of annihilation to come back armed with those lucrative *siddhis,* testifies more to decadence than to orthodoxy. In Yoga the ancient trance-sacrifice-initiation-mysticism drama of soul-loss and recovery is side-tracked into the final solution of soul annihilation. Durkheim has shown in his study of altruistic suicide that self-annihilation was at one time taken so literally as a goal in Hinduism that older Brahmins were expected to kill themselves.[83] Brahmins who performed suicide as stunts were sent to Rome as gifts, according to Fedden.[84] This persisted in the Jain sacrifice of starvation unto death.

The yogin's path is an ascent to god. This reproduces the universal theme of ascent to the heavens, to obtain divine power, in magicians' initiations. Where, after all, did Yoga come from? Figurines of yogins in the lotus posture have been dug up at Mohenjo-Dari.[85] In his last chapter, "Yoga and Aboriginal India,"[86] Eliade links the practice with shamanism and primitive magic. He specifically links its ideal of "freedom" with exemption from social forms, which is the magician's prerogative.[87] The aboriginal is recaptured especially in Tantric Yogas that go beyond good and evil. Eliade links Tantric rites in particular to primitive magicians' initiations.

Eliade is not completely explicit, but the following explanation can be pieced together. It is well-known that Yoga had ancient roots but became prominent only after the rise of Hinduism per se, that is, after the Brahmins' response to the Buddhist challenge. The Buddhist challenge was primarily magical—promising the average person an escape from the social system through powerful personal magics of meditation. Hinduism in part represented the revival of aboriginal magic on a Brahminical base to meet this challenge. Against this background, we could speculate that what Yoga essentially is, what it comes from, is the aboriginal Indian magical profession. Before the Aryan invasion, before the rise of the Brahmins, there were Dravidian magicians, and like most primitive magicians they derived their social power and their main symbolic techniques from their elaborate initiation rites. When the Aryans conquered India, a peculiar thing happened: their magicians (the Brahmins) took charge of *religious* life; Aryan magicians instead of priests commanded India's spiritual development. And they were a special kind of magician, too, namely, heralds, the singers and later the literate carriers of the sacred texts. They tended to rationalize magic, but they were interested in all forms of magic. When Buddhist meditation magic challenged them and the caste system which their rationalizations supported, they reached into the aboriginal tradition for additional magical weapons. One weapon which they dredged up was Yoga, which was originally none other than the formation and initiation of the aboriginal Dravidian magician.

Actually, Eliade says much that would support and nothing that would refute this explanation. Consider his discussion of Yoga's relationship to shamanism.[88] He has written elsewhere that classic shamanism is a north European circumpolar medical magic influenced by Buddhism.[89] This classic shamanism in turn influenced the Yoga-Tantric traditions. But Yoga itself was built out of symbolism from the initiation rites of an archaic Dravidian "shamanism" (in the lowercase sense where shamanism means any medicine-man magic based on trance ecstasy). Yoga is the cultivation of this primitive shamanic trance ecstasy. The question is complicated by Eliade's wish to distinguish shamanism from ordinary magic. But he does draw attention to fakiric *siddhis* associated with Yoga, such as the rope trick—the rope trick in turn seems very much like a myth that reflects an ancient rite, namely, the initiatory ascent of the magician to heaven. (In the original versions, his body is cut to pieces, just as in magical initiations; the "limbs fall to ground one by one" and are reconstituted.[90]) Thus some miracles are "romances" that recall magic "rituals."[91] And just as Rasmussen reports that the Eskimo shaman attains full power when he can see himself as a skeleton, the yogin also tries to "burn" his physical being as part of his magical ascent.[92] Again, the similarity to basic initiation drama enacting ritual death and rebirth is striking. Magical, shamanic and yogic traditions can, however, be distinguished and Eliade does so.[93] But he is also interested in showing their interrelations. Ecstasy, freedom as deliverance, immortality are ideas born in all these magical rites. It is true that in allying itself with philosophy classical Yoga attempts to purify itself of its magical origins; but one effect is to rob the individual initiate of the magical rewards for his spiritual labors and thus ensure the extinction of the self rather than its recovery at the end of the orthodox ritual. Yoga is rationalized by the Brahmin caste, so that it is not a technique of ecstasy at last, like shamanism, but rather of lucid calm trance. But it does preserve its immemorial symbolism of magical initiation. And Eliade repeats at the end of his book the insight with which it began:

> Yoga takes over and continues the immemorial symbolism of initiation; in other words it finds its place in a universal tradition of the religious history of mankind: the tradition that consists in anticipating death in order to ensure rebirth in a sanctified life—that is, a life made

real by the incorporation of the sacred. But India went particularly far on this traditional plane. For Yoga, the initiatory rebirth becomes the acquisition of immortality or absolute freedom. It is in the very structure of this paradoxical state, which lies outside of profane existence, that we must seek the explanation for the coexistence of "magic" and "mysticism" in Yoga.[94]

I believe that the similarity of Yoga to a magician's initiation is a key for understanding many patterned mysticisms. And Eliade's whole book is full of the recognition that the entire matter concerns *magic*. Of great importance here are the Hermetic-like elements in Yoga, the "mystic physiologies" and correspondences between bodily parts and parts of the universe they reflect and may affect. Yoga is also viewed as the result of a philosophical-scientific attempt to understand and explain magic which has the effect of augmenting magic.[95] (Magic is like mathematics: any generalization, rationalization or reflection on it generates more of it.) Eliade reports that Vedanta scorns Yoga as a quest for *magic;* that Yoga is putting the relation between man and gods on a magical level;[96] that Yoga is a *magic* that helped pull Brahmin atheist monism, via primitive Bhakti, toward theism;[97] that the *Ghita* suggests that man can *magically* participate in creation by turning all his acts into sacrifices[98] (detaching oneself from the fruits of one's action as magical sacrifice); that Yoga as a way of thinking and acting colored all Hindu practice and showed how to turn all religious ritual, all human action and thought into *magic;* that the Buddhist "path" also is equivalent to *magical* initiation;[99] that Tantra-Mantra, sudra-mandala mechanical meditation is the ultimate logical development of yogic *magic.*[100]

Thus mysticism, like sacrifice, is magical in at least the weak sense.

3. Myth

Myth is similar. Like initiation and sacrifice, it is mainly a religious phenomenon but it seems to give off magic. And myths tend to become more magical with time; eventually they are used by magicians. But even when still part of religion they seem "magical" in the weak sense, and in this way they model their magical potential.

Malinowski once wrote that all myths are creation myths.[101] Without taking so categorical a position, we might say that creation myths are among the most important and primary of myths, and that many of the other types are products of decay.[102] We have seen how healthy communities preserve some memory of their historical construction—this is the function of creation myths. They preserve social history, not prehistorical wonders; they enshrine agreements about how people shall live together, not mystical archetypes. Initiation and sacrifice are interrelated and both turn on the same idea of *membership,* which arises as groups consciously constitute themselves. Initiation becomes significant because membership is significant; sacrifice becomes important because fealty is important—myths preserve memory of the social contracts that create membership. But the memory can fade, and myths, like all sacred materials, can be expropriated by magic and applied to other purposes.[102] Myth is vital to magic because it preserves recognition that man makes the power magic uses: hence it is man's "charter" for magic, as Malinowski puts it. And myth embodies that "generalization of mana" that magic requires—for myth consists of general propositions asserting relations between whole classes of sacred objects. The inevitable paradox is that, in wrenching mythic scripts from community and turning them into fragmentary formulae of efficacy, magic plays a part in that darkening of memory which is the fall of myth and the alienation of man.

Our century has seen the formulation of many striking theories of myth, and almost all of them contain some truth. They only fail, as Barthes and Caillois put it, because no one theory says it all,[103] says all that myth is and becomes. Therefore, instead of expositing and criticizing the theories and picking favorites, we can arrange many of them in a way that shows their truth. For each of the classic anthropological theories of myth tends to be especially true at one of the several temporal stages in the life cycle of a myth. And each theory, moreover, asserts a different temporal relation of myth to rite—whether *before* it, *accompanying* it, or *after* it. But these two temporal sequences are isomorphic to each other so they can be laid out together. For myth begins by preceding rite; later it accompanies rite; and as myth ages it comes after rite. At its birth, myth comes *before* rite, for it is simply the history of a social contract; later, as the contract is ceremonialized with initiation and sacrifice, and religion thus begins, myth *accompanies* the rite as its script; still later it comes *after* the rite as a magical application, decay product or rationalization. To each stage corresponds some theory—myth as accompanying script (Lévy-Bruhl[104]), myth coming after rite as magic (Jensen[105]) or rationalization (Harrison[106]) or romance (Weston[107]). And the whole sequence once again provides us with that haunting and persistent image of the fall of man, the descent of symbolism into literalness, the forgetfulness of creation which the *Urmonotheismus* writers identified with forgetting god and which we should instead recognize as the gradual forgetting of the social creation of reality. At the beginning of their life cycles myths are not even religious; they are history. As they become scripts for rites that ceremonialize history and its arrangements, they become part of religion. As their sympathetic effects are modeled, recognized and expropriated for other efficacies, they become scripts for magic.[108]

We can detail this sequence a bit more, breaking it down more finely:

A. Creation myths (stressed by Eliade,[109] Malinowski,[110] Campbell,[111] etc.). These record social history. Not all societies are equally in touch with their past, but most have some creation myths, or creation is present as one of several themes in myth. And as Radin,[112] Lévi-Strauss,[113] Kroeber,[114] Diamond,[115] and others have so often demonstrated, some societies do have striking creation myths that reflect recent events, such as migrations or changes in social structure only a few generations back. Davy,[116] Lévi-Strauss,[117] Mauss,[118] etc., demonstrate that the historical event recalled is often a contract that reunited split lineages or tribes, or some other alliance or contract, which was solidified with gift exchange and marital alliances. Myths at this stage may make use of the typical religious symbolism and imagery of the cultic area, but they are more social-historical than religious in and of themselves.

B. *Myths as pure projection—cosmic myths* (theories of Durkheim,[119] Dumézil,[120] Feuerbach,[121] Mauss,[122] etc.). Here we are at the beginning of religion, or any new religion, *ceremonializing* a constituted or reconstituted social order with what Durkheim calls "representative rites."[123] These myths are the secondary representations projected on to sacred objects symbolizing the mana of subgroups; the myths come together to form a worldview that is an elaboration of the projection of social morphology. At first, cosmic myths seem like little more than a collection of elements that mirrors social morphology. Thus they practically coincide with the primitive classification systems from which they emerge by elaboration. This is the kind of basic cosmic myth that Dumézil[124] often writes about when he describes, for example, the principal characters in Indo-European myths as three tiers of gods which reflect the original three-class system of the Aryan peoples.

Creation myths and cosmic myths are very close and both may precede rites. But it is more likely for pure creation myths that memorialize a social contract to be in circulation before relevant rites fully develop. Then the myth is history and the group practice is purely social, not yet ceremonialized into religion: Creation myths may be ritually inert, like otiose high gods. Cosmic myths, by contrast, are often the product of incipient religious ceremonialization.

C. *Myth as a charter for rite* (theory of Malinowski[125]) might be said to come next. Often this is a creation myth which has been extended to include an account of the creation of the particular religious or magical rite to which it is attached as a preface. In an interesting circularity which Malinowski noticed, the relevant part of the creation myth used as a charter myth is the part that tells about the creation of the particular magic used in the rite. This charter myth is often recited before the rite, as authorization for its effects, the way administrative rulings may cite their legislative authorization in a preface. Citing a myth about the creation of the ritual authorizes the doing of the ritual and helps its effects to work.[126] What is happening here, it seems, is that the memory of man's social creation, though fading, is still partly present, and citing it has the effect of: *we can do it again.*

D. *Myth as the animating, creative "script" for a rite* (Lévy-Bruhl's last three books,[127] also Eliade,[128] Hubert[129]). Here the *content* of oral rites consists of myths, which are recited like scripts during the actual performance of the ritual actions. Just reciting the myth, saying its words, is thought to have efficacy by itself (and therefore it does). This is very common. Much of the script of the Catholic mass, for example, consists in reciting the story of Christ's life.

In this case, memory of creation is fading, but myth is still history and has its effect partly because it is a reminder of that original making which founded the group or the sect, and a reminder of its ideals, purposes and aims. Eliade has shown how the basic idea is that repetition of the story of creation repeats creation. By turning time back to "creation time" it makes reality plastic to creation again. Eliade[130] builds in turn on Hubert's demonstration[131] that myth time, as creation time, is *before* the making of time and therefore *outside* time.

Already we have advanced a long way in the modeling of the magical effects of social-religious symbolism. Myths as powerful charters for rites, myths as scripts in ritual have striking effects—they strengthen social ties and move the participants. All this "models" their symbolic powers and their social-moral effects, which are deeply felt by people, and from this they infer the possibility of using these formulae for achieving other effects. Lévy-Bruhl and Hocart[132] were quite correct in pointing out that myth is already being used instrumentally in religious rites before being expropriated by magic.

E. Myth that parallels rites (Frazer, Jane Harrison, Gilbert Murray,[133] Cornford,[134] Gaster[135]). In addition to myths as scripts for rituals, there are also early myths that grow directly out of rites not yet as aetiological myths that explain rites but in the sense of *paralleling* rites. This occurs, most piquantly, when a raw social ceremony like initiation is being ceremonialized; then the derivative myth can be conceived, as Jane Harrison writes, as a parallel expression of the ceremonialization. Thus the myth of rebirth grows out of initiation rites, in which the individual ceremonially dies to one role to be born to another. Thus the *"Titanes"* or "white-clay men" are just the elders ceremonially painted for the ceremony. It was a great discovery to point out how many primal myths (and deities) derive from rites as parallel expressions of their meaning.

F. Aetiological myths and culture-ideal myths. This is a later stage. Myths and deities that parallel rites are fairly immediate expressions of the original ceremonialization. But aetiological and culture-ideal myths are decay products:

i. Aetiological myth comes later when meaning has become problematical. Aetiological myth is an attempt to explain symbols which are no longer clear for they derive from rituals which are no longer understood or are not performed at all.

ii. Another kind of myth that springs up later when meanings are partly forgotten but mythic scenarios are still whole is *myth as a cultural ideal*. As aetiological myths speculate on meanings, cultural ideal myths rationalize the material further and prescribe moral archetypes. Thus Indian girls until recently were taught, "Be like Sita."[136] The Sita figure in turn derives from aetiological myths, worked over in romance and epic, which attempt to explain certain ritual practices (fertility rites of the field furrow, maybe suttee) whose original meaning is forgotten. Theories of myths as social archetypes (Nietzsche,[137] Zimmer,[138] Joseph Campbell,[139] etc.) usually refer to this later development, when myths are being rationalized simultaneously in several ways—as aetiology, as moral philosophy. This is the kind of myth that Bergson and Caillois have in mind[140] when they say it takes the place that instinct plays in animals in regularizing social behavior. But myths as archetype are far from being archetypical myth. Often they are products of a fairly ripe stage of development, where several related mythic ideas are synthesized as archetypes in syncretistic civilizations. At this stage, myth may be once again in touch with part of social structure; it may reflect the cultural ideals of a creative class or ruling elite.

G. *Mere fragments of myths as scripts for magic* (Jensen,[141] Mauss,[142] Barthes,[143] etc.). Harrison[144] has shown that initiation rites and their emerging myths get used, very early, for magical purposes, above all fertility rites. The *Urmonotheismus* thinkers from Schmidt to Jensen also think of agricultural fertility as a first "magical application" of myths that are originally religious and preserve memory of god's creation . In both schools, there is the feeling that fertility magic is a "natural" or "high" magic; we would say that it is "ceremonial magic," done officially on behalf of the whole community, aimed at giving "life" to all (Hocart[145]). But the magical possibilities of religious myths, having been modeled by religion itself, are more and more obvious and myth is extrapolated more and more for *all* kinds of magical rites. In the end, mere fragments of myths may be recited, mumbo-jumbo style, for their dimly remembered effects by practitioners who have forgotten their meaning, even by magicians of later civilizations who do not understand the language in which the myth fragment is cast. To the *Urmonotheismus* school, this is the final descent in man's forgetting of god; we would say that this is a forgetting of the original historical meaning of the myth as an account of social man making himself.

H. *Myth as romance* (Jessie L. Weston,[146] Grimm, Vladimir Propp,[147] etc.). But myth may be saved from fragmentation in degraded magic formulae by a diversion; it may be reworked and revivified as romance, folktale, etc.

Romance seems an innocent attenuation of myth, but what it too really involves is taking the symbolism of myth literally. It is a literary analogue, therefore, of the general thrust of magic toward the literal, but one that prevents fragmentation. These cycles have their own rules and forms, which may serve to preserve coherently some elements of the myth. The structural study of these forms (cf. Lévi-Strauss on Propp) is another matter. As frames upon which they are reconstituted, cycles of romance, folktale, etc. extend the lives of myths though their historical meanings are forgotten. But sometimes, if the form is congenial, the original sense of the myth can be revived—the way Gilbert Murray showed that Homer used various myths that had gotten detached from their social-ritual origins due to the *Völkerwanderung* of the Ionian peoples, and that these regained some of their original ritual power and meaning when the Athenian dramatists put them back inside of theatrical forms emerging from the same fertility-initiation rituals in which the figures had been born.[148] And so, as Jessie L. Weston put it, we go from ritual to romance; but myth begins several stages before ritual, at least logically.

In creation myths (which preserve memory of social contracts), cosmic myths (which project society), charter myths, and script myths (used in ceremonies), myths that parallel rites, aetiological myths and so on, we see a progress which describes that increasingly explicit modeling of magic which goes on in religion. Myth is at first part of the social contract or the original religious projection of society in worldview; it must be affirmed if it is to be sustained; affirming it takes the form of telling it, and this emerging narrative has a social-moral effect; this potentially efficacious instrument of magic is modelled even more flauntingly when religion uses recitation of its own myths to try to produce some physical effect analogous to moral-social uplift (such as renewing nature's fertility). Later, when myth is used as script in rites, just saying it, telling it, is seen to produce striking effects, and so the possibility of magic is increasingly modeled by religion.

Once again we discover that a core religious phenomenon is "magical"; and we explain this by saying that 1. it is magical in "the weak sense" and 2. that the link between magic in the weak sense and magic in the strict sense is explained by saying that religion models the possible magical effect, thus prompting people to take over myths and use them in peripheral ceremonies that are magical in the strict sense.

4. Prayer

Mauss' incompleted doctoral dissertation, *La Prière et les Rites Oraux*,[149] illustrates the difficulty of this subject—which may be why he did not finish it. Mauss recognized some of the problems: No religious phenomenon is more complex than prayer. It is part of what is most primitive in religion and what is most modern. Originally just the spoken part of rite, prayer is now associated with modern and personal religion. Prayer is part of both rite and belief. In a rite it is not just words but the act of saying them in a certain attitude that counts. Prayer is also credo, a belief.[150] It is often narrative in form, so Mauss thinks that it is additionally the beginning of myth. Prayer presents other difficulties: it is both oral and mental. But despite all these recognitions there is a further complexity which he does not mention and which is the heart of the problem: prayer is both magical and religious. He does notice that there are prayers to demons, that some prayers are constraining while others supplicate, etc. But his attempt to distinguish prayer from incantation is muddled, and the essay breaks down completely right after his involved and unconvincing demonstration that the Intichiuma ceremony, by which the Arunta try to renew their totemic species, does contain true prayer and not just incantation. The problem is that distinctions of prayer and incantation are hard to make because prayer is a religious phenomenon in which the "magical" element is extremely conspicuous. If, as Cazeneuve says, sympathetic magic is inherent in the nature of language, verbal rites model it strikingly. Prayer is primitive and modern, oral and mental, a rite and a belief, a credo and a myth...but the real problem is that it is both magical and religious. This is the problem that Mauss did not solve, despite his having written a theory of magic. His usual methods failed and after a long wind-up he gave up in confusion.[151]

If anything, the magical nature of prayer seems to increase with its sophistication, its personalization, its modernity. Keith Thomas has suggested[152] that

Protestant "prayer magic" rushed in to fill the vacuum created by the Reformation's destruction of man's magical defenses. Much prayer, of course, is frankly for some benefit. Even if the prayer is not answered, praying is thought to strengthen the personality. In more self-conscious sophisticated Protestant usage, where any hint of manipulation is avoided, there is a good deal of vagueness about the very object or end of prayer. The very vagueness of the object serves further to mystify the act of prayer. Sometimes prayer almost takes on the form of talking with the divinity, in what Thomas called a kind of "oracular trance." The idea of "faith" itself takes on magical overtones, as a state of mind that somehow makes one victorious and immune to disaster. All these suggestions of power, personality change, influence over events—plus the increasing emphasis on *individual* prayer, private and personal prayer—strongly suggest magic.

More to the point, prayer can be used as a hypnotic to relax the objective frame and produce magical, paranormal or trance experiences. The Catholic Church plays down the magic of prayer by rigidly formalizing prayer; it categorizes and names a dozen or so different kinds of acceptable prayer; it encourages group prayer and scripted prayer. On the other hand, for specialized orders it tolerates prayers intended to produce mystical states (e.g., the Jesus prayer, meditating on the crucifix, etc.).

At its modern extreme, prayer becomes a mental magic whereby an individual who may be socially isolated nonetheless draws strength from community through an internal dialogue with his idealization of community (god). The "dialogue," the openness to community are the only remnants of the religious foundations of the act; the emphasis now is on sheer expropriation by an ego which is literally feeding itself on its own superego. At its modern limit, prayer becomes individual autonomy magic, whereby every individual can do what previously only the shaman could do in his drama of superego conquest—i.e., draw strength for autonomy by sucking on his own superego. This superego is part of the community, which flows through the person in his stream of consciousness. By drinking of that stream he can acquire, even in temporary isolation, symbolic power and authority. The expropriation from the superego may be so enormous as to result in "inspiration," "charisma" and a seizure of moral authority. But often charisma is routinized, as with businessmen who pray for inspiration before or even during board meetings, thereby symbolically reinforcing their already considerable social authority.

Yet prayer *is* religious. It begins in group rites. But more than most central religious phenomena, it has its magical aspect, too. How can we deal with this? Again, by making use of my subsidiary concept of magic in the weak sense, and relating this to magic in strict sense through the concept of modeling. Prayer tends very strongly to be magical (in the weak sense) because of the basic magical coloration of all human symbolic speech and thought (in the weak sense). In religious oral rites par excellence, members of a society see the possibility of magical efficacy modeled for them.

5. Core Religious Rites in General

It should be apparent that virtually all core religious rites have this quality of modeling magic. Warner gives the best global example of this in his study of the Murngin of Australia.[153] Warner agrees with Durkheim about religion, but does not think magic can be distinguished from it; he is wrong but his demonstration is interesting: All Murngin tribes believe in magic, but the tribes of the northern region have no witch doctors. When individuals here experience some magical attack or danger (e.g., sorcery), they use a religious rite instead of magic as a defense. This proves, according to Warner, that religion and magic are interchangeable. Religion is implicit, he says, in all magical operations, and the whole group is behind the white magician, who works on behalf of the community, just like a priest. Religion even has its black magic side, for all social ritual can kill as well as cure, as when, for example, someone is pronounced incurable and succumbs to the suggestion.

But all of these points can be accepted without entailing that it is either fruitless or impossible to distinguish magic from religion. What Warner's interesting demonstrations show us is that religion puts its own rites to magical purposes, and thereby models magic for the community. Religion tends to use its own ceremonies instrumentally the more it becomes conscious of their sympathetic effects.[154]

We can explain all this by saying that religion "models" magic. Before formalizing this hypothesis, consider alternatives. What are the other theoretical explanations of this overlap of magic and religion?

Theories Explaining Overlap of Magic and Religion

1. Magical-Religious Identity

Some writers simply say that all magic is religion and all religion is magic: perfect identity. It has already been shown that this position renders all statements about magical-religious interaction uninteresting. It can now also be proven that this position is wrong. The simplest *reductio* is to point to black magic, with its florid hostilities to religion: in what sense is black magic identical with religion? True, some try to include black magic within religion. Kluckholn[155] attributes to witchcraft a religious "bogeyman" function in enforcing moral laws. But this cannot cover *all* black magic, which is often dysfunctional. And we have seen that writers who postulate identity do not always mean it literally or without qualification.[156] So the identity formula (M = R) simply dodges the problem.

2. Polar Ideal Types

Dorothy Hammond[157] and the Waxes[158] tell us that, in practice, most anthropological field workers between the wars were using some rough and ready "polar ideal type," which presumed that magico-religious phenomena ran a continuum from a most magical pole to a most religious pole. Many, according to Hammond, preferred something like Ruth Benedict's continuum,[159] which, using Marett's term "animatism" for mere impersonal efficacy, scaled "magico-religious" phenomena on a continuum of animatism-animism. In actual fact, however, quite a number of rough-and-ready antinomies or polar ideal types have been in use, each one the precipitate of some grand theory about the distinction of magic from religion. 1. Thus Frazer's distinction of prayer from incantation on the basis of whether the rite was "supplicative" or "manipulative" has remained in active use. 2. Durkheim's distinction of *individual* vs. *collective* ends is often used. 3. *Instrumental* vs. *ultimate,* or ends vs. means is another schema. It was perhaps inevitable that someone would finally attempt to weld all these distinctions together into a multiple polar ideal type, just as Parsons turned the key antinomies of classical sociological theory into his "pattern variables."[160] The hazards were even greater when Goode[161] did this, however, because he did not imagine a two- or three- or N-dimensional matrix of cells in the Parsons manner, but simply assumed that there would be such strong correlations between all the sets of opposites on their respective positive and negative poles that he could just clump them all together. His ideal type became one more clumsy sociological scale reification, a blurred pattern in logical space to enable lazy writers to decide which nomenclature, magical or religious, to affix to otherwise inadequately analyzed phenomena. The Goode scale, moreover, links together measures that are on different logical levels of reality—magic in the weak sense, and magic in the strong sense, and so on. Most of the scale, in fact, being mentalist rather than descriptive (e.g., "supplicative vs. manipulative, " "goal vs. instrument," etc.) refers to magic in the *weak* (i.e., social-psychological coloration) sense. Perhaps that is its best use: it might be employed to grade religious rites to determine how explicitly they are modeling magic.

The Goode polar ideal type rates a sacred phenomenon as leaning more toward magic or religion depending on its position on these separate continua: 1. concrete vs. general goals (from Mannheim?); 2. manipulative vs. supplicative attitude (from Frazer); 2. professional-client vs. shepherd-flock relationship (from Durkheim); 4. individual vs. collective interest (from Durkheim); 5. private vs. collective action; 6. greater vs. lesser concern over success; 7. impersonality vs. emotional affects; 8. rite initiated by practitioner vs. rite pre-arranged on a sacred calendar; 9. magic at least potentially used against society or a group in it; 10. magic used only instrumentally, and so forth. There is a general casualness about the index, and in fact the author does not tell us *how* to use it. One trouble with such a polar ideal type is that it generalizes from diverse *theories,* not from facts, and though seemingly based on continua it actually emphasizes extreme contrasts. For example, Goode contrasts religious festivals which allegedly have fixed times, with magical rites that do not. No such distinction is even tenable, according to Hubert and Mauss' investigations, which show that magical ceremonies often have their appropriate times and places,[162] just like religious rites: full moons, solstices, when somebody is sick, when it does not rain, etc. Many of these paired oppositions apply mainly to magic in the weak sense and provide little real distinction between religion and magic in the strict, institutional sense.[163]

3. Class Inclusion Theories

More interesting because they attempt to say something about magic in the strict sense are theories which predicate that one phenomenon is included within the other. These theories use A or I propositions to say that *all* X is Y or *some* X is Y. Of the A propositions, there are two types: those that say that all magic is a sub-province of religion, and those that say all religion is a sub-province of magic. These are interesting and potentially testable propositions.

Dorothy Hammond[164] makes the clearest formulation of the first position: all magic is part of religion.[165] Her statement is interesting and not trivial because she simultaneously maintains a clear distinction between religion and magic. Her solution is to say that the two are on different levels. Magic is not a higher order institutional entity like religion; it is a subset of cultic practices entirely included within religious institutions. Her position, which she unfortunately does not document, is defensible up to a point. Even the peripheral provinces of magic such as medical magic and the occult sciences could be conceptualized as provinces of religion if "religion" were in turn broadened to comprise "the religious culture" of a society as a whole. I have already suggested that magical protest sects are indeed patterned somewhat this way, by culture complexes and expectations which religion projects. It would be easy to assimilate the magical medical complex conceptually to religion, as a kind of semi-detached parish psychiatry. But the attempt breaks down against the *reductio* of black magic. Perhaps black magic could be conceived of as sick religion, as the inevitable decay of declining religions (George Steiner has suggested that the decay of religion releases "toxins"). And there is certainly a sense in which religious worldview makes black magic possible. But it is too extreme to try to include obdurate black magic institutions inside religion. They are separate institutions, separate organizations. So the A proposition, that all magic is part of religion, fails.

More interesting is the alternative A proposition that "all religion is part of magic," which Douttée set forth in his book on North African religion.[166] According to Douttée, *magic* consists of two vast provinces—religion and black magic.[167] This is reminiscent of Lévy-Bruhl's overview of the sacred as superstition, which in turn comprises both religious and magical rites; it is as if Douttée had applied the term "magic" to supernatural thought in general, and then discovered religion to be a part of it. Though he makes these statements in a brief chapter, this is perhaps why, in dealing with what is allegedly the least magical of world religions, Islam, Douttée chooses for virtually all his chapters titles which have the word magic in them. According to him, both sorcery and religion use the collective and obligatory representations of society but sorcery puts them to ends that are more individual or maleficent. All this recalls Hubert and Mauss on expropriation of the sacred, except that Douttée calls the core collective sacred "magic" rather than religion.

What does Douttée mean? Partly he means that religion never quite outgrows magic, not even when it seems to. The Muslim saints, or marabouts, are virtually indistinguishable from the illicit magicians or primitive shamans. He often appears to make use of the preanimist position that religion has its roots in magic. His point is that an animism born so clearly of magic is still magical: "Like magic, theism has a practical end; it is a matter first of all of immediate physical needs, then of moral needs..."[168] Sorcery is not therefore different in kind from religion, both are magic; the crime of sorcery is really a crime of heresy—i.e., it consists of the sorcerer's attributing to himself powers which belong only to god and so behaving like a god.[169] We have seen a similar interpretation by Christian dogmatists reported in the works of Lea.[170]

But in addition to these two weak senses (religion as derived from magic and religion as always retaining something of its magical origins) there is a stronger sense in which Douttée is trying to say that all religion is magic: that is, magic and religion both are a matter of wishful thinking. In pure religion, in monotheism, the basic intention of all magic is stripped back to its original core: to mere wish. Muslim monotheism, the most severe on earth, so accomplishes this reduction that in the end Allah is nothing other than the personification of man's wish.[171]

Douttée suggests that Islam is a fruitful subject of study precisely because it is so pure and simple—simpler in dogma than Catholicism, virtually lacking in myth, less syncretistic or assimilative than any other world religion, so hostile to magic that it partly resists subcult formation. But even this religion has simply repressed obvious magic, for it remains as the hidden meaning of certain rigid ritual prescriptions such as the veil (this wards off the evil eye, he claims), the pilgrimage, circling the Ka'ba, etc. Magic also hides in the "cult of saints." But the main point is that the religion itself, and its core representations, are but the objectification of desire, and this is magic in Douttée's formulation.[172] He resembles Malinowski in imagining that magic erupts out of human desire; finding religion full of desire, he equates it with magic. The god thus crystallized out of mana in the preanimist manner remains an "objectification of human desires" for Douttée, so that the aim of the highest religion is linked to the original source of the magical impulse, which is magic desire, magic hope.[173] It is precisely because orthodox Islam rejects obvious magic that it so simplifies itself as to make clear that the inner aims of religion are themselves magical.[174] Douttée is working a series of simple equations in which magic = desire; religion = desire; therefore, religion is part of magic.

Many writers really say the same thing, that all religion is magic: Lévy-Bruhl, for example, with his idea of "superstition" or "prelogical thinking." This is also part of Frazer's thrust. Exposing the magical elements in religion can lead to the formulation that all religion is magic. But this is not my position. It is an interesting idea, however. It would help explain why new religions begin with magical demonstrations and why magical protest cults seem to renew religion: i.e. religion languishes when its magic dies and it then needs new magic to come back to life. But there are difficulties with this position. As Cazeneuve points out, it is contrary to general usage.[175] This is serious, because general usage tells us a good deal about magic. Also, it is too easy to point out elements in religion that are not magical. There is, for example, the institutional shell, religion as organization, what Durkheim calls the "church." There is also the realm of credo, belief, worldview, what becomes philosophy.

Maurice Pradines emphasizes this element of "philosophy" as the non-magical pole in religion.[176] In everything else, magic and religion can be similar. Pradines assures us that magic as well as religion undergoes rationalization; both are "part of human reason," like science. Modern science advanced only when it freed itself from pure empiricism and created abstract categories, and magic as well as religion were part of this process. (Magic errs in having a distorted cognitive viewpoint: it fails to see that world reason is a collective vision. Magic is the error of the monad taking itself for the whole.)

Pradines' formula would be: religion = magic plus philosophy. Again, this is too partial a view. At very least religion equals some magic plus philosophy plus collective organization plus sympathetic rites that are *not* magical except in the weak sense.

In Cazeneuve's *Sociologie Du Rite*[177] I find a statement closer to my position. Cazeneuve is struggling with the same problem of magic-religion overlap. His solution is similar to my "magic in the weak sense." He uses the term "sympathy" in that sense. Rituals in general (magic, taboo and religion) use "sympathy" because symbolization in general is based on sympathy. He means that those affinities between words which Frazer called sympathetic magic are intrinsic properties of human symbolization. Cazeneuve[178] leans heavily on Hubert and Mauss in showing how sympathy works, how the word links are traditional rather than free-associated.[179]

Solution: Religion Models Magic

Keeping in mind Cazeneuve's position we might say that the ceremonialization of social customs which constitutes initial religious rites immediately enhances their sympathetic reverberations; and as the rite is used more instrumentally, the sympathetic magic potential of rites and of symbolism becomes more obvious. But instead of saying that we are therefore sliding along some mental continuum toward a magical pole, we might simply say that religion is demonstrating or modeling the potential for magic by displaying these sympathetic symbolic effects with increasing explicitness.

Religion models magic by demonstrating the sympathetic effects of rites, which depend on symbolic affinities deep in each culture's language. They appear to derive ultimately from primitive classification systems. Religion makes sympathy more explicit by using its own ceremonials in a more instrumental way. This demonstration provokes the creation of institutions outside religion that are magical in the strict sense.

To show what I mean, begin at the beginning. Here is a polysegmental society

of loosely connected clans; as its members work and play together they sometimes feel an eerie sense of their own collective power and they symbolize this
"mana feeling" with objects which become "sacred" on that account—a tree,
sparrows, grubs and so forth. A dominant symbol projected by one clan, for
example, might be the falcon, which eventually becomes their totem; but other
symbols are used, too, including, as it happens, ants and the east wind. All the
other clans are projecting symbols, too, and in time a classification system
develops that reflects this polysegmental social structure, and in it the east wind
and ants are included under the falcon class because all three objects have been
used to symbolize the mana of that clan. Later, during the generalization of
mana at the tribal stage, myths become more inventive, and they may somewhat
rationalize these now problematical affinities, asserting a relation, for example,
between ants found in the falcon class and bees found in the owl class, if such
provocative coincidences have been projected. Myth may be so creative that the
very word for *falcon* may come to be something like "bird that lives with
ants," as philological research will one day record. Later still, a divination procedure of this society that works upon its classification system may attain an
impressive coherence, so that it is taken over by a more advanced society and
further rationalized into an "occult science" like the I Ching. Or perhaps this
society itself may become civilized and radiate its cosmic myths across a
continent. The result is that quite distant peoples will one day have some dim
notions about the connections of bees to owls and ants to falcons, all the more
mysterious since original class meanings have been forgotten. Poetry will work
this over, and metaphors will turn into new words. Theosophies may later arise,
and this civilization may develop its own Jung or Lévi-Strauss, who will some day
mysteriously assert that "bees are to owls as ants are to falcons." Or that bees
with their obvious interest in honey contrast with the well-known relation of
owls, falcons and all other raptors to death and hence to ashes. Or that the raptors embody the Shadow while the industrious ants and bees are Animus figures
—and other profound wisdom.

But the main result is that for centuries, perhaps millennia, the connection
of bees to owls and ants to falcons will be a "sympathetic" link in language;
whenever this link is strummed, something will reverberate in the unconscious
mind. Religions may work upon this imagery with falcon altars or amulets with
emblems of bees attacking falcons, and thereby further model the magic potential. Taking the hint, shamans may eventually arise to cure people of "bee complexes" or "ant cathexes" by working through their underlying "falcon or owl
character structures." And no one could possibly now remember that the falcon
clan originally identified also with ants because there were enormous ant hills
near their winter quarters in their lost society six millennia ago.

The sympathy effects of religious rites are part of what is sustaining and
miraculous and full of hope in religion. When this element atrophies, the institution may become sterile and offer no efficacy; it may take some "miracle" to
renew it. But the point for this chapter is that the "magic" (weak sense) that is

coined within religion constantly moves out of religion. Now magic in the strict sense grows up—institutions of magic outside religion. By what routes do we get to this?

1. Expulsion. One way magic moves out of religion is by ejection. According to Idries Shah, as religions grow ethical they expel their magical elements or drive them underground. Baroja and Lea suggest that even some black magic patterns derive from dead religions. European witch beliefs are colored by remnants of a cult of Diana, perhaps. The very propensity of religion to be an organization leads to boundaries, routinization of charisma and exclusions.

2. Growing complexity. It is notorious that the religion of the stranger is considered magic. The religions of conquered and subject peoples, the diffused cults of neighboring tribes, even the subcults of a large religion may be branded as magic and come to play that part. Sheer complexity of religion leads to marginality of some less favored cults. Hocart[180] claims, for example, that the *lower castes* in Ceylon derive from priesthoods of debased rites—fallen gods or "Titans" now considered demons. "Drummers," "barbers" and other such "occupations" still center on these rituals which have a social place on certain social occasions ("barbers" for example perform a ritual before weddings).

3. Social conflict and change. Even simple societies have a latent pluralism, and undergo change through conflict. Gurvitch[181] emphasizes the importance of the men's houses which prepare young men for initiation. They develop sacred practices of their own, often dramatize a mock or real hostility to the clan-oriented religion. During social change, such as a transition from matriarchy to patriarchy, which does sometimes happen, the magic of the men's house may be opposed to the central religion based on matriarchy. Similarly, in societies beset by sorcery and witchcraft, quasi-magical sects spring up to fight the danger. And so on.

4. Sheer expropriation. Finally, there is sheer expropriation of religious rites by magicians who take them over and copy them. But sometimes it is almost as if religion were inviting people to take over its rites and put them to instrumental purposes. The rites are sympathetic in the first place; then they are put to frankly instrumental ends within religion itself. Religion often employs the first practitioners of ceremonial magic: headmen, official magicians. (Religion precedes magic but there may be magicians before there are priests; they may work for the public good at first.)

And so, religion seems not merely to "model" magic but to have emitted it in the first place. It is therefore not enough to state that "some magic is religion," or to diagram this with Venn circles showing an overlap, like this:

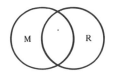

This is still too static. We must imagine *moving* Venn circles, describing, for example, magic being expelled from an ethical religion (Figure I); or a magical protest sect lodging in the periphery of an existing religion (Figure II):

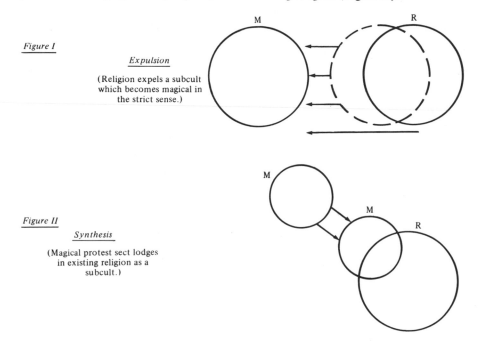

Figure I

Expulsion

(Religion expels a subcult which becomes magical in the strict sense.)

Figure II

Synthesis

(Magical protest sect lodges in existing religion as a subcult.)

We can also imagine the magical circle penetrating more deeply into the religious circle, or swelling in comparative size, during ages when the magical coloration of religion grows more pronounced, as in the Hindu revival (Figure III-a, III-b).

Figure III-a   *Figure III-b*

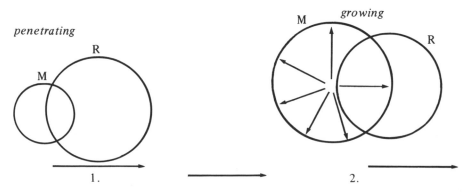

penetrating   growing

1.   2.

(Magical subcult penetrates religion deeply, grows in importance, almost swamps religion.)

We can also imagine religion creating, by modeling, expulsion, expropriation and social change, a whole series of magics—all seven major provinces of them, each overlapping the other, as if religion were blowing magical bubbles (Figure IV).

Figure IV

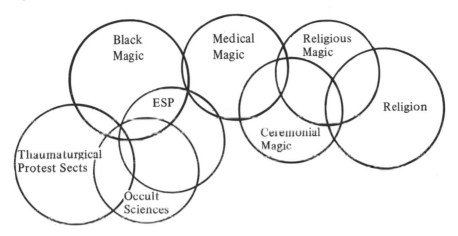

Imagine all these bubbles in motion; imagine not one but several bubbles of each type, representing different sects, cults, witch patterns, medicines, etc.

To make the diagram even more perspicuous, we could shade those sections of the non-intersected parts of the religion circle which might be characterized as "magic in the weak sense" (i.e., those which make demonstrative use of sympathetic effects and so model magic for the community). The shaded area would then be distinguished from that "shell" of religion which is conceptually free of magic altogether (such as organization, cosmic projective map of society, philosophy, etc.) See Figure V:

Figure V

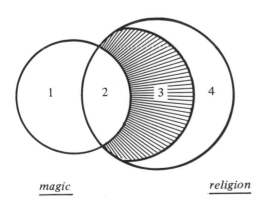

magic   *religion*

1 = Magic in the strict sense, institutions separate from religion
2 = Religious magic (exorcism, cult of saints, etc.)
3 = Core religious rites that are magical only "in the weak sense" but thereby "model" sympathy effects (sacrifice, initiation, etc.)
4 = "Pure" religion (organization, cosmos, etc.) having no magical coloration

The size and positions of the circles could be varied to map any particular society; Evans-Pritchard[182] and Lowie[183] have shown how, depending on world-view, one province of magic may expand so that it takes over functions of others and even of religion (as witchcraft provides Zandeland with worldview and theodicy). A series of diagrams could show current direction. Is religion rationalizing itself, expelling magical sub-cults and even its own sympathetic rites? Are magical protest sects springing up like bubbles in boiling water and then exploding into nothing or amalgamating with the central religion? Is religion shrunk to a small, non-magical circle, with no shading of sympathetic magic? Or is the magic within a religion moving deeper into its core (as with Protestant churches in the Seventies)? We can perhaps use the diagrams also to test "steady state" hypotheses about sacred experience. When some bubbles contract, do others always expand to fill the vacuum? When religion's worldview is impoverished, does magic also decline, or expand to take its place?

Summary: Magic As Symbolism From Religion

It would be useful to summarize the findings so far. We began, like Hubert and Mauss, with the assumption that magic is a real social fact because it possesses some visible anchors in social reality, including: 1. definitely formed institutions with professional practitioners and formed practices; 2. a long tradition in many societies of common speech identifying these institutions as magical; 3. a penumbra of metaphorical statements in many languages also identifying certain aspects of human speech and action as somehow magic. We noted that there were seven or so main provinces of magic, including 1. religious magics, such as exorcism; 2. ceremonial magic, such as community rain making; 3. medical magic; 4. the magic of new cults and witch-finding movements, etc.; 5. black magic; 6. the magic of ESP and paranormal states; and 7. the divinatory occult sciences and their derived theosophies. Hubert and Mauss, concentrating on professional magicians, had restricted themselves mainly to religious magic, ceremonial magic, medical magic and black magic. I wanted to include the magic of new cults, covered so well by Weber; also ESP and the occult sciences. I wanted, moreover, to explore the persistent penumbra of magical metaphor about human speech and action. I sought what Louis Schneider[184] called "gains to analysis" by widening definition, and what Solomon Snyder[185] called "strategic" formulations that would cover all the empirical facts. The risk of a too-wide explicit definition was triviality; but there was a greater risk in avoiding definition: implicit equivocation and the pseudo-discoveries from using a word simultaneously in two senses. I sought to avoid this by using two conceptions of magic—an initial explicit definition of magic in the strict (institutional) sense; and an open usage of the word "magic" in the weak sense to which meaning would accumulate during the study via comparison of suggestive data with magic in the strict sense. Two definitions, one strict and one left open to catch and explore metaphors of magic, were used in other words to avoid equivocation; to avoid "category errors" I specified that where references were made simultaneously to magic in both senses some kind of functional relationship must be asserted between the two.

To avoid incorporating conclusions into initial definitions, I tried to begin with a minimal, tentative, working definition of institutional strict-sense magic. Common report of mankind was weighted in this definition. But a few definite abstract postulations had to be incorporated as well to give it some rigor of reference. Since I support the Durkheim position about the undifferentiated nature of mana and sacred experience in general (while insisting that magic and religion *can* be distinguished), this clearly implied usage of something like the Robertson Smith-Durkheim-Mauss "peripheral hypothesis" with the implication that we were going to witness a dialectic between society's central religion and its peripheral magical protests. The suggestion that magic is related to religion dialectically was of necessity implied in the definition because I must deny that there is any phenomenological basis for an absolute distinction of religious mana or experience from magical mana or experience. The occupational distinction (membership vs. professional-client relationship) was thought to be suggestive but not always reliable; it was incorporated with reservations (e.g., it does not fit ceremonial magic). The notion of serving individual ends was broadened (in response to Weber's ideas) to include fractional ends of all kinds: those of subgroups as well as individuals.

I then formulated and attempted to document empirically some postulates about magic in the strict sense, always watching for light they also might shed on magic in the weak senses, and gradually saying more about these senses. The first four postulates constituted a phenomenology of magic, exploring its symbolism and showing how it gets its effects. Thus I showed that magic is a real form of social action (Postulate 1); that it consists of symbolic performances and that verbal symbolism is central (Postulate 2); that magical symbolic action is highly scripted, more rigid even than religious action (Postulate 3); that magical scripts achieve their social effects largely by agreement (Postulate 4). The evidence for all these postulates was significant for the weak senses of magic. The next four structural postulates were about the relation of magic institutions to religion and they showed more definitely how the weak senses of magic might be defined. They demonstrated that magic derives from religion rather than vice versa (Postulate 6); that magic borrows much of its symbolism from religion and uses it to argue with religion (Postulate 5); that magic makes use of symbolism projecting society and its power that has become generalized so it can be "expropriated" and "applied" to instrumental purposes (Postulate 7). Finally, in the present section, I showed that religion stimulates these applications by its own example, and thereby models magic for society. And here the weak sense of magic becomes clearer: it has to do with the sympathetic nature of social language, based originally on social classifications and myth, but also probably related to the sensitivity social beings have to each other[186]—"Symbolism plus mana," Hubert and Mauss call it. In religion these sympathetic effects become more visible; their capacity to organize collective action and will and strengthen the sense of life is demonstrated—and from that it is an easy step to "expropriation" (Huvelin) and "application" (Jensen). (But there will be more to say about magic in the weak sense in chapters that explore the origin of the self.)

Thus religious projections of society create the possibility of magic by 1. projecting a world view in which magical efficacy is possible (Durkheim), and 2. modeling the sympathetic properties of symbolism (Cazeneuve), and 3. even creating small magical institutions and then expelling or separating them. (Lea, Baroja, etc.) This is so important a function that one is almost tempted to define religion in terms of it: "religion is the institution that creates and models magic for society." (But of course it has some other functions, too.) By modeling sympathetic effects of rites that are magical in the weak sense, religion invites formation of peripheral institutions that are magical in the strict sense.

Relating the weak sense of magic to the strict sense makes it possible to anchor—in ways that commit neither category errors nor equivocations—all the myriad and rich strata of social experience in which metaphors of magic leap inevitably to human lips whenever an attempt is made to characterize them—to an explanatory base. The "magic" of propaganda, of "bad faith," of rhetoric, of legal sentences handed down by judges, of performative sentences creating states of marriage, war, outlawry, damnation and voodoo death . . . all these suggestive metaphors can finally be gathered into a frame that helps us to understand how and to what extent human social experience is magical. For such experiences really are magical, in the weak senses, and these senses can be made meaningful if they are provably linked to magic in the strict sense—i.e., to real magic institutions that once were powerful. For magic in the strict sense, when it arises, makes language *more* "magical" in the weak sense. Symbolism that already had built-in sympathetic effects is worked over, first by religion, then by magic, and this *accentuates* these properties. Ages of magic shape human speech and its use. Languages in which half the vocabulary was created by mythic metaphors originally used to rationalize sympathy links stratified in symbolism are then made *more* "magical" still by being put to instrumental magical uses. The very sentence forms may be shaped by these uses and by ancient assumptions about their effects.

Religion is not the only institution that creates and models magic for society, it is only the first. The magical origins of most professions are thoroughly researched—less attention is given to how medicine, law, etc., continue, even in civilized times, to create and model new magics.[187] In a secular age the miracles of medical research, the reifications of social science, the fiats of law, the dramaturgic uses of politics probably emit more new magical forms than religion does. The magic which religion manufactures tends to get stereotyped and grow dull; today the occult imitates science to develop new magics that are less dull—such as the "wild psychologies" of biofeedback, T-groups, etc.

Magic, though it rigidifies its scripts, reflects the conflict and fluidity of social reality while religion is associated with its order. The sociology of religion has had the effect of emphasizing and perhaps of claiming more order than actually exists. Nisbet has portrayed the classics of sociological theory, because of their concern with religion, as importing a conservative undertow through possibly anachronistic categories such as "the sacred," "status," "community," etc. (He traces the roots to ultramontanist reaction to the French Revolution.[188]) Sometimes sociology seems to be saying: if anything changes, people get sick. A sociological theory of magic might be an antidote to these reifications of order and of wholes.

Religion is not only order, but also chaos, reflecting the chaos in society as surely as Feuerbach thought it projected human misery; at the same time it strives for order by idealizing a tradition. We need not become neo-corporativists because we like Durkheim, or call as he did for the reconstitution of "intermediary groups" in which the Hegelian-Rousseauist ideal of reason would be further refracted by what Rousseau called "the accursed corporations." There is already enough chaos in society without introducing the artificial chaos of corporativism, and a sociological theory of magic will help to explain the chaos, by revealing religions to be the half-incoherent, undigested syntheses of ages of dialectical struggle between groups and their sacred projections and sects.

No one, for example, not even the most learned historian, possesses a map or index to the whole of the Hindu religion. Just as only parts are known to members of particular varnas, castes, subcastes and biradiris, only a fraction of the whole has been unraveled by the combined industry of philologists, anthropologists, sociologists, etc. Is this RTA, is this order? Parsons[189] sometimes writes as if modern society were still at the stage of simple "mechanical solidarity"; but not even primitive societies are simple. Magic is an engine of their latent pluralism. And the dialectic of religion and magical peripheral protest is not Hegelian: there is no complete synthesis; instead there is a mess, there is a zoo, an "inherited menagerie," as Gilbert Murray once called it.[190] Durkheim has shown that in primitive society religious symbolism is the one thing that is most plastic; it moves as easily as ideas move in the unconscious; it turns in every fantastical direction—and the sacred is a miscellany precipitated by these fancies. Ethical religions often begin as protests against this chaos, against this inherited menagerie, and as attempts to cleanse it and put it into decent order. For protest is as outraged at confusion as it is at magic; it rails at obsessional proliferation of rites and incoherent catalogues as much as it condemns superstition.[191] But the new protest sects usually promote themselves with new magics of their own; their victory is usually partial, not complete; they become subcults and so the menagerie and the confusion grow. Religions begin sometimes as "vast laundering enterprises," Camus wrote[192] (thinking no doubt of the Baptist's simple rite of forgiveness), providing magical simplifications to overcome the fear of magic and the guilt instilled by existing religion; usually they have the result of creating new canons of guilt and add to the sum total of magic. Although Durkheim specifically minimized the effect that religious projections could have on social morphology, he did not deny them altogether, and a dialectical theory based on his school is quite possible; but what it and a sociological theory of magic should emphasize are the complications and the chaos, rather than the order, in religious projections. As such, religious and magical representations can be used to help understand the disorder and conflict in society. As religion models magic, it also models the language of protest, and the forms which social struggle can take. (Engels had the sense of this in his work on the Peasant Wars.[193])

Conclusion: the solution to the problem of distinguishing magic and religion, and of showing how magic in the weak and strict senses fit together, then, is to say that religion "models" the magical potential of symbolism and invites the emergence of magical institutions. As E.O. James puts it, the rituals of religion are efficacious in themselves and hence have magical effects, even while fitting into a religious ceremony.[194] But this solution brings us to the edge of history, to real events, above all to the emergence of the individual, for religion enters into its magic-modeling phase at a particular point in human development.

After the first four somewhat phenomenological postulates about magic's symbolic texture, the second four structural chapters, now concluding, about the interaction of magic and religion, refer mainly to the dialectic of subgroups with the community. In the next four somewhat more functional and historical postulates, we will consider the dialectic of community and individual—and the drama of the emergence of the individual out of the community with the assistance of magic.

Prelude to Individuals: Rites of Membership

Religion is the institution that models magic for society, but this modeling becomes especially conspicuous when the grand operas of sacrifice and initiation rites begin. This happens when societies grow bigger, have more internal parts, so that *membership* in parts and the whole becomes problematical. Sacrifice and initiation help join the parts, but they also toughen individual members so they can pass through elaborate new role transitions without being torn apart. As such, they are a prelude to the birth of the individual. But before discussing this, consider first some remarkable affinities between these two master religious rituals.

We saw that, in sacrifice, the victim symbolizes the sacrifier. But look closely at what that interpretation of the symbolism entails: Once again, as in initiation, a subject is "dying" (symbolized by the sacrificial rite) and then being "reborn" (in the renewed strength the sacrifier derives from the rite). All this strongly suggests that sacrifice was initially not a gift to the gods, not a communion feast, not a sacred bridge—*but part of an initiation rite.* Initiation rites are often gruelling contests; in some of them, perhaps, the candidate accidentally died. Fraternity boys still die every few years during their hazing. If one out of a dozen candidates for manhood died during his ordeal, imagine the heightened power thereby lent to the others by this acting out of the symbolism of death and rebirth to a new role. Imagine the Mau-Mau-like bond created among the *Brüderbund* of survivors. From such accidents perhaps rites of human sacrifice would develop. And it is extremely suggestive that so many investigators have considered human sacrifice to be the primal form of sacrifice. It is also extremely interesting that the human victim in such rites—whether Minoan or Carthaginean or from the mythology of many other peoples—have typically been youths and maidens, young people of initiation age. From the accident of death through hazing, to the ceremonialization of regular human sacrifice from among the initiates, it could have been an easy step to substitute animal victims.

Many writers have made *some* connections. But who has connected sacrifice with initiation? Jane Harrison trembles on the brink of this recognition, but she never postulates a fundamental relation.[195] In a contributing chapter in her book *Themis* ("The Origin of the Olympic Games", ch. 7), F. M. Cornford is more explicit: The rite of initiation became a magic tool for the regeneration of the seasons and sacrifices *were associated with* these secondary magical applications of initiations. Cornford finds evidence in myths like that of Tantalus, of children served up for dinner, eaten, put back together. This is the old initiation symbolism of death and rebirth, but now someone is eating the victim and we have sacrifice.

Harrison and Cornford came closest. However, they failed to shout Eureka. Perhaps they did not recognize how significant it would be to show that sacrifice in its earliest forms was linked with the application of initiation rite symbolism to magical purposes. For consider: between the two of them sacrifice and initiation seem to be starting points and archetypes for most important magico-religious rituals.

A. Initiation: Jane Harrison has shown how merely social initiation becomes ceremonialized;[196] its forms are immediately expropriated by magic to become the magician's initiation rite. Mauss has confirmed how a magician's initiation resembles ordinary initiation.[197] Jensen[198] has shown how shamanic trance drama repeats the symbolism of the magician's initiation—his soul leaves the body, struggles with demons, ascends to heaven and so forth. I have extended this to magic's symbolic tools in general—they are often *fragments* of the magician's initiation (trance, magic initiation substance, possession, etc.). Eliade[199] has shown how Yoga resembles initiation, and I have extended this to mysticism in general.

B. Sacrifice: Other writers have shown that sacrifice is no less fertile as a source of ritual forms. Most of the other sacraments come from it, perhaps. Hocart[200] has tried to show that government and social classes grew out of various ritual roles in sacrifice.

If initiation and sacrifice can be homologized, then these two vast provinces of ritual that spring from them can be unified. In both there is symbolism of death and rebirth. In both initiation and sacrifice an individual ego is being worked upon. And is there not a similarity between the "entry and exit rites" of sacrifice (Hubert and Mauss[201]) and the "limens" (Van Gennup[202]) or "betwixt and between periods" (Turner[203]) in initiations and other rites of passage? The fact that both ceremonies get used as all-purpose rites is also interesting. Jane Harrison shows us initiation rites being used for fertility; Lienhardt and Evans-Pritchard show us sacrifice being used for fertility, for curing, etc.[204] Eliade's study of Australian religions[205] shows us tribes in which, when they want to attain some magical end, like curing an illness or catching game, they simply initiate someone! It is as if a university scheduled someone's Ph.D. orals or defense as good luck magic whenever it started a fund-raising drive or put in for government money. (In truth, universities make good public use of their initiation ceremony: graduation exercises become national platforms.)

Initiation-sacrifice seems to be the primal ritual machinery of magico-religion, or of religion modeling its "magical" effects and inviting the emergence of magic. Other things besides rituals perhaps emerged from initiation and sacrifice. Implicit in Frazer's accounts of sacrificial kings[206] is the possibility that kings and governments arose from the victim in sacrifice. Hocart's vision that the ritual apparatus of sacrifice is taken over as the apparatus of incipient government is similar. Less well known is Hocart's secondary suggestion that the class system, originally a caste system, came out of the division of roles in sacrifice.[207] In primitive society sacrifice was like a major oratorio, or Wagnerian opera, or a Berlioz symphony with 200 instruments in the orchestra; it was the greatest show in earth. All the magics of the society fed into it: personal magic, sympathetic magic, also taboos; there were complicated entry and exit rites; the materials used had to be medicated in advance. Division of magical labor might very well have begun here. Becker[208] has suggested that it even stimulated economic activity; surpluses were required for sacrifice.

Many basic religious and magical practices thus seem to use the same few principles, maybe only one idea. What would the underlying idea behind all of this be? I think the key idea is of the group as constituted by membership. This is quite conscious in later political-religious movements based on some social contract, such as an Apiru "tribe." But even in primitive societies, membership becomes a problem very early, for most primitive societies are not monolithic.

In a number of publications, half a dozen French writers have set forth bits and pieces of a powerful theory of the growing social complexity that calls this ritual apparatus into being. The drama begins with what Durkheim calls "polysegmental society"—those amorphous mosaics of clans or gentes, only loosely connected together, with virtually no overarching social structure, endlessly repeating the same design like wallpaper. Ultimately, under population pressure, these simple lineages split: As David Mandelbaum and William Goode have shown in India,[209] and Turner in Africa,[210] consanguineal families must eventually split when there are too many people in the household. Then the sons or grandsons of the patriarch must pack their bags and move their wives and offspring to form new lineages. But in many primitive societies, this fission poses a problem, because strangers are a problem: Some Australian societies, meeting a stranger, must either incorporate him into their kin system or kill him. What often happens therefore is that the severed halves of the split lineage form some kind of a compact to avoid war and remain brothers.

Davy was one of the first to study this, in his Ph.D. dissertation published as *La Foi Jurée*. His aim was to show that contracts, as a category of the human spirit and as a legal form, were born in these split-lineage agreements. Since there were no "individuals" yet, these had to be "total contracts," uniting whole groups.[211] Mauss was building on this study when he wrote *The Gift*.[212] The "total prestations" (mass gift exchanges) which he showed preceded individual gift-giving were symbolic actions to perpetuate the social contract between the reunited halves of the split lineage. Primitive ideas of the circulation of blood, of semen and of spiritual substances were at work in these exchange arrangements. Later, Lévi-Strauss also built on Davy's total contract and Mauss's total prestations when he showed, in *The Elementary Forms of Kinship*,[213] how marriage alliances were also contracted to keep semen and blood and spiritual substance circulating so the reunited social segments would remain one. (Lévi-Strauss perhaps became a structuralist when he discovered primitive marriage contractors discovering that various arrangements had logical consequences.)

During these changes, the idea of membership became a category of the human spirit: Two brothers who take their wives and children to different houses must establish a new kind of bond between them. Alterations in descent also complicate the problem. A child, brought up by the women, must eventually make the transition to the men's house. The idea arises that people are or become *members* of different groups and not just occupants of relational positions toward one another. (Membership ideas perhaps assisted the development of the category of "classes" or sets.)

Initiation has to do basically with membership. It is an action sequence by which the group is augmented. There is a germ of creation in it. The inculcation of a new member is a microcosmic reenactment of the creation of social reality that occurs in grand contracts and alliances. Society both creates its members and is "membered" by their addition. In an initiation, a new member is created, but the social group is also recreated and enlarged. Similarly, in sacrifice a member symbolically offers up his very self to the group, and gets it back strengthened, and the social group is also strengthened by the ritual of fealty. In sacrifice and initiation, in other words, the member is symbolically *dis*membered so that he can be *membered*—and the group is *re-membered* by his addition to it. No wonder sacral-magical phenomena abound along all these fissures. Taboo and magic crackle around these borders and limens (Van Gennup[214]) because they define membership, which is the creation of social power and mana.

Social reality is adventitious, full of holes and cliffs of fall because it is made up continuously by agreement about membership. It is more agreeing than precipitate of agreement, because even the august weight of tradition that we think we can lean on is there because we continue to agree to it. Paradigms of alienation catch only one part of agreement when they postulate that social reality is created by agreements which then become facticities because we forget their origins. I am suggesting something more radical: that we do not entirely forget. These facticities seem to be substantial only because we continue to agree to their existence. We agree that we are agreeing that we have agreed and can agree; we agree to agree that there is agreement even when there is not, and we paper over considerable disorder and disagreement by our agreement always to assume that there is some agreement. All forms of authority—traditional, legal-rational, charismatic—are based on our still agreeing to go along, and deep down, we know it. There is more "bad faith" than "alienation" in the social constraints and membership rules we consent to.

Agreements about membership and its rules are not merely the existential texture of everyday life. Agreements are major events; they happen as history all the time; they constantly create and alter social structure far more than we currently agree to notice. The socialization idea has become a dull stereotype that blinds us to the ferment and self-construction of societies. Even primitive societies have their own equivalents of Dumbarton Oaks, Yalta, Versailles. Typically, they make their own history in almost every other generation. They are not static. The typical primitive tribe trekked to its present habitat from a distant location a few generations ago; upon arriving it entered into a social compact changing its marital arrangements, patterns of gift exchange, territorial layout and social structure. It was driven to migrate and restructure by war, overpopulation, famine, real events in other words—and in recent centuries (as Lévi-Strauss told in *Tristes Tropiques*[215] and Vidich[216] in his critique of the Dubois Alorese study) these societies were badly wounded by the advancing whites. All this recent constitutional history is recalled in creation myths which are used as scripts in magical and religious ceremonies that seek to perpetuate the membership arrangements.

In initiations, all the members of a society are invited to recall the agreements and partly reenact their creation of social reality. The smaller the group the keener is the sense that the group itself is re-membered as a new initiate is membered. All small societies are like partnership papers that have to be redrawn when a new partner is admitted. A fraternity inducting a new pledge class, or a small law firm taking in a year's pick of the graduates, is poignantly aware that the group itself, its ethos and mood, will be fundamentally re-membered by these additions. As Frank Young[217] puts it, new members pose a threat to the community; initiation is a "sacred drama" that enables the group to assimilate the threat. It does this by recreating itself to a small degree. In the rite all the members are invited to become aware again of creation; in the microcosmic social contract of augmenting membership they are reminded of the grand contracts of membership on which their being depends. These are powerful techniques for keeping alive spontaneity and creativity.

And so, as more populous tribes are forced to tinker with their social structure and membership becomes problematical, simple practices of induction become "ceremonialized" (Mendenhall); they take on the aspect of religious rites (Harrison); and these new rites model the possibility of magical application. They can be "expropriated" (Mauss), "detoured" (Huvelin) and "applied" (Jensen) to other purposes, the first one probably being fertility (Harrison, etc.). For membership and membering, initiation rites and rites of loyalty (sacrifice) are powerful metaphors that demonstrate "the sympathetic potentials of symbolism" (Cazeneuve). A child is leaving the woman's house, joining the men's lodge; finally he is initiated as a member. The symbolism dramatizes his death to one role, his rebirth in another. This is powerful symbolism; it is quickly applied to nature, to bring the world back to life in the spring. But behind the whole dramatic apparatus and its elaborate theology lies the simple idea that membership creates a world of power. (In the *Bhagavad Ghita*, we are taught how, by turning our every action into a sacrifice, renouncing its fruits, we can participate continuously in creation.)

So the two rites that strongly model magic, initiation and sacrifice, are born together when membership becomes problematical. They smooth transitions for the group, making its re-membering easier; they also strengthen group members, so that they can pass through successive roles without being torn apart. In this, they are *preludes to the birth of the individual.*

We can conclude with a diagram showing the grand unification that is possible if the theories of these various French writers are fitted together.

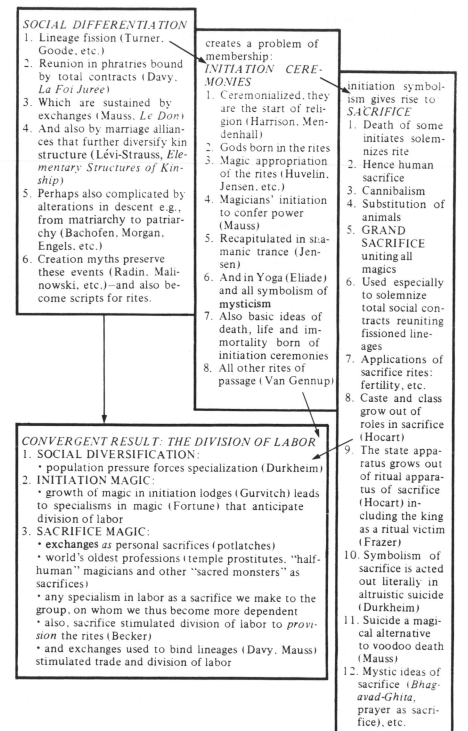

SOCIAL DIFFERENTIATION
1. Lineage fission (Turner, Goode, etc.)
2. Reunion in phratries bound by total contracts (Davy, *La Foi Juree*)
3. Which are sustained by exchanges (Mauss, *Le Don*)
4. And also by marriage alliances that further diversify kin structure (Lévi-Strauss, *Elementary Structures of Kinship*)
5. Perhaps also complicated by alterations in descent e.g., from matriarchy to patriarchy (Bachofen, Morgan, Engels, etc.)
6. Creation myths preserve these events (Radin, Malinowski, etc.)—and also become scripts for rites.

creates a problem of membership:
INITIATION CEREMONIES
1. Ceremonialized, they are the start of religion (Harrison, Mendenhall)
2. Gods born in the rites
3. Magic appropriation of the rites (Huvelin, Jensen, etc.)
4. Magicians' initiation to confer power (Mauss)
5. Recapitulated in shamanic trance (Jensen)
6. And in Yoga (Eliade) and all symbolism of **mysticism**
7. Also basic ideas of death, life and immortality born of initiation ceremonies
8. All other rites of passage (Van Gennup)

initiation symbolism gives rise to:
SACRIFICE
1. Death of some initiates solemnizes rite
2. Hence human sacrifice
3. Cannibalism
4. Substitution of animals
5. GRAND SACRIFICE uniting all magics
6. Used especially to solemnize total social contracts reuniting fissioned lineages
7. Applications of sacrifice rites: fertility, etc.
8. Caste and class grow out of roles in sacrifice (Hocart)
9. The state apparatus grows out of ritual apparatus of sacrifice (Hocart) including the king as a ritual victim (Frazer)
10. Symbolism of sacrifice is acted out literally in altruistic suicide (Durkheim)
11. Suicide a magical alternative to voodoo death (Mauss)
12. Mystic ideas of sacrifice (*Bhagavad-Ghita*, prayer as sacrifice), etc.

CONVERGENT RESULT: THE DIVISION OF LABOR
1. SOCIAL DIVERSIFICATION:
   • population pressure forces specialization (Durkheim)
2. INITIATION MAGIC:
   • growth of magic in initiation lodges (Gurvitch) leads to specialisms in magic (Fortune) that anticipate division of labor
3. SACRIFICE MAGIC:
   • exchanges *as* personal sacrifices (potlatches)
   • world's oldest professions (temple prostitutes, "half-human" magicians and other "sacred monsters" as sacrifices)
   • any specialism in labor as a sacrifice we make to the group, on whom we thus become more dependent
   • also, sacrifice stimulated division of labor to *provision* the rites (Becker)
   • and exchanges used to bind lineages (Davy, Mauss) stimulated trade and division of labor

Notes

1. Lloyd Warner, *A Black Civilization* (N.Y., 1958), p. 232ff.
2. E. E. Evans-Pritchard, *Nuer Religion* (Oxford, 1956, 1970), chs. 8, 10, 11.
3. A. M. Hocart, *Kings and Councillors* (Chicago, 1970), p. 32ff.
4. Mircea Eliade, *Cosmos and History* (N.Y., 1959), pp. 49–92.
5. Godfrey Lienhardt, *Divinity and Experience, The Religion of the Dinka* (Oxford, 1961), pp. 291–292.
6. Durkheim, *The Elementary Forms...* (London, 1954), Book 3, ch. 5, "Piacular Rites...," pp. 389–414.
7. Mary Douglas, *Purity and Danger* (Baltimore, 1970), difficulty of distinguishing magic from religion, pp. 29, 33, 84, etc. *Natural Symbols* (N.Y., 1973), association of magic and ritual, pp. 35–39.
8. Arnold Van Gennup, *The Rites of Passage* (Chicago, 1969), p. 13.
9. See Introduction to this paper.
10. Samuel Dill, *Roman Society in Gaul in the Merovingian Age* (London, 1926; N.Y., 1966), pp. 395–430.
11. T. K. Oesterreich, *Possession, Demoniacal and Other* (Secaucus, N.J., 1974), p. 101.
12. Oesterreich, *op. cit.,* p. 102.
13. Henry Charles Lea, "Sorcery and Occult Arts," ch. 8 in *A History of the Inquisition in Spain* (N.Y., 1906–7, 1966).
14. Most polar ideal types with their dichotomies of means vs. ends, etc., actually catch part of this penumbra of magic in the weak sense, though they cannot explain strictly magical institutions.
15. Douglas, *Natural Symbols* (N.Y., 1973), p. 35ff, etc.
16. Arnold Van Gennup, *Rites of Passage* (Chicago, 1908), ch. 1, pp. 1–13.
17. Jean Cazeneuve, *Sociologie du Rite* (Paris, 1971), ch. 9.
18. Van Gennup writes: "These theories constitute *religion,* whose techniques (ceremonies, rites, services) I call *magic.* Since the practice and the theory are inseparable—the theory without the practice becoming metaphysics, and the practice on the basis of a different theory becoming science—the term I will ... use is the adjective *magico-religious.*" (p. 13, *op. cit.*)
19. Maurice Pradines, *Esprit de la Religion* (Paris, 1941), cf. preface. Cazeneuve, however, reports that, in another book which I did not consult, *Traité de Psychologie Générale,* Pradines disputed the idea that religion had no technique of its own. Cazeneuve, *op. cit.,* ch. 9.
20. Alfred Loisy, *Essai Historique Sur Le Sacrifice* (Paris, 1920), ch. 1.
21. Van Gennup, incidentally, is doing something similar; in effect he is characterizing one element of sacrifice as the key magical rite in religion. I refer to his attempt to treat most rites as variations of rites of passage. These are difficult and dangerous role transitions that must be negotiated by magic. I suspect that he got the idea from Hubert and Mauss' account of the "rites of entry and exit" which surround sacrifice. Entry and exit rites bridge the dangerous gaps between sacred and profane, just as rites of passage bridge dangerous roles. Hubert and Mauss' monograph on sacrifice came out in 1898, a decade before Van Gennup's *Rites de Passage* (1908). Van Gennup's influential idea of "sacred borders," "limens," etc. in turn has stimulated many others. (E.g., Victor W. Turner's idea of "liminality" in ch. 3, *The Ritual Process* (London, 1914), pp. 80–118; and ch. 4, *The Forest of Symbols* [Ithaca, 1967], pp. 93–111.)
22. Max Weber, *The Sociology of Religion* (Boston, 1964), cf. index under any of those terms.

23. *Ibid.*, p. 55.

24. A. M. Hocart, *Kings and Councillors* (Chicago, 1970). Hocart demonstrates that the "life" sought in religious rites is not immortality, but a life lived in peace and prosperity to the end of its natural course. (p. 32ff.)

25. Ernest Becker, *Escape From Evil* (N.Y., 1976), ch. 1, pp. 6–25.

26. C. S. Lewis, *Mere Christianity* (N.Y., 1964).

27. Dorothy Hammond, "Magic: A Problem in Semantics," *American Anthropologist*, vol. 72, 1970, pp. 1349–1356.

28. Thomas Luckmann, *The Invisible Religion* (N.Y., 1970).

29. H. Hubert & M. Mauss, *Sacrifice* (Chicago, 1964), p. vi, etc.; and for explicit statement of this point, their "Introduction à l'Analyse de Quelques Phénomènes Religieux" (1906), Mauss, *Oeuvres*, vol. I, pp. 3–65.

30. Hubert & Mauss, *Sacrifice*, ch. 2, pp. 19–49.

31. Hubert & Mauss, Prologue to *General Theory of Magic* (N.Y., 1972), pp. 7–10.

32. Durkheim organizes his entire account of religious ceremonies around sacrifice in *The Elementary Forms . . .*, Book Three, "The Principal Ritual Attitudes," pp. 299–414. Sacrifice (the model is the Arunta Intichiuma ceremony) is the key example he uses of "positive cult" (chs. 2, 3, 4 of Book III). Negative cult (ch. 1) is purely taboos related to such ceremonies. Durkheim actually synthesizes Tylor's gift theory, and Smith's communion feast theory, to say, in effect, that life is given to the gods and other symbols of community in the communal feast.

33. W. Robertson Smith, *The Religion of the Semites* (N.Y., 1972).

34. Georges Gusdorf, *L'Expérience Humaine du Sacrifice* (Paris, 1948).

35. Alfred Loisy, *Essai Historique Sur le Sacrifice* (Paris, 1920).

36. Sir Edward B. Tylor, *Anthropology*, abr. ed. (Ann Arbor, 1970).

37. Andrew Lang, *Magic and Religion* (London, 1901, 1969).

38. M. Mauss, *Essai Sur les Variations Saisonnières des Sociétés Eskimos, L'Année Sociologique*, 1904–5; reprinted in C. Lévi-Strauss, *Marcel Mauss Sociologie et Anthropologie* (Paris, 1950, 1966), pp. 389–475.

39. E. E. Evans-Pritchard, Intro. to R. Hertz, *Death and the Right Hand* (Aberdeen, 1960), pp. 9–24.

40. Hubert and Mauss are writing about high sacrifice, using Vedic horse sacrifice as their "natural ideal type," and this is so dangerous it must be performed by specialists. So they distinguish the "sacrifier" (*Sacrifice*, p. 10), the person for whom the rite is performed, from the "sacrificer" (p. 22), the specialist who performs the ceremony. I think the victim symbolizes the sacrifier, or client. Note also that sacrifice is an elaborate rite, and (as Hocart reminds us) there may be many functionaries involved in it. In Hocart's schema, the sacrificer is the person who kills the beast; he is usually a chieftain and out of his role grows the Kshatriya caste. The heralds (kerux) who speak the oral rites, the prayers or incantations, become the Brahmins. The attendants who provision the rites become the Vaisya caste of farmers and husbandrymen. (A. M. Hocart, *Kings and Councillors*, Chicago, 1970), pp. 86ff, 102ff, 115–129.

41. In fairness, Hubert and Mauss are close to saying sacrifice symbolizes surrender and renewal of self. In ch. 6 they say the main unity of the ceremony is its 1. *procedure* and 2. *its effect of sanctifying the sacrifier.* Late passages hint at the great trick sacrifice performs: "The sacrifier gives up something of himself, but he does not give himself . . ." (*Sacrifice*, p. 100. See sequence: pp. 100–101).

42. Ernst Becker, *Escape From Evil* (N.Y., 1975), p. 104.

43. Cf. E. O. James, *Origins of Sacrifice*, cited by Evans-Pritchard in *Nuer Religion* (Oxford, 1956), p. 282. See the chapters on sacrifice in the latter book, esp. ch. 11, "The Meaning of Sacrifice," (pp. 272–286) for a discussion suggesting the giving and returning of the self, strengthened.

44. Georges Gusdorf, *L'Expérience Humaine du Sacrifice* (Paris, 1948), chs. 1–2.

45. Godfrey Lienhardt, *Divinity and Experience, The Religion of the Dinka* (Oxford, 1961), ch. 7.

46. E. E. Evans-Pritchard, *Nuer Religion* (Oxford, 1956), ch. 11, pp. 272–286.

47. *Ibid.*, p. 275.

48. *The Elementary Forms of Religious Life* (London, 1954), Book III, ch. V, "Piacular Rites," pp. 389–414.

49. ". . . any sacrifice involves ends which go quite beyond any particular end which may be its special proximate occasion. It is made not only and specifically for one sick man . . . it is made for and on behalf of the sacrificing community." Lienhardt, *Divinity and Experience, The Religion of the Dinka* (Oxford, 1961), 291-2.

50. Evans-Pritchard, *Nuer Religion,* chs. 8, 10, pp. 197-230, 248-271.

51. Marcel Mauss, "La Prière et Les Rites Oraux," in *Oeuvres,* vol. 1, e.g., p. 369, 379, etc.

52. W. Lloyd Warner, *op. cit.,* ch. 7, 8, p. 193ff.

53. P. Huvelin, "Magie et Droit Individuel," *L'Année Sociologique,* 1905-6, pp. 1–47. Cf. p. 46.

54. One way the church attempted to tame mysticism was to pattern it as something brief and sanitary, noetic and ineffable, reducing it to a mere single psychic experience. It is in this spirit that Angus writes that even Plotinus had only one or two mystical experiences in his life, and each of them mild. S. Angus, *The Mystery-Religions* (N.Y., 1975), pp. 214, 266.

55. Rudolf Otto, *Mysticism East and West* (N.Y., 1970), ch. 2, pp. 33–46.

56. Max Weber, *The Protestant Ethic and the Spirit of Capitalism* (London, 1948). The term is a chapter title: "The Religious Foundations of Worldly Asceticism," ch. 4, pp. 94-154.

57. Arnold Toynbee, *A Study of History,* D. C. Somervell Abridgment (N.Y., 1947), p. 217, *seq.*

58. Eliade thinks this literalness is the source of such strange phenomena as the Thugee. They are acting out symbolic dramas—literally. Eliade claims that in Hindu eschatology, such literalness is associated with the Kali Yuga—the Urmonotheismus school would say it is associated with the fallen world that has descended into magic. (Eliade, *Yoga,* Princeton, 1969). References to be discussed.

59. I. M. Lewis, *Ecstatic Religion* (London, 1971), pp. 18-36.

60. Morton Smith, *The Secret Gospel* (N.Y., 1973), chs. 10-13, pp. 78-114.

61. Marcel Mauss' *L'Origine Des Pouvoirs Magiques Dans Les Sociétés Australiennes,* now reprinted in vol. 2 of the Karady-edited *Oeuvres* (Paris, 1968, pp. 319-369), was written shortly after Hubert and Mauss did *L'Esquisse d'Une Théorie Générale de la Magie* for *L'Année Sociologique* and continued its argument. First published in *Rapports Annuels de l'Ecole des Hautes Etudes* in 1904, it was one of the few Mauss monographs to appear in book form during his lifetime, since he and Hubert picked it for inclusion in their joint collection *Mélanges d'Histoire des Religions* (Paris, 1909). Mauss' monograph on Australian magic is inferior to the *Esquisse,* but was perhaps included for balance: the volume already had one joint piece, and Hubert's article on how time is shaped by religion. So Mauss' own piece on magic was picked over their superior joint monograph on the subject.

62. Mircea Eliade, *Yoga* (Princeton, 1969).

63. There is a beginning of mana words in Australia, he writes, but it is hesitant; there is more than one such word, or the word only refers to one aspect of power (e.g., *arungquiltha* as *evil* magical power of magical rites, substances and things among the Arunta). Durkheim perhaps got his idea of the generalization of mana from these remarks but Mauss does not possess this concept, so he does not explicitly state the significance of this finding: i.e., magic here is incipient; mana has not yet been *generalized.* This would help explain why the so-called magician actually functions as an official of the Arunta religion. Mauss does observe that Frazer had difficulty with this picture of apparent magicians working like priests and that is why he (erroneously, according to Mauss) called the Arunta religion a "confederation of magic." But it is hard to suppose that this is a primordial magic just on the point of emerging within clan religion; it is too complex. Eliade, noting its similarity to magic patterns found throughout the world, has suggested a different explanation: diffusion of the magician complex from outside Australia. Mircea Eliade, *Australian Religions, An Introduction* (Ithaca and London, 1973), ch. 4.

64. Jane Ellen Harrison, *Themis* (Cambridge, 1927), ch. 3.

65. Mauss notes that this is an old Hindu classification (*A General Theory of Magic,* p. 40). Here again Mauss draws on a native theory or concept, just as he used Melanesian "mana" as a causal explanation in the *Esquisse* (section 4), and Polynesian "hua" as explanation in *The Gift,* ch. 1.

66. Cf. Robert Lowie, *Primitive Religion* (N.Y., 1924, 1970), pp. 4–15.

67. Diogenes Laertius, *Lives of Eminent Philosophers,* vol. II, p. 357.

68. Eliade, *Shamanism* (Princeton, 1972), p. 60ff.

69. James Henry Breasted, *Development of Religion and Thought in Ancient Egypt* (Gloucester, Mass., 1970), pp. 10, 34–35, 45.

70. In Cynic and Stoic meditation this begins to be taken more literally. By the time we get to the Neo-Platonists, the mystic experience and the path to it are increasingly patterned.

71. Eliade, *Yoga* (Princeton, 1970), pp. 295–301.

72. Morton Smith, *Clement of Alexandria and A Secret Gospel of Mark* (Cambridge, Mass., 1973), pp. 219–221.

73. *"Remplir son personnage":* Conclusion of Australian magician essay, Mauss, *Oeuvres,* vol. 2, p. 369.

74. William James, *The Origins of Religious Experience* (N.Y., 1902), e.g., Lecture 11. The term "moment of illumination" is, I believe, from Virginia Woolf.

75. The reference is to Mauss' "Les Techniques du Corps" in the Lévi-Strauss-edited collection, *Sociologie et Anthropologie* (Paris, 1950, 1966), pp. 365–386, and to Jacques Ellul's concept of "technique" in *The Technological Society* (French title *La Technique ou l'Enjeu du Siècle*) (N.Y., 1964), cf. pp. 3–23.

76. Cf. Zimmer, Eliade, Dumézil, *ops. cit.*

77. Naranjo and Ornstein distinguish the traditional "paths" in meditation: 1. the negative way of emptiness, 2. concentration of forms, 3. the expressive way (hedonism, surrender, etc.). Claudio Naranjo and Robert E. Ornstein, *On The Psychology of Meditation* (N.Y., 1971). Ornstein shows that all these are merely a matter of diverting attentionality to control the stream of consciousness or even alter brainwaves, as by a ganzfeld (p. 142ff). My section on altering the frame of objective reference has shown how easily any one of dozens of methods do this. We might associate all these practices by saying that there are *mechanical* approaches to mysticism. The milder methods that cultivate the foothills are the techniques of meditation; the methods that storm the heights are the more advanced yogas.

78. Archie J. Baum, *Yoga, Union with Ultimate—A New Version of the Yoga Sutras of Patanjali* (N.Y., 1961).

79. Mircea Eliade, *Yoga* (Princeton, 1970). Discussion and references follow.

80. *Ibid.,* p. 6 (Italics added.)

81. Marcel Mauss, "A Category of the Human Spirit," *The Psychoanalytic Review,* vol. 55, no. 3 (1968), pp. 457–481.

82. Mauss has shown how the personal "person" begins out of what is most impersonal in the individual but is developed by Western law and philosophy to support a true subjective individualism. In India, by contrast, the impersonal *Atman* is surrendered *back to* the ritual impersonality of *Brahman.* Thus Hinduism is a vast circular religious confederation eliciting and patterning endless magical pseudo-revolts against itself which have always the end result of imploding the self and shortcircuiting the development of individualism or of true social revolt.

83. Emile Durkheim, *Suicide* (Glencoe, Ill., 1951), p. 224.

84. Henry Romilly Fedden, *Suicide, A Social and Historical Study* (London, 1938), ch. 4.

85. Eliade, *Yoga,* p. 355.

86. *Ibid.,* p. 293ff.

87. *Ibid.,* p. 294.

88. Eliade, *Yoga,* p. 318ff.

89. Eliade, *Shamanism* (Princeton, 1972), ch. 14, "Conclusions," pp. 495–507.

90. Eliade, *Yoga,* p. 322.

91. Cf. Jessie L. Weston, *From Ritual to Romance* (N.Y., 1957).

92. Eliade, *Ibid.,* p. 325.

93. *Ibid.,* p. 334ff.

94. Eliade, *Yoga,* pp. 363–364.

95. *Ibid.,* p. 109.

96. *Ibid.,* p. 145.

97. *Ibid.,* p. 153.

98. *Ibid.*, p. 157.

99. *Ibid.*, p. 199.

100. *Ibid.*, ch. 6.

101. Bronislaw Malinowski, *The Foundations of Faith and Morals* (London, 1936, 1969), ch. 2, also pp. 30, 45, etc.

102. This is Adolf E. Jensen's position.

103. Roland Barthes, *Mythologies* (N.Y., 1975), cf. pp. 134–140; Roger Caillois, *Le Myth et l'Homme* (Paris, 1938), ch. 1.

104. Lucien Lévy-Bruhl, esp. *La Mythologie Primitive* (Paris, 1935).

105. Adolf E. Jensen, *Myth and Cult Among Primitive Peoples* (Chicago, 1963, 1973), pp. 242–243.

106. Jane Ellen Harrison, *Themis; Prolegomena to the Study of Greek Religion*, p. 6.

107. Jessie L. Weston, *From Ritual to Romance* (N.Y., 1957), *passim*.

108. The schema by no means includes a complete catalogue of theories of myth. For example, it leaves out the "meta-language" dimension of those who speak of myth's "rainbow of meanings" (Plutarch), its infinity of suggestions (Caillois) which, together with its use of bits of narrative instead of words as its vocabulary, cause it to be a "meta-language" (Barthes) which explores various logics of possibility (Lévi-Strauss), and so on. Here we examine just those theories which say something about the *relation of myth to rite*

109. Mircea Eliade, *Cosmos and History* (N.Y., 1959); *Myth and Reality* (N.Y., 1968); *The Two and the One* (N.Y., 1965); *Images and Symbols* (N.Y., 1969); *Patterns in Comparative Religion* (N.Y., 1963).

110. Malinowski, *op. cit.*, ch. 2.

111. Joseph Campbell, *Hero With a Thousand Faces* (Princeton, 1972); *Myths, Dreams and Religion* (N.Y., 1970), pp. 138–145, etc.

112. Paul Radin, Works, esp. *Primitive Religion* (N.Y., 1957), pp. 241–249, 262–266.

113. C. Lévi-Strauss, *Structural Anthropology Volume Two* (N.Y., 1976), ch. 9.

114. A. K. Kroeber, *An Anthropologist Looks at History* (Berkeley & L.A., 1966).

115. Stanley Diamond, *Primitive Views of the World* (N.Y., 1964); *In Search of the Primitive* (New Brunswick, N.Y., 1974).

116. George Davy, *La Foi Jurée* (Paris, 1922).

117. Lévi-Strauss, *Elementary Structures of Kinship* (Boston, 1969).

118. Marcel Mauss, *The Gift* (N.Y., 1967).

119. Emile Durkheim, *The Elementary Forms of Religious Life.*

120. Georges Dumézil, *Les Dieux des Indo-Européens* (Paris, 1952).

121. Ludwig Feuerbach, *The Essence of Christianity* (N.Y., 1957).

122. Durkheim & Mauss, *Primitive Classification* (Chicago, 1967).

123. In the layout of Durkheim's book, sacrifice is the key "positive" rite; "imitative" (i.e., sympathetic) rites and representative rites (i.e., myth and cosmos-elaborating rites) are secondary positive rites built upon it. Taboos are related, as defenses of the profane against the sacred. Only piacular rites are treated separately.

124. Georges Dumézil, *Les Dieux des Indo-Européens* (Paris, 1952). For a useful summary of his other books see C. Scott Littleton: *The New Comparative Mythology: An Anthropological Assessment of the Theories of Dumézil* (Berkeley, L.A., 1973).

125. Bronislaw Malinowski: many references to this in his works but esp. in *The Foundations of Faith and Morals* (London, 1936, 1969), ch. 2, p. 11ff.

126. Malinowski is usually writing about "ceremonial magic": official, on the periphery of religion, often done by clan officials, performed for the public good.

127. Lucien Lévy-Bruhl, *L'Expérience Mystique et Les Symboles* (Paris, 1938); *La Mythologie Primitive* (Paris, 1935); *Primitives and the Supernatural* (N.Y., 1935).

128. Mircea Eliade, *Cosmos and History* (N.Y., 1959), pp. 21–27, etc.

129. Henri Hubert, "Etude Sommaire de la Représentation du Temps Dans la Religion et la Magie," Hubert & Mauss, *Mélanges d'Histoire des Religions* (Paris, 1909).

130. Eliade, *Ibid.*, pp. 73–93.

131. Henri Hubert, *op. cit.*, pp. 206–207.

132. A. M. Hocart, *The Life-Giving Myth* (London, 1952), ch. 1.

133. Gilbert Murray, "An Excursus On The Ritual Forms Preserved in Greek Tragedy," an insert after Ch. 8 in Jane Ellen Harrison, *Themis* (Cambridge, 1927), pp. 341–363; also *The Rise of the Greek Epic* (Oxford, 1907, 1967).

134. Francis Cornford, *The Origin of Attic Comedy* (Garden City, N.Y., 1961); also *The Origin of the Olympic Games,* ch. 7 in Harrison, *Themis.*

135. Theodor H. Gaster, *Thespis* (N.Y., 1950, 1961), pp. 24-25, etc.

136. Santha Rama Rau tells me that Indian girls, when she was growing up, were so admonished.

137. Friedrich Nietzsche, *The Birth of Tragedy From The Spirit of Music,* in *The Philosophy of Nietzsche* (N.Y., 1927), pp. 951-1088.

138. Heinrich Zimmer, *Myths and Symbols in Indian Art and Civilization* (Princeton, 1946, 1974).

139. Joseph Campbell, *The Hero With a Thousand Faces* (Princeton, 1949, 1968), pp. 318-364.

140. Henri Bergson, *The Two Sources of Morality and Religion* (N.Y., 1935); Roger Caillois, *Le Myth et l'Homme* (Paris, 1938).

141. Adolf E. Jensen, *Myth and Cult Among Primitive Peoples* (Chicago, 1963, 1973).

142. Hubert & Mauss, *A General Theory of Magic:* see the passage on "mythical spells" derived from fairy tales or epics and their if-he-can-I-can logic, on p. 56 of the English edition.

143. Roland Barthes, *Mythologies* (N.Y., 1973); *Critical Essays* (Evanston, Ill., 1972); *Writing Degree Zero* (N.Y., 1968).

144. Harrison, *Themis,* chs. 3-4.

145. A. M. Hocart, *Kings and Councillors* (Chicago, 1970), p. 32ff; *The Life-Giving Myth* (London, 1952), ch. 1.

146. Jessie L. Weston, *From Ritual to Romance* (Garden City, N.Y., 1957).

147. See the account of Propp's *Morphology of the Folktale,* in Lévi-Strauss, "Structure and Form: Reflections on a Work by Vladimir Propp" (1960), ch. 8 of *Structural Anthropology—Volume Two* (N.Y., 1976).

148. This is in the Gilbert Murray chapter in Harrison, *Themis.*

149. In *Marcel Mauss Oeuvres* (Paris, 1968), vol. I, pp. 357-477.

150. "Elle est un rite, car elle est une attitude prise, un acte accompli en face des choses sacrées. . . . Mais en même temps, toute prière est toujours, à quelque degré un Credo. . . . La prière est une parole. Or le langage est un mouvement qui a un but et un effet; il est toujours, au fond, un instrument d'action. . . . Parler, c'est à la fois agir et penser." (Mauss, *op. cit.,* p. 358.)

151. The prefatory remarks on method that often appear near the beginning of Mauss' monographs this time almost turn into a short disquisition on epistemology. The usual critical survey of previous theories becomes painfully long. All during this 80-page, many-sectioned methodological wind-up, he plays with tentative definitions. He has great trouble distinguishing prayer from incantation. The manuscript breaks off before a real exposition has started to track. Karady claims that Mauss gave up his studies of the sacred after this failure, because it convinced him that these studies were unprofitable. But Mauss wrote notable short pieces on magic after this, including several that related money to magic. All that the monograph's failure shows is that even the Hubert and Mauss theory of magic is not fully adequate; otherwise the ambiguity of prayer would not have defeated him.

152. Keith Thomas, *Religion and the Decline of Magic* (N.Y., 1971), ch. 5, pp. 113-150.

153. W. Lloyd Warner, *A Black Civilization,* Rev. ed. (N.Y., 1958), chs. 7-8.

154. When religion becomes conscious of itself as symbolism, then its latent functions become manifest functions (Merton). As this happens, religion becomes more magical in coloration.

155. Clyde Kluckholn, *Navaho Witchcraft* (Boston, 1944, 1967), p. 112ff.

156. E.g., Mary Douglas, whose M = R position in *Purity and Danger* is qualified in *Natural Symbols,* as previously explained.

157. Dorothy Hammond, "Magic, A Problem in Semantics," *op. cit.*

158. Rosalie and Murray Wax, articles cited.

159. Ruth Benedict, "Religion," ch. 14, Franz Boaz, ed., *General Anthropology* (N.Y., 1938), pp. 627-665.

160. Talcott Parsons and Edward A. Shils, eds., *Toward a General Theory of Action* (N.Y., Cambridge, Mass., 1951). Parsons defines a pattern variable as a dichotomy, one side of which must be chosen by an actor before the meaning of a situation is determinate for him; and he builds up whole systems of ideal types for social structures, cultures and what

have you, from these dichotomies. More notorious is his practice of running one against another, to create a 2 X 2 matrix of four cells in which institutional types can be classified. This approach is really quite primitive, a return to mere classification, and also primitive in the sense that it is put together by means of *miscellaneous* rather than systematic rules. The dichotomies come from different sources, and are not always on the same logical level. Behind each of these lifeless counters lies a theory of classical sociology that was more interesting. Thus Parsons' "universality vs. particularity" perhaps comes from Mannheim's remarks on how law varies between general and specific stipulations (in *Ideology and Utopia, Diagnosis of Our Times*, etc.). "Ascription vs. achievement" is from Linton's role theory in *The Study of Man* (N.Y., 1936). "Private vs. collective" is the great orientation of the Durkheim school, and so forth. These distinctions are emptied of content, then run together as matrices without any question raised about whether they are logically isometric. In Parsons we see virtually a regression to *totemic* classification thinking.

161. William J. Goode, *Religion Among the Primitives* (Glencoe, Ill., 1951), pp. 50–55.

162. Hubert & Mauss, *A General Theory of Magic*, English ed., p. 45.

163. Far from helping to distinguish magic from religion, they help confound them. For on the one hand polar ideal types are bound to overvalue the "magic" (weak sense) *content* of *religion*, yet they have little to say about magical *institutions* per se. Thus they will minimize the differences between religion and magic.

164. Dorothy Hammond, "Magic, A Problem in Semantics," *American Anthropologist*, vol. 72, 1970, pp. 1349–1356.

165. I.e., $\left(R_{\textcircled{M}}\right)$ All M is R but *not* all R is M.

166. Edmond Douttée, *Magie et Religion Dans L'Afrique du Nord* (Algiers, 1908). I.e.,

$\textcircled{M}\,\textcircled{R}$

167. "Ainsi naît, à côté de la magie licite et même obligatoire qui soutient la vie de la société, une magie nuisible ou tout au moins inutile à celle-ci et comme telle réprouvée et interdite ou à peine tolérée. Nous appelons la première *religion* et la second *sorcellerie*." Douttée, *Ibid.*, pp. 334–5.

168. Douttée, *Magie et Religion . . .*, p. 331.

169. *Ibid.*, pp. 337–340.

170. Henry Charles Lea, esp. *Materials Toward a History of Witchcraft* (London, 1957).

171. Douttée, concluding chapter.

172. ". . . magic, invented under the pressure of need, is nothing but the objectification of desire . . ." Douttée, p. 330 (my translation).

173. "Theism keeps many of the traits of magic. . . . What then is the character which distinguishes theism from magic? Just one: the personification of magic as a distinct will. . . ." (*Ibid.*, p. 331) ". . . In a word, the character of Islam has been to reduce the role of rites that risk stifling consciousness of the desire . . . we say even that God is nothing but this desire which it objectifies, which it projects outside of us, as the savage does with his mana." (*Ibid.*, my translation, p. 595).

174. "Orthodox Islam . . . has pushed back as much as it could complicated rituals and systems of belief that attach themselves to it, i.e., myths: Moslem mythology is excessively poor . . . it has tended to eliminate the manual rite . . . to develop oral rite. It has tended to move rite into oral language, then into interior language, and that is the most simple expression of desire. . . . This desire which mounts toward God, is it really different from God? (p. 603) . . . And so from this desire . . . the Moslem has made Allah, the perfect being to whom he abandons himself. . . . He is nothing but the consciousness of the continual effort that is in us." (*Douttée*, my translation, p. 604).

175. Jean Cazeneuve, *Sociologie du Rite* (Paris, 1971), ch. 9.

176. Pradines, *Esprit de la Religion* (Paris, 1941), preface.

177. Cazeneuve, *op. cit.*, ch. 9.

178. Cazeneuve's 1971 book is only the latest example of the continuing vitality of the *Esquisse d'Une Théorie Générale de la Magie* in France. His ideas on sympathetic magic repeat the position of that monograph of three quarters of a century before. When you consider that the monograph was not published in book form for 50 years, that it could only

be found in the crumbling pages of back issues of *L'Année Sociologique,* the fact that it influenced so many philosophers, sociologists, historians, etc., is interesting.

179. But just as Hubert and Mauss themselves do not explicitly link sympathy effects to primitive classification systems in the *Esquisse* (that is a connection I made using Mauss' later book on classification systems), so Cazeneuve does not provide an ultimate explanation of sympathy.

180. A. M. Hocart, *Caste* (London, 1950), pp. 12–17ff.

181. Georges Gurvitch, *La Magie, La Religion et le Droit,* in *La Vocation Actuelle de la Sociologie* (Paris, 1963), vol. 2, pp. 59–174; cf. pp. 160–170.

182. *Witchcraft, Oracles and Magic Among the Azande.*

183. Robert A. Lowie, *Primitive Religion* (N.Y., 1924, 1970), pp. 3–98.

184. Louis Schneider, "The Scope of 'The Religious Factor' and the Sociology of Religion: Notes on Definition, Idolatry and Magic," *Social Research,* vol. 41, no. 2 (Summer, 1974), pp. 340–361. Schneider balances the risk of flabby equivocations that seem to extend the meaning of concepts but result in pseudo-discoveries and make concepts imprecise against strategic expansions that discover something: e.g., Sutherland's concept of "white collar crime." In this spirit, he thinks that the definition of religion should be enlarged so as to take in and include magic; this would help make magic more understandable. Cf. pp. 359-361.

185. Solomon H. Snyder, *Madness and the Brain* (N.Y., 1974). Snyder, writing about schizophrenia, surveys a century of research on every aspect: clinical, pharmacological, psychometric, etc. (chs. 4-8). He wants to find strategic explanations that can cover as much of these data as possible. He feels that the dopamine hypothesis does this: sensory overload caused by excess dopamine would explain the breakdown of abstractions, the confusing world that creates terror, the hallucinations, the flattened affect, etc. Cf. pp. 224-254.

186. Just as collective action is organized chemically among social insects–e.g., Derek Wragge Morley's identification of "excitement center" ants whose initiation of action chemically stimulates other ants to imitate their behavior–the possibility of collective human behavior depends in part on this mutual susceptibility plus the sympathy effects of symbolism that work upon it to provoke and organize group action. Morley, *The Ant World* (London, 1953). Cf. pp. 73, 76ff.

187. Ivan Illich has written of the new medical magics that have led to the "medicalization of life"; he suggests that the magic of modern scientific medicine is less healthy than the old-fashioned medical magic modelled out of religion because it is more mechanical, delivered, non-participative. Medical magic "has today turned black." Instead of mobilizing self-healing powers, it makes people depend on treatment. They lose the power to cope. Meanwhile the "miracles" of medicine are broadcast via the media all over the world, even to poor people who could never afford modern medicine. It is all very alienating. Etc. Ivan Illich, *Medical Nemesis* (Cuernavaca, 1975), *passim.*

188. Robert A. Nisbet, *The Sociological Tradition* (N.Y., 1966), pp. 21-47.

189. Esp. in Talcott Parsons, *The Social System* (N.Y., 1951).

190. Gilbert Murray, *Five Stages of the Greek Religion* (Garden City, 1955).

191. It takes the determination of a Freida Fromme-Reichmann or a Harry Stack Sullivan, patiently trying to find the hidden meaning of schizophrenic communication, to make sense of some of the "holy books," where the text sometimes disintegrates into near "word-salads."

192. Albert Camus, *La Chute* (Paris, 1956).

193. Friedrich Engels, "The Peasant War in Germany," collected in Engels, *The German Revolutions* (Chicago, 1967), pp. 3–119.

194. E. O. James, *Comparative Religion* (London, 1961), p. 67.

195. Jane Harrison insists that sacrifice is magic (*Themis,* p. 138), and she has shown that primal magic is born of the initiation rite; and in criticizing gift theories of sacrifice she emphasizes that the rite predates the gods. This suggests that it is of the same age as initiation, but she does not make the connection. She observes that sacrificial meals are another source of deities; gods emerge from sacrifice rites just as they arise from initiation rites (*Ibid.,* pp. 142-144ff). She does come very close indeed in Chapter Six, on the Dithyramb, in discussing bull sacrifices held to commemorate a new year. The Dythrambos of this rite are the same as the Kouretes or Corybantes of Zeusian rites, she says. Both are

groups of youths at their initiation stage. And she notices that Cumont has observed that initiation rites took place in the spring among the Mithraic cult. So she is demonstrating here that initiation rites, as an all-purpose magic, get used for fertility purposes, to celebrate and inspirit the new year, *and she finds sacrificial rites associated with all this*. And there is a chorus of initiation-age youths involved in the sacrifice, just as in the rite of initiation proper. The song of the Dithyrambos chorus that accompanies the bull sacrifice is similar to the song of the Kouretes; both are groups of initiation youths; and etymologically both words are linked to Zeus. Conclusion: She makes many connections but no formal statement.

196. Harrison, *Themis*, "The Kouretes, The Thunder Rites and Mana," ch. 3.

197. Mauss, "L'Origine des Pouvoirs Magiques . . . ", vol. 2, *Oeuvres*, pp. 319–369.

198. Jensen, *Myth and Cult* . . . (Chicago, 1963), pp. 219, 221, and chs. 11–12 *passim*.

199. *Yoga*, p. 363, etc.

200. *Kings and Councillors*, chs. 8–10.

201. *Sacrifice*, ch. 2.

202. *Rites of Passage*, pp. 18, 20–25, etc.

203. *The Forest of Symbols; The Ritual Process; Dramas, Fields, and Metaphors*, etc.

204. See Lienhardt on the Dinka, Evans-Pritchard on the Nuer, Lloyd Warner on the Murngin, previously cited.

205. Eliade, *Australian Religions, An Introduction* (Ithaca & London, 1973), chs. 3, 4.

206. Frazer's *The Divine King* became chapters in *The Golden Bough*.

207. With the heralds or Brahmins being those who spoke the incantations, the Kshatriyas the sacrificers, the Vaisyas the provisioners, who provided the animals for slaughter, etc. (And what about the untouchables to clean up after the exit rites?) Cf. *Kings and Councillors*, ch. 9, pp. 102–127.

208. Ernest Becker, *Escape From Evil* (N.Y., 1976), chs. 2, pp. 26–37.

209. David G. Mandelbaum, "The Family in India," *Southwestern Journal of Anthropology*, vol. 4, no. 2 (Summer, 1948). William Goode, *World Revolution and Family Patterns* (N.Y., 1963, 1970), pp. 238–247.

210. V. W. Turner, *Schism and Continuity in African Society* (Manchester, 1957). Turner's focus, however, is on *village* fission. Cf. ch. 6.

211. Georges Davy, *La Foi Jurée* (Paris, 1922), Introduction and ch. 1.

212. M. Mauss, *The Gift* (N.Y., 1967), p. 3.

213. C. Lévi-Strauss, *The Elementary Structures of Kinship* (Boston, 1969), pp. 52–68.

214. *Rites of Passage*, chs. 2–3.

215. Lévi-Strauss, *Tristes Tropiques* (N.Y., 1969), *passim*.

216. In Introd. by Arthur Vidich, to Paul Radin, *The Method and Theory of Ethnology* (N.Y., 1966), pp. xcii to xcix.

217. Frank W. Young, *Initiation Ceremonies* (Indianapolis, 1965), chs. 1, 8.

BOOK THREE

INDIVIDUALS AND SELVES

Postulate 9: MAGIC TRIES
TO PROTECT THE SELF.

Summary

Many theories associate magic with the individual and religion with society. In *Magic and Schizophrenia* Géza Róheim[1] took a great step forward—he suggested that magic *defends the individual against society,* against the superego. I have found this hypothesis enormously productive; it helps explain a great deal about the endless dialectic of magic and religion. Magic often seems to be opposed to religion, yet is made of material torn out of it, just as the individual who sometimes opposes society can only exist in its embrace. Róheim's posthumously published book is not a sport of old age, but the logical outcome of his life's work. More than that, it can be shown that he built on the orthodox psychoanalytic theory of magic. This section will begin by reconstructing the psychoanalytic theory of magic, as an introduction to the assertion that magic aided the evolution of the self. In Part Two I will suggest that, as a result of this, the human self and ego continue to have magical attributes, and that this is a further explanation for the "weak sense of magic" metaphors in psychological usage.[2] Part Three will examine phenomena like voodoo death as extreme cases to prove that what magic ultimately defends the self against is psychic death, extinction of the ego.[3] Finally, Part Four will attempt to determine *how* magic protects the ego—through its aggressive abstractions that mobilize self for action, through action itself which overcomes helplessness, through expropriated social symbolism that provides will and autonomy, through a struggle for meaning and through actual conquest of superego symbols.

In this chapter, then, we will examine the psychological side, "the self." In the next chapter we will look at the institutional framework supporting it, "the Individual," a legal-political-social complex. This section inevitably becomes a further exploration of "magic in the weak sense," in this case ego magic, while the next relates this to real magical institutions fostering individuation. Here we draw on the one discipline outside sociology which possesses an interesting *social* theory of magic: that is, psychiatry. (Paradoxically, many anthropological theories seem to be more psychologistic: such as Frazer's associationalism, Malinowski's confidence theory, and Radin's psychopathology explanation.)

PART ONE: FROM PSYCHOANALYSIS—A THEORY OF MAGIC AND SELF

In psychoanalysis there is a frequent association of magic with both symptom and ego, both illness and autonomy—the result is ambivalence. There is a strong sense that magic is infantile, dysfunctional or regressive, struggling with insights that magic is protective, saving and part of man's natural development. On the one hand Freud, Fenichel,[4] Nunberg,[5] Ferenzci,[6] Arieti,[7] etc., parallel Lévy-Bruhl, Storch [8] and Heinz Werner[9] in the formula: magic = infantile = primitive = psychotic. Thus the thinking of both small children and of primitives is "early"; neurotics are "stuck" at an early stage and psychotics "regress" to it; and it is all infantile, narcissistic, omnipotent magic thinking.[10] The infant passing from the "magical" thinking of infancy, to the "religious" formation of the Oedipal stage and the "scientific" thought of maturity (cf. Weston La Barre[11]) transparently repeats the ethnocentric ideology of evolutionary progress crystallized for Western thought by Hegel. But on the other hand, Freudian psychiatry shimmers with insights about the positive contributions of magic: in "regression in the service of the ego" (Kris[12]), in the "dynamisms" that are ego-syntonic when they work (projection, repression, etc.), in growing self-consciousness about the magical nature of curing itself.

There is a powerful sociological theory of magic in all this. Despite its ambivalence about magic, this psychoanalytic theory can be shown to be consistent (in a dialectical way). Moreover, it is sustained—just as in the Durkheim-Mauss tradition, Freudian analysts keep using their theory of magic generation after generation and keep making discoveries with it. The psychoanalytic theory of magic converges with the sociological theory—and enriches it by discovering what magic defends *against*. It is little appreciated because it is scattered through dozens of works by different authors, with an even wider surrounding penumbra of insightful metaphors of magic in general psychiatric usage for describing symptoms, ego operations, etc. The few attempts at general statement (e.g., *Totem and Taboo*[13]) have usually been failures. One exception is Róheim's *Magic and Schizophrenia*. I will try to pull this scattered theory together, beginning necessarily with the numerous references in Freud.

1. Freud's Theory of Magic

A. *Freud on Institutional Magic*

Though his greatest contributions concerned magic in the weak sense (his works on ego magic and sympathetic magic) Freud also wrote about real magic institutions, what I call the seven main provinces of magic. He used psychoanalysis to "explain away" five provinces, kept an open mind about a sixth, and self-consciously practiced within a seventh:

i. Black Magic. In "A Neurosis of Demonical Possession in the 17th Century," Freud explained away black magic as delusions projecting Oedipal ambivalence onto father symbols.[14] Primitive god figures are ambivalent, uniting good and evil, because gods are father figures to Freud and men are Oedipally ambivalent toward fathers. Therefore demons and so on are projections of the hate and fear in father-superego formations. Elsewhere, in comments on obsessionalism, Freud added that the demonic is also a projection of repressed atavism.

ii. Religious Magic. In "Obsessive Acts and Religious Practices"[15] Freud explained away religion (and hence religious magic) as obsessional neurotic ritual. In *Future of an Illusion*[16] he called religion "the universal obsessional neurosis" of mankind. He showed what he meant in *Totem and Taboo*[17]: religion works like repression in keeping down impulses to incest and cannibalism through ambivalent rituals—the way obsessional neurotic rituals both repress and express forbidden atavisms and lusts. In *Civilization and Its Discontents*[18] he described how religion derives from the father and supports with rituals the instinct deprivations on which civilization is built.

iii. The Occult Sciences.[19] This is my term for the province of the pseudo sciences, which are often generalized divination systems (I Ching, Astrology, and so on) and which further generalize into the theosophies. Freud explained all this away in the concluding chapter of *The Psychopathology of Everyday Life.*[20] There he observed that "superstition" is just psychological knowledge of inner reality projected onto outer reality. Inner reality consists of repressions and their sympathic associations—these may appear as "coincidences" when projected onto the outside world. Projecting this can be useful: for instance, divination procedures which warn a general not to fight may reflect unconscious irresolution and weakness and save him from defeat. Freud's use of an example from divination, followed by his statement that "metaphysicians merely extend superstitions,"[21] covers the whole sequence of this province: from divination to occult sciences to theosophy.[22]

iv. Ceremonial Magic. This is covered by his reductive explanation of religious magic.

v. The Magic of New Sects. Freud said little directly on this, but his account of how followers pathologically identify with a leader (in *Group Psychology and the Analysis of the Ego*[23]) is very useful in understanding the psychology of some charismatic magic movements.

vi. The Paranormal. About this province, Freud remained open-minded. In several papers on precognition and telepathy he showed[24] how most—but not all—of these phenomena could be explained away. Prophetic dreams are probably nonsense, and anyway the matter is unfalsifiable. But telepathic dreams may exist, though dreams and telepathy cannot explain each other[25] (the dream state is just more susceptible to ESP). At first Freud[26] hesitated to admit this possibility because he feared the rising occult tide as anti-scientific. Interestingly, he recognized in it an attempt to restore religion and perceived that it was bad for his movement's reputation, would ultimately be hostile to it, and was a distraction from its true rational mission. But in the later papers he admitted a possible core of reality in ESP—probably some physical mechanism, hidden by "an encrustation of fraud and superstition." But his examples were naive. He proposed, for example, that the best way to study ESP was in accounts of fortune tellers whose predictions did *not* come true: what you study is how they "telepathically" divined their clients' wishes.[27] But the medicine man's insight into this is an old folk art; sheer community gossip tells him most of what he needs to know. It is curious Freud should overvalue such data.

vii. Medical Magic. Finally, Freudian psychoanalysis had the social effect of reviving magical curing and the movement expressed some self-consciousness of this. Fenichel[28] frankly traced the magical lineage of psychoanalysis back through hypnosis to Mesmerism. (Mesmerism in turn had links to spiritualism, Swedenborg and a tradition of "strokers" going back to "the king's touch.") Freud and Fenichel claimed they were simply digging out the buried irrational in man's psyche and their techniques would grow less magical and more scientific in time. This may have happened in orthodox Freudian institutes, but culturally, Freudian psychiatry was the opening wedge for the revived prestige of magical curing.

Freud's scattered observations on the seven provinces of magic are inadequate to explain these social institutions because they are psychological reductions. They just deepen the English psychological theory of magic of the nineteenth century.[29] And Freud's attempt to provide a *general theory* of institutional magic—in *Totem and Taboo*—was a failure. This book is Freud's *"Timaeus,"* his myth of origins. *Totem and Taboo* purports to be a theory of the origin of religion, but it is also his *Genesis* of magic. The book is full of references to Frazer and sympathetic magic. It abounds in identifications between magical ritual and obsessional symptoms. Freud's theory is that religion and its magical rituals arose out of a widely repeated prehistoric crime in which a band of brothers overthrew the hominid patriarchal horde, killed and ate the father— and then established formal kinship rules (exogamy) to achieve by design what natural selection had previously achieved by instinctual savagery. They also created the totemic religion whose magic, like an obsessional neurosis, both celebrated and decried the crime, and in it they ambivalently worshipped the slain father in the form of the totem animal who gave them life when they ate it. And Freud says he means it: all this literally happened.

A priori, unfalsifiable, undocumented, the book is an exercise in mythic thinking. Since psychological reductionism cannot give an adequate account of institutional origins, myth of some sort is perhaps inevitable.

But Freud had another, less mythic theory of magic. It is more relevant to ego "magic" but has also been used to explain institutional magic reductively. This is the *narcissism* theory and it is an advance beyond mere genetic sequence. In the paper entitled "Narcissism,"[30] Freud wrote about what he called secondary narcissism. This is the stage when the incipient ego, frustrated, withdraws some cathexis from the mother and cathects itself. It is this self-love that produces the sense of omnipotence from which the magic of words and thoughts is born. Infants do this in growing up; neurotics cling to it; psychotics return to it. In "Neurosis and Psychosis"[31] and "On the Mechanism of Paranoia,"[32] the dangers of too much self-cathection are made apparent: removing love entirely from the world makes it seem unfamiliar, dangerous, demonic; moreover, the

magic no longer works. When it does work magic achieves its effects by exploiting what Baldwin calls "adualism," the confusion of inner and outer; it
works on outer by working on inner. But when a psychotic pulls it all in, when
there is nothing hanging out, he cannot get any traction on the outside by his
inner manipulations. With narcissism goes "magic thinking," the overestimation
of the power of thought and of words. These are stimulating ideas. But they are
more relevant to "magic in the weak sense," which is where Freud made his
greatest contribution, and to which we next turn.

B. Freud on Magic in the Weak Sense

Freud's best contributions were to "magic in the weak sense." These might be
classed as 1. negative (the narcissistic theory of magic as infantile thinking); 2.
neutral (his explorations of sympathetic magic); and 3. positive (how magic helps
the ego).

i. Sympathetic Magic in Freud. Consider Freud's theory of sympathetic magic
first. It is contained mainly in four monographs: *Psychopathology of Everyday Life,*[33] *Wit and Its Relation to the Unconscious,*[34] *The Interpretation of
Dreams,*[35] and *The Uncanny.*[36] The basic idea is that sympathetic magic works
because of repression—symbolic associations are dodges to escape the censor.
Freud's treatment is not only more explanatory (because psychodynamic)
than Frazer's, it is more sensitive and it contains many additional dynamisms
besides Frazer's "contiguity" and "similarity."

Consider his account of "the dream work" in chapter 6 of *The Interpretation
of Dreams.*[37] Here we find the tools of "condensation," "displacement" and
"agreement" ("just as") assisting "contiguity" and "similarity" in creating symbolic disguises to get repressed material past the censor. Also "identifications,"
"composite formations," "transformations into opposites" and "inversions."
Dreams are wish fulfillments of repressed material that slip into thought by using
the sympathetic magic associations to assume disguised form. Similar processes
are at work in the "wit work" described in *Wit and Its Relation to the Unconscious.* "Double meanings," "plays on words," "indirect expressions" and
"omissions" are additional sympathetic magic principles cited in this book as
means whereby repressed material gets past the censor.

Coincidences are also based on sympathetic magic links. In chapter 12 of *The
Psychopathology of Everyday Life*[38] Freud writes that coincidences are really
overdetermined subjective associations along sympathy links. For example, no
one can "pick a number at random" or "make up a name" for a character in a
book without the choice being overdetermined by psychic influences which
show up in free association. (Free association, by the way, might be described
as a kind of reverse sympathetic magic which exposes sympathy links in order
to dissolve their power.)

Eerie affects like "uncanniness" are also caused by repressed material
breaking through—again it slips along sympathy links to sneak into consciousness. "The uncanny"[39] is an affect accompanying this return of the repressed.

ii. Magic in Neurotic Symptoms. Freud's *negative* account of weak-sense magic is to be found in his theory of the narcissistic origin of magic—and in his idea that all neurotic symptoms *are* magic.[40] They differ from magico-religious rituals only in that they are private rather than public. Again and again, Freud designates neurotic symptoms as magic in their formation and function. The two activities that *cause* all symptom formation—"undoing" and "isolation"—are characterized as magical in both *The Problem of Anxiety* and *The Ego and The Id.*[41] In "The Wolf Man" Freud characterizes neurosis as regression to magical ideas about omnipotence of thought.[42] In *A General Introduction to Psychoanalysis,* a symptom is described as a "magical ceremony,"[43] and as "magical precautions."[44] In *Totem and Taboo,* taboos are described as repressions, above all of the *délire du toucher*[45] that expresses both sex and aggression. And there is a marvelous account here of how the repressed *spreads* in symbolic form, *along sympathetic links,* necessitating new repressions.[46] In *The Meaning of Anxiety* there is a further description of this, with each symptom symbolically expressing both the repression and the repressed.[47]

iii. Positive Ego Magic. But there is also a positive theory of psychological magic in the works of Freud. This strain is found whenever he discusses the mental dynamisms, which he characterizes both as magical and as vital to ego's equilibrium and survival. Freud has positive things to say about the effectiveness of *negation;*[48] about how *repression* is also useful when it works;[49] about *projection* as a possible road to recovery from psychosis.[50] These positive statements culminate in his ego psychology.

Freud recognized as clearly as Róheim what magic is all about—it is a defense against psychic death. I do not mean physical death (or the "denial of death" that Rank[51] and Becker[52] write about). Freud himself was quite ambivalent about Rank's idea and said, in *The Ego and the Id,* that ego has no experience of death to go on; what it fears is castration which it uses as a symbol of death.[53] And since his narcissism theory showed that the ego is born in the transfer of libido to itself, castration must be a symbol for the death of ego, not of the body. Rollo May has outlined how Freud's successive theories of anxiety shifted from fear of one's inner instincts to fear of social retaliation for their expression,[54] but Freud went further than this. At the end of *The Problem of Anxiety,*[55] he showed that anxiety is basically a return to *helplessness* (such as Spitz found children experience at eight months when they first notice separation from the mother[56]). Seligman has shown that helplessness *is* ego death and can cause physical death.[57] I will return to this.

Especially in "The Uncanny," Freud shows that what magical operations like repression fight against is psychic death. Consider the various themes that cause uncanniness. The sandman[58] or bogeyman is a father figure threatening castration. Dismemberment also suggests castration. The double also perhaps refers to the dethroned father of the repressed Oedipus complex, another castration threat.[59] And Freud has written that castration is a symbol of death. Incidents of repetition suggest the repetition compulsion which, because it can override the pleasure principle, evokes the death wish.[60] The uncanny is also evoked by anything which reactivates magical structures of consciousness. Freud does not say *why* but it may be because both the threat and defenses against it evoke memory of one another. Magic always reminds us of magic's original purpose, which was to defend us from psychic death, so magic itself seems uncanny. Our affect is uncanniness rather than fear because of repression: the uncanny is something swarmingly familiar that has been made mysteriously unfamiliar by repression. But what we are afraid of in all these manifestations is psychic death, and this is what magic mechanisms fight in their defense of the ego.

2. Some Orthodox Freudians

Other psychoanalysts developed Freud's theory of the magical nature of neurotic symptoms. In a standard psychoanalytic text, Otto Fenichel emphasized the striking social effects of infants' speech in building faith in the omnipotence of words and thought.[61] Some words retain magic power in later ages: obscenities, oaths. Magical operations like undoing and isolation are the root of all mental symptoms, which in turn are seen as magical rituals (p. 153). Especially interesting is his analysis of the perversions as magical (p. 459). All this magic is infantile narcissism: phobics become helpless children again; masochists show infantile helplessness, etc. And all patients expect magic of their analysts (p. 562), whose magical powers they hope to pick up. Fenichel acknowledged that psychoanalysis itself grows out of magical healing, though it makes progress toward science (pp. 2-6). Here is a technical, influential Freudian text that uses the idea of magic as a category of explanation throughout.

Some analysts developed their own theories of magic. Sandor Ferenczi proposed[62] that children advance through four stages of increasingly adaptive magics: 1. the "unconditional magic" of the womb; 2. the "magical hallucination stage" where every wish is gratified (as in dreams); 3. magic omnipotence of gestures (childlike kicking and screaming); 4. the omnipotence of word magic. In other words, from primal to image to motor to verbal magic. On this framework Nunberg erected[63] a paradigm of mental illnesses as regressions, with the most serious, schizophrenia, corresponding to regression to square one, the helpless magic of the womb; paranoia as regression to square two, magical hallucination; hysteria going back to the magical gesture stage and obsessions regressing to thought and word omnipotence.

Like Fenichel, Nunberg produced an orthodox text, *Principles of Psychoanalysis*,[64] and it is interesting that he reconstructed Freud's narcissistic theory of magic in his chapter on the ego.[65] Neurotic regression takes the form, Nunberg writes, of acting increasingly on oneself in order to affect the world, returning thereby to the magical omnipotence of childhood "dual unity." All magic is accompanied by feelings of omnipotence which reveal its origins in childhood narcissism. Omnipotence is always a sign that "objects are missing," that ego is withdrawing love from the world and putting it on itself. To Nunberg, magic is thoroughly regressive and dysfunctional; he associates it with the id. In extreme magical regression, id conquers ego and the schizophrenic experiences his instincts as overpowering magic to which he must submit; he feels magically influenced, Nunberg writes, whereas healthy people get along without magic.[66] But many people renounce childhood magic only conditionally; they hope to get it back when they grow up. Neurotics seek it through treatment. Nunberg repeats Freud's idea that neurotic symptoms are magical rituals and that they in turn are created by the magical activities of undoing and isolating.[67] In another paper,[68] Nunberg views homosexuality as a magic device to develop power, an idea we encounter also in Rank,[69] Becker[70] and others. Both magical symptoms and ego magic are viewed darkly by Nunberg, as regressions to childish, pleasure-driven structures of consciousness. This is typical of most orthodox Freudian analysts.

The "Magic Thinking" Group

The negative thrust is also found in the students of "magic thinking," though some are French and influenced by Durkheim and Mauss. One whole issue of *Revue Française de Psychanalyse* (1934)[71] was devoted to the subject, with articles on "magic thought among primitives" (Marie Bonaparte[72]), "magic thought in daily life" (H. Codet[73]), "magic thought in religion" (R. Laforgue[74]), "magic thought in neurosis" (J. Leuba[75]). Charles Odier's *L'Angoisse et la Pensée Magique*[76] built on Baldwin's "adualism" and Piaget's "infantile realism" idea — the infant's confusion between himself and his mother — to define magic as working on the inside world to get effects on the outside. Sartre built his theory of his emotions[77] as magical action performed on the self on similar ideas.

More positive was Bastide's *Sociologie et Psychanalyse,*[78] which propounded a dualism of social representations and organic libido and suggested that magic thinking was a necessary "libidinization" of symbolism which gave it spontaneity. This theory intimately associated magic with the springs of human action, as Róheim did. Magic does derive from collective representations, as Mauss explained, with sympathy links given by tradition; but sex is also "deep," rooted in biology, Bastide writes. Through the "magical" libidinization of symbols (in narcissism), social symbolic networks are kept alive and lively. Magic is therefore a strategic subject for understanding individual spontaneity.

This is certainly a positive note, but most "magic thinking" students stressed the infantile or the pathological. In *The Child's Conception of Physical Causality,*[79] Piaget showed how children advance from magic conceptions to mechanical-logical ones; in *The Moral Judgment of the Child,*[80] they advance from "animistic" to abstract ideas of morality;[81] in *Play, Dreams and Imitation in Childhood,*[82] magic is associated with the egocentrism a child must outgrow to progress from "preconcepts to concepts."[83] In Odier this viewpoint is most severe. Magic is regression to infantile adualism in which the patient confuses self and other, inner and outer, and so acts maladaptively on himself instead of the real world. Magic is *not* an effective defense against anxiety, but more a symptom of it, so dysfunctional in fact that it can *cause* anxiety. This is Sartre's view, too: magic is like taking drugs, acting on one's own mind instead of the world. It just does not work. It is very important to keep these dysfunctions in mind during the argument about positives that will follow: No doubt about it, there is a sick magic, and probably most magic is sick, at least today. The magic of neurotic symptoms is conspicuous in a sick society where individuals have lost their symbolic powers and magic is turned against the self to make it "sit still" (T. S. Eliot). In a rationalized, bureaucratic society magical action will not even communicate. If you are fired by the computer or the management-cost committee, expressing emotions or assaulting magical-mental images of your opponents in your own mind—or even making threats—will not get you anywhere.

3. Róheim's Positive Theory of Magic

Some analysts responded to the positive theory of magic implicit in Freud. It remained for Róheim to pull it all together in a powerful book published after his death: *Magic and Schizophrenia.*[84] Róheim's career developed against a background of growing concern that psychoanalysis itself might somehow weaken the ego. Stekel purposely attempted to shorten the course of treatment lest the ego be weakened; Ferenczi and Franz Alexander[85] for similar reasons experimented with brief psychotherapy. Rank[86] wrote of the ego impairment and cultural loss of nerve as psychoanalysis exaggerated self-consciousness about the self. Szasz suggested that psychoanalysis in the courtroom, by undermining due process, might weaken the institution of the Individual which supports the self.[87] Róheim's own increasing concern was with the superego, which he identified with the death wish and which he found constantly strengthened by the institutions of this world. In a remarkable passage in *Psychoanalysis and Anthropology,*[88] he identified the ethical "reformist" world religions that Weber celebrated for driving out magic with the paternal superego that punishes the child's magical pleasures.[89] In *The Gates of the Dream*[90] he attributed anxiety dreams to the superego overcoming the dream work's necessary job (of rebuilding ego's world through infantile regression) by reminding it of infantile helplessness. All this implies a critique of culture; Róheim met the challenge in *The Origin and Function of Culture*[91]; all culture is neurosis and "national character" is just superego distortion. (This is close to Wilhelm Reich's position.[92]) In *Psychoanalysis and Anthropology,* Róheim anticipated Marcuse's idea that while civilization may be based on repression, the repression becomes excessive,[93] more than necessary. In a concluding chapter Róheim became shrill, identifying superego with death itself.[94] In death, he writes, superego is finally triumphant: a corpse can neither fight nor love nor think.[95] In *Magic and Schizophrenia,* therefore, Róheim reminded psychoanalysts of their original mission to work against the superego, with the id.[96]

Rank, Stekel and Róheim were voices crying in the wilderness. An inexorable social process was assimilating psychoanalysis to the medical establishment and allying it with the superego. The average length of psychoanalytic treatment increased; neurotics were increasingly diagnosed more gravely as "neurotic characters" and in America especially the category of "pseudo-neurotic psychotic" became popular.

Róheim's concern over superego pressure was one mainspring of his theory of magic. Here is a parallel point: Róheim remained like Reich, like the original Freud, basically an id-psychologist. He developed even his ego theory mainly out of id components.[97] His theory of magic curing is an id psychology in terms of oral, anal and genital fixations; his dream theory is an id theory. This emphasis, too, made him willing to find positive values in magic.

It is wrong therefore to suppose that *Magic and Schizophrenia* was a break in Róheim's thinking. Róheim was an orthodox Freudian analyst who was also a Ph.D. professor of anthropology. He began his anthropology as an armchair theorist in the 19th century manner; then late in life did extensive fieldwork, thus combining "the best of both worlds," as Robinson put it[98]: bold theorizing with first-hand empirical detail. In the field he psychoanalyzed primitives, observed their sex lives, analyzed their dreams. The fertility of psychoanalytic insight reaches one of its peaks in Róheim: his brilliant interpretations of myths, dreams, art and culture, which are so convincing because the outcomes are overdetermined, remind us what an advance in human understanding was provided by Freud's method. Robinson claims that Róheim gradually drifted away from Freud's Oedipus toward Malinowski's functionalism; I find little evidence for this, unless Robinson is misinterpreting Róheim's great interest in pre-Oedipal stages, typical of his generation. In late books we still find him using Oedipal theory to explain the Adam and Eve myth,[99] the Job story,[100] the Faust legend.[101] The truth is that Róheim remained an orthodox Freudian and that is why he was able to discover a positive theory of magic, for the thing was implicit in Freud's writings. It was this that enabled him to go "beyond Malinowski," as he put it.

The roots of his theory are there in his earlier researches. To summarize: 1. One element was his growing concern with superego pressure, developed especially in *Psychoanalysis and Anthropology.* 2. Another was his idea, in *The Origin and Function of Culture,* that mankind's long infancy constitutes an extended foetalization that makes him susceptible to both neurosis and civilization.[102] (The implication is that there is something creative in infantilism.) 3. A third trend was Róheim's positive valuation of the primary process, of the id, which shows up in his books on dreams.[103] From Ferenczi's theory of *Thalassa* (sexual intercourse as return to the womb), he derived a theory of id regression in the service of the self.[104] 4. A fourth interest was his long-term preoccupation with magic curing, interpreted in id psychology terms in *Animism, Magic and The Divine King.*[105] Here Róheim, in his attempt to understand magical thinking, practically adopted it himself, rephrased in psychoanalytic language. The medicine man, he wrote, is correct to interpret illness as "soul loss"—for libido is soul and it *is* diffused and "lost," locked up in bad fixations. It needs to be released in the sexualized transference of the patient to the witchdoctor.

In ideas like these, Róheim found positive functions for id magic, for regression. Therefore Freud's theory that magic is narcissism, or a throwback to the infantile, did not condemn magic in his mind. To Róheim, in fact, most myths are about fruitful magical regressions that evade the superego's punishment in order to gain independence: Job overcomes the good-bad father (Lucifer and Yahweh are really one), by his good-little-boy sacrificial stance.[106] Faustian pacts with the devil are really magical treaties with the superego to allow the self to experience infantile pleasure for a little while longer—until guilt overwhelms it.[107] What is at issue in Adam and Eve is the emerging ego's attempt to become independent and to act.[108] Superego, the "internal saboteur," forever says to ego: "You cannot. You must not." And ego forever goes on trying to act independently, because magical narcissism has made it able to withstand separation anxiety. Superego pursues ego all through life as thanatos pursues eros. In modern civilizations, superego becomes embodied in cold reason, Blake's "Urizon," the "sedimented rationality" of Marcuse.[109] Modern man revolts against Urizon and turns to magic, to "the resurrection of the body" (Brown[110]), to the deliberately irrational (Marcuse), even to the psychopath (Mailer[111]). Magic remains the "home brew" (Ernest Becker) of the ego, its first and also last recourse in its struggle to be. Thus magic forever fights the sense of helplessness that superego keeps trying to instill, and ego forever lives by magic and loves by magic.

Róheim finally pulled this all together in *Magic and Schizophrenia.* Just as Marx believed that Marxism was the outcome of Western philosophy, I believe that Róheim's theory of magic—and not the occultism of Jung on the one hand or the watered-down pragmatism of the psychiatric practitioner on the other—is the logical outcome of Freud's meta-psychology of id and ego: a theory of the magic self.

Róheim's Magic and Schizophrenia. In this work, Róheim puts his ideas together in a theory of ego magic. If sexualization of the self gives ego the courage to withstand separation, if the magic omnipotence of thought which this narcissism inspires gives ego confidence in his projects, then perhaps magic is the mid wife that assists at the birth of the ego. If mankind's long foetalization produces a creative neotony; if magical self-love enables the ego to act creatively despite the superego; if action on the inner world somehow rehearses action in the real world, then magic is not futile. It is the superego, enshrined at last as cold reason, that tells us we cannot and must not, that we must give up our projects; but just as the id warms us with pleasure and nourishes our will to live, the narcissistic magic it passes on to us gives us the courage to act spontaneously in the dangerous real world. Magic, therefore, is the very beginning of action; action begins in the magic protoaction of fantasy, delusion, dream and magical thinking.

In this book Róheim goes beyond Malinowski's notion that magic gives confidence in uncertain actions, to say that ego operations he calls "magic" are performed *before action of any kind whatsoever.* They give the actor confidence in his ability to perform in the real world. Róheim even goes further and portrays magic as the basis of all human *thought* and *speech* as well as *action.* Man's prolonged "refoetalization" makes him dependent and in constant danger of ego collapse. Magic thought, speech and imaginary action push outward against all that. *"Magic is...the counterphobic attitude,"* he writes, *"the transition from passivity to activity."* As such it is probably the basic element in thought and the initial phase of any activity.[112]

Róheim is in the mainstream when he speaks of the "magic" of infantile speech. Many psychologists, such as Selma Fraiberg,[113] characterize the child's experience of witnessing his speech affecting others as "magical": The child utters sounds, and the mother reacts.[114] Róheim portrays this in romantic language which interestingly lapses into metaphors about religion.[115] And thereby he gives hints of what magic defends against—hints that are more explicitly developed in Stekel.[116] In both there is talk of "winning over the superego." These ideas represent, in psychiatric language, the same discoveries made by the Durkheim school, that magic "expropriates" social symbolism on behalf of the ego:

> It is the superego that tells the ego, "You are a coward or have no heart or brain." But if the superego is won over, all is well again. (Róheim, *op. cit.,* p. 46)

Róheim finds authority in Freud to formulate a theory of magic as the basis of action:

> Freud (1911) has defined thinking as "an experimental way of acting." Hermann (1940) has described thinking as the process in which the mental image is separated from the object and independently manipulated. (p. 201). . . . We suggest, therefore, that *thinking,* which at its apex is very much an ego activity, is deeply rooted in the libido, and that in between the two we must place the mental image as magic. It means both "away from the object" and (by means of the image) "back to the object". . . . Words constitute the path to reality, to the world of objects. (p. 203). . . . Magic is the counterphobic attitude, the transition from passivity to activity. (p. 18, Róheim, *op. cit.*)

The infant is totally dependent on the mother, almost a part of her. Then he begins to separate, and inevitably experiences some frustration. The ingested "bad mother" who frustrates him is "the first superego formation" (the later one will be Oedipal). The child reacts against frustration with aggression. But of what aggression is an infant capable? All he can do is to remove some love from the mother. And where can he "put" this libido, having no world beyond his mother? He puts it on himself and so discovers himself; he "cathects" himself and so begins his ego. Róheim formulates this in psychiatric apocalyptic language: "At the stage of secondary narcissism, the ego withdraws libido from the mother and cathects itself . . . " And that is the beginning of the self, and of its biological rootedness that gives it a place to stand as against the social symbolic consensus.[117]

This primal act of self-love is the basis for the later importance of the castration complex: Castration fear easily translates into the threat of psychic death, because the self originally took nourishment from this sexual base in resisting society at the moment of its emergence.[118]

Róheim (and other analysts) are reporting that something which they must call "magic" arises at the moment when an individual monad separates from the cosmos of mother-society. Van Gennup[119] has shown that magic arises along fault lines where groups split apart; Marwick has shown[120] that it crackles in such areas of separation as lineage fission. It is not surprising that it also arises when an individual is coming into being from the womb of society. Magic fights separation anxiety by counterphobic action, Róheim tells us.[121]

The "Magic Principle." Magic works by exploiting the "dual unity situation," the fact that in early years the child cannot well distinguish himself from his mother, or his inside world from the outside world. Róheim uses this in his definition of what he calls the *magical principle*, which stands between the pleasure principle and the reality principle.[122] It works precisely by dealing with the outside world as if it were governed by our own wishes or thoughts. This attitude, unrealistic at a limit, is the only way we can achieve something in reality: "Certainly, if we do not believe that we *can* get what we want, even that we can get it *because* we want it, we could not get it simply on the basis of realistic action (alone)." Thinking of Durkheim's "Homo Duplex" essay,[123] we might add that "adualism" is to some degree realistic because what happens in one's mind really is, partly, "out there" it is part of the social system inside of us.

The magical principle works because it *is* action, mental "action" in the Weberian sense, which is already the beginning of "social action," mental action directed against the first outposts of social reality which are inside us. For example, a man embarking upon a course of aggression against someone with whom he has been close, has already begun to act when he attacks his own mental representations of that person and tries to undo his grip upon him. This explains the common report that shamans achieve their magical powers initially through the conquest of severe psychological illnesses: this can be understood as a partial conquest of the social part of themselves.

Only at a limit does the magic strategy fail. To Róheim, schizophrenia is the pure magic which is sterile magic because adualism has been abandoned for pure solipsism. Obsessional magic is half successful magic that has become rigid and repetitive. The implication is that there is also a "normal" magic in which the magical principle turns passivity into activity, develops mental symbolic plans of action which issue into the outside world. Historically, magic has shrunk, falling back before the priests and then before the scientists. The implication is similar to the suggestion of Stanley Diamond: In complex civilizations in which man's symbolic powers are alienated, magic retreats, crippled, to its psychological base, and the obsessional-compulsive neurosis spreads rampantly.

4. Stekel: Magic Fights Religion As Superego

The idea that magic fights social pressure, superego, even religion, is more explicit in Stekel, especially in *Compulsion and Doubt*,[124] his study of the obsessional-compulsive neurosis. Many psychiatrists have felt it natural to describe the spectacular symptoms of this neurosis in metaphors of magic. Harry Stack Sullivan[125] alleged that the compulsive was once a child who had frightening and unpredictable parents and learned that he could "magically" control their behavior with words—*up to a point*. Thus compulsives try to control events through word formulas— and hence always the "doubt," because "it doesn't always work."[126] Freud's interpretation of obsessionalism went in terms of the degradation of the impulse due to damage in repression, with consequent unbinding of the aggressions (Thanatos) and return of the repressed.

Out of so many rich ideas, the one to hold on to for the moment, because Stekel's argument is built on it, is Freud's idea that religion is the obsessional neurosis of mankind and conversely that the neurosis itself is a kind of "private religion" for the obsessional, devoted to trying to constrain his aggressive impulses. But to Stekel the obsessional is just anti-social enough to be *sorry* that his private religion succeeds in containing his aggressions (and that is another reason for doubt[127]). For Stekel this private religion is an apostasy. As shorthand I will call it a "pseudo-superego" though Stekel does not use this term. Taking off from Freud's emphasis on the atavism of obsessionals, Stekel speculates that the obsessional is not fully socialized; he borrows energy to build his pseudo-superego from what would have developed into the legitimate superego (which is strongly reminiscent of Mauss-Huvelin ideas of magic as the expropriation of the sacred). He is only to a small degree less out of step than the psychopath: not having a true social conscience, he builds a fake one. For one thing, it is at all times conscious; and it is at the heart of his structure of symptoms. Its main purpose, the one the neurotic will speak about, is to prevent "harm to other people"; but behind this, as Stekel, Freud and Rollo May[128] report, is his real fear, which is of the counter-aggression that his aggressions would provoke. The structure has some survival value; it is a "private religion" that disciplines behavior to keep the obsessional out of trouble. In his heart, however, he hates society, and—Stekel cannot avoid the metaphor—he hates "religion."[129] His associate, Gutheil, underscores this:

> The basic attitude of the compulsive neurotic is directed against religion. He counters established religion with a religion of his own coinage. (p. 18) . . . The stronger the resistance to inner anti-social and anti-moral impulses, the greater the inclination to blasphemy. . . . This often results in a fear of entering the house of worship. (p. 19, Emil Gutheil, Preface & Introd. to *Compulsion and Doubt*, pp. 1–34)

Stekel's account of the individual forming itself as a logos against the totality is striking—and it is followed by other passages which imply that compulsion neurosis is magic, and that *it entails stealing the sacred power of the deity:*

> The life of the compulsive neurotic is but a series of oracles. A small change of posture or of an everyday routine may be good or bad luck. (*Ibid.*, p. 45). . . . By adherence to superstition man endows himself with mystical power. He steals the power of the Deity. (p. 49)

Róheim and Stekel have rediscovered in man's psychology what sociologists find on the institutional level: 1. That magic steals sacred symbolism and authority from religion and society (in this case, from the superego). 2. That it then turns this apparatus against religion, against society. But the psychiatric theorists have in addition discovered something that the sociologists missed, namely, a *reason* for the struggle with religion. French sociologists such as Huvelin, who speaks of magic's *"detouring"* of religious mana, or Hubert and Mauss, who speak of magic's "expropriation," are not completely clear on why the theft occurs. The reason for giving so much attention to the psychiatrists is that they have found the answer: Magic expropriates religious power and uses it against religion, *in order to defend the self against religion, against society, against the superego, which at all times threaten to implode the self and snuff it out.*

Róheim and Stekel emphasize that magical expropriation is used to defend the self against social pressure. Hubert and Mauss only have inklings of this; they speak glancingly of magic being used to *"échapper à la pression social,"*[130] but they do not make much of it. That is why the frequently reported, massively documented clinical evidence from the psychiatrists that magical symptoms are defenses against the superego and hence society itself, are so important. Sociology has already shown us that magic steals fire from religion and uses it to fight religion. Now psychiatry shows us why: magic fights to defend the individual ego against the social group from which it is born but which is capable of disintegrating it by the least pressure. The stolen fire, as the Prometheus legend tells us, is used to defend man, individual man—against the gods, the logos, the nomos, the superego, the society—to defend man's spontaneity against his socialization.

What it comes down to is a matter of life or death. At a limit, in a showdown, what magic defends the self against is death. But before demonstrating that, it is necessary to examine what the self is.

PART TWO: WHAT IS THE SELF THAT MAGIC DEFENDS?

What is the self? The self tends to be what the historically evolving "person category" says it is—and speculation about it affects its nature, in the Heisenberg manner.[131] Nonetheless, most cultures have converging ideas about the contents of the self, and empirical evidence does suggest that "something is there." But the models are bewilderingly diverse, especially in our time—Freud's "ego, id and superego"; Reich's three tiers of "natural, nasty and nice" with nice sitting on top wearing its forced smile; Jung's "shadow, anima, animus," etc. These models have to be sorted out just to agree on *nomenclature*. The entities proliferate; they seem unreal; yet each school has its tests to prove they are there—ego disturbances to reveal the unconscious id for the Freudians, loaded verbal instructions to reveal the latent person for "personalists" like Gordon Allport, etc. Rapaport,[132] Gordon Allport,[133] Anna Freud[134] have summarized some of this empirical evidence, much of it self-fulfilling, guaranteed by the circularity of definitions-and-tests. In the end one is tempted to treat these "scientific" paradigms as data in the Margaret Mead manner.[135] Like Mauss, we should seek to show how self ideas evolve historically.[136] Like Rank,[137] we should ask whether present-day ego models strengthen or weaken the self.

The self was originally a collection of magical metaphors derived from religious ritual that helped elicit a spontaneity society then required: soul recovery for soul loss, etc. Today "Oedipus," "ego," "identity" etc. are at very least equally effective metaphors that bring forth something which our culture agrees can pass as healthy self behavior.

The self is usually thought to consist of several "institutions" on different planes of consciousness. Thus we have the conscious, preconscious and unconscious (not to mention Jung's collective unconscious, various hyperconscious states and Sartre's pseudo-unconscious plane of "bad faith"). Peopling these planes we find some collection like ego, superego and id. Id is unconscious, and ego is partly conscious, partly unconscious. (In early Freud, ego is entirely conscious; in late Freud it is both conscious and unconscious; to Anna Freud it becomes more unconscious in operations in which it gradually buries itself; to Hartmann,[138] by contrast, ego *emerges from* an unconscious biological root. Erikson[139] finally buries ego totally in the unconscious.)

The partial derivation of ego psychology from romantic German philosophy (with its Eastern influences) reminds us of the outcome of Hindu Atman-philosophy, in which a feverish preoccupation with self puffed up the self and everted it.[140] Rank warns that ego psychology could pose a threat to the self.[141] He claims that Freud showed neurosis is based on pathological self-knowledge (the weakness of the repression mechanism) and worries that psychiatric self-knowledge feeds this neurotic self-consciousness. Rank links the soul to magic[142] (through its link to will, which he identifies with mana) and suggests that insight therapy is destructive of the magical will that powers the self. Therefore the patient's final separation from psychoanalysis is "the really human step, away from all that binds."[143]

It is perhaps no coincidence that the no-Atman of Wittgenstein, Ryle and "philosophical psychology" appears in the same generation as ego psychology,[144] just as the no-Atman philosophy of Buddhism appeared along with the puffed-up "self" of Hinduism. Mauss wondered what the self might become tomorrow. It might become something that is worried to death and then abandoned as non-existent.

Convergence of Models

Despite confusions about details, there are transcultural convergences. We find in most civilizations and even in primitive societies the following regularities in models of the self:

1. Most societies postulate that the self is multiple. Storch thought this a sign of the ego weakness of primitives, but it is found in world civilizations as well.

Ancient Egypt had the *ka* (a corporeal double, guardian genius in the hereafter) and the *ba* (a soul released at death that came to mean logos, life, breath[145]). Hertz[146] alleges universality for two souls: one is a duplicate of the body, another spiritual which cannot be released until the body has wasted (then the second burial[147]). Populating a self with several different "institutions" such as id, ego, superego is not a modern eccentricity.

2. *The multiple selves are generated by a few universal dichotomies.* Lévy-Bruhl[148] and Durkheim[149] on personal vs. group totems illustrate the fundamental dualism, which is the personal vs. the social individual. That always gives rise to two souls. But two is only the minimum number. Roger Westcott[150] explores some of the other dichotomies: e.g., mortal vs. immortal. Gnostic dualisms also multiply souls: we have good and bad selves. (Not all are isomorphic to one another.) Minimal philosophical consciousness also produces the I/Me discovery in both East and West: Augustine, Plato, James, Mead, Sartre, etc. in the West, Atman philosophy in the East. There is a kind of logic of possibility here, and selves continue to be multiplied by philosophical analysis. Thus the medieval philosopher Avicebrun, pondering Aristotle's distinction of form vs. matter and the Christian distinction of soul vs. body, crossed them so that both soul and body *each* had a form and a matter, thereby producing four entities. This was called "universal hylomorphism."[151] It might be said, there is a lot of "universal hylomorphism" going around, multiplying ideas of self. Such ideas affect what the self is felt to be and comes to be.

3. *Most cultures link the different institutions of self to different grades of consciousness.* Freud was not the first to speak of an "unconscious" id, a "conscious" ego and so on.[152] The new research on "altered states of consciousness" reminds us how old such ideas are. Thus Upanishadic thought identified the highest state of self (*Brahman*) with dreamless sleep, the conscious self with the ego as a role in *Mâya*, and meditation with transcendent consciousness.[153] Formulations waver, however. Westcott attempts a modern synthesis linking ego to the waking state, *Brahman* to deep sleep, id to dreaming REM sleep, superego with trance, and the oversoul or "Atman" to "released" or higher states.[154] He even relates the different grades of consciousness to phylogenetic stages: with sleep (low torpid consciousness) coming first in man's evolution; then the entranced state of trance dancers and group action (e.g., pyramid builders); then ego, with the released state waiting the future superman.[155]

4. *There is a time dimension in the multiplication of selves.* Totems are *ancient* guardian spirits. Archetypes are *old.* Freud stresses that the superego is the "transmitter of tradition." More schematic is Erikson's distinction of superego from Freud's virtually interchangeable term, "ego ideal." In Erikson's [156] usage, superego is really "the superego of one's parents"; it is a totally unconscious archaic element. Ego ideal is a more "historical" dimension. It tends to be preconscious; it gets influenced by each generation's experiences. To this we might add Lecky's ideas about the self-image,[157] which cover the *biographical* part of the self's time dimension, and is conscious. Finally, in the instantaneous present, there is the "I," which is pure "now" and time-transcendent. We could construct a

coordinate system with grade-of-consciousness on the Y axis (unconscious, preconscious, conscious, transcendent) and the time dimension on the X axis (archaic, historical, biographical, immediate). Then we could imagine a function of the form X = Y intersecting a series of squares to give us the "temporal-consciousness vector" of ego, running from *archaic unconscious superego,* through *historical preconscious ego ideal,* to *biographical conscious self image,* to *instantaneous pure-conscious I.*[158]

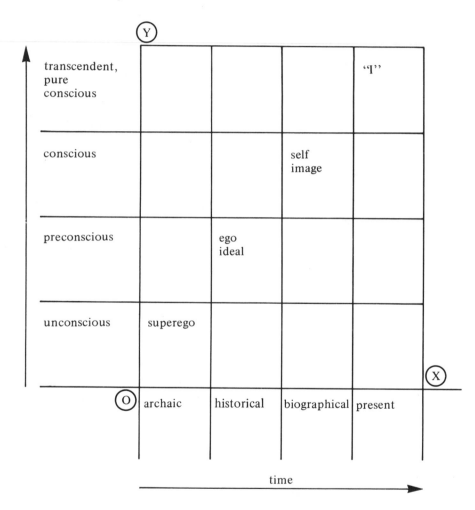

The Self Model of Modern Ego Psychology

It is sometimes suggested that there is no self, or hardly any self, just a collection of processes, as Gilbert Ryle[159] and the philosophical psychologists slice it. Or perhaps there is just barely enough self organization to cope interpersonally, and too great an inner reality is pathological, as the behaviorist sociologists and psychiatrists sometimes suggest (Becker, Sullivan, Laing, etc.). But these formulations, for all their seeming agnosticism, are no less dogmatic-metaphysical or self-fulfilling than other self models. The no-Atman demonstrations of Wittgenstein require an attitude as artificial as old-fashioned introspectionist psychology, with its "stimulus error" rules.[160] And behaviorist ego psychology, such as Ernest Becker's,[161] is pure abstract interactionism, built up from ideal types. Behaviorism, under attack on its own ground for operationalist circularities, conceptual tautologies and solipsistic self-confirming experimental design (e.g., Merleau-Ponty's critique[162]), is born again in sociology through the mediation of prestigious philosophy (e.g., Becker gets it from G. H. Mead and Dewey[163]). The behaviorist, black-box, virtually-empty self is perhaps more descriptive of primitive, psychotic or infantile selves in which ego is little developed than of constituted adult modern selves.

For this and other reasons, I will build on orthodox Freudian ego psychology, which, despite didactic detail, is more agnostic than it is usually represented. Psychoanalytic models have some advantages: they attempt to describe complex, modern, constituted selves. They are the empirical products of a scientific psychotherapy. Their creators also explicitly drew on man's philosophical heritage, East and West. They were sensitive to anthropological knowledge as well. Psychoanalytic models therefore incorporate convergences in self concepts found throughout history. Another advantage: Freudian ego concepts are the most influential currently in our culture; therefore they help shape what the self here actually comes to be. Whether or not there really *is* a self, Freudian therapy produces it; it produces spontaneity, will, conflict resolution, integration of behavior—just as primitive magic produced what passed for selves in primitive societies. Psychoanalysis may be self-fulfilling, but it fulfills itself by producing what it says is there, just as primitive ego magic did. Let us therefore pick out some key points from Freudian ego psychology that will at least help develop a model of nomenclature for discussing selves:

1. *The psychoanalytic model takes account of gaps in the self.* The three Freudian "institutions" of the self—ego, id, superego—have become so familiar that the popular mind tends to think of the Freudian self as a snug house filled up with fully furnished rooms. But the Freudian self is really more like a barely explored continent: The id is unknown territory which we can only infer, from distortions it causes in the ego, as Anna Freud showed.[164] The superego is either deeply unconscious and hence equally unnoticeable (Freud[165]), or else it is so "in synch" with the ego that it is not noticed (Anna Freud[166]), so it too must usually be inferred. Id, superego and the unconscious part of the ego together make up most of the self—most of the self is therefore inaccessible to consciousness. Much of it, moreover, has no organization: the id has no structure at all except a few earthworks thrown up in the dark here by ego against the instincts. These hidden ego constructions grow wobbly, come apart; then the debris spreads, via sympathetic magic, and magical symptoms erupt from the depths ("return of the repressed"). Borders between the institutions collapse; ego is an organ of the id, a surface perhaps; but it easily slips back into the id (in psy-

chosis) or the two extravasate into each other in character disorders. And there are large areas totally unknown, about which Freud often said, "We don't know."

The picture the model conveys is of a mostly submerged continent, whose shores are partly colonized by an abstract ego structure feebly trying to extend some organization inland but always at the expense of building underwater, alienating itself in the unconscious, a largely unknown continent where the sullen superego lies buried like a minefield, where drives conflict and where ego has built its sandcastles of repression pitting pleasure against pain. Conclusion: the Freudian self model takes considerable account of gaps, uncertainties and sheer amorphism in the self.

2. *How odd the ego.* There is something very strange about an entity that builds itself out of nothing. Although later Freudian ego psychologists (Erikson, Hartmann) accorded the ego independent genetic roots, Freud's earliest ego theories defined that entity as having virtually no resources of its own. The ego has to make itself, "magically," out of other things. Basically it is constituted out of its identifications, a process similar to Mead's "mirroring of significant others,"[167] but more elaborate, with actual love involvement, followed by withdrawal from the object with its image taken into the personality as a modification of the ego. How can ego, with no energy of its own, repress anything? Freud's solution was "withdrawal of cathexis,"[168] removal of love and interest from a topic. But how could ego persuade the id to give up its attachments? Freud regarded anxiety as an ego signal working via the pleasure principle (*unlust*) to whip the id into line. At first anxiety was supposed to be created by sheer transformation of libido, denatured by repression. Later this position was reluctantly given up for the idea that ego emits the painful anxiety signal by purposely *remembering* previous painful anxieties[169] — above all, the separation anxiety of eight months (Spitz). Ego was also supposed to develop its own energies in the form of auto-cathexis (which required desexualization of libido with the inconvenient result of unbinding the death instinct). The problem of ego energy puzzled psychoanalysis, with Hartmann[170] finally claiming that ego has inborn energies of its own. But even in Hartmann, we get a picture of a *bricoleur* ego, magically synthesizing bits and pieces of experiences. The conscious part of ego's repressions, for example, remains as autonomous structures put to other uses; Hartmann complacently calls these the "secondary adaptation processes;" Anna Freud offers an example in the "intellectualization" with which ego fights masturbation during latency, which is available as a tool of thought. But what about the inconvenient links these badly-wired structures maintain with the repressed?

It is not surprising that a jerry-built structure so flimsy, made of borrowed energies, discarded loves and fragments of outdated defensive operations should be subject to amazing vicissitudes. The most remarkable is sudden death: ego can just up and die and take the living organism to the grave with it (voodoo death). Ego structures can turn into their opposites; libido and affects can be transformed; ego can give up and join the id (in psychosis).

But there are deeper paradoxes which perhaps proceed from Freud's philosophical preoccupations. The ego is the sensitive, outward-turning, perceptive tip of the id, but in *Beyond the Pleasure Principle* Freud also likens it to an external membrane, like a fingernail, that gets so "baked through" by stimuli in its job of screening out stimuli that it "dies" or almost dies, becoming a quasi-inanimate layer protecting life (shades of Mâya ideas, or Reich on the "deadness" of character). Freud literally suggests that nerve cells perhaps grew out of membrane cells and notes that the cerebral cortex is a kind of membrane of the brain. Alive but also somehow "dead," ego is subject to other paradoxes as well: It expresses Eros and seeks self-preservation, but works partly through ego energies derived from desexualizing libido with consequent unbinding of the death impulse. The result is that Freud associates ego with death.[171] The reverberations of German romantic philosophy in that idea continue today in ideas of consciousness as a killer,[172] in Rank, Dewey,[173] etc. The ego is alive but dead, a life-preserver but also a killer. In addition, it is both personal and impersonal. It is impersonal because it is in touch with reality, guided by the "reality principle" and gradually filled up by the "secondary process" (society's logicalization of symbols).

There is actual chaos here. The ego can take a lifetime to get itself organized and there are many botches. Conflict is the rule. "Secondary adaptation structures" which derive from old defensive operations maintain secret conflicts of interest to old repressions. Identifications conflict with each other; and the superego punishes some of them (in melancholia). Ego erects both repressions and reaction formations in the unconscious id; the successful ones are out of its reach; the unsuccessful ones proliferate symptoms. Ego takes some of these symptoms into itself as part of its own Gothic architecture; and Erikson has shown how every story of the building can be warped by unsuccessful resolution of life's key conflicts. And all its life, ego collects objects. It sucks them in like a black hole. Freud relates the way ego takes in objects to eating. Ego fashions symbols of the objects, tokens with which ego can think; others are hurled into the unconscious. Ego is a ramshackle structure.

Barely coherent and barely awake, ego is forever drugging itself with libido. Every abandoned object releases cathexis which is temporarily put on the ego with resultant euphoria, but every identification is liable to superego punishment with resultant depression. And every disturbing id impulse causes ego to shock the self with the anxiety signal. Ego begins by flooding itself with cathexis in infantile narcissistic withdrawal from the mother and it almost dies of an overdose right then: too much can produce the magic *liebestod* of schizophrenia. Whenever reality frustrates ego, it is tempted to withdraw again, dope itself with self-love and sink into psychotic sleep in the bosom of the id. Externally, the ego is easily trapped in fascinations: in hypnotic love ("overvaluation of the sex object," a kind of erotic latah), in loyalties too easily given to groups and their leaders, in dangerous idealizations. The ego is easily invaded magically and taken over from outside.[174] It is easily hypnotized, stolen, fascinated, entranced. And like magic itself, ego is permeated with the feeling that it has constructed itself out of crimes—the destruction of the father buried in the Oedipal repression, the abandonment of loved objects, the release of the death instinct to strengthen itself.

Ego is a magician riding wild horses, doing a balancing act, making itself out of things it throws away, full of conflict and increasingly complicated and barely adequate in focusing the action of the self. And thus the Freudian ego, like the self as a whole, is full of holes; the model is dogmatic but agnostic enough almost to fit behaviorist formulations in terms of pure action and response. You might say that the ego is what barely focuses action, making it barely consistent and adequate. And all these Freudian hypothetical constructs are themselves metaphors of "magic" used to whip sick persons back into spontaneity and autonomy.

3. *The ego defends itself.* The ego cannot really be said to defend the self as a whole: what it defends is its own integrity and equilibrium. That may have the effect of preserving the self.[175] But ego's struggles can be detrimental to the self as a whole; ego's attempt to keep its own pilot light burning at all costs can torment the self with pain and injury. In some suicides, for example, ego is really trying to kill the tormenting superego; this primitive abortive magical act of self-defense incidentally destroys the self.

4. *The ego's organization is rooted in unconscious repression.* The formulation I am driving toward is this: The ego is a structure of repression which acts by means of the magic principle. Freudian ego psychologists took different positions on whether the ego is conscious, but the trend was increasingly to call more and more of the ego unconscious and to identify this part with repression.[176] Anna Freud put a finishing touch on Freud's own account of repression: To control the id, she wrote, ego buries part of itself in the unconscious. Ego energy and symbolic content remain locked up there, inaccessible downward from ego's conscious part, but in touch upwards in disguised form through symptoms. As Anna Freud put it, ego inroads into the id are unconscious but id inroads into the ego are conscious. In psychoanalysis, perceiving that the analyst at first "works with the primary process," ego throws up resistances because it fears that analysis will destroy its very core. I think the implication is that the core of ego's precious organization is unconscious, rooted precisely in those energy investments it has made in its repressions.[177] To save this buried system of itself ego fights the analyst with transference resistance, repetition compulsion and Reichian body resistance. And the particular resistances encountered in each neurosis relate to the manner in which ego has constituted itself in repression. [178]

There is some evidence that Freud perhaps intended some such notion. In *Beyond the Pleasure Principle,* he writes that the core of the ego is its unconscious repressions, and that resistance arises from this unconscious core.[179] In *The Ego and the Id,* he writes that the superego or ego ideal is the primal basis of the ego and it is woven out of the resolved Oedipal conflict and its identifications which are then repressed.[180] Freud's frequent assertion that repressions require continual inputs of energy also suggests that a large percentage of ego's energy is invested in these unconscious repressions.

All this perhaps offers a way around the biosocial dualisms that are precipitated whenever anyone tries to synthesize the Durkheimian and Freudian positions: for example, Bastide.[181] It is not necessary to postulate a dualism of symbolism and biological libido as he does. Freud's theory of ego organization as rooted in unconscious repression suggests how a "pure sociology" explanation is possible, which however does not have to evaporate or dismiss ego as Sullivan and Reich do. The nascent ego is a social idea, but this idea gets grafted deeply onto a genetically receptive biological organism through repression. Thus ego develops its own independent rootedness, separate from society. This rooted apartness is not pure biology, however, but something society arranges as it needs it. Social patterns dig deep roots into a receptive biological medium through the process of unconscious repression.

   5. *The action of the ego is magical.* To speak of ego "magic," as Freudians inescapably do, is more than a metaphor. Consider Rapaport's reconstruction of Freud's theory as a simple model.[182] As Rapaport formulates it, in the "primary process," a drive reaches a threshold, attaches to an object, is acted on and is satisfied. But in the secondary process, when the reality principle rules, the scenario is altered. Now, when a drive reaches a threshold, a derivative ego drive is mobilized, the counterdrive is used to produce a structured delay until the drive can be diverted into some other satisfaction more compatible with ego survival, and meanwhile ego engages in *thinking* as "experimental action" before finally action is emitted. There are many variations: drive can be repressed, object can be unavailable, drive can be diverted into fantasy. But the basic model holds—i.e., ego is associated with delayed behavior, with thinking as experimental action, with use of derived drives to deflect drive.

   Imagine all this as a visual image: Something primitive gushes up from the depths; during its rise something channels, translates, purifies it into conscious form so that ego can perceive it, get purchase on it, delay it, change its expression. A biological urge has to be translated into something conscious, more than that, into manipulable *symbols,* so that ego can turn it over mentally, devise a plan and act on it. How is this translation performed?

   Freud gave the beginnings of the answer when, in *The Ego and the Id,* he reported that the superego did much of this job in ego's early stages.[183] Superego is a powerful unconscious structure created out of remnants of the Oedipus complex; once it is set up as a kind of shield against the id, the ego really begins to grow rapidly.[184] I.e., superego is pushed underground like a kind of storm drain (or filter) just as ego is really getting started; it partly insulates ego from the id. Ego grows above it, on the other side, and the unconscious superego *screens* and *filters* a good deal of the id drives that pass up to ego. This is suggestive. If superego, man's first considerable unconscious repression, screens and shapes what passes up to ego, then perhaps in general we may find that ego is a structure of unconscious repression which translates id drives to consciousness with the aid of its repressions. Perhaps all those unconscious drains and dams and pipes that channel the flow into consciousness together constitute ego's coherence. And if this is so, then the structural foundations of ego's integrity will be found in these unconscious repressions.

Róheim had the genius to see that this process of transforming unconscious drives into thought and action is "magical" (in at least the weak sense). Without going into his theory again, let us simply say that ego is a structure rooted in repression, which transforms passivity into activity. We know that this process was once assisted by magic because there was a literal magical chorus out there in the social world waiting for this symbolic performance—in those primordial eras when society was first creating egos. Magical rituals, dances, shamanic ecstasies were demanding that translation of confused or passive biological drives into appropriate symbolic action—these demands and expectations were grafted onto the self and *became* the ego that produced the performance on demand. The ego retains a magical nature; its whole function is to translate passivity into action, to translate inarticulate biological urges into that just barely appropriate social action which we call spontaneity.

Everything about ego remains miraculous or magical. Imagine a structure that continuously creates itself out of rejected or lost loves, burying bits of itself beyond recall in the unconscious; fighting fire with fire in the sympathetic magic of unconscious id struggles; "undoing" things by ritualistically repeating them; "denying" objects and thereby stripping them of affect so they can be used as counters for thought; using religious rituals to strengthen resistance to instincts; using bodily musculature as ritual symbols of ego resistance. The truth is that psychoanalysis is indeed Magian, as Gide said, and Jung is perhaps a natural offshoot, blocked only by what Rieff called "the triumph of the therapeutic," which might be interpreted as the triumph of white therapeutic magic over the other magics: occult, religious, black magic, etc. As a basically Magian view of the self it is not surprising that psychoanalysis in effect presents a picture of a self with a magical core: the ego, whose coherence is in repression and whose action is magic. The magic action of the ego gears together both kinds of magic, ego magic and social magic, magic in the weak and strict senses. As drives are translated into consciousness by ego's unconscious structures of repression, and then into symbolic form by conscious ego according to the magical principle of thought as experimental action, this weak-sense magic produces a performance—ego *acts*. It projects action by the "I" out into the real social world—which is receptive to such spontaneity because of patterning by institutions some of which were originally magical in the strict sense. After man "fell into the deep well of himself" (Loren Eiseley), into the symbolic social world with its "cliffs of fall" (Gerard Manley Hopkins), individual action at first could only be organized by ritual. Men at first could march only in serried ranks. Mauss has shown how many human gestures trace back to rituals.[185] It is amazing how much of ordinary social interaction today is still patterned by rituals. Magic ritual on the outside, the magic principle on the inside, make it possible for that frail pilot light of ego to produce spontaneity when society requires it, without scaring itself to death.

Toward a Nomenclature Model: The Problem of Other Terms

It seems likely, then, that Freudian ego psychology will fit the theory of magic, and provide a model of the self which magic defends. I can at very least offer a "model of nomenclature," to show how terms like ego, self, id, etc., fit together. It may also show where some non-Freudian terms fit in, such as the I/Me dichotomy of philosophy, the "self-image" of social psychology, etc.

To construct a model of nomenclature, I start with a segment of the diagram (on p. 280) in which I plotted time against level of consciousness to show the temporal/consciousness sequence of superego, ego-ideal, self-image and "I":

Unconscious ...	Preconscious ...	Conscious	... Hyperconscious
Superego	*Ego ideal*	*Ego*	*I*
(archaic)	(historical, cultural)	(Biographical)	(immediate)

The self segment of this coordinate map would include the present and the bio-graphical past, but not the historical or the archaic eras, which *precede* the self. And we can simplify the time dimension (by collapsing preconscious into un-conscious and making hyperconscious just a limit of conscious). The self diagram will then have four cells: Lecky's conscious self-image and the hyperconscious "I" will fill the two upper, or conscious, cells. And we will add the terms "ego" and "id" and "Me" to the two lower, or unconscious cells:

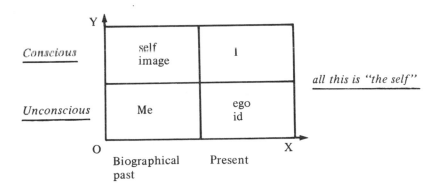

It is a bit more complicated than that, for the diagram must show that the ego is partly conscious though its roots are in the unconscious id. Moreover, ego has tentacles in the biographical past—and it also digs into the biological substrate by transforming drives. So ego might be drawn like a little octopus with its tentacles digging in unconsciousness (and partly in pastness, and also below the Y axis into the biological substrate which is not part of the self). But its head pokes up into the conscious sphere, like this:

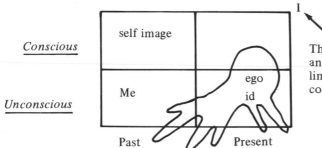

Now the "I," which the ego emits, is the instantaneous present, a limit, so it is veered over to the right end of the chart.[186] It is also pure or "hyper" consciousness, so it is moved to the very top. Outside of these four cells we can show the past roots of self. They lie to the left of the 0 origin. They are therefore *not* a part of the self, but can be used to show its prehistory. Thus the diagram shows the archaic superego transmitting through the historical ego-ideal, to the biographical self-image. But note that the superego is also found in the present unconscious—as a residue of the Oedipal struggle, which is supposed to reenact and transmit this archaic heritage.

The diagram already shows us how to avoid confusing ego, a complex, vested structure, with the instantaneous "I"—or with the inert "Me" precipitated by ego's past actions. The "I" is the action-of-an-actor that comes out of the ego. The "Me" is the precipitate that ego-I leave behind in the biographical past. Putting these pieces together, we get the following temporal-consciousness model of the self. (See facing page.)

The diagram could be used to sort out numerous other terms used in social science. For example, "selves" as Erikson calls them, unconscious role precipitates, can be shown in the biographical unconscious, coalescing into the more integrated, more pre-conscious "Me." The biographical "self-image" (Lecky's term), in turn, is close to Erikson's "social identity," so both could be put in one cell.

The self is all four squares, but nothing more. It is "inside the skin," but it is not biological. The self is the social actor. It is symbolic-mental and it exists in the present and biographical past, not in past history, eternity or any Platonic realm of ideas. It is shaped by history but does not exist before its own formation; it is a social construct epigenetically drafted onto a biological organism but it is not that organism.

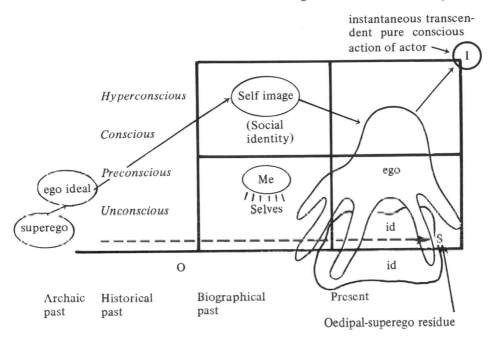

instantaneous transcen-
dent pure conscious
action of actor →

The Y dimension can be used to express both degrees of consciousness and the degree of activity. The ego is shown rooted in repression and in id-passivity, but it thrusts, via the magical principle, first into consciousness and then into action as the "I."

The Me is a system of past precipitates of action; it is also unconscious like most of the ego, but different processes work in the two. In the Me, this system is largely memory, biography. It is not completely inert. A process which Halbwachs[187] and Schachtel[188] and Bartlett[189] have separately described goes on here, i.e., the transformation of individual memory into social stereotypes. It is like the process of historical memory described in Eliade,[190] where historical events are assimilated to the stereotyped plots of myth. Thus memory clusters around social rallying points like birthdays, Christmas, graduation, occupation. The Me, in other words, is biography transforming into history transforming into myth. It has a strong past dimension. The ego roots, by contrast, while laid down in the past, are more active in the present. Libido must be constantly pumped into the unconscious repressions that constitute these roots. Messages are constantly sent up through the roots, too.

There is a great deal of entropic, deadweight, downward pull in the whole system. Ego creates its coherence only by going underground into the unconscious, and the unconscious id constantly threatens to collapse ego down into it altogether. The preconscious Me is constantly being transformed into a stereotype by socialized memory processes. The self image works well only when it neatly fits into a social identity related to the historical ego ideal. With the transformation of the Me into social stereotype, and the over-identification of self image with ego ideal, the biographic hemisphere of the self tends to become inert, heavy, passive, unconscious, and pulls downward.

The ego-I system, meanwhile, may be weak. It can be weak on account of several defects: 1. Bad genetic endowment of character, will, intelligence, etc., and other "primary structures of autonomy," genetically given, which inhabit the ego's "conflict-free sphere" (Hartmann). 2. Excessive conflict between the "institutions" of the self, on which coherence of ego identity depends. (Conceivably, an ego can still be strong while the self is weak—an ego housed in a self that is badly educated, forced to play defective roles, etc., but this is difficult.) 3. But ego can be weak in another way—it can be rudimentary, barely formed, *primitive* in other words. The most important reason is *the relative shallowness of repression.*

Ego weakness is often associated in the literature with magic, but it has to be grasped that magic is an old defense of ego, building it up. If ego is primitive, or regresses to a primitive stage, we see magic more visibly at work because magic, as ego's oldest defense, is also its last line of defense. Ego is not weak because it is magical; it is because some egos are weak that they have little else but magic to work with. We see magic thinking, Werner tells us,[191] in primitives, infants and psychotics, but it is a necessary defense of their weak egos that can be a step forward for them. Storch,[192] who is an early source (1924) for the Werner, Sullivan, Arieti, etc., equation of primitive, psychotic and infantile thought as magical, makes a similar insistence. Kris[193] shows how the artist makes positive use of magic thought, and unlike the psychotic stays in command of it.

Besides shallow repressions, there is another basic reason why primitive egos are weak—the social structures for accepting and supporting "I" behavior have not sufficiently developed. (Margaret Mead's famous movie of "washing-the-baby" rituals in three different cultures suggests what I mean.) Extremely primitive societies do not train, expect, elicit or subliminally cue deeply autonomous ego-I behavior. Categories of selfhood are only partly developed. "The Individual" is not yet established in law, polity, economy. The secondary process may also be weak in primitive cultures.

In some ways the magical principle works *with* the secondary process. But when the secondary process and the social institutions of logicalization that back it grow stronger, ego's security is strengthened, and its actions do not have to depend so much on magic. The two are substitute defenses of ego more than they are antithetical. But even the civilized ego must remain capable of some magic in the weak sense just to overcome the inertial weight of social processes. For along with society's logicalization, which builds the secondary process into ego, goes the objectification of mind in the outside world, which makes it weightier, harder to fathom and more oppressive to ego. The conscious ego, then, balances the magical principle and the secondary process: too much logic and ego's magic dies; too much subjective magic and ego dies. (The latter case is schizophrenia.)

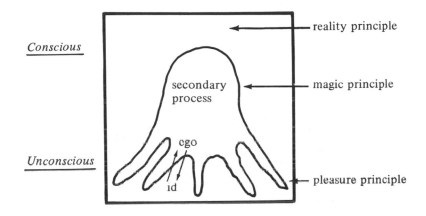

Róheim's magical principle, then, is to be put alongside the other Freudian "regulatory principles" (Hartmann's term)—i.e., the "pleasure principle," the "reality principle" (and later the "nirvana principle," with perhaps the "repetition compulsion" on the same level). The primary process governs the id (and early ego); the secondary process governs the mature conscious tip of the ego. Ego in turn controls the id with the pleasure principle, deals with reality with the reality principle, and translates from drive into symbolic-social action with the magic principle. Thus the magic principle is "in between the pleasure and reality principles" as Róheim wrote: it translates from passivity to activity, from drive to symbol, from pleasure to reality, from thought to action. Moreover, it translates from magic in the weak sense to magic in the strict sense. For although it may be merely a metaphor to call ego action magical now, this action originally geared outwards into real institutions and patterns of acceptance in the social world which at one time were magical in the strict sense. These often took the form of rituals, as Mauss pointed out: sheer rituals to enable people to act, the way they still have to get elocution lessons, assertiveness lessons, dancing lessons, swimming lessons or sex therapy lessons, etc., when they feel awkward. Work party rituals, sex party rituals, play rituals—at first men could only act "in serried ranks," because the ego was frail and terrified. The primitive ego was vulnerable because its secondary process was weak; this in turn because society's supportive logics were weak. Yet the whole social world had become a cauldron of symbols when man "fell into the deep well of himself" (Loren Eiseley). The conscious ego could be easily snuffed out by mere social signals, as in voodoo death. It was then that magic ritual organized action and gave groping individuals lines to say and gestures to perform.

The ego begins in consciousness, as an interface between reality and the id; but it burrows into unconsciousness. This strongly suggests social selves being grafted onto biological natures. Tollman,[194] Adler, Mauss,[195] Hertz,[196] etc., have shown again and again that the social can graft directly onto the biological; Wolfgang Wickler[197] has shown that mere usage can rapidly change bodily morphology in many species. And the Freudian theory of identification as withdrawal, intake and repression, Freud's notion of ego as a structure of unconscious repressions erected in the biological id, take us away from the superficiality of mere *mirroring* (G. H. Mead). The Freudian model shows that, even though ego is something society grafts onto a biological individual, it gets *deeply* grafted. Ego as a structure of repressions digging into the biological substrate sinks down to a different level from the social-symbolic sphere. Ego begins to become individual by cathecting itself in narcissism; it develops an idiosyncratic personal style rooted in its repressions and their deforming effects on biological instincts. Ego's biographical development can indeed be regarded as epigenetic. That is, with some built-in predispositions (Hartmann), ego takes in a social model, goes through developmental stages that are psychosexual (Freud, Erikson) and creates biological roots for itself in repression. But the development is also a matter of "genetic epistemology" (Piaget[198]) because in its successive equilibria ego assimilates more and more of the secondary process and this means internalizing those "categories of the human spirit" (Mauss, Durkheim) which represent man's "logicalization" of his experience in society (Lévi-Strauss). Human action and spontaneity remain possible, even after this logicalization has produced a tight web, because ego can still operate via the magic principle (Róheim) bringing some libido to its symbols (Bastide[199]).

In the conscious ego, therefore, the secondary process and the magical principle can work together to produce what Arieti calls "the magical synthesis," concepts for action that embody as "moments" (Hegel[200]) in their synthesis the more primitive "endocepts" and "paleological concepts" (Arieti[201]) that are more in touch with libidinal energies and ego's own idiosyncratic structure of repression.

Ego has two jobs—integration and the passage over to action. It integrates itself on the basis of its repressions, and it passes over to action with the magical principle that was nourished in infantile omnipotence. And always ego dreams of a return to that omnipotence;[202] its very propensity to action is motivated by a desire to recover this mana.

The Self in the Individual

There are separate centers of consciousness in the self: ego consciousness; the "I" as pure consciousness; self-image consciousness; plus successive conscious tokens from the preconscious (aspects of the "Me"). The self, then, is not fully organized, not even the conscious parts, and this self is not ego alone. The entire self is, however, inside the skin. As we will see, this model of the self is only the core of a larger model of the Individual. But the Individual, the "person," etc., are entities that do go outside of the skin. One of the weaknesses of behaviorist ego psychology (e.g., G. H. Mead) is its tendency to extend the boundaries of the self outside the skin, by confusing the "self" with the "person" and the "individual" with the ego and even with his reputation, etc.[203] To handle these matters we must move on to a broader diagram with larger entities, the organs of "the Individual." We cannot do more than define these terms here, however, for the Individual is the subject of the next chapter.

Definitions:

1. The Individual. The Individual with a capital letter is a complex of institutions, including: A. individual law (property, contracts, persons, conveyances, etc.); B. political citizenship; C. economic relations of production and the roles they produce; D. "the idea of the person" as a "category of the human spirit"; E. institutions of "conscience" which support this archetype, such as meditation techniques, the confessional, mysticism and so on; F. the *ideology* of individualism. (Durkheim has traced its rise; Durkheim and Luckmann suggest it may be the "new religion" projected by an age of individualism.)

2. The Person Category. This is Mauss'[204] "category of the human spirit." It reflects all the other institutions of the Individual and focuses their influences to form cultural archetypes that guide the socialization of individual selves. The person category might be said to plug the self into the institution of the Individual, and we can even say where the "plug" is located. While the person category surely affects all four "cells" of the self, it especially influences the particular subcultural historical *"ego ideal"* (Erikson) which in turn mediates its influence into the self via the *self image*.[205] Strictly speaking the person category is an organ of the Individual-as-an-institution, so it will be studied in the next chapter.

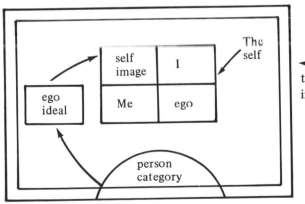

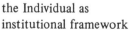

the Individual as
institutional framework

3. The Actual Individual. This is the actual human being who fits into the institution of the Individual. The actual individual embraces the self, but much more, too, and its boundaries go far beyond the skin. The actual individual includes the following: 1. the self; 2. the prehistory of the self (archaic superego, historic ego ideal, and also the individual's genealogy and heredity); 3. the reputation, the dossier, all the social imprints left by this individual; 4. his property, power, net worth, legal rights, economic activity; 5. his investments in family, marriage, friendship, voluntary associations; his citizenship and other identifications; 6. his *persona,* masks, roles, role enclaves, etc.; 7. his "personality," which is a particular impression formed of him through his roles, *personae* and actions. At its widest extent (in great civilizations), the actual individual can become a great power, with a huge household of relatives, servants and retainers; vast economic and political strength; a huge net worth; a charismatic personality; a towering reputation; a biography that may be studied for centuries; a heritage of literary or artistic creations; a plethora of attachments, involvements and roles; an infinity of experience; a partly corporate entity perhaps; with a powerful self at the core of it all directed by a strong and coherent ego that is animated by a world-conquering magic.

How the self fits into the Individual and what the Individual's various organs are is suggested by another fanciful diagram (see facing page).

But the core of all this elaborate architecture of Individual and self remains the half-conscious ego, an entity which is organized by unconscious repressions and acts through the magic principle. The magic principle enables it to translate passivity into activity, mute drives into symbolism, impulses into a plan or model of action that governs action—and thereby to emit that barely appropriate action which is called spontaneity, that unique performance of the transcendent "I" which society accepts as the appropriate action of a "self."

PART THREE: AGAINST WHAT DOES MAGIC DEFEND THE SELF?

Once again, extreme cases are illuminating. Bizarre phenomena like "voodoo death," "soul loss" and even suicide demonstrate that, at the extreme, what magic defends the self against is simply—death. In extreme cases the self can take the biological organism into extinction with it. To pinpoint this precisely, we might say that extreme social pressure can put out the self's "pilot light," the ego. Even more precisely, we might say that this takes the form of overthrowing the "I." In voodoo death or malignant anxiety or extreme depression, the spontaneous transcendent "I" can no longer perform that barely appropriate action we call spontaneity. Its actions are either inappropriate, causing anxiety to escalate (Goldstein[206]), or stereotyped and depressive; or else the "I" recognizes that it cannot act correctly and freezes in catatonia (Sullivan[207]). But paralyzing the "I" has an effect on the ego equivalent to cutting down the supply of oxygen to the brain: for the ego *is* the translation of passivity into activity, of repression-channeled impulse into appropriate symbolic action. When the "I" is paralyzed the "magic principle" fails. Ego may attempt to work autistically, withdrawing into a protective psychotic hibernation, but it is damaged by this.

Institution of the Individual

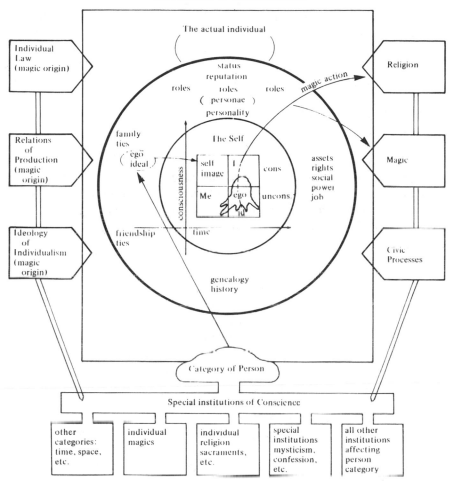

If ego dies, the self becomes disorganized. The "Me" and the "self-image" become fantasms, the amorphous id cannot regulate its own functions. The whole self may die while the organism survives in the slow degradation of hebephrenia. But if ego death is sudden, the biological organism may go to the grave as well in the extreme case of voodoo death. (Sociologically, this also entails the death of "the individual": the eventual liquidation of his estate, his relationships, his rights, his political status and social roles.) Extreme shocks to the self are also capable of killing the biological organism *before* the self dies (i.e., "psychosomatic" death)—but whichever goes first can pull the other into the grave. There are many variations, but the paradigmatic formula is this: the death of the "I" kills the "ego" which kills the "self" which can kill the organism and hence the "individual." Let us study these extreme cases, beginning with voodoo death.

1. Voodoo Death

Voodoo death has generated a considerable literature since Mauss' pioneering essay. Metais' bibliography[208] indicates its extent. In addition, epidemiological studies of social stress and illness are also relevant—such as the work of Holmes,[209] Beck,[210] etc., on illness and death after job loss, divorce, etc., or the Rochester studies of Engel, Schmale and Green on sudden death after loss of a parent or spouse[211] and similar studies in Britain.[212] An article in *Science*[213] suggests that the constructs need refinement, but preliminary findings are striking. Rene Dubos' *Mirage of Health*[214] was an early orientation, reminding us that Pasteur regarded his microbial approach as a strategy rather than a final cause, and suggesting that disease occurs at weak points when stress increases susceptibility. Studies of deaths after birthdays and holidays (as if people waited to die) are part of the accumulating data waiting for a "Keynesian revolution" in conceptualization that will readmit the biosocial to medicine.

Social statistics as recently as the nineties used to enumerate millions as dying of "fevers" (at least in places like India[215]). When we consider methodological problems of defining causes of death, it is unlikely that current epidemiological techniques have the last word. We may be on the eve of a realignment in our conventional wisdom about how people die, which may bring us closer to the primitive emphasis on psychic (really social) causes. Because the modern ego is stronger than the primitive, it is unlikely that as many of our people die for these reasons, but it is also likely that we have complacently underestimated this phenomenon. If we knew how vulnerable we really are to evil tongues, malevolent associates and social traps, we might be more worried.

Mauss: "Death Suggested by the Collectivity." Mauss was one of the first to gather these cases and use them to display the extreme fragility of the emerging self, in his 1926 essay *Effet Physique Chez l'Individu de l'Idée de Mort Suggérée Par La Collectivité.*[216] Perfectly robust natives, he reported, upon breaking a taboo or being cursed, take to their huts, waste away and die within a few days. Sixteen years later, in 1942, Walter Cannon would call this phenomenon "the voodoo death."[217] Mauss called it "the physical effect on the individual of the idea of death suggested by the collectivity." Mauss' term is far more suggestive, but "voodoo death" is convenient short-hand, so I will use it. Mauss studied the phenomenon among the Maori and some Australian aborigines and it took two different forms in these two areas. But the key to understanding his study is to recognize that the two cases are the same: The Maoris are religious and voodoo death comes to them mainly through something close to the religious sense of sin, i.e., breaking a taboo. Whereas among the Australians the death seems more magical, for it is caused by a magician. But the two cases assimilate to each other, for the Australian magician often kills by causing a person to break a taboo;[218] and, anyway, when he orders a man to die he often speaks for the collectivity.[219] In both cases it is the moral weight of society that kills. These are religious assassinations, not magical ones, and in fact magic is the only defense against this pressure.

In all these cases, someone is killed by religious-moral pressure. What is the point of this finding? It is an illustration of the social nature of homo duplex and its consequent vulnerability to social implosion. When a primitive breaks a taboo or a magician curses him, then his spirit grows heavy, and he "feels an alien spirit inhabiting him," Mauss reports. His conscience is "completely invaded by ideas and sentiments which are entirely collective in origin" — and this is enough to kill him. What physically destroys the organism could be some form of killer anxiety,[220] a panic that disorganizes the ego by removing the social supports that are 99 percent of homo duplex. Mauss is not clear. But what he finally suggests (something Tollman has formulated elsewhere[221]) is that, in man, the social is in direct contact with the biological—it can kill it. The whole Durkheim school is full of such suggestions—e.g., Hertz's speculations on the social origin of handedness;[222] Mauss on the "techniques of the human body,"[223] etc. And in some programmatic essays in the twenties Mauss would call for a "tridimensional approach," studying how social forces directly shape biological material with psychological experience as a mere epiphenomenon.[224]

The Sympathetic-Adrenalin Hypothesis. In 1942 Walter Cannon did a similar study which gathered data from a much wider area and speculated in more detail about how voodoo death might be physiologically mediated.[225] Cannon found reports of voodoo death from every continent, going back to 1587 (Soares de Souza). Voodoo death is most often caused by breaking a taboo or by sorcery in these reports. As a physiologist, Cannon took seriously one possible interpretation; the reports might be in error, based on faulty observation. He dismissed the idea, however, because many trained doctors had observed voodoo deaths and done autopsies. The natives died after either sorcery (as when a medicine man "pointed a bone" at someone) or the breaking of a taboo.

Cannon assembled impressive data showing that the only defense against voodoo death is magic. In one case a Rockefeller Foundation scientist and a missionary threatened the witchdoctor, who removed the spell: the dying man thereupon recovered. In other cases, a curing magician, by palming imaginary or planted missiles, convinced the patient that the spell had been lifted and he recovered. The point is important. Some writers on voodoo death loosely call it a "magical" phenomenon based on "magical" beliefs. But voodoo death is a religious phenomenon; the *defense* against it is magic.

Cannon's interpretation: Belief is so strong that breaking a taboo or being ensorcelled can cause deadly physiological processes. These are sympathetic-adrenalin processes: the fight-or-flight reaction which, if prolonged, does damage. He cites experiments with decorticate cats provoked to continuous rage: it killed them. Death is due to persistent, excessive activity of the sympathetic-adrenalin system. This works through high sugar concentration, lower blood pressure, tachycardia and other crisis reactions.

Other investigators have emphasized other physical mediations. One is sudden cardiac accidents that occur during stress, emphasized by George Engel.[226] This may be a different kind of event from voodoo death, however, though no less illustrative of human frailty.

A Social Ostracism Hypothesis. Most investigators emphasize the *social* invitation to die, like Mauss. Wolfgang Winkler finds it even among lower organisms: for example, cockroaches persistently mounted by other cockroaches afterwards die, with no identifiable physical signs on autopsy.[227] Voodoo death occurs even in pluralist modern settings of role distance—for example, in bureaucratic situations when individuals who have internalized too much of a particular rat race cannot stand being sidetracked, scapegoated or otherwise cursed.

Lloyd Warner[228] notes that there are two "movements" in these social executions among the Murngin, one "away from" the patient, then one back to him. First, friends and family accept the definition, place the unfortunate in a new category and withdraw from him. He is a "walking dead man," as they say in the Mafia. He is shunned as an outcast (in modern bureaucratic settings, as a "loser," "someone who isn't going anywhere"). As he sickens the group keeps suggesting death to him. In primitive society, they may speak of returning to his ancestors. (In modern bureaucracy they may speak of early retirement.) In primitive societies this is done solemnly. (In modern settings it may be done with the killer wit which the new "gamester" executives use like a scourge.) The individual himself accepts the verdict, and withdraws. Cannon observes that this is a kind of suicide, for withdrawal has physiological consequences such as not eating, dehydration, etc.

In the second act, the primitive group "returns" and "mourns" the individual while he is still alive. Even in modern societies, Cannon observes, this can have a deadly effect: Catholic "last rites" may hasten death. (Job's "miserable comforters" are another example and their analogues are found in corporate settings. Sometimes the comforter has been delegated by the management. His rituals are ostensibly consoling, but the message is: die. Often, the result is just that. The individual not only lets go of the job, he dies.[229])

It is possible that most deaths in primitive society are indeed of this sort. Life is markedly shorter in primitive societies as a whole but longevity varies too strinkingly among them to be explained entirely by physical causes. In Western society life is much longer, but is this entirely the result of modern medicine? Ivan Illich[230] has summarized evidence casting doubt on that. Longevity was low in the nineteenth century, still suffering the scars of that greatest forced draft of labor since the pyramids—what we call the industrial revolution. It may have been higher earlier on. I am suggesting that longevity may have increased in Western societies because *selves* are tougher, giving extra protection against voodoo death. Perhaps civilization arose in societies sufficiently healthy psychologically so that longevity advanced and so enabled the adult work force to accumulate a surplus.

Every Man A Voodoo Assassin. Eliane Metais,[231] a French anthropologist influenced by Mauss, found that among the Canaques of New Caledonia even ordinary people can kill each other by things they say. (Black magic beliefs here are a collective response to corporate disintegration under colonialism, but the price is dissemination among a people with weak egos of terrifying ideas which frequently kill them. Metais should be read as corrective to the easy functionalism which insists that black magic abreacts group tensions.)[232]

One does not have to wait to break a taboo or run afoul of a witchdoctor to meet one's end here: A threat of black magic by a close friend is enough to cause death. Canaques would probably not survive one minute in modern America, where the level of daily verbal aggression is extremely high, according to Bandura.[233] Mere threats, mere hints, mere life-negating statements cause death. People die even as a result of arguments. Metais presents vivid case histories: An argument occurs, a threat is uttered, a man falls sick, goes to the hospital, will not eat, dies.[234] A man with a dormant TB infection is threatened during a quarrel; he gets sick, despairs, refuses a doctor's help.[235] Whole families sicken and die when a powerful member, who had protected them, dies.[236] Metais is a convinced "tridimensionalist," adopting Mauss' later "biosocial approach" in which social forces work directly on physical organisms.[237] Evidence marshalled by this study raises the suspicion that voodoo death is more widespread than has ever been reported.

Recent Research. Some modern cases are assembled by Seligman under his theory of "helplessness." A businessman cursed by his mother falls sick, is treated by a psychoanalyst and starts to recover; he is cursed again and dies for no discernible physical reason. Seligman believes that voodoo death by cursing is related to death through helplessness—the individual dies because he thinks he can do nothing against the curse.[238] Thus Cannon's cases would be similar to old people who die if the decision about sending them to old people's homes is made by others (Ferrari[239]); or Spitz's "anaclitical depression" and death from "hospitalism" in children.[240] Helplessness was indeed Freud's final interpretation of anxiety[241]; Seligman also relates it to depression as a premorbid condition in mysterious deaths. This would help explain how magic wards off voodoo death—it not only fights to lift the curse; it is something to *do* and that overcomes the sense of helplessness. "Action is the counter-phobic attitude," as Róheim put it. A Portland zoo keeper advocated putting manipulanda in animal cages to cut down the enormous death rate caused by helplessness in zoos.[242] Considering the "iron cage" of bureaucracy where most of us wind up these days, and the bleak "destination suburbs" like Crestwood Heights[243] where we go to die, and the built-in values that lead us to expect to "peak" in our forties, if not sooner; and the inherent pressure toward early retirement implicit in pension funds so huge they could buy out the economy (Berle[244]), men and women increasingly experience helplessness, and this may be why, despite one of the highest incomes per capita, America has one of the lowest rates of longevity in the West.

Our contemporary category of psychosomatic illness covers a lot of unexplained phenomena. It may be urged that a large percentage of mankind has always died from some kind of biosocial shock of which voodoo death is the most striking example, that the longevity of civilized man is greater partly because his ego is better defended against these dangers, that magic contributed to this defense, but that we are still susceptible to social assassination to a much greater degree than we now imagine.

2. Suicide

And what about suicide? Neither Durkheim's social integration theory[245] nor the psychoanalytic theory of misplaced aggression deflected against the self[246] adequately explains this puzzling phenomenon. Even the neat axiomatic integration of the Durkheim and psychoanalytic theories accomplished by Henry and Short in *Suicide and Homicide* provides mere correlational schemas without sufficient explanation.[247] It is possible that voodoo death may help to illuminate the mystery of suicide.

What is most praised in Durkheim's study of suicide, the statistical method, is most flawed, for the constructs that are manipulated statistically incorporate his conclusions.[248] But what is most criticized is most valuable—for the behavior maxims that incorporate his conclusions contain remarkable insights. These come closest to uncovering what this mysterious business is all about. Durkheim makes us aware of suicide's eerie impersonality (from a social dimension) when he writes of "suicidal currents" running through social tissue and killing vulnerable cells. Today an emerging phenomenology of suicide is beginning to expose this constrained impersonality from the *individual* viewpoint.

Suicide is related to voodoo death. The idea occurs to several students of voodoo death, such as Cannon, who makes occasional reference to suicide. Sylvia Plath's idea of "the bell jar"[249] and Alvarez's idea[250] of suicide as a "closed world with its own irresistible logic" suggest the same mysterious external compulsion. Schneidman and Farberow write of the catastrophic logic or "catalogic" that takes over in the pre-suicide state.[251] Mauss, too, dropped some hints at the end of his voodoo death essay, suggesting a link to suicide. This is significant, for he had helped his uncle three decades earlier with the statistical research for *Le Suicide* (1897). Now he was dealing with voodoo deaths that occurred automatically, without self-infliction, but the two were deeply related in his mind. In this essay, I believe, Mauss' argument contains the hint that voodoo death is the primitive phenomenon that precedes suicide and that suicide in modern society takes the place of voodoo death. He concluded the essay by saying that his findings somehow "confirm" Durkheim's discoveries about anomic suicide.[252]

Why should he link voodoo death to *anomic* suicide? Is not it closer to *altruistic* suicide? Since Mauss did not complete these connnections, I will speculate about them.

Let us take a closer look at Durkheim's book *Suicide.* Nowhere does he say that his entire study could be used as a demonstration of the fragility of the individual ego, but the work can be interpreted in this fashion. Nisbet[253] writes that Durkheim, far from having no theory of the individual, has the best sociological theory of all. In fact, why is it not recognized that Durkheim's main preoccupation was with the social emergence of the individual? (Why is it not recognized that Mauss' main preoccupation was with magic, a closely related issue?) Of Durkheim's four major works, *The Division of Labor in Society*[254] is about the emergence of the individual; *The Elementary Forms of Religious Life*[255] is about the cognitive-transcendent nature of society that makes this emergence possible; and *Suicide* is a demonstration of the continued social dependence and fragility of the individual.

Durkheim finds that officially counted suicides are just the tip of the iceberg. Many acts that are dangerous or self-destructive result in death. So how does one define suicide? It is surprisingly hard to do. Durkheim has to put something subjective into his definition: Suicide is defined by the "certainty" the victim has that his act will result in death.[256] But this is vague, since unsuccessful suicide attempts far outnumber successful suicides; and Durkheim's postscript about them[257] does not avoid this circularity. The truth is that a suicide attempt is defined *post hoc* by the authorities out of the much larger number of deliberate and quasi-deliberate destructive acts that people commit. It is an old metaphor to call habits like alcoholism suicidal (e.g., Menninger's "chronic suicide"[258]). But huge provinces of destructive behavior exist whose outcome is far more immediate, such as accidents, which are among the ten leading causes of death. We cannot even be sure that voodoo death has disappeared. "Psychosomatic" illness is more often socio-somatic. Cases of death from "disappointment" or "a broken heart" are still turned up by the most casual studies. When all these deaths are taken together—disguised voodoo death, frank suicide, slow self-destructive actions—we see how hard it is for the human self to remain upright. As Ernest Becker[259] puts it, the self is always anxious over the fact that it "sticks out" just by being. Suicide is merely the most conspicuous sign of the extreme difficulty human egos have in tolerating their own free-floating existence.

Freud's concept of Thanatos, or death wish, could perhaps be reconceptualized on a sociological basis.[260] Instead of being a mysterious urge of biological life to return to inanimate matter, it could be the individual's urge to return to social *koinomia*. Many, perhaps most, human acts perhaps have a suicidal component. Most acts are tension-reductive, and most in some way pay respect to the society. Camus, in *Le Mythe de Sisyphus,* suggests that the decision to live is a problematical decision. The mystery of suicide in advanced societies, and of voodoo death in primitive societies, is perhaps a key to understanding the magical nature of the self.

In Durkheim's theory, suicide is a lesion on the social body; it is mediated to individuals on a probabilistic basis by "suicidogenic currents." What is implied by this metaphor? First of all, forget Durkheim's mysticism about the stability of suicide rates; statistics were new in his day and stochastic systems seemed more surprising than they do now. Also, penetrate his organicist analogies and one sees that they are really cognitive. Suicidogenic currents are simply *moral ideas* circulating through the social system. Durkheim's whole aim was to deny any causative property in individuals (the sole exception being suicides caused by mental illness, grudgingly included as a residual or fourth class that did not fit under the others).[261] Otherwise, the only individual susceptibility he allows is the *"length and degree of exposure"* to *suicidogenic currents*. That is as impersonal as Jeremy Bentham's felicific calculus which measured pleasure by "duration," "intensity," etc.[262]

In an important sense, Durkheim is right. There *is* an impersonality element in suicide; it is a "something" that "gets" you. It is part of the natural attitude to deny this: it can't happen to me; when it happens to other people it was foreordained from their earliest childhood, etc. Until it *does* happen to you. Durkheim stresses the impersonality factor from a collective point of view. But there is an impersonality element in suicide even from the individual point of view as well. The newest researches on the mysterious "acute depressions" that precede suicide indicate this. I am suggesting that there exists a property in human egos which makes them susceptible to suicide. Human selves are vulnerable to suicide because they are extremely frail emergents which are mostly social-impersonal in nature.

"Suicidogenic currents" explain only the cognitive part of ego's jeopardy. What Durkheim had in mind are movements of ideas—such as *"Kulturpessimismus,"* or the romantic cult of the doomed individual in De Vigny's *Chatterton*[263] and Villiers de l'Isle Adam.[264] With altruistic suicide, he was thinking of the pressure of moral ideas, such as duty and honor; with egoistic and anomic suicide, he spoke of isolating ideas or conflicting ideas. Not enough is said in all this about the sheer vulnerability of the ego. Not enough is said about how suicidogenic currents work as pressures *within* homo duplex—anomic conflicts like ego splits; altruistic currents like sheer superego pressure.

Durkheim alleges that what protects against suicide in religion is *community*, but his results would also correlate with the degree of *magic*. Catholicism, for example, is more magical than Protestantism; this and not community could explain its greater protection. The fact, tortuously buried under Durkheim's subcorrelations, that the family as a "community" does *not* afford much protection against suicide impairs his attribution of a protective quality to "community." (But Judaism remains as problematic to my interpretation as to Durkheim's.)[265]

Durkheim's definitions are really his conclusions, but they are more interesting than his statistics. His definitions of the main types of suicide should be read for their insights into how society presses on individuals. It is in these definitions that he digs most deeply into the extreme frailty of the self.

"Altruistic suicide," for example, is internalized social pressure, an excess of loyalty that demands death for breaches of honor. Durkheim's examples suggest it is most prominent in archaic civilizations, neither primitive nor modern: the Brahmins' suicide in ancient India, Samurai suicide in old Japan. Is it possible that altruistic suicide is transitional between voodoo death and modern egoistic and anomic suicides? Durkheim himself does not say this. But he does observe that, outside of institutions perpetuating archaic values, such as the military, altruistic suicide is rare in modern society. It characterizes archaic civilizations and subcultures with archaic values. This suggests that it derives from a stage in which society already requires individuals, but does not yet provide sufficient supports for this precarious state. Durkheim does relate it to *insufficient* individuation.[266]

Durkheim even specifies what particular social pressures cause altruistic suicide—this is found in his sensitive subclassification. Let me interpret his subtypes of altruistic suicide: 1. *"Obligatory altruistic suicide."* Typical example: Samurai codes requiring compulsory suicide for loss of face. Surely this is close to the voodoo death that occurs as the result of breaking a taboo. Loss of face and breaking a taboo are similar. And the automaticity of voodoo death is close to the compulsoriness of obligatory suicide—both have a mechanical quality. There are cases where it is hard to say which is which: cases where loss-of-face suicide is so obligatory that we wonder whether psychic death might not occur if the individual refused to obey the code. But the difference is in the more deeply sculpted selves of archaic civilizations: More autonomy was expected of them than of primitive man; they had tougher hides and might not swoon away on breaking a taboo. So they had to do the deed of death themselves. 2. *"Religious altruistic suicide."* Typical examples: Ancient Brahmins' suicides, Jain starvations unto death. This type is obviously related to sacrifice. We have seen that in sacrifice the self is symbolically offered up to the community. In this kind of suicide, the drama is acted out literally. 3. *Optional but prestigious suicide.* Typical example: "Who would bear the whips and scorns of time...when he himself might his quietus make with a bare bodkin?"[267] "Sticking out" is hard work; the courage-to-be falters under social pressure; the "death wish" is an urge to return to koinomia. In Greece and Rome, before Christianity, an individual simply applied to the state for permission, and then his suicide was perfectly legal.[268]

All three can be understood as social pressure, religious pressure. And all pertain to a partial but incomplete stage of individuation. It is likely that altruistic suicide wanes as society evolves toward a greater division of labor. Durkheim calls this the transition from "mechanical solidarity" (society united by common beliefs) to "organic solidarity" (society united by the division of labor). When people do not have to carry so many common values around in their heads, society's pressure on the ego is lessened. Altruistic suicide may then decline. On the other hand, in complex economies, individualism grows excessive and some people get lost. "Egoistic suicide" ensues.

It is remarkable that Durkheim did not explicitly link his three types of suicide with the useful categories developed in *The Social Division of Labor,* but we can do it for him:

1. Voodoo death is associated with "mechanical solidarity"—Durkheim's term for the primitive state in which society is integrated by beliefs. Everyone must believe exactly the same things. So much social content, heated up by group conviction, makes social-religious pressure powerful enough to cause voodoo death automatically.

2. *Magic death* (homicide) is associated with transitional societies (tribes, chiefdoms). Now homicide protects the self from voodoo death. It still occurs, but is partly checked by the counter threat of a witch-accusation-and-execution or a sorcery murder that a person charged with a moral breach might hurl back at the "moral entrepreneur" making the deadly charge.

3. *Altruistic suicide* is associated with the first states and archaic civilizations. Society is moving away from "mechanical solidarity" to division of labor. The impulse to die when "honor" or taboo is broken is still strong, but now ego, too, is tougher, so the individual does not die automatically. He has to kill himself. But there is still a burden of collective moral ideas, especially among cultivated elites.[269] Altruistic suicide persists as a survival among the military castes in later civilizations.

4. *Egoistic suicide* is associated with full "organic solidarity," when consensus is much lessened and individuals are integrated by the division of labor. Now some people become too independent and detached. Excessive moral isolation causes egoistic suicide.

5. *Anomic suicide* is associated with what Durkheim called "the abnormal division of labor,"[270] imperfect or post-organic solidarity. Now society is a chaos,[271] and conflicting values tear people apart, causing anomic suicide.

Suicide, then, is a lesion on society's objective, symbolic hide, which kills a certain number of cells every year. But it is the existence of *so many* "susceptibles" that really needs to be explained.[272] I associate it with the vulnerability of the self, which magic attempts to protect. (See diagram next page.)

What really happens in suicide? What is Durkheim's drift? Durkheim factors correlations to show suicide is a function of *relatedness* to society—"too related" produces altruistic suicide; too *un*related produces egoistic suicide; confusingly related produces anomic suicide. But behind these literal interpretations of correlations lies the deeper theory, hidden in the definitions: Suicide is caused by tides in the moral-symbolic social stuff out of which individual egos are made— if the stuff is too strict, egos are snuffed out by altruistic suicide; if it is too loose, egos sink into egoistic suicide; if it is confused, they are torn apart and succumb to anomic suicide. This is still the most promising approach, but hiding the real explanation in definitions blunts the analysis so it does not go deep enough. Durkheim did not bite down into this because he feared "psychologism." As a result he rested with a cognitive or idealist theory, i.e., "suicidogenic currents" as currents of ideas.[273]

The psychoanalytic theory, supplementing Durkheim, points to deeper social causes; and Freud's explanation of depression (superego punishing a taken-in identification within the self[274]) suggests ego's ectoplasmic frailty. It also suggests a link to homicide, though the notion of "suicide as displaced homicide" is Stekel's, not Freud's, and too simplistic.[275] But the attempt of Henry and Short[276] to link suicide and homicide (and Durkheim with Freud) by mere sta-

DEATH FROM SOCIAL PRESSURE

Stage of society	*Typical form*
1. Primitive Society—*"Mechanical Solidarity"* (Integration by intensely shared common beliefs)	VOODOO DEATH (Automatic religious death upon breaking a taboo or being officially cursed by community spokesmen)
2. Transitional Societies—*Mechanical Solidarity"* (Integration by intensely shared common beliefs)	MAGIC DEATH (Voodoo deaths continue. But they are now fought by countermeasures: witch accusations and executions, sorcery, homicides, i.e. magic that kills the accuser)
3. Early states and archaic civilizations—*Early Organic Solidarity* (Greece, Rome, India, Japan, etc. Markets and some division of labor)	ALTRUISTIC SUICIDE (Compulsory, sacrificial or optional)
4. Modern Societies—*Mature Organic Solidarity.* (Integration based on advanced division of labor. Early modern societies through mature capitalism)	EGOISTIC SUICIDE (The lonely, uprooted individual)
5. Postmodern Societies—*Organic Solidarity Breaking Up.* (Durkheim's "abnormal division of labor." Central values disintegrating, extreme cultural conflicts, discontinuities)	ANOMIC SUICIDE (The individual as nexus of value conflicts)

tiotional correlation is superficial. ("Suicide varies inversely and homicide directly with 'external restraint.' ") And there are too many important exceptions. For example, since women are socially weaker than men (that means subject to more "external restraint") they should commit homicide more often—they do not. *Both* suicide and murder increase in some periods[277]—they should not move together.

Durkheim's orientation is right but not deep enough; psychoanalysis can deepen it; but "external restraint" theory is too superficial to harvest these suggestions and produce a synthesis. Perhaps it is time to recognize that correlational analysis is just a first stage; fixation on it had a deadening effect on some of Durkheim's followers, Alvarez claims,[278] adding that psychoanalysis similarly failed to deepen its initial insights (with some conspicuous exceptions).

Recently a new kind of research emerges out of suicide-prevention centers. It seems to reveal, even more than statistics, how suicide is caused by social pressure. Hot line groups in the U.S. sponsor research with depth interviews of victims. This research[279] indicates: 1) Suicide is associated with a sudden acute depression. For example, a new type of suicide is reported among women, associated not with protracted depression but with sharp breakdowns under stress.[280] 2) This depression correlates with social stress as defined in recent indices (e.g., the Holmes scale). The Los Angeles Institute for the Study of Self Destructive Behavior emphasizes that the depression is associated with immediate, overwhelming *social* pressures—not just personal problems, but social problems. 3) Often this depression is a passing or temporary episode. (The Samaritans in England have cut the local suicide rate by one-third, proving that it is a preventable death.) 4) Seligman and others mention a sense of helplessness. Some kind of social trap or pressure has paralyzed an individual's capacity to act. 5) Alleviation seems to depend not on mere attention or comforting, but on getting the would-be victim to take action. 6) This works best if another person helps him, in a one-to-one relationship, like the shaman.

People seem to commit suicide, then, when they get into some kind of value trap or situation of excruciating social pressure which produces helplessness. Andics speaks of social failure, injured self esteem.[281] This condition is not necessarily a byproduct of classical depression; antecedents may be hard to find. When the social problems are cleared up the depression abates.

Suicide As a Magical Act. Some analysts have sensed the complexity of the act, which goes deeper than Stekel's "displaced aggression." Menninger[282] claimed to see three components in suicide: the wish to kill, the wish to be killed and the wish to die—and Alvarez reports that the Melanie Klein group finds each of these processes to be highly complex. Malinowski[283] notes that suicides have complex motives all mixed together: self-punishment, escape, aggression against an accuser.

The suggestion is heard that in many suicides the individual attempts to kill *part* of himself. This may take several forms. 1) The suicide may be trying to kill the part of himself that is an identification with someone he once loved— this is the case Freud examined.[284] 2) But he may also be trying to kill something in himself which he hates or fears:

> For we must drink deep, deep from Lethe's spring,
> Ere that which we least wish to behold will sleep.
>
> *(Byron, "Don Juan")*

The typical case reported by the Samaritans in their early years was of this sort: e.g., a person with a sexual perversion combined with a religious conscience. 3) But I want to suggest that a third case is quite prominent and colors the others. Very often the part of himself that the suicide tries to kill is *precisely the social superego which is causing him to die.* It is not unusual, writes Glasser, for a depressed person to commit suicide in order to completely remove the anger (hostile, self-attacking) from his ego.[285]

All this reminds us that suicide is already a step away from voodoo death;

perhaps it is partly a defense against it, though hardly a successful one. Fedden[286] emphasizes the defiant, anti-social aspect of suicides in primitive society. Similar is Malinowski's[287] memorable description of the Trobriand ritual suicide. A transgressor has been publicly accused by someone; he climbs to the top of a palm tree and accuses his accuser of killing him by this obloquy, then leaps to his death. (Would he have died of voodoo death anyway if he had not acted? Interestingly, this "magic" counterattack on consensus has some effect: it sometimes compels the accusing moral entrepreneur to commit suicide in turn.)

All this suggests that suicide is itself a defective magical defense, as well as one of the pressures against which magic defends. William Wahl explored this possibility in his essay "Suicide As A Magical Act."[288] He found typical "magical" goals in suicide, such as 1. making another person feel guilty; 2. reducing personal guilt by self-punishment; 3. disarming fear of death by embracing it; 4. superstitious hopes of appealing to the deity for justice after death; 5. unconscious ideas of killing the world by killing oneself.

Even in voodoo death, it should be remembered, the victim takes some action. It is not much action, but it is decisive as Warner has shown:[289] the accursed person acquiesces in his fate, isolates himself, refuses nourishment, etc. In suicide, ego also acquiesces, but it dies in a more magical way: it attacks and tries to kill the society that is killing it by destroying a piece of it, that is inside itself. This shows most nakedly in the allegedly rare suicides that do occur in primitive society. Fedden[290] reports that depressive, egoistic suicide is unknown there; and such suicides as occur are vengeance suicides. They aim at shaming a social group, or forcing someone else into suicide. They also saddle the social system with the extreme inconvenience of a disgruntled ghost. Statistics about primitive suicides are hard to get; Lunde suggests that primitive societies vary widely on this score. But we do see accounts of revenge suicide in archaic epics, in Homer, in Sophocles' Ajax, etc. Revenge suicides are terrible aggressions that dislocate order, invite the gods to retaliate, let loose a dangerous ghost, activate feuds and blood vengeance systems. The feeling that suicide is magical, impious, sacrilegious and mystically dangerous is what overcame the initial Christian impulse to go along with classical tolerance, and reestablished the primitive horror of the act, according to Alvarez and Fedden.

All this supports the idea of a progression from voodoo death through the various forms of suicide. The advance reflects in an odd and dysfunctional way the growing power of the individual. The "person category" almost comes to include the trait: "will commit suicide if dishonored." A bureaucrat thinks twice about firing an employee with a Samurai name who might cut open his guts on the doorstep. In archaic civilizations, this was one more magical protection of the self. If gossip, slander or social oppression were heaped on a Roman, he would not quietly retire to his hut and conveniently waste away. He might "take arms against a sea of troubles and by opposing end them." He might open his veins and shame his adversaries to death. Duelling was probably developed as an escape clause or defense against honor suicide in turn. From voodoo death, to revenge suicide, to honor duelling, to sorcery and homicide, we see the individual self growing tougher and more dangerous. The rare and heroic primitive who committed revenge suicide was perhaps a herald of the future independence of the self.

This continuity of voodoo death and suicide suggests that the two may have other similarities. The new studies of depression as the larval state of suicide point this way. It is almost as if psychiatry were discovering a new kind of depression that does not fit classic syndromes of depression, in which perhaps the pre-suicide experiences the psychic catastrophe that used to cause voodoo death. A few poets have told us about the experience. Sylvia Plath speaks of the "bell jar" that descends, shutting out the normal social atmosphere. Alvarez speaks of "the closed world of suicide,"[291] and of suicide's irresistible "logic,"[292] Schneidman of "catalogic." Writing of suicidal depressions, Beck notes that "previously inanition due to lack of food and secondary infection were occasional causes of death but with modern hospital treatment such complications are unusual."[293]

More phenomenological research is needed concerning these peculiar acute depressions. But notice already how many of their symptoms resemble the mysterious symptoms that Mauss and Cannon studied in voodoo death: 1. There are reports of extreme psychic pain and some suggest it is so intense that suicide is performed just to stop it. This is reminiscent of the "killer anxiety" conjectures which observers have made about the extreme discomfort preceding voodoo death. 2. Beck's suggestion that acute depression, if untreated, would lead in many cases to death from inanition and lack of food is significant. This suggests that total "disorganization" of function found in voodoo death. Perhaps something goes on inside the "bell jar" similar to the mysterious processes in voodoo death. In many cases, these depressions can still kill, all by themselves. In other cases, the individual acts and takes his own life, to ease the terrible pain. As for the "internal logic" Alvarez speaks of, logic means implication, and this is provided by the value traps, the "predicaments" that frail egos get into: "if this, then that," "if I am this kind of person, then I must do this."

Suicide and Homicide. All this suggests that a stronger link could be discerned between suicide and homicide than Henry and Short's inverse correlations. I think Stekel's idea that suicide is murder transferred to the self can more often be reversed: Many murders are magical acts displacing suicide onto another person. In murder the actor often tries to kill a part of himself that he hates *without* killing himself.[294] It may be a superego figure at whom he strikes. The boy who kills his father, and the criminal who kills a father figure are familiar case histories. It is surely suggestive that most homicides are committed against family, relatives, neighbors or close friends, just like witch accusations. In intense small groups, anyone can play the role of the oppressive superego to anyone else, and speak for the social chorus. Also suggestive are the facts that the killers usually do not try to escape, that they confess, that homicide has the highest "police clearance rate" of any crime, that the victim so often provokes the crime and even provides the weapon—facts neatly marshalled in a recent study by Lunde.[295] (But, as this author reminds us, there are many other factors in murder and the rates are quite volatile,[296] so we should not try to explain too much. Other factors include alcohol, hand-guns, "subcultures of violence."[297])

As for Henry and Short's inverse correlations of suicide and homicide, this suggests that many cases could go either way. We may now be approaching a situation in which many individuals experience both the frustrating external restraints that provoke murder and the maddening unstructured freedom that correlates with suicide. Modern bureaucracy is confining professionally, yet increasingly indifferent about private lives. We can be totally frustrated from nine to five, then allowed quietly to go to hell the rest of the time. Perhaps this is one reason why, as Lunde reports, the U.S. homicide rate now equals the suicide rate (which used to be twice as high).[298] Borderline cases that could go either way force themselves on our attention. I once heard a desperate person repeatedly threaten suicide by saying (quite unselfconsciously), "I'm going to get into my car and drive a hundred miles an hour and crash into a bus." Our streets are full of individuals who attack police hoping to be shot, and of suicides who kill themselves in ways that border on homicide. Even the murder of strangers, the so-called "felony murders" committed during some other crime, which are now on the rise,[299] often contain a suspiciously suicidal element in carelessness of risk, etc.[300]

Both suicide and murder have "magical" dimensions. In both a physical act is performed to change a psychological condition—to alleviate psychic pain, destroy the superego, fight voodoo death. When we add together murder, suicide, self-destructive accidents, psychosomatic illnesses, sick lifestyle, Menninger's "chronic suicides" and continuing undetected voodoo deaths, human selves still seem to die in vast numbers from social pressure, or in destructive "magical" attempts to fight against it. We may have reached the point where, with modern medicine enjoying diminishing returns, longevity rates are now more elastic to these social pressures, thus producing, at the margin, the predicament of primitive society.[301] Among American teen-agers, the suicide rate doubled in the seventies, becoming the third leading cause of death. According to some journalistic reports, the other two leading causes for this age group are accidents and homicides. Then we have the psychosomatic and lifestyle diseases of the despairing middle aged, not to mention the helplessness-induced deaths of the marginalized old. Despite the tough modern ego, people still die of social pressure. Maybe most people ultimately die for social reasons, if the truth were known.

Where does magic fit in? How does it prevent these deaths? Let us recall first that suicide itself is often a magic act[302] that defends against another, more helpless death: voodoo death, sheer destruction by society. Suicide obviously is a *defective* defense; but botches are nothing new in magic. And magical institutions in turn weave more elaborate defenses against magic's own hazards. It seems possible that duelling customs, which have roots no doubt in earlier magical contests, are a defense, an alternative, against altruistic suicide. More advanced magic, in addition, fights the root social pressure that leads to suicide.

In part four of this chapter we shall see *how* magic, in general, fights such social pressure on behalf of the ego. Above all it does so by restoring ego's main function, which is to translate passivity into action. The shaman teaches the patient to continue to act. He "will not cease from mental fight."

3. Soul Loss

Social pressure can wound a primitive as well as kill him; it can cause sickness as well as death. Primitives have a term for sickness which they also apply to the pre-morbid condition preceding voodoo death: They often call it "soul loss." Magic defends against soul loss.

Why was soul loss such a problem for primitives, why should physical illness be so easily induced by social pressure? De Martino[303] suggests an answer. To translate his idea into my terms: the primitive self was extremely vulnerable because it lacked the protective armature of "the Individual," a legal-rational supportive institution not yet constituted. There was no individual law, no citizenship, no "advanced" religion institutionalizing "soul" to back up the self. Therefore, the self depended almost exclusively on magic to defend its slender being.

Today our fortified egos lack the excitement and aliveness of challenges unto psychic extinction. Gilbert Murray once remarked that one fascination in studying the ancient world was that men in those times did not have the massive moral institutions of 19th century Europe to guide them, so the moral struggles of a Themistocles or a Pericles had a heroic quality. The same is true of the mere struggle to be, among more primitive peoples. In De Martino's view, magic is not just a struggle for the self, but a struggle for reality, for that too must be constituted to provide the individual with a home. (Remember, the "secondary process" has not yet put the world in order.) World as well as self are precarious, both are mâya, both have not yet been fully constituted.[304] Primitives who fight for life with magic are therefore also fighting for reality, and they are more aware than we that social creations are mâya.

De Martino dramatizes the fragility of primitive ego by describing the widely reported propensity of primitives to get fascinated by any prepossessing sight around them. In some societies, individuals caught by such fascinations compulsively imitate them: they imitate waves, birds. As late as the nineteenth century whole Cossack regiments would be seized with this compulsion and endlessly mimic an officer. Such phenomena are called "olon" in Siberia, "latah" in Malaya, "atai" among the Mota, according to Codrington. But words like this are found virtually everywhere, De Martino claims, like mana words. This phenomenon dramatizes how permeable social monads were to each other, how little inner autonomy they had.

At this primitive stage, the self is so vulnerable, that it often simply dies, or is "lost." De Martino claims that "soul loss" is the magical illness par excellence, involved in all mental disturbances. Anxiety, on the other hand, is a sign of resistance to the *fascinans,* to the indiscriminate *koinomia* of olonism and latah. Magic is the tool of this resistance. It fights against soul loss.

And magic is real. De Martino means this on several levels. 1. First, it works. 2. Secondly, magic uses real paranormal phenomena which are not yet scientifically explained. 3. But in addition, beyond ESP, De Martino claims that magic possesses true spiritual powers because the universe is spiritual and magical. De Martino is a true believer, in other words, but one who commands great knowledge of social science. Drawing especially on Rasmussen, Bogaraz, Shirokogoroff and other Slavic scholars of shamanism, he makes the interesting claim that paranormal powers of magic, still active in primitive societies, get screened out by Western anthropologists and so are under-reported.

The threat magic fights is collapse of ego back into the *koinomia* or community from which the monad emerged: latah is surrendering to outside fascination, becoming what you see.[305]

Magic, according to De Martino, does not merely win time for the ego to emerge; through its creations it builds up social structures of self that guarantee it. (He does not, however, demonstrate the historical process whereby this happens.) He is now writing about the beginnings of the person category, but using existential language. Our Christian rational civilization assumes a soul; it is based on centuries of Christian philosophy, institutions, legal guarantees, the reward of a long struggle. In the magic world of the primitive, soul is *not* guaranteed, but must be fought for in an heroic struggle.

Originally the *dasein,* the presence, the being-there of the person was threatened by the *fascinans.* At first the presence did not have the power to crush the fascinating object by mastering its emotional charge—so it attached itself to it. Thus the initial magical method of protection was to personify any fascinating object and then enter into relations with this personification. The shaman showed the community how to do this (when he entered into a relationship with the spirits that first possessed him). In this manner, surrender is avoided; insight is gained; the presence stands. The shaman, once attacked and recovered, repeatedly acts out his drama of soul loss and recovery to strengthen the group by his example.

Any illness is interpreted as soul loss because any illness can *become* soul loss. It has been shown[306] how this can cause panic among primitives. Any illness striking an Eskimo is potentially a psychic illness, because it is a dangerous *fascinans,* a potential source of mass hysteria. In some Eskimo work groups, illness starts and one by one all the members are seized. They drop in lethargy, depression; they cease to hunt and fish. They would all die of starvation did not the culture contain the prescription: a shaman. If none is present someone is coopted to go through the shamanic experience. He then personifies the illness as a spirit, experiences a painful possession by the spirit, but finally conquers it and by his example cures the group.

Thus cultural redemption of the presence begins; it is narrated in myths, repeated in dreams, acted out in rites. The self grows in strength through such dramas, grows in its power to resist the koinomia. The shamanic drama may be institutionalized in some societies as an experience *all* are expected to go through to deepen selves: e.g., vision quest among the Plains Indians, the spiritual quests of young Brahmins, certain drug cults, experiments in hedonism during the German *wanderjahr.* Cults of mysticism perpetuate the archaic human experience of strengthening the self through jeopardy and loss.[307] (Thus Kierkegaard writes of gaining power through facing dread.)[308]

To many primitives, most illnesses are potentially diagnosable as soul loss: either they are caused by social pressure or their terrifying example *creates* social pressure (panic, hysteria). Some modern psychoanalysts such as Róheim and Ferenczi have attempted to cast these ideas into modern terms, suggesting diffusion of libido and libido fixation in particular organs in psychosomatic illness—libido as "soul" that has become "lost" (diffused, locked up in complexes).

4. Anxiety

Related to voodoo death and soul loss (though on a different plane conceptually) is the mysterious phenomenon of anxiety. Many psychiatrists (e.g., Sullivan) have considered anxiety to be the cause of virtually all mental symptoms, which the Freudians in turn frequently characterize as magical rituals. Therefore anxiety is seen to cause magic (or else magic is portrayed as a defense against anxiety). Some consider this defense to be quite positive—Róheim, for example. Some go further and regard the mere presence of anxiety as a positive sign that ego has gone over to the offensive against psychic death (De Martino). But others, such as Odier, regard magical operations as defective protections against anxiety, "too little and too late"; so magic is just a symptom that anxiety is swamping the ego. Against such disagreements, it is hard to say anything definite. And Lévi-Strauss has warned us that the concept of anxiety is far too vague to explain magic.[309] (The Oxford linguistic philosophers would agree: "A pang of anxiety" is one of their favorite examples of a virtually incommunicable experience.) Lévi-Strauss comments: "As affectivity is the most obscure side of man, there has been the constant temptation to resort to it, forgetting that what is refractory to explanation is *ipso facto* unsuitable for use in explanation. A datum is not primary because it is incomprehensible."[310] He means that magic cannot be explained causally as a defense that arose against anxiety. In fact, Lévi-Strauss observes, magic often causes anxiety[311] (an insight as old as Lucretius). These iatrogenic effects are probably just as uncertain as magic's alleged cures.

Perhaps no definite formulation about anxiety and magic can be made. But there are some interesting contrasts in the disagreements about it, which are suggestive. For example, psychiatrists who put a grave interpretation on anxiety are often people who work with extremely sick mental patients, especially schizophrenics. Whereas psychiatrists and philosophers who address themselves to robust modern selves seem to think we can stand anxiety, even profit from it. Thus Heidegger[312] preaches "resoluteness" against it; Kierkegaard[313] and the existentialists urge that man is not fully human unless he experiences the ontological version of anxiety, *"angst."* Freud, treating robust upper-middle class Viennese neurotics, complacently imagined that ego could use anxiety routinely as a signal to scourge the id and maintain psychic control. Tillich associates it with the courage to be,[314] and elsewhere asserts it is controlled by symbolism, by "the right word."[315] Charles Frankel writes of the "love of anxiety."[316] Rollo May writes that it is indeed a fear of death, but that it can also be an ally of the reality principle that leads to a creative integration of individual and society.[317] And to Mowrer, anxiety is "guilt trying to return from repression and produce overdue growth."[318]

There exists today a Boy Scout rhetoric of anxiety—anxiety is good for you. But this cheerful approach is not often used by psychiatrists who work with truly desperate patients, people whose egos have been virtually destroyed, such as psychotics or autistic children. Bruno Bettelheim[319] considers "panic anxiety," caused by extreme stress, to be a common denominator and a causative factor in autism. Nicholas Tinbergen[320] thinks autism is rising because extreme social stresses are increasing and are causing intense affect.

The issue, with anxiety as with magic, seems to be psychic death, and this is a more urgent threat with weaks egos. But ego is always at stake, even in neurosis. Eugene Levitt[321] reminds us that all the basic ego dynamisms work against anxiety; Vaillant[322] grades dynamisms by how effective they are against anxiety. In studies of psychosis, in which ego is actually overthrown, there is a greater emphasis on anxiety. Federn[323] does a sensitive phenomenology of its erosion of ego boundaries. Freeman, Cameron and McGhie formulate that anxiety causes cognitive deterioration,[324] disturbances of attention[325] that break ego boundaries, with loss of object relations and identity.[326] Mednick[327] views schizophrenia as a catastrophic defense against anxiety which uses irrelevant associations to defeat drive generalization so that cognitive disorganization is reinforced. Many psychiatrists today seem to suggest that anxiety is the "violent chronic affect" that Jung[328] conjectured caused schizophrenic deterioration and what Janet[329] called "lowering of the mental level." (Snyder's[330] dopamine hypothesis is only the latest attempt to discover a physiological base for such a disorganizing affect.[331])

Even with psychotics, however, the picture is ambivalent. Bender[332] asserts that anxiety is the key problem with childhood schizophrenia, but that it also gives the schizophrenic his only weapon to control behavior that is already disorganized (probably due to an inborn lability). According to Klein,[333] the main task of the child is to master anxiety; in this sense anxiety stimulates growth of the ego, but if too intense it can retard it. Whittaker and Malone[334] speak of positive and negative anxiety. And behind "overwhelming anxiety" there is often a real threat—Rheingold[335] suggests actual fear of annihilation,

Goldstein[336] suggests a catastrophic reaction to one's inability to cope, as does Fromme-Reichmann[337] (but she also thinks the affect can be mobilized to help the patient[338]). Goldstein[339] also writes of an anxiety-fear continuum; fear focuses and controls anxiety; conversely excessive fear always threatens to turn back into swamping anxiety (anxiety is the "sting of fear," Tillich writes[340]). These ambiguities are neatly sorted out by the Yerkes-Dodson theorems in experimental psychology.[341] Anxiety is a curvilinear function: a little bit stimulates learning (and presumably ego growth); too much swamps both.

While some who treat psychotics assert that even here anxiety can be helpful in mild intensities, Sullivan's absolute terror of anxiety is perhaps more typical of those who work closely with these desperate people. Sullivan in fact defines the self[342] in such a way as to lead to the conclusion that anxiety is utterly destructive of it. The self in his definition *is* "anxiety-free consciousness" which struggles desperately to *stay* free of anxiety. Sullivan does not like the self very much, precisely because it is so intrinsically susceptible to anxiety; this makes it the Achilles' heel of the whole personality. A few writers have attempted to generalize this conviction at a philosophical level—Fingarette,[343] for example, declares that anxiety is nothing other than the disintegration of the personality. It is the pain felt when the ego begins to tear.

We see that the destructive potential of anxiety is especially grave with weak egos, such as we find in schizophrenics, autistic children, brain-damaged individuals—and perhaps primitives. And despite Lévi-Strauss' warning about the vagueness of the term, there is no doubt that anxiety is associated with magic. Magic fights helplessness with action. It appears, both as a symptom and a defense, in psychotics, primitives and small children, whose egos are weak. The reason is that it is ego's first defense and therefore also its last-ditch defense. The ambiguous relation to anxiety may also tell us something about the iatrogenesis that dogs magical cures. In religious rites like sacrifice, human *angst* is experienced, faced down, resolved. By contrast, while some magic abreacts, much magic simply flees or binds anxiety. Kierkegaard's concept of the "demoniacal as the dread of the good"[344] may also be relevant, since the deadly danger magic often fights is the pressure of religion, of the moral community, of conscience. (Whereas healthy dread is like a "grand inquisitor," relentlessly examining the soul for imperfection.)

The magician lives with anxiety, De Martino writes. His magical actions counter anxiety; they may also cause anxiety, as everyone from Lucretius to Schipkowensky[345] has pointed out. It may barely work, and it may fail. Although the matter is far from clear, then, we can probably speak of anxiety as one of those extreme conditions with which magic tries to cope.

PART FOUR: HOW DOES MAGIC DEFEND THE SELF?

Magic accoutres the fragile emerging self with its earliest and flimsiest armor—correct gestures and acceptable speeches that lock into collective rituals to give the self a presence. These frail devices facilitate the ghostly ego magic of the "magical principle," encouraging the diffident transformation of pleasure-principle drives into reality-principle action. Psychological ego magic is the fountain and the sword's point of self; it is also the first redoubt and in regression it may again become the last and only defense. But real magic is not just a bundle of subjective tendencies. It is an historic complex of real institutions out there in plain view in the flaming headdresses of the ritual choruses, the solemn work magic of the yam gardens, the sullen lore and antic paraphernalia passed down to the shaman. Even those shadowy ego operations which I call "magical-in-the-weak-sense" can work only because they gear outwards into this colorful, heartening, massified drama of symbolic mumbo-jumbo. These institutions helped create ego in the first place; and now they hold up to it all those cues and stimuli and encouraging signals of receptivity for "I-behavior" through which alone ego magic can translate outward into successful individual action.

How magic increasingly encourages the behavior which we call "self" might be diagrammed as a series of ever wider concentric circles around the ego as history progresses. First there is only frail ego magic playing to an immediate magic chorus of ritual expectations; but gradually more solid supports are built around this core. Religion creates the religious magics, especially the rites of membership (sacrifice and initiation) that redraw boundaries for the self. Ceremonial magic uses these gestures to hearten not only the work gang but the individual in it. Later, medical magic reworks the old symbols to cure sick souls. Still later, magic transforms into powerful secular institutions and the institution of the Individual is born as a redoubtable outer fortification around the self.

But under pressure the battle so easily collapses back to the inner redoubt. For the ego remains a ghostly wraith, rather like the frail naked Martian who crept out of the gigantic space ship in H. G. Wells' *War of the Worlds*. The Moloch-like institutions of Western individualism are like that space ship. But the ego remains like the naked Martian who crept out of it, killed by the common cold. The armor is far from invulnerable; voodoo death still stalks the land in new guises; and weak selves are easily killed by lucky shots. So let us spend more time on the inner battle, on the sheer defensive ego magic of self, but let us look at it now from a sociological view.

I. The Psychoanalytic Theory Fits and Confirms the Sociological Theory of Magic

The psychoanalytic theory I reconstructed from Róheim and Freud can be fitted into the sociological theory of magic. Mauss' work contains some anticipations of the discovery that what magic fights is superego pressure threatening ego collapse:[346] e.g., his idea of *"expropriation"* (and Huvelin's idea of *"detouring"*[347]). "Et nous serons amenés à l'idée que ces individus non fait que s'approprier des forces collectives."[348] It was this statement about "expropriating" that Huvelin picked up to develop his theory of the "detouring" of the sacred in magic. And Huvelin specifically related this *"détournement"* to the protection of the individual. (Specifically, he depicted magic curses and oaths as the original sanctions protecting the individual in his property.)

Consider in sociological terms some of the strategies whereby magic saves the self:

1. *Magic protects the self from the social.* Durkheim[349] emphasized that the profane must be protected from the sacred, *because the sacred would destroy it.* Extraordinary symbolic precautions (taboos) are needed, for the sacred spreads along its sympathetic-symbolic pathways, just like the repressed. Even to think of what must not be mixed is dangerous. The suggestion is that to some degree the person is profane—and society is sacred and taboo protects the profane ego from the mortal danger of the sacred-social.[350] Thus Durkheim anticipated the psychoanalytic discovery that magic defends the ego from destruction by the social.

Studies of witchcraft confirm this: The accused witch is often what Howard Becker[351] calls a "moral entrepreneur," who brings an accusation against ego on behalf of the social chorus, working like an external superego. The witch accusation (which is the magical act) neutralizes this pressure, and defends the self from the social.

Immoderate magical resistance to social life can lead to complete disconnection and the psychic death of schizophrenia. But inadequate magical defenses make the individual susceptible to voodoo death. The seance drama of medical magic is a struggle against it. Someone has cursed a man, or perhaps the person's own superego attacked after he broke a taboo. The witchdoctor struggles on his behalf, using the "surplus meaning" of his spectacular abundant symbolism to objectify into defeatable symbols the diffuse meaning-illness that has beset him. Since, as Hegel showed, magic always operates "by getting things on their weak side,"[352] sorcerers, witches and the superego usually attack where there is already a physical susceptibility. But the struggle is over the will to live. And it is a moral struggle. The witchdoctor's symbols challenge the moral authority of the social pressure that is killing his patient. And all the while, the victim's underlying rupture with community is treated symbolically in an attempt to reintegrate him into the nomos before it kills him.

2. *Magic nurtures man's spontaneity against his socialization.* Even before magic, religion nourished the emerging ego. From religion came the first ideas of a personage, of a soul. Religion even fostered spontaneity to some degree. Just projecting the social in religious representations helped people get it in hand. I do not wish to assert a Huvelin-like dichotomy of magic/religion related to individual/social any more than Hubert and Mauss[353] did. Magic, too, is social, even when helping the individual; and on the other hand religion has, as one of its main functions, the creation and socialization of selves. But selves as spontaneous actors cannot be fully programmed in advance—the very rules that set them spinning can snuff them out if taken too literally in some situations. So religion's byproduct, magic, fights for breathing space on their behalf, fights

against religion and all the rules of existence where necessary. The drama *Antigone* illustrates the value conflicts that can lead to death; magic provides escape hatches against this. Among the Trobrianders, Malinowski found magic providing all sorts of off-sets for religious rules and their supernatural sanctions.[354]

Therefore the formula is: 1. Religion is the core of the socialization process. 2. Magic is man's first defense against his own socialization, when it interferes with his spontaneity. Without its contrapuntal resistance to religion, the superego would crush all initiative; any departure from the norm would strike terror; and anyone accidentally caught in value conflicts would die of voodoo death.

Whether magic is an adequate defender of the ego is another question. After all, it uses the same sacred-social symbolism that can frighten us to death when it appears in religion. One feels that magic works for a while, but becomes symptomatic or even iatrogenic if overly indulged, and that it is less adaptive in modern than in primitive societies. Lévi-Strauss' image of the *"bricoleur"*[355] is apposite here: the magician is like a handyman who keeps patching things up, repairing old machines out of the debris of wrecked machines, patching up broken egos with some of the sacred symbols that smashed them—the whole thing barely works and there are never any fresh or permanent solutions; it is all conservative, defensive, just adequate, or an actual botch.

The shaman typically has no lasting cures except "analysis interminable"; his clients become anxiously attached to him as half-cured, half sick, lifetime dependents, like the permanent members of Alcoholics Anonymous or Synanon. Magic is by nature a kind of avoidance behavior, so it can seldom solve anything, but it can buy time. Historically, magic bought time for the Individual to emerge and develop more lasting defenses for the self.

3. Magic uses meaning to defend the self from terror. A witch, a sorcerer, a taboo, a superego has attacked someone. He is going to die because he is supposed to die, because he believes he is supposed to die, because, by all the rules, he *must* die. To this, magic says, "Yes...but..." The nomos is reinterpreted; the taboo contains an exception; the sin is forgiven; the sorcerer is forced to retreat; the busybody is branded as a witch. And if the patient is already overwhelmed by his helplessness and sunk in unutterable horror, the shaman uses his spectacular vocabulary to *make* it utterable and get control of it. The patient is all affectivity with insufficient symbolism so he cannot explain his feelings, Lévi-Strauss writes. The shaman, by contrast, bubbles over with surplus symbolism; he has interpretations to spare, interpretations to sell. The shaman blots up the patient's excess affectivity with his surplus symbolism. In one childbirth scene described by Lévi-Strauss,[356] the Indian shaman simply tells a fantastic tale about a group of heroes travelling through the dreaded birth canal; this gives meaning to the contractions the woman experiences; meaning lessens her anxiety and this controls her pain. The contemporary Lamaze method of childbirth is perhaps no less magical: the Pavlovian metaphysics that comes with it is perhaps not much more relevant than the Indian myth—but just having some meaning[357] seems to control anxiety and thereby pain.

Magic controls anxiety with meaning; it steals the meaning from religion; it changes it for its own purposes. Just giving any kind of interpretation helps to transform the anxiety into fear, which is more manageable. The true pain in any fear is the threat of de-objectification—the danger that the fear will spread and turn into object-less, overwhelming anxiety. Just tying the anxiety up with something, giving it an object, helps turn it back into fear. And then the fear in turn can be dealt with by manipulating the object symbolically. So the shaman palms a dart and then removes the planted object from the patient's body—this magic dart, he asserts, was the cause of the illness. Seeing the dart, the patient focuses on it and fears it—this drains off some of his anxiety.

But the shaman digs deeper with his symbolism. His ability to understand the social "network" of the patient (currently being rediscovered as a psychiatric art[358]) seems so sensitive to us that Freud identified it with ESP.[359] But the shaman simply knows who accused the patient of being unsocial, what rival might have tried to frighten him, what rules he may be breaking. He also knows the man's vices, weaknesses and reputation. (In Cebu, sorcerer-witchdoctors conduct an active, open investigation into the social background of a client's case, according to Lieban.[360]) All this information is embroidered in the songs the magician sings, the tales he tells, the prayers he prays, in an attempt to weave the man back into the social fabric.

Health is the ability to respond to meaning with meaning. Magic is one of the older, cruder, lower-order strategies in this struggle for meaning. It is never quite adequate by itself though it may buy time. Too obsessive a grubbing for meaning is more a symptom of sickness than it is a defense of health. Goldstein has shown how a pathological craving that everything be meaningful appears in brain-injured patients.[361] Impaired in abstraction and cognitive control, they cannot tolerate anything that is unstructured, undefined, open or provisional. They grub for meaning, even in details, to control terror. Lévi-Strauss similarly observes that a sick and terrified primitive feels distress mainly because of the emptiness and inadequacy of his response to the "storm of meaning" outside him in the social world.[362] His confused affectivity *is* his sense of the inadequacy of his symbolic response. We know that strong egos can tolerate hypotheses, suspension of judgment, openness, provisionality. An excessive craving for meaning may indeed be a sign of ego weakness. And therefore magic, with its orgy of identification, is a symptom but also a cure, a way of coping (Arieti[363]).

4. *Magic fights helplessness with action.* "Magic is the counterphobic attitude," Róheim wrote,[364] and this is true of real magic as of ego magic. There has been a lot of convergent research in recent decades on helplessness as the cause of anxiety, depression, etc. Consider first the "learned helplessness" experiments in academic psychology, in which an animal learns that its responses are independent of any outcome. A dog repeatedly exposed to unavoidable shock gives up and does not avoid. A rat held helplessly in a harness and then dropped into water gives up and drowns while other rats swim for hours. The source of helplessness is the *unpredictability* of an outcome that our actions cannot affect.[365]

This produces anxiety at first, and finally causes the same symptoms found in clinical depression: such as fewer voluntary responses, lowered aggression, loss of appetite, etc. Seligman has summarized this evidence and inferred from it that "learned helplessness" and depression are probably the same; that the key to both is the ultimate formation of a hypothesis (or an "expectation") that our responses will not have any effect.

A special issue of the *Journal of Abnormal Psychology*[366] was recently devoted to the learned helplessness model. Aaron Beck has criticized the model, but his own model of negative cognitive set[367] is perhaps similar. In both theories, it is not just the frustrating outside situation, but something "inside," something taking place in the "dynamic assessment" (MacIver[368]) which the person makes before any action, which causes helplessness. People with past experience of accomplishment are more immune to the deadly hypothesis of personal helplessness. All this reminds us that helplessness can be induced by an attack on our nerve as well as by objectively frustrating situations. The rival who tells us "You'll fumble it," like the sorcerer who says, "Things will go wrong," can induce helplessness. And that is also where positive magic comes in, of course. When effective action seems blocked, magic says: "Something can be done after all. We can finesse it." Even today, every popular magic from Coué to assertiveness training attempts to change our "negative cognitive set" (Beck) or destroy our hypothesis of helplessness (Seligman). The basic message of magic is: We can do it. Magic in practice consists of *new hypotheses* which say: act and something will happen. Even sick magic has that quality. Paranoid projections say: You can do it, and the paranoid at least *does* something, however crazy, that causes things to happen.

And it is interesting to me that at least one of the helplessness studies lapses into metaphors of magic. Seligman characterizes various predictable pairings of response and outcome (where something expected happens and one is *not* helpless) as "magic moments."[369] A voluntary action or "operant" that has an effect (e.g., push button, elevator comes), or one that is *predictably in*effective and will "extinguish" (push button, no elevator) are both "magic moments."[370] His metaphor seems to suggest that, by contrast, helplessness is the state of being utterly *un*magical.

B. F. Skinner's[371] classical study of "superstition" seems to confirm this and even to suggest that magic is a defense against anxiety. Skinner found that when pellets were dropped into pigeon boxes at short intervals, the pigeons would start repeating whatever behavior they had engaged in just before the first few pellets arrived. Skinner called his study "Superstition in the Pigeon" and thought it helped explain how magic gets stamped into behavior.[372] Suppose a pigeon was whirling around counter clockwise when the first pellets arrived. It would then continue to turn and turn. Even if very few pellets came while the pigeon did this, that would be enough to "reinforce" the behavior—in fact, as many studies have shown, "periodic reinforcement" (irregular rewards) makes a response virtually invulnerable to "extinction" (because, as it were, the organism "remembers" that the action is *sometimes* rewarded, and "you never know").

But this experiment really explained a lot more than the "superstitious" quality of magic. I suggest that what these pigeons were really doing was getting their helplessness under control. Whirling and turning was like a magic hypothesis about the arrival of the pellets. It was as if the pigeon had seized control of the experiment from the psychologist and turned it into a set-up for "periodic reinforcement"! And this action favorably changed their predicament, which had been adverse. If the helplessness situation they escaped had been more punishing, then doing this might have saved the pigeons' lives.[373]

I am forcing Seligman and Skinner, of course, but look at the remarkable parallels in real institutional magic. The rain maker knows that he does not really make the rain. His dance is a "metaphor of mastery" as Stanley Diamond puts it.[374] He dances "with the rain," as Suzanne Langer puts it,[375] so as to have some control over its unpredictable coming, like the pigeon that whirls and whirls. This may focus his attention, as Lienhardt puts it,[376] so that later he may notice that rain comes after certain weather signals appear, and this will give him still more control. As Tillich[377] writes, anxiety is helplessness and the lack of intentionality, of something to do. The original purpose of rain-making was to control the terror of helplessness by taking action in a metaphor of mastery.

5. *Magic goes on the offensive.* "The courage to be," Tillich wrote, "is self-affirmation 'in-spite-of,' that is, in spite of that which tends to prevent the self from affirming itself."[378] The in-spite-of is the superego, man's socialization. It is a struggle for being, against non-being, against anxiety. Heidegger reminds us that the verb "to be" in primitive Greek derived from a verb meaning "to stand up, to shine forth."[379] Every time someone opens his mouth to speak, a "magical" act can take place as he uses consensual representations skillfully or ineptly, acceptably or unacceptably, to enhance his position in "quality space" (Osgood).[380]

Magic does not just *defend* the self, it aggrandizes the self; in magic the self goes over to the offensive, against the superego. It begins by capturing what is social within itself. Hubert and Mauss write that the magician is a popular hero who is admired above all for the power that he has over himself: this power-over-self is the basis of his other powers.[381] Later they note a universal theme in magic: the *"dédoublement."*[382] But obviously this doubling has to do with homo duplex, and getting control over oneself means getting control over the social side of homo duplex—which is already a first step toward control over the social.[383] The arena in which the magician first expropriates social power is inside his own superego—this is what Róheim means when he writes that, "But if the superego is won over, all is well again."[384] The first collective-religious symbols which he learns to manipulate are, necessarily, those that he has ingested. He demonstrates his control by overcoming spectacular magical illnesses and by this demonstration he acquires power over others.

Hubert and Mauss have shown how the witch's familiar is probably an outgrowth of the personal totem—it is mastered by the magician.[385] But since even a personal totem is just an avatar of the clan totem[386] getting control of a familiar or totem animal expresses and at one time actualized the magician's seizure of religious power through mastery of the social in his own personality. Among the Eskimos,[387] the shaman usually returns from his initiatory trance with one or more spirits who are now his servants and give him power; these are animal spirits and possibly totemic remnants. In many cultures the magician after initiation has spirits at his command. These are avatars of society itself, which he now partly masters. His relationship to them is ambiguous: they remain powerful and dangerous; they are not fully tamed; they may turn on him. Moreover, in some societies the candidate for magician has no choice for he cannot resist the spirits' insistent offers of help. He begins to become a magician by getting "infected" by them. They enter him, "possess" him, make him "sick"; he "conquers" them and gets well and thereafter they are his dangerous "allies." In this symbolic drama, the magician has begun to conquer the social that is within him.

6. *Magic seizes control through the power of abstraction.* In magic man begins to exploit his first abstractions, which were forged in religion. Becker has defined an abstraction behavioristically as a pragmatic arrangement of objects for action,[388] and this is useful. To abstract is to "refer the object to one's intended use." There is a strong sense in which abstraction does violence to reality. Kris, writing of creativity,[389] observes that abstractions and creative representations *dismember* or replace reality. Heinz Werner,[390] though identifying magic thinking with what is infantile or psychotic, has shown how magic sympathetic associations are nonetheless the beginnings of abstraction. Arieti[391] similarly portrays magical thinking as an intermediary stage between primitive concreteness and full abstraction, when he speaks of its "concrete abstractions," "endocepts" and "paleologic." Phenomenologies of action (Heidegger, Schutz) write of the prefiguring of action in a mental "plan" or "model" or "project" which changes perception of external reality and then is used to act upon it and change it in actuality. And we have seen that some degree of abstraction is intrinsic to magic; that it only arises with the "generalization of mana" (Durkheim); that its operations of *extrapolation* (Huvelin) and *implication* (Mauss) and *application* (Jensen) depend on generalization that can work from one case to another. There is sense in which magic is man's original bag of abstractions for the purpose of doing violence to reality.[392]

The first abstractions were created in religion, which numerous studies by the Durkheim school have shown to be the original factory of the categories. Magic takes over these earliest abstractions and applies them. But then it quickly develops self-conscious theories of what it is doing and these theories create new abstractions which make further magical applications possible. In this sense, magic is like mathematics, which expands every time a theory of how it works is generated (e.g., Gödel numbers, used to propound Gödel's proof, produced a new branch of mathematics[393]). Magicians always have theories about what they are doing, and the theories themselves are often incorporated into spells the way "charter myths" are.[394] Religion supplies the classifications, magic and myth begin the *propositions* based on this proto-logic of classes. In his theory and praxis, the magician perennially uses abstractions; in fact he invents some of the race's earliest concepts. That may be one reason why, as Eliade reports, the shaman's vocabulary is often enormously larger than that of the average person.[395]

But there is also something reminiscent of magic in Goldstein's account of sick behavior where abstraction is impoverished—the meaning-grubbing of his brain-injured people somehow suggests magic. Instead of speaking of sick vs. healthy magic, perhaps we could instead say, as primitive man does, that some magic is more powerful than other magic. Power seems correlated with the degree of abstraction and generality. The most powerful magic words are often theory words, concept words, like "mana." Other magics, less abstract, more concrete, purely defensive, are simply weaker magic. In schizophrenic magic, which is failed magic, abstraction fails completely. (See Solomon Snyder's summary of three generations of evidence on the collapse of the abstract attitude in schizophrenia.[396]) Obviously, the "magic" of a phobia which unleashes anxiety automatically to avoid a situation of more serious anxiety is much weaker than the "magic" of seers who figure out from the stars how to predict the rising of the Nile and use their knowledge to become Pharaohs in Egypt.

Magic tends to be implicative while religion is ontological. And it is curious that extreme implication in logic, the so-called "paradoxes of implication"[397] wherein everything seems to imply everything else, seem to confirm the magical monistic view of the universe. The assumption of unity is one of magic's first bold ideas in getting hold of the world; it is an accurate assumption, for what it really intuits is the moral unity of the social group, which makes it possible for the monad to take the attitude of the "generalized other" (G. H. Mead) and to influence almost anything in the culture through almost anything else.

7. How magic is alienated. One reason we associate magic more with its weaker manifestations is that the more powerful magics have been reduced to sciences in our civilizations. But, like most public property, magic turned into science seems somewhat alienated from man, as Feuerbach claims religion to be. Magic also gets alienated in official religions that monopolize magic and of course professions try to do so, too. But magic does not just get away from the individual it began by serving; it also piles up around him and becomes oppressive to him. Magical institutions, traditions and lore become part of the environment with which he must cope through his own feeble ego magic. As more and more magic is objectified in scientific knowledge, rigidified in religions, vested in learned occult establishments and sheer tradition, it is harder and harder for the magical attitude to "size things up" and form an abstract model for an attack on reality. "Reality" now is not just "listless nature," as Goethe called it, but also "objectified mind" in Hegel's phrase, and it bristles.

Through millennia, man as the magic animal has turned back the environment with his powerful abstractive magic again and again, but each time he acted magically, he precipitated *more* objective mind. Now the meaning of the towering social structures that surround him is virtually unfathomable, and it is harder and harder for the magician to get a fix on it, to abstract it and wrench it into a plan enabling one to attack it. After a point individuals and civilizations grow sick from their magical "cures." Sullivan reports that sometimes a successful obsessional neurosis grows weary with age; the cobwebs woven by a lifetime of symbolic magical operations become too complicated to compute, and the tired obsessional drifts into schizophrenia. So too, perhaps, do certain primitive cultures, whose magic grows more elaborate until the whole culture becomes a disease: e.g., sorcerer-ridden Dobu, whose residents are more comfortable visiting foreign islands than exposed to the magic terrors of home. The compulsive expansion of meaning is visible in many provinces of culture—and what Wittgenstein called "the accursed fertility of philosophy" is true of magic, too. What William Irwin Thompson calls "Pythagorean science,"[398] what Joseph Needham similarly calls the "Taoist" mentality,[399] can be lively and inventive in dawning ages like the Renaissance or the Han Dynasty, but gradually the cobwebs accumulate, the *"bricoleur"* becomes an obsessional and the vision darkens into a complex heavy gnosticism or an astral pessimism in ages of decline. One could make an analogy to the schizophrenic "trip." Often it is numinous, inspired, and some like Laing think it could be put to positive use. But usually its magic inspirations usher in a long period of confusion.[400] Storch writes vividly of this sequence, in haunting language that could apply to magic as to psychosis, and to civilizations as to individuals:

> But this fabulous efflorescence . . . is transitory, usually only a single phase of an ominous disease process. The glowing experience is dissipated like a vapor; the return to the world of reality is barred; there remains only one way out and that leads through rending torments, rambling confusion, apathetic waste, to imbecility or empty torpidity. But even beneath the hard and sterile stones of fixed catatonic reactions . . . seethe and murmur the springs . . . of experiences now almost extinguished, which at one time carried the being higher and higher . . . until, in Promethean temerity he grasped for the highest of all—and fell.[401]

Ethical religions often arise in protest against the pain of magic's accumulated meaning—"dung heaps" Veblen called such traditional "wisdom." In a sense, "organic solidarity" (Durkheim) is a partial protection against this; the Yellow Pages image of society limits the amount of collective representations (and hence magic) we each must carry. But in ripe, archaic societies, the burden of magical knowledge is so intolerable as to provoke the rise of ethical religions as one more drastic cure. Angus, Lucretius and others have written of the sheer fear that magic and religion engender. Perhaps the division of labor itself is partly stimulated by this motive of escape from the burden of meaning—irrational magical meaning used as particularistic defense against anxiety but constantly expanding and constantly, with iatrogenic side effects, creating the need for continued expansion of new cures for diseases created by old cures. The continuing popularity of primal magical experiences which symbolize a blotting out of consciousness—such as trance and Yoga—may also owe something to this motive. The "dung heap" (Veblen) of ever-accumulating symbolic "knowledge" may help explain the perennial fascination of *le néant,* the cloud of unknowing, reality as non-being, to the religious imagination.

Fortunately, the human ego, though nurtured in magic, eventually finds firmer supports in legal, political, philosophical institutions based on man's sedimented rationality. But reason can become oppressive too, just like magic. For both manufacture more culture, more objective mind, more meaning and can eventually swamp the egos they set out to support. Lévi-Strauss has shown how it is the very superfluity of meaning in possession of the magician that enables him to have effect. But as the outside social world grows in density of meaning, as man's impersonal principle is increasingly objectified in rationalized institutions, and as man increasingly confronts not other men but the corporate nonpersons which are themselves the embodiment of unfathomable complexes of meaning, ego magic's spontaneous power to generalize and abstract is enfeebled by comparison. The need of the nonpersons to nourish the systems of "knowledge" on which they depend[402] requires them to impose increasingly long periods of education on the people, which further weaken their natural symbolic powers. For these reasons, magic is increasingly marginalized, or driven back, crippled, to its psychological base in the formation of neuroses, in which, for example, the obsessional uses it to control his own behavior, rather than to communicate with or to influence others. Magic ultimately is frozen entirely— into patterned deviancies such as drug cults, or the rigid symptoms of mental illness.

II. Magical Institutions Help Defend the Self

Ego does not have to fight alone. Magical strategies are professionalized by elaborate magical institutions that struggle on its behalf. They have just as much massed symbolism at their disposal as any other cultural province. Now objectified mind fights objectified mind in ego's defense. Shamans and psychoanalysts have their own "depth," their own traditions, mysteries and accumulated weapons and arts to counterpoise against the unfathomable superego structures of religion, education, socialization. The basic magical strategies of abstraction, separation, doubling and conquering the superego do not have to be rediscovered by each individual or performed extemporaneously without props. These tested devices are embedded in towering symbolic complexes staffed by myriad caretaker professions—diviners, soothsayers, medicine men, shamans, wizards, headmen, priests. All seven provinces of magic work on ego's behalf, and their trained personnel are in fact man's earliest learned professions, but obviously medical magic is the strategic arena of struggle.

Every witchdoctor cure is a struggle with public opinion. The medicine man counterattacks, on behalf of his client, against the legitimacy of the spiritual attack that has been made upon him, and thereby attempts to disarm the super-ego that is killing him. The magic of the attack (by sorcerer, evil spirit, broken taboo, etc.) is weighed against the magic of the witchdoctor by the deeply con-cerned chorus of onlookers and by the patient himself. A battle of symbols ensues. If the invitation to die was issued legitimately or officially—by a headman or a broken taboo, for example—defense is difficult. But sometimes the broken taboos can be atoned for, or the moral entrepreneurs can be neu-tralized by witch accusations. Sorcerers can be identified and counterattacked. Some of the guilt resulting from whatever separation from community lies behind the affair can be drawn off and the patient reintegrated to koinomia. The shaman who has saved his own soul tries to save the patient's.[403]

Primitive medical magic has been partly misconceived by Western man. It is thought of as merely a superstitious form of medicine, or an elementary psychotherapy. It *became* these things, but our modern analogies lead us to miss the awesome atavism of the original function, and can be misleading in suggesting too many similarities with psychiatry's repair of rugged, constituted modern selves. Primitive medical magic grew when the self was problematical and barely in existence. The first practitioners were probably just ecstatics who could do little more than demonstrate that a self *could be*—could dare to "stick out" (Becker) and get away with it. Later, the ecstatic became a sorcerer, as the exuberant overflow of his magic led him to turn his counterattack on the superego against other people (perhaps those who represented superego to him). Even today most fieldworkers report that medicine men are suspected of being sorcerers, and many really are. Some are consulted in both capacities. In Cebu today there are sorcerer-witchdoctors who are openly consulted by clients seeking not just magic cures of illness, but also black magic illness to inflict on enemies.[404] The curing function probably grew out of primal *rivalries between sorcerers*—they would show off their strength by curing someone whom a rival sorcerer had attacked. (The duels of powerful sorcerers are a universal theme in the myths and epics of early civilizations.) And so, from ecstatic to sorcerer to a medicine man curing his rival's victims, the medical magician had at first only incidental interest in illness. And even when illnesses drew his attention, they were interpreted spiritually. Moreover, physical illness only threatened society *as* a spiritual problem. Primitives were quite accustomed to see their relatives die. What threatened society as a whole was the occasional chain reaction that an uncanny death could cause—when someone's shocking demise might fascinate others and set them to mimicking his symptoms in a deadly collective hysteria.[405]

It is above all Rasmussen's account of Iglulik Eskimo shamanism that prompts these speculations. Aua told him, "We do not believe, we fear";[406] and every fifth Eskimo, it seemed, had developed shamanic powers to fight these fears. But each shaman was feared by the others. They seemed to use their powers ecstatically to fight their own fears, and then to attack other people when their powers overflowed. But in the same accounts, Rasmussen shows shamanic powers being coopted, dragooned into social service. One shaman cures a rival's victim to show his powers. Soon others come for help. Then a terrifying illness strikes someone. Suggestible relatives begin contracting sympathetic symptoms; the precarious Eskimo ecology comes to a standstill and the people start dying. At that point, one of the shamans is pressed into service to cure the mass hysteria. And if no acknowledged shaman is present, someone is socially pressured to "fulfill his personage" as Mauss puts it.[407] Curing the sick man gives the illness meaning and arrests the panic of the group. This is the wisdom of Lienhardt's remark that magic medicine which treats one sick man among the Dinka really strengthens the whole society.[408]

The Classical Shaman Pattern. One typical medicine man is the shaman. The word is sometimes used too loosely to mean any kind of witchdoctor or magician. But it has two acceptable uses, not just one. It seems legitimate to accept a broad usage referring to any magicians who use trance techniques. But in addition, "shaman" refers to a definite culture pattern—classical or circumpolar shamanism, which diffused across northern Russia, Siberia and Scandinavia, and may or may not have diffused much more widely. (Idries Shah[409] suggests that it diffused to the Middle East; Kapelrod[410] believes the Hebrew prophet complex was shamanic; and some North American Indian witchdoctors resemble circumpolar shamans.)

Classical shamanism is not just an ideal type; it is something that happened. It is a collection of roughly similar movements that importantly affected the culture of large parts of the Eurasian continent. Shamanism is a prehistoric complex, but its impulses continued into the historical period. Evolutionary theories[411] that regarded shamanism as one more example of the "magical origin of religion" have been superseded by more careful research, especially by Scandinavian and Soviet scholars, who treat shamanism instead as a medical magic complex diffused from one society to another. Eliade has emphasized interaction with various primitive religions and with Buddhism.[412]

Recognition is dawning that shamanism has perhaps been a force of historical importance. Joseph Needham regards it as one of the main roots of Taoism, which he in turn portrays as the most characteristic expression of Chinese religion and culture and the origin of Chinese science.[413] In China, perhaps, we see a great civilization with important shamanic roots. And E. R. Dodds has suggested possible shamanic roots for Apollonian and Dionysian trance cults of importance in the Orphic-Pythagorean-Platonic tradition that helped shape Western intellectual culture.[414] All this suggests *a magical revolution sweeping across the world just prior to the emergence of civilizations,* which increased the magical coloration of existing religions and strengthened the individual.

Ethnological data reveal that usually shamanism is *not* the religion of a society; there is a separate religion and often other magical cults present as well. This may help to solve the spurious problem some writers (such as La Barre in *The Ghost Dance*) have raised about the shaman—whether he is a "priest" or a "magician," and if a magician does not his priority prove that magic comes first, etc. Shamanism appears to be a medical magic complex that spreads by diffusion (as so many do), coming into individual societies to *supplement existing religion* (and magic). It may of course assume great importance in some societies, swamping other magical and religious phenomena, the way the witch complex does in Zandeland.[415] Shamanic medical magic appears to diffuse at a time when social evolution is producing individuals; it serves a useful function in helping to protect their frail, emerging egos. The shaman is therefore felt to work for the community, and his magic may to varying degrees become official.

But basically a shaman is just one kind of magician; he is above all a medical magician. According to Gustav Rank[416] this is the Russian view: shamanism with its long prehistory is regarded by writers like Zelenin as a natural primitive magic of curing, to which ecstasy was added later. (Eliade suggests the trance elements may later have been colored by Buddhist meditation ideas.[417]) But of course ecstasy, with its frequent symbolization in magical ascent to heaven, is perhaps just a natural reproduction of something ancient in magic: i.e., the magician's initiation with its symbolism of rebirth to a new status. Shamanic trance as an outgrowth of the magician's initiation suggests that the pattern could have very ancient roots. Needham[418] also emphasizes the shaman's creative role in dawning pseudo-sciences beginning with rainmaking magic. But all field reports emphasize that the shaman is above all a healer. Erik Holtved[419] and Rasmussen[420] show us a still primitive curer who has no official capacity, even though he may act for the group. Ake Hultkrantz[421] notes that intense shamanism (e.g., of the Arctic kind) requires trance every time the shaman practices, but there is always a tendency for its magic to be democratized and trance then becomes less frequent. Special seances like "spirit lodge" or "shaking tent" he sees as intermediary.

Trance serves several purposes: 1. It is a dramatization and renewal of the perennial initiation symbolism (death to old role, rebirth to another) by which society conferred the magician's powers. 2. This ceremony strengthens egos, for the drama of soul loss and recovery which it enacts suggests to the onlookers the path of ritual submission to superego followed by a heightened courage-to-be. 3. Trance relaxes the objective frame of the paramount reality, so collective definitions of ensuing paranormal events can renew the faith on which curing depends. 4. This definition process can also change the social situation and hence affect social symptoms. 5. In addition, trance has a psychodynamic dimension: e.g., Odd Nordland[422] uses Kris' term,[423] "regression in the service of the ego," and speaks of insight into the social through access to the unconscious. As Jurgen Ruesch[424] points out, regression can sometimes mend communication by going to a lower level where contact can be reestablished.[425]

Techniques that extend the shamanic experience, such as use of drugs, may produce new religious congregations, but this is not always the outcome. In India, the typical social structure of ecstatic instruction remains the guru and his disciples, which is not a congregation. The yogin is often a solitary. Castenada's *brujo* Don Juan and his student do not form a church. Castenada has shown that *folie à deux* will suffice to establish what he calls "the special consensus about non-ordinary reality."[426] Harner's group[427] demonstrates cases in which shamanic drug experience renews religious vision. The Jivaro believe that all "can become shamans" through use of the hallucinogenic drugs which shamans teach. Gerald Weiss stresses the transition from magic to religion through drugs.[428] But the transition to religion does not always happen: people can simply turn it into a kind of mass magic. Some of the drug cults in the Western world remain at the magical level; they do not become religions. If a new community is not created, it is to be questioned whether this kind of mass-magic really helps egos.[429]

Another possibility must always be considered. Certain types of mass magic, instead of representing new religion or even a transition to it, are, in effect, failed magic. Sometimes magic fails to protect the emerging self; in some cultures the self dies and magic flickers on as an afterglow. The whole thrust of Buddhist and Hindu thought is to avoid hurt by abandoning the self. Here, the object magic set out to protect is abandoned while magic itself is preserved. The *no-atman* of Buddhism and the *atman* = *brahman* of Hinduism protect the self only by denying that it exists. The sick magic of neurotic symptoms which turn magic against the self to make it "sit still" is mirrored in the failed mass magics that drug the self or train it to seek altered states of consciousness which are then overvalued as substitute status.

Sometimes whole classes lose their symbolic powers: they are trapped in speech codes that ensure defeat (as Basil Bernstein,[430] and before him Hoggart,[431] showed). Or bureaucratization destroys the public language, as Steiner[432] and Mueller[433] demonstrate. Or expropriating specialisms commandeer sectors of consensual symbols: as Illich shows the medical profession strips the people of defensive folk magic. There are countermovements, of course, especially among socially strong classes that retain some command of symbolism—such as the upper-middle class Lamaze and LeBoyer counterrevolution against the over-medicalization of childbirth.[434] Magic often fails, in other words, because it gets alienated; the magic that once protected selves sets up on Park Avenue and invents new evil spirits to attack them.

The Danger in Magical Curing: Iatrogenesis. Disease always suggests the idea of death, and so therefore does any cure. Illich[435] claims that the "medicalization" of society is iatrogenic precisely because it preoccupies the mind with illness. Schipkowensky[436] suggests that all medical encounters today, whatever the specialty, are either psychotherapeutic or iatrogenic, and more likely the latter in the West. In our self-consciously "therapeutic society" (Rieff), Sullivan[437] can easily write that most formal interviews are experienced as "psychiatric interviews," with the same psychodynamic invasions—and no wonder since nowadays interviewers are taught such "magical" techniques as the Carl Rogers device of always "responding to statements of feeling" and recklessly apply them in the most mundane transactions. Today writers like Perle suggest that most human encounters are either nourishing or iatrogenic; the point is that in medicalized society we grow more conscious of this dimension and accentuate it, thus wearing the lining off each other's egos and primitivizing one another.

The medical profession with its enormous prestige leads us in these preoccupations. The institutionalization of the "annual physical check-up" in a society noted for unnecessary operations, overprescription of drugs and high documented rates of iatrogenesis[438] becomes a ritual that reminds the fragile ego that the doctor will harvest it in the end. Meanwhile, medical practices that remove autonomy from the patient also strip him of his personal magic, such as it was. While primitive magical cure consists of an oversupply of meaning, the modern medical profession maintains its social power through a monopoly of information and creates hospital procedures in which nurses are not allowed to answer questions and the family is separated from the death in an absolute vacuum of meaning. They sit in the solarium for hours, speculating about the outcome, but they are not told much about what is happening. This humiliating demonstration of social weakness no doubt communicates the *"idée de mort suggérée par la collectivité."*[439]

But on the other hand the iatrogenic backfires of primitive medical magic were often more severe: For one thing, each successful cure confirmed belief in spiritual power whose ability to kill depended precisely on belief. The trouble with spiritual healing is that the cure creates the disease, which is one reason why it lingers. Medicine literally creates diseases, defines syndromes and tells people how to "do" these diseases. This is certainly more evident to us in primitive societies than in our own. In rural Greece today, for example, the Blums[440] find, associated with magical cures, a number of mysterious diseases like "the wandering navel," "to be black like a crow" and "the waist" (the victim of the latter gets very fat and uncomfortable). Una MacClean[441] reports that, in Ibadan, even elites still use primitive healing; Hsu shows how Chinese urban elites in the forties used both modern and primitive practices. He writes that they do so to hedge their bets. A better explanation is that they use both, because they are still susceptible to both, because they still use both...

Magical institutions that try to defend the self also add to its problems. Witchcraft ideas grow out of witch accusations aimed at neutralizing the superego—but they spawn a universe of black magic nightmares that torment the imagination of mankind. Shamanism emerges to fight soul loss, but spreads the idea of possession like a mass hysteria. Religions and magics literally invent some of the psychopathologies of mankind, including perhaps some perversions as Rank has shown, and spread them by diffusion. New sect magic may fight religion for ego, but it precipitates *more* religion. In the end, ego is better protected by the nonmagical institutions that grow out of magic, such as individual law.

But ego at heart is still an occult creature, a "Martian," subject to deadly colds and mysterious fits. If his protection is too purely abstract and mechanical, he dies—or invents new magics. Psychoanalysis arose in the West because institutions of individualism were insufficient by themselves to protect the moody, occult self. Magical curing had all but vanished but magical *illnesses* remained.

But just as all medicine is iatrogenic, psychoanalysis inevitably helped to create some new illnesses (e.g., "neurotic character" disorders as a byproduct of lucrative "analysis interminable"[442]) while wiping others off the map of civilization (e.g., transparent symbolizations like "hysterical inactivization"). Its very attempts at control through abstraction (e.g., its syndromologies) created new damnation categories, new Platonic ideas which, like Durkheim's "suicido-genic currents" "get" their victims. In addition, Freud's public statements of pessimism about the curability of some of these syndromes have been criticized for alleged iatrogenic effects by Horney, Bergler, others. Schilder[443] also noted that excessive self-observation fostered by psychiatry can itself encourage the partial withdrawal of cathexis from the world that ushers in every neurosis and psychosis. Rank expressed similar misgivings about the effect on the ego. And from the beginning, orthodox psychoanalysts contraindicated the psychoana-lytic method in certain syndromes because it did *harm:* the most notorious was pseudoneurotic "latent schizophrenia," where it was felt that free associa-tion would precipitate a psychotic "blowup."[444] Apparently, a person already afflicted with an excess of defective ego magic is hurt by further magical inter-vention.

To summarize: The ways in which medical magic fail are several. First, a lot of it is just too frightening for the patient. Second, success confirms belief in the spiritual illnesses magic fights, and so sustains their virulence. Third, there is routinization of charisma; magic becomes religion and joins the superego. The "vast laundering operation," as Camus calls any pristine religion (in *La Chute*), turns into the institutionalized religion that punishes the ego more than ever. Thus the length of the average psychoanalysis and perhaps the severity of diag-nosis have been increasing all during this century with the growing acceptance of psychoanalysis by the establishment.[445]

The same happens in primitive magic, where diagnosis can kill. But in small primitive communities, the patient and society work together in the formula-tion of new definitions. Lévi-Strauss observes that in psychoanalysis there is only one abreaction instead of the three that occur in primitive medical magic (those of the patient, the medicine man and the onlookers). Thus it lacks real social power to change things for the individual.[446] Magic adapts the group to the patient and his problems; psychoanalysis only adapts the patient to the group. It is sometimes experienced therefore as so much additional ego pressure.

Propensities to iatrogenesis are abundantly present in all magic. Today's landscape is filled, not just with reports of magic, but with widespread reports of the failures of magic. New psychotherapies keep cropping up in part because others are felt to fail: The sense of helplessness grows and there is an urgent feeling that we must somehow regain our symbolic powers. Therefore, even though magic tries to defend the ego, its failures make it hard to believe, as De Martino claims, that it successfully *established* it. Often it makes a botch, and even when it succeeds and buys time, it does so at the expense of reinforcing belief in magical dangers and threats. De Martino does not explain how magic goes beyond defense and actually establishes ego in an historical sequence. It seems more fruitful to look for the establishment of the Individual in the social infrastructure of society, rather than in its religious and magical projections. This will be considered in the next section.

Notes

1. Géza Róheim, *Magic and Schizophrenia* (Bloomington, Ind., 1955, 1962), post-humously edited by Dr. Warner Muensterberger with the assistance of Dr. S. H. Ponsinsky.

2. My position is the opposite of Malinowski's "eruption theory." Instead of supposing that human psychology with its emotions and drives "erupts" and then gets shaped into social institutions of magic, I suggest that the social evolution of egos depended so much on magic that magical attributes are built into human psychology as survivals.

3. The recognition that magic is the protector of the self is no doubt one source of the universal feeling (reported, for example, by Malinowski) that primitives have concerning magic: i.e., that it is *for man*, associated with man, made either for him or by him. Religion is for society, nature and god; magic is man's special province.

4. Otto Fenichel, *The Psychoanalytic Theory of Neurosis* (N.Y., 1945), pp. 2-6, 46-47, 209, 272, 315-319, etc.

5. Herman Nunberg, *Principles of Psychoanalysis* (N.Y., 1955), esp. ch. 5, "The Psychology of the Ego," pp. 114-177.

6. Summarized in Nunberg, *Ibid.*, pp. 124-126.

7. Sylvano Arieti, *The Intrapsychic Self* (N.Y., 1967, 1976), and *Creativity: The Magic Synthesis* (N.Y., 1976). To be discussed.

8. Alfred Storch, *The Primitive Archaic Forms of Inner Experience and Thought in Schizophrenia* (N.Y. & Washington, 1924), p. 20, etc.

9. Heinz Werner, *Comparative Psychology of Mental Development* (N.Y., 1948), pp. 337-378.

10. Identification of psychotic material with "archaic" or primitive thought goes back to some 19th century figures, according to de Martino: Gustav Carus (1831), Eugenio Tanzi, Morselli. (E. de Martino, *The World of Magic*, Hong Kong, 1972, pp. 161-162.)

11. La Barre associates magic with the narcissistic, pre-Oedipal stage, religion with the Oedipal stage of struggle against the father, science with the post-Oedipal individual who is himself a creative father, reconciled to society. Some such metaphysics is implicit in much of the Freudian school's approach to magic. Weston La Barre, *The Ghost Dance* (N.Y., 1972), ch. 3, pp. 93-120.

12. Ernst Kris, *Psychoanalytic Explorations In Art* (N.Y., 1952, 1964), pp. 47-56.

13. Freud, *Totem and Taboo* (N.Y., 1950), pp. 15-95 & *passim*.

14. Sigmund Freud, "A Neurosis of Demonical Possession in the 17th Century," (1923), in *The Collected Papers of Sigmund Freud, Studies in Parapsychology* (N.Y., 1963), ch. 3, pp. 91-125.

15. Freud, "Obsessive Acts and Religious Practices," (1907), in *Collected Papers: Character and Culture* (N.Y., 1963), ch. 1, pp. 17-26.

16. Freud, *The Future of An Illusion* (Garden City, N.Y., 1964), pp. 69-73.

17. Freud, *Totem and Taboo* (N.Y., 1950), ch. 2.

18. Freud, *Civilization and Its Discontents* (Garden City, N.Y., 1954), p. 13ff, etc.

19. Freud actually used the word "occult" to refer to a *different* province of magic, the one I call the "paranormal."

20. Freud, "Determinism, Chance and Superstitious Beliefs," *Psychopathology of Everyday Life* (N.Y., 1951), ch. 12, pp. 136-168.

21. *Psychopathology of Everyday Life*, p. 153.

22. Just as religion is the obsessional neurosis of mankind, "philosophy" assimilates to paranoia, he writes. In all three stages psychological associations between symbols are projected onto the world as mysterious coincidences. In fact, Freud writes, superstition occurs *because* primitive people do not know about psychological determinism; the implication

is that psychoanalytic knowledge will dissolve this province of magic.

23. Freud, *Group Psychology and the Analysis of the Ego* (N.Y., 1960), pp. 46–53, 62–77.

24. Discussed here: a. "Dreams and Telepathy," 1922, *Collected Papers: Studies in Parapsychology* (N.Y., 1964), ch. 2, pp. 63–90. Also b. "Psychoanalysis and Telepathy," written 1921, published in London, 1941; c. "The Occult Significance of Dreams," 1925; d. "Dreams and the Occult," 1933. All collected as chs. 5–8 of George Devereux, ed., *Psychoanalysis and the Occult* (N.Y., 1953, 1970), pp. 56–112.

25. "Dreams and Telepathy," in Devereux, ed., *op. cit.,* pp. 76–78.

26. 1921 and 1922 papers, footnote 24.

27. "Dreams and the Occult," Devereux, ed., *op. cit.,* p. 98.

28. Otto Fenichel, *op. cit.,* pp. 2–6.

29. Freud renews Darwin-Tylor-Frazer reductionism in the 20th century. 1. Freud's genetic sequences keep Darwinian evolutionism alive. 2. His ideas on the psychic unity of mankind perpetuate Tylor's notion of universal "animist" stages. 3. His psychological reductions simply substitute psychodynamic explanations for Frazer's associationalist account of magic.

30. Freud, "On Narcissism, An Introduction," 1914, *Collected Papers; General Psychological Theory* (N.Y., 1963), pp. 56–82. See also ch. 3, *Totem and Taboo,* pp. 75–95.

31. "Neurosis and Psychosis", 1924, in Freud, *op. cit.,* pp. 185–189.

32. "On the Mechanism of Paranoia," 1911, Freud, *op. cit.,* pp. 29–48.

33. Sigmund Freud, *The Psychopathology of Everyday Life* (N.Y., 1951).

34. Collected in *The Basic Writings of Sigmund Freud* (Modern Library ed., N.Y., 1938), pp. 633–806.

35. *The Interpretation of Dreams,* collected in *The Basic Writings of Sigmund Freud,* pp. 181–549.

36. "The Uncanny," 1919, in *Collected Papers: Studies in Parapsychology,* pp. 19–62.

37. "The Dream Work", ch. 6 in *The Interpretation of Dreams,* pp. 319–467.

38. "Determinism, Chance and Superstition," ch. 12 of *The Psychopathology of Everyday Life,* pp. 136–168.

39. "The Uncanny," 1919, *Ibid.* In several *other* works Freud further contributes to the theory of sympathetic magic. In "The Occult Significance of Dreams," (1925, *Ibid.*), Freud writes that symbolism is a problem of archaic thinking (p. 87). This recalls the theory I reconstituted from Mauss that sympathy links derive from primitive classification systems. In his postscript to the Schreber case, Freud writes of mytheopic propensities inherent in human religion, neuroses and symbolism. ("Psychoanalytic Notes Upon an Autobiographical Account of a Case of Paranoia," 1911, postscript, in Freud, *Collected Papers, Three Case Histories* [N.Y., 1963], pp. 183–184.) In *A General Introduction to Psychoanalysis* (N.Y., 1949) he writes, "Words and magic were in the beginning one and the same thing . . ." (p. 19).

40. "Idealization" is described as an "enchantment" of ego, a "hypnosis" leading to "overvaluation of the sex object" (love) or the endowment of a leader with mana (in *Group Psychology and the Analysis of the Ego,* N.Y., 1960, pp. 54–62).

41. Freud, *The Ego and the Id* (London, 1957); *The Problem of Anxiety,* Norton ed., ch. 6, "The Undoing and Isolation Mechanisms in Compulsion Neurosis," pp. 53–58.

42. Freud, "From the History of an Infantile Neurosis," 1918, *Collected Papers: Three Case Histories* (N.Y., 1963), pp. 187–316. This regression also makes the patient more vulnerable to the demonic magic of coincidences, suggestive dreams, etc.

43. *A General Introduction to Psychoanalysis* (N.Y., 1949), p. 237.

44. *Ibid.,* p. 242.

45. *Totem and Taboo* (N.Y., 1950), p. 27.

46. *Ibid.,* ch. 3, "Animism, Magic and the Omnipotence of Thoughts," pp. 75–99.

47. *The Problem of Anxiety,* p. 102ff.

48. S. Freud, "Negation," 1925, *Collected Papers: General Psychological Theory* (N.Y., 1963), pp. 213–217.

49. S. Freud, "Repression," 1915, *Collected Papers: General Psychological Theory* (N.Y., 1963), pp. 104–115.

50. S. Freud, "On the Mechanism of Paranoia," 1911, in *Collected Papers: General*

Psychological Theory (N.Y., 1963), pp. 29–48.

51. Otto Rank, *Psychology and the Soul* (N.Y., 1950); also "Fate and Self Determination," ch. 6 in Clark E. Moustakas, ed., *The Self* (N.Y., 1956, 1974), pp. 70–75.

52. Ernest Becker, *The Denial of Death* (N.Y., 1973); *Escape From Evil* (N.Y., 1976); *The Revolution in Psychiatry* (N.Y., 1964); *The Birth and Death of Meaning* (N.Y., 1971); *The Structure of Evil* (N.Y., 1968); *Angel in Armor* (N.Y., 1975).

53. Freud, *The Ego and the Id* (London, 1957), pp. 85–88.

54. May, *The Meaning of Anxiety* (N.Y., 1950). May himself accorded importance to a helplessness theory of anxiety, both in his account of Horney's work (pp. 138–145) and in his own synthesis (ch. 8).

55. Freud, *The Problem of Anxiety*, pp. 114, seq.

56. René A. Spitz, *La Première Année de la Vie de l'Enfant* (Paris, 1963), pp. 49–63.

57. Martin E. P. Seligman, *Helplessness* (San Francisco, 1975), ch. 8, pp. 166–188.

58. "The Uncanny," in *Studies in Parapsychology*, pp. 31–37.

59. *Ibid.*, p. 39. Mauss, incidentally, notices the theme of "doubling" running rampant in magic (*General Theory of Magic*, pp. 34–36).

60. A compromise with Rank and Becker might be found in Freud's idea (in *Beyond the Pleasure Principle*, N.Y., 1959, p. 71ff, etc.) that ego is obsessed with death because ego itself is a mechanism that helps to detour physical death. Ego wants to die, but in its own time. Ego works by decathecting libido and releasing thanatos, etc. Freud does say that religion denies the horror of death (*Future of an Illusion*, p. 22ff.). So the ego is a death-fascinated, death-driven, denial-of-death mechanism but it fights to keep *itself* alive. It is the psychic death of ego which magic fights; it fights physical death only incidentally. As Freud puts it (in *The Ego and the Id*, pp. 85–88), ego has no personal knowledge of physical death. As I put it in sociological terms, immortality as escape from physical death is a (late) cultural *projection* of the work of fighting *psychic* death.

61. Otto Fenichel, *The Psychoanalytic Theory of Magic* (N.Y., 1945), p. 46.

62. Ferenczi's theory of magic is outlined in Herman Nunberg, *Principles of Psychoanalysis* (N.Y., 1955), pp. 124–125.

63. Nunberg, *op. cit.*, pp. 125–126.

64. Nunberg, *op. cit.*, N.Y., 1945.

65. *Ibid.*, "The Psychology of the Ego," ch. 5, pp. 114–177.

66. *Ibid.*, p. 127.

67. *Ibid.*, pp. 240–241.

68. "Homosexuality, Magic and Aggression," in Nunberg, *Practice and Theory of Psychoanalysis* (N.Y., 1943), ch. 10.

69. Otto Rank, *Psychology and the Soul* (N.Y., 1950, 1961), p. 40.

70. Ernest Becker, *The Denial of Death* (N.Y., 1973), pp. 230–231.

71. 7e année, 1934, no. 1, *Revue Française de Psychanalyse*.

72. *Ibid.*, Princess Marie Bonaparte, "La Pensée Magique Chez le Primitif," pp. 3–18.

73. *Ibid.*, H. Codet, "La Pensée Magique dans La Vie Quotidienne."

74. *Ibid.*, R. Laforgue, "La Pensée Magique Dans La Religion," pp. 19–31.

75. *Ibid.*, J. Leuba, "La Pensée Magique Chez le Névrosé," pp. 32–50.

76. C. Odier, *L'Angoisse et la Pensée Magique* (Neuchatel, 1947), (English trans., N.Y., 1956).

77. J.-P. Sartre, *The Emotions, Outline of a Theory* (N.Y., 1948). With a phenomenological twist. Cf. ch. 3.

78. Roger Bastide, *Sociologie et Psychanalyse* (Paris, 1950, 1972), cf. ch. 1, 6.

79. Jean Piaget, *The Child's Conception of Physical Causality* (Totowa, N.J., 1965).

80. Jean Piaget, *The Moral Judgment of the Child* (London, 1932, 1950).

81. Laurence Kohlberg continues these researches.

82. Jean Piaget, *Play, Dreams and Imitation in Childhood* (N.Y., 1962).

83. *Ibid.*, p. 257.

84. Géza Róheim (Bloomington, Ind., 1955).

85. Cf. Franz Alexander & Thomas Morton French, *Psychoanalytic Therapy* (N.Y., 1946).

86. Otto Rank, "Fate and Self-Determination," ch. 6 in Clark E. Moustakas, ed., *The Self* (N.Y., 1974), pp. 70–75.

87. Thomas Szasz, *Law, Liberty and Psychiatry* (N.Y., 1963), e.g. ch. 18, pp. 212–222.

88. Géza Róheim, *Psychoanalysis and Anthropology* (N.Y., 1950), p. 479.

89. He even proposed a dialectic along these lines: Excessive super-ego pressure drives ego to invent new magic to find relief. This in turn provokes a new attack by the paternal superego in the form of a Puritan reformist religion that drives out magic.

90. Géza Róheim, *The Gates of the Dream* (N.Y., 1952), p. 63.

91. Róheim, *The Origin and Function of Culture* (Garden City, N.Y., 1971), p. 28, etc.

92. Reich, esp. *The Mass Psychology of Fascism* (N.Y., 1970). Also, *The Sexual Revolution* (N.Y., 1945, 1969); *The Function of the Orgasm* (N.Y., 1942, 1961); *Sex-Pol, Essays, 1929-1934* (N.Y., 1972); *Character Analysis* (N.Y., 1976); For Critique: Paul A. Robinson, *The Freudian Left* (N.Y., 1969), pp. 9–73; P. Rieff, *The Triumph of the Therapeutic* (N.Y., 1968), ch. 6, pp. 141–188.

93. Herbert Marcuse, *Eros and Civilization* (Boston, 1955), p. 79ff, etc.

94. G. Róheim, *Psychoanalysis and Anthropology*, ch. 11, "Psychology and History," 461–87.

95. *Ibid.,* pp. 475–476.

96. *Magic and Schizophrenia*, p. 47.

97. He suggested, for example, that regression was initially an id function, before there was regression in the service of the ego (*Gates of the Dream*), p. 545, etc.

98. Paul A. Robinson, *The Freudian Left* (N.Y., 1969), pp. 75–146.

99. *Psychoanalysis and Anthropology*, p. 462.

100. *Ibid.,* pp. 470–471.

101. *Ibid.,* pp. 482–486.

102. Infancy prolongs the "dual unity situation," so separation from the mother becomes especially traumatic for humans. Róheim portrays civilization as a colossal effort by the aging child to protect himself against this loss. Prolonged infancy produces neurosis and also culture, but that is more neurosis, just "fixation clusters" blocking some feared impulse: e.g. Kwakuitl economic exuberance in the potlatch is just an anal problem, etc.

103. *The Eternal Ones of the Dream* (N.Y., 1970), *The Gates of the Dream* (N.Y., 1969).

104. Sleep is regression to the uterine position, but this threatens death. So the dream is an attempt to recreate the world (the way the psychotic delusion tries to recreate the world abandoned). There is a "basic dream" in which the body as a whole is libidinized to represent a phallos, so going into sleep mimicks sexual intercourse. (Thus Róheim reverses Ferenczi, who identified sexual intercourse with return to the womb.) (*The Gates of the Dream,* N.Y., 1969) In *The Eternal Ones of the Dream* Róheim states that culture is created when dreamers tell each other their dreams. Curing, religion and all ideate culture are products of "the dreaming" (as the Arunta call it)—and therefore of id processes.

105. Géza Róheim, *Animism, Magic and the Divine King* (London, 1930). Here Róheim adopts Freud's idea that the ego can have no experience (and hence no fear) of physical death and fears castration instead because castration effectively symbolizes psychic death to an institution *built up on* the genitals: Freud's theory of narcissism is used to explain the origin of the ego and it is interpreted in literal sexual terms. The child, frustrated by the mother, withdraws some libido from her and puts it on himself, auto-erotically, and *that* to Róheim is the-origin of the ego. The soul is originally a symbol for the penis; the penis is the foundation of the self (cf. pp. 19–20ff, etc.).

106. *Psychoanalysis and Anthropology*, ch. 11, pp. 461–487.

107. *Ibid.,* p. 473.

108. *Ibid.,* pp. 461–470.

109. Herbert Marcuse, *Reason and Revolution* (Boston, 1960); *One Dimensional Man* (Boston, 1964); *Five Lectures* (Boston, 1970); *An Essay on Liberation* (Boston, 1969); *A Critique of Pure Tolerance* (Boston, 1969); *Eros and Civilization* (Boston, 1955).

110. Norman O. Brown, *Love Against Death* (N.Y., 1959).

111. N. Mailer, "The White Negro" (N.Y., 1957).

112. *Magic and Schizophrenia*, p. 18.

113. Selma H. Fraiberg, *The Magic Years* (N.Y., 1968).

114. *Magic and Schizophrenia*, p. 46, etc.

115. "We grow up through magic and in magic . . . Our first response to the frustrations of reality is magic; and without this belief in ourselves . . . we cannot hold our own against

the environment and against the superego.... The ultimate denial of dependency comes from the all powerful sorcerer. (p. 46)... Magic is also a revolt against the gods.... The analyst, in giving interpretations, actually ... takes the side of the primary process.... We actually move with Acheron against the Gods. And, in analyzing others, we are fighting their superego and our own.... In magic, mankind is fighting for freedom. (p. 47)... We might therefore say that mankind functions mainly according to the magical principle.... It would be wrong, therefore, to say that the goal of analysis is to eliminate magical thinking. We cannot form a species with a prolonged infancy into a calculating machine (Róheim, *op. cit.,* p. 83).

116. Wilhelm Stekel, *Compulsion and Doubt* (N.Y., 1949, 1962). To be discussed.

117. Withdrawal of libido from the world seems perhaps a step in *any* magic–the weak-sense magic of neurotic symptoms, also the strict-sense magic of a magician's training. For example, initiation into magic power often involves abstention from sex.

118. Róheim and Stekel both report that an important magical symbol in the ancient world was the *fascinium,* a simulacrum of the penis carried about on one's person. Touching the penis is still considered an antidote to the evil eye in some peasant societies. Stekel, *op. cit.,* p. 47; Róheim, p. 31ff.

119. In *Rites of Passage,* ch. 2.

120. Max G. Marwick, *Sorcery in Its Social Setting* (Manchester, 1965), pp. 146–147.

121. "Magic... is our great reservoir of strength against frustration and defeat and against the superego." (Róheim, *op. cit.,* p. 45).

122. *Ibid.,* pp. 82–83.

123. Emil Durkheim, "The Dualism of Human Nature and Its Social Conditions," in Kurt H. Wolff, ed., *Essays on Sociology and Philosophy by Emile Durkheim et al.* (N.Y., 1964), pp. 325–340.

124. Wilhelm Stekel, *Compulsion and Doubt* (N.Y., 1949, 1962).

125. Harry Stack Sullivan, *Clinical Studies in Psychiatry* (N.Y., 1956), p. 229ff.

126. Sullivan, *Ibid.,* ch. 12, "Obsessionalism," pp. 229–283. The verbal obsessional operations would proliferate, in other words, because the patient could never be sure that his "spells" worked. In *The Interpersonal Theory of Psychiatry* he specifically associated ideas of "magical potency" with situations in which "we have an exceedingly inadequate grasp on all that is actually happening ..." (Sullivan, N.Y., 1953, p. 69.)

127. "The compulsion neurotic is never sure that he has carried out the rituals correctly, because parallel to an ego compulsion which wishes to carry them out there exists a second ego-compulsion which does not wish to carry them out ..." (Stekel, *op. cit.,* p. 60)... "Doubt is the endopsychic perception of bipolarity" (p. 114).

128. Rollo May, *The Meaning of Anxiety* (N.Y., 1950), pp. 118–122ff.

129. From Stekel's *Compulsion and Doubt:* "The compulsion neurotic ... hates the Logos.... He obeys the secret laws of his own psyche. He maintains a Logos of his own (p. 40).... The compulsive neurotic is asocial, and his disturbance is ... as a protest against society. The compulsion neurotic is proud of his affliction, which he alone has created and he alone fully comprehends. (p. 40).... The compulsion neurotic, in order to preserve his individual religion, struggles against the foreign religion with which his environment confronts him. (p. 43).... For compulsion neurosis is originally a protest against religion.... The child creates his own religion.... Fundamentally it is the belief in one's self, in the divine in one's self." (p. 142)

130. Henri Hubert et Marcel Mauss, "Introduction à L'Analyse de Quelques Phénomènes Religieux," in Mauss, *Oeuvres,* vol. 1, p. 25, line 1.

131. Psychoanalysis arose when magical defenses against magical illness were weak, and the first analytic paradigms tried to restore spontaneity (early emphasis on id psychology). Ego psychology was a new strategy for producing spontaneity *with adjustment,* in a more turbulent age. Group psychologies attempted to elicit the cooperative inter-social self required for occupational settings in which most elites spend their working days in meetings. Primitive magics similarly not only defended the self but produced on order what was required *as* a self. To an important degree, magic consists of ritual metaphors to elicit the behavior that society agrees to define as a self.

132. David Rapaport, *The Structure of Psychoanalytic Theory, A Systematic Attempt, Psychological Issues,* vol. II, no. 2, monograph 6 (N.Y., 1960). See also D. Rapaport,

"Historical Introduction," to Erik Erikson, *Identity and the Life Cycle, Psychological Issues,* vol. 1, no. 1, monograph 1 (N.Y., 1959), pp. 1–17.

133. Allport, *Personality and Social Encounter* (Boston, 1964); *The Person in Psychology* (Boston, 1968).

134. Anna Freud, *The Ego and the Mechanisms of Defense* (N.Y., 1976), ch. 1.

135. The way Margaret Mead and Wilhelm Reich studied child-rearing manuals of different countries as empirical evidence of national character traits and sex repression. In Mead & Wolfenstein, eds., *Childhood in Contemporary Cultures* (Chicago, 1955), chs. 9–12, pp. 145–230; Reich in *The Sexual Revolution* (N.Y., 1969), chs. 2–5, pp. 30–79.

136. Mauss, "Une Categorie de l'Esprit Humaine: La Notion de Personne, Celle de "Moi'," in Lévi-Strauss, ed., *Marcel Mauss Sociologie et Anthropologie* (Paris, 1950, 1966), pp. 333–364.

137. Otto Rank, "Fate and Self Determination," in Clarke Moustakas, *op. cit.,* p. 71.

138. Heinz Hartmann, *Ego Psychology and the Problem of Adaptation* (N.Y., 1958), ch. 1.

139. Erickson's model crosses the I-Me dichotomy of the philosophers with the Freudian "institutions" and grades of consciousness to produce the following picture: The "Me" which the I reflects upon is really the "selves," or role memories. It is preconscious and its "counterplayers" are the other social roles in the social world. The ego is totally unconscious and its counterplayers are the unconscious id and superego but also all those other unconscious egos in the *lebenswelt* who unconsciously perceive and measure each other. The transcendent "I" alone is pure consciousness, and its only possible counterplayer is the source of all consciousness and life, the creator, god. Erik Erikson, ch. 5, "Theoretical Interlude," *Identity, Youth and Crisis* (N.Y., 1968), pp. 208-231.

140. "Une Catégorie de l'Esprit . . ." *Mauss,* in Lévi-Strauss, ed., *op. cit.,* pp. 348-9, but my interpretation.

141. Otto Rank, *Psychology and the Soul* (N.Y., 1950), pp. 31-32, etc.

142. Rank in Moustakas, *op. cit.,* ch. 6.

143. *Ibid.,* p. 71.

144. E.g., Gilbert Ryle, *The Concept of Mind* (N.Y., 1969); Donald F. Gustafson, ed., *Essays in Philosophical Psychology* (Garden City, N.Y., 1964); V. C. Chappell, ed., *The Philosophy of Mind* (Englewood Cliffs, N.J., 1962).

145. James Henry Breasted, *Development of Religion and Thought in Ancient Egypt* (Gloucester, Mass., 1970), pp. 51-57.

146. Robert F. Hertz, "A Contribution to the Study of the Collective Representation of Death," *Death and the Right Hand* (London, 1960), pp. 29-88.

147. The immortality of the more spiritual soul must be saved to save the immortality of the group.

148. Lévy-Bruhl, *The "Soul" of the Primitive* (Chicago, 1971), p. 52ff.

149. Cf. Durkheim, *Elementary Forms of Religious Life* (London, 1915), Book II, ch. 4, "The Individual Totem and the Sexual Totem," pp. 157-167.

150. Westcott, *The Divine Animal* (N.Y., 1969). He also recognizes several types of impersonality: a. the "prepersonality" of animals; b. the "transpersonality" of transcendence; c. the "depersonality" of alienation. Cf. pp. 236-239.

151. Gordon Leff, *Medieval Thought, St. Augustine to Occam* (London, 1958), pp. 162-64. You might say that there is a lot of "universal hylomorphism" going around, especially in philosophical thought, which tends to multiply distinctions and then run them against each other, like x and y coordinates, producing mental matrices promiscuously.

152. Models are "pictures," as Wittgenstein contemptuously says; and certainly Freud's "level of consciousness" model implies entities in space. What kind of space? Rapaport suggests that Freud's theory has a topographical dimension. Its spatiality is not explicit but is seriously intended, I think, and can be pieced together from hints. Thus he keeps comparing ego to a surface, a membrane, while speaking of id as "deep." Ego as the cerebral cortex, id as the mid-brain come to mind.

153. Robert Ernest Hume, "An Outline of the Philosophy of the Upanishads," in *The Thirteen Principal Upanishads* (Oxford, 1921, 1971), pp. 1-72.

154. Westcott, pp. 216-258.

155. More recently, Julian Jaynes also speculates that both consciousness and ego come

late in civilization. *The Origin of Consciousness in the Breakdown of the Bicameral Mind* (N.Y., 1976). Part of his inspiration appears to come from Dodds' idea of external "monitions." Cf. p. 330 ff, etc.

156. Erikson, "Theoretical Interlude," *Identity, Youth and Crisis* (N.Y., 1968), pp. 208–231. Nunberg splits superego and ego ideal on other grounds. Analyzing passages in *The Ego and the Id*, etc., in which Freud seems to prefer one term or the other, he notes that superego is ingested because of love as well as fear, and that as the repression of the Oedipus complex it includes father as well as mother. He then identifies "ego ideal" with the *love* motive and the maternal side of conscience formation, and superego with the fear motive and the paternal side, while admitting they are hard to separate. Herman Nunberg, *Principles of Psychoanalysis* (N.Y., 1955), pp. 145–148.

157. Such as Lecky's "individuality record" and "self-consistency." Cf. Prescott Lecky, *Self-Consistency, A Theory of Personality* (Garden City, N.Y., 1969), chs. 3, 8.

158. Sec tables, pp. 282, 289.

159. Gilbert Ryle, *The Concept of Mind*, ch. 1.

160. E.g., see Edna Heidbreder, *Seven Psychologies* (N.Y., 1933, 1961), ch. 4, "Titchener and Structuralism," pp. 113–151.

161. Ernest Becker, e.g., *Revolution in Psychiatry* (N.Y., 1964).

162. In *The Structure of Behavior* (Boston, 1963).

163. In behaviorist psychiatry, of course, there is a basis of clinical evidence. Sullivan and Laing get some therapeutic results. It is interesting that metaphors of magic occur in their writings: e.g., Sullivan on the self-system as a series of "linguistic tricks" and most symptoms as verbal or mental magic. Personalist models (e.g., Gordon Allport) also allege empirical verification. But the verbal instructions, questionnaires and other tricks used to prove that "something is there" are too transparent; they practically tell the subject how to "do" a scene of ego pain or status panic.

164. Anna Freud, *The Ego and the Mechanisms of Defense* (N.Y., 1966), pp. 5–10.

165. S. Freud, *The Ego and the Id* (London, 1957), p. 35ff and *passim.*

166. Anna Freud, *op. cit.*, p. 5.

167. George Herbert Mead, *Mind, Self and Society* (Chicago, 1934), chs. 20–22.

168. Sigmund Freud, "Repression," 1915, in *General Psychological Theory* (N.Y., 1963), ch. 5, pp. 104–115.

169. *The Problem of Anxiety*, pp. 71ff.

170. Heinz Hartmann, *op. cit.*, ch. 1.

171. In *The Ego and the Id* (London, 1957), pp. 66–67.

172. E.g., consciousness or knowledge about power, where it lies, tends to cause power to weaken and disintegrate.

173. John Dewey, *Human Nature and Conduct* (N.Y., Modern Library ed.).

174. In *Group Psychology and the Analysis of the Ego* (N.Y., 1960), Freud writes that while in identification ego enriches itself by incorporating a rejected objective, in idealization (of a loved person or a leader) ego is impoverished by surrendering itself to the object and substituting it for its own ego ideal. (p. 56)

175. "From the pleasure principle to the instinct of preservation is a long way," Freud wrote (quoted in Hartmann, ch. 3). Pleasure can disturb adaptation. But the ego's reality principle also has a way to go before it can translate into self-preservation. (To Freud, it is itself an outgrowth of the pleasure principle, though Hartmann thinks it is an independent genetic endowment.) For one thing, the ego knows the social situation imperfectly and its own unconscious even less perfectly. It makes mistakes.

176. As Rapaport writes (Introd. to Erikson, *Identity and the Life Cycle*, pp. 6–7ff), Freud at first identified ego with perception and confounded it with ideas of consciousness, self or the dominant mass of conscious ideas. Later (in *The Ego and the Id*) Freud still identified ego with perception, also with the "reality principle" and the "secondary process" which both imply consciousness, but ego now also included structures that are responsible for resistances and are unconscious. (Thus, Freud's later position is: ego partly conscious, partly unconscious.) The later orthodox ego psychologists—those who retained the Freudian orientation (Hartmann, Anna Freud, Lowenthal, Krist, Erikson, Rapaport) and remained "biological, genetic, dynamic, economic and topographical," as Hartmann put it (*op. cit.* ch. 1), as distinguished from the sociocultural ego psychologists Fromm, Horney,

Sullivan, Kardiner—gave even greater attention to *unconscious* ego roots, in attempting to ground ego more in a genetic endowment independent of id.

177. Radical psychiatrists like Reich or Sullivan considered ego itself a kind of sickness.

178. Thus hysteric resistance related to direct, simple repression; obsessional resistance to the "isolation" and "undoing" so prominent in that neurosis (hence hysterics go silent and obsessionals get loquacious as they resist analysis). The implication is that in some sense ego *is* its repressions, or is partly so.

179. *Beyond the Pleasure Principle* (N.Y., 1959), p. 41ff.

180. *The Ego and the Id* (London, 1957), ch. 3, pp. 34–53.

181. In *Sociologie et Psychanalyse* (Paris, 1950), Bastide proposed a dualist position—sexual instincts vs. social symbols. Society cannot be derived entirely from libido as Freud imagined, Bastide claims, but neither is the self a mere avatar of the social as Durkheim supposed. It has also its independent biological base. Just as the individual is constantly socialized, filled with social "secondary process" symbols, social symbolic networks are also constantly libidinized. Bastide fears the superficialities of the Horney-Fromm cultural approach in psychiatry, so he clings to Freud's instinct theory. But he underestimates the depth of the Durkheim school's sociological determinism, which is quite capable of explaining how even biological patterns have social roots—e.g., Hertz on left-handedness. Bastide considers magic strategic for the Freudo-Durkheimian synthesis he proposes: Freudianism itself, he recognizes (quoting Gide),has a "Magian" dimension, the positive side of which is its ability to describe individual spontaneity.

182. David Rapaport, *The Structure of Psychoanalytical Theory, Psychological Issues,* vol. 2, no. 2, monograph 6 (N.Y., 1960), pp. 39–72.

183. (London, 1957), pp. 39, 45, etc.

184. Superego forms a kind of platform for the ego, on which it builds. Nunberg introduces a new term to put it this way (*op. cit.,* 1955, pp. 126–7): the childish "ideal ego" (a proto-ego that is purely magic and omnipotent) is in direct touch with the id and barely distinguishable from it. Then the superego decisively interposes itself, separates this magical "ideal ego" from the id and enables ego now to grow into a structure more in tune with reality principle and secondary process. Note that Róheim, like other analysts of his generation, was interested in pre-Oedipal stages and he thought superego began much earlier than the Oedipal conflict: in the infant's first experience of frustration by the mother. Ego begins at the same instant for Róheim: when the outraged infant withdraws cathexis from the frustrating mother and cathects itself. So superego and ego are born together, in the world's first great "No," and the child's autoerotic magical refusal to accept it. But Nunberg's terms could be used to square Róheim's position with Freud's: The "ego" which the infant forms in secondary narcissism to fight frustration is really only the primitive "ideal ego": no wonder it is magical. And the "superego" set up by the first frustrations is also but a primitive prototype of the complex machine that the Oedipus complex will later construct.

185. In "Les Techniques du Corps," in C. Lévi-Strauss, ed., *Marcel Mauss Sociologie et Anthropologie,* pp. 363–386. Cf. p. 370ff.

186. On the transcendence of the "I", see J.-P. Sartre, *The Transcendence of the Ego* (N.Y., 1957).

187. Maurice Halbwachs, *Les Cadres Sociaux de la Mémoire* (Paris, 1925); *La Mémoire Collective* (Paris, 1950).

188. Ernest G. Schachtel, "On Memory and Childhood Amnesia," *Metamorphosis* (N.Y., 1959), ch. 12, pp. 279–322.

189. F. C. Bartlett, *Remembering* (Cambridge, 1932, 1964), pp. 202–214.

190. Mircea Eliade, *Cosmos and History, The Myth of the Eternal Return* (N.Y., 1959), pp. 37, 39–48, 107.

191. Heinz Werner, *Comparative Psychology of Mental Development* (N.Y., 1940, 1948), "The Fundamental Ideas of Magic as an Expression of Primitive Conceptualization," ch. 11, pp. 337–376.

192. Alfred Storch, *The Primitive Archaic Forms of Inner Experience and Thought in Schizophrenia* (N.Y. & Washington, 1924), pp. 38, 60 and *passim.*

193. Ernst Kris, *Psychoanalytic Explorations in Art* (N.Y., 1952, 1964), pp. 53ff, 61ff.

194. Ernest Chace Tollman, "Physiology, Psychology and Sociology," 1938, collected in *Behavior and Psychological Man* (Berkeley, 1961), pp. 179–189.

195. "Rapports Réels et Practiques de la Psychologie et de la Sociologie" (1924) col-

lected in *Marcel Mauss Sociologie et Anthropologie*, pp. 285–310.

196. Hertz, *Death and the Right Hand*, p. 90ff., etc.

197. Wolfgang Wickler, *The Sexual Code* (Garden City, N.Y., 1973), p. 37ff, etc.

198. This is the title of a book: Jean Piaget, *Genetic Epistemology* (N.Y., 1971).

199. Roger Bastide, *Sociologie et Psychanalyse* (Paris, 1950, 1972), pp. 256–257, 283–293.

200. G. W. F. Hegel, *The Phenomenology of Mind* (N.Y., 1967), Preface, pp. 67–130.

201. Sylvano Arieti, *The Intrapsychic Self* (N.Y., 1967), pp. 83–93, 124–126, 274–277, etc.

202. Ego's magical nature is unconsciously sensed by most peoples, and as a result many of the conceptualizations of the self have been magical ("the occult self" of the mystery religions, for example).

203. G. W. Allport, *Personality and Social Encounter* (Boston, 1964), e.g., chs. 2, 3, 5, 9 and *The Person in Psychology* (Boston, 1968), ch. 15.

204. "Une Catégorie de l'Esprit Humaine," *Marcel Mauss Sociologie et Anthropologie* (Paris, 1966), pp. 331–362.

205. The person category also affects the Me, for when the I reflects upon it, it has cultural expectations. Thinking about the Me, examining one's stream of consciousness, is a highly self-conscious operation which is culturally patterned. Ego as well is shaped by the person category, for obviously this category influences which repressions each culture expects ego to execute in building its coherence. Gorer, Mead, Bateson, etc., have shown how ego repression structures fit a range of possibilities within each culture (how anality is repressed, how aggression is repressed, Russian swaddling, etc.). Reich has radicalized this to say national character is a particular repression model.

206. Kurt Goldstein, *Human Nature in the Light of Psychopathology* (N.Y., 1963, 1971), pp. 85–119; *The Organism* (Boston, 1963), pp. 291–307; "Concerning the Concept of 'Primitivity,' " in Stanley Diamond, ed., *Primitive Views of the World* (N.Y., 1964), pp. 1–19.

207. H. S. Sullivan, *Clinical Studies in Psychiatry* (N.Y., 1956), pp. 312–324.

208. Eliane Metais, *La Sorcellerie Canaque Actuelle: Les "Tuers d'Ames" Dans Une Tribu de la Nouvelle-Caledonie* (Paris, 1967), cf. bibliogrpahy.

209. T. H. Holmes and R. H. Rahe, "The Social Readjustment Rating Scale," *Journal of Psychosomatic Research,* 1967 (11), pp. 213–218.

210. Aaron T. Beck, *Depression. Causes and Treatment* (Philadelphia, 1967); *Cognitive Therapy and the Emotional Disorders* (N.Y., 1976).

211. Cited in Martin E. P. Seligman, *Helplessness: On Depression, Development and Death* (San Francisco, 1975), pp. 177–8.

212. Seligman, *Ibid.,* p. 180.

213. "Ethology and Stress Diseases," *Science,* July 5, 1974, pp. 20–27 and May 2, 1975, pp. 401–406.

214. Rene Dubos, *Mirage of Health* (Garden City, N.Y., 1959), pp. 61–112.

215. S. Chandresekhar, *India's Population, Facts and Policy* (N.Y., 1946).

216. First published in 1926 in *Journal de Psychologie Normale et Pathologique.* Reprinted in C. Lévi-Strauss, *Marcel Mauss Sociologie et Anthropologie* (Paris, 1950, 1966), pp. 311–330.

217. Cannon, " 'Voodoo' Death," *American Anthropologist,* n.s., vol. 44, no. 2 (April–June, 1942), pp. 169–181.

218. Provoking another person to sin is one of the oldest themes in myth and literature. Dodds reports Homeric Greeks had so little innerness that they thought ideas and moods came from the gods. (*The Greeks and the Irrational*, Berkeley, 1973). The idea perhaps lingers in Christian "grace," the gift from heaven that gives one the will to do the right thing. Those who sin are seen, conversely, as cursed. Or, as Menander wrote, "Whom the gods would destroy they first make mad."

219. In primitive religions the first religious functionary may be a ceremonial magician (headman) or a "witchdoctor." Religion precedes magic, but magicians who work for religions often come before priests.

220. Lévi-Strauss, ed., *Marcel Mauss Sociologie et Anthropologie*, p. 329.

221. Edward Chace Tollman, "Physiology, Psychology and Sociology," *Psychological Review,* May, 1938, reprinted in *Behavior and Psychological Man* (Berkeley, 1961), pp.

179-189.

222. Robert Hertz, "The Pre-eminence of the Right Hand," *Death and the Right Hand* (Aberdeen, 1960), pp. 87-160.

223. Mauss, "Les Techniques du Corps," *Journal de Psychologie,* 32, nos. 3-4 (1936); reprinted in Lévi-Strauss, ed., *Marcel Mauss Sociologie et Anthropologie,* pp. 363-386.

224. The "tridimensional" program was announced several times, but the most complete theoretical statement was in Mauss, "Rapports Réels et Pratiques de la Psychologie et de la Sociologie," *Journal de Psychologie et Pathologique,* 1924, reprinted in Lévi-Strauss, ed., *op. cit.,* pp. 281-310.

225. Cannon, " 'Voodoo' Death," p. 176ff.

226. George L. Engel emphasized cardiac accidents in a summary of many cases, historical and current (with a current bibliography) in "Sudden and Rapid Death During Psychological Stress—Folklore or Folk Wisdom?" in Charles A. Garfield, ed., *Rediscovery of the Body* (N.Y., 1977), pp. 297-328.

227. Wickler, Seligman (*ops. cit.*), etc. have reported similar sudden deaths in situations of helplessness.

228. Warner, *A Black Civilization: A Social Study of an Australian Tribe* (1937, rev. 1958).

229. Mankind perhaps has a stamped-in propensity to return to a local group or work group of 30-40 people; that about corresponds to the size of the average corporate "department." In these parochial settings, "for reasons beyond our control," the word often comes down to "kill" someone. If he is fired, fast and mercifully, he usually survives physically. But increasingly, in the quasi-paternalistic, quasi-authoritarian multinational corporations in which men spend their lives, he is instead "sidetracked" or allowed "to rot on the vine." He may in fact sicken and die. Since, as Cannon has shown, even careful autopsies do not turn up a clear physical process in voodoo death, we are perhaps misdiagnosing thousands of such deaths.

230. Death rates for major diseases started down this century before vaccines were developed. He suggests that the cause was public health and hygiene, and that may indeed be so. But how much does public health include? What about mental health? Ivan Illich, *Medical Nemesis,* advanced proofs edition (Cuernavaca, 1975).

231. Metais, *La Sorcellerie Canaque Actuelle . . . op. cit.,* pp. 211-214.

232. Writing in the tradition of Durkheim on funerary rites, Lienhardt on individual curing, Rasmussen on shamanic curing—studies showing that curing the individual bolsters the whole group—Metais focuses on the contrasting situation in which magic serves the group *at the expense of the individual.* Similar are the findings of some family therapists like Nathan Ackerman, David Cooper, who say the modern family succeeds nowadays only by sacrificing or destroying some of its members. Cf. David Cooper, *The Modern Family* (N.Y., 1968); Philip Slater, *The Pursuit of Loneliness* (Boston, 1970); Uri Bronfenbrenner, *Two Worlds of Childhood* (N.Y., 1970); R. D. Laing, *The Politics of Experience* (N.Y., 1965); Andrew Ferber, Marilyn Mendelsohn, Augustus Napier, *The Book of Family Therapy* (Boston, 1973).

233. Albert Bandura, *Principles of Behavior Modification* (N.Y., 1969); *Aggression* (N.Y., 1973); ed., *Psychological Modeling, Conflicting Theories* (Chicago, N.Y., 1971), etc. Also taped interview on modeling and aggression, Palo Alto, Cal., 1974.

234. E. Metais, *op. cit.,* p. 211.

235. *Ibid.,* p. 212.

236. *Ibid.,* p. 213-214.

237. *Ibid.,* pp. 364-365.

238. Martin E. P. Seligman, *Helplessness* (San Francisco, 1975), p. 176ff.

239. Cited by Seligman, p. 185.

240. René A. Spitz, *La Première Année de la Vie de l'Enfant* (Paris, 1963), p. 117ff.

241. Sigmund Freud, *The Problem of Anxiety,* Norton hardcover ed., p. 119.

242. Seligman, *op. cit.,* p. 174.

243. John R. Seeley, R. Alexander Sim & E. W. Looseley, *Crestwood Heights, A Study of the Culture of Suburban Life* (Toronto, 1956, 1971), pp. 67-68ff.

244. Adolph E. Berle, Jr., *Power Without Property* (N.Y., 1959); *The American Economic Republic* (N.Y., 1965).

245. Emile Durkheim, *Suicide* (Glencoe, Ill., 1951). To be discussed.

246. A. Alvarez, in *The Savage God* (N.Y., 1973), attributes this formulation to a statement by Wilhelm Stekel at an April, 1910, meeting of the Vienna Psychoanalytic Society: "No one kills himself who has never wanted to kill another, or at least wished the death of another." Freud was skeptical of this simplistic interpretation, according to Alvarez; he is supposed to have suggested that suicide could not be understood until more was known about melancholia. Cf. pp. 98–99ff.

247. Suicide is "inversely related to external restraint" and homicide is "directly related to external restraint." Andrew F. Henry and James F. Short, Jr., *Suicide and Homicide* (N.Y., 1954, 1964), p. 75ff, etc. In further axioms they define "relatedness" as a correlate of external restraint; they also correlate low social class with external restraint. (Cf. chs. 5–6). A person in the lower classes has a lot of people sitting on him, as it were. If he is frustrated he can find plenty of targets. But if he is rich, independent, Protestant and free of restraints, he has nobody to assault but himself, so he elects suicide instead of homicide. As epidemiological studies in social psychiatry go, this synthesis of Durkheim and Freud is a masterpiece of economy. Homicides and suicides are easier to operationalize than the notoriously shifty constructs of mental illness used in August B. Hollingshead and Fredrick C. Redlich, *Social Class and Mental Illness* (N.Y., 1958), or Srole, Langner, Michael, Opler and Rennie, *Mental Health in the Metropolis: The Midtown Manhattan Study* (N.Y., 1962), vol. I. But does the Henry and Short study really *explain* anything about suicide?

248. Although MacIver (*Social Causation*, Boston, 1942, pp. 140–143; also lectures, 1949, but note his reservations) and others tout it as an exemplar of sociological method, Durkheim's study is deeply flawed in method. (For some recent critiques see Jack D. Douglas, *The Social Meanings of Suicide* [Princeton, 1967, 1970]; Whitney Pope, *Durkheim's Suicide, A Classic Analyzed* [Chicago, 1976]; Jacques Choron, *Suicide* [N.Y., 1972]). The most remarkable defect is his adoption of what he calls the "reverse order of study." (p. 146) Confronted with phenomena which are difficult to sort out, Durkheim astonishingly announces that he will classify them according to their causes, thus incorporating what he sets out to prove in his initial definitions. (This is just the opposite of what he called for in his *Rules of Method.*) This is the "latent hermaneutic" in his work that Goldmann speaks of. (Lucien Goldmann, *The Human Sciences and Philosophy* [London, 1969], pp. 36–48) It takes the form of an elaborate series of behavior maxims deduced from each other. These deductions are then put to "statistical tests." They fit pretty well, but it is likely that facts were made to fit theory via the "reverse sequence."

249. Sylvia Plath, *The Bell Jar* (N.Y., 1975).

250. Alvarez, *The Savage God*, p. 115ff.

251. Edwin S. Shneidman and Norman L. Farberow, "The Logic of Suicide" in Shneidman and Farberow, eds., *Clues to Suicide* (N.Y., 1957), ch. 4, pp. 31–40.

252. "Vous me permettrez, pour terminer, de mentionner encore que ces faits confirment et étendent la théorie du suicide anomique que Durkheim a exposée dans un livre modèle de demonstration sociologique." Mauss, "L'Idée de Mort . . .", p. 330.

253. Robert A. Nisbet, *The Sociology of Emile Durkheim* (N.Y., 1974), pp. 105–113.

254. Glencoe, Ill., 1933, 1949. First published as *De la Division Social du Travail* (Paris, 1893).

255. London, 1915, 1954. First published as *Le Suicide* (Paris, 1897).

256. *Suicide*, p. 44.

257. *Ibid.*, p. 45.

258. Karl Menninger, *Life Against Death*, cited in A. Alvarez, *op. cit.*, pp. 102, 127.

259. Ernest Becker, *Escape From Evil* (N.Y., 1975), p. 34.

260. *Beyond the Pleasure Principle*, p. 71ff.

261. *Suicide*, pp. 147–8.

262. Jeremy Bentham, *An Introduction to the Principles of Morals and Legislation* (Oxford, 1948), ch. 4, "Value as a Lot of Pleasure or Pain, How to Be Measured," pp. 151–154.

263. Alfred De Vigny, *Chatterton* (Paris, 1956).

264. Cf. Edmund Wilson's account in *Axel's Castle* (N.Y., 1931), p. 259ff.

265. Judaism is associated with urbanism, intellectualism, individualism, mobility, etc., yet has lower suicide rates than even Catholicism. Durkheim says it is because of the sense of community experienced in a ghettoized group, but the answer seems forced. On the other hand, it would be hard to imagine that Judaism in practice is more magical than Catholicism.

266. To excessive *or* rudimentary individuation. *Suicide,* p. 221.

267. *Hamlet,* Act III, Scene 1.

268. Henry Romilly Fedden, *Suicide: A Social and Historical Study* (London, 1938), p. 89.

269. Fedden, *Ibid.,* ch. 4.

270. Anomic suicide is an unclear concept. Writing of it Durkheim almost sounds like the Lord Krishna in the *Ghita,* warning Arjuna of the confusion and unhappiness that result if people do not stay within their caste roles. For Durkheim associates anomic suicide with the social mobility of capitalism: caste and class systems produce stable expectations and people are satisfied; with social mobility no one is satisfied (*Suicide,* pp. 254–5). Once again, we encounter the unattractive side of Durkheim, the side that makes the reader want to cry out "anomie is good for you!" The distinction of anomic from egoistic suicide is vague. In egoistic suicide the individual has no collective social *integration,* by membership or belief, to protect him. In anomic suicide, there is no social *restraint* on the individual, norms are lacking or contradictory. Perhaps we can say that egoistic suicide responds to overly-individualistic, pessimistic ideas; and anomic suicide to contradictions and gaps in social morality.

271. On this cf. also Durkheim, *The Social Division of Labor* (Glencoe, Ill., 1947), Book 3, "Abnormal Forms," pp. 353–410.

272. Durkheim admits this factor of the susceptibility of the human monad to suicide when he admits that there are always "more than enough susceptibles" for the "suicidogenic currents" to take their toll. (*Suicide,* p. 324).

273. On a cognitive level, suicidogenic currents may be close to what Parsons called "patterned deviancies." (Talcott Parsons, *The Social System,* Glencoe, Ill., 1951, p. 267ff, etc.) This is the hypothesis that there exists in every culture a latent but ascertainable hierarchy of escapes, arranged in order of ignominy, which individuals can opt for when the heat is too much for them.

274. In Freud, "Mourning and Melancholia" (1917), *Collected Papers: General Psychological Theory* (N.Y., 1963), pp. 164–179.

275. According to Alvarez, *The Savage God* (N.Y., 1973), pp. 98–99.

276. In *Suicide and Homicide* (N.Y., 1954, 1964), ch. 5, pp. 69–81.

277. According to Donald T. Lunde, *Murder and Madness* (Stanford, 1975), p. 33.

278. Alvarez, *op. cit.,* p. 90.

279. For this paragraph I am relying on journalistic accounts in current newspapers and magazines, and some interviews with reporters. I cannot vouch for *all* the many *ad hoc* hot lines that have sprung up in American cities. I have heard of at least one that uses an answering service during evenings and holidays.

280. Cima Star and Shari Steiner, "Why More Women Are Committing Suicide," *McCall's Magazine,* N.Y., Jan. '76, p. 47ff.

281. Cited in Alvarez, pp. 92–95.

282. *Ibid.,* p. 102.

283. B. Malinowski, *Crime and Custom in Savage Society* (Totawa, N.J., 1976), pp. 85–99.

284. "Mourning and Melancholia," p. 170ff.

285. William Glasser, *Mental Health Or Mental Illness?* (N.Y., 1960, 1970), p. 132.

286. Fedden, *op. cit.,* ch. 3.

287. Bronislaw Malinowski, *op. cit.,* pp. 78–79. Also *Sexual Life of Savages* (N.Y., 1929), pp. 119–120.

288. Charles William Wahl, "Suicide As a Magical Act," ch. 3 in Edwin S. Schneidman and Norman L. Farberow, eds., *Clues to Suicide* (N.Y., 1957), pp. 22–30.

289. W. Lloyd Warner, *A Black Civilization* (N.Y., 1958 rev. ed.), p. 241.

290. Fedden, *op. cit.,* p. 42.

291. This is his title for Part Two of *The Savage God,* pp. 73–132.

292. *Ibid.,* p. 119.

293. Aaron T. Beck, *Depression: Causes and Treatment* (Philadelphia, 1967), p. 56.

294. For example, Paul Roazen, after repeating Stekel's theory of suicide as displaced murder as relevant to Tausk's case, makes it equally plain that this rejected young disciple of Freud did not really want to die, but sought to *kill something inside himself that would not be still.* Paul Roazen, *Brother Animal, The Story of Freud and Tausk* (London, 1973),

pp. 128–9 & ch. 5 *passim*. Incidentally, in this book and in *Freud and His Followers* (N.Y., 1976), Roazen comes close to suggesting that Freud acquired a kind of (unconscious) shamanic power to cause voodoo death among his colleagues, a number of whom committed suicide after rejection by him. Cf. pp. 320–21, etc.

295. Donald T. Lunde, *op. cit.*, p. 11.

296. Homicide has risen tenfold in this country since the turn of the century, but not steadily: it rose practically to its present height (10 per 100,000 per year) in the 1920's, then fell below 1910 records between 1935 & 1955, then started up again, and has doubled since 1968. Lunde, *op. cit.*, pp. 13–18ff.

297. The murder rate, in general high, is 50 times higher among young males in these subcultures: e.g., new immigrants. Lunde, *op. cit.*, p. 19.

298. Lunde, p. 33.

299. According to numerous newspaper reports.

300. Felony murders are often the response, to direct social pressure, of primitive individuals with weak egos and virtually no superegos (the poorly socialized "psychopath"). They strike back directly at symbols of the social pressure that oppresses them rather than hitting symbols of their own internalized identifications. Here we get closer to the early primitive "magical" murders—witch executions and sorcery murders.

301. Studies announced by the U.S. Surgeon General (1977, 1979) attribute the recent increase in longevity rates in the U.S. (after some years of stagnation) to the public drives aimed at curbing tobacco, cholesterol, inactivity, destructive lifestyles in general. In primitive societies, the effect of the religious-magical balance on longevity must surely have been significant. People do not live long lives among Canaques, where everyone seems capable of bringing voodoo death down on everyone else. By contrast, consider the rock-like institutions of the Greek and Roman sibs described by de Coulanges (*The Ancient City*, N.Y., 1954, Book II). Except for the besetting problem of warfare, one suspects that longevity (at least among the dominant males) would be higher here than in some other places. Perhaps primitive societies with comparatively greater longevity are the ones that evolve toward higher civilization (thanks to the economic surplus and leisure that longer life makes possible).

302. Fedden's own peculiar confession of bias in favor of suicide reveals something of its magic flavor. He writes that all men die anyway and when it is over, it is over: "eventually, why not now." Do-it-yourself makes you master of your fate, etc. Alvarez notes that the ready access to modern painless means of suicide (sleeping pills and gas) makes it seem even more magical: an easy act of self-determination which painlessly changes destiny. Cf. Alvarez, *op. cit.*, pp. 131–132.

303. Ernesto de Martino, *The World of Magic* (Hong Kong, 1972). Discussion follows.

304. "Therefore, corresponding to the magical risk of losing the soul, there exists the danger of losing the world. (de Martino, p. 129) . . . In a civilization such as ours, where the decision of the self and of the world is no longer a . . . problem . . . we are, ourselves, 'given facts,' and the objects and events of the world are therefore considered by our empirical minds as given facts." (*Ibid.* p. 136)

305. Sartre, in *The Transcendence of the Ego* (N.Y., 1957), noted this vulnerability of the "I": its tendency to *reflect* what it sees; the tendency of the other person therefore to be more real than oneself (p. 48ff. and *passim*).

306. Knud Rasmussen, *Intellectual Culture of the Hudson Bay Eskimos*, which is part 1 of vol. 7 of Report of Fifth Thule Expedition, 1921–24 (Copenhagen, 1930). Cf. ch. 5. See also discussion of Shirokogoroff report in de Martino, *op. cit.*, pp. 102–3.

307. Today R. D. Laing calls for consideration of schizophrenic episodes as voyages of discovery, as trips which should be socially guided to aid reintegration of the personality. This is an old idea in European psychiatry, conceptualized by the Polish psychiatrist Dabrowski, with his concept of creative disintegration. (Kasimierz Dabrowski, *Positive Disintegration*, Boston, 1964) The idea has a certain fascination to the totalitarian mind; Hannah Arendt, in *The Origins of Totalitarianism*, speculated that the concentration camp was intended to become a universal experience for all members of Nazi and Communist society; all were to be broken and reassembled by this crucible in order to produce better citizens (Cleveland & N.Y., 1951, 1958), pp. 457–9, etc.

308. Søren Kierkegaard, *The Concept of Dread* (Princeton, 1957), ch. 4, pp. 99–138.

309. Claude Lévi-Strauss, *Totemism* (Boston, 1963), pp. 66–69.

310. Ibid., p. 69. More: "Before a recourse to anxiety could supply even the outlines of an explanation, we should have to know what anxiety really is, and then what relations exist between, on the one hand, a confused and disordered emotion, and, on the other, acts marked by the most rigorous precision. . . ." (p. 68).

311. ". . . while one anthropological theory is that magic and religion give men confidence, comfort and a sense of security, it could equally well be argued that they give men fears and anxieties from which they would otherwise be free" (p. 67). Lévi-Strauss is here quoting Radcliffe-Brown.

312. Martin Heidegger, *Being and Time* (N.Y., 1962), p. 343, etc.

313. *The Concept of Dread* (Princeton, 1957); *Fear and Trembling* (Garden City, N.Y., 1954), etc.

314. Paul Tillich, *The Courage to Be* (New Haven, 1952, 1959), *passim*.

315. Paul Tillich, "Anxiety-Reducing Agencies in Our Culture," ch. 1 in Paul H. Hoch and Joseph Zubin, *Anxiety* (N.Y., 1950), pp. 17-25.

316. This is the title of a book of Charles Frankel's essays (N.Y., 1967).

317. Rollo May, *The Meaning of Anxiety* (N.Y., 1950), pp. 232-234, 355-356.

318. O. Hobart Mowrer, "Pain, Punishment, Guilt and Anxiety," ch. 3 in Hoch and Zubin, *op. cit.*, pp. 27-40.

319. Bruno Bettelheim, *The Empty Fortress* (N.Y., 1967, 1972), pp. 63-74.

320. Nikolaas Tinbergen, "Ethology and Stress Disease," *Science*, Vol. 185, July 5, 1974, pp. 20-27.

321. Eugene E. Levitt, *The Psychology of Anxiety* (Indianapolis, 1967), ch. 3, pp. 34-36ff.

322. George E. Vaillant, *Adaptation to Life* (Boston, 1977), pp. 75-192.

323. Paul Federn, *Ego Psychology and the Psychoses* (N.Y., 1952), pp. 189-191ff, etc.

324. Thomas Freeman, John L. Cameron, Andrew McGhie, *Studies on Psychosis* (London, 1965), p. 54ff.

325. *Ibid.*, ch. 4, pp. 72-87.

326. *Ibid.*, ch. 5, and p. 46ff.

327. Sarnoff A. Mednick, "A Learning Theory Approach to Research in Schizophrenia," ch. 3 in Arnold H. Buss and Edith H. Buss, eds., *Theories of Schizophrenia* (N.Y., 1969), pp. 76-95.

328. Carl Jung, *The Psychology of Dementia Praecox* (Princeton, 1974), p. 190ff.

329. Cited in Jung, *op. cit.*, p. 28, etc.

330. Solomon H. Snyder, *Madness and the Brain* (N.Y., 1975), pp. 225ff., 255ff.

331. For earlier attempts to find a physical base, cf. survey in Roy Hoskins, *The Biology of Schizophrenia* (N.Y., 1946).

332. Lauretta Bender, "Anxiety in Disturbed Children," ch. 7 in Paul H. Hoch and Joseph Zubin, *Anxiety* (N.Y., 1950), pp. 119-139.

333. Melanie Klein, *The Psychoanalysis of Children* (N.Y., 1960).

334. Carl A. Whitaker and Thomas P. Malone, "Anxiety and Psychotherapy," in Arthur J. Vidich and David Manning White, eds., *Identity and Anxiety* (N.Y., 1960), pp. 166-180.

335. Joseph C. Rheingold, *The Mother, Anxiety and Death* (Boston, 1967), pp. 155-193.

336. Kurt Goldstein, *The Organism* (Boston, 1963), pp. 35, 117, etc. Also *Human Nature In The Light of Psychopathology* (N.Y., 1963), pp. 92-94.

337. Frieda Fromm-Reichmann, "Psychiatric Aspects of Anxiety," in Vidich and White, eds., *Identity and Anxiety, op. cit.*, pp. 129-143.

338. Frieda Fromm-Reichmann, *Psychoanalysis and Psychotherapy* (Chicago, 1959), pp. 102-4, 315-6.

339. Kurt Goldstein, *Human Nature in the Light of Psychopathology*, pp. 92-94.

340. Paul Tillich, *The Courage To Be*, p. 37.

341. Eugene E. Levitt, *op. cit.*, ch. 7, "Anxiety and Learning," pp. 108-138.

342. Esp. in papers 13 & 14 in the collection, Harry Stack Sullivan, *The Fusion of Psychiatry and Social Science* (N.Y., 1964), pp. 198-254.

343. Herbert Fingarette, *The Self in Transformation* (N.Y., 1965), ch. 2, "Anxiety and Disintegration," pp. 71-112.

344. Søren Kierkegaard, *The Concept of Dread* (Princeton, 1957), pp. 105-121.

345. Nikola Schipkowensky, *Psychotherapy Vs. Iatrogeny* (Detroit, 1977), *passim.*

346. In the Introduction to *Mélanges,* Hubert and Mauss write: "Magic in effect has furnished to the individual the means to make himself valuable in his own eyes and the eyes of others, or to escape the crowd, to escape social pressure (s'échapper à la pression sociale) and routine." H. Hubert and M. Mauss, "Introduction à l'Analyse de Quelques Phénomènes Religieux," Mauss, *Oeuvres,* vol. I, pp. 24–25. (My translation.)

347. P. Huvelin, "Magie et Droit Individuel," in *L'Année Sociologique,* 1905–1906, pp. 1–47.

348. Hubert and Mauss, "Esquisse d'Une Théorie Générale de la Magie", in Lévi-Strauss, ed., *Marcel Mauss Sociologie et Anthropologie,* p. 83.

349. *The Elementary Forms of Religious Life,* pp. 317–325.

350. "Owing to the contagiousness inherent in all that is sacred, a profane being cannot violate an interdict without having the religious force, to which he has unduly approached, extend itself over him and establish its empire over him. But as there is an antagonism between them, he becomes dependent upon a hostile power, whose hostility cannot fail to manifest itself in the form of violent reactions which tend to destroy him. This is why sickness or death are considered the natural consequences of every transgression of this sort . . ." (*The Elementary Forms . . .,* p. 320).

351. Howard S. Becker, *Outsiders: Studies in the Sociology of Deviance* (N.Y., 1963), pp. 135, 147–163.

352. Hegel, *Lectures on the Philosophy of Religion* (N.Y., 1962), vol. I, part 2, ch. 1, "Immediate Religion," pp. 290–317.

353. Huvelin was criticized by them for overschematizing and dichotomizing magic and religion, in "Introduction à l'Analyse de Quelques Phénomènes Religieux," 1906, collected in Mauss, *Oeuvres,* vol. I, Paris, 1968, 3–39. Cf. pp. 22–26.

354. Bronislaw Malinowski, *Crime and Custom in Savage Society* (London, 1926; Totowa, N.J. 1976) pp. 80–81 etc.

355. Lévi-Strauss, *The Savage Mind* (Chicago, 1966), pp. 16–33.

356. Lévi-Strauss, *Structural Anthropology* (vol. 1) (N.Y., 1963), ch. 10, "The Effectiveness of Symbols," pp. 186–205.

357. Adulatory accounts of this metaphysics appear in, for example, Irwin Chabron, *Awake and Aware* (N.Y., 1966); Marjorie Karmel, *Thank You Doctor Lamaze* (Garden City, N.Y., 1959).

358. See R. Speck and C. Attneuve, "Network Therapy," ch. 22 in Andrew Ferber, Marilyn Mendelsohn, & Augustus Napier, *The Book of Family Therapy* (Boston, 1973), pp. 637–665.

359. Freud suggested that fortune tellers use telepathic powers to divine the secret wishes of their clients. See chs. 5 & 8, by Freud, in G. Devereux, *Psychoanalysis and the Occult* (N.Y., 1953, 1970), pp. 56–68, 91–112.

360. Richard W. Lieban, *Cebuano Sorcery* (Berkeley, 1967, 1977), p. 39.

361. Goldstein, *Human Nature In The Light of Psychopathology* N.Y., 1963), ch. 4 *passim* and pp. 79ff, 106, etc.

362. Lévi-Strauss, Introd. to *Marcel Mauss Sociologie et Anthropologie* (Paris, 1950, 1966), pp. IX–LII.

363. Sylvano Arieti, *Creativity, The Magic Synthesis* (N.Y., 1976), pp. 264–6.

364. *Magic and Schizophrenia,* p. 18.

365. Martin E. P. Seligman, *Helplessness* (San Francisco, 1975), p. 108ff.

366. *Learned Helplessness As a Model of Depression,* special issue, *Journal of Abnormal Psychology,* vol. 87, no. 1, Feb. 1978.

367. Aaron T. Beck, *Depression* (Philadelphia, 1967), cf. index.

368. Robert MacIver, *Social Causation* (N.Y., 1942), chs. 11, 12, pp. 291–350.

369. Seligman, *Helplessness,* pp. 14, 16, 18.

370. Seligman's precise definition of helplessness is scattered through his chapters but it is acute. Helplessness is a learned expectation that may result (affecting behavior, cognition and emotions) when an organism learns that events are uncontrollable. Uncontrollability, in turn, is mathematically defined as situations of equal probability of outcomes: responses are just as likely to have no effect as some effect. It occurs to me that this situation of "response contingency" or equal probability corresponds to the strategy which

game theorists consider to be appropriate in non-zero-sum games with no saddle points: Utterly randomizing one's responses is the only possible way to beat the other fellow. But of course he will do the same thing if he has any sense. Sometimes I think we are all engaged in too many non-zero-sum games with no saddle points and everyone is randomizing his responses and it is driving us crazy.

371. B. F. Skinner, "Superstition in the Pigeon," *Journal of Experimental Psychology,* 1948 (38), 168–172.

372. Skinner writes: "The experiment might be said to demonstrate a sort of superstition. The bird behaves as if there were a causal relation between its behavior and the presentation of food, although such a relation is lacking. There are many analogies in human behavior. Rituals for changing one's luck at cards are good examples. A few accidental connections between a ritual and favorable consequences suffice to set up and maintain the behavior in spite of many unreinforced instances." *Ibid.,* p. 171.

373. Magic metaphors of mastery, stolen from religion and projected onto the cosmos, give man similar defense against helplessness, just as the whirling pigeon seized control of the experiment from Skinner.

374. Stanley Diamond, lectures and conversations, 1967.

375. Suzanne K. Langer, *Philosophy in a New Key* (N.Y., 1948), p. 129.

376. Godfrey Lienhardt, *Divinity and Experience: The Religion of the Dinka* (Oxford, 1961), ch. 7, e.g., p. 280.

377. Paul Tillich, *The Courage To Be* (New Haven, 1959), ch. 2, pp. 32–63.

378. *Ibid.,* p. 32.

379. M. Heidegger, *An Introduction to Metaphysics* (Garden City, N.Y., 1961), ch. 2, pp. 43–62.

380. C. E. Osgood et al., *The Measurement of Meaning* (Urbana, 1957), *passim.*

381. French ed., *Esquisse . . .,* pp. 26–28.

382. *Ibid.,* p. 28.

383. Reviewing Eduard Seler's paper (1899) on magic in ancient Mexico, Hubert and Mauss note that the mana-like word *nagual* means "magic," but also mystery, hidden, disguise or double. (*Oeuvres,* vol. 2, p. 389).

384. *Magic and Schizophrenia,* p. 47.

385. French edition, pp. 29–31.

386. See Durkheim on personal totems. The personal totem as magical servant recalls also the "genius" who, in the case of brilliant men such as Socrates, did not so much possess as serve the man, while not being quite under his control. *The Elementary Forms of Religious Life* (London, 1915, 1954), p. 157ff.

387. Rasmussen, *op. cit.,* ch. 5.

388. Ernest Becker, *The Revolution in Psychiatry* (N.Y., 1964), p. 24.

389. Ernst Kris, *Psychoanalytic Explorations* in Art (N.Y., 1952, 1964), p. 52ff.

390. Heinz Werner, *Comparative Psychology of Mental Development* (N.Y., 1940, 1948), p. 357ff.

391. Silvano Arieti, *Creativity, The Magic Synthesis* (N.Y., 1976), pp. 264–266.

392. Goldstein has suggested somewhere that abstraction involves not just a wrenching of reality, but also a separation: one imagines oneself as separate from reality to move it. Magic's alleged impiety and skepticism derive in part from this role-distance.

393. Ernest Nagel & James R. Newman, *Gödel's Proof* (N.Y., 1958), pp. 68–75.

394. It is common for a magical ceremony to contain a straightforward "theoretical" account of how the magic works. Repeating this explanation is supposed to increase the efficacy.

395. M. Eliade, *Shamanism* (Princeton, 1972).

396. Solomon H. Snyder, *Madness and the Brain* (N.Y., 1975), chs. 4–8.

397. L. Susan Stebbing, *A Modern Introduction to Logic* (N.Y., 1931, 1961), p. 194.

398. William Irwin Thompson, *At The Edge of History* (N.Y., 1971), pp. 58–61, 102ff, etc.

399. Needham, *Science and Civilization in China,* vol. 2, Section 10, esp. pp. 89–98.

400. Cf. Malcolm B. Bowers, Jr., on the numinous illuminations that sometimes usher in psychotic disintegration: *Retreat From Sanity* (Baltimore, 1974), pp. 25–48.

401. Alfred Storch, *The Primitive Archaic Forms of Inner Experiences and Thought in Schizophrenia* (N.Y. & Wash., 1924), p. 106.

402. See Fred Hoyle on the growth of knowledge as "The Thing," in *Man and Materialism* (N.Y., 1956).

403. As Róheim has shown, he even doubles for the patient's soul, maintaining his vigil while the sick man sleeps.

404. Richard W. Lieban, *Cebuana Sorcery* (Berkeley, 1967, 1977), p. 23ff.

405. The magical psychological complex becomes a medical complex because of the experimental nature of magic. Attempts are made ultimately to cure the physical disease as well as the spiritual attack that provoked it or preyed on it, and a lore of drugs and other treatments accumulates as a secondary development.

406. Knud Rasmussen, *Intellectual Culture of the Iglulik Eskimos, Report of the Fifth Thule Expedition,* vol. VII (Copenhagen, 1930), p. 56.

407. Marcel Mauss, "L'Origine des Pouvoirs Magiques Dans les Sociétés Australiennes," *Oeuvres,* vol. 2, p. 369.

408. *Divinity and Experience,* pages cited.

409. Idries Shah, *Oriental Magic* (N.Y., 1973), p. 3.

410. Arvid S. Kapelrud, "Shamanic Features in the Old Testament," ch. 6, C.-M. Edsman, *Studies in Shamanism* (Stockholm, 1967).

411. E.g., Weston La Barre's account in *The Ghost Dance* (N.Y., 1972), pp. 93–120.

412. In *Shamanism* (Princeton, 1972), p. 499ff.

413. Joseph Needham, *Science and Civilization in China,* vol. 2, section 10.

414. E. R. Dodds, *The Greeks and the Irrational* (Berkeley, 1951, 1973), ch. 5, "The Greek Shamans and the Origins of Puritanism," pp. 135–178.

415. The fact that shamanism sometimes *turns into* religion is no problem—our analysis of Weber's work has shown how most magic has this propensity. Just because later shamans sometimes turn into priests, it is not necessary to postulate that shamanism is some kind of vague primordial MR or "magico-religion" preceding religion. Priests are a late development which G. Weiss (in Harner's *Hallucinogens and Shamanism,* London, 1973, pp. 40–48) identifies with state systems. The dangers of polar ideal types are illustrated by these persistant pseudo-problems of dichotomies. Religion comes before magic but the first religious functionaries are headmen magicians and there is no contradiction in that—only polar ideal types make it seem so.

416. Gustav Rank, "Shamanism as a Research Project," In Carl-Martin Edsman, *Studies in Shamanism* (Stockholm, 1967).

417. Eliade, *Shamanism* (Princeton, 1972), pp. 498ff.

418. Needham, *Science and Civilization in China,* vol. 2, pp. 132–139.

419. Erik Holtved, "Eskimo Shamanism," in Edsman, *op. cit.*

420. Rasmussen, ch. 5.

421. Ake Hultkrants, "Spirit Lodge, A North American Shamanistic Seance," in Edsman, *op. cit.*

422. Odd Nordland, "Shamanism as an Experience of the Unreal," in Edsman, *op. cit.*

423. Ernst Kris, *Psychoanalytic Explorations in Art* (N.Y., 1952, 1954).

424. Jurgen Ruesch, *Disturbed Communication* (N.Y., 1957), p. 71.

425. The shaman is like the modern-day "family therapist," who treats the whole "network." Critics of American society like Philip Slater (*The Pursuit of Loneliness*), and Richard Sennett (*Families Against the City, The Uses of Disorder*) claim that in fleeing one another into new self-made ghettoes of age, income and occupations, we flee our natural networks with the result, since they remain inside of us, that our original integrations can never be set right. Out in the suburbs, people live so far away from parents and relatives that no "shaman" can assemble the "chorus" that shaped them for purposes of dramatic redefinition.

426. Don Juan told his pupil what to expect and so pre-patterned the drug experience, and he guided interpretation of it afterwards. He also conveyed it within a special conceptual frame. Castenada outlined the system as having four units: 1. the "man of knowledge" (who respectfully "learns" this special cognitive experience which is thought of as a form of "knowledge"); 2. the "ally" or drug he uses; 3. the "rule" that goes with the ally; 4. the corroboration of the rule by the "special consensus" (of two people). Carlos Castenada, *The Teachings of Don Juan: A Yaqui Way of Knowledge* (N.Y., 1969), Part 2, "A Structural Analysis," pp. 199–255.

427. Michael J. Harner, ed., *Hallucinogens and Shamanism* (London, N.Y., 1973).

428. Harner, *op. cit.,* ch. 4, pp. 40–48.

429. Useful here is Erika Bourguignon's distinction of ordinary trance from "possession trance" and the finding of her group that possession trance correlates with situations in which there is both 1. complexity in social structure (many roles and hierarchy) and 2. rigidity in the system. So people are locked into their fixed roles. Possession trance enables them to play other roles. Bourguignon, ed., *Religion, Altered States of Consciousness and Social Change* (Columbus, Ohio, 1973), cf. Introduction.

430. Basil Bernstein, *Class Codes and Control* (N.Y., 1974), *passim.*

431. Richard Hoggart, *The Uses of Literacy* (Boston, 1961).

432. George Steiner, *Language and Silence* (N.Y., 1967).

433. Claus Mueller, *The Politics of Communication* (Oxford, 1973).

434. Or Masters and Johnson daring to tell childless couples, in popular magazine articles, commonsense principles such as varying frequency during fertile periods, information every primitive possessed but which, until recently, was dispensed at great expense and only after prolonged tests by standard medical practice in New York City.

435. Ivan Illich, *Medical Nemesis* (Cuernavaca, 1975).

436. Nikola Schipkowensky, *Psychotherapy Vs. Iatrogeny* (Detroit, 1977).

437. Harry Stack Sullivan, *The Psychiatric Interview* (N.Y., 1953).

438. Cf. older studies summarized in "Iatrogenic Disease: The Scourge of Doctor-Caused Disease," in Martin L. Gross, *The Doctors* (N.Y., 1966).

439. Title of Mauss' essay on voodoo death.

440. Eva and Richard Blum, *The Dangerous Hour* (London, 1970), ch. 9.

441. MacClean, *Magical Medicine, a Nigerian Case-Study* (London, 1971).

442. From the title of Freud's essay, "Analysis Terminable and Interminable," 1937, British ed. of *Collected Papers,* James Strachey, ed., vol. 5 (London, 1957), ch. 30, pp. 316–357.

443. Paul Schilder, *Medical Psychology* (N.Y., 1953).

444. Cf. Paul Federn, *Ego Psychology and the Psychoses* (N.Y., 1952).

445. Psychiatry seems to become more stigmatizing as it gains acceptance. There seems to be a virtual epidemic of "neurotic character" disorders in America. There is also a notorious epidemic of "pseudo-neurotic latent psychosis". Snyder observes that American psychiatrists are especially fond of diagnosing mental illness this way. Of course, it is quite possible that individuals are getting much sicker than before. It is also possible that the increasingly accepted psychiatric profession is taking the attitude of the superego instead of going against it as Róheim said it should. It is possible that magic is turning into religion, once more, as always. There is already a "magical revolt" against psychoanalysis as an establishment religion going on within the profession. Thomas Szasz objects to psychiatry's alliance with the legal profession; in his view this not only turns the doctor into a superego figure but corrupts due process of law. R. D. Laing goes so far as to identify with the patient's symptoms, in order to restore magical efficacy. After Hollingshead and Redlich showed in their study that psychiatrists tend to diagnose non-establishment people more severely than they do upper-class people, *Srole et al.* went them one further by diagnosing *most* of the inhabitants of New York City as crazy. It is interesting that the evaluations in the New Haven study were made by social scientists mainly while those in New York were made by psychiatrists.

446. Instead of the immediate "chorus" of onlookers at the magical seance, psychoanalysis gets incorporated into the *weltanschauung* of the whole society so there is a kind of remote or implied audience participation, but the result is different: "When this happens . . . the treatment, . . . far from leading to the resolution of a specific disturbance within its own context, is reduced to the reorganization of the patient's universe in terms of psychoanalytic interpretations." (*Structural Anthropology,* p. 183) When it works, psychoanalysis does refer to an audience: "the friends of psychoanalysis" as an informal supportive cultural milieu. But this may be a waning subculture today.

Postulate 10: MAGIC HELPED DEVELOP THE INSTITUTION OF THE INDIVIDUAL.

MAGIC not only defends the self—once upon a time it helped fabricate the institutional shell within which the self now snugly resides.[1] In the last chapter I considered the "self" in isolation, a ghostly psychological concept; now I look at this institutional shell, which is a bristling sociological facticity. We call this shell the "Individual." It is an *institution*—in fact, a whole complex of institutions. And magic helped shape the origins of most of these sub-institutions of the Individual—private property, law of contracts, individualist religion, the idea of the person. Many studies reveal parts of this; all we lack is the general recognition that puts these pieces together. But to pull this together properly it will be necessary first to trace the original emergence of magic and the Individual together in the Neolithic, and follow their conjoined fortunes through the evolution from band to tribe to chiefdom to empire and finally to cities.

The Individual is a recent event, so if magic helped create it, this suggests that perhaps magic itself is not primevally primitive after all. And there is indeed evidence that man had already walked down a long road by the time he fashioned the main magics with which history and anthropology are familiar. Durkheim, Gurvitch, Halbwachs and others of the French school related the rise of magic to the "generalization of mana"[2]—new religious symbols which reflected society's advance from a ramshackle mosaic of "polysegmental" local groups, each with its own kindred religion, to a more articulated and hierarchical "tribal" structure. I believe that this is a brilliant intuition.

Neolithic Barbarism

Let me admit my own speculations: I think it likely that the first major religious projections of society arose in the Paleolithic, in social stages that Tyler,[3] Morgan,[4] Engels and Childe[5] called "savagery." Of course religion *keeps on arising anew*— with every new social contract, with every new form of society— but quite probably many of the first religious practices appeared in Paleolithic savagery. Perhaps some black magic was also present then, perhaps some rudimentary work and curing magic. But the *main* bodies of magic, I think, split off from religion in the Neolithic, during "middle and high barbarism."[6] (Both magic and religion then continued to evolve, right into the civilized period.) At some key points in the Neolithic, after technological and ecological changes sustained larger work groups and complex social contracts began linking clans together into tribes, the religions reflecting this went into eruption, modeling magic with such intensity that they started a perturbation within *koinomia* leading to articulation and separation of parts. Spectacular new ceremonies commemorated the complex new social contracts; soul-transforming initiation rites and the grand opera of sacrifice created a fireworks display of the sympathetic-magic potentials of social ritual. That is when real magical institutions began to crystallize within religion and later to separate out of it.[7] As social contracts and consequent role transitions became more complex, requiring young men to recapitulate the social history of their societies in successive initiations into sib, phratry and tribe, selves had to be made hardier to endure such shifting about and consequent contradictions. It was then that black magic grew more aggressive in sorcery, and sorcery in turn gave rise to medical magic to protect the self. Still later, the occult sciences emerged from divination procedures in medical magic. All these magics sustained the frail emerging self— ceremonial magic focused his attention and made his work more effective, black magic and medical magic protected him from the whiplash of social contradictions, and the occult sciences enabled him to withstand uncertainty.

Where the classical magics persist today they still aid the core of self, however ineptly in our time. But the birth of magic also saw the start of solider institutions no longer considered magical that more securely support the Individual, the self's lasting institutional shell. These included some new occupations that emerged from the division of labor, which was originally a division of magic.[8] Specialized *magics*, specialized *knowledge* and, finally, specialized magical occupations gave individuals a special standing and integrity against the community. The learned professions that descend from them still enfold a core of magic as we shall see.

In this chapter we will concentrate on institutions closest to the Individual, using studies by the French school especially to consider how individual law, law of contracts, individualistic religion and the idea of the person grew partly out of magic and constituted the infrastructure of individuality. In the last chapter I will return to the division of labor and show how magic helped accelerate it, how magic, indeed, seems to "fit" organic solidarity.[9] There I will wrestle with the seeming paradox of magic's continued growth during civilization. Does the world perhaps become more magical with man's advance, rather than less?

PART ONE: MAN'S TURNING POINT

The question is: when did the major magics of the world start? Functionalists and nominalists like Goldenweisser[10] long ago cautioned anthropologists: don't ask. Suspension of evolutionary conjectures was hailed as a timely antidote to imaginary prehistory. But since then archeological findings have filled in many gaps in our knowledge.[11] We now know how ecological changes after the last glaciation made larger work groups possible, and that this altered family structure and demanded more of the human mind. Just having to name, know and interrelate with 500 people, instead of 25 or 50, stimulated man's already impressive gift of symbolic speech. We have collateral evidence from physical anthropology of a dramatic expansion in brain size about this time. Loren Eiseley has suggested that natural selection required this sudden adjustment as man "fell into the deep well of himself" and had to survive in a perilous new environment of talk and symbols that his big new groups, intensely interacting, had created. We have learned more, too, about the long prehistories of agriculture and other Neolithic technologies. The three movements occurred within a comparatively brief band of man's long term on earth: denser social groups, the explosion of symbolization and the Neolithic revolution in technology...let the Marxists and the Durkheimians debate which of the three was the trigger.

Synopsis and synthesis: At some momentous point in this Neolithic ferment, a human transformation occurred that Caillois,[12] Jensen[13] and Frazer[14] link to agriculture and Engels[15] to animal husbandry; that Bachofen,[16] Morgan,[17] Engels and Millett[18] associate with an overthrow of matriarchy by a patriarchy which established property and government; that Gurvitch, Granet,[19] Harrison,[20] etc., link to mixed situations where a matriarchal clan religion overlaid by patriarchal tribal society required elaborate ritual transitions; that Van Gennup[21] and Gurvitch associate precisely with those magic rites of passage that protected the ego from conflict during his precarious progress between the two rites; and which the Durkheimians connect with the stage when loose confederations of sibs consolidated into real tribes.... At some such turning point, the first steps were taken simultaneously toward the separation of magic from religion and the emergence of the individual from community. Shortly thereafter suicide and homicide begin to replace voodoo death; sorcery makes individuals too dangerous to push around; and initiation lodges turn into magical associations teaching them medicines, psychic defenses, powerful new crafts. The new associations provide the individual with multiple memberships and multiple footings, a new Archimedian place to stand from which he can act on society. Now he has honor, mana, reputation and rank. Now true magic begins; now heroes emerge as *daimones* from rites that strengthen individuals; and now animism begins to replace totemism as anthropomorphic gods appear in the sky reflecting the emergence of individuals on earth. And soon, within the hothouse homosexual atmosphere of those magic initiation lodges, something stranger than the bull-roarer is heard—the buzz and hum of a new kind of human interaction based on desperate competition, non-kinship hierarchy, reckless potlatching and domination. A tumult of forbidden games, dangerous parties, antinomian heresy provides a curiously stimulating atmosphere for breeding new magics, new techniques and crafts of combat, curing, leadership. And from within the agitated swarm, a new human personality emerges, a "leader" who dominates others by magic force of personality and with whom others magically identify (cf. Freud[22]); one day he leads his *Brüderbund* out of the lodge and overthrows the kinship elders and the clan religion. Now war begins, now clans can be galvanized into tribes and led into battle, with the lodge brothers serving as the first armies and police forces, like the "dog soldiers" of the Plains Indians.[23] Now man's expanded mind can take account of 500 people, a tribe-sized universe, instead of the 25 or 50 of the band world of monkeys or Paleo-lithic savagery.[24] Man now also lives in "secondary groups" where the higher flim-flams of advanced magic are possible, and the possibility of secret knowledge appears. Now specialized occupations appear that are at first speci-alisms in magic—the shaman, the magical war leader, the Promethean seer; later come the magic crafts and secret societies that possess them. The *Kalevala,* the *Niebelungenlied* and all the epics of barbarism commemorate the competi-tions of these magical craft fraternities in myths of contests with magic weapons which preserve traces of the half-potlatch half-warfare clashes of smithies and shamans, of sword-makers and medicine men that Granet,[25] for example, re-constructs in ancient China.

What was the strategic change? Where exactly, on what base point, can we pin the emergence of magic from religion? I discard two possibilities—patriarchy and technology—to accept a third, the passage from band to tribe.

Not Patriarchy. The thesis of a patriarchal revolution has been discussed by Bachofen, Engels,[26] Morgan,[27] Millett.[28] They presupposed that some new form of subsistence which was naturally man's work—possibly animal husbandry —produced a surplus and made patrilineal descent of tools and wealth seem necessary. Now patriarchy took over; property and sexually exclusive family relations were rigidified because patrilineal descent is uncertain biologically; and the state later emerged to protect these institutions. As a universal evolu-tionary sequence the theory is discredited in anthropology today. But I do not doubt that occasional transitions from matriarchy to patriarchy (*or* vice versa) do occur. And like any social transition, this can stimulate magic. We know of such sequences in particular culture areas; e.g., the Dorian conquest. And such transitions still occur today, though they are less dramatic. In Austra-lian societies described by Elkin,[29] or among Plains Indians described by Lowie,[30] or Northwest Indians described by Drucker,[31] or tribes in India described by Lévi-Strauss,[32] we find both patrilineal and matrilineal groups living side by side. All four authors suggest some groups have switched from one to the other line of descent. Elkin described the "intertribal meetings" when adjacent clans get together; the elders immediately sit down and begin com-paring notes on their social structure. Lévi-Strauss describes how new marriage rules are endlessly created as these groups form alliances. Drucker and Lowie infer that matrilineal and patrilineal descent diffuse from one group to another. Making a switch from matriliny to patriliny or vice versa is not apparently a bloody revolution; it happens for reasons of convenience, alliance, adjustment. Lowie[33] describes one Plains Indian tribe in which a new hunting technology based on horses and guns has given men preponderance but the matriarchal clan religion is still retained. Here transition of young men from the matriarchal clan to the tribal world will be perilous and will require impressive religious rituals that strongly model magic. But these revolutions are reversible and can go either way. We cannot postulate a universal patriarchal revolution as a definite stage of evolution and use it as our base point for the emergence of magic.

Not Technology. The related Engels-Morgan-Childe thesis of stages of technological advance linked to a particular social form is not definite enough either. Morgan and Engels claimed that patriarchy, private property, the family, the state all began when animal husbandry was developed. Now as a matter of fact, "middle barbarism," as Morgan[34] called this stage (using an older term of Tylor's), is a fair conjecture about when magic emerged, for Tylor defined it broadly to include animal husbandry, *and* irrigation agriculture, *and* the development of permanent stone villages and towns. That inclusive definition would make it the fulcrum of the Neolithic.

Such ideas are influential. Recently Cohen and Middleton propounded that bands are gatherers, while tribes arise with husbandry and agriculture.[35] But insistence on a definite technological sequence as decisive is narrow; for one thing, it leaves out ecological factors which also affect subsistence. The Northwest Indians, for example, have a rich, thickly settled society on its way to tribal structure—yet no agriculture and no animal husbandry.[36] Instead, an abundant ecology based on rivers choked with salmon and woods full of trees for building houses enables them to catapult to population density and incipient tribes, with settled villages, complex institutions and spectacular magic. Thus they resemble Morgan's "barbarians" socially and culturally, but their technology, fishing, fits his category of "middle savagery." Morgan and the others have not allowed for sheer natural abundance in some ecologies. I have little doubt that, within broad limits, human technology is decisive in determining subsistence, hence population, hence social organization—but those limits must be broad enough to allow for ecological factors and for historical accidents. Conclusion: level of technology is not a precise enough base to pinpoint the magical revolution.

1. From Band to Tribe

I prefer to use, as the basing point, the transition from "bands" to "tribes." This idea can be derived from the Durkheimians.[37] Behind it lies a commonsense idea: level of subsistence, however determined by ecology and technology, decides how dense population can be and therefore how complex the social structure is likely to become. If bands are permitted by subsistence conditions to live near one another, they are likely to form alliances; as lineages grow too large and split they are now able to reunite as phratries; phratries may later join together in tribes or "nations." In short, population density (determined by technology *and* ecology[38]) determines the "moral density," Durkheim's term for the degree of complexity of groups. And magic is created, according to Durkheim, when societies advance from a "polysegmental" collection of "clans", each with a clan religion, to a "hierarchical tribal structure" with a tribal religion reflecting it: this tribal religion "generalizes" the mana into broader symbols (e.g., heroes, gods) which are easier to manipulate, expropriate.

The Band

What meaning and status do these terms "band" and "tribe" have in the anthropology of today? There is a reasonable consensus about what a band is. It is the "local group" or "work group." Among nomadic peoples it is the traveling group. Among sedentary peoples, Lowie notes,[39] it may correspond to the small village (but a big village could be a tribe). Linton[40] notes that bands (and families) are as old as mankind and are also found among primates; Pfeiffer[41] claims that the 25-member band is typical of monkey troops as well (and Reichard[42] claims to see local groups even among some insects). Firth[43] reminds us that the band is a face-to-face group, a "primary group" (Cooley[44]). The band is mankind's natural home, Linton writes; even today we live much of our lives in such local groups as neighborhoods, big families, corporate departments. But extremely primitive peoples supposedly lived almost entirely in "integral bands," Firth's term for bands that are self-sufficient.

The band stage was a limitation imposed by narrow subsistence. Low food supply forced early man to disperse. Lowie notes that some Cheyenne bands consisted of just one family; in the winter of 1837 the Cheyenne got bored living this way, tried to stick together and almost starved.[45] Pfeiffer tells how small bands of Bushmen occupy a camp for a few weeks, literally eat their way out of it and have to move on. Mauss notes that Eskimo settlements have to be far apart and thin subsistence necessitates frequent outmigrations.[46]

Internal Composition. What is the social structure of a band? It is usually a collection of families, probably related. Ideal-typically, it is a "lineage," several families descended from one ancestor—five families, say, of 25 people under one grandfather and his five sons.[47] Pfeiffer and Birdsell,[48] who offer this as typical, speak of the "magic numbers," 25 for a band, 500 for a tribe; they claim statistical averages cluster at 25 with a low standard deviation. But band size depends on subsistence and will be larger in agricultural societies—up to 100 or 200 according to Linton. Lowie even finds roving bands of 80 to 160 among the Kiowa.[49] Internal composition varies, too. Instead of a lineage, a large band might be a phratry, or more distantly related families with some stragglers and guests.

Band organization is based on kinship, with the lineage head or oldest male in charge, though there may be rival elders and factions (cf. Turner[50]). Traditions and rules are self-enforcing, face to face; life is communalistic, reciprocal and religious. Even bands that are dependent parts of tribes[51] tend to have their own distinct culture, Lowie notes, with special dress and even a dialect. "Integral" bands[52] may have their own religions.

Most purely band societies have disappeared. Even in cultures where the band is primary, it is no longer "integral" but part of looser, larger units, such as an acephalous "tribe." Only a few band cultures survive, such as the Kalihari bushmen. Among these people, sharing is vital, reciprocity is intense, babies are suckled until four or five, Pfeiffer notes.[53]

Band Religion. This is the kind of society I associate with early, pure religion in the Paleolithic, before the major magics emerged. The Pygmies are one surviving band society, and Father Trilles[54] reports they are theistic and nearly devoid of magic. The Tikopei, Firth tells us in one book,[55] also consist of self-sufficient local groups, and in another book[56] he notes they have almost no magic.

Magic is meagre in these tiny societies. A prophet is without honor in his own country. Durkheim was really writing about band religion in *The Elementary Forms;* he called it a "clan" religion because lineage relations appear to be remembered while Australian bands may change due to accidents of history and ecology so the two no longer quite correspond.[57] But his citation of totemism with its particularization of cults is a good example of the fragmented religions projected by such polysegmental societies, with their endless chains of self-sufficient groups resembling one another like wallpaper.[58] Each family or clan has its own rites. Mana is locked up in the idiosyncratic symbols of particular families, so the possibility of magical expropriation is limited. The Joneses cannot easily use the Smiths' rites, and one Jones trying to turn his own family's rites to a private magical purpose might be laughed at. Mana must first be generalized, concentrated in more abstract symbols of broader reference, before it can be expropriated; this happens when the clans are united in tribes which project more general sacred symbols.

The Tribe

For tribes to emerge there must be enough subsistence that bands can live closer together, so when lineages split the brothers can remain in touch. Even in pure band societies local groups maintain some relationships; in tribes these are so sustained they result in social contracts.

"A tribe is an association of kin groups which are themselves composed of families...[It] is a much larger, more segmented society," writes Sahlins,[59] who thinks tribal organization was made possible by the expanded subsistence of the Neolithic.[60] Tribal numbers are a human phenomenon; there are no groups of 500 among monkeys or primates.[61] The tribe is man's first "secondary group." In tribes men must know and relate not only to a larger group of people but to persons who are not always present, and this stimulates memory, symbolization and mind.

Greater population density often means "unite or fight." Split lineages living near one another reunite to avoid fratricidal strife. But their tribal unions make real war possible. Linton claims that the earliest function of the tribe was war.[62] Often bands are tightened to tribal intensity by the demands of defense (e.g., the Iroquois and Algonquin federations). Subsistence bands are too small for sustained conflict; they have less territorial identification and small capacity for assimilating surpluses, slaves or other booty. But tribal barbarism is the heroic age of war. This may be one reason why the warrior males often come to predominate in barbarian patriarchy.

New Structure Principles. Partly, tribal organization is just an extension of the kin principle; but partly, it is also a break with that mode of organization. For now other principles come into play to hold structures together. Elkin, White, Linton,[63] mention that the tribe has a more pronounced *territorial identification.* Dumont,[64] Lévi-Strauss,[65] Davy,[66] Mauss, etc., stress *contractual agreements* between groups. Gurvitch, Tiger,[67] Mauss, etc., stress the increased role of *"class associations."* Finally, Freud, Gurvitch etc., stress the new *leadership principle.* In centralized tribes ("chiefdoms" and incipient states) leaders try to replace the whole chain of kin authority with appointed officers. In the more typical loose or "acephalous" tribes, leaders dominate by generosity (magic potlatching), oratory, personality, etc.[68] All this is "charisma," magic.

Most so-called primitive societies which anthropology studies are somewhere between pure band and full tribe. Fortes and Evans-Pritchard[68] therefore speak of three types instead of two: bands, loose tribes and "centralized tribes." Cohen and Middleton[70] use the word "tribe" for the loose form, and reserve "chiefdom" for the centralized tribe.[71] Some societies fluctuate depending on the food supply, functioning like tribes when the living is easy and breaking up into bands in the leaner months.

Segments and Classes. There are intermediary groups inside a tribe, including both "segments" and "classes." Segments are kin structures: lineages, phratries, moieties, etc.[72] Theoretically one builds up to tribes by uniting lineages into phratries, phratries into tribes. De Coulanges[73] shows that this was done in Greece and Rome. But tribes are big, unwieldy structures and need extra mortar; this is where the "class associations" come in. In a short, little-known essay, Mauss[74] showed how this additional set of links, cross-cutting the kinship segments, further united society.[75]

Tribes differ from bands because they are 1. bigger; 2. contain more sub-units; 3. make greater use of class associations; 4. use other integrating principles besides kinship—including territory, contractual alliance, leadership principle. 5. They also "generalize" mana in symbols. 6. Also, tribes are secondary groups (though they may briefly become primary during feasts when they concentrate[76]). Secondary groups make magical flim-flam more possible; there are constant rumors of miracles performed in the lineage just over the hill. 7. And tribes are "hierarchical," Durkheim and Gurvitch tell us.

What is meant by "hierarchical"? One aspect of it is apparent among the Northwest Indians. Drucker says, for example, that the Tsimshian are "more tribal" than the Tlingits because their lineages are *ranked.*[77] By custom, some families are "better" than others and the chief of the highest lineage is chief of the tribe. One function of peaceful potlatches is to renew these ranking positions as new chiefs come to power[78]—potlatches are like their coming-out parties where everyone "pays the respect," as they say in the Mafia. And one cause of competitive potlatching, such as the spectacular Kwakuitl displays, is to establish a new rank order between unacquainted tribes newly settled together who have not yet established precedence—this happened when they clustered around the white man's trading posts.[79] Ranking lineages is one aspect of hierarchy. Another is the emergence of a class system, impossible at the band stage. 1. First, the leadership principle born in the initiation lodges provides the top class, the *chiefs* and subchiefs who replace the kinship elders. 2. In addition, tribal wars generate *slaves.* 3. Further, a class of *aristocrats* is a mathematical product of the more complex kin systems and taller lineages that can be propped up by the mortar of tribal organization. Among the Northwest Indians as among the Romans described by de Coulanges,[80] aristocratic rank is derived from relatively direct descent from the distant lineage founder. 4. Tribal warfare can also lead to conquest, which may create a conquest state with a new class of *helots,* and even turn the demobilized occupying army into yet another class of *bureaucrats.* So the class system begins in tribal barbarism, with its chief, nobles, commoners, slaves, helots and officials.

Ranking of lineages, creation of ordinal classes...there is more to tribal hierarchy than just these structural factors. A new competitive personality emerges from the magical contests and potlatches of the initiation lodges, and man in Ardrey's term comes to resemble a prairie dog society,[81] bristling with territoriality, establishing non-instinctual pecking orders, constantly challenging, "joking," intimidating, magically hexing, facing down and overawing rivals; creating out of nothing all sorts of new magical "values" and then competing to obtain these crests, headdresses, signs of honor, *Renommiergeld,* coppers...yes, and finally money, the most naked symbol of all these new magical values. Hierarchy becomes a universal principle of human interaction at the tribal stage.

Tribal Religion. As Halbwachs once pointed out,[82] "There are religions of clans, tribes, cities and peoples." Every social form "projects"; where society is polysegmental we get something like totemic fragmentation; where society pyramids through successive agglomerations of clans, phratries, tribes, cities, there are concentric religious projections of each;[83] and where society is a chaos and a mystery so are its ghostly shadows in the sky, as Feuerbach[84] has claimed and as the nightmare of Hinduism vividly demonstrates. So when tribes emerge there will be tribal symbols along with the totemic symbols of clans; as tribes become coherent these will coalesce into tribal religions. When Durkheim wrote of the "generalization of mana" at this stage, he meant that religious symbols (e.g., gods instead of totems) will now refer to broader groups of people (the tribe as a whole), and to larger groups of rites (mana in general). But in what concrete ways does tribal religion differ from the clan religion?

1. First, tribal religious rites are much more magical in the weak sense. Sacrifice and initiation in particular demonstrate the magical capacities of ritual with special frankness. 2. Second, tribal rites are increasingly performed by specialists rather than headmen—by magicians, witchdoctors, shamans, etc., rather than elders. 3. Finally, tribal religion is *more animist* than clan religion, and this needs discussion.[85]

The preanimists have accustomed us to associate animism with pure religion and "preanimist" mana ideas with primitive magic, in an evolutionary sequence in which man "advances" from magic to religion. I want to suggest that precisely the opposite is true (and even obvious), that anthropomorphic symbols are a sign that man is divinizing himself with magic, and that gods appear as projections in the sky when individuals begin to emerge on earth. Great individuals have always seemed striking phenomena to men of early civilizations. The ancient world was so fascinated by figures like Timoleon and Cleomenes that it raised altars to them. Pantheons of historical hero gods are quite common, from Jainism to Voodoo and Santería.[86] The cult of saints came as easily to Moslems as to Christians.[87] Gods and heroes are easily associated. Harrison[88] has shown that the first product of an initiation rite at the tribal stage is a daimon who represents the rite, becomes a hero, is later considered a god. The idea of gods is created by sacrifice as well, which begins before gods exist.

In short, animism, the worship of gods, is under suspicion of being magical because it is anthropomorphic; totemic symbols are more impersonal, referring to classes or species in nature. As man approaches the tribal stage, he grows interested in ghosts, which are the persistence of memories of powerful persons; this happens because persons are growing more powerful. He begins to worship his own ancestors instead of totemic animals. When leaders emerge from the initiation lodges and make themselves chiefs and kings, it is hard to dismiss them after death; they persist as ideas of gods. (Frazer was close to formulating that animism reflects magic with his theory of the "divine king"—the magician who used his wiles to conquer kingly power and is worshipped after death as a god.)

Man's worship of gods is not a sign of advancing humility. The gods who "dethrone nature" (as Redfield said of the Hebrews[89]) are personifications of man's magical rites; later man will dethrone these gods in turn and take charge in person. (In modern times, the Protestant god becomes a Cheshire cat; we "transcend theism" as Tillich[90] wrote, yet still have the god idea as a powerful personal resource.) The god idea is one of man's cleverest magics and the more deist, the more pure and *absconditus* he is made the more powerful is the Archimedean trick of magically moving the social world. Animism is the appropriate religion for this heroic age of tribal barbarism. God figures are the perfect example of "generalization of mana," and much easier to manipulate by magic than are totemic mana symbols; one can pray to them, talk to them, sacrifice to them, make deals with them.

Tribal Magic. But gods in the sky not only reflect individuals emerging on earth, they help them emerge. Gods, daimons, heroes emerge in the initiation rites that help make individuals. Later, these projections serve as models for personhood. Every anthropomorphic god or hero invites an *imitatio.* Just as Hindu girls were told during their upbringing to "be like Sita," Greeks strove to be like Hercules or the half divine Achilles, and so fulfilled their personhood.

The major provinces of magic emerge at this stage. Tribal religion, being much more complex and rich, better models the sympathetic potentials of ritual. And tribal complexity requires individuals who are tough enough to make role transitions without breaking. Religious rites like sacrifice and initiation try to assist them, but are not enough. They cannot allow for deadly value contradictions (like the one Sophocles dramatized in the *Antigone*) which can literally kill people. So magic institutions are spun off as the dramatically modelled sympathetic rites are expropriated to help save the individual.

Magic is further stimulated by the great gatherings of tribalism. These much larger festival crowds raise more mana than tiny bands can generate. They are great occasions for fun and games, for *homo ludens* and magic tricks. Such magical vibrations as arose in the Paleolithic were made possible by interclan meetings, whether for collective hunts or sociability. But in the Neolithic, population is more concentrated; there are longer, more frequent gatherings; eventually whole tribes live together in large villages and some tribes party all summer (or all winter) long. In the buzzing hive, the individual is paradoxically more individuated; his multiple memberships give him balance; his access to multiple rites makes magical extrapolation in self-defense easier.

Most "primitive" cultures are in some transitional stage between band and tribe. The level of magic is related to the advance of tribal organization, it seems. The Australians, American Indians and Africans might be ranked on a continuum of increasing magical coloration this way: a. Most *Australian* societies are not full tribes, but incipient, shadowy confederations. For example, the "Murngin" did not really have much identity, not even a tribal name, when Warner studied them[91] (he arbitrarily called them the Murngin after their principal group); though when the Berndts restudied them 20 years later[92] they had progressed in cohesion and identity and now called themselves the Walamba. Elkin found that Australian clan bands are more likely to feel affinity for neighboring bands of other tribes than for their more distant tribal cousins.[93] This tribal looseness is perhaps reflected in their magic, which is limited to witchcraft (the earliest, simplest magic to appear), some ceremonial magic, and the merest beginnings of sorcery and medical magic. (Ceremonies to increase the totemic species, such as the Intichiuma, are profoundly religious rather than magical.)[94] b. *American Indian tribes* possess all the provinces of magic—the ceremonial magic of rain making, the medical magic of shamanism, the religious magic of exorcism, the magic of protest sects, black magic both primitive (witchcraft) and advanced (sorcery), etc. But some of this material seems fresh and unelaborated (e.g., the occult sciences). This reflects a culture area where we have everything from isolated bands to "nations" (confederations of tribes), but where the general picture is band life embedded in strong tribal structures with a tribal religion already well developed. c. Finally, many *African tribes* have gone all the way to full chiefdoms and beyond that, to proto-states. And here we find not only every province of magic, but magic richly advanced, with a full panoply of occult sciences elaborated all the way to theosophies (e.g., the Dogon systems), magical pharmacopias as complex as the American drug industry, etc. We may conclude that magic arises with the tribe and correlates with degree of tribal organization.[95]

II. The Revolt of the Magical Individual

Just as magic derives from religion, many institutions begin in religion and then go through a transitional magical phase before they are consolidated. This is true of the individual. His nature was born in the membership rites of the tribal religion, but his independence was won by the tribal magic spun off from those rites. The tribal religion laid the foundation. Tribal society is complex and membership becomes problematical; people are constantly being membered into new groups by initiation rites, and then re-membered into the moral whole by sacrificial dramas. In these rites is born the atomic idea of the individual as a detachable personage who maintains his integrity through successive rebirths into new roles. Accumulation of initiation names shows that he is one-person-who-passes-through-roles. In most societies individuals have several names, some not conferred until initiation, while others are relinquished. Where societies disperse, he may have a winter name and a summer name (the Kwakuitl). The names represent his successive roles and memberships, but increasingly, in the tribal stage, he retains all his names and bears all at once (Quintus Fabius Maximus Cunctator!) as a sign that he is one, and he is powerful. Tribal rites help concentrate this identity.

De Coulanges has noticed that the successive initiations a young tribesman goes through recapitulate the confederative history of his society,[96] the way the embryo recapitulates evolution. Greek and Roman cities were made by successive agglomerations and each had its separate religion: There were altars and gods for gens, phratry, tribe and city, and the child was successively initiated into each religion in the same chronological order as the federations were established. Traces of these initiation rites persist. Baptism recalls the newborn's ritual acceptance into the clan. Holy Communion at seven or eight could be a remnant of his initiation into the phratry. Catholic confirmation perpetuates puberty rites initiating young men into the tribe. And in some countries the twenty-first birthday is still a ceremonial occasion for young gentlemen: this is perhaps an echo of initiation into the polis, the political life of the state.

As membership and "passages" became important,[97] class associations developed greater influence. Perhaps Paleolithic bands had rudimentary class groupings based on age, sex and generation, each with its own rites. But now, as age groups of males must be initiated successively into the sib, the phratry and the tribe, the initiation classes draw together and their identification is intensified by the prolonged preparation they must receive to negotiate these passages with a minimum of dissonance. Turner[98] and Mauss[99] dwell on the fellow-feeling that develops in them, though they perhaps exaggerate the "liberty and equality" of such "liminal" groups—initiation lodges are also training grounds in magic competition and hierarchy. The class associations in any event proliferate—Australia has its men's houses, American Indians have their medicine lodges,[100] some African societies have outright sorcery clubs. Important religious ceremonies often get taken over by these associations. The women's groups or a secret society or a lodge among the Arunta, the ancient Chinese,[101] the Iatmul[102] or the Kwakuitl[103] will put on one ceremony, the men or another lodge, another. The Wikeno have eight orders of dance societies within their shaman's society, according to Drucker;[104] each ceremony is owned by a particular dance society, which keeps it partly secret. Here we have religious rites parceled out so they take on a magical coloration. The associations grow in influence. Daryll Forde finds some among the Yako in Africa that resemble voluntary associations: e.g., a club formed to combat theft.[105] "Ward associations" spring up, which are territorially based prestige clubs of the local patriciate, and the government must get their cooperation to act. There is even one such association, the Ikpungkara, made up of 40 members who have settled land disputes and expropriated similar judicial authority. Forde insists that the associations constitute an additional force, along with kin relations and political sanctions, that helps integrate society. (Mauss has made the same point.[106]) Simmel[107] has familiarized us with the idea that the modern self owes some of its autonomy to multiple memberships; this begins already in the tribal stage.

The associations arise from initiation lodges; they probably provide the template for many of the others. Jane Harrison,[108] Lowie on vision quest,[109] have shown how the transition to tribal membership requires preparation. It is typical of American Indians for the novitiate to be spent in a separate building where the boy is instructed by the men. These initiation lodges pullulate with magic. We have testimony on that from Boas on the Kwakuitl,[110] Radin on the Winnebago, Gurvitch,[111] Lowie,[112] Drucker,[113] Malinowski, Margaret Mead,[114] Ruth Benedict, Reichard,[115] Schapera,[116] Millet,[117] Tiger[118]—too many to summarize. Eliade[119] finds the puberty rites of tribal initiation to be the archetype for other types: secret society initiations, and mystic vocation initiations (e.g., the magician's initiation). It is a lively topic in Europe, too, and Gurvitch cites many continental sources, including Steinmetz, Frobenius, Peschuel, Juno, Jofstra and Schurtz's *Alterklassen Und Männerbunde*.[120] Granet and Needham have shown how the secret society, a form perhaps derived from initiation lodges, continues to be the vehicle of magical religions like Taoism and magical-political protest in China. It is almost as if magic were invented in the initiation lodges and the idea spread. From the churning, rebellious men's houses of the magical revolution to the more settled medicine lodges of later times and thence to the trans-societal medicine cults, the pattern is similar. It blends into the magical protest sects that form one of the main provinces of magic. So even if we do not accept the Harrison-Tiger-Gurvitch-etc. theory of magic originating in the initiation lodges, it seems probable that at least one major province of magic found its archetype there.

Several writers have developed complete theoretical scenarios for a magical revolution issuing out of the initiation lodges. Lionel Tiger[121] makes many of these connections in his theory of male bonding. The initiation lodges reek of magic in his descriptions. Initiation itself is always anti-family, he claims; charismatic male-bonding leaders like Christ always tell people to sever family ties.[122] The lodges inculcate principles of hierarchy, of leadership. They are revolutionary, they will overthrow the old community. Tiger grasps in all this that magic is used *against* religion.[123] But he tries to explain it on a biological basis, and there I cannot follow him. He claims that men team up in lodges and fight the kin society because they have a propensity to "male-bonding," which leads to domination, leadership, homosexuality, a revolt against kinship, etc. Tiger considers this propensity to be an instinct that got stamped in because it had survival value. Perhaps he is thinking of the long Paleolithic when division of labor was far simpler but more radical: the women stayed in camp with the babies while the men hunted and depended on one another's support. In that case the magical revolution of the initiation lodges would be a *counterrevolution* against Neolithic diversity with its greater sexual equality based on agriculture. Tiger's biological speculations cannot be evaluated here, but certainly he makes his case more difficult by neglecting simpler and more provable evidence that social-structural imperatives of tribal organization made initiation lodges prominent.

Freud's *Totem and Taboo*[124] can be read the same way, except that in the first act the *Brüderbund* gathers in outcast isolation in the brush. Presumably, after its primal crime, the take-charge generation can then provide more comfortable quarters for its own progeny to be taught the father-worshipping religion Freud claims totemism to be. Kate Millet[125] has a similar theory of the men's houses as the homosexual breeding grounds of the patriarchal revolution that Morgan and Engels wrote about. And maybe Engels was telling the same story with his account of how democratic military assemblies of the whole people (are these not class associations of able-bodied men?) eventually overthrow the gentile society under the leadership of kings.[126]

All these observers make some of the connections; Gurvitch[127] makes them all. He associates together: 1. The emergence of hierarchical tribal organization above clan society. 2. Durkheim's "generalization of mana," that Plutarchian process[128] whereby from the broader tribal perspective men recognize that falcon, crow, north star and Dingo Dog are all sacred similarities, all have mana, and proceed to invent "condensation symbols" (Turner[129]), "translation symbols" (Mauss), "logical operators" (Lévi-Strauss) and finally mana words, words for the *whole* mana experience. 3. The resulting invention of magic. 4. The rise of individuals with the help of this magic. 5. The division of labor in new magic crafts. All these changes develop from the magic initiation lodges; Gurvitch also associates with them the beginnings of potlatching, the leadership principle and states (thus linking Mauss' magic theory to Frazer's magician-king study).[130] Even the patriarchal revolution theory feeds into this synthesis, for where tribal patriarchy is imposed on clan matriarchy the struggle of lodges against clans is more intense.

But Gurvitch's main achievement was to link magic to the rise of the individual in a way that fits empirical data. Mauss always had trouble with the seeming paradox that magic serves individuals yet is eminently *social.* Gurvitch's solution was to conceive of magic as the agency that performs the social manufacture of individuals. The lodges are public institutions, embodied in the tribal religion, yet they breed anti-religious magical attitudes that foster the individuality, leadership, spontaneity and independence which society now requires.

Submerged in homosexuality and onanism (like Róheim's self-cathecting ego at the stage of secondary narcissism), thumbing their noses at their mothers and the clan religion, learning and practicing white and black magic, making war and potlatching wildly, establishing pecking orders and hierarchy and identification with a leader, the boys also start to invent the new occupations of warrior, magician, smithy and seer. And one day, Gurvitch fantasies, they will stream out of their lodges under the leadership of the chief they have made and overturn the hereditary headmen, the kinship society and its religion. Thereafter the chief will use the lodge associations as his police, army and administrators in a new order that will reach through competition, conquest and war toward kingship. The most successful tribal leader will conquer other tribes and establish a state. This leader, a product of the magic lodges, will lead by personal force, charisma and magic—he will in effect *be* a magician. And when he dies, his ghost will be a problem to social memory, so in myths he will mount into the sky and sit there as a god.

Thus Gurvitch derives the apparatus of government from a magical ritual apparatus (the initiation lodges), just as Hocart[131] derives it from a religious apparatus (the social organization of sacrifice). His theory throws a spotlight on the often overlooked pluralism of so-called primitive societies. It reveals another tension between magic and religion that fuels their creative dialectic besides the struggle of the individual with the group: magic is also ignited by the struggle of subgroups within a community. Despite the excessive dualisms of his method (too many absolute dichotomies of magic vs. religion, mana vs. the sacred, lodges vs. clans, "action vs. submission," "fear vs. anxiety," etc.), it is an impressive synthesis.[132]

The Neolithic revolution of magic still haunts the myths of man. It is remembered in stories of the fall, of an exile from a Paleolithic Eden where society was a sacred family. It is transmuted into acosmic millenarianism in the world-wide image of the cracking of the cosmic egg (found, for example, in Taoist China,[133] ancient India,[134] also in gnosticism[135]). The primal egg was really social *koinomia,* which burst into pieces at the tribal stage with division of labor, class associations and private magics. In Valentinian gnosticism,[136] cosmic unity was said to split because of an inner perturbation—this could be the spectacular heating up of tribal religion, reflecting social complexity, which modeled sympathetic magic so dramatically it invited expropriation. Or the myths say the perturbation in the cosmic egg begins when the weak side of god fails, because it is female, or because it loves or thinks. (This could reflect the temporary relative sexual equality of the early Neolithic, with agriculture bringing men and women's work closer together, thereby offending the male-bonding instincts surviving from Paleolithic hunting.) Thereafter cults and myths and epics of bruderbund-like friendship dominate man's culture all through barbarism and into civilization, until destroyed by the capitalist and Protestant emphasis on capital accumulation and the conjugal unit.

III. Magic Continues to Advance

For how long does magic keep advancing? In the next pages we will consider: 1. Chiefdoms. 2. States and empires. 3. Cities.

1. The Competitions of the Confraternities. We left off with the young men streaming out of the initiation lodges, following their leader of the day. But gentile society is not overturned in an afternoon. And the lodge leaders still have to struggle with one another before any fixed new order is created. They have to compete and establish an ordinal, pecking-order rank. How? Since their power is magical, they compete in magic. The lodges were the forcing beds of new magical technologies: sorcery, medicine-man magic, divination, but also crafts, armorers, smiths, potters. The leaders of these groups competed in displays of their magic. From the lodges arose wealth and potlatching, and potlatching contests are still used to rank social groups.[137] We may suppose that the lodge captains competed in hocus pocus, games of skill, potlatches, tests of endurance and demonstrations of magical crafts.

Granet gives us a striking picture of this stage in ancient China,[138] after the lodges have erupted and produced leaders, but before one of them has become high chief or king. Deciphering ancient Chinese myths of magic struggles,[139] he reconstructs contests of rival brotherhoods of smiths, husbandmen, potters and shamans fighting for primacy through their magical knowledge and crafts. He tells of magic contests at winter gatherings of the tribe, of competitive seven-day drinking bouts, of deadly chess games, bloody jousts, suicidal potlatches and dances unto death. This rival-brotherhood phase led from the old polysegmental clans and moieties to hierarchies, chiefdoms, cities and states, he writes. The purpose of competitions in magic was, like Tsimshian potlatching, to establish rank. The power of chiefs grew out of these *homo ludens* contests of the rival men's houses, for the results were signs from heaven. One contest was to shoot arrows at the sky: he with favor of heaven won; he without it was killed by his own falling arrow. Incidentally, Needham and Granet stress how important *divination* was in Chinese magic and how many games and sciences developed out of it (chess, backgammon, I Ching). Here divination was used not just in medical diagnosis but in magical contests of election. These dangerous games led in time to war, and the hierarchy of winners led to chiefdoms, cities and states. Potlatching was such a big part of primeval Chinese magical competition that Granet and Needham suggest it persists in the much noted Chinese customs of competitive obsequiousness.

Reading Granet reminds me that much of the so-called national epic of Finland, the *Kalevala,* consists of contests between two magicians, Vainamoinen, aged wizard of Finland, and Yokahainen, young magician of the north country.

They fight with all kinds of magic weapons, which could represent early arts of magical craft brotherhoods. (Vainamoinen enlists Ilmarinen, the smith, to produce the sampo, a mill that creates riches.) Or consider the elaborate fashioning of Achilles' new armor before the fight with Hector, and the divine elements in it, especially the shield. (Harrison has suggested[140] that Pallas Athena herself arose as a projection of the palladion or shield, a daimon of the armorer's skill.) Or consider the "sword in the stone" that only young Arthur can remove because he has some special virtue. Special virtues linked with magical weapons were magical rather than moral. So much in these epics is about magic weapons, forged by magician smiths or smithy gods—and also about magic treasures like the Rhinegold. Deciphering myths Casaubon-style[141] is, as Socrates said in the *Phaedrus*, an enterprise that attracts a "very curious, painstaking and not very happy man"[142]; I may lack one of those traits, for I find myth interpretation a slippery business. I will go no further; but I want to suggest that, wherever magic weapons appear in barbarian epics, they may be elements from still older myths reflecting the stage when magic brotherhoods that emerged from the initiation lodges fought it out.[143] In the Prometheus myth we see the final solution of this struggle—the war magician founds a state and binds the other magicians, including Prometheus the seer, Hephaestus the smithy, and so on.[144]

2. The Magic-Monopolizing Chiefdoms. Chiefdoms substitute territorial for kinship administration and use officials in place of headmen.[145] The officials are drawn from the brotherhoods. The chief's bodyguards, police and armies usually come from something like the "dog soldiers," the warrior lodges of the Plains Indians.[146] Linton reminds us that the earliest bureaucracies were demobilized occupying armies.[147]

Students of political anthropology notice another remarkable tendency in centralized chiefdoms and incipient states. The new chiefs try to monopolize magic. They try to take it away from the people. In Africa, Max Gluckman finds this tendency among the Zulu[148]; L. Schapera among the Ngwato[149]; K. Oberg among the Ankola[150]; and Fortes among the Tallensi.[151] In Zululand the chief was in charge of all magic, and the great Shaka expelled rainmakers from his kingdom saying that only he could control the heavens. He also possessed important therapeutic medicine, and all skilled leeches had to teach the king their cures.[152] The king's witchdoctors had to confirm all verdicts of sorcery before sentence could be executed. The Ngwato king monopolized all war magic.[153] In Ankola the king gathered magicians at his court like Louis XIV so he could keep an eye on them, and they lived together in their own kraal, with diviners, sorcerers, white magicians, etc., organized into departments. Any magician who got a reputation in the country might get a command from the king to come live in court.[154]

Why should the king centralize magic? Because his own power is magically derived and he cannot allow competition. Fortes and Evans-Pritchard hint at this when they note that the chief's power mysteriously persists even under colonialism when chiefs lose political power. Why? Because of the "mystical powers" associated with the office, the authors write. But to focus on the "magical mentality" of African organization is not explanation enough, they write.[155]

3. The Hydraulic Molochs and Alienated Magic. Magic continued to grow, even after states and empires emerged. The empires tried to monopolize magic, just like African chiefdoms. "The magic powers of the commonwealth," Wittfogel writes, "tended to converge."[156] But this did not stop magic; it served to subsidize it, as priestly bureaucrats pursued astrological, alchemical and sorcery researches at state expense. And new popular magics kept emerging.

The empires, dependent on huge irrigation systems, necessarily became bureaucracies, Wittfogel writes. They therefore attached themselves to the country's dominant religions and recreated them as priestly bureaucratic instruments.[157] Religious officials abound in these empires but they are "benefit-of-clergy" types, clerks in Holy Orders working as officials. And the state uses its religious bureaucracy to control magic as well. Magic is collected like gold and centralized in academic departments in the governing Sumerian "temples" and the prebendary Egyptian priesthoods. At the same time, Childe claims,[158] the empires also somehow "encourage" magic and superstition among the people as a tool of domination. I think he is referring to the new state cults they fashion out of religions they take over. The state religions are truly "superstitious" for they now project the state and its official myths rather than any true community in the underlying *pays réel.* Mendenhall has shown how some of their gods (e.g., Ashur) and the god symbols (e.g., the aegis) stand for nothing but the state.[159] In time, these official religions become academic amalgams of diverse religious traditions, with strong and conscious infusions of priestly magic. The founders of the Ptolemaic Empire, for example, hired a task force of philosophers to fashion a religion that would unite both Asiatic and Greek populations; the resulting cult of Sarapis incorporated the most magical ideas of both Greek mystery religions and Asiatic corn god cults.[160] And typically these state religions are astral cults, as Bloch demonstrates.[161] It is almost as if, in putting the gods up in the sky, the conquest states with their oppressive bureaucracies alienated religion and magic altogether from the community.

But there is no stopping magic. Childe finds archeological evidence of continued expansion all during the Neolithic—more magic amulets, more Venus figures, more apparent trade in magic substances.[162] Magic keeps advancing for many reasons: 1. First, imperial concentration and subsidy of magic stimulate it. The magic arts of a hundred captive nations become academic researches within temple priesthoods. As Weber has shown, priestly "rationalization" usually goes in an *irrational* direction,[163] making the data more magical. It is now that priestly researchers transmute the divination techniques of subject peoples into the first "occult sciences." (The rationalizing temple priests are the first *social base* for the magical province I call the occult sciences, just as initiation lodge brotherhoods provided the original social form for magical protest sects.) Chaldean astrology, for example, begins this way, augmented by astrological observation. 2. Meanwhile, rebellious new magics arise among subject and enemy populations. 3. In addition, conquest which destroys some societies wounds or kills their religions, and the dying religions release toxins for black magical brews. 4. Empires create wider publics and faster diffusion of magic along imperial roads, with clash of cultures. The other man's religion is always a gold mine of magic. 5. Technology is mystified as magic. There are many motives, including war. (The Mitanni kept Armenian iron-mongers working in secret for generations to keep a military advantage.) 6. Finally, writing enables emperors to preserve magic in imperial academies.

It is remarkable how much magic was openly practiced in these bureaucratic empires. Breasted,[164] Budge,[165] Frankfort,[166] Thorndike[167] and Shah[168] testify that Egypt had a notorious reputation as the home of the world's most powerful magicians. Budge reports Egyptian magic was the most ambitious in the world: its whole thrust was to give man power over the gods. Egyptian magic was a *ceremonial magic* to command gods of nature in ritual metaphors that celebrated Egypt's victory over its environment. It was priest magic: Idries Shah[169] tells us Egyptian priests were miracle workers. It was a verbal magic, magic of the word: The ancients thought that Egyptian priests could restore the dead, raise storms, transform beings by a word. Much primitive magic is fearful and defensive, but Pharaoh's magic was bold and ambitious. He instructed his priests to find for him the secret of real immortality. And the king's ambition was then imitated by the masses; Breasted reports that with the Osirian revolution magical powers including immortality were won by the people too, a development which anticipated Christianity.[170]

It was in Egypt that Frazer's imaginative scenario of the magician king was perhaps acted out,[171] and that may help explain the magical cast of his state. In Frazer's scenario, a magician used his arts to dupe the people and become king, founding a state. When he died, his presence lingered in memory, so instead of a mere ghost he became a god.[172] Pharaoh transmuted myth into state ideology by divinizing himself and declaring his immortality during his lifetime.[173]

Childe[174] suggests that the first Pharaoh was a chief of the Falcon clan who managed to identify himself with the totem of his clan and monopolize communion with its mana. (Talk about "expropriation of the sacred.") This is speculation and debatable of course (Frankfort[175] claims no evidence of totemism here), but the argument continues persuasively. A caste of magicians had already won power by magic: decisive were the astronomical observations that had enabled them to predict the rising of the Nile, so important for the irrigation system. They mystified this knowledge to increase their power. Then Menes, chief of the Falcon clan, identified himself with its totem, the divine Falcon Horus, conquered the Delta and created a state as a single household.[176] Its head was himself, a god "made immortal by magic rites and guaranteeing by his own magic the fertility of flocks and crops." And here is an indication that Pharaoh was a magician: Instead of a temple, he concentrated his treasure in a tomb, in his magical aim at immortality.

By contrast, the first Sumerian states were born of social contracts in which large groups of colonists possibly from different lands banded together to clear the marshes. Their enormous cultic apparatus, set up to symbolize complicated social agreements, provided the nucleus of the state, and the corporate "temples" that concentrated capital directed economic activity. It is interesting that the Sumerian cities, organized on a religious basis, did not preach the magic goal of immortality as did the magician kings of Egypt. The Akkadian Gilgamesh epic is pessimistic on this subject.[177]

So magic advanced, but after a point stopped serving the individual. As Hegel said, only the king was now free. Magical chiefs born of the initiation lodges had become kings who centralized magic, and emperors who turned magic back into religion, celebrating the state. And the new technologies and crafts that magic had originally stimulated were finally choked by it. Childe claimed this explained the "Neolithic paradox"—why dozens of basic inventions occurred in the first millennium after the urban revolution (4,000-3,000 B.C.), but only a few in the next (3,000-2,000 B.C.).[178] It was not just that state cults and writing broadcast superstition. More decisive, magical kings created parasitical new classes of warriors, priests and scribes, and degraded primary producers to serfs and slaves.

And so the domination born in magical bruderbunds with their leadership principle led to the hyperorganization of empire and an oppressive new umbrella of symbolic culture that stagnated technology. The astral religions that alienated magic reflected not only the state, but human misery, as Feuerbach wrote.[179] Bloch claimed[180] that magic elements in astral cults nonetheless still held out magic hope and this was potentially revolutionary. But the only revolutions that left a mark were antimagical, seeking to pull down the astral projection along with the slave states: e.g., the Apirus, the Hebrews. And in the end deliverance came from outside, from wars and invasions, as prematurely hyperorganized empires with weak roots in underlying communities succumbed to the "semi-barbarian states of the periphery" (Toynbee[181])—first to the Hyksos, Gutti, Amorites, Kassites, Elamites and others their barbarian trading partners who had learned the secrets of bronze age metallurgy from them—and a second time to Dorians, Chaldeans, Aramaeans, etc., who had discovered the cheap iron that made every freeman a knight. Each time empires arose anew, more prosperous than before, sometimes reestablished on a more popular base. The Persians, for example, allowed more autonomy to their subject satraps. And on the periphery of Near Eastern empires, tribes formed themselves into political confederacies as a means of defense and began participating in the widening world commerce. It was then that a new kind of state began, the *polis* or city, with momentous consequences for magic and the Individual.

IV. Stadluft Macht Frei

At a time when our own cities have blurred so much that we cannot even visualize them any more, so that even urban theory fails and lacks images,[182] we have trouble understanding what the first cities were, and what momentous changes they unleashed. The Graeco-Roman city originally was something very determinate, well organized, and extremely clear to all its members—it was the *cultic center* of a religious *confederacy of tribes.* As such, Western cities were religious in constitution, and they made creative use of the gentile kinship structure. In city constitutions one can almost discern a counterrevolution of gentile religion and community self-determination against the magical usurpation that led to bloated empires and alienated astral state religions in the East. Cities became strong precisely because they organized and harnessed the solid underlying gentile communities. They "smashed" this structure only in the sense of using it, modifying it, but in so doing they kept it in the action, they kept a link between community and state, whereas kinship communities in the East were often bypassed or destroyed by imperial hyperorganization. (And the so-called "magical barriers" between the urban sibs that Weber writes of were really religious, totemic barriers, which Western families themselves overcame by their social contracts.)

Weber tells us[183] that the first cities grew out of fortresses and markets. This is true of many early Eastern cities that never became polises. When absorbed by empires they became administrative centers with little self-determination. But many of the historically decisive Graeco-Roman cities began neither as markets nor as fortresses but as the cultic centers of political-religious confederacies of free tribes. De Coulanges, Morgan and Maine have diagrammed the process neatly.[184]

Greek and Roman religions were originally swarms of separate ancestor-worshipping cults of individual patriarchal families, the *gentes,* which pyramided as follows:

1. *Gentes.* Each extended family had its own private religion, complete with ancestor gods buried under the doorstep, home altars built around the fireplace, and sacrificial meals shared with its dead.

2. *Phratries.* When families united in larger fraternal associations, called phratries in Greece (and *curiae* in Rome), this religious pattern was self-consciously repeated as a tool to solemnize the new social contracts. A new religion of the phratry was now above the individual family religions to hold the larger group together. It was based on what Maine called the "legal fiction" of everyone in the phratry agreeing to say they were descended from the same ancestors. (De Coulanges claims this might indeed be the case, that families who felt an affinity might dimly remember splitting off from a single lineage.[185]) The common ancestors they either remembered or invented became the gods of the new phratry religion, and just like family gods they had their own altars and rites, centered on a shrine where all could periodically assemble.

3. *Tribes.* The same kinship building blocks and religious symbols were used when phratries united in still larger units for military defense. Just like the Middle East confederations described by Mendenhall,[186] these political associations would organize themselves as "tribes" after traditional kinship. Once again they would agree on common ancestors and then set up a tribal religion to strengthen their union, with its own altars and rites to honor ancestral gods, and also a very large shrine or sanctuary where the entire tribe could gather for celebrations.

4. *Cities.* Finally, when several tribes confederated, a city came into being. For now the cultic center would have to be very large (e.g., the Acropolis at Athens, the temple at Jerusalem). Athens began as the cultic center of the confederation of tribes in Attica. The city gods might include the famous men who arranged the tribal confederacy, or they might pick popular gods from the composing tribes or gentes. De Coulanges alleges that Athena Acropolis had been a goddess of the Butadae family; when she was adopted as goddess of Athens the Butadae became her hereditary priests.[187] In any event, the new city gods were more abstract, representing a wider social union: Athena, emerging from the shield, worshipped by the Butadae, came now to mean *Athens.*

The Greeks and Romans organized tribes and then cities this way wherever they settled or conquered.[188] This system built powerful but self-determining social structures, stronger than empires but freer for individualism to develop, at least among the secure and dominant males who had absolute power (*patria potestas*) over minors, women, slaves and clients but met with other men as equals in democratic councils.

It is true that the gentile organization began to be modified almost immediately in Graeco-Roman cities, and that in the end families changed much more drastically here than in the East. But the families were themselves active associations, themselves effected the first modifications; and the new social forms (wards, demes, tribunican assemblies) retained family feeling, structures and names. The creation of the city itself was already a deliberate modification. Maine and de Coulanges have shown how even the basic unit, the patriarchal family, was used pragmatically, with legal fictions like adoption augmenting numbers. Lévi-Strauss and Elkin have shown us how even primitive men sit down in their palaver houses and tinker with their marriage alliances. This process continued in barbarian cities, whereas it was partly bypassed in the East as a result of premature hyperorganization. When Eastern empires arose, whether because of technological imperatives (Wittfogel) or magical cunning (Frazer), they used personnel from the magical class associations to create a new bureaucratic order separate from the kin structure. In ancient Egypt and Assyria there are vast armies and bureaucracies but the underlying community structures are not engaged. For centuries they might be taxed and bullied but otherwise bypassed. Later, in the hypertrophy of despotism, whole nations are uprooted and transplanted to stamp out resistance; or they are subjected to genocide. Enslavement, transportation and war destroy the gentile communities of many peoples whose remnants might later reorganize as Apiru "tribes." But even where gentile communities survived, the point is they were seldom engaged; they were subjugated and bypassed; at best they might be left alone.[189]

The Graeco-Roman cities, then, were religious in several ways. 1. First, they were *communities*, freely created by confederations of smaller communities—they were not the pseudo-communities assembled under a monolithic conquest state with its alienated astral religion. 2. The founding was a religious act, as Eliade[190] and de Coulanges have shown. 3. The gentile religion was intact at the founding, and was self-modified rather than smashed. Even when it was changed fundamentally, gentile forms and symbols were still used. So the families formed the state; and even after they were transformed into demes and tribunican assemblies, the demes and assemblies still *participated*, by their votes. Participation of the families gave Western cities a religious cast; it was reflected in Roman *virtus* and *gravitas*, in Greek *arete*. It was not the mere "superstition" of the bypassed Eastern village.

When Greek and Roman cities first appeared, their families were already strikingly different from those in the East. For one thing, private property was already conspicuous here, whereas in India for example land was often owned collectively by the village.[191] Maine thought this was because village elders were more "religious" in India,[192] but de Coulanges showed that family property was guaranteed *by* the Graeco-Roman *religion*, in which revered ancestors were buried in each family's sacred ground.[193] Nor was this property often violated and centralized by the state, as in some Near Eastern empires.[194] It remained a powerful religious support for independence. Trade was freer here; free capitalists emerged; there were powerful social classes independent of the state. The Roman Empire began as a web of alliances with neighboring cities, and even when the allies were reduced to subjects after the Social War, the cities governed their own affairs. By contrast, every tax-farming empire in India from the Guptas to the Moghuls skimmed off virtually the entire surplus of the community without being constituted by that community.

In the West, with families constitutive of states, the dominant males who ran these states were perhaps the most secure and self-determining selves history had seen. They had a powerful social structure as a solid platform for individuality. Together these men would create the contractual order of legal-rational processes that consolidated the Individual.

What about magic? In the East, bypassed community religions decayed, emitting magic toxins. And other religious cults swept in easily, for the community had little cultural resistance. Eastern village communities were simultaneously bypassed at a primitive level of gentile development yet exposed to all the tradewinds of cosmopolitan conquest states with their roads, caravans and traveling magicians. The result was what I would call "superstition": the helpless man's mixture of feeble magic, outmoded tradition and credulous belief in alienated religions. Western communities, by contrast, defended their religions and regulated against foreign influences, at least at first. The Romans constantly passed laws[195] outlawing foreign magicians, forbidding astrology, crushing the Priscillians.[196] Christianity was attacked in part because it was thought to be magical.[197]

But as the gentile system altered itself, its religion began to break, and some magic oozed out. At first, some of this magic continued to help the individual. Typically, some quasi-magical bumpkin rite was revived and refashioned as a mystery religion with emphasis on personal salvation and other magical goals, as Angus has demonstrated of the Dionysian cult, and E. O. James of the Eleusinian mysteries.[198] They helped strengthen the self in the transition between the destructuring of religious communities and the creation of legal order. I agree with Mauss, Hubert and Davy that we must not exaggerate (in the manner of Frazer and Huvelin) the contribution magic made to individual law in the cities. The gentile *religion,* creatively reshaped, was the real foundation. But Mauss and Davy do agree that there was an intermediary stage when magic provided transitional protection. I want to examine this next. But first I have to show that magic did not retard the Individual.

Max Weber writes of the "magical barriers between the sibs" which were broken down by "rationalization," whereas these barriers defeated civic life in the East.[199] But the (totemic or sib-religion) barriers he writes about were more religious than magical, and they were altered by a change in the social structure, not by a movement of ideas. Weber himself calls the taboos "totemic." But he follows the erroneous Frazerian usage of regarding totemism as "magical." Admittedly, as Weber demonstrates, the ascendency of a caste of magicians intensified these family barriers in India. But the real reason totemic barriers remained in the East was that families there were no longer in control of their own destinies. Under the empires they did not have the freedom to confederate; to confederate was to revolt. In the West, where this freedom existed, it was the self-determining confederative action of the families themselves that erased totemic barriers.

V. The Legal Process

Social self-determination accelerates with the legal process. It begins with the first written codes, such as the Twelve Tables at Rome. Codes appear all over the Graeco-Roman world about the same time.[200] Maine and de Coulanges associate them with resolution of civil conflicts, when founding families which had closed their membership books (the "patricians") are forced to admit late-coming "plebians" (*'plebes gentes non habeunt'*) to the family-structured constitutions. The new codes were *written.* Law must now be public, known to all, political rather than religious—and the result was to accelerate the process of social contracts that had already been turning kinship into a new political order. As Maine observes,[201] with written law the new expedients of case law, and equity (e.g., *ius gentium*), and legislation are added to legal fictions as devices to speed new social contracts that transform society.

Of course the roots of the legal process go much further back. At the band and clan religion stage, law is entirely custom and virtually self-enforcing. Malinowski identifies primitive law with "reciprocity rules" and makes a persuasive case for their self-enforceability (each side having an interest in the outcome): these reciprocal obligations, based on exchange agreements, have more powerful *built-in* sanctions than the religious obligations the Durkheimians emphasize, he argues (*Crime and Custom in Savage Society*). But, however tightly they may compel in showdowns and breaches of reciprocity, these rules are still much more informal than what we consider law to be. At the more magical tribal stage of secondary groups, law, if not written, is increasingly *said,* in myth and maxims. But where do we draw the line between a custom or a maxim and a law? Some anthropologists (e.g., Hoebel[202]) today borrow the criteria of the American legal realists who identify law with what courts decide.[203] The trick is to look for something like courts in primitive society, and Radcliffe-Brown[204] warns us that these may be quite informal. At first they might be groups of elders; but at the tribal stage we may see magical class associations at work, as when, for example, the initiation lodges or the Elk Soldiers decide to punish a member.

Another place to look is in the magical medical complex. The elaborate witchcraft machinery is really a grievance mechanism. In Zandeland, for example, when someone believes he is harmed, he goes from diviners and witchdoctors to oracles and ultimately to the king's oracles working like an appelate court to determine who is guilty. If the higher oracle confirms the judgment, he goes to the accused witch and gets him to apologize. This is not just a primitive medical system but a primitive legal system as well.[205] Malinowski discerned another prototype of law in primitive myth.[206] He noticed that parts of a myth were often owned by different clans and represented charters of the rights of these owners. (Elkin found myths that extended over hundreds of miles in Australia, with tribes along this route owning the local segments of the story.[207]) Lévi-Strauss found[208] confirmation: again and again he deciphered myths to show they were really stories about some major historical tinkering with a tribe's marriage alliances that altered its social constitution. Just as Malinowski roundly declared that all myths were originally creation myths, it could be said that all law in the beginning is constitutional law.[209]

When law is finally written it speeds up the transformation of gentile society so much that it seems magical. Writing itself is regarded as a magic at first. There does seem to be something mysterious about the legal process, but it is really more religious than magical in origin. Consider legal reasoning, for example, which curiously mixes rationality and irrationality in a way that the layman has difficulty following. Something like deduction goes on here, but there are sacred-sounding traditional premises and *a prioris,* and seeming *non sequiturs,* too. Something like induction also goes on, too, but the rules so derived often seem arbitrary. "Rules are changed as the rules are applied," Edward Levy writes.[210] Judges infer rules from previous cases, but the choice of precedents and of rules derived from them is partly up to the judge. This is reminiscent of the magician who expropriates a religious principle or bit of myth and recasts it as a tool to accomplish something in a particular situation. Is law then the "expropriation" (Mauss) or *"détournement"* (Huvelin) of the sacred, just like magic? No, because the process is public and the public is defended by an adversary procedure in which "competing analogies" are put before the court.[211] Probably legal thinking traces back to the practical rationality whereby primitive man used religious symbols to create social contracts in palaver houses. The universe of discourse of a palaver house, or of an interclan meeting to arrange a new marriage alliance, is "symbolic interaction," humanistic speech with echoes and shaded meanings. But the talk results in social contracts that are quickly discovered to have logical consequences: *if this, then that.* If cross-cousin marriage, then such and such will follow. And very often it is back to the old palaver house to talk it out again, or consider some other precedent and its consequences. From palaver houses to the founding of cities to *ius gentium*, we see in law the same practical rationality whereby earlier societies used religious representations actively to constitute themselves.

But law also went through a magical stage. It still retains mystical concepts like natural rights. It clings to its sacred language the way magicians try to recite the religious scripts they borrow letter-perfect, because that way they work. Performing the verbal legal rite with exactitude is as important as saying the *Brahmanas* correctly. Magical spells said wrong can cause death; a trivial error in legal form can lose a case. Like magic incantations, law achieves some of its effects by means of power prescriptive and performative sentences that bring about states of affairs just by being uttered: "I now pronounce you man and wife." These sentences can create powerful new beings, such as corporations and estates. Spoken correctly they can change a person's status, his fortune, even his identity. They can remove citizenship, declare a man an outlaw or legally incompetent or legally dead. Legal sentences can free, imprison, marry, divorce, disconnect, stigmatize or degrade, if spoken in the course of a correct procedure which demonstrates the decision to derive correctly from a legal heritage alleged to embody the social consensus.

But from the beginning law makes exceptions to sacred consensus through its legal fictions, as Maine has shown—the legal fictions of adoption, of common descent, of treating early wills as "sales," and so on. Here we see a bending if not a "detouring" of the sacred. The Roman *mancipium*, for example, was a quasi-sacred rite to *de*-sacralize something *religious* (family property) so it could be sold. In modern societies law itself is sold and it makes its exceptions increasingly for powerful individuals and corporations, again, an expropriation of the sacred, perhaps. The special-pleading lawyer cites a precedent and extracts a rule that sounds like social consensus in order to bend that consensus for his client. Law is public, but it comes to be owned in part by the legal caste. The original constitution of Indiana gave every free adult male the right to practice law; but today the legal profession itself certifies new members, just like collegia of magicians initiating a novice. Plato, as a religious thinker, was as suspicious of lawyers as he was of other magical professions (doctors and poets). Something that was constitutive and alive in religious representations seems to get alienated, and so Hocart suggests[212] that being ruled by law instead of custom in the religious *koinomia* of primitive society is like having social relations ordered magically. It is interesting that Dumézil finds a perennial doubling of the upper-class deity in the widespread Aryan three tiers of class gods—a god of law and contract (like Mitra) sitting alongside a god of magic (like Varuna) and the two confounded by the understanding that the magic god Varuna is the one who "ties and binds."[213]

Law retains some magical coloration partly because some branches went through a transitional stage of magic sanctions when they broke loose from religious moorings but had not yet been consolidated politically. Originally, for example, property was collective and religious and was defended by automatic religious sanctions and self-activating community reciprocity arrangements; today individual property is defended by legal-political sanctions. But in between, when property first became private and individual, what defended it? Henry Sumner Maine,[214] who initiated some of the issues pursued by the French school, who pioneered the historical method and even pointed to religious origins of law, could not answer this because he gave no attention to magic.[215] What were the motives which first induced men to respect each other's private property? It remained for Frazer and the French school,[216] in a number of studies of different branches of law, to demonstrate a transitional stage when law, breaking free of religion, was helped by magic. Since this was also one more instance of magic helping the individual, I will examine these studies.

PART TWO: MAGICAL HELP TO INSTITUTIONS FOSTERING INDIVIDUALS

I. Legal Institutions

1. Individual Law, Law of Property. In 1908 Westermarck reported[217] that the Kouis of Laos place a magic object in their fields and if anyone steals from the crops he develops a shaking fit and gets so sick he cannot leave the spot. This is the kind of example that studies of legal magic employ. Folklore and fiction are full of them—the idol's eye, monkey's paw, Rhinegold, moonstone, Maltese falcon or other sacred object that will mystically kill any thief who takes it. Archeology finds that magical objects of this kind which defend property not surprisingly grew with the advance of civilizations, which often fostered private property. Dodds,[218] for example, finds an increase in the *defixionum tabellae,* or cursing tablets, in later centuries in the Greek world:[219] These curses, inscribed on lead tablets or potsherds and placed in the ground, perhaps in a grave, have sometimes been interpreted as aggressive sorcery. But Huvelin,[220] in "Les Tablettes Magiques et le Droit Romain" (1900), suggested they protected property. Examination of the written formulae on the tablets showed they were often designed to 1. punish a thief (automatically, magically), and 2. get property back. Gurvitch also cites magic rites performed at a creditor's door (up to and including suicide) in Ireland, India, Persia, as additional examples.[221]

I call this "whoever magic." It "gets" *whoever* steals the object or hurts the individual. It works partly by "psyching him out": Just as a religious taboo can kill automatically through voodoo death if it is infringed, a magical *defixio* aims at the same outcome and just knowing this can make a primitive sweat. And a *defixio* is also an appeal to public opinion, a call for vigilantes and a hue and cry, though it is an unofficial call, like a Mafia "open contract." But the thief or transgressor at least knows that there is one family around who would thank anyone who killed him.

Frazer summarized anthropological reports about whoever magic, in *Psyche's Task*,[222] with his usual catalogues of instances. Besides property, he wrote, whoever magic protected the individual in other ways. His marital rights were strengthened by magical beliefs that adultery could blight the crops.[223] And the individual's personal magic provided protection from homicide: fear of a vengeful ghost could work as a deterrent.[224] Typically, Frazer saw all this as one more example of base magic paradoxically advancing mankind by its deceptions, in this case fostering morality—but the French school faulted him for superficiality.[225]

The great French statement on magical sanctions was made some years earlier (1905) than Frazer by Huvelin,[226] who in "Magie et Droit Individuel" ambitiously aimed at making a contribution to general theory with a hypothesis he deduced from Hubert and Mauss' theory of magic and sought to prove empirically. From Mauss' "expropriation" of the sacred, he derived the idea of a magical "turning" (*détournement*) of social power to the advantage of the individual. What "whoever magic" does, in other words, is to grab hold of awesome religious symbolism, social taboo ideas and such deadly stuff, and use it to *protect* the emerging individual. Huvelin felt he was not only enlarging Hubert and Mauss' idea of magical expropriation, but *proving* it by showing how it worked in individual law. At first all property is public, sacred, guaranteed by taboos, Huvelin wrote. But then private property begins to appear—e.g., the individual's tools and furnishings come to belong to him and law must individualize itself somewhat to protect these goods. And first the protections of private property take the form of punitive magic: *"maledictions, conjurations, envoutements, etc., qui servent à punir les voleurs."*[227] Huvelin also cites again the *tabellae defixionum* of his previous study. All this magic *works*. He cites an example among the Fijis where the thief actually dies from it.

Huvelin declares that even black magic is often a proto-legal defense against an attack on the individual. Sorcery performed against a calumniator, for example, preceded the law of slander. Creditors who had no overarching law to support their claims put moral pressure on debtors through dangerous magic. (There are remnants of this in *The Merchant of Venice*.) Magical practices were especially effective in enforcing early contracts, before a public law of contracts existed. Magical symbols exchanged in contracts, like the Germanic *Wadium* or Old French *gage* (often a glove), were believed to have dangerous magical properties derived from the persons of the contractors which would attack the other party if he failed to live up to the agreement. Still another magical device to bind agreements was the oath or vow.

Huvelin calls all these whoever magics "conditional maledictions," and says they are a magical detouring of religious symbolism. Oaths, for example, demonstrate the *détournement* at work, because they often wish down *un jugement de Dieu* if the obligation is not fulfilled.[228] When writing is invented, oaths and maledictions can be put on *defixiones*. Just being written increases their magic power: *c'est écrit!*[229] Even after a public law of individuals and property is established, traces of magic persist in it, e.g., Roman *quaestio lance licioque*, etc. Huvelin even claims that our preoccupation with fingerprints and footprints grew out of a magic which sought to curse the traces of the thief so as to wound him sympathetically. And though individual law remains a public rite, it is often set in motion by the individual rather than by the public officers.[230] Huvelin further speculates that natural rights ideas trace back to the mana worth of the individual.[231]

Huvelin's position was immediately qualified by other Durkheimians, who characteristically felt he neglected the larger role *religion* played in shaping individual law. Was not religion after all the source of magic? Had not de Coulanges demonstrated[232] that individual families possessed property at Rome because the Roman *religion* required this (for burial of sacred ancestors)? In 1920, in *La Responsabilité,* Paul Fauconnet developed evidence that *new* religious projections, reflecting society's further evolution, were also decisive at later stages in individual law. For example, magic provided only partial protection against homicide, for it protected murderer and victim alike. Only when advanced religion redefined homicide as revolt against the gods and a sin was a rule against it collectively enforced.

Among the first to object to Huvelin's position were Hubert and Mauss, from whose theory of magic he had in part deduced it. They criticized Huvelin's monograph in a 1906 article (which later became the preface to a collection of several monographs by Hubert and Mauss in 1909, the one book by Mauss published during his lifetime[233]). Their whole purpose in studying magic in the first place had been to demonstrate how something as seemingly individual as magic is really social.[234] Now they feared Huvelin's excessive identification of magic with the individual might undercut this. In the new manifesto they conceded his main point that magic can turn the sacred to individual ends. Magic does indeed help nascent individuals and protect the self against social pressure;[235] it makes freedom of action and inquiry possible.[236] But magic is not always antisocial; there are also religious and ceremonial magics, for example. Their main objection, however, was that some of the institutions supporting individuals that Huvelin called "magical" were really religious. Mauss and his graduate student Davy developed this idea further in their studies of contracts, leading to a theory in which first religion and then magic help develop individual law, a typically Durkheimian R...M sequence. Since Davy and Mauss developed their argument about contracts, we can move to that topic next.

2. Law of Contracts. Maine had proposed that society evolved "from status to contract." Now Davy suggested how first religion—and then magic—set this process in motion. In a nutshell, contracts began as religiously sanctioned *collective* agreements between large groups of people—and later, magic helped back contracts between lone individuals. It was the typical Durkheimian religion-to-magic sequence. And once again it was used to show how a religious form provided a model that magic could use later in fostering individual spontaneity.

Mauss prepared the way for Davy's work with some studies of his own,[237] which also debouched into his work on the gift, *Essais Sur le Don,* published in the second series of *L'Année Sociologique* for 1923–24, when it briefly resumed under his editorship.[238] Before the war he had begun to study law of contracts with Davy, perhaps stimulated by his dispute with Huvelin, and in 1921 he published a short paper on the evolution of such law among the ancient Thracians.[239] This was one year before Davy's *La Foi Jurée*[240] came out in 1922; and the next year, in his essay on *The Gift,* Mauss wrote that his study of gift exchange had developed out of his collaboration with Davy on this research.[241] It was in the 1921 Thracian study that the idea was first publicly introduced that ancient contracts and exchanges were collective "total contracts and total prestations" between large groups of people. Apparently, what happened was that Mauss had read Boas' account of "potlatches"[242]—those spectacular, agonistic giveaway contests between competing Kwakuitl Indian chiefs in Northwest America—and then recalled suspiciously similar scenes from his Greek classics. Had not Thucydides tersely reported, concerning the familiar Greek pattern of giving and then expecting gifts, that among the Thracians it was important to give *more* than you got? Mauss speculated that perhaps all ancient peoples had gone through a potlatching stage—but he imagined that, before that, came an earlier stage of "total prestations" between groups, in which whole collectivities would trade with each other *as units.* In particular, Mauss scrutinized the story Xenophon told in *The Anabasis,* about hiring out the remnants of his "Ten Thousand" Greek mercenaries to a Thracian king for a civil war, and how the king had promptly solemnized the contract with an orgy of feasts, gift-giving, entertainments and marriage alliances. These "sumptuary contracts" had a religious coloration, for they were conducted by heralds, and involved a communal feast. And they set off exchanges not just of goods but of "women, children, food, rites, heritages."

In a few years, Mauss would study these exchanges as the origin of economic exchange; in the forties Lévi-Strauss[243] would study the concomitant exchanges of women and the social structural consequences of these marriage alliances. Davy concentrated on *the contracts that underlay the whole arrangement.* Since the social contract was fundamental Davy's study puts all the pieces of the broader picture together—more than the more specialized studies of the exchanges by Mauss or the marriage alliances by Lévi-Strauss. Thus Davy's 1922 book, unfortunately never translated, helps us understand a trend in two generations of French social theory, and one link between Mauss and Lévi-Strauss.

The root image[244] in Davy (and Mauss and Lévi-Strauss) is that primitive society builds up through social contracts reuniting the severed halves of families that have split apart after growing too big. This is one speculative interpretation of the widespread discovery by anthropologists of "dual organization"–societies composed of two halves or "moieties" which constantly exchange gifts, wives, ceremonies. Davy supposed that population pressure caused the extended family to split; then, to prevent war between brothers, they formed a contract, reuniting as "phratries" or moieties and later as still larger units including tribes. (There is some evidence of this splitting still at work today: Victor Turner[245] on lineage fission in Africa, Goode[246] on family splits in India, etc.)

Davy supposed that *groups* rather than individuals would be the parties to these primal contracts. He thought the law of contracts grew out of these primordial agreements. So here we have a school of modern French sociologists who revive the social contract theory of the 18th century, not as political ideology, but as a scientific hypothesis of some plausibility in organizing some compelling facts.

When split lineages reunified as phratries, one first symbol of their union was blood; men would cut their arms and mix the blood and adopt each other as relatives–and this is to be interpreted as a religious bond, because in primitive totemism the religion is the projection of the kinship system.[247] Another natural symbol that united the groups in these contracts was semen; they were bound together by marriage alliances, in which, for example, members of the two lineages reunited as phratries agree to marry each other's women. Originally, these were group rites, everyone marrying at once to effectuate the contract–events perhaps dimly remembered in such myths as the rape of the Sabine women. And Davy marshalled evidence that the contracting groups also held together by mass exchange of gifts.[248] A very primitive idea of union is at work in all this–the notion that if vital substances like blood or women or magical gifts keep circulating between two groups, they are one.[249]

The thing to grasp in Davy is that these marital and gift exchanges are *religious* rituals to sustain and perpetuate social contracts between groups. Davy emphatically insists that the process begins as collective and religious rites, and only later becomes individual and magical. This transition is evident in the transformation of total prestations into potlatching. At first, gifts are solemn, *collective*, mass exchanges, one whole group giving to another and then receiving. But gradually, as magic matures in the initiation lodges and chiefs emerge, the chiefs begin to give on behalf of their lineage or tribe as a whole; and the giving becomes individualistic and competitive. Wild potlatching contests are staged as religion begins to break down, dangerous games in which not only wealth but also religious symbols, titles, crests, even memberships, statuses and families can be recklessly given away, like a Ross MacDonald character gambling away his wife at the tables at Las Vegas. And this corresponds to *a magical stage of contracts* in which contracts are enforced by magical means:

> The institution (of contracts) evolves more and more toward magic and imprecation; and the religious idea of communion in a same substance disappears . . . (Davy, *op. cit.,* p. 79, my translation).

In other words, the stage which Huvelin and Frazer wrote about, in which the "whoever magic" of curses and oaths enforced individual law and contracts, was a *secondary and intermediate* stage coincident with emerging individualism. In the beginning, contracts were collective and enforced by *religious* sanctions. And later still, as society advanced further, came a *third* stage in which contracts were enforced by law. *Thus magic is an intermediary stage in between religious and true legal sanctions.* Mauss would later sketch a similar sequence for the development of the law of exchanges. This is the underlying sequence of the later Durkheim school: We go from religion to magic to law. Translating this into Max Weber's terms, this would be a progress from "traditional" to "charismatic" to "legal-rational authority," a sequence Max Weber often found historically. (As when, for example, charismatic authority challenged tradition, and then later there was "routinization of charisma.")

Davy also insisted that individualism gains and grows through contracts. Contracts, which magic helps push, are a new "category" of action that buttresses the individual by extending the outgo and influence of the individual human personality.

3. Law of Conveyances, Exchange. Economic anthropology has accumulated much data on the magical coloration of primitive gift giving, trade and accumulation. Childe, Jane Jacobs, Sombart have noted how the earliest trade was often in magical substances;[250] Drucker and Boas have described the magic of competitive gift-giving (potlatch).[251] Fortune has shown[252] how different Dobuan clans have *property* in specialized magic; and anthropologists in Africa have shown[253] how this shades into outright monopolies in certain industries reserved for particular families. Radin[254] stressed the economic side of magic, noting that shamans make people sick and then charge fees to cure them; in Africa magical medicines are sold and taught for a fee, and a lively trade in protective magic is carried on. Historically, the types of property that first exchanged were often magical—the Kwakuitls potlatch magic coppers, symbolic crests, names and titles, but usually not food or other necessities. The Durkheimians are therefore not alone in noting the magic coloration of property and exchange. The Boas school finds it at every turn, but notices *variety* of forms rather than an evolutionary sequence.[255] The magical basis of property and trade is vividly clear in Malinowski's Trobrianders: property here means magical power and is backed by magical power. Chiefs can get rich because they are chiefs, able to command 30 to 70 percent of the symbolic wealth, but they *must* get rich and stay rich to uphold their magic power. Apparently they prevent the emergence of other rich men by death sorcery.

It is also clear in many studies that one important purpose of trade is reciprocity, the establishing of social ties; this is the "religious coloration." Social ties appear in "trading partners"[256] and special relationships, such as jajaminis in India, where the tradesman's tie to particular customers is almost sacred.[257]

The Boas school speaks of trade in sacred objects providing a *"ceremonial framework"*[258] making other trade possible. Malinowski shows how this works for the Trobrianders.[259] They are already great traders at home, with barter, potlatch, sacred and profane trade. But when they travel overseas, to alien islands with dangerous sorcerers, they establish safe ties in these places by reverting to gift-giving. Gift-giving is originally a religious activity and the kula objects given to the foreign tribes have religious value—as if they were reaching out with religious symbolism to establish safe ties.[260]

Barter was always present, but barter did not lead anywhere. (Mauss admits that barter goes back to the beginning, in his Thracian essay; just as he insists that contracts and markets were also present from the beginning, in *The Gift.*) Barter did not lead to anything, but the symbolic exchanges created the social support for wider trade in necessities. Among the Trobrianders, for example, a lot of trade in *gimwala* goods (secular objects) goes on as a sideline during a kula-exchange voyage.

Later on, the ceremonial framework evolves into the law of exchanges, what John R. Commons called "the legal foundations of capitalism,"[261] the legal framework of economic activity. The ceremonial framework eventually *becomes* the law of business, both substantive and remedial, with its prohibitions, mandates and licenses, its laws of conversion, trespass, interference and other torts; its laws of real property, personal property and contract; its laws of agency, of organization, of corporation, or marketing with performances, warranties and titles; its laws of fraud, of employment, of guarantee and suretyship; its laws about the security of property and person and the administration of justice and the social control of the whole process. And to many of these laws, symbolic elements cling for many ages that are reminders of the magico-religious ceremonial exchanges out of which they emerged—such as the wadium or gage still thrown down in exchanges in the Middle Ages.

The ceremonial framework was religious at first, because it was collective. The magical element came in later to provide something additional: movement, individual action. Purely religious goods like land will not trade at all in the beginning; it is sacrilegious to part with them; they are "priceless." But sometimes religious property can be blasted loose by a special rite—like Roman *mancipium.*[262] *Mancipium* could be thought of as a religious rite that makes an exception, or as a magical rite that "turns" the sacred by desocializing it, so individuals can buy and sell it. A lively trade also grows up in property that is *outside* the heavy hand of collective-religious ownership. Very often this free trading stuff is loose because it is anti-religious or magical: amulets, charms, "medicines," spells, songs, disease magic. So we might sum it up this way: religious exchanges (such as obligatory gift giving) provide the ceremonial framework, and then magical exchanges provide the electricity to make the wheel turn, to push individual action, create movement and spontaneity.

Here then is another legal institution that begins in religion and goes through a magical stage before it is consolidated in legal form. Just as Davy showed this sequence with contracts, Mauss attempted to do it on exchanges in his essay, *The Gift.* And he tried to place the evolution of exchanges within Davy's theory of primeval social contracts. Again there is first a religious and collective stage, corresponding to Davy's "total contracts" between the groups. One whole group exchanges with another. And they exchange everything, not just goods, but also courtesies, entertainments, rituals, women, children, dances, feasts, everything under the sun. For this reason, Mauss calls these exchanges "total prestations."

The rules of gift circulation are enforced at first by religious ideas but then, in transition, these become magical. Among the Samoans, for example, every gift has *hua,* a spiritual urge to return to its original owner, and it turns on a trader who holds a gift, and makes him sick. Among the ancient Teutons, a gift that is held too long turns to poison, which perhaps helps explain why the German word for gift, *das Gift,* also means poison. *Hua* is related to mana words, and to Mauss and Durkheim mana ideas are the source of both religion and magic. It is plain that Mauss thinks of *hua* as a mainly religious sanction, a collective idea enforcing the rules of exchange. But Gurvitch insists that these ideas come to have a magical coloration during the later stage of individual exchange.[263] Pledge symbols like the French *gage* or the Teutonic *wadium,* exchanged during contracts, seem magical. *Wadium* and *gage* are something personal, like a glove, symbolically part of the individual who gives the gift or makes the loan. Sometimes the pledge was split in two and a half kept by each partner. "When I give, I give myself," runs an old saying. But something of *me* in your possession, on *your* person, can be magically dangerous to you if you wrong me or keep it too long. A gift puts a person under obligation; it gives someone else power over him; it is dangerous to accept a gift from an enemy; it is uncomfortable to hold a gift from someone with whom one has grown angry. Lévy-Bruhl later noticed[264] a similar magical symbol used in the earliest Roman form of contract, the *nexum.* Mauss mentioned the *nexum,* but not the magic token exchanged in it. Lévy-Bruhl in 1934 pointed it out: It was a bronze ingot or slug called the *aes rondusculum,* that changed hands in the *nexum.* "It represents the person of the lender; it is the (magic) symbol of him. It is delivered to the borrower at the same time . . . as the object . . . and it is this same bronze slug which is returned to the lender at the moment of repayment. More exactly it is the return of the *aes* which operates the repayment."[265]

Magical sanctions like these helped enforce rules of exchange during the transition from religious to legal sanctions. Gurvitch cites charts from the Frankish period showing catalogues of threats, anathemas, imprecations and other curses to enforce deals. Mauss admits that a "magical sanction may intervene,"[266] but insists the symbol is religious in origin because it *must* be given.[267] But Davy, Huvelin, Gurvitch suggest that the coloration becomes *more* magical when we come to individual trading. A similar "magic" enforces deals that are outside the law today. Gambling markers, for example, if unpaid, could be traded to gangsters who might work *maleficium* outside the law. Deals are backed up by oaths (*Omerta!*), promises of "a pound of flesh," fearsome gestures of sworn faith.

Roman law often tried to stop magic, and that is interesting. We have already seen how first chiefdoms and later empires tried to centralize magic. The curious attempt of Roman law from its beginnings in the 12 Tables to restrict magic was perhaps similar. In Rome we see a long trend of laws against magic promulgated by a people who practiced magic at every level of society.[268] Not black magic alone was proscribed, but all kinds of magic outside the official, ceremonial magic of the state. Even (foreign) forms of divination were proscribed, which seems unusual since, as Massonneau and Thorndike have shown, the Romans made a distinction between divination and magic and tended to incorporate divination in their religion (e.g., the official *haruscipes,* etc.). But against foreign divination or magics of any kind, Rome repeatedly legislated, outlawing at one time or another the *mathematici* and *Chaldaei* (astrologers), the *Magi* (Persian magician priests), the *Malifici, Venefici* and *Goetes* (charlatans who practiced sleight of hand) and the *striges* or sorcerers.[269] (But the *Vates,* or official diviners, were accepted and consulted on state occasions.) Magical cults like the Bacchanales and the Priscillians were proscribed,[270] and Morton Smith [271] claims that Christianity was persecuted in part because it was considered magical. Eventually, oriental religions swept the populace. But to the end of the empire, superstitious men running the government, themselves practicing magic, continued through law to try to control magic.

Why did law try to control, limit, centralize magic? The Romans believed in the power of magic and the crime of magic was often confounded with the crime of *lèse-majesté,* Massonneau writes.[272] That is part of it. But I suspect also that it happened because law was replacing magic; law was becoming the new order. There is something faintly surreptitious about *ius gentium,* as about magic; it grows up outside the normal community. The idea of natural law to which it gives rise and which became a guiding ideal in Roman law is a mana idea, perhaps. The *actions* at law are remarkably similar to magical actions, and they made use of magical symbols at first, such as the *aes* and the *wadium.* Law could accomplish transformations of social status, of identity, of social structure, by writ, as magic does by spells. Law is about all these *actions,* as magic is above all a *factum,* a doing. Both Maine and Maitland in fact aver that law in general is secreted by its own procedures, by what Maitland calls "the forms of action."[273]

The legal state attempted to replace magic and fill its function. No more spells are allowed except the imperative of writs like *habeas corpus,* in other words. In the modern era the legal state would become the ally of the individual.

4. Money. In two short essays written twenty years apart, Mauss remarked on a curious fact. The word for "money" in a number of primitive languages is the same as the "mana" word. In "Les Origines de la Notion de la Monnaie,"

1914,[274] he noted that the Algonquin mana word, which is "manitou," also designates their pearl money. Similarly, nations of the Togo region use the word *dzo* to mean something like mana; and a derivative word, *dzonu,* meaning "magic thing," also means money. He even claimed that the Melanesian word *mana* itself is sometimes used to mean money, too. In another article twenty years later,[275] Mauss added to the list: The Iroquois also use their mana word, *orenda,* to mean money, he claimed, and the Sioux use *wakan* the same way.

Others have observed magical meanings in money. Desmonde,[276] for example, noted references in the Freudian tradition. What does all this mean? Mauss provided a hint in an earlier piece,[277] where he remarked on Spencer and Gillen's finding that the Arunta sometimes used their sacred churinga symbol as money. The churinga is *religious,* he observed; it figures in the totemic religion. (I think the implication is that money is an individual manipulation of religious symbols, like magic itself.) In the 1914 essay Mauss insisted on a literal, logical interpretation. If *mana* words for social power also mean *magic,* and are additionally used to mean *money,* then money means magic and vice versa.

Many investigators have noticed that the earliest trade often began in magical substances—e.g., Jane Jacobs,[278] V. Gordon Childe. Desmonde mentions use of charms, amulets, religious medals as money. Mauss reported[279] that the quartz crystals ingested in Australian magicians' bodies during their initiations were used as money. Even a Marxist writer like Ernest Mandel notes that the first "universal equivalent" used as money was apt to be either something in pragmatic use (like wheat, rice, tools) or else a collection of ornaments "the first use of which may well have been magical"[280] (though Marxists would assert that money, once established, became an independent engine of mystification, separate from magic).

The magical objects used as money *retained* their magical powers. With Kwakuitl coppers, Trobriand kulas and Teutonic *Renommiergeld* ("money of renown")[281] not only did individual pieces of money have names and histories and myths attached to them, they had particular properties, including magical medical powers. Some were used to cure particular illnesses. Many, like the Kwakuitl copper called "bringer of coppers," had the property of magically attracting more money, and money retains this property. ("To them that hath shall be given.") Malinowski reported that some kula money (the actual objects, or vaygu'a, consisting of armshells and necklaces) were used as instruments in magical and religious rites.[282] The magic power of money, moreover, grows in exchanges: Iroquois wampum, for example, grew in value as each owner might add a new figure of pearls to it.[283] Malinowski reported the same for kula money; it grew in action as it was traded and this was physically marked, by added decoration.

Perhaps we could trace for money the same three stages we see with contracts: Early wealth consisted of religious objects, such as the churinga; originally these were "priceless" heritages of the community and could not be traded. But then, in a "magic stage," they *were* traded, at first surreptitiously, and the first money was, like magic itself, expropriated religious symbols. And as magical objects *per se* appeared, these were traded from the start: amulets, talismen, ritual objects, "medicines." It is the very nature of magical objects to be exchanged, to be sold—from African "medicines"[284] to modern good luck charms. With the generalization of mana at the tribal stage, more universal symbols were used. Money is, precisely, the sacred good that will trade for all other sacred objects, and some object to which the most universal mana ideas attached was picked as the universal standard of measure, which is perhaps why the mana word often became the word for money. But magical qualities still adhered to these more universal objects—Trobriand coppers, kula shells, even gold could bestow health, fight witchcraft and perhaps ensure immortality. Faustian alchemy sought gold not just for its own sake, nor even just for its Hermetic significance; it hoped to find in gold magic invincibility and a victory over death.

In the magical stage money fostered the activity and spontaneity of the individual. Like a Master Charge card, it enabled him to go anywhere, buy anything, do anything; its universality of value enabled him to translate his status, position, identity. Money gave him power over others. Finally, came a legal-rational stage when money was coined. Once again, this was in part an attempt by empires and states to centralize magic. But even after coins were minted they were still thought to have magic powers that reflected the hands they passed through: e.g., the "thirty pieces of silver." Numismatics is full of such lore.

Money always retains some of its magical meaning, which is the sharing out to individuals of what cannot really be shared, i.e., the total sacred value created by the community. As such money acts out the individual's drama of the magical expropriation of mana. Money's value is always a fragment of the total social value and it fluctuates with it. Money always tries to turn into hard cold coin, but like magic it is human activity, and it expands with human activity. The money supply increases when entrepreneurs are sufficiently moved by magic hope to take out bank loans to create new action. What money represents is a piece of the action, being in the social action: hoarding money causes other money to disappear through a contraction in aggregate demand. Mankind has always been fascinated by the ambiguous image of the miser, who hoards money only to have it turn back into dross, only to live in poverty because money is action and removing it from exchange causes it and the owner to wither. Magic values can be illusory. We have "money illusions" when an increase in money supply causes a decrease in its value; and Kuznets[285] has shown that GNP is full of imaginary wealth.

Like magic, money is subversive of the social order. Kwakuitl potlatches undermine the kinship society the way Spanish gold dissolved European feudalism. So we say, "The love of money is the root of all evil." Psychoanalytic anthropologists perpetuate the myth in their attempts to associate acquisitive societies with obsessionalism and "anality." "In muck there's money," they say in Yorkshire. The idea of money as a mysterious evil that makes something out of filth broods over the Thames in Dickens' *Our Mutual Friend.* Marx and Engels merely added to the conservative sacred chorus when they cried: "All that is solid melts into the air; all that is holy is profaned."[286]

I do not just mean that money was originally magical, or even merely that magical ideas still cling to it. I want to say more: money is still partly magical in nature; it is still a means whereby individuals expropriate social symbolism and power—some, just enough to act and live their lives, others enough to dominate. I think that economic theory keeps having to revise itself because it keeps bumping into the magical properties of money which it prematurely excludes. Just as Gödel showed[287] that the properties of numbers cannot all be deduced as a logical system from any set of axioms, that other unexpected properties will always turn up; similarly, axiomatic economics by its narrow exclusions keeps underpredicting the properties of money. This keeps popping up in pseudo-rediscoveries of spurious remainders—e.g., the enormous surprise that economists registered two decades ago at Theodore Schultz's discovery of the importance of "intangible capital."[288] (As if anyone should be surprised that wealth consists of human skill, knowledge, action, spirit! "The only wealth is life," Thoreau wrote in *Walden.*) Veblen was closer than many to recognizing all this. He showed the magic side of money in *The Place of Science.*[289] He showed how money turns objects into magical "goods," in *Theory of the Leisure Class*[290]; how magic motives fuel the quest that creates value, in *The Instinct of Workmanship*[291]; how the magic superstructure dominates production, in *The Engineers and the Price System*[292]; and how magic values are periodically puffed up and liquidated in business cycles, in *The Theory of Business Enterprise.*[293]

Eventually, states centralize money as they centralize all magic. (But even minted coins retain magical properties; they are still used as medicine.) In coinage, states enter into a permanent alliance with individuals. By putting more money into circulation, states make the movement of individuals freer. (When the Roman state collapsed, society moved back to a religious phase of frozen property and status again in feudalism.) Money is one more legal institution that emerges out of a religious and then a magical background, and by its emergence helps to consolidate the Individual.

II. Other Institutions Help Consolidate the Individual

Besides the new legal props, other institutions develop that support the Individual:

The political process evolves new, non-magical foundations for the Individual: citizenship, suffrage, bills of rights and rights of man, the ideology of individualism as the policy of the modern state.

The economic process, built up from the ceremonial framework, develops new props, too: "free enterprise," increasing occupational choice, more professions with long formations that deeply sculpt proud identities.

Medical institutions, sprung from magic, strengthen the Individual. It takes time to become a real person (as Shaw[294] insisted in *Back To Methuselah*) and now people live longer. Medical attitudes increasingly affirm self and Individual. In the religious stage, illness was a judgment for sin (e.g., "Job's comforters"). The magical idea that someone hexed you was already a step away from passivity and resignation. Finally, rational medicine removes all stigmas for illness.[295]

Personal Religions. Magical revolts are precipitated back onto religion, making religion more magical, giving it a human face, making it more helpful to the Individual. Later, after daimones and ancestors and hero gods succeeded totems, and then the tribal religions were in turn disintegrated in the cities they created, atomized urbanites turned to the even more magical mystery religons that promised to save the Individual. States kept coopting these magics as official religions, alienating them from the people, but more sprang up to fill the vacuum. Christianity attempted to restore personal magic to the masses, with its forgiveness, its prolific mental magic, its original transcendence of the social system, its magical hope and magical promises (redemption, immortality, divinity). It handily fit societies that increasingly required individuals to take care of themselves. In religious projections society first transcended itself in self-consciousness, and these projections, incorporated in the socialization of the young, assisted in the transcendence of the self. (Luckmann[296] even goes so far as to regard socialization itself as therefore intrinsically religious and spiritual, but his attempt to turn the water back into wine rests on an equivocation about the meaning of the word "transcendence.") Religion was always interested in stamping in some minimal social identity. But after the daring, independent self emerged with the help of tribal magic, and magic increasingly colored religions, magical technologies of vision quest, trance, meditation and mysticism became standardized religious experiences through which everyone passed in becoming a person.

There is not space to study all the institutions of the Individual. But one more is worth special attention, what Mauss called "the category of the person."[297]

"The Category of the Person." This is the consensual idea of what a self is supposed to be, which emerges in every culture.[298] The person category is not part of the self: it is a social institution, part of "the Individual," but it mediates that whole complex to the self. I imagine that it flashes its picture into the self especially through the self image, but obviously it also affects ego through whatever cultural fashions in repression it bolsters. The person category is in touch with all other institutions of the Individual—like a lens it focuses supportive attitudes from individual law, citizenship, personal religion, exterior formations buttressing the Individual which it reflects as ideas and interiorizes. But it also casts its own likeness back onto individual law, personal religion and citizenship as a unifying "logical operator" (Lévi-Strauss). In its early career it was embodied in mythic images. (Caillois[299] characterized myth as "the highest branch of the superstructure," so it receives vibrations "from every other part." He, Bergson, Campbell and Frazer claimed mythic archetypes of personality serve man the way instincts serve animals, providing models to live by.) The

person category helps consolidate the Individual by fitting parts coherently together; it also helps inspire confidence in the frail self that cowers inside the institutional shell by teaching him that he is *"Civis Romanus,"* or "the citizen of no mean city" as Paul said, or "a being made in the likeness of god," etc.

But to call the idea of the person a "category" as Mauss did is something of a joke today. It is not a clear and distinct idea in our time. It has become a rag-bag of concepts and theories, including all those murky entities—ego, me, id, self-image—that I tried to mock up into a "model of nomenclature" to sketch the actual self.[300] In Christian Rome, perhaps, ideas about personhood emerging in law, religion, kinship, etc. did concentrate to form a synthesis as Mauss claimed. But this synthesis repeatedly broke down when challenged by new currents in religion and philosophy reflecting changes in the Individual.

III. The Career of the Person Category

No full history of the Western person category has been written, though some studies of particular eras are helpful. Histories of philosophy do cover the full sequence (Brehier,[301] Randall,[302] Father Copleston,[303] Windleband[304]), but the person category cannot be understood by a history-of-ideas approach alone. Of course, being an idea it responds to other ideas, and some philosophical studies are useful—Bruno Snell[305] on the "discovery of mind", A. E. Taylor[306] on Socrates' idea of soul, Nock[307] on conversion, Randall[308] and Robinson[309] on the "making of the modern mind." But the person category is a complex nexus between self and Individual, between ideas and institutions, and can be understood only in an institutional context. It is a collection of official or dominant ideas which A. reflect other institutions of the Individual (law, economy, religion), and B. inculcate them into selves, C. through the mediation of particular carriers ("caretakers," confessors, repairers of selves, and so on) and particular self technologies (mysticism, meditation, psychotherapy, etc.). Few studies of this exist. (The "national character" studies in anthropology, the "personality" studies in psychology or the "personality-in-culture" studies in sociology take still-life snapshots, ignoring history, and they mix up self, person category, ego and Individual.) More heuristic is the Durkheimian view that with patience the person category can be penetrated as a clear and distinct idea, a "category" like the Aristotelian categories of time and space, whose inner coherence enables it to serve as a "translation symbol" (Mauss) or "logical operator" (Lévi-Strauss) communicating between different symbolic provinces of meaning so that, for example, the Christian idea of "the soul" fits into the legal conception of "the person." Maybe the way to study the person category is from two extremes simultaneously. It is, or becomes, a pure idea. On the other hand, it mediates ideas through particular institutions to biosocial selves.

Several people have studied it this way—including Durkheim, Mauss, Colin Morris, Michel Foucault, Benjamin Nelson, Karl Mannheim. Most have specialized in one epoch. I will assemble some of their studies to suggest what a full evolutionary account of Western personhood might look like—using the Durkheimians to describe the primitive religious and magical stages when those formations still retained "affective" (Lévy-Bruhl) and even psychomotor (Heinz Werner) elements.[310]

The Durkheim school had a program of studying the categories as social products: Mauss's monograph was part of this.[311] As usual, his study is elliptical; it will be better understood if I demonstrate, with help from his colleagues, that once again we see an institution of the Individual going through first a religious stage, then a magical stage and finally a legal stage, though Mauss does not say this.

The Religious Stage

Although "the person" seems a taken-for-granted reality, it is an "idea" and of recent origin, so recent we can trace its history. But ancestors of the idea appear in totemic clan names which are mere positional indicators in a kinship system. This was the religious stage. Mauss gives it little attention here, but Lévy-Bruhl devoted several books to it and Durkheim gave it two chapters. In *The Soul of the Primitive*,[312] Lévy-Bruhl shows primitives used group images in place of person ideas. Thus, a man of the wolf totem *was* a wolf—his idea of himself was the idea of a species. This meant person ideas were shadowy, affectual and impersonal, but totemism also gave the person duality and bipresence (he could send his totem, like a witch's familiar, on errands). In *Primitive Mentality* Lévy-Bruhl[313] showed that diffuseness of person ideas was one source of the "mystic participations" and "mystic causality" to which selves were subject: e.g., there were no natural deaths.

Durkheim[314] found that totemic systems already projected glimmerings of a notion of a soul—through reincarnation theories and through individual totems. Take reincarnation first. What it really represents is the filling of social spaces by available positional names—like a problem of vector spaces in matrix algebra. Totemism is thus a fertile source of metempsychosis ideas. (Spencer and Gillen had found reincarnation ideas in Australia[315] and Durkheim suggested they appear wherever there is totemism.) Reincarnation is almost a *reductio* illustration of the personal as impersonal[316] —the idea that a person can become a completely different person and still be somehow the same person shows how impersonal his personhood was. (Current attempts to test metempsychosis ideas "empirically," are among the most amusing trends in pseudo-science.)

Another source of soul ideas in the religious stage is the individual totem,[317] which differs from clan totems: 1. It is a single guardian animal, not a species. 2. The relationship to it is one of friendship, not descent. 3. While clan totems are inherited, individual totems may be acquired by deliberate act such as initiation or vision quest. Though perhaps transitional, the individual totem is a religions cult, a reflection or avatar of the clan totemic religion. I believe, along with

Nisbet,[318] that Durkheim is here describing a mirroring process whereby the self emerges as a reflection of society, just like George Herbert Mead's mechanics of the "generalized other."[319] The personal totem idea is so appealing that it is preserved across the ages in tales of animal helpers (Androcles' lion, Mowgli's friends) and personal spirits (like Socrates' "genius").

The Magic Stage

But personal totems are probably transitional toward a magical stage, in which the person idea gets loose from the totemic system. For they make possible individual manipulation of the sacred. You can send your nagual or manitou to do something to somebody, and because of it you have mana. Witches' familiars are probably remnants of personal totems, and in central American "nagual" figures we see perhaps something intermediate between a totem and a familiar. In some Australian tribes (e.g., the Euahlavi) only the magicians have personal totems, which is also suggestive.[320]

Mauss gives little explicit attention to a magical stage, but he cites elements which other Durkheimians identify as such a stage: He describes, for example, the vertiginous name exchanges in Kwakuitl potlatches when individuals swap their seasonal names, secret society names, etc. He is emphasizing the impersonality of such temporary names, but Gurvitch identifies those potlatches with a magical stage in which religious symbols are shaking loose. Names are lost in Kwakuitl potlatches, almost as if role name impersonality were being burlesqued on the way out. Mauss also emphasizes that theater contributed to the person category, even to its name, with the *persona* or theatrical mask. But he mentions that beneath theater lay older institutions of ritual dramas of the confraternities, and the relation of theater to magical fertility rites is well known. In the magical stage the mana of the individual strongly developed; Huvelin suggests this is one source of later natural law ideas.

The Legal Stage and Synthesis

Mauss concentrates mainly on the legal stage, as it solidified personhood ideas in Graeco-Roman cities in which individuals were initiated successively into a family, a phratry, a tribe and a city. Names now *accumulated to* the person, instead of his passing from one to another as he passed through roles.[321] And the person idea was now founded at law for all but the slave (*"servus non habet personam"*). This is a crystallization, a synthesis. For the new legal concept of the person incorporates old kin positional name ideas, with magical ideas such as the *persona* derived via theater from initiation rites and religious ideas: Christian concepts of the soul influence it in the late empire.

Mauss looks ahead briefly, observing that later on philosophy will greatly influence the idea of the person: e.g., notions of ego that developed with Kant, Fichte, etc. The synthesis is not permanent; he wonders what the person category might become tomorrow.

East vs. West

Person ideas developed also in India, though with a different outcome. In Atman-philosophy the self was finally identified with the world, with Brahman.[322] The Upanishads follow the *tat vam asi* (that thou art) of the *Ghita*. And Buddhism considers the individual ego to be an illusion: no Atman. Mauss' implication is that this aborted a trend toward a person category. This is interesting since some Atman philosophy and its yogas were very ambitious. According to Zimmer,[323] the demiurge or world god of each yuga is a yogin who *thought* himself up into the sky. It is as if the attempt of the magic self to puff itself up when the actual self was quite weak helped to *evert* the self. The weak self that stormed heaven became part of heaven in Hinduism and part of nothingness in Buddhism. In "Atman equals Brahman" the Hindu person *surrendered* to the primal impersonality of person ideas just as later Indic sacrifice went all the way (in Brahmin suicides and Jain starvations unto death) instead of sacrificing symbols of self to strengthen self.

Why did this happen? *Not* mainly because of a different movement of ideas as Weber[324] supposes (with monism the inevitable, "logical" result of acceptance of metempsychosis, etc.). It happened because social structure in India was different. Margaret Cormack[325] and Gardner and Lois Murphy[326] have described the enveloping Indian extended family with its depressive boys and ghostly little girls. V. S. Naipaul[327] has shown how resulting ego weakness fosters an obsessional magic that ritualizes all the details of everyday life.[328] Maine has shown the trend away from private property, and the *Cambridge History of India* shows the weakness of cities, the absence of political citizenship. In India the impotent patriarchal families of wrack-rented villages, bypassed by empires, offered their young men few arenas for social action; even in the village panchayats the caste barriers of this wounded society limited reciprocity and effective individual action.

By contrast Graeco-Roman social structure was more self-constituting: This was more decisive than philosophical movements in developing strong ideas of personhood

Originally, Greek self concepts were actually quite fragile. The typical idea that "virtue is knowledge" (cf. Plato's *Protagoras*) means that it comes to the fragile self from *outside,* just as Homeric Greeks believed that passions and even ideas ("monitions") came from gods.[329] In other words, both self and person category were shallow. The self-constituting urban political process strengthened the Individual but led to a breakdown of the gentes which caused anxiety and guilt. Dodds interprets this as Oedipal guilt. The negative effect was the flight into magic. But Dodds also hints a positive effect: this revolution transformed Hellas from a "shame culture," into a "guilt culture." In Freudian language those are loaded terms: guilt is mature, shame is immature. This suggests a deepening of the ego due to Oedipal struggle and its repression in the form of a superego structure.

Of course dissolution continued. The Graeco-Roman world passed from breakdown of the gentes to breakdown of the cities; men experienced that "failure of nerve" which Gilbert Murray saw as the beginning of overwhelming superstition. But cities never fully lost their self-constituting roles. Leagues of cities stood up against Diodachs and Romans, Cleomenes even revived Sparta.[330] And the Roman state preserved cities as local self-government, up until Diocletian's corporativism. By then Caracalla had extended Roman citizenship[331] to the whole empire, and Roman law had guaranteed the person. Person ideas never totally lost their roots in self-constituting institutions.

The Christian synthesis that followed declared that souls were created in the image of god but were in no way part of god: from Athanasius to Barth mainline Christian theology has denied immanence. And Western self-magic has been more successful than Eastern in widening the scope of man's actions instead of helping him withdraw. Hindu meditation typically aims at emptying the stream of consciousness of content (turning on the alpha wave, as we now understand it), whereas some Western mysticisms have explored the contents of mind.[332] We forget this because this approach is so productive that it spins off sciences we no longer think of as part of meditation. The Cambridge Platonists developed optics partly out of introspective techniques; "psychophysics," introspectionist psychology (Tichenor), phenomenology and Freudian free-association are more modern techniques of treating the contents of meditation as objective. Content-oriented mysticisms augment the strategems and powers of ego and hence are self-strengthening magic, whereas alpha wave manipulation can lead back to the impersonality of the original person idea.

Medieval and Early Modern Syntheses

The Roman synthesis was not permanent. Rome fell; some institutions of the Individual contracted (money, citizenship); the person category blurred. But Western Europe in the long run retained its heritage and in the Middle Ages developed new institutions fostering the Individual and reflected in person ideas. Colin Morris[333] stresses the personalism of feudal ties as a source. Morris and Foucault[334] both emphasize the importance of the confessional as one of the typical institutions inculcating new person ideas. Its rituals of "examination of conscience," "true repentence" and "sincere resolution" not to sin again were subjective exercises but could be objectively examined by the confessor. Foucault calls confession a "ritual of discourse" that transformed the West into a "confessing society"; it was the archetype for many other institutions including the current models of therapeutic confession. Annual confession was made compulsory for all Christians in 1215, the same year as Magna Carta. The Inquisition was also active in these years and the two kinds of examination of subjectivity are related. The haunting anecdotes in Lea's[335] histories, in which men are pursued by the Inquisition's dossiers through many countries and several decades, are terrifying enough, but they hardly suggest that the individual person was anonymous or unimportant.

Institutions like confession do not just "carry" or "inculcate" person ideas; they also *witness* and demonstrate what persons are supposed to be. In our time, the psychoanalytic stream of free association and the stenographic transcript of jury trials do the job confession once did of providing Western civilization's main demonstrations of its ideas of the person—as something formed, knowable and infinitely recoverable; responsible and rational but also "deep," integral, capable, etc.[336] (Witnessing is always profoundly important in any magical or religious undertaking; one of the latent functions of shamans was to witness and demonstrate that selfhood *can exist.*)

The new institutions were complex; society changed rapidly; personhood was constantly remade. Benjamin Nelson wrote speculatively about the successive syntheses; his analysis sometimes mixed together person, ego, Individual and self, but it is frequently enlightening. These elements stand out: a. Subjective person ideas were always linked to *objective institutions*—to "caretakers" (e.g., pastoral care); but also to "courts" (e.g., the Inquisition); and to institutions of "conscience" (such as the confessional); and to "self technologies" (medita-tion, mysticism, etc.) b. There was a *series* of these syntheses. c. *Both rational and irrational elements* entered into them. d. All these processes are reversible.[337]

Consider the successive syntheses: a. Popular mysticisms broke in on the early Middle Ages' settled system of "casuistry and conscience," and deepened the person concept.[338] b. These mysticisms were then assimilated into a new synthesis[339] of "conscience, casuistry and cure of souls," buttressed by monastic philosophy and its great *"imitatios."*[340] In the *Imitatios* of St. Bernard, etc., a "faith structure of consciousness" deepened ideas of self (and perhaps actual selves) through disciplines aligning them with god and Christ by imitation rather than total identification and merger in the Hindu manner. c. But now this new synthesis was challenged by a new (scholastic) rationalism based on the recovery of Aristotle and Roman law. A faith structure of consciousness gave way to (and synthesized with) a rational structure of consciousness centering on the idea of individual responsibility. This was the age of the first catechisms, of fine debates on moral responsibility and of the Fourth Lateran Council ruling in 1215 making confession compulsory at least once a year. Now the self was linked with objectively-oriented institutions demonstrating its personal res ponsibility, with ecclesiastical courts and the Inquisition growing in impor-tance.[341] d. But this is not a simple sequence running safely from faith to rationa-lity; it is dialectical and precarious. For now this predominantly rational struc-ture of consciousness was in turn challenged by friar mysticism and later by Protestant illuminism.[342]

There was an interplay between objectively-oriented institutions supporting selves ("courts and casuistry") and subjectively-oriented institutions (e.g., mysti-cism) which enriched both. Objective courts and rational casuistry embodied increasingly sensitive *subjective* content harvested from mysticism: thus, ideas of personal responsibility advanced in acuteness and innerness. New "irrationalities" were incorporated into later rational syntheses as well. Nelson suggests that some eighteenth century ideals of "Reason" can be traced to revived Neoplatonic concepts, for example.[343] Mysticisms in turn were increasingly guided in a rational way—an *imitatio Christi* is more structured than *nirvana,* and it was succeeded by the even more disciplined "worldly asceticism" of the Calvinist sects.[344]

Persistence of Occult Person Ideas

But retention of mystic content in person ideas would ultimately pose a problem. Western person ideas had extensive occult roots to begin with. Dodds traced some to Greek contacts with shamanism. Alongside Thracian *group* ecstasy cults (of Dionysios) came the shaman-like *individual* ecstasy of early Apollonian cults (before the Greek temper tamed them) which derived, he thought, from real shamanism through Greek Black Sea settlements. Their synthesis in a sequence running from Eleusinian Mysteries and Orphism through Pythagoreanism[345] and Platonism into Christianity consolidated a foundation of occult content in Western personhood. New mystic inputs in the Middle Ages were added to an already mystical tradition. It finally evolved into Faustian ideas of self that first celebrated the birth of modern science and later unleashed the beyond-good-and-evil romantic self that resisted it.

Because of reversibility and instability, the outcome is uncertain. When rapid change upsets the "generic order of existence," it can make the world seem absurd or grotesque.[346] These contradictions could lead the masses to withdraw into "trances of action," "disaster politics," "dances of death,"[347] Nelson writes, in an analysis mixing together person category and self. It is not clear whether Freudian psychology is the undertaker of the occult self or its continuator.[348] Or even how much it *can* help, for when the cues given actors become too disorganized by rapid change, anomie must result.[349]

Increasingly, rationality is spread by collectivist movements and no longer depends on the selves and individualities that first carried it.[350] Even capitalism apparently no longer needs structures of faith to undergird it.[351] Does the Western person become an antithesis of the modern world? If we speak strictly of the person category I think that something else happens: fragmentation.

The Final Crack-Up of the Person Category

The modern era witnesses fragmentation in person ideas, a process that begins in philosophy and spreads to psychology. There is no single "category of the person" any more. We have many different concepts and few people use them the same way. What happened? I find a hint in Mannheim.[352] He speaks of free intellectuals replacing clergy and challenging official worldview; as a result, objective world images break down. When this happens, intellectuals look for subjective supports. When Sophist skepticism disintegrated worldview, Socrates tried to reconstruct order through a subjective approach (epistemology). Similarly, Kant attempted to fight the modern skepticism of British empiricists by reconstructing "the order of the knowing subject." But the Kantian revolution unleashed a storm of subjective self-analysis in German philosophy which exploded the person category, seeding a shower of new concepts: the ego, the self, etc. Mannheim tells us that the unity of mind was lost in philosophy and psychology, that psychology turned atomistic. He demonstrates how the deadly "unmasking and nihilating procedures" of competing ideologies destroyed the integrity of mind.[353] But Mannheim does not say enough[354] — he gives a hint, which I must develop further.

I think that the deep logical contradictions inherent in the Western person category (the unstable mixture of rational and irrational ideas) made it extremely vulnerable to the disputatious new philosophical subjectivisms. Modern subjectivism discovers, in philosophical reflection upon Western ideas of personhood, conflicting logical tendencies, which it hypostasizes.[355] Philosophical dissection of concepts produces new constructs for self-fulfilling clinical confirmation. I think it is likely that the self *does* contain separate parts, but these are socialized into it partly by society's own ideas of how many parts *should* be there—and subjective philosophy always rediscovers the perennial dichotomies of good/bad, personal/impersonal, I/me, etc. A socialization that anticipates inner multiplicity and conflict will help produce it. Psychoanalysis, which began as a demonstration of depth and character, becomes a witness to fragmentation, confirming chaos.

The ego psychology of Fichte and Schelling was initially a self-consciousness of strength, but by the time we come to Freud, the self has fragmented badly. Eventually, a Western version of Buddhist no-Atman philosophy appears in Wittgenstein[356] and the Oxford analysts who attempt to demonstrate that "mind" is not present (Ryle[357]) or to reduce "persons" to the way we talk about the idea of persons (Strawson,[358] Ayer[359]), or to show that in important mental operations like reading we do not even have to suppose that a subject is at work. That this is a Western no-Atman movement like Buddhism is being discovered backwards. With typical Western ethnocentricity, students like Stcherbatsky[360] and "Bharati"[361] are discovering that Buddhist logics or Tantric psychologies are really sophisticated "analytical philosophy," just like white man's wisdom. It might be better to consider Western analytical philosophies as our own no-Atman movements and possibly the final solution of the person problem. Just like Buddhism, they appear after excessive preoccupation with self ideas had both fractioned it and puffed it up, threatening to evert it. No-Atman philosophies then work like garbage collectors, cleaning up the wreckage.

In the 19th century, person ideas began to break up while the actual self continued to grow in coherence. Eventually, however, disintegration of person ideas may open a breach in the Individual that exposes the self. In the meanwhile, disintegration of the person idea releases its irrational elements; the id, the shadow and the occult self speak up for themselves. An idea that went through religious, magical and legal stages retained all its earlier elements, and today occult archetypes of personhood are in the vanguard of every occult revolution. In a later chapter we will explore the persistence of magic in the modern world and its continuing threat to rational structures of consciousness and social order.

Conclusion and Summary. Magic helped develop the Individual as a social institution that protects the self. Of great importance were the tribal initiation lodges whose magical professions gave individuals a social standing. Along with them came institutions of medical magic, magical protest cults, etc. First chiefdoms and later empires tried to centralize this magic, alienate it, but more magics kept emerging. Finally, in the self-determining Graeco-Roman gentile cities, new secular institutions consolidated the Individual. Several of these—law of contracts, of property, of exchanges—went through a magical stage. Eventually they were secured on a legal-rational framework guaranteed by the state. The Individual was also secured by certain cognitive institutions that were less stable and more reversible: these include personal religion and the person category.

So magic advanced with human progress, with civilization and the Individual, at least for a while. For how long does magic continue to advance? That is the topic of the remaining chapters. Magic might be said to persist in several ways:

1. As a stress index. Magic at very least reflects social tensions, conflicts of groups and pressure on the Individual and the self. That is the subject of the next chapter, which examines black magic as a "strain gauge" of tensions in society.

2. Actively. But magic also continues to play an active role in society; perhaps it even has a certain appropriateness as an expression of the fragmenting modern world. That will be the subject of the last chapter: the relation of magic to "organic solidarity."

3. Independently. Finally, magic persists because it accumulates as a literary tradition which piles up in libraries, is constantly consulted, has historical effects on movements of ideas and is always stirred up again in occult revivals. That will be discussed in the Postscript (i.e., Postulate 13).

Notes

1. The modern self has a very prickly shell indeed to sustain its determined presence. It is encased in a thick weave of legal identity, political citizenship and rights—and if you trespass on them, it can sue you at law. It surrounds itself with outer walls of secure property; it can negotiate binding contracts and pass on lasting testaments. It has, moreover, clear blueprints of what it is supposed to become—ambitious archetypes of "personality" and "soul" are officially stamped into it by a prolonged education. Its gritty presence is deepened and rooted by institutions of meditation, psychotherapy, sacraments and prayer. It has immortal longings, and it is egged on by individualistic religions that exalt personal salvation (and other magical goals) above community. It is supported by the official ideology of individualism, and backed ultimately by the state. The primitive self was an unstable wraith compared to this armored, modern monolith.

2. Gurvitch, *La Magie, La Religion et Le Droit, op. cit.;* M. Halbwachs, *Sources of Religious Sentiment* (N.Y., 1962), pp. 70–74.

3. Edward B. Tylor, *Anthropology,* Abr. ed. (Ann Arbor, 1970).

4. Lewis Henry Morgan, *Ancient Society* (N.Y., 1971), pp. 3–45.

5. Gordon Childe, *What Happened in History; Man Makes History,* etc.

6. What about Paleolithic rituals that seem magical, such as those dimly glimpsed in Mousterian burial sites or Aurignacian and Magdalenean cave paintings? I think these were more communal and religious rites; they were "magical" in the weak sense that religious

rites model magic effects. (Though some cave paintings do suggest ceremonial work magic to organize the hunt: cf. Arnold Hauser, *The Social History of Art,* vol. I, N.Y., 1951, pp. 3–15.)

7. One early province was the still quasi-official "ceremonial" magic that extrapolated sympathetic effects of sacred-social rituals to rainmaking, agriculture and work gang coordination. The first magicians who practiced it were still kin leaders, headmen, agents of the full community.

8. In societies like Dobu, evolutionists might well claim to see a stage when division of labor was anticipated by division of magic. Different Dobuan clans specialize in the black magics of various diseases and the medical magics of their cures and this incites a lively commerce in spells and antidotes. In the primitive "sciences" of societies like the Dogon, reported by Griaule, we can perhaps also discern the division of labor being prepared by the division of magical *knowledge.*

9. A rudimentary division of labor of course preexisted, at the band stage, in the Paleolithic: that between the sexes. It was extreme in hunting and gathering cultures, with women stuck home in camp and men roving. Agriculture brought women's work closer to men's (and raised their prestige); it also increased social density and helped stimulate specialized occupations.

10. A. A. Goldenweisser, *Early Civilization* (N.Y., 1922), ch. 17 and *passim.*

11. There has been a reaction against the excesses of a historical functionalism, which at its worst confounded function with both effective cause and origin. (Cf. David Bidney on Malinowski, in *Theoretical Anthropology,* N.Y., 1953, 1967, pp. 223-236.) There is a revival of interest in charting of diffusion paths on the one hand, and social evolution on the other. Bastian and Boas implied that evolutionary stages confounded logic and history, and at very early stages evolution and logic often do coincide (Bidney). There is, for example, a Simmel-like logic in what is possible in a group of 500 vs. what is possible among 50 people. Bidney's idea that, at early stages, logic and history do coincide, helps cast the work of the Durkheim school in a favorable light. Durkheim and Mauss, like Hocart, bracket the question of evolutionary stages or diffusion paths. But in their work they seem implicitly to assume that such stages and pathways exist. The stages are just not spelled out. When we enter the world of Mauss, Hocart, Gurvitch and the others, we enter a mysterious time warp where everything is written in what might be called the Marxist present tense, with assertions to the effect, for example, that the stage of tribal organization "follows" clan organization, etc. No stipulation as to *when* this happens, or where diffusion pathways lie, just the feeling that both pathways and early logical stages of development did exist. And since, as Ratzel said, "the world is small," this assumption is perhaps not unreasonable.

12. Roger Caillois, *L'Homme et le Sacré* (Paris, 1950), ch. 3 & *passim.*

13. Adolf E. Jensen, *Myth and Cult Among Primitive Peoples* (Chicago, 1963), *passim.*

14. *The Golden Bough,* ch. 11, p. 40, etc.

15. Frederick Engels, *The Origin of the Family, Private Property and the State* (N.Y., 1971), pp. 21-22, 47-54.

16. J. J. Bachofen, *Mother Right,* excerpts from *Myth, Religion and Mother Right* (Princeton, 1967), pp. 69-210.

17. Lewis Henry Morgan, *Ancient Society* (N.Y., 1971), Part III.

18. Kate Millett, *Sexual Politics* (N.Y., 1971). Millett stresses the discovery of paternity, cf. p. 28.

19. Marcel Granet, *Etudes Sociologiques Sur la Chine* (Paris, 1953); *Chinese Civilization* (N.Y., 1958); *La Pensée Chinoise* (Paris, 1968).

20. Jane Harrison, *Themis.* This is what makes the initiation rite so fraught. Cf. ch. 1.

21. Arnold Van Gennup, *The Rites of Passage* (Chicago, 1960), ch. 6 and *passim.*

22. *Group Psychology and the Analysis of the Ego* (N.Y., 1965), pp. 46–53.

23. Robert H. Lowie, *Indians of the Plains* (Garden City, 1963), p. 105ff.

24. See discussion in ch. 16, John E. Pfeiffer, *The Emergence of Man* (London, 1970), pp. 332-352.

25. Marcel Granet, *Chinese Civilization* (N.Y., 1958), Part II, Book 2, ch. 4, pp. 194–204.

26. *The Origin of the Family, Private Property and the State,* p. 48ff.

27. *Ancient Society, passim.*

28. *Sexual Politics,* ch. 2.

29. A. P. Elkin, *The Australian Aborigines* (Garden City, N.Y., 1964).

30. *Indians of the Plains,* pp. 96–97ff.

31. Philip Drucker, *Indians of the Northwest Coast* (Garden City, N.Y., 1963), pp. 102ff.

32. C. Lévi-Strauss, *The Elementary Structures of Kinship* (Boston, 1969), pp. 98–117, 218, 303, etc.

33. *Indians of the Plains,* pp. 96–97.

34. *Ancient Society,* p. 11.

35. Ronald Cohen and John Middleton, eds., *Comparative Political Systems* (Garden City, N.Y., 1967), Introd. by eds., pp. ix–xiv.

36. Drucker, *op. cit.,* Introd., esp. pp. 1–8.

37. It is true that in *The Division of Labor in Society* (Glencoe, Ill., 1933, pp. 256–282) Durkheim made population his "final cause" and suggested it forced division of labor. Social organization (a reflection through subsistence of both technology and ecology) is Durkheim's strategic variable. Mauss cautioned against too great an emphasis on ecology as unilinear, and typically looked for a "total social fact" as he later called it, that would cluster together all the important variables. ("Essai sur les Variations Saisonnières des Sociétés Eskimos," collected in *Marcel Mauss Sociologie et Anthropologie,* pp. 389–475). What was most interesting to the Durkheimians was not technology or ecology, but level of social organization. Determined by history and natural forces, it is itself a nexus of determination to them. This is their "sociologism," their "pure sociology." Durkheim's association of magic with the transition from band to tribe is a typical application of this approach.

38. Lévi-Strauss also emphasizes human cognitive skills that respond to these opportunities in forming social contracts where subsistence conditions permit. Cf. *The Elementary Structures of Kinship* (Boston, 1969), pp. 485ff; and *Totemism* (Boston, 1963), ch. 4, "Toward the Intellect," pp. 72–91.

39. *Indians of the Plains,* p. 91ff.

40. Ralph Linton, *The Study of Man* (N.Y., 1936), chs. 13–14, pp. 209–252.

41. John E. Pfeiffer, *op. cit.,* pp. 332–335.

42. Gladys A. Reichard, "Social Life," Franz Boas, ed., *General Anthropology* (Boston, 1938), pp. 409–486.

43. Raymond Firth, *Elements of Social Organization* (Boston, 1961, 1972), ch. 2, "Structure and Organization In a Small Community," pp. 41–79.

44. Charles Horton Cooley, *Social Organization* (N.Y., 1909), ch. 3.

45. Lowie, *Indians of the Plains,* p. 92.

46. Mauss, "Essai Sur les Variations Saisonnières des Sociétés Eskimos," *Année Sociologique,* 1904–5, collected in *Marcel Mauss Sociologie et Anthropologie* (Paris, 1966), pp. 389–475.

47. Lineages are families that trace descent in one line only, father or mother, not both like our own "bilateral" families. They are typical of many primitive societies and may be produced by a division of labor that favors one sex over another, the requirements of some kind of local residence, or exogamy, according to Leslie White, *The Evolution of Culture* (N.Y., 1959), pp. 150–182.

48. Birdsell thesis discussed in ch. 16, John E. Pfeiffer, *The Emergence of Man* (London, 1970), pp. 332–333.

49. Lowie, *Indians of the Plains,* p. 92.

50. V. W. Turner, *Schism and Continuity in an African Society* (Manchester, 1957).

51. Firth calls these "sectional" bands, as distinct from "integral" bands. Raymond Firth, *Elements of Social Organization* (Boston, 1972), ch. 2, "In a Small Community," pp. 41–79.

52. *Ibid.*

53. Pfeiffer, *The Emergence of Man,* pp. 334, 347ff.

54. R. P. Trilles, *Les Pygmées de la Forêt Equatoriale* (Paris, 1931).

55. Raymond Firth, *We, The Tikopia* (Boston, 1936, 1957), pp. 61–197.

56. Firth, *Tikopia Ritual and Belief* (Boston, 1967), ch. 9, "The Sociology of Magic," pp. 195–212.

57. The Australians are perhaps at an early stage of the transition to tribes; some groups have shadowy tribal names and symbols. And Durkheim says that, technically, totemism is a religion (and classification system) projected by the tribal universe as a whole. But it is a

religion fragmented into clan cults, as the society itself is still centered more in the bands than in the tribe. The symbols of the tribe as a whole are fewer and weaker.

58. Ancestor worship as described by de Coulanges at the beginnings of Greece and Rome provides another good example of a religious particularization at the later stage Morgan called "higher barbarism." Here the *gentes* still have private family cults. The gods of the Claudii are not the gods of the Fabii, etc.

59. Marshall D. Sahlins, "The Segmentary Lineage," ch. 5, in Ronald Cohen & John Middleton, eds., *Comparative Political Systems* (Garden City, N.Y., 1967), pp. 89–120.

60. "By a tribe we usually mean an economically independent group of people speaking the same language and uniting to defend themselves against outsiders," writes Reichard. Gladys A. Reichard, "Social Life," Franz Boas, ed., *General Anthropology* (Boston, N.Y., 1938), ch. 9, p. 413. Elkin writes that a true tribe entails territory, identity (a name) and also a separate culture of customs, rites, beliefs and even dialect. (A. P. Elkin, *op. cit.*, p. 27).

61. Pfeiffer, *The Emergence of Man*, p. 333.

62. Ralph Linton, *The Study of Man* (N.Y., 1936), ch. 14, "Tribe and State," e.g., pp. 233, 238.

63. Linton, *op. cit.*, p. 232.

64. Louis Dumont, "The Marriage Alliance," ch. 11 in Paul Bohannan and John Middle ton, eds., *Marriage, Family and Residence*, pp. 203–214.

65. *The Elementary Structures of Kinship, passim.*

66. *La Foi Jurée* (Paris, 1922.) To be discussed.

67. Lionel Tiger, *Men In Groups* (N.Y., 1970), ch. 6.

68. Sahlins, in Cohen & Middleton, *Comparative Political Systems*, p. 96.

69. M. Fortes and E. E. Evans-Pritchard, eds., *African Political Systems* (London, 1966), Introd., pp. 1–23.

70. Cohen and Middleton, eds., *Comparative Political Systems* (N.Y., 1967), Introd., pp. ix–xiv.

71. Another term often heard for the looser structure is the "acephalous" or headless tribe, the tribe that lacks a powerful chief

72. *Phratries* are groups of lineages that "sing together," as Northwest Indians say; they feel a sense of fellowship which *may* be based on vague memories of common descent from lineages that split with population growth. (White uses the term "named clans" for phratries where this memory of common descent is more conscious.) *Moieties* are phratry-size segments found in the widespread dual organization of tribes; e.g., a tribe split into two complementary phratries that exchange gifts, wives, festivals, courtesies, rites, etc. *Lineages* are extended families that count descent in one line only, patrilineal or matrilineal, unlike our own bilateral family. I prefer to follow the traditional Boas and Reichard usage of the term *sib* for both kinds of lineage, reserving *clan* for matrilineage and *gens* for patrilineage. But it should be recognized that "clan" is also used in at least two other ways. First of all, common speech, and some anthropologists like Ashley Montague (*Man, His First Two Million Years,* N.Y., 1969, pp. 174–177), turn away from the unfamiliar word *sib* and use *clan* instead to mean either kind of lineage, patri or matri. Secondly, Montague, Leslie A. White (*The Evolution of Culture,* N.Y., 1959, ch. 7, pp. 142–204), and some others also use "clan" to refer to a *collection of lineages* that are linked together; this sounds like a phratry but perhaps White makes the distinction with his more precise term, "the named clan." I.e., this is a group of lineages with the same name, like the great gentile houses of Rome that contained thousands of members and many lineages, or like the Scottish "clans." This kind of named clan is almost a tribe, or at least a large province of a tribe.

73. Fustel de Coulanges, *The Ancient City* (Garden City, 1955), pp. 117–120.

74. "La Cohésion Sociale dans les Sociétés Polysegmentaires," 1931, collected in *Oeuvres,* vol. 3, pp. 11–27.

75. Daryll Forde, in Cohen and Middleton, *op. cit.*, pp. 121–142, makes the same point, suggesting that the integrating role of the cross-cutting associations is intermediary between the "mechanical solidarity" of kin links and the latter "political integration" of chiefdoms and states. Mauss distinguished the "polymorphism" of families from the "amorphism" of the class associations. He meant something like Turner speaking of the *"communitas"* found in "liminal" (transitional, initiation) groups. (Victor W. Turner, "Betwixt and Between, the Liminal Period in *Rites de Passage*," ch. 5, *The Forest of Symbols,* Ithaca,

1967, pp. 93-111. Also, chs. 3, 4, 5 of *The Ritual Process,* London, 1969, pp. 80-154). Mauss writes of the equality and the freedom within communities of age, sex and generation classes (p. 18, *op. cit.*), the direct identification of fellow candidates with one another. The idea is that the class associations, by providing respites of community, liberty and equality from the positioned roles of kinship, give extra heart and loyalty to solidarity.

76. In the "crowd excitement" Durkheim discerned on *jours de fête,* the tribal religion is renewed by a primary group experience.

77. Drucker, *Indians of the Northwest Coast,* p. 118.

78. *Ibid.,* pp. 131-143.

79. *Ibid.,* pp. 137-139.

80. De Coulanges noted that this process at Rome was intensified by the phenomenon of "charter families" (those who signed the constitution, as it were), originally swollen by the legal fiction of adoption, who then closed their books to new members and declared: *Plebes gentum non habeunt.* Maine had a similar insight. (De Coulanges, *op. cit.,* p. 127ff).

81. Robert Ardrey, *The Territorial Imperative* (N.Y., 1970), p. 155.

82. Maurice Halbwachs, *Morphologie Sociale* (Paris, 1970), p. 18.

83. Fustel de Coulanges, *The Ancient City,* pp. 120-166.

84. Ludwig Feuerbach, *The Essence of Christianity* (N.Y., 1957).

85. It was surprising that this was not grasped, for the insight that the evolving religious process has something to do with the development of the person hovered over the whole animist debate. It lurked in the assumptions of Tylor and Spencer with their studies of dreams, shadows, ghosts; in Wilhelm Wundt's idea that gods originate in heroes, and the whole revival of Euhemerist theory from its late Hellenistic sources; in Hegel's deflection of philosophy into the study of the evolution of religion as the emergence of spirit. (Hegel portrayed history as the evolution of succeeding social structures which permitted larger and larger numbers of people to become "free," i.e., individuated. *Philosophy of History* (N.Y., 1900).

86. Cf. Migene González-Wippler, *Santería* (Garden City, N.Y., 1975).

87. Cf. Douttée, *op. cit.* (Algiers, 1908), ch. 1.

88. *Themis,* ch. 1, "The Hymn of the Kouretes."

89. Robert Redfield, *The Primitive World and Its Transformations* (Ithaca, 1965), pp. 95, 101-104.

90. In ch. 6 of *The Courage To Be* (New Haven, 1959) Paul Tillich defines Protestant confidence as the courage to accept being accepted without necessarily being acceptable and possibly without someone who accepts. Absolute faith transcends theism and accepts the possibility that there is no god (or that god is non-being). (pp. 164-165). Bultmann, Bonhoeffer, Altziger and the like play with atheism in god-language; yet these are *popular* theologies consumed by masses of people seeking *personal resources.* One Bultmann critic spoke of leaving out "an angle thrown out for the half believer." (Austin Farrer, "An English Appreciation," pp. 212-223 in Rudolf Bultmann and Five Critics, *Kerygma and Myth,* N.Y., 1961, p. 212). Martin E. Marty speaks of "ersatz faiths" (*Varieties of Unbelief,* Garden City, N.Y., 1966), p. 56.

91. W. L. Warner, *A Black Civilization* (N.Y., 1937), ch. 7, p. 193ff.

92. R. M. and C. H. Berndt, cited in A. P. Elkin, *The Australian Aborigines* (Garden City, N.Y., 1964), p. 45-46.

93. A. P. Elkin, *The Australian Aborigines,* pp. 39-46.

94. The existence in Australia of a class of magicians complete with apprenticeship and collegia presents a problem in this formulation. For although they appear to be coopted into religious functions (they do ceremonial magic for the community, even lead religious rites), their initiation rites project archetypes universally found in more advanced magic, as Mauss has shown ("L'Origine des Pouvoirs Magiques . . .," 1904, *Oeuvres,* vol. 2, pp. 319-369). And their curious relationship to a cult of astral high gods (described by Eliade, *Australian Religions, An Introduction,* Ithaca & London, 1973, p. 129ff) needs explanation. But the simplest explanation would be diffusion, and Eliade himself leans toward it, insisting that Australia has not been hermetically sealed off from the rest of the world and is full of cultural influences from outside.

95. The schema will not fit exactly; and there are exceptions. For example, how about the advanced medical magic of shamanism found among Eskimos who live in bands? Did Eskimos regress to a band stage, after their migration northward, from a more advanced

tribal society further south, and retain medical magic as a defense against Arctic terror? Or did shamanism, which diffuses remarkably well, come to them from other societies further south that evolved into the tribal stage?

96. Fustel de Coulanges, *The Ancient City* (Garden City, N.Y., 1955), p. 128.

97. Gail Sheehy recently dramatized the perilous "passages" of adult life (*Passages,* N.Y., 1976). Earlier, Ruth Benedict spoke of "cultural discontinuities" which can be painful in modern societies lacking "rites of passage." (Ruth Benedict, "Continuities and Discontinuities in Cultural Conditioning," in Mead & Wolfenstein, eds., *Childhood in Contemporary Cultures,* N.Y., 1955, pp. 21–30).

98. Victor W. Turner, *The Forest of Symbols* (Ithaca, 1967), ch. 4; & *The Ritual Process* (London, 1969), chs. 3, 4, 5.

99. Mauss, "La Cohésion Sociale dans les Sociétés Polysegmentaires," 1931, *Oeuvres,* vol. 3, pp. 11–27.

100. In Australia, the initiation lodges are marked by frank hostility to women. This is less true of the Plains Indians societies, which often have women's auxiliaries. (Lowie, p. 105ff.)

101. Marcel Granet, *Chinese Civilization* (N.Y., 1958), Part II, Book 2, ch. 4.

102. Gregory Bateson, *Naven* (Stanford, 1958), pp. 6–22.

103. Franz Boas, *The Social Organization and Secret Societies of the Kwakuitl Indians . . .* (Washington, 1897).

104. Drucker, *Indians of the Northwest Coast,* p. 166.

105. Daryll Forde, "The Governmental Roles of Associations Among the Yako . . .," in Cohen & Middleton, eds., *Comparative Political Systems* (Garden City, N.Y., 1967), pp. 121–142.

106. "La Cohésion Sociale . . ." *op. cit., Oeuvres,* vol. III, pp. 11–27.

107. *The Sociology of Georg Simmel,* K. Wolff, ed. (Glencoe, Ill., 1950), Part 4, "The Secret and the Secret Society," chs. 1–4, pp. 307–378.

108. Harrison, *Themis,* ch. 1.

109. *Primitive Religion* (N.Y., 1924, 1970), ch. 1, "Crow Religion," pp. 3–32.

110. F. Boas, . . . *Secret Societies . . ., op. cit.*

111. Gurvitch, "La Magie, La Religion et Le Droit," in *La Vocation Actuelle . . .* vol. 2 (Paris, 1963).

112. Lowie, *Indians of the Plains,* pp. 105–113.

113. Drucker, *Indians of the Northwest Coast,* ch. 6, pp. 163–172.

114. Margaret Mead, *Sex and Temperament in Three Primitive Societies* (N.Y., 1950), pp. 53–64.

115. In Boas, ed., *General Anthropology* (N.Y., 1938), ch. 9, pp. 409–486.

116. I. Schapera in Fortes and Evans-Pritchard, *op. cit.,* pp. 70, 74.

117. *Sexual Politics,* pp. 48–50.

118. Lionel Tiger, *Men in Groups,* ch. 6. "Men Court Men: Imitations and Secret Societies."

119. Mircea Eliade, *Rites and Symbols of Initiation* (N.Y., 1958), pp. 2–4.

120. Cited in Gurvitch, *La Magie, la Religion et le Droit,* in *La Vocation Actuelle de la Sociologie.* (Paris, 1963), vol. II, pp. 160–170.

121. Lionel Tiger, *op. cit.,* ch. 2.

122. *Ibid.,* p. 173.

123. Werner Cohn (cited in Tiger, p. 170) also associates male-bonding clubs with magic.

124. Sigmund Freud, *Totem and Taboo* (N.Y., 1950), pp. 141–142.

125. Kate Millett, *Sexual Politics,* pp. 48–51.

126. Engels, *The Origin of the Family, Private Property and the State,* pp. 148–150.

127. Gurvitch, in *La Magie, La Religion et le Droit,* p. 158–170ff, *passim.*

128. I am referring to Plutarch's deciphering of common themes in different religions and myths in *The Moralia.*

129. Victor Turner, *The Forest of Symbols* (Ithaca, 1967), pp. 28–30.

130. *Magic and the Divine King,* cf. *The Golden Bough,* abr. ed. (N.Y., 1960), chs. 1–27.

131. Hocart, *Kings and Councillors* (Chicago, 1970), p. 34ff and *passim.*

132. There is a germ of truth in all these myths of social science. For the *brüderbund* that streams out of the initiation lodges to overturn the gentile religion is the perennial band of young Turks (or young Nazis) who everywhere spread fear with their wave-of-the future

fallacy and superannuate the old. In paleolithic communities, religious societies and even some trade unions, the headman is simply an elder. The "leader," by contrast, is often the one who can mobilize the young against the old, even though he may be of the older generation himself. The magical chief emerging from the initiation lodge lives on in the middle-aged executive today who, with the help perhaps of a youthful claque, wins the rat race among his own age group, and then fires, sidetracks, early retires, or drives out his own generation so that he can run the show like Boys Town with a staff of much younger, lower-paid people—and then *boasts* about what he has done to Madison Avenue and Wall Street. In military systems, this practice is institutionalized: "Up or out" means up fast or out early. Whenever this happens, this is a victory of the young over the old, of domination over kinship, of magic over religion, of power over authority, of class over segment, of society over community, of potlatch and money over reciprocity, of achievement over ascription and of war over peace. It is also the victory of the future over the past, of charisma over tradition, of progress over Eden. Society will now become increasingly "cofigurative" and even "prefigurative" rather than "postfigurative," to use Margaret Mead's terms; the old will learn from the young, the elders from the magicians; the end result cannot help but be an acceleration of social change.

133. Joseph Needham, *Science and Civilization in China,* vol. 2, section 10.

134. Eliade, *Yoga,* p. 92, etc.

135. Hans Jonas, *The Gnostic Religion* (Boston, 1963), p. 58ff and *passim.*

136. Jonas, *op. cit.,* ch. 8, pp. 174-205.

137. Drucker, *Indians of the Northwest Coast,* pp. 131-143.

138. Marcel Granet, *Chinese Civilization* (N.Y., 1958), Part II, Book 2, ch. 4, "Rivalries of Brotherhoods," pp. 194-204.

139. Needham's interpretation of Granet's method, in *Science and Civilization in China,* vol. 2, p. 119, etc.

140. Jane Ellen Harrison, *Themis* (Cambridge, 1927), pp. 86-88.

141. I refer to the minister in George Eliot's *Middlemarch,* who endlessly gathers research notes for an ambitious general theory of mythology, which he never writes.

142. Plato's *Phaedrus,* quoted R. Graves, *The White Goddess* (N.Y., 1948, 1972), p. 10.

143. Incidentally, what are dragons in these epics? In Java, in the East, they fight witches. They often bury themselves deep underground, guarding a magic treasure. As snake creatures, they are phallic and fertility symbols. Obviously they served some ancient good, such as fighting witches, conserving some treasure. But sometimes they run amok, lay waste the land, and have to be fought by heroes. Could dragons be symbols of sorcerers?

144. Reading accounts of Aeschylus' trilogy in Gilbert Murray's *The Rise of the Greek Epoch* (Oxford, 1934, 1967), Hugh Lloyd-Jones' *The Justice of Zeus* (Berkeley, 1971), Denis Donoghue's *Thieves of Power* (N.Y., 1974), and Aeschylus' extant *Prometheus Bound* (Oates and O'Neill, *The Complete Greek Drama,* N.Y., 1938, vol. 1), I think it likely that Aeschylus, in dramatizing a rationale for the state emerging from the Athenian tribal confederacy, drew on elements of earlier myths from the days of the competing confraternities. For all the characters in *Prometheus Bound* are specialized magicians; Zeus is all powerful but does not know the future; Prometheus is omniscient but not all powerful (perhaps he was a diviner); Hephaestus uses a magic craft, etc. All these magicians helped Zeus the war magician to overthrow the kinship order symbolized by Kronos; and now they are bound and tied by the new arts and domination they have created. Hence the ambiguity of "the Promethean" as a category, according to Donaghue: he is like Christ in one way, like Satan in another. Howard Nemerov views the Promethean as a western category expressing the rise of individual imagination and consciousness, with the presentiment that they are divine powers that are stolen, and are therefore, as Rilke wrote, "always against." (Howard Nemerov, *Figures of Thought,* Boston, 1978).

145. The victory of deliberate design over biological kinship goes back farther. Dumont states that the marriage alliance is primal. The contract creates the affinal tie, and a contractual structure whereby that tie is passed down through the generations. (Louis Dumont, "The Marriage Alliance," in Paul Bohannan and John Middleton, eds., *Marriage, Family and Residence,* Garden City, 1968, ch. 11.) This was recognized 100 years ago by Maine, who demonstrated that kinship was increasingly contractual, stretched by legal fictions (*Ancient Law,* London, 1861, republ. Boston, 1963, p. 126). In one place (p. 127) Maine seems to suggest that, in principle, social contracts preceded pure kin structures. A Kwakuitl

reductio ad absurdum demonstrates the degree to which marriage is not an extension of consanguinity, but an alliance. Drucker reports that Kwakuitl marriages touch off a potlatch in which the sibs try to return the bride price, and an exchange of valuable coppers thus begins. This exchange was such a valued goal that during the period of population shrinkage when there were few candidates for marriage, the Kwakuitl would arrange fictitious marriages, betrothing a young chief to the arm, leg or housepost of another chief so as to trigger the exchange of brideprice and the counterpotlatch ... in other words, so as to set up an exchange alliance. (Philip Drucker, *Indians of the Northwest Coast,* Garden City, 1963, pp. 144–145.)

146. Lowie, *Indians of the Plains,* p. 106.

147. Linton, *op. cit.,* p. 248.

148. Max Gluckman, "The Kingdom of the Zulu of South Africa," M. Fortes and E. E. Evans-Pritchard, eds., *African Political Systems* (London, 1940, 1966), pp. 25–55.

149. I. Schapera, "The Political Organization of the Ngwato of Bechuanaland Protectorate," in Fortes & Evans-Pritchard, *op. cit.,* pp. 56–82.

150. K. Oberg, "The Kingdom of Ankole in Uganda," in Fortes & Evans-Pritchard, *op. cit.,* pp. 121–164.

151. M. Fortes, "The Political System of the Tallensi of the Northern Territories of the Gold Coast," in Fortes & Evans-Pritchard, *op. cit.,* pp. 239–271 (esp. 259).

152. Gluckman, *op. cit.,* p. 31.

153. Schapera, *op. cit.,* p. 70.

154. K. Oberg, *op. cit.,* p. 145.

155. Fortes and Evans-Pritchard, *op.cit.,* Introd., p. 19.

156. Karl A. Wittfogel, *Oriental Despotism* (New Haven, 1957, 1967), p. 90.

157. Wittfogel, *Oriental Despotism,* pp. 87–96.

158. V. Gordon Childe, *What Happened in History* (London, 1942, 1964), pp. 174–5; *Man Makes Himself* (N.Y., 1951), pp. 83–4.

159. George E. Mendenhall, *The Tenth Generation* (Baltimore, 1973); see esp. "The Mask of Yahweh," ch. 2, pp. 32–68.

160. W. W. Tarn, *Hellenistic Civilization* (N.Y., 1961), pp. 355–7.

161. Ernst Bloch, "Man's Increasing Entry Into Religious Mystery" in *Man On His Own* (N.Y., 1970), pp. 147–240.

162. Childe, *Man Makes Himself,* p. 85, etc.

163. Weber, *The Sociology of Religion,* 1922 (Boston, 1964).

164. James Henry Breasted, *Development of Religion and Thought in Ancient Egypt* (Gloucester, Mass., 1970), pp. 94–95. See also comment in Lynn Thorndike, *op. cit.,* p. 10.

165. E. A. Wallis Budge, *Egyptian Magic* (N.Y., 1971), pp. 4, 5, 6, etc.

166. Henri Frankfort et al., *Before Philosophy* (London, 1951), *passim.*

167. Lynn Thorndike, *A History of Magic and Experimental Science,* vol. I, (N.Y., 1923), ch. 1.

168. Idries Shah, *Oriental Magic* (N.Y., 1973), ch. 5, "Egyptian Magic," pp. 35–49.

169. Shah, *Oriental Magic,* p. 36.

170. Breasted, *Development ... in Ancient Egypt,* "The Osirianization of the Hereafter," Lecture 5, pp. 142–164. Henri Frankfort disagrees with Breasted's sequence. The Egyptian masses always had an immortality hope, through identification with Pharoah who would lead them into the beyond. In times of instability, when there were conflicting Pharoahs, they transferred this hope and identification to Osiris, who had been a Pharoah symbol. In one book Frankfort's account of the imagery of so-called "immortality" suggests more poetic acceptance of a return to inanimate nature. (*Ancient Egyptian Religion,* N.Y., 1948), pp. 3–29.

171. J. G. Frazer, *The Divine King,* incorporated in *The Golden Bough* (N.Y., 1960, abridged). See chs. 1–27.

172. Hertz, Codrington and Cassirer suggest that ghosts derive from very strong individuals who are hard to forget after their death.

173. Perhaps, in Durkheimian terms, all this is just a projection of the immortality of the state, and perhaps there is some policy behind it.

174. Childe, *What Happened in History,* pp. 124–129.

175. Henri Frankfort, *Ancient Egyptian Religion* (N.Y., 1948, 1961), p. 9.

176. *What Happened in History*, p. 124.

177. *The Epic of Gilgamesh*, in Isaac Mendelson, *Religions of the Ancient Near East: Sumero-Akkadian Religious Texts and Ugaritic Epics* (N.Y., 1950), pp. 47–115. For an interesting commentary see Cyrus H. Gordon, *The Common Background of Greek and Hebrew Civilizations* (N.Y., 1965), pp. 60–85, 142–145, 267–273.

178. *What Happened in History*, pp. 84–5, 277; *Man Makes Himself*, p. 182.

179. *The Essence of Christianity, passim.*

180. *Man on His Own*, pp. 226ff, 233–238.

181. Arnold Toynbee, Somervell abridgment of vols. I–VI, *A Study of History* (N.Y., 1947), pp. 403–425.

182. Cf. James M. Beshers, *Urban Social Structure* (N.Y., 1962), pp. 3–8; Scott Greer, *The Emerging City* (N.Y., 1962), pp. 5–19. Kevin Lynch, in *The Image of the City* (Cambridge, 1960), shows residents have no image, either.

183. Max Weber, *The City* (N.Y., 1966), pp. 65–80.

184. Fustel de Coulanges, *The Ancient City*, 1864 (N.Y., 1955). Lewis Henry Morgan, *Ancient Society*, 1877 (N.Y., 1971). Henry Sumner Maine, *Ancient Law*, 1861 (Boston, 1963). To be discussed.

185. De Coulanges, *The Ancient City*, Book Third, ch. 1, "The Phratry and the Curia. The Tribe," pp. 117–119.

186. George E. Mendenhall, "Covenant Forms in Israelite Tradition," *Biblical Archeologist Reader 3* (Garden City, N.Y., 1970), pp. 25–53; "Tribe and State in the Ancient World," ch. 7 in *The Tenth Generation* (Baltimore, 1973), pp. 174–197.

187. De Coulanges, *op. cit.,* p. 124.

188. When Epaminondas defeated Sparta, he attempted to reduce her by *deurbanizing* her. This was far worse than Sparta's humiliation of Athens by requiring her to pull down her long walls. (Anyway, proud Sparta had no walls.) What it amounted to was breaking up the Spartan confederation that constituted the city and its empire, turning the Lacedaemonians and their allies back into a collection of separate tribes living in villages. J. B. Bury, *A History of Greece* (N.Y., Modern Library ed.), ch. 14, "The Hegemony of Thebes," pp. 576–612.

189. Of course there were exceptions, especially in the Syriac area, and the trouble they gave the empires is indicative of the strength of these communities. From Ebla to Roman times they kept rebuilding their confederations and cultic centers. Alexander had to spend time reducing them on his way to Egypt. On the ancient "temple states," cf. W. W. Tarn, *Hellenistic Civilization* (N.Y., 1961), p. 138ff.

190. Mircea Eliade, *Cosmos and History* (N.Y., 1954, 1959), p. 10ff.

191. Henry Sumner Maine, ch. 8 in *Ancient Law* (London, 1861; Boston 1963), pp. 237–294. Frederick Pollach (Introd. to Beacon ed. of Ancient Law, Boston, 1963) observes that with limited data then available Maine did not know that there were several types of Indian land tenure. Pramathanath Banerjea (*A Study of Indian Economics*, London, 1944), for example, distinguished the landlord joint villages from the "Raiyatwari villages" of Madras, Bombay and Central India, which had private small landholders with or without tenants. (The existence of separate endogamous castes within even small villages poses additional problems.) Maine hinted later, in *Village Communities and Miscellanies* (N.Y., 1881, pp. 65–174), that Indian villages were not that uniform. But in *Ancient Law* he had spoken also of *trend:* he claimed that the trend in India (and Russia) was always toward joint ownership; whereas the trend in the Graeco-Roman cities was away from it.

192. "The religious element in the East tended to get the better of the military and political" (*Ancient Law*, p. 10). Similar quotes throughout. He is referring to the crushing of the Kshatriyas, the rise of Brahmins and emperors, etc. That is one way of looking at it. Indian villages, split by castes, with the gentile religion overlaid by Hindu theosophy, were self-determining only at the level of the village Panchayat. They were tax-farmed helot or serf communities milked by empires; the families could not confederate. At best, sub-castes as corporations could negotiate slightly hypergamous marriage alliances to raise their caste prestige.

193. *The Ancient City*, Book Second, ch. 6 "The Right of Property," pp. 60–71.

194. Wittfogel, *op. cit.,* pp. 78–81.

195. Eliane Massonneau, *Le Crime de Magie et le Droit Romain* (Paris, 1933).

196. Massonneau, Part II, ch. 2.

197. Morton Smith, *Jesus the Magician* (N.Y., 1978), pp. 21–80.

198. E. O. James, *Comparative Religion* (N.Y., 1961), "Greece and the Mystery Religions," ch. 5, pp. 119–140. The Mysteries were an old corn god cult of Eleusis in Attica, going back to Mycenaean times and predating the political religions of the Attic Confederacy. In the new version encouraged by the "tyrant" Pisastratus, the perennial "rebirth" symbolism of initiation (which had already been magically extrapolated to agriculture by the ancient Eleusinians) underwent a further "translation toward the literal" (so typical of magic) in promises of literal rebirth in immortality.

199. Weber, *The City* (N.Y., 1966), pp. 99–104.

200. Henry Sumner Maine, *Ancient Law,* ch. 1, cf. p. 2ff.

201. *Ancient Law,* pp. 21–27ff.

202. E. Adamson Hoebel, *The Law of Primitive Man* (N.Y., 1954, 1968), pp. 23–25ff.

203. Thus Cardozo writes that law is a "principle or rule of conduct so established as to justify a prediction with reasonable certainty that it will be enforced by the courts if its authority is challenged." (B. N. Cardozo, *The Growth of Law,* New Haven, 1924, p. 52, quoted in Hoebel, p. 22.) Or Holmes: "The prophecies of what the courts will do in fact, and nothing more pretentious, are what I mean by law." (O. W. Holmes, Jr., "The Path of the Law," *Harvard Law Review,* 10:457, 1897, quoted in Hoebel, p. 22). Or Max Radin: "But there is an infallible test for recognizing whether an imaginary course of conduct is lawful or unlawful. This infallible test in our system is to submit the question to the judgment of a court." (Quoted in Hoebel, p. 23). Hoebel thinks this approach sounder than using the definitions of natural law thinkers, or idealist definitions like those of Austin, or the legal positivist definitions that emphasize logic and "pure science" of law.

204. A. R. Radcliffe-Brown, Preface to Fortes & Evans-Pritchard, eds., *African Political Systems* (London, 1940, 1966), pp. xi–xxiii.

205. It is true that even in Zandeland there exist separate courts and the Azande distinguish between grievances that should go to court and those that go to the witch complex. But it is easy to imagine the courts grew out of these more primitive grievance procedures. Hoebel notes the criminal justice system in Zandeland serves the nobles, the conquest stratum, implying that the witch complex is the proto-legal system of the people. (Hoebel, *op. cit.,* ch. 10, pp. 257–274.)

206. Bronislaw Malinowski, *The Foundations of Faith and Morals* (London, 1936, 1969), pp. 11, 25, etc.

207. A. P. Elkin, *The Australian Aborigines* (Garden City, N.Y., 1964), p. 45.

208. E.g., in *Structural Anthropology* (N.Y., 1963); in "The Story of Asdiwal," ch. 9 in *Structural Anthropology Volume Two* (N.Y., 1976).

209. Maitland has shown how British common law was built up from the foundation of constitutional law. *The Constitutional History of England* (Cambridge, 1950), *passim.*

210. Edward H. Levy, *An Introduction to Legal Reasoning* (Chicago, 1948, 1961), p. 3.

211. It is more like the consensus-bending enthymenes of rhetoric, which must be certified by the audience.

212. A. M. Hocart, *Kings and Councillors* (Chicago & London, 1970), ch. 10, "The Law," pp. 128–155.

213. Georges Dumézil, *Les Dieux des Indo-Européens* (Paris, 1952). See also C. Scott Littleton, *The New Comparative Mythology* (Berkeley, 1973).

214. Mauss, Davy, Huvelin, Durkheim, Fauconnet and others in the French school developed many of their ideas through studies of Roman law, and in this they followed Maine. He showed that Roman law itself consisted in part in the reflexive study of law by itself, with successive praetors' edicts and later commentaries on them. The earliest theory of what law is derived this way, i.e., the "natural law" ideas that emerged from successive jurisconsults' comments on *ius gentium,* the "equity" or exceptional law applied to colonies of foreign traders at Rome. But Maine's big step was to turn away from natural law explanations that still colored *modern* theorists like Bentham and Austin and use the historical method. And where historical forms were hard to understand, he frequently suggested looking for religious origins, an approach developed with great penetration by the French school. Many of the issues and subjects the Durkheimians studied were introduced by Maine: Maine pioneered the analysis of the gentile constitution of Greece and Rome, which de Coulanges perfected a few years later, and on which Weber in turn built *The City* (not to mention the influence on Morgan and Engels). He raised questions about the Roman *mancipium* which

Davy, Mauss and the others would pursue. This was a ritual conveyance which enabled sacred (family) property to be sold. Maine thought the first contracts developed from it (as *delayed* sales), and the first wills, too (through the "legal fiction" of regarding the will as a "sale" to the heir). Like the French, Maine often traced the growth of laws out of primal customs which were religious. However, he gave no attention to the intermediary stage of magical sanctions, and as a result had to confess in several passages that he could not explain why private property or individual rights were respected when they *first* emerged.

215. Even Maine's emphasis on religious origins was challenged: e.g., by A. S. Diamond (*Primitive Law,* London, 1935), who said ancient extant legal codes were innocent of religion (cited in Hoebel, p. 258). Julius E. Lips' chapter on primitive government and law in the influential Boas textbook *General Anthropology* (N.Y., 1938, ch. 10, pp. 487–534) makes no mention of magic, emphasizes economic origins instead and is critical of the French "deductive method" in tracing origins of law. Malinowski repeatedly suggests (in *Crime and Custom in Savage Society*) that the Durkheimians overestimate religious sanctions, which are not very strong (p. 57ff) and are offset by magical loopholes (e.g., pp. 80–81). Reciprocity (i.e., economic) sanctions are what really cause primitive "law" to be obeyed. Some later texts on primitive law, like Max Gluckman, *Politics, Law and Ritual in Tribal Society* (N.Y., 1965), and Hoebel's *Law of Primitive Man,* do cite, if not the Durkheimians, British anthropological fieldwork inspired by them which demonstrated magical sanctions enforcing early law (e.g., Evans-Pritchard's study of Azande justice is discussed, pp. 254–6).

216. The Durkheim school took up the matter eagerly, for it had inherited from Durkheim himself the 19th-century European preoccupation with explaining how individuals had come to be. All the great social distinctions of classical social theory – Spencer's "industrial vs. military society", Tönnies on "community vs. society", Maine's "from status to contract" – really turned on distinguishing the kind of social structure that made individuals possible. An increasing number of critics are coming to recognize that Durkheim's real subject was the emergence of the individual – these include Lukes, Robert Nisbet, Tiryakian, Thomas Luckmann, Joseph Neyer; and some older critics did too, like Alpert, Imogen Seger and Charles Elmer Gehlke. And Durkheim had pointed toward the evolution of law as his data of choice for understanding this process. Some of the best sociological research has in fact been done by using legal codes (instead of, say, the artifacts of questionnaire construction) as data: e.g., Durkheim's *Division of Labor In Society,* Bouglé's *Essais Sur le Régime de Castes,* Mauss' study of *The Gift,* some of Weber's shorter pieces, and so on.

217. E. Westermarck, *The Origin and Development of Moral Ideas* (London, 1908), pp. 59, 69. Cited by Frazer in *Psyche's Task* (London, 1913), p. 32.

218. E. R. Dodds, *The Greeks and the Irrational* (Berkeley, 1951, 1973), pp. 194, 204, 206.

219. Angus finds a growth in magical inscriptions of all kinds, cf. *The Mystery Religions* (London, 1928; N.Y., 1975), pp. 64, 94ff, etc.

220. 1900, reproduced in Lévy-Bruhl, ed., *Etudes d'Histoire du Droit Commercial Romain* (Paris, 1929), pp. 219–272, cited by Gurvitch, *La Magie, La Religion et le Droit,* p. 133ff.

221. Gurvitch, *op. cit.,* pp. 133–140.

222. J. G. Frazer, *Psyche's Task* (London, 1913), pp. 20–43.

223. *Ibid.,* ch. 4, pp. 44–110.

224. *Ibid.,* ch. 5, pp. 111–153.

225. On the one hand, Gurvitch wrote that Frazer's examples all *presupposed* the existence of moral values already. And he had actually neglected outright contributions magic made to the *content* of law (for example, mystical ideas about the "worth" of the individual developed from mana concepts). And on the other hand, Fauconnet observed that magical protection was feeble; it protected murderers as well as victims, for example; and it was not until a new advance in *religion* made homicide a sin that protection was socially guaranteed.

226. P. Huvelin, "Magie et Droit Individuel," *L'Année Sociologique,* 1905–1906, pp. 1–47.

227. Huvelin, "Magie et Droit Individuel," p. 13.

228. *Ibid.,* p. 31.

229. *Ibid.,* p. 34.

230. Individual law itself can be a form of sorcery. H. D. F. Kitto reminds us of the aggressive side, of lawsuits, and reports that the Athenians were extremely litigious and burdened one another's lives with fearsome suits at law. Kitto, *The Greeks* (N.Y., 1950).

231. Huvelin, *op. cit.,* p. 44–45. "Individual law" covers many branches. Maine showed how *the law of persons* derived from the *patria potestas* of the Roman religion and the legal fictions used in it, according to which women were defined as daughters of their husbands and wards of their sons, foreigners could become brothers and agnates by adoption and slaves became members of the family because they were admitted to the sacrifices. ("Clients" were freedmen who continued membership in the family religion they had joined as slaves, according to Maine.) The law of persons is an important prop for the individual. Consider, for example, the statuses of "citizens," ex-citizens, minors, wards, legal incompetents, etc. Or how vital citizenship or its lack proved to be in Europe during the Hitler period (as Hannah Arendt and Reinhold Bendix have shown). Citizenship in the ancient world originally meant membership in the religion of the tribal confederation.

232. Fustel de Coulanges, *The Ancient City,* pp. 60–72.

233. Mauss & Hubert, "Introduction à l'Analyse de Quelques Phénomènes Religieux," *Revue de l'Histoire des Religions,* 58 (1906), 163–203; repub. as the preface of Hubert & Mauss, *Mélanges d'Histoire des Religions* (Paris, 1909); repub. in vol. I, Mauss *Oeuvres* (Paris, 1968), pp. 3–39.

234. As they explain in the prologue to the *Esquisse;* cf. English ed. *A General Theory of Magic* (Boston, 1972), pp. 7–10.

235. Mauss, *Oeuvres,* vol. I, pp. 24–25.

236. "In the shelter of magic not only are juridical audacities possible, but also experimental initiatives. Savants are the sons of magicians." (*Ibid.,* p. 25, my translation.)

237. In 1896 he had written a longish paper entitled "La Religion et les Origines du Droit Penal d'Après un Livre Recent" (by Steinmetz), in which, in the manner of the Durkheim of *The Division of Labor in Society,* he traced the evolution of some penal law out of religion. Repub. in *Oeuvres,* vol. 2, pp. 651–698.

238. Republished in Lévi-Strauss, ed., *Marcel Mauss Sociologie et Anthropologie* (Paris, 1950, 1966): *Essais Sur le Don Forme et Raison de l'Echange Dans les Sociétés Archaiques,* pp. 145–280; English ed. *The Gift* (N.Y., 1967).

239. Mauss, "Une Ancienne Forme de Contrat Chez les Thraces," 1921, *Revue des Etudes Greques,* now in vol. 3, *Oeuvres,* pp. 35–43.

240. Georges Davy, *La Foi Jurée* (Paris, 1922); the subtitle is *Etude Sociologique du Problème du Contrat.*

241. In the Introduction to *The Gift* (Norton paper ed., N.Y., 1967, p. 3), Mauss writes: "This work is part of the wider research carried out by M. Davy and myself upon the archaic forms of contract, so we may start summarizing what we have found so far." He then cites, in a footnote, both Davy's *La Foi Jurée* and his own "Une Forme Archaique de Contrat chez les Thraces," in *Revue des Etudes Greques,* 1921 (now republ. in *Oeuvres,* vol. 3, pp. 35–43). *La Foi Jurée* was Davy's Ph.D. dissertation; it was published as a book a year later, in 1922. The implication is perhaps that Mauss collaborated on research for it. *The Gift* in turn was published about one year after that, in *Année Sociologique,* 2nd series, 1923–24, as a long journal article, and did not appear in book form until Lévi-Strauss's posthumous collection of some of Mauss' essays in 1950, entitled *Marcel Mauss Sociologie et Anthropologie.*

242. See bibliography of Boas on the Kwakuitl at end of Franz Boas, "Literature, Music and Dance," in Boas, ed., General Anthropology (N.Y., 1938), ch. 12, pp. 589–608. Also Helen Codere, ed., Franz Boas, *Kwakuitl Ethnography* (Chicago, 1966, 1975), pp. 423–432.

243. *The Elementary Structures of Kinship.* Davy is thanked for his help, p. xxvi.

244. See Stephen G. Popper, *World Hypothesis* (Berkeley, 1942, 1970).

245. Turner, *Schism and Continuity in an African Tribe* (Manchester, 1957).

246. William J. Goode, *World Revolution and Family Patterns* (N.Y., 1963, 1970), p. 238ff.

247. Strangers, too, are handled this way; in some Australian tribes strangers must be immediately adopted or rejected (some say, killed).

248. Maine thought that contracts, wills and exchanges all go together, with both wills

and contracts growing out of *mancipium,* the special Roman rite for conveyances. The Durkheimians in effect extend the cluster, showing that marriage alliances as well as economic exchanges and contracts go together. But for them the ancestor of all these things is the social contract that united groups. *Mancipium,* after all, is just a ceremony needed to desacralize collective property so it can be traded. Maybe this form in Roman law was creative, but it was hardly the origin of the whole development. It seems in fact to correspond to the magical phase, in between religion and law. For is not *mancipium* a kind of social magic to *desacralize* property that is too religious to trade? With the help of *mancipium,* property began circulating rapidly, at potlatch speed, and bred social revolutions in Italy as the peasantry were bought out.

249. It is not an exclusively primitive idea. One model for the strong nuclear force in the fifties supposed that particles were held together by continual exchange of mesons. (Today gravitons, vector bosons and gluons are supposed to power gravitation, weak nuclear force and "color force" by similar exchanges.)

250. Childe, *What Happened in History; Man Makes Himself.* Werner Sombart, *The Quintessence of Capitalism* (London, 1915); *Luxury and Capitalism* (Ann Arbor, 1967); Jane Jacobs, *The Economy of Cities* (N.Y., 1969), pp. 18-20ff.

251. Philip Drucker, *Indians of the Northwest Coast* (N.Y., 1955, 1963), pp. 131-143.

252. R. F. Fortune, *Sorcerers of Dobu* (N.Y., 1963), p. 144, etc.

253. Ruth Bunzel, "The Economic Organization of Primitive Peoples," in Boas, ed., *General Anthropology* (N.Y., 1938), ch. 8, pp. 327-408, esp. p. 349.

254. Paul Radin, *Primitive Religion* (N.Y., 1937, 1957), ch. 3, pp. 48-58.

255. Bunzel summarizes: Property and exchange may convey magical-social power, but in a variety of ways— by making domination of others possible (e.g., the Chuckchee); by purchasing women (certain African tribes); by simply reinforcing prestige (Kwakuitl). But in one way or another, if property and trade do convey power, then what is traded is magical, i.e., some mana symbol of social power. (*op.cit.,* pp. 341ff., 349, 363-7.)

256. Bunzel, *op. cit.,* p. 398.

257. E. A. H. Blunt, *The Caste System of Northern India* (Oxford, 1931). Jajaminis, fixed supplier-customer relationships, are even *inheritable.* Cf. ch. 13, "The Economic Aspect of Caste."

258. Bunzel, *op. cit.,* p. 366.

259. Bronislaw Malinowski, *Argonauts of the Western Pacific* (N.Y., 1961), ch. 21, pp. 494-508.

260. Trade between nations in the ancient Middle East established publics out of which later emerged confederations with closer ties. By contrast, Lévi-Strauss has shown how in the crumbling civilization of India, "withdrawal of reciprocity" between tribes and nations helped create the endogamous castes with their magical barriers. *Elementary Structures of Kinship,* p. 417ff.

261. John R. Commons, *Legal Foundations of Capitalism* (N.Y., 1924).

262. Maine, Davy, Mauss, Gurvitch all have passages studying *mancipium.*

263. Of course this is easier for Gurvitch to do because of his forced distinction of mana from the sacred. The latter is the source of religion while mana ideas are purely magical to him.

264. Lévy-Bruhl, "Quelques Problèmes du Très Ancien Droit Romain," 1934, pp. 144, quoted in Gurvitch, *op. cit.,* p. 137-138.

265. *Ibid.,* Gurvitch, pp. 137-138, my translation.

266. *The Gift,* p. 60.

267. The religion-to-magic-to-law sequence is not explicit in *The Gift.* Two things obscure it. 1. Mauss here introduces his idea of the "total social fact." (pp. 76-81) He is tired of unilinear approaches such as economic determinism, or even religious determinism. He insists that important institutions are economic, political, magical and religious all at once. But Mauss is still describing a sequence in which total social facts that are *mainly* religious, are succeeded by total social facts that are *mainly* magical, etc. 2. Mauss gives most attention to the *first* stage, the *religious* stage of total prestations (using evidence from the later magical potlatching stage mainly to infer and reconstruct it, for total prestations are prehistoric). The legal stage is barely discussed. But there are passages in which he explicitly refers to transitional sanctions as magical, or implicitly adumbrates part of a religion-to-

magic-to-law sequence (e.g., p. 48). Gurvitch insists that *The Gift* is largely about magic, while Karady claims that Mauss is trying to get away from his earlier emphasis on magic in it. I think the solution is that Mauss is building on his magical studies to show how religion and magic together build up a new order of society, based on division of labor and a legal framework, which then moves away from sacral-magical institutions.

The Gift is really volume two in a half-century-long French trilogy on the prehistory of "organic solidarity" (the division of labor). In *Division of Labor* Durkheim imagined that tiny, self-sufficient "polysegmental" clans would break down under population pressures in cities, where sheer crowding would break weak cognitive walls and overpopulation would force specialization for survival. But this was to derive social progress from disorder. Mauss instead portrays the division of labor arising out of systematic exchanges between bands that unite to form phratries and tribes. So the process is orderly and occurs earlier than the urban stage; it begins at the transition to tribes. Later, Lévi-Struass would stress the conscious human thought that went into devising contracts between groups, with specialization in economic function growing out of marital alliances at a still earlier stage. Much of French twentieth-century social thought can be understood if we keep in mind this Durkheim-Mauss-Lévi-Strauss trilogy on organic solidarity, for which Davy's bold speculations on social contracts provide the master key. In it we catch glimpses of the magical foundations of economic civilization.

We can tell Mauss is really following Davy's religion-magic-law sequence by looking at the way his paper is laid out. He moves from "hua" (ch. 1) and "kula" (pp. 18-31) to potlatch (pp. 31-37) to Roman law (pp. 47-53), in a way that suggests many societies go through these three stages: 1. Trobriand kula trade is used as a demonstration of the original *religious* framework, when "total prestations" between whole groups solemnized an alliance. (Actually, no pure total prestations still exist; kula is already somewhat competitive, transitional to potlatching; but with the help of Samoan *hua* ideas Mauss *infers* the earlier stage of total prestations from kula.) 2. Kwakuitl *potlatching* is an example of more agonistic individual exchanges with *magic* sanctions. 3. Then Mauss briefly studies early Roman law of conveyances.

The original religious contracts entailed three exchange obligations: obligation to give, obligation to receive and obligation to repay. A break with any caused war. How close together are festival and war, feast and battle, Mauss observed. (Many examples come to mind—such as the ambushes and assassinations that break out at feasts in barbarian epics like the *Niebelungenlied*.) Gift-giving prevents war by establishing new relationships. In early trade one always has partners in jajamini, silent trade or kula; the partners are the people with whom you want to form an alliance. Neoclassical economists today still write of abstract markets run by a hidden hand, but American firms abroad know better: they give "gifts" to set up trading partners! Following Mauss, Wilton S. Dillon in *Gifts and Nations* (The Hague, 1968) tried to show how American gift giving in the postwar Marshall Plan helped to create an Atlantic community. (Richard M. Titmuss in *The Gift Relationship* [N.Y., 1971], showed how blood donations create communities in blood banks.)

268. Eliane Massonneau, *Le Crime de Magie et le Droit Romain* (Paris, 1933), ch. 2.

269. Massonneau, *Le Crime de Magie . . .,* "The Main Names for Magicians," ch. 3.

270. *Ibid.,* Part II, "The Repression of Magic."

271. Morton Smith, *Clement of Alexandria and a Secret Gospel of Mark; Jesus the Magician,* chs. 4, 5, etc.

272. Massonneau, *op. cit.,* p. 119.

273. Maitland quotes Maine: "So great is the ascendency of the Law of Actions in the infancy of Courts of Justice, that substantive law has at first the look of being gradually secreted in the interstices of procedure." Maine, *Early Law and Custom,* p. 389; quoted by F. W. Maitland, *The Forms of Action at Common Law* (Cambridge, 1968), p. 1.

274. Mauss, "Les Origines de la Notion de Monnaie'" *Oeuvres,* 1914, vol. II, p. 106-112.

275. "Débats Sur les Fonctions Sociales de la Monnaie," *L'Année Sociologique,* 1934, *Oeuvres,* vol. II, p. 116-120.

276. William H. Desmonde, *Magic, Myth and Money: The Origin of Money in Religious Ritual* (N.Y., 1962), ch. 1.

277. "Sur la Notion de dzô en Afrique Centrale, in *L'Année Sociologique,* 1910, republished in Mauss, *Oeuvres,* vol. 2, p. 112-113.

278. Jane Jacobs, *The Economy of Cities* (N.Y., 1969), ch. 1, pp. 3–48.

279. In the 1914 essay on magicians' initiations, Mauss, *Oeuvres*, vol. II, p. 319ff.

280. Ernest Mandel, *Marxist Economic Theory*, vol. I (N.Y., 1970), p. 75.

281. Mauss, *The Gift*, p. 43.

282. Malinowski, *Argonauts . . .*, p. 90.

283. Mauss, *Oeuvres*, vol. II, pp. 106–120; *The Gift*, pp. 43–45.

284. Cf. Evans-Pritchard, *ops. cits.*, etc.

285. Simon Kuznets, *Economic Change* (N.Y., 1953), pp. 152–158.

286. Marx and Engels, *The Communist Manifesto*, in Max Eastman, ed., *Capital, The Communist Manifesto and Other Writings by Karl Marx* (N.Y., 1932), cf. p. 324.

287. Ernst Nagel & James R. Newman, *Gödel's Proof* (N.Y., 1964), p. 99ff.

288. Walter Heller reported on this research to the Joint Economic Committee of the U.S. Congress in 1959: *Hearings Before the Joint Economic Committee (. . . Maximum Employment . . . Adequate Rate of Growth . . . Stability of the Price Level . . .)*, 86th Congress, first session, S.Con.Res. 13, Part 9A pp. 2988ff. A special issue of *The Journal of Political Economy*, supplement: Oct., 1962, vol. LXX, no. 5, part 2, *Investment in Human Beings*, was also devoted to it.

289. Thorstein Veblen, *The Place of Science in Modern Civilization and Other Essays* (N.Y., 1919).

290. Veblen, *The Theory of the Leisure Class* (N.Y., 1899, 1931).

291. Veblen, *The Instinct of Workmanship* (N.Y., 1914, 1942).

292. Veblen, *The Engineers and the Price System* (N.Y., 1921, 1963).

293. Veblen, *The Theory of Business Enterprise* (N.Y., 1904, 1932).

294. George Bernard Shaw, *Back to Methuselah* (N.Y., 1947).

295. Margaret Mead summarized the contemporary American attitude: Illness is no reflection on the individual, provided he does his best to get better.

296. Thomas Luckmann, *The Invisible Religion* (N.Y., 1967). He identifies the old philosophical problem of the "transcendence" of the "I," which goes back to Augustine, with the spiritual transcendence of souls that religion allegedly effects.

297. Mauss, "Une Catégorie de l'Esprit Humain: La Notion de Personne, Celle de 'Moi'," in Lévi-Strauss, ed., *Marcel Mauss Sociologie et Anthropologie* (Paris, 1950, 1966), pp. 333–364.

298. The devotions, *imitatios* and inner dialogues associated with it often enable quite simple people to round out lives of decency and fortitude.

299. Roger Caillois, *L'Homme et le Myth* (Paris, 1938), ch. 1, *passim*.

300. In Postulate Nine. The *self* is a real biosocial entity. It has a somewhat shadowy texture, but obviously something is there. The *Person Category* is a social idea about this something. In our time it is a *collection* of ideas, terms and concepts. I used these terms to construct a model of nomenclature of the actual self.

301. Emile Bréhier, *The History of Philosophy*, some volumes: *The Hellenic Age* (Chicago, 1963, 1965); *The Hellenistic and Roman Age* (Chicago, 1965); *The Seventeenth Century* (Chicago, 1966).

302. John Herman Randall, Jr., *The Career of Philosophy* (N.Y., vol. I, 1962, 1970; vol. II, 1965, 1970).

303. Frederick Copleston, *A History of Philosophy*, numerous volumes (Garden City, N.Y., paperback editions, 1964).

304. W. Windleband, *History of Ancient Philosophy* (N.Y., 1900, 1966).

305. Bruno Snell, *The Discovery of the Mind* (N.Y., 1960).

306. A. E. Taylor, *Socrates* (N.Y., 1954).

307. A. D. Nock, *Conversion* (Oxford, 1933, 1961).

308. John Herman Randall, Jr., *The Making of the Modern Mind* (N.Y., 1940).

309. James Harvey Robinson, *The Mind In the Making* (N.Y., 1921, 1950).

310. On persisting "body ego" ideas cf. Robert Fliess, *Ego and Body Ego*, vol. I (N.Y., 1961); Paul Federn, *Ego Psychology and the Psychoses* (N.Y., 1952); Paul Schilder, *Medical Psychology* (N.Y., 1953), p. 229.

311. A translation appeared in *Psychoanalytic Review:* "A Category of the Human Spirit," vol. 55, no. 3 (1968), pp. 457–481.

312. Lucien Lévy-Bruhl, *The Soul of the Primitive* (Chicago, 1966, 1971), chs. 1, 5, etc.

313. Lucien Lévy-Bruhl, *Primitive Mentality* (Boston, 1966), pp. 129–131, 445–446.

314. Emile Durkheim, *The Elementary Forms of Religious Life* (London, 1915), Book II, chs. 1, 2, 3, 4, 8, 9.

315. B. Spencer and J. Gillen, *The Northern Tribes of Central Australia* (London, 1904). Persistence of reincarnation ideas in India perhaps reflects a society regressed to something close to tribalism: endogamous subcastes withdrawing from reciprocity with each other through particularistic rites and totem-like purity barriers. Lévi-Strauss points to "withdrawal of reciprocity" in Hindu caste formation in *The Elementary Structures of Kinship* (Boston, 1969), ch. 25, pp. 406–421.

316. Durkheim keeps stressing that the first idea of the person was precisely what was most *impersonal* in him, his clan positional name. The generation of the personal out of the impersonal is one of the dozen strikingly *dialectical* ideas in Durkheim, usually overlooked, which operate his theory of the generation of the individual from society.

317. Durkheim, *op. cit.*, Book II, ch. 4, "The Individual Totem and the Sexual Totem," esp. pp. 157–164.

318. Robert A. Nisbet, *The Sociology of Emile Durkheim* (N.Y., 1974), pp. 55–61.

319. *Mind, Self and Society* (Chicago, 1934, 1963).

320. Durkheim, *The Elementary Forms . . .*, Book II, ch. 4.

321. The Roman citizen now has the right to the *nomen, praenomen* and *cognomen.* The *praenomen* designated the birth order of the ancestor who begot him (Primus, Quintus, etc.); it seems merely positional but the point, I think, is that now it is retained, as his family membership is retained. The *nomen* is the sacred name (*nomen* is *numen*) of the *gens*—but remember at Rome this is already a very large group, several thousand people of related conjugal families. Mauss does not tell us whether Roman youth received curial and tribal names as well, the way Roman Catholics in our society get confirmational names at puberty. He concentrates on the *cognomen* which had another history. *Cognomen,* the appelation one could bear, got confused with the *imago,* the mask of wax moulded on the face of a dead ancestor. The *cognomen* also ran in families. The Roman Senate, Mauss claimed, was regarded as made up of a fixed number of *cognomenes* representing the images of famous ancestors.

322. Robert Ernest Hume, Intro. to *The Thirteen Principal Upanishads* (London, 1921, N.Y., 1971), "An Outline of the Philosophy of the Upanishads," pp. 1–72.

323. Heinrich Zimmer, *Myths and Symbols in Indian Art and Civilization* (Princeton, 1972), pp. 51–52.

324. Max Weber, "The Social Psychology of the World Religions" and "India: The Brahman and the Castes," chs. 11 & 16 in Gerth and Mills eds., *From Max Weber* (N.Y., 1958), pp. 267–301, 396–415.

325. Margaret Cormack, *The Hindu Woman* (N.Y., 1953).

326. Gardner Murphy, *In the Minds of Men* (N.Y., 1953).

327. V. S. Naipaul, *India, A Wounded Civilization* (N.Y., 1977), cf. ch. 5, pp. 101–9ff.

328. Right down to what Mauss somewhere called "la position de la main dans la miction." Cf. "Les Techniques de Corps," in *Marcel Mauss Sociologie et Anthropologie,* pp. 365–388.

329. The best source on this is E. R. Dodds, *The Greeks and the Irrational* (Berkeley, 1951, 1973). It, and the new right-hemisphere research, seem to be inspirations for Julian Jaynes' *The Origin of Consciousness in the Breakdown of the Bicameral Mind* (N.Y., 1976).

330. Cf. Paul Cloché, *La Dislocation d'Une Empire* (Paris, 1959); M. Cary, *A History of the Greek World 323-146 B.C.* (London, 1932, 1972); W. W. Tarn, *Hellenistic Civilization* (N.Y., 1961); J. B. Bury *et al., The Hellenist Age* (N.Y., 1923, 1970); Bury, *A History of Greece* (N.Y., Modern Library ed.), chs. 26–28.

331. Maine refers to the strengthening of family, property and self by extension of Roman citizenship—with it went the *patria potestas.* (*Ancient Law,* pp. 136, 140–144.)

332. On similarities and differences, cf. Rudolf Otto, *Mysticism East and West* (N.Y., 1932, 1960).

333. Colin Morris, *The Discovery of the Individual: 1050-1200* (N.Y., 1972).

334. Michel Foucault, *The History of Sexuality,* vol. I (N.Y., 1978), pp. 57–67.

335. Henry Charles Lea, *The Inquisition of the Middle Ages,* Selection: "Its Organization and Operation" (N.Y., 1954, 1967), pp. 61, 75, etc.

336. Secondary demonstrations are also provided in popular culture by dramatizations of the jury trial and psychoanalytic processes. Films from "Spellbound" to "Sybil"

dramatize the psychiatric transcript to teach the infinitely recoverable and determinate nature of self's experience. Concepts of great subtlety about self experience (some derived from the confessional) are incorporated into the legal process: e.g., the McNaughton rule.

337. Papers by Benjamin Nelson which I consulted:

i. *The Idea of Usury* (Chicago, 1949, 1969).

ii. "Weber's Protestant Ethic: Its Origins, Wanderings and Foreseeable Futures," ch. 2 in *Beyond the Classics?* (N.Y., 1973), C. Y. Glock and P. E. Hammond, eds., pp. 71–130.

iii. "Actors, Directors, Roles, Cues, Meanings, Identities: Further thoughts on Anomie," 1964, *Psychoanalytic Review,* 51: 1, 135–160.

iv. "The Games of Life and the Dances of Death," in Edith Wyschogrod, ed., *The Phenomenon of Death* (N.Y., 1973), pp. 113–131.

v. "The Omnipresence of the Grotesque," *Psychoanalytic Review,* vol. 57, no. 3 (1970), pp. 505–518.

vi. "The Future of Illusions," in Robert Endleman, ed., *Personality and Social Life* (N.Y., 1967), pp. 563–578.

vii. "Civilizational Complexes and Intercivilizational Encounters," *Sociological Analysis,* vol. 34, no. 2 (Summer, 1973), p. 79ff.

viii. "Communities, Societies, Civilizations: Post-Millennial Views on the Masks and Faces of Change," in Manfred Staley, ed., *Social Development: Critical Perspectives* (N.Y., 1972), pp. 105–133.

ix. *"Eros, Logos, Nomos, Polis:* Their Changing Balances and the Vicissitudes of Communities and Civilizations," in A. W. Eister, ed., *Changing Perspectives in the Scientific Study of Religion* (London, 1974), 85–111.

x. "Scholastic Rationales of 'Conscience,' Early Modern Crises of Credibility and the Scientific-Technocultural Revolutions of the 17th and 20th Centuries," 1968, in *Journal for the Scientific Study of Religion,* VII, 2: 157–177.

xi. "Perspectives on the Therapeutic in the Context of Contemporary Sociology: A Dialogue Between Benjamin Nelson and Dennis Wrong," 1972 in *Salmagundi,* vol. 20 (Summer-Fall, 1972), pp. 160–195.

xii. "Self-Images and Systems of Spiritual Direction in the History of European Civilization," from S. Z. Klausnor, ed., *The Quest for Self-Control* (N.Y., 1965), pp. 49–103.

xiii. "The Legend of the Divine Surety and the Jewish Money Lender," (with Joshua Starr) *Annuaire de L'Institut de Philologie et d'Histoire Orientales et Slaves,* vol. VII (1939-1944), Brussels, pp. 289–338.

338. Nelson, "Self Images and Systems of Spiritual Direction."

339. Nelson, "Eros, Logos, Nomos, Polis."

340. Nelson, "Scholastic Rationales of 'Conscience.' "

341. Lea (*op. cit.*) demonstrated the inexorable power of the first written dossiers begun by the Inquisition, pp. 75, etc.

342. Nelson, "Weber's Protestant Ethic."

343. Nelson cites Carl L. Becker, *The Heavenly City of the Eighteenth Century Philosophers* (New Haven, 1970).

344. This evolution can be viewed as part of that sinking of the Christian ethos into the masses, which Huizinga demonstrated to be a later medieval development. In Christianity we also see certain psychological magics which are superior to archaic and folk magics. The Christianization of the masses therefore resulted not merely in making the people more religious, but giving them access to the more powerful psychological magics of this superior religion. One of the main functions of the so-called "higher" (mass) religions is to repackage the sophisticated psychological magics of elites for the transformation of masses.

345. Dodds regarded Pythagoras and Empedocles as typical shaman figures. *The Greeks and the Irrational,* ch. 5, "The Greek Shamans and the Origins of Puritanism," pp. 135–178.

346. Nelson, "The Omnipresence of the Grotesque."

347. Nelson, "The Games of Life and the Dances of Death."

348. Nelson, "Perspectives on the Therapeutic."

349. Nelson, "Actors, Directors, Roles, Cues, Meanings, Identities."

350. Nelson, "Civilizational Complexes and Intercivilizational Encounters."

351. Nelson, "Weber's Protestant Ethic."

352. Karl Mannheim, *Ideology and Utopia* (London, 1936); *Freedom, Power and Democratic Planning* (London, 1951); *Man and Society in an Age of Reconstruction* (London,

1940); *Diagnosis of Our Time* (London, 1943); *Essays on the Sociology of Knowledge* (N.Y., 1952); *Essays on Sociology and Social Psychology* N.Y., 1953).

353. "The Problem of a Sociology of Knowledge," ch. 3, in *Essays on the Sociology of Knowledge.* The Marxists discredit the thinking capacity of opponents with concepts like false consciousness; the Freudians discredit the thinking of allegedly "sick" people, etc., pp. 84–133.

354. Mannheim mostly used a history-of-ideas approach. He was often vague about the concrete social structures that determined ideas. But he is useful because on the one hand he studied category ideas clearly and on the other insisted on social determinism. In actual practice, to avoid a liar's paradox extremity of relativism, he often fudged. He did not want to say that mathematics was socially determined and hesitated about the sciences, though a potential for declaring rationality itself to be socially determined, as Lukacs did, was perhaps inherent in his work and could repel Popper's attack. Mannheim's hedging made his formulations indeterminate. In practice he tended to say that social circumstances affect mental productions—except when they do not.

355. The person category contains irrational elements. When philosophy starts self-consciously picking at the idea it quickly discovers these contradictions and splits the person into ego, id, superego, anima, shadow. This only partly reflects clinical discoveries. Partly it is just logic working on ideas.

356. I refer to the Ludwig Wittgenstein of the *Philosophical Investigations* (N.Y., 1958).

357. Gilbert Ryle, *The Concept of Mind,* etc.

358. P. T. Strawson, *Individuals* (Garden City, N.Y., 1963). Strawson actually tries to reconstruct the person as a "primitive" (i.e., unitary, irreducible) concept, but in no-Atman language, I think.

359. A. J. Ayer, *Language, Thought and Logic* (London, 1950).

360. F. Th. Stcherbatsky, *Buddhist Logic,* vol. I (N.Y., 1962).

361. Agehananda Bharati, *The Tantric Tradition* (N.Y., 1970).

Postulate 11: MAGIC—
ESPECIALLY BLACK MAGIC—
IS AN INDEX OF SOCIAL PRESSURES
ON SELVES AND INDIVIDUALS.

BLACK magic is extreme magic and earliest magic; it best reveals what magic is really about. As such, it provides a test of the last two postulates which assert a relation of magic to the self and to the Individual. For we find that black magic springs up when either the self or the Individual is stressed, even in modern times. (Black magic also expresses pressures on subgroups in a society, and so indirectly tests earlier propositions about the interaction of protest sects with religion.)

In most societies, black magic correlates with social tensions, especially those pressing on the self. Today, when pressures on selves are intense, there is even a cultist revival of black magic in Western civilization. It may turn out to be superficial. But in most past societies black magic has sprung up so readily in response to social upheaval that Max Marwick says it can be used as a "social strain gauge."[1] It is studied this way at some British universities, especially the Oxford Institute of Social Anthropology which has sometimes shown Durkheimian interests. And in recent years a tradition in historical studies crystallized by Wallace Notestein[2] in America and transferred to Oxford after he became Emeritus at Yale and joined the Oxford faculty—a scholarly method of correlating witch accusations in modern Europe with social relationships—has made productive contact with the Oxford anthropologists. The result has been a group of new studies by the younger Oxford historians MacFarlane[3] and Keith Thomas[4], which now gather impressive data to support hypotheses about modern European witch persecutions similar to those employed by the anthropologists in Africa. The viewpoint of these converging schools is Durkheimian: they seek to understand sorcery and witchcraft by relating them to stresses in the social structure. I will be reviewing all these studies.

PART ONE: HOW THESE TERRORS BEGAN—MY THEORY

The Strangest Subject
In many ways, black magic is both the strangest and the most typical province of magic. The mind resists the very idea of it, especially the modern

414

mind, which wonders how such a thing could even be, and is astonished at the virtually universal distribution of consistent witch and sorcery complexes throughout the world. And yet black magic is magic at its most typical—expropriating the sacred, protecting the self, hostile to religion. Quite possibly it is the oldest magic. Paradoxes abound: black magic seems at the very antipodes of religion, and yet it is the most mystical of magics; it approaches religion in its 100-proof "sacred" intensity; and Kluckhohn has shown how its black-and-white value reversals and its bogeyman sanctions curiously support the religious values.

The darkest form of black magic, witchcraft, is a purely "imaginary crime" as Evans-Pritchard put it: There simply cannot be persons who fly through the air and eat our inner organs and so on. Witches do not use magic, which is real, but kill by mystical means. So at first I wondered: how could witchcraft have anything to do with magic? Yet witch beliefs always come embedded in magical complexes: A great deal of magic is little more than a *defense against witches*. Later I came to recognize that the *accusation* of witchcraft is the magical act, perhaps the earliest and most primitive magic, in which an individual escapes voodoo death by turning the tables on a moral entrepreneur who is putting superego pressure on him. Someone says you are violating the group's morality; this could kill you in a primitive society. But instead you accuse him of being a witch, of being the very opposite of every value the group stands for, and this may save your life. It marshals your courage against the superego and maybe it swings public opinion. The fear of the witch is the fear of the group's power to kill by its moral judgments.

Witch beliefs seem strongest in small, face-to-face communities, where relations are total and intense and almost anyone can serve as a superego figure for anyone else. We often see black magic in very simple societies barely above the band stage. Conversely, we find black magic complexes begin to wane as third world populations move into cities where relationships are more instrumental or partial, rather than total and face-to-face. How account for witch beliefs, then, in early modern Europe? When we look at the hard data which Notestein and MacFarlane turn up from Tudor and Stuart Assize records, we find we are still in small face-to-face communities, villages out of the great society's main stream. And the people they accuse of witchcraft are close to them: wives, relatives, next-door neighbors.

The Spiritual Kill

Why *should* there be a form of black magic which actually uses no magic at all, but is purely imaginary, or "spiritual"? Why should there be witches? Kluckhohn,[5] Monica Wilson[6] and others claim this is really a *religious* complex, which "reverses" the normal values and beliefs of society in a vivid, bogeyman manner, thereby dramatizing what they are. But why should religion broadcast its values this way? Witch and sorcery beliefs are destructive; some societies (e.g., Dobu,[7] the Canaques[8]) seem to be demoralized by them. The crime of witchcraft is imaginary, but it does kill. The person who believes himself cursed by a witch can die of it. In documented cases, no physical cause of death can be found, just as in voodoo death. This strongly suggests *a connection between witchcraft and voodoo death,* and I believe that line of inquiry will provide the right answer.

The fact that witches kill *without* magic suggests that witch fears arose *before* magic. And we do find black magic complexes in quite primitive societies that have little or no other kind of magic. I am thinking of the Ndembu described by Turner,[9] and certain Australian tribes. In the Pygmies, we perhaps see a people so primitive they have *no* magic at all, not even black magic. This was Father Trilles' claim,[10] and Colin Turnbull[11] provided some confirmation, with personal accounts of Pygmies resisting the black magic beliefs of their Negro neighbors. But even Father Trilles had to admit rudiments of black magic in occasional beliefs in "evil spirits,"[12] which some Pygmies considered the cause of some illnesses.[13]

Witches, evil spirits, ghosts, demons—all these agencies kill without magic, which suggests they arose before magic. I think they arose out of religion and relate to voodoo death. I think the deadly fear of spiritual murder which they reflect refers to voodoo death. Primitives often witness voodoo death caused by social condemnation. Witch fears are "projections" of primitive man's nascent awareness of the killing power of social consensus.

Very Old Beliefs

Several factors suggest that these are very old beliefs. A. *Absence of magic.* Witches killing without magic suggests they arose before magic, i.e., before "the generalization of mana" at the tribal stage, perhaps at the Paleolithic band stage. B. *Relation to totemism.* Witch beliefs seem connected with totemism, also a very old complex. Hubert and Mauss noticed as early as 1902 that the witch "familiar" resembles a totemic animal. Witch variants found in lycanthropy and vampirism are also animals.[14] Vampires and werewolves are people who can turn into bats and wolves, the way Lévy-Bruhl said primitives confound the individual with the totemic species.[15]

There is striking confirmation in recent studies of "nawalism," a Central American institution that appears to be a missing link between totemic animals and witches' familiars. Manning Nash, in "Witchcraft as a Social Process in a Tzeltal Community,"[16] finds some men are believed to have animal counterparts, called nawales; the nawal gives them magical medical power; and at whim they can transform themselves into the animal. Some use their nawal power to cure; others use it to harm and these people are considered witches.

In "The Concept of 'Bewitching' in Lugbara,"[17] John Middleton explicitly relates the witch complex to one's "nagual," or personal bird spirit, and characterizes this as a totemic survival. He roundly asserts that ideas like familiars, transformation into animals, and naguals are basic to witch beliefs in general. Benson Saler prefaces another study of these beliefs in a Quiche village with a useful summary of this literature,[18] citing George Foster (1944), Kaplan (1956), Holland (1961), Wagley (1949), Lewis (1951). He notes that two themes appear in nawal or nagual ideas: 1. The nagual as "companion" or "guardian spirit," and 2. "the transforming witch." In some cases the nagual is just a spirit helper; in others the witch turns into his nagual. I think we can trace these two themes back to personal totems and clan totems.[19] The clan totem is a species, and individuals belong to it, *are* it, by "mystic participation" (Lévy-Bruhl). Whereas the personal totem is an individual animal helper, not a species; a friend, not an ancestor or group soul. Transformation ideas may descend from the religious clan totem, helper ideas from the more magical personal totem.[20]

Recalling Rasmussen[21] on the Hudson Bay Eskimos, I am also reminded that the shaman's power derives from spirits that seize him and which he then overcomes. Asen Balikoi[22] finds the same among Netsilik Eskimos, and in both the possessing spirit conquered by the shaman is often an animal figure of some sort. The shaman conquers these spirits and then they become allies. This suggests that shamanism may have begun in an experience of overcoming voodoo death or witch attack. In the witch accusation, man counterattacks the superego and turns the tables on the moral entrepreneur who put him down. But in shamanic possession, trance struggle and victory, he goes further—he conquers a totem and turns it into an ally. The spirits that torment the Iglulik are not totemic, yet we may suspect a totemic background, for these are animals the people eat. In withstanding their attack and then converting them into allies, the shaman in effect converts something like an attacking clan totem into something like a supporting personal totem. This, I think, is the form that what I called shamanic "conquest of the superego," "of the social inside the self" actually takes.[23] What began as mere defense against voodoo death, the counterattack of the witch accusation, in shamanism goes further and becomes a conquest of the social. This is the transition from witchcraft to sorcery.

Now we can be more precise about the sense in which witchcraft is "religious." Witch *fears* are "religious projections," part of the religious worldview. (They project something in social reality, namely voodoo death. They reflect the mortal subjugation of individual egos to the collective conscience.) But witch *accusations* are magical. They are the first magical act. Witch accusations are defenses against witch fears, which are religious; hence they are defenses against religion. This resolves the paradox. It shows how witchcraft ideas can reinforce religion by supplying black-and-white dramatizations of what *not* to do, and yet be the blackest, foulest province of magic, of anti-religion. The formula is simple: witch fears are religious; witch accusations are magic.

Witch accusations are the beginning of ego resistance; they are a sign that egos and selves are beginning to be there. In a totemic society, in which mana is particularized, diffused into subcults, ego is very weak. Individuals have no magic, but they have mana; they are all sacred religious objects. Norms are self-enforcing through religious taboos that work automatically. Voodoo death is very common. There are no priests or officials, just headmen; and therefore, in these face-to-face groups in which everyone is sacred, any person if he speaks right can speak for the consensus and so act as superego for any other person. So these are shame rather than guilt cultures. And everyone is very touchy, easily hurt; joking patterns are carefully controlled; and words can kill. It is very likely that the pattern Metais found among the Canaques—voodoo death caused by *anyone* else—is rather common. Even in more advanced societies, such as Azande, people are very sensitive to critical remarks.[24] So we may suspect that a lot of illness really is caused by "spiritual forces" as these peoples believe. When, for example, a man has broken a taboo, if a "significant other" speaks critically to him at that vulnerable moment, he takes the role of the "generalized other" and his words might very well cause the offender to waste away and die.

And as he begins to die, is he not likely to dream that the man who criticized him is killing him? After all, he possesses as yet no concept of "society" as a moral, abstract entity. All he has are totemic representations of that reality. And is it not likely, in fact, that *the afflicted man will dream that the totem animal of his critic has attacked him?*

What attacks the guilty person is the moral force of society; but this force is always personified in an individual who speaks on its behalf. Howard Becker calls such a person a "moral entrepreneur."[25] (Malinowski showed how his moral initiative could force a Trobriander to kill himself.[26]) Among very primitive peoples, the moral entrepreneur's power will perhaps be conceptualized as a totem. It is an easy step from this to suppose that the guilty person may imagine that his critic has sent his totem animal to attack him—and this would certainly help explain why witch beliefs all over the world include the idea of the witch sending her familiar to attack her victims in the night. The man condemned to die by group morality may indeed imagine, during the throes of that "killer anxiety" or "disorganizing depression" or whatever the precise process of voodoo death is, that he is being destroyed by a bat or a black cat or a werewolf or some other totem whose taboo he infringed, or the totem representing the clan he offended, or the personal totem of the person who criticized him.

We can suppose a long era of totem fears but no witch accusations, a period when those who died defenselessly of "mortal sins" felt that they were killed *by totems.* The very *idea* of a witch is already a defense, a transition toward an accusation, just as, in Freud's system, a psychotic delusion is already the struggle to get well. There was probably a long period in Paleolithic times when witch projections did not exist. Men experiencing voodoo death instead imagined that they were attacked by totem animals. We see remnants of this in ideas of vampires, werewolves, etc., which may be older than witch ideas. Similar perhaps are the fearful animal spirits that torment primitive Arabians, the *jinn* reported by Robertson Smith.[27] Among the Azande, some animals (notably cats) still have mangu,[28] or witchcraft, all by themselves, without being any witch's familiar.

All this would explain how witchcraft, which is action without magic, belongs within magic. For witchcraft as a social institution is built, not around the delusions but around the accusation, not around the religious fear, but around the magical antidotes.

Other provinces of magic develop later around this nucleus. Medical magic begins here. At first one just accuses the witch; later, medical magic is used against him. Divination develops to identify the witch and this leads to the occult sciences. Etc.

Witch ideas still waft denatured religious vapors, with their uncanny totemic archetypes, their chill reminders of the killing power of consensus. But they are also antipodal magic, blackest, foulest, most anti-social magic. This unsurpassed inner contradiction adds to their mystery and terror. By contrast, sorcery is much more thoroughly magical, anti-social and individualistic. It may be presumed to have emerged somewhat later.

De Martino[29] suggests that sorcery was the first activity of shamans. Once they conquered the spirits, they then attacked persons. It is easy to imagine *whom.* They probably first attacked the same people whom witch accusations attack: moral entrepreneurs who kill by talking in the management voice when they morally condemn a person. Only later do shamans start curing people, de Martino says, and he supposes they begin by trying to cure the victims of their *rivals,* in contests of magical strength.

Sorcerers are the opposite of witches. They are people who have beaten back witch attack or something like it. They survived the crushing power of social consensus, and even conquered some of it. They have expropriated a clan totem, a spirit symbolizing society itself, and turned it into a personal totem. And they have invented other magic. Thus the sorcerer is a person who "wins over the superego," as Róheim[30] put it. Most societies suspect their witch doctors or shamans of also doing sorcery on the side, and in some societies they do so openly (e.g., Cebu).[31]

Cast of Characters

Sorcerers are ambiguous figures. As they move toward the more anti-social pole, they become more imaginary and in some societies get confounded with witches. Sorcery becomes an "unlikely crime" to set alongside the "impossible crime" of witchcraft, as Evans-Pritchard put it. And as sorcerers move toward curative, white magic, they become witchdoctors and partly pass out of the black magic province and into medical magic. Yet sorcerers are important for they are the only *real* members of the black magic cast and that is interesting. This province is peopled by many other dangerous characters, but they are all imaginary, like witches; they kill by mystical means, like witches. First, there are werewolves and vampires, related to witch familiars. Vampirism strongly homologizes to the common idea that witches slowly devour the vital inner organs (e.g., Zandeland[32]). In addition, there are ghosts, evil spirits, demons. The ego pressure of evil eye is related to ideas of witches and werewolves.[33] All these characters are imaginary. What Evans-Pritchard said of witches is true of them too: theirs are "impossible crimes." And what I have said is also true: they all reflect voodoo death. Just like witch ideas, they are projections of society's terrible power to kill. As such they are *religious* personifications.

All of these various points apply to evil spirits, too. They are imaginary, kill by mystical means, and reflect society's killing power. Evil ghosts are, in some societies, the spirits of dead witches or sorcerers (e.g., Azande). Hubert and Mauss have proposed some other sources for them as well. An evil spirit might be generated by a black magic ritual,[34] the way Jane Harrison[35] showed religious rituals generate spirits. Douttée claimed that genies are generated this way in Muslim magic.[36] Finally, there are major demons, usually conceived of as deities. They may be generated out of conquered or outlawed religions. The Hebrews declared the gods of the gentiles to be demons; the Christians did the same with the pagan gods.

Why Two Bogeymen?

Sorcerer and witch start from different points: one is a resistance against society's pressure while the other *is* that pressure: one is late and one is early. And the two retain big differences: sorcerers use magic while witches kill by imaginary means. Even so, the two approach each other; many people confound the terms; some languages have only one word for both (e.g., French, *le sorcier*). Why should two similar complexes *persist?* Why do many societies have both?

John Middleton and E. H. Winter attempt a hesitant answer.[37] They first admit both serve some identical functions: both work as a theodicy, both supply sanctions to underline good vs. bad behavior[38]; both express and maybe abreact social tensions. Even so the authors discern some slight differences in function: One pattern often fills out logical gaps left by the other. If witch power is associated with the maternal line, sorcery may express tensions between men. (Similarly, where sorcerers are accused of misfortunes that befall individuals, witches may be considered the cause of *general* misfortunes.) But the authors suspect that that full answer is deeper and more difficult. They examine other clues somewhat miscellaneously: 1. Witch ideas seem to predominate in unilineal kinship societies, sorcery in non-lineages. 2. Accused witches are often kin of the accusers, while accused sorcerers are more often rivals. 3. Sorcery is often practiced by the weak against the strong, while witchcraft is sometimes imputed to chiefs who abuse their position. 4. Witch accusations are always public, while sorcery detection is more private.

These hints are tantalizing. Let me try to explain them. Recall that witch fears are religious, while witch accusations and sorcery are anti-religious magic. The two patterns persist because they *continue* to express these two different tensions. Witchcraft remains closer to religion and expresses persisting human fear of the killing power of society—whereas sorcery fears reflect the hostile action of *rivals*. Magic is used to defend against both, both consensus and competitors, but sorcery itself is already magic—*your rival's magic*.

All of Middleton and Winter's observations will fit this interpretation. Sorcerers are often rivals while witches are often relatives, because relatives are close enough to us to exert oppressive moral authority. There is more witchcraft in lineages because these can be tighter moral structures than bilateral families. Chiefs are suspected of witchcraft because they are powerful moral figures whose quick tongues deal out voodoo death—whereas sorcerers are rivals who use dirty tricks, a different kind of danger. Dirty tricks by rivals are a private problem. Witch accusations, by contrast, must be tried in public if voodoo death is to be averted. Some anthropologists report that witch death is often a slow process, whereas sorcerers kill suddenly. Again, this would fit my proposal that the real witch fear is of something like voodoo death, which Cannon and Mauss say is a wasting away that takes a few days or weeks—whereas sorcery is often a swift murder by physical means: The Barotse bushwack their victims with bush guns.[39] The Bunyoro burn down their enemies' houses, according to John Beattie.[40] Poisoning is quite common: there was a great fear of women poisoners among the Roman imperial family, according to Tacitus,[41] Robert Graves.[42]

Witch accusations must be public because they are really counterattacks against moral authority, and can only work if tried in the court of public opinion. A person who accuses a relative or neighbor of witchcraft is trying to undo a moral entrepreneur by publicly inverting him. The serious business involved in adjudicating witch accusations makes them the beginning of criminal justice. Fighting sorcery remains more private; one modern descendent is feuding, which remains outside the law. But witches, allegedly, have violated fundamental values, and this is public business. The very accusation of witchcraft is itself a serious matter, and quite possibly a crime if it is misplaced. The whole procedure has some of the august solemnity of a murder trial, and that is suggestive.

Anthropologists (e.g., Nash[43]) hear reports of witch trials that took place *after* the witch was slain. Usually these occurred before colonial and modern governments squelched the witch-finding machinery. We may suspect that originally murder of the witch usually preceded the accusation. The dealer in voodoo death was simply killed, and then the killer tried to justify himself. Primordial witch trials may have been murder trials conducted after the sentence had been passed. Then the accused, like Orestes before the Areopagus,[44] attempted to escape kin retribution and automatic voodoo death by charging unnatural crimes upon the deceased "witch" to justify killing him. And if all this is so, then since the witch accusation is man's first magical act, magic begins in murder.

These public issues could be one reason for the widespread preference in Africa for divination of witchcraft by *mechanical* oracle. In Azande the verdict of a mechanical oracle is considered more "legal" than the diagnosis of a live diviner or witchdoctor. Why? Evans-Pritchard says an oracle has greater "objectivity." What does that mean? It is likely that in mechanical, binary, she-loves-me-she-loves-me-not oracle we see a social rallying point (Schelling[45]) for objectivity. It makes a hard decision easier for a riven, small society. A divination procedure is the primitive equivalent of a scientific experiment: both are due processes for the promulgation of moral or cognitive legislation. In a divination procedure a society agrees to agree (Wittgenstein[46]) on how it will reach agreement.[47]

Summary: Origins of Black Magic

That is my theory of how black magic began. Witch fears are religious projections of society's power to kill. The witch accusation is the individual's first *magic,* his first counterattack on social consensus. Voodoo death is experienced in dreams and hallucinations as an attack by a totemic animal. The victim beats off the attack by accusing the moral entrepreneur who criticized him of being the exact opposite of every social value, of being a witch. The accusation is made openly, in the court of public opinion. Later, some individuals beat off voodoo death all by themselves. They dramatize it as a trance struggle against possessing totemic spirits, which they overcome and then turn into personal servants. They are the first sorcerers. They proceed to attack other people, beginning with the moral entrepreneurs whom others brand as witches. They also attack other sorcerers. Eventually, some of them cure the victims of rival sorcerers in contests of magic strength. Soon tormented primitive societies cajole or force them to use this demonstrated ability to cure magical illnesses. Then sorcerers become medicine men and the magic medicine complex emerges to fight magical illnesses, of which black magic remains the most important kind.

PART TWO: WHY THESE TERRORS HAVE A PATTERN CONSISTENCY— THE VALUE OF SOME OTHER THEORIES

But some of the other theories are useful. They can help explain pattern consistency. My theory suggests how black magic *began.* But how to account for the worldwide regularities it shows? I think other theories (which *try* to explain origins) can sometimes help explain why black magic forms are so similar over wide areas. Let us review some of them.

1. Drug Theories

These have an old pedigree. Suspicions were voiced in the ancient world and the Middle Ages that witches took some kind of drug. Lea reports[48] the Spanish Inquisition at first held that witches' flight was a hallucination caused by the "inunction of drugs." Harner cites[49] medieval reports that European witches rubbed their skins with ointments before their magic flights; or that they used plants like belladonna, Mandrake, henbane, which contain atropine that can be absorbed through the skin. These drugs cause hallucinations of a "trip," he asserts. Margaret Murray also refers to "flying ointments"; so did Tylor and others.

Some current experimental research lends support to this view. Carlos Castenada reports experiences of magic flight when he first used the drug Jimson weed, or Datura, before Don Juan fully patterned the experience.[50] The German scholar Karl Kiesewetter, reading of witch ointments, applied atropine to his skin and had a hallucination of flying.[51]

There is considerable research today into several drugs as possible sources of magical and religious experiences. R. Gordon Wasson[52] tried to identify a drug allegedly used in the Eleusinian mysteries as a mushroom drug, possibly similar to peyote. Wasson[53] also attempted to identify the "soma" of the Rig-Veda with the mushroom fly-agaric. The widespread figurines of toadstools with elves sitting on them are supposed to suggest visions produced by the magic mushrooms. The intoxicant was passed in the urine, and often drunk by the intoxicated guru's disciples; Zoroaster condemned the "urine of drunkenness." John Allegro[54] claimed evidence for a widespread cult of fly-agaric throughout the Near East and traced it to Sumeria. He claimed that both the Eleusinian Mysteries and the esoteric religion of Christ used the drug. But Allegro suggested that Datura was probably the source of the ferocious imagery of the witch complex.

Michael Harner summarized this evidence to suggest that the consistency of the witch complex and some other cults is based on the consistent psychological effects of several drugs.[55] It is suggested that witchcraft was a movement of drug shamanism, which some see as a transition from the "magical" complex around the entranced shaman to a "religious" community based on the sharing of trance through drugs. Whether or not this is true, it seems likely that drugs could help pattern witch experiences consistently.

2. Cult Diffusion Theories

Several investigators explain the consistency of witch ideas as a diffusion of outlawed religious cults. Margaret Murray's[56] theory is the best known. She imagines a Paleolithic religion of a horned god of hunting and husbandry diffused through Europe and Africa, driven underground, branded by the Church as demonic. But Keith Thomas[57] reports little evidence of the cult she alleged in the actual documentation of European witch trials and confessions.

Michelet[58] propounded something similar, but more reasonable: He did not imagine an organized cult, just a reaching back to superstition by an oppressed peasantry. Michelet derived witchcraft from the despair of the peasantry. When the Church persecuted these folk beliefs as devilish, the revolting peasantry accepted the challenge and patterned their practices after the charges of the accusers. So Michelet alleges, like Margaret Murray, and both on thin evidence, that sabbats really existed; but to him they were communes of revolt rather than the old time religion of Margaret Murray.

Baroja takes a slightly different tack. He links witches to real religious cults that were well known in the ancient world.[59] Scanning classical literature, he finds many references to witches, associated with night, the moon, the dead, women, the moon goddess, etc. Factoring out this material, he concludes that European witch ideas derived from the *imagery*[60] of by-passed matriarchal cults, especially those of Diana, Hecate and the White Goddess,[61] which lost prestige to the male-dominated pantheons but were still tolerated. After the Christian conquest, paganism lost official status and was condemned as demonic by the church. And so it became.[62]

The heritage of Judaic intolerance and Hellenic exclusionary logic intensified the natural process whereby fallen gods are condemned to become demons. In India, according to Dumont,[63] cults are *ranked* rather than excluded, and Hocart[64] even suggests that the caste system consists of a hierarchy of cults, with so-called "drummers," "potters," "washermen" and "barbers" actually the priests of fallen rites of *asuras*, or demons, or, as Hocart calls them, "Titans." Each has a priestly function for a debased *rite de passage* which the higher castes, as priesthoods of *devas* (gods of light) cannot handle: washermen preside over girls' first menstruations, for example. Every occupation is a priesthood, a sacrifice (the *Puranas* use the word *bali*, sacrifice, to designate subcastes.) Judeo-Hellenic Christianity, by contrast, excludes rather than ranks fallen cults, accentuating the demonological, and this has the effect of a self-fulfilling prophecy. Carlos Ginzburg[65] finds a dramatic example in the Benandanti, a 16th and 17th century witch-finding cult in Friule which, branded as witches by the Inquisition, began to act out witch stereotypes, including sabbats and pacts with the devil.

3. Patterning By Persecution

A closely related and popular theory is that black magic was an artifact of deluded persecutors and their self-fulfilling prophecies. Baroja's account[66] gives importance to this factor, with demonology ideas crystallized by the Paris theologians and the Inquisition. Trevor-Roper is perhaps the most extreme exponent of the persecution theory.[67] He denies that *any* real elements were present at all to abet this paranoid synthesis. The entire thing was imaginary. This is an extremely cognitive position, typical of the British tradition.

The classical persecution theory was written by Henry Charles Lea,[68] a busy Philadelphia publisher who employed copyists at major European libraries to do research for him.[69] His posthumous editor Arthur C. Howland reports[70] that Lea originally meant to study black magic. He may have been trying to write a general theory of magic. Twice he began and twice he was deflected into studies of the Inquisition, partly because the topic of magic proved so enormous he had to study particular issues first, and partly because he broke down, at least the first time. His several breakdowns were attributed to overwork, but Howland reports he was deep in the study of Hindu philosophy and magic when he broke down the first time. (Weber, by contrast, turned to the study of religion and magic *after* a nervous breakdown.[71]) Lea's original quest was to understand "man's assumed control over spiritual forces"; this led him first into the study of the origin of evil in different religions. He got deep into oriental religions, cracked up, and upon recovery avoided orientalism and worked on his monumental *Inquisition of the Middle Ages*, published in 1888.[72] But apparently he still thought of it as a preparation. Later he tried again to study black magic, this time in Europe, but he got into the contrasts between the persecutions in different countries (e.g., fewer persecutions in Spain) and this diverted him again, to his second Inquisition book, *History of the Inquisition of Spain*. But the second book did contain two chapters on his original interest (ch. 8, "Sorcery and Occult Arts," ch. 9, "Witchcraft"). He tried a third time to write a theory of black magic shortly before his death in 1909. The notes he and his copyists had assembled were posthumously published by Howland as *Materials Toward a History of Witchcraft.* These included a finished excursus on transalpine European witchcraft left out of the Spanish Inquisition book, for space, and notes toward a new history of witchcraft in the West. (Nowhere could be found his unfinished "History of Magic," begun in the 1870's.)

Lea's basic theory is a cross between "patterning by persecution" (like Trevor-Roper), and "magic as a decay toxin released by dying religions" (like Steiner[73]). His root idea, according to Burr, is that as religion succeeds religion, the superseded faiths become the forbidden magics of later cultures. In Lea's view,[74] the classic world was heir to a mass of superstitions from dead or foreign religions—decisive was Iranian dualism filtered through the Judaic religion by the Babylonian captivity. Christian theologians, rationalizing what they rejected as well as what they accepted, cast all the dead religions together and used as their core the Persian Ahriman figure, transformed through Hellenic Judaism into Satan. Theologians followed a logic, turning this demonology into the reverse of Christianity (just as witch beliefs in many cultures reverse accepted values).

Christian theology assumed the fall of man and the fall of the angels (a theodicy to rationalize Persian dualism). The devil was "the prince of the earth,"[75] but Christ gave man control over him; Morton Smith goes farther,[76] noticing that Christ gave his esoteric inner circle dominion over specific hosts of demons (Luke IX, 1). Lea gives much attention to this demonological core, to Christian thaumaturgy, to Simon Magus, etc. Cohn similarly speaks of "Europe's inner demons."[77]

For centuries this dangerous core was quiescent; church rationalism subdued it. Augustine attacked the whole gnostic drift of the fall of the angels; and Church councils at least threw out the Canaanite version that the angels had fallen because of congress with the daughters of man. But the cleaned-up version (i.e., the angels fell through "pride") remained as a potential gnostic eschatology, and angelology pullulated with rank fertility. Davidson's *Dictionary of Angels*[78] contains thousands of names around which myths, legends, literature grew. Hocart[79] has suggested that angel figures derive from Iranian heralds, who homologize to magicians. Since angels are just one slip (or "fall") away from demons, angelology kept the demonological potential alive.

It was the persecution of gnostic-Manichean heretics that let the demons out of the Christian bag. The obsession of the heretics themselves with dualism and the devil[80] drew attention to these ideas and stirred up Christianity's own repressed. And the either-or, black-or-white logical thinking of the Paris schoolmen contributed mightily to the crystallization of demonology ideas.

For years, the Inquisitors brought in reports of black magic as well as heresy. Finally, in 1326, Pope John XXII in *Super Illius Specula,* lamented the invocation of demons and ordered that all who do so be punished as heretics. Thus the church officially declared that witches were real. A logical juggernaut was unleashed that culminated in 1398 when the University of Paris declared that there was an implied pact with the devil in all superstitious observances.

And the persecutions elicited the imaginary phenomena they sought to punish. The Inquisition itself became aware of this sociological basis of black magic.[81] No land was more exposed to witch fears than Spain, where for 100 years the masses had clamored for a persecution. The Inquisition resisted; it was run by rational men who clung to earlier medieval ideas that witchcraft was a delusion induced by drugs. But when popular pressure forced the Inquisition briefly to persecute, they quickly discovered that the examiners created the confessions and the confessions created the mass hysteria that led to more accusations. The Suprema was briefly captured by some true believers; there were witch convictions and these fed the delusion.

Later, skeptics again gained the upper hand; an inquisitor named Salazar was sent into the field to study the phenomenon; he spent a year, returned in 1612, did a report citing extorted confessions and mass delusions. The Suprema was finally convinced; it cracked down; it actually punished people for witch accusations. Meanwhile, it continued to punish sorcery (as late as the eighteenth century) and even such minor magic as fortune telling. Like Evans-Pritchard, it declared in effect that magic was real but that witchcraft was an impossible crime.

In Lea's *Inquisition of the Middle Ages* we are reminded of the great extent to which this whole phenomenon was a consequence of writing and bureaucratic procedures. The church, possessing literate clerks, and wealth to support a bureaucracy, was unopposed as it shaped these damnation categories, first heresy and then witchcraft. And its dossiers might pursue a man for decades, from one kingdom to another. Persecution did not create black magic ideas, but Lea's histories demonstrate with vivid detail how it stamped pattern consistency on them for Western Europe.

4. Functionalist Theories

Some investigators claim witch ideas persist because they help society in various ways. The classic example is Kluckhohn's study of Navajo witchcraft. Kluckhohn is really quite miscellaneous about all the functions he assigns to Navajo witchcraft.[82] There are so many they have to be enumerated: a. Witch beliefs underline the social values by providing a mirror image of them through their reversals. b. They also help to force conformity; deviants know they can be branded as witches if they go too far. c. They are a vehicle for expressing and abreacting social tensions. d. They also provide a moral explanation of the world, a theodicy. e. Witch beliefs are an outlet for marginal people, getting them some attention. f. Witchcraft is also like Roman circuses for the people; it keeps them entertained. g. It helps build conviction in the efficacy of cures. h. It helps express deviant impulses. i. It handles the frustration-aggression problem by offering the witch as scapegoat. j. It helps verbalize and hence abreact anxiety. Other functionalists add to this list: Some have noticed, for example, that witch beliefs force decent social behavior on conformists as well as non-conformists; the latter fear witch accusations, but the former fear witch attacks if they are too unkind to poor or deviant people.

The trouble with this is several-fold: a. The system is assumed to be totally functional. But it is quite possible that witchcraft beliefs often create more social tensions than they abreact. b. A mere list of functions, without weights, without internal logical articulation, is not a satisfying explanation. c. No attempt is made to relate the particular form that witch beliefs take among the Navajo to their social system.

More satisfying is the functional interpretation of Paiute sorcery attempted by Beatrice Blyth Whiting.[83] Using the anthropological theory of social control, she set out to prove (via statistical tests worked on the Yale Cross Cultural Survey) that social control is the function of black magic.[84] Among the Paiute, social control is "informal," based entirely on fear of retaliation, which takes three forms: a. direct retaliation; b. retaliation through sorcery; c. the *accusation* of sorcery. All three serve to control deviant, anti-social or unfriendly behavior. Most feared is sorcery.

Unlike Kluckhohn, she looks for correlation of belief with social pattern at every turn. She finds that the particular kind of spirit affliction suffered correlates with age. This is a marginal society which must control aggression to survive, she concludes. Fear of one's own aggression, trained in by the family, is the key. Overt aggression does in fact break out: drunken husbands beat their wives, wives club one another and their children; there is a high suicide rate. When one's own aggression breaks out, there is a terrible fear of loss of help and support in a society where everyone depends on everyone else. Sorcery ideas project these fears; and fear of sorcery controls aggression.

This kind of study is a step in the right direction; it is marred only by its inexactitudes. The nature of the Paiute family is not clear enough; her remarks on aggression are ambiguous (fear of it is instilled yet there is a lot of it); she omits African societies from her search of the Cross Cultural Survey for proof. Finally, her definitions are none too exact: Paiute "sorcery" sounds more like witchcraft. These "sorcerers" kill mystically, just by thinking bad thoughts abut their victims, consciously or even unconsciously, or in dreams. Perhaps it is a mixed case.

The trouble with functionalist theories of black magic is that they overlook its dysfunctions. Some societies are torn apart by them. Metais finds witchcraft ideas among the Canaques[85] to be a group response to danger that is devastating for the individual. Like Merton's critique of functionalism,[86] this study asks, "functional for *whom?*"

R. F. Fortune's study of Dobu[87] presents a similarly bleak picture of sorcery. Here is a society in which sorcerers really exist: families here own sorcery spells for specific diseases; poisoning is also practiced. Fortune relates sorcery to the overpopulated, competitive culture. The rich and successful are thought of as thieves. They are the envied targets of sorcery but they are also presumed to have used sorcery to become successful. Fortune finds only one functional value in this cruel theodicy—it explains away failure; failures learn that they were cheated. But he makes no claims that sorcery constrains this conflict; it seems rather to *reflect* it. He is more typical of the later generations of British Durkheimians than the early functionalists. The Dobuans are so frightened of their own magic that they are more relaxed when they visit among the Trobrianders, one of the few instances in the literature where primitives feel safer among strangers than at home.

It was in opposition to "unilinear" theories like these that Mauss proposed instead the study of "total social facts."[88] Nonetheless, some unilinear theories of black magic—especially those pointing to drugs, ancient cults and persecutor's delusions—do usefully organize large bodies of data. They do not tell us the origins of black magic as they claim, for they are too one-sided; but each one sheds a little light on why black magic patterns have remained consistent. My theory tells how these terrors *began.* These theories help explain their consistency.

But why do they persist? The answer is that they reflect social stress, and we turn now to the Evans-Pritchard group which studies this.

PART THREE: GETTING DOWN TO REAL CASES—
EVANS-PRITCHARD'S MODEL

Two generations ago, British anthropologists influenced by Durkheim and Mauss turned away from unicausal theories of origin for black magic. Instead, they tried to recreate the "total social fact" by analytical description of striking cases. The turning point was Evans-Pritchard's *Witchcraft, Oracles and Magic Among the Azande* in 1937. It is a perfect example of the "method of extreme cases" Mauss recommended. I call it a "natural ideal type."[89] This trend in anthropology sometimes is misunderstood in nominalist America. Sometimes people say British fieldworkers abandoned theory and turned to purely factual studies of single societies. That is a misrepresentation. We know Evans-Pritchard was reading Lévy-Bruhl and other French theorists as he worked.[90] He praised Mauss' work on magic before his major Azande study.[91] He later prefaced or caused to be translated several books of the French school.[92] In his introductions to Hertz,[93] Mauss,[94] and Hubert and Mauss[95] he applauded (with reservations[96]) their method of "descriptive integration."[97] He said Mauss could do more "without leaving his flat in Paris,"[98] through his method of focusing on the totality, than some fieldworkers trapped in "mere empiricism."[99] I do not mean that Evans-Pritchard consciously set out to create a model in Azande witchcraft; in another place he strongly emphasized how institutions differ according to the worldviews of different societies.[100] But it is not surprising that his study became a model.[101] He, too, aimed at "descriptive integration." The real proof is the aftermath: two generations of British fieldworkers have used his Azande study as a model type and standard of comparison, with brilliant results.

A natural ideal type is empirical; it bores into what is really there; it pulls it together through a descriptive integration that takes account of complexity.[102] And what is there is unimaginably complex. You could never have guessed at it by an abstract ideal type; and you could never have seen the woods for the trees if you just described it without "analytic integration." Before Evans-Pritchard, we had only bits and pieces of black magic: medieval demonology, witch beliefs among primitives, some dim knowledge of sorcery and witchdoctors, studies of divination. Evans-Pritchard's natural ideal type showed us how they all fit together: Divination is the diagnosis of black magic; witchdoctors are therapists; magic is used against witches who do not use magic themselves; witchcraft is imaginary but sorcery uses magic. Evans-Pritchard showed us how two vast provinces of magic overlap and fit together: medical magic and black magic.[103] Before his study there was no unification of parts; for all the decades of grand theorizing it was all too narrow and the parts remained fragmentary. Evans-Pritchard revealed more by studying the real social facts in a single society. His study has been confirmed by many others. I do not mean that other investigators found exactly the same complex. They found divergences; but every one could be related to special social features to discover where the tensions and conflicts were in each society.

A Universal Pattern

My own theory of black magic[104] is generalized from these natural ideal types and the research they stimulated. Evans-Pritchard said witches and sorcerers are different. This is confirmed. Witches kill mysteriously, but sorcerers attack by means of magic. This is confirmed. His numinous account of Azande magic has lit up what is apparently a near-universal human culture pattern. Almost everywhere we look we now expect to see black magic and medical magic overlapping, with death and disease attributed largely to mystical causes, especially witchcraft, evil spirits, ghosts or broken taboos, also sorcery, and with the relative prominence of each determined by local stresses. Usually we expect that the afflicted individual will first test public opinion; he will go to a diviner, or consult a mechanical oracle, or seek diagnosis from a witchdoctor who also treats illness. The diviner or witchdoctor will be sensitive to community factions and feuds; he will be aware of any breach of reciprocity. He will offer a tentative diagnosis. If the diagnosis gets some kind of confirmation from public opinion, the witch or sorcerer will be confronted, asked to apologize or to confess. If he does so, and symptoms disappear, there will be resolution of social conflict as well as of illness. If the illness persists, the victim and his advisors may decide that they are dealing with an unknown witch or sorcerer; in that case vengeance magic may be directed at "whoever" the enemy is. A particularly inveterate witch or sorcerer will finally be named; public opinion will be tested; if it goes against the accused he will be tried, driven out or killed.

Azande Peculiarities

This pattern is of near universal value as a standard of comparison, even though Azande black magic has certain peculiarities: a. Witchcraft *dominates* here. It is the most frequent cause of illness and death; it swamps other magic and even religious phenomena: It provides a theodicy, a causality that explains the world, etc. This makes Zandeland an "extreme case." b. Azande witchdoctors are of secondary importance in divination: mechanical oracles, especially the poison oracle (widespread in Africa), have greater objective validity. This is a common pattern but pushed to an extreme. c. Witchcraft has a curiously banal, commonplace quality to it here. People are irritated but not frightened by it; possibly because they have so many defenses against it.[105] That is unusual. d. Azande witchcraft is thought to be an inherited physical endowment (another common idea), taking the form of a physical appurtenance visible upon autopsy. (Evans-Pritchard believes that this is nothing other than the small intestine happening to be distended by the passage of food at the time of death and autopsy.[106]) Individuals do not know that they possess this capacity; witch attack is thought in many cases to be unintentional. Though physical, witchcraft works spiritually. It is not witchcraft itself, *mangu,* this growth inside the body, that attacks; rather, it is *mbisimo mangu,* the spirit of witchcraft, that rises from the sleeping witch, flies to seek its victim, and kills by eating not the inner organs themselves, but the spirit of the inner organs, *mbisimo palio.* Characteristically, witch illness is a wasting illness, whereas sorcery kills quickly. Most of these ideas are found elsewhere. e. Sorcery and magic seem almost *de trop* in this complex,[107] and that is unusual. There is a hint that the decline of sorcery is an index of social decline, first under the conquering Vongaras, then under the British.[108] The witchdoctor's symbolic powers are used only where a witch cannot be found, or the illness persists despite apologies.[109] Altogether, it does not sound like particularly efficacious magic. f. Because anti-witch magic is weak, it is supplemented by other means. The country is swamped by the influx of new medicines[110]; moreover, thaumaturgical movements also crowd in,[111] filling the vacuum caused by government's outlawing of the witch ordeal.

So the Azande witch complex has special features. Nonetheless this superbly *formed* "extreme case" has served as a useful natural ideal type and yardstick. Anthropologists typically correlate variations from it with peculiarities in social structure and social tensions. But this was not Evans-Pritchard's own approach; he was more interested in the witch complex as a theodicy, a world-view. His approach was cognitive, like Kluckhohn's. His main interest was to show how and why the system persists—i.e., because it presents an air-tight explanation of everything that happens, and because it cannot be falsified, cannot be disproven.

Fragmentation Fosters Belief

The system persists because it explains evil, death and illness in a manner satisfying to the people. As Evans-Pritchard formulates it (drawing on Lévy-Bruhl), it does not so much explain *how* a death occurs as *why* it occurs: why an injured man happened to be in the dangerous spot at the moment the accident happened to him. But the main reason the system persists is that it is virtually unfalsifiable, and this is so mainly because it is fragmented.[112] This is Evans-

Pritchard's great contribution to the sociology of knowledge; it can be used to understand why belief in other fragmented systems, such as Hinduism, remains so strong.

People here simply do not generalize. They talk about a particular family which has been hexed; they have only pragmatic interest. Constantly they hear their neighbors accused and constantly they hear of their public apologies ("If I am, I am sorry"). But as each incident is settled, it is closed. The Azande joke nervously about witches all the time but do not reveal their own personal encounters. Of course, the witch accusation is public. But if it fails, and defensive or vengeance magic is resorted to, the whole thing goes underground. This secrecy further fragments knowledge.

In a typical case, family X has had an illness, and has been unable to stop it through the due process of oracle and witch confrontation. The family member dies. Family X now consults a witchdoctor for further diagnosis, and family Y is indicated. Family X now secretly buys vengeance magic against family Y. (The witchdoctor eats "medicines" while he speaks spells against family Y.) Meanwhile, family Z has also lost a member. They have completely failed to identify the witch, whether by oracle, diviner *or* witchdoctor. So family Z has bought "whoever" magic from a witch doctor, vengeance magic aimed at *whoever* did it. Later, someone in family Y dies. Now the members of family X believe that their vengeance magic, directed against family Y, worked. And members of family Z also believe that they have finally discovered the witch who afflicted them, and killed him. But now members of family Y decide that witchcraft has struck *them,* and they consult oracles, and so continue the cycle.

This calls to mind Hinduism, which has proven remarkably resistant to conquest or acculturation. Does its resistance have something to do with the fact that the system as a whole is too complicated for any individual to know? Or consider totemism.[113] Each totemic clan knows a particular subcult thoroughly, the way the citizens in Ray Bradbury's *Fahrenheit 451* have each memorized a book. This makes the total knowledge more deeply ingrained. Each one assumes that the other clans are authorities about their subcults. In a modern society, diversity of specialized knowledge helps to make the system more resistant. We assume the other person is doing his job and knows his business; we assume, moreover, that the whole thing hangs together and we can always look it up in the Yellow Pages.

Another reason why the Azande system is unfalsifiable is that all the parts support one another. If the oracle indicates someone is the witch and you confront him, he does not call you a damned fool; he would not dare. Instead, he says, "If I have *mangu* unbeknown to myself, I will 'cool' it."[114] The accusation is not falsified. The system is unfalsifiable, moreover, because what is alleged is unfalsifiable. It is not *how* someone got sick or died but *why* he was so unlucky. Such statements cannot be proven or disproven.[115]

In this whole system, magic is a defensive matter. Witches do not use magic. They have no medicines, no spells. They kill spiritually, almost by a kind of conscious or unconscious intention, it seems. Magic is the defense against witch-craft.

Sorcerers, if they exist, *do* use magic—medicines, spells, poison, dirty tricks. It is quite possible for some people to be doing this sort of thing and imagining it to have an effect; so Evans-Pritchard says that sorcery is a "possible" crime.[116] But it is an "improbable" crime, he says, on shaky evidence, perhaps. Medicine bags are mysteriously found outside houses of people under attack, he admits, but maybe they are just collections of twigs which somebody thinks is medicine. His attempts to explain sorcery away seem weak; but in Azande, perhaps sorcery is rare. Real magic reduces to the witchdoctor. And most of his job is to fight witches. Once again, the natural ideal type provided by an extreme case is illuminating: it dramatically focuses for us *the main function of magic: which is to defend the ego and the individual.*

The witch himself is just a symbol for the moral consensus in such a primitive society. The Azande seem almost to grasp this themselves, with their idea that the witch capacity may lie in all of us, that we may all bewitch our neighbors unintentionally. It is even possible to envy the Azande their system, and to wish, if one is trapped in a huge bureaucracy crackling with personal animosities, group tensions, secret "contracts" out on individuals, and so on, to wish that one could consult an oracle, find out what is wrong, confront the hostile superior whose unconscious anger is responsible for one's social malaise (i.e., the witch), or the jealous competitor whose dirty tricks are responsible (i.e., the sorcerer), and get him to climb down peacefully.

New medicines and new thaumaturgical movements based on easy initiation and membership keep coming into Zandeland from other societies. Some collegia of magicians admit laymen who clamor to join. Again, the natural ideal type has picked up something: In primitive society there is a tendency for every man to turn into a magician. There are some societies where one in five is a magician. Everyone needs magic to defend against the witch—i.e., the superego's totemic killer, religion's assassin. The result is that:

> . . . every Zande, except small children, whether young or old, is to some extent a magician. At some time or other a man is sure to use some or other medicine. Throughout life men are constantly associated with medicines . . . (Evans-Pritchard, p. 432)

Evans-Pritchard's conclusion is that the witch complex is about death. In Zandeland (and in most places) witches kill.[117] The witch kill is slow, like voodoo death. I have already shown Mauss hinting that voodoo death is related to suicide. I now want to suggest that *witchcraft, voodoo death and suicide are all related.* Voodoo death in societies of mechanical solidarity is commonplace; witch accusations are probably among the first defenses against it. As ego is more deeply sculpted, voodoo death is replaced by suicide. Witch fears bespeak enormous social pressures exerted on egos; witch accusations attempt to resist these pressures. Witch accusations, like most serious magic, are a matter of life or death.

PART FOUR: WHY THESE TERRORS PERSIST—
A SOCIAL STRAIN GAUGE

Confirmation of EP's Model

How does one confirm a natural model that has to admit of variation from case to case? By showing that its central tendencies are usually present and that variations are overdetermined, related to social structure and conflicts. Lucy Mair concluded[118] that the model is confirmed in this sense, even though Azande witchery is in some ways eccentric (e.g., the curious lack of fear of witches), and other elements are mostly African (witchcraft as a physical organ inherited in the body, etc.). The key tendencies, however, are almost universally present, she found: the distinction of witch and sorcerer, with the witch killing by spiritual means rather than magic; the whole zoo of magic professions that fight the witch, and so on. Parrinder found[119] the model especially apt for Africa: witches here fly by night, suck spiritual organs, often attack unconsciously, etc. But some parts apply all over the world, especially the existence of two patterns, witch and sorceror. One will predominate, but in every society there will be at least vestigial remains of the other. Middleton and Winter,[120] surveying 30 years of such investigations, also concluded that the model holds up, especially the distinction of the sorcerer who uses magic and the witch who kills without it. One investigator after another finds both patterns, though they are called by different names ("day witch versus night witch" among the Lobedu,[121] or sorcerers and "real sorcerers" among the Cewa[122]). Even where only one pattern, say sorcery, seems to predominate, one looks closer and there are myths or rumors of "flying witches," too (e.g., Dobu[123]). Even fieldworkers not conversant with the model can be shown to confirm it: for example, two French investigators with unidentified credentials, J. Kerhara and A. Bouquet,[124] distinguish "intentional" from "unintentional sorcery" in some French African societies—obviously, these correspond to sorcerer and witch. These authors also find numerous other magical professions—including "fetichers, prophets, clairvoyants, etc.," but these can be classified as witchdoctors or diviners, i.e., as curers or diagnosticians. (Fetichers, with their knowledge of special plants, are obviously witchdoctors.[125]) That is the value of the model: it enables us to "read" ethnographic data on black magic from almost any society, and identify the cast of characters.

One important element in the model has been challenged: this is Evans-Pritchard's idea that sorcery, while possible, is an "improbable crime," imaginary just like witchcraft. In some societies real sorcerers have apparently been found, and many use physical aggression as well as magic. Besides the Barotse,[126] with their bushguns and poison, and the disease-owning Dobu,[127] there are, for example, Bunyoro sorcerers who burn down people's houses and use poison.[128] Isaac Schapera found[129] that sorcery was so real in Bechuanaland that in 1943 native courts were given the right to deal with such cases. The Tswana here especially used poison.[130] Threats of sorcery are also a very real form of aggression and often effective: Beattie found them among the Bunyoro. This is not to deny that in some societies sorcery may be quite as imaginary as witchcraft; Max Marwick finds sorcery beliefs distinct from witches among the Cewa,[131] yet no evidence that such persons exist.[132] In Cebu, witchdoctors routinely treat patients who are ill and also take clients who want sorcery done on enemies, reports Lieban,[133] but he describes no such case first hand. But there are many societies in which there is at least evidence of father-to-son training in sorcery (e.g., the Konkomba[134]). Moreover, witchdoctors clearly do exist and they can and sometimes do use their magic malevolently. A lesser problem is posed by claims that witchcraft also exists. This usually takes the form of finding some alleged elements of a witch pattern (e.g., flying, killing by spiritual means, cannibalism) among real sorcerers, as Schapera did in Bechuanaland, Whiting among the Paiute,[135] and so on. Victor Turner[136] notes witch patterns among convicted Barotse "witches"[137] and uses them to carp at the sorcerer-witch distinction in nominalist fashion. But the seeming existence of witch patterns could be explained: a. *By confusion of archetypes and nomenclature.* Especially where sorcery *is* imaginary, or partly imaginary, it is easy for witch elements to get mixed into it. Even where sorcery exists, it is mostly underground, and rumors may attribute witch elements to it. b. *By acting out.* Sorcerers may feed these rumors, may try to act out witch patterns to increase their frightfulness. The result is mixed cases, such as Paiute sorcery, in which some real black magic is practiced by a few individuals but around it has grown up a penumbra of rumor and myth that leans more toward the witch archetype.

But, aside from his idea that sorcery is improbable, Evans-Pritchard's model of black magic stands up.

Different Ways the Model Is Used

Some anthropologists use the model cognitively, as Evans-Pritchard did, showing how black magic provides a theodicy, supports a worldview, underlines values. Philip Mayer[138] stresses theodicy: black magic beliefs help answer the problem of evil. To Monica Wilson,[139] witch beliefs are "the standardized nightmare" of the group. The Nyakyusa, for example, among whom rich and poor live side by side, characterize witches as ravenously hungry; while the Pondo, who inhibit sex, imagine witches as driven by lust. J. Krige[140] finds witch beliefs give people an excuse for failure; Fortune reports[141] the same of Dobu sorcery beliefs. The very idea of witch and sorcerer, Krige writes, presupposes a just, ordered world in which evil is outlawed and overcome by man-made techniques. Jean Buxton[142] on Mandari witchcraft reports much witch interest in sexual perversions, a dramatic way of underlining what behavior is unacceptable. This was Kluckhohn's approach.[143]

But most British anthropologists who use Evans-Pritchard's model have deemphasized his cognitive approach and instead correlate black magic with social conflict: e.g., Fortes explains Tallensi witchcraft in Ghana as related to uterine conflicts in a patrilineage.[144] Several students similarly find women accused as witches in Africa when they become traders and accumulate wealth. Middleton and Winter assert[145] that this is a more sociological approach. Max Marwick thinks[146] that moving from static functionalist to dynamic models this way better captures the change going on in Africa and the primitive world generally.

The "social strain gauge" studies in turn could be broken down several ways: 1. *Pressure on groups vs. pressure on individuals.* The studies of modern European witchcraft give more attention to social stress on the individual; the African studies stress group conflicts more. This is understandable: selves are more evolved in an advanced civilization. 2. *Conservative vs. revolutionary effects.* The older studies showed black magic reflecting social tensions but helping to contain them, hence having conservative effects. But increasingly, students like Max Marwick, Crawford,[147] Lucy Mair[148] show how black magic fosters social change.

Strategic in these studies is the valuable new focus on the *accusation* of witch-craft (in Marwick, Turner, Crawford, etc.)—who accuses whom and what this reveals about social stresses and changes. Lineage fission gets special attention (by Beattie, Turner, Marwick, etc.) as an engine of social change; so do rising classes getting involved with white man's money economy such as migrant workers, market women, money lenders, who are all sometimes accused of witchcraft.

Social Stress and Black Magic in Africa

Max Marwick[149] coined the expression "social strain gauge" for witchcraft; I think black magic in general reveals where group conflicts lie.

1. Economic Conflicts Are One Kind. For example, Nadel reports[150] the Nupe believe their witches are organized and the leader of the women traders is at their head: this expresses husbands' discomfort at wives' commercial success in the growing money economy. Similarly Scarlett Epstein,[151] writing of a Mysore village in India, finds it is women rising as money lenders who are most often considered witches. Max Marwick[152] comments that, in general, where relative status is not ascribed but is up for competition, black magic accusations often result. David Tait,[153] on Konbomba sorcery, finds that wealthy people are suspected of sorcery; the thinking is that they must have used dirty tricks to succeed. Beattie[154] reports the familiar finding that it is one's rivals who are suspected of sorcery, those who have become successful and powerful. *Economic* rivals are probably more often suspected of sorcery than of witch-craft, though there are exceptions.

2. Political Conflicts. By contrast, witch fears are often projected at authority figures, which would fit my own theory of counterattacking the superego. Robert Gray,[155] reporting on the Mbugwe, finds witch accusations (but not sorcery accusations) are made against chiefs. Bad chiefs are thought to use their witchery to do general damage. That is the conservative side of the complex; it helps restrain power. But *weak* chiefs are also accused of witchcraft by rivals who expropriate their power: that is the revolutionary side. (There is a possible connection here to Frazer's evidence that weak or wounded kings are thought to have a maleficent effect on prosperity.[156])

3. Cognitive Conflicts. Black magic can also reflect value conflicts, cultural discontinuities. Mary Douglas,[157] Middleton and Winter, and many[158] have emphasized that black magic is often socially disruptive and dysfunctional. This may be the case especially with cognitive conflicts. Joyce Bednarski[159] analyzes a modern case that way, tying the Salem witch trials to the new royal charter which ended theocratic rule in Massachusetts: the wounded religious community felt itself to be disintegrating and projected witch fears. Norman Cohn[160] and Trevor-Roper[161] take this approach: in tying European witch beliefs to demonology ideas provoked by heresy they emphasize cognitive conflict. S. H. Hooke finds evidence[162] that demonic ideas of black magic were bred out of derogated religious cults as far back as Babylonia and Assyria. Black magic is probably at its nastiest, least functional and most disruptive when it reflects fundamental value conflicts.

4. Conflicts In Kin Structure. Certain conflicts seem built into kin systems, and sorcery-witchcraft fears reflect them. Black magic accusations often go against women in patrilocal groups. R. G. Willis[163] finds one society (Ufipia) in which the young accuse the old of sorcery. Mary Douglas finds the same among the Lele: accused sorcerers are weak, neglected old people. The real problem is that they hang on too long and the young want their own day. Something similar happens in U.S. corporations.

Lineage Fission

Turner studied witch accusations in family splits.[164] When Ndembu families grow too big, the sons start accusing each other of black magic and that helps grease the skids. The extended lineage finally splits, and afterwards the witch accusations serve as *post hoc* justifications for what had to happen anyway because of population pressure. Turner calls these family crackups "social dramas." Villages also split after long struggles in which rivals who hope to become headmen seek allies as tensions build. The final ruptures explode with open accusations of witchcraft. After the split, a new equilibrium is established. But what seemed revolutionary here is really conservative; the society has the same form as before.

Turner describes several typical "social dramas" he witnessed first hand. A village headman is aging; competitors for the succession build influence by warning followers that their present neighbors are bewitching them and inviting them to come live nearby, thus prefiguring new villages. The tensions are usually brought to a flash point by some natural calamity like an epidemic; then rumors escalate into open accusations of witchcraft and the family or village splits. Yet the society, fragmentary on the local level, keeps its basic outlines; the witch accusations help let off steam and facilitate adjustments that are basically conservative.[165]

Who Accuses Whom

Today British anthropologists give special attention to the direction of black magic accusations. This approach makes the "social strain gauge" a sensitive tool indeed. It was direction-of-accusation that revealed tension between the sexes in Ufipia, conflict with chiefs among the Mbugwe, and so on, in studies already cited. It gave me my idea that "the accusation is the magical act," and helped me see how witchcraft, which is non-magical, fits into magic. As Marwick pointed out,[166] there can be three parties in an accusation: the victim, the accuser (who may be somebody else, a kinsman or friend) and the accused witch. Statistical studies of their sociograms usually show what is going on. I think that direction of accusation can help show whether a black magic complex is conservative or revolutionary. We see accusations in Africa directed more often against strong people—chiefs, headmen, powerful rivals—whereas modern European witch accusations went more against the weak and the poor. Attacking the powerful is not revolutionary; as Turner showed,[167] it is part of a normal process of friction and change within stability (e.g., lineage fission); others have shown how it maintains community by making even the powerful obey the rules. Whereas attacks upon the weak usually indicate a fundamental break with basic values (such as traditional reciprocity rules). In Tudor England, the poor were accused of witchcraft just as the enclosure movement and capitalist investment in land were beginning. These accusations helped force revolutionary changes.

One student of direction-of-accusation was Max Marwick, whose study of the Cewa, *Sorcery in Its Social Setting,*[168] used the strain gauge sensitively and backed it with impressive verification. Marwick employed statistical tests on 194 incidents to test his hypothesis that accusations correlate with social change and conflict. He confirmed it. One target of accusations was people who worked for the whites for cash wages but did not share with relatives according to old reciprocity rules. He also found, like Turner, that accusations help force inevitable lineage fission during population expansion. Most Cewa accusations are between cousins in the matrisib; and it is along these fault lines that the families will split. Sorcery charges are used in two stages: 1. Politically, as rivals jockey for power within the extended family; 2. later, to confirm the split. Co-wives also attack each other and so do competitors for the favor of a chief. Accusers tend to be men on the make. Shrewd diviners study social ties and animosities in deciding their diagnosis. The Cewa are allegedly good sociologists and seem to understand that sorcery is connected with social conflicts. Marwick's conclusion: black magic accusations arise in close groups, as a safety valve, when there is no other between people who relate intensely, in total rather than segmental roles. The pressure is insufferable. Sorcery serves to keep people in line with the norms (both fear of attack and fear of accusation are sanctions).

Marwick studied alternative explanations to solidify his proof; for example, he found no statistical correlation between accusations and how near people lived to each other. Sorcerer-victim links he takes to reflect knowledge the public has of open quarrels (diviners point a victim to a particular "sorcerer" according to conflicts they know about). But the accuser-sorcerer links reflect real hostilities (people accuse their actual enemies). Victim-accuser links merely reflect affiliations. (Your friends or family may accuse on your behalf.) Sorcery is a moral force; as a rule *both* victims and accused have done something wrong. So sorcery upholds moral values. In this sense it is conservative. It also expresses conflict, but Simmel[169] and Coser[170] have shown that conflict can sometimes help bind society together.

In a collection of articles he edited, Max Marwick gathered similar studies and observed that dynamic models like direction-of-accusation are better able to capture changes going on in Africa. Now doing field work in Oceania himself, he noted that in this culture area accusations are more likely to go outside one's own group than is the case in Africa.[171] He is not sure what this means, but thinks that possibly the accusations outside the group could be connected with war.

The most exciting essay in this collection is J. R. Crawford's "Consequences of Accusation."[172] I have already said that the accusation is the real magical act; Crawford's study would help confirm this. The accusation is not a mere indicator of strain, he writes. It is dynamite. It is what really blasts the "witch"; aggressive magic is secondary. The accusation assaults his social being. It sets in motion the whole apparatus of diviners, oracles, witchdoctors and their hard-to-stop procedures. Crawford says it is a political act, a bid for power, above all a manipulation of public opinion for private ends. This is reminiscent of Huvelin's idea that magic is the "detouring" of community symbolism to serve an individual.

Like Marwick, Middleton edited (or coedited) several collections of studies[173] using the Evans-Pritchard model as a social strain gauge, with direction-of-accusation often the guide. Middleton and Winter's *Witchcraft and Sorcery in East Africa* is perhaps the definitive volume of the social morphology school of black magic. Victor Turner wrote an evaluation of the collection[174] in which he called for rethinking these matters in terms of the new structuralism and the new process theories. He was perhaps thinking of his own study of lineage fission, stability encapsulating constant change as a process. But he applauded the increasing attention to the accusation, and the vectors between accuser, victim and witch or sorcerer; the productive research of the future lies in this direction, he wrote.

In *Magic, Witchcraft and Curing* Middleton gathered studies which tested the method further afield, not just in Africa but also in South and North America, India, the Arctic. In this volume Manning Nash reports[175] on witchcraft among the Tzeltal of Central America, and this is one of the striking cases where the witch is killed *before* the trial. If enough men come to believe that a person is an inveterate witch, they ambush him and kill him. Usually a victim does this with the help of his kin. But then a problem faces the community which threatens to cause blood feuding: was the killing justified? So a trial is held, *after* the witch is killed, to decide whether he was indeed a witch. He who kills a witch runs the risk of death at the hands of the community if he misjudges the character of his victim or public opinion, or is not himself well liked or accepted. I have already suggested that witches were probably dispatched this way in many societies before colonialism; Evans-Pritchard, Reynolds, many others, have heard reports. Perhaps this was how the witch-finding apparatus began, after the fact, after the periodic murder of moral entrepreneurs whose criticisms, gloominess and generally accusing demeanor had activated moral pressure.

Black Magic and Moral Consensus

Witchcraft, seemingly at the antipodes of magic, is close to religion. It possesses no intrinsic magic; rather, magic is used against it. It works by spiritual means, as religion does; no wonder its persecutors imagine witches' sacrifices, witches' gods, sabbats of witches, witchcraft as a demonic religion. Witchcraft is more concerned with morality than most magic; it inverts morality to reinforce the value system. Witchcraft, moreover, is a projection of voodoo death, which is execution by religion; witchcraft becomes a theodicy explaining death because it is originally about death. psychic death. The witch kill is the totemic symbolization of the voodoo death; and the witch accusation is man's first magic to fight religious assassination. In this sense, all witch accusations are a form of sorcery, in which another human being is hit because he symbolizes or speaks for the oppressive consensus. That is why there is a strain or a suspicion of sorcery in *all* magic[176] : because all magic has something to do with protecting the self by counterattacking the moral order. Usually it attacks another person as the symbol of that order. The witch accusation is the perfect paradigm of magic, because, as Crawford shows, it takes the form of manipulating public opinion for private ends, by accusing the moral accuser of inverted moral values. So witch accusations are the perfect illustration of Mauss' "expropriation"[177] and Huvelin's "detouring"[178] of the sacred for private ends.

The accusation was originally defensive; but in more complicated societies, when the self goes on the offensive, witch accusations can be attempts by individuals to seize power by manipulating consensual values so as to downgrade rivals. In modern bureaucracies, the "sorcerer" is the deadly rival who proceeds by foul means of rumor, innuendo, destruction of one's work and other secret measures to ruin ego as a competitor.[179] While the "witch" is the person who speaks in the management voice, clothes himself with the moral values of the group to attack weak or marginal individuals as unworthy, or to brand dissenters as immoral. In modern organizations, however, there are no "diviners," no accepted oracles, no tribunals of public opinion, no magical grievance procedures to handle cases in which some individuals make others get sick and even die. Modern bureaucrats allegedly protect themselves by "role distance" and role diversity; but in American society, occupational role is so much more greatly weighted, and is so determining of other roles, that the totalism of primitive kin groups is approached again. Work groups in bureaucracies tend to number the familiar 30 to 50 individuals found in band societies; in corporate bureaucracies these tend increasingly to be "parochial" groups who stay together for long periods, perhaps whole dreary lifetimes; unconsciously these groups are internalized as moral orders, even by scoffers who protest more skepticism and distance than they actually achieve. In many cases, the odd man out, the person who loses the partly competitive, largely cooptative and often dishonest status game, literally sickens and may die. Primitive ideas of the moral nature of illness are never far from the minds of the participants, moreover. And when one person who has been isolated, marginalized, has finally sickened to the point that he drops off, quits or dies, some remarkable things happen. First, despite the secular milieu, the event is interpreted with almost primitive realism and moralizing theodicy. "He was slipping." He deserved to die. It is a moral judgment which teeters on the edge of causal explanation and sociological insight. And secondly, an even more remarkable thing happens. Once he is gone, somebody else gets "sick," as if the system generated its own tensions and required scapegoats to withstand its own terrible internal moral pressures.

PART FIVE: THE SOCIAL STRAIN GAUGE FITS MODERN EUROPE TOO

Black magic continues to provide a strain gauge of pressures on selves and individuals, even in modern civilization. An important group of historians have used the new methods on witchcraft in Tudor and Stuart England. Early members of this group independently invented their own strain-gauge methods; later members frankly adopted techniques from the anthropologists.[180] Increasingly they emphasize direction-of-accusation as the key tool for understanding black magic as a social phenomenon. With it, they have produced some of the best explanations so far of the persistence of black magic into modern civilization.

I am talking about some Oxford historians who eventually cross-fertilized with Oxford anthropologists at the Institute of Social Anthropology. But their own tradition began elsewhere, in America, and then crossed the ocean. Henry Charles Lea's researches may have stimulated them, but I date the new approach to 1907, when Professor George Lyman Kittredge published a paper entitled, "Notes on Witchcraft" in the *American Antiquarian Society Proceedings.*[181] This paper contained a much more scrupulous use of the evidence than previous studies. And it quickened and stimulated the work of a young history graduate student at Yale named Wallace Notestein, who had been spending summers in Oxford and London carefully sifting primary documents of witch trials.[182]

Notestein

Most previous students of witchcraft had a. studied all periods at once and spread themselves thin; b. studied all countries at once even though the persecutions varied significantly (e.g., less demonology in England, restraint by the Inquisition in Spain, etc.). c. In addition, previous studies had relied on second-hand or literary sources, such as pamphlets attacking the witches or describing their trials. Notestein instead went to the legal record.[183] He thus pioneered a new technique in witch studies: he focused on the court record of the actual trials to see who accused whom of exactly what. And he focused on a small area (one country, one period).

Notestein's Ph.D. dissertation was accepted in 1908, and published as a book in 1911.[184] He became a professor at Yale, and his subsequent historical investigations (e.g., *The English People on the Eve of Colonization*) frequently took him to England. After he became emeritus at Yale, he became a professor at Oxford.[185] There some younger historians who have continued to use his methods for studying Tudor and Stuart witchcraft, notably A. D. J. MacFarlane and Keith Thomas, have also been influenced markedly by the Evans-Pritchard group over on South Park Road. The result was a most fruitful cross-fertilization of methods, with old court records searched, above all to discover the identity of the accuser, the accused, the victims and their social relationships with each other. The results parallel the discoveries of the African area anthropologists that black magic accusations correlate with social tensions.

Notestein's method led him gradually toward a sociological interpretation of witchcraft, the first impressive such interpretation made on English materials. The sixteenth and seventeenth centuries in England could not be understood without a grasp of this "ugly movement" which involved all classes, threatened everyone. And Notestein insisted, as he said the Elizabethans had, on the distinction of witch and sorcerer. The witch has abandoned Christianity, worshipped Satan as god, etc. Witchcraft was a very old idea, yet in a sense comparatively modern, the modern element being the devil idea which was seeping in from the continent. This demonology element was late to reach England; like Lea, Notestein traced it to Southern Europe, and before that to Byzantium, referring to the Manicheist tradition (see Steven Runciman on the path of these ideas[186]). When it reached England it came through theology and from there influenced law; law in turn influenced the action of prosecutors which influenced public opinion.

New laws punishing witchcraft were watersheds unleashing not only numerous trials but epidemics of accusations, as if legal validation helped to foster it. From the opening of Elizabeth's reign, the people knew a law would be passed. The crime of *sorcery* had previously been tried, and was used as a political weapon, tried in council. Henry VIII had passed a harsh statute about black magic which remained on the books only six years; now Henry's law was to be renewed under Elizabeth. It was finally passed in 1563. It provided that anyone causing death by witchcraft, enchantment, charm or sorcery was to pay the penalty of death as a felon. Anyone merely causing harm by such means would get one year's imprisonment for a first offense, death for a second.

Why was it passed? The Protestant crown, under attack by Spain and the Catholics, genuinely feared conjuration against the queen's life, the way we fear presidential assassination.[187] The Renaissance had provoked an upsurge of magic, and the country was full of mystic humanists, "cunning men," astrologers and wizards. In this atmosphere of rising magic the crown felt threatened and took the initiative; the church was quietly dampening the matter in canon law proceedings with mild penalties, while Cecil's detective service sought out conjurers the way secret police seek out dissidents.

The first important trial following the new law was an Assize case, in Essex in 1566, in which the Privy Council intervened. Women employing cat familiars were accused in Chelmsford. In England, torture was not used, but captious cross-examination and all-night third degrees broke many witnesses. Repeated alarms in Chelmsford brought further trials, and the trials seemed to touch off waves of accusations in other areas: Notestein attempted to connect them chronologically to emphasize this.

Notestein's narrative method is a careful reconstruction of each "social drama" (Turner), using details about accusers, accused and victims developed directly from the primary court records. In most English cases the accused were women, often poor or mendicant. And Notestein finds what Lea found in Spain: although the central administration stirred up the mania by its inquisitions and trials, the populace overresponded, and the shaken central authority eventually tried to quiet the uproar it had provoked. The Privy Council began issuing pardons; assize judges grew more lenient; in the latter part of Elizabeth's reign half the trials ended in acquittal. This Notestein partly attributes to the growing movement of skepticism; books like Reginald Scot's *Discoverie of Witchcraft* influenced the educated and hence the judges. Then James I revived the persecutions with a harsher law, and his demonological opinions swayed the courts.

Now new demonological theories and cruel methods of interrogation were coming in from the continent and the confessions they exacted temporarily overwhelmed the growing skepticism. There were more trials, but also more acquittals. As before, each trial bred more accusations; extorted confessions named still other witches. And now traveling witch finders like Matthew Hopkins went from town to town like their counterparts in Africa, stirring up the mania. But in the end, skepticism triumphed. When the ruling classes withdrew their belief, judges stopped convicting. Lack of convictions in turn stopped certifying the masses' delusion, and the accusations themselves gradually waned.

Much of Notestein's book is history of ideas: The ruling class becomes superstitious; their actions stir up the masses; the ruling class recoils and stops convicting; and the superstition wanes. But Notestein also offers sociological interpretations: He links black magic accusations especially to the political struggle. And the sociological implications of Notestein's data went further than his explicit conclusions. Studying the legal records of real trials inevitably exposed social patterns which later historians would interpret: such as the poverty and social weakness of the accused, the close relationships between victim, accused and accuser, and so forth.

Ewen and Kittredge

Even Notestein's study was spread thinner than some which came later, inspired by his labors. He tried to cover the whole of England for 160 years; and to cover that ground he had to stick to cases in print. He included some local as well as central courts, but admitted that no history would be final until someone had been round the English counties to study municipal archives. In 1929 C. L. Ewen attempted some of this: he published the Home Circuit Assize court indictments for witchcraft, 790 of them, of which only a few had been turned up by Notestein.[188]

In 1929, George Lyman Kittredge published *Witchcraft in Old and New England,* making somewhat looser use of the new method to compare witch persecutions in Massachusetts with those in England. Kittredge, in his 1929 study, stressed cognitive elements and gave great attention to the skeptics whose publications turned educated opinion. Kittredge also emphasized political conflict as Notestein had: At the time of the Salem trials, Massachusetts had just emerged from a crisis which had threatened its very existence; Increase Mather had been the colony's representative in London during these negotiations. Witch ideas are common, Kittredge concluded, but they come to the fore in sporadic outbursts related to political conflict.

MacFarlane

It remained for a younger Oxford historian who had been influenced by the Oxford anthropologists as well as by Notestein to take the sociological spotlight away from the elites and the political struggle, and focus it on the common people and their class conflicts. A. D. J. MacFarlane did his doctoral dissertation on this subject,[189] with advice from the Oxford anthropologists. He used the Notestein method on court cases and the anthropologists aided him with interpretations. He concentrated on a single county, Essex, where there had been a good deal of commotion, and did a micro-examination of petty court records there—borough courts, quarter session courts and ecclesiastical courts as well as the Assizes, building in part on the earlier researches of Ewen. He concentrated, moreover, on a somewhat shorter time period than Notestein, 120 years, apparently. By digging into local and ecclesiastical courts, he was able to show that each big secular trial was the culmination of a long grass roots process of suspicion, gossip, slander and lower court accusations; he was able to embed the political trials in underlying social conflicts. His main emphasis was not the struggle of political elites but the socio-economic circumstances of the humble players in these social dramas: the accused, the accusers and the victims. His findings are interesting.

The accused witches were generally poorer than their accusers, in contrast with many African societies where the accused witches might be superior persons, possibly a chief; and the explanation is in the wrenching social changes going on in Europe. The accused witch, moreover, was typically not just poor, but downwardly mobile; her estate had been higher. She might be a widow reduced to penury, or a wife of a family that had gone down economically. In an earlier, more community-minded England, these unfortunate people from decent families could expect to be looked after by their neighbors.

Witches were not the usual stereotype—not ugly, lame or squint-eyed—but they were irritating, for they did not suffer in silence. Instead of living lives of quiet desperation they complained, muttered and grumbled. Their real sin was that they begged and would not take no for an answer; when turned down they scolded people and upset them. Many were old women who cursed their better-off relatives and made them feel guilty.

MacFarlane interpreted these tensions against the socioeconomic changes in England, changes Max Weber wrote about in *The Protestant Ethic.*[190] Old community values of reciprocity, kin-ties and friendship were giving way to a new acquisitive ethic. Go-getting individuals now preferred to invest their profit in additional land instead of sharing it out with poor relatives, beggars or friends.[191] The immediate conjugal family was becoming the main focus of economic loyalties, as Benjamin Nelson showed in *The Idea of Usury.*[192] This abetted the transition to capitalism by downgrading economic claims by most other relatives.

In such a struggle, women, being mother symbols, were extremely troubling to conscience. Women remained a coordinating element in society, embodying the older ethic of village reciprocity. Accusing them of witchcraft was one way of neutralizing their terrible pressure on the selfish ego, a pressure exerted no doubt both externally and internally, as shame before public opinion and as guilt before conscience.

Trial records revealed that it was almost always the victim of witchery who had committed the breach of reciprocity. He refused food or beer or help or comfort to someone who perhaps had a right to expect it, and her grumbling made him feel guilty. And it was this disappointed person who was then accused of witchcraft.[193] Furthermore, the trial records show the accusations most often occurred between close neighbors and kin, people in the same village, on the same street.[194]

A disappointed old woman would make a threatening remark, and later someone would get sick. MacFarlane does not stress possible psychosomatic effects, but I have no doubt that a poor old woman's taunts could make some selfish people sicken with guilt. Then the victim would recall some suspicious circumstance—perhaps the old woman had given him a gift or her cat had been seen nearby. He would then accuse her of witchcraft to protect himself.[195]

MacFarlane concludes that in a rapidly changing society, witchcraft accusations can have revolutionary effects, instead of stabilizing effects as in primitive societies. He dismisses the political strife Notestein and Kittredge stressed as of lesser importance. Law cannot make such beliefs, only religion can. Witch beliefs surged up from grass roots distress during a period of moral confusion, the transition from old communitarian norms to a capitalist ethic. Interestingly, MacFarlane associates the ultimate waning of the witch mania with the final victory of Puritanism. Once in power Puritanism at last provided a theodicy to justify the new ethic of acquisitiveness, and so filled the moral gap. The new morality taught that the poor were *not* entitled to indiscriminate aid. Polanyi[196] has traced this process in detail. The workhouse ethic that condemned indiscri-

rising middle classes from the terrors of a social conscience that had, in primitive times, been capable of producing voodoo death. The net effect was that the moral authority of the poor was destroyed, and with it, their ability to hinder the new classes.[197] With this pressure removed, it was no longer necessary to brand the poor as witches.[198] A further factor in ending the epidemic was the population shift to the cities, away from the intense small communities which are the natural moral climate of witch fears.[199]

The law provided an institutionalized framework, that is all. The system itself was based on popular beliefs, and MacFarlane puts himself in the Durkheim tradition by insisting that these are magical ideas which derive from religion.[200]

Keith Thomas

Keith Thomas continued the tradition[201] even though he did not do original research in court records. His contribution was to place this new research in the context of a broader history of magic and religion. His approach is mostly cognitive, history of ideas, like Notestein's, but with a secondary emphasis on social stresses. He is extremely skillful at untangling the dialectical relationships between magic, religion, science and rationality. His work is notable for the emphasis given to the Renaissance theosophies, above all Hermeticism, Neo-Platonism and astrology, in providing a canopy of belief making witch doings seem possible to the intelligentsia. Like Kittredge and Notestein he traces the decline of the witch mania to a refusal of judges to convict, which began when these theosophies were undermined by modern science. But more than the others Thomas also gives attention to the canopy of belief provided by religion itself. In Durkheimian fashion, he exposes witchcraft as an offshoot of Christian theology. His interpretation goes in terms of gnosticism; it is almost as extreme as Eric Voegelin's characterization of Calvinism as a modern gnosticism.

In fighting its gnostic-manicheist heretic wing, Thomas writes, the Catholic Church patterned the ancient complex of maleficium as demonological. But this constituted, in effect, a concession to gnosticism, for it surrendered much of the world to the devil, and thereby abetted the feeling of helplessness already growing in the dislocated masses. And Protestantism was often a reflex quite similar to such demonology: Did not Luther call the world the "province of the devil"? In denying the dominion of the Roman world church (declaring it, in fact, to be evil, as some early gnostics had declared Jehovah to be the devil), in condemning earthly pleasures, in preaching transcendental rapport with a distant deity who could not be mediated through worldly institutions, Protestantism had the same gnostic effect as demonology: abdication and helplessness. This was a great age of conversions, reversals. Often, people who converted to Protestantism had felt an impulse, just before, to convert to demonology and satanism, Thomas reports. This was a time of hysteria, and a common illness was a morbid compulsion to blurt out blasphemous statements during mass.[202] It is true that Protestantism later had a very *this*-worldly effect, due to the "worldly asceticism" (Weber) which later generations cultivated to give themselves some outer signs of election and allay their terrible fears about predestination. But in the beginning, Protestantism almost as much as demonology seemed to propose that the world was occupied by the legions of evil.

This abdication fostered a sense of helplessness, which was intensified when both Protestantism and Catholicism removed popular defenses against black magic. The same driven logic and mad rationalization that led Catholicism to give a demonological interpretation to witchcraft led it in the end to condemn *all* magic, and so weaken popular defenses against maleficium. Similarly, Protestantism was a movement against magic to begin with, provoked in part by the excesses of the occult revival in the Renaissance. So both religions simultaneously removed popular defenses against maleficium while intensifying belief in black magic with their pessimistic, gnostic, demonological views of the world.

The result was an upsurge of witch accusations among the people. Whereas on the continent the witch persecutions had been initiated from above (as part of the church's drive against heresy, or Protestantism's drive against magic), Catholic England had possessed no Inquisition, no theology of demonology, at first. England's upper classes, therefore, did not, at least under Catholic rule, initiate mass prosecutions. They came from the masses. The prosecutions did not begin on a large scale until Protestant monarchs came to power. Then there were some sorcery cases among the threatened Protestant ruling classes. And then the witch laws were passed under Henry VIII, Elizabeth and James, expressing the Protestant antipathy toward magic in general, including witchcraft. (It was the extreme Protestants who called for the death penalty for *all* kinds of magic.)

The new laws provoked an explosion of witch accusations among the people by providing them with certified official forms. But black magic fears and tensions had already been building among them for a hundred years. Stripped of traditional defensive magic by rising Protestantism and Catholic rationalism, pressured by social change and conflict, the populace was tormented by old fears of maleficium. Priests heard their tales in confession. Doctors heard their charges when they came to surgery complaining that they had been bewitched and made ill. Church courts and the courts of the gentry had been pressed by these complaints for decades. The gentry were skeptical and resisted. But when the Protestant monarchs passed laws condemning all magic, mass witch fears now had a focus. Accusations that were tried and resulted in official convictions and executions certified these beliefs and bred more accusations. Almost immediately, as in Spain, the ruling classes drew back in horror at what they had stirred up. Resistance began very early, and took the form of judges refusing to convict, or refusing to pass sentence of death.

But it was the weakening of the worldviews that supported belief in witchcraft which finally made these laws dead issues before they were ever repealed. The Newtonian synthesis destroyed the prestige of the Hermetic-Neoplatonic-Astrological worldview that had captured the intelligentsia since the Renaissance (even if, as Frances Yates has suggested, that modern scientific synthesis grew out of Hermetic roots).

Keith Thomas also makes it quite plain that it was the waning of religion, as well as of magical theosophy, that cooled the witch persecutions. He notices that witch beliefs are curiously related to religion, are almost part of it, in fact. For example, he cites the Judeo-Christian tradition according to which Satan is an agent of god. He cites the fact that the church has spoken officially on the matter of witchcraft again and again. Whenever religion is all-pervasive, it is apt to engender a sense of evil like this, because of the profound pressure which it itself exerts on conscience. So, working with MacFarlane's findings and pushing them up to higher levels of generalization, *Thomas' main finding is that witchcraft is created by religion.*

And the church itself practiced black magic. For example, it frequently used prayers in ways that implied curses: such as praying for the downfall of thieves and wrongdoers. Even fasting was sometimes used as a maleficium, the so-called "black fast" as mystical social pressure against an enemy to make him sicken and die. The practice became so widespread that it had to be condemned. (Black fasts are still used in our own era, for political purposes.) So while the church patterned maleficium with its demonology concepts, it modeled maleficent magic itself with its curses, black fasts, masses for the dead and prayers for vengeance.

Thomas takes over many of MacFarlane's findings and adds broader historical perspective. For example, in discussing MacFarlane's discovery that witches were often poor old women, he puts his finger on a special circumstance: the legal weakness of old women in England.[203] They were allowed some gleaning and stubble rights on community land, but these were hurt by the enclosure movement. Polanyi has shown how such forces created rootless, landless people whom it was easy to brand as deviant as a way of controlling them.

Conclusion: Expansion or Contraction of Individuals and Selves

In these English studies we see witch beliefs arising in a modern society at a time of pressure on the individual; but in this case the pressure was generated by the *expansion* of individualism. It pressed outwards; this caused it to collide with older reciprocity values, and superego pressure against the self was generated and felt. Among the relatively developed selves of this era, social pressures caused by change were experienced more as pressures on egos than as conflicts between groups. We do not have witch dramas of lineage fission here; we have instead individual dramas of single ambitious farmers turning away requests for charity and then hurling the witch accusation at those who made them feel guilty. Today cultic black magic returns, perhaps because of stress caused by the *contraction* of the individual. But in Renaissance England we discover that stress is also experienced when individualism attempts to expand, because the self is brought into moral conflict with older value systems.

In a sense, a witch accusation adds insult to injury: it is often an attack against someone whom one has already harmed and who has thereby made one feel guilty. And it invites further injury: it is an appeal to public opinion which by itself harms the witch and calls for still greater sanctions against her. It used to lead to murder or executions, and often, perhaps, the witch accusation was made *after* the murder had been committed. The person who was thus injured, insulted or murdered was someone who stood for the moral order of society, often an old woman precisely because she is a mother figure, that first focus for the "generalized other." The real enemy, however, is the generalized other, the superego. A man who gets sick in Zandeland will first wonder whether he has perhaps broken a taboo, and if not, *then* he will suspect witchcraft. The two are very close.

Witchcraft, voodoo death and suicide are related. Every moral criticism potentially challenges the very existence of that frail, transcendent steering mechanism called the self which society creates by socialization in order to build the atoms of autonomy it needs for its own functioning. Criticism, since it mobilizes both public opinion and superego pressure, both shame and guilt, is always potentially deadly, especially in the beginning of the Individual, when homo duplex is perhaps 99.99 percent social, and the self hardly dares to be. The first magic that occurs to man, then, is probably the very idea of witchcraft, the simple idea that the moral entrepreneur or social critic could be *wrong*. Shamans and sorcerers emerge later, as mana is generalized and individuals grow stronger, but even then, most new magic is still put to work fighting witchcraft and voodoo death. Social institutions eventually evolve that defend the individual against untimely death; Frazer has shown how magic defends him against murder. But the idea of death remains in the "suicidogenic currents" that run through the value system—altruistic suicide flourishes in early civilizations, for society still claims the right to decide who shall be. And even when the *Individual* is secured, the self as a transcendent construct (Luckmann[204]), as a metaphor that is made up in socialization (Gardner[205]), or as an analog device in consciousness (Jaynes[206]) . . . even then the self is still frail. If too much autonomy is demanded of it, it may succumb to egoistic suicide; if it gets caught in crossfires of value conflict, anomic suicide may put it out.

Whenever individualism attempts to expand or is forced to contract, cognitive dissonance and moral pressure are felt by the self. It usually responds with magic. Sometimes it merely defends itself with magic; sometimes it tries to puff itself up with magic, going against the trend of institutions. But magic is an extreme recourse and a primal regression in our times, for the self that was created in magic has been long since secured by more reliable institutions. Any serious recourse to magic defense of the self now—especially black magic—is evidence of severe regression indicating extreme pressure, indicating, perhaps, that the institutional walls have been breached.

When the determined world suddenly reveals itself as not determined, Sartre wrote,[207] the recognition may be experienced as horror. The effect may be regressive. Individuals may become suspicious, inclined to wonder, like primitive man, "who" is doing it, instead of "what" is doing it. Conspiratorial theories then abound, and what Hofstadter calls "the paranoid style" may prevail in politics as institutions are suspected of being less solid than they seem. Then "each minate charity, which we see in full flower in Dickens' novels, protected the

thing meets in mere repugnance" (*Coriolanus*) and *homo homini lupus* implies that every man is also a sorcerer. Then desperate men try to regain their magical powers, first through status symbols, later through mystifications and deceit, but such attempts are confessions of weakness and vulnerability, rather than of strength, and they aggravate social conflict.

And meanwhile, those who would defend the self with magic too easily abandon the outer walls of the institution of individualism. New magics of the self, if they grow inward, turn away from the legal and political order which provides a more lasting protection of personal autonomy. But since this is where we all began, and since magic still struggles clumsily for personal freedom, it is hard to be totally unsympathetic with those who now pursue this path, however hopeless or even disastrous it may now be.

Notes

1. Max Marwick, "Witchcraft as a Social Strain Gauge," ch. 24 in Marwick, ed., *Witchcraft and Sorcery* (London, 1970), pp. 280-295.

2. Wallace Notestein, *A History of Witchcraft In England* (N.Y., 1911, 1968).

3. A. D. J. MacFarlane, *Witchcraft in Tudor and Stuart England* (N.Y., 1970).

4. Keith Thomas, *Religion and the Decline of Magic* (N.Y., 1971)

5. Clyde Kluckhohn, *Navajo Witchcraft* (Boston, 1944, 1967).

6. Monica Hunter Wilson, "Witch-Beliefs and Social Structure," ch. 22 in Marwick, ed., *Witchcraft and Sorcery* (London, 1970), pp. 252-263.

7. R. Fortune, *The Sorcerers of Dobu* (N.Y., 1963).

8. Eliane Metais, *La Sorcellerie Canaque Actuelle* (Paris, 1967).

9. Victor Turner, *The Forest of Symbols, The Ritual Process, Schism and Continuity in an African Society, Dramas, Fields and Metaphors.*

10. R. F. Trilles, *Les Pygmées de la Forêt Equatoriale* (Paris, 1931), pp. 61-197.

11. Colin M. Turnbull, *The Forest People* (N.Y., 1962), pp. 80, 145 and *passim*.

12. Trilles, *op. cit.*, ch. 6.

13. *Ibid.*, ch. 11.

14. *A General Theory of Magic*, pp. 36-37.

15. Lucien Lévy-Bruhl, *The Soul of the Primitive* (Chicago, 1966), chs. 1-2, pp. 15-109.

16. In John Middleton, ed., *Magic, Witchcraft and Curing* (N.Y., 1967), ch. 7, pp. 127-133.

17. In John Middleton, ed., *Magic, Witchcraft and Curing*, ch. 4, pp. 55-68.

18. Benson Saler, "Nagual, Witch and Sorcerer in a Quiché Village," in John Middleton, ed., *Magic, Witchcraft and Curing*, ch. 5, pp. 69-100.

19. Cf. Durkheim, *The Elementary Forms of Religious Life* (London, 1915, 1954), Book II, chs. 1-4, pp. 102-166.

20. There are four essays that give considerable attention to nawalism in the Middleton volume. Yet few links are drawn between them. Some of these points are my own inferences.

21. Knud Rasmussen, *The Intellectual Culture of the Hudson Bay Eskimos.*

22. Asen Balikei, "Shamanistic Behavior Among the Netsilik Eskimos," in John Middleton, ed., *Magic, Witchcraft and Curing*, ch. 11, pp. 191-209.

23. It is similar to Menes' feat of identifying himself with the totem of the Falcon clan, in Childe's account of the first Pharoah—or to the leader's feat of getting the horde to identify with him, in Freud's *Group Analysis and the Psychology of the Ego* (N.Y., 1965), pp. 46-53.

24. E. E. Evans-Pritchard, *Witchcraft, Oracles and Magic among the Azande* (Oxford, 1937), p. 111.

25. Howard S. Becker, *Outsiders, Studies in the Sociology of Deviance* (N.Y., 1963), pp. 147-163.

26. Malinowski vividly demonstrates the role of the moral entrepreneur among the Trobrianders. When a taboo is broken, the culprit does not die; his neighbors disapprove but take no action against him as a rule. But if any one person does speak up and denounce him for his infraction his death is certain: he commits ritual suicide. (*Crime and Custom in Savage Society*, pp. 78ff.)

27. W. Robertson Smith, *The Religion of the Semites* (N.Y., 1972), pp. 119ff.

28. Evans-Pritchard, *op. cit.*, diagram on p. 423: Witchcraft, or *mangu*, is a physical characteristic possessed by witches, but also by cats and certain deformed individuals called "bad teeth men" and "gall bladder men," also other similar evil agents (p. 423).

29. Ernesto de Martino, *The World of Magic* (Hong Kong, 1972), Part II, pp. 81-178.

30. Géza Róheim, *Magic and Schizophrenia* (Bloomington, Ind., 1955).

31. Richard W. Lieban, *Cebuano Sorcery* (Berkeley, 1967), pp. 23-27, etc.

32. Evans-Pritchard, *op. cit.*, ch. 3. Western dualism colors our understanding of these phenomena. It has been suggested by Helene Moglen, formerly Professor of English at SUNY, Purchase, that the vampire-zombie idea of the Victorian age is a dualist remainder: a fear of the body after the soul is gone. In older cultures, vampires are probably just one particular totemic incarnation of witch fears. And zombies may have something to do with the persistence of the dead before the second burial which Hertz has described. The Western mind-body split complicates all this.

33. Cf. Frederick Elsworthy, *The Evil Eye* (N.Y., 1958, 1970), p. 29, etc.

34. *A General Theory of Magic* (London and Boston, 1972), pp. 104-6.

35. *Themis*, ch. 1, etc.

36. Edmond Douttée, *Magie et Religion dans l'Afrique du Nord* (Algiers, 1908), pp. 117-119.

37. John Middleton and E. H. Winter, Introduction to Middleton and Winter, eds., *Witchcraft and Sorcery in East Africa* (N.Y., 1963), pp. 8-14ff.

38. Witch ideas work morally in several ways. Besides dramatizing the difference between good and evil, the fear of witch accusation keeps grumblers and rebels in line (lest they be accused of witchcraft). And fear of attack by witches keeps the greedy from too outrageous a break with the community reciprocity. It is surprising how often, one way or the other, *both* witches and witch accusations seem to attack *guilty* consciences. In Elizabethan England, the witch *victim* was often a rich farmer who refused to help his poorer neighbors; whereas the accused *witch* was often an eccentric grumbler.

39. Barrie Reynolds, *Magic, Divination and Witchcraft Among the Barotse of Northern Rhodesia* (Berkeley & Los Angeles, 1963), ch. 2.

40. John Beattie, "Sorcery in Bunyoro," in Middleton and Winter, eds., *Witchcraft and Sorcery in East Africa* (N.Y., 1963), ch. 1.

41. Tacitus, *Annals*, in Modern Library *Complete Works* (N.Y., 1942).

42. Robert Graves, *I Claudius, Claudius the God.*

43. Manning Nash, "Witchcraft as a Social Process in a Tzeltal Community," ch. 7 in John Middleton, ed., *Magic, Witchcraft and Curing* (N.Y., 1967), pp. 127-134.

44. Aeschylus, *The Eumenides.*

45. Thomas G. Schelling, *The Strategy of Conflict* (N.Y., 1963), p. 91ff, etc.

46. Ludwig Wittgenstein, *Remarks on the Foundations of Mathematics* (Cambridge, Mass., 1967), pp. 94-98, etc.

47. The very fact that the cast of bones or dice is a matter of chance that allegedly cannot be affected by the manipulator makes the outcome a rallying point on which all can agree.

48. Henry Charles Lea, *A History of the Inquisition of Spain* (N.Y., 1906-7, 1966), "Witchcraft," ch. 9.

49. Michael J. Harner, "The Role of Hallucinogenic Plants in European Witchcraft," in Harner, ed., *Hallucinogens and Shamanism* (London, N.Y., 1973), ch. 8, pp. 125-150.

50. Carlos Castenada, *The Teachings of Don Juan: A Yaqui Way of Knowledge* (N.Y., 1968), cf. Part II, pp. 201-255.

51. Cited by Harner, ch. 8, p. 139.

52. R. Gordon Wasson, chs. 6-7 in Peter T. Furst, *Flesh of the Gods, the Ritual Use of Hallucinogens* (N.Y., 1972), pp. 185-213.

53. Wasson, *op. cit.*, pp. 201-213.

54. John M. Allegro, *The Sacred Mushroom and the Cross* (N.Y., 1970), chs. 1–3. Fly agaric was widely used as a fly repellant to dispel the noisome insects which inevitably made bloody religious sacrifice an unpleasant experience. Sometimes a second beast was slaughtered nearby to draw them off: thus "the Lord of the Flies," as Beelzebub was called.

55. "Probably the single most important group of plants used by mankind to contact the supernatural belongs to the order Solanaceae (the potato family).... Besides the potato, tomato, chile pepper and tobacco, the family includes a great number of species of the genus Datura ... called by a variety of names, such as Jimson weed, devil's apple, thorn apple, mad apple, the devil's weed ... and all are hallucinogenic. Datura has been used widely and apparently from ancient times in shamanism, witchcraft and vision quest.... Other hallucinogens in the potato family ... include mandrake [Mandragora], henbane [Hyoscyamus] and belladonna or deadly nightshade [Atropa belladonna]." Harner, *op. cit.,* p. 128.

56. Margaret Murray, *The God of the Witches* (London, 1952).

57. Keith Thomas, *Religion and the Decline of Magic* (N.Y., 1971), pp. 514–517, 525.

58. Michelet, *La Sorcière* (Paris, 1964), pp. 45–64.

59. Julio Caro Baroja, *The World of the Witches* (Chicago, 1965, 1973), pp. 17–40.

60. Baroja thinks that magic originates in religion and separates via myth, which is then put to various applications in rites.

61. Baroja, *op. cit.,* ch. 4, "The Witches' Goddess," pp. 58–68.

62. Baroja eclectically weaves together cult diffusion, the decayed-religion idea, Michelet's peasant misery theme, and even incorporates the drug theory.

63. Louis Dumont, *Homo Hierarchicus* (Chicago, 1970), p. 191ff.

64. A. M. Hocart, *Caste* (London, 1950), pp. 12, 16–17.

65. Cited by Mircea Eliade, p. 74ff in *Occultism, Witchcraft and Cultural Fashions* (Chicago, 1976), pp. 73–78.

66. Baroja, *op. cit.,* ch. 8, "The Definitive Form of the Crime of Witchcraft," pp. 112–121.

67. H. R. Trevor-Roper, *The European Witch-Craze* (N.Y., 1956, 1967), ch. 3.

68. For this section I am using three main works of Henry Charles Lea: a. *The Inquisition of the Middle Ages,* Citadel press selections from the three-volume edition (N.Y., 1954, 1963); b. *A History of the Inquisition of Spain* (N.Y., 1906–7, 1966), vol. 4, ch. 8, "Sorcery and Occult Arts," and ch. 9, "Witchcraft;" and c. *Materials Toward A History of Witchcraft* (London, N.Y., 1957). The last book contains useful introductions by the editor, Arthur C. Howland, and by George Lincoln Burr.

69. *American Authors,* 1960, p. 456.

70. In Howland's Introduction to Lea's posthumously published *Materials Towards a History of Witchcraft* (London, 1957).

71. Arthur Mitzman in *The Iron Cage* (N.Y., 1969) suggests that Weber was fighting his father in his early works on the Prussian Junkers, and broke down when his father died after being ordered from his house during a quarrel (pp. 148–152). Weber wrote the books on religion during his long recuperation while he held no university post, as if in these very dialectical books he were working something through. Some recent books have suggested that Charles Darwin's illnesses were psychosomatic, and grew worse while he was writing *The Origin of the Species,* which, as an assault on god the father, was an Oedipal issue.

72. In a letter to Burr, Sept. 7, 1907, Lea wrote: "Many years ago I commenced researches into man's assumed control over spiritual forces and this led me back into investigating the theories of the origin of evil in the various great religions, oriental and occidental. I had a book about half completed on the subject when nervous exhaustion condemned me to intellectual idleness for some four years, and when I gradually emerged, I felt it risky to resume where I had broken off in a study of the Vedanta philosophy.... So I turned to the Inquisition, for which I had already made collections, as a simple and less brain-fatiguing amusement. Now ... I am occupying my old age with recurring to witchcraft." (Quoted p. xxiv, *Materials Toward A History of Witchcraft*)

73. George Steiner, *In Bluebeard's Castle* (New Haven, 1971, 1973), pp. 53–56.

74. What follows in the text summarizes *Materials Toward a History of Witchcraft.*

75. At first the Hebrews had no evil principle; Yahweh did both good and evil. Later, when Yahweh chastised Israel, he had Satan do it—for the Hebrews, imbibing dualism from Persia, were now squeamish about seeing god do evil. But in Job Lucifer was just an official

of god; "the adversary" or accuser in god's court. The Job story is old, going back to Nippur, but the idea of a high god who sends evil spirits to punish is new in this culture area. The Sadducees refused to believe in Satan or any spirits at all; but the new exotic Pharisee doctrine admitted angels, spirits and finally demons. In *Genesis* was the idea of the fall of man; later the fall of the angels is invented as a compromise between Hebrew ideas of the moral Jehovah and the challenge of Persian dualism. Canaanite myths of angels put to watch over earth who fall in love with the daughters of men and so fall may have suggested the idea. By the time the Book of Jubilees, about 135 B.C., Satan is substituted for god as tempter of David; now Satan, not god, is the worker of evil, but god *allows* it as a test of man.

76. Morton Smith, *The Secret Gospel* (N.Y., 1973), cf. Luke IX, i.

77. Norman Cohn, *Europe's Inner Demons* (N.Y., 1975), cf. pp. xv–xvi.

78. Gustav Davidson, *A Dictionary of Angels, Including the Fallen Angels* (N.Y., 1967). On a rough estimate, this book lists 3500 angels in alphabetical order, from A'albiel to Zuriel.

79. A. M. Hocart, *Kings and Councillors* (Chicago, 1970), pp. 20–21.

80. Cf. Hans Jonas, *The Gnostic Religion* (Boston, 1963), ch. 10, etc.

81. Lea, *A History of the Inquisition of Spain*, chs. 8 & 9.

82. Clyde Kluckhohn, *Navajo Witchcraft* (Boston, 1944, 1967), pp. 76–113.

83. Beatrice Blyth Whiting, *Paiute Sorcery* (N.Y., 1950).

84. There are six types of social control, she writes: conscience, public opinion, reciprocity, religious or supernatural sanction, retaliation and institutional sanctions.

85. Eliane Metais, *La Sorcellerie Canaque Actuelle* (Paris, 1967).

86. Robert K. Merton, *Social Theory and Social Structure* (Glencoe, Ill., 1949): pp. 21–82, "Manifest and Latent Functions."

87. R. F. Fortune, *Sorcerers of Dobu* (N.Y., 1963).

88. In the last pages of *The Gift* (N.Y., 1961), pp. 77–78ff.

89. That is, instead of an abstract model of an institution, like Max Weber's 11-page "ideal type" of bureaucracy (*The Theory of Social and Economic Organization*, London, 1947, pp. 302–12), you pick one society where the institution is strikingly formed, and use *that* real case as your model for comparison. Thus, instead of Weber's ideal type of bureaucracy, we could use the Prussian or Chinese civil service, real cases (which he really had in mind anyway). Having it out in the open that way makes the details testable and correctable. And a real model is more apt to catch the complexity of social institutions.

90. Evans-Pritchard took up Lévy-Bruhl's idea of (what I call) "why causality," developed it empirically, and Lévy-Bruhl expanded his idea in a later book with acknowledgment. Lévy-Bruhl set the idea forth in *Primitives and the Supernatural* (N.Y., 1935), ch. 6, pp. 153–154ff. Evans-Pritchard cited this idea in his 1937 book on Azande witchraft, and gave examples (pp. 67ff). Then Lévy-Bruhl reciprocated and cited Evans-Pritchard's examples in his later book *L'Expérience Mystique et les Symboles Chez les Primitifs* (Paris, 1938), ch. 1. Still later, E-P hailed Lévy-Bruhl's "last volumes," which include these two, as unsurpassed in "depth and insight," Introd. to Robert Hertz, *Death and the Right Hand*, p. 24.

91. Evans-Pritchard, "Witchcraft Among the Azande," in *Sudan Notes and Records*, vol. 12, 1929, pp. 163–249; excerpted in Marwick, ed., *Witchcraft and Sorcery* (London, 1970), pp. 27–37.

92. *The Gift* by Mauss, *Death and the Right Hand* by Hertz, *Sacrifice* by Hubert and Mauss.

93. *Death and the Right Hand* (London, 1960), Evans-Pritchard Introduction, pp. 9–24.

94. *The Gift* (N.Y., 1967), Evans-Pritchard Introduction, pp. v–x.

95. *Sacrifice* (Chicago, 1964), Evans-Pritchard Introduction, pp. 1–8.

96. I would dispute his claim that the Durkheimians analyzed systems of ideas as if they were independent. (Introduction to *Death and the Right Hand*, pp. 17ff). The Durkheimians analyzed systems of ideas because they were the kind of real social fact most accessible to them. But they made it clear that these ideas were *projections* of social structure. There is even a vivid passage in *Suicide*, already cited in chapter 5, in which Durkheim wrote that social structure shapes ideas but the reverse process is minimal or feeble (which would make him more determinist than the Marxists). *Suicide* (Glencoe, Ill., 1951), p. 227.

97. ". . . in their equally fine essay on sacrifice [Hubert and Mauss] . . . show us the pat-

tern of sacrificial acts so that we perceive how the whole rite and each part of it make sense. Hertz's essays exemplify this descriptive integration. . . ." (Introduction to Hertz, *Death and the Right Hand*, p. 15).

98. Evans-Pritchard, Introd. to *The Gift*, p. viii.

99. Introd. to *Death and the Right Hand*, p. 24.

100. Evans-Pritchard, *Nuer Religion* (Oxford, 1956), ch. 13, esp. p. 315.

101. He is on record as criticizing nomothetic, unilinear theories, in *Theories of Primitive Religion* (Oxford, 1965); and I have just shown his appreciative remarks on Mauss' natural ideal types.

102. An abstract ideal type, by contrast, besides being notoriously biased, can leave a lot out. Someone can always go back to Zandeland and repeat Evans-Pritchard's study and find out things he missed and thus enrich the model. But two generations of students experience only frustration in trying to enrich the Weber model of bureaucracy. New material accumulates showing the model to be inadequate; this is interesting, but the model itself can never be modified. Its rigidities, prejudices and gaps continue like a force field to deflect empirical research. Above all, the defects of surreptitious induction that close the operation of induction, transcendent typication and premature elaboration of theory dog the ideal-type method.

103. To put it simply, the purpose of medical magic is protection against black magic.

104. Outlined in Part I of this chapter.

105. The Azande have many means to control these terrors. a. First, for real social injuries, the commonsense Azande go to court. b. There is also minor magic they can apply themselves. c. Preventive medicine abounds, in the form of membership in thaumaturgical associations, and even in collegia of magicians. d. But if a real witch attack is suspected, the individual can consult one of the various heads-tails binary mechanical oracles. e. If a witch is indicated, confirmation can be sought via an additional more powerful oracle, or via a consultation with a witchdoctor. f. A first public step is a public oration warning the witch without naming him. g. If illness continues, the witch may be confronted. To do this, the poison oracle must be used. The wings of a dead bird, killed by the poison test, are taken to the doorstep of the accused witch, and he is asked to blow upon them to "cool" his witchcraft. h. If the illness continues, other witches may be identified. It is now politic to seek confirmation of this diagnosis by having it repeated by the poison oracle of the prince. i. If the diagnosis is confirmed, it is considered appropriate to use magic. A witch doctor is now called in. He may undertake just defensive magic at first. j. But finally, if illness continues, it is possible to buy offensive magic; if death occurs, the family of the deceased will buy vengeance magic. If a witch is known, it will be directed against him; if the witch is unknown, it will be directed against "whoever." k. Sometime later on, maybe years later, someone will die. And then the family of the bereaved will feel that justice has been done.

106. Evans-Pritchard, *op. cit.*, p. 22.

107. Yet, curiously, sorcery is more feared. It is felt that at one time it was stronger than now. The nobles of the overbearing Vongara house look down with contempt at witch beliefs (though they administer the witch finding system for social equilibrium). But they fear sorcery.

108. At one time they had powerful magicians, powerful shamans, great symbolic powers of their own; then sorcery was feared. Now it is peripheral, and their witchdoctors are socially weak. (It would in fact be legally precarious to proceed against a witch just on *their* say so.) Perhaps conquest and defeat have regressed them to more primitive ego structures, so the witch accusation, man's earliest magical defense, is their instrument of choice.

109. Evans-Pritchard, *op. cit.*, Part II, chs. 1, 2, 3.

110. *Ibid.*, Part Four, "Magic," esp. chs. 2, 3, 4.

111. *Ibid.*, Part IV, ch. 4.

112. *Ibid.*, pp. 26ff, pp. 475–478.

113. It is a curious and possibly fundamental contradiction that Durkheim applied to primitive societies the concept of "mechanical solidarity," which meant that they are allegedly held together by everyone believing exactly the same thing (in *Social Division of Labor*), and then, in a later book (*The Elementary Forms*), characterized, as the most primitive religion, totemism, which is precisely a religion in which the fragmented separate parts, i.e., the clans, each have *separate* cults.

114. The psychological experience of the accused person is interesting. He is always surprised; he never thought anything like this could happen to him (though it has probably happened to practically everyone else); he has no cognitive resistance. He supposes either that it is a mistake which will iron itself out (meanwhile it is judicious to be polite and cooperative); or else, if he is a bit more imaginative, he speculates that perhaps he might have *mangu* after all, and not know about it; and that is interesting.

115. Those are the main reasons the Azande system cannot be disproved. But starting on page 475, Evans-Pritchard gives a remarkable list of about two dozen other reasons why Azande belief in witchcraft cannot be disproved by experience. Skepticism is one defense of belief, paradoxically. The Azande are quite skeptical of the whole thing, and this insulates them from disbelief; weakly held beliefs are less brittle to contradiction. (One wonders what other empires skepticism wins for faith.) Also, contradictions in their beliefs are not noticed because the beliefs are not all in play at once. Another point: the Azande are socialized to believe these things. Also, there are mystical secondary explanations for the failure of a particular rite. Also, magic is often used to produce events which are likely to occur anyway, such as rain. Not too much is claimed for magic. Magic does not work by itself but is associated with empirical action (e.g., the accusation) that *does* produce social results. Political authority supports the system of magic. Rumors circulate about effective magic. Many of the medicines used are foreign and the Azande assume the other peoples had experience of their efficacy. Azande beliefs are so vaguely formulated and something so vague is difficult to disprove. And so on.

116. Evans-Pritchard, *op. cit.*, pp. 404–406.

117. "It is in connection with death that Zande belief in witchcraft, oracles and magic is most intelligible to us . . . for it is death that answers the riddle of mystical beliefs. . . . It is with death and its premonitions that Azande most frequently and feelingly associate witchcraft and it is only with regard to death that witchcraft evokes violent retaliation. It is likewise in connection with death that the greatest attention is paid to oracles and magical rites. . . . Thus death evokes the notion of witchcraft; oracles are consulted to determine the course of vengeance." Evans-Pritchard, *op. cit.*, pp. 540–544.

118. Lucy Mair, *Witchcraft* (N.Y., 1969, 1971), pp. 18–24 and *passim.*

119. Geoffrey Parrinder, *Witchcraft, European and African* (London, 1958, 1963), pp. 13–14, 132–138.

120. John Middleton & E. H. Winter, eds., *Witchcraft and Sorcery in East Africa* (N.Y., 1963), Introduction.

121. J. D. Krige, "The Social Function of Witchcraft," in Max Marwick, ed., *Witchcraft and Sorcery* (London,1970), pp. 237–251.

122. Max Marwick, *Sorcery in Its Social Setting* (Manchester, 1965).

123. R. Fortune, *op. cit.*, pp. 150, 152.

124. J. Kerharo and A. Bouquet, *Sorciers, Feticheurs et Guérisseurs de la Côte D'Ivoire-Haute-Volta* (Paris, 1950), ch. 1.

125. More problematical are some French African studies in which magic has a more theurgic or religious function: such as Marcel Griaule on the Dogon (*Dieu d'Eau, Entretiens Avec Ogotemmeli*, Paris, 1948; *Les Masques Dogon*, etc.); or Jean Rouch on the Songhay (*La Religion et la Magie Songhay*, Paris, 1960), where there is a further problem of diversity (this society has many different magical and religious "paths to god", cf. ch. 1). But even here the model helps pick out and identify those adepts who play familiar roles in the medical magic complex (several castes of magicians, especially the Schantye magicians, who make a kind of magic cake, called "korte," which is a cross between a medicine and a fetich, and use it to cure). And, sure enough, the agents of spiritual afflictions here include the familiar cast of characters: flying witches that "eat souls," and so on.

126. Barrie Reynolds, *Magic, Divination and Witchcraft among the Barotse of Northern Rhodesia* (Berkeley, 1963), chs. 1–2.

127. R. Fortune, *op. cit.*, p. 144, etc.

128. John Beattie, "Sorcery in Bunyoro," in Middleton & Winter, eds., *Witchcraft and Sorcery in East Africa*, ch. 1.

129. Isaac Schapera, "Sorcery and Witchcraft in Bechuanaland," in Max Marwick, ed., *Witchcraft and Sorcery*, esp. pp. 109–110.

130. *Ibid.*, p. 113.

131. Max G. Marwick, *Sorcery in Its Social Setting* (Manchester, 1965).

132. Witches here kill for meat hunger, sorcerers for anger. They use real magic consciously. It sounds like a clear distinction of sorcerer and witch, but actually the two patterns blur into each other. The sorcerers use some mystic means; some witches use magic, too. Sorcery here is imaginary in part, one feels, precisely because it blurs into witchcraft.

133. Richard W. Lieban, *Cebuana Sorcery* (Berkeley, 1977). His evidence is second hand or circumstantial, however. Cf. p. 48ff.

134. David Tait, "Konkomba Sorcery," in John Middleton, ed., *Magic, Witchcraft and Curing* (N.Y., 1963), pp. 155-160.

135. Beatrice Blyth Whiting, *Paiute Sorcery* (N.Y., 1950).

136. Victor Turner, "Witchcraft and Sorcery, Taxonomy Versus Dynamics," *Africa*, XXXIV, No. 4 (October, 1964), collected in Turner, *The Forest of Symbols* (Ithaca, 1967), pp. 112-127.

137. In the trials, human remains were found in many households; many people committed suicide. In other ways, too, Barotse sorcerers acted out witch patterns that enhanced their frightfulness.

138. Philip Mayer, "Witches," in Marwick, ed., *Witchcraft and Sorcery*, pp. 45-64.

139. Monica Hunter Wilson, "Witch-Beliefs and Social Structure," in Marwick, ed., *Witchcraft and Sorcery*, pp. 252-263.

140. J. D. Krige, "The Social Function of Witchcraft," in Marwick, ed., *Witchcraft and Sorcery*, pp. 237-251, cf. p. 248.

141. *Sorcerers of Dobu*, pp. 136, 176, etc.

142. Jean Buxton, "Mandari Witchcraft," in Middleton and Winter, *Witchcraft and Sorcery in East Africa* (N.Y., 1963).

143. Clyde Kluckhohn, *Navajo Witchcraft* (Boston, 1967), Part II, section 3.

144. Cited by Middleton and Winter, *Witchcraft and Sorcery in East Africa*, Introd.

145. *Ibid.*, pp. 5-8.

146. Max Marwick, ed., *Witchcraft and Sorcery*, Introd. by Marwick.

147. J. R. Crawford, "The Consequences of Allegation," in Marwick, ed., *Witchcraft and Sorcery* (London, 1970), pp. 305-318.

148. Lucy Mair, *Witchcraft* (N.Y., 1969), p. 158.

149. Max Marwick, "Witchcraft as a Social Strain Gauge," 1964, collected in Marwick, ed., *Witchcraft and Sorcery*, pp. 280-295.

150. S. F. Nadel, "Witchcraft in Four African Societies" in Marwick, ed., *Witchcraft and Sorcery*, pp. 264-279.

151. Scarlett Epstein, "A Sociological Analysis of Witch Beliefs in a Mysore Village," in John Middleton, ed., *Magic, Witchcraft and Curing* (N.Y., 1967), pp. 135-154.

152. Max Marwick, *Sorcery in Its Social Setting* (Manchester, 1965), ch. 11, p. 288, *passim*.

153. David Tait, "Konkomba Sorcery," in Middleton, ed., *Magic, Witchcraft and Curing*, pp. 155-170.

154. In *Witchcraft and Sorcery in East Africa*, Middleton and Winter, eds. (N.Y., 1963), ch. 1.

155. Robert F. Gray, "Structural Aspects of Mbugwe Witchcraft," in Middleton and Winter, eds., *op. cit.*

156. *The Golden Bough*, ch. 17, etc.

157. Mary Douglas, "Techniques of Sorcery Control in Central Africa," in Middleton and Winter, eds., *op. cit.*

158. Eliane Massonneau, Victor Turner, etc.

159. Joyce Bednarski, "The Salem Witch-Scare Viewed Sociologically," in Marwick, ed., *Witchcraft and Sorcery*, pp. 151-163.

160. Norman Cohn, *Europe's Inner Demons* (N.Y., 1975).

161. H. R. Trevor-Roper, *The European Witch-Craze* (N.Y., 1956, 1967).

162. S. H. Hooke, *Babylonian and Assyrian Religion* (Norman, Okla., 1963), pp. 25ff, 35ff.

163. R. G. Willis, "The Kamcape Movement," in Marwick, ed., *Witchcraft and Sorcery* (London, 1970), pp. 184-198.

164. V. W. Turner, *Schism and Continuity in an African Society* (Manchester, 1957), chs. 5-12.

165. Ndembu villages are weak and frequently split. Local fragmentation perhaps streng-

thens the emerging central tribe or "state," but it is still largely ritualistic (the king is a ritual king). But the society is integrated nonetheless; e.g., cross-cutting memberships in ritual groups bring together different factions and villages. Cf. Turner, *op. cit., ch. 5.*

166. Max Marwick, "Witchcraft as a Social Strain Gauge," ch. 24 in *Witchcraft and Sorcery,* pp. 280-295.

167. *Schism and Continuity in an African Society,* ch. 12.

168. Max Marwick, *Sorcery In Its Social Setting* (Manchester, 1965).

169. Georg Simmel, *Conflict and the Web of Group Affiliations* (N.Y., 1955, 1964).

170. Lewis A. Coser, ed., *Georg Simmel* (Englewood Cliffs, N.J., 1965), Introd., pp. 1-26.

171. Max Marwick, ed., *Witchcraft and Sorcery* (London, 1970), ch. 24, p. 289ff.

172. J. R. Crawford, "The Consequences of Accusation," in Max Marwick, ed., *Witchcraft and Sorcery,* pp. 305-318.

173. John Middleton, ed., *Magic, Witchcraft and Curing* (N.Y., 1967), and Middleton and Winter, eds., *Witchcraft and Sorcery in East Africa* (N.Y., 1963).

174. Reprinted as ch. 5, *The Forest of Symbols* (Ithaca, 1967), pp. 112-127.

175. Manning Nash, "Witchcraft as a Social Process in a Tzeltal Community," ch. 7 Middleton, ed., in *Magic, Witchcraft and Curing,* pp. 127-133.

176. Freud perhaps had this insight when he noticed the aggressive component in the character makeup of many doctors. Psychiatrists as wounded surgeons, doctors as perpetrators of iatrogenic diseases, medical men as people who constantly demand, and sometimes expropriate, the "high jurisdiction"—all these matters are extremely suggestive. Lawyers do not demand the right to execute criminals.

177. M. Mauss, *Esquisse d'une Théorie Générale de la Magie,* in Lévi-Strauss, ed., *op. cit.,* p. 83.

178. P. Huvelin, *Magie et Droit Individuel, L'Année Sociologique* (1905-6), p. 46.

179. Rivals still practice sorcery. A humorous article in a 1972 *Advertising Age* reminds older executives there are ways of dealing with a competitive young tiger: Such as leaving a note on his desk reading, "Your psychiatrist called and it's all right to spend the weekend with Myron." A listing in *Red Channels* was an older joke. The propensities most people have toward each other are relatively inertial, even in a complex bureaucratic setting. Someone who can figure them out and reverse them, who can change the sociogram to his advantage by means of "dirty tricks," as it is called in "tradecraft," is a sorcerer.

180. These historians emphasize pressure on *egos* more than group conflict: egos are more deeply sculpted in modern societies than in Africa.

181. N.s., XVIII, 1907, pp. 169-176. Cited in Notestein, pp. ix-x, 298, 383.

182. If Notestein felt any special debt to Lea, he did not acknowledge it in his study, though he did footnote him three times. Lea's own documentation, while using mostly secondary sources and covering an enormous sweep in time and geography, did include some records of trials.

183. Like so many in the Durkheim tradition, like Bouglé using the Code of Manu (in *Essais sur le Régime des Castes*), or Durkheim on society's move from punitive to restitutive law (*The Social Division of Labor*), or like Mauss studying the consolidation of individualism in Roman law (*The Gift*), and like many other productive sociologists (Maine, Weber, etc.), Notestein went to the *legal* fact as the preeminently *real social fact.* I think that legal facts are closer to the Durkheim-Mauss criteria for real social facts than are statistical facts, especially those made up by experimentor design (e.g., questionnaire research).

184. Wallace Notestein, *A History of Witchcraft in England from 1558 to 1718* (N.Y., 1968).

185. My source for this is DeWitt Wallace. Notestein was his great uncle.

186. Steven Runciman, *The Medieval Manichee* (Toronto, 1947), *passim.*

187. Moreover, Protestant Churchmen exiled by Mary had spent time in Zurich and Geneva, where witch killings were in full cry, and had talked with continental theologians.

188. Cited in A. D. J. MacFarlane, *Witchcraft in Tudor and Stuart England* (London, N.Y., 1970), pp. 5-6.

189. *Ibid.,* Acknowledgements, p. xiv.

190. Max Weber, *The Protestant Ethic and the Spirit of Capitalism* (London, 1930), *passim.*

191. A whole class which previously had a moral claim for reciprocity was morally nul-

lified and psychologically neutralized. The philosophy of Undershaft triumphed and the poor were blamed for their poverty.

192. Benjamin Nelson, *The Idea of Usury*, rev. (Chicago, 1969).

193. New studies suggest that psychological depression in status loss can be a temporary process leading to adjustment. The individual attacks his own self-image; that causes the depression; it is over when he comes to equilibrium accepting himself at a lower status level. Prolonged depression, however, is always read socially as a sign of rebellion, a refusal to accept a lowered status. (George Maclay & Humphry Knipe, *The Dominant Male*, N.Y., 1972, pp. 62-64).

194. But kin *by itself* does not seem to have been the main element in Essex: It was not so much families as *neighbors or kin living nearby* who were distressed during the transition "from community to society."

195. So here we see witch-accusation magic defending the ego as usual. MacFarlane does not pursue this point and the court records would not tell him anyway whether victims of psychosomatic illness generally got better after they projected their guilt by accusing some old lady of witchcraft.

196. Karl Polanyi, *The Great Transformation* (Boston, 1957), *passim.*

197. Ritual attacks on the powerful are normal safety valves in every society; they are abreactive rather than revolutionary. Accusations of sorcery against headmen during lineage fission, of witchcraft against chiefs during generational change, are part of a process of stability-within-renewal found in conservative primitive societies. But when a society begins to attack its weak, a Nietzschean process of fundamental moral change is under way, for the weak are always carefully defined in any society's theodicy. When the weak are attacked, basic values are changing.

198. ". . . witchcraft prosecutions may be seen as a means of effecting a deep social change, a change from a 'neighborly' . . . interdependent village society to a more individualistic one. . . . Thomas Cooper . . . warned the godly in 1617 to forego indiscriminate charity and be especially hard on suspected witches, 'to bee straight handed towards them, not to entertaine them in our houses, nor to relieve them with our morsels: not to fear the spiritual consequences. . . .' Witchcraft beliefs provided both the justification for severing contact and an explanation of the guilt and fear still felt by the individual when he did so . . . this was witchcraft, and thus evil, rather than punishment for his own shortcomings . . . through the idiom of witchcraft prosecutions, the older values were undermined or changed. . . . Witchcraft prosecutions, therefore, may have been principally important as a radical force which broke down the communal pattern inherited from the medieval period." (MacFarlane, *op. cit.*, p. 197).

199. In a closer, between-the-lines reading of MacFarlane, we can see still other fascinating patterns about which he did not generalize. For example, a child was sometimes the witches' victim; the witch was often an old woman—and the accuser was usually of the hard-pressed, striving, *middle* generation.

200. MacFarlane, *op. cit.*, pp. 201-203.

201. Keith Thomas, *Religion and the Decline of Magic* (N.Y., 1971).

202. See Stekel on the relation of this compulsion to magic in the obsessional-compulsive neurosis. Wilhelm Stekel, *Compulsion and Doubt* (N.Y., 1962); passages discussed in Postulate 9.

203. We see this even among the upper classes hundreds of years later in the widows' dower houses, reported, for example, in the novels of Anthony Trollope, especially in *Is He Popenjoy?*

204. Thomas Luckmann, *The Invisible Religion* (N.Y., 1967), p. 49.

205. Howard Gardner, *The Shattered Mind* (N.Y., 1975), pp. 410, 422-3, 451-6.

206. Julian Jaynes, *The Origin of Consciousness in the Breakdown of the Bicameral Mind* (Boston, 1976), pp. 62-65.

207. Jean-Paul Sartre, *The Emotions, Outline of a Theory* (N.Y., 1948), pp. 84-86.

Postulate 12: MAGIC PERSISTS
AS AN EXPRESSION OF
CERTAIN ASPECTS OF CIVILIZATION.

MAGIC persists. Repeatedly driven underground, it repeatedly surfaces to become part of events—in the early modern witch-mania, in the magnetism-spiritualism-theosophy sequence of the 19th century. It is dismissed as superstition, anachronism, survival, subcultural idiosyncracy, deviance and lag. But today magic again flares up, so insistently that it commands attention from a surprised intelligentsia which had not noticed that the occult underground has been seething for 150 years. Now our perspective changes: It is perhaps *part* of the present "occult revival" to notice at last that Renaissance science was stimulated by magic, that the Reformation had magic offspring, that subterranean magic currents have continued to influence modern thought.

In this chapter I will explore the possibility that magic bears some intrinsic relationship to modern society. To put it roundly in social theory language: magic may be the natural projection of advanced "organic solidarity" (society held together by division of labor). Today post-industrial society, in splitting the "formal rationality" of its complex systems off from the "substantive rationality" of individuals, makes the world seem uncanny to the self. This could have the same effect that "withdrawal of love" (Freud[1]), or withdrawal of action (Ernest Becker[2]) has in psychosis: i.e., it could make objects seem demonic. And Storch,[3] Werner,[4] DeMartino[5] and Lévy-Bruhl[6] have shown that "magical thinking" is the only way of coping when the world becomes (or seems) demonic. In addition, magic may express the friction of individuals fighting contraction—and also their continued attempts to expand along with the magical possibilities of the modern world.

Magic is probably more than cultural lag. It even goes beyond persistence of occult elements in the person category and the ego. Quite possibly the "invisible religion" of organic solidarity is not merely "situation ethics" or "private religion," as Luckmann[7] thought, but the occult itself, as Ellul suggests.[8] Perhaps the occult is the natural expression of a society in which we live surrounded by machines, bureaucracies, technologies and planning systems made by human rationality but unfathomable to us personally.

458

Certainly there is no doubt that magic persists. Currently it seems to advance, and that is true of all seven provinces. Planetary civilization with its eclectic tastes throws open all antiquarian magics of every society in history to mass consumption. Anthropology even makes available the magics of bypassed primitive societies for jaded cosmopolitan publics. Medical magic constantly develops new formulae and never forgets an old remedy. Occult sciences develop out of every divination system ever known to man, and also by imitating every new science. New ESP phenomena are "discovered" and old ones never forgotten. Magical protest sects sweep the Third World and the internal proletariats of Western civilization. Libraries preserve it all; nothing is lost; every successive revival feeds on past revivals. And modern sciences themselves pursue Faustian aims and invade magical territories with new investigative techniques that create new magical technologies.

At times of great social stress—in the Renaissance, the Reformation and the twentieth century—literal black magic is acted out again. But here I want to explore magic as a still active process, rather than just a symptom. Here we will study magic as a possibly intrinsic expression of our society.

PART ONE: MAGIC AS AN EXPRESSION OF MODERN SOCIETY

Magic and the Division of Labor

Modern society is in large part "integrated," glued together, by the division of labor. We are all specialized and sell one another goods and services; that is what makes us hang together. Durkheim calls that "organic solidarity"[9] and distinguishes it from primitive "mechanical solidarity" (society glued together by fanatical adherence to religious ideas). But the division of labor began during a magical revolution, the tribal revolt of the men's houses. It was preceded by a division of magic and magical knowledge. Most of the new crafts and professions were magical at first; later they cooled and there was "rationalization of charisma." But many kept magical residues or are magical in some weak sense— in their language or traditional symbols or ceremonies. Who is to say these cooled secular institutions could never heat up and erupt again? Medicine gives off crank magic like decay particles. Priesthood seethed with suppressed demonology in the nineteenth century (Huysmans[10]). In Nazi Germany, the legal profession invented such abominations as "phenomenological law" (Neumann[11]), and psychiatry treated fimosis by castration (Wertham[12]). Any institution that is magical in the weak sense could heat up again, especially those that minister to the "self." For the self was nurtured in the magic explosion and took magical elements into its basic constitution, above all its pilot light, the ego, which is a structure that is organized by repression and acts by magic.

Consider how magical the new occupations were when they first emerged. Many studies have documented the magic origins of the arts and crafts. Pottery, metallurgy, arms-making, etc. were developed by magical brotherhoods who mystified their work: surrounded praxis with magic and kept the formulae secret. Chemistry started as occult alchemy in Egypt, and got a later boost from magical research in the Renaissance, according to the Warburg Institute researchers (Frances Yates, D. N. Walker, Peter French). Crafts were later democratized but sheer explosion of modern knowledge forces specialization and the equivalent of secrecy again. Or consider the arts: Hauser[13] has shown how the plastic arts began as magic, pursuing magical ends. Gilbert Murray,[14] Harrison[15] and Gastor[16] have shown how Attic comedy and tragedy grew out of magic ceremonies of an initiation spirit or *Einautus Daimon* (later a corn god), with tragedy celebrating his death and comedy his wedding feast. Robert Graves[17] suggests that poetry derives from sacred myth and remains magical when it still works.

What Does "Organic Solidarity" Become?

It is the insight of the great sociologists that the rationality of our society depends on its social structure. We witness in recent centuries a great progress called "secularization," which "disenchants"[18] the world of superstitious ideas, substitutes scientific explanation, displaces religious authority, and substitutes legal-rational institutions. Secularization in turn is part of a broader process sometimes called "rationalization," which is nothing less than logicalization of thought and life, including bureaucratization of professions, the rationalization of production and so on. Rationalization and secularization are confidently linked by most observers to industrialization, to the continued progress of the division of labor and mass production. But Luckmann and other Durkheimians remind us that the link of our industrial system to rationalization is *indirect*— it works through organic solidarity.[19] Precisely because society is integrated by the reciprocal dependencies of the division of labor, it does not require fanatical adherence to religious beliefs to hold together; therefore rational ideas can prevail. If the Valkyries are not to return, therefore, we must hope to see a healthful continuance of organic integration. But what in fact happens to organic solidarity in our time?

As Lukes[20] and others have shown, Durkheim was unsure, and took several different positions on this. (I count four.) Durkheim had to deal with the fact that modern society often seemed not integrated but riven, not peaceful but at war with itself. He called these difficulties the "abnormal forms" of the division of labor[21] and distinguished the "forced division of labor" of class war and depressions, and the "anomic division of labor" of unfree occupational choices, excessive specialization that causes alienation, and other failures of integration. Were these difficulties temporary, permanent or symptoms of something worse yet to come? Durkheim took different positions: 1. In gloomier moments, he seemed to suggest that such problems were endemic to the system. 2. But more often and most characteristically, he said that they were temporary difficulties, that "full" organic solidarity had not yet come and when it did come it would integrate society harmoniously. 3. An overlapping position was his call for state economic intervention to help speed this process.[22] 4. But Durkheim occasionally hinted at a much darker vision. He worried that organic solidarity might fission into complete chaos. Would economic interrelationships alone be enough without a core of common values?

Talcott Parsons made much of this concern in *The Structure of Social Action*,[23] claiming that Durkheim turned to the study of sacred institutions late in his life to determine how social values are developed. I think he exaggerated. But Durkheim was concerned. He worried whether there would be enough common beliefs to provide a stable framework. John R. Commons (in *The Legal Foundations of Capitalism*) and others have shown that economic inter-relationships are grounded in law and laws in turn depend on common beliefs. Durkheim hoped that a moral consensus would develop naturally in economic society, that organic solidarity would project an appropriate "religion." Since the very coherence of modern society did not depend on fanatical beliefs, the new "religion" would be reasonable. Optimistically, he noted that a religion of organic solidarity had already been evolving historically—individualist Christianity was a step toward it, Protestant conscience was a further step, and he regarded the political ideologies of individualism as "religions" too, projected by the social structure.

But look at that social structure: warring monopolies, extreme specialization in jobs and quasi-anonymous roles, anomie and alienation, economical retribalization perhaps. Suppose people did not even believe in the rights and responsibilities which individualism entails? Durkheim's solution: responsible, social-minded individualism must be taught as a kind of moral religion by the state-administered educational system. Just like Robespierre, just like Comte and like the kings of ancient empires, Durkheim suggested that a nation should have a state-sponsored cult to hold society together, in this case a cult of reason and individuality. The anti-clerical French Third Republic virtually adopted his suggestion, coopting Durkheimianism itself as a quasi-official theory of moral pedagogy to be propagated through its normal schools. (This caused one former colleague, Gaston Richard, to charge that "atheism in the guise of sociology" had become the moral philosophy of the state.[24]) Behind this move lay the early twentieth century fear of social chaos as religious consensus faded. Fascist movements tried similarly to advance state cults of social morality, but these were collectivist, based on adulation of folk or state.[25] Durkheim, by contrast, had diagnosed that the appropriate "religion" of modern society was individualism, and that moral education should try to teach people how to become responsible individuals.

The fears of social dissolution that haunted the early twentieth century panicked several European nations into totalitarian solutions which led to a world conflagration. Out of this disaster came some new "diagnoses of our times"[26] that went deeper than Durkheim into the possibility that organic solidarity might contain some fundamental contradictions.

"Organic Solidarity" and "Formal Rationality"

A pessimistic new forecast about the predicament of the modern individual was carried out of central Europe during the Nazi era by social scientists who fled to England and America. They said it in many ways, but it came down to the same thing: Something had happened to human reason. Under modern organic solidarity reason had somehow gotten away from the individual, impoverishing him, or it had fragmented, or perhaps it had actually turned on him. This culminated in the great distinctions of "formal" or institutional rationality from "substantive" or individual rationality, with the implication that the former was advancing at the expense of the latter. Horkheimer[27] warned of the "eclipse of reason," of "automatons of formal reason."

Röpke wrote[28] of the "aberrations of rationalism." Horkheimer and Adorno saw instrumental reason as the most decisive of all dominations. Marcuse called it "one-dimensionality." Adorno wrote[29] of "the divergence of social order and personality" and of methodological decisionism as the mask of ideology. Kahler wrote[30] of the disintegration of the individual as his "communities" are replaced by "collectivities."[31] Fromm wrote[32] of a "lack of synchronization" between the individual's "freedom from" and his "freedom *to*," with the result that he sought an "escape from freedom" through blind loyalty to large organizations. Mannheim[33] blamed this on the alienation of reason by these large organizations themselves, which reduced individual decisions to trivial choices, thus rendering "freedom to" virtually insignificant. And the Frankfurt school expressed fear that once reason was buried in technological imperatives (Habermas[34]), it was beyond debate or discussion (Marcuse[35]) so it might actually become irrational, a blind "behemoth" (Neumann[36]).

The Weber-Mannheim distinction of individual reason from the "formal" or institutional reason of the system is still the best logical tool for getting at this problem.[37] Mannheim clearly thought that the institutional reason of science and systems had marginalized individual responsibility and intelligence, and that the result could be *ir*rationality. Reason develops too fast in the technologies, he wrote, and the rest of culture cannot keep up.

The refugees were also in agreement that this process harmed the individual. Later writers spoke of the individual becoming anachronistic (Adorno), or superfluous (Luhmann[38]), or bypassed (Nelson[39]). There were darker prophecies. No longer participating in the public discourse of reason, the individual might give vent to his irrational unconscious. He might turn to "destructiveness" (Fromm[40]) or become a useless ghost (Adorno[41]). Perhaps this outcome can be understood by an analogy to the Freudian theory of psychosis. In a psychosis, a person withdraws "cathexis" (love, interest, caring) from the world and its objects. (Behaviorist psychiatrists like Becker[42] say that he withdraws "activity" from objects.) When one withdraws interest and activity from objects, they become unfamiliar in time, and may start to appear strange, even uncanny. Psychosis results when the world is so completely abandoned by the individual that it appears demonic to him. As Storch,[43] Werner,[44] Arieti,[45] etc., have shown, this causes a breakdown of the secondary process. Then all objects can lose their normal boundaries, and become threatening. In such circumstances, magical thinking returns as the only defense, the only way to cope with demonic or unbounded objects. In primitives and infants, magical thinking is the frail self's only defense; in psychotics it is the last ditch defense to which ego retreats.

If the world becomes strange to the masses because they have withdrawn from the rational processes of society (or because they have been edged out of active participation in them), they may start to behave magically just to cope. And behind the diagnosis of many of the refugees, we see something like that. Ortega y Gasset[46] spoke of "the rebellion of the masses," Heiden of the "armed bohemians,"[47] Mannheim of "negative democratization,"[48] Neumann and Marcuse of "plebiscitory democracy,[49] Adorno of "disaster politics," Voegelin[50] of susceptibility to "gnostic movements," Norman Cohn of "millennial" movements,[51] Nelson[52] of "dances of death." Not so long ago chiliastic political movements like Nazism were seriously characterized as "religions" by social scientists—in fact, as magical religions. Neumann in particular sketched the magical worldview and practice of Nazism.[53] Then two semi-barbarian powers on the periphery, as Toynbee might call them,[54] stamped out these movements, but in their own antagonism and cold war balance of power were unable to set up a "universal state," so European civilization was restored. As a result, the concern about magical mass movements was partly forgotten (Daniel Bell even announced "the end of ideology"[55]). But I want to suggest that the refugees' diagnosis was important, that a splitting of rationality which makes the world seem uncanny to the masses can be a fundamental property of advanced "organic solidarity." It does not even matter if the Frankfurt school exaggerates the degree to which alienated rationality structures can themselves go off the track—if the public loses touch with reason and lapses into magic, that is serious enough.

The refugees did exaggerate, for after all there is a positive side to formal rationality. If social integration depended on our subjective powers alone, there would be chaos. The person category disintegrates in our time; yet the institutions of the Individual are not immediately disorganized by this. Something else integrates citizenship, property, individual law and so on. And what could this be but what the refugees call "formal rationality"? It is precisely legal-economic-rational processes sedimented in these institutions that hold them together even when ideas about selves blur.

But the long-run danger remains, if formal rationality is not renewed by participation. And one difficulty in our era is that formal rationality is not concentrated but diffused. Ultimately its seat is not the individual who evolved with rational institutions, nor is it any longer the liberal state. Instead, as Durkheim predicted, rationality is sedimented into a "web" of "legal and economic interrelationships." This is similar to that "embedding in the infrastructure" which the Frankfurt sociologists recognized as the alienation of rationality.[56] The rising power of administrative tribunals is typical of this diffusion; so are quasi-independent government corporations.[57] Meanwhile, the individual is now allowed quietly to go to hell in his private life; bureaucracy no longer cares very much what he does with himself in his off hours; this reflects his declining importance. The individual, in turn, would be the last to know if the "rationality" embedded in the system went completely off the track. Does it? We do know that "strange things happen," as Ortega y Gasset put it. In Germany, the psychiatric profession began killing its patients. In America, we almost had thermonuclear war when NORAD's radar twice bounced off the moon in the 1960's, and its computers showed imaginary squadrons of Russian planes passing our fail-safe point (fortunately there were a few rational individuals still left in posts of command who said it just was not possible).

To summarize: When "objective mind" (Hegel) becomes too complicated, when man's "impersonality principle" (Lévi-Strauss), his "formal rationality" (Weber, Mannheim), his "instrumental reason" (Horkheimer, Adorno, Wellmer), his "accursed corporations" (Rousseau), his "collectivities" (Kahler), his "techniques" (Ellul), his bureaucratic "iron cage" (Weber)—when they blot up his own reason and leave him with only "minimal choices" (Mannheim), with just "a series of performances of highly anonymous specialized social roles" (Luckmann[58]); then the individual withdraws love and activity from unfathomable institutions he can no longer understand or participate in—and as a result they come to seem strange to him. Then he may rebel against this "Urizon" (Blake), become "retribalized" (McLuhan[59]), turn "destructive" (Fromm), unbind the death wish (Marcuse), participate in "disaster politics" (Adorno), politics of the irrational (Lasswell[60]), "millenarian politics" (Norman Cohn), "gnostic movements" (Voegelin). The net result could be that the appropriate religious projection of disintegrating organic solidarity is . . . magic.

Why Magic Persists In the Modern World

No satisfactory explanation has been offered of why magic persists in the modern world. To say magic persists because the people are "superstitious" is almost as tautological as the old "phlogiston" explanation for combustion. I have already broached the possibility that magic persists because it fits social reality. But before developing that, let us consider another related matter which partly explains the persistence of magic: the persistence of religion.

A. Religion As a Reservoir of Magic Infection. Magic persists in part because religion persists and magic derives from religion. Religion persists both as anachronistic cultural lag, and as the perennial new ceremonialization of any new social contract. *1. New projection.* Whenever a new social system is erected, it projects religious symbolism like an atmosphere. Especially if alienated, its own ceremonialization of itself can turn into a kind of religion (e.g., Bellah's "civic religion"[61]). 2. *Lag.* Religions have built-in propensities for cultural lag which derive from their special properties. First, religions are deeply involved in the socialization of the young, so they can sometimes transmit beliefs fanatically across generations in societies these beliefs no longer fit. Second, religious representations are so vague, equivocal and confused, that they are easily made to fit new social situations. Martin E. Marty[62] observes that many people join a denomination and identify with it without knowing much about its beliefs: they feel that is the job of the religious professional. The average religious person has such a limited understanding of what he thinks he believes, and parishioners in general experience religion in so many diverse ways that it is not hard for the thing to bend and change color to fit new situations. The usual historical situation is this: some monstrously disordered traditional religion persists as an inherited menagerie (Gilbert Murray[63]) to which elites pay nominal allegiance and from which diverse classes derive different magical supports; new cults constantly arise within this menagerie to reflect and express new structures in social life.

The incoherence of the religious menagerie not only gives it flexibility; increasingly it comes to express the underestimated and constantly growing incoherence of most large societies and civilizations. The diverse subcults help express the dissatisfactions and conflicts of subgroups within these civilizations. Through dialectic reabsorption of magical protest sects, the world religions become increasingly magical and incoherent, thereby reflecting the increasingly incoherent civilizations. Toynbee and Spengler have accustomed us to recognize that various world civilizations are in part created by certain great world religions. But some of these are so magical that we might also seriously consider a catalogue of civilizations based on different kinds of *magic*. In China, for example, we perhaps see a great civilization built on the beneficent white magic of shamanism, if Needham's syllogism about the fundamental importance of shamanism in Taoism, and the centrality of Taoism in turn to Chinese culture, is accepted.[64] In India we see another civilization based on the ceremonial magic of the Brahmins. Western civilization grew out of, and advanced with, the continued career of magical protest sects.

However tame a religion may seem in some eras, it is always a potential reservoir of magical eruption. Some religions include outright magical institutions, such as official church exorcism in Catholicism. Even relatively antimagical religions like Mohammedanism contain the possibility of magical decay. If religion is to be compared to the DNA of society,[65] magic might be thought of as an RNA byproduct; and just as DNA and RNA can reconstitute each other, magic and religion each provide the possibility for the other. Any occult upsurge can turn into a religious revival, and any religious revival enhances the potential of magic, with new credibilities and sometimes new outright magical techniques. Religious revivals enhance magical experience immediately by causing sacred symbolism to saturate a culture more thoroughly—the way Huizinga[66] showed the Christian religion to sink down into the ethos and saturate the everyday life of the people in the late Middle Ages. One outcome was a renewed upsurge of the religious magic of hagiolatry, sacred amulets, benedictions, sacraments, etc. Dill[67] has shown how magical was the cult of saints in the Merovingian period. If anything, the saint cult now became more magical. When St. Thomas Aquinas died with the Monks of Fossanuova, they boiled, decapitated and preserved his body.[68] In 1000 A.D. Umbrian peasants wanted to kill St. Romuald the hermit to acquire his magical bones.[69] Other saints became the objects of frankly magical cults—some were thought to cure and *cause* diseases. (Thus Rabelais reported that some lower-class preachers taught that St. Sebastian was the author of the plague.[70])

But even anachronistic, fading religions can release extra magic as decay particles. Like Ben Franklin's analogy between fish that is kept too long and guests who overstay their welcome, old religions begin to stink. Then they start to emit "toxins," as Steiner[71] puts it. Steiner even speculates that the holocaust derived in part from poisons emitted by a dying Christianity.[72]

B. What Is the Religion of Organic Solidarity? But the persistence of religion explains only part of the persistence of magic. Is it possible that magic in some way fits or expresses the present social system? And what *is* the appropriate religious projection of organic solidarity?

The answer depends on the future of organic solidarity—will it be solidarity or will it be fragmentation? On the one hand, the magic of money and exchange knits economic society together as never before; all subcultures are dragged into the market. On the other hand, the social system becomes so big, the parts so diverse, that individuals do not even know them all any more. What they do know is that they can look most things up: the "Yellow Pages" image of society. For example, most laymen are dimly aware of many specialisms within medicine; but all of this is potentially knowable; we could go to a library and read up on any specialism. Beyond that, however, we do not really know very much; we do not know whether those specialisms are always working very hard for the common good, whether reciprocity and the profit motive cause them to make a real contribution; whether they are productive or parasitical; or how much their members share the minimal remaining common values that allegedly make the center hold. On the other hand, we are uneasily aware that some large companies are owned by Mafiosi or anti-social cults; that some American corporations are multinationals which speculate against the dollar and export jobs; that some Western intelligence agencies have gone beserk; that some doctors privately claim and exercise the power of euthanasia; that some new "professions" define their ethics in self-serving ways—in short, that there can be *systematic* disharmonies before we even consider the individual deviancies.

As for rationality, my own substantive rationality diminishes; I cannot fix my car or my oil burner or many of the appliances I rely on; instead, I send for someone to help me; and I could not repair a social breakdown in my community, either. Rational control does not reside at the center any more than with individuals; the old French ideal of a rational state allied with rational individuals is doubly vitiated by the pluralization of reason, the parcelling out of power, rationality and authority among a host of quasi-governmental and private bodies. Society, as Durkheim said, is integrated by a "web" of law and contracts—and it is a spider web that entangles us all. Rationality has not only "sunk down" into the technostructure, as the Frankfurt writers say, it has also diffused through this spider's web of anonymous administrations and corporations. The Enlightenment believed that reason had to *concentrate* to be clear (e.g., "voter watching"); today it is spread out and thinned out and parcelled out to administrative tribunals and "gatekeepers" and bureaucratic barons and such senseless lifeless rigid rules that it no longer seems like "reason." Is this an "organic" society or a *fragmented* society? Will its appropriate religious projection be something universalistic—or something fragmented, like totemism, or the individual rites of the Hindu castes, or a congeries of magical sects reflecting different populations?

I think the answer is that there will be several religions in ripe organic solidarity, some expressing unity and participation for elites who still experience the world that way, others expressing fragmentation and despair for those left out. We might discern three main types of religious expression.

1. For Elites. First, the universalistic, rational, ethical, non-superstitious religion that Durkheim predicted for organic solidarity really does exist in a dozen guises—"humanism," scientism, "demythologized" Protestant sects like modern Quakerism. These are often the religious orientations of many of the elites who, by running the system and manning its key levers, still participate to some degree in the "formal rationality" that has sunk into it. Many of these people either espouse such attenuated and universalistic religions, or have no religion (except maybe what Bellah calls "the civic religion") or else they continue a nominal affiliation with one of the older Jewish or Christian sects but experience this as a universalistic, rational, ethical religion. In a country like the United States, the elites who still participate can include a large number of people.

2. For Middle Classes. Secondly, the "middle classes"—by definition those who do not run things but are treated well in return for their loyalty (and in the United States that is the majority)—will continue nominal-to-intense affiliations with Catholic, Protestant or Jewish sects. I have demonstrated that the world religions are somewhat magical;[73] on the other hand, secularization has worked on them, as Herberg,[74] Cox,[75] Berger,[76] Marty[77] and others have documented. This seeming contradiction presents no difficulty. We wind up with religions that are practical in approach, and which are experienced as practical magic by their members. What is difficult about that? Magic is always practical. These religions use god language as self language, and seek sacramental and pastoral help to enable them to adapt to the socioeconomic system and its alienated formal rationality. Herberg and Cox stressed the secular side of these religions; but they overlooked the magical reservoirs, the "rumors of angels," the sympathetic potentials of the rites and symbols still kept alive by these churches.

3. For the Alienated. In addition, there will be other kinds of religion for those who feel left out, for those who experience formal rationality as the alienation of reason, and organic solidarity as fragmentation. Instead of community, these religions will express the individual's lonely private life, and his need to create his own world.

A. Benign Outcomes. Cox and Berger focus on relatively benign forms of so-called "private religion." These include "situation ethics," Bultmann's "demythologizing" Protestantism, Bonhoeffer's "grown-up Christianity," and even various brands of "atheistic" Christianity such as Altizer's. Existential philosophies which try to deal with the "predicament" of the lone individual caught in some anonymous role might also be cited. Luckmann[78] suggests that something like these movements constitutes the "invisible religion" of organic solidarity. Luckmann himself does not spell out what this religion might be, but I think Berger does[79] when he often writes of the "private *nomos*" that sensitive, intelligent people nowadays try to create in their private lives, often without much traditional religious content. These private *nomoi* often center on the institution of marriage, in which, as Berger and Kellner[80] have shown, individuals create a private moral order. It often begins in the conversation of courtship, when, like F. Scott Fitzgerald's "The Rich Boy" and his fiancée, the young couple talk earnestly and endlessly about what they "believe." As they discover and create agreement, they create a micro-moral order in their marriage, and it may in turn become the only "sacred canopy" that their unchurched offspring will grow up with.

B. *Less Benign Outcomes.* But this idealization covers only the most favorable outcomes. Castles in the air that are created in the conversation of courtship and marriage can be disintegrated very quickly by the conversation of divorce. For many people, the private religion is a *folie à deux.* And overall, the invisible religion tends to be a *fragmented* religion, just like totemism, ancestor worship or Hinduism, with rich couples, poor couples, gay couples, psychopathic couples, counter-culture communes, deviant subcultures, predatory gangs and criminal families each projecting quite different "private religions."

The "invisible religion" has many provinces, including some inside established churches which are experienced differently by different individuals. And private religions also shade into occult religions, which deserve special consideration here.

The Occult As a Religious Projection of Society

For 150 years, the "occult underground" (Webb's term[81]) has been in such eruption that it has become an "occult establishment" (Martin Marty's term[82]). Not only have magical sects been precipitated back into religion, giving it a magical coloration: some magics have turned into religions. Spiritualism has become a church, while remaining spiritualism, for example.[83] Historically, protest magic gets embedded as subcults inside religions, or else turns into a church itself. But in some cults charisma is not routinized—it remains magic, and magic takes the place of religion (e.g., snake handling cults[84]). I think that for large numbers of people in America today, traditional magic itself is experienced religiously, just as traditional religion is experienced magically. People say they "believe in" astrology, and some of them believe in little else. A preoccupation with ESP, which takes the form of reading and perhaps membership, fills a religious vacuum for some people—it is what they "do with their privateness," in Whitehead's phrase. In a society where consensus is no longer often required and community is not always experienced, the typical shaman-to-client, one-to-one relationship of magic is enough for some people. They do not require or seek community or membership or a church. Magicians typically do not form churches with their clientele; they work alone on a one-to-one basis with them; when they form collegia it is with their colleagues, and clients are not admitted. But for some people that is fine; just going to the fortune teller or the astrologer or the deviant psychotherapist and getting his "personal" attention for their private predicament is enough. In this way the occult is increasingly experienced religiously in America. There is a theurgic element in contemporary magic and many have remarked on it.

This is not necessarily a protest against modern society; it may be an expression of it. This is how many people experience the modern world. Living in insecure microworlds, often members of deviant, antisocial, criminal or atavistic subcultures, practicing occupations that increasingly break free from consensus, define their roles to suit their pocketbooks and prey on the community, many people experience the modern world as unsafe, irrational, unpredictable; and they seek magical defenses. Magic for them is not just a defense against a demonic world, but a religious expression that "tells it as it is," that *reflects* the world as they experience it, so they recognize it and feel more comfortable with it.

How accurate are these magical projections of society? Later I will discuss the magical texture of modern society, with its propaganda, its symbolic politics, its media myths, its secrecy and irrationality. But we must nonetheless recognize that much of the "magic" which millions of people see in the world today and project in occult sects is really in the eyes of the beholders. It partly reflects the degree to which they have withdrawn from participation in the great society[85] (or have been driven out of participation). It is not an entirely objective matter. Nonetheless, their perceptions, illusions or not, reflect the split of reason in organic solidarity that causes their symptoms. In that sense, the occult is a natural "religious" projection of modern society as it is experienced by many marginalized, dropped out or deviant groups.

An extreme statement about the appropriateness of occult movements in modern society is made by Jacques Ellul in his book *The New Demons*.[86] Ellul claims that modern society is Dionysian and the occult revival is not a protest against it but its natural expression. Ours is not a secular society at all; it pullulates with magic in every sphere. A new demonic religion is arising here which reflects the amoral, magical and ritualistic civilization in which we live. This is a society pervaded by the "anonymous discourse" of myth (Lévi-Strauss' term—the announcer's voice fits that image perfectly). Even in rational France, Ellul finds, there are 6,000 fakirs, soothsayers and fortune tellers, and 10,000,000 people who follow horoscopes.[87] The media increasingly reflect mass interest in the occult. Often a once forbidden theme is first broached in comedy or satire; a film appears spoofing vampirism, for example; box office reaction is overwhelming; and more earnest vampiric films are produced. In effect, the media discover the popular magical religion of the masses by discovering what will pay, and so help bring this demonic religion to consciousness; but the latent magical religion is already there and it really reflects modern industrial society. It is amoral, anti-social and magical, just like that society. It wants to celebrate; it calls for *festivitas*, drugs, hard rock music and "Strength Through Joy."

I believe that Ellul already began to demonstrate that modern society is magical in several earlier books. 1. In *The Meaning of the City*[88] he proposed that the trouble began at the beginning, with the Promethean foundation of cities—"man's high-handed piracy of creation," he called it[89] (in a swipe, perhaps, at Eliade's theory of the religious foundation of cities.[90]) Using biblical statements as revelation in a manner seldom seen in modern discourse, Ellul observed that god damned cities as nowhere places ("East of Eden"), places of wandering ("in the land of Nod") where man is captured by his own magics and "embedded in structures of sin and evil."[91] Living in this occult enclosure of his own symbols, man is soon enslaved by the "dominations, thrones, principalities and powers" of his own self-alienating magic. 2. In *Propaganda*,[92] he showed that cities lead to demonic states and their most demonic product is propaganda which, by preaching pseudo-community, actually isolates the individual, destroys both his communities and his reason, and profanes and ruins language; so he is utterly impotent. Mannheim[93] after World War II had proposed that democracies should fight fire with fire and use propaganda to defend freedom. He seemed unaware that, as Lasswell[94] had shown, the democracies (the United States especially) had already done just that with great success in the First World War and had actually provided Hitler with a model. Ellul's claim now is that all propaganda is self-defeating because it ruins language and mind and makes them hopelessly magical, so reason cannot function. 3. In *The Political Illusion*[95] Ellul showed how even infrastructural actions disintegrate into magical superstructural gestures in our society—rather the way Thurman Arnold[96] and Murray Edelman[97] had shown, for example, that antitrust suits become mere symbolic gestures to allay public anxiety about the inexorable advance of monopoly. Politics becomes a circus on television that preoccupies individuals who are no longer able to think clearly about their own needs, and so on. 4. In *The Technological Society*[98] Ellul showed how these symbolic overdoses of magical politics and magical propaganda so ruined communication and made men so passive, that they turned in self-defense to the magic of personal rituals. Modern society as a whole seeks the reduction of all spontaneous activity back into ritual. Ellul cites Mauss' essay on the "techniques of the body,"[99] his observation that individual action in primitive society begins "in serried ranks," in collective ritual that overcomes anxiety. But now civilization returns to the ritualization of everything: from Taylorian, de-skilled assembly-line production to the psychological technologies of meditation, Yoga, etc. *Conclusion:* Modern man lives in a fragmented, Faustian, thoroughly ritualized society, where language is ruined by too many mythic, propagandistic and other magical communications, where real events disintegrate into symbolic gestures. Free individual action becomes difficult and the anonymous, anarchic dominations, thrones, principalities and powers take over in a Dionysian struggle for power. Magic is the natural religious projection of this society, in Ellul's view.

But this is true only for a minority—at least so far, in my opinion. The elites who still participate in formal rationality are numerous; the middle classes who still benefit are the majority. The center holds, so far, and the universalistic "religions" that Durkheim predicted for organic solidarity—various humanisms and secularized religions—do indeed predominate. And in this process the mass media often play a positive role. The European refugees, startled at how successfully millenarian movements had manipulated the media in Europe, came to America preaching that the media isolated and atomized the individual. Empirical observers like Bramson,[100] Lazarsfeld[101] and Arendt[102] disputed this, demonstrating that Americans experience media inputs in small, critical groups who evaluate this information. And ideally, the media *involve* the masses, enlist their interest, and prevent their withdrawal by communicating to them the concerns and internal debates of those who operate the central institutions of formal rationality. Thus formal rationality is not totally alienated. The Watergate experience suggests that this media function of augmenting participation is still working. But the American optimistic counterargument against the refugees' diagnosis fluctuates in conviction. Television habits are a current worry. Bronfenbrenner[103] and Marcuse[104] score telling points in demonstrating the degree to which the media have taken over the socialization of the young from working mothers and commuting fathers. The media, moreover, broadcast the occult messages of deviant minorities as well as the rational debates of the great society. For example, *Life* Magazine in effect mailed out millions of invitations to Haight-Ashbury during the height of the Hippie insanity. So the old European fear returns. There were special conditions in Germany—an undefeated feudal class, a *völkisch* ideology,[105] a peculiar constitution,[106] etc., but no society is without special conditions. The real danger is not publicity about the occult beliefs of deviant minorities but the special susceptibility of our whole civilization to millenarian movements (a susceptibility based on the fact that this civilization was constituted by such a movement). If the center holds, above all, if the civic democratic process stands, then only a minority of the people will experience the modern world as demonic.[107] The real danger arises when competing elites support or create quasi-occult millenarian movements[108] like Nazism to win a majority and overturn the system.[109]

PART TWO: HOW MAGICAL IS MODERN SOCIETY?

Extreme statements are useful in commanding attention for fresh questions. How just is Ellul's Old Testament-style indictment of the modern world? Precisely how magical is our world, and in what sense?

"Post-modern," "post-organic" or "post-industrial" society, as it is variously called, is magical in the weak sense mostly, and it can also *seem* more magical to those who withdraw from it—but it does not have too many outright magical institutions, though there are some. With its shift from goods to services (Bell[110]), from "tangible" to "intangible" capital (Schultz[111]), from ownership to management to fiduciary trust (Berle[112]), from tangible products to knowledge products (Machlup[113]), from economic goals to identity goals (Glaser[114]), it does tend to dematerialize itself, to translate infrastructure into superstructural gesture, property into symbols, wealth back into (magic) money[115] and everything into mana, so it is not surprising that it *seems* magical in many facets to many observers. But if we talk of magic in the strict sense, if we say modern society is *really* magical, we have to point to magical institutions. There are some; consider the following:

1. Traditional Magical Institutions That Persist

What passes as quaint or ethnic in the way of soothsayers, fortune tellers and the like is real magic. The gypsy palm reader and the old lady who peers at tea-leaves are consulted by credulous people who use them as diviners. Characteristically they diagnose magical illnesses and then prescribe magical cures, often sending clients to herbalists, "white witches," etc. Observers who have attempted empirical estimates of the numbers of these hard-core magical professionals at work in modern society—from Adorno[116] to Truzzi[117] to Ellul[118]— have come up with enormous figures. Truzzi in 1969 reported 10,000 full-time and 175,000 part-time astrologers alone in the U.S., for example.

All seven major provinces of magic persist in underground or marginal institutions. Paranormal phenomena (ESP, etc.) seem more active than in primitive society; perhaps a smaller percentage of the population believes in it, but there is more going on: more commotion from the pseudo-events of self-confirming "scientific" experiments. Protest cult magic is beginning to thrive in the West again. Religious magic enjoys new prestige and every church takes the charismatics seriously. Only ceremonial magic and black magic seem relatively quiescent, though there are disturbing rumors of an underground in the latter. In short, traditional magic institutions persist but they are marginal, "underground," bypassed and until recently successfully ignored.

2. New Modern Institutions That Are Magical

What of distinctly modern institutions? We do find some that are frankly magical; and the majority of these are within the medical magical complex.

A. New Psychotherapies. Freudian analysis, itself scientific, opened the floodgates. Today we have "Dianetics," the Process Church and all kinds of commotions in psychotherapy. Most are modern because they apply or mimic modern science; but many are thoroughly magical in social structure, confirmational procedures and goals. Some of these are disaster psychotherapies, which not only psychologically cripple the participants, but model magical behavior for millions. Adorno has said that certain kinds of psychiatry become a sickness that leads straight to the concentration camp, and in Germany this was literally true.[119] In our times, the psychotherapist not only turns into a medicine man, he sometimes recapitulates his phylogeny completely and becomes a deadly sorcerer. Certain radical therapies (e.g., Reichian persuasions) declare the ego itself to be a sick growth and actively seek to destroy it. These disaster psychotherapies furthermore transmit quit-self ideologies of personal nihilation via the media throughout the culture. Psychotherapy and other magical services to the body and mind today constitute a significant percentage of those "service industries" which increasingly replace hard economic goods in GNP.

B. Intelligence Agencies. Modern intelligence agencies seem to have an "elective affinity" (Weber's term[120]) for the occult, and a propensity to engage in sorcery, and perhaps a built-in tendency to go off the tracks and turn on the nations that support them. At least one intelligence agency began murdering the people of its country so promiscuously that it had to be disbanded (Rumania).[121] At least one other worked for the enemy (Austria-Hungary). In the United States the C.I.A. made an alliance with the Mafia whose ramifications have still not been adequately exposed.[122] Today intelligence agencies support occult research in both the Soviet Union and the United States, so prodigally that at least one writer, John Wilhelm,[123] has suggested that they are the natural "carriers" of the occult, the way Max Weber said Buddhism was carried by world-traveling monks, Mohammedanism by world-conquering warriors, and so on.[124] The secrets and meta-secrets and dangerous games intelligence agencies play with one another, which destabilize the politics of the world, develop in them a natural interest in secrecy, deception and occult knowledge. And do they not practice sorcery, with their poisons, assassinations and other "dirty tricks"? The various attempts on Castro's life and public image perpetrated by Operation Mongoose and the Amlash connection, as detailed by the Schweicker subcommittee,[125] surely earn the title of sorcery. Putting a drug on Castro's shoes to make his beard fall out, putting LSD in someone's soup so he will make silly speeches and lose his charisma—what could be more magical?[126] "From those wonderful folks who gave us the Leninist revolution" might be the title of a chapter on the similar world-destabilizing sorcery of (German) intelligence activities during World War I. And surely it contributes to the "demonic" atmosphere of the modern world that two-thirds of the American people (according to polls) do not believe the Warren Report and that many suspect that an intelligence agency, *somebody's* intelligence agency, executed a successful coup d'état against the American people in Dallas, November 22, 1963.

3. Some Borderline Institutions

Some new institutions of the modern world are borderline. They seem magic, and it is a bit more than just being magical in the weak sense; but it is more their coloration or effects than their constitutions which are magical. We might characterize them this way: these are institutions which increase magical thinking among the population. Among them are propaganda, advertising, public relations and so forth.

Advertising consciously exploits, activates, strengthens and adds to the sympathetic magical links in everyday language. It also employs expensive psychological technologies like Osgood's semantic differential and Dichter's "depth research"[127] precisely to *discover* what *are* the masses' magical associations so as to exploit them. And it forces the media to cater to the masses' hunger for magic and to take their magical thinking seriously. Today, as a result, a torrent of poison is disseminated by the same media that we also depend on for minimal participation in the central rational processes of society. Bandura's group[128] has repeatedly demonstrated how even a half-hour's exposure to moderate television violence will cause children to test as more violent than controls on Stanley Milgram pseudo-experiment tests[129] of aggression administered six months or even a year later. "Here is the house that the Ding Bat campaign bought," a friend told me as we drove past a luxurious suburban house which a young ad executive had purchased with his profits from a singularly offensive campaign selling a harmful product to the public. Poisoning the public atmosphere so we may retire to the brush or the suburbs with our private gain is the magical mentality at its purest, and the result, as Slater has shown,[130] is more loneliness.

4. The Oldest Professions

These began in magic, but are magical today "in the weak sense." The sympathetic magic of their symbolism has cooled. But they can always heat up again. In the agonistic competition of advanced monopoly capitalism, moreover, the professions increasingly expropriate to themselves the particular cultural province in which they are based. For example, the legal profession monopolizes law and uses this social heritage to struggle for special interests. Gilb, in *Hidden Hierarchies*,[131] tells how modern occupations go through three stages which sound like Huvelin's "expropriation of the sacred." A. In the United States, lawyers, surveyors and many other professionals found their first employment with the state. B. Then, as economic development speeded up, they separated themselves, acquired the right to practice independently, setting up their own trade associations. C. But still later they moved back into the public arena to try to capture enough social power to regulate their private affairs with public authority—to restrict entry and to expropriate the cultural province in which they practiced. And of course economic enterprise attempts the same thing—as Selznick showed in his book on TVA,[132] as Neumann showed in his study of "totalitarian monopoly capitalism."[133] *Ad hoc* contracts between individual powers replace the general rule of law and general reason, according to Neumann.[134] Kariel,[135] Spitz,[136] Presthus[137] and other antipluralists sound like Rousseau in their attack on this parceling out of public power. The pluralist fragmentation of power resembles the expropriation of social mana that is magic—but only in the weak sense.

PART THREE: MAGIC IN THE WEAK SENSE—THE SOCIAL TEXTURE

Those who are left out withdraw from the world, so it comes to seem strange to them. But there are some eerie dimensions to the modern world even for those who remain active in it. These dimensions are magical only in the weak sense, but they are new dimensions that come with modernity.

Money and Secrecy

Ours is a money society and the magic of money gives it some eerie properties. For one thing, as Simmel[138] showed, the possibility of "secrets" grows with money (because it is abstract, compact and acts at a distance[139]). Solid economic institutions are undercut today by conspiracies of money, as when, for example, a corporation's banker reveals its vulnerable financial situation to a predatory conglomerate and even helps finance that conglomerate's take-over bid. Money helps keep secret societies flourishing and mobile, and we live in a world criss-crossed by mafias, tongs and troads, some descended from remote times, and most in turn penetrated by secret intelligence agencies. Thomas Pynchon caught some of this flavor in his novel *The Crying of Lot 49*, which imagined a private postal service from the Austro-Hungarian empire still in existence, killing those who would expose it.[140] The Garrison investigation in New Orleans stumbled on a dozen secret societies that were no joke—some were fascist or communist in orientation, many were multiply infiltrated by intelligence agencies. It even found a homosexual religious cult with origins as a breakaway Catholic splinter in the Netherlands of the eighteenth century.[141]

Magical Products

We live, also, with magical products. Arthur Clarke[142] has said that the products of any scientific technology carried beyond a certain point are virtually indistinguishable from magic. We live with thousands of products our ancestors would have considered magical, which we ourselves cannot explain, without any sense of wonder. Not even the most hackneyed journalist uses the adjectival phrase "push-button" any more, the way it was used just 25 years ago to express a still lingering faint sense of wonder. But unconsciously, all this is a magical current in our perception of the modern world. Meanwhile, Faustian science grows even more daring in its goals, and announces them in programmatic manifestoes, which instill a Faustian expectation toward the future in us all. In our time "futurology" becomes an academic discipline.

Modern Myths and Magical Language

The news increasingly becomes magical spectacle, with its hypnotic reports of disaster psychotherapy and disaster politics, intelligence agencies practicing sorcery, gladiators and hit men as celebrities, Iron Guardists taking over the Rumanian American church, the cult of insanity as a lifestyle, illnesses turning into cognitive minorities and later into affirmative action groups, and so forth. And as the agenda of issues is partly manipulated by special interests and political cliques, we lose control of our attentionalities.

One long-term result of the overload of magical messages is the effect on language. Barthes[143] speaks of the cluttering up of modern language and thought with new "myths"; Ellul of the destruction of language and mind by propaganda.[144] To understand what they mean, let us go back to the beginning:

Cazeneuve[145] has demonstrated that sympathetic magical effects are intrinsic to any language; with the help of Mauss[146] I have traced these back to dim memories of associations between words in the primitive classification systems that underlie languages. These echoes grow weak in civilization, but certain practices in the recent modern world turn the volume up again. Propaganda, advertising, millenarian ideological movements all recharge the magical batteries of language. And some believe that churning up the magic in language's depths makes it too unclear to work effectively for a rational world. Orwell on Newspeak,[147] Steiner[148] on conscience-numbing totalitarian euphemisms, Kahler[149] on "abstractions" as junk that turns into machines (Martin Gardner shows[150] that this is literally true; certain abstractions do turn into machines), Boorstin on pseudo-events,[151] McLuhan[152] on the linear compulsion of print, Spengler[153] on printing as "Faustian distance-tactic" for long-range bombardment of the intellect, Marcuse on one-dimensionality,[154] Schroyer,[155] Habermas[156] and Mueller[157] on "repressive communication" pick up various facets of this abuse of language. There is little doubt that advertising, propaganda, etc., not only reanimate sympathy links but build new "magical" associations into language. We reach a point where the mind is stuffed with mythic images and everything suggests something else, so we are distractable, easily manipulated, unable to think clearly.

Barthes refers to this heaping up of too much "knowledge," too much propaganda, too many associations as "myths."[158] In an early book he wrote of the modern weariness with this burden of magical associations and of a need for artists to "write degree zero,"[159] in the limpid indicative, without special effects, so as to minimize these deceptions. (He even suggested this was what the new French novelists like Nathalie Sarraute[160] were up to.) But "degree zero writing" produces its own magical effects (e.g., the *faux naif*) and later Barthes admitted that it is virtually impossible to avoid mythic effects in language[161] (just as Cazeneuve said it is impossible to avoid the inherent sympathetic-magical associations of language[162]). Even if a Rudolf Carnap invents a logical language, Carnap and his enterprise become a "myth," a multiple association that can be put to magical ends. Ellul said prolonged education makes us more susceptible to propaganda and Barthes said the same about myths. We are burdened with our knowledge of "facts"; propaganda and myth both deal in transparent "facts" and seek to instill not orthodoxy but "orthopraxy," Ellul said, action that validates the facts. Barthes had a somewhat similar idea with his notion that myths "naturalize" events. Seeing something *done* (Barthes) or *doing it* yourself (Ellul) "certifies it" (Walker Percy) and makes it seem natural.

Barthes uses the word "myth" in a curious way—the way Walter Lippmann used "stereotypes"[163] or Boorstin "images" or Bacon "idols"[164]; but there is genius in calling these modern ideas "myths," because this exposes the compressed narratives that are curled up inside them, thereby establishing a link to primitive myths (and overturning the notion that we are superior to primitives). Barthes gives an example of what he means. During a French newsreel, the image of a black man saluting the French flag flashes on the screen.[165] This is a fragment of a myth, and then something is asserted under its aegis (about the French Empire). Here a rather complex situation, possibly even a long story about that black man and how he got into uniform, is compressed into a single image which is then used as a "word" in a proposition that asserts something.

Because the words thus used in myth are often condensations of whole stories, Barthes called myth a "metalanguage," intending the meaning used in logic; this is probably a misuse of Tarski's term,[166] but we know what he means. Plutarch[167] spoke of the "rainbow" effect of a myth, which seems to suggest many different meanings; Freud spoke of "overdetermination," and Caillois[168] suggested that this shimmer effect enables a myth to seem to speak to each individual personally.[169] In this vein, Lévi-Strauss calls myth "anonymous discourse" and Barthes cites the announcer's voice as a modern example. Does not the announcer tell me about "*my* deodorant"? Caillois and Barthes believe that myths "naturalize" conflicts in society, just by turning them into stereotypes of the mundane. It is like the old joke about the combat pilot telling the shaky beginner during his first mission under fire, "It's o.k., son, they're *allowed* to shoot at us." Myth is transparently clear and that is its deception; it does not so much hide its manipulation as stun us by it. What the myths of the mass media do is to naturalize a crazy world and make us believe that its contradictions are only natural.

I think all this is magical in a special way. Magic is symbolism stolen from what Berger[170] calls "the sacred canopy" of religion. Today the sacred canopy is rent; some people sit under smaller private tents, many of us have no canopy at all. But with pop culture myths we put up little parasols and umbrellas to strike sacred attitudes for personal objectives. A person refers to some current cultural myth like "middle America," for example; immediately he has put up his sacred parasol and we all piously take off our hats while he delivers the punch line of his enthymeme, his manipulative magical rhetorical syllogism. We darken one another's light with our sacred parasols all day long, switching on mythic relevancies the way we switch dials, and we keep fascinating and being fascinated, apparently going in and out of momentary minor trances, according to Hilgard.[171] The rainbow effect of magical myths torn from the rent sacred canopy enables them to speak to anyone, so we stun someone we want to manipulate by hauling up the flag of middle America or the parasol of motherhood, and then deliver our low punch while he stands in its shadow. Myth is always effective immediately, as Lévi-Strauss said. Hitler, addressing the army before war in the East, told them that terrible suffering would be inflicted, "*but such are the fortunes of war.*" No one asked "says who." He was using a tattered sacred parasol to naturalize horrors before they had even occurred; this helped to unleash them.

Barthes' work is part of a worldwide discovery that modern society and its major institutions skate on the thin ice of illusion. Daniel Boorstin's discovery[172] that pseudo-events drive real events from public attention, Walker Percy's idea[173] that a real event does not exist until it is "certified" by a pseudo-event (such as a follow-up reaction story in the press), Murray Edelman and Thurman Arnold and Jacques Ellul on the vaporization of political action into symbolic gesture over the head of the immediate situation to the mythic ideals whereby men are bound and tied to their society—all show how the clouding of communication by magical myth baffles and defeats real collective action. One result of all the propaganda, the advertising, the millenarian movements, the decaying religions, the prolonged education, is that in advanced industrial civilization there is a considerable amount of deception going around and "You could die from it." It is cleverly served up, in striking mythic forms and powerful "natural symbols" that, as Caillois wrote, have "an objective capacity of direct action of the affectivity."[174] As magical communication drowns out rational communication, as magical action defeats praxis, there is a great potential for domination; and lately even the Marxists grasp that ideology is just as safely hidden in the deceptive "daylight" myths of superstructure as in the dark ground of technostructure. A society that is increasingly magical in its communications, its public gestures, its very language, is a society that may be easy to dominate.

Recently, some groups have pointed out the dangers which the occult uprising poses to *science*. But a good deal more is at stake than that. The real danger is not pseudo-science but something much more horrid, something like Nazism or the Hindu caste system. Some groups would in effect censor mendacious publishers who pander to occult tastes by persuading them to check everything with scientists. But science is not a sacred cow, nor is it the be all and end all of human existence. (Some so-called science *is* magic—arrogant, false, self-confirming.) More important than science is the decent, secular, democratic social structure that underlies it and makes science possible. The real danger is that this could be undone by a millenarian movement which in effect organizes a political alliance between the occult minority, some disadvantaged classes and some ambitious elites. It has happened before . . .

PART FOUR: MAGIC AS AN EXPRESSION OF PRESSURE ON INDIVIDUAL AND SELF

Magic persists, then, partly because it expresses modern social structure—the fragmentation of organic solidarity, the splitting off of formal rationality, the alienation of many left-out groups, distorted communications. But in addition, since magic's emergence was tied up with the fortunes of the Individual and the self, it persists as an expression of pressure on those two institutions.

The position of the Individual today is paradoxical. On paper he is buttressed by powerful social supports in the great society, but in real life he lives in thousands of particular microworlds. The light of reason does not shine in all those places; some are dark or full of holes; and many individuals are trapped in special situations, "predicaments," as the existentialists say. A man whose employer secretly discriminates against him, whose divorce destroys his home, whose socialization bequeathed to him a crippling neurosis or its opposite, has limited protection of selfhood. The existentialists remind us how much such end-game predicaments are the result of previous choices: and no doubt such pious admonitions "build character." But when flaws and weaknesses appear throughout millions of individual microworlds in a *systematic* manner, then we are permitted to sociologize.

Certainly economic insecurity and family disintegration are systematic weak spots in the Individual today. Bensman and Vidich[175] speculate that the upper middle and professional classes in postwar America have enjoyed affluence out of proportion to their social power and that they are being "carried" by the system to prop up the consumption function. But one side effect is the insecurity of people whose salaries include a lot of economic rent exceeding their transfer value, and whose usefulness to the system may be running out. After Marcuse hailed the upper middle classes as the revolutionary wave of the future, Hermann Kahn overheard and warned his institutional clients; and in two recessions government fiscal policy and business practice seemed almost calculated to humble this class. In many fields footing lost is never regained and there are derogated occupations to which they must sink: advertising men to trade association work, editors to public relations. The fact that C. Wright Mills saw[176] bureaucratization of the professions coming 25 years ago, or that a torrent of popular books by William Whyte,[177] Vance Packard,[178] David Riesman,[179] John Galbraith,[180] Peter Drucker,[181] Alan Harrington,[182] (largely consumed by this class) helped "naturalize" the new insecurity by providing pop-sociology images for it, does not make this position any less precarious or painful. The growing insecurity of these favored middle-class loyalists is perhaps a warning signal.

The fragmentation of cities, the growth of anonymous organizations, the reduction of occupations to anonymous roles, are some of the other systematic forces turning individual microworlds into perilous predicaments. They are responsible in part for the new images of helplessness that flood sociological literature—such as Rollo May[183] on "loss of innocence" through loss of power, Howard Becker,[184] Garfinkel[185] and the ethnomethodologists on spectacular deviant subcultures, Fourcault[186] on madness as a metaphor about the futility of human knowledge, Lasswell[187] on politics as simply the process whereby the "irrational bases of society are brought into the open"—and Edelman, Boorstin, Ellul and the others on how efficacious action disintegrates into futile symbolic gesture. De Martino has shown that primitive magic was a response to helplessness in a mysterious world. Today, besides images of helplessness, we get images of our world as dematerial and mysterious. Even economy, capital and production have turned into "knowledge," as Drucker, Machlup, Schultz show.

But what happens to families perhaps best typifies the insecurity of the private individual. Goode[188] has shown that the post-Roman bilateral Western family was already radical; when the Reformation and modern industralism further stripped it down (to "what you can fit into a station wagon," Margaret Mead wrote), this freed individuals from their indigent uncles, crazy aunts, reactionary elders and hidebound traditions. In the Third World the Western family pattern still sells itself as an ideology of freedom. But the stripped down families also strip dominant members of some social powers that for some were unparalleled (e.g., *patria potestas*). Today, with the divorce rate passing 50 percent, we seem to split down to subatomic particles of the conjugal atom: the enormous welfare budget is perhaps more a reflection of this family disintegration than of strictly economic problems. "Private religions" are cancelled in the divorce courts along with much of the biographical past of the individual, his previously assumed future, and most of the family-centered person's sense of reality. In *Women in Divorce,* Goode[189] found a remarkable consistency about the time divorce takes: The whole thing averages (median) 23.8 months; but the time from first "serious consideration" to "final decision" is only 4.6 months, while the median time from decision to filing is only 3.2 months. Goode found very little variation in these two intervals, no matter what the "cause" of divorce.[190] In another study[191] I found that these two phases, especially the first, are when the "conversation of divorce" takes place; it destroys the marriage so swiftly precisely because many modern marriages are little more than conversational castles in the air, or "private *nomoi,*" as Berger calls them. I suspect that where subcultural supports that correlate with lesser divorce rates actually come to bear is in short-circuiting this conversation. ("We can't, we're Catholic; we can't even discuss it.") But many American marriages, with few kin supports or economic supports and little economic usefulness as an alliance, are conversational structures based on bricks no solider than the saying, "It can't happen to us," which disintegrate in a few chill minutes once earnest divorce talk begins. *"Plebs gentem non habet,"* the Roman aristocrats used to say:[192] "The plebes don't have families." If we smash up our little families, destroy our little havens of safety and affection, break up with our babies and our old folks will we all become powerless again? If the majority some day is fatherless, born yesterday, solitary or gay, and calls that freedom, will it be freedom indeed or a sign that people are getting socially smashed, preparatory to a final enslavement?

The forces contracting the Individual are great—but there are also new social demands and elaborate training for even tougher individuals to man elite posts of great responsibility. Political innovators, astronauts, corporate C.E.O.'s, daring medical scientists are sought and rewarded for almost superhuman faculties of self-directed action. Meanwhile, movements of role radicalism press for undreamed of new freedoms for women, children, the old, all marginalized groups. Advances in fundamental law protecting minorities are enormous. We find the same paradoxes when we move from the Individual to the self. Charges of "preformation of the ego in the media," "decline of superego" and "impoverishment of self" must be balanced against spectacular new psychological technologies with ambitious aims to aggrandize the self.

Magic As Reflection of Expansion OR Contraction

In the last chapter we saw that even extreme (black) magic has erupted in modern Europe when selves came under pressure. In general we may expect to see an eruption of some kind of magic phenomena whenever *either* the self *or* the Individual is *either* expanding to new powers *or* is under pressure to contract. That sounds like a simple argument to be organized under four sub-heads: Self Expanding, Self Contracting, Individual Expanding, Individual Contracting—but that would oversimplify and ignore cross elasticities. The self resides *in* the Individual and feels any pressure to which it is subjected; the Individual in turn is subverted if the self succumbs. Moreover, there are imbalances the most common case being an attempt to puff up the self by "psychological technologies" when the walls of individualism are collapsing. And some institutions, such as the person category and magical religion, affect both self and Individual alike. In most historical crises, moreover, both Individual and self are experiencing pressure, and sometimes both kinds simultaneously: pressure to expand and pressure to contract. Most cases are mixed. The important point is that magic erupts whenever either Individual or self start moving, whether forwards or backwards.

Renaissance magic, for example, coincided not only with the advance in science it helped stimulate, but also with a spectacular age of great individuals with vast opportunities for power and exploit. Magic erupted also in the Reformation, when the self was on the march to new realms of private power and integrity.

But magic also erupted in the late Roman Age when Christianity was *expanding* the *self* but social forces were meanwhile *contracting* the *Individual*. Even the latter case was mixed, for Roman codification was quietly expanding the Individual's integrity at law (for a future harvest) while far greater forces were weakening him. Economic and administrative pressure on the *curiales* had begun early, at least in the time of Nero, according to Dill.[193] By the reign of Diocletian, as Gibbon[194] and Rostovtzeff[195] have shown, this class (and others) were permanently locked into place by the corporate state. The burden was so great many fled into vagabondage or attached themselves to powerful magnates. Ferdinand Lot[196] has shown that serfdom began that way, long before Rome fell. The enormous bureaucracy and army together with subvention of the urban proletariat raised taxes so high that manufacturers moved out to the *latifundiae,* as Rostovtzeff has shown, and in the company towns and farms of rural space individualism sunk to a nadir. Vivid individuals like Symmachus or Ausonius or Sidonius still remained at court and in places of privilege, as Dill[197] and Bury[198] show, but individualism was no longer a way of life for lower, middle or upper middle classes.

Magic reflects both pressures to expand and pressures to contract, but I suspect it reflects the self more directly than the Individual. The self contains a "magical" institution within it, the ego; "magic" in the weak sense is one of its typical responses to pressure. Whereas pressures on the Individual probably cause magical phenomena through the indirect pressure this puts onto the self. (Example of direct pressure on the self: destructuring of families that weakens socialization. Examples of indirect pressure on the self caused by contraction of the Individual: bureaucracy, job insecurity.) What often happens historically is that pressure which contracts the Individual helps provoke counterpressure from within the self to expand its psychic powers as a compensation. In late Rome, Christianity armed the self with a soul, immortality, personal magic and promises of divinity[199] at a time when politics and economics were actually collapsing the outer walls of the Individual.

This frequently happens, and it can backfire; if immoderate it can lead to a sidetracking of energy. In India, where similar pressure contracted the (feeble) institutions of the Individual, the self was so puffed up by a magical counterattack that it deflected individual effort thereafter into a spiritualism that actually eviscerated the self, everted its contents, declared Atman to be Brahman (Hinduism) or Atman not to exist (Buddhism) and so killed the self. In the West, the revolt of the self against the contraction of the Individual did not have this effect, because the Christian revolt was measured and because Roman law and feudal institutions preserved some walls for the Individual.

What is happening today? Is the self expanding or contracting; is the Individual expanding or contracting? The answer is that *all four movements* are taking place at once and it is hard to assess the "weights." There seems to be a tremendous effort to aggrandize the self, to endow it with "higher" consciousness, occult faculties and Faustian powers. At the same time, some of the magic seems distinctly defensive, as if responding to pressures to contract: deviant psychotherapies, meditation techniques, drop-out cults. Is the space age self a new Renaissance Faust bent on conquest, or is it simply counterattacking desperately, responding to its own socialization weaknesses and to pressure passed inward by collapsing individualism?

Pressure on the Individual

The condition of the Individual is mixed. He experiences pressures in both directions: New capacities, freedoms, expectations, rights, institutions, exploits drive him upwards. Yet constricting webs of bureaucracy and economy limit his options. We can only guess the weights, but for most classes right now the pressures contracting the Individual probably outweigh those expanding him. Since C. Wright Mills' *White Collar* we have known how even the professions were becoming bureaucratized[200]; for decades small businesses have been gobbled up by giant corporations.[201] Property also has grown more abstract; most of it now is paper; ownership carries little power. Tax laws press hard on the modern *curiales* who seek to become independent; it is hard to do it. The corporate state moves into more areas, such as education; state-engineered inflation cuts down many areas of autonomy (e.g., working one's way through college becomes impossible). Durkheim's idea that organic solidarity would become a mesh of legal ties becomes a corporativist nightmare, as legal wizards devise more and more enclosures for us.

Finally, one institution of the Individual has already cracked. The person category has fragmented, turned into a bagful of disparate concepts—ego, self, identity, self-image, person, etc.

Pressure on the Self

Here, too, pressures come both ways—to expand, to contract. Pressures to expand are mostly magical, but should not be thought of as merely defensive. Magical technologies like mysticism and meditation have engineered lasting advances for the self in the past. But the self can also expand through structural changes: such as a deepening of the Oedipal struggle, successful repression, apt socialization. Today pressures to expand the self seem to be mostly a matter of psychological technologies, if not outright magic, so the expansion is *probably* a reaction, a defense, a counterattack. (And that is a clue to contractive pressures on the Individual probably outweighing expansion.)

Pressure to contract the self are of two kinds: indirect (i.e., the self experiencing pressures on the Individual) and direct. The direct pressures are more serious. Various writers have charged that key "institutions" of the self are crumbling:

Crumbling Superego? Sorokin[202] called ours a "sensate" age. Spengler called it[203] moving from "culture" to "civilization"; Toynbee spoke of the weakening of the "mass drill" whereby the values of the "creative minority" are instilled. Nisbet[204] wrote of the "twilight of authority," Riesman[205] of the decline of "inner-directed" men. They were all talking about the superego, and Marcuse put it most clearly. In a later book he seemed to turn his back on the whole Wilhelm Reich-Frankfurt tradition, which in *The Mass Psychology of Fascism,*[206] *The Authoritarian Personality,*[207] etc., had charged that strict families produced submissive characters who joined totalitarian movements. Now, in "The Obsolescence of the Freudian Concept of Man," Marcuse wrote[208] with nostalgia and regret of the decline of fatherly authority, because this ended the Oedipal struggle through which the individual became a free person. Marcuse's argument also concerns the ego, but we should remember that in orthodox psychoanalytic theory the superego *is* the unconscious, resolved and buried Oedipus complex. No more Oedipal struggle means no more superego.

Collapsing Ego? Closely related is the ego, which has its roots in repression. No more Big Daddy means no more repression. Marcuse charges[209] that ego today is "preformed in the media," stamped in as a shallow pop image, rather than deepened by a freedom-giving Oedipal struggle. Bandura[210] and Bronfenbrenner[211] back this empirically: more hours in front of TV than in the classroom. Others diagnose ego impairment other ways. Charles Fair[212] uses an old-fashioned brain physiology[213] to identify ego with the cortex, which he says is stimulated to grow by community, religion, objectivity—as these decline, the lower-brain id dominates culture. Rollo May[214] discerns regression to id-control coming through excessive ego frustration in the modern world (the old Dollard-Doob frustration-aggression hypothesis[215] used to diagnose magic as a symptom of frustration). Bettelheim[216] and Tinbergen[217] speculate that increasing thousands of egos are nipped in the bud by childhood autisms as a result of the thickening web of social frustrations. But at the same time a host of *anti*-ego ideologists claim ego is retreating because it is a destructive dinosaur that deserves to die. Roger Wescott[218] is a moderate who speaks of imbalance: he thinks ego is receding because it grew too large. But wilder voices are heard and they are part of the pressure on the ego. The message of Wilhelm Reich—that ego is a disease, a neurotic body armor[219]—is broadcast as widely in America as the similar message of Buddha was broadcast in India. Today shrill, hopeful books become best-sellers, which suggest that "self" can expand by sacrificing the ego, shedding its "heavy armor"—the old Hindu trick of everting Atman into Brahman. The several Maslow schools[220] teach temporary use of magical experiences to strengthen oversoul dimensions that will replace narrow ego. Robert Hunter,[221] Roger Poole,[222] Joseph Chilton Pearce,[223] Stan Gooch[224] in various ways preach something like the Hindu doctrine of mâya or the old shamanic trick of soul loss for recovery with greater strength. But where individualism continues to contract, soul loss can become literal, without recovery, as the Hindu example shows. Soul loss then becomes a "patterned deviancy" (Parsons) which adjusts to a social system of reduced individuality; in extreme cases, like Hinduism, techniques to efface the self become part of the ideological and religious support of the oppressive social system. But the puffed-up self at a time of contracting individualism *has* worked in the West in the past;[225] this time, moreover, it arms itself with all the accumulated spiritual techniques of the ages together with the new "wild sciences." In the U.S., moreover, the counter-culture maintains its ties with the tradition of protest, which indeed it absorbed after 1968.[226] It is possible that adventurous pursuit of old and new magics to puff up the self might accomplish something.

A Postscript on the Person

One strategic, integrating institution has already collapsed, one that mediates other institutions of the Individual to the self: this is the person category. As we saw in Chapter 10, the person category becomes incoherent in our time; it fragments into concepts like the id, me, identity.[227] But the self lives on, and the Individual for a while seems to get stronger. What happened? Dozens of shrill books announcing the death of the self are written by pale-faced men who emerge from their libraries surprised to discover that people still endure even when ideas about them fall apart. Writers like Charles Fair[228] and the others have simply mixed up the person category with the self, or the Individual, and what happens in philosophy with what happens in real life. But should not confusion about what persons are cause some disorganization in the other institutions of the Individual? Not immediately, for these are not integrated subjectively or at a superstructural level. Have not the Frankfurt Marxists[229] told us that rationality is "sedimented" into the techno-economic-legal system? Disintegration of the person category need not disorganize the self immediately either. Its integration is also accomplished differently, *by the ego,* whose powers depend on natural endowment, Oedipal resolution and repression, and only partly on cognitive factors. The ego continued to grow in strength during the nineteenth century, while the person category splintered, because Western socialization deepened repression and public life offered a free arena for growth.

But *how long* can ego and self remain unaffected by confusion in society's person ideas[230]? If egos *are* increasingly preformed in the media and the peer group as Marcuse claims[231] and Bronfenbrenner partly demonstrates,[232] with six daily hours of television replacing an Oedipal struggle with a father who is now too weary commuting to fight, then they depend more on cognitive coherence and surely confused person ideas in the media will affect the self.[233] It is theoretically possible for a nation to be entirely socialized by television and still produce reasonable if shallow selves, provided media messages about personhood are reasonable. But the contents of television today are more incoherent and perverse about personhood than any previous socialization medium. Moreover, the person category is mediated to selves by caretakers; if deviant psychotherapists and insane gurus foist demonic ideas of personhood on young people, by modeling, persuasion, therapeutic assault and physical intervention including drugs, who is to say that confused ideas of personhood will not affect selves? For weak selves and perhaps societies, this could tilt the balance.[234] Today's confused ideas of personhood could produce the first tears in the secondary process for selves and for the civilization itself as a structure of consciousness.

The Tear in the Fabric

Person ideas become contents of the "intrapsychic self" (Arieti[235]), for they saturate the lexical forms of language, and sediment deep structures of social memories that frame conventionalized biographies (Halbwachs,[236] Schachtel[237]). So what do today's confused person ideas inside the self do to its organization; and how could they affect its organizer, the ego? They could tear rents in the fabric of the secondary process, enabling primary process material to break through. This is usually fought by magical thinking. Both the eruption and the antidote weaken the reality framework and change the structure of consciousness.

Of course, a controlled inruption of primary process material is part of normal self functioning. We see this most clearly in the "extreme" case of creativity. Kris,[238] Arieti,[239] etc., show how in the creative act ego dips into the primary process (the unconscious) and then repackages its materials in secondary process forms for a public. Arieti calls this "the magic synthesis." (Cazeneuve claims[240] all magic does that: it crosses the border from order into chaos and returns strengthened.) Thus Kris speaks[241] of regression in the service of the ego, Dabrowski[242] of "positive disintegrations," Laing[243] of voyages of discovery, and psychoanalysts of the creative process like Kubie[244] and Arieti,[245] of tapping the unconscious, or the primary process. The idea goes back at least to Vico, and certainly well before Freud, as Lancelot Whyte has shown in *The Unconscious Before Freud.*[246] But creativity studies in turn merely dramatize what the normal ego always does. Ego's main function is to channel the inruption of primary process materials and translate them into secondary process symbols and action via "the magic principle" (Róheim). In this sense, all normal human action is creative.

But an excess of primary process eruption can overwhelm structures of ego and self. Demonic person concepts that promote this are Trojan horses in any logical universe of discourse. Similarly, sheer fragmentation of the person category may be the Achilles heel of the secondary process; and it may help regress the secondary process of the civilization itself back toward more magical structures of consciousness. "The jewel is in the lotus," the occultists tell us, and they know their business. Excessive self-scrutiny could be the magic carpet back to the enchanted world of mankind's childhood.

The secondary process is conscious thought guided by reality, whereas the primary process (in Freud's works) means the primitive, pleasure-driven thought typical of the unconscious.[247] The secondary process increasingly reflects man's logicalization. In growing up modern selves gradually fill up with secondary process concepts that are abstract, universalistic and logical; these aid ego in its perennial task of constructing abstract plans for action. In this, socialization recapitulates the historical development of culture. As Hegel has shown, a child of ten might take in logical structures in a few months that represent a whole century's advance, the way we learn the fifteenth century's trigonometry in a semester.[248] Socialization also recapitulates prehistory, as "affectual categories" (Lévy-Bruhl[249]), crude paleological "endocepts" (Arieti[250]), or "psychomotor" constructs (Werner) typical of primitive thought give way by adolescence to truly abstract concepts.[251]

Throughout Western history, until its disintegration by contemporary subjectivism, the person category tended toward extreme logicalization. Husserl, in describing the intersubjectivity of the "life world," wrote that we come to think of ourselves and of others as if we were each the O origin of an X-Y-Z-T coordinate system in spacetime.[252] In Einstein's sense,[253] we even assume these coordinate systems are "Galilean," i.e., we could extrapolate from one to another if we knew the "transformation equations" (Lorentz[254]), and hence all person experience is potentially completely rational and knowable. But there is an inherent limitation in this development: As Arieti points out, an ego with pure secondary process contents, no access to the unconscious and no use of magic thinking would lose all spontaneity.[255] I say more: it would lose the ability to act altogether, it would die. Human beings cannot be automatized, for their integration requires ego and its magic action. When real selves are excessively automatized they often lose all integration and go haywire.

But the secondary process can collapse altogether and with it the ego and the self. As far back as Karl Gustav Carus in 1831,[256] psychologists have made an analogy between childish thought that precedes the secondary process biographically, and primitive thought that precedes it historically, and psychotic thought that regresses to a childish or primitive level.[257] It is not surprising that ego, self and person category are all weak in all these cases. Nunberg,[258] for example, speaks of the reciprocal relation of ego and secondary process: ego helps establish the secondary process (by repressing primary process thoughts, adjusting to cultural reality); on the other hand ego has organization partly because it is ruled by the secondary process. To this trilogy of infantile, primitive and psychotic structures of consciousness (all dependent on a weak or regressed secondary process), I want to add a fourth analogue: the breakdown of a civilization as a structure of consciousness.

World Collapse and Magic

Today, at a time when both self and Individual are under pressure, the secondary process in which both subsist is also subjected to hammer blows. Primary process eruption is cultivated as a lifestyle through drugs, hard rock and techniques of ecstasy. Occult messages about personhood bombard the logical universe of discourse; psychoanalysis as a lifelong training in magical thinking makes the culture sensitive to omens[259]; other cultural waves tear rents in the secondary process of the civilization itself. Discourse thickens, images coarsen and we see ugly reflections of our mutated souls on the covers of *People* Magazine. I want to press the analogy between the breakdown of the secondary process in an ego (that is, psychosis) and the world collapse that seems to threaten when a civilization as a structure of consciousness becomes addicted to unleashing the primary process.

Psychotic breakdown is often visualized as disintegration of the secondary process. Frustrated (all too easily) by its environment, a (weak) ego withdraws all love ("cathexis") from the world, so the world's objects lose all interest.[260] Secondary process conceptions of these objects then collapse. The ego weakness that undermines secondary process thinking this way can be caused by "weak ego boundaries" (Tausk[261]), insufficient "ego intentionality" to sustain the objective frame (Kronfelt[262]), arrested ego growth due to failure to solve previous problems (Erikson[263]), failure of ego defenses (Anna Freud[264]), weaknesses in ego's genetic endowment (Hartmann[265]). Or psychosis can be conceptualized the other way round as well, with some external factor overthrowing the secondary process directly and *that* paralyzing the ego. The secondary process could be overthrown by some overwhelming affect (Jung[266]), such as extreme chronic anxiety that disturbs attention (Freeman *et al.*[267]), or some powerful lust from the unconscious (Storch[268]), or too much dopamine (Snyder[269]), or some other chemical (Roy Hoskins[270]), with a hereditary basis (Kalmann twin studies), and perhaps even by a cultural disorganization (this crazy world). An intermediary case is suggested where there is some fundamental cognitive problem making ego inept at adapting to secondary process logic, such as "concrete" thinking and weakness in abstraction (Goldstein[271]), faulty associations (Bleuler[272]), "loose" associations, "magic speech operations," (Sullivan[273]), "acausal reasoning" (Cameron[274]), weak conceptualization (Kasinin[275]). Since egos and civilizations are intimately connected structures of consciousness, all these concepts suggest analogies.

Whatever the cause, the outcome is the same when the walls start crumbling down. There is a failure of abstract thinking (Goldstein), causing a "lowering of the mental level" (Janet[276]), with inruption of primary process materials (Freud), "archaic thinking" (Sullivan), "archetypes" (Jung), "prelogical thought" (Lévy-Bruhl). Storch[277] notes striking resemblances between such content (especially in schizophrenics) and primitive religio-magical representations. Both are archaic philogenetically: emotional, subjective, expressing desire, inclining toward pantomime, visual rather than abstract, asserting excessive sympathy links between ideas, disorganized and vague. Both primitives and schizophrenics are obsessed with fears of external influences, which reflect weak egos that *are* easily influenced. And in both there are masochistic symbols of ego capitulation: including themes of transformation of identity, mystic union, cosmic identification and rebirth. Storch uses the word "magic" but seems to be writing more about primitive religion. For example, he identifies mystic ecstasy with catatonic stupor and notes similarities between gestures in Vedic rites and schizophrenic episodes. On the other hand, he asserts that magic *defends* weak egos of primitives and psychotics against psychic death.[278] For Storch the psychotic episode begins in a larval stage of agitation, often caused by a strong drive conflicting with a weak ego; then comes the moment of euphoria when ego gives in, joins the primary process and opens the floodgates to primitive thought.[279]

Werner and Arieti paint a more vivid picture of logical collapse in psychosis because they first build up the secondary process philogenetically, then reverse the sequence dramatically. Werner[280] recognizes (like the later Lévy-Bruhl, whom he frequently cites) that civilization means not just logic but the logicalization of objects through concepts with sharp cutting edges. By contrast, primitive proto-concepts for objects were much vaguer; they contained not just "affectual" content as Lévy-Bruhl[281] said, but also psychomotor elements. This world corresponds to the primal mana world of primitive religion, Werner writes. (He will later show that magic is the first step out of it, toward our world.) Here space, for example, is non-isotropic as Lévy-Bruhl demonstrated[282]; action is ritualistic, bound to traditional stimuli; this is a passive "religious world."[283] And psychotic breakdown is a throwback to this primitive "religious" world.

Arieti traces the intermediary stages between primitive-religious and modern-logical thought (and their reversal in psychosis).[284] The first step is a mere "image," a memory that serves the self as a crude direct symbol but cannot communicate to others. A slight advance is the "paleosymbol," a crude *private* construct that stands for something in external reality, but is solipsistic. A further step is the "endocept," the first class symbol, which however is still too personal to communicate clearly because it contains affectual meaning. This is like Lévy-Bruhl's "affective categories" with their "mystic participations." Images, paleosymbols and endocepts together constitute the "paleologic" that precedes the fully abstract concepts of the modern secondary process. In psychosis, this evolutionary sequence is reversed: concepts give way first to endocepts, then regress to paleosymbols, and finally to the phantasmagoric inner world of mere images. This is a regression from abstractness, objectivity and communicability all at once.[285]

Kronfelt's[286] idea of "rents" in the secondary process (found in pre-psychotics) is useful. In borderline cases archaic primary-process thought breaks in only here and there; most of the time rationality still prevails. But new rents are made, so mythic primary process thinking *grows,* side by side with rational thought, until at last it overwhelms it. I want to add: the existence of some rents predisposes to new ones, just the way a torn fabric easily tears further.

Many people walk around with large holes in their secondary processes, which may be hidden by mental blocks or refusal to discuss certain matters or seeming *idées fixes.*[287] These holes may seem minor but they are deep ("'Tis enough, 'twill serve"); they are like black holes with time reversal inside them because here the logical rules of timespace and secondary process stop.

Today certain cultural processes are blasting gaping holes in the secondary process, both for individuals and for the civilization, that may function like expandable tears. For example, a decade ago many young people were encouraged to undergo LSD experiences which left permanent scars in their secondary process in the form of ineradicable memories of blackhole space trips. Today they are subjected to deviant and occult psychotherapies that purposely assault the self as the enemy. Nonordinary experience is validated by guided drug trips. Not only are individual egos affected—these experiences are dramatized, and enter the cultural stream. Commune experiences which dramatize structures of self and consciousness antithetical to secondary process serve as communicative models broadcasting occult messages over the heads of the media (though often with their fascinated cooperation) to millions. I think the fabric tears. The fact that many people pass into psychosis as a result of drug trips, deviant psychotherapy and anti-ego T-groups is well documented. Less certain is the degree to which the uproar tears holes in the secondary process of the civilization itself.

In this process, magic plays an ambivalent role. Recourse to magic is part of the recourse to the primary process, but it is also part of the fight against it. Magic is not so much the illness as a regression to a primitive line of defense which the illness causes. There is a better analogy between religion and primary process, perhaps, and if the civilization breaks, perhaps a new faith structure of consciousness will succeed it; but meanwhile desperate magic is part of the fight for reality, just as it is in psychosis, just as it was for primitives. When the secondary process collapses in psychosis, magic thinking returns as the only possible way of dealing with a world of shadowy, mystical, incoherent and demonic objects. Werner therefore regards magic as intermediary in man's development, and even identifies truly primary-process materials with *religious* phenomena.

Magic is already an advance beyond primitive "religious" thought, which is holistic, concrete, diffuse, affectual, in which action is ritualistically bound to a concrete situation. Magic, by contrast, detaches ritual, extrapolates and travels. The primary process world is passive, as religion is passive, whereas in metaphors of magic, Werner shows, man moves forward to action.[288] Passivity is domination by the concrete diffuse field; at first there is no planfulness or even much inner motivation.[289] Primitive action is diffuse just as religious ceremonies are labile.[290] Primitive thought is phenomenal and so is its causality: the explanation for everything is "in the beginning," when some exceptional event gave the rule for present structures.[291] Magical action gradually emerges out of this, initially taking advantage of its blurred identities and adualism to act. Magic is not this primitive sacral-holistic content but the exploitation of it.

As such, magic is a step to the secondary process. It begins with analogies as stratagems of control. Magic arises initially because it has to, to defend the ego against the demonic entities of the holistic-religious world; it is the only way of coping with such entities, but it has the effect of gradually changing them.[292] Magic creatively groups entities by analogies, then uses the analogies to link together action and result. So magic is transitional to logical thought, and reappears as a progressive stage in that direction in children. (Werner traces two magical stages: the first merely adualist and primitive, the second more imaginative and creative in rearrangement by analogy.) And magic thinking reappears when the world collapses and ghostly and indefinite objects return that can only be grasped and controlled by magic thought. Then magic, like much of the symbolic content of psychosis, is part of the process of trying to get well by getting back in touch with the world.[293] In a late book Susanne Langer advanced similar evidence, based on dream symbolism as a kind of logical neotony.[294] And Arieti, who builds on Werner, also agrees that magic is an intermediary step. The same idea is implicit in Lévy-Bruhl's later works on mythic reasoning, on "affectual categories" such as ideas of "luck" and "dispositions." In *l'Expérience Mystique et les Symboles . . .*, he writes that the "affective category of the supernatural" is the *origin* of abstract thoughts. And he also insists that such magic thinking is initially *the only way* to manipulate the vague unformed entities that people the unmade world of the primitive.[295] And of course Lévi-Strauss built upon Lévy-Bruhl's work his own interpretation that mythic and magic thinking contain prototypes of "logical operators," whereby primitives grope toward systematic thought. Here then is one more sense in which magic helped the Individual and the self. *It helped begin the "secondary process"* in which both subsist.

The ambivalence of magic makes it hard to interpret its reappearance. We have already seen that it arises when the self and the Individual are contracted, but also when either expands. And its effect on the secondary process in which both subsist is paradoxical. On the one hand, I cannot help but feel that any recourse to magic is regressive and may tear further rents in society's rational structure of consciousness. At the same time, magic is clearly a defense against rents that are already present; magic is clearly an effort at reconstitution of order, however iatrogenic the effects may often be.

The Critical Nexus: Individual and State

The secondary process of the civilization seems to tear, but so far both Individuals and selves register forces driving them in both directions—pressures to expand, pressures to contract. Which holds the key to the future? It is the weights that matter. Jürgen Habermas made a significant attempt to assess them in *Legitimation Crisis*.[296] Habermas begins by recognizing that the classic sociology of Weber and Durkheim was precisely about society as a *moral* entity that gives birth to individuals. Self is dependent on the Individual as a social institution, and he in turn depends on a moral social order: "The unity of the person requires the unity-enhancing perspective of a lifeworld that guarantees order and has both cognitive and moral-practical significance."[297]

A great deal depends therefore on the coherence of world-maintaining interpretive systems which overcome chaos and contingency. But the paradox of organic solidarity poses again the problem of disorder: When only minimum consensus is needed to integrate society, society is integrated with only minimum consensus and with insufficient meaning. Worldviews become impoverished, and so does the inner direction of the individual person. The "repoliticalization of theology" (e.g., Pannenberg, Bultmann, etc.) is one attempt to reestablish a moral community, according to Habermas. But most current philosophy is more pessimistic. And there is a trend toward elitist theories in most social sciences. What these secretly express is the hope that technicians will do the job of integration in the absence of moral consensus and substantive reason, on which the nurturing of individualism depends. But without some core of moral consensus, individuals could become so robbed of substantive rationality as to function like homologues of the social insects.

In the end, Habermas comes down to one issue as strategic, and that is the question whether, in growing social complexity, the political steering system can remain responsive to the society as a whole, to its members and its interest groups. In other words, he challenges the whole question of elites and of technocracy. There have probably been a dozen separate "literatures" on the issue of elites—the classical elitist theorists Mosca,[298] Michels,[299] Pareto; the American "technocrats"[300] cresting with Veblen's *Engineers and the Price System*[301]; the 1940's English "planning" literature of Barbara Wooton,[302] Ernest Davies,[303] etc.; the "pluralists" such as G. D. H. Cole; American sociological studies of elites by C. Wright Mills, Galbraith, Polsby,[304] Baltzell,[305] Floyd Hunter,[306] Arnold M. Rose,[307] Robert A. Dahl[308]; there is even an active antipluralist opposition in writers like Henry Kariel, David Spitz, Philip Selznick,[309] and Andrew Hacker.[310]

What is new in Habermas is the insistence that the issue be considered in moral terms, in its effect on moral formation of the individual. Habermas gives most attention to the formulation of his associate Luhmann,[311] and although he dismisses it at the end, Luhmann's vision is clearly intended as an archetype of what might happen. In Luhmann's model, the political steering mechanism gradually becomes free of the society, and *must* do so because of the system's increasing complexity. To escape from disorder brought on by its own problem-solving ability, the steering system must detach itself from the underlying society via nonparticipatory planning. Planning must hereafter be conceptualized in systems-analysis terms, not in terms of the "old European" idea of some minimal moral consensus, which, in the reality of modern democratic states, is up for grabs in a daily struggle of interest groups. But when the system does not even presuppose a core of moral consensus, when it is held together by non-participatory planning based on systems-analysis models, then there is no *nomos* at the center for individual monads to reflect, there is no more core for socialization, and the individual is dead. Luhmann accepts this: the individual must instead be socialized for utter open-endedness and indeterminateness.

Designs for this kind of socialization already exist in new models of "formal organization" which, in certain industries, have been superseding the older models based on the normative order lying behind the Weberian ideal type of bureaucracies. The so-called "organic model" of formal organization[312] found in some economic sectors (e.g., "continuous flow industries," upper management, etc.) is utterly open-ended in its demands on each participant: the very lack of definition of responsibilities poses a totalitarian burden. C. S. Lewis' *That Hideous Strength* and Joseph Heller's *Catch-22* best convey the flavor of this "organic" model of formal organization, perhaps. Completely "other directed," without the shield of bureaucratic norms which Crozier[313] has had the wit to see protect individuals, the new group-think forms are apparently efficient, as perhaps Japanese management experience illustrates.

A Demonic Self?

Luhmann and Habermas recognize that if the political process is run according to systems-management design, the self, the Individual, will atrophy. Another possibility, lightly touched on by Habermas (who in turn cites Adorno's *Negative Dialectic*[314]), is that the individual may remain but as a useless entity, possibly as a form of consumption. If lifestyles will be diverse and freely chosen in the future, a lifestyle involving old-fashioned moral socialization and inner-directedness will be one which many members of the leisure class will still choose, if only for its prestige. But Habermas does not discuss another possibility: If deeply-formed selves persist when they no longer fit the social system, they might turn demonic. As Dodds has shown, the Western self is somewhat demonic to begin with. From Crimean shamanism[315] came the idea that dreams reflect occult powers in man, giving birth to the concept of the soul as the occult self, and to cults of magic puritanism.[316] It fed into the Apollonian religion, into the Eleusinian Mysteries (with their initiation magic literalized into the idea of rebirth to eternal life *through* death[317]), into Orphism, and, through Pythagoreanism, into Platonism and Christianity. The psyche of the West retains in part this occult heritage: *the Christian soul is purest when the body is dead.* One can feel this visiting churches in Spain that are virtual tombs, criss-crossed with sepulchres, one of them guarding the remains of the Spanish Civil War general who cried, "Long live death!"

Occult ideas of self, Dodds wrote in a later book,[318] are one reason why there was always a great gnostic potential in Greek thought, even in the classic period. It is still with us. Wilhelm Reich and counterculture figures who attack Western ego in effect say that the Western self is already demonic. Historically, when Western individualism is cramped, it often retreats into romanticism or worse. Babbitt's *Rousseau and Romanticism,*[319] Praz's *The Romantic Agony,*[320] De Vigny's *Chatterton*[321] show the beginnings of such pressure; De Rugieri[322] and Sartre[323] show that modern existentialism is a romanticism of the cramped ego. So was the religious "enthusiasm" of middle classes dependent on but impotent under the old regime, according to Ronald Knox[324] and Lucien Goldmann.[325] Jonas[326] goes further and shows similarities between existentialism and gnosticism. In modern algolagnic gnosticisms we may again see the mirror image of a demonic self, for the self that in Hellenistic gnosticism projected the god of this world (even Jehovah, god of justice) as a *devil* inevitably had a demonic face.[327] So there is not only the possibility that the self may contract (of which impotent magic is the symptom), but the chance that the self might persist anachronistically in an unattractive, demonic form.

Automatons or demonic selves—those are among the risks of continuing to replace society's small remaining moral consensus with nonparticipatory planning. Since the society we make socializes our children, they inevitably take shape in its image. The old Bolshevik prisoner in Koestler's *Darkness at Noon* was troubled that he had helped produce a generation of "Gletkins" (his bloodless, faceless interrogator). Some former Cold Warriors feel the same about a generation of "Calleys." Modern grey-flannel selves already reflect the chill impersonality principle we have built into society. But so perhaps does Charles Manson. A demonic revolt is perhaps just as likely as further automatization simply because the human self probably will not bend further without extinction. The person idea is already the most occult category in the secondary process and the human ego still works by a kind of magic. Unless it is lobotomized, as in Zamiatin's *We*[328] (where an operation was performed to remove human "fancy"), it is just as likely to turn demon as robot.

In Adorno, Reich and Marcuse, we sometimes even hear explicit calls for a demonic self that will revolt against the impersonality principle that rules the world—just as Norman Mailer, on similar grounds, praises psychopaths[329] (and R. D. Laing, schizophrenics[330]).

Non-persons vs. Selves

Even without nonparticipatory planning being official state policy, it already rules much of the economy and its bureaucracies. The magical ego is already forced to its limit of toleration of impersonality. The main problem confronting moral community today is the growing power of anonymous organizations that decide our lives. We increasingly live and work in corporate groups of which we are not true members and in which we have few or poorly defined rights.[331] Even government tends toward corporative organization by function rather than membership; local government especially fragments into special-service authorities. Fragmentation is greatest in cities, where paradoxically government is densest, closest and somehow most anonymous; and this is reflected in the inability of urban theory even to form an image of the city any more.[332]

Either chaos results or there is accommodation between these forces; again, it is a *system* rather than a community. The corporate non-persons man has been creating by legal fictions for several millennia embody his impersonality principle. These non-persons are systems that tend toward boundary-maintenance and in the end adjust to one another only through a systems dynamic. The organization of organizations, rather than a moral order, regulates society.

But paradoxically, the logical impersonality of man's institutions is partly a precipitate of his past attempts to use *magic* to get them under control. In magic, symbolism is wrenched from consensus and used to make some pragmatic device or procedure—a model to manipulate social reality, a drill to focus attention and effort. It usually precipitates some new abstraction or mechanism. The categories and philosophy may grow out of religion as the Durkheimians claim, but I suspect that the anarchic non-persons, abstractions on the loose, are born in magic with its legal fictions, enthymemes and special designs. And does not magical organization—beginning with the class associations and culminating in magicians' collegia in which clients have no membership—provide a blueprint for the impersonal organization which spreads alienation? Hegel wrote that all action contains, through the objectifications it creates, the possibility of alienation: in magic man alienates himself more than in many of his works—and then he creates new magic to fight alienation.

How Odd the Corporation. Consider some of the strange attributes of the dominant corporate non-persons of our era, "magical" attributes built into them by legal fictions. For one thing, these "legal persons" are almost ectoplasmic in their increasing independence: they are independent of people. (First stockholders wither away with the "managerial revolution," as Burnham showed;[333] then managers lose power as it "passes down into the technostructure," as Galbraith[334] shows; finally, with automation, many workers are not needed either.) Corporations are independent also of place, of nationality, of stated purposes (no more *ultra vires* suits) or anyone's goals. During World War II, some split so their subsidiaries could fight on both sides, to reunite later. Prolific, they spawn other corporations. The first, according to Maine, were created by the state. (John P. Davis[335] thought they were created by the church; Mauss and Maine have noticed their beginnings in certain legal fictions attending Roman testamentary arrangements.) In the end, they even become free of the profit motive; they cause governments to prop them up (e.g., Lockheed). They have mysterious powers that ordinary individuals do not possess: Their taxes are lower; they do not liquidate their property at death but are immortal; they have limited liability while individuals do not. They started as voluntary associations but become governments that evert individuals from membership. Instead of being regulated by governmental authorities, they often capture these and turn them into additional independent, policy-free, autonomous, impersonal entities. Today the form runs away with itself. The *inter vivas* form, which Maine thought the original legal fiction, can now be summoned by any citizen like a genie from a bottle. Even without a lawyer, any citizen of the United States, simply by using the forms contained in books like Dacey's *How to Avoid Probate*, can create dozens of nonpersons who are recognized at law, have to file tax returns, and can outlive him, can live forever, in fact.[336] The population of nonpersons exceeds the population of persons. Increasingly they influence our basic political thought: John Locke, who was so influential with the men who drafted the U.S. Constitution, wrote political philosophy at night but in the daytime, in his regular employment, he drafted corporate charters. In our daily lives, we increasingly confront or work for, or are entangled by, these legal nonpersons, and they feed our growing helplessness. In the 1930's, as the TNEC Report showed, any businessman in the glass industry had to contend with a formidable non-person called the Hartford Empire Company, which was nothing but a collection of paper assets manipulated by some legal fictions controlling a patent monopoly.[337] Non-persons are invulnerable to all of our magics except legal magic. Most of our symbolic powers are disarmed this way.

The non-persons create their own social force fields, thereby defeating the "general will" or "reason" or the rational state, just as they baffle the individuals who at one time projected this state. They refract law like power prisms; they bend general rules to particular cases. Increasingly they are ruled by compacts, agreements with other powers rather than general laws, as Neumann showed for pre-Nazi German big industry.[338] They fight law, then settle out of court on an *ad hoc* basis that reflects their power, thus refracting law.

Originally corporations were powerful engines that individuals or groups of people used to get rich; they still provide a living but personal control wanes (Berle charts a progress from "real stockholder control" by one or a few until 1900, to "working control" by a group in 1914-1928, to "management control" after 1929, to "emerging fiduciary control" in the 1960's.) For long periods, some people are on top of these organizations, they ride the lion, they have power; but even they are retired or fired or early retired or forced out in the end. Meanwhile, they try to amass enough money to be "independent." Wealth increasingly turns back into pure money (which is mana) as ownership evaporates, what Barzelon calls "the paper economy."[339] Berle has shown that the percent of personal wealth held in cash, securities or other paper has grown enormously; real property passes into the hands of non-persons. Thus property, power, status translate back into mere money, which derives from *mana*, from magic, and is simply some fractional value notation for a quality-space position in a consensus that is no longer there. The dream of the strivers, however, increasingly becomes a matter of simply trying to amass enough of this money to get free—free to do what? Simply to be free of the system, of the non-persons, of the organization of organizations, of the helplessness built in. Community and nomos have vanished so thoroughly that egos strive increasingly just to amass enough coined and minted magical power to escape from pseudo-community into private worlds. The desire for capital to escape arises at a time when engineered inflation and government tax policies make such escape increasingly difficult, but the urge feeds the transformation of property into paper, of capitalism into finance capitalism,[340] with all its heightened potential for magical manipulations. Economic status and economic wealth are pursued as economic power slips out of the hands of even the managerial class.

This is one reason, perhaps, why they applauded as their own children in the 1960's attacked the non-persons—and thereby discovered the surprising vulnerabilities of these powers and at the same time rediscovered the potential for community in the political process. In participation and in activism, a fairly sizeable portion of the population recovers its symbolic powers in a fight that shores up the Individual as a social institution. In doing so they may indeed stay healthier than the groups who try instead to puff up the self while abandoning defense of the outer walls.

Magic as Reflection of Impotence: Impersonality and Helplessness

Sociological theory arose as a backlash from society's contracting moral consensus. That is one reason for its obsession with religion, for its moral, almost theological, almost prophetic tone. From the beginning, the sociological imagination has been filled with jeremiad images of helplessness which infect its main concepts. Even "structure" is just another aspect of that "embeddedness" which Reich and the Frankfurt school discern as the alienation of reason, which is in turn a new metaphor for the Fall of Man. The Frankfurt Marxists think reason gets embedded, beyond discussion, in the scienitific technostructure; Barthes and the structuralists think it is just as easily hidden in the logics of the cultural superstructure. Whether they are in the sky or in the ground, we "go to meet" these ideas, the way Christians go to meet their creator; but they are only our own abstract ideas of society. Forgetting that we create "nature" this way, beginning with projections of society which get rationalized, scientized and operationalized for useful feedback, we descend into the ultimate idolatry of worshipping what Hegel calls "objective mind." But it is only our own impersonality principle that we go to meet, and we should not let it intimidate us. We need not turn it into a machine of non-participatory planning as Luhmann suggests, nor suppose that it is a Moloch which cannot be addressed but only blown up as the modern Nechayevs insist. All these allegedly "embedded" or "inherent" structural propensities are remarkably vulnerable to free discussion and criticism, just like all previous sacred structures in history.

Does "the sociological imagination" help us, or paralyze us with premature "hypotheses of helplessness" (Seligman)?

Whether it calls itself left or right, the sociological imagination tends to be conservative and pessimistic. So-called Marxists like Adorno tell us that everythng is terrible but nothing can be done. Even attempts to help the individual are criticized as snares that embed him more deeply in a hopeless system. For example, C. Wright Mills, Adorno and other critics of a psychotherapeutic approach to individual problems claim this merely takes the mind off the social problems that lie behind personal problems (and which cannot be solved anyhow).[341] Adorno cries that psychology as a cult perpetuates the illusion of the helpless that their fate lies in their own hands. But meanwhile the Kulturpessimismus of the Hegelian Marxists, who preach that revolution is essential but impossible, invites a Kamakazi response from the demonic self. Reich[342] and Habermas are more optimistic than Adorno about such constructive magics as we still possess: e.g., psychoanalysis as a sociological psychology. They think it can help the self because it is "dialectical."[343]

Is it possible that despite its conservative, pessimistic, backlash mentality sociological insights can help to protect the self? The Marxists say: only if they are translated into action; but in Marxist action we "go beyond" philosophy, beyond thought[344] and lose our way again. In mere Hegelian insight, we go to Nirvana. Perhaps there is an affinity between social science and magic which condemns both to sit poised between action and thought. Perhaps our thought is part of a further process of "generalization of mana," and perhaps we will regain our symbolic powers after all.[345] But in magic, I fear, mind alienates itself faster even than in religion. This is also true of social science. "From those wonderful people who gave us Taylorism" might be the advertising slogan for social science. Just as magic has iatrogenic effects, and precipitates into new cults and new alienated bodies of knowledge, social science is busily at work chipping away at our basic human freedoms—by deskilling workers, micro-dividing labor (Friedmann[346]); inventing new social barriers (e.g., testing[347]); creating diseases ("overachievers," "minimal brain dysfunction," etc.); undermining due process of law (Thomas Szasz[348]), etc.

Durkheim's idea of supporting the individual by shoring up intermediary groups also fails if these in turn are run by elites (Dahrendorf[349]). If on the contrary they are more inclusive communities, then corporativism could take us back to feudalism (for Simmel has shown[350] that our freedom is based on the loose organization of the organizations). In communities individuals can have effects again, helplessness is overcome, individual magic is reanimated and feeds back into group nomos; but aside from therapeutic communities, total communities do not fit the requirements of modern society. Durkheim obviously had the professional communities in mind and he and his school entertained the idea of corporativist legislatures. But formal experiments in this direction under Italian Fascism and the NRA show that quasi-anonymous corporate groups profit most from such arrangements.

A better defense is to be found in the political process itself, provided we cure it of some engrained liberal habits of solving every problem by creating a new machine. Among some liberals, conservatives and even Marxists, a new consensus is brewing that final solutions are the enemy, that final formulations are impossible, that we must be patient and serious enough to keep patching things up and to keep all issues permanently open for discussion. This is the real sense of Jefferson's idea of continuous revolution; it helps restore the healthy primitive situation of continuous creation of social reality in a community. It abolishes not only all absolutes but all privileged expertises. The distinction between policy and administration, romanticized[351] in the British "parliamentary question" where the minister always protects the loyal career administrator, is abolished. Everyone is accountable. The fine print is abolished. Leaving it to the experts is abolished. "Although only a few may originate a policy, we are all able to judge it," said Pericles. Even that should be abolished. We are all able to originate a policy, and this we must believe.

From Popper's *Open Society*[352] to Habermas' latest call that everything be thrown open to discussion, the individual's path to salvation has been clear, if too arduous to be appealing. The trouble is, it is hard work. Spengler predicted that the media would overexpose issues and make the masses bored. We *must* all have opinions on Alaskan oil and the rachet effect, but it is hard to keep the discussion going with the television on. Actually, the television can help a lot, if we do not keep turning to another channel.

And in a world dominated by non-persons who can buy whole channels, full and open discourse to perpetuate a core of nomos is difficult. It was the genius of the critical school, of Adorno, Horkheimer, Neumann, Habermas, Marcuse, to decipher how ideals of rationality were being used to cover assumptions that were no longer shared—or, to put it into Wittgenstein's terms, that we were agreeing to agree that we agreed, without taking the trouble really and continuously to agree. The functional rationality of the political-economic-technological system, in addition to being an ideology as the Frankfurt school shows, is also a predication of more order than there actually is. Order is partly faked in the midst of disorder, and always has been. The ideal of reason is partly a pious hope about ability to agree that we can agree, and the rationality of the system is something that we breathlessly pray is there. Because of such doubts, we must applaud Habermas' attempt to reconstitute the individual's substantive rationality by throwing everything open to discussion, and we may even hope that "the system" is too chaotic to prevent this.

Dominations, principalities, powers and thrones that are not even human, that bend law in their private force fields, do not wish to engage in such discussions, for they know that power is often disintegrated by mere knowledge of it. But that effect (Sartre) is a measure of their ultimate vulnerability. R. W. Boyder[353] reminds us that corporations have receded in the past; they have become too arrogant before and have been curbed; their power is disorderly and illusory. In such a chaos, organizing society via a nonparticipatory steering mechanism would produce just an accommodation of powers, what Neumann calls a "Behemoth," rather than even "formal" rationality.

A Stratification of Selves?

If the picture on the institutional level is chaotic, a clown show of rationalized irrationality, of compacts between anarchic powers at the expense of weak publics, perhaps the situation of egos will be the same. One possibility is diversity. Instead of contracted Individuals and selves; or puffed-up selves pushing against contracted individualities and everting the self; instead of expanding selves and Individuals, *we might have a chaos of all types at once*. The system's very indifference to the private realm makes diversity possible. Bureaucracies now care less and less how crazy we are in our spare time.[354] In fact, the system may have a vested interest in the continual increase in privacy, if certain managerial prophets like Peter Goldmark and Herman Kahn are correct. Some of these prophets imagine a totally decentralized society in which exurban masses will teleport their labor inputs from consoles instead of commuting to work. In which case, why should we ever meet at all? Philip Slater[355] and Richard Sennett[356] collect evidence that Americans *like* to live this way, and flee diversity as they flee one another. With no one down town, and no quorum for solemn assemblies, the nonpersons could easily take over and run things according to some system model which actually reflected their differential powers.

But what kinds of human beings would live out in exurbia, sending their work into town by television, and what would their children be like? It is possible that they would be very diverse. Some would still be quite civilized. Cultivation of self as an artistic, privatized item of consumption has appeared before in history: the Chinese literati whose arts gave their bureaucracy style but were otherwise a solipsistic extra world; the cultivated Kshatriya nobles of India and the Albigensian gentry of Provence. Mass consumption of patterns of auto-cultivation of great delicacy is possible. In addition, some old-fashioned inner-directed egos would still be socialized and would still strive to gain heights within the corporativized world from which they might exercise at least the illusion of temporary power.

The evidence seems to suggest that the upper-middle classes are actually intensifying their historic role as creators of deeply sculpted egos. On the baby farms of suburbia, the sheer investment in special training, special stimulation, special lessons has been greatly magnified since this class tuned in to the new evidence from academic psychology (e.g., Jerome Bruner, J. McVicker Hunt, Piaget, etc.) that early cognitive stimulation of children can raise lifelong intelligence. This new knowledge is added to the previous generation's digestion of psychodynamic wisdom. Along with it is imparted the liberal political understanding of many of the parents. The results have already been seen in the student revolts of the 1960's led by young people who, according to good evidence,[357] are from privileged families, are not seeking personal rewards, are not mentally ill, etc.

These new selves seem strong enough to have launched a successful counter-attack on behalf of the contracting institution of individualism; they sallied out from the self to reoccupy the walls of the Individual. But their effect is paradoxical, as Habermas points out. Without being demonic, these are critical selves, in the neo-Kantian, Frankfurt sense—and their effect, really, is to disintegrate much of the small remaining consensus that a society in organic solidarity still sustains. Each temporary victory is bought at the expense of exposing, not just arrant power (which always regroups), but the weakness and untruths of part of the assumptive moral frame which led to beliefs that it cannot happen here. If power constantly regroups, then the critical attacks of these heroic selves will produce a succession of Pyrrhic victories that disintegrate the remaining nomos of the fly-apart society. Needless to say, these highly self-conscious people will be among the first to recognize this and to try to rethink the problem. Their solution will probably be some sort of universalistic ethics, just as Durkheim's solution pointed in this direction. But attempts of various members of the Piaget school (e.g., Laurence Kohlberg) to root such a universalistic ethic in the genetic epistemology of the human being's normal developmental cycle are unconvincing. Universalistic ethics really represent anachronistic shadows of old projections of bygone social agreements; the consensus of most societies has contained this penumbra; a retreat to it is a retreat to a watered-down consensus which even then will be dated. Since morality, like religion, reflects social morphology, universalistic ethics may be taken to do so, too, and what they will reflect increasingly is the isolated but deeply socialized individual attempting to pass his own lonely socialization on to his children. But since the "child-centered family" of the fifties (Barzun[358]) has given way to the peer-centered, media-centered family of the seventies (Bronfenbrenner), this will be possible only for the most determined.

Selves As a Caste System

We may see a stratification of selves, just as there is a stratification of classes. Personal character has always reflected class, but now the gulf may become enormous, more like a caste system of selves. It would include the following: 1. *Inner-directed activists.* There will still be some of the old-fashioned, inner-directed, deeply socialized upper and upper-middle class professionals, embued with critical consciousness, still striving to be effective in the world but all too often tending to disintegrate minimal remaining nomos by their critical attacks. 2. *Cultivated private souls.* In addition, there will be highly cultivated souls who relax and enjoy the privacy of extreme organic solidarity, the isolation, even the lack of nomos, but who elect to invest effort and resources in the aesthetic cultivation of self. These modern equivalents of the Kshatriya or Provençal literati will in many cases produce whole and happy children whose very psychological health will be a post-modern form of privilege. 3. *Demonic selves.* Besides these, gazing eerily out at the divided world, will be the occult selves of those who have grasped the gnostic alienation of the world, the ab-

solute severence between any social moral order and the highly privatized individual and who accept the occult implications of this split. In a way, these
ghostly spirits will not be much more strange than the cultivated private souls
or the activist strivers—all will have something of Symacchus, Sidonius, Ausonius and strangers in a fallen world about them. 4. *Preformed selves.* Beneath
will lie the broad middle class of souls who are indeed "socialized in the masses"
or "by the peer group," as Bronfenbrenner and Marcuse describe it, or whose
egos are "preformed" by the media. These egos will indeed be considerably
shallower than were the egos of ordinary middle-class, lower-middle-class and
working-class people a hundred years ago. But with highly technical training
they will be quite capable of manning important posts in the industrial system.
5. *Crippled selves.* Below, the already numerous tribes of the psychologically
deformed will have been greatly augmented in number and variety. They will be
supplemented by new patterned deviancies, as illnesses increasingly organize
themselves into cognitive minorities and marginal protest groups and hence greatly enhance the usual processes of recruitment. The mentally ill, the addicted,
the vagabonds of various sorts, and all the other tribes of poorly socialized individuals will perhaps more accurately reflect the chaos of society than any of
the groups above them. Moreover, it is quite likely that the "organization of
organizations" (Simmel), the system as a system model (Luhmann), will find a
way to work with these individuals, so they can quietly go to hell on their own
time while providing "necessary social labor" (Marx) and not upsetting the
status quo.

In other words, we may have a virtual caste system of selves, with intermarriage between types virtually unthinkable, and cultural contamination avoided
at all costs. In such circumstances, the perennial elitist theories of a Yeats, of a
Radhakrishnan,[359] of the mentality that believes some men are Brahmins by
nature or slaves by birth (Aristotle) will be rankly fertilized.

Of course it is possible that one of the types might get control and change
things. The inner-directed activists, operating on a strong political system, might
reestablish a social consensus with continuing open discourse restoring substantive rationality. Or the magic self, instead of turning demonic, might indeed
discover new ways of "increased sweetness, increased light, increased sympathy,
increased life" that would reestablish harmonies between the individual and the
system. Revolts of the self have not always failed—for instance, Buddhism under
the Mauryas.[360] Out of the magic revolt of the self against contracting individualism a new community is a possibility. But it is not one on which to give odds.
What Adorno, Habermas, Horkheimer on the one hand, and conservatives like
Schumpeter on the other hand all recognize is that all these new types of selves
(for which "the intellectual" is the paradigm in Schumpeter) tend to disintegrate
nomos and consensus.[361] Or, as Habermas puts it, the bourgeois order has
nothing intrinsic that renews its own motivations in successive generations.
Moreover, it should be recognized that the new magics, as they are invented or
rediscovered, are in the common domain and can just as easily be used by sys-

tems to engineer consent as by individuals to change consensus. Take "behavior control," for example. One can now buy books or take classes in behavior control, and learn how to stop a cigarette habit, turn off gloomy thoughts, or control an unquenchable thirst for strong drink. But behavior control is also used in prisons, in advertising. The new magics of the "wild sciences" can just as easily be used for systems maintenance as for the magical protection of the self.

Summary

We are having magical revivals now because both the psychological self and the institution of the Individual are under pressures—pressures to expand and pressures to contract. The important question is what are the weights and these cannot be guessed at, but must be determined empirically. The evidence indicates that the pressure to contract individualism is probably the most significant force, and that it provokes resistance, including the magical revolt of the self as counter-pressure. The outcome cannot be predicted. But one possibility is a diverse outcome—with broken egos, shallow preformed egos, demonic egos, and old-fashioned deeply-sculpted egos, this diversity in turn reflecting the diversity and chaos of advanced organic solidarity. It is quite likely, as Luhmann imagines, that state institutions using systems models will try to control this disorder, probably *without* attempting to destroy democratic feedback, at least consciously. In so doing the managers will make the best use of such egos as they find, and will tolerate even more privatization, personal disorder and personal diversity. But even the order imposed by the systems managers will be more faked than real. To a large extent it will consist of official spokesmen asserting that there *is* order.

It seems quite possible that such fragmentation will have a regressive effect on cultural representations. In this sense, magic is a true reflection of this society, but it is only one among many, for this is a diverse society. If the center holds, and that means the political process, magic will remain a sideshow: but one of *our* sideshows, a natural reflection of one aspect of a disorderly, quasi-Dionysian society.

PART FIVE: CONCLUSION—
A GENERAL SOCIOLOGICAL THEORY OF MAGIC

The issue is the self-constitution of man through his own symbolic apparatuses which constantly threaten a crushing alienation. In religion, a nascent sociological imagination produces representations that give men some self-consciousness of his social nature and a vocabulary with which to forge new, self-determining social contracts. But the projections pile up, they literally tower into the skies; their social roots are forgotten and religion torments man with an astral pessimism and a moral pressure that can cause death. Next, in magic, man expropriates symbolic operators from religion to survive its moral pressure and to dare to think and speak and act as individuals; but this theft embeds him in structures of domination and evil which still further mystify his religious representations and darken his understanding. Later, in legal-rational institutions, man constitutes communities again, but retains his self-determining spontaneity, and disenchants his world. But in time these institutions rigidify into lifeless bureaucracies and inquisitorial moral agencies which often become oppressive. As these devices successively slip in his hands, man substitutes one for the other; sometimes recourse to a religious or magical device is only temporarily regressive, like "regression in the service of the ego;" and so man's capacities to reconstitute community through religion and to protect the self through magic are never entirely given up.

Therefore magic is found in almost every age and society; it advances with civilization for long periods instead of declining; and it is inextricably woven with other human institutions, including the ego itself. Magic as one of man's most typical resources is a ganglionic human institution, a total social fact of enormous complexity. It cannot be grasped by single hypotheses which skim the surface. On the other hand, a formal general theory would be premature. I have attempted, therefore, a preliminary *descriptive* general theory which analyzes the best ideographic studies in several fields and organizes them around 12 very general but falsifiable postulates.

Book One: Symbols

The potential for magic is inherent in several aspects of the symbol world man creates as his "species-specific environment." These dimensions are magical "in the weak sense." Postulate 1: Once man "falls into the deep well" of his symbolic self, action becomes symbolic; statuses, situations and identities can be changed by words. We have no trouble therefore fitting magic into various theoretical schemas of social action theory; magic is real action indeed; and the suspicion in fact arises that symbolic action itself has a dimension which is "magical in the weak sense." Postulate 2: Inherent properties of symbolism make magic possible. First, even single words can have magic effects, for most words are concepts that appresent something transcendent. Second, there are mysterious affinities between words in the lexical structures of languages which make sympathetic magic possible: these trace back to primitive classification systems, which in turn are those end-product cosmologies of religious projection which in fact map social morphology. Later, mythic and magical sentences work like a logic of classes on these classification systems, and perhaps sentences as cognitive structures originally arose from such pragmatic, magical-religious functions. Postulate 3: Magic expropriates religious scripts, with their powerful, abstract symbols, then rigidifies them to retain their efficacy. Magical-religious language is therefore different from praxis talk or symbolic interaction talk; even more than religion, magic consists of fixed scripts that provide certainty, organize action, give the speaker confidence. Magical operators helped individuals emerge from the social chorus, and, despite the terrors of man's new symbolic world, helped them to think, speak and act for themselves. The "categories," forged in religion, illustrate how such operators can quicken individual thought. Postulate 4: But symbolism alone cannot explain how magic works. For its efficacy, it depends on another attribute of man's social symbolic environment: the fact that things are as they are (or seem) by agreement. Magic derives its efficacies not from interaction fireworks, not from persuasion, not from logic or illogic but from traditionally patterned techniques which systematically relax the frame of the paramount reality so that supernormal experiences will ensue, and from traditionally patterned agreements to define these experiences a certain way.

Book Two: Religions

But symbolism, social action—all the dimensions of the *lebenswelt* that are magic in the weak sense—will not by themselves *explain* magic, which consists of real institutions. We must turn to religion, for magic is above all a religious institution, saturated with religious elements—prayers, sacrifice, initiation, mysticism, gods. Postulate 5: Magic constantly challenges religion, amalgamates with it, changes it, thus helps it stay in touch with social reality. The world religions are confederations of many subcults that began as magical protest movements reflecting social conflict; that is why Buddhism, Christianity and the others grow more magical throughout much of history, despite routinization of charisma. Postulate 6: Magic emerges out of religion, not vice versa, though protest sects may precipitate new cults within religion. (The relation to science is less determinate. Magic is not a proto-science; magic empiricism may at times feed into science but is not its engine. Studies show magic both impeding and stimulating science at different periods: we need more knowledge of weights.) Postulates 7 and 8: Religion arises in the Paleolithic or earlier as collective representations of society which have survival value in integrating small human groups. Most magics arise later, in the Neolithic, at the tribal stage of "generalization of mana," when more complex societies use more general symbols (e.g., gods instead of totems) which are easier to expropriate, extrapolate and apply to individual or profane ends. Just before this happens, religion itself becomes more magical in the weak sense, modeling the inherent sympathetic-magic potential of symbolism and rite, above all through the grand opera rituals of sacrifice and initiation. Both of these have to do with membership, which becomes problematical when society is more complicated. Some of the earliest magic is modeled on these rites. Thus we go from tribal initiation to the specialized initiation of magicians, to the trance dramas that recapitulate the magicians' literal experience of initiation symbols which they now use as all-purpose curing devices. Sacrifice in turn models all the more magical sacramental forms. The new magics precipitate back on and color religions, which become more magical in means and goals; world religions offer magical benefits to individuals, including salvation, immortality, gnosis, power, peace, escape from social conflict—more than primitive religions offered. In all this magic assists religion's great task of creating selves; it provides safety hatches, easements for conflicts like Antigone's; it defends man's spontaneity against his socialization at a time when more complex societies require that barely acceptable behavior we call spontaneity.

Book Three: Individuals and Selves

Magic aided the emergence of both the self and the Individual. Postulate 9: Ego is an interface between weak-sense magic and strict institutional magic, as it is between passivity and action, affect and symbols, primary process and secondary process. Ego can only act because of something that seems magical in the weak sense, something Róheim metaphorically called "the magical principle," that hopeful, magical rehearsal of action before it is emitted, that partly narcissistic working on inner as if it were outer. And early egos, emerging when men could "only act in serried ranks," played to expectant choruses in real magical institutions: religious magic, ceremonial magic, medical magic, which elicited on cue the ego action society was beginning to demand. But magic is feeble, not merely alienated, but easily botched, iatrogenic. It is so inept that it seems to some theorists to be the illness, not the cure. I think it is rather the earliest defense of nascent ego and hence the last ditch defense when the world of the secondary process breaks down. Postulate 10: The self therefore only succeeds when consolidated by the Individual, a congeries of legal-rational institutions. But magic also helped develop *these* more solid institutions and left residues and warps behind in them, in law, money, medicine, not to mention modern religions. Postulate 11: Magic flares up whenever the Individual or the self is under pressure. Black magic, man's earliest and most ego-intimate magic brew, best illustrates this. Witches use no magic but kill by spiritual means; witch fears are religious (a projection of voodoo death, of society's power to kill), but the witch accusation is magic, possibly man's first magic, certainly his first counter-attack on the superego. Black magic or something curiously like it arises even in modern times when the Individual or the self is under stress. Postulate 12: For these reasons, magic continued to grow through most of civilization. Magic, then, is no prehistoric survival: There was little of it in the Paleolithic when religion had already displayed its group-binding contribution to survival; perhaps some black magic. The main provinces of magic split off from religion in the Neolithic. But even then magic was not perfected. The main provinces were further rationalized in archaic civilizations: Divination systems were worked up into occult sciences and then into theosophies, those theologies of magic; thaumaturgical protest sects gave way to organized magical religions; even black magic advanced in civilizations with their rationalized demonologies. In modern times magic is marginalized, along with its factory, religion, by the "rationalization" that disenchants the world. The small community group that bred black magic maismas is uprooted and thrown into bidonvilles. Meanwhile, the prestigious scientific worldview defeats the theosophies of Hermeticism and Neoplatonism that fostered early modern belief in magic. Yet magic persists and its revivals threaten that worldview. First, there are reservoirs of infection: the so-called world religions, and magical residues in the ego and the person category. Second, the old magical institutions persist in the shadows of subcultures. Third, magic as a planetary literary heritage is never lost and easily revives under stress with the avid cooperation of publishers. Magic also persists because people have need of it. The magical illnesses persist so magic medicine must be reinvented whenever it is forgotten. The decline of religion creates nomic vacuums which the occult fills. Finally, instrumental reason, by crowding people out of participation, invites them to withdraw interest from the great society with results similar to the withdrawal of cathexis in psychosis. The secondary process is torn and the world comes to seem demonic to the masses.

In magic, man is forever rebelling and then enslaving himself. Magic technologies are possessed by specialists rather than by individuals or the community; there is more alienation in magic than in religion; there is indeed tragedy that could perhaps be better expressed in existential, theological or pathetic language. This is man's passion play in which the self emerges through means which embed it in structures of evil and alienation. Creation myths are full of this insight: cosmic eggs that split, Edens abandoned, self-consciousness or creation as itself a fall. In *Prometheus Bound,* Aeschylus no doubt worked with fragments of older myths from the tribal stage which Granet has described, when magical brotherhoods of smiths, diviners, weapon-makers and warriors competed until one dominated the others. For in Aeschylus' play every character is a specialized magician, and now they are all bound by the war chief magician and the domination that emerges from their magical revolution. Aeschylus views this as tragic necessity and looks toward the legal-rational polity emerging at Athens that will succeed the magic tribal stage.[362] But in the magic tyrants of the Near East empires, in the magic revolt of the self which overthrew the legal-rational Individual in Nazi Germany, and in the near permanent victory of the heralds in India, we see reminders that the outcome is not always that happy.

Are the unhappy outcomes perhaps the *inevitable* result of magic's criminal expropriation of the sacred and of the individual's hubris? Part of us wants to say so, just as part of us still feels guilty over the audacity of our emergence, over the decision to be, over the separation from parents, events still perceived by the unconscious as Oedipal crimes. And all of us can perhaps understand what Kierkegaard[363] meant when he called the demoniacal "the dread of the good." Since magic arises to defend the self against the pressure of too much community, too much religion, too much moral consensus, since magic is forever defensive and evasive and so condemned to live with anxiety, magic is therefore always assuming postures of anti-social estrangement. It is against the logos, as Stekel wrote. It fears the religious nomos. As such, it may indeed become a "dread of the good" and fall into the demoniacal.

In a secular age when the ego is cramped for breath, magic can seem releasing; it can remind us of the transcendent and miraculous in everyday life which we are inured to ignore; in psychoanalysis it can force us to recognize symbolic constraints that block us like enchantments. Certain specialists still witness the miraculous, but report it in stereotyped languages that blunt the wonder. Clergymen constantly change status, create new entities, transform identity, but talk about it in a churchly language that has become banal. (Occasionally an H. A. Williams[364] will break through our slumber by pointing to the commonplace experiences of "true resurrection" all around us.) Psychoanalysts similarly see people released from enchantments and spells, but report it in a specialized language which has also grown familiar. Magical revivals today consist partly of new vocabularies to remind us of the transcendent all around us. But the transcendent is nothing more or less than the remarkable social-symbolic realm which we ourselves partly make, and every magical victory is potentially alienating by mystifying this. Every magical cure, whether "medical" or "religious," is potentially self-defeating by increasing our belief in spiritual dangers. But even by themselves, before any iatrogenesis, the victories of magic somehow seem in part to be victories against humanity, icons that derogate men. One wishes that, more often, the individual or the group could have saved itself. Especially since that is what really happens anyhow, under the aegis of the self-inflating miracle.

At some point, a patient decides that he is cured and leaves analysis, and that, as Rank wrote, is the truly human act. And some men of great courage forgive or heal themselves. Similarly, peoples of great courage create their own social orders by constitutions, as the Attic tribal confederacy did, as the Americans did in 1787. In prehistory, religious symbols assisted such self-determination, but in later ages, as Mendenhall wrote, religion, as the *ceremonialization* of the social order, is already the beginning of the fall. If the bureaucratic net of modern life so tightens that individuals are socialized to helplessness, they will try to build pseudo-communities of escape through religious cults, and to regain the illusion of having an effect, through magic. If the sociological imagination collapses into the arid empiricism of chi square, people will seek new social insight in theology, as so many non-theist people do now. But if, on the contrary, social thought and collective action rediscover the miraculous in our symbolic-social universe—the possibility of continuous self-creation of our individualities and our world—we will remain self-constituting and engaged.

So far, the modern world is experienced as demonic only by a large minority. Elites who still participate are numerous; the middle classes who benefit and are content with the tamed personal magics of the traditional religions are the majority. Whether magic returns in conquest to pull down the world it once helped build depends mainly on whether the political process holds, and in one form or another remains in touch with the sedimented instrumental reason of the infrastructure. That process is weakened; in Germany within living memory a magical movement overthrew it; today it is undermined by magical communications and certain vested interests such as intelligence agencies with their elective affinity for magic and their world-destabilizing dirty tricks. But it is remarkable how much does hold, how mankind still expresses itself, often in huge numbers, successfully through the various forms of the political process. If men can still influence their fates through these civic capacities, then they will not have to regress to the desperate, last-ditch and self-defeating defenses of magic.

Notes

1. Cf. Sigmund Freud, "On the Mechanism of Paranoia," 1911; "Neurosis and Psychosis," 1924; "The Loss of Reality in Neurosis and Psychosis," 1924, in *Collected Papers, General Psychological Theory* (N.Y., 1963), pp. 29–48, 185–189, 202–206.

2. Ernest Becker, *The Revolution in Psychiatry* (N.Y., 1964), pp. 46–53.

3. Alfred Storch, *The Primitive Archaic Forms of Inner Experiences and Thought in Schizophrenia* (N.Y. & Washington, 1924).

4. Heinz Werner, *Comparative Psychology of Mental Development* (N.Y., 1940, 1948), pp. 357ff.

5. Ernesto de Martino, *The World of Magic* (Hong Kong, 1972), pp. 160–175.

6. This is implicit in the lack of the principle of contradiction in the world of *How Natives Think*, in the blurring of individual and species in *"The 'Soul' of the Primitive,"* in the affectual categories of his last three books, and in the objects poorly defined in *Les Carnets*, etc.

7. Thomas Luckmann, *The Invisible Religion* (N.Y., 1967, 1970), ch. 6.

8. Jacques Ellul, *The New Demons* (N.Y., 1975), pp. 140–143 and *passim*.

9. This is the argument of *The Division of Labor In Society* (Glencoe, Ill., 1947).

10. J. K. Huysmans, *Là-Bas* (Paris, 1950s, Livre de Poche ed.)

11. Franz Neumann, *Behemoth* (N.Y., 1942, 1966), p. 453.

12. Frederick Wertham, *A Sign for Cain* (N.Y., 1969), ch. 9, "The Geranium in the Window," pp. 150–186. The life-hating, black magic side of some psychiatry is shown in such publications as Eugene Kahn's *Psychopathic Personalities* (New Haven, 1931), which defines what it calls "constitutionally inferior, psychopathic personalities." According to Wertham and Reitlinger (*S.S. Alibi of a Nation*, N.Y., 1957), the euthanasia of the mentally ill program began within this German psychiatric profession, rather than in the Nazi Party. Cf. Reitlinger, pp. 270–272.

13. Arnold Hauser, *The Social History of Art*, vol. I (N.Y., 1951), ch. 1.

14. Gilbert Murray, chapter in Jane Harrison, *Themis* (Gloucester, Mass., 1974 reprint), "An Excursus on the Ritual Forms preserved in Greek Tragedy," pp. 341–363.

15. Jane Ellen Harrison, *Themis* (Cambridge, 1927), ch. 2, "The Dithyramb and the Drama".

16. Theodor H. Gastor, *Thespis* (N.Y., 1950, 1961), *passim.*

17. Robert Graves, *The White Goddess* (1948, 1972), pp. 9–45. We think the poetic art is inborn, he writes, but the ancients felt you could train it by teaching secret themes, encouraging the student to memorize sacred verses and putting him through a (magic) initiation. Poets were precisely the technicians who understood the sacred myths. All real poetry, poetry that still works, that makes your hair stand on end, still produces "magical" effects.

18. These are mostly Max Weber's terms, from *Ancient Judaism, The Protestant Ethic, Theory of Social and Economic Organization*, etc.

19. Thomas Luckmann, *The Invisible Religion* (N.Y., 1967, 1970), *passim.*

20. Stephen Lukes, *Emile Durkheim, His Life and Works* (London, 1972), pp. 29ff, 165ff.

21. Emile Durkheim, *The Division of Labor In Society* (Glencoe, Ill., 1933), Bk. III, pp. 353–409.

22. In this he resembled the Marxists, who seek to "help" what is inevitable in the historical process. As a democratic socialist Durkheim felt that the state should regulate especially against the "forced" or exploitative division of labor, against the microdivision of labor.

23. Talcott Parsons, *The Structure of Social Action* (Glencoe, Ill., 1937, 1949), chs. 8–12, pp. 301–450.

24. Gaston Richard, "L'Athéisme Dogmatique en Sociologie Religieuse," *Revue d'Histoire et de Philosophie Religieuse* (Paris, 1923), pp. 125–136.

25. Durkheim's books were apparently popular in Salazar's Portugal and under some other Latin regime governments, however.

26. This is the title of a typical book of this period by Karl Mannheim (London, 1943).

27. Max Horkheimer, *Eclipse of Reason* (1947, 1974), *Critical Theory* (N.Y., 1968, 1972).

28. Wilhelm Röpke, *The Social Crisis of Our Time* (London, 1942, 1950).

29. Theodor Adorno essays, "Sociology and Psychology," Parts I & II, *New Left Review,* vol. 46 (1967), pp. 67–80; vol. 47 (1968), pp. 79–97.

30. Erich Kahler, *The Tower and the Abyss* (N.Y., 1967), p. 15ff.

31. Of course the latter go back to the class associations of magic's revolt in tribal society.

32. Erich Fromm, *Escape From Freedom* (N.Y., 1941).

33. Karl Mannheim, *Man and Society* (London, 1940).

34. Jürgen Habermas, "Technology and Science as Ideology," mimeographed translation by Claus Mueller (N.Y., 1969).

35. Herbert Marcuse, *One Dimensional Man* (Boston, 1964, 1968); *A Critique of Pure Tolerance* (Boston, 1969).

36. Franz Neumann, *Behemoth* (N.Y., 1942, 1966).

37. Weber first distinguished the *"formal* rationality" of the economic system (he meant its quantitative accounting of values) from the *"substantive* rationality" that concerns individuals (he meant an empirical attention to actual goals of economic action). (Max Weber, *The Theory of Social and Economic Organization,* London, 1947, pp. 170ff.; 190, and cf. pp. 44–45 of Talcott Parsons' Introduction.) He was writing the way a Keynesian or institutional economist might write in noticing that while the economic system on paper maximized economic values it did not serve the real needs of actual individuals because, as partial equilibrium analysis would later show, there were depressions, maldistributions of goods, poverty, etc. Mannheim generalized this idea from the economic sphere to apply to reason in social life in general. Much of *Man and Society* (London, 1940) is devoted to this idea (cf. esp. pp. 39–78.) Mannheim wrote that with progress, more and more of man's reason gets embedded in the social-legal-economic institutions he created. (Mannheim called this "functional" rationality, whereas Weber called it "formal" rationality.) The result is that individual rationality gets stunted. (Mannheim's translator called this "substantial" rationality.) In a crisis, when social life collapses, the individual "cannot repair it by his own insight." Originally, early organic solidarity *did* foster individual rationality; the early liberalism of small businesses and farms required many individuals to think and use their wits. But now we all work for big organizations, and our choices are shrunk to minimal options, so we lose the habit of thinking rationally. We depend on the rationality of the system. So Mannheim says that a third stage has arrived, *after* organic solidarity—a new stage which he does not name.

38. Niklas Luhmann is discussed in Jürgen Habermas, *Legitimation Crisis* (Boston, 1975), esp. pp. 130–142.

39. Essays on the person category and the self by Benjamin Nelson are discussed in Chapter 11.

40. Erich Fromm, *The Anatomy of Human Destructiveness* (N.Y., 1973).

41. Theodor Adorno, *Negative Dialectics* (N.Y., 1973) Part III, ch. 1; and cf. in Habermas, *op. cit.,* pp. 126–7.

42. Ernest Becker, *The Revolution in Psychiatry* (N.Y., 1964), pp. 46–53 and *passim.*

43. *The Primitive Archaic Forms . . .,* etc.

44. Heinz Werner, *Comparative Psychology of Mental Development* (N.Y., 1948), *passim.*

45. Sylvano Arieti, *The Intrapsychic Self* (N.Y., 1967, 1976), pp. 265–298; *Creativity, the Magic Synthesis* (N.Y., 1976), pp. 180–186, etc.

46. Ortega y Gasset, *The Rebellion of the Masses* (N.Y., 1932, 1964), *passim.*

47. Konrad Heiden, *Der Führer* (N.Y., 1936), *passim.*

48. K. Mannheim, *Man and Society* (London, 1940), pp. 71ff, 85ff.

49. F. Neumann, *Behemoth* (N.Y., 1942, 1966), pp. 54–55.

50. Eric Voegelin, *The New Science of Politics* (Chicago, 1952); *Science, Politics and Gnosticism* (Chicago, 1968), *passim.*

51. Norman Cohn, *The Pursuit of the Millennium* (N.Y., 1961), *passim.*
52. Benjamin Nelson, "The Games of Life and the Dances of Death," in Edith Wyschogrod, ed., *The Phenomenon of Death* (N.Y., 1973), pp. 113–131.
53. Neumann, *Behemoth*, esp. pp. 92–97.
54. Arnold Toynbee, *A Study of History* (D. C. Somervell abridgment of vols. I–VI, N.Y., 1947), esp. p. 423ff.
55. Daniel Bell, *The End of Ideology* (Glencoe, Ill., 1960).
56. But whereas the Durkheimians stressed legal and economic interrelationships, the Frankfurt school stressed first technology, and later science as the infrastructure.
57. On this, for example, see Philip Selznick, *TVA and the Grass Roots* (New York, 1966), *passim.*
58. T. Luckmann, *The Invisible Religion* (N.Y., 1967), p. 95.
59. Marshall McLuhan, *Understanding Media* (N.Y., 1964, 1965), *passim.*
60. Harold Lasswell, *Psychopathology and Politics* (Chicago, 1930).
61. Robert N. Bellah, "Civil Religion in America," *Beyond Belief* (N.Y., 1970), ch. 9, pp. 168–192.
62. Martin E. Marty, *Varieties of Unbelief* (Garden City, N.Y., 1966), ch. 9. In Marty's terms, this often makes churches citadels of "unbelief," p. 165.
63. Gilbert Murray, *Five Stages of the Greek Religion* (Garden City, N.Y., 1955), *passim.*
64. *Science and Civilization in China*, vol. II, sect. I.
65. As Parsons does in "Durkheim on Religion Revisited," in Glock & Hammond, eds., *Beyond the Classics?* (N.Y., 1973), pp. 156–180.
66. J. Huizinga, *The Waning of the Middle Ages* (Garden City, N.Y., 1956). "All life was saturated with religion . . ., people were in constant danger of losing sight of the distinction between things spiritual and things temporal. If . . . all details of ordinary life may be raised to a sacred level . . ., all that is holy sinks to the commonplace . . ." (p. 156).
67. Sir Samuel Dill, *Roman Society in Gaul in the Merovingian Age* (London, 1926; N.Y., 1966), ch. 2, "Saints and Miracles," pp. 395–438.
68. Huizinga, *op. cit.*
69. *Ibid.*, pp. 166–167.
70. *Ibid.*, pp. 173–174.
71. George Steiner, *In Bluebeard's Castle* (New Haven, 1971), pp. 55ff.
72. "The structures of decay are toxic." (p. 55, Steiner, *In Bluebeard's Castle*). The holocaust had many roots, but there are insistent reports of religious imagery connected with it. Survivors of *Einsatzgruppen* mass murders report hearing sermons condemning the Jews for Christ's execution read just before S.S. men began firing. The Poles came out of their churches shaking their heads at the judgment of god as the Jews of the Warsaw ghetto were rounded up. This is a subject of serious study among some Christian conferences today.
73. In Postulate Five.
74. Will Herberg, *Protestant, Catholic, Jew* (Garden City, N.Y., rev. ed., 1960), *passim.*
75. Harvey Cox, *The Secular City* (N.Y., 1965), *passim.*
76. Peter L. Berger, *The Noise of Solemn Assemblies* (Garden City, N.Y., 1961).
77. Martin E. Marty, *Righteous Empire* (N.Y., 1970, 1977).
78. Thomas Luckmann, *The Invisible Religion* (N.Y., 1970).
79. Peter L. Berger, *The Sacred Canopy; The Noise of Solemn Assemblies; Social Creation of Reality; Invitation to Sociology; The Precarious Vision; A Rumor of Angels.*
80. Peter L. Berger and Hansfried Kellner, "Marriage and the Construction of Reality," *Diogenes*, Summer, 1964, No. 46, pp. 1–24.
81. This is his title: James Webb, *The Occult Underground* (LaSalle, Ill., 1974).
82. Martin Marty, "The Occult Establishment," *Social Research*, vol. 37, 1970, no. 2, pp. 212–230.
83. Cf. Irving I. Zaretsky, "In the Beginning was the Word: The Relationship of Language to Social Organization in Spiritualist Churches," in Irving I. Zaretsky and Mark P. Leone, eds., *Religious Movements in Contemporary America* (Princeton, 1974), pp. 166–219.
84. Cf. Weston La Barre, *They Shall Take Up Serpents* (N.Y., 1969).
85. This expression comes from a title: Graham Wallas, *The Great Society* (London, 1914), cf. ch. 1, pp. 1–20 for definition.
86. Jacques Ellul, *The New Demons* (N.Y., 1975), p. 143ff.

87. *Ibid.*, p. 133.

88. Ellul, *The Meaning of the City* (Grand Rapids, Mich., 1970), ch. 1, pp. 1–43.

89. *Ibid.*, p. 7.

90. E.g., Eliade, *Cosmos and History* (N.Y., 1959), pp. 5–17.

91. Cf. Harvey Cox summary, "The Ungodly City, A Theological Response to Jacques Ellul," *Commonweal*, July 9, 1971, pp. 351–357.

92. Jacques Ellul, *Propaganda* (N.Y., 1968), ch. 4–5.

93. Karl Mannheim said this in *Freedom, Power and Democratic Planning* (London, 1951), *passim.* Tutorial discussion with John Plamenatz, 1951.

94. Harold D. Lasswell, *Propaganda Technique in the World War* (N.Y., 1927).

95. Ellul, *The Political Illusion* (N.Y., 1967), *passim.*

96. Thurman W. Arnold, *The Folklore of Capitalism* (New Haven, 1937), ch. 9, pp. 207–229.

97. Murray Edelman, *The Symbolic Uses of Politics* (Urbana, Ill., 1967), pp. 40–43.

98. Jacques Ellul, *The Technological Society* (N.Y., 1964), pp. 24–27 and *passim.*

99. Mauss, "Les Techniques du Corps," in Lévi-Strauss, ed., *Marcel Mauss Sociologie et Anthropologie* (Paris, 1950, 1966), pp. 365–386.

100. Leon Bramson, *The Political Context of Sociology* (Princeton, 1961, 1969), ch. 2 & 6, pp. 27–46, 121–139.

101. Elihu Katz and Paul F. Lazarsfeld, *Personal Influence* (N.Y., 1955, 1964), Part I, pp. 15–133.

102. Hannah Arendt, *The Origins of Totalitarianism* (Cleveland, 1951, 1958), p. 316.

103. Urie Bronfenbrenner, *The Two Worlds of Childhood* (N.Y., 1970), pp. 102–103.

104. Herbert Marcuse, "The Obsolescence of the Freudian Concept of Man," in *Five Lectures* (Boston, 1970), pp. 44–61.

105. Cf. George L. Mosse, *The Crisis of German Ideology* (N.Y., 1964), chs. 3, 4 and *passim.*

106. Cf. S. William Halperin on this: *Germany Tried Democracy* (N.Y., 1946, 1965): e.g., the federalism, pp. 2, 14–16.

107. Neumann has seriously suggested that the formal rationality of the modern economy persisted (even advanced) under Nazism, but it was certainly bent to some irrational ends. *Behemoth* (N.Y., 1944), Part II, cf. pp. 249–251.

108. Sokka Gakkai attempts this in Japan today.

109. Magic power is what is sought in the substitute status of sects, in the primal scream of Pentacostalist logolalia. Totalitarian movements which use magical symbolism to win the masses but smash personal magic once in power are an accentuation of the perennial tendency of magic to begin as a protest sect and then become the religious establishment. Modern totalitarian movements even tend to bring back the primeval three-caste system that Dumézil discerned among the Aryans: with the party as the Brahmins, the military as the Kshatriyas, the businessmen and workers as the loyal, twice-born Vaisyas, and the conquered people as the Sudras, and the untouchable Jews and gypsies burned. Djilas has shown that communism produces the same class structure, right down to the slave laborers. Capitalism for a while seemed to disintegrate the Brahmins and Kshatriyas (so Marx thought it could not be all bad), but they come back in a time of imperialism and monopoly.

110. Daniel Bell, *The Coming of Post-Industrial Society* (N.Y., 1973), ch. 2, "From Goods to Services," p. 121–164.

111. Theodore Schultz's thesis was discussed by Walter Heller in *Hearings on . . . Employment . . . Growth . . . and . . . Stability of the Price Level*, Joint Economic Committee, 86th Congress, First Session, 1959, Part 9A, pp. 2988–3018; and in a special issue of *Journal of Political Economy* supplement, Oct. 1962, vol. LXX, no. 5, part 2, *"Investment in Human Beings."*

112. Adolph A. Berle, Jr., *Power Without Property* (N.Y., 1959); *The American Economic Republic* (N.Y., 1965); *The 20th Century Capitalist Revolution* (N.Y., 1954).

113. Fritz Machlup, *The Production and Distribution of Knowledge in the United States* (Princeton, 1962), *passim.*

114. William Glasser, *The Identity Society* (N.Y., 1972, 1976), pp. 3–24.

115. Cf. David T. Bazelon, *The Paper Economy* (N.Y., 1959), ch. 4, "Money, Credit and other Magic," ch. 5, "More Paper Magic," pp. 68–122.

116. "The Stars Down to Earth," *Telos*, Spring 1974, no. 19, pp. 21ff and *passim.*

117. Marcello Truzzi, "The Occult Revival as Popular Culture . . ." *Sociological Quarterly*, vol. 13 (Winter, 1972), pp. 16–32.

118. Jacques Ellul, *The New Demons* (N.Y., 1975), p. 133ff.

119. Reitlinger, Wertham and others have shown that the euthanasia of the mentally ill began within the German psychiatric profession (admittedly it had been reorganized by the Nazis and that it later provided the administrative core, the technologies and some personnel for the Final Solution. Gerald Reitlinger, *S.S., Alibi of a Nation* (N.Y., 1957), p. 270–277; F. Wertham, *The Show of Violence* (N.Y., 1969), pp. 150–186.

120. "The Social Psychology of the World Religions," in Gerth & Mills, eds., *From Max Weber* (N.Y., 1946), pp. 267–301.

121. On another way in which Rumania went off the tracks cf. Raul Hilberg, *The Destruction of the European Jews* (Chicago, 1961, 1967), pp. 485–509.

122. *Alleged Assassinations Involving Foreign Leaders*, Interim Report of Select Committee to Study Governmental Operations with Respect to Intelligence Activities, U.S. Senate (N.Y., 1976), pp. 74–85, 94, 106–107, 125–132.

123. John Wilhelm, *In Search of Superman* (N.Y., 1976).

124. Weber, *op. cit.*, pp. 268–269ff.

125. This was reported by the full committee as *The Investigation of the Assassination of President John F. Kennedy, Performance of the Intelligence Agencies*, Book V of Final Report of the Select Committee To Study Governmental Operations with Respect to Intelligence Activities, U.S. Senate, April 23, 1976, cf. pp. 2–21.

126. *Alleged Assassinations of Foreign Leaders* (N.Y., 1976), *Ibid.*, pp. 72–73.

127. This was the subject of Vance Packard's *The Hidden Persuaders* (N.Y., 1957).

128. Albert Bandura, *Principles of Behavior Modification* (N.Y., 1969), pp. 159ff, 196.

129. Stanley Milgram, *Obedience to Authority* (N.Y., 1974), pp. 13–27.

130. Philip Slater, *The Pursuit of Loneliness* (Boston, 1970). Cf., for example, ch. 3, pp. 53–80.

131. Corinne Lathrop Gilb, *Hidden Hierarchies* (N.Y., 1966), pp. 27–46.

132. Philip Selznick, *TVA and the Grass Roots* (N.Y., 1966), *passim*.

133. Franz Neumann, *Behemoth* (N.Y., 1942, 1966), p. 221ff.

134. *Ibid.*, Part two, pp. 221–364.

135. Henry S. Kariel, *The Decline of American Pluralism* (Stanford, 1961), p. 89ff.

136. David Spitz, *Patterns of Anti-Democratic Thought* (Glencoe, Ill., 1949), p. 43ff, *passim*.

137. Robert Presthus, *The Organizational Society* (N.Y., 1962), p. 59ff.

138. *The Sociology of Georg Simmel*, ed. Kurt Wolff (Glencoe, Ill., 1950), pp. 330–344.

139. *Ibid.*, p. 335.

140. I once noticed a listing for "The Pythagorean Society" in the Manhattan directory and called up to ask whether this was the well-known secret society of ancient Crotona. I was told by a heavily accented voice that "This is just a Greek club." But who knows? *They* were "not supposed to tell."

141. Joachim Joesten, *The Garrison Enquiry* (London, 1967); *La Vérité Sur le Cas Jack Ruby* (Paris, 1967), etc.; Rosemary James & Jack Wardlaw, *Plot or Politics, The Garrison Case and Its Cast* (New Orleans, 1967); Jim Garrison, *A Heritage of Stone* (N.Y., 1970); Harold Weisberg, *Oswald in New Orleans* (N.Y., 1967), etc.; Paris Flammonde, *The Kennedy Conspiracy* (N.Y., 1969), etc.

142. Speeches, conversations.

143. Examples in Roland Barthes, *Mythologies* (N.Y., 1972), pp. 15–105, theory on pp. 109–159, and in *Writing Degree Zero* (N.Y., 1968). Cf. pp. 76–77ff.

144. Jacques Ellul, *Propaganda* (N.Y., 1968), pp. 163–192, esp. p. 180ff.

145. Jean Cazeneuve, *Sociologie du Rite* (Paris, 1971), ch. 9.

146. Durkheim and Mauss, *Primitive Classification* (Chicago, 1963, 1967), *passim*.

147. George Orwell, *1984* (N.Y., 1949), p. 9.

148. George Steiner, *Language and Silence* (N.Y., 1967), "Language Out of Darkness," pp. 95–168.

149. Eric Kahler, *The Tower and the Abyss* (N.Y., 1967), pp. 10, 21, etc.

150. Martin Gardner, *Logical Machines, Diagrams and Boolean Algebra* (N.Y., 1968), *passim*.

151. Daniel Boorstin, *The Image, A Guide to Pseudo-Events in America* (N.Y., 1964), pp. 7–44.

152. Marshall McLuhan, *Understanding Media* (N.Y., 1964, 1965), p. 33ff.

153. Oswald Spengler, *The Decline of the West* (N.Y., 1962), Modern Library, Abridged, p. 372ff.

154. Herbert Marcuse, *One-Dimensional Man* (Boston, 1966), p. 84ff.

155. Trent Schroyer, *The Critique of Domination* (N.Y., 1973), p. 33ff.

156. Jürgen Habermas, "Technology and Science as Ideology," mimeographed translation by Claus Mueller (N.Y., 1969), pp. 1-2.

157. Claus Mueller, *The Politics of Communication* (N.Y., 1973), pp. 19, 86-101, etc.

158. Barthes, *Mythologies* (N.Y., 1972), pp. 9, 11-12.

159. Barthes, *Writing Degree Zero* (N.Y., 1968), p. 76ff.

160. She gave her own explanation in Nathalie Sarraute, *L'Ere de Soupçon* (Paris, 1956), *passim.*

161. Roland Barthes, *Mythologies* (N.Y., 1972), p. 132ff.

162. Cazeneuve, *Sociologie du Rite,* see "Magie, Sympathie, Accessoires Magiques," ch. 9

163. Walter Lippmann, *Public Opinion* (N.Y., 1922, 1960), pp. 79-158.

164. Francis Bacon, *Novum Organon,* in *The English Philosophers From Bacon to Mill* (N.Y., 1939), pp. 24-128, esp. pp. 31-45.

165. *Mythologies,* p. 116-117.

166. A. Tarski introduced the idea that logical antinomies like the "liar paradox" could be solved by speaking of them in a "meta-language" outside ordinary language. Like Barthes, Lévi-Strauss used the metaphor of "meta-language" to describe myths and even called his "structuralist" analysis of myth a meta-metalanguage, thereby giving it oracular status. But Wittgenstein showed there are no meta-languages; at best we just jump in and out of different "language games." Meta-languages are pretend Platonisms.

167. In *The Moralia.* Cited by Cazeneuve, *op. cit.,* ch. 9. Similar idea in Barthes, *op. cit.,* p. 140ff, etc.

168. Roger Caillois, *Le Myth et l'Homme* (Paris, 1938), ch. 1.

169. Caillois, following Frazer and Bergson, saw a social function for magical myth. Usually it celebrated a culture hero who solved a social contradiction and so naturalized it . . . with the result that myths rivet men in their roles and stations the way instinct rivets animals.

170. Peter L. Berger, *The Sacred Canopy* (Garden City, N.Y., 1967), title and cf. ch. 2.

171. Ernest Hilgard on hypnosis, taped interview, Stanford, May, 1974.

172. In *The Image, op. cit.,* pp. 7-44.

173. *The Movie Goer* (N.Y., 1967).

174. Roger Caillois, *Le Myth et l'Homme* (Paris, 1938). The reference is in the chapter on "The Praying Mantis," ch. 2.

175. Joseph Bensman and Arthur J. Vidich, *The New American Society* (Chicago, 1971), *passim.*

176. C. Wright Mills, *White Collar* (London, N.Y., 1951, 1956), pp. 113-143.

177. William H. Whyte, Jr., *The Organization Man* (Garden City, N.Y., 1957), *passim.*

178. Vance Packard, *The Status Seekers* (N.Y., 1959); *The Pyramid Climbers* (N.Y., 1962), etc.

179. David Riesman, *The Lonely Crowd* (New Haven, 1950), *passim.*

180. John K. Galbraith, *American Capitalism* (N.Y., 1952); *The Affluent Society* (N.Y., 1957); *The New Industrial State* (Boston, 1967), cf. esp. pp. 60-71.

181. Peter F. Drucker, *The New Society* (N.Y., 1949, 1962).

182. Alan Harrington, *Life in the Crystal Palace* (N.Y., 1959).

183. Rollo May, *Power and Innocence* (N.Y., 1972), *passim.*

184. Howard S. Becker, ed., *The Other Side* (N.Y., 1964), *passim.*

185. Harold Garfinkel, *Studies in Ethnomethodology* (N.Y., 1967), *passim.*

186. Michel Fourcault, *Madness and Civilization* (N.Y., 1968).

187. Harold D. Lasswell, *Psychopathology and Politics* (Chicago, 1930).

188. Cf. William J. Goode, *World Revolution and Family Patterns* (N.Y., 1963, 1970), pp. 6-23.

189. William J. Goode, *Women in Divorce* (N.Y., 1956).

190. *Women in Divorce,* p. 139.

191. Daniel O'Keefe, "Cognitive Breakdown in Two Frail Cognitive Structures," unpublished paper, 1966.

192. Henry Sumner Maine, *Ancient Law* (Boston, 1963), p. 195. But de Coulanges reports they tried to form gentes: *The Ancient City, op. cit.,* p. 101.

193. Samuel Dill, *Roman Society From Nero to Marcus Aurelius* (London, 1904, N.Y., 1957), Bk. II, ch. 2, pp. 196-250; *Roman Society in the Last Century of the Western Empire* (London, 1899, N.Y., 1958), Bk. III, ch. 2, pp. 245-281.

194. Edward Gibbon, *The Decline and Fall of the Roman Empire* (N.Y., 1932), vol. I, ch. 13.

195. M. Rostovtzeff, *Rome* (N.Y., 1960), ch. 22, cf. p. 277ff.

196. Ferdinand Lot, *La Fin du Monde Antique et le Debut du Moyen Age* (Paris, 1968), ch. 6, "Le Régime des Castes," pp. 109-136.

197. I am thinking of his portraits of Symmachus, Ausonius and Sidonius, in Dill's *Roman Society in the Last Century of the Western Empire,* Bk. II, chs. 2, 3, 4, pp. 143-223.

198. J. B. Bury, *History of the Later Roman Empire From the Death of Theodosius I to the Death of Justinian* (N.Y., 1958), vol. I, pp. 55-62.

199. According to C. S. Lewis, anyway, in *Mere Christianity* (N.Y., 1952).

200. C. Wright Mills, *White Collar* (N.Y., 1951, 1956), pp. 112-141.

201. A new sophistication seems complacent about monopoly but the reason is that the voices opposing it have been stilled; their *sitz-an-leben* is gone; whole strata have disappeared; a whole range of companies have been gobbled up by the conglomerates. The "new conservatism" is a projection of the corporate giants that won, and of their desire to seem respectable. It is like saying, in a science fiction scenario, "No one worries about the Martians anymore," and not noticing that most people nowadays are Martians and almost no one else is left. Ionesco's *Rhinoceros* says it.

202. Pitirim A. Sorokin, *Social and Cultural Dynamics* (N.Y., 1937-41), cf. summary by Hans Speier in Harry Elmer Barnes, ed., *An Introduction to the History of Sociology* (Chicago, 1948), pp. 892-898.

203. Oswald Spengler, *The Decline of the West,* Modern Library, Abridged Edition (N.Y., 1962), pp. 24-26.

204. Robert A. Nisbet, *The Twilight of Authority* (N.Y., 1975), *passim.*

205. *The Lonely Crowd* (New Haven, 1950), pp. 13-30.

206. Wilhelm Reich, *The Mass Psychology of Fascism* (N.Y., 1970), cf. chs. 1, 7, 12.

207. T. W. Adorno, Else Frenkel-Brunswick, David J. Levinson & R. Nevitt Sanford, *The Authoritarian Personality* (N.Y., 1964), e.g. Part I, ch. 10.

208. In Herbert Marcuse, *Five Lectures* (Boston, 1970), ch. 3, pp. 44-61.

209. *Ibid.,* pp. 47-48.

210. Albert Bandura, taped interview, Palo Alto, Cal., May 1974, and works previously cited.

211. Urie Bronfenbrenner, *Two Worlds of Childhood* (N.Y., 1970), pp. 109-115.

212. Charles M. Fair, *The Dying Self* (Garden City, N.Y., 1970), p. 22ff.

213. To build on brain physiology is to build on sand, for theories change even faster in this "hard" science than in psychology: a fallacy of misplaced concreteness.

214. Rollo May, *Power and Innocence* (N.Y., 1972), ch. 1 and p. 155ff.

215. John Dollard *et al., Frustration and Aggression* (New Haven, 1939), *passim.*

216. Bruno Bettelheim, *The Empty Fortress* (N.Y., 1967, 1972), pp. 63-85.

217. Nikolaas Tinbergen, "Ethology and Stress Diseases," *Science,* Vol. 185, no. 4145, July 5, 1974, pp. 20-27.

218. Roger W. Wescott, *The Divine Animal* (N.Y., 1969), pp. 210ff, 219-235.

219. Wilhelm Reich, *The Function of the Orgasm* (N.Y., 1942, 1961), pp. 114-129. *Character Analysis* (N.Y., 1976), pp. 171-175.

220. Cf. Abraham H. Maslow, *Toward a Psychology of Being* (N.Y., 1962, 1968), *passim.*

221. Robert Hunter, *The Storming of the Mind* (Garden City, N.Y., 1972), *passim.*

222. Roger Poole, *Toward a Deep Subjectivity* (N.Y., 1972).

223. Joseph C. Pearce, *The Crack in the Cosmic Egg* (N.Y., 1971), *passim.*

224. Stan Gooch, *Total Man* (N.Y., 1972).

225. It *has* worked in the East, too; e.g., Buddhist sensibility under the Mauryas.

226. Daniel Jankelovich, polls for *Fortune* Magazine, 1972.

227. Some modern person ideas are so rationalized they could fit onto a coordinate system in spacetime. Yet in the same culture, we exalt other, Faustian self ideas which make "non-negotiable demands" on the world and render identity adjustment difficult by "trying to get more out of life than there is in it," as humorist Don Herold once put it. It was these inner contradictions that caused Western person concepts to fission, and the result is there is no clear concept of *arete* in this culture, no *virtus*, no *imitatio Christi*, no Rama or Sita, to model—just an endless invitation to look inward and multiply self concepts.

228. Charles M. Fair, *The Dying Self* (N.Y., 1970), pp. 11–37.

229. For summary see: Martin Jay, *The Dialectical Imagination, A History of the Frankfurt School and the Institute of Social Research 1923-1950, passim.*

230. For a hundred years it has been folk wisdom that the modern world makes people mad. The epidemiology of mental illness offers no proof of this; if anything, the contrary. Studies by Goldhammer and Marshall, Eaton and Weil, etc. suggest that mental illness has remained steady or dropped in the last century. But the unoperationalized nature of data in this field is notorious; and, anyway, compensating factors (such as better nutrition and physical health, better treatment, etc.) may have cancelled out any evidence of a trend toward mental illness that might correlate with fragmentation of society's ideas about personhood.

231. "The Obsolescence of the Freudian Concept of Man," in *Five Lectures* (Boston, 1970), pp. 44–61, cf. pp. 47–48ff.

232. *Two Worlds of Childhood* (N.Y., 1970), pp. 100–119.

233. Confused self-images resulting from crazy cultural ideas of personhood must surely destabilize ego's *long-term* efforts at *biographical stabilization* and meaning. This is the crisis of "identity," Erikson writes about. In effect, he warned us some time ago (*Identity, Youth and Crisis*, N.Y., 1968, pp. 15–19) that an identity crisis in a young person should be treated like a psychosis because it is that serious; unresolved, it will block sucessful negotiation of typical conflicts of later life stages that ego must manage to keep on growing.

234. For example, Erikson's work shows that ego-syntonic processes succeed through identification: the ego has to adapt the self to some variant of a socially acceptable identity. If society's ideas of personhood fragment or include demonic or insane options, the identification side of ego-syntonic processes may be hurt.

235. Sylvano Arieti, *The Intrapsychic Self* (N.Y., 1967, 1976), pp. 8–14.

236. Maurice Halbwachs, *Les Cadres Sociaux de la Mémoire* (Paris, 1925); *La Mémoire Collective* (Paris, 1968), p. 35ff.

237. Ernest G. Schachtel, "On Memory and Childhood Amnesia," *Metamorphosis* (N.Y., 1959), pp. 279–322.

238. Ernst Kris, *Psychoanalytic Explorations in Art* (N.Y., 1952, 1964), pp. 47–63.

239. Sylvano Arieti, *Creativity, the Magic Synthesis* (N.Y., 1976), pp. 12–13.

240. Jean Cazeneuve, *Sociologie du Rite* (Paris, 1971), p. 168 and *passim*.

241. Ernst Kris, *op. cit.*, p. 61ff.

242. Kazimierz Dabrowski, *Positive Disintegration* (Boston, 1964), pp. 1–32.

243. R. D. Laing, *The Politics of Experience* (N.Y., 1967), p. 81ff.

244. L. S. Kubie, *Neurotic Distortion of the Creative Process* (Lawrence, Kans., 1958), *passim.*

245. Sylvano Arieti, *Creativity, the Magic Synthesis* (N.Y., 1976), pp. 180–187.

246. Lancelot Law Whyte, *The Unconscious Before Freud* (Garden City, N.Y., 1962), *passim.*

247. Freud, *The Interpretation of Dreams*, ch. 7, see esp. pp. 535–6, in *The Basic Writings of Sigmund Freud* (N.Y., 1938). See also Arieti's comment on the secondary process in *Creativity, the Magic Synthesis*, pp. 12–13.

248. *The Phenomenology of Mind* (N.Y., 1967), preface, pp. 67–130.

249. *L'Expérience Mystique et les Symboles chez les Primitifs* (Paris, 1938), ch. 2.

250. *The Intrapsychic Self*, pp. 83–93.

251. Assimilation of secondary process in socialization fits "epigenetically" into the heredited maturational process, as Piaget and Erikson have shown. Piaget proposes that the whole secondary process itself ultimately derives from the sensorimotor sphere so the

developmental process unfolds a biological structure that is "ready" for the secondary process. (Jean Piaget, *Structuralism* N.Y., 1971, p. 75ff) Piaget's "structuralism" is neither Lévi-Strauss nor Durkheim; it is an empirical-foundation-of-logic theory like Mill's. But Piaget's account seems to converge toward an abstract logic, just like Lévi-Strauss's structuralism; and he even equates his two main principles of adaptation and growth, "accommodation and assimilation" (cf. *The Origins of Intelligence in Children,* N.Y., 1963, Part I, pp. 21–144) with Hegel's "antithesis" and "synthesis" respectively (*Structuralism,* ch. 4, cf. p. 71ff). But these ideas in turn *derive,* via a logic of possibility, from sensorimotor interaction with the physical environment. Sociocultural processes are not neglected in Piaget's developmental psychology. He was present at the conference in which Mauss re-outlined the Durkheim program for studying the categories as social history (cited in Mauss, *Oeuvres*), and he did himself do this in part in some of his studies of *The Moral Judgment of the Child* (London, 1932); *The Child's Conception of Physical Causality* (Totowa, N.J., 1965); ... *of Number* (N.Y., 1952); ... *of Space* (N.Y., 1956), etc. The overall approach is *Genetic Epistemology* (N.Y., 1970). Piaget writes that whereas Durkheim views social structure as cognitive, his emphasis is on autonomous structures developing epigenetically between developmental capacities of the organism and the symbolic species-specific environment in which it lives (*Structuralism,* p. 107).

252. Edmund Husserl, *Cartesian Meditations* (The Hague, 1960); *Ideas* (London, 1962), *passim.*

253. Albert Einstein, *Relativity, The Special and General Theory* (N.Y., 1961), p. 11.

254. *Ibid.,* pp. 30–34.

255. In *Creativity, The Magic Synthesis,* pp. 264–266, etc.

256. Cited by Ernesto de Martino in *The World of Magic* (Hong Kong, 1972), pp. 161–162.

257. This approach is pursued by Storch, Werner, Arieti, Lévy-Bruhl and Harry Stack Sullivan, among others.

258. Herman Nunberg, *Principles of Psychoanalysis* (N.Y., 1955), pp. 118–9.

259. Magic thinking is necessary, apparently, to overcome magical illnesses. But does not psychoanalysis promise that it is a learning experience which lasts a lifetime, that the former analysand will automatically, in situations of difficulty, free-associate and think his way through? Some analysts (Stekel, Rank, Alexander) have insisted all along that a prolonged exposure to psychoanalysis can weaken the ego. Surely one way is by teaching it to watch for and be alarmed by "sympathetic" connections and social omens. Pre-schizophrenics break down under psychoanalysis. In them the secondary process is already weak; they are already tormented by sympathetic connections. Could psychoanalytic ideas tip the balance for the culture as a whole and weaken the secondary process by heightening attention to omens and interpretations driven by primary processes?

260. Esp. in "Neurosis and Psychosis," 1924; "The Loss of Reality in Neurosis and Psychosis," 1924; "On the Mechanism of Paranoia," 1911, collected in Freud, *General Psychological Theory,* ed., Philip Rieff (N.Y., 1963), pp. 29–48, 185–189, 202–206.

261. Discussed in Paul Roazen, *Brother Animal: The Story of Freud and Tausk* (N.Y., 1973), p. 173. Applied by Tausk's colleague and friend Paul Federn in *Ego Psychology and the Psychoses* (N.Y., 1952), ch. 6.

262. Discussed in A. Storch, *The Primitive Archaic Forms of Inner Experiences and Thought in Schizophrenia* (N.Y. & Wash., 1924), section 3, p. 103ff.

263. *Identity and the Life Cycle* (N.Y., 1959), pp. 122–146.

264. Anna Freud, *The Ego and the Mechanisms of Defense* (N.Y., 1966, 1976), chs. 6–10.

265. H. Hartmann, *Ego Psychology and the Problem of Adaptation* (N.Y., 1958), pp. 1–21.

266. C. G. Jung, *The Psychology of Dementia Praecox* (Princeton, 1974), p. 175ff, 190–193.

267. Thomas Freeman, John L. Cameron and Andrew McGhie, *Studies on Psychoses* (London, 1965), pp. 54, 72–73ff.

268. Alfred Storch, *op. cit.,* p. 104ff.

269. Solomon H. Snyder, *Madness and the Brain* (N.Y., 1974, 1975), pp. 238–254.

270. Roy Graham Hoskins, *The Biology of Schizophrenia* (N.Y., 1946).

271. Kurt Goldstein, *The Organism* (Boston, 1963), *passim; Human Nature in the Light of Psychopathology* (N.Y., 1963, 1971), pp. 69–119.

272. Discussed in Snyder, *op. cit.*, p. 80.

273. Harry Stack Sullivan, "The Language of Schizophrenia," in J. S. Kasanin, ed., *Language and Thought in Schizophrenia* (N.Y., 1946). pp. 4–16.

274. Discussed in Kasinin, p. 52.

275. J. S. Kasinin, ed., *Language and Thought in Schizophrenia* (N.Y., 1964), p. 41ff.

276. Synopsis in Jung, *op. cit.*, pp. 158–159ff.

277. Alfred Storch, *op. cit.*, pp. 92–94.

278. Like Werner, Storch gets some of his ideas from the German preanimists (Vierkandt, Preuss).

279. Two recent summaries of investigations (by many schools) of psychotic breakdowns, written by Malcolm Bowers (*Retreat From Sanity*, Baltimore, 1974), and Solomon H. Snyder (*Madness and the Brain*, N.Y., 1974, 1975), provide ample confirmation of this euphoric stage when ego, having withdrawn from the social-symbolic world, attempts to reconstruct its own world with primary process materials.

280. Heinz Werner, *Comparative Psychology of Mental Development* (N.Y., 1948), Bk. II.

281. *L'Expérience Mystique et les Symboles,* etc. Werner is obviously conversant *both* with the early Lévy-Bruhl's ideas about "prelogical" primitive thought and his last books on "affective categories."

282. Lucien Lévy-Bruhl, *How Natives Think* (N.Y., 1966), pp. 102–103.

283. Behaviorist self models, in psychiatry (Harry Sullivan), philosophy (Dewey, Mead), and sociology (Ernest Becker), with their minimum of structure, absence of an unconscious and emphasis on mere response clusters are inaccurate for modern selves, because they leave out the patterning of experience in civilization by the secondary process and the person category, and because they ignore the rootedness the modern ego attains through repression. Becker's self model in *The Revolution in Psychiatry* (N.Y., 1964) is just a collection of "objects," "actions" and "rules," which are all circularly interdefined. Behaviorist models like this are actually assaults on the modern self rather than accurate pictures of it. These books might be titled *Denial of Self.* They do not fit modern selves, but they *do* suggest what primitive selves were like. Primitive selves were indeed little more than "clusters of action." Without the anchor of an ego-repression structure, without the stabilizers of the secondary process, primitive selves were indeed organized by social "objects"—and by magical cues to elicit and guide their responses.

284. In *The Intrapsychic Self* (N.Y., 1967), pp. 274–289.

285. In a later book (*Creativity, the Magic Synthesis,* N.Y., 1976, ch. 5) Arieti contrasts primary and secondary process cognition more precisely. Secondary process thought follows Leibnitz's law: It establishes identity only on the basis of identical subjects. But paleological thinking accepts identity if just a few *predicates* are identical. This is typical of sympathetic magic. Just a few identical predicates are enough to link objects in an "orgy of identification." Cf. pp. 68–69ff.

286. Cited in Storch, *op. cit.*, pp. 103–4.

287. Sullivan tells how psychiatrists frequently do not recognize that a patient is psychotic until a sensitive area is discussed and he then begins to talk, for example, about how "the sun is somehow mixed up in it." Harry Stack Sullivan, *Clinical Studies in Psychiatry* (N.Y., 1956), p. 260.

288. Heinz Werner, *Comparative Psychology of Mental Development* (N.Y., 1948), ch. 11, pp. 337–378.

289. *Ibid.*, ch. 7, pp. 191–198.

290. *Ibid.*, ch. 8, pp. 199–212.

291. *Ibid.*, p. 305.

292. "The basic tendencies of magic behavior proceed out of a kind of thinking which, although deviating from the Western man's point of view, is quite intelligible and in no sense is of mysterious import to the native himself. It is a type of thinking calculated to deal with the syncretic and diffuse objects . . ." *Ibid.*, p. 352.

293. "The intermediate genetic position of the sphere of magic is based on the fact that the concrete and emotional fullness of primitive thought is preserved. . . . The genetic sig-

nificance of magical-mythical apperception lies above all in its power to systematize. Long before the development of scientific abstract concepts of the world, creative magic (magical apperception) had formed relatively closed, universal systems." (*Ibid.*, p. 357).

294. Susanne K. Langer, *Mind: An Essay on Human Feeling* (Baltimore, 1972, 1974), vol. II. Langer shares Werner's conviction that human thought advances in magic. Her early writings about magic as a byproduct of conceptualization have already been reviewed (*Philosophy in a New Key*, N.Y., 1948, pp. 28-30, 129ff, 160-162, discussed in ch. 2). In this later book she speculates that imagination begins in the dream, which is a process similar to the clearing of a computer. Then excess symbolism is created because incompleted perceptions that get finished off-duty provide extra images. Dream clearing of the mind creates surplus symbolic connections as a kind of neotony. In dreams the images detach from the dream sequence to become symbols. So symbolism grows up outside of the rational-instrumental sphere. Here we have ideas similar to Werner's notion that sympathetic connections and analogies give men some control over diffuse entities of cognition and perception, and form man's first ("concrete") abstractions. Cf. ch. 17, esp. p. 283ff.

295. Werner, *Comparative Psychology . . .*, ch. 11, pp. 337-378.

296. Jürgen Habermas, *Legitimation Crisis* (Boston, 1975), Part III, ch. 4, "The End of the Individual?" pp. 117-129.

297. *Ibid.*, p. 118.

298. Gaetano Mosca, *The Ruling Class* (N.Y., 1939), pp. 50-102.

299. Robert Michels, *Political Parties* (Glencoe, Ill., 1949), pp. 25-36 and *passim*.

300. Stuart Chase, conversations, 1953.

301. Thorstein Veblen, *The Engineers and the Price System* (N.Y., 1921, 1963), Cf. ch.3.

302. Barbara Wootton, *Freedom Under Planning* (Chapel Hill, N.C., 1945), *passim*.

303. Ernest Davies, *National Enterprise* (London, 1946), chs. 4-5.

304. Nelson W. Polsby, *Community Power and Political Theory* (New Haven, 1963).

305. E. Digby Baltzell, *The Protestant Establishment* (N.Y., 1966).

306. Floyd Hunter, *Community Power Structure* (Garden City, N.Y., 1963).

307. Arnold M. Rose, *The Power Structure* (N.Y., 1967).

308. Robert A. Dahl, *Who Governs?* (New Haven, 1961).

309. Kariel, Spitz and Selznick, cited earlier.

310. Andrew Hacker, *The Corporate Takeover* (Garden City, N.Y., 1965).

311. Habermas, *op. cit.*, pp. 130-143.

312. Cf. accounts in Theodore Caplow, *Principles of Organization* (N.Y., 1964); Joan Woodward, *Industrial Organization Theory and Practice* (London, 1965); Victor A. Thompson, *Modern Organization* (N.Y., 1961); Tom Burns & G. M. Stalker, *The Management of Innovation* (London, 1961).

313. Michel Crozier, *The Bureaucratic Phenomenon* (Chicago, 1964), pp. 108, 203-208.

314. Theodor W. Adorno, *Negative Dialectics* (N.Y., 1979), pp. 66ff, 361-368 and Part III, ch. 1.

315. E. R. Dodds, *The Greeks and the Irrational* (Berkeley, 1951, 1973), pp. 140-149.

316. *Ibid.*, "The Greek Shamans and the Origins of Puritanism," ch. 5, pp. 135-178, and ch. 7, "Plato, the Irrational Soul and the Inherited Conglomerate," pp. 207-235.

317. E. O. James, *Comparative Religion* (N.Y., 1961), ch. 5, "Greece and the Mystery Religions," pp. 119-140.

318. E. R. Dodds, *Pagan and Christian in an Age of Anxiety* (N.Y., 1970), ch. 1. See also ch. 2, "Man and the Demonic World," pp. 37-68.

319. Irving Babbitt, *Rousseau and Romanticism* (N.Y., 1955).

320. Mario Praz, *The Romantic Agony* (N.Y., 1970).

321. Alfred de Musset, *Chatterton* (Paris, 1950s).

322. Guido de Ruggiere, *Existentialism* (London, 1946).

323. Jean-Paul Sartre, *L'Existentialisme Est une Humanisme* (Paris, 1947).

324. Ronald Knox, *Enthusiasm* (Oxford, 1950), *passim*.

325. Lucien Goldmann, *Le Dieu Caché* (Paris, 1959), *passim*.

326. Hans Jonas, *The Gnostic Religion* (Boston, 1958, 1963), pp. 320-340.

327. Arthur Lyons has shown (*The Second Coming: Satanism in America*, N.Y., 1970), how black mass satanism appealed to by-passed 18th century aristocrats: cf. p. 69ff.

Huysmans (*Là-Bas*, Paris, 1950) has shown it growing rankly among bypassed Catholic Church intellectuals in the Third Republic.

328. Eugene Zamiatin, *We* (N.Y., 1959).

329. Norman Mailer, "The White Negro," *Advertisements for Myself* (N.Y., 1959).

330. R. D. Laing, *The Politics of Experience* (N.Y., 1967), pp. 68–90.

331. Cf. David W. Ewing, *Freedom Inside the Organization* (N.Y., 1977).

332. Urban theory seems to be withering away just as society becomes urbanized. Scott Greer (*The Emerging City*, N.Y., 1962, pp. 5–13) has written of the collapse of the urban image, and the current urban crisis as partly an intellectual crisis; urban studies, like the city itself, fragment into separate specialties of stratification, demography, mass society, urban pathology. Kevin Lynch shows that people in most American cities literally have no map picture of their towns' layouts (*The Image of the City*, Cambridge, Mass., 1964). Attempts to reconstruct the city via theories of subcultures fail—e.g., James M. Beshers, *Urban Social Theory* (N.Y., 1962).

333. James Burnham, *The Managerial Revolution* (New York, 1941), *passim*.

334. John Kenneth Galbraith, *The New Industrial State* (Boston, 1967), pp. 60–71.

335. John P. Davis, *Corporations* (N.Y., 1897, 1961), ch. 3, pp. 35–87.

336. Norman F. Dacey, *How to Avoid Probate* (N.Y., 1965).

337. David Lynch, *The Concentration of Economic Power* (N.Y., 1946), pp. 273–279.

338. Franz Neumann, *Behemoth* (N.Y., 1942, 1966), Part Two, cf. pp. 255–292.

339. David T. Bazelon, *The Paper Economy* (N.Y., 1959), *passim*.

340. V. I. Lenin, *Imperialism, The Highest Stage of Capitalism*, in Henry M. Christman, ed., *Essential Works of Lenin* (N.Y., 1966), pp. 177–270.

341. C. Wright Mills, *The Sociological Imagination* (N.Y., 1959), p. 8ff.

342. Wilhelm Reich, "Dialectical Materialism and Psychoanalysis," article translated 1966 by Anna Bostock.

343. Reich cites all the dialectic mechanisms in psychoanalysis (return of the repressed, identification, transformation into opposites, i.e., no absolutes).

344. This is Henri Lefebvre's interpretation in *The Sociology of Marx* (N.Y., 1969), pp. 3–5.

345. Voegelin sees in social science generally a revival of the realistic civic discourse that enabled men in Greek city states to recreate wholeness of life. Eric Voegelin, *The New Science of Politics* (Chicago, 1952, 1971); *Science, Politics and Gnosticism* (Chicago, 1968).

346. George Friedmann, *The Anatomy of Work* (Glencoe, Ill., 1961).

347. Banesh Hoffmann, *The Tyranny of Testing* (N.Y., 1960); Martin L. Gross, *The Brain Watchers* (N.Y., 1962).

348. Thomas S. Szasz, *Law, Liberty, and Psychiatry* (N.Y., 1963).

349. Ralf Dahrendorf, *Class and Class Conflict In Industrial Society* (Stanford, 1959), p. 193ff.

350. Georg Simmel, *Conflict and the Web of Group Affiliations* (N.Y., 1955, 1964), p. 140ff.

351. E.g., by Harold E. Dale, *The Higher Civil Service of Great Britain* (London, 1941).

352. Karl R. Popper, *The Open Society and Its Enemies* (Princeton, 1950), *passim*.

353. R. W. Boyden, "The Breakdown of Corporations," in Andrew Hacker, ed., *The Corporate Takeover* (Garden City, N.Y.), pp. 40–58.

354. Cf. Habermas, *Toward a Rational Society* (Boston, 1971), p. 112.

355. Philip Slater, *The Pursuit of Loneliness* (Boston, 1970).

356. Richard Sennett, *Families Against the City* (N.Y., 1970); *The Uses of Disorder* (N.Y., 1970).

357. Habermas, *op. cit.*, p. 121.

358. Jacques Barzun, *The House of Intellect* (N.Y., 1959), ch. 3.

359. S. Radhakrishnan, *Eastern Religions and Western Thought* (Oxford, 1939; N.Y., 1969). See ch. 9, pp. 349–385.

360. For several centuries, Buddhism created a national religion, which, allied with a strong state, greatly ameliorated life. Buddhism failed in the end because it was purely a revolt of the self; no attempt was made to save and form an alliance with the Individual. Buddhist acceptance of Hindu monist and reincarnation ideas made that impossible. (C. Bouglé, *Le Régime des Castes*). Moreover, the Buddhist no-atman theory ultimately everted

the self (Mauss). But it is pure wisdom of hindsight to say "therefore" Buddhism failed. It also failed because the Indian state was overwhelmed in wars, conquered and divided by invaders, ruined by bad economic policies.

361. Joseph A. Schumpeter, *Capitalism, Socialism and Democracy* (N.Y., 1942, 1950), pp. 145–155.

362. For this comment on the Prometheus story: Aeschylus, *Prometheus Bound.* Hugh Lloyd-Jones, *The Justice of Zeus* (Berkeley, 1971). Gilbert Murray, *The Rise of the Greek Epic* (London, 1967). Denis Donoghue, *Thieves of Fire* (New York, 1974).

363. Søren Kierkegaard, *The Concept of Dread* (Princeton, 1957), pp. 105–138.

364. H. A. Williams, *True Resurrection* (London, 1972).

POSTSCRIPT

HISTORY

Postulate 13: MAGICAL SYMBOLISM TRAVELS EASILY AND ACCUMULATES A HISTORY.

IN a monograph begun with Durkheim in 1913 entitled *Note Sur La Notion de Civilization,*[1] Mauss proposed a survey to show which cultural facts "travel easily" and which do not. He observed that myths, money, technology, tools, scientific knowledge all travel. He wondered what the common denominator might be. His studies of logic might have provided part of the answer: The level of generality of a cultural pattern has something to do with its transmissibility. Mauss did not indicate which patterns do *not* travel easily, but probably these would include parochial folk customs and religious practices of peoples at a low level of social organization. Ndembu rituals, for example, might not travel very far. Yet some sacred symbolism does travel—world religions with generalized messages, for example. And I think that much of magic should be added to this list. If we follow Durkheim on "the generalization of mana," magic already possesses a degree of generalization. And when we examine the evidence we find that magic does indeed travel; even quite primitive magic, by common report, travels to neighboring societies.

PART ONE: A BURDEN OF HISTORY

One result of the ease with which much magic travels is that it accumulates a history; many magics have known histories, even among quite primitive people. Field workers report the constant influx of new methods of divination, witchfinding cults, medicines, from adjacent societies. These events are well-known, as a kind of oral history. New magics and the social changes they cause must be among man's first experiences of history.

A Burden of Knowledge

When writing is invented and magics accumulate in cosmopolitan civilizations, the burden of knowledge about origins becomes greater; moreover, it is never completely set down. Antiquarian interest keeps alive virtually every magic ever committed to writing by any people anywhere. The ancient world "knew" that much magic was the gift of the Magi from Iran,[2] as did the early Middle

523

Ages.[3] However accurate, this was not mythic knowledge but historical knowledge, stemming in part from historical events, such as the presence at Rome of collegia of Iranian magi. The Middle Ages also "knew" that alchemy came from Egypt; the Renaissance knew that Cabala word-and-number magic was a Jewish invention; everyone knew that astrology was a product of Babylonia, etc.

The development of a sense of history is much touted as a sign of religious maturity; Weber and some other German commentators have seen a link between Judaism's self-conscious historical sense and its alleged poverty of magic. It is a curious paradox, therefore, that among the earliest significant events to evoke the historical consciousness were the incursions of new magics and the social changes they caused or reflected.

Occult Revivals: One Historical Sequence

As eclectic magics accumulate from one civilization to another, a counter-cultural heritage grows. The anti-magical obsessions of Christianity, perhaps caused by its own repressed, led it to categorize all these magics as demonic, and hence unify them intellectually as a kind of opposition party. In the West, therefore, magic becomes an underground, anti-establishment tradition, which occasionally erupts, and some scholars like Tiryakian[4] think its eruptions play a creative part in Western cultural change. An occult upsurge in the Renaissance perhaps changed the course of science; the current upsurge seems aimed at expanding the powers of the individual mind. Because the Western establishment patterns magic as the opposition, it tends to hang together so that when one aspect wins acceptance this accrues to the benefit of the others. Thus we have "occult revolutions" and these historical sequences resemble each other. What usually happens is the following: 1. There is some magical outburst, resulting from some seemingly new (but usually old) method for weakening the objective frame. The people involved have often been dipping into the old magical literature. 2. The prestige of the new phenomena accrues to all other magics. These are tried out again and new phenomena are produced and widely reported. 3. If the civilization is ripe, there are large numbers of semi-literate masses who are alienated. They provide a market for a publishing boom. What James Webb[5] calls "the secret traditions" are searched anew for titles. They are translated and published in cheap editions. This happened in the Renaissance, in Nazi Germany, in the Soviet Union and in the United States at the present time.

It will be interesting to trace one 19th century sequence to show the typical patterning at every stage by the occult tradition as a literature. This is the sequence that runs from Mesmerism through spiritualism through ESP to today's occult boom. But before it, as Slater Brown[6] reveals, was a long tradition of healing by touching and stroking. The first outbreak perhaps was Valentine Greatrakes, called "the stroker," born 1628; other popular healers followed him. But certainly this upsurge could be connected to the waning of the institution of the "king's touch" during the Puritan era—Keith Thomas has suggested as much.[7] Marc Bloch in *Les Rois Thaumaturges*[8] has shown how the king cured certain diseases by his royal touch in France and England throughout the Middle

Ages. Interruption of this custom perhaps led to popular outbursts. Mesmerism in turn, as the rediscovery of trance, was influenced by this background: hence the early emphasis on the passage of hands and the concept of "magnetism." But there was another influence: Mesmer himself had been reading the old Hermetic literature—specifically Paracelsus.[9] Reports of his activities burst upon a public already influenced by the books of Swedenborg, who also had been dipping into the Hermetic texts before his own visions began. It is not surprising, therefore, that the relaxation of the frame which hypnotism produced was immediately accompanied by reports of paranormal phenomena. French magnetists influenced by Swedenborg, such as Alphonse Cahagnet, began to use hypnotized subjects as mediums to contact the dead. This was not common in the ancient world;[10] it was something new elicited by relaxing the frame with Swedenborgian expectations.[11]

All this preceded the Rochester rappings which finally gave birth to the spiritualist movement. The publicity which the two young girls received for their apparent ability to decipher "spirit messages" helped not merely to spread the phenomenon but to give it form. But the chain of history continues. Madame Blavatsky visited the scene and her experiences there led her to form the Theosophical Society which became later an instrument for the transmission of oriental magic into the West. The Society for Psychical Research was also founded for the express purpose of investigating the new spiritualist phenomena—it in turn invented a new kind of "ESP" experiment which slowly but inexorably, as a brain-washing technique for winning a new agreement about the categories, began to wear down the positivistic frame. ESP research is of minor importance now in the current occult explosion; but for many years, as a source of intellectual prestige, and as a worldwide publishing venture and generator of attention-getting pseudo-events, it kept the impulse alive. And so we can trace a path from the king's touch, to the popular strokers, to Mesmerism, to spiritualism, to theosophy, to ESP, to the current "occult revival." And we find the links and transmissions decisively influenced by antiquarian readers, by people like Mesmer and Blake and Swedenborg who dip back into the perennial stew for the trans-civilizational patterns that seem to travel best.

A Bookish Business

Magic is a bookish business and always has been since writing was invented. The grimoires of the Middle Ages, the voluminous publications of the alchemists, the dream books of the ancient world pour forth like a torrent, and few titles are ever permanently lost. There are eras when magic is quiescent, but the accumulated tradition is kept alive by antiquarian or eccentric interest, by underground cults, by the Vatican library, or the Warburg Institute in London, or the secret societies or each era's equivalent of New York's Sixth Avenue in the forties:

> The occult is rejected knowledge; that is, an Underground whose basic unit is that of Opposition to an Establishment of Powers That Are.[12]

Webb traces the Western occult tradition back to the syncretisms of the Ancient World, finding a core in Neo-Platonism, Gnosticism, Hermeticism and the Mystery Religions. The tendency toward unity is also provoked by its sustained role as opposition party.

Again and again magic belief is renewed when someone goes to the library and consults the tradition. In effect Kramer and Sprenger received a reading license from Innocent VIII after his bull *Summis Desiderantes Affectibus* in 1484 deploring the spread of witchcraft in Germany. It authorized the two Dominican inquisitors to study it and extirpate it.[13] They delved into the grimoires, and were later suspected of heresy themselves precisely because of the forbidden knowledge they thereby obtained. The *Malleus Maleficarum*,[14] which they published in 1486 was the first of many handbooks. Bookish, pedantic, heavy and musty is the atmosphere of the magical heritage:

> O, Faustus, lay that damnèd book aside,
> And gaze not on it, lest it tempt thy soul.[15]

Magic is in a significant sense a *publishing venture*, competing with the official worldview and patterning expectations among quasi-literate masses sufficiently as to obtain the "synthesized a prioris" that feed popular credence.

Occult Sciences and Mass Audiences

The learned "occult sciences" thus play the role on a public level that magical seances play in smaller societies in patterning confirmatory experience. The small group that weakens the objective frame systematically and agrees to agree on the definition of the outcome is mirrored by the popular publication of marvels which elicit further reports of marvels from a superstitious mass audience. In America, as Keynes once wrote, average opinion spends much of its time "anticipating what average opinion expects the average opinion to be,"[16] and the bandwagon effect confirms many marvels. Just *reading* that other people have such experiences is perceived as confirmation.

Many occult sciences derive from the divination procedures of some ancient or primitive society, which have been rationalized later on in a civilization. Durkheim and Mauss[17] also note that many derive originally from primitive classification systems—I Ching, astrology, etc. The classifications are used as oracles for divining through some mechanical principle which works on the association of nouns in the system. Astrology, of course, was related to an early astronomy, but the popular version that passed to the West and was rationalized by the Greeks was a form of fortune telling and divination based on a rationalized classification system. Thorndike[18] claimed that divination proceeds to science more rapidly than other magics because it is a form of forecasting and hence gets tested. But Evans-Pritchard[19] has shown how, when associated in the circularities of the whole magical medical complex, the outcomes of divination are quite unfalsifiable. Similarly, alchemy may have historically stimulated some chemistry, but as Jung, Eliade,[20] Burckhardt[21] and so many others have shown it was a primarily mystic knowledge of magical correspondences (again based on old classification systems), a kind of theurgy, and when revived it is revived as such. The mystic correspondences of alchemy (e.g., mystic physiologies relating every bodily organ to some element) reflect the perennial magic worldview synthesized in Hermetic theosophy of "as-below-so-above." Burckhardt and Eliade[22] characterize alchemy as an erudite symbolism used as a path to mystic union. Alchemy, then, is a kind of magical gnosis.

So is astrology, besides serving as a divination system. In astrology, in fact, we can see the whole sequence in this province of magic, from divination to occult science to theosophy; for this remarkable system is used at all three levels of generalization. It is still a divination system for millions of horoscope readers; they use it as pragmatically as the Azande use their poison oracle. But it is also an occult science of great complexity; some people spend years studying it. In addition, astrology has been used as a general theosophy, or magical theology, a complete worldview, just like Neo-Platonism, Gnosticism and Hermeticism. At several decisive phases in history, astrology has been an important part of the over-arching canopy of belief supporting the magic worldview. Angus showed it was as important as Neo-Platonism during the Hellenic world's long occult siege. Keith Thomas has shown how it played a similar role in the Renaissance; it was astrology, along with Hermeticism, that made belief in witches possible for the educated. It apparently has a similar centrality in the current occult revival; according to Truzzi it is by far the biggest seller among occult subjects.

But in our time we do not just witness the revival of history's planetary heritage of occult sciences. New occult sciences are created more rapidly than ever before, in imitation of prestigious science. ESP research is a new version of the perennial magic seance, modelled on the social design of scientific experiments, used to create raw magic experience through relaxing the frame and agreeing about the result. The sciences themselves appear increasingly willing to create occult sciences and give them official blessing. The social structure of psychedelic experience, which recreates shamanic drug seances with a patient guided by a witchdoctor, began as a Harvard psychology experiment with subjects reporting their experiences to experimenters (Leary and Alpert). The T-group movement, which has spun off numerous new social forms for eliciting and validating paranormal experience, also began in academic social science (Perls, Lewin, etc.) Each new wild science from academic psychology consists of some new way to weaken the frame (via verbal instructions, cognitive-social pressure, drug intervention, hypnotic manipulation, etc.) to provide the raw paranormal experiences, together with new methods to engineer group agreement in interpreting and overvaluing these results (i.e., the ritualistic, self-confirming "experimental designs.")

But psychology is not the only modern science spinning off new occult sciences. Physics is another notorious source. The number of eminent physicists who have dabbled in oriental esoterica (Oppenheimer, Schroedinger, the new "Tao" group, etc.) is large, and many have propounded occult theories (Konecci's "personal psi plasma fields," Pauli's Kammerer-derived "synchronicity" theory of coincidences, etc.). Arthur Koestler[23] wrote a credulous summary of coincidence theories, in which, despite learned references to Freud's telepathy papers, he did not mention that Freud had propounded a far more elegant, non-occult theory of coincidences as unconscious associations.[24] Today all the sciences emit occult movements just as they are bedeviled with the problem of fraud—both are symptomatic. Enormous postwar expansion of recruitment, funding and goals, careerist stresses in a competitive society, and increasing attention from the media put science under continual pressure to gratify the mass hunger for news, excitement, help and magic. When a new occult movement splits off from an established science, the orthodox can piously disclaim responsibility. But there may be a connection between a society that values scientism and a public fascinated by the occult sciences which imitate science. Magic does not evolve into science as Frazer thought; it evolves into pseudoscience—but so do some sciences themselves.

The occult sciences create a kind of macro version of the typical small experimental magical group, as they demonstrate their stunts before literate mass publics instead of face-to-face onlookers. But there are some differences from the face-to-face magical seance. For one thing, failures and exposed frauds have more serious consequences. When confirmation is second-hand, failures, instead of being reinterpreted on the spot, become news. Fraud plays a big role in magical movements within mass civilizations, possibly because the monetary rewards are so great, and exposure of fraud plays a big role, too, often a decisive historical role that protects the objective reality frame from occult assault.

Here are some examples: 1. In 1888, Maggie Fox confessed: she and her sister had produced the spirit rappings by cracking leg joints. This confession coincided with the cresting of the movement, which then became encapsulated within a cognitive minority in the form of the Spiritualist Church. 2. Madame Blavatsky was forced to confess that some of the magical phenomena she produced were fraudulent;[25] losing face she retired from India and soon after, upon her death, the Theosophical Society took a somewhat different path under her successors. 3. Koestler,[26] reporting sympathetically on attempts by some physicists to explain ESP in terms of "psi fields," time reversals, "psitrons" and Neo-Machian reformulations of the old magical worldview of a unified universe of instantaneously interactive symbolic entities ("holons" as emergents, with "synchronicity" explaining seeming chance), builds less than convincingly since he builds on an Austrian biologist named Kammerer who committed suicide in 1926 when it was discovered that he had cooked evidence in an attempt to prove a Lamarckian hypothesis in an experiment. This event no doubt cooled somewhat the mystic impulses unleashed by the frame-bursting revolution of the new physics, though some, like Schroedinger,[27] Duhem and Heisenberg[28] continued to dabble in the occult. 4. For years when the occult frontier was relatively quiescent, the endowed parapsychologist Rhine at Duke University continued to pump sustaining cc's of magical protest into the collective conscience via rigidly controlled psychological experiments that impressed a scientized public which was unaware of how strikingly self-confirming laboratory psychology itself resembles magical seances to begin with. Despite the successful results he obtained within his experimental design, his successor felt impelled to fake his own data and was recently exposed. This timely news somewhat weakened the current assault on the social frame of objective reality. 5. Yuri Geller's experiments have been studied by the prestigious Stanford Research Institute; the attempt of some SRI scientists to get their (positive) evaluations of Geller published in the prestigious journals *Science* and *Nature* were viewed as strategically important in winning acceptance for the competing worldview. But enthusiasm cooled when claims were published that several of the scientists involved were also Scientologists,[29] and that this institute has been characterized as a "this-gun-for-hire" think tank which receives "black money" research contracts from intelligence agencies.

The spread of macro-magic seems associated with literacy; Angus and Dodds have spoken of the mass literacy of the ancient world creating a market for pseudo-science; Webb has noticed that spiritualism arose in an area of high literacy, upstate New York during the Lyceum movement.[30] A recent French study suggests occult beliefs find a home among educated urban classes.[31] Convinced occultists are perhaps somewhat impermeable to experience that falsifies their beliefs, but they *are* more likely to confront such contradictions in the form of the printed word than are primitive participants in self-validating groups. It was news when Blavatsky, Maggie Fox and Kammerer were exposed; it was news when Reginald Scott[32] attacked witch beliefs. George Lyman Kittredge[33] has an interesting chapter on the gradual build-up and finally the torrent of books that denounced witch beliefs in Western Europe when the tide was turned. As the opposition grew more courageous the attack on these beliefs grew more total, from Johan Wier (who still believed in demons) to Reginald Scott (who still believed in evil spirits) to John Webster (who still believed in ghosts) to true skeptics like Balthasa Bekker in 1693. The failures, too, became part of the historical record, and Reginald Scott was also revived and sold in New York's Eighth Street Bookstore in the seventies along with a wall of witch books.

Another differentiating mark of macro-magical movements before mass publics is the vesting and funding of magic and magical research, though there are analogues in primitive societies. Magic is often associated with money, which develops out of magic. Even in primitive societies virtually bereft of cash markets, charms, amulets, spells, medicines and initiations are sold, and bequeathed as wealth. Medicine men and diviners are fee-paid professionals and magic is often a money-making proposition.

In cosmopolitan civilizations, however, magic is *capitalized*. Alexander the Great had to pause to conquer a Syria that was balkanized by a proliferation of tiny states created by funded magics turning themselves into religions. These temple states persisted as local governments under the Seleucids.[34] Diem struggled with similar enterprises in South Vietnam; new magical Buddhisms grow rich in postwar Japan and bid for political power. Wilhelm Reich went to jail for "medical fraud" when he sold orgone boxes through the mail, but J. Ron Hubbard turned Dianetics into the Church of Scientology and got rich. Magical cults that successfully incorporate as religions in the United States not only escape prosecution for fraud, they escape taxes, fair business practice laws, labor relations rules and many other restrictions that give them a keen competitive edge. Reactionary or dotty wealth funds research foundations that pump news of miracles into the public bloodstream. The foundations, the magical churches and the lucrative cults are better able to capture and ghettoize their own publics as cognitive minorities with the untaxed funds they can devote to publicity; the ghettoized publics in turn provide a stable source of income. Many of these movements have the get-rich appeal of chain letters for members as well as elites: become a "clear" and you can "audit" others, for a fee. This was always true of magic, of course; the initiation fee was willingly paid so the new magician could begin a moneymaking practice; but in cosmopolitan civilizations with international markets, the *capitalization* of magic always potentially threatens to swamp the economy, just as its rival, religion, not merely threatens but frequently succeeds in doing. Mattingly[35] has shown how the wealth of the Spanish Empire went into "hospitals" and other religious endowments; only when such a process is reversed, as by a Henry the Eighth, do we see how much land the sacred has gobbled up.

PART TWO: SOME HISTORICAL OCCULT REVIVALS

The structure of occult revivals deserves study. Several ideas from Weber provide initial hypotheses: A. Excessive rationalism in elites can drive the masses into irrationality.[36] For example, Weber contrasts sophisticated Brahmin metaphysics and Confucian rational ethics with pullulating popular magic in India and China.[37] B. But when magic breaks through such a fragile rationalism, it is often rationalized in turn.[38] (This increases its ability to travel.) In addition, I have outlined some hypotheses: C. New paradigms appear that protest the rational frame and provide authorization for accepting magical experience. Protest paradigms may be scientific (ESP research, psychoanalysis), philosophical (neo-mystic philosophies) or religious. D. Validation of any magical experience increases the credibility of others and so the revival spreads from province to province. E. This reactivates the general magical worldview, often under the aegis of a traditional theosophy. F. The whole revival is a publishing boom. Let us examine some real historical revivals as ideographic types.[39]

1. The Occult Siege of the Ancient World
For several centuries, the rationality of the Graeco-Roman world was besieged by mounting tides of magic: first by mystery cults springing from rural magic; then by invading oriental religions heavily freighted with exotic magic;

then by occult sciences which Greek rationality spun out of foreign divination systems; and finally by master theosophies which generalized magic to challenge religion. We need to understand both the magic and the nature of the rationality which it challenged.

Brittle Rationality. Gilbert Murray[40] has traced the successive retreats of Hellenic rationality before this onslaught. Murray offered three explanations, though the public remembers one best, his "failure of nerve" idea. That is, the decline of free, self-determining city states (together with the devastations of the Roman peace) made the Greeks lose confidence in reason and themselves. But in addition, Murray stressed the extreme reliance of Greek rationalism on "subjective criteria of fitness" (always susceptible to changes in consensus) rather than on objective experience, with the result that all the rational systems (except Epicureanism) left "curious little side doors" open through which superstition could creep back in. (And his third explanation is similar to Weber's ideas: Greek rational philosophy, by killing off the "inherited menagerie" of popular religion, created a vacuum.)

There is considerable evidence for this view of Greek rationality. Stoic monist ideas were not too different from the perennial magical worldview. (Stoicism easily succumbed to astrology.) The personal salvation aims of many systems made them vulnerable to magical shortcuts to the same goals. And a gnostic potential was perhaps inherent in Greek rationality from the beginning, with its dualism, its essentialisms and the (Aristotelian) celestial worldview common to some systems which implied the derogation of the "sublunar" world in which man lives. Certain gnostic theories and images can be traced back to Greek philosophy, Jonas[41] and Dodds[42] have shown. Plotinus' idea that "all the world's a stage" and its people puppets, for example, appears in Plato's *Laws*.[43] In general, I think, the dualism that the Greeks derived from logic and the problem of ideas blended easily into the ethical dualism from Persia to create the sense of a fallen world.

Perennial Hellenic Magic. Not only was intellectualist Greek rationality vulnerable, the ancient world itself never lacked for magic. The Eleusinian Mysteries, for example, were developed from a ceremonial agricultural magic in Eleusis which E. O. James[44] traces back to Mycenaean times. Richard and Eva Blum[45] in turn have shown how tenacious this Greek rural magic has been, even into our own times, with evil eye, medical magic, ideas of "vulnerable periods," sorcery, etc. persisting in patterns quite like those found in classical antiquity. Lynn Thorndike[46] ridicules notions that the Greeks were somehow less given to magic than other peoples: the rich, fantastical nature of Medieval magic *derived* from Hellas. Greek literature was full of it even at high noon; the *Timaeus* was not an aberration but Plato's attempt to write a natural theory of magic (like Ficino and Pico in the Renaissance). Pliny's *Natural History* and the works of Ptolemy, Philo, Galen, etc. were like vast encyclopedias of magic, according to Thorndike, transmitting the ancient lore to the grimoires of the Middle Ages. Magic was so conspicuous that scholars studied it: Plutarch syncretized it in *The*

Moralia like an ancient *Golden Bough;* Apuleius accumulated the occult wisdom of various peoples; and St. Cyprian was a learned philosopher trained in the Athenian schools who both studied and practiced magic like Faust, before becoming Christian bishop of Antioch.

The ancient world did not just witness magic overcoming reason but also Greek imagination rationalizing magic and turning it into something more powerful and dangerous. Rites that were originally magic only in the weak sense, such as corn rituals of folk religion, became more magical *as* they were rationalized—more useful to individuals, more Faustian, more antinomian. One of the last great rationalizations was Neo-Platonism, which Julian used as the official Pagan theosophy to oppose the Christian-gnostic synthesis. The crystallization of pagan magics in such theosophies as Neo-Platonism and Hermeticism made it easier for Christians to "know their enemies." Christian intolerence further crystallized the occult as a unified, rejected, underground knowledge sure to break out again. The demonology of the modern witch mania was a late harvest of this ancient synthesis.

The Mystery Religions. Angus[47] notes that the mystery religions derived from rural folk cults. Jane Harrison[48] marshalls evidence that Dionysios with his thiasos was just a bumpkin avatar of the Zeus of the *Kouretes* who had been rationalized into an Olympian. Some elements came from overseas, but the Eleusinian Mysteries and the Dionysian religion apparently derived from the very hinterlands from which the new urban people had come. It was almost as if tribal society, unsettled by the incipient urban process, had reached back into the countryside for tribal religious support. For these newer, more magical religions arose at a time when the gentile society was being disturbed by city life. Pisastratus endowed the Eleusinian cult while his dictatorship was temporarily postponing further reform of the gentile structure that Solon had cautiously begun and Cleisthenes would later complete by reorganizing the tribes into political wards (*demes*).[49] Certain elements prominent in the mystery religions perhaps show us what was being lost and what people were reaching back for. Central to these cults were rites of sacrifice and initiation rites. Since both have to do with membership, we may surmise that the whole issue of membership was becoming problematical.[50] Later, when urban masses were deracinated and city states absorbed into Hellenistic empires, communal sacrificial meals became a central element in the "clubs" (or magical lodges) that proliferated at Athens.[51]

Problems of membership: that is the social side of it. The lostness of the individual is the personal side. Membership rituals like sacrifice and initiation were put to new, more magical, more individual uses. They became redemptive, salvationist. There was an emphasis on purification, beatitude, personal happiness. Obviously they were increasingly serving individual needs. Several scholars have speculated about what those needs were. Dodds[52] suggests that the overthrow of the gentile society was experienced as killing the father and engendered Oedipal guilt. In another book[53] he suggests that the disavowed patriarchal superego broke through in experiences of disassociation (dreams, hallucinations) that fostered belief in magic: hence the new emphasis on trance, possession and dream interpretation. Gouldner,[54] following Nietzsche, portrays Hellas as an extreme "contest culture," with non-zero-sum games, fame for the winners, disgrace for the losers, tensions that drove losers to homosexuality and treason. Kitto[55] emphasizes the litigiousness, factional enmities and wearying controversies that the secular political life created. But since Thucydides[56] we have known that the main stress was the politicized class struggle. Finley,[57] Friedmann,[58] Cowell,[59] Rostovtzeff,[60] etc., show us how advanced were the capitalist and political processes that underlay it. Behind the *"miasma"* feelings Dodds attributes to Oedipal guilt alone was a more socioeconomic sense of dislocation, something similar to Hindu horror at the "Kali Yuga" when caste barriers are breached (when merchants and mere freedmen like Trimalchio[61] rise in the social scale).

Increased Susceptibility to Magic. Oedipal guilt is painful, it is also an advance over a shame culture. The mystery religions reflect both the pain and the pride of selfhood; there is something exultant in them. Yet their coming seems to cast a shadow on the free political society that is fostering selves and institutions of individualism to protect them. They carry a hunger for the mystical that becomes in time an escape from freedom. Angus has shown that the mystery religions increased the susceptibility of the masses to other magic. Their coming ushers in the beginnings of a new age of faith that will one day submerge individualism.

Almost immediately, more exotic elements ride in on the coattails of the mystery cults. James[62] has shown how the Orphic cult quickly merges with the Dionysian, but originally they were quite different. Otto[63] insists Dionysus was indigenous and very ancient in Greece (moreover, Otto's own attempt to write a new theogony celebrating the god simply serves to confirm, in its detail, Harrison's impression that the myth of his strange birth and career symbolizes a rural initiation rite). In short, the Dionysus cult is an old community rite that is revived in more urban times and mutated into a magical personal religion. By contrast, some have suspected that Apollo, and hence the whole Apollonian-Orphic-Pythagorean sequence, had quite exotic roots. Dodds[64] traces it to classic shamanism diffused into Hellas from Greek settlements on the north shore of the Black Sea. (Bury[65] and Jean Bérard[66] have shown that the same Euboan cities were involved in colonizing *both* the Crimea and Magna Graecia, which might help explain the Pythagorean connection.) Guthrie,[67] Nilsson[68] and Dodds have shown that Apollo, seemingly so purely Greek, may have come from quite a distance. Nilsson notes some roots in Asia Minor, but Dodds thinks they derive in turn from Siberian shamanism and that Apollo is really the god of individual or shamanic trance. From the collective trance or ecstasy of Dionysus to the individual trance of Apollo is a further step from religion to magic. Apollo's Pythia used either drugs or autohypnosis to answer questions entranced like a shaman.[69] Greek rationality cleaned this up, but Apollonian calm remains suspiciously like an entranced state. It was perhaps more a matter of elective affinity, and not historical accident and irony as Gilbert Highet[70] thought, that Apollo's face became the model for images of the Buddha in that previously iconoclastic cult after Alexander's raid into India.

Oriental Religions into Magical Cults and Occult Sciences. Softened up by the mystery religions and the new mystical philosophies of the Orphics and Pythagoreans, the literate Hellenic masses were extremely vulnerable to the tide of oriental religions that swept westward as a backlash from Alexander's conquest.[71] These religions brought new magics. And once again the Greek mind went to work rationalizing primitive magic into something more sophisticated. The first result was to fashion out of traditional Eastern religions and alienated imperial astral cults new mystery religions of personal redemption. Thus Sarapis was deliberately fashioned out of Ishtar, Sol Invictus[72] out of Syrian and Egyptian solar cults. And sometimes selection did the work of invention, for the Greeks could pick and choose among cults. Thus they imported the redemption version of Zoroastrianism, Mithraism, which arose under Macedonian occupation and influence and already had a Hellenic flavor, but not the parent religion. In several books Cumont[73] has traced the impact of these magical cults on the Graeco-Roman world and shown how they replaced traditional religions.[74] But not enough attention has been paid to how Greek rationalization made this material more individualized, more redemption-oriented and more magical.

Oriental magics were also rationalized into occult sciences. The Greek world easily succumbed to astrology, but it also elaborated it into a far more complex "science," bequeathing this to the world. (The deliberate Seleucid revival of Babylonian religion assisted this process.) Astrology served as a kind of ecumenical theology,[75] providing the overarching framework for all magic, and Angus[76] suggests that consequent astral determinism contributed to the pessimism of the later ancient world. Kabbala begins in Neo-Pythagorean Judaic-Hellenic rationalization of Jewish occultism during this period.[77] The first systemization of Egyptian alchemy dates from the Hellenistic age.[78] The occult sciences are part of Hellas' legacy to the world.

Magic imported to sustain the self becomes a burden to it as it accumulates densely. When Lucretius wrote of the terrible fears inspired by religion he was really writing about magic too:

> Whilst human kind
> Throughout the lands lay miserably crushed
> Before all eyes beneath Religion—who
> Would show her head along the region skies
> Glowering on mortals with her hideous face . . . [79]

The Theosophies. In most civilizations theoretical systems eventually develop which rationalize occult knowledge to produce the typical monistic, magical worldview. Huxley calls this the "perennial philosophy."[80] These systems are the theologies of magic. I will use the word "theosophy," though it has other associations,[81] to refer to them. Because they are magic at its most general, they travel with great ease and affect planetary culture for millennia. Hellenism bequeathed at least two grand theosophies to the world which were influential in later occult revivals, gnosticism and Neo-Platonism. (Manicheism and Hermeticism, as special types of gnosticism, are worth mentioning too.)

How are occult sciences, themselves rationalized from divination systems, further rationalized and synthesized into theosophies? Hermaneutic, the higher criticism and allegorizing of myths, is a common path. For example, the Eleusinian Mysteries were secret but many initiates dropped hints; generations of philosophers produced allegorical interpretations of these rituals; this sedimented a soil of hermaneutic out of which gnosticism grew, according to Eliade.[82] (Since the Eleusinian Mysteries used initiation symbols of death and rebirth this movement was the typical magical literalization of symbols.) Sandmel[83] reports that Philo initiated a similar allegorizing of scripture; it fed the gnostic synthesis. According to John Dart[84] and Jean Doresse,[85] some tracts at the Dag Hammadi gnostic library appear to allegorize myths from the book of *Genesis.* Francis Cornford[86] has described early Greek philosophy as the "analysis of religious ideas," and I have noted that this analysis moved away from mana words toward scientific concepts; but in hermaneutic a counter-trend set in: Nilsson[87] finds that much later Greek philosphy allegorized back to magical ideas (e.g., the Stoic concept of universal "sympathy."). Meyer Abrams[88] has discerned a similarly hermaneutic-gnostic allegorizing in German romantic philosophy. The modern scientific study of religion can go this way; Eliade[89] reminds us that it feeds the occult upsurge; and the psychoanalytic interpretation of myths and dreams also has a hermaneutic potential for gnostic outcomes. What Howard Nemerov calls "associative reasoning", which is implicit in these techniques, makes them akin to magic thinking; therefore gnostic outcomes are not surprising. This is one reason why I do not often try to interpret myths in this paper.

Neo-Platonism was the pagan magical synthesis; gnosticism was the Christian rationalization of magic. There were also pagan gnosticisms (Hermeticism), oriental gnosticisms (Manicheism) and Judaic gnosticisms besides the Christian and pseudo-Christian gnostic heresies of Marcion and Valentinian. But most gnosticisms were colored by Christianity, and the central movements were so close to that religion as to inspire continuing speculation[90] that gnosticism was its esoteric doctrine. Gnostic syncretism reflected many elements that went into Christianity's own synthesis; the Christian religion was explicitly gnostic during the third century struggle with paganism; and the final orthodox credo retained some gnostic elements (the fall of the angels, the evil of the world).

It is perhaps a bit forced to call all Neo-Platonism a theosophy. This diverse movement was in part a revival of Platonism at the Academy and among the gentry, as Bréhier[91] has shown. Both Bréhier[92] and Jonas[93] suggest that the Neo-Pythagorean movement began first and stimulated the Platonic revival and Neo-Platonism both; and the movement always bore traces of its rational origins. But there was an early synthesis with occult elements in Plotinus and after him the movement increasingly consisted of using Platonic conceptualization to rationalize magic. As early as Plotinus "an extraordinary power (was) attributed to rites which gradually transformed any religious practice into a magical act."[94] Later Neo-Platonists used their ideas about the unity of being as a philosophical foundation to explain sympathetic magic.[95] Neo-Platonic operators like "the One" came to play the role that "mana" plays in primitive cosmologies. In general, Neo-Platonic magic tended to be theurgic rather than antinomian.

Neo-Platonism retained a philosophical syntax and some of the rationalism of its Platonic heritage; it remained in part a natural philosophy. It considered matter inferior to spirit, but not evil. Hence an earthly ethic and a scientific rationality were still possible. In the struggle of Neo-Platonism and gnosticism, the two moved closer to each other.[96] Pagan philosophy accepted more magic and Christianity took on more philosophy to communicate to the educated. But a gulf remained between them. The pagan philosophers affected to dislike the irrationality of gnosticism and Christianity. Pagan philosophy retained its loyalty to the state, its belief in a rational, knowable world. Platonists feared that Christianity pitted faith and obedience against reason. These fears led to Plotinus' attack on gnosticism, in which he criticized its rejection of the world and its lack of an ethics and said the two went together. Acosmic, antinomian gnosticism, in its most extreme forms, so rejected this world that asceticism and libertinism were equal options. But by the time of Julian's state cult (Gilbert Murray's "fifth stage" of the Greek religion) Neo-Platonism has become a full-blooded theosophy; later, in the Renaissance, it would have a baleful influence in helping make witch beliefs possible.

The origin of gnosticism is still debated.[97] Jonas concludes that it is syncretistic, yet somehow embodies the ideal of the systems it synthesizes, what they have in common. He speaks of the "underlying unity" and "representativeness of gnostic thought," as the key to the epoch.[98] Since many of its constituents are occult, it seems to me that the "unity" of gnosticism derives from the fact that it is a philosophy of magic synthesizing all the magic sciences: Babylonian astrology, Egyptian theurgies, esoteric Christianity, Greek mysticism, Iranian dualism, etc. And certainly gnosticism embodied perennial principles we find whenever magic reaches this degree of self-consciousness: above all, the unity of the magical universe with all parts able to affect one another, and, second, a marked anti-religious, even anti-social strain. In gnosticism we find an acosmic, antinomian rejection of this world and its religious representations. Jehovah is portrayed at best as a petty judge (in Marcion), or at worst as the satanic demiurge who made the world (in Valentinian.) Gnosticism really rejects god, for it does not say that Jehovah is a false god; he is indeed the lord and creator of this universe. In other words, *god* is evil. He is rejected in favor of a distant "god" who did not make us, has little concern for us and is not a god of this universe. Even man's inwardness is rejected as suspect (as "false consciousness?"); it is a construction of demonic trickery and an instrument of domination over man's true, submerged self. The soul, god, the world all the way up through the heavens are rejected; the planets and stars are ruled by evil Archons who try to keep man's spirit from escaping his prison to the *Deus Absconditus* beyond the universe.

All religious symbols are social projections and it should be apparent what gnosticism reflects. Implicit in all magical theosophies East and West is a recognition of the artificial ("magical") and oppressive nature of social reality. Magic theosophies arise when the social weight becomes too heavy, and they teach man to fight magic with magic. There are analogies in India, where Varuna was the magician god who "ties and binds," and Vishnu, his successor, the magical demiurge who creates each cosmic age out of mâya, or magical illusion.[99] To the gnostics the world is an evil creation that enslaves man; here, expressed in mystic terms, is a dawning consciousness of the social creation of reality. In the late Roman Empire, the sociocultural edifice was oppressive and it sat on people; above it towered its gloomy religious projections reinforcing despair. In Valentinian and Manichean accounts of creation we find an almost Hegelian interpretation of alienation through objectification. In various gnostic myths, creation is an accident that happens when a perturbation in the cosmic egg causes god to reflect upon himself: the objectification of his *I* as a *Me* is the first escape of the light, the first alienation. In Valentinian systems, the great chain of accidental being is unleashed because god's weak or feminine side (*Sophia*) thinks, or it loves; this produces a progressive fall with more emanations sent from god's light to recapture the *pleroma*. In dualist Iranian versions, by contrast, light and dark are coequals; the fall begins when dark sees the light and attacks it; the light, being pacifist, does not fight but throws out some of itself as creation to provide a diversion. In all these myths, something is lost by virtue of being created. All this sounds very much like modern Hegelian ideas of social reality as alienation.[100] Jonas notices a similarity between gnosticism and existentialism: both romanticize the lostness and "thrownness" (Heidegger) of the individual in a world he did not make.

Gnosticism is an anti-religious theosophy, a theology of magic masquerading as a religion. It attacks god and religion as projections of an oppressive society, as many magic protest sects do. Once crystallized, gnosticism became the perennial philosophy of antinomian revolt for Western society; heretic and messianic movements in Christendom usually contained a gnostic streak. But magic theosophies like gnosticism (and Neo-Platonism) do not just rationalize magic. They do not provide a sacred canopy of belief for it. They also create more magic and themselves work as magic directly:

> The Hermetic treatises, which often take the form of dialogues between master and disciple, usually culminate in a kind of ecstasy in which the adept is satisfied that he has received illumination and breaks out into hymns of praise.[101]

The sing-song, repeated refrains of the Upanishads provided similar immediate, magical gratification:

> Now that which is subtle essence, in it all that exists has its self.
> It is the True. It is the Self, and thou, O Svetaketu, art it.[102]

Even conventional religious literature approaches these effects on a continuum, beginning with mere capitalizations of "Him" and "God" and "His Kingdom" and veering through archaisms to increasing disintegration of normal cognitive discourse until quite plainly it is magical (trance) effects that are being sought. Malinowski has shown us that reciting myths can be magic; in China[103] scripture was read publicly to fight plague. Magic is created by the generalization of mana; new magics emerge in the rationalization of divination systems into the occult sciences; and the further abstractions of theosophy not surprisingly produce new magic ideas, symbols and sacred texts for concrete applications. Thus gnosis is the theosophy of magic, but it is magic too, by itself, just as the philosophy of mathematics produces more mathematics.[104]

Rational Outcome. In the end, a quasi-theosophical religion captured power in the Graeco-Roman world: the gnostic-Christian movement—and yet the occult tide eventually waned, as it often has in the West. The victorious religion restored more personal magic to the masses, with its immortal self, magical sacraments, techniques of magical puritanism, etc. Yet the new Christian monopoly caused a net reduction in magic. Christianity's heritage of Judaic intolerance, Hellenic exclusionary logic derived from political polemics and Roman legalism caused it to outlaw exotic practices rather than "rank" them as Hinduism more tolerantly does (Dumont[105]). Christianity suppressed pagan, oriental and folk magics—it even cast out some of its own magic heritage, condemning gnosticism (and Manicheism) as heresies. Joachim Kahl[106] claims that it was as diverse and syncretistic as Hinduism, but this is an exaggeration for the sub-sects were bureaucratically subjugated to dogma. And while it fostered belief in its own considerable magic, the shield of Christian intolerance repelled oriental magic for a millennium or more. Hellenism had not repelled Near Eastern cults, and Radhakrishnan[107] and others have suggested that even Hinduism was leaking into the West during the Hellenic era. There were "gymnosophists" (yogin) at Athens; the thread of metempsychosis (otherwise alien to the West) running through Orphism-Pythagoreanism-Platonism is suggestive, as is the emphasis on meditation in Cynicism. Christianity (and feudal isolation) absolutely repelled all that. With the dissolution of the shield of Christian intolerance, Pauwels[108] and others speculate that Hinduism and Buddhism are again leaking into the West, attempting through their theosophies to recreate the perennial Aryan four-estate system Dumézil[109] shows to have been our heritage (with, for example, the Nazi or Communist party or the gurus as the Brahmins, the *Wehrmacht* or Red Army as Kshatriyas, the industrialists as twice-born Vaisyas, labor as Sudras and concentration camp labor as untouchables).

Dumont, Dumézil, Weber use Hinduism to show how religious ideas, as social ideology, can affect social structure; at very least, like "switchmen" (Weber)[110] or "gear wheels" (Mauss), they deflect social outcomes according to their "elective affinities" (Weber) to each other and to social structures they fit well. Thus Weber proposes that once Hinduism accepted metempsychosis, monism was inevitable. (And Bouglé[111] showed how acceptance of monism undercut the Buddhist revolt against caste by perpetuating vulnerability to Hindu ideas of reincarnational advantage.) Where religious ideas dominate, they do influence events, but this is somewhat circular. Whether they dominate is determined less by ideas and more by social structure. There was little inherent resistance to the occult in Greek rationalism. Most Greek systems succumbed to it, and the whole society was taken over by gnostic Christianity. It was social structure that provided resistance to occultism and eventually threw it off. The self-constituting gentes had established a political order in which the Individual was consolidated. The heritage of Roman law, the ideal of universal citizenship perpetuated in church membership, the continued charter rights of depopulated but independent cities were among the legal-rational elements that persisted in the social structure.

But to understand this outcome, compare it to what happened in India, where a different social structure supported a more lasting occult establishment.

2. Hinduism As a Permanent Occult Revolution

That is one way of looking at it—India swept by successive waves of magic-fostering theosophy. A. The first "occult revolutions" came with the Upanishads, which started as a coda to the liturgical Brahmanas.[112] Here, an impulse toward natural philosophy was deflected into magic theosophy because its carriers were magician priests and its terms of reference were ritualistic; the result was that the discourse did not get beyond the analysis of mana, which Ionian physics eventually did transcend.[113] The Hindu mana word, *Brahman,* derived from words meaning magic power of rite.[114] The point is that it remained a mana word; even when used to designate the substrate of the universe, it continued to mean magic power; no wonder the world itself was considered mâya, illusion. The discovery that Atman (personal mana) equals Brahman (universal mana)[115] was just the typical magic worldview in which mana is mana and all is one.[116] B. Very quickly followed the first great anti-caste renunciation cults (Jains, Buddhists). They had magical aims, developed powerful new magics (super-meditation), and accepted the magical-monist worldview. C. Then came the new theosophies (*Samkhya,* etc.) of "Hindu revival," when the Brahmins reached down into aboriginal magic (e.g., Yoga) to compete with Buddhist magic. Thereafter, all renunciation sects[117] followed credos that were some variant of the old or new theosophies (Upanishads, Samkhya,[117a] Vedanta, etc.). Though some sects were mildly theist, the basic trend was monist gnosis under guidance of a perennial theosophy of mana: i.e., personal escape through magic knowledge or power.

The theosophies are only part but an important part of Hindusim; they take the place of theology in providing unification of the sacred canopy. But theosophies are worldviews which markedly encourage belief in magic. The outcome was an intensely religious culture which seems to us both atheistic and magical. Religious intensity, if ethical, often controls magic and repels atheism, but Hinduism is a religion of mana. Why this outcome? Magic struggles clumsily for the self and its presence indicates pressures on selfhood. In classic Hinduism, the self is crushed, struggling for freedom but forever trapped because the escape routes are patterned by monist theosophies that demonstrate escape is impossible. It is as if the rigid caste system had almost suffocated the self whose minimal spontaneity society requires: so the system had to pattern self-struggle as resuscitation and safety valve. Yogic self-technologies and renunciation sects denied caste but thereby made it tolerable. Why should theosophies of mana take the place of theology? The answer has something to do with domination by a caste of fee-paid magicians. Magic theosophies and the Brahmins are the two unifying elements in Hindu diversity.

The Hindu Menagerie. Bouquet's analogy[118] between classic Hinduism and the ripe menagerie of late Roman religion is apt; let me extend it. The Upanishads, Vedanta, etc., might be lined up against Neo-Platonism and gnosticism as theosophies that rationalize magic into the perennial mana worldview. Other Hindu schools parallel the Hellenistic ethical philosophies: Skepticism (Buddhist logic), Stoicism (the *Ghita*), etc. The renunciation sects parallel the competing salvation religions of the ancient world. In the background would be, not the Vedic gods, but the syncretistic Graeco-Roman pantheon, with industrious rationalizers like Plutarch abetting the monist undertow. If Christianity with its intolerance and exclusionary logic had not pruned this jungle, it might have grown (or remained) closer in nature to Hinduism.

But the cultic menagerie is not all of Hinduism. The core is something even more fragmented. Indians call the religion *Arya Dharma*,[119] Aryan duty, which the *Ghita* showed means caste duty.[120] The dharma of each caste (prayers, rituals, duties) differs, and Weber shows that all these practices are deeply influenced by magic.[121] It is like the separate rites of totemic clans in Australia, or the individual family religions of primitive Rome. What counts in Hinduism are the caste rituals, taboos, distances, duties. In this intensely religious culture, religion really does mould the social system: It sells the social system like an ideology, says Dumézil;[122] the Brahmins actively design caste arrangements, says Weber;[123] the caste prescriptions translate into socioeconomic reality even against the grain of economy, says Dumont.[124]

But even in India, religion was more projection of society than vice-versa. To understand its permanent occult revolution we must look at the social structure that supported it. Whereas Graeco-Roman society dissolved totem-like barriers between sibs with its self-constituting urban process, legal rational institutions, strong supportive states and ultimate religious cleansing by intolerant Christianity, Hindu society instead froze totem-like barriers between sib communities into the caste system. Studies by Blunt,[125] Hutton,[126] Bouglé,[127] Ghurye,[128] Dumont,[129] Weber,[130] Lévi-Strauss,[131] Hocart,[132] Bouquet[133] make it clear that the caste system is the morphological basis of Hindu occultism. (While Margaret Cormack,[134] Gardner Murphy,[135] V. S. Naipaul,[136] David Mandlebaum,[137] etc., show how the dovetailed Hindu family produced a character structure resigned to caste duty and monist-magic worldview).

What is Caste? Castes are 1. *ranked,* 2. *occupationally interdependent,* but 3. *mutually repellant* hereditary kinship communities. Not enough attention is paid to the contradiction between these last two attributes.[138] On the one hand each caste prohibits marital exchange with outsiders (endogamy), or any personal contact, by obsessive, mana-related purity taboos. Yet all castes are forever locked together in a web of reciprocity based on extreme and uneconomic microdivision of labor fixed by religious tradition. Mutual abhorrence but total interdependence—curious! From a kin-structure viewpoint caste may indeed reflect a historic "withdrawal of reciprocity," as Lévi-Strauss[139] speculates; but economically, reciprocity under the caste system seems as total as under socialism (Dumont).[140]

The contradiction strongly suggests something wounded and regressed. Because of cult fragmentation, totem-like taboos between sibs and reincarnation ideas, a comparison with totemism is sometimes made, as if a broken civilization had regressed urban guilds, gentile tribes, subject nations, religious sects and all other groupings to something resembling totemic sibs. And certainly, with its endogamous communities, the system has fallen back on kinship organization[141] (perhaps because the Indian family unit is solid and "harmonious"— patrilocal, patrilineal, patriarchal). But the form is not totemic, for several reasons: 1. Castes are endogamous; totemic clans are usually exogamous. 2. Castes have tribal, occupational, religious, etc., names; seldom totemic names.[142] 3. Totemic clans are polysegmental identities, each economically self-sufficient; whereas castes are hyperspecialized by division of labor. 4. Totemism is prior to the generalization of mana, with limited magic; whereas Hindu caste is saturated with magic.

If castes are regressions, it is to something further along than totemism, perhaps to *the tribal stage* with its division of labor, strong magic and endogamous marriage within the tribe.[143] At the tribal stage, remember, division of labor was just beginning, as a *division of magic* between the confraternities. If Hinduism is a regression to tribal endogamy, the caste system could be a regression to early division of labor on magical principles.

Hocart's evidence that many seemingly occupational castes are really priesthoods of fallen rites would suggest this. In a remarkable book entitled *Caste*[144] he reports that in Ceylon "drummers" are really people who officiate at funerals and other low rites, and for this they are pariahs. The "barber" is not just a man who shaves heads; his important role is to perform certain rites at festivals and weddings.[145] Washermen are really menstrual priests who officiate at a rite connected with a girl's first menses. In South India, "potters" sometimes officiate as priests; they make a sepulchral urn; they heal bones and fractures but leave boils, wounds and tumors to barbers.[146] Throughout the world the theme of a primordial struggle of gods and giants appears; in India the forces of dark (Asuras) are defeated by those of light (Devas). Hocart equates Asuras and Titans. (Perhaps Titans and Asuras are gods of fallen matriarchal rites.) Vanquished cults are not abolished in India, but "ranked," as Dumont[147] shows, and given some function. Hocart observes that Devas, as gods of life, cannot be involved with death, so priests of fallen Asuras rites are enlisted. Their status is low *because* they perform a wholly unclean function, and also because they do so as priests of a fallen, demon rite. (I think, in general, they get involved with "exit" rites in sacrifice and other sacraments: they clean up pollution, death, etc.)

This priestly, ritualistic, sacrificial underlay of so many seemingly economic occupations provides support for my point: If Hinduism is regression to tribal endogamy, the caste system regresses division of labor to its earlier magical basis and principles. This would help explain the paradox of mutual exclusivity combined with economic interdependence between the magically demarcated castes and occupations.

Caste Fragmentation. But though most castes have fixed occupations, caste is a miscellany. Molony compared it to dividing England into "families of Norman descent, clerks in Holy Orders, noblemen, positivists, iron-mongers, vegetarians, communists and Scotsmen."[148] In most Indian language areas before partition there were up to 200 or so castes of *diverse* nature: about 5 to 15 represented *crafts* associated with towns; but 5 to 15 were formed by *primitive tribes;* most of the rest had *religious or tribal* names.[149] The subcastes, which may be more important,[150] had *occupational* or *territorial* names, but also religious, customal, adventitious or mixed names.[151]

New subcastes constantly formed, by mésalliance, by change of occupation, but mostly by status fission as some families rose and cut others. Endogamous systems must have some exogamous arrangements within them; in subcastes these are handled by rules,[152] and also by marriage classes, the exogamous "gotras" inside subcastes.[153]

And the remarkable thing is that in most subcastes the gotras are already sorting themselves out by status; some will not intermarry, others will marry only with certain others; this leads to fission and new subcastes.[154] One prime way new castes are formed is religious; gotras of families that fall off in observances may be rejected by others in the subcaste and so form a new and lower endogamous caste; conversely, ambitious families may increase observances (e.g., become vegetarian) and then split from others to form a higher subcaste.

The core of the system is magical repulsion, tempered by magical offsets (e.g., the five cow products) so that status positions have a relativity and the hierarchy system has overlapping laminations,[155] and varying purity distances.[156] There was even a 1932 report of a caste of "unseeables" who were polluting even to look at, so they could come out only at night—they washed the clothing of untouchables.[157] Race may have something to do with it; racial repugnance is expressed openly: some Brahmins claim their purity derives from the original Aryan race purity which they best preserved, and Blunt,[158] Bouglé, Ghurye and Weber take this claim seriously. Ghurye did cephalic indexes and other race measures and found Brahmins did tend to be more Caucasian in the north though not in the south.[159] There is outspoken racism in some Indian interpretations of caste, e.g., S. V. Viswanatha's.[160] Radhakrishnan's justification of caste by the inherent "virtues" of the several varnas is more subtly racist.[161] Yet the impression is inescapable that race is secondary to magical purity ideas rather than vice versa.

Further proof that these ideas are magico-religious: even upper castes are to some degree impure to lower castes, the way a mixture of sacred and profane can hurt both. The lower pollutes the sacred upper because lower is profane; but the sacred can also pollute and destroy the profane: *sacer* means polluted as well as sacred in Latin. Hutton reports that there is even some repulsion between individuals. Blunt confirms it, noting the custom of Rajput soldiers each to eat alone. And in every linguistic area there *are* some castes which in the memory of man *have* been generated by mésalliance; this further demonstrates the power of magic purity.

Another point to grasp: castes are self-conscious communities. That is one way they differ from classes.[162] Castes have councils (Panchayats) with rules and a judicial process to try offending members. There is no doubt that caste is integrative as Hutton stresses, as well as fragmentary. The proof is in the pudding: no jacquerie, no rebellions from below. India is a diverse group of populations never fully digested by its unstable states; caste locks these populations together by "ranking diversity."[163] Each caste has different rites and these are graduated, with Vedic rites for the twice-born only and debased rites for untouchables.

And these communities *compete*—but as groups. A group of families decides to risk an occupational change, not lone individuals. There *is* mobility, but by groups. Some methods are quite blatant. One subcaste will start calling itself Brahmins to the census enumerator and hope to "pass." Other efforts are more systematic and they involve: 1. liberality (gifts to Brahmins who in return may do favorable genealogies); 2. observance (stricter religious rules); 3. rupture of reciprocity with less mobile caste members (stop marrying the Joneses who do not keep up). Education can increase status; a British official in 1917 called it "a despotism of caste tempered by matriculation."[164] But any new occupation undertaken must be no less pure than the old, or status will be lost.[165] Hypergamous marriage of daughters into the upper crust can increase status—but if the marriages are too morganatic they will be considered mésalliances and the whole pack of social climbing families will be expelled by the Panchayat to tumble down the social scale as a new fallen subcaste.

Origins of Caste. For some time it has been clear that caste is not to be explained by any one of the unilinear theories—such as Brahmin exploitation (a popular theory among Indians), kingly design (Ghurye), guilds (Dahlmann), race (Viswanatha), Aryan clan (Senart), value of higher occupations (Nesfield[166]), etc. Caste is the result of many forces. But most attempts at theoretical synthesis have not truly penetrated the phenomenon yet.

The simplest synthesis is just to assemble all the factors eclectically, as Hutton does.[167] Similar is Bouglé's idea[168] of a piling up of divisive elements in Hindu society (race, hierarchy, conquest, etc.), which finally caused fragmentation. Weber has a similar idea of cumulative pressures causing a break.[169]

This will not work because it is just not true to say that all these elements were not present together elsewhere. Hierarchy, hereditary priests, purity, guilds, conquest, race mixture—all were present at the same time in most civilizations. Pile-up of factors is important. But even synthesizers began looking for a *strategic factor*, something accentuated in India which crystallized the other factors.

1. *Purity*. One early emphasis was on religious purity ideas. Hutton[170] and Bouglé,[171] while noting pile-up of factors, both pointed to purity ideas as strategic. Of Bouglé's three main caste principles—hierarchy, division of labor and mutual impurity[172]—the last is the key. Dumont shows[173] how his other two factors reduce to impurity ideas. And this purity obsession is obviously religious rather than hygienic. But it is not enough to say that ritual purity is the linch pin, for that does not explain why something so common should be so exaggerated here.

2. *Hierarchy*. In later syntheses, Lévi-Strauss and Dumont looked for distinct "operators" fissioning groups on purity lines. Lévi-Strauss[174] proposed that competitive "hypergamy" is the operator, and Dumont that status competition is. Both thereby shifted emphasis toward hierarchy as the cause of purity ideas more than vice versa:

Dumont proposed that it was Aryan status mania which produced caste fission. He formulated a precise operator, what I will call the "high-hat effect." A group of families in a marital-alliance system rises in status; it is always these top dogs who then stop exchanging wives with lower status families and force endogamy on them. When families maritally "high-hat" other families, castes or sub-castes split, thereby forming new endogamous groups. (For example, Risley found a district where the clans were held in such low esteem that no one would give them daughters in marriage. So they were condemned to marry among themselves and stagnated into a new endogamous caste.)[175]

Lévi-Strauss also proposed a precise operator, "hypergamy." This is the practice of marrying women to higher-status men; it was accepted in India because women were thought inferior, so brideprice was lessened, etc. Especially in the north, there were whole subcastes of Rajputs who used to marry their daughters to subcastes of Brahmins.[176] Hypergamy may begin informally, but it becomes an organized exchange between groups, and eventually new castes are precipitated.

Lévi-Strauss has an interesting theory about how caste evolved out of system overload and pathology. Studying other marriage systems in Southeast Asia,[177] he finds that the usual pattern is generalized exogamous marital exchange, and that this is unstable. Societies evolve complex exchange systems to organize it, but there are signs of pathology: e.g., rural indebtedness caused by moneylender loans for brideprice or weddings is a sign that reciprocity is breaking down. What finally collapsed generalized marriage exchange in India was that extra Aryan preoccupation with status which Dumont stresses. Given status mania, generalized marital exchange meant that "good" marriages would convey enormous advantage; this tipped the system toward hypergamy; hypergamy in turn led to closed marriage classes and eventually to endogamous castes.

Therefore, comparing India's with nearby marital systems, Lévi-Strauss infers a momentous historical "withdrawal of reciprocity." At some point large groups of people stopped marrying each other, stopped exchanging gifts, wives, courtesies. (Yet *economic* reciprocity remained in the frozen division-of-labor of the caste system. Lévi-Strauss does not explain the contradiction.) Continued status competition led to further fissioning. Aryan society had been organized into the four varnas ("colors"): Brahmin (priest), Kshatriya (warrior), Vaisya (farmer, artisan) and Sudra (worker). Originally these were not hereditary, apparently. They became hereditary and later they split into castes. But it did not stop there: the castes split into thousands of subcastes which many consider the basic unit. And either the high-hatting effect (Dumont) or hypergamy (Lévi-Strauss) or competition with mésalliance keep fissioning castes into smaller groups.

But again, to attribute the whole movement to a "hierarchical principle" as Dumont does is no more satisfying than to say that purity obsession is the key. Both are phenomenological explanations of a sociological fact, and as feeble as Hocart's saying that the Brahmins came to power because Indians are impressed by words.[178] As a matter of fact, hierarchy and purity ideas are closely related and collapse into each other: *Both purity and hierarchy are magical ideas.*

Weber has shown[179] that ranking is usually by power, class or status; but *all three* go back to magical ideas of mana, money and face.[180] At what stage do we find this preoccupation with ranking by *purity?* Again, it strongly reminds me of the tribal stage, when the lodges have erupted and there is magic everywhere, the magic of chiefs and shamans, of lodges and class associations. Every individual at the tribal stage has mana; everyone is dangerous or impure to everyone else. Evans-Pritchard observes a tendency for every man to become a magician.[181] And everyone is *ranked.* Hindu hierarchy mania and occupations that are really fallen priesthoods remind me of the craft brotherhoods competing in magic games to establish precedence in Granet's picture of ancient China.[182] Or of Kwakuitl clans competing in potlatches to establish rank.[183] Hindu economic reciprocity on close inspection appears to be a kind of frozen potlatch; some castes are still paid for their services by *gifts.*[184]

Both purity and hierarchy seem related to tribal society, as if Indian civilization had regressed to this stage. When we ask why this happened, we fall back on ideas of system overload and pile-up of stress. Suppose that Lévi-Strauss is correct about system pathology in underlying kin structure. Suppose Aryan status mania overtaxed this system, producing panic at competitive hypergamy. Meanwhile failures in the macro-society complicated these stresses. India endured the same premature hyperorganization of empires as the Near East, with the result that the gentes were not engaged in active social change as in Greece and Rome, but bypassed. In addition, Indian states collapsed and were succeeded by generations of conquest states which tax-farmed the entire surplus of the country. The cities were ruined.

But the Near East also endured hyperorganization and conquest states under Assyrians, Persians, Greeks, Romans, Moslems; it often experienced disengagement of the gentes in places, yet developed no caste system, despite historical affinities between Sumerian and Mohenjo-Dari and Harappa culture. (Of course, it did have one experience in common with the West: a housecleaning of the inherited menagerie by an intolerant religion.) Even synthesis theories so far have not been penetrating enough.

A Caste of Magicians

A more penetrating synthesis can perhaps be formed by centering on the Brahmins. For the outcome obviously has something to do with the rampant magic of the system, and the Brahmins are magician-priests. Moreover, they are the lodestar and guide of *both* the hierarchy and purity systems which recent syntheses stress.

Hierarchy: The upper class orients any hierarchy system. After the Hindu revival,[185] the Brahmins were clearly top rank. Other castes were ranked by how much the Brahmins ministered to them and by their liberality toward Brahmins.

Brahmins are also the lodestar of the *purity* system.[186] Before the Buddhist revolt, purity obsessions clung mainly only to Brahmins.[187] It is plain to see what they were. The Brahmins were the "sacrificers," to use Hubert and Mauss' term, i.e., the technicians who performed the collective sacrifice ritual for the "sacrifiers" or sponsors, who were the kings. Sacrifice, a ritual on the border between religion and magic, is perceived as a dangerous, quasi-criminal act. It must be hedged by elaborate "entry and exit rites"[188] to prevent spiritual backfire of released mana. The Brahmins were in charge of getting these rites done letter perfect.

Hocart[189] thinks the Brahmins were more specialized than that. All three Aryan castes participated in sacrifice: the Vaisyas or farmer-artisans were the *provisioners* of sacrifice, the kings were the principal performers. The Brahmins spoke the prayers of the *oral rite*.[190] They had to say their lines just right lest they mingle sacred and profane and blast one or the other.[191]

Purity ideas apply with special puissance to food, what is eaten in sacrifice.[192] The *Ghita* propounded the idea of turning all action into sacrifice; it is almost as if Hinduism took this so literally that all meals became sacrificial meals.[193] Hindu food purity obsessions fasten especially on the *preparation* of food:

contamination is most likely during cooking. I suggest that food preparation here is homologized to entry rites in sacrifice.

Why Did the Brahmins Win? But the mana and sacrifice ideas which Hindu purity obsessions exaggerate are found in all societies at the tribal stage. And Brahmin-like classes existed in other tribal societies, too. History sometimes misses them because this was not usually a full-time occupation. In "Flamen-Brahmin,"[194] Dumézil identified the Roman flamens with Brahmins. Elsewhere he tried to show that the Celtic Druids played this role, and that the Persians had a similar class, the Baresman.[195] The evidence is hazy.[196] But certainly many peoples had classes of hereditary priests: Egypt, Sumeria, Israel.[197]

Hocart attempts a similar identificaiton of Brahmins with the Greek herald (*kerux*).[198] There were heralds in the state and in the Eleusinian mysteries. They convened the assemblies of the people but also religious ceremonies. Iranian heralds were the model for angel ideas ("the herald angels"). Originally, Hocart said, heralds were the officials who spoke the oral rite in sacrifice; later they were messengers taking the oral word from gods and kings to men. Herald and Brahmin symbolism had striking similarities: both carried staffs as insignia; both were messengers of gods and kings, both were peacemakers; both were inviolable. There were similarities between their gods: Hermes in Greece, Agni in India. If heralds were Brahmins, their different evolution in Greece is striking. Whereas they became all-powerful magicians in India, in Athens they were ultimately reduced to town criers.[199]

We could generalize Dumézil and Hocart to suggest that the magician class is a natural product of the magical revolution of tribalism. When the lodges erupt, they produce hordes of magical leaders. In the magic competitions of these brotherhoods, one lodge leader comes to power as the king. For a long time his election remains magical, and depends on continued display of his magical powers, as Frazer demonstrates.[200] In many African transitional societies, the king used to be overthrown or killed if he weakened. All the myths of the wounded king, reported in Jessie L. Weston,[201] T. S. Eliot,[202] Frazer, etc., really point to magical weaknesses, not physical ones, and what they suggest is a long transitional period, before kingship became fully hereditary, when kings were still thrown up from a caste of magician leaders.

But why did tribal magicians become so powerful in India? A partial answer is that India retained in many ways (or regressed to) the character of a transitional tribal society. Urban and governmental processes that disintegrate tribalism's magician-priests were interrupted in India. On the other hand, India did advance to civilization, so that a class which is part time in primitive tribal society could be supported full time by an economic surplus. Eskimo shamans must hunt and often can barely support themselves;[203] probably Aryan heralds were also part time. But civilizational surplus enabled Brahmins to become full-time priests in India, while fragmentation of the society prevented their concentration in state collegia and temples as in more stable Egyptian regimes.

Special conditions in India tipped the scales toward the Brahmins. After the pro-Buddhist Maurya dynasty, India was invaded by Greek, Persian, Chinese, Hun and Kushan armies between 200 B.C. and 500 A.D.[204] The Kshatriya appeal to the masses against Brahminism perished with the Maurya state and the destruction of this literary warrior gentry. The successor "pseudo-Kshatriya" Rajputs were illiterate and did not challenge the Brahmins. The Vaisyas declined with the ruin of many cities.

Meanwhile, Brahmins had fallen heir to some functions that flamens, Druids and heralds elsewhere did not retain. For one thing, they took on the role of sophists. Ionian physics was begun by merchant intellectuals;[205] and even when Greek sophism became a full-time, fee-paid profession, it was secular.[206] The reasons were urbanism, citizenship and democracy. The sophists were secular teachers training young men for participation in the civic process, training them above all in rhetoric.[207] From Isocrates on, philosophy was subordinated to this more practical art. Roman education built on this secular foundation, for even with empire there was political office for the patriciate under the Augustine compromise, not to mention the lively municipal life of the provincial *curiales*. In India, the sophists were also priests, and they produced in the theosophies influential ideas that contributed to their power. Weber refers to the "socially anchored unshakeability of certain metaphysical presuppositions."[208] Monist theosophy was a vested interest in India, broadcast by the theosophies that saturated all education, and backed by the endowed Brahmin caste, and thereby all Hindu thought fell into this black hole so that resistance was intellectually impossible. Only Neo-Platonism rivals Upanishadic thought as the crystallization of the magical worldview for planetary culture.

Victory Through Magic

Weber reports that the power of the Brahmins depended on increasing the significance of magic in all spheres of life. And they did seem to grow more powerful the more they used magic.

1. At first they were specialists in the congregational rites of sacrifice, part of a religious ceremony. But then Aryan sacrifice became so complicated that the Kshatriyas could not keep up with their specialism: "Brahminism" became a complicated liturgical knowledge. We do not know why sacrifice, the great magic-modeling religious rite of tribalism, became so prominent in the age of the *Brahmanas,* but possibly these rites were a badge of unity for groups of city-destroying Aryans dispersed among the conquered population like Dorian and Lombard bands and possibly uneasy about race mixture.

2. Next, the Brahmins used the prestige and leisure which their specialism earned them to rationalize tribal sacrificial magic—all the way to theosophy. The Upanishads dominated Indian thought after this and forever accrued to the prestige of the Brahmins.

3. When the Kshatriyas appealed (in Buddhism, Jainism, etc.), over the heads of the Brahmins to the masses with promise of deliverance from caste and powerful personal magic to save the self, the Brahmins tried to compete with this magic.[209] During the Buddhist ascendancy under the Mauryas, when the

Brahmins did not always enjoy prestige in court but continued to earn good livings as local magician-priests, they dipped down into aboriginal magic; they adopted techniques from Dravidian shamans. It seems possible that the Aryans did not penetrate the south except culturally,[210] and that many "Brahmins" in the Deccan *were* local shamans who adopted Hinduism.

4. During the Hindu revival the Brahmins literally "wrote" the caste system that put them on top. We have the texts: the *Code of Manu,* the *Puranas.* Like Solons they drew up social constitutions, but instead of destructuring tribes into political wards, they restructured incipient urban masses back into something like tribes, into "occupational" castes hierarchically arranged according to purity rules, no doubt using the Aryan four-tiered structure as their nuclear idea.

5. Then, after the death of Harsha in 650 A.D. (a kind of Hindu Charlemagne), came the Indian "Middle Ages," with the country broken up into small states ruled by Rajput kings (foreign conquerors or mercenaries originally), with trade almost impossible and travel difficult to all but Brahmins. With the Kshatriyas destroyed, with no unifying state (until the Moslem conquest in 1200), the Brahmins with their caste blueprints and justifying theosophies were the only force providing cultural unity. It was during this period that the Brahmins gradually imposed the caste system and completed their own evolution from participants in the collective Vedic *religious* rite of sacrifice to independent fee-paid *magicians* working on a one-to-one relationship with clients and serving no congregations.

Observers report the Hindu masses believe the Brahmins imposed the caste system. Bouglé objected because they were never organized enough to do any such thing.[211] But in the Weber scenario,[212] they did not have to be organized. Their blueprint was organized; it was in writing, in the *Code of Manu.* One by one the little Rajput conquest states, seeking legitimacy, would begin to ape Hindu observances, then call in Brahmin genealogists who, for a fee, would discover that they descended from Kshatriya or even Brahmin castes, and impose a caste order on their subjects to make them docile. Vaisyas and Sudras often resisted, according to Ghurye, but they were helpless against the alliance of Brahmins with illiterate Rajput kings who seldom challenged their ascendency.[213]

So the Brahmins won through magic, by alienating the magic of the whole people.[214] They developed such a monopoly that only they could pray.[215] Strict rules determined what rites each caste was entitled to: only the high-born castes could even *hear* the Vedas. Brahmin magic theosophy with its pseudo-profundity of mana monism overwhelmed all intellectual opposition. Brahmin theosophies took the place of higher ethical religions; and even when these began to appear (e.g., in Buddhism), mana-monist presuppositions undercut their ethical potential.[216]

A fit was established between the monist worldview and actual social fragmentation. Brahman-Atman ideas denied differences, denied separations, denied barriers, declared all was one, and so perpetuated and even justified actual separations and barriers. Magical theosophies with their false hope filled a religious vacuum created by the regression of a civilization to the stage of tribal fragmentation. In place of theology, of theism, of ethical religions, we have the mind-stunning litanies of one-ness. In place of priests: Brahmins; in place of sophists and philosophers: Brahmins; in place of teachers: Brahmins. Magicians as priests, philosophers and teachers ensured total saturation of the culture by mana theosophy. And this had the curious result that a caste of magicians, practicing magic and preaching magical theosophy, reinforced a *particularized religion* (i.e., *Arya Dharma*). Instead of protesting it, overthrowing it, magic reinforced it by patterning all protest into a perennial short-circuit of withdrawal, denial and acceptance. Part of it was the continued emphasis on selfhood, which is the obsessive preoccupation of tribalism and Hinduism, but in India it leads nowhere. The self that is cultivated in theosophy and Yoga, in gnosis and practice, is everted in paradigms of withdrawal and renunciation that divert revolt into resignation.

The futility of individual Hindu self strategies is matched by the collective futility of Hindu revolutions, which attempt to accomplish by magic what can only be accomplished by law, as Naipaul[217] puts it. Gandhi's revolution (like Buddhism) was too magical in its means to succeed, according to Naipaul; his nonviolence easily degenerated into the opposite of what he sought, into quietism, into the traditional ideal of self-realization, into karma, "the Hindu killer."[218] The magical nature of Gandhi's movement is more clearly seen in his follower, Vinobe Bhave, whose celebrated "walks" put mass pressure on landowners to give some land voluntarily to the poor—but served to set back true land reform. Bhave's real message was: obedience. Bhave and Gandhi both appeared to villagers as magicians; their Congress party was run by the landowners who were the centers of local power; Gandhi's revolution "masked the underlying violence of Indian life." As Dumont[219] reminds us, the center of power was the landowner (who often achieved domination by violence, warfare)—the Brahmin rationalizes this domination and freezes all around it. Hinduism is saturated with magic: in place of a social contract, magic; in place of revolutionary reform, magical movements. Magical ideas saturating religion and education deflect most revolts into non-productive directions[220] and so defend the social system against change.

Western Contrast. In the West, by contrast, social evolution had apparently gone too far for the political collapse to undo it completely. The empire fell, but the gentes had grown up. They had reconstituted themselves in the liberating urban process; they had stripped down from extended patriarchal sibs into the smaller bilateral families of the Middle Ages, with free, generalized exogamy, and social mobility was great—through the clergy, through force of arms, eventually through the armed, oath-sworn confederacies of merchant adventurers. And the spiritual movement that substituted for political unity was a centralized *church* rather than a caste of magicians. Constantine established it as the state religion a century and a half before Rome's collapse; it modeled itself bureaucratically on the empire, whose ghost it became, as Gibbon wrote. The church preserved Roman ideas of citizenship in the universal Christian commonwealth. Christianity was a congregational religion, with membership for priests and laity alike, and priests as servants of the community.

In the Middle Ages, with cities reduced to mere forts or ecclesiastical centers,[221] the perennial Aryan three-class system did return in the form of nobles, priests and serfs, but the magical barriers of caste were never raised and all were citizens in the universal congregation. The barons, moreover, held their own against the priests, and they managed to create in feudalism a rational system based on land tenure that had great logical consistency (cf. Maitland[222]). Also, the cities were never quite eliminated; in their ancient charter power,[223] their territorial basis and their concept of citizenship in the Holy Roman Empire,[224] the idea of an empire of universal citizenship persisted. The universal church, meanwhile, underwent a process of rationalization during which, if only briefly, it adopted Augustine's idea that the powers of the magician are illusions.

But most of the time the Church remained a reservoir of magic and all classes practiced it. Historians like Viktor Rydberg[225] remind us that the medieval Christian cosmos, taken over from Aristotle, Plato and the Alexandrians, is an approximation of the classic magical worldview. All energies and motions are directed by angels; everything on earth is guided by a particular angel under the influence of the stars, and above them, the Platonic archetypes. The church pours forth a never-ending stream of magical protections from cradle to grave. Masses are said for the crops; insect pests are excommunicated; scripture is used as verbal magic against enemies; monasteries are "magical fortresses" fighting demons and "occupying" the land.

3. The Renaissance Occult Revival As a Publishing Phenomenon

It is against this background of monopolized, controlled, partly rationalized official Christian magic that the occult revival of the Renaissance occurs. This second major occult upsurge in the Western world has many similarities to the one that stormed Graeco-Roman civilization, but also some differences: 1. Once again this is largely a publishing venture, with a determinate history: e.g., the recovery of classical texts after the fall of Constantinople, and especially the immediately influential translations of the Hermetic books by Ficino under the orders of Cosimo de Medici.[226] Maguses are men who, like John Dee, possessed large libraries. (His was one of the largest in England, according to Peter French.[227]) The Renaissance outburst, basically, consists in the gradual recovery of much of the cosmopolitan occult knowledge assembled during the Graeco-Roman period—Hellenic, Roman, Persian, Chaldean, Egyptian, Hebraic magics then syncretized into occult sciences. The only major addition is the considerable Jewish magic accumulated during the Middle Ages (and some Arabic magic): the far Orient does not open up as a source of cosmopolitan magic in an occult revival until after the age of exploration. 2. Trance, interpretation of dreams and similar psychological magic do not get even the mild emphasis they had in the ancient world much less the greater interest in the current occult revival; rather, the recovered magical texts are studied as *scientific* wisdom in an experimental attitude. 3. On the other hand, there is a frank appreciation in the Renaissance that all these studies *are* really a matter of magic. Despite the church's continuance of the Roman policy of proceeding against magic legally, so many prestigious writers in fact develop explicit theoretical defenses of *magic as a natural science* (e.g., Ficino, Pico, Campanella,[228] etc.) that at least one observer, Robert Leon-Wagner,[229] has noticed that the word magic begins to lose some of its negative valence and acquire some prestige in the early modern era. 4. In the ancient world magic in the form of occult sciences erupted into an excessively rationalized philosophical climate (Hellenistic philosophy) and overthrew it. The same thing happened in the Renaissance, as the magic from the ancient world overthrew the Aristotelian scientism of the late schools. (John Hermann Randall, Jr., has shown how close to the modern scientific and philosophical temperament the Averroist Aristotelians and the Occamites had come.[230]) 5. But there is a lively literature in history today (e.g., Frances Yates, D. P. Walker, Peter French) suggesting that in this particular case a dawning youthful age used the antiquarian occult sciences of an older, falling world not just to overcome a sterile rationalism but to develop the dynamic of the modern scientific movement that would go beyond philosophical rationalism. But *this* historical literature is in turn perhaps part of the twentieth century occult upsurge! The perennial antiquarian nature of magic bookishness is vividly illustrated in all this. Thus scholars like Frances Yates, operating out of the occult collections of the Warburg Institute in London, seek to prove that modern science was stimulated by the Renaissance occult revival.

Why did an occult revival take place at this time? There was a complex interplay between rationality, magic, religion and emerging science. Keith Thomas[231] has shown how the rationalizing drive of Christianity, its assault on magic during the high Middle Ages left a vacuum for magical revolt. In this the schoolmen played a part, yet as Lea has shown, they also rationalized in a magical direction: they propagated the new demonological theories that justified the witch persecutions. Hiram Hayden[232] and Wayne Shumaker[233] have depicted Renaissance magic as a revolt against the tedious excesses of scholastic rationalism. But Frances Yates has shown that when this development caused the Papacy to dabble in magic arts, this deviation was one of the factors touching off the anti-magical movement of Protestantism.[234] The Protestant victory in turn led to new extremes of anti-magic (some sectarians attacked even prayer as magic) but also to new forms of magic—"divinatory prayer," Protestant confidence magic, etc.

Four Occult Sciences

The magic theosophies and occult sciences so swamped the intelligentsia that common folk easily confused learning and magic. ("Thou art a scholar; speak to it, Horatio."[235]) Two theosophies and four occult sciences dominated the period. The theosophies were Neo-Platonism and Hermeticism, a Pagan gnosticism from Alexandria. The four occult sciences were astrology, cabala, *"magia"* and alchemy. But my classification is a bit arbitrary for there were overlaps: astrology worked like a theosophy as well as an occult science, helping create the overarching magic worldview. And Hermeticism merged with *magia* as a theory of magic. Let us consider the occult sciences first.

1. *Astrology,* never entirely absent form the Aristotelian-Ptolemaic cosmos taken over by Christianity, revived as an occult science early in the Renaissance, but counterattacks appeared at once. Early Christianity had attacked astrology as part of the rival ecumenical theology of all the non-Christian religions of the ancient world. And now once again, as Burckhardt[236] shows, after an initial fad swept Renaissance Italy, important figures spoke out against it. The first was Petrarch. Later, even Pico, an influential propagandist for "natural magic," exposed astrology for its bad logic and worse physics, and for its empirical inaccuracies. However, D. P. Walker[237] has shown that Pico had reservations: there was a "good astrology" and a bad astrology just as there was good and bad magic. The good astrology was free of demons and somehow did not undermine God's freedom of action or man's free will. (Walker, incidentally, is another who has labored in the Warburg Institute collection, whose founder insisted that occult works and philosophical treatises be shelved together, according to Peter Gay.[238]) Wayne Shumaker[239] speculates that perhaps Pico attacked astrology because Bellanti of Siena took his horoscope and predicted his early death: it made him vomit. And he did die at 33. (Was this a kind of voodoo death from suggestion?) Though weakened as an occult science by such early attacks, astrology remained part of the sacred canopy due to the ascendency of Neo-Platonism and Hermeticism, part of the worldview of most intellectuals right up until the Newtonian synthesis, according to Keith Thomas.[240] It was implicit in the magic correspondences of Hermeticism's "as above, so below" and in Platonism's "great chain of being."[241]

2. *Alchemy* did not so much revive in the Renaissance as quicken its progress. It had been active during the Middle Ages. Now it was stimulated by the ideas of Renaissance "magia"; so the spiritual alchemists expanded their symbolism and the "charcoal burners" furthered the experiments that led to modern chemistry. This progress began to be felt in the later Renaissance; Frances Yates[242] reports that it became an influential part of general intellectual culture toward the end of the 16th century. Revival of alchemical correspondences (alchemy was a magical classification system as well as an experimental science[243]) enhanced the prestige of astrology.

3. *Cabala.* With astrology immediately attacked, and the influence of alchemical progress coming later, the two occult sciences that were most decisive in the early Renaissance were magia and Cabala (Kabbala). Both were associated with the new interest in Hermeticism. The association of Cabala with Hermeticism was congenial, for Cabala had begun in the same intellectual environment, especially in Alexandria among Jewish writers influenced by Neo-Pythagorean-

ism. Seligmann reports it was later developed further in Babylon.[244] Cabala is several things: 1. A Neo-Pythagorean worldview, with numbers shaping the cosmos, but also astrological and Aristotelian elements. 2. A number magic and numerology, used to predict the future, etc., based on the fact that the Jewish language used its letters for numbers, so all words have some "numerical weight." 3. An emphasis on Iranian angelology: troops of angels run the seven heavens taken over from Aristotle and numerological classification techniques are worked on them.[245] After Renaissance scholars discovered that ancient magical lore could be recovered in the Greek language, they next learned Hebrew to gain access to Cabala and Jewish magic.[246] Pico pioneered this influence and associated the study of Cabala with the recovered Hermetic books. As guest peoples outside the Christian law, Jewish communities had preserved much Hellenistic magic; typically, as Trachtenberg has shown, Jewish magic in practice was theurgic, devotional.[247] But Cabala's angelology had a demonic potential, and its Neo-Pythagorean number mysticism had a scientific potential. Later maguses would use angel magic to command demons,[248] while Yates claims that number magic led to the mathematicalization of modern science.[249] Due to the connection with Cabala, mathematics was suspect in the English Renaissance; Peter French[250] has shown how Bacon and Dee kept quiet about their knowledge of it, and mathematics was no longer taught at Oxford.

4. *Magia.* The most prominent occult science of the Renaissance was called simply *magia,* or *magia naturalis.*[251] We do not think of plain "magic" as an occult science any more, though Roszak[252] so lists it as part of the "Aquarian frontier" today. *Magia* in the Renaissance referred to a particular body of ideas which constituted a kind of meta-science of magic, at once an explanation of it and a program for its development which aimed at opening the natural world to human exploitation. Garin[253] characterizes it as practical activity exploiting nature through hypotheses derived from magical ideas of nature's unity. *Magia* as such was more open to empirical modification than astrology, Cabala or even the spiritual kind of alchemy, which all tended to freeze back into primitive classification systems. *Magia* was both theory and the practice, both a collection of experimental enterprises (some of which became sciences) and a general theory of how these activities worked. Ficino and Pico thought they were writing general theories of magic just like Hubert and Mauss; the difference was they believed such theories would show man how to exploit the magic correspondences in nature; they did not recognize that magic was a symbol system derived from projections of society. Campanella, Bacon and the others hoped to reduce magic to science[254] and the combination of experimental *magia* with numerological Cabala prefigured and stimulated the combination of empirical science with mathematics, according to Yates. Bronowski[255] similarly suggests that modern science as an irreversible cultural process was begun by Renaissance *magia* or natural magic. Both science and *magia* are integrated, active world pictures; *magia* served as a proto-ideal that led to science. Bronowski

thus asserts of early Renaissance *magia* what Rossi[256] sees in the later Baconian program—it is a new thrust emerging from magic which becomes collective, public and social, rather than elitist and secret, allies itself with the mechanical arts, and seeks to learn and cooperate with nature's laws instead of forcing nature, as older, vainer esoteric magics attempted.

The impulse for the theoretical side of *magia* was provided by the recovered Hermetic books, which were themselves, like all theosophies, attempts to write general theories of magic and of the magical universe, and which in rationalizing the occult sciences actually invented new magics. Magic always advances by means of theories of itself, just like mathematics. (David Hawkins[257] writes that: mathematical truth is analytic, but it is analytic of conditions implicit in the expansion of mathematics itself—so mathematics expands.) From the first "generalization of mana," through the rationalization of divination systems into occult sciences, to the grand syntheses of all these sciences in the theosophies, theories about magic provide new formulae for magical actions. From the Hermetic generalizations ("as above, so below") came ideas of influencing one phenomenon by manipulating another, etc. The theoretical part of *magia* consisted of: 1. general propositions about how magic worked—through nature's unity, through Hermetic correspondences; 2. classifications of the different kinds of magic with programs for their development. Thus Ficino and Pico wrote influential classifications of magic adopted by many later maguses: 1. "Natural magic," related to the natural qualities or "virtues" of things and substances. 2. "Celestial magic," related to astronomy and astrology (but also, on its darker side, to angels and demons.) 3. Divine magic, preferably theurgic but potentially manipulatory like the ambitious magic of the ancient Egyptians who sought to command the gods. Intersecting this classification was the distinction of good vs. bad magic. In general good magic worked via natural causes, while bad magic worked by manipulating angels. The danger with angels was demons, or the demonic use of angels. Natural magic as propounded in the Renaissance was a dawning of empirical science; but natural magic was constantly tempted by angel magic, a regression to magic as sacred rite, working on primitive social classification systems instead of on nature. As Renaissance maguses became more daring, they practiced angel magic more openly—Trithemius, Agrippa, Paracelsus, Campanella—which contributed to the scandal of magic and the Protestant revolt against a Church establishment that dabbled in it. With the classifications went also programs and ideologies. The general view, as Garin[258] puts it, was of man as having no particular nature, an unfinished animal, between god and devil, order and chaos, the conditioned and the contingent. This has been the cant of magic humanism ever since. The new Warburg library researchers trace how it merged into the Baconian program for modern science. Before discussing this later transition, I want to mention the romance of the Hermetic books which stimulated both *magia* and Cabala and their cooperation in ways that prefigured mathematicalized experimental science.

The Hermetic Books

In the Renaissance many books were junked. The scholastic treatises were bypassed; hundreds of volumes of alchemy were superseded by newer researches. But history was made mainly by the *recovery* of lost Graeco-Roman books and no incident was more dramatic or strategic than the recovery of the Hermetic books. They were probably written in the third century A.D., perhaps in Alexandria, and though cast in a pseudo-Egyptian form were clearly Greek.[259] There was a large literature written around the figure of "Hermes Trismegistus," or the thrice-praised Hermes, who was identified with the Egyptian god Thoth yet was also conceived of as an historical character. Alexandrine Euhemerist thought was comfortable with the idea of a magician scientist who had become a god after his death, and the Greeks further identified him with Hermes, their own god of magic and heralds. Ambitious, god-commanding Egyptian magic[260] had prestige. The Hermetic books collected this magic, but also the magic of Persian magi, Chaldean astrology, Indian gymnosophists, Greek mysteries with typical late Hellenic eclecticism, and several collections attempted to generalize this into a theosophy. This amalgam apparently was influenced by Neo-Platonism, Gnosticism and Neo-Pythagoreanism; the latter was probably decisive. Hermeticism is a kind of pagan Gnostic theosophy, with a Neo-Pythagorean flavor. To the Renaissance it bequeathed what William Irwin Thompson[261] called "Pythagorean science," what Joseph Needham[262] called "the Taoist mentality," a mystical but ambitious approach to natural science. It also contributed what we think of as the Leonardo view of man; the Asclepius begins: "Man is a great miracle, worthy of honor and veneration."[263] Early church fathers had been impressed by this viewpoint, though Augustine attacked the Hermetic defense of magic.[264]

The theosophical Hermetic books came in two collections: 1. The *Asclepius,* which purported to be an account of ancient Egyptian magic, telling how the Egyptians could draw down the power of the cosmos and the gods into their statues. 2. The *Corpus Hermeticum,* 15 dialogues in Upanishad style between master and pupil, beginning with the *Pimander* which, like *Genesis,* tells of the creation of the world.

Now the dialogues were romantically dated in the distant past; though written in the third century of the Christian era, they were supposed to take place several millennia earlier, when Thoth was alive on earth. They owe their curious influence in the Renaissance in part to the fact that Ficino, their translator and editor, took this romantic dating literally, and made an opera out of it. This is curious, for the early Christian fathers had known the works; and as Garin points out, they were not unknown in the Middle Ages.[265] Some parts were available; there were also rumors and perhaps a subterranean cult. Then, in about 1460, manuscripts of 14 of the 15 dialogues came, from Macedonia and the dying Byzantine empire, into the hands of Cosimo de Medici. He ordered Ficino to put aside his translation of Plato and translate these first. In his preface Ficino broadcast the legend of the *"prisci theologi,"* the ancient sages who had anti-

cipated Christian wisdom. Because he accepted the romantic dating of the dialogues at several millennia B.C., he could portray them as remarkable anticipations of Greek and Christian scientific and spiritual wisdom. In citing Orpheus,
Zoroaster, Plato and Moses among the ancient sages, he was simply repeating
popular traditions of the Middle Ages. For over a hundred years European scholars believed in the prehistoric origins of these revelations. One of the perennial
ideas in magic thought is the theme of ancient wisdom; gnosis is not so much
discovered as rediscovered. The error about dating contributed to the prestige
of the great programs of natural magic which Pico, Ficino and later maguses
built on the recovered Hermetic books. Hermetic mysticism was interpreted
in a Neo-Pythagorean spirit that set the tone for an ambitious positive, optimistic kind of magic. Renaissance magic was not the defensive magic of trance, possession, withdrawal or protection of self. It was world-conquering magic
transforming itself into marvels of technology and science.

Transition to Science

Finding occult origins for modern science is itself a kind of occult "new
science" today. Some of its practitioners date the true start of modern science
out of magic to a later stage in the Renaissance, what Yates calls the "Rosicrucian Enlightenment"[266] and what Haydn[267] calls the "Counter-Renaissance."
This was a period at the start of the Reformation when newer syntheses of
occult sciences attacked not just medieval scholasticism but also the increasingly arid new humanistic studies of the early Renaissance. In England,
according to Peter French,[268] where mathematics was no longer taught at
Oxford and a didactic humanism prevailed, maguses attempted to restore England's late medieval heritage of Platonic science (the Cambridge Platonists,
optics, Roger Bacon) Frances Yates[269] notes the important role that mathematics
and the newer alchemical studies played in the new occult syntheses, also
the great emphasis on mechanical marvels. In the Elizabethan era, maguses
like John Dee and Robert Fludd had great influence at court, and Yates
claims that the travelling English players' companies, including Shakespeare's,
subtly propagandized for the new worldview of magical science[270] (e.g., the
"magical atmosphere" of Shakespeare's plays[271]). The emphasis on magical
technology on the one hand (the marvelous machines, fountains and devices
of John Dee, Robert Fludd, Inigo Jones, used in palaces, theaters, etc.) and on
Hermetic mysticism about mathematics on the other hand, prefigured the alliance of mathematics and empirical observation aimed at practical results in
modern science. The uproar over the anonymous publication of the "Rosicrucian manifestos" in Germany (which Yates portrays as propaganda for the Anglo-
Palatinate mystical liberal Protestant movement toward German reunification
that touched off the Thirty Years War) is shown to have elicited numerous other
manifestos announcing programs for the launching of modern science: e.g.,
Francis Bacon's. Descartes and Leibnitz were affected by the movement. This
was also the background of Newton's occult interests. The movement's leader,

John Dee, applied *magia* to mathematics, expounding that there were three worlds of numbers like the three worlds of magic: 1. A physical world of applied mathematics; 2. a celestial world of abstract mathematical laws; 3. a divine world of mathematical essences. He proposed that science concentrate on the middle mathematics of abstract laws and ally it with mechanical technology. His program and Bacon's program, both derived from the new occult synthesis, led to the Newtonian revolution and to modern science, Yates claims.

Magic and Science: Help or Hindrance to Each Other?

The works of Frances Yates, Peter French, D. P. Walker, J. Bronowski, Paolo Rossi, Wayne Shumaker, Hiram Hayden, etc., in building on earlier accounts of Renaissance magic (e.g., Burckhardt) to show a relationship to modern science, in effect constitute a new hypothesis about the relation of magic to science (i.e., M . . . S, or magic leads to science). As such they must be put next to the other theories and tested as thoroughly by empirical research before a definite evaluation can be made. Weber's hypothesis[272] about the stimulation which the "worldly asceticism" of Protestantism gave to capitalism (and thereby to science) (R . . . S) and the rival theories (such as Sombart[273] on the growth of a capitalist class *independent* of religion, or Von Martin[274] on the contribution of increasing Catholic rationalism to that class) have led to extremely thorough empirical studies.[275] The technological progress that preceded and underlay the growth of modern science has also been painstakingly studied by scholars like Lynn White,[276] Lefèbre des Noëttes,[277] William Carroll Bark,[278] who demonstrate that even the so-called Dark Ages was a period of striking technological innovation. (It included the stirrup from China that underlay the cavalry basis of feudalism for Brunner, the horse collar that revolutionized agricultural transport and market for des Noëttes, the heavy iron plough that underlay the manorial system for White, the rudder and compass that stimulated the age of exploration for Mattingly.[279]) Merton's[280] attempt to synthesize studies of technological advance with Weberian accounts of facilitating Protestant attitudes helped create a new branch of sociology, the sociology of science and technology, pursued by scholars like Bernard Barber,[281] Ian G. Barbour,[282] Leo Marx,[283] etc.

The bold hypothesis of dM . . . dS (increments of magic stimulate increments of science) of the new Renaissance scholars has had *nothing like this degree of testing*. Nor has the new reverse theory that *science* can stimulate magic (as in the current occult upsurge). Pauwels and Bergier[284] suggest that the recent overturning of old scientific worldviews has unleashed a sense of magical possibility. In Thomas Kuhn's[285] sense, perhaps any "paradigm revolution" causes flux in the categories that underlie the objective frame of the paramount reality. According to Pauwels and Bergier, the nineteenth century positivistic synthesis was especially flat, anti-magical and physicalist, while the wonders of twentieth century physics strongly suggested a universe closer to the classical magical worldview. Certainly the universe of Mach and of Einstein's general theory of relativity (in which, for example, as Sciama[286] has shown, my weight is determined by the mass of all the stars in the universe; and the sky is dark at night, as Olbers[287] has shown, because the universe expands) strongly resembles the perennial magical worldview of the universe as an interconnected unity of forces. Relativity, time reversal, black holes threaten the objective framework, and meanwhile, as Arthur Clarke[288] has said, new technology constantly appears which is virtually indistinguishable from magic. But the hypothesis of dS ... dM is also too new for adequate confirmation to have provided a basis for evaluation.

It might be useful at this point, however, to admit that there are a number of different possible interconnections between magic and science in sociological theory, which provide a logic of possibility for further investigations. It may be that there is no determinate or even predominate relation between magic and science; they do appear to react on each other but all possible permutations and combinations may be found in history. Thus: 1. *Magic may depress science.* M. Cary,[289] for example, summarizing his account of the stagnation of Greek science, dismisses several other explanations and attributes it at last to the rise of interest in magic and astrology caused by the Hellenistic failure of nerve. This is the position of Max Weber: magic impedes science by blocking rational structures of consciousness. 2. *Magic may stimulate science:* The Renaissance studies of Frances Yates, Peter French, D. P. Walker, etc., point in this new direction. 3. Conversely, *science may stimulate magic:* Pauwels, Roszak and other Aquarians today suggest that rapid scientific advance opens vistas of magical possibility. 4. Alternatively, *scientific advance may discourage magic.* Keith Thomas and George Lyman Kittredge show how the modern scientific outlook emerging in the seventeenth century weakened magic by destroying the overarching worldview of Neo-Platonism and astrology that made it possible.

The older theories are better documented, but the newer researches which evidence the opposites are by so much offsets to these proofs. My own feeling is that no determinate relationship between magic and science has yet been established. Not only can magic both stimulate or depress science, and science both stimulate or depress magic, but all four trends are often present at once, though with different weights. For the interrelation between magic and science is not as intimate as that between religion and magic, which is one reason why I have concentrated on the latter in this study. Magic and religion are complicated enough in their dialectic, but they are each other's lifeblood; their interaction is intimate and it is possible to generalize about it. Whereas science and magic are *two different systems* that have sometimes interacted in history. In general, magic is a system of social symbols borrowed from religion; it is used on religion and on selves—and also, to some degree, on the natural world. There is frequently a sequence from religion to magic to science (rather than from magic to religion to science as Frazer thought); representations of society forged in religion (ideas of order like *Ma'at, Rta, Moira*) are projected on to the natural world in religion and magic does to some degree try to manipulate the natural world by working with these social symbols. But that is far from being the origin of science, which grows out of rational-purposive action, out of work. Magic, as Hubert and Mauss put it, leads to the development of some *technologies* that interact with science (pharmacology, alchemy, etc.) And certain *religious* ideas (above all "the categories") ally themselves with empirical praxis in the beginnings of science. But mostly magic is a system of religious symbols. Very often, as in our own time, it tries to seem like science, but its reference is social and its effect is psychological.

Magic and science are different systems which are similar in some ways and sometimes interact. Both are largely recent (i.e., historical), useful knowledge that is preserved as a planetary heritage. Both are collective representations which are augmented by individual action upon them (e.g., experiments.) In recent centuries science advances faster and discards more, but both make progress, both empirically and in rationalization. Both borrow from each other and from time to time are stimulated or retarded by each other. But it is probably safe to say that these effects in many periods are slight, even when provable. The Renaissance was perhaps a great exception. Hermetic propaganda apparently heartened nascent Renaissance science, but even so it seems likely that in its absence the age would have found some other vocabulary to express its restless curiosity. Conversely, I think it a bit doubtful that the magical content of a culture would be an absolute bar to science—though the social structure which projects this culture might be. And often, the so-called "magical" bars to progress are posed by religion, which is more collective and sometimes conservative. As for the idea that a certain kind of religion is necessary to bring forth science, this may be a Western conceit. There was never any absence of fundamental scientific discovery or invention in India or in China. In some disciplines they ran at most a few centuries behind the West, and in others they were ahead. The endless musing of Western philosphy on why we were so wonderful as to develop science while lesser breeds failed to do so is really rather rank. In some cases we might better ask: what were the social structural differences in the West that enabled it to destroy superior scientific cultures in war and put an end to their progress? That is extreme, but we need a respite from our own ethnocentrism.

What enabled science to advance, what held it back, is more likely to be found in social structures than in ideas, for science is a complicated social system. Rostow[290] has shown, for example, how development of science depends on a cluster of interlinked "social propensities"; Merton[291] has demonstrated how this configuration worked in modern England. It is not just innovations, but the propensity to accept innovations, a market to distribute them and so on that count. All these in the end link down to social structures. And even when ideas are important, these are related to social structures. Needham,[292] for example, links the lack of Chinese ideas of "scientific law" to the ruination of the legalist school which interrupted positive law and to the lack of a logical theology. Fung Yu-Lang,[293] Granet and Needham have shown that what the

Chinese found newest in Western philosophy, what they most lacked, was a logic that tied itself down to the principle of contradiction. But I think Aristotelian logic, however true it may be, can be shown to have derived from the public process of political debate in free and self-constituting Greek city states, i.e., from *polemos,* as Heidegger wrote. In short, it came from the social structure which made such ideas possible in one civilization, less so in another.

Millennial Movements

Hermeticism was a gnosticism; so was the Manicheism of modern heresies. Their revival had consequences not just for science and religion; they also renewed the propensity toward millennial political expression with which Christian culture had begun. Ronald Knox[294] writes of the great movements of "enthusiastic" religion, his wide term including both those with gnostic roots and those going back to early Christian sects practicing extreme simplicity or rigorism, such as Montanism and Donatism. Norman Cohn[295] traces them to the Christian and gnostic Apocrypha. Both Knox and Cohn give insufficient attention to the degree to which orthodox Christianity itself was gnostic. In Cohn there is an interesting picture of how Messiah figures and millennial ages in these prophecies are both split into double forms as myths elaborate.[296] At work, perhaps, is a dialectic of magic and religion. It even finds its way into modern philosophies of history: what is the "universal state" that caps each civilization in Spengler[297] or Toynbee[298] but the Joachimite "Empire of the Last Days," before the fall? Nelson has shown how millennial thinking saturates Western political philosophy.[299] Hobsbawn[300] and Engels[301] have shown how the first modern revolutionary movements began as quasi-gnostic sects. Voegelin[302] finds gnostic millenarianism even in liberalism and Protestantism. Western culture has not outlived its magic origins in a gnostic religion.

4. The Modern Occult Upsurge: 19th and 20th Centuries

The 19th century occult revival which continues today was stimulated in part by the classic theosophies revived in the Renaissance: Mesmer, Blake and Swedenborg had all dipped into Hermetic and Neo-Platonic literature. But the theosophies' influence never quite recovered from the loss of prestige suffered after the 17th century victory of the Newtonian worldview. The attempt at revival through mathematical mysticism at the end of the nineteenth century was partly neutralized by the *Principia Mathematica* and Wittgenstein. Meanwhile, as planetary civilization increasingly gave access to alternative cultures, *oriental* theosophies came to play in the 20th century revival the role that Neo-Platonism and Hermetic gnosticism played in the Renaissance: The Hindu monisms in particular are so irrational that they are not repelled by rational discourse—they are like attack planes that fly *under* radar nets. The example of the early success of main-line Hindu theosophy in the U.S.—Vivekananda's import of the Arya Samaj rationalization of the Upanishadic tradition into the U.S. in the nineteenth century,[303] the prestige here of Vedanta and the Upanishads in the first half of the twentieth century—has been followed by the importation of Tantric, Mahayana and mechanical Buddhisms and still more irrational theosophies once the lesson was learned about the relative invulnerability of cults that refuse to engage in the language game of logical discourse.

The present occult revival has been going on since the nineteenth century, with peaks in the magnetism-spiritualism-ESP sequence already mentioned, and localized upsurges in late Czarist Russia, Nazi Germany, the Soviet Union and the United States today. But those commotions have never overcome the positivist worldpicture; they have remained peripheral, and "occult" has continued to have the connotation of secret, condemned or unorthodox knowledge. On the other hand, there were often occult motives *behind* movements of ideas that *did* translate themselves into the objective framework—for example, the occultisms involved in recreating dormant nationalism. Irish, Polish, Provençal, Breton and Norman nationalisms were often allied with occult interests in such figures as Yeats, Wronski, etc.[304] (The Serbian nationalist secret society to which Gavrilo Prinzip belonged was occultist.) There were also some occultist roots for Utopian socialism (Fourier dabbled in the Hermetic literature, Robert Owen in spiritualism, and Thomas Davidson,[305] one of the founders of the Fabian Society, in Platonism). Also pronounced was the interest which French Catholic and Russian Orthodox reaction took in the occult, as shown by Webb,[306] Huysmans,[307] etc. Even Lourdes had its political, anti-Republican side according to Webb.[308]

And if a mechanist, physicalist, positivist worldview dominated 19th century society, there was great ennui in it (as Steiner has shown[309]), and a Stendhalian hunger of the imagination for violence and irrationality. This imagination was fed by a romantic literature that often contained occult elements, as shown by Irving Babbitt,[310] Graña,[311] Mario Praz,[312] and so many others; Edmund Wilson[313] has demonstrated that in the symbolist culmination romanticism became frankly occult. The cult of the artist in Chatterton,[314] Mallarmé, Jarry,[315] de Lisle-Adam, recalls the occult self of shamanism, the mystery religions and the alchemists (who also referred to themselves as "the artist"). There were occult as well as anti-Semitic elements in the German *Völkisch* movement as George Mosse[316] has shown; the two often went together, with occultism showing up in the French anti-Dreyfusard movement just as ancient gnosticism had often been anti-Semitic. (Hannah Arendt[317] has shown that the revival of anti-Semitism in the nineteenth century was partly due to the identification of the Jews with the rational modern state which gave them citizenship and employment and which was often an enemy of quasi-occult micro-nationalisms). Steiner sees these occultist strains renewed by the debris of a dying Christianity and thinks that they culminated in the Nazi concentration camps:

> It is to the ambiguous afterlife of religious feeling . . . that we must look, to the malignant energies released by the decay of natural religious forms. . . . *L'universe concentrationnaire* has no true counterpart in the secular mode. Its analogue is Hell. The camp embodies, often

down to minutiae, the images and chronicles of Hell in European art and thought . . . To have neither Heaven nor Hell is to be intolerably deprived and left alone in a world gone flat. Of the two, Hell proved the easier to recreate . . . The structures of decay are toxic. [318]

Occult theories also lay hidden in academic philosophies and even lodged in sciences. Meyer Abrams[319] has traced much of German romantic philosophy to Neo-Platonic and Hermetic roots. Scientific paradigms, themselves idealist constructions using categories derived originally from the sacred, sometimes seemed to emit metaphysical messages. Logic and mathematics are notorious reservoirs of infection, and their "messages" sometimes set intellectuals to reading the Hermetic tradition again.

It is also hard to escape the impression that while the occult in the ancient world was associated with "a failure of nerve," but in the Renaissance with scientific adventure, in our more mixed time it is associated with psychological exploration but also with cultural reaction. The right-wing political preferences of certain mystically-inclined 20th century physicists are perhaps significant. Occult revivals do not start in cosmopolitan civilizations because miracles just "happen." Paranormal experiences abound at all times; what is needed are categories and acceptable philosophical-scientific draftings to get them past "the rules committee." These are usually provided by a movement in philosophical thought. An advance in science that shatters old paradigms, or an economic movement of society that upsets old social certainties often provokes reaction in the form of "new" philosophical statements which actually draw on the old theosophical traditions. From their syntheses may emerge conceptualizations that make it possible to take notice of the irrational or the paranormal again. H. Stuart Hughes[320] has shown the relation of the "Southwest Germans" Rickert and Weber and their decisionist, idealist theories to theology in a time of challenging social change. Modern philosophical movements of a relativizing nature seem to open gaps in the positivist worldview that may readmit the possibility of miracles. Thus the so-called "philosophy of science" and the "sociology of knowledge" seem to offer superposing overviews of scientific wisdom, but they can lead to "a rumor of angels."[321]

Goethe's renewal in the 19th century of the Renaissance Faust myth (*"Faustus,"* or "favored one," was apparently an epithet applied to Simon Magus) helped to inspire the influential Faustian psychologies of Nietzsche and Freud. Freud found it necessary to employ magical myths to create conceptual language capable of recovering primitive psychological wisdom.[322] But the paranormal phenomena which fascinated Freud led one whole wing of his movement back to Hermetic theosophy and alchemy: Jung's archetypes represent a modern renewal of the spiritual-symbolic side of alchemy. By and large, however, the objective frame withstood these onslaughts.

In the twentieth century occultist movements did sometimes attain or were allied with political power. It has long been known that there were occult elements in Nazism (e.g., Von Eckhardt, the SS race mythology, Himmler's occult researches).[323] In recent years many popular books, which are themselves part of the occult revival,[324] have perhaps exaggerated in suggesting that these elements were central to the Nazi movement. Anyway, the military destruction of Czarist Russian[325] and Nazi regimes ended these experiments.

Occult America. This country, to a degree that is little recognized, has provided a fertile soil for magic movements—so much so that the United States has been a net exporter of mysticism for the last one hundred years. Missionaries of "enthusiastic" U.S. Protestant sects, spiritualism, Pentacostalism, Mormonism and other positive items in our spiritual balance of trade have attained such a volume that American-derived "churches" are part of the magical zoo of many Asian, Latin American and African primitive societies.[326] We have even exported to India:[327] e.g., the Theosophical Society was derived from U.S. spiritualism and helped reawaken classical Hindu theosophies. Nonetheless the American "civic religion" (Bellah[328]) has been virtually untouched by all these movements; American philosophy has remained predominantly rational (pragmatist, classical realist, positivist, analytical), and public discourse between leaders and masses has continued to operate in the objective frame. Herberg[329] has shown that the major religions became something almost secular here, instruments of assimilation, and later the three secularized "religious establishments" that are an unofficial part of the political system. Berger has shown that the church membership boom of the fifties partly expressed this assimilation to the rationally constituted political society,[330] for which President Eisenhower's famous, oft-quoted prescription is the clearest charter:

> Our government makes no sense unless it is founded in a deeply felt religious faith—and I don't care what it is.[331]

The failure of previous occult commotions to effect permanent changes in the social frame should be considered in evaluating the present-day outburst. Another reason for discounting its long-term expectations is its rather adventitious roots. Basically, the present occult revival is an interaction between a youth movement and the publishing industry. Briefly, what happened is this: Mobilized to mass action by the sit-ins, the Vietnam war protests and the "modeling"[332] effect such behavior had via lavish media attention, American college youth enjoyed a series of dramatic "summers" similar to the great *journées* of the French Revolution. There was the "Mississippi summer" when the civil rights movement peaked in 1964, hundreds of college students went south and thousands more identified with them. There was the 1967 "summer of love" when the rival, more apolitical counter-culture drew attention away from the New Left to a new modeling of shaman-like protest behavior in the East Village and in Haight-Ashbury. When the diggers (leaders of the latter community) announced that "love is dead" (complete with televised funeral), they told the Hippies to "gather into tribes and disperse," forming communes.[333] And so they did, though few noticed at the time, for the political tide of interest was rising again. 1968 was supposed to be the political summer, with New Left students again active, manning the Kennedy and McCarthy primary campaigns —but meanwhile the communes were growing, sending out seed pods from their origin in the California hills to other states. 1969 was called "the summer of the communes."[334] The press piously hoped that 1970 would be another political summer when "young people would rechannel their dissent into the political process" by getting out the vote for the fall's midterm election. But fewer turned out than were predicted, and meanwhile, more and more slipped off to the communes. 1971 was supposed to be the "summer of the farms," a constructive compromise of ecology and counter-culture movements similar to 1942 when students went to work pitching hay to help the war effort. But this time mystic ideas and new lifestyles predominated and many young people did not come back from their summer; they joined the communes. By December 1970, *Time* was estimating that there were about 3,000 communes (vs. only a few hundred intentional communities of all kinds in 1965.)

Counting young people who trooped through on weekends, perhaps only a hundred thousand or so have ever even been to a commune, but for millions of others in the early seventies these movements modeled new behavior. A Yankelovich study in 1972[335] showed 36 percent of college students were interested in joining communes; it also showed radical attitudes rising at a time of apparent political inaction among young people. Yankelovich speculated that the New Left, discouraged by the political process, had joined the counter-culture, and colored it.

The new communes differed radically from the nineteenth-century experimental communities. 1. There were many more of them, thousands vs. at most a few hundred in the nineteenth century; and they provide vicarious experience via the media for millions of others, as Brook Farm never did. 2. Nineteenth-century communes were larger, better organized and better capitalized; they were run by adults who brought to them their whole, intact families; they were political *communities.* The 1970's communes were small, undercapitalized, often populated by single young people; they resembled large *families.* 3. The nineteenth-century communes were political experiments promoting liberal or socialist changes; the new communes sought instead to change micro-institutions, above all the family and the constitution of the self.

In the close, small-group interaction of the communes, sometimes with help of drugs, magical experience was renewed. It was virtually inevitable that occult phenomena would emerge from these intense, seance-like groups. Some communes turned occultist by plan; others by evolution and small-group interaction. (Slater has demonstrated how even an "encounter group" can project a kind of religion, like the Durkheimian religion that emerged among a group of shipwrecked English boys in William Goldings's novel *The Lord of the Flies;* however, Slater's own researches are somewhat suspect since he "seeded the mine" by assigning Golding's book to his experimental classes.[336]) Other small-group movements produced magic phenomena: group therapies and "sensitivity training" groups. Many of these were products of academic psychology, such as Perls' gestalt psychology therapy and Kurt Lewin's small-group studies. These experiments helped restore the ancient money-making element so important to magic, by providing an academically-legitimized financial framework. But even the million or so couples who allegedly engage in "swinging" are reported frequently to get involved in occult experiments, perhaps as a result of no more mysterious a process than *folie à deux* (or *à quatre*).

The interest of fad-setting young people and academics in the occult provided a ready-made initial market for the publishing industry and a source of legitimizing reviews. Once again, as in past occult revivals, antiquarian libraries were searched and old titles translated and reset. Because planetary culture had brought Asia nearer than in the Renaissance, while anthropology had translated the religions and magics of primitive cultures, the 1970's publishing explosion was far richer than any previous in human history. Every book influential in the Renaissance was a potential paperback; and so were oral or secret traditions from remote Tibet, sent westward by the Chinese invasion. Thousands of gurus have followed in the footsteps of Vivekananda; Transcendental Meditation is taught in suburban high schools and the millions in proceeds are untaxed. Meanwhile the continued difficulties of the American political and economic processes and bad memories of Vietnam continue to weaken the competing prestige of the rational, positivist tradition.

Will the present commotion continue, will it have lasting effects? In view of the dissipation of previous occult revivals in America, it is easy to doubt this, but there are reasons for not sharing the complacency of students like Truzzi. To Truzzi, all this is merely history repeating itself as comedy. His conclusion: This is not a search for new spiritual meaning but a final expression of disenchantment with religious orthodoxy. It *plays* with the occult, and so abreacts it.

But magic is always in some measure a game of "acting as if;" even the magician is skeptical. And students like Adorno have shown that even playing at astrological concerns can cause some personality change.

Theodore Adorno's papers on the occult,[337] written long before the present revival, were part of his studies of the "culture industry." Aside from his Marxist conceptions about occult interests as a symptom of regression in the face of social helplessness, and magic as a projection of "commodity fetishism," and the occult as alienation in a proto-fascist oppressive social world, Adorno also observes, in a more down-to-earth manner, that occult wisdom is "the metaphysics of the dopes." "The dull naturalist content of the supernatural message gives away its untruth . . . They provide feeblemindedness with a Weltanschauung."[338] His main point is that, like any astral religion, astrology (even when only half-believed) teaches resignation and conformity. Occult science today is a parody of official materialism, of scientific reification, which is the contemporary official "religion." In his content analysis of the post-war Los Angeles *Times* astrology column[339] he notes that readers only half believe it, do not take it seriously—yet they do magically follow it. Readers think they are totally skeptical, but unconsciously they align their behavior with the predictions or interpret it *post hoc* in light of them. Such columns, moreover, help induct many readers into a more serious involvement with astrology; some subscribe to the technical magazines and learn the system. No doubt the columns are often used as oracles. The Los Angeles *Times* columnist, like many diviners, is purposely vague to reduce risks of falsification, Adorno writes. He also keeps promising "narcissistic" satisfactions and indirectly threatening anxiety. His advice is basically conformist. The depersonalized, merciless, abstract latent threat of the astral system of course reflects the abstract, anonymous, overdetermined, "fatalistic," impersonal social order. Perhaps the basic message—obey the rules, trust the stars, the social system is solid and will protect you and you will be happy—is needed by alienated, potentially unruly people. Perhaps also its magic helps weak egos to act by helping them make decisions. But if they act with its help they must surely decline in insight and become more dependent and Macawberish. Irrational intuition is praised as against thinking things out; abilities are treated as magical assets (e.g., "charm"). There is the constant appeal to "anal regression" (the notion that weak, uneducated people with miserable assets can somehow triumph by *rearranging* them—e.g., "first make a list"). Luck is emphasized, as is the helpful agency of "mysterious strangers" or "powerful friends" (usually higher-ups with whom one is thus taught "identification with the aggressor"). Astrology provides even those who merely play at it with a thorough training in magical thinking, just as gambling cultivates the addiction to magical hope.

Astrology was the ecumenical worldview of all the Hellenistic magics; it functioned like a major theosophy in the overarching sacred canopy of Renaissance magic; so perhaps it is significant that it plays so big a role in today's upsurge. Astrology is apparently the core of the current occult revival. According to Truzzi 68 percent of occult books published in 1969 were on astrology and he estimates the existence of 175,000 part-time astrologers in the United States.

The classical gnostic and Neo-Platonic theosophies are only wanly revived today, but there are additional sources of magical worldview; above all theosophical versions of contemporary scientism (e.g., "Scientology") and the imported oriental theosophies. Today Tantrism[340] perhaps bids to take the place that Hermeticism had in the Renaissance; this eclectic Mahayana and Hindu magic has some of the same idea of microcosmic correspondence to the macrocosm which it attempts to manipulate via mantra-mandala-yantra-sudra (sudra, gesture; yantra, symbol; mantra, mystic syllable). Self-conscious definitions of magic as the art of effecting changes in consciousness by will (Richard Cavendish[341]) or magic as the search for power (Crow,[342] Levay,[343] Arthur Lyons,[344]) magic as the recovery of ego from social illusion (Regardie,[345] Freedland,[346] Laing) easily fit into the Tantric systems. In general the theurgical element is strong in today's revived magic. As Roszak[347] formulates it, it was precisely the magical worldview and magic itself which were the most valuable elements in the old religion; when secularization leached magic out of religion, new magical religions had to emerge to overcome man's alienation.

The objective frame rooted in science and secular democracy has proven highly resistant to this sort of thing for the past 150 years. However, there are some new factors in the current upsurge which suggest that it may continue for at least a while; and I will mention just a few of them:

1. One is the increasing iatrogenesis of modern medicine, which makes magical medicine seem a sensible alternative. Keith Thomas has shown how orthodox medicine in the English Renaissance was so rankly iatrogenic (e.g., bloodletting) that the common people consciously knew this and preferred to be treated by white magicians for quite sensible reasons. Today a modern medicine that until recently prescribed deadening anesthetics for childbirth, and mere diagnostic techniques with death rates as high as 10 percent, is rationally perceived in many situations to have a higher marginal disutility than magical medicine.[348] The public has genuine and sensible reasons to be frightened of biopsies, catheters, transplants, dialysis and other interventions—not to mention the illicit, bureaucratically motivated euthanasia practiced informally on "unpromising" cases in many hospital situations. In 1971, between 12,000 and 15,000 malpractice suits were lodged in U.S. courts, and 7 percent of all hospitalized patients suffer compensatable injuries according to a U.S. Department of Health estimate.[349] Ivan Illych further estimates that one out of every five patients admitted to a typical research hospital acquires an iatrogenic disease, 1 in 30 of which leads to death. Thousands of articles have been published in medical journals about iatrogenic illnesses. Magical medicine arises in part because the public is driven away from conventional medicine. The fact that magical medicine has its own long and sorry record of iatrogenesis is too easily forgotten.

2. Another factor is the huge incidence of "magical" illnesses in times of social distress. The epidemiology of mental illness, which measures such things, has many conceptual and methodological weaknesses that make estimates uncertain.[350] But whether incidence of mental disorders is actually rising, the absolute levels for all kinds of psychological illnesses are strikingly high. This fuels the high demand for magical cures.

3. The increasing financial capitalization of magic is another reason why the current boom may continue. Magic is big business; when practitioners succeed in avoiding taxes by having their ventures declared religions or charitable foundations they prosper. Magical products have cross-elasticities with all other goods and services in the economy; if other goods are taxed at up to 46 percent federally, and subjected also to regulation of all kinds, then magical goods may partly drive non-magical goods out of circulation. If Transcendental Meditation is permitted to sell nonsense syllables for $150.00 a morpheme in every state in the union without a single regulatory agency lifting a finger, while a manufacturing company can be prosecuted for literally thousands of infringements of six centuries of business law, which product will prosper more? Magic also obtains large infusions of capital from crazy or reactionary sections of

America's rich. This money, poured into advertising, publicity and propaganda, helps recruit the cognitive minorities that become markets for magical products, and even the cognitive ghettoes in which slave laborers enrich the cults.

4. Another factor is the heavily endowed new magical foundations and research centers. Many have learned how to use the paradigm of the scientific "experiment," with its agreement to agree, to manufacture news reports of magical findings as pseudo-events; they also subsidize the writing and publishing of books and articles favorable to the occult and critical of its opposition. The heavy government investment in such research, some of it by the intelligence agencies which have an elective affinity for secret and esoteric knowledge, is a further resource. Academic psychology, with its own self-confirming experimental designs, has become another vested source of new occult findings, spawning new shamanic professions for its graduates, producing wizards for consulting, testing, personality screening and other devices of divination. A new social basis for magic is perhaps developing in these tax-free foundations, wild psychotherapies, government research and academic psychology.

5. Another reason why the current commotion may continue for some time is that, whether they are artifacts or not, the new experimental designs have been producing results. There may indeed exist some discoverable phenomena that have been screened out in the past. Such findings will accrue to the prestige of the occult, at least temporarily.

6. Finally, a continued weakening of the political process in the United States may delay the recovery from guilt and lost confidence produced by the Vietnam War. Occultists indict rationalism, positivism, liberalism and Marxism as leading to My Lai, conveniently forgetting the magical hetacombs of past ages. What Goffman calls "looping"[351] (declaring inmates to be ill on the basis of the distress they show when they are abused) is also a current factor, as is the "wave of the future" fallacy so conveniently used by totalitarian movements.[352] If the political process recovers, however, the rational political and scientific frames seem likely to withstand this upsurge as they have withstood 150 years of magical religions among the people.

Summary. Magic symbolism travels easily. Every rigid script wrenched from a past religion, every device for relaxing the objective frame through agreement to agree, every magical defense of timorous selves is potentially transmissible and immortal. The magical heritage accumulates as a growing burden in cosmopolitan civilizations. It discards less than science does, or it only seems to discard or forget, only to revive everything in the next occult upsurge. Even when civilization reaches great heights of rationality, science and secular order, something like the Nazi movement can spring up in a few years and threaten to bring the Valkyries back. The magical heritage that man creates out of his daring and his weakness casts a threatening and possibly permanent shadow over all his other creations. As the burden of his maturity grows heavy, there is always a limited but real danger that his unshakeable occult heritage might overwhelm civilized cultures and change their nature.

Notes

1. Marcel Mauss, with Emile Durkheim, "Note sur la Notion de Civilisation," *L'Année Sociologique,* 12, 1913, in Mauss, *Oeuvres,* vol. II, pp. 451–455.
2. Eliane Massonneau, *Le Crime de Magie et le Droit Romain* (Paris, 1933), ch. 2.
3. Viktor Rydberg, *The Magic of the Middle Ages* (New York, 1879), pp. 36–38.
4. Edward A. Tiryakian, "Toward the Sociology of Esoteric Culture," *American Journal of Sociology,* 78, November, 1972, pp. 491–512. Reprinted in Tiryakian, ed., *On the Margin of the Visible* (N.Y., 1974), pp. 257–280. Tiryakian relates the occult to cultural change, to modernity, to liberation from the past, and thinks it intervenes to break up established beliefs and aid scientific and cultural revolutions. He notes its association especially with the avant-garde, with Bohemianism and with the ideology of modernity, in the symbolists, surrealists, etc.
5. James Webb, *The Occult Underground* (LaSalle, Ill., 1974), p. 191ff.
6. Slater Brown, *The Heyday of Spiritualism* (New York, 1972), pp. 1–28.
7. Keith Thomas, *Religion and the Decline of Magic* (New York, 1971), pp. 198–204.
8. Marc Bloch, *Les Rois Thaumaturges* (Paris, 1961), *passim.*
9. Webb, *Ibid.,* p. 23.
10. According to E. R. Dodds. See *The Greeks and the Irrational* (Berkeley, 1951, 1973), pp. 70–73, etc. on mediums, and *Pagan and Christian in an Age of Anxiety* (N.Y., 1965, 1970), p. 54ff for the distinction.
11. For example, Andrew Jackson Davis of Poughkeepsie, who after a magnetism exhibition developed the ability to diagnose illness while in a trance state, had read Swedenborg. Webb, *Ibid.,* p. 28.
12. Webb, *op. cit.,* p. 192.
13. H. R. Trevor-Roper, *The European Witch Craze* (N.Y., 1969), p. 101.
14. Heinrich Kramer and James Sprenger, *The Malleus Maleficarum,* ed. by Montague Sommers (New York, 1971).
15. Christopher Marlowe, *The Tragical History of Doctor Faustus,* Scene 1.
16. John Maynard Keynes, *The General Theory of Employment, Interest and Money* (New York, 1936), Ch. 12, cf. p. 156. There was even a television quiz show in the sixties, called "The Match Game," in which the participants tried to guess, not the correct answer, but the answer which the other participants would guess.
17. Durkheim and Mauss, *Primitive Classification* (Chicago, 1967), pp. 67–76.
18. Lynn Thorndike, *A History of Magic and Experimental Science* (New York, 1923), Vol. 1.
19. E. E. Evans-Pritchard, *Witchcraft, Oracles and Magic Among the Azande* (Oxford, 1937), p. 475ff.
20. Mircea Eliade, *The Forge and the Crucible: The Origins and Structures of Alchemy* (New York, 1962), *passim.*
21. Titus Burckhardt, *Alchemy* (New York, 1967, 1971), chs. 2–3.
22. Eliade has written often of the occult sciences. Besides *Yoga, Shamanism,* and *The Forge and the Crucible* already cited, I consulted *The Two and the One* (N.Y., 1965); *Patterns in Comparative Religion* (N.Y., 1963); *Images and Symbols* (N.Y., 1969); *Myth and Reality* (N.Y., 1968); *Rites and Symbols of Initiation* (N.Y., 1965); *The Quest* (Chicago, 1969); *Myth, Dreams and Mysteries* (N.Y., 1967); *Occultism, Witchcraft* and *Cultural Fashions* (Chicago, 1976).
23. Arthur Koestler, *The Roots of Coincidence* (New York, 1972).
24. In the last chapter of *The Psychopathology of Everyday Life.* Here, coincidence is portrayed as the projection, onto the outer world, of sympathetic magic connections from the unconscious.
25. Webb, *op. cit.,* pp. 89–91.
26. Arthur Koestler, *The Roots of Coincidence* (N.Y., 1972), *passim.*
27. Schroedinger's *What Is Life* espoused the philosophy of the Upanishads.

28. E.g., Werner Heisenberg, *Across the Frontiers* (New York, 1975).

29. John L. Wilhelm, *The Search of Superman* (New York, 1976), pp. 234–235ff.

30. Webb, *op. cit.*, p. 32.

31. "Le Retour des Astrologues," cited in Tiryakian, *op. cit.*, p. 257ff.

32. Reginald Scott, *The Discoverie of Witchcraft* (London, 1584, repub., N.Y., 1972).

33. George Lyman Kittredge, *Witchcraft in Old and New England* (Cambridge, Mass., 1956,), Ch. 18.

34. W. W. Tarn, *Hellenistic Civilization* (N.Y., 1961), pp. 138–141.

35. Garrett Mattingly, Lectures, Columbia University, 1957.

36. Max Weber, "The Social Psychology of the World Religions," Ch. 11 in H. H. Gerth and C. Wright Mills, *From Max Weber: Essays in Sociology* N.Y., 1958), pp. 267–301.

37. "The Brahmin and the Castes" & "The Chinese Literati" Chs. 16 & 17 in *From Max Weber*, pp. 396–444.

38. Max Weber, *The Sociology of Religion* (Boston, 1964). See references to magic and to rationalization in index.

39. Cf. Heinrich Rickert, *Science and History, A Critique of Positivist Epistemology* (Princeton, 1962), pp. 44, 81 and *passim*.

40. Gilbert Murray, *The Five Stages of the Greek Religion* (Garden City, N.Y., 1955), cf. ch. 4.

41. Hans Jonas, *The Gnostic Religion* (Boston, 1963), ch. 3.

42. E. R. Dodds, *Pagan and Christian In An Age of Anxiety* (New York, 1970), pp. 8–11.

43. Dodds, *op. cit.* Early Stoics used it as a moral metaphor about playing one's role, but as the sublunar world grew darker, the image was used to suggest unreality. To Marcus Aurelius it visualized the futility of human action. Plotinus used it pessimistically to interpret human misery.

44. E. O. James, *Comparative Religion* (New York, 1961), Ch. 5, cf. p. 125ff.

45. Richard and Eva Blum, *The Dangerous Hour* (London, 1970), pp. 11–21 and *passim*.

46. Lynn Thorndike, *A History of Magic and Experimental Science* (New York, 1923), Vol. 1, ch. 1.

47. S. Angus, *The Mystery-Religions* (London, 1928, New York, 1975), p. 43ff. H. Jeanmaire summarizes evidence of Thracian origin in a footnote, *Dionysos, Histoire du Culte de Bacchus* (Paris, 1951), p. 488.

48. Jane Ellen Harrison, *Themis* (Cambridge, 1927), Chs. 1, 2.

49. J. B. Bury, *A History of Greece* (New York, Mod. Library), Ch. 5. The cult was later endowed by the state: cf. p. 446.

50. With citizenship becoming more important than birth, *demes* replacing tribes, slaves and freedmen belonging to gentes by legal fiction, metics without civic membership residing in cities, etc.

51. W. W. Tarn, *Hellenistic Civilization* (New York, 1961), Ch. 3, cf. pp. 92–94.

52. E. R. Dodds, *The Greeks and the Irrational* (Berkeley, 1951, 1973), ch. 2, cf. pp. 44–50.

53. E. R. Dodds, *Pagan and Christian In An Age of Anxiety* (N.Y., 1965), pp. 38–53.

54. Alvin W. Gouldner, *The Hellenic World, A Sociological Analysis* (N.Y., 1965, 1969), pp. 47–63.

55. H. D. F. Kitto, *The Greeks* (Baltimore, 1951), p. 217ff.

56. Thucydides, *The Peloponnesian War*, e.g. Ch. 10, on the Corcyraean revolution. (pp. 173–192 in N.Y., 1934 Modern Library ed.)

57. M. I. Finley, *The Ancient Economy* (Berkeley, 1973), pp. 80–92, etc.

58. Georges Friedmann, *The Anatomy of Work* (N.Y., 1961, 1964), pp. 2–3 of Introd.

59. F. R. Cowell, *Cicero and the Roman Republic* (London, 1956), ch. 4.

60. M. Rostovtzeff, *Rome* (New York, 1960), p. 101ff. and *passim*.

61. Petronius, *The Satyricon* (New York, 1960), ch. 5, pp. 38–83.

62. E. O. James, *Comparative Religion* (N.Y., 1961), Ch. 5, cf. p. 136ff.

63. Walter F. Otto, *Dionysus, Myth and Cult* (Bloomington, Ind., 1965), pp. 52–64. The "nurses" who reared the newborn god, the maturation of his fetus in Zeus' body, his descent to Hades, his being torn apart and other details mirror the familiar death-dismem-

berment-rebirth initiation rites in a patriarchal men's house superimposed on a primal matriarchy. The special direction the myth takes, however, perhaps indicates a continuing or renewed tension between matriarchal and patriarchal principles, and also the new uses the primal cult was put to as a magical mystery religion for deracinated urban individuals.

64. *The Greeks and the Irrational*, Ch. 5, "The Greek Shamans . . .," pp. 135–178.

65. Bury, *A History of Greece*, Ch. 2 "The Expansion of Greece," cf. p. 82–98.

66. Jean Bérard, *La Magna Grecia, Storia delle Colonie Greche dell'Italia Meridionale* (Turin, 1963), ch. 2.

67. W. K. C. Guthrie, *The Greeks and their Gods* (Boston, 1955), pp. 73–86.

68. Martin P. Nillson, *A History of Greek Religion* (New York, 1964), p. 203; *Greek Piety* (New York, 1969), p. 41ff.

69. But Delphism was itself a local cult, though a missionary one. Cf. Marie Delcourt, *L'Oracle de Delphes* (Paris, 1955), p. 11ff.

70. Gilbert Highet, *Man's Unconquerable Mind* (New York, 1954).

71. This is Angus' idea in *The Mystery-Religions* (N.Y., 1975), pp.16, 31.

72. Gibbon, *Decline and Fall of the Roman Empire*, Ch. 6.

73. Franz Cumont, *Oriental Religions in Roman Paganism* (N.Y., 1911, 1956); *The Mysteries of Mithra* (N.Y., 1956); *Astrology and Religion Among the Greeks and the Romans* (N.Y., 1912, 1960).

74. Oriental religions were experienced *as* mystery religions by the Greeks. Cf. (on Attis, Isis, etc.) O. E. Briem, *Les Sociétés Secrètes de Mystères* (Paris, 1951), p. 297ff.

75. Cumont, *Oriental Religions in Roman Paganism*, Ch. 7, "Astrology and Magic," pp. 162-195.

76. Angus, *The Mystery-Religions*, pp. 164-169.

77. Joshua Trachtenberg, *Jewish Magic and Superstition* (N.Y., 1961), pp. 117-120.

78. Kurt Seligmann, *Magic, Supernaturalism and Religion* (N.Y., 1948, 1968), pp. 120-166.

79. Lucretius, *The Nature of Things* (N.Y., 1957), p. 4.

80. Aldous Huxley, *The Perennial Philosophy* (New York, 1944, 1970), *passim*.

81. The O.E.D. defines theosophy as "any system of speculation which bases the knowledge of nature on that of the divine nature." The term has historical reference to Boehme and to Blavatsky's Theosophical Society. In a vague sense it means a mystic philosophy. I am using it in a special way, to mean theologies of *magic*. This usage is defined by the text.

82. Mircea Eliade, *Rites and Symbols of Initiation* (N.Y., 1965), pp. 109-115.

83. Samuel Sandmel, *We Jews and Jesus* (N.Y., 1977), pp. 67-69.

84. John Dart, *The Laughing Saviour* (N.Y., 1976), p. 55ff.

85. Jean Doresse, *The Secret Books of the Egyptian Gnostics* (London, 1960).

86. Francis Cornford, *From Religion to Philosophy* (N.Y., 1957), p. 125.

87. Martin P. Nilsson, *Greek Piety* (N.Y., 1969), p. 103ff.

88. M. H. Abrams, *The Mirror and the Lamp* (London, 1971); *Natural Supernaturalism* (N.Y., 1971), ch. 4.

89. Mircea Eliade, "The Occult and the Modern World" in *Occultism, Witchcraft and Cultural Fashions* (Chicago, 1976), pp. 47-68.

90. In for example, Morton Smith's works, already cited.

91. Emile Bréhier, *The Hellenistic and Roman Age* (Chicago, 1965), p. 167ff.

92. Bréhier, pp. 171-172.

93. Hans Jonas, *The Gnostic Religion* (Boston, 1958, 1963), p. 25.

94. Bréhier, p. 199.

95. *Ibid.*, p. 201.

96. E. R. Dodds, *Pagan and Christian In An Age of Anxiety*, p. 120-122ff.

97. Jonas tells us: The revival of gnostic studies in the 19th century led first to Von Harneck's formulation of traditional church theory: gnosticism as "the acute Hellenization of Christianity." The discovery of Iranian, Babylonian and Judaic contents in Mandean and Coptic texts weakened this and led to the theory of oriental origins. This, in turn, weakened when philosophical content could not be traced to the Orient. The oriental thesis was renewed when mythic contents were seen to derive from there so gnosticism appeared to be (like astrology) the Hellenistic rationalization of oriental ideas. But latest discoveries emphasize Judaic and esoteric Christian content. The present trend is to interpret gnosticism as syncretistic with strong attention to Judaeo-Christian elements. Jonas, preface, pp. XVff.

98. Jonas, *op. cit.*, p. 26.

99. Heinrich Zimmer, *Myths and Symbols in Indian Art and Civilization* (Princeton, 1972), pp. 13–17, 23–26, 35ff, 44, 51–52.

100. There is some recognition of Hegel's gnostic strain in Voegelin.

101. Frances A. Yates, *Giordano Bruno and the Hermetic Tradition* (N.Y., 1969), p. 4.

102. Chhandogya Upanishad, in Nicol MacNicol, ed., *Hindu Scriptures* (London, 1938), Max Muller trans., p. 117ff, and excerpted in Lin Yutang, ed., *The Wisdom of China and India* (N.Y., 1942), p. 38.

103. Francis L. K. Hsu, *Religion, Science and Human Crises* (London, 1952), ch. 2.

104. Cf. S. Körner, *The Philosophy of Mathematics* (N.Y., 1962).

105. Louis Dumont, *Homo Hierarchicus* (Chicago, 1970), pp. 191–192.

106. Joachim Kahl, *The Misery of Christianity* (London, 1971), pp. 25ff, 121ff.

107. S. Radhakrishnan, *Eastern Religions and Western Thought* (Oxford, 1959), pp. 115–152.

108. I. Pauwels & J. Bergier, *The Morning of the Magicians* (N.Y., 1968), p. 214ff, 208, 292ff and *passim.*

109. In *Les Dieux des Indo-Européens*, etc.

110. "The Social Psychology of the World Religions," in Gerth and Mills, *From Max Weber*, pp. 267–301.

111. Celestin Bouglé, *Essais Sur le Régime des Castes.* I used the Felix Alcan 1935 Paris edition. Dumont has interesting information on previous editions and versions, in *Homo Hierarchicus*, p. 349.

112. The first *Upanishads* are continuations of the sacrificial rules and discussions of the *Brahmanas*, in which the Brahmins rationalized their ritual knowledge. Robert Ernest Hume, *The Thirteen Principal Upanishads* (Oxford, 1921, 1971), Introduction, p. 5.

113. The Ionian *physoloigoi* also began with mana words and *Rta* words to explain the universe's substrate, e.g., words like *moira*, moral destiny. Philosophy did indeed start as "the analysis of religious ideas," as F. M. Cornford put it (*From Religion to Philosophy*, N.Y., 1957, p. 125). But the merchant intellectuals of Miletus did not stop there; they advanced to natural philosophy, with their emphasis on change, differentiation, pluralism, etc. They were not priests but "active practical men" (Benjamin Farrington, *Greek Science*, London, 1953, 1961, p. 35ff).

114. According to Hume, the Rig-Veda *brahma* meant first "hymn, prayer, sacred knowledge, magic formula." (Hume, *op. cit.*, p. 14) According to Hubert and Mauss, *bráhman* (neuter) meant prayer, formula, rite, the magic or religious power of the rite. Brahman is that which activates men and gods, referring particularly to the voice. (*A General Theory of Magic*, p. 116). Hocart has shown that the Brahmins were those who performed the spoken rites in sacrifice (*Kings and Councillors*).

115. Or brahman as *social* mana: "atman = brahman" is like saying the individual totem reflects the clan totem.

116. A discovery that creates in some an impression of profundity by stunning the mind with traditional tautologies and equivocations repeatedly.

117. This is Dumont's term: e.g., *op. cit.*, pp. 184–186. But the idea is in the *Bhagavad-Gita.*

117A. There is an account of the relation of Yoga to Samkhya in Eliade's *Yoga* (Princeton, 1970), pp. 367–377.

118. A. C. Bouquet, *Comparative Religion* (London, 1949), Ch. 7 and *Hinduism* (London, 1948), p. 13.

119. A. C. Bouquet, *Hinduism* (London, 1948), pp. 10–12.

120. *Bhagavad-Ghita*, Part I.

121. Max Weber, *The Religion of India* (N.Y., 1958), *passim.*

122. Summary in C. Scott Littleton, *The New Comparative Mythology* (Berkeley, 1973). See "ideology" in index.

123. *The Religion of India*, pp. 15–17, 131, etc.

124. *Homo Hierarchicus*, ch. 4, "The Division of Labor." A surprising percent of Hindus will follow their prescribed caste occupations even when there is minimal demand. Even a small village will have "sweepers," etc. pp. 92–97.

125. E. A. H. Blunt, *The Caste System of Northern India* (Oxford, 1931).

126. J. J. Hutton, *Caste in India* (London, 1946).

127. C. Bouglé, *Essais Sur le Régime des Castes* (Paris, 1935).

128 G. S. Ghurye, *Caste and Race in India* (London, 1932).

129. Louis Dumont, *Homo Hierarchicus* (Chicago, 1970).

130. Max Weber, *The Religion of India* (N.Y., 1958).

131. Claude Lévi-Strauss, *The Elementary Structures of Kinship* (Boston, 1969), ch. 25, "Clans and Castes," p. 406-421.

132. A. M. Hocart, *Kings and Councillors* (Chicago, 1970).

133. Bouquet, *Hinduism* (London, 1948), pp. 35ff, pp. 11-13, and *passim*.

134. Margaret Cormack, *The Hindu Woman* (N.Y., 1953).

135. Gardner Murphy, *In the Minds of Men* (N.Y., 1953).

136. V. S. Naipaul, *India, A Wounded Civilization* (N.Y., 1977).

137. David G. Mandelbaum, "The Family in India," *Southwestern Journal of Anthropology*, vol. 4, no. 2, summer 1948.

138. Most definitions of caste focus on these three attributes: hierarchy, purity-separation-with-endogamy and occupational specialization. E.g., Bouglé's definition which Dumont also follows. Blunt stresses only separation and occupational specialization in his definition, but then gives *empirical* attention to hierarchy.

139. *Elementary Structures of Kinship*, ch. 25.

140. Dumont, *op. cit.*, ch. 4. Dumont claims the caste system modifies exploitation, guarantees all a share, provides security. Elsewhere, he frequently suggests that hierarchy is an inevitable consequence of having any values at all. In Dumont, the tendency of Durkheimianism to turn into reactionary ideology is prominent. Cf. pp. 106-108. Cf. also A. M. Hocart, *Caste* (London, 1950), p. 140.

141. Hocart tells us that in Ceylon, *jati* or caste means birth, lineage. But *bali*, subcaste, means sacrifice. A. M. Hocart, *Caste* (London, 1950), pp. 16-17ff.

142. Only some very primitive castes derived from aboriginal tribes have totemic names, according to Blunt.

143. Yet the analogy to totemism, however inaccurate in detail, is understandable impressionistically. Given the frozen inertness of the kin structure, these tribe-like endogamous groups lack the self-constituting confederative capacity of Roman gentes and tribes, for example. Religious taboos prevent them from forming wider unions.

144. A. M. Hocart, *Caste* (London, 1950), cf. Ch. 1.

145. In some ethnic European subcultures in the U.S., there were still customs about the barbershop before the wedding in this century.

146. In *Kings and Councillors* Hocart suggests some occupations derive from division of labor in sacrifice. Cf. p. 102ff. In *Caste* he notes that in the *Puranas*, subcastes are called *bali*, which means sacrifice, pp. 16-17.

147. Louis Dumont, *Homo Hierarchichus*, pp. 191-192.

148. He used the caste table for Madras, 1911. Cited in Hutton, p. 153.

149. According to Ghurye, *op. cit.*, ch. 1.

150. Kingsley Davis, *Human Society* (N.Y., 1949), pp. 378-385. Dumont, *op. cit.*, pp. 61-64, 280-281, 198-99.

151. Ghurye, *op. cit.*, ch. 1.

152. Blunt enumerates 1. *Sapinda* rules which forbid union of any two with common ancestors not more than six degrees removed on the male side, four on the female. (This is said to exclude 2,121 kinds of relatives.) 2. The avuncular rule: you cannot marry anyone in the line of paternal or maternal uncle or aunt. 3. The "memory-of-man" rule: you cannot marry anyone if anybody can remember the two families intermarrying before. With endogamy limiting marriage outwards and strict exogamy limiting it inwards, marriage choice is constricted. This partly explains child marriage: parents try to get there first. Cf. E. A. H. Blunt, *op. cit.*, ch. 4.

153. Gotras appear to be superclans. Perhaps they were once phratries.

154. Hutton, Dumont, Blunt, etc. all remark on this.

155. Thus Ghurye notes that one way to classify the castes is in five groups as follows: 1. The "twice-born" (initiated) castes of the top three Aryan varnas (Brahmin, Kshatriya, Vaisya). 2. Those castes from whom the twice-born can take pakka food (food cooked in ghee—cf. Blunt, ch. 5). 3. Those from whom the twice-born cannot take any kind of food but can take water. 4. Those from whom the twice-born cannot take water but which are

not untouchable to them. 5. The untouchables. This classification has overlaps, because, for instance, Brahmins cannot take ordinary food from some other twice-born Vaisya castes.

156. Cf. Davis' list, *op. cit.*, p. 380.

157. Hutton, *op. cit.*, p. 81.

158. Blunt writes, "Intermarriage in such circumstances cannot have been free and unrestrained. It began: it ceased as soon as possible. As cadets of the full and half blood pushed further afield, it began again; and again ceased. The result would be the formation of groups of all shades of color, all degrees of mixed blood—all with a strong tendency to endogamy." Blunt, *op. cit.*, p. 14.

159. Ghurye, *op. cit.*, ch. 5.

160. S. V. Viswanatha, *Racial Synthesis in Hindu Culture* (London, 1928).

161. Radharkrishnan, *Eastern Religions and Western Thought* (Oxford, 1939, 1959), ch. 9, "The Individual and the Social Order in Hinduism," cf. pp. 358–370.

162. But Marx believed classes tend to *become* self-conscious. Cf. Stanislow Ossowski on this, *Class Structure In the Social Consciousness* (N.Y., 1963), pp. 72–73.

163. Dumont, *op. cit.*, pp. 191–192.

164. Quoted in Hutton, *op. cit.*, p. 113.

165. Occupations were not hereditary in the Vedic period, according to Hocart. Even Brahmin was a career open to talent. Occupations are not exactly closed now, either, according to Ghurye; it is just that 1. the castes in control of a job will try to block entry; 2. a job switch can cause a fall in status if the new job is considered less pure than the old.

166. Précis of Dahlmann, Senart and Nesfield's theories are found in works cited by Bouglé, Hutton, Blunt, Dumont.

167. ". . . caste appears to be an institution of highly complex origin, an origin so complex indeed that in its very nature it must be limited to a single area; and that, no doubt, is why it is only found in India. For although social institutions that resemble caste in one respect or other are not difficult to find elsewhere . . . yet caste in its fullest sense, caste, that is, as we know it in India, is an exclusively Indian phenomenon. . . . If it were a simple institution it could hardly fail to be more widely distributed . . . caste could only arise within a limited area in which all the elements contributing to it were associated over a long period of time." (Hutton, p. 46).

168. "Lorsq'ils se sont rencontrés, il est probable qu'Aryens et Aborigènes étaient les uns et les autres divisés en tribus; leur choc a sans doute redoublé l'intensité de cette repulsion pour l'étranger dont chacun de ses groupes primitifs portait en lui le germe." (Bouglé, *op. cit.*, p. 63).

169. *The Religion of India*, cf. p. 131.

170. J. J. Hutton, *Caste In India* (London, 1946), *passim*.

171. *Essais Sur le Régime des Castes*, p. 63 and *passim*.

172. *Ibid.*, cf. Introduction.

173. Louis Dumont, *Homo Hierarchicus* (Chicago, 1970), p. 43ff.

174. *The Elementary Structures of Kinship*, ch. 25, pp. 406–421.

175. Risley, 1891, cited in Lévi-Strauss, *op. cit.*, p. 417.

176. Frequently mentioned in Blunt, etc.

177. Lévi-Strauss, *op. cit.*, chs. 23–28.

178. A. M. Hocart, *Kings and Councillors*, p. 195.

179. In "Class, Status, Party," Part III, ch. 4, *Wirtschaft und Gesellschaft*, pp. 631–40. Excerpted in Gerth and Mills, *From Max Weber* (N.Y., 1946), p. 180–195. Essays discussing this distinction are collected in Reinhard Bendix and Seymour Martin Lipset, eds., *Class, Status and Power* (N.Y., 1966).

180. *Status* is most obviously magical. Veblen has shown that even in economic-rational societies most status criteria are magical; all the more so in societies based on "face" and other magical ideas. *Power* also is originally magical, a matter of charisma and mana, as we see in the tribal stage when the first leaders emerged. And even *"class,"* which Weber and the Marxists define strictly in terms of income, is magical: because *money* is a magical system, as I have shown (Ch. 10). As against the latently fascist position of Durkheimians like Dumont who postulate that hierarchy is a logical and necessary condition of *any* value system, I pose the proposition that *any* system of hierarchy or any elitism whatsoever can be demonstrated to reduce to some arbitrary magic criterion and to magic thinking aimed at

inducing overvaluation of this criterion. Every form of elitism is some kind of magical flim-flam based on agreement-to-agree that some vague, self-defining or *absurd* criterion like "education," "birth," "intelligence" or "achievement" will be allowed to rank human beings and limit their life chances across the boards.

181. E. E. Evans-Pritchard, *Witchcraft, Oracles and Magic Among the Azande*, p. 432.

182. Marcel Granet, *Chinese Civilization* (N.Y., 1958), Book II, ch. 4, pp. 194–204.

183. Philip Drucker, *Indians of the Northwest Coast* (Garden City, N.Y., 1963), pp. 137–140.

184. Mauss noticed that the conservative Brahmins are still theoretically paid only by gifts (*The Gift*, pp. 53–8). Much later Dumont discovered (*Homo Hierarchicus*, ch. 4) that *other* castes in Indian villages depend on similar distributions—everyone from the sweeper to the Muslim dancing girl is entitled to some share of the harvest and to small fixed gifts on certain holidays.

185. The original three-tiered Indo-European structure had status ambiguity; Brahmins and Kshatriyas were rivals for first rank. The Kshatriyas were wiped out in war. And Bouquet claims (*Hinduism*, p. 73) that Buddhism discredited the agriculturalists (Vaisyas) because they destroyed life. Kshatriya apostasy in Jainism and Buddhism was also a factor (the Brahmins said they were destroyed "for their sins").

186. Dumont tries to demonstrate an underlying purity logic which goes like this: Brahmin = cow. Impurity is fought by Brahmin rites and the five cow products. The other end of the spectrum, the untouchable, is preeminently the man who eats beef and works with dead cows. So untouchable is the opposite of Brahmin. This was intensified when the Brahmins adopted vegetarianism to compete with Buddhist renunciation asceticism. Dumont, *op. cit.*, p. 53.

187. Cf. A. C. Bouquet, *Hinduism* (London, 1948), p. 72–75. Testimony also of Bouglé.

188. Cf. Hubert and Mauss, *Sacrifice* (Chicago, 1964), pp. 20ff & 45ff.

189. A. M. Hocart, *Kings and Councillors* (Chicago, 1970), ch. 9, etc.

190. Hocart goes further to claim that the caste system, classes in general and the division of labor originated in specialization of function during the grand opera of sacrifice.

191. Dumont even shows, Caillois-style, how the whole system can be generated by a binary purity logic. First we have the pure Brahmins against all other castes. But the kings are participants in sacrifice, too; so the two top castes stand apart in purity from the others. But then the three-tiered Aryan tribes conquer the Dravidians, and the "good black" (*sat Dasu*) becomes a fourth, servant class, the Sudras. So now the three "twice-born castes" of Brahmins, Kshatriya and Vaisya are set apart from the aboriginal Sudra caste. Finally, the untouchables are generated by mésalliance and absorption of savage tribes. Now the four varnas stand in opposition to the untouchable castes. Then, hypergamous marriages between the varnas (or the "high-hatting effect" within them) generates the castes. Sacred vs. profane ideas cause a continuing process of fission in which the subcastes are generated.

192. Criticizing Senart's derivation of purity from communal sacrifice, Hutton suggests that conmensalism based on purity notions could be causally prior to endogamy—obviously it would be inconvenient to marry a woman who could not cook your food.

193. Hindu mana ideas frequently translate into alimentary concepts: some Upanishads speculate that the universal substrate is some kind of food. The five cow products are magic purifiers and ghee protects all meals from magical contamination.

194. Apparently on better historical than etymological grounds. Georges Dumézil, "Flámen-Brahman," *Annales du Musée Guimet*, vol. 51, Paris, 1935; Discussed in C. Scott Littleton, *The New Comparative Mythology* (Berkeley, 1973), pp. 54–56.

195. Littleton, *op. cit.*, pp. 56.

196. The apparent absence of such a class among the Teutons weakens the argument.

197. The Levites were such, and Hocart observes that before centralization of the cult in Jerusalem, they were spread among the people like the Brahmins, serving the local cults. But the Levites took a different turn because, as Weber put it, "they sided with The Mountain," (i.e., with the revolutionary ideology of freedom.) *Ancient Judaism* (Glencoe, Ill., 1952), p. 170ff.

198. *Kings and Councillors*, pp. 16–22.

199. What happens to the heralds' god Hermes in Greece is another contrast. Originally the Greek version of the Trickster (see Paul Radin, *The Trickster*, N.Y., 1972), the embodi-

ment of magic as illusion and trickery and possibly a deified magician, this patron-god of the heralds became the god of the emergent bourgeoisie. Hermes was the god of the limens, of the boundary stones, because heralds passed borders (also as Van Gennup shows, magic is experienced as one passes borders—*The Rites of Passage*, Chicago, 1969, ch. 2). He later became a god of thievery — an early form of systematic trading. Norman O. Brown (*Hermes the Thief*, N.Y., 1969) interprets the Homeric hymn of Hermes stealing the sacred cattle of Apollo and then getting reconciled to his brother as a charter for the social acceptance of the rising commercial classes. By contrast, in Hesiod's dark view (*Theogony*) Hermes has become sinister; this is like the Hindu idea of the "Kali Yuga," or stage of the fallen world— it corresponds to the caste disorder which occurs when a money economy elevates the Vaisyas. So the god of magic becomes the god of the money class and yet *remains* a god of magic, for money is the new magic which conquers the world.

200. *The Golden Bough*, chs. 5, 14, 17, 24, 25.

201. Jessie L. Weston, *From Ritual to Romance* (Garden City, N.Y., 1957), p. 8–11.

202. T. S. Eliot, *The Waste Land*.

203. Knud Rasmussen, *Intellectual Culture of the Hudson Bay Eskimos* (Copenhagen, 1930), Part I, ch. 5.

204. I follow here Blunt, *op. cit.*, ch. 2.

205. Cf. Benjamin Farrington, *Greek Science* (London, 1953); Francis Cornford, *op. cit.*, G. S. Kirk & J. E. Raven, *The Presocratic Philosophers* (Cambridge, 1960); W. K. C. Guthrie, *A History of Greek Philosophy* (Cambridge, 1962).

206. W. K. C. Guthrie, *The Sophists* (Cambridge, 1971), *passim*.

207. Cf. Quintilian, *On the Early Education of the Citizen-Orator* (Indianapolis, 1965).

208. *The Religion of India*, p. 147.

209. The later Upanishads perfected the identity of Atman and Brahman during the same period that the Kshatriya systems of Buddhism and Jainism arose; possibly this was already a competition in ideas; some observers have even claimed that some later Upanishads were written by Kshatriyas.

210. Ghurye, *op. cit.*, ch. 5.

211. Bouglé, *op. cit.*, Part I, ch. 1.

212. *The Religion of India*, "Diffusion Patterns of Hinduism," pp. 9–21.

213. The Brahmins always allied themselves with power, Dumont writes. One more fragmenting force in India was the lack of any ethic of state legitimacy. Domination was by force, and Brahmins would organize all other classes around it.

214. The Brahmins won, it is said, because of race purity; but that is a myth and symbol of their magic. They won because of *spiritual* purity, Bouglé said; unlike popes they did not confound their spiritual authority with political authority. But that is just one more measure of their magician stance, which withdrew so far from community that the top Brahmins are typically above even the caste system, beyond good and evil. The Brahmins really won by virtue of their observances: to compete with the Buddhists they adopted vegetarianism, they do not touch alcohol and so on. Again, this is magic, the magic puritanism which seeks mana power by not dispersing one's "vital bodily fluids," as the mad general said in *Dr. Strangelove*.

215. *La Prière*, in Mauss, Oeuvres, vol. I, pp. 357–477.

216. This is Bouglé's idea and many echo it.

217. V. S. Naipaul, *India, A Wounded Civilization* (N.Y., 1977). Indian life is saturated with magic, Naipaul writes. Conversation at any gathering quickly trails to magic. Magic solutions and short-cuts abort real effort in every sphere. The resulting poverty is more dehumanizing than any industrial system. "Hindu speculation can soar high but . . . spirituality for most people is . . . magic." (*op. cit.*, p. 181).

218. Naipaul, *Ibid.*, p. 17.

219. *Homo Hierarchichus*, p. 153ff.

220. As effectively as "Big Brother's" control of "The Underground" in *1984*.

221. Cf. Henri Pirenne, *Mohammed and Charlemagne* (N.Y., 1957); *Economic and Social History of Medieval Europe* (N.Y., 1937). Cf. also Gideon Sjoberg, *The Preindustrial City* N.Y., 1960), and Pirenne, *Medieval Cities* (Princeton, 1952), pp. 58–69ff.

222. F. W. Maitland, *A Constitutional History of England* (Cambridge, 1950), "Retrospect on Feudalism," pp. 141–164.

223. For example, cf. Ferdinand Schevill, *Siena, The History of a Medieval Commune* (N.Y., 1964), ch. 2; Gino Luzzatto, *Breve Storia Economica Dell'Italia Medievale* (Turin, 1965), ch. 5.

224. Cf. Joseph Calmette, *Le Reich Allemand Au Moyen Age* (Paris, 1951), ch. 9.

225. Viktor Rydberg, *The Magic of the Middle Ages* (N.Y., 1879), ch. 1.

226. Cf. Frances A. Yates, *Giordano Bruno and the Hermetic Tradition* (N.Y., 1969), pp. 12-13.

227. Peter J. French, *John Dee: The World of an Elizabethan Magus* (London, 1972), ch. 1.

228. Cf. D. P. Walker, *Spiritual and Demonic Magic From Ficino to Campanella* (Notre Dame, 1975), chs. 1, 7; also Yates, *Giordano Bruno and the Hermetic Tradition*, pp. 62-83, etc.

229. Robert-Léon Wagner, *"Sorcier" et "Magicien," Contribution à L'Etude du Vocabulaire de la Magie* (Paris, 1939).

230. John Herman Randall, Jr., *The Career of Philosophy* (N.Y., 1979), Vol. I, Book II, ch. 2.

231. Keith Thomas, *Religion and the Decline of Magic* (N.Y., 1971), ch. 3, etc.

232. Hiram Haydn, *The Counter-Renaissance* (N.Y., 1950), pp. 176-177.

233. Wayne Shumaker, *The Occult Sciences in the Renaissance* (Berkeley, 1972), cf. chs. 3, 4.

234. Yates, *Giordano Bruno and the Hermetic Tradition*, p. 143.

235. Keith Thomas uses this quote from Hamlet this way: *op. cit.*, p. 227.

236. Jacob Burckhardt, *The Civilization of the Renaissance in Italy*, Vol. II (N.Y., 1958), Part IV, ch. 4, pp. 484-509.

237. D. P. Walker, *Spiritual and Demonic Magic from Ficino to Campanella* (London, 1958), pp. 54-59.

238. Peter Gay, *Weimar Culture* (New York, 1970), pp. 30-34.

239. Wayne Shumaker, *The Occult Sciences in the Renaissance* (Berkeley, 1972), ch. 1.

240. Keith Thomas, *op. cit.*, chs. 10, 11, 12, 22.

241. Arthur O. Lovejoy, *The Great Chain of Being* (N.Y., 1960), ch. 2.

242. Frances A. Yates, *The Rosicrucean Enlightenment* (London, 1972), preface and ch. 16.

243. Titus Burckhardt, *Alchemy* (Baltimore, 1971), chs. 1, 2.

244. Kurt Seligmann, *Magic, Supernaturalism and Religion* (N.Y., 1968), pp. 338-358.

245. Leo Schaya, *The Universal Meaning of the Kabbalah* (London, 1973), pp. 76-78.

246. Seligmann, *op. cit.*, p. 340; Yates, *Giordano Bruno and the Hermetic Tradition*, ch. 5.

247. Joshua Trachtenberg, *Jewish Magic and Superstition* (Cleveland, 1961), pp. 11-13, 15-17, 45.

248. D. P. Walker, *op. cit.*, e.g., pp. 103-104, 234-236.

249. Yates, *The Rosicrucean Enlightenment*, chs. 3-5.

250. Peter J. French, *John Dee, The World of an Elizabethan Magus* (London, 1972), chs. 1, 2.

251. Yates, *Giordano Bruno and the Hermetic Tradition* (N.Y., 1964), ch. IV, e.g., p. 80; ch. 5, p. 87ff.

252. Theodore Roszak, *Unfinished Animal* (N.Y., 1975), p. 27.

253. Eugenio Garin, *Science and Civic Life in the Italian Renaissance* (Garden City, N.Y., 1969), p. 146ff.

254. Garin, *Ibid.*, last chapter, "Magic and Astrology . . .," cf. pp. 146-147.

255. J. Bronowski, *Magic, Science and Civilization* (N.Y., 1978), *passim* and cf. pp. 25-37.

256. Paolo Rossi, *Francis Bacon From Magic to Science* (Chicago, 1968), pp. 29-36.

257. David Hawkins, *The Language of Nature* (N.Y., 1967), p. 36.

258. Garin, *op. cit.*, pp. 149, 152-153.

259. Frances A. Yates, *Giordano Bruno and the Hermetic Tradition* (N.Y., 1964), Ch. 1, cf. pp. 2-6.

260. E. A. Wallis Budge, *Egyptian Magic* (N.Y., 1971), pp. viii-xii.

261. William Irwin Thompson, *At The Edge of History* (N.Y., 1971), pp. 19, 58, 61, 100, 102, 105, 135, 141, 151.
262. Joseph Needham, *Science and Civilization of China,* Vol. II, sect. 10, pp. 33–34.
263. Quoted by Garin, *op. cit.,* p. 150.
264. Yates, *Giordano Bruno . . .,* pp. 9–10.
265. Garin, *op. cit.,* p. 151.
266. Frances A. Yates, *The Rosicrucean Enlightenment* (London, 1972), ch. 16.
267. Hiram Haydn, *The Counter-Renaissance* (New York, 1950).
268. Peter French, *John Dee, The World of an Elizabethan Magus* (London, 1972), defined, p. 14ff.
269. The Rosicrucean Enlightenment, *preface.*
270. Frances A. Yates, *Theater of the World* (Chicago, 1969), passim.
271. Frances A. Yates, *Majesty and Magic in Shakespeare's Last Plays* (Boulder, 1978), pp. 87–105.
272. Max Weber, *The Protestant Ethic and the Spirit of Capitalism* (London, 1930), pp. 155–183.
273. Werner von Sombart, *The Quintessence of Capitalism* (N.Y., 1915), *passim.*
274. Alfred von Martin, *The Sociology of the Renaissance* (N.Y., 1963), ch. 1.
275. E.g., Nelson's documentation of new lending activity immediately after various rationalist Protestant leaders fended off radical fundamentalist sects by officially declaring that the New Testament with its interdiction of usury was not meant to serve as a civil constitution for the world. Benjamin Nelson, *The Idea of Usury* (Chicago, 1969), pp. 82ff. See also Nelson's bibliography of studies testing Weber's Protestant ethic hypothesis, in Block and Hammond, *Beyond the Classics?,* pp. 113–130.
276. Lynn White, Jr., *Medieval Technology and Social Change* (N.Y., 1964).
277. Lefèbre des Noëttes: references in Lynn White, *op. cit.,* pp. 26, 59ff.
278. William Carroll Bark, *Origins of the Medieval World* (N.Y., 1958), pp. 125–141.
279. Garrett Mattingly, lectures, Columbia University (N.Y., 1957).
280. Robert K. Merton, *Science, Technology & Society in 17th Century England* (N.Y., 1970).
281. Bernard Barber, *Science and the Social Order* (N.Y., 1952).
282. Ian G. Barbour, *Issues in Science and Religion* (N.Y., 1966).
283. Leo Marx, *The Machine in the Garden* (N.Y., 1964).
284. Louis Pauwels & Jacques Bergier, *The Morning of the Magicians* (N.Y., 1968), Part I, ch. 1.
285. Thomas S. Kuhn, *The Structure of Scientific Revolutions* (Chicago, 1970), p. 43ff.
286. D. W. Sciama, *The Unity of the Universe* (Garden City, N.Y., 1961), p. 71ff.
287. For a critique see Stanley L. Jaki, *The Paradox of Olbers' Paradox* (N.Y., 1969).
288. Arthur C. Clarke, conversations and addresses.
289. M. Cary, *A History of the Greek World 323 to 146 B.C.* (London, 1972), pp. 352–353.
290. W. W. Rostow, *The Process of Economic Growth* (N.Y., 1962), pp. 16, 20–54.
291. Merton, *op. cit.,* ch. 5.
292. *Science and Civilization in China,* Vol. II, Section 18, cf. pp. 581–583.
293. Fung Yu-Lan, *A Short History of Chinese Philosophy* (N.Y., 1966), pp. 12–13, 328–331.
294. Ronald Knox, *Enthusiasm* (Oxford, 1950), defined, ch. 1.
295. Norman Cohn, *The Pursuit of the Millennium* (N.Y., 1961), *passim* and cf. pp. 13–21.
296. At first there is just the anti-Christ followed by the Messiah and the millennium. But gradually both are split to produce four phases in prophetic futurology: 1. The Last Empire, the worst. Its leader is sometimes called "the false prophet." 2. Then comes the "Emperor of the Last Days," who is the reborn form of some hero king like Constans, Charlemagne, Baldwin, Frederick II, etc. He rules for about 100 years, a last golden age, establishing an empire from Jerusalem. 3. Then the anti-Christ raises the forces of Gog and Magog and overthrows him. 4. Finally, the anti-Christ is overthrown by the Messiah, who is also a warrior king; he sets up a "millennium" which, like the Joachimite Thousand Year

Reich, lasts precisely a thousand years culminating in the last judgment and the heavenly kingdom which in some versions is here on earth as it is in heaven. In this doubling, the original anti-Christ has been split to produce a weak and a strong version: the false prophet and the anti-Christ proper; the Messiah is similarly doubled into hero king and Messiah. (My interpretation, based on N. Cohn, *op. cit.*)

297. Oswald Spengler, *The Decline of the West* (Modern Library abridged ed., N.Y., 1962), pp. 81-83, 235-244, 27-29.

298. Arnold Toynbee, *A Study of History,* D. C. Somervell abridgement (N.Y., 1947), pp. 31, 33, 112, 361, 374, etc.

299. Benjamin Nelson, "The Future of Illusions" in R. Endleman, *Personality and Social Life* (N.Y., 1967), pp. 563-576.

300. E. J. Hobsbawn, *Primitive Rebels* (N.Y., 1959), cf. chs. 4-6.

301. Friedrich Engels, *The Peasant War in Germany* in *The German Revolutions* (Chicago, 1967), pp. 1-119.

302. Eric Voegelin, *The New Science of Politics* (Chicago, 1952, 1971), pp. 133ff., 175.

303. James Webb, *The Occult Underground* (LaSalle, Ill., 1974), pp. 58-60.

304. James Webb, *op. cit.,* pp. 245ff, 316-319, 331, etc.

305. *Ibid.,* p. 353.

306. *Ibid.,* Ch. 5.

307. J. K. Huysmans, *Là-Bas.*

308. Webb, *op. cit.,* p. 297.

309. George Steiner, *In Bluebeard's Castle* (New Haven, 1971), pp. 3-25.

310. Irving Babbitt, *Rousseau and Romanticism* (N.Y., 1947), pp. 72, 124ff.

311. César L. Graña, *Modernity and Its Discontents* (N.Y., 1964), *passim.*

312. Praz, *The Romantic Agony* (N.Y., 1933), *passim.*

313. Edmund Wilson, *Axel's Castle* (N.Y., 1931), *passim.*

314. Cf. Alfred de Vigny, *Chatterton.*

315. Cf. Chapter on Jarry in Roger Shattuck, *The Banquet Years* (Garden City, N.Y., Doubleday Anchor paperback), p. 223ff.

316. George L. Mosse, *The Crisis of German Ideology* (N.Y., 1964), chs. 1, 2, pp. 13-51.

317. Hannah Arendt, *The Origins of Totalitarianism* (Cleveland, 1958), pp. 11-53.

318. Steiner, *op. cit.,* pp. 53-55.

319. Meyer H. Abrams, *The Mirror and the Lamp* (N.Y., 1971); *Natural Supernaturalism* (N.Y., 1973), chs. 3-4.

320. H. Stuart Hughes, *Consciousness and Society* (N.Y., 1958), pp. 190-200.

321. This is the title of a book by Peter L. Berger: *A Rumor of Angels* (Garden City, N.Y., 1969), in which he showed that sociology of knowledge tricks could be used *against* the positivist frame that excludes the miraculous.

322. Cf. Jacques LeCan on this necessity in *Yale French Studies,* nos. 36-37, *Structuralism* (1966), "The Insistence of the Letter in the Unconscious," pp. 112-147.

323. On Nazi occult interest, cf. Pauwels and Bergier, *The Morning of the Magicians,* pp. 246-299.

324. E.g., Trevor Ravenscroft, *The Spear of Destiny* (N.Y., 1974); J. H. Brennan, *The Occult Reich* (N.Y., 1974).

325. On reaction, anti-Semitism and occultism as movements in Czarist Russia, see Norman Cohn, *Warrant For Genocide* (N.Y., 1969), Ch. 4, pp. 77-107.

326. Cf. accounts of American "churches" as thaumaturgical movements in Africa in Bryan Wilson, *Magic and the Millennium* (N.Y., 1973), ch. 2.

327. But Hinduism was also imported as early as the Transcendental movement in New England. Van Wyck Brooks, *The Flowering of New England* (Cleveland, 1946), pp. 292-293.

328. Robert N. Bellah, *Beyond Belief* (N.Y., 1970), Ch. 9, "Civil Religion in America," pp. 168-192.

329. Will Herberg, *Protestant, Catholic, Jew* (Garden City, N.Y., 1960), ch. 3.

330. Peter L. Berger, *The Noise of Solemn Assemblies* (Garden City, N.Y., 1961), pp. 30-39ff.

331. Bellah, *op. cit.,* p. 170; also quoted in Herberg, *op. cit.,* p. 84.

332. The sense intended is the way "modeling" is used in the social learning theory of Albert Bandura.

333. Many of the first were formed immediately around San Francisco.

334. Media attention rose that year and no doubt helped to encourage the phenomenon.

335. Daniel Yankelovich, Inc., *Changing Values on the Campus* (N.Y., 1972), *passim.*

336. Philip E. Slater, *Microcosm* (N.Y., 1966), pp. 21, 47, 57–58.

337. Theodore Adorno, "Theses Against Occultism" and "The Stars Down to Earth," no. 19, *Telos* Spring, 1974, pp. 7–12, 13–90.

338. Adorno, *Ibid.,* p. 9, 10.

339. Adorno, *op. cit.,* "The Stars Down to Earth," his data explained, pp. 17–21ff.

340. Cf. Agehananda Bharati, *The Tantric Tradition* (Garden City, N.Y., 1970), *passim.*

341. Richard Cavendish, *The Black Arts* (N.Y., 1967), pp. 6–8.

342. W. B. Crow, *Witchcraft, Magic and Occultism* (Los Angeles, 1972).

343. Anton S. LaVey, *The Satanic Bible* (N.Y., 1969).

344. Arthur Lyons, *The Second Coming: Satanism in America* (N.Y., 1970), p. 9.

345. Israel Regardie, *The Tree of Life, A Study in Magic* (N.Y., 1971), ch. 1.

346. Nat Freedland, *The Occult Explosion* (N.Y., 1972).

347. Theodore Roszak, *Where the Wasteland Ends* (Garden City, N.Y., 1973), pp. 101–130. Cf. also *The Making of a Counter Culture* (Garden City, N.Y., 1969), pp. 239–268; *Sources* (N.Y., 1972); *Unfinished Animal* (N.Y., 1975), *passim.*

348. Cf. Alex Comfort, *The Anxiety Makers* (London, 1967); Martin L. Gross, *The Doctors* (N.Y., 1966), pp. 234–285; Ivan Illich, *Medical Nemesis* (London, 1975), pp. 15–30.

349. Ivan Illich, *op. cit.,* p. 25.

350. As compared with suicide and homicide, where there are bodies to count, so that data language of different studies is comparable and theory can cumulate, it is almost impossible to agree on the operationalization of constructs in the "epidemiology of mental illness," so successive studies are not commensurable, there is little progress and constructs remain mired in low and uncertain empirical estimates with meagre theoretical advance. Thus Faris and Dunham (*Mental Disorders in Urban Areas,* Chicago, 1965) talk about "anomie" but their data are only operationalized to things like housing. Several studies have cast doubt on the notion that mental illness is increasing: Herbert Goldhamer and Andrew Marshall (*Psychosis and Civilization,* Glencoe, Ill., 1949) claim to prove that mental illness was just as great in Massachusetts a century ago as it is today; and Joseph W. Eaton and Robert J. Weil (*Culture and Mental Disorders,* Glencoe, Ill., 1955) show serious mental illness prevalent among the Hutterites, a *gemeinschaft* society for which previous theories would predict immunity. On the other hand, the overall incidences are quite high. The Midtown Study of Srole *et al.,* (*Mental Health in the Metropolis,* N.Y., 1962) had perhaps some built-in biases leading to its astonishing estimate that some 80 percent of the population of Manhattan was to some degree impaired by mental illness (p. 137ff). It used questions derived from that notorious reification, the MMPI, nonprofessional interviewers trained to watch for superficial quirks, second- and third-hand bureaucratic grading of results that magnified reifications. Nonetheless this was a thorough poll based on door-to-door, in-depth interviewing and the statistical results are striking.

351. Erving Goffman, *Asylums* (Garden City, 1961).

352. E.g., by the left and right in the Weimar Republic and the French Third Republic, when their own pressure made center coalitions impossible, so that they could say that democracy was "unworkable."

DATE DUE